D0380205

Middle East

T 20110

Andrew Humphreys **Virginia Maxwell**
John R Bradley **Richard Plunkett**
Paul Greenway **Grace Pundyk**
Anthony Ham **Deanna Swaney**
Paul Harding **Jenny Walker**
Siona Jenkins **Pat Yale**

LONELY PLANET PUBLICATIONS
Melbourne • Oakland • London • Paris

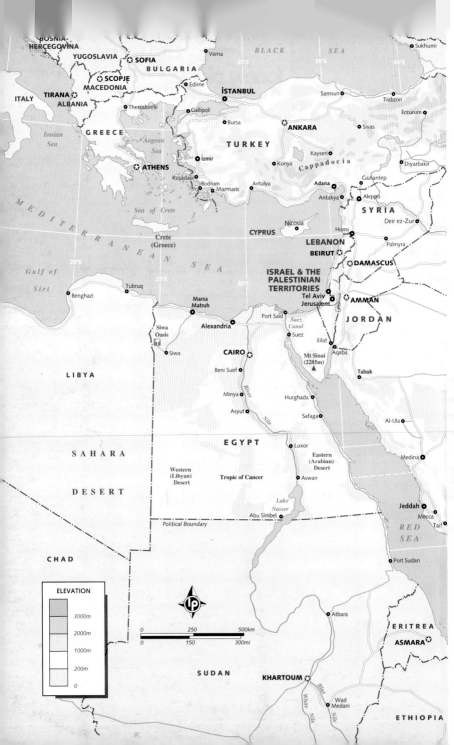

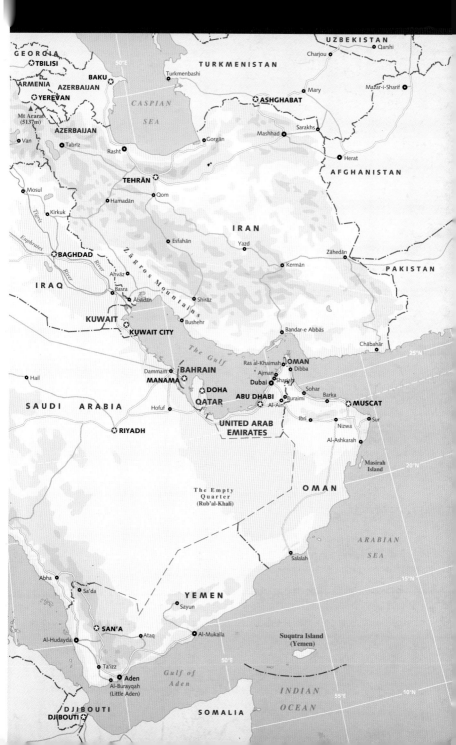

Middle East
4th edition – January 2003
First published – April 1994

Published by
Lonely Planet Publications Pty Ltd ABN 36 005 607 983
90 Maribyrnong St, Footscray, Victoria 3011, Australia

Lonely Planet Offices
Australia Locked Bag 1, Footscray, Victoria 3011
USA 150 Linden St, Oakland, CA 94607
UK 10a Spring Place, London NW5 3BH
France 1 rue du Dahomey, 75011 Paris

Photographs
Many of the images in this guide are available for licensing from
Lonely Planet Images.
w www.lonelyplanetimages.com

Front cover photograph
Silhouetted arm holding a sheer scarf, dusk, İstanbul, Turkey
(Will & Deni McIntyre, Getty Images)

ISBN 1 86450 349 1

text & maps © Lonely Planet Publications Pty Ltd 2003
photos © photographers as indicated 2003

Printed through Colorcraft Ltd, Hong Kong
Printed in China

Contents – Text

IRAN 205

IRAQ 277

ISRAEL & THE PALESTINIAN TERRITORIES 290

Middle East
4th edition – January 2003
First published – April 1994

Published by
Lonely Planet Publications Pty Ltd ABN 36 005 607 983
90 Maribyrnong St, Footscray, Victoria 3011, Australia

Lonely Planet Offices
Australia Locked Bag 1, Footscray, Victoria 3011
USA 150 Linden St, Oakland, CA 94607
UK 10a Spring Place, London NW5 3BH
France 1 rue du Dahomey, 75011 Paris

Photographs
Many of the images in this guide are available for licensing from
Lonely Planet Images.
w www.lonelyplanetimages.com

Front cover photograph
Silhouetted arm holding a sheer scarf, dusk, İstanbul, Turkey
(Will & Deni McIntyre, Getty Images)

ISBN 1 86450 349 1

text & maps © Lonely Planet Publications Pty Ltd 2003
photos © photographers as indicated 2003

Printed through Colorcraft Ltd, Hong Kong
Printed in China

Although the authors and Lonely Planet try to make the information as accurate as possible, we accept no responsibility for any loss, injury or inconvenience sustained by anyone using this book.

Contents – Text

JORDAN

KUWAIT

LEBANON

OMAN

THE UNITED ARAB EMIRATES 706

YEMEN 743

LANGUAGE 781

GLOSSARY 792

THANKS 796

INDEX 806

Contents – Maps

6

MAP LEGEND
back page

METRIC CONVERSION
inside back cover

The Authors

Andrew Humphreys

Andrew coordinated this book and updated the introductory and Syria chapters. He has been living, travelling and working in the Middle East on and off since 1988 when he arrived in Cairo on holiday and took three years to leave. Originally trained in London as an architect, he slid into writing through a growing fascination with Islamic buildings. Following a spell in mainstream journalism based for several years in the Baltic States, Andrew hooked up with Lonely Planet and has since authored or co-authored guides to Russia, Central Asia, the Middle East, Israel and the Palestinian Territories, Jerusalem, Egypt, Cairo and Syria. He currently divides his time between London and way-stations throughout the Arab world.

John R Bradley

John updated the Saudi Arabia and Iraq chapters. While studying English at University College, London, Dartmouth College and Exeter College, Oxford, John wrote book reviews for the *Independent on Sunday* and the *Times Literary Supplement*, founded a national cultural magazine called the *London Quarterly* and published three books on Henry James. After travelling extensively in the Middle East he decided to study Arabic intensively in Cairo while working as an editor on *Al-Ahram Weekly*. He stayed for 18 months. Afterwards, he moved to Saudi Arabia to become news editor at Jeddah-based English-language daily, the *Arab News*. He has since written for Salon.com, and his articles on Saudi Arabia for the news wires regularly appear in dozens of international publications. He is also a columnist for one of Saudi Arabia's Arabic language dailies, *Al-Madinah*, and occasionally contributes to the mass-circulation, pan-Arab *Al-Watan*.

Paul Greenway

Paul updated the Yemen chapter. Gratefully plucked from the blandness and security of the Australian Public Service, he has worked on about 20 Lonely Planet titles, including *Jordan*, *Bulgaria* and *Botswana*. During the rare times that he's not travelling (or writing, reading or dreaming about it) Paul relaxes to (and pretends he can play) heavy rock, eats and breathes Australian Rules Football, and will go to any lengths to avoid settling down.

Anthony Ham

Anthony updated the Jordan chapter. He worked as a refugee lawyer for three years, during which time he completed a Masters degree in Middle Eastern politics. After tiring of daily battles with a mean-spirited Australian Government, he set out to see the world and restore his faith in humanity. Sitting on the running boards of a train in Thailand, he decided to become a writer and ever since has been travelling throughout the Arab world, India and Africa. Whenever circumstances permit, he heads for the Sahara desert and now lives in Spain. For Lonely Planet, Anthony has worked on *Middle East, Africa, Iran, India, North India, Jordan* and his most satisfying project, the 1st edition of *Libya*.

Paul Harding

Paul updated the Iran chapter. Born in Melbourne, he worked as a newspaper reporter and editor of a London travel magazine, then backpacked around the world a bit before finally joining Lonely Planet's Melbourne home for wayward travellers. After a soul-searching period of editing other people's manuscripts, he swapped his red pen for a blue one and now works as a full-time writer and researcher. Paul has contributed to Lonely Planet's *Istanbul to Kathmandu*, *Australia*, *New Zealand*, *India*, *South India*, *South-East Asia* and *Read this First: Europe*.

Siona Jenkins

Siona updated the Egypt chapter. She arrived in Egypt for six months of Arabic language study in 1989 and is still based there. After giving birth to her son Leo in 1993 she began working as a freelance journalist and hooked up with Lonely Planet to work on its *Egypt* guide. Since then she has also authored or co-authored guides to Lebanon, Africa and the Middle East and Lonely Planet's *Egyptian Arabic phrasebook*. When not working for LP she contributes to the *Irish Times* newspaper and a number of magazines. She has also worked as a researcher, producer, travel guide, translator and 'destination expert' for a number of documentary films, and has appeared in a variety of guises (including Pharaonic slave girl and Graeco-Roman mourner) in several others.

Virginia Maxwell

Virginia updated the Lebanon chapter. Her background is in editing, architectural journalism, museum curating and film-festival programming. Since being drawn into the travel publishing business, she's developed a fascination with all things Middle Eastern, read lots of travel fiction and clocked up an impressive tally of frequent-flyer points. When she's not travelling with her partner Peter and young son Max, she works at Lonely Planet's Melbourne headquarters as a Series Publishing Manager in charge of country guides to the Middle East, Africa, the Indian subcontinent, Asia and the Australia-Pacific region.

Richard Plunkett

Richard updated the UAE chapter. Richard grew up on a farm and vineyard near Avenel, Australia. He's been a stock-market reporter, rock-concert reviewer (a veteran of no less than three Bon Jovi tours), farm labourer, sub-editor for the *Big Issue*, and once very briefly had the job of cleaning the mincer at a butchers. Since becoming a travel writer he's visited places like Turkmenistan, the Deccan, Karakalpakstan and Bangladesh. When he's not travelling or travel writing, he writes screenplays.

Grace Pundyk

Grace updated the Bahrain, Kuwait and Qatar chapters. A perpetual traveller, Grace has always made it a point to make sure, no
matter what, travel is on her agenda. As a result she has worked
as a cook on a prawn trawler, a flight attendant, an actor in a travelling theatre troupe and now as a writer with Lonely Planet.
Permanently exiled (by choice) from Australia, she spent four years
in the desert country of Kuwait working, among other things, as
editor of the *Kuwaiti Digest* and correspondent for a number of
international publications. She then packed up and moved on to
tropical and very green Singapore, where she works as a freelance
editor and writer, and is discovering the delights of Ashtanga yoga.

Deanna Swaney

Deanna updated the Israel & the Palestinian Territories chapter.
After graduating from university, she made a circuit of Europe and
the Middle East, and has been addicted to travel ever since. Despite
an erstwhile career in computer programming in midtown Anchorage, at first opportunity she made a break for South America to
write Lonely Planet's *Bolivia* guide. Subsequent travels steered her
through a course of paradise destinations and resulted in six more
1st editions of Lonely Planet guides: *Tonga*; *Samoa*; *Iceland, Greenland & the Faroe Islands*; *Zimbabwe, Botswana & Namibia*;
Norway; and *The Arctic*. She has also updated *Brazil*; *Mauritius,
Réunion & Seychelles*; *Madagascar & Comoros*; and *Russia, Ukraine
& Belarus*; and contributed to guides to Africa, South America and
Scandinavia. Deanna now divides her time between travelling,
hiking, writing and looking for time to work on various construction
projects around her home base in Alaska's Susitna Valley.

Jenny Walker

Jenny updated the Oman chapter. This was her first assignment for
LP, but she's no stranger to the series, having used editions in the 70
countries she's travelled in. She's no stranger to the Middle East
either, having studied the perception of the Arabic Orient for degrees
at Stirling and Oxford universities and having visited all parts of the
region for reasons as diverse as butterflying in Saudi and milking
goats in Syria. Jenny spent many years as an art agent arranging exhibitions in the Far East. After a night on the Mekong, she packed a
folding book into a knapsack and badgered the artists of the Silk
Route to contribute pages. Spending her last pound diverting to the
Frankincense Trail, she fell in love with Oman and stayed there.

Pat Yale

Pat updated the Turkey chapter. She first visited Turkey in 1974
in an old van that didn't look as if it would make it past Dover.
Since throwing up sensible careerdom (ie, teaching), she has co-
authored several editions of Lonely Planet's *Turkey* as well as
worked on other Lonely Planet titles. At the time of writing she
was living in a restored cave house with all mod cons and many
cats in Göreme, Cappadocia.

FROM THE AUTHORS

Andrew Humphreys Thanks to my fellow authors for rendering a potentially fraught project relatively painless.

John R Bradley Thanks to Khaled al-Maeena, editor-in-chief of *Arab News*, for giving me time off to undertake research for the Saudi chapter. Peter Harrigan provided useful advice that made my trips to Medain Saleh, Najran, Abha and the Farasan Islands much smoother than would otherwise have been the case. Saeed Haider introduced me to Khobar and shared with me the knowledge of the Eastern Province that he has acquired while reporting for *Arab News* from there for the last two decades. Roger Harrison helped with the boxed text on Red Sea diving, the entry on Jubail and with some of the nitty-gritty research. Javid Hassan was my guiding light in Riyadh. And Keith Birmingham introduced me to Jeddah's Afghan souq.

Paul Greenway I would mostly like to thank Yousuf Mohageb, who went far beyond the call of duty, eg, helping me to retrieve lost luggage and smoothing over ridiculously suspicious officials at the airports in Aden and San'a. In the process, he became a good friend. Also, thanks to the Deputy Minister, Mohamed M Qaflah, and the Tourism and Environment Minister, Abdul Malik A Al-Eryani.

Anthony Ham As always in the Arab World, I made many new friends in Jordan and so many people gave their assistance without asking anything in return.

Special thanks must go to Fayez al-Kayyali, Ra'ed Agrabawi and Dr Suheil Twal for their friendship and invaluable insight in Amman. Thanks also to the following for their patience, information and the warmth of their welcome: Ahmad al-Omari at the Umm Qais museum; Nowa Nasser at the Jordan Tourism Board in Amman; Deeb Hussein for his avuncular help in Pella; Ahmed Mansour in Irbid; Charl al-Twal and Osamah Twal in Madaba; Hayat for her charming tour around Hammamat Ma'in; Zac and Jan for feeding me so well in Amman – sorry that illness prevented me making it back to say goodbye; Jihad al-Sawalqa for being such an inspirational host in Dana and for sending me the information as promised; Jihad Amarat at the visitors centre in Petra; Sabah at Wadi Rum visitors centre; Attayak Ali, Difallah Ateeg and Osama Musa in Wadi Rum; Mater Saqer in the Public Information Office of UNRWA; and the urbane Mazhar and soul man Khalil (Dreads) at the Books@cafe, Amman. Finally, a very special thank you to 'Ruth' who was hugely generous with her assistance as she is to all travellers who visit Jordan.

Back home, a massive thank you to my family and friends for their patience, understanding and warmth despite my long absences, especially Jan, Ron, Lisa, Greg, my very special nieces Alexandra and Greta, Rachael, and Damien and Quetta for such a chilled wedding in Vanuatu on the way home. In the LP office, grateful thanks to Virginia Maxwell for her Jordan insights, and Brigitte Ellemor and Meredith Mail for their support during days of upheaval.

Paul Harding Thanks, as always, to the people at Lonely Planet who allow me to continue travelling for a living, this time Michelle Glynn and Brigitte Ellemor among others. In Iran I was constantly amazed by the hospitality, generosity and goodwill of the Iranian people. In particular, thanks to Ms Roosta and Ali Reza at Arg-e-Jadid in Tehrān; to the brilliant Komeil Noofeli and the guys at Pars in Shiraz; Mehdi and Hossein in Esfahān, and everyone at Nomad Carpet Shop in Esfahān; to Jalal in Kermān (a big thanks), and also to the Akhavan brothers; Nasser Khan, the consummate guide, in Tabriz; Mr Khatib and Hassan at Adibian Tours in Mashhad; Akhbar in Bam; Sima Shahraki in Zāhedān; Amir Norouzi from Tehrān; Hassan in Yazd; Abbas on Kish; Michael Lynch at the Australian embassy in Tehrān; and Gol Assadi in Canberra. I'm also indebted to Pat Yale and Anthony Ham not only for their solid research in the latest Iran guide, but for freely sharing their advice and contacts. Finally, thanks to the handful of travellers I met for their input – particularly Richard Rutter, one of the few who was braving the overland trail from Kathmandu.

Siona Jenkins Thanks to Andrew for his expert but laid-back coordinating and to editor Bethune Carmichael for understanding the demands of school-holiday travel. Many thanks to Abdallah Baghi, Mounir Neamatallah and John Grainger for hospitality and environmental updates, and to James for lugging my prehistoric laptop. As ever, big kisses to Leo for putting up with the inconvenience of his mother's deadlines.

Virginia Maxwell The Lebanese are probably the most friendly and helpful people I've ever encountered; so many of them helped me when I was researching my chapter that it's impossible to list them all here. Particular thanks go to Mrs Boushra Haffar at the Ministry of Tourism in Beirut, Mrs Salwa Abdo at the Ministry of Tourism in Tripoli, Raja Saad, Samar Kadi, Alex Fallaha and Joe Hayek. Esther Charlesworth shared her knowledge of great places to sleep, eat and drink in Beirut.

Also in Lebanon, Ambassador John Fennessy and staff at the Australian embassy answered lots of my questions and supplied me with invaluable background information.

LP authors Andrew Humphreys, Cathy Lanigan, Diana Saad and Andrew Burke gave me great advice and tips. Elizabeth Maxwell, Matthew Clark and Lara Dunston sent me regular Middle East dispatches and put me in contact with Lebanese friends and contacts.

At LP's Melbourne headquarters, Brigitte Ellemor, Meredith Mail, Mandy Sierp and Bethune Carmichael helped me juggle my schedule with the book's tight deadlines. Thanks guys.

Finally, the biggest thanks of all must go to my two favourite travelling companions of all time, Peter and Max.

Richard Plunkett Special thanks to Sophie Morell for her company and sense of humour. Thanks also to Inger Rasmussen at Orient Tours; Siobhan and Adrian at the Sandy Beach Diving Centre; Valerie Upham, Louise Mulshaw and Kathy Mitchell in Dubai; Paul Hofman in Ras al-Khaimah; Peter Deakon and Sohrab Motiwalla at the Victorian Government Export Centre; Ajay Rajguru at the DTCM; and to Colin Richardson, Mohammed Odadi, Marcela Maximova, Samir Ozturk, Tim Gane, Laetitia Sadier and Mary Hansen. Thanks to Finola Collins in the LP London office for help with flight prices and to all the people who wrote to LP about the last edition. Back home, thanks most of all to the ever-lovely and charming scientician, Rebecca Ryan.

Grace Pundyk In Kuwait, thanks to my dear friends Rob and Anne Barker for their hospitality and generosity; also my appreciation and love goes to the following people: my adopted Kuwaiti family, the Al-Meas, for their kindness and trust and for bringing me into their family; Laila Nasrallah for her fantastic cooking and love of the world, her children and all things good; Hassan Nasrallah for our heated debates; Bassima and Farhan al-Farhan for their generosity; and Saad Qulfat and Omar Shawar for their never-ending support and integrity.

In Bahrain, thanks go to Majeed for sharing with me his love of the island; Alison and Emoke for being like me – an ex-hostie who also loves the Arabian Gulf; and to Ahmad for his excellent Arabic spelling.

In Qatar, thank you to Jan Sjoukens for his kind assistance and enthusiasm; Nikolas Maratos and Bonnie Day-Cook for taking the time to meet with me; and Dahabiya Gabi and Abdul Hamid al-Ansari for allowing me an insight into the Qatari people.

Thanks also to Sayid and Mohammed at the Saudi Commercial office in Singapore for their Arabic translation and to my husband Robert for his never-ending support and patience.

Deanna Swaney Any reputation for surliness that Israel and the Palestinian Territories may have is wholly unsubstantiated! Though the country was embroiled in tragedy on all sides, the friendliness, tenacity and faith of its people – from the Mediterranean to the Jordan River, and from the Good Fence to Taba – more than mitigated any political or official unpleasantness during my research. Some people stood out, however, by providing their invaluable assistance, expertise and optimism.

Thanks especially to Chris Wright and Dave Cohen at IsraWorld in Tel Aviv – this book would have been considerably diminished without their apparently boundless willingness to keep me abreast of changes. Danny Flax at Allenby 2 in Jerusalem made great cheese-and-olive toasted sandwiches and went beyond the extra mile to ensure that I didn't miss some of Jerusalem's most wonderful sites and experiences. Amichay Neeman at Kikar Dizengoff Apartments provided useful information and Hebrew vocabulary, as well as a comfortable pad in Tel Aviv. Semir at Old Jaffa Hostel in

Jaffa made mean cups of tea and helped with new Arabic script. With his unbounded enthusiasm, Ze'ev at Port Inn went out of his way – and took lots of time out of his busy schedule – to instil in me a new appreciation for Haifa and points north; love also to Rachael and Jordanna. Russel Kibel at Villa Kibel should be commended for creating such a lovely and relaxing place to stay in Eilat. Thanks to Erez and Josa at Desert Eco Tours in Eilat for their appreciation of their fabulous desert country. Thanks also to Alexis, for good food and good company in Mitzpe Ramon. Thanks to the lovely Sarah and Israel Shavit at Shavit B&B in Arbel (my stay with you was a major highlight of my time in Israel). Thanks also to Sinead from Australia, who was great company on the road in Jerusalem and southern Israel, and Zehava Bakeman of Tarzana and the Universe, who widened my appreciation of her native country. I also appreciated the long conversations with Sergio, Chaim, Guy and Wanda, Ralph, Cyntia, Sam, Lee and all the other folk around the table at Allenby 2.

Finally, love and best wishes to Earl, Dean, Kim, Jennifer and Lauren Swaney in Fresno; Rodney, Heather, Bradley and Eric Leacock in Colorado Springs; Keith and Holly Hawkings in Anchorage; and especially to Dave back home in Alaska. Finally, many thanks to the Lonely Planet production team in Melbourne.

Jenny Walker Oman is a wonderful country of delightful people and I'm heartily grateful to have had the opportunity to discover many corners of it. In particular, I want to thank Khamis Mabrook and Nasser Suleiman (the 'jebel rebel') for being such excellent cultural resources. Mr Melton at NTT was very helpful, too. A thank you to everyone involved in this edition at LP, specially Brigitte Ellemor, for making it such an enjoyable experience. Thanks also to Lou Callan, whose groundwork in Oman I've enjoyed updating. I reserve the biggest thanks of all, however, for my dearest husband, Sam Owen, who has been unstinting with his time, energies and encouragement – not to mention the patient driving.

Pat Yale Where would I be without all the people who routinely help me on my way around Turkey? Inevitably there are too many to mention by name, but particular thanks are owed to Aydın Şengül in Bergama; Zafer Küstü in Bodrum; Uğuur Çelikkol in Bursa; Corinne Parry in Fethiye; the Kiğuılı family in İstanbul; Mike and Karen Belton in Kaş; Şahin and Sami Sağuıroğulu in Köceğuiz; Sezgin Sağulam in Kuşadası; Rifat Koray, Ertan and Hakan Senkron in Pamukkale; Alison, Derviş, Jimmy and Shannon in Selçuk; Penny and Ali Yeşilipek in Side; and Remzi Bozbay in Van. In Cappadocia I owe a special *teşekkür ederim* to great friends Ahmet Diler in Avanos; Dawn Köse, Ruth Lockwood, Mustafa Güney and Ali Yavuz in Göreme; and Suha Ersoz and Aydın Güney in Ürgüp. Finally, Lisa Raffonelli, Golnaz Assadi and Paul Stockley went way beyond the normal demands of friendship in helping me track down plane fares from afar.

This Book

This book originally grew out of the Middle East section of Lonely Planet's *West Asia on a shoestring*. Many people have helped to create this 4th edition. Among the major contributors to past editions were Tom Brosnahan, Lou Callan, Geert Cole, Paul Greenway, Rosemary Hall, Anthony Ham, Paul Hellander, Andrew Humphreys, Ann Jousiffe, Cathy Lanigan, Leanne Logan, Gordon Robison, David St Vincent, Damien Simonis, Perti Hämäläinen, Diana Saad, Neil Tilbury, Tony Wheeler, Jeff Williams and Pat Yale.

From the Publisher

This edition of *Middle East* was coordinated in Lonely Planet's Melbourne office by Bethune Carmichael with editorial assistance from Susie Ashworth, Lou Callan, Melanie Dankel, Liz Filleul, William Gourlay, Kim Hutchins, Lara Morcombe, Gina Tsarouhas, Louise McGregor, Tom Smallman and Tasmin Waby. The project was commissioned by Brigitte Ellemor and Michelle Glynn and managed by Brigitte, Meredith Mail, Lynne Preston and Robert Reid. Amanda Sierp coordinated the mapping and was helped by Tessa Rottiers, Helen Rowley, Sarah Sloane and David Wenk. Pablo Gastar took care of design and eased the book through layout under the guidance of Adriana Mammarella and with help from Nick Stebbing, Tamsin Wilson, Anna Judd and Mark Germanchis. Hilary Ericksen lent her fresh eye for layout checks. Special thanks to Emma Koch for the language section and foreign script, and to Simon Bracken for designing the cover.

THANKS
Many thanks to the travellers who used the last edition and wrote to us with helpful hints, advice and interesting anecdotes. Your names appear in the back of this book.

Foreword

ABOUT LONELY PLANET GUIDEBOOKS

The story begins with a classic travel adventure: Tony and Maureen Wheeler's 1972 journey across Europe and Asia to Australia. There was no useful information about the overland trail then, so Tony and Maureen published the first Lonely Planet guidebook to meet a growing need.

From a kitchen table, Lonely Planet has grown to become the largest independent travel publisher in the world, with offices in Melbourne (Australia), Oakland (USA), London (UK) and Paris (France).

Today Lonely Planet guidebooks cover the globe. There is an ever-growing list of books and information in a variety of media. Some things haven't changed. The main aim is still to make it possible for adventurous travellers to get out there – to explore and better understand the world.

At Lonely Planet we believe travellers can make a positive contribution to the countries they visit – if they respect their host communities and spend their money wisely. Since 1986 a percentage of the income from each book has been donated to aid projects and human rights campaigns and more recently, to wildlife conservation.

> Although inclusion in a guidebook usually implies a recommendation we cannot list every good place. Exclusion does not necessarily imply criticism. In fact there are a number of reasons why we might exclude a place _ sometimes it is simply inappropriate to encourage an influx of travellers.

UPDATES & READER FEEDBACK

Things change – prices go up, schedules change, good places go bad and bad places go bankrupt. Nothing stays the same. So, if you find things better or worse, recently opened or long-since closed, please tell us and help make the next edition even more accurate and useful.

Lonely Planet thoroughly updates each guidebook as often as possible – usually every two years, although for some destinations the gap can be longer. Between editions, up-to-date information is available in our free, quarterly *Planet Talk* newsletter and monthly email bulletin *Comet*. The *Scoop* section of our website covers news and current affairs relevant to travellers. Lastly, the *Thorn Tree* bulletin board and *Postcards* section carry unverified, but fascinating, reports from travellers.

Tell us about it! We genuinely value your feedback. A well-travelled team at Lonely Planet reads and acknowledges every email and letter we receive and ensures that every morsel of information finds its way to the relevant authors, editors and cartographers.

Everyone who writes to us will find their name listed in the next edition of the appropriate guidebook, and will receive the latest issue of *Comet* or *Planet Talk*. The very best contributions will be rewarded with a free guidebook.

We may edit, reproduce and incorporate your comments in Lonely Planet products such as guidebooks, websites and digital products, so let us know if you don't want your comments reproduced or your name acknowledged.

How to contact Lonely Planet:
Online: e talk2us@lonelyplanet.com.au, w www.lonelyplanet.com
Australia: Locked Bag 1, Footscray, Victoria 3011
UK: 10a Spring Place, London NW5 3BH
USA: 150 Linden St, Oakland, CA 94607

Introduction

Welcome to a realm where history lives and breathes. The Middle East is where three continents meet, where empires have waxed and waned, merchants have long traded and warriors have long clashed. The result is a region rich with the accumulated detritus of five millennia's worth of major civilisations and cultures. Every town, valley and hillside is a living museum of humankind's history: that's the field on which Ramses triumphed over the Hittites; this is where Alexander the Great sought the Oracle's advice; here is where Cleopatra bathed; this is the route walked by Christ; that's where Richard the Lionheart set up camp; and this is where Napoleon put ashore. It's no wonder the Middle East is prone to turbulence when so much of its territory means so much to so many.

Tumultuous politics, a handful of scary extremist organisations, a religious devotion that inspires incomprehension and a correspondingly unflattering media profile have done the Middle East few favours when it comes to selling the place as a destination to potential Western visitors. Even Egypt, Israel and Turkey, all long-standing staples of the European and American package-tour trade can't completely escape the blight. All three still occasionally fall victim to shrill headlines and the knee-jerk 'stay away' responses they inspire in too many. Which is all a pity, because for anybody who can see beyond those headlines the countries of the Middle East are some of the most welcoming in the world.

In setting our boundaries, we've chosen a modern political definition of the Middle East, hence the inclusion of Turkey and Iran. It makes for a fascinating area, stretching from the vast sand seas of the Sahara in the southwest, up to the mountainous wooded shores of the Caspian and Black Seas in the north. Africa (in the form of Sudan and Libya), Asia (in Pakistan and Afghanistan) and Europe (Greece and Bulgaria) are all neighbours.

Although it helps, it isn't necessary to have any appreciation of history to be awed by much of what there is to see here. The Pyramids and temples of Egypt speak for themselves, as do the ghostly ruins of the Roman desert cities in Jordan and Syria, the towering mud cities of Yemen and the elegant tiled mosques of Iran. And the scenery can be stunning. Captivated by the desert scenes in *Lawrence of Arabia* and *The English Patient*? Then head off to Jordan, Egypt or Oman. Sand and sea more your thing? The beaches of Sinai and along Israel's and Turkey's Mediterranean coasts are pure paradise, while the underwater landscapes of the Red Sea are equal to anything above sea level. And after exploring the sites you will discover the food is excellent, costs are low, the people are extremely hospitable and getting around will prove to be very easy. A few bureaucratic problems aside, the main difficulty most visitors find when visiting the Middle East is that with such a large and diverse region, so densely packed with must-see sites, how do you decide where to go and what to leave out? As problems go, that's not a bad one to face.

Facts about the Middle East

HISTORY
This section sketches out the broadest sweeps of Middle Eastern history – for further details see the more specific History sections in the individual country chapters.

Cradle of Civilisation
If Africa is the birthplace of humanity, the Middle East can make strong claims to being the birthplace of civilisation. The fertile crescent of Mesopotamia (ancient Iraq) and the valley of the Nile River were sites of some of the earliest known organised societies.

About 5000 BC a culture known as Al-Ubaid first appeared in Mesopotamia. Little is known about it except that its influence eventually spread down what is now the coast of the Gulf but was then a string of islands. Stone Age artefacts have also been found in Egypt's Western Desert, Israel's Negev Desert and in the West Bank town of Jericho.

Sometime around 3100 BC the kingdoms of Upper and Lower Egypt were unified under Menes, beginning 3000 years of Pharaonic rule in the Nile Valley; the fact that there were two kingdoms for Menes to conquer implies that a relatively organised society already existed in Egypt at that time. The earliest settlements in the Gulf also date from this period and are usually associated with the Umm an-Nar culture (centred in today's United Arab Emirates), about which relatively little is known. The Levant (present-day Lebanon, Syria and Israel & the Palestinian Territories) was well settled by this time, and local powers included the Amorites and the Canaanites. In Mesopotamia it was the era of Sumer, arguably the world's first great civilisation.

In the late 24th and early 23rd centuries BC, Sargon of Akkad conquered much of the Levant and Mesopotamia. At its southern edge Sargon's empire contended with a powerful kingdom called Dilmun, centred on the island of Bahrain in the Gulf. Dilmun's civilisation arose around 3200 BC and was to continue in one form or another for nearly 2000 years.

The patriarch Abraham also came from Mesopotamia, having been born, according to tradition, in Ur of the Chaldees on the Euphrates River. His migration from Ur to Canaan is usually dated around 1800 BC. Other powers in the region at that time included the Hittite and Assyrian empires and, in Greece and Asia Minor, Mycenae and Troy.

The 7th century BC saw both the conquest of Egypt by Assyria and, far to the east, the rise of the Medes, the first of many great Persian empires. In 550 BC the Medes were conquered by Cyrus the Great, usually regarded as the first Persian *shāh*, or king.

Over the next 60 years Cyrus and his successors Cambyses (r. 525–522 BC) and Darius I (r. 521–486 BC) swept west and north to conquer first Babylon and then Egypt, Asia Minor and parts of Greece. After the Greeks stemmed the Persian tide at the Battle of Marathon in 490 BC, Darius and Xerxes (r. 486–466 BC) turned their attention to consolidating their empire, though Xerxes launched another invasion of Greece in 480 BC.

Egypt won independence from the Persians in 401 BC only to be reconquered by them 60 years later. But the second Persian occupation of Egypt was brief. Little more than a decade after they arrived, the Persians were again driven out of Egypt, this time by the Greeks.

The Hellenistic World
In 336 BC Philip of Macedon, a warlord who had conquered much of mainland Greece, was murdered. His son Alexander (see the boxed text) assumed the throne and began a series of conquests that would eventually encompass most of Asia Minor, the Middle East, Persia and northwest India.

Under Alexander, the Greeks were the first to impose any kind of order on the Middle East as a whole. Traces of their rule ring the eastern Mediterranean from Ephesus in Turkey south and around to the oasis of Siwa in Egypt's Western Desert. Far greater than the archaeological evidence are the legends and tales of the Greeks, the *Iliad* and the *Odyssey*, and the descriptions left by their historians such as Strabo, Herodotus and Pliny. Taken together, all of these writings present us with strong clues to the state of the Middle East 300 years before Christ and 900 years before the coming of Islam.

Empire Builders: Alexander the Great

One of the greatest ever figures to shape the Middle East, Alexander (356–323 BC) rode out of Macedonia in 334 BC to embark on a decade-long campaign of conquest and exploration. His first great victory was against the Persians at Issus in what's now southeast Turkey. He swept south conquering the Phoenician seaports and thence into Egypt where he founded the Mediterranean city that still bears his name. From Egypt he returned north, heading for Babylon. Crossing the Tigris and the Euphrates he defeated another Persian army before pushing his army up into Central Asia and northern India. Eventually fatigue and disease brought the drive to a halt and the Greeks turned around and headed back home. Alexander succumbed to illness and died in Baghdad. The whereabouts of his body and tomb remain unknown.

TRUDI CANAVAN

Following Alexander's death, his empire was promptly carved up by his generals. This resulted in the founding of three new ruling dynasties: the Antigonids in Greece and Asia Minor; the Ptolemaic dynasty in Egypt; and the Seleucids, who controlled the swath of land running from modern Israel and Lebanon through Mesopotamia to Persia.

That is not to say that peace reigned. Having finished off a host of lesser competitors, the heirs to Alexander's empire then proceeded to fight each other. The area of the eastern Mediterranean splintered into an array of different local dynasties with fluctuating borders as different parts were conquered and lost. It took an army arriving from the west to again reunite the lands of the east – this time in the shape of the legions of Rome.

Romans & Christians

Rome's legionaries conquered most of Asia Minor in 188 BC, then Syria, Palestine and the North African territories of Carthage in 64 and 63 BC. When Cleopatra of Egypt, last of the Ptolemaic dynasty (see the boxed text 'Cleopatra' in the Egypt chapter), was defeated in 31 BC, the Romans controlled the whole of the Mediterranean world. This left the area covered by this book divided largely among two empires and their client states until the coming of Islam. Asia Minor, the Levant and Egypt were dominated by Rome (known, after AD 395, as the Eastern Roman, or Byzantine, Empire), while the Sassanians, a dynasty based in what's now Iran, ruled the east. Only the

nomads of the desert and the frankincense kingdoms of South Arabia remained independent of the great powers of the day.

While the mighty empire of Rome suffered no great external threats to its eastern Mediterranean empire, there was plenty of trouble fomenting within. The Jews went into open revolt in AD 66 and it took four years for the legionaries to quell the uprising. In retaliation, Jerusalem was razed to the ground and rebuilt as a Roman city and the Jews were sent into exile (an exile which could be said to have ended only with the creation of the state of Israel in 1948).

One of the rebellious orators who had been stirring up anti-Roman sentiments was Jesus of Nazareth, but it wasn't until almost 300 years after his death that his preaching fully manifested itself. In AD 331 the newly converted emperor Constantine declared Christianity the official religion of the 'Holy Roman Empire', with its capital not jaded, cynical Rome but the newly renamed city of Constantinople (formerly Byzantium, later to become İstanbul).

The Coming of Islam

Constantinople reached its apogee during the reign of Justinian (AD 527–65), whose reign saw the Byzantine Empire consolidate its hold on the eastern Mediterranean, while also recapturing the lost domain of Italy. But the Sassanian Empire to the east was constantly chipping away at Byzantine holdings, creating a fault line between the two empires running down through what we know as the Middle East. Meanwhile, far to the south, in lands that were independent of the two great empires, a new force was preparing to emerge.

A merchant named Mohammed, born around AD 570 in the Arabian town of Mecca (now in Saudi Arabia), had begun preaching against the pagan religion of his fellow Meccans, who worshipped many gods represented to them by idols. As a result, in 622 Mohammed – the 'Prophet' – and his followers were forced to flee to Medina, an oasis town some 360km to the north. In Medina, Mohammed rose to become a successful religious, political and military leader. He brought all the region's tribes into his fold and eventually gathered an army of 10,000 troops and conquered his home town of Mecca.

Mohammed died in 632 but under his successors, known as *caliphs* (from the Arabic word for 'follower'), the new religion continued its rapid spread, reaching all of Arabia by 634. Egypt, Syria and Palestine were wrested from the Byzantines by 646, while most of Iraq, Iran and Afghanistan were taken from the Sassanians by 656.

Arguments over the leadership quickly arose and just 12 years after the Prophet's death a dispute over the caliphate opened a rift in Islam that grew into today's divide between Sunni and Shiite Muslims (see the Islam section under Religion later in this chapter). Civil war broke out, ending with the rise to power of Mu'awiyah, the Muslim military governor of Syria and a distant relative of Mohammed.

Early Islam

Mu'awiyah moved the capital from Medina to Damascus and established the first great Muslim dynasty called the Umayyad (or Omayyad) dynasty.

The Umayyads were descended from a branch of the Quraysh, the Prophet's tribe, known more for expediency than piety. Mu'awiyah's father was one of the last people in Mecca to embrace Islam and had long been Mohammed's chief opponent in the city. By moving the capital to Damascus the Umayyads were symbolically declaring that they had aspirations far beyond the rather ascetic teachings of the Quran (Koran).

The Umayyads gave the Islamic world some of its greatest architectural treasures, including the Dome of the Rock in Jerusalem and the Umayyad Mosque in Damascus. History, however, has not been kind, remembering them largely for the high living, corruption, nepotism and tyranny that eventually proved to be their undoing.

In 750 the Umayyads were toppled in a revolt fuelled by accusations of impiety. Their successors, and the strong arm behind the revolt, were a dynasty called the Abbasids. The Abbasid caliphate created a new capital in Baghdad and the early centuries of its rule constitutes what's often regarded as the golden age of Islamic culture. The most famous of the Abbasid caliphs was Haroun ar-Rashid (r. 786–809) of *The Thousand and One Nights* fame (see the boxed text of the same name in the Arts section later in this chapter) – a warrior king who led one of the most successful early Muslim invasions of Byzantium, almost reaching Constantinople. He also presided over an extraordinary burst of creativity in the arts, medicine, literature and science. Al-Maamun, Haroun's son and main successor, founded the Beit al-Hikmah, or 'House of Wisdom', a Baghdad-based academy dedicated to translating Greek and Roman works of science and philosophy into Arabic. It was only through these translations that most of the classical literature we know today was saved for posterity.

After Haroun's death the empire was effectively divided between two of his sons. Predictably, civil war ensued. In 813 one son, Al-Maamun, emerged triumphant and reigned as caliph for the next 20 years. But Al-Maamun's hold on power remained insecure and he felt compelled to surround himself with Turkish mercenaries. Over time the caliph's Turkish bodyguards became the real rulers of an empire that itself was rapidly shrinking.

By the middle of the 10th century the Abbasid caliphs were the prisoners of their Turkish guards, who spawned a dynasty of their own, the Seljuks (1038–1194). The Seljuks extended their reach throughout Persia, Central Asia and Afghanistan. They also took control of Armenia, Azerbaijan and a large part of Anatolia where the Seljuk Sultanate of Rum made its capital at Konya. The resulting pressure on the Byzantine Empire was intense enough to cause the emperor and the Greek Orthodox Church to swallow their pride and appeal to the rival Roman Catholic Church for help.

The Crusades

In response to the eastern empire's alarm, in 1095 Pope Urban II called for a Western Christian military expedition – a 'Crusade' – to liberate the holy places of Jerusalem. Rome's motives were not entirely benevolent: Urban was eager to assert Rome's primacy in the east over Constantinople.

After linking up with the Byzantine army in 1097, the Crusaders successfully besieged Antioch (modern Antakya, in Turkey) and then marched south along the coast before turning inland, towards Jerusalem. A thousand Muslim troops held Jerusalem for six weeks against 15,000 Crusaders before the city fell on 15 July 1099. The victorious Crusaders then massacred the local population – Muslims, Jews and Christians alike – sacked the non-Christian religious sites and turned the Dome of the Rock into a church.

These successes were short-lived. It took less than 50 years for the tide to begin to turn against the Crusaders and only 200 before they were driven out of the region once and for all.

The Muslim leader responsible for removing the Crusaders from Jerusalem (in 1187) was Salah ad-Din al-Ayyub, better known in the West as Saladin (see the boxed text). He and his successors (a short-lived dynasty known as the Ayyubids) battled the Crusaders for 60 years until they were unceremoniously removed by their own army, a strange soldier-slave caste, the Mamluks.

The Mamluks ran what would today be called a military dictatorship. But the only way to join their army was to be press-ganged into it. Non-Muslim boys were captured or bought outside the empire, converted to Islam and raised in the service of a single military commander. They were expected to give this commander total loyalty, in exchange for which their fortunes would rise (or fall) with his. Sultans were chosen from among the most senior Mamluk commanders, but it was a system that engendered vicious, bloody rivalries, and rare was the sultan who died of natural causes.

The Mamluks were to rule Egypt, Syria, Palestine and western Arabia for nearly 300 years (1250–1517) and it was they who succeeded in ejecting the Crusaders from the Near East, prising them out of their last stronghold of Acre (modern-day Akko in Israel) in 1291.

Empire Builders: Saladin

Saladin – or to give him his proper Islamic name, Salah ad-Din ('restorer of the faith') al-Ayyub – was born to Kurdish parents in 1138 in what is modern-day Tikrit in Iraq. He joined other members of his family in the service of Nureddin (Nur ad-Din) of the ruling Zangi dynasty. By the time Nureddin died in 1174, Saladin had risen to the rank of general and had already taken possession of Egypt. He quickly took control of Syria and in the next 10 years extended his authority into parts of Mesopotamia, careful not to infringe too closely on the territory of the now largely powerless Abbasid caliphate in Baghdad. In 1187 Saladin crushed the Crusaders at the Battle of Hittin and captured Jerusalem, precipitating the Third Crusade and pitting Saladin against Richard I 'the Lionheart' of England. After countless clashes the two rival warriors signed a peace treaty in November 1192, giving the coastal territories to the Crusaders and the interior to the Muslims. Saladin died three months later in Damascus, where he's now buried.

The Ottoman Turks

In 1258, just eight years after the Mamluks seized power in Cairo and began their bloody dynasty, a boy named Osman (or Othman) was born to the chief of a Turkish tribe in western Anatolia. He converted to Islam in his youth and later began a military career by hiring out his tribe's army as mercenaries in the civil wars then besetting what was left of the Byzantine Empire. Payment came in the form of land.

Rather than taking on the Byzantines directly, Osman's successors (the Ottomans) deliberately picked off the bits and pieces of the empire that Constantinople could no longer control. By the end of the 14th century the Ottomans had conquered Bulgaria, Serbia, Bosnia, Hungary and most of present-day Turkey. They had also moved their capital across the Dardanelles to Adrianople, today the Turkish city of Edirne. In 1453 came their greatest victory when Sultan Mehmet II took Constantinople, the hitherto unachievable object of innumerable Muslim wars almost since the 7th century.

On a battlefield near Aleppo 64 years later an army under the sultan Selim the

Empire Builders: Süleyman the Magnificent

Sultan of the Ottoman Empire from 1520 to 1566, Süleyman I truly earned his honorific of 'the Magnificent'. He shattered the army of the Kingdom of Hungary and laid siege to Vienna, and his navy challenged the Portuguese in the Indian Ocean. He was responsible, too, for building many public works – mosques, aqueducts and bridges – particularly in İstanbul, but also elsewhere. For instance, the surviving walls and some of the gates of Jerusalem were built under his patronage. Of even more relevance to today's traveller is the fact that it was via the Constantinople of Süleyman that coffee was first introduced to Europe.

Grim routed the Mamluks and, at one stroke, the whole of the eastern Mediterranean, including Egypt, was absorbed into the Ottoman Empire.

The empire reached its peak, both politically and culturally, under Süleyman the Magnificent (see the boxed text), who led the Ottoman armies west to the gates of Vienna, east into Persia, and south through the holy cities of Mecca and Medina and into Yemen. His control also extended throughout North Africa.

After Süleyman, however, the Ottoman Empire went into a long, slow period of decline. Only five years after his death Spain and Venice destroyed virtually the entire Ottoman navy at the Battle of Lepanto (in the Aegean Sea), a loss which eventually cost the Ottomans control of the western Mediterranean. North Africa soon fell under the sway of local dynasties. The Ottomans were driven out of Yemen in 1636, and conflict with the Safavids – Persia's rulers from the early 16th century to the early 18th century – was almost constant.

Enter Europe

Europe's colonial expansion into the Middle East had begun in 1498 when the Portuguese explorer Vasco de Gama visited Oman's northern coast, the Strait of Hormuz (then the seat of an independent kingdom) and the Sheikhdom of Julfar, near modern Ras al-Khaimah in the United Arab Emirates (UAE). In 1507 Portugal annexed the Yemeni island of Suqutra and occupied Oman. Its power eventually extended as far north as Bahrain. Although Portugal retained control of Bahrain until 1602, and was not driven out of Oman until 1650, the area was important to it only as a way-station on the route to India. Little, if any, effort was made to penetrate Arabia's interior.

But in the late 18th century the European powers began further chiselling away at the ailing Ottoman Empire. In 1798 Napoleon invaded Egypt in what he planned as the first step towards building a French empire in the Middle East and India. The French occupation of Egypt lasted only three years, but left a lasting mark: until very recently French was the second (sometimes the first) language of choice for the Egyptian upper classes. Even today, Egypt's legal system is based on a French model.

The British, protecting their own Indian interests, forced the French out of Egypt in 1801, and several years of unrest followed. In 1805 Mohammed Ali, an Albanian soldier in the Ottoman army, emerged as the country's strongman and became the vassal of the sultan in Constantinople. He set about modernising the country, and as time passed, it became increasingly obvious that Constantinople was becoming ever more dependent on Egypt for military backing rather then the reverse. Mohammed Ali's ambitions grew. In the 1830s he invaded and conquered Syria, and by 1839 he had effective control of most of the Ottoman Empire. Constantinople itself would probably have been his next target had not the European powers, alarmed by the idea of the Ottoman government collapsing, forced him to withdraw to Egypt. In exchange, the Ottoman sultan gave long-overdue acknowledgment of Mohammed Ali's status as ruler of a virtually independent Egypt and bestowed the right of heredity rule on his heirs (who continued to rule Egypt until 1952).

In 1869 Mohammed Ali's grandson, Ismail, opened the Suez Canal. But within a few years his government was so deeply in debt that in 1882 the British, who already played a large role in Egyptian affairs, occupied the country.

At the same time, the Ottoman Empire was becoming increasingly dependent on the good will of the European powers and was weakening its own position by ceding authority over its subjects to various foreign governments. In 1860 the French sent troops to Lebanon after a massacre of Christians by the local Druze. Before withdrawing, the French forced the Ottomans to set up a new administrative system for the area guaranteeing the appointment of Christian governors, over whom the French came to have great influence. In 1911, after a short struggle between Rome and the Turks, Tripoli and Cyrenaica (Libya) went to the Italians.

The Modern Middle East

With the outbreak of WWI in 1914 the Ottoman Empire sided with Germany, and Sultan Mohammed V declared a jihad, or holy war, calling on Muslims everywhere to rise up against Britain, France and Russia. To counter the sultan, the British negotiated an alliance with Hussein bin Ali, the Grand Sherif of Mecca. In 1916 Sherif Hussein agreed to lead an Arab revolt against the Turks in exchange for a British promise to make him 'King of the Arabs' once the conflict was over. It's within this context that the story of Lawrence 'of Arabia' takes place.

The British never had any serious intention of keeping this promise. At the same time that they were negotiating with Sherif Hussein, they were holding talks with the French on how to carve up the Ottoman Empire. Britain had also given the Zionist movement a promise, known as the Balfour Declaration (named after the then-British foreign secretary), that it would 'view with favour the establishment in Palestine of a national home for the Jewish people' after the war. (For more on the background to Zionism and the Arab-Israeli conflict, see the Israel & the Palestinian Territories chapter.)

In the closing year of the war the British occupied Palestine and Damascus. After the war a settlement modelled on the Sykes-Picot Agreement – the secret Anglo-French accord that divided the Ottoman Empire into British and French spheres of influence – was implemented and given the formal rubber-stamp approval of the newly created League of Nations. France took control of Syria and Lebanon, while Britain retained Egypt and was given control of Palestine, Transjordan and Iraq. These territories were formally held under 'mandates' from the League of Nations, but in practice the system amounted to little more than direct colonial rule.

The war also meant the end of the Ottoman dynasty. Stripped of its Arab provinces, the Ottoman monarchy was overthrown and a Turkish Republic was declared under the leadership of Mustafa Kemal 'Atatürk', a soldier who became Turkey's first president in 1923. (For more on Atatürk see the Turkey chapter.)

Atatürk's drive toward secularism (which he saw as synonymous with the modernisation necessary to drag Turkey into the 20th century) found an echo in Persia. There, in 1923, Rezā Khān, the commander of a Cossack brigade who had risen to become war minister, overthrew the decrepit Ghajar dynasty. To emphasise his nationalist credentials, he changed his name from Khān to the more Persian-sounding Pahlavi, which also happened to be the name of the language spoken in pre-Islamic Persia. He initially moved to set up a secular republic on the Turkish model, but after protests from the country's religious establishment he had himself crowned *shāh* instead. In 1934 he changed the country's name from Persia to Iran.

Independence & Pan-Arabism

The Middle East was only of marginal importance during WWII. Egypt and Libya were briefly central to the war, with decisive battles fought at Tobruk and El Alamein in the desert west of Alexandria. But the region's problems began in earnest soon after the war was over.

Since taking control of Palestine in 1918, the British had been under pressure to allow unrestricted Jewish immigration to the territory. With tension rising between Palestine's Arab and Jewish residents, they had refused to do this and, in the late 1930s, had placed strict limits on the number of new Jewish immigrants.

Several plans to partition Palestine were proposed during the 1930s and '40s, but WWII (briefly) put an end to all such discussion. When the war ended, Britain again found itself under pressure to allow large-scale Jewish immigration, particularly in the wake of the Holocaust.

In early 1947 the British announced that they were turning the entire problem over to

Gamal Abdel Nasser: Arab Hero

Nasser's dreams weren't imperial, but his dream and pursuit of the ideal of a united Arab nation make him arguably the most important Arab world figure of the 20th century. The first president of the newly independent republic of Egypt was regarded as a pharaoh, with a touch of Che Guevara. He stood defiantly against the old regional rulers of Britain and France, while playing off the new super powers – the Soviet Union and the USA – against each other.

Under Nasser, Egypt became a beacon for all those countries in Africa and Asia that had recently thrown off European colonial administrations. His rousing pan-Arab speeches gave the nations of the Middle East and North Africa the belief that together they might not only free themselves of Western dominance, but even achieve political and economic parity. From Algeria to Iraq and Yemen, Nasser was a bona fide hero.

But all real attempts at any kind of political union failed and the brave new Egypt came crashing down on 5 June 1967 when Israel wiped out the Egyptian air force in a surprise attack. With it went the confidence and credibility of Nasser. He never recovered and died of heart failure three years later.

the newly created United Nations (UN). The UN voted to partition Palestine, but this was rejected by the Arabs. Britain pulled out and the very next day the Jews declared the founding of the state of Israel. War broke out immediately, with Egypt, Jordan and Syria weighing in on the side of the Palestinian Arabs.

The disastrous performance of the combined Arab armies in the 1948 Arab-Israeli War had far-reaching consequences. Recriminations over the humiliating defeat and the refugee problem it created laid the groundwork for the 1951 assassination of King Abdullah of Jordan. Syria, which had gained independence from France in 1946, became the field for a seemingly endless series of military coups in which disputes over how to handle the Palestine problem often played a large part. In Egypt the army blamed the loss on the country's corrupt and ineffective politicians. In July 1952 a group of young officers toppled the monarchy. Initially an aged and respected army general was installed as the country's president, but it soon emerged that the real power lay with one of the coup plotters: Gamal Abdel Nasser (see the boxed text). By 1954 he was the country's acknowledged leader. After facing down the combined powers of Israel, Britain and France over the Suez Crisis of 1956, Nasser also emerged as the pre-eminent figure in the Arab world and a central player in the politics of nationalism, socialism and decolonisation that gripped much of the developing world throughout the 1950s and '60s.

The Arab-Israeli Wars

Arab opposition to the creation of the state of Israel again came to a head (helped along by Nasser's fiery speeches) in 1967. In May of that year the Egyptian army moved into key points in the Sinai and announced a blockade of the Straits of Tiran, effectively closing the southern Israeli port of Eilat. The Egyptian army was mobilised and the country put on a war footing.

Israel responded on 5 June 1967 with a pre-emptive strike that wiped out virtually the entire Egyptian air force. The war lasted only six days (hence the 'Six Day War'), and when it was over Israel controlled all of the Sinai Peninsula and the Gaza Strip. The West Bank, including Jerusalem's Old City, had been seized from Jordan and the Golan Heights from Syria.

The year 1970 saw the ascension of new leaders in both Egypt (Anwar Sadat) and Syria (Hafez al-Assad). The decade also began with the last remnants of colonial rule departing from the Middle East when the British, in late 1971, pulled out of the Gulf.

Preparations were also well under way for the next Middle Eastern war. The Arab states were constantly under pressure from their citizens to reclaim the land lost in 1967. The war began on 6 October 1973, when Egyptian troops crossed the Suez Canal, taking Israel (at a standstill, observing the holy day of Yom Kippur) almost entirely by surprise. After advancing a short distance into Sinai, however, the Egyptian army stopped, giving Israel the opportunity to concentrate its forces against the Syrians on the Golan Heights and then to turn back towards Egypt.

When the war ended in late 1973 the Israelis actually occupied more land than they had when it began. Months of shuttle diplomacy by the US secretary of state, Henry Kissinger, followed. Pressure on the USA to broker a deal was fuelled when the Gulf States embargoed oil supplies to the West 10 days after the war began. The embargo was relatively short-lived but if the goal was to get the West's attention, it succeeded.

The embargo also led to a huge, and permanent, increase in the price of oil, which in turn led to a flood of money landing in the laps of the Gulf sheikhs. An enormous building boom began throughout the Gulf, and free-spending Arabs started to become a fixture in the West.

All of this shifted the balance of power in the Middle East. The oil states, rich but underpopulated and militarily weak, gained at the expense of poorer, more populous countries. Huge shifts of population followed the two oil booms of the 1970s as millions of Egyptians, Syrians, Jordanians, Palestinians and Yemenis went off to seek their fortunes in the oil states – including Iraq where, in the late 1980s, over a million Egyptians alone were working.

Peace & Revolution

Anwar Sadat's dramatic visit to Jerusalem in 1977 opened the way for an Egyptian-Israeli peace process which culminated, in March 1979, with the signing of a peace treaty between the two countries at Camp David in the USA. In response, Arab leaders meeting in Baghdad voted to expel Egypt from the Arab League.

Meanwhile, one of the few friends Sadat had left in the region had troubles of his own. Discontent with the Shāh of Iran's autocratic rule and his personal disregard for the country's Shiite Muslim religious traditions had been simmering for years. Political violence slowly increased throughout 1978. The turning point came in September of that year, when Iranian police fired on anti-*shāh* demonstrators in Tehrān, killing at least 300. The momentum of the protests quickly became unstoppable.

On 16 January 1979 the *shāh* left Iran, never to return (he died in Egypt in 1980 and is buried in Cairo). The interim government

set up after his departure was swept aside the following month when the revolution's leader, the hitherto obscure Āyatollāh Ruhollāh Khomeini, returned to Tehrān from his exile in France. (For more on Khomeini and the Islamic Revolution, see the Iran chapter.)

After the Revolution

Iran's Islamic Revolution seemed to change everything in the Middle East, ushering in a period of instability that lasted until nearly the end of the 1980s.

In 1979 militants seized the Grand Mosque in Mecca – Islam's holiest site – and were only ejected several weeks later after bloody gun battles inside the mosque itself. In November of that year student militants in Tehrān overran the US embassy, taking the staff hostage. In 1980 Turkey's government was overthrown in a military coup, capping weeks of violence between left- and right-wing extremists. Further east, Iraq invaded Iran, launching what would become the longest, bloodiest and, arguably, most pointless war in modern history.

Tensions were further cranked up in 1981 when President Sadat of Egypt was assassinated by Muslim militants. The following year Israel invaded Lebanon, further contributing to the cycle of chaos and destruction that had gripped that country since 1975. In 1986 clashes between the USA and Libya came to a head with the American air strikes on Tripoli, while the following year saw an escalation in violence in Israel & the Palestinian Territories with the beginning of the *intifada* (the grass-roots Palestinian uprising).

There were the occasional bright spots. Turkey returned to democratic rule in 1983, albeit with a new constitution barring from public office anyone who had been involved in politics prior to the 1980 coup. In 1985 the Israelis withdrew from most of Lebanon. In 1988 Iran and Iraq grudgingly agreed to a cease-fire. The following year Egypt was readmitted to the Arab League and Jordan held its first elections in more than 20 years.

Moves Towards Peace

In August 1990, Iraq invaded Kuwait. A nervous King Fahd of Saudi Arabia requested help from the USA. The result was a US-led coalition that, under the operational moniker 'Desert Storm', engaged in a six-week bombing campaign and a four-day ground offensive that drove Iraq out of Kuwait. (See History in the Kuwait chapter for more details.) In the process Iraqi president Saddam Hussein (previously supported by the West in his war against Iran) became world public enemy number one.

While attempting to solicit Arab support for the anti-Iraq coalition, then-US president, George Bush, had promised to make a new effort to achieve Arab-Israeli peace once the Iraqis were out of Kuwait. This took the form of endless shuttling between Middle Eastern capitals culminating in a US-sponsored peace conference in Madrid in October 1991. It achieved little, and two years of further negotiations seemed similarly fruitless until in the late summer of 1993 it was revealed that Israel and the Palestinians had been holding secret talks in Norway for 18 months. The 'Oslo Accord' was cemented with a handshake between Yasser Arafat and Israeli prime minister Yitzhak Rabin on the White House lawn in September 1993.

A new era of hope for peace in the Middle East seemed on the horizon. Lebanon had just held its first democratic elections for 20 years and the internecine fighting seemed at an end. In 1994 Jordan became the second Arab country to sign a formal peace treaty with Israel. At the same time Egypt seemed to have succeeded in putting a lid on the terrorist activity of Islamic extremists that had been plaguing the country since the assassination of Sadat more than a decade previously.

The Middle East Today

Tragically, the nascent Arab-Israeli peace process was derailed by the November 1995 assassination of Rabin and the subsequent election to power of hardline candidate Binyamin Netanyahu. A blip of hope re-emerged when Netanyahu lost office to Ehud Barak, a prime minister who expressed willingness to pull his troops out of occupied South Lebanon, to talk with the Syrians on the issue of occupied Golan, and to reopen negotiations with the Palestinians. Although the first of these things happened, Barak was unable to curtail the violence closer to home. He was unseated by a vicious campaign of Palestinian bombing, and in his place Israel elected the frightening figure of Ariel Sharon. Since Sharon became prime minister the violence has escalated into what is vir-

tually all-out warfare in the Gaza Strip and West Bank paired with endless bloody suicide attacks on Israeli population centres.

The events ongoing in Israel & the Palestinian Territories dominate the current Middle Eastern scene. But away from the horror the story is considerably more upbeat. In recent years both Jordan and Syria have gained new young leaders, educated in the West and who are already displaying a reformist bent – and it can't be long before Egypt's President Mubarak, in power since 1981 and now in his 70s, is succeeded by a more youthful figure. It's unlikely that Yasser Arafat or Saddam Hussein will be with us much longer, either. Turkey is looking to tie its fortunes to those of the West, actively pursuing membership of the European Union.

The indications are that there is a sea change ahead for the region. That said, in a neighbourhood as traditionally volatile as this, it's impossible to predict what the coming years will bring. But, considering that only three of the 16 countries in this book existed as independent entities at the start of the 20th century, one has to make a few allowances for growing pains.

GEOGRAPHY

The Middle East is a somewhat vaguely defined area where the three continents of the Old World meet. The region could essentially be defined as southwest Asia, but because present international borders and age-old cultural exchanges draw Turkey and Egypt into the picture, Europe and Africa are also included.

The core of the Middle East consists of the Arabian Peninsula and the Levant, but the region can be said to extend north to the natural boundaries of the Black and Caspian seas and the Caucasus Mountains.

On hearing the term Middle East, many people immediately visualise sand dunes, but the reality is that sand deserts form only a tiny percentage of the whole area – mainly in Egypt, Oman and Saudi Arabia. Mountains and high plateaus abound in many countries: in Turkey, Iran and Yemen much of the area rises above 1000m. The highest mountains in the Middle East include the 5671m-high Mt Damāvand in Iran, the 5137m-high Ağrı Dağı (Mt Ararat) in Turkey and the 3660m-high Jebel an-Nabi Shu'ayb in Yemen.

The biggest rivers in the area include the Nile, bringing African waters through Egypt, and the Euphrates and Tigris, flowing from the Anatolian highlands through Syria and Iraq to the Gulf. Otherwise, with the exception of those in Turkey and northwest Iran, rivers flowing all year round and reaching the sea are a rarity in the region, due to the arid climate.

CLIMATE

This section gives an overview of the Middle East's climatic pattern and characteristics. Of course, within a region as vast as this there are considerable variations and these are discussed in the individual country chapters. More details on how the climate affects travel are given under When to Go in the Regional Facts for the Visitor chapter.

Temperatures & Humidity

Temperatures vary wildly depending on the time of year and location. The low-lying coast lands of the Red Sea, Arabian Sea and the Gulf are hot in the extreme throughout the year, with humidity continuously exceeding 70%. Expect daytime temperatures between 40° and 50°C during the summer, and way above 30°C in the winter, with nights not much cooler. Along the southern coasts of the Black and Caspian Seas the mild climate resembles that of Central Europe.

On the other hand, temperatures drop consistently as altitude increases. The rule of thumb is that for every 100m of ascent the temperature drops by 0.5° to 0.7°C: many high plateaus are quite hot during the summer days but still freezing cold at night.

Mountains with snow caps are to be seen in Turkey, Iran and even as far south as Lebanon and northern Israel. Winters are regularly snowy in the nonarid highlands of Turkey and Iran, and in the coldest winters it can snow in the highest spots of the Hajar Mountains in northern Oman and as far south as the mountains of Yemen.

Rainfall

Most of the Middle East is arid or semi-arid, including the greater part of the Arabian Peninsula and Egypt, and most of Jordan, Iraq and Iran. In many regions annual rainfall hardly reaches 100mm. Most of Egypt, southeast Saudi Arabia and western Oman are extremely arid, with years often passing

without rain. Dasht-e Kavir, or the Great Salt Desert of Iran, is the largest area in the world with absolutely no vegetation. However, mountain ridges and two separate moist climate systems guarantee that considerable variation occurs within most of the countries.

The coastal areas of Turkey, Syria and Lebanon all get an ample amount of rain from the Mediterranean climatic system. So do northeast Iraq and northwest Iran, where a narrow slip of this type of climate extends from the Black Sea, along the western Zāgros Mountains, all the way to Khuzestān and beyond, bringing cyclonic rains in winter. Annual rainfall can reach 600mm in some areas, while in others it can even go up to 2000mm. Further south there tends to be less rain, although southernmost Arabia and, occasionally, southeast Iran are affected by the Indian monsoon system.

ECOLOGY & ENVIRONMENT

When it comes to the environment the Middle East has an ever-increasing litany of woes. Perhaps the single biggest problem is the lack of water. Resources throughout the region are either stretched to their capacity or beyond it. In Jordan, for example, a very visible result of diminishing water resources is the virtual disappearance of the Azraq oasis in the east of the country, and all the wildlife that went with it. It is estimated that 20 species of fauna have disappeared from the country in the last two decades or so, and even more are threatened with extinction. Much of Iran was gripped by drought in 2000–2001. Saudi Arabia will run out of ground water long before it runs out of oil. Bahrain's freshwater underground springs have already dried up leaving the country to rely on expensive desalinated water.

It's a problem that has great political ramifications: Syria and Iraq have protested to Turkey over that country's building of dams at the headwaters of the Tigris and Euphrates Rivers, while Egypt has threatened military action against Sudan or any other upstream country that endangers its access to the waters of the Nile. Demand far exceeds supply, and wastage on the land and in the cities exacerbates the situation. Experts often predict that the next big Middle Eastern conflict will be triggered not by rival land claims but over water rights.

Beyond the water shortage problem, ecological and environmental issues relevant to the Middle East are similar to those elsewhere in the world. Air pollution (already critical in Cairo and Tehrān), water pollution, deforestation, soil erosion, habitat and wildlife destruction, and conservation of natural resources are all becoming increasingly pertinent.

When discussing environmental matters there is often a danger of over-simplification. It is easy to regard the issues in isolation when, in fact, they are all inter-related and linked to wider economic, social and political situations on a national, regional and global scale.

For example, in countries such as Yemen and Egypt, an ever-increasing human population puts great demands on the land and other natural resources. One of the ways of combating this is to lower the rate of population growth. However, to suggest that the solution simply involves contraception or a change in cultural attitudes represents a narrow view. Conservationists who prefer a broad perspective point out that the rapid population growth is closely linked to poor living conditions, which in turn is linked to social issues such as lack of education and healthcare. They argue that it is not reasonable to expect people with little money or food to worry about conservation in its widest sense; the root of the problem – poverty – desperately needs to be addressed.

However, in this respect the Middle East straddles the environmental dilemma. Israel, which is by no means a poor country, has been damned by criticism from Greenpeace for fouling the Jordan River with industrial sewage. This came on the heels of a 1997 disaster when a bridge over the polluted Yarkon River collapsed during an international sporting event and two of the fatalities occurred as a result of the athletes swallowing the toxic water.

There are bright spots. The UN Environmental Programme has singled out Oman as a country with exemplary conservation measures; it was the first Arab country to set up a ministry exclusively concerned with the environment, and every year on 8 January the sultanate celebrates 'Environment Day'. Other Middle Eastern nations are slowly following suit. In recent years Egypt has appointed a minister of the environment and

begun investing money in protectorates, while in the UAE the fight against desertification has resulted in much 'greening' of the region. The UAE, along with Israel, Jordan, Oman and Qatar, also has active breeding programmes for endangered species (see the Flora and Fauna sections later in this chapter). See also the boxed text on Kuwait's Japanese Garden in the Kuwait chapter.

Tourism & the Environment

As one of the Middle East's largest industries, tourism itself is a major environmental issue. **Greenpeace Mediterranean** (✆ *961 1 785 665;* **e** *supporters@greenpeace.org.lb; PO Box 13-6590, 1102 2140, Beirut)* considers tourism to be one of the major causes of coastal destruction in Lebanon, and that's certainly the case in Egypt and Turkey. It cites the dozens of yacht ports, 'land reclamation' projects and hotels that have been established illegally along the coast.

Problems also arise when destinations cannot cope with the number of tourists they attract, so that natural and social environments quickly become damaged. The prime example of this is the Red Sea coral reefs, which are under enormous threat from irresponsible tourism and opportunistic development. Also, sites such as Petra are now having to consider limiting the number of visitors to lessen the human wear and tear on the monuments and surrounding landscape.

The gradual erosion of traditional life as a result of mass tourism is also a problem. Sexual promiscuity, public drunkenness among tourists and the wearing of unsuitable clothing are all of concern. For information on how to reduce your environmental impact, see Responsible Tourism in the Regional Facts for the Visitor chapter.

FLORA

Not surprisingly, Middle Eastern flora tends to be at its lushest and most varied in the north, where the climate is less arid. That said, after millennia of woodcutting much of Turkey and Syria is now largely denuded. Only the Mediterranean coast west of Antalya, the Black Sea area and northeast Anatolia still have forests of considerable size. Yew, lime and fir trees predominate in areas where vegetation has not been reduced to scrub. The Iranian landscape is far more pristine and large areas – especially the Alborz

Mountains region – remain densely forested with broad-leaved deciduous trees.

In Lebanon, the Horsh Ehden Forest Nature Reserve is the last archetype of the ancient natural forests of Lebanon and is home to several species of rare orchids and other flowering plants. The cedars which Lebanon is famous for are now confined to a few mountain-top sites, most notably at Bcharré and near Barouk in the Chouf Mountains.

The forests of the north give way to the cultivated slopes of the Jordan Valley where cedar, olives and eucalyptus are dominant.

South towards the Dead Sea the vegetation gives way to mud and salt flats. South and west of the Dead Sea the only other spread of greenery is Egypt's Nile Delta, a fertile agricultural region.

Although much of the Arabian Peninsula is desert, the varied terrain of the UAE and Oman (the latter with plentiful fertile wadis irrigated by spring water) makes for an equally wide variety of plants. In the UAE, outside of the mountain areas, much of the vegetation you are likely to see is, in fact, not indigenous but rather part of the local government's 'greenery' programme. Even in the Buraimi oasis natural groves of date palms have been supplemented by hectares of grass and trees planted in municipal parks.

FAUNA

Due to its position at the junction of three natural zones, the Middle East was once a sanctuary for an amazing variety of larger mammals, including leopard, cheetah, oryx (see the boxed text 'Saving the Arabian Oryx'), aardwolf, striped hyena and caracal. Crocodile used to inhabit the Nile River, and lions roamed the Iran of old. Unfortunately, all of these are either now extinct in the region or on the brink of extinction due to intense hunting and the spread of human settlement. These days you'll be lucky to see any mammals other than domesticated camel, donkey and water buffalo, although in Sinai and the southern desert regions of Israel there are ibex, gazelle and rock hyrax. In Saudi Arabia colonies of wild baboons inhabit the highlands of Asir province.

Turkey and Iran have similar animal life to that in the Balkans and much of Europe (including bear, deer, jackal, lynx, wild boar and wolf). In the hotter, southern

Saving the Arabian Oryx

The Arabian oryx is a herbivore. Adapted well to its natural desert environment, the oryx is said to have an uncanny ability to sense rain on the wind. One herd is recorded as having travelled up to 155km, led by a dominant female, to rain. In times of drought, oryx have been known to survive 22 months without water, obtaining moisture from plants and leaves. The animal's white coat offers camouflage in the searing heat of the desert, but it's a pelt that has also been traditionally highly prized by hunters, as have its long curved horns. So the last time oryx was seen in the wild in Jordan was in 1920 when hunting drove the animal to extinction. In 1972, the Arabian oryx was declared extinct in the wild anywhere in the world.

The nine lonely oryx left in captivity were pooled and taken to the Arizona Zoo for a breeding programme. They became known as the 'World Oryx Herd'. In 1978, four male and four female oryx were transported to Jordan, and three more were sent from Qatar the following year. In 1979, the first calf, Dusha, was born and Jordan's oryx began along a precarious road to recovery. By 1983, there were 31 oryx and they were released into large enclosures at the Shaumari Wildlife Reserve. Similar breeding programmes are ongoing elsewhere in the region, including in Oman and, fittingly, in Qatar where the oryx is the national emblem.

In a significant landmark for environmentalists the world over, but especially in Jordan, five oryx were reintroduced into the wild in the Wadi Rum Protected Area in July 2002 – a small, tentative step in what is hoped will be the start of the recovery of the wild oryx in Jordan and the Middle East.

ANN JEFREE

regions of the Middle East the only largish mammals likely to be seen are ibex, a member of the goat family.

Desert regions are full of small rodents such as the desert fox, sand rat, hare and jerboa, but most of these are nocturnal. You may well spot lizards, possibly scorpions and the occasional snake, although these rarely present a problem – just check your shoes or any clothing that has been on the ground before you get dressed.

National Parks & Wildlife Reserves

Your best chance of spotting something lies in visiting a reserve, although in the Middle East these are few and far between. It's possible to see gazelle and oryx, once common features of the desert landscape, at the Shaumari Wildlife Reserve in the east of Jordan.

In Lebanon there are about 30 different species of mammal at the **Al-Chouf Cedar Reserve** (☎/fax 05-503 230; e carzshouf@cy beria.net.lb), including the mountain gazelle, striped hyena, lynx and hyrax. One of the best Israeli reserves to visit for wildlife is Ein Gedi on the shores of the Dead Sea. In Bahrain the uninhabited Hawar Islands are an important breeding ground for migratory birds, and the surrounding waters are rich with marine life such as dugong and turtles; local tour operators can organise visits – see the Bahrain chapter for further information.

Birds

In contrast to the region's lack of any high-profile wildlife, the variety of bird life is exceptionally rich. As well as indigenous species, the Middle East serves as a pit stop on migration routes between Asia, Europe and Africa. Israel claims to be the world's second largest fly way (after South America) for migratory birds and the **Society for the Protection of the Nature of Israel** (SPNI; ☎ 03-638 8677, fax 688 3940; e tourism@ spni.org.il) has an excellent map and guide, *The Bird Trails of Israel*, detailing 14 bird-watching centres. Egypt's Sinai Peninsula and Al-Fayoum Oasis, Wadi Araba in Jordan and the tidal wetlands around Dubai (ie, the Khor Wildlife Sanctuary) also receive an enormous and varied amount of ornithological traffic – both Egypt (visit W www .birdingegypt.com) and Dubai have recorded sightings of over 400 different species.

Contact the following organisations for more information:

Israel International Birdwatching Centre (☎ 08-6335319, fax 08-637 6922) PO Box 774, Eilat 88106, Israel
Oman Bird Records Committee PO Box 246, Muscat, Oman
UAE Emirates Bird Records Committee (☎ 9714-472 277, fax 472 276) PO Box 50394, Dubai, UAE
Yemen Ornathological Society (☎ 01-207 059, e cyos@y.net.ye) San'a, Yemen

Marine Life

The Red and Arabian Seas, as well as the Gulf, are teeming with an amazing spectacle of colour and form. Reef sharks, stingrays, turtles, dolphins, colourful corals, sponges, sea cucumbers and a multitude of molluscs all thrive in these waters.

Coral is what makes a reef and, although thought for many centuries to be some form of flowering plant, it is in fact an animal. Both hard and soft corals exist, their common denominator being that they are made up of polyps – tiny cylinders ringed by waving tentacles that sting their prey and draw it into the stomach.

During the day corals retract into their tube and only at night do they display their real colours.

There are about a thousand fish species in the Red Sea, many of them are endemic. Most of them closely associated with the coral reef, and live and breed in the reefs or nearby beds of seagrass. These include grouper, wrasse, parrotfish and snapper. Others, such as shark and barracuda, live in open waters and usually only venture into the reefs to feed or breed.

When snorkelling or diving, the sharks you are most likely to encounter include white or black-tipped reef sharks. Tiger sharks, and the huge, plankton-eating whale sharks, are generally found in deeper waters only. No divers or snorkellers have ever been killed by sharks in the Red Sea and there are no sea snakes here.

Green turtles are a world famous attraction of the Arabian Sea. Oman has one of the largest nesting sites at Ras al-Jinz (see the Oman chapter). The green is just one of five endangered species supported by the coasts of Oman; all species are protected by royal decree.

GOVERNMENT & POLITICS

Leaving aside the non-Arab nations of Israel, Turkey (the only two countries in the region that even come close to being democratic) and the widely unloved Iran, the countries of the Middle East are still far from being a homogeneous bunch. Territorial disputes and rival claims on water rights, as well as ideological clashes, not to mention the wedges driven in by external influences, have all combined to ensure that the postcolonial notion of a powerful Pan-Arab union has rarely ever looked like becoming a reality.

The Pan-Arab dream has its origins in 1945 with the convening of the Arab League of Nations, which brought together in a proposed political and economic union the seven independent Arab states of the time (Egypt, Lebanon, Transjordan, Syria, Iraq, Saudi Arabia and Yemen). Although the league has since swollen to 21 members, the unified front that the organisation aimed to present has constantly been undermined by internal dissension to the extent that the whole idea of a political merging of the Arab world has been completely discredited.

In 1979 Egypt, home of the Arab League, was ostracised from the organisation after signing a peace treaty with Israel at Camp David. Its respectability has since been restored, but the downgraded Egypt now vies for the mantel of regional superpower with Jordan and Syria. Relations between the three, especially Jordan and Syria, have traditionally been, at best, lukewarm, although there has been improvement with young blood acceding to power in both countries.

Ranks were split by Iraq's invasion of Kuwait. During the bloody war against Iran, Iraq had enjoyed the support of most of the Middle East's Arab nations (Syria alone has good relations with the Persian mullahs), but Saddam Hussein found himself out of sympathy when he committed his act of aggression against a fellow Muslim Arab state. Only Jordan, Yemen and the Palestinians abstained from joining the US-led Desert Storm coalition during the Gulf War.

The 1991 Desert Storm affair also served to illustrate just how large an influence the oil-producing Gulf States had acquired in the politics of the region. Had the super-rich Saudi Arabia not itself felt threatened by Saddam and made an appeal for help, it is unlikely that the USA would have moved to directly intervene. And without coercion from the White House, it is also almost certain a country like Egypt would have remained inactive: many of the region's poorer nations still resent the Gulf States for their perceived failure to share around the dividends of their oil wealth.

ECONOMY

The Middle East is an area of great economic disparity. At one end are those citizens of the Gulf States – notably Kuwait and the UAE – who have per capita incomes comparable to those of citizens in the richest Western countries. At the other end of the spectrum lies Yemen, by almost any measure one of the poorest countries on earth.

Two industries dominate the economic life of most of the countries covered by this book: oil and tourism. This is something of an oversimplification, but while there are exceptions to the rule (agriculture, for example, remains a key sector of the economy in many countries), oil and tourism are the Middle East's main sources of income.

The Middle Eastern oil industry got its start in Persia (present-day Iran), where oil was found in commercial quantities in 1908. The next major strikes were in the Kurdish region of northern Iraq in 1927 and in Bahrain in 1932. By the time WWII broke out in Europe, the Middle East in general, and the Gulf in particular, was known to contain some of the richest oil fields on earth.

Today, oil is the economic mainstay of Iran, Iraq and all the Gulf States. It is also an important source of income for Egypt, Syria and Yemen. Many of the region's countries that do not possess oil remain indirectly dependent on it in the form of remittances sent home by nationals working in the oil states.

The only countries that have neither oil of their own in significant quantities nor large numbers of their citizens working in the oil states are Israel, Lebanon and Turkey. In the case of Israel, decades of political isolation have led the Jewish state to look beyond the Middle East for its economic strategies, and the country has developed a variety of industries such as chemicals, plastics, electronic equipment, military technology and computers.

Lebanon's once-thriving economy, traditionally based on free trade, banking and service industries, is slowly being rebuilt after it was thrown into turmoil by 17 years of fighting, but it's still struggling, with about 50% of the national budget being spent on debt servicing. Lebanon's major source of income is remittances from nationals abroad, which accounts for an extraordinary 25% of the GDP, with agriculture and industry other significant contributors.

Turkey has traditionally relied on agriculture (it's a net exporter of food and the biggest wool producer in Europe). However, manufacturing and services have now come to dominate the economy. In this respect Turkey has provided something of a model for other Middle Eastern states such as Egypt and Jordan, which have long been struggling to reform and modernise their ageing industrial bases. Both are at last starting to make some headway, largely by opening up former big state monopolies to privatisation. The same process is also going on in Syria, though there the shackles are coming off at a much slower rate.

Turkey also benefits more than most from the very lucrative tourism industry that annually brings billions into the region. Its government, along with those of Egypt and Israel, has worked hard to convert the country's natural beauty and vast wealth of religious and archaeological treasures into cash in the bank. And while Saudi Arabia may forbid tourism and Iran and Iraq make little effort to attract foreign visitors, most countries in the region have caught on. Tourism is a rapidly growing industry in Jordan, Syria, Yemen, Bahrain, Oman and the UAE.

Tourism, however, is an uncertain source of income. The Gulf War destroyed the 1990–91 tourist season throughout the region, a double whammy of high-profile terrorist attacks crippled Egypt in 1997, and at the time of writing tourism is down again all throughout the region as a result of the fallout from 11 September combined with the ongoing cycle of violence in Israel & the Palestinian Territories.

The region's political troubles also negatively impact upon national economies in the form of military spending. In Israel and Syria severe strain is placed on the economy by defence spending, which in each case swallows up over 50% of the national budget. Iran, Iraq and Egypt also spend well beyond their means on military resources, in the case of the latter as a result of an en-

trenched military elite that objects to any attempt to scale back its privileges, even though regional tensions have eased.

It's often said that the Middle East is potentially one of the richest regions of the world, but it's unlikely that its potential wealth will ever be fully realised in the present turbulent political climate.

POPULATION & PEOPLE

The most populous countries in the Middle East are Iran (approximately 75 million), Turkey (approximately 68 million) then Egypt (approximately 61.5 million). The combined population of the remaining countries is around 100 million; the smallest – Bahrain and Qatar – have less than three-quarters of a million each.

The people of the Middle East are descendants of those who built many ancient civilisations. While the Turks and Persians (Iranians) are distinctive groups with their own countries, customs and languages, for Arabs the picture is less clear.

Arabs

The question of who the Arabs are exactly is still widely debated. Are they all the people speaking Arabic, or only the residents of the Arabian Peninsula? Fourteen centuries ago, only the nomadic tribes wandering between the Euphrates River and the central Arabian Peninsula were considered Arabs, distinguished by their language. However, with the rapid expansion of Islam, the language of the Quran spread to vast areas.

Although the Arabs were relatively few in number in most of the countries they conquered, their culture quickly became established through language and intermarriage. The term 'Arab' came to apply to two groups: in addition to the original nomadic Arabs, the settled inhabitants of these newly conquered provinces also became known as Arabs.

In the 20th century rising Arab nationalism legitimised the current blanket usage of the term to apply to all the peoples of Middle East – except the Persians and Turks. That said, many Egyptians bridle at the label as it conflicts with claims to a Pharaonic heritage.

Bedouin The most romanticised group of Arabs is no doubt the Bedouin (also called Bedu). While not an ethnic group, they are

Ponder times past at some of the region's spellbinding highlights: lounging at the Pyramids, Egypt (top); an ancient arch frames the library at Ephesus, Turkey (middle left); sensuous reflections at Emām Khomeini Mosque, Esfahān, Iran (middle right); and the sun-burnished Urn Tomb, Petra, Jordan (bottom).

Unsurpassed friendliness and generosity make travel in the Middle East special. From the traditional cloth vendor in Iran (top) and the drinks seller in Lebanon (bottom left), to the purveyor of tea and snacks in Iraq (bottom right), the people of the region are open and welcoming.

An Arab from Cairo dressed in a turban and the full-length robe known as a *jalabiyya*

the archetypal Arabs – the camel-herding nomads who travel all over the deserts and semideserts in search of food for their cattle. From among their ranks came the warriors who spread Islam to North Africa and Persia 14 centuries ago.

Today, Bedouin are found mainly in Jordan, Iraq, Saudi Arabia, Yemen, Egypt's Sinai Peninsula and in the Wahiba Sands in Oman, as well as settled in Kuwait and Qatar. Their numbers are unknown due to their habit of wandering in regions where no census-takers venture.

While some have settled down to enjoy the facilities of modern life, many maintain semitraditional lifestyles. Their customs derive from the days of early Islam, and the hospitality towards strangers that Arabs are so famous for (and proud of) certainly takes its most genuine forms among the Bedouin.

For more information see the boxed text 'The Bedouin' in the Jordan chapter.

Persians

Persians are descendants of the Elamite and Aryan races (from southern Russia) who first settled in the central plateau of what is now Iran in the 2nd century BC. The Persians, or Farsis, retained their own language even though they were among the first to adopt the new religion of Islam and welcomed the Arabic script for writing Persian. Although Iran is the home of the Persian people, a significant percentage of the population south of the Gulf in Bahrain, Oman and Qatar is also of Persian descent.

Turks

The Turkish peoples originated in Central Asia where they ruled several empires before being pushed westwards by the Mongols. At first they were shamanist nomads, but at one time or another these early Turks followed each of the great religions of the region including Buddhism, Nestorian Christianity and Judaism. During their western migrations they became familiar with Islam and it stuck. The Turks kept their own language even after conversion. During the 600-year Ottoman Empire, when Turks ruled most of the Middle East, they became known as Shimaliyya (Northerners) throughout the Arab world.

Kurds

The Kurds are spread across a large area of the Middle East, including a good part of eastern Turkey (with a Kurdish population of maybe 12 million), Iran, northeastern Iraq and Syria. Although they have been around longer than any other people in the region (since at least the 2nd millennium BC), the Kurds have never had a nation of their own. For more information on the Kurds see the boxed text 'The Kurds' in the Iraq chapter.

Druze

The Druze have no homeland or language of their own and their nation, such as it is, is defined by their religion, an off-shoot of Islam. Like Muslims, the Druze believe in Allah and his prophets but they believe that Mohammed was succeeded by a further divine messenger, Al-Darazi – from whose name the term Druze is derived. The Druze also hold the non-Islamic belief of reincarnation.

Most of the Druze nation lives in Lebanon and Syria and a few villages in the Galilee and Golan regions of Israel & the Palestinian Territories. Having never had a state of their own the Druze tend to give allegiance to whatever country they live in.

Jews

The most high-profile non-Arab ethnic group in the Middle East, is of course the Jewish people. Following their exile from Jerusalem at the hands of the Romans, the Jews spread far and wide, many settling in neighbouring countries. Until the middle of the 20th century and the creation of the Jewish home-state, Egypt, Syria, Iran and Iraq were all home to significant Jewish populations. For more background on the Jewish people in the Middle East see the Israel & the Palestinian Territories chapter.

Armenians & Others

Armenians, like Kurds, form a small group badly treated by history. They have lived in eastern Anatolia for millennia, almost always as subjects of some greater state such as the Byzantines, Persians, Seljuks or Ottomans. In the early 20th century the Orthodox Christian Armenian minority made the error of siding with the Russians against the Muslim Turk majority. The Armenians were massacred; hundreds of thousands died and they were almost wiped out in Turkey. Elsewhere in the Middle East there are significant Armenian communities in Syria, Iran and Israel.

At its southernmost fringes, the Middle East also includes African peoples. Most notable of these are the Nubians, the dark-skinned people of Nubia, the region between Aswan in the south of Egypt and Khartoum in Sudan, which was known in ancient times as Kush. Since the drowning of their homelands caused by the creation of Egypt's High Dam, many Nubians have migrated north to the cities of Cairo and Alexandria in search of a livelihood.

A sizable number of Swahili-speaking Africans have also been integrated into the Omani population, originally through slavery and then through colonisation, particularly of Zanzibar and other East African trading ports

See also the boxed text 'Expatriates' in the UAE chapter for a discussion of the region's guest workers.

ARTS
Architecture

Architecture in the Middle East begins with the egotistical monoliths raised to the glory of Egypt's pharaohs and comes bang up to date with the soaring hi-tech wonder of Dubai's Burj al-Arab, a modern-day monument to all that money can buy.

It's in the Middle East that you see the first transitions from the classical column-and-lintel way of building (employed by the Ancient Egyptians, Greeks and Romans) to a more fluid architecture based on arches, vaults and domes. This new style of construction, facilitated by the supplanting of stone with the smaller and far more malleable unit of the brick, developed under the Byzantines based in Constantinople. Their legacy is best illustrated by Justinian's great cathedral of Aya Sofya in İstanbul, and a scattering of more modest structures dotted throughout Syria, most notably the 5th-century Qala'at Samaan north of Aleppo.

Byzantine forms carried through into the early Islamic period, and some of the earliest Muslim monuments (the Dome of the Rock in Jerusalem, the Umayyad Mosque in Damascus) owe their form to eastern Christianity. Over time, Islam developed its own building vocabulary (for more information see the special section 'Mosques' later in this chapter). An egalitarian religion, its mosques simply required a single, large, open space with as little clutter as possible. A domed central chamber proved to be the best way of achieving this. Slender minarets provided a platform for the daily call to prayer.

In addition a subsidiary set of buildings evolved including the Quranic school (madrassa), monastery (khanqah), fountain (sabil), mausoleum (turba) and public bathhouse (hammam).

The Middle East's medieval architectural glory – the accumulated great mosques, palaces and old quarters – is one of the region's greatest draws (best seen in the old cities of Aleppo, Cairo, Damascus and Jerusalem) but tragically, for the most part, the peak was as early as the 16th or 17th century. By this time the finest structures were built, including the Turkish architect Sinan's great masterpieces in Edirne and İstanbul and the shimmering complexes of Esfahān.

From the 17th century, as the political clout of the Ottomans – overlords of much of the Middle East – declined, so their buildings became more modest. European influence also began to make itself felt. Europe had undergone a flirtation with baroque, so

[Continued on page 40]

MUSIC OF THE MIDDLE EAST

In most countries of the Middle East music is all pervasive. Egypt, Lebanon, Syria, Jordan, the Arabs of the Palestinian Territories – these are not societies that recognise the concept of personal space. You will be bombarded with tinny pop blasted out of shop doorways or from street traders' cassette decks, thumping from the interiors of passing cars, or wafting down from the balconies of apartment blocks. In taxis it's not uncommon to have to ask the driver to turn the music down.

As in the West, the diversity of music is huge and it's impossible to do it justice in such a brief space, and although we make the division here into three broad musical types – Arabic classical, pop and traditional music – there are many, many artists who fail to fit neatly under any of these headings or conversely crossover into all three.

Arabic Classical

Tonality and instrumentation aside, classical Arabic music differs from that of the West in one big respect: in the Middle East the orchestra is always there primarily to back the singer.

The all-time voice of classical Arabic music is Egyptian-born songstress Umm Kolthum, who was at her peak in the 1940s and '50s but whose voice remains ubiquitous on radios and cassette decks throughout the Middle East today (see the boxed text 'Umm Kolthum' in this special section).

The kind of orchestra that backs such a singer is a curious cross-fertilisation of East and West. Western-style instruments, such as violins and many of the wind and percussion instruments predominate, next to such local species as the oud and tabla – see the illustrations. The sounds that emanate from them are anything but Western. There is all the mellifluous seduction of Asia in the

Umm Kolthum

From the 1940s through into the '70s, the voice of Umm Kolthum was the voice of the Arab world. To the uninitiated she can sound incredibly rough and raucous, but her protracted love songs and *qasa'id* (long poems) were the very expression of the Arab world's collective identity. Egypt's love affair with Umm Kolthum (where she's known as 'Kawkab ash-Sharq', or 'Nightingale of the East') was such that on the afternoon of the first Thursday of each month, streets would become deserted as the whole country sat beside its radios to listen to her regular live-broadcast performance. When she died in 1975 her death caused havoc, with millions of mourners pouring out onto the streets of Cairo. Her appeal hasn't been purely confined to the Arab world either; former Led Zeppelin vocalist Robert Plant was reported as saying that one of his lifetime ambitions was to re-form the Middle Eastern Orchestra, Umm Kolthum's group of backing musicians.

Inset: A Baluchi man playing the *sorna*, a woodwind instrument, Iran (Photo by Patrick Ben Luke Syder)

Middle Left: The oud (meaning 'wood' in Arabic) can be tuned in different ways

Middle Right: The tabla is one of the most commonly played percussion instruments

backing melodies; the vaguely melancholic, languid tones you would expect from a sun-drenched and heat-exhausted Middle Eastern summer.

Although they never achieved the heights scaled by Umm Kolthum, the 1950s – the golden age of Arabic music – gave rise to a lesser pantheon of stars that notably included Abdel Halim Hafez and Syrian-born Farid al-Atrache, two male crooners who owed much of their popularity to their omnipresence on cinema screens in countless Cairo-produced romantic movies. As with Umm Kolthum, both of these male artists remain loved and widely listened to.

Of all these golden-era singers, only one is still active and that's Fairouz (see the boxed text 'Fairouz' in this special section).

Pop

Arabic Characterised by a clattering, hand-clapping rhythm overlaid with synthesised twirlings and a catchy, repetitive vocal, the first true Arabic pop came out of Cairo in the 1970s. As the Arab nations experienced a population boom and the mean age decreased, a gap in popular culture had developed that the memory of the greats couldn't fill. Enter Arabic pop. The blueprint for the new youth sound (which became known as al-jeel, from the word for generation) was set by Egyptian Ahmed Adawiyya, the Arab world's first 'pop star'. But to untrained ears, the Arabic pop of the 1980s is music to be driven insane to. It's cheesy and one dimensional and much of it sounds like it came preprogrammed out of a Casio keyboard – hunt down a copy of the excruciating 'Lo Laki' by Ali Hameida, which was played everywhere nonstop for several years after its release in 1988, like an uptempo electronic version of Chinese water torture.

During the 1990s there was a calculated attempt to create a more upmarket sound. Tacky electronics were replaced with moody pianos, Spanish guitars and thunderous drums. Check out Amr Diab, whose heavily produced songs have made him the best-selling artist ever in the Arab world (achieved with his 1996 album Nour al-Ain).

Diab is Egyptian but in recent years the Egyptians have been beaten at their own game and many of the current biggest selling artists come from elsewhere. Heading the current crop of megastar singers (and the

---

Fairouz

A Lebanese torch singer with a voice memorably described as 'silk and flame in one', Fairouz has enjoyed star status throughout the Arab world since recording her first performances in Damascus in the 1950s. Along with her writers, the Rahbani brothers, Fairouz embraced a wide range of musical forms, from flamenco to jazz, and during the 1960s and '70s became the perfect embodiment of free-wheeling Beirut, then often referred to as the 'Paris of the Middle East'. During the civil war she became a symbol of hope and an icon for Lebanese identity (though, in disgust, she sat out the fighting in Paris). At the end of the hostilities, in 1994, she returned to give a concert to 40,000 in downtown Beirut. Now in her late 60s, she has resettled in her homeland, living in the hills above Beirut, but she rarely performs as her voice is no longer up to it.

Arabic music scene is totally dominated by solo vocalists, there are no groups) are Majida al-Rumi of Lebanon and Iraqi-born Kazem al-Saher. Unfortunately, in the largely shrink-wrapped world of pop, regional influences are minimised and most artists have a tendency to sound the same, no matter where they come from.

Turkish In Turkey there is a thriving indigenous pop culture, with some of the leading artists breaking out from the Turkish ghetto and making a splash in countries like France as well. Tarkan, for example, first recorded *Simarik*, a track better known to Western audiences as *Kiss Kiss*, courtesy of a cover by chart popper Holly Valance. Other super-popular pop stars include 'arabesque' star İbrahim Tatlises (also a constant fixture on Turkish TV) and the more versatile female singer Sezen Aksu (writer of *Simarik*).

Turkish folk music has also undergone a revival in recent years, as 'Türkü' – an updated, modern version often using electronic instruments but traditional songs.

Traditional Music

Each of the Arabic countries of the Middle East has its own minority groups – ethnic, regional or religious – and most of these groups have their own musical traditions. The most high-profile is the Nubian music of southern Egypt.

Unlike much Arabic music, with its jarring use of quarter tones, the Nubian sound is extremely accessible, mixing simple melodies and soulful vocals, and with a rhythmical quality that's almost African and a brass sound that's almost New Orleans. About the biggest name is Ali Hassan Kuban, who has toured all over Europe as well as in Japan, Canada and the US. He has several CDs out on the German Piranha label, including *From Nubia to Cairo* and *Walk Like a Nubian*. There's also a loose grouping of musicians and vocalists recording under the name Salamat who have several CDs out, also on Piranha, including the highly recommended, explosively brassy *Mambo al-Soudani*.

Not as high profile as the Nubians, other notable Arabic folk music comes from the Bedouin (for details on these people see the boxed text

Right: Bedouin dancing to traditional music, United Arab Emirates

CHRISTINE OSBORNE

A Listening Guide

Arabic Classical

In the last couple of years some of the big Western record labels have begun systematically releasing the best of Arabic music on well-packaged CDs. As a consequence, it's now fairly easy to find high-quality recordings by classic Arab artists in the world-music sections of record stores such as HMV, Virgin or Tower. (In the Middle East you'll be able to get all the following on humble cassette.)

Fairouz There is lots available by this popular singer on various small labels, but a good place to start is with a compilation CD *The Legendary Fairouz* put out by EMI records in its Hemisphere series.

Abdel Halim Hafez EMI Arabia is in the process of releasing a superb series of original soundtracks to Abdel Halim's films from the 1950s and '60s. One in particular to look out for is *Banaat al-Yom* (Girls of the Day) with music by Mohammed Abdel Wahab, one of the great classical composers.

Umm Kolthum This Egyptian-born songstress is well served by a collection called *La Diva* that presently runs to four CDs; although for her best single performance, *Inta Omri* (You are My Life), you'll have to search for a CD put out by Golden Records of Beirut.

Also highly recommended is a series put out by Virgin France called *Arabian Masters*. It includes CDs devoted to Umm Kolthum, Fairouz, Abdel Halim Hafez and Mohammed Abdel Wahab. It has a double CD called *Les Plus Grands Classiques de la Musique Arabe* with a track from each of these artists plus half a dozen others, including the wonderful 'Batwanes Beek' by Algerian-Lebanese singer Warda.

Arabic Pop

Modern Arabic pop is far less well represented on CD, as the people it appeals to most – the lower waged majority of the population – don't own CD players. However, some of the upmarket artists with an eye on the international market are beginning to venture into this format. Golden boy Amr Diab has a slickly done 'best of' package released on EMI Arabia, while Kazem al-Saher is represented by a CD in Virgin France's *Arabian Masters* series. *Camelspotting* (complete with spoof 'Trainspotting' sleeve) is a compilation album put out by EMI showcasing platinum-selling singers from the Arabic-speaking world – it's all sugary, soul-free stuff, although there's a great track by Yemeni singer Osama al-Attar.

Otherwise, you'll have to pick up cassettes while in the Middle East. Ask for the albums *Kalimat* or *Tawq al-Yasmeen* by Majida al-Roumy (anthemic); *Zahma* by Ahmed Adawiyya (groundbreaking); *Shababik* or *Al-Malek* by Mohammed Mounir (jazzy); *Nazra* by Hakim (streetsound); *Awedony* or 'Nour al-Ain' by Amr Diab (chic); *Ana w'Leila* by Kazem al-Saher (classy) or anything by George al-Rassy (earthy).

'The Bedouin' in the Jordan chapter). Whether produced by the Bedouin of Egypt, Jordan or Syria, the music is raw and traditional with little or no use of electronic instruments. The sound is dominated by the *mismar*, a twin-pipe clarinet, and the *rabab*, a twin-stringed prototype cello.

Much more refined than the Bedouin sound, but equally dominated by traditional instrumentation, is what's known as Sufi music. Sufis are religious mystics who use music and dance to attain a trance-like state of divine ecstasy.

TRUDI CANAVAN

The music is bewitchingly hypnotic – a simple repeated melody usually played on the *nay*, accompanied by recitations of Sufi poetry. Sufi music (and dance) can be experienced in Konya, Turkey. There's a fascinating two-CD set called *Sufi Soul* with an accompanying booklet available on German label NetworkMeiden GMBH.

The Music Scene

Sadly, it's very difficult to get to see live music almost anywhere in the Middle East. Artists don't generally perform gigs and there are no live-music clubs as such.

Other than the odd festival, like Lebanon's Baalbek Festival or the Bosra Festival in Syria (see those chapters for details), your best chance of catching a performance is at a wedding or party, which is the scene on which nearly all Arab singers and musicians get their start. Thursday night is the big wedding night and favoured venues are open-air restaurants or hotels. The exception to this is İstanbul, which has a vibrant live music scene centred on the backstreets of the Beyoğlu district (see İstanbul in the Turkey chapter for details).

Anyway, when it comes to Arabic pop, its true home is not on stage but on cassette. Artists have traditionally had little regard for production values and the music is slapped down in the studio and mass produced on cheap tapes in their thousands. Few people can afford quality tape decks anyway, so who cares about the quality of sound? Every town and city has numerous kiosks and shops selling tapes of whatever's the flavour of the moment, plus a selection of the classics. Shopkeepers are usually only too happy to play cassettes before you buy, although at only a dollar or two a pop you can afford to take risks.

Top: The *qanun* has at least 81 strings stretched across its length

[Continued from page 34]

to the simplicity of Arab and Turkish architecture was wedded the decorative excesses of imported stylings, visible in İstanbul's various palaces, the grand houses of Damascus and Aleppo, and in a great number of gaudy Ottoman monuments in Cairo.

European influence increased in the 19th century. Most Middle Eastern cities bear evidence of this with an assortment of churches, embassies and public buildings fashioned in Gothic or Florentine or Slavic or some other such imported style, all examples of (rival) foreign powers asserting their presence in the region through architecture. It was only in the mid-20th century that anything like a movement toward regional identity in architecture was to reemerge; and it was only at the close of the millennium that domes, courtyards, adobe and whitewash (all traditional elements of centuries past) once again returned to vogue.

Decorative & Fine Arts

The arts of the Middle East are largely the arts of Islam, typified in the minds of the non-Muslim by exotic curves and arabesques, and by intricate geometric patterning. Artistic tradition in the Western sense of painting and sculpture has historically been largely absent, as Islam has always regarded the depiction of living beings as idolatrous. There have been some exceptions. The long-standing figurative art traditions in Asia Minor, Persia and further east were never completely extinguished by Islam; the Turks and Iraqis continued to produce beautiful illuminated manuscripts, while the Persians retained their art of miniature painting – which is still practised today in places like Esfahān in present-day Iran.

Since the pervasive influence of Europe in the region, beginning in the 19th century, Western-style painting and sculpture have come to take their place in the Middle Eastern artistic repertoire, but few artists have been able to reconcile these mediums with their heritage, and all too often results rely heavily on ill-appropriated European models.

In the areas of calligraphy, metalwork, ceramics, glass, carpets and textiles, however, Islamic art has a cultural heritage of unsurpassable richness – one that, in turn, has had great influence on the West. Middle Eastern artisans and craftspeople (Armenians, Christians and Jews as well as Muslims) have for more than 1200 years applied complex and

PATRICK BEN LUKE SYDER

Islamic calligraphy on a wall of the Emām Mosque, Esfahān, Iran

sumptuous decorations to often very practical objects to create items of extraordinary beauty. Plenty of such items are on view in the region's museums such as the Topkapı Palace in İstanbul or the Islamic Museum in Cairo. However, to appreciate the achievements of Islamic art, just visit one of the older mosques in which tiling, wood carving, inlaid panelling and calligraphy are often combined in exaltation of Allah. Islamic art is, for a Muslim, foremost an expression of faith.

Literature

Poetry has traditionally been the pre-eminent literary form in the Middle East and all the best-known figures of classical Arabic and Persian literature are poets – men regarded as possessing knowledge forbidden to ordinary people, supposedly acquired from demons. The favourite demon seems to have been alcohol. Abu Nuwas, faithful companion to the 8th-century Baghdadi caliph Haroun ar-Rashid, and a rather debauched fellow, left behind countless odes to the wonders of wine, as did the Persian Omar Khayyām, famed 11th-century composer of *rub'ai* (quatrains). (The current Iranian regime prefers to celebrate Khayyām for his work as a mathematician.)

The tradition continues today, maintained by figures of international standing such as Syrian-born Adonis and Mahmoud Darwish. Darwish is the Arab world's best-selling poet; a recent recital in a Beirut stadium drew 25,000 people. He has been translated into more than 20 languages, and is the bestselling poet in France.

Arab literature in the form of novels and short stories is only as old as the 20th century. An increased exposure to European influences, combined with nascent Arab nationalism in the wake of the Ottoman Empire's decline, led to the first stirrings. The Egyptians and Lebanese have been most active in the field, but much of the credit for the maturing of Arabic literature can be credited to one single author, Naguib Mahfouz, who was unquestionably the single most important writer of fiction in Arabic in the 20th century.

A life-long native of Cairo, Mahfouz began writing in the 1930s. From Western-copyist origins he went on to develop a voice that is uniquely of the Arab world and that draws its inspiration from storytelling in the coffee houses and the dialect and slang of the streets. His achievements were recognised internationally when he was awarded the Nobel Prize for Literature in 1988. Much

---

The Thousand and One Nights

After the Bible, *The Thousand and One Nights* (in Arabic, 'Alf Layla w'Layla', and also known as *The Arabian Nights*) must be one of the most familiar yet unread books in the English language. It owes its existence in the popular consciousness almost entirely to the Disneyfied tales of *Aladdin*, *Sinbad* and *Ali Baba & the 40 Thieves* that appear in children's books, animated films and Christmas pantomimes.

That the actual text itself is largely ignored is unsurprising considering that in its most famous English-language edition (translated by the Victorian adventurer Sir Richard Burton), it runs to 16 volumes. In fact, an old Middle Eastern superstition has it that nobody can read the entire text of *The Arabian Nights* without dying.

But what constitutes the entire text is a matter of academic debate. *The Thousand and One Nights* is a portmanteau title for a mixed bag of colourful and fantastic tales, and the many historical manuscripts that carry the famed title collectively contain many thousands of stories, sharing a core of exactly 271 common tales. They all, however, employ the same framing device – that of a succession of stories related nightly by the wily Sheherezade to save her neck from the misogynistic King Shahriyar.

Sheherazade and her tales have their origins in pre-Islamic Persia, but over the ages (and in endless retellings and rewritings) they were adapted, expanded and updated, drawing on sources as far flung as Greece and India. As they're known to us now, the stories are mainly set in the semi-fabled Baghdad of Haroun ar-Rashid (r. AD 786–809), and in Mamluk-era (1250–1517) Cairo and Damascus. Regarding the last two cities in particular, *The Arabian Nights* provides a wealth of rich period detail, from shopping lists and prices of slaves, through to vivid descriptions of types and practices of assorted conjurers, harlots, thieves and mystics. *The Thousand and One Nights* is revered as much by medieval scholars as it is by Walt Disney's animators.

Recommended Reading

Much Middle Eastern literature is still narrow and overly-political in comparison to that coming out of, say, Latin American. It's also hampered by political and religious censorship, and low literacy rates throughout the region. Why write books when there's so few people to read them? Hence, its low profile in the West. However, there is plenty of good stuff out there, and the following is a shortlist of 10 must-read books, all of which are available in English-language translations.

Arabic Short Stories translated by Denys Johnson-Davies. An excellent primer with tales from all over the Middle East gathered by the world's foremost translator of Arabic literature.

Beirut Blues by Hanan al-Shaykh. A novel dealing with the fallout from the Lebanese civil war, as seen through the eyes of a young woman trying to decide whether to stay or flee abroad following in the steps of friends and family.

The Black Book by Orhan Pamuk. The Kafkaesque tale of an abandoned husband's search for his wife in İstanbul.

Cities of Salt by Abdelrahman Munif. The first in an epic series detailing the loss of a way of life as an unnamed Arab emirate goes from humble beginnings (good) to wealthy oil-producing state (bad). Enthralling, and banned in several Gulf countries.

The Harafish by Naguib Mahfouz. The desert island choice if we were allowed only one work by Mahfouz, but everything he's done is worth reading.

The Map of Love by Ahdaf Soueif. Best-selling historical novel by London-based Anglo-Egyptian writer about love and clashing cultures.

Mehmet My Hawk by Yaşar Kemal. The Nobel laureate's most famous (and very readable) work, which deals with near-feudal life in the villages of eastern Mediterranean Turkey.

Rubaiyat of Omar Khayyām Written in the 11th century, translated into English in the 19th when they became a sensation throughout Europe and America, and a major influence on Western poetry ever since.

Samarkand by Amin Maalouf. Lebanese by birth, Maalouf lives in Paris and writes in French. He's the author of several excellent historical novels, and this particular highly romantic tale begins with Omar Khayyām and ends on the *Titanic*.

The Thousand and One Nights It's an anonymously written, mixed bag of colourful and fantastic tales as related nightly by the wily Sheherezade to save her neck from the misogynistic King Shahriyar.

---

of his work has since been made available in English-language translations.

After Cairo, the other beacon for Arab literature is Beirut. As well as being the focus of Lebanese literary life, Beirut has been the refuge of Syrian writers escaping their own repressive regime and of refugee Palestinians. Of the latter category Liana Badr, who fled to Beirut after the Israelis captured her home town of Jericho in 1967, has two books available in English: *The Eye of the Mirror* and the short story collection, *A Balcony over the Fakihani*. Both draw heavily on her first-hand experiences of upheaval.

Of the native Lebanese writers, the most famous is Hanan al-Shaykh, who writes extremely poignant but humorous novels (*Beirut Blues, The Story of Zahra* and *Women of Sand and Myrrh*) that resonate beyond the bounds of the Middle East.

The literary scenes of the more cloistered countries of Yemen and the Gulf States are unsurprisingly much less developed than elsewhere in the Middle East, although now and again they do throw out the odd surprise. In 1988 a book called *Cities of Salt* by Abdelrahman Munif, a relatively unknown author even in his own homelands of Saudi Arabia and Iraq, caused a stir by being picked up by a major US publishing house. The book (and its two successors) have sold extremely well and remain firmly in print.

Turkey's best-known writer is probably Yaşar Kemal, winner of the 1998 Nobel Prize for Literature. Author of the moment is Orhan Pamuk, widely published in a great number of languages, including English, whose books are walking out of the bookshops in record numbers.

Cinema

Of all the Middle East countries only Egypt, Lebanon, Iran and Turkey have any strong film-making traditions. Of these, Egypt's film industry is reckoned to be in serious decline. In its halcyon years, Cairo's film studios would be turning out more than 100 movies annually, filling cinemas throughout the Arab world, but these days the average number of films made is around 20 a year. Most of these are genre movies relying on moronic slapstick humour and hysterics rather than acting, and usually a little belly-dancing thrown in for spice. The one director of note is Yousef Chahine, a staple of international film festivals (which are virtually the only places you'll get to see his work) and recipient of a lifetime achievement award at Cannes in 1997.

Lebanon's small film industry is showcased each year at the Beirut International Film Festival. Some of the well-known filmmakers include Maroun Baghdadi (who won an award at the Cannes Film Festival), Samir Nasri, Mohammed Sweid and Paris-based Jocelyn Saab who made the popular *Once Upon a Time Beirut*. If you get a chance, see *West Beyrouth* (1998), the story of three teenagers. The film begins on 13 April 1975, the first day of the Lebanese civil war; the cinematography is supremely slick, which is not surprising given that first-time director Ziad Doueirim was formerly Quentin Tarantino's cameraman.

It's a shame that the best-known film about Turkey is the American-made, racist *Midnight Express* when Turkish directors have produced so much better and more interesting portrayals of the country. Nor are these particularly uncritical. Yilmaz Güney's Palme d'Or-winning *Yol* (The Road) was not initially shown in Turkish cinemas; its portrait of what happens to five prisoners on a week's release was too grim for the authorities to take. Güney's *The Herd* has also been shown in the West. More recently, Reis Çelik's *Hoşça Kal Yarın* (Goodbye Tomorrow) told the story of the three student leaders of Turkey's revolutionary left in the 1970s.

The real success story of the region is Iranian cinema. Despite serious straitjacketing by the authorities regarding content, Iranian directors have been turning out some extremely sophisticated and beautifully made films that have won tremendous plaudits on an international level. Their accent on character and story stands in refreshing contrast to much of modern cinema, particularly that which comes out of Hollywood. Such is the standing of Iranian cinema in Europe and America that new films by Iranian directors are regularly given first-run screenings in cities like London, Paris and San Francisco. Names to look out for are Abbas Kiaorstami, regarded as Iran's pre-eminent film-maker and whose *The Taste of Cherry* won the Palm d'Or at Cannes in 1997, Mohsen Makhmalbaf (and equally talented daughter Samira) and Jafar Panahi, whose *The Circle* (2000), a brave and powerful account of the way women are oppressed in present-day Iran, is the most recent addition to an extraordinary body of work.

SOCIETY & CONDUCT

With the notable exception of Israel, the whole of the Middle Eastern region is predominantly Muslim. Religious values still greatly dictate social life. There is a strong emphasis on family and hospitality, and women tend to take a back seat to men in all matters other than the domestic.

This expression of religious values is at its most extreme in Saudi Arabia, which is one of the most insular societies on Earth. Alcohol and pork are illegal, as are theatres and cinemas. At prayer time all shops must close. The public profession of all faiths other than Islam is banned. Non-Muslims may not enter mosques, are barred from Mecca and may visit only the outskirts of Medina. Public observance of the Ramadan fast is *mandatory* for Muslims and non-Muslims alike, with prison sentences for anyone caught smoking, drinking or eating in public.

Even Iran looks positively liberal compared with Saudi Arabia; although the dress restrictions are, if anything, stricter, especially as regards women (see the boxed text 'The Big Cover Up' in the Iran chapter for more details).

Other than Saudi Arabia and Kuwait, the Gulf States are more relaxed, and social etiquette for visitors is fairly much in line with that in countries like Egypt, Jordan, Lebanon, Syria and Turkey. Alcohol and pork are available, though rarely obvious, theatres and cinemas are popular, and the only time most shops close is possibly for noon prayers and on Friday, the holy day of the Islamic week.

Social Graces

People are generally very easy-going towards foreigners and forgiving of any social errors. Having said that, there are a few things that genuinely do cause offence, including inappropriate dress and open displays of affection – kissing and hugging in public are taboo and even holding hands is frowned upon. Vocal criticism of the government or country is also to be avoided.

Dress Advice for women on how to dress is given in the Women Travellers section in the Regional Facts for the Visitor chapter, but what men wear is important too. Look around you: the only people wearing shorts or tatty clothes are kids, labourers or the poor. Locals consider exposing the skin to the blistering sun at best odd and at worst silly. No-one is going to stop a tourist for walking around in shorts and a sleeveless T-shirt, but it's about as appropriate as walking around wintry London in a thong. Shorts are only appropriate in the coastal resort regions of Turkey, Sinai, the Red Sea and in Israel, where pretty much anything goes. The further away from the tourist areas and the big cities you go, the more conservative Middle Eastern society is, and the more you need to be aware of what you wear.

Alcohol Despite the popular impression of the Middle East as an abstemious region, the only countries to ban alcohol outright are Iran, Kuwait and Saudi Arabia. In all the other countries booze is tolerated to some degree. In most Gulf States alcohol is restricted to hotel restaurants and bars, but elsewhere you'll find it served in small local bars and nightclubs. That said, Middle Eastern bars are always very discreet. Other than in Israel and Turkey, drinking in public is rarely possible and most countries will impose a fine on anyone openly carrying alcohol on the streets.

RELIGION

The Middle East is the birthplace of the big three monotheistic world religions: Judaism, Christianity and Islam. The followers of these religions worship the same God, the main difference between them being their understanding of when God's revelations ceased. While Judaism adheres to the Old Testament, Christianity adds on the teachings of the New Testament, and the Muslims claim that their holy book, the Quran, contains the final revelations of God, clearing up the points not made clear by earlier prophets.

Islam

Islam was founded in the early 7th century by the Prophet Mohammed, who was born around AD 570 in the city of Mecca. At the age of 40 Mohammed began to receive revelations from the archangel Gabriel containing the words of Allah (God). The revelations continued for the rest of Mohammed's life and they were written down in the Quran (from the Arabic word for 'recitation') in a series of *suras* (verses).

Unlike the Torah and Bible, which are the interpretative work of many individuals, the Quran is said to be the direct word of Allah. Since its transcription by Mohammed, not one dot of the book has been altered.

By Mohammed's time religions such as Christianity and Judaism had become complicated by factions, sects and bureaucracies, to which Islam offered a simpler alternative. The new religion did away with hierarchical orders and complex rituals, and instead offered believers a direct relationship with Allah based only on their submission ('Islam' is derived from the Arabic word for submission) signified by observance of the five pillars of the faith:

Shahada Muslims must publicly declare that 'there is no God but Allah and Mohammed is his Prophet' (in Arabic).

Salat Pray five times a day: at sunrise, noon, mid-afternoon, sunset and night. It's acceptable to pray at home or elsewhere, except for Friday noon prayers, which are performed at a mosque (for details on the workings of a mosque see the special section 'Mosques'). The act of praying consists of a series of predefined movements of the body and recitals of prayers and passages of the Quran, all designed to express the believer's absolute humility and Allah's sovereignty. Before praying, the believer washes to indicate a willingness to be purified – there are ablution fountains in mosques for this purpose.

Zakat Muslims must give alms to the poor to the value of one-fortieth of a believer's annual income. This used to be the responsibility of the individual, but zakat now usually exists as a state-imposed welfare tax administered by a ministry of religious affairs.

Ramadan Fast during daylight hours in the month of Ramadan. During this month, Muslims abstain from eating, drinking, smoking and sexual

Islam & the West

Islam has been much maligned and misunderstood in the West in recent years. Any mention of it usually brings to mind one of two images: the 'barbarity' of some aspects of Islamic law such as flogging, stoning or the amputation of hands; or the so-called fanatics out to terrorise the West (an image that has been greatly strengthened post 11 September 2001).

For many Muslims, however, and particularly for those in the Middle East, Islam is stability in a very unstable world. Many of them are keenly aware that Muslims are seen as a threat by the West and are divided in their own perceptions of Western countries. Not without justification, they regard the West's policies, especially towards the Arab world, as aggressive and they often compare its attitudes to them with those of the medieval Crusaders. Despite this view that Western culture is dangerous to Muslim values and the growing influence of anti-Western religious groups, many Muslims still admire the West. It is common to hear people say they like it, but that they are perplexed by its treatment of them.

If the West is offended by the anti-Western rhetoric of the radical minority, the majority of Muslims see the West, especially with its support of Israel, as a direct challenge to their independence.

Although the violence and terrorism associated with the Middle East is often held up by the Western media as evidence of blind, religiously inspired bloodthirstiness, the efficient oppression of the Palestinian Arabs by Israeli security forces has, until fairly recently, barely rated a mention. The sectarian madness of Northern Ireland is rarely portrayed as a symbol of Christian 'barbarism' in the way political violence in the Middle East is summed up as simple Muslim fanaticism. It is worth remembering that while the 'Christian' West tends to view Islam with disdain, if not contempt, Muslims generally accord Christians great respect as believers in the same God.

Just as the West receives a distorted view of Muslim society, so too are Western values misread in Islamic societies. The glamour of the West has lured those able to compete (usually the young, rich and well educated), but for others, it represents the bastion of moral decline.

These misunderstandings have long contributed to a general feeling of unease and distrust between nations of the West and the Muslim world, and often between individuals of those countries. As long as this situation persists, Islam will continue to be seen in the West as a backward and radical force bent on violent change, rather than as simply a code of religious and political behaviour that people choose to apply to their daily lives, and which makes an often difficult life tolerable.

intercourse from sunrise to sunset. The purpose of fasting is to bring people closer to Allah. (For more details on Ramadan see Public Holidays & Special Events in the Regional Facts for the Visitor chapter.)

Haj Every Muslim capable of affording it should perform the haj, or pilgrimage, to the holiest of cities, Mecca, at least once in his or her lifetime. The reward is considerable: the forgiving of all past sins.

Muslims also believe in the angels who brought Allah's messages to humans, in the prophets who received these messages, in the books in which the prophets expressed these revelations, and in the last day of judgment. The Quran mentions 28 prophets, 21 of whom are also mentioned in the Bible. Adam, Noah, Abraham, David, Jacob, Joseph, Job, Moses and Jesus are given particular honour, although the divinity of Jesus is strictly denied. The Quran also recognises the Scriptures of Abraham, the Torah of Moses, the Psalms of David and the Gospels of Jesus as God's revelation.

Shiite & Sunni Despite Mohammed's original intentions, Islam did not remain simple. The Prophet died leaving no sons, which led to a major dispute over the line of succession. Competing for power were Abu Bakr, the father of Mohammed's second wife Aisha, and Ali, Mohammed's cousin and the husband of his daughter Fatima. Initially, the power was transferred to Abu Bakr, who became the first caliph, or successor, with Ali reluctantly agreeing.

Abu Bakr's lineage came to an abrupt halt when his successor was murdered. Ali reasserted his right to power and emerged victorious in the ensuing power struggle,

[Continued on page 50]

MOSQUES

Embodying the Islamic faith, and representing its most predominant architectural feature is the mosque, or *masjid*, or *jamaa*. The building was developed in the very early days of the religion and takes its form from the simple, private houses where the first believers gathered to worship.

The house belonging to the Prophet Mohammed is said to have provided the prototype for the mosque. It had an enclosed oblong courtyard with huts (housing Mohammed's wives) along one wall and a rough portico providing shade. This plan developed with the courtyard becoming the *sahn*, the portico the arcaded *riwaq* and the houses the *haram* or prayer hall.

The prayer hall is typically divided into a series of aisles. The centre aisle is wider than the rest and leads to a vaulted niche in the wall called the *mihrab*; this indicates the direction of Mecca, towards which Muslims must face when they pray.

Before entering the prayer hall and participating in communal worship, Muslims must perform a ritual washing of the hands, forearms and face. For this purpose mosques have traditionally had a large ablutions fountain at the centre of the courtyard, often fashioned from marble and worn by centuries of use. These days, modern mosques have just rows of taps.

The mosque also frequently serves the community in other ways: often you will find groups of small children or even adults receiving lessons (usually in the Quran), people in quiet prayer and others simply enjoying a peaceful nap – mosques provide wonderfully tranquil havens from the hustle and bustle of the streets outside.

SARA-JANE CLELAND

Inset: Minaret of a mosque in Al-Muharraq, Bahrain (Photo by Phil Weymouth)

Left: Ablutions fountain in the courtyard of the Mosque of ibn Tulun, Cairo, Egypt

Visiting Mosques

With the exception of those in Saudi Arabia and Yemen, non-Muslims are generally quite welcome to visit mosques at any time other than during Friday prayers.

You must dress modestly. For men that means no shorts; for women that means no shorts, tight pants, shirts that aren't done up, or anything else that might be considered immodest. Some of the more frequently visited mosques provide wrap-around cloaks for anyone who is improperly dressed. Shoes have to be removed or, again, some mosques will provide slip-on shoe covers for a small fee.

In Yemen some historic mosques that are not in active ritual use can be entered but you must remember never to do so without asking permission first.

Stylistic Developments

The earliest of the grand mosques inherited much from Byzantine models (the Dome of the Rock is a basilica – see also Mosques Not to be Missed, later), but with the spread of the Muslim domain various styles soon developed, each influenced by local artistic traditions. The Umayyads of Damascus, for example, favoured square minarets; the Abbasids of Iraq built spiral minarets echoing the ziggurats of the Babylonians; and the Fatimid dynasty of North Africa made much use of decorative stucco work.

The vocabulary of mosque building quickly became very sophisticated and expressive, reaching its apotheosis under the Mamluks (1250–1517). A military dynasty of former slaves ruling out of Egypt, the Mamluks were great patrons of the arts. Their buildings are characterised by the banding of different coloured stone (a technique known as *ablaq*) and by the elaborate carvings and patterning around windows and in the recessed portals. The best examples of their patronage are found in Cairo but impressive Mamluk monuments also grace the old cities of Damascus and Jerusalem.

Top Right: Early Mamluk minaret featuring a square base and pepperpot dome, Mosque of Beybars al-Jashankir, Cairo, Egypt (1307)

Middle Right: The pencil minaret of the Ottoman style, Mosque of Suleiman Pasha (1528), The Citadel, Cairo, Egypt

Bottom Right: Lavish detail and three tiers characterise the late Mamluk minaret of the Mosque of Amir Qurqumas, Cairo, Egypt (1506)

The Mamluks were eventually defeated by the Ottoman Turks who followed up their military gains with an equally expansive campaign of construction. Designed on the basic principle of a dome on a square, and instantly recognisable by their slim pencil-shaped minarets, Ottoman mosques can be found throughout Egypt, Israel & the Palestinian Territories, Lebanon, Syria and Iraq. The most impressive monuments of this era, however, were built at the heart of the empire – the Süleymaniye Mosque in İstanbul and the Selimiye Mosque at Edirne, both the work of the Turkish master architect Sinan.

Of all the non-Gulf regions of the Middle East, Persia was the one area that did not fall to the Turks. The Persian Safavid dynasty proved strong enough to hold the Ottomans at bay and thus Iran, and neighbouring Afghanistan, have a very

ILLUSTRATIONS BY LPP

different architectural tradition from elsewhere in the Middle East. Persian architecture has its roots not in Arab or Turkish forms but in those of the eastern lands occupied by the Mongols who swept down from Central Asia. Their grand buildings are very simple in form but made startling by the sumptuous use of cobalt-blue and turquoise tiling, which often covers every available surface.

Mosques Not to Be Missed

Azim-e Gohar Shād Mosque (1418), Mashhad, Iran This is the jewel at the heart of this pilgrimage city's holy shrine complex, built by the wife of the son of the Central Asian warlord Tamerlane. It shows a clear kinship with the Mongol-dynasty mosques of Samarkand and Bukhara. (See page 252.)

Dome of the Rock (688), Jerusalem, Israel & the Palestinian Territories One of the earliest mosques built and with its octagonal plan and mosaic-encrusted exterior, one of the most unique of all Islamic structures. (See page 317.)

Emām Mosque (1638), Esfahān, Iran The grandest and most ornate of the garish Persian mosques, with almost every surface covered by shimmering turquoise-blue tiles and the whole thing topped by a great 54m-high dome. (See page 238.)

Mosque of Ibn Tulun (879), Cairo, Egypt This may be the first building to ever employ the pointed arch that has since come to typify Islamic architecture. It also has a wonderful spiral minaret based on the Iraqi model. (See page 152.)

Mosque of Qaitbey (1474), Cairo, Egypt The most exquisite of the region's vast legacy of Mamluk buildings with, perhaps, the best carved-stone dome to be seen anywhere. (See Greater Cairo map, page 147.)

BRADLEY MAYHEW

Left: Azim-e Gohar Shād Mosque, Mashhad, Iran

MARTIN MOOS

Selimiye Mosque (1574), Edirne, Iran More modest and not as well known as his İstanbul mosques, but architectural historians rightly regard this, the most harmonious and elegant of Sinan's works, as his masterpiece. (See page 660.)

Süleymaniye (1557), İstanbul, Turkey Sinan was the master builder of the Ottoman Empire and his work is found throughout the region, but fittingly the grandest of his mosques, the Süleymaniye, dominates the skyline of the former imperial capital. (See page 650.)

Umayyad Mosque (705), Damascus, Syria An adaptation of a Christian cathedral (itself built on the site of a Roman temple), this mosque is notable for its age, size and the stunning Byzantine-style golden mosaics that cover the courtyard walls. (See page 593.)

Top: Emām Mosque, Esfahān, Iran

[Continued from page 45]

moving his capital to Kufa (later renamed Najaf, in Iraq), only to be assassinated himself in AD 661. The Umayyad dynasty, after defeating Ali's successor, Hussein, in AD 680 at Kerbala, rose to rule the vast majority of the Muslim world, marking the start of the Sunni sect. Those who continued to support the claims of the descendents of Ali became known as Shiites.

Beyond this early dynastic rivalry, there is little difference between Shiite Islam and Sunni Islam, but the division remains until today. Sunnis comprise some 90% of the world's more than 800 million Muslims, but Shiites are very close to being a majority of the population in Iraq and constitute a clear majority in Bahrain and Iran. There are also Shiite minorities in almost all Arab countries.

Judaism

The foundation of the Jewish religion is the Torah, or the first five books of the Old Testament. The Torah contains the revelation from God via Moses more than 3000 years ago, including, most importantly, God's commandments (of which there are 613 in all). The Torah is supplemented by the rest of the books of the Old Testament, of which the most important are the prophetic books, giving much of the substance to the religion.

These books are complemented by the Talmud, a collection of another 63 books, written in the early centuries AD and containing most of what separates Judaism from other religions. Included are plenty of rabbinical interpretations of the earlier scriptures, with a wealth of instructions and rulings for the daily life of a Jew.

The Talmud was written when the Jewish Diaspora began. After the Romans crushed the Jewish state and destroyed the Temple in Jerusalem in AD 70, many Jews were either exiled or sold into slavery abroad. The Jewish religion was kept intact, however, within families, who passed the teachings from generation to generation.

Unlike Christians or Muslims, Jews have never actively sought converts from the followers of other religions.

Christianity

Jesus preached in what is present-day Israel & the Palestinian Territories, but Christians form only minority groups in all Middle Eastern countries. Their numbers range from zero in Saudi Arabia (only Muslims can have Saudi nationality) to about 13% of the population of Egypt and Syria.

Lebanon and Jordan have sizable Christian populations too, and the former's one million Maronites also have followers all over the world. By far the biggest Christian sect in the region is formed by the Copts of Egypt, who make up most of that country's Christian population. Originally, it was the apostle Mark who established Christianity in Egypt, and by the 4th century it had become the state

The Bible as History

Unlike Egypt, where the wealth of tomb and temple texts and papyri has enabled historians to work out a detailed historical framework, the 'Holy Lands', where the earliest events as related in the Old Testament of the Bible are said to have taken place, have yielded little in the way of written archives. Historians cannot say for sure whether characters such as Abraham, Moses or even Solomon existed. The Old Testament was compiled from a variety of sources, and probably set down in script no earlier than the 6th century BC. The stories it contains might have some grain of truth in them, but then again they may have been no more than folk tales.

When it comes to the New Testament and episodes related in the Gospels by Matthew, Mark, Luke and John, we do have some means of corroboration. This was the Roman era and there are plenty of other sources in the form of written accounts, inscriptions and works of art so that we can say with certainty that figures such as Herod, Pontius Pilot and a man called Jesus, from Nazareth, did exist. Where history moves into the realm of conjecture again is in associating particular places with biblical events. Many sites commonly held to be of biblical significance were only fixed in the 4th century AD by the empress Helena, some 300 years after the death of Christ. They owe their status more to tradition than historical veracity.

religion. The Coptic Church split from the Byzantine Orthodox Church in the 5th century after a dispute about the human nature of Jesus, with Dioscurus, the patriarch of Alexandria, declaring Jesus to be totally divine. Internationally, the most famous Egyptian Copt today is the former UN secretary-general, Boutros Boutros-Ghali.

Otherwise, the Arab Christians of the Middle East belong to many churches in all main branches of the religion – Orthodox, Catholic and Protestant. This richness reflects the region's location on major routes along which the religion spread to Europe and Asia, and by which people and ideas have flowed into the area for centuries.

However, the number of Christians in the Middle East is definitely in decline. The reasons are predominantly demographic. Over the centuries Christians, in Egypt and Syria in particular, have moved from the country to the city and this urbanisation has led to a fall in birth rates. Also, traditionally Christian church schools have provided a better education than Muslim state schools, which again has had the effect of lowering the birth rate. The professional qualifications resulting from the better education and subsequent wealth have also meant that Middle East Christians are far more able to emigrate. Syrian and Egyptian churches have found it impossible to stem the flow of parishioners to Australia and the USA.

For a fascinating exploration of Christianity in the Middle East today read William Dalrymple's *From the Holy Mountain*.

Regional Facts for the Visitor

SUGGESTED ITINERARIES

The hardest part of planning a trip to the Middle East is deciding what to leave out. Do you go for a single country, a combination of two or three neighbouring countries, or a grand once-in-a-lifetime odyssey like Turkey all the way down to Egypt over a couple of months? Does a side trip to Beirut mean that there's no time for Jerusalem? There are some tough decisions to be made.

Given that travel around the region is fairly straightforward, most people elect to visit two or three countries in the one trip. The favourite combination is with the countries that ring the eastern Mediterranean – Turkey, Syria, Lebanon, Jordan, Israel & the Palestinian Territories and Egypt. It's easy to devise a straightforward north-to-south or south-to-north itinerary, with no backtracking (although be aware of the Israeli stamp issue – see the boxed text 'The Israeli Stamp Stigma' later in this chapter). This, of course, necessitates buying an open-jaw air ticket, by which we mean you fly into one airport and out of another.

Iran is popular, but it involves a big detour. The only open land border is with far, far eastern Turkey. Plus the country itself is big and takes time to get around. People who go to Iran tend to limit their trip to just that country, or possibly Iran and Turkey. Unless that is, you fly.

The countries of the Gulf are rarely visited in conjunction with countries that are non-Gulf. They occupy their own insular universe. Oman may trade visitors with the UAE, but rare is the itinerary that takes in Oman, say, and then Egypt. As for Saudi Arabia and Yemen, they're such 'niche' destinations that the kind of people who go there tend to be almost fetishistic in their single-minded fixation on the country at hand.

The all-important factor is time. A few suggested itineraries, based on given lengths of time, follow.

One Week

If one week is all that you have in total, then limit yourself to a single country (especially if it's somewhere big like Egypt, Iran or Turkey – in each of these chapters we give suggested itineraries within the country).

Even then, don't try to cram in too much – if you aren't careful then all you'll remember of the trip is a succession of transport interchanges and the blurry flashing by of scenery half-glimpsed though grimy bus windows. For those suggested individual country itineraries see the relevant country chapter.

Ten Days to Two Weeks

Plan carefully and you can cram plenty into 10 to 14 days. Stick to the part of the region where inter-capital distances are least (Beirut, Damascus, Jerusalem, Amman and Cairo are all within easy reach of each other) and you could quite easily take in the best of two, possibly three, of the following countries: Egypt, Jordan, Israel & the Palestinian Territories, Syria and/or Lebanon. Sample itineraries might be:

Egypt, Jordan & Israel Fly into Cairo and spend the first two days ogling the Pyramids and Egyptian Museum. Take a train down to Luxor for the monuments of Ancient Egypt. Then spend two days travelling via Sinai to Aqaba in Jordan and then to Petra. Carry on to Amman and spend a couple of days there before crossing into Israel & the Palestinian Territories. Make a base in Jerusalem and from there visit the Dead Sea. Fly out of Tel Aviv.

Jordan & Syria Fly into Amman and spend the first four days around Wadi Rum and Petra. Head north to Damascus (calling in at Bosra en route) and allow five or six days for visits to Crac des Chevalier, Palmyra and Aleppo. If there's time you could even make an overnight visit to Baalbek in Lebanon.

Turkey & Syria It's tight, but in eight days you could fly into İstanbul, explore for three days, scoot down the coast to Ephesus for one day/night, carry on along the Med breaking the journey at somewhere like Fethiye and then Antakya before making for the Syrian border. You'd then hit Aleppo (two days), Hama (one day, including a trip to Crac des Chevalier) and then finish up with a final two or three days in Damascus (possibly squeezing in a trip to Palmyra). Fly home out of Damascus thoroughly exhausted, but happy.

Three to Four Weeks

With this amount of time you can up the ante and do Egypt, Israel & the Palestinian Territories and Jordan properly, or Syria, Jordan and Lebanon, or, if you're prepared to crack the whip, Turkey down through Syria and Jordan to Egypt. It's easy to get open jaw tickets that allow you to fly into, say, İstanbul, and out again from Amman or Cairo.

İstanbul to Cairo

To do the whole İstanbul to Cairo thing you're looking at a minimum of four weeks, but ideally five or six. Even then, if you also wanted to take in Lebanon and Israel & the Palestinian Territories you would be looking at something more like seven or eight weeks. Our breakdown of such a trip would be as follows:

Turkey (14 Days) Fly into İstanbul (3 days), travel down the Aegean Coast to Çanakkale (2 days), Selçuk (2 days) and Bodrum (1 day), then spend two days at either Fethiye (Butterfly Valley, Ölüdeniz) or Kaş (Olympos, Chimaera). Detour inland to see Cappadocia, resume travels along the coast by taking a bus back south to Adana and then head east to Antakya.

Syria (Eight Days) Arrive at Aleppo (2 days) and head south to Hama (2 days). De-tour to Palmyra (1 day), kick back in Damascus (2 days) with maybe an overnight trip to Baalbek, then continue south stopping at Bosra on the way to the Jordanian border.

Jordan (Seven Days) Visit Jerash on the way down to Amman (2 days) from where you can daytrip to the Dead Sea. Continue south via Madaba to Petra (2 days) and Wadi Rum (2 days), overnight in Aqaba and move on the next morning.

Egypt (12 to 14 Days) Arrive via the ferry at Nuweiba in Sinai (2 days) then push on across the Eastern Desert down to Luxor (3 days) and further south still to Aswan (2 days), including an excursion to Abu Simbel. Head back via the Western Oases (4 days) or directly by train to Cairo (3 days). Fly out from Cairo.

Following an itinerary like this would still constitute something of a breakneck tour, allowing for highlights and major sites only.

PLANNING
When to Go

When planning a trip to the Middle East, the two main things to keep in mind are the weather and the religious holidays that can sometimes make travelling difficult.

Is It Safe?

Safety is a very subjective subject. Perceptions of the issue as far as the Middle East is concerned are shaped for most people by ever-present news stories of conflict, killings and bombings. It's a lopsided picture. Imagine somebody whose image of the USA is built solely on CNN reports of Waco and Columbine High–style incidents, or a person whose view of the UK has been formed purely on the evidence of the behaviour of its football fans abroad. Just as mainstream society in the USA and UK has little to do with the headline-making elements mentioned, so day-to-day life in the Middle East rarely involves shootings, explosions and other elements of terror. There are trouble spots (most notably at the time of writing the Palestinian territories of the West Bank and Gaza Strip), but these are well-defined areas that are easily avoided.

In our experience the people of the Middle East are perfectly able to distinguish between governments and their policies and individual travellers. You might receive the occasional question ('Why does the West support Israel?'), but you'll never be held personally accountable. Once in Tehrān we stood, obviously Westerners, with cameras and pasty complexions, and watched a crowd march by chanting 'Death to America! Death to Britain!' – several marchers grinned, waved and broke off to come over and ask how we liked Iran.

So, while right now we'd advise against visits to Gaza City or Hebron, rarely should events in the news make you reconsider your travel plans. Keep abreast of current events and if you need to phone your embassy for travel advice then do, but otherwise, just go.

Weather Most of the Middle East is best visited in autumn and spring (September to November and March to May). Though the stereotypical images are of a baking blood-red sun, in fact December and January can be fairly bleak and overcast everywhere in the region save for southern Egypt, Yemen, Oman and the Gulf. On the other hand, unless you really are an avid sun-worshipper or water-sports freak, the summer months of June through to September should definitely be avoided. It's just too hot to do anything. This particularly applies the further south you head – in July and August visitors to the Pharaonic sites at Aswan and Luxor in Egypt are obliged to get up at 5am to beat the heat.

There are exceptions. For example, you should not venture into the northeast of

Turkey before May or after mid-October unless you're prepared for the cold, as there will still be lots of snow around, perhaps even enough to close roads and mountain passes. Parts of Syria and northern Iran also suffer from miserable weather between November and March or April.

There are more details on weather conditions under Climate in the individual country chapters.

Religious Holidays & Festivals The main holiday to avoid is Ramadan. Although non-Muslims are not bound by the fasting, most restaurants and cafés throughout the region (with the exception of those in hotels) will be closed. Transport is on a go-slow and office hours are erratic to say the least.

Highlights

One person's highlight is another's major disappointment. But while the highlights of any trip (anywhere, not just the Middle East) are such a subjective matter, there are certain places that simply must be seen. For the Middle East we've come up with a top-twelve list of the most magnificent, the most stunning, the simply unmissable, the most awesome... These sights are all given special treatment in this guide, presented as double-page spreads with illustrations. Our list runs:

- Baalbek (Lebanon) *See page 484*
- Crac des Chevaliers (Syria) *See page 605*
- The Dead Sea (Israel & Jordan) *See pages 257 & 404*
- Ephesus (Turkey) *See page 670*
- Old city of Jerusalem, Haram ash-Sharif & the Dome of the Rock (Israel & the Palestinian Territories) *See page 317*
- Meidun-e Emām Khomeini (Iran) *See page 238*
- Palmyra (Syria) *See page 618*
- Persepolis (Iran) *See page 247*
- Petra (Jordan) *See page 410*
- The Pyramids (Egypt) *See page 160*
- San'a (Yemen) *See page 756*
- Topkapı Sarayı (Turkey) *See page 651*

In addition to the above, each regional chapter begins with boxed text highlighting what we consider the best dining, nightlife, walk, view and activity in that particular country. This is complemented by a 'What to See' box, which

offers a brief summary of the places that most visitors find interesting, rewarding or enjoyable, along with some ideas on suggested itineraries.

All of this is fine from a geographical point of view, but if you're interested in structuring a trip around more specialised interests then the following is our list of where's good for what:

Activities
- Diving the Red Sea (Egypt) *See page 140*
- Hiking through Wadi Shab (Oman) *See page 510*
- Pearl diving (Bahrain) *See page 113*
- Steaming in a *hammam* AKA Turkish bath (Syria and Turkey) *See pages 596 & 637*
- For more ideas see the Activities section later in this chapter.

Arts & Culture
- Tel Aviv Museum of Art (Israel) *See page 330*
- Whirling Dervishes in Islamic Cairo (Egypt) *See page 151*

Beaches
- Southern Sinai (Egypt) *See page 196*

Chilling Out
- Dahab (Egypt) *See page 200*
- Hama (Syria) *See page 608*
- Esfahān (Iran) *See page 234*

Dining
- Aleppo (Syria) *See page 611*
- Beirut (Lebanon) *See page 453*

If you're visiting Turkey, you might also want to avoid Kurban Bayram, which lasts a full week. Hotels are jam-packed, banks closed and transport booked up weeks ahead.

The other big Muslim feasts only last a day or two and shouldn't prove too disruptive to most travel plans. In fact, it's worth trying to time your visit to tie in with something like Eid al-Adha (the Feast of Sacrifice, which marks the Prophet's pilgrimage to Mecca) or the Prophet's Birthday, as these can be colourful occasions.

Iran also has a couple of festivals to avoid during Moharram, the month of mourning, and the Persian New Year celebrations, while in Israel & the Palestinian Territories quite a few religious holidays such as Passover and Easter cause the country to fill up with pilgrims, prices to double and public transport to grind to a halt. There are several Jewish holidays in autumn that also make it tricky to get around.

See the Public Holidays & Special Events section later in this chapter for details of all these events. See also the When to Go sections in the individual country chapters.

Maps

A general Middle East map is not going to be of much use for anything except the broadest of planning. You really need separate country maps. There's no shortage of these on the market but we've found the best of what's available to be those produced by Freytag & Berndt and GeoCenter. Once you are in the region, you will also

---

Highlights

- Dubai (UAE) *See page 724*
- İstanbul (Turkey) *See page 642*

Hotels (Budget but Brilliant)
- Al-Haramein & Ar-Rabie, Damascus (Syria) *See page 596*
- Malek-o-Tojjar, Yazd (Iran) *See page 249*
- Shali Lodge, Siwa Oasis (Egypt) *See page 181*

Hotels (Landmark & Luxury)
- Abbāsi Hotel, Esfahān (Iran) *See page 237*
- Adrére Amellal, Siwa Oasis (Egypt) *See page 182*
- Al-Moudira, Luxor (Egypt) *See page 171*
- Baron Hotel, Aleppo (Syria) *See page 617*
- Beit al-Wakil, Aleppo (Syria) *See page 617*
- Jumeira Beach Hotel, Dubai (UAE) *See page 730*
- Four Seasons Hotel, İstanbul (Turkey) *See page 658*
- Hotel Albergo, Beirut (Lebanon) *See page 461*
- Mir Amin Palace, Beiteddine (Lebanon) *See page 483*
- Old Cataract, Aswan (Egypt) *See page 177*
- Old Winter Palace, Luxor (Egypt) *See page 170*

Museums
- Egyptian Museum, Cairo (Egypt) *See page 150*
- Israel Museum, Jerusalem (Israel) *See page 322*
- National Jewels Museum, Tehrān (Iran) *See page 225*
- National Museum, Beirut (Lebanon) *See page 457*
- Topkapı Sarayı, İstanbul (Turkey) *See page 651*

Nightlife
- Beirut (Lebanon) *See page 453*
- Bodrum (Turkey) *See page 676*
- Dubai (UAE) *See page 724*
- İstanbul (Turkey) *See page 642*
- Tel Aviv (Israel) *See page 329*

Scenery
- Jebel Shams (Oman) *See page 516*
- Wadi Rum (Jordan) *See page 415*

Shopping
- Dubai (UAE) *See page 724*
- Damascus & Aleppo souqs (Syria) *See pages 590 & 611*
- İstanbul's Grand Bazaar (Turkey) *See page 650*

For the best of Islamic architecture see the Mosque special section *(see page 46)*.

Remember, though, that in the Middle East the atmosphere of the places and the activities of the people are often more interesting than the tangible 'sights'. In Damascus, for example, you could rush around the city's recognised attractions in half a day, but if you spend more time here strolling through the souq, sitting in a coffee house, or just talking to locals, you'll get far more out of the visit.

With that in mind, you could have a memorable trip through this part of the Middle East without seeing any of our highlights. In fact, some travellers may want to avoid these places precisely because they are in this book.

Latest Travel Advice

Lonely Planet's website (**W** www.lonelyplanet.com) contains information on what's new etc, and any new safety reports. See Digital Resources in this chapter for more information.

The US State Department's Bureau of Consular Affairs (Washington DC 20520, USA) offers periodically updated Consular Information Sheets, which include entry requirements, medical facilities, crime information and other topics – however, it has to be said these err heavily on the side of overcaution and are often out of date. They also have recorded travel information on ☎ 202-647 5225. You can subscribe to an online mailing list for all State Department travel advisories by sending a message containing the word 'subscribe' to **e** travel-advisories-request@stolaf.edu (St Olaf College, Northfield MN, USA). You can check out current and past advisories at **W** www.stolafedu/network/travel-advisories.html.

You can get British Foreign Office travel advisories from the Travel Advice Unit (☎ 020-7270 4129, fax 7270 4228), Foreign & Commonwealth Office, Room 605 Clive House, Petty France, London SW1H 9HD. Regularly updated Foreign Office travel advice is also displayed on BBC2 Ceefax, pp 564 ff.

Australians can ring the Department of Foreign Affairs and Trade in Canberra (☎ 02-6261 3305) for advisories, or visit the Consular Travel Advice website (**W** www.dfat.gov.au/consular/advice).

find that every country has piles of locally produced maps available, which vary in type and quality – from government survey maps to free tourist-office hand-outs.

Also check out Lonely Planet's city map series: Cairo, İstanbul and Jerusalem are currently available.

What to Bring

Clothes Temperatures are generally hot, so you won't need many clothes. Bear in mind the modesty issue though (see the Society & Conduct section in the Facts about the Region chapter and the Women Travellers section later in this chapter), and bring some light, (long-sleeved) baggy tops and trousers. Should you need to, you'll have no problem buying clothes anywhere in the Middle East, in Egypt, Israel and Turkey especially.

Note that in most places, especially in cities, local people dress smartly if they can afford to, so it might be worth taking a lightweight shirt and a pair of chinos or a skirt that you can keep clean and wear when the occasion demands it. They will be useful when it comes to visa applications or crossing borders, or if you are invited to somebody's house. Also, a lot of hotel bars and nightclubs have some kind of loose dress code. Military-style clothing or baggage is definitely not a good idea.

And don't forget the sunglasses and hat.

Equipment There are very few camping grounds in the Middle East, so it's not worth lugging a tent and camping gear around. A sleeping bag is useful in the cooler months, particularly if you're sleeping outside (for example on the roofs of hostels) or staying at some of the more rough-and-ready budget-accommodation options like tree houses in Turkey or beach camps in Sinai; a lightweight, one-season bag will do. Otherwise, bring a sheet liner at least.

Other useful items include a basic medical kit, mosquito repellent, sun cream or block, torch/flashlight and spare good-quality batteries, and eight to 10 passport-sized photos – because every time you apply for a visa you're going to need at least two or three. A universal washbasin plug is a good idea, as is a small padlock to secure the contents of your pack, a compact travel alarm, a Swiss Army–style knife and a length of cord for drying clothes.

Women should bring preferred sanitary protection – you can't always find what you want and when you do it's pricey (two boxes of tampons in Tehrān costs the same as a flight to Esfahān).

Outside big cities and traveller haunts, English-language reading matter can be hard to come by so make sure you bring your own paperbacks.

RESPONSIBLE TOURISM

Tourism is one of the Middle East's largest industries, and the impact on environment and culture can be great. A British organisation called **Tourism Concern** (☎ *020-7753 333;* w *www.tourismconcern.org.uk; Stapleton House, 177-281 Holloway Rd, London N7 8NN)* has come up with some guidelines for travellers who wish to minimise any negative impact they may have on the countries they visit. These guidelines include:

Save Precious Natural Resources Try not to waste water. Switch off lights and air-conditioning when you go out. Avoid establishments that clearly consume limited resources such as water and electricity at the expense of local residents.

Support Local Enterprise Use locally owned hotels and restaurants and support trade and craft workers by buying locally made souvenirs.

Ask Before Taking Close-Up Photographs of People Don't worry if you don't speak the language. A smile and gesture will be understood and appreciated.

Respect for Local Etiquette Earns You Respect Politeness is a virtue in most parts of the world but remember that different people have different ideas about what's polite. In many places, tight fitting wear, revealing shorts or skimpy tops are insensitive to local feelings. Loose lightweight clothing is preferable. Similarly, public displays of affection are often culturally inappropriate.

Be Informed Learning something about the history and current affairs of a country helps you understand its people and helps prevent misunderstandings and frustrations.

Be Patient, Friendly and Sensitive Remember that you are a guest.

To which we would add:

Leave It as You Found It As long as outsiders have been stumbling over the ancient monuments of the Middle East, they have also been chipping bits off or leaving their own contributions engraved upon them. When visiting historical sites, consider the irreparable damage you inflict upon them when you climb to the top of a pyramid, or take home an unattached sample of carved masonry.

Don't Litter Resist the local tendency of indifference to littering and bin your rubbish or, if there are no bins, carry it with you until you can dispose of it properly.

Do as Requested Strange to say, but despite warnings and posted signs to the contrary, divers and snorkellers continue to destroy coral by touching it and treading on it, and despite instructions to the contrary, drivers in national parks still insist on heading off the beaten track, in some cases causing great damage to the fragile environment.

See also the boxed text 'Footprints in the Sand Only, Please' in the Egypt chapter, which deals with good behaviour in desert environments.

TOURIST OFFICES

Most countries in the region have tourist offices with branches in big towns and at tourist sights. However, don't expect much. Usually the most the offices can stretch to is a free map; help with booking accommodation or any other service is typically

The Israeli Stamp Stigma

Israel is, of course, the venue for that popular Middle Eastern game that involves entering and leaving Israel without picking up any 'incriminating evidence' that one has been there. In the Middle East, only Turkey, Egypt and Jordan recognise Israel – all other countries in the region refuse to admit anyone whose passport is tainted by evidence of a visit to the Jewish state. Israeli immigration officials will, if asked, stamp only your entry permit and not your passport. This is fine for those flying to and from Israel, but if you're crossing into Egypt or Jordan overland, the entry stamps into those countries at an Israeli border crossing will be considered no less incriminating than an Israeli stamp. Travellers leaving Israel have managed to get Jordanian officials to stamp a separate piece of paper leaving passports untainted, but Syrian border officials usually want to see your Jordanian entry stamp and if they don't find one they are likely to bar your entry.

Visiting Israel from Jordan, many travellers have convinced Jordanian immigration officers (especially at the Allenby Bridge crossing) to stamp a separate piece of paper, thus entering and leaving Israel via Jordan without accruing any stamps. But this is still risky. Get a pig-headed immigration officer and there go your chances of visiting Syria, Iran, Yemen et al. In this case, your only option is to 'lose' and replace your passport in Jordan or Egypt. Even then, foreign passports issued in these countries may raise suspicions and your entry may still be barred.

The only sure way is to arrange your itinerary so that a visit to Israel comes after those countries that discriminate against the Jewish state.

beyond the resources of the often nonetheless amiable staff. (The exception to this is some of the offices in Israel, which are in fact very useful.) You will usually get better results relying on the knowledge and resourcefulness of your hotel reception. Tourist office locations are given in the individual town and city sections.

VISAS & DOCUMENTS
Passport

Some countries require that your passport is valid for at least three months beyond the time you plan staying in their country, so renew yours if it's near the end of its life-span. Make sure it has plenty of blank pages too – at least two for every country you intend visiting (one for the visa, one for the entry and exit stamps).

Visas

You can either get them before you go or along the way, or increasingly frequently, at the airport or border – a brief summary of requirements is given in the table 'Visas at a Glance', but for more information see the relevant country chapter.

The advantage of predeparture collection is that it doesn't waste travelling time and 'difficult' embassies are sometimes less dif-

Visas at a Glance

For full visa costs and exactly how and where to get your visas, see the Visas & Documents section in the relevant country chapters.

country	visa required?	visa available on arrival?	any special requirements?	visa available in the Middle East?
Bahrain	Yes	Yes	None	n/a
Egypt	Yes (unless just visiting Sinai)	At airports & seaports only	None	Yes, in all capitals plus Aqaba & Eilat
Iran	Yes	No	Must not have visited Israel	Yes, in all capitals
Iraq	Yes	No	Must not have visited Israel	Possibly, but don't count on it
Israel	No	n/a	None	n/a
Jordan	Yes	Yes (except at King Hussein Bridge)	None	n/a
Kuwait	Yes	No	Local sponsor	May be possible from Egypt but still need sponsor
Lebanon	Yes	Yes	Must not have visited Israel	n/a
Oman	Yes	Yes	Israeli nationals may not enter	n/a
Qatar	Yes	Yes	None	n/a
Saudi Arabia	Yes	No	Must not have visited Israel	Possibly, but don't count on it
Syria	Yes	No*	Must not have visited Israel	Bahrain, Egypt, Kuwait, Qatar, Turkey
Turkey	(See Turkey chapter)	Yes	None	n/a
UAE	Yes	Yes	Must not have visited Israel**	n/a
Yemen	Yes	No	Must not have visited Israel	Only in Egypt (one week), Qatar (one day) and the UAE (three to five days)

* If your home country has no Syrian embassy you may obtain your visa at the border.
**But see the UAE chapter for a note on this.

ficult when you are in your own country. There is also never any guarantee that the Iranians and, sometimes, the Syrians, are going to grant you a visa; if you apply from home first, you at least know where you stand before setting off. If you are turned down in your home country, there's usually nothing to stop you trying again while on the road.

Some embassies request a letter from an employer or, if you're applying abroad, a letter of introduction from your embassy, while if the Israeli officials don't like the look of you they may ask to see that you have a sufficient amount of money to cover your stay. Some embassies also ask to see a 'ticket out', which means that before you can obtain a visa to get into a country you must have a ticket to prove that you intend leaving again.

Travel Insurance

Travel insurance covering theft, loss and medical problems is a good idea. Some policies offer lower and higher medical-expense options; the higher ones are chiefly for countries such as the USA, which have extremely high medical costs. There is a wide variety of policies available, so check the small print.

Some policies specifically exclude 'dangerous activities', which can include scuba diving, motorcycling, even trekking. A locally acquired motorcycle licence is not valid under some policies.

You may prefer a policy that pays doctors or hospitals directly rather than you having to pay on the spot and claim later. If you have to claim later make sure you keep all documentation. Some policies ask you to call back (reverse charges) to a centre in your home country where an immediate assessment of your problem is made.

Check that the policy covers ambulances or an emergency flight home.

Driving Licence & Permits

If you plan to drive, get an International Driving Permit from your local automobile association. They are valid for one year only. If you plan to take your own car you will need a *carnet de passage* (a booklet that is stamped on arrival in and departure from a country to ensure that you export the vehicle again, after you've imported it) and third-party insurance or a Green Card (see Car & Motorcycle in the Getting Around the Region chapter for more information).

Student Cards

An International Student Identity Card (ISIC) can come in useful in the Middle East. Egypt, Israel and Turkey have various student discounts on flights and rail travel, and reduced admissions at museums, archaeological sites and monuments of anything between 25% to 33% for card holders. A student card also gets the holder 50% off admissions to museums and cultural sites in Iran, while in Syria it slashes admissions to almost all historical sites to about a tenth of the normal foreigners' price. Bear in mind that a student card issued by your own university or college may not be recognised elsewhere: it really should be an ISIC.

Copies

All important documents (passport data page and visa page, credit cards, travel insurance policy, air/bus/train tickets, driving licence etc) should be photocopied before you leave home. Leave one copy with someone at home and keep another with you, separate from the originals.

EMBASSIES & CONSULATES

It's important to realise what your own embassy – the embassy of the country of which you are a citizen – can and can't do to help you if you get into trouble. Generally speaking, it won't be much help in emergencies if the trouble you're in is remotely your own fault. Remember that you are bound by the laws of the country you are in. Your embassy will not be sympathetic if you end up in jail after committing a crime locally, even if such actions are legal in your own country.

In genuine emergencies you might get some assistance, but only if other channels have been exhausted. For example, if you need to get home urgently, a free ticket home is exceedingly unlikely – the embassy would expect you to have insurance. If you have all your money and documents stolen, it might assist with getting a new passport, but a loan for onward travel is out of the question.

Some embassies used to keep letters for travellers or have a small reading room with home newspapers, but these days the mail holding service has usually been stopped and even newspapers tend to be out of date.

For the addresses and contact details of embassies and consulates abroad and in the

Middle East, see the Facts for the Visitor sections in the individual country chapters.

CUSTOMS

Customs regulations vary from country to country, but in most cases they aren't that different from what you'd expect in the West – a couple of hundred cigarettes and a couple of bottles of booze. The exceptions are, of course, in dry countries like Iran, Kuwait and Saudi Arabia, where it is strictly forbidden to take alcohol into the country.

Electronics always arouse plenty of interest too, especially in Egypt, Syria and Iran. Items like laptop computers and especially video cameras may incur heavy taxes, or they may be written into your passport to ensure that they leave the country with you and are not sold. If you are carrying this sort of thing, it's better not to be too obvious about it.

In many Middle Eastern countries, particularly those in the Gulf and Iran, video and even audio cassettes come in for scrutiny and may be taken off you for examination. In Iran and Saudi Arabia books and magazines will also be given a careful going through for any pornographic or other incendiary material. Even something as innocuous as *Newsweek* may be confiscated because, for example, a woman in an ad is deemed to be wearing a dress that's too low cut. The simple rule is don't take in any print material that you're not prepared to lose.

MONEY

Details on the currencies used in each country, places to change money and advice on specific exchange rates are given in the individual country chapters. Throughout this general section we have quoted prices in US dollars (US$) as these rates are more likely to remain stable than local currencies, which may go up and down.

Exchanging Money

Check around when looking to exchange your cash as rates do vary. A good general rule is to never change cash at borders or airports. Also be on the lookout for hidden extras like commission. Official money-changers rather than banks often offer the best deals. Throughout the Middle East avoid accepting torn or particularly tatty notes as you will have difficulty disposing of them.

Cash & Travellers Cheques Most travellers carry a mix of cash and travellers cheques. Cash is quicker to deal with, can be exchanged almost any place and gets better rates, but it cannot be replaced. Travellers cheques are accepted everywhere in the Middle East except for Iraq and Iran; it's also difficult to find places to cash them in Yemen, though it's not impossible. If your travellers cheques are lost or stolen you get a refund. When you buy your cheques make sure you are clear about what to do when the worst happens – most companies give you a 24-hour international phone number to contact. Well-known brands of cheque such as American Express (AmEx) and Thomas Cook are better to deal with as they're the most widely accepted; both companies have offices in the Middle East.

It's worth carrying a mix of high and low denomination notes and cheques so that if you're about to leave a country, you can change just enough for a few days and not have too much local currency to get rid of.

ATMs Most of the larger banks in the region (with the exception of those in Iran, Iraq, Syria and Yemen) now have Automated Teller Machines (ATMs) linked up to one of the international networks (eg, MasterCard/ Cirrus or Visa/Plus or GlobalAccess systems). In countries like Bahrain, Egypt, Israel & the Palestinian Territories, Lebanon, Oman, Qatar, Saudi Arabia, Turkey and the UAE it's possible to completely avoid having to bring wads of cash and/or travellers cheques – just bring your plastic. Major credit and credit/debit cards, especially Visa and MasterCard, are readily accepted and many machines will also take bank-issued cash cards (which you use at home to withdraw money directly from your bank account). Make sure you remember your PIN (personal identification number), and it is also a good idea to check out what sort of transaction fees you are likely to incur from both your own bank and the banks whose machines you will be using while you travel. See Money in the individual country chapters for more details.

Credit Cards Countries like Iran and Yemen aside (where your plastic is useless), credit cards are fairly widely accepted in the Middle East, although in Syria and Jordan their use is often restricted to top-end hotels. Israel & the

Palestinian Territories, Lebanon and the Gulf States, on the other hand, are fully plastic societies where almost everything can be paid for by credit card, right down to your morning coffee. Visa, MasterCard and American Express are the most popular. It's possible to get cash advances on credit cards in several countries in the region including Egypt and Israel – see Money in those individual country chapters for more details.

International Transfers Bank-to-bank transfers are possible but, unless your home bank has links with a banking group in the country you're travelling in, it is a very complicated, time-consuming and expensive business, especially when you get outside the major capitals. Unless you are going to be in that one place for at least a couple of weeks don't attempt it. A cash advance on a credit card is much simpler. Alternatively, Western Union Money Transfer has representatives in quite a few Middle East countries including Bahrain, Egypt, Israel, Qatar and Turkey.

Black Market There is still black-market activity in some Middle Eastern countries, notably Iran. If you do play the black market don't do it on the street – a dealer with a front, a travel agent or tailor shop, for example, is safest. Big notes are worth much more than small ones – 100 US$1 bills are worth less than one US$100 bill.

Security
The safest place to carry your money is right next to your skin. A money belt, pouch or an extra pocket inside your jeans will help to keep things with their rightful owner. Remember that if you lose cash you have lost it forever, so don't go overboard on the convenience of cash versus the safety of cheques. A good idea is to put aside a separate emergency stash, say US$50, for use if everything else disappears.

Costs
The Gulf States, Lebanon and Israel & the Palestinian Territories aside, travel in the Middle East is cheap. Daily travel costs in Bahrain, Kuwait and Qatar range from between US$70 (Bahrain) to US$150 (Kuwait) for the average-budget traveller. In Lebanon you could limit yourself to US$20 a day on the tightest budget, while to travel more comfortably would see you spending around US$40 a day. In Israel & the Palestinian Territories, budget travellers could keep things down to $US35 per day.

Elsewhere real shoestringers could pare living expenses down to no more than US$10 to US$15 a day, although a more realistic budget that allows for site admissions, a varied diet and an improved chance of getting hot water at your hotel might be US$30 a day.

When estimating your own costs, take into account extra items such as visa fees (which can top US$50 depending on where you get them and what your nationality is), long-distance travel, plus the cost of organised tours or activities such as camel trekking, snorkelling or diving.

More details of costs are given under Money in the individual country chapters.

Tipping
Tipping is expected in all Middle Eastern countries except to some extent in Oman, and in Yemen where this practice simply does not exist. Called 'baksheesh', it is more than just a reward for having rendered a service. Salaries and wages are much lower than in Western countries, so baksheesh is regarded as an often essential means of supplementing income. To a cleaner in a one- or two-star hotel who might earn the equivalent of US$50 per month, the accumulated daily dollar tips given by guests can constitute the mainstay of his or her salary.

For Western travellers who are not used to continual tipping, demands for baksheesh for doing anything from opening doors to pointing out the obvious in museums can be quite irritating. But it is the accepted way. Don't be intimidated into paying baksheesh when you don't think the service warrants it, but remember that more things warrant baksheesh here than anywhere in the West.

One tip: carry lots of small change with you but keep it separate from bigger bills, so that baksheesh demands don't increase when they see that you can afford more.

Bargaining
In Middle Eastern countries, bargaining over prices is a way of life. People from the West often have difficulty with this concept, and are used to things having a fixed

value, whereas in the Middle East commodities are typically considered worth whatever their seller can get for them.

In markets selling basic items like fruit and vegetables *some* sellers will put their asking price high when they see you as a wealthy foreigner. If you pay this – whether out of ignorance or guilt about how much you have compared to locals – you may be considered foolish, but you'll also be doing fellow travellers a disservice by creating the impression that all foreigners are willing to pay any price named. Having said that, many sellers will quote you the same price that locals pay, particularly away from cities or tourist areas. It is very important not to go around expecting *everybody* to charge high. It helps of course to know the price of things. After the first few days in a country (when you'll inevitably pay over the odds a few times) you'll soon get to learn the standard prices for basic items.

Bazaars & Souqs In the bazaars and souqs, where many of the items are specifically for tourists, bargaining is very much expected. The vendor's aim is to identify the highest price you're willing to pay. Your aim is to find the price below which the vendor will not sell.

People have all sorts of formulas for working out what this should be but there are no hard and fast rules. The vendor will always first quote you a price inflated anywhere between two-fold and four-fold. Decide what you want to pay or what others have told you they've paid, and your first offer should be about half this. At this stage, the vendor may laugh or feign outrage, while you plead abject poverty. The vendor's price then starts to drop from the original quote to a more realistic level. When it does, you begin making better offers until you arrive at a mutually agreeable price. Tea or coffee might be served as part of the bargaining ritual, but accepting it doesn't place you under any obligation to buy.

If a seller won't come down to a price you feel is fair, it either means he really isn't making any profit, or that if you don't pay his price, he knows somebody else will. Remember the sellers are under no more obligation to sell to you, than you are to buy from them. You can go elsewhere, or (if you really want the item) accept the price.

POST & COMMUNICATIONS

Post and telephone services are quite reliable in most of the Middle East, though in rural areas the service can range from slow to nonexistent – it definitely pays to make your calls or send your mail from the main centres. For more specific details, such as rates and prices, see Post & Communications in the individual country chapters.

Sending Mail

Letters sent from a major capital take about a week to reach most parts of Europe, and anything between a week and two weeks to reach North America or Australasia. If you're in a hurry, either DHL or Federal Express has offices in almost every capital city in the Middle East.

Receiving Mail

If you need to receive mail, you can use *poste restante* services. Have letters sent to a post office (usually in a capital city or major town) for you to collect. Letters should be addressed in this form:

Your NAME
Poste Restante
General Post Office
City, Country

To collect your mail, go to the main post office in that town and show your passport. Letters sometimes take a few weeks to work through the system, so have them sent to a place where you're going to be for a while, or or to a place you will be passing through more than once.

Some hotels and tour companies operate a mail-holding service, and AmEx customers can have mail sent to AmEx offices. Details are given under Post & Communications in the individual country chapters.

Telephone & Fax

Most cities and large towns have public telephone offices (either part of the post office, or privately run) where you can make international calls and send faxes and telegraphs. Card phones are starting to appear in many countries, including Egypt, Jordan, Syria, Turkey and Yemen, from which you can direct dial internationally, but at present the service is limited. The exceptions are Bahrain, Israel, Oman, Qatar and the UAE, where virtually all public phones offer international direct dial.

Costs for international calls start at about US$3 per minute, and only a few countries offer reduced rates at night. The other problem is the waiting time between placing your call with the operator and actually getting through, which can be minutes or hours depending on the locality and time of day.

Mobile Phones Throughout the Middle East the use of mobile phones is widespread (not to say obsessive) and every country has its own networks. Some of these networks run on the GSM system, like Europe, so if your phone works on GSM and your account allows you to roam, then you'll be able to use your mobile (this is the case in Egypt and Oman). In other places you'll have to buy prepaid sim cards. Beware though: the cost of using a mobile in some countries is up to three times as high as a call on a land line. See individual country chapters for further details.

Email & Internet Access

The Middle East is joining the communications revolution, but as yet hooking up your laptop is still difficult throughout most of the region. If you plan to carry your notebook or palmtop computer with you, remember that the power supply voltage in the Middle East may vary from that at home, risking damage to your equipment. The best investment is a universal AC adaptor for your appliance, which will enable you to plug it in anywhere without frying the innards. You'll also need a plug adaptor for each country you visit (see Electricity later in this chapter) – often it's easiest to buy these before you leave home.

Also, your PC-card modem may or may not work once you leave your home country (and you won't know for sure until you try). The safest option is to buy a reputable 'global' modem before you leave home. Keep in mind that there are a variety of telephone sockets used in each country, so ensure that you have at least a US RJ-11 telephone adaptor that works with your modem. For more information on travelling with a portable computer, see **w** www.teleadapt .com or **w** www.warrior.com.

AOL (**w** www.aol.com) and **CompuServe** (**w** www.compuserve.com) have dial-in nodes only in Egypt, Israel and Turkey. If you access your Internet email account at home through a smaller ISP or your office or school network, your best option is either to open an account with a global ISP, like those mentioned above, or to rely on Internet cafés and other public access points to collect your mail.

If you intend to rely on Internet cafés, you'll need to carry three pieces of information with you to enable you to access your Internet mail account: your incoming (POP or IMAP) mail server name, your account name and your password. Your ISP or network supervisor will be able to give you these. Armed with this information, you should be able to access your Internet mail account from any Net-connected machine in the world, provided it runs some kind of email software (remember that Netscape and Internet Explorer both have mail modules). It pays to become familiar with the process for doing this before you leave home.

You'll find Internet cafés throughout the Middle East (even Iran, Syria and Saudi Arabia are now online big time). But while getting access is usually no problem, connection speeds can be painfully slow. Addresses are given in individual town and city sections.

DIGITAL RESOURCES

The Internet is a rich resource for travellers. You can research your trip, hunt down bargain air fares, book hotels, check on weather conditions or chat with locals and other travellers about the best places to visit (or avoid).

There's no better place to start your explorations than the **Lonely Planet website** (**w** www.lonelyplanet.com). Here you'll find succinct summaries on travelling to most places on earth; travel news; postcards from other travellers; the Thorn Tree bulletin board, where you can ask questions before you go or dispense advice when you get back; and subWWWay, which links you to the most useful travel resources elsewhere on the Web.

Much of the Middle East has been slow to embrace the Internet – governments in the region are wary of encouraging a system that allows for an unregulated flow of information. As a result the best Arab-oriented websites tend to emanate from Europe or America, developed largely by Middle Eastern expatriates, students or trade associations dealing with the Middle East. There's some good stuff out there – whether you want to find out the current prayer times or arrange yourself a marriage... Of course, there's a lot of dross too, but the following sites are some of the better ones.

ArabCafe A lively message and discussion board on Arab-world related issues. Sample topics on our last visit: 'The Fate of the city of Jerusalem'; 'Arabic concerts in the USA'; 'Can't we all just get along?'.
W www.members3.boardhost.com/arabcafe/
Arabnet Excellent Saudi-run online encyclopaedia of the Arab world, collecting together news and articles plus links to further resources organised by country.
W www.arab.net
ArabStars The online Arab-world equivalent of Hello! – lots of gossip and news on Middle Eastern pop stars and film idols. Strangely addictive.
W www.arabtop.net
Al-Bab Arab-world gateway ('Al-Bab' means 'The Gate') that covers the entire Arab world with links to dozens of news services, country profiles, travel sites, maps, profiles, etc. A fantastic resource.
W www.al-bab.com/arab/countries/egypt.htm
BBC News Follow the links to the Middle East section for comprehensive and excellent regional news that's constantly updated. You can also access the archives of old stories and follow links to topical in-depth features.
W www.news.bbc.co.uk
Great Buildings Online Download then explore digital 3D models of the Pyramids and İstanbul's, Aya Sofia, plus lots of other info and images of monuments throughout the Middle East.
W www.greatbuildings.com
Al-Mashriq A repository for cultural information from the Levant (Israel, Jordan, Lebanon, Palestine, Syria, Turkey). This site hasn't been added to for a long time, but nevertheless collects a host of articles on everything from ethnology to politics.
W www.almashriq.hiof.no

BOOKS

Most books are published in different editions by different publishers in different countries. As a result, a book might be a hardcover rarity in one country while it's readily available in paperback in another. Fortunately, bookshops and libraries search by title or author, so your local bookshop or library is best placed to provide you with information on the availability of the following recommendations.

The books listed here contain general information about the Middle East. Other books more relevant to individual countries are listed under Books in each chapter.

Lonely Planet

Lonely Planet has several detailed guides to the Middle East *(Bahrain, Kuwait & Qatar; Egypt; Iran; Israel & the Palestinian Territories; Jordan; Lebanon; Libya; Oman & the UAE; Syria; Turkey; İstanbul to Cairo;* and *Yemen)*. There are also city guides *(Cairo, Dubai* and *İstanbul)* World Food guides *(Morocco* and *Turkey)*, a diving guide *(Diving & Snorkeling the Red Sea)* and phrasebooks *(Egyptian Arabic, Farsi, Hebrew* and *Turkish)*.

Lonely Planet's travel-literature series, *Journeys*, includes stories from Syria *(The Gates of Damascus* by Lieve Joris), Jordan *(Kingdom of the Film Stars* by Annie Caulfield), Iran *(Black on Black: Iran Revisited* by Ana Briongos), and Israel and the Palestinian Territories *(Breaking Ranks: Turbulant Travels in the Promised Land* by Ben Black).

Arts & Culture

Architecture of the Islamic World edited by George Michell. Its gazetteer approach (what's where) makes this a very useful volume for the traveller. It's well illustrated, generally avoids stuffiness and remains pretty much the standard work on the subject.
Islamic Arts by Jonathan Bloom & Sheila Blair. Part of Phaidon's beautifully formatted Arts & Ideas series, this is an excellent introduction to the subject; the text is lively and concise, and there are some great photos.
Oriental Rugs & A Buyer's Guide by Essie Sakhi. As well as colour photographs, the book includes useful information on the history of Persian carpets, how they are made, and even more importantly, what to look for when buying one.

History & Politics

The Arab World: Forty Years of Change by Elizabeth Fernea & Robert Warnock. A wide-ranging and very readable overview of trends and events in the recent history of the Middle East. It makes a great primer for a trip to the region.
Arabia Without Sultans by Fred Halliday. A detailed and accurate account of the development of the Arab Gulf countries in recent decades, with some 180 pages devoted to Yemen.
From Beirut to Jerusalem by Thomas Friedman. The recent history of the Middle Eastern conflicts as witnessed by a Pulitzer prize-winning journalist.

Fascinating remains from past civilisations abound throughout the region. The cliff-hugging bridge at Shihara, Yemen (top left); the tombs at Jebel Hafit, UAE (top right); the desert castle at Qusayr Amra, Jordan (middle right); and the city of Bam, Iran (bottom) – all speak of an ancient heritage.

PHILIP GAME

BETHUNE CARMICHAEL

OLIVIER CIRENDINI

PAUL GREENWAY

Middle Eastern cities are exciting places to be. From traditional Jeddah, Saudi Arabia (top left) and ultra-modern Dubai, UAE (top right), to Egypt's dynamic Cairo (middle left), cosmopolitan İstanbul in Turkey (bottom left) and Lebanon's chic Beirut, the recurring themes are colour, grace and vitality.

The book is an excellent read for anyone seeking a fuller understanding of the causes and effects of the strife that afflicts the region.

A History of the Arab Peoples by Albert Hourani. While not exactly holiday reading, this is possibly the single best book on the development and sociology of the modern-day Arab world.

The Middle East by Bernard Lewis. A recent and very erudite overview of Middle Eastern history from the rise of Christianity to the present day.

Money For Old Rope; Tribes With Flags by Charles Glass. Two collections of articles and essays on Levantine politicking by veteran journalist Glass. Both include accounts of his kidnapping and subsequent escape from pro-Iranian guerrillas in Beirut.

A Peace to End All Peace: Creating the Modern Middle East, 1914-1922 by David Fromkin. For some background on how the Middle East came to be the mess that it is, this book is absolutely essential. Fromkin defines the region broadly, even taking in Central Asia, as he details the Western machinations during and immediately after WWI that laid the groundwork for the Middle Eastern politics of today.

People & Society

The Hidden Face of Eve: Women in the Arab World by Nawal el-Saadawi. The author is an Egyptian psychiatrist, feminist, novelist and writer of nonfiction. Her books are well worth reading for the insight they provide into the lives of women in the Arab world. This one considers the role of women in world history, Arab history and literature.

Nine Parts of Desire by Geraldine Brooks. An investigation into the life of women under Islam. As befits a Wall Street Journal correspondent, the book succeeds in maintaining a degree of objectivity, and interview sources range from village girls to Queen Noor of Jordan and the daughter of President Rafsanjāni of Iran.

Price of Honour by Jan Goodwin. The blurb on the back of this book includes the terms 'horrific', 'abused', 'oppressed' and 'restrictions', and that's all within a single sentence. Goodwin has clocked up the miles and the hours in her quest to expose the Muslim world's mistreatment of women, but you can't help but suspect she already had her script written long before she set about her research.

Literature

For literature by Middle Eastern writers see the Arts section in the Facts about the Region chapter.

Travel

Arabia Through the Looking Glass by Jonathan Raban. One of the most readable of English travel writers, Raban, in this early book, visits the Arab Gulf countries during the oil boom. His observations on expatriate life in the region are as valid today as they were when he visited in early 1979.

Arabian Sands by Wilfred Thesiger. The author was one of the last great adventurers. As much anthropologist and ethnographer as traveller, in this book he lovingly records the desert life of the Gulf nomads in the last years before the discovery of oil was to change the region forever.

Baghdad Without a Map by Tony Horwitz. Should really be subtitled, 'the trials and misadventures of a freelance journalist awash in the Middle East'. Among other places, Horwitz trips up in Baghdad, Beirut, Tehrān and Yemen. Sober reading for anyone who thought they might make some easy cash by flogging their travel diary on getting back home.

East is West; Valleys of the Assassins; Beyond the Euphrates by Freya Stark. Probably the most famous of a number of distinguished women travellers in the Middle East, Stark wrote more than 20 books recounting her travels throughout the region.

Expats by Christopher Dickey. A side of the Middle East that's rarely written about – expatriate life in Libya, Egypt and the Gulf. Well observed and fluidly written by a former *Newsweek* correspondent.

From the Holy Mountain by William Dalrymple. An ambitious attempt by the most fêted travel writer of the moment to revisit the roots of Christianity in the troubled spots of eastern Turkey, Lebanon, Palestine and middle Egypt. Beautifully written and highly recommended.

Pillars of Hercules by Paul Theroux. The normally acerbic and grumpy Theroux lightens up a little as his exploratory jaunt around the fringes of the Mediterranean takes in seaside Turkey, Syria, Israel and Egypt.

Sandstorms by Peter Theroux. A memoir of the author's seven years stationed as a journalist in Riyadh, bookended by stays in Cairo.

Travels With a Tangerine by Tim Mackintosh-Smith. A modern account (published 2001) of a journey in the footsteps of Ibn Battuta, a 13th century Arab Marco Polo, starting in Morocco and taking in several countries of the Middle East.

FILMS

Murder, war and horror. Those three words pretty much sum up the role of the Middle East in modern cinema as portrayed by Western film makers. Despite the often stunning scenery and fantastic monuments, it's always some terrible scene that plays out here on celluloid. It's partly Agatha Christie's fault – she set the ball rolling with a murder on a train as it sped to İstanbul *(Murder on the Orient*

Express) and foul play involving little old ladies on a cruise ship in Egypt *(Death on the Nile)*. Both books were filmed in the '70s with all-star casts.

The cinematography was lush in both cases, but never has the region looked better than in David Lean's explosive epic *Lawrence of Arabia* (1962), shot around Wadi Rum in Jordan (with Seville standing in for Cairo). Peter Weir's harrowing *Gallipoli* (1981) is the same war but stripped of romance, as Australian troops train in the Egyptian desert before being cut to ribbons in the Turkish Dardanelles.

Horror of a different kind can be found in *The Exorcist* (1973), which opens with a very eerie prologue filmed in Iraq. This kicked off a genre trend: *Damien: Omen II* (1978) opens in Akko (Israel) and Brian DePalma's *The Fury* (1978) begins the bloodletting in Caesarea (also in Israel).

James Bond has been a frequent visitor to the region, first in *From Russia with Love* (1962), which made excellent use of İstanbul locations, then in *The Spy Who Loved Me* (1977), which has Egypt provide the Martini-glamorous backdrops for the campy, smirking antics of Roger Moore. In *The World Is Not Enough* (1999) Bond is back in İstanbul.

The most recent filmic trend is the 'US army whups the towelheads' movie, eg, *Three Kings* (1999) set in post-Desert Storm Iraq and *Rules of Engagement* (2000) where Yemeni folk are shown to be all bloodthirsty gun-wielding terrorists – and that's just the women and children.

For the work of Middle Eastern directors see Cinema in the Facts about the Region chapter.

NEWSPAPERS & MAGAZINES

There are no English-language daily or weekly newspapers that cover the whole of the Middle East or have any kind of regional distribution. Instead, almost all the countries have their own English-language press. These vary greatly in quality. Many papers are state-run and contain little for anyone with interests beyond those of what the president did this week. Nongovernment papers are, in most Middle Eastern countries outside of Israel, subject to censorship, but as long as they stay away from military topics, wayward interpretations of Islam and say

only good things about the country's leaders, this doesn't affect the reporting too much. About the best English-language paper in the region is the *Daily Star*, published out of Beirut. It's only available in Lebanon, but it does have a good website – see Digital Resources in the Lebanon chapter. For details of other English-language papers see Newspapers & Magazines in the individual country chapters.

PHOTOGRAPHY & VIDEO
Film & Equipment

Most types of film are available in the Middle East, though they may not be easily found outside of the big cities. Colour-print processing is usually quite adequate, while B&W and slide processing is not that good.

Film prices are usually similar, if not more expensive, to prices in Western countries, so you may want to bring your own supply. In some countries, film may have been stored for ages in less than ideal conditions, so always check the 'use by' date.

Cameras and lenses collect dust quickly in desert areas. Lens paper and cleaners can be difficult to find in some countries, so bring your own. A dust brush is also useful.

Technical Tips

In most Middle Eastern countries, early morning and late afternoon are the best times to take photographs. During the rest of the day, sunlight can be too bright and the sky too hazy, causing your photos to look washed out. There are a few remedies for this: a polarisation filter will cut glare and reflection off sand and water; a lens hood will cut some of the glare; Kodachrome film, with an ASA of 64, and Fujichrome 50 ASA and 100 ASA are good slide films to use when the sun is bright.

Many religious sites and other buildings are not lit inside and you'll need long exposures (several seconds), a powerful flash or faster film. A tripod can be very useful, too.

Restrictions

In most Middle Eastern countries, it is forbidden to photograph anything even vaguely military in nature (bridges, train stations, airports and other public works). The definition of what is 'strategic' differs from one country to another, and signs are not always posted, so err on the side of caution.

Photography is usually allowed inside religious and archaeological sites, unless there are signs indicating otherwise. As a rule, however, do not photograph inside mosques during a service.

Many Middle Easterners are sensitive about the negative aspects of their country, so exercise discretion when taking photos in poorer areas.

Also, be aware that certain countries, like Iran, are very suspicious of video cameras and may not allow you to take one into the country. See Photography & Video in the individual country chapters for further details.

Photographing People

As a matter of courtesy, don't photograph people without asking their permission first. Children will almost always say yes, but adults may say no. In the more conservative Muslim countries, such as Iran, Kuwait and Saudi Arabia, you should not photograph women. In countries where you can photograph women, show them the camera and make it clear that you want to take a picture of them.

TIME

Egypt, Israel, Jordan, Lebanon, Syria and Turkey are two hours ahead of GMT/UTC.

Bahrain, Iraq, Kuwait, Qatar, Saudi Arabia and Yemen are three hours ahead; and Iran is 3½ hours ahead. See the boxed text to find out what the time is in your city when it's noon in the Middle Eastern capitals and which countries have daylight saving.

Time is something that Middle Eastern people always seem to have plenty of – something that should take five minutes will invariably take an hour. Trying to speed things up will only lead to frustration. It is better to take it philosophically than try to fight it.

ELECTRICITY

The electric current in most Middle Eastern countries is 220V AC, 50 Hz, though in some both 220V and 110V are in use in different areas – see the boxed text 'Electrical Conversions'. Bring along an adapter and transformer if necessary because these sorts of things are hard to find locally.

WEIGHTS & MEASURES

All the countries in this book use the metric system. There is a standard conversion table at the back of this book.

In Iran, you may still come across the *sir* (about 75g) and the *chārak* (10 *sir*) in some remoter places. Gold and other precious

---

Time Differences

When it's noon in the following Middle Eastern capitals, the time elsewhere is:

city	Paris	London	New York	LA	Hong Kong	Sydney	Auckland	daylight saving
Amman	10am	9am	4am	1am	5pm	7pm	9pm	yes
Baghdad	10am	9am	4am	1am	5pm	7pm	9pm	n/a
Beirut	11am	10am	5am	2am	6pm	8pm	10pm	yes
Cairo	11am	10am	5am	2am	6pm	8pm	10pm	yes
Damascus	11am	10am	5am	2am	6pm	8pm	10pm	yes
Doha	10am	9am	4am	1am	5pm	7pm	9pm	no
Dubai	9am	8am	3am	midnight	4pm	6pm	8pm	no
İstanbul	11am	10am	5am	2am	6pm	8pm	10pm	yes
Kuwait	10am	9am	4am	1am	5pm	7pm	9pm	no
Manama	10am	9am	4am	1am	5pm	7pm	9pm	no
Muscat	9am	8am	3am	12am	4pm	6pm	8pm	no
Riyadh	10am	9am	4am	1am	5pm	7pm	9pm	no
San'a	10am	9am	4am	1am	5pm	7pm	9pm	no
Tehrān	9.30am	8.30am	3.30am	12.30am	4.30pm	6.30pm	8.30pm	yes
Tel Aviv	11am	10am	5am	2am	6pm	8pm	10pm	yes

The above times do not take into account daylight saving.

Electrical Conversions

country	voltage	plug
Bahrain	230	3-pin UK-style
Egypt	220	round 2-pin
Iran	220	round 2-pin
Israel	220	round 2-pin
Jordan	220	round 2-pin
Kuwait	220, 240	2-&3-pin UK-style
Lebanon	220, 110	round & flat 2 pin
Oman	220, 240	3-pin UK-style
Qatar	230	3-pin UK-style
Saudi Arabia	220, 110*	3-pin UK-style
Syria	220	round 2-pin
Turkey	220	round 2-pin**
UAE	240 & 220***	3-pin UK-style
Yemen	220	3-pin UK-style

* Both 220 and 110 are found at various places in the kingdom, but the latter is more widespread.

** There are two sizes of plug in use in Turkey. The most common one is the small-diameter prong; the other is the large-diameter, grounded plug used in Germany and Austria.

*** The current is 240V in Abu Dhabi and 220V in the rest of the Emirates.

metals are still measured by the *mesghāl*, equal to 4.7g.

In the souqs of Oman, silver jewellery is often sold according to weight measured in *tolas*. Tolas are sometimes called *thallers* after the Maria Theresia dollar, an 18th-century Austrian coin which became the model for Arabia's common currency of the 19th and early 20th centuries. One *tola* is equal to 11.75g.

HEALTH

Travel health depends on your predeparture preparations, your daily health care while travelling and how you handle any medical problem that does develop. While the potential dangers can seem quite frightening, in reality few travellers experience anything more than an upset stomach.

Predeparture Planning

Immunisations Plan ahead for getting your vaccinations: some of them require more than one injection, while there are some vac-cinations should not be given together. Note that some vaccinations should not be given during pregnancy or to people with allergies – discuss with your doctor.

It is recommended you seek medical advice at least six weeks before travel. Be aware that there is often a greater risk of disease with children and during pregnancy.

Discuss your requirements with your doctor, but vaccinations you should consider for this trip include the following (for more details about the diseases themselves, see the individual disease entries later in this section). Carry proof of your vaccinations, especially yellow fever, as this is sometimes needed to enter some countries.

Diphtheria & Tetanus Vaccinations for these two diseases are usually combined and are recommended for everyone. After an initial course of three injections (usually given in childhood), boosters are necessary every 10 years.

Polio Everyone should keep up to date with this vaccination, which is normally given in childhood. A booster every 10 years maintains immunity.

Hepatitis A Hepatitis A vaccine (eg, Avaxim, Havrix 1440 or VAQTA) provides long-term immunity (possibly more than 10 years) after an initial injection and a booster at six to 12 months. Alternatively, an injection of gamma globulin can provide short-term protection against hepatitis A – two to six months, depending on the dose given. It is not a vaccine, but is ready-made antibody collected from blood donations. It is reasonably effective and, unlike the vaccine, it is protective immediately. However, because it's a blood product, there are current concerns about its long-term safety. Hepatitis A vaccine is also available in a combined form, Twinrix, with hepatitis B vaccine. Three injections over a six-month period are required, the first two providing substantial protection against hepatitis A.

Typhoid Vaccination against typhoid may be required if you are travelling for more than a couple of weeks in most parts of Asia, Africa, Central and South America and Central and Eastern Europe. It is now available either as an injection or as capsules to be taken orally. A combined hepatitis A/typhoid vaccine was launched recently, but its availability is still limited – check with your doctor to find out its status in your country.

Meningococcal Meningitis Vaccination is recommended for travellers to certain parts of Asia, India, Africa and South America. It is also required of all haj pilgrims entering Saudi Arabia. A single injection gives good protection against the major epidemic forms of the disease for three years. Protection may be less effective in children under two years.

Hepatitis B Travellers who should consider vaccination against hepatitis B include those on a long trip, as well as those visiting countries where there are high levels of hepatitis B infection, where blood transfusions may not be adequately screened or where sexual contact or needle sharing is a possibility. Vaccination involves three injections, with a booster at 12 months. More rapid courses are available if necessary.

Rabies Vaccination should be considered by those who will spend a month or longer in a country where rabies is common, especially if they are cycling, handling animals, caving or travelling to remote areas, and for children (who may not report a bite). Pretravel rabies vaccination involves having three injections over 21 to 28 days. If someone who has been vaccinated is bitten or scratched by an animal, they will require two booster injections of vaccine; those not vaccinated require more.

Malaria Medication Antimalarial drugs do not prevent you from being infected but kill the malaria parasites during a stage in their development and significantly reduce the risk of becoming very ill or dying. Expert advice on medication should be sought, as there are many factors to consider, including the area to be visited, the risk of exposure to malaria-carrying mosquitoes, the side effects of medication, your medical history and whether you are a child, an adult or pregnant. Travellers to isolated areas in high-risk countries may like to carry a treatment dose of medication for use if symptoms occur.

Health Insurance Make sure that you have adequate health insurance. See Travel Insurance under Visas & Documents earlier in this chapter for details.

Travel Health Guides Lonely Planet's *Healthy Travel Africa* is packed with useful information including pretrip planning, emergency first aid, immunisation and disease information and what to do if you get sick on the road. It's particularly useful in Egypt. *Travel with Children* from Lonely Planet also includes advice on travel health for younger children.

There are also a number of excellent travel-health sites on the Internet. From the Lonely Planet home page there are links at **w** www.lonelyplanet.com/weblinks/wlheal .htm to the World Health Organization and the US Centers for Disease Control & Prevention.

Other Preparations Make sure you're healthy before you start travelling. If you are going on a long trip make sure your teeth are OK. If you wear glasses take a spare pair and your prescription.

If you require a particular medication take an adequate supply, as it may not be available locally. Take part of the packaging showing the generic name rather than the brand, which will make getting replacements easier. It's a good idea to have a

Medical Kit Check List

Following is a list of items you should consider including in your medical kit – consult your pharmacist for brands available in your country.

☐ **Aspirin or paracetamol (acetaminophen in the USA)** – for pain or fever
☐ **Antihistamine** – for allergies, eg, hay fever; to ease the itch from insect bites or stings; and to prevent motion sickness
☐ **Cold and flu tablets, throat lozenges and nasal decongestant**
☐ **Multivitamins** – consider for long trips, when dietary vitamin intake may be inadequate
☐ **Antibiotics** – consider including these if you're travelling well off the beaten track; see your doctor, as they must be prescribed, and carry the prescription with you
☐ **Loperamide or diphenoxylate** – 'blockers' for diarrhoea
☐ **Prochlorperazine or metaclopramide** – for nausea and vomiting
☐ **Rehydration mixture** – to prevent dehydration, which may occur, for example, during bouts of diarrhoea; particularly important when travelling with children
☐ **Insect repellent, sunscreen, lip balm and eye drops**
☐ **Calamine lotion, sting relief spray or aloe vera** – to ease irritation from sunburn and insect bites or stings
☐ **Antifungal cream or powder** – for fungal skin infections and thrush
☐ **Antiseptic (such as povidone-iodine)** – for cuts and grazes
☐ **Bandages, Band-Aids (plasters) and other wound dressings**
☐ **Water purification tablets or iodine**
☐ **Scissors, tweezers and a thermometer** – note that mercury thermometers are prohibited by airlines

legible prescription or letter from your doctor to show that you legally use the medication to avoid any problems.

Basic Rules

Food Local-style food is usually safer than Western-style food because it's cooked much longer (sometimes all day) and the ingredients are invariably fresh. On the other hand, food in a smarter restaurant may have been lingering in a refrigerator.

Even travellers with sensitive stomachs can usually eat traditional Middle Eastern food if they ease themselves in gently to the change of diet. In any kind of restaurant, you might get a bit of stomach trouble if plates or cutlery aren't clean, but that can happen anywhere, and it doesn't happen often.

Water The number one rule is *be careful of the water* and especially ice. If you don't know for certain that the water is safe, assume the worst. Reputable brands of bottled water or soft drinks are generally fine, although in some places bottles may be refilled with tap water. Only use water from containers with a serrated seal – not tops or corks. Take care with fruit juice, particularly if water may have been added. Milk should be treated with suspicion as it is often unpasteurised, though boiled milk is fine if it is kept hygienically. Tea or coffee should also be OK, since the water should have been boiled.

Medical Problems & Treatment

Self-diagnosis and treatment can be risky, so you should always seek medical help. An embassy, consulate or five-star hotel can usually recommend a local doctor or clinic. Although we do give drug dosages in this section, they are for emergency use only. Correct diagnosis is vital. In this section we have used the generic names for medications (check with a pharmacist for brands available locally). It's worth bearing in mind that pharmacists throughout the Middle East are often staffed by highly knowledgeable graduates who can often give very good advice on medicines and drugs. They frequently speak good English and stay open late. Every town and city neighbourhood will have one pharmacy that stays open 24 hours.

Note that antibiotics should ideally be administered only under medical supervision. Take only the recommended dose at the prescribed intervals and use the whole course, even if the illness seems cured earlier. Stop immediately if there are any serious reactions and don't use the antibiotic at all if you are unsure that you have the correct one. Some people are allergic to commonly prescribed antibiotics such as penicillin; carry this information (eg, on a bracelet) when travelling.

Environmental Hazards

Heat Exhaustion Dehydration and salt deficiency can cause heat exhaustion. Take time to acclimatise to high temperatures, make sure you drink enough – don't rely on feeling thirsty to indicate when you should drink – and do not do anything too physically demanding.

Salt deficiency is characterised by fatigue, lethargy, headaches, giddiness and muscle cramps; salt tablets may help, but adding extra salt to your food is better.

Anhidrotic heat exhaustion is a rare form of heat exhaustion that is caused by an inability to sweat. It tends to affect people who have been in a hot climate for some time, rather than newcomers. It can progress to heatstroke. Treatment involves removal to a cooler climate.

Heatstroke This serious, occasionally fatal, condition can occur if the body's heat-regulating mechanism breaks down and the body temperature rises to dangerous levels. Long, continuous periods of exposure to high temperatures and insufficient fluids can leave you vulnerable to heatstroke.

The symptoms are feeling unwell, not sweating very much (or at all) and a high body temperature (39° to 41°C or 102° to 106°F). Where sweating has ceased, the skin becomes flushed and red. Severe, throbbing headaches and lack of coordination will also occur, and the sufferer may be confused or aggressive. Eventually the victim will become delirious or convulse. Hospitalisation is essential, but in the interim get victims out of the sun, remove their clothing, cover them with a wet sheet or towel and then fan continually. Give fluids if they are conscious.

Prickly Heat Prickly heat is an itchy rash caused by excessive perspiration trapped under the skin. It usually strikes people who have just arrived in a hot climate. Keeping cool, bathing often, drying the skin and using a mild talcum or prickly heat powder or resorting to air-conditioning may help.

Sunburn In the tropics, the desert or at high altitude you can get sunburnt surprisingly quickly, even through cloud. Use a sunscreen, a hat, and a barrier cream for your nose and lips. Calamine lotion or a commercial after-sun preparation are good for mild sunburn. Protect your eyes with good quality sunglasses, particularly if you will be near water, sand or snow.

Infectious Diseases

Diarrhoea Simple things like a change of water, food or climate can all cause a mild bout of diarrhoea, but a few rushed toilet trips with no other symptoms is not indicative of a major problem.

Dehydration is the main danger with any diarrhoea, particularly in children or the elderly as dehydration can occur quite quickly. Under all circumstances *fluid replacement* (at least equal to the volume being lost) is the most important thing to remember. Weak black tea with a little sugar, soda water, or soft drinks allowed to go flat and diluted 50% with clean water are all good. With severe diarrhoea a rehydrating solution is preferable to replace minerals and salts lost. Commercially available oral rehydration salts (ORS) are very useful; add them to boiled or bottled water. In an emergency you can make up a solution of six teaspoons of sugar and a half teaspoon of salt to a litre of boiled or bottled water. You need to drink at least the same volume of fluid that you are losing in bowel movements and vomiting. Urine is the best guide to the adequacy of replacement – if you have small amounts of concentrated urine, you need to drink more. Keep drinking small amounts often. Stick to a bland diet as you recover.

Gut-paralysing drugs such as loperamide or diphenoxylate can be used to bring relief from the symptoms, although they do not actually cure the problem. Only use these drugs if you do not have access to toilets, eg, if you *must* travel. Note that these drugs are not recommended for children under 12 years.

In certain situations antibiotics may be required: diarrhoea with blood or mucus (dysentery), any diarrhoea with fever, profuse watery diarrhoea, persistent diarrhoea not improving after 48 hours and severe diarrhoea.

These suggest a more serious cause of diarrhoea and in these situations gut-paralysing drugs should be avoided. A stool test may be necessary to diagnose what bug is causing your diarrhoea, so you should seek medical help urgently. Where this is not possible the recommended drugs for bacterial diarrhoea (the most likely cause of severe diarrhoea in travellers) are norfloxacin 400mg twice daily for three days or ciprofloxacin 500mg twice daily for five days. These are not recommended for children or pregnant women. The drug of choice for children would be co-trimoxazole with dosage dependent on weight. A five-day course is given. Ampicillin or amoxycillin may be given in pregnancy, but medical care is necessary.

Two other causes of persistent diarrhoea in travellers are giardiasis and amoebic dysentery.

Giardiasis is caused by a common parasite, *Giardia lamblia*. Symptoms include stomach cramps, nausea, a bloated stomach, watery, foul-smelling diarrhoea and frequent gas. Giardiasis can appear several weeks after you have been exposed to the parasite. The symptoms may disappear for a few days and then return; this can go on for several weeks.

Amoebic dysentery, caused by the protozoan *Entamoeba histolytica*, is characterised by a gradual onset of low-grade diarrhoea, often with blood and mucus. Cramping abdominal pain and vomiting are less likely than in other types of diarrhoea, and fever may not be present. It will persist until treated and can recur and cause other health problems.

You should seek medical advice if you think you have giardiasis or amoebic dysentery, but where this is not possible, tinidazole or metronidazole are the recommended drugs. Treatment is a 2g single dose of tinidazole or 250mg of metronidazole three times daily for five to 10 days.

Fungal Infections Fungal infections occur more commonly in hot weather and are usually found on the scalp, between the toes (athlete's foot) or fingers, in the groin and on the body (ringworm). You get ringworm (which is a fungal infection, not a worm) from infected animals or other people. Moisture encourages these infections.

To prevent fungal infections wear loose, comfortable clothes, avoid artificial fibres, wash frequently and dry carefully. If you do get an infection, wash the infected area at least daily with a disinfectant or medicated soap and water, and rinse and dry well. Apply an antifungal cream or powder like tolnaftate. Try to expose the infected area to air or sunlight as much as possible and wash all towels and underwear in hot water, change them often and let them dry in the sun.

Hepatitis Hepatitis is a general term for inflammation of the liver. It is a common disease worldwide. There are several different viruses that cause hepatitis, and they differ in the way that they are transmitted. The symptoms are similar in all forms of the illness, and include fever, chills, headache, fatigue, feelings of weakness and aches and pains, followed by loss of appetite, nausea, vomiting, abdominal pain, dark urine, light-coloured faeces, jaundiced (yellow) skin and yellowing of the whites of the eyes. People who have had hepatitis should avoid alcohol for some time after the illness.

Hepatitis A is transmitted by contaminated food and drinking water. You should seek medical advice, but there is not much you can do apart from resting, drinking lots of fluids, eating lightly and avoiding fatty foods. Hepatitis E is transmitted in the same way as hepatitis A; it can be particularly serious in pregnant women.

There are almost 300 million carriers of **hepatitis B** in the world. It's spread through contact with infected blood, blood products or body fluids, for example through sexual contact, unsterilised needles and blood transfusions, or contact with blood via broken skin. Other risk situations include shaving, tattoo or body piercing with contaminated equipment.

The symptoms of hepatitis B may be more severe than type A and the disease can lead to long-term problems such as chronic liver damage, liver cancer or a long-term carrier state. Hepatitis C and D are spread in the same way as hepatitis B and can also lead to long-term complications.

There are vaccines against hepatitis A and B, but there are currently no vaccines against the other types of hepatitis. Following the basic rules about food and water (hepatitis A and E) and avoiding risk situations (hepatitis B, C and D) are important preventative measures.

Schistosomiasis Also known as bilharzia, this disease is transmitted by minute worms and is a big problem in Egypt (see the Health section in that chapter). The worm enters through the skin and attaches itself to your intestines or bladder. The first symptom may be a general feeling of unwell, or a tingling and sometimes a light rash around the area where it entered. Weeks later a high fever may develop. Once the disease is established abdominal pain and blood in the urine are other signs. The infection often causes no symptoms until the disease is well established (several months to years after exposure) and damage to internal organs irreversible. A blood test is the most reliable way to diagnose the disease, but the test will not show positive until a number of weeks after exposure.

Insect-Borne Diseases

Malaria This serious and potentially fatal disease is spread by mosquito bites. If you are travelling in endemic areas it is extremely important to avoid mosquito bites and to take tablets to prevent this disease. Symptoms range from fever, chills and sweating, headache, diarrhoea and abdominal pains to a vague feeling of ill-health. Seek medical help immediately if malaria is suspected. Without treatment malaria can rapidly become more serious and can be fatal.

There is a variety of antimalarial medications (eg, mefloquine, Fansidar and Malarone). Before travelling, seek medical advice as to the right one and dosage for you. If medical care is not available, malaria tablets can be used for treatment. You must use a malaria tablet which is different from the one you were taking when you caught malaria.

Travellers are advised to prevent mosquito bites at all times. The main messages are:

• Wear light-coloured clothing.
• Wear long trousers and long-sleeved shirts.
• Use mosquito repellents containing the mosquito repellents containing the compound DEET on exposed areas (prolonged overuse of DEET may be harmful, especially to children, but its use is considered preferable to being bitten by disease-transmitting mosquitoes).
• Avoid perfumes or aftershave.
• Use a mosquito net impregnated with mosquito repellent (permethrin).
• Impregnating clothes with permethrin effectively deters mosquitoes and other insects.

Dengue Fever This viral disease is transmitted by mosquitoes and is fast becoming one of the top public health problems in the tropical world. Unlike the malaria mosquito, the *Aedes aegypti* mosquito, which transmits the dengue virus, is most active during the day, and is found mainly in urban areas, in and around human dwellings.

Signs and symptoms of dengue fever include a sudden onset of high fever, headache, joint and muscle pains (hence its old name, 'breakbone fever') and nausea and vomiting. A rash of small red spots sometimes appears three to four days after the onset of fever. In the early phase of illness, dengue may be mistaken for other infectious diseases, including malaria and influenza. Minor bleeding such as nose bleeds may occur in the course of the illness, but this does not necessarily mean that you have progressed to the potentially fatal dengue haemorrhagic fever (DHF). This is a severe illness, characterised by heavy bleeding, which is thought to be a result of second infection due to a different strain (there are four major strains) and usually affects residents of the country rather than travellers. Recovery even from simple dengue fever may be prolonged, with tiredness lasting for several weeks.

You should seek medical attention as soon as possible if you think you may be infected. A blood test can exclude malaria and indicate the possibility of dengue fever. There is no specific treatment for dengue. Aspirin should be avoided, as it increases the risk of haemorrhaging. There is no vaccine against dengue fever. The best prevention is to avoid mosquito bites at all times by covering up, using insect repellents containing the compound DEET and mosquito nets – see the Malaria section earlier for more advice on avoiding mosquito bites.

Cuts, Bites & Stings
Cuts & Scratches Wash well and treat any cut with an antiseptic such as povidone-iodine. Where possible avoid bandages and Band-Aids, which can keep wounds wet. Coral cuts are notoriously slow to heal and if they are not adequately cleaned, small pieces of coral can become embedded in the wound.

Bedbugs & Lice Bedbugs live in various places, but particularly in dirty mattresses and bedding, evidenced by spots of blood on bedclothes or on the wall. Bedbugs leave itchy bites in neat rows. Calamine lotion or a sting relief spray may help.

All lice cause itching and discomfort. They make themselves at home in your hair (head lice), your clothing (body lice) or in your pubic hair (crabs). You catch lice through direct contact with infected people or by sharing combs, clothing and the like. Powder or shampoo treatment will kill the lice and infected clothing should then be washed in very hot, soapy water and left in the sun to dry.

Bites & Stings Bee and wasp stings are usually painful rather than dangerous. However, in people who are allergic to them severe breathing difficulties may occur and require urgent medical care. Calamine lotion or a sting relief spray will give relief and ice packs will reduce the pain and swelling. There are some spiders with dangerous bites but antivenins are usually available. Scorpion stings are notoriously painful and in some parts of Asia, the Middle East and Central America can actually be fatal. Scorpions often shelter in shoes or clothing.

Ticks You should always check all over your body if you have been walking through a potentially tick-infested area as ticks can cause skin infections and other more serious diseases. If a tick is found attached, press down around the tick's head with tweezers, grab the head and gently pull upwards. Avoid pulling the rear of the body as this may squeeze the tick's gut contents through the attached mouth parts into the skin, increasing the risk of infection and disease. Smearing chemicals on the tick will not make it let go and is not recommended.

WOMEN TRAVELLERS
Middle Easterners are conservative, especially about matters concerning sex and women (and by that read local women, not foreign women).

An entire book could be written from the comments and stories of women travellers about their adventures and misadventures in the Middle East. Most of the incidents are nonthreatening nuisances, in the same way a fly buzzing in your ear is a nuisance: you can swat him away and keep him at a distance but he's always out there buzzing around.

Attitudes Towards Women

Some of the biggest misunderstandings between Middle Easterners and Westerners occur over the issue of women. Half-truths and stereotypes exist on both sides: many Westerners assume all Middle Eastern women are veiled, repressed victims, while a large number of locals see Western women as sex-obsessed and immoral.

For many Middle Easterners, both men and women, the role of a woman is specifically defined: she is mother and matron of the household. The man is the provider. However, as with any society, generalisations can be misleading and the reality is far more nuanced. There are thousands of middle- and upper-middle-class professional women in the Arab World who, like their counterparts in the West, juggle work and family responsibilities. Among the working classes, where adherence to tradition is strongest, the ideal may be for women to concentrate on home and family, but economic reality means that millions of women are forced to work (but are still responsible for all domestic chores).

The issue of sex is where the differences between Western and Middle Eastern women are most apparent. Premarital sex (or, indeed, any sex outside marriage) is taboo, although, as with anything forbidden, it still happens. Nevertheless, it is the exception rather than the rule – and that goes for men as well as women. However,

Tips for Women Travellers

There are a number of things that you can do to lessen the harassment, but top of the list is to dress modestly. The woman wearing short pants and a tight T-shirt on the street is, in some local's eyes, confirmation of the worst views held of Western women. Generally, if you're alone or with other women, the amount of harassment you get will be directly related to how you dress: the more skin that is exposed, the more harassment you'll get – although it has to be said in some places nothing you can do short of garbing yourself in full Saudi-style chador is ever going to completely leave you free of unwanted attention. For more on the dress issue see the What to Wear section.

Other helpful tips include the following:

- Wear a wedding band. Generally, Middle Eastern males seem to have more respect for a married woman.
- If you are unmarried but travelling in male company say you are married rather than girlfriend/boyfriend or just friends.
- Don't say that you are travelling alone or just in the company of another female friend – always say that you are with a group.
- Avoid direct eye contact with local men; dark sunglasses help.
- Don't respond to any obnoxious comments – act as if you didn't hear them.
- Be careful in crowds and other situations where you are crammed between people, as it is not unusual for crude things to happen behind you.
- Don't sit in the front seat of taxis unless the driver is a woman.
- On public transport, sit next to a woman if possible.
- Be very careful about behaving in a flirtatious or suggestive manner, it could create more problems than you ever imagined.
- If you need help for any reason (directions etc), ask a woman first. That said, local women are less likely than men to have had an education that included learning in English – you'll find this a major drawback in getting to meet and talk with them.
- If dining alone eat only at Western-style restaurants and cafés. Ask to be seated in the 'family' section, if there is one.
- It is perfectly acceptable for a woman to go straight to the front of a queue or to ask to be served first before any men that may be waiting.
- Going to the nearest public place, such as the lobby of a hotel, usually works in getting rid of any would be 'admirers'. If they still persist however, then ask the receptionist to call the police. This will usually frighten them off.

for women the issue is potentially far more serious. With the possible exception of the upper classes, women are expected to be virgins when they get married and a family's reputation can rest upon this point. In such a context, the restrictions placed on a young girl – no matter how onerous they may seem to a Westerner – are intended to protect her and her reputation from the potentially disastrous attentions of men.

The presence of foreign women presents, in the eyes of some Middle Eastern men, a chance to get around these norms with ease and without consequences. That this is even possible is heavily reinforced by distorted impressions gained from Western TV and, it has to be said, by the behaviour of some foreign women in the country – as one young man in Egypt remarked when asked why he persisted in harassing every Western woman he saw, 'For every ten that say no, there's one that says yes'. So, as a woman traveller (even when accompanied by a male partner or friend) you can expect some verbal harassment at the very least. Sometimes it will go as far as pinching bottoms or brushing breasts but physical harassment and rape are not significant threats.

Treatment of foreign women tends to be at its best in strictly Islamic societies such as Iran (providing of course you adhere to the prevailing social mores; see the boxed text 'Women in Iranian Society' in the Iran chapter), and at its worst in Egypt, Israel and Turkey, where sexual harassment can be a real holiday-souring nuisance.

What to Wear

This differs from country to country, though on the whole a certain amount of modesty is advisable.

In Egypt, Iraq, Israel & the Palestinian Territories, Jordan, Lebanon, Syria and Turkey attitudes towards women are more relaxed than in Iran, Yemen and the Gulf countries. In the former group of countries, women can generally wear what they like at beach resorts and in big cities – within reason. Outside of these areas, however, it is better to ensure that legs, arms, shoulders and the neckline are covered. Baggy T-shirts and loose cotton trousers or long skirts won't make you sweat as much as you think and will protect your skin from the sun as well as from unwanted comments. Wearing a bra will avoid count-

less unwelcome confrontations, and a hat or headscarf is also a good idea.

As with anywhere, take your cues from those around you: if you're in a rural area and all the women are in long, concealing dresses, you should be conservatively dressed.

In the very traditional societies of Iran and Saudi Arabia, although it is not necessary for foreign women to wear the *chador* (the one-piece cloak associated with Muslim countries), it is essential for them to cover all parts of the body except the hands, feet and face (from hairline to neckline), and to ensure that the outer layer of clothing gives no hint of the shape of the body. For more on this see the boxed text 'The Big Cover Up' in the Iran chapter.

For information on local women's attitudes to the practice of wearing a headscarf (or *hejab*), see the boxed text 'Boys, Girls & the Veil' in the Egypt chapter.

GAY & LESBIAN TRAVELLERS

With the exception of Egypt, Lebanon, Turkey and Israel & the Palestinian Territories, homosexuality is illegal in all Middle Eastern countries. Penalties include fines and/ or imprisonment, and in Iran, Saudi Arabia and Yemen the death penalty may be invoked (although this doesn't prevent activity online. Check out ⓦ www.welcome.to/gayiran).

Even in those countries in which homosexuality is not prohibited by law, it remains fairly low key, with a few exceptions (İstanbul in Turkey and Tel Aviv in Israel both have vibrant gay scenes). However, in general, as a Westerner, you are unlikely to encounter prejudice or harassment as long as you remain discreet, although this may not be the case if you become involved with a local.

For more information on gay-friendly bars and hotels see the *Spartacus International Gay Guide* and Gay & Lesbian Travellers sections in the individual Egypt, Israel & the Palestinian Territories, Jordan, Lebanon and Turkey chapters.

DISABLED TRAVELLERS

Generally speaking, scant regard is paid to the needs of disabled travellers in the Middle East. Steps, high kerbs and other assorted obstacles are everywhere, streets are often badly rutted and uneven, roads are made virtually uncrossable by heavy traffic, while many doorways are low and narrow. Ramps and specially equipped lodgings and toilets are an extreme rarity. You will have to plan your trip carefully and will probably be obliged to restrict yourself to luxury-level hotels and private, hired transport. The happy exception is Israel & the Palestinian Territories – see the Disabled Travellers section in that chapter. There are also agencies in Oman and the UAE specialising in making arrangements for disabled travellers – see those chapters.

Otherwise, before setting off for the Middle East, disabled travellers could get in touch with their national support organisation (preferably with the travel officer, if there is one) – in the UK contact **RADAR** (☎ 020-7250 3222; 250 City Rd, London EC1V 8AS) or the **Holiday Care Service** (☎ 01293-774 535).

SENIOR TRAVELLERS

Few countries in the Middle East subscribe to the cult of youth worship that exists in the West, and traditionally the region's older citizens are accorded great respect. The family remains the single most important thing in the lives of most Middle Easterners and if you bring along some photos of your children and (even better) grandchildren, they'll act as a great icebreaker.

Respect yes, but concessions no; unlike in many Western countries, there are rarely discounts on public transport, museum admission fees and the like for senior travellers.

The major thing to be wary of is the heat. It can be crippling – not just to senior citizens but to travellers of any age. A lightweight folding stool might be a good idea if you are prone to tiring quickly. Plan ahead and don't try to do too much in too short a time – advice good for travellers of all ages.

TRAVEL WITH CHILDREN

Taking the kids can add another dimension to a trip to the Middle East, although there are a few provisos that should be born in mind. Firstly, it's a good idea to avoid travel in the summer as the extreme heat can be quite uncomfortable and energy sapping. With infants, another problem may be cleanliness. It is impractical to carry more than about a half dozen washable nappies around with you, but disposable ones are not always that easy to come by – although in Egypt, Israel, Lebanon and Turkey there should be no problem. Powdered milk is widely available, as is bottled water. As for

hotels, you are going to want something with a private bathroom and hot water, which will normally preclude most budget accommodation. The good news is that children are made a big fuss of in the Middle East. They'll help break the ice and open doors to closer contact with local people.

For more comprehensive advice on the dos and don'ts of taking the kids in your luggage, see Lonely Planet's *Travel with Children* by Cathy Lanigan.

DANGERS & ANNOYANCES

The Middle East has a reputation for being a dangerous area because of political turmoil, the Arab-Israeli conflict and the emergence of Islamic fundamentalism in many countries. Don't let this deter you from travelling. The trouble spots are usually well defined, and as long as you keep track of political developments, you are unlikely to come to any harm (see the boxed texts 'Is It Safe?' and 'Latest Travel Advice' at the beginning of this chapter).

In general, theft is not really a problem in the Middle East and robbery (mugging) even less of one, but don't let the relative safety lull you. Take the standard precautions.

Always keep valuables with you or locked in a safe – never leave them in your room or in a car or bus. Use a money belt, a pouch under your clothes, a leather wallet attached to your belt, or internal pockets in your clothing. Keep a record of your passport, credit-card and travellers-cheque numbers separately; it won't cure problems, but it will make them easier to bear.

However, beware of your fellow travellers; there are more than a few backpackers who make their money go further by helping themselves to other people's.

BUSINESS HOURS

With just a few exceptions, the end-of-week holiday throughout the Middle East is Friday. In Israel it's Saturday (Shabbat), while in Lebanon and Turkey it's Sunday. In countries where Friday is the holiday, most embassies and offices are also closed on Thursday, though private businesses and shops are open on Thursday mornings and many stores will reopen in the evening on Friday.

In many countries, shops have different hours at different times of the year, depending on the season (they tend to work shorter

Open Sesame

Where possible, throughout this book we give the opening times of places of interest. The information is usually taken from notices posted at the sites. However, often the reality on the ground is that sites open pretty much as and when the gate-guard feels like it. On a good day he'll be there an hour early, on a bad day he won't turn up at all. Who can blame him when in little-touristed countries like Syria or Oman he may never see a visitor for days anyway? With the exception perhaps of those countries with a more Western concept of time keeping (Israel and Turkey, for example), all opening hours must be prefaced, therefore, with a hopeful *insha'allah* (God-willing).

hours in winter) and during Ramadan (the month-long fast for Muslims) when almost everything shuts down in the afternoon.

PUBLIC HOLIDAYS & SPECIAL EVENTS

All Middle Eastern countries, save Israel, observe the main Islamic holidays listed below. Countries with a major Shiite population also observe Ashura, the anniversary of the martyrdom of Hussein, the third imam of the Shiites. Most of the countries in this book also observe both the Gregorian and the Islamic New Year holidays. Every country also has its own national days and other public holidays – for details refer to the individual country chapters.

Islamic New Year Also known as Ras as-Sana, it literally means 'the head of the year'.

Prophet's Birthday This is also known as Moulid an-Nabi, 'the feast of the Prophet'.

Lailat al-Mi'raj This is the celebration of the Ascension of Prophet Mohammed.

Ramadan Ramadan (Ramazan in Iran and Turkey) is the ninth month of the Muslim calendar, when Muslims fast during daylight hours. How strictly

the fast is observed depends on the country, but most Muslims conform to some extent. Foreigners are not expected to follow suit, but it is impolite to smoke, drink or eat in public during Ramadan – in the more strictly Islamic countries flaunting your nonobservance of the fast will get you into trouble, especially in Saudi Arabia where jail sentences are handed out to anyone seen so much as smoking during daylight hours. Business hours tend to become more erratic and usually shorter, and in out-of-the-way places you may find it hard to find a restaurant that opens before sunset. As the sun sets each day, the fast is broken with *iftar* (breakfast), at which enough food is usually consumed to compensate for the previous hours of abstinence.

Eid al-Fitr (Şeker Bayramı in Turkey) This feast marks the end of Ramadan fasting; the celebrations last for three days.

Eid al-Adha (Kurban Bayramı in Turkey) This feast marks the time that Muslims make the pilgrimage to Mecca.

Islamic Calendar

All Islamic holidays fall according to the Muslim calendar, while secular activities are planned according to the Christian system, except in Saudi Arabia, where the Muslim calendar is the principal one used, and in Iran, where the Iranian solar calendar is used.

The Muslim year is based on the lunar cycle and is divided into 12 lunar months, each with 29 or 30 days. Consequently, the Muslim year is 10 or 11 days shorter than the Christian solar year, and the Muslim festivals gradually move around our year, completing the cycle in roughly 33 years.

Year zero in the Muslim calendar was when Mohammed and his followers fled from Mecca to Medina (AD 622 in the Christian calendar). This Hejira, or migration, is taken to mark the start of the new Muslim era, much as Christ's birth marks year zero in the Christian calendar.

ACTIVITIES

Although the Middle East is a region not generally associated with activities, its wide

Islamic Holidays

Hejira Year	New Year	Prophet's Birthday	Lailat al-Mi'raj	Ramadan Begins	Eid al-Fitr	Eid al-Adha
1424	04.03.03	12.05.03	21.09.03	25.10.03	24.11.03	01.02.04
1425	22.02.04	01.05.04	10.09.04	14.10.04	13.11.04	21.01.05
1426	10.02.05	19.04.05	31.08.05	03.10.05	02.11.05	10.01.06

variety of terrain – from deserts to beaches to snow-capped mountains – does offer quite a few opportunities to do things other than visit museums and old stones.

Cycling

See the Bicycle section in the Getting Around chapter for details about cycling around the Middle East, including practicalities and organisations to contact.

Desert Safaris & Drives

One of the most striking topographical features of the region is the desert. The easiest place to experience stunning sand landscapes is Wadi Rum in Jordan. There are plenty of operators there who organise anything from afternoon camel treks to safaris and hikes lasting several days. Oman is the other great desert exploration country – see the Activities section in that country chapter.

In Egypt there are plenty of small Bedouin operators who lead groups into the Sinai interior on overnight or two or three day camel treks – see the Sinai section for more details. It's also possible to head off into the less-visited Western Desert as part of a 4WD safari.

Israel's Negev desert is less attractive than deserts elsewhere, but there are some fun truck tours organised by Desert Eco Tours in Eilat (see Activities in the Israel & the Palestinian Territories).

Diving

The Red Sea is one of the world's top diving sites. Its waters are teeming with a dazzling array of colourful coral and fish life, supported by an extensive reef system. The best place to experience the Red Sea is from one of the resorts on southern Sinai or south along Egypt's Red Sea coast. Eilat in Israel and Aqaba in Jordan also have dive centres but the underwater scenery up here isn't half as spectacular as in Egypt's waters. Diving is also a possibility in Kuwait and Oman.

Most of the clubs in these places offer every possible kind of dive course. The average open-water certification course for beginners, either with CMAS, PADI or NAUI, takes about five days and usually includes several dives. The total cost varies between US$280 and US$400 depending on the operator and location. A day's diving (two dives), including equipment and air fills, costs US$50 to US$95. An introduc-

tory dive is around US$60. Full equipment can be hired for about US$20 per day.

For more details see the Activities sections in the relevant country chapters.

Pearl Diving For an unusual slant on underwater exploration see the Activities section of the Bahrain chapter.

Fishing

Big game fishing is a possibility in southern Egypt – see Activities in the Egypt chapter.

Golf

It's strange but true: golf has caught on in a big way in the Middle East (despite the chronic shortage of water, and blistering heat). Egypt now has several international courses, as do Qatar, Bahrain and the UAE. See the Activities section in the relevant country chapters for further details.

Hammams

One of the great sensual indulgences of the Middle East, the *hammam* (or *hamam in Turkey*) is better known in the West as a 'Turkish bath'. Whether you submit to a massage or not, it's worth a session in the steam room and then tea afterwards swathed in towels if only for the unique architecture of some of these places. The best *hammams* are found in İstanbul, Damascus and Aleppo (see these sections for further details).

Hiking & Trekking

There's a wealth of superb hiking opportunities, both leisurely and more strenuous, though you have to be careful in picking the right time of year for your visit. In Jordan, from June to August it's too hot for any walking, but outside the summer months Dana Nature Reserve and the area around Petra offer have great walks among superb desert scenery. The Upper Galilee and Golan regions of Israel have plenty of trails through semi-mountainous, wooded terrain with a good series of hostels providing accommodation. (For more on hiking in Israel & the Palestinian Territories, see the Activities section in that chapter.) In Iran, the Alborz Mountains are a popular destination for walking, though the region lacks any infrastructure and places to stay are rare. Hiking and mountain trekking are also becoming increasingly popular in Turkey, particularly in

Desert Hiking

While the Middle East offers a host of hiking opportunities, the conditions are quite different to those most visitors are accustomed to. It's especially important to note that hiking isn't recommended during the heat of the summer months, when temperatures can exceed 40°C.

In the summer, hiking can be extremely dangerous, and in 40°C heat most hikers will go through 1L of water every hour. Even in the cooler months, your main issue will be water, and hikers should have available at least 4L per person per day (an excellent way to carry water is in 2L plastic soft drink bottles, which are available in many places).

The most effective way to conserve water isn't necessarily to drink sparingly, as this tends to psychologically focus attention on water availability, and may lead to an unhealthy hysteria. Before setting off in the morning, flood your body's cells with water. That is, drink more water than you feel you can possibly hold! After a few hours, when you grow thirsty, do the same again from the supply you're carrying. Believe it or not, with this method you'll actually use less water and feel less thirsty than if you drink sparingly all day long.

Another major concern is the desert sun, which can be brutal. Wear light-coloured and lightweight clothing; use a good sunscreen (at least UV Protection Factor 30); and never set off without a hat or Arab-style head covering that shelters your neck and face from the direct sun. You'll also need a light, semitransparent veil to protect your eyes, nose, mouth and ears from blowing sand and dust.

If the heat is a major problem, it's best to rise before the sun and hike until the heat becomes oppressive. You may then want to rest through the heat of mid-day and begin again after about 3pm. During warmer months, it may also be worthwhile timing your hike with the full moon, which will allow you to hike at night.

Because many trails follow canyons and wadis, it's also important to keep a watch on the weather. Rainy periods can render normally dry wadis impassable, and those with large catchment areas can quickly become raging – and uncrossable – torrents of muddy water, boulders and downed trees. Never camp in canyons or wadis and always keep to higher ground whenever there's a risk of flash-flooding.

the northeast. See the Activities section in the relevant country chapters for further details.

Water Sports

The Red Sea resort of Eilat in Israel is possibly the Middle East's water-sports capital, although places like Sharm el-Sheikh and Hurghada in Egypt, Aqaba in Jordan and many of Turkey's Mediterranean beach resorts all offer ample opportunities for year-round sailing, snorkelling, water-skiing and windsurfing. For the region's best windsurfing spot though, head to Moon Beach in Sinai. Water sports are also popular throughout the UAE, and the tourist industry is increasingly pushing the country as a winter 'sea & sun' destination. However, most water-sport facilities are tied either to a big hotel or a private club and are not generally accessible to nonguests and non-members.

For more on water sports see the Activities sections in the Egypt, Israel & the Palestinian Territories and Turkey country chapters.

Yacht Cruising

Turkey has lots of possibilities for yacht cruising, from day trips to two-week luxury charters. Kuşadası, Bodrum and Marmaris are the main centres, with more resorts developing yachting businesses all the time. You can hire crewless bareboats or flotilla boats, or take a cabin on a boat hired by an agency. Ask anywhere near the docks for information.

LANGUAGE COURSES

Various institutes and colleges in Egypt, Jordan, Kuwait, Lebanon and Yemen offer short intensive courses in Arabic and there are plenty of places in İstanbul at which to study Turkish. It's also possible to take up Hebrew and biblical studies in Israel. See Courses in the specific country chapters for more details.

WORK

It is quite possible to pick up work in the Middle East in order to extend your stay and eke out your savings – but you have to know where to look and what you are looking for. Forget places like Iran and Syria or the Gulf countries (although it is quite possible to work in the latter if you can secure a job in advance); realistically, your best options are Egypt, Israel and Turkey, that is the places where other foreigners gather in numbers.

See the Israel & the Palestinian Territories chapter for information about working on a kibbutz or a moshav.

Tutoring English

Teaching centres – both of the respectable kind and cowboy outfits – can be found throughout the Middle East. Cowboy outfits are often desperate for teachers and will take on people whose only qualification is that their mother tongue is English. Pay is minimal and you'll probably have to stay on a tourist visa, which will be up to you to renew. However, many long-termers finance their stays this way, particularly in Cairo and İstanbul.

In Cairo your first port of call should be the **International Language Institute** *(ILI; ☎ 02-291 9295, fax 02-415 1082; e ili@idsc.net .eg; 2 Sharia Mohammed Bayoumi, Heliopolis)*, which is a privately run English-language school. Otherwise, visit the British Council for a list of schools to contact.

In İstanbul, again, visit the British Council. Your chances of getting a job are greatly improved if you have a certificate in Celta (Certificate in English Language Teaching to Adults). This is what used to be known as TEFL and, basically, it's your passport to work abroad. To get the qualification you need to attend a one-month intensive course, which you can do in your home country via an English-language training centre. In the UK contact **International House** *(IH; ☎ 020-7491 2598; w www .ihlondon.com)*, which runs more than a dozen courses a year (in 2002 the course cost UK£1010). IH has 110 affiliated schools in 30 countries worldwide, including Egypt (Cairo) and Turkey (İstanbul) and then, once you have completed the course, you can apply for any advertised positions.

Alternatively, you could fly out to Cairo and do the Celta course at Cairo's ILI, Heliopolis (for contact details, see earlier in this section). The cost of the course in 2001 was the equivalent of UK£650. Depending on the price of your flight, this is a cheaper way to do it than at IH in London.

The other big employer of English-language teachers is the British Council. Its overseas teaching centres don't often take on people who just turn up at the door as most recruiting is done in the UK – contact the **Information Centre** *(☎ 0161-957 7755, fax 957 7762; w www.britishcouncil.org)*, but you may be lucky. For British Council addresses in the Middle East see Cultural Centres in the capital city sections throughout this book.

Qualified teachers should also check w www.eslcafe.com for regular job postings.

Working at a Backpackers

In Israel (Jerusalem, Tel Aviv and Eilat) and various places in Turkey (particularly İstanbul, Selçuk, Bodrum, Fethiye and Cappadocia), it's usually possible to pick up work in a hostel, typically cleaning rooms or looking after reception. It doesn't pay much, but it does usually get you a free room, a meal or two a day plus some beer money. The only way to find this kind of work is to ask around.

Copy Editing

There are literally dozens of English-language newspapers and magazines published in the Middle East. Unless you have the proper training and experience you're unlikely to be offered any work in the way of journalism but there's often a need for people with good English-language skills who can copy edit. The amount of work available and money to be made obviously depends on whether the paper or magazine is daily, weekly or monthly – whatever the case, you aren't going to make much, but it may be enough to cover the cost of your accommodation. The only way to find such work is to pick up the newspapers and phone.

ACCOMMODATION

In most of the countries covered in this book, you'll find a wide range of places to stay, from international-class Hiltons and Sheratons in the capitals and resorts, through reasonably priced, comfortable, mid-range hotels, down to the most basic lodging houses out in the sticks or in the rough end of town.

Camping

Camping in the Middle East is possible, but it's always better to stick to officially sanctioned camp sites because many areas that are military or restricted zones aren't always marked as such. There are official camping grounds in Egypt, Iran, Israel & the Palestinian Territories, Lebanon and Saudi Arabia.

Hostels

There are youth hostels in Bahrain, Egypt, Israel & the Palestinian Territories, Qatar, Saudi Arabia and the UAE. It's not usually necessary to hold a HI card to stay at these places, but it will get you a small discount.

Hotels

Standards vary between countries but quality generally reflects price – although in some countries, such as the Gulf States, it can be difficult to find really cheap accommodation at all. Hotels at the top end of the range have clean, air-con, self-contained rooms with hot showers and toilets that work all the time. In the mid-range, rooms are self-contained, but there may not always be hot water, and there will probably be fans instead of air-con. Near the bottom end, hotel rooms are not always clean, in fact they are sometimes downright filthy, showers and toilets are usually shared and they're often in an appalling state. The very cheap hotels are just dormitories where

you're crammed into a room with whoever else fronts up. Some of the cheapest places are probably too basic for many tastes and not always suitable for women travelling alone.

For further details and other types of accommodation see the individual country chapters.

FOOD

The quality of food varies considerably from country to country – in terms of local cuisine, the best is in Lebanon and Turkey, the worst is in Egypt and some of the Gulf States. For an overview of the kind of food to expect see the special section 'Middle Eastern Cuisine'.

Where to Eat

A pleasant feature of Middle Eastern travel is the easy availability of street food – ideal if you're on the move, or prefer to eat little and often. In the Mediterranean arc of countries from Turkey down to Egypt, small eateries peddle kebabs, shwarma, felafel and other types of sandwiches, all usually served with some form of salad. These sorts of things are cheap, quick, nearly always cooked in front of you and rarely involve plates or knives.

As well as restaurants serving the sort of cuisine described in the special section, every

Eating Like the Locals

Middle Eastern eating habits are not wildly different from those in any city in Europe and America. Here too people consume a standard three meals a day, based largely on vegetables, beans, pulses and meat, with pasta and rice thrown in for variety. However, bread and bread products account for 60% of the average caloric intake. Middle Easterners consume far less fast food or frozen meals than Western counterparts (a result of economics rather than health awareness), which might translate into a more life-prolonging diet if it wasn't for the fact that most cooking is slathered in lethal amounts of clarified butter *(samna)*, like Indian ghee.

When it comes to breakfast, Kelloggs have yet to make a great impact – for much of the populace the morning meal consists of bread and cheese, maybe olives, maybe a fried egg taken at home, or a *fuul* (fava bean paste) sandwich on the run. Lunch is the day's main meal, taken from 2pm onwards, but more likely around 3pm or 4pm when dad's home from work and the kids are back from school. Whatever's served, mama will probably have spent most of her day in the kitchen preparing it (Middle Eastern cooking always seems to be very labour intensive); it'll be hot and there'll probably be plenty to go round. Whatever's left over will probably be served up again later in the evening as supper.

Although quite happy to patronise the local *fuul*-and-felafel stands and buy grilled chicken or baked fish, most locals (other than the middle and upper classes) treat restaurants with suspicion. Why pay hard-earned money when they know mama does it better? Hence the rather disappointing dining out scene in most countries. The exceptions are the Arab Gulf States such as Bahrain, Qatar, Kuwait, and Dubai in the UAE, which have an extensive and well-patronised eating-out scene.

Those who do dine out do so late and wouldn't dream of taking a table before 10pm. It's not unusual for families to be out working their way through dinner at one or two in the morning.

country in the region also has a plethora of Western-style eateries, which range from burger bars (McDonald's, KFC, Pizza Hut etc are all present in the region) to five-star haute cuisine establishments (top UK chef Gordon Ramsey recently opened a restaurant in Dubai). In fact, throughout the region, mid-range and up restaurants invariably dish up some form of international cuisine because eating Chinese, Indian or Italian carries connotations of sophistication, which appeals to the moneyed classes who can afford to dine out. Our advice though is to stick with the indigenous cuisine, which is invariably done better than local attempts (even when executed at five-star establishments) at the likes of lasagne or chicken tikka. The exception here is in the Gulf States; the Western cuisine here is excellent at the many international restaurants, and a sizeable Indian population means that you're never wanting for a decent curry.

When to Eat

Most restaurants tend to open around noon, or just before, and keep the kitchens going until the last customer leaves, which can be long past midnight. Although we give opening times in our listings, treat them as a guideline, not gospel. Apart from in the few cases noted, reservations are rarely necessary. Other than snack joints, few places ever get busy at lunchtime and proper restaurants don't fill up until maybe 9pm or later, Middle Easterners being late eaters. Once tables are taken though, they stay taken – the local way is to linger over dinner and make an evening of it.

Vegetarian Food

The main difficulty faced by nonmeat eaters travelling the Middle East is boredom. Avoiding meat is not a problem as most mezze are vegetable based – salads (tabouleh, fattoush, *shinklish*) or purees (hummus, *baba ghanoug, muttabel*), while stuffed vegetables *(mahshi)* feature heavily on most restaurant menus, and there's always the fall-back of the ubiquitous felafel. But it's not a very varied diet and after even just a week, it can become very repetitive. One of the authors working on this book, normally a committed vegetarian, found herself having to give way and succumb to chicken. The issue is even more acute in countries like Iran, where it can seem that the entire cuisine is based on the kebab.

The best country for veggies is Israel, where kosher dietary laws don't permit the mixing of meat and dairy products, resulting in a lot of 'dairy' restaurants where no meat of any form is served. There are also plenty of cheap, decent vegetarian restaurants in the Gulf States serving southern Indian cuisine.

Elsewhere, dedicated vegetarian restaurants are rare. There are several in İstanbul, including **Badehane** *(☎ 0212-249 0550; General Yazgan Sokak No 5, Tünel; open 10am-2am)*, **Nature and Peace** *(☎ 0212-252 8609; Büyükparmakkapi Sokak 21/23 , Beyoglu; open 11am-11pm daily)*, **Nuh'un Ambari** *(☎ 0212-292 9272; Yeni Çarsi Caddesi 54, Galatasaray; open noon-7.30pm Mon-Sat)* and **Parsifal** *(☎ 0212-245 2588; Kurabiye Sokak 13, Beyoglu; open 11am-11pm Mon-Sat)*.

In Cairo, **L'Aubergine** *(☎ 735 6550; 5 Sharia Sayyed al-Bakry, Zamalek; open 10am-2am daily)* also has a strongly veggie menu. Beyond that we're struggling.

DRINKS
Nonalcoholic Drinks

Tea & Coffee In the Middle East, tea *(shai)* and coffee *(qahwa)* are drunk in copious quantities and are served strong.

Tea comes in two sorts: there's the tea bag type (often called *shai libton* – Lipton tea – whatever the brand) and local tea. Local tea is made with green leaves (often imported from China) and is served in small glasses, often with *na'ana* (mint). It's incredibly sweet unless you ask for only a little sugar *(shwayya sukkar)* or medium *(wassat)*. If you want no sugar at all, ask for it *bidoon sukkar* (without sugar), but it tastes bitter and has a strong tannin aftertaste.

Coffee is usually Turkish coffee in small cups and is also sweet. If you want less sugar ask for it *mazboota*; without sugar ask for *sada* (plain). It is very thick and muddy so let it settle a bit before drinking. Don't try and drink the last mouthful (which in cups this size is only about the second mouthful) because it's like drinking silt.

The traditional Arabic or Bedouin coffee is heavily laced with cardamom and drunk in cups without handles that hold only a mouthful. Served without sugar, it is poured from a silver or brass pot and your cup will be refilled until you make the proper gesture

[Continued on page 87]

MIDDLE EASTERN CUISINE

This section describes the kind of indigenous food that you're likely to encounter throughout much of the region, Iran and the Gulf States aside. Iran has its own very distinctive cuisine, which is briefly described in that chapter, while the Gulf States have never been known for their cuisine and almost everything on the menu in these countries is imported. Note that while many dishes described on the following pages are found in Turkey, they often go by a different name – see the Food section in the Turkey chapter.

Street Food

Street food in the Middle East is good and cheap, although often limited; the two main staples are felafel and shwarma.

Felafel is mashed chickpeas and spices balled up and deep fried. Egyptians, instead of chickpeas, use ground black-eyed beans mixed with parsley, and, in Cairo especially, the term *ta'miyya* is used instead of felafel. You usually buy felafel in the form of a sandwich, with several balls stuffed inside a pocket of pita-type bread along with salad and perhaps hummus. Shwarma is the Middle Eastern equivalent of the Greek *gyros* sandwich or the Turkish *döner kebap* – strips are sliced from a vertical spit of compressed lamb or chicken, sizzled on a hot plate with chopped tomatoes and garnish, and then stuffed in a pocket of pita-type bread. In Israel & the Palestinian Territories, shwarma stalls usually invite customers to help themselves to free salad, while in Syria the shwarma is an anaemic affair, popped into a sandwich toaster and served with a dollop of sour cream.

In Egypt you'll also encounter *fuul* – black-eyed beans mashed into a thick, lumpy paste, usually ladled into a piece of pita-type bread. *Fuul* is also occasionally offered in a more refined version, often flavoured with garlic and lemon, on Lebanese-style menus. Another Egyptian favourite is *kushari*, a mix of noodles, rice, black lentils, fried onions and tomato sauce. The ingredients are served together in a bowl for sit-down meals, or spooned into a polythene bag or plastic tub for takeaway. You can recognise *kushari* joints by the great tureens of noodles and rice in the windows.

Inset: *Kaymak*, a thick cream from cows fed on opium poppies (Photo by Greg Elms)

Right: *Döner kebap* sliced from the spit at a stall on Ribtim Caddesi, Karaköy, İstanbul, Turkey

JEFF GREENBERG

MIDDLE EASTERN CUISINE

Mezze

A traditional Middle Eastern meal starts with *mezze*, which is a selection of hot and cold starters. In a good restaurant the number of *mezze* offered can run to 50 or more. Order as many or as few as you choose. It is quite acceptable to make a meal of just *mezze*. If there are, say, two of you dining then a spread of maybe six *mezze* plus bread will usually make for a satisfying meal. Note that because of the imprecise nature of transliterating Arabic into English, spellings will vary; for example, what we give as *kibbeh* may appear variously as *kibba*, *kibby* or even *gibeh*.

baba ghanoug – a lumpy paste of mashed baked aubergine (eggplant), typically mixed with tomato and onion and sometimes, in season, pomegranate; done well, it has a delicious smoky taste

batata hara – diced potatoes fried with spices such as coriander, garlic and peppers (capsicum); served hot

börek – little pastry pockets stuffed with either salty white cheese or spicy minced meat with pine kernels; also known as *sambousek*

fatayer – small pastry triangles filled with spinach

fattoush – a fresh salad of onions, tomatoes, cucumber, lettuce and shards of crispy, thin, deep-fried bread

hummus – cooked chickpeas ground into a paste and mixed with tahini, garlic and lemon; the test of a good restaurant is its hummus – woody tasting and watery or thick and creamy?

kibbeh – minced lamb, burghul wheat and pine nuts shaped into a lemon-shaped patty and deep fried

kibbeh nayye – minced lamb and cracked wheat served raw

kibda – liver, often chicken liver (*kibda firekh* or *kibda farouj*), and usually sautéed in lemon or garlic; done correctly they should have an almost pâté-like consistency

labneh – a cheesy yogurt paste which is often heavily flavoured with garlic or sometimes, even better, with mint

loubieh – French bean salad with tomatoes, onions and garlic

mashi – various vegetables, such as courgettes (zucchinis), vine leaves, peppers, or white-and-black aubergines, stuffed with minced meat, rice, onions, parsley and herbs and then baked

mujadarreh – a traditional 'poor person's' dish of lentils and rice garnished with caramelised onions, served hot or cold

muttabel – similar to *baba ghanoug* but the blended aubergine is mixed with tahini, yogurt and olive oil to achieve a creamier consistency

shinklish – a salad of small pieces of crumbled tangy, eye-wateringly strong cheese mixed with chopped onion and tomato

soujuk – fried, spicy lamb sausage

tabouleh – a bulgur wheat, parsley and tomato based salad, with a sprinkling of sesame seeds, lemon and garlic

tahini – a thin sesame seed paste

GREG ELMS

Left: Mezze tray at the Meze Meyhane in Taksim Square, İstanbul, Turkey

Bread

Known as *khobz* or *aaish*, bread is eaten in copious quantities with every meal. It's unleavened and comes in flat disks about the size of a dinner plate. It's used in lieu of knives and forks to scoop up dips and ripped into pieces that are used to pick up the meat. You can also often get *aaish bi zaatar*, which is bread with spices, seasoned with thyme and a mixture of other herbs.

Main Courses

Meat *Kofta* and kebab are the two most popular main dishes throughout much of the Middle East. *Kofta* is ground meat peppered with spices, shaped into small sausages, skewered and grilled. Kebab is skewered, flame-grilled chunks of meat, usually lamb (this is known as sheesh or shish kebab).

There are a few regional variations and specialities – although nothing that strays too far from the norm: *kebab halebi* (Aleppan kebab) is a standard kebab but served in a heavy, chopped tomato sauce; *kebab İskenderun* is a spicy kebab; *kebab yogurtlu* is kebab in a yogurt sauce.

Equally ubiquitous is *shish tawouq*, which is a kebab with pieces of marinated, spiced chicken instead of lamb.

Meat usually comes on a bed of *badounis* (parsley) and may be served in upmarket restaurants with grilled tomatoes and onions. Otherwise you eat it with bread, salad and tahini.

Chicken *(farouj* or *firekh)* is very common, typically roasted on a spit and, in restaurants, ordered by the half. In Egypt, also look out for *hamam* (pigeon), which is usually served stuffed with rice and spices. It's also served as a stew cooked in a deep clay pot, or *tagen*, with onions, tomatoes, and rice or cracked wheat. Less common is quail *(saman)*.

Stews Stews are usually meat or vegetable or both and, although not available everywhere, make a pleasant change from chicken and kebabs. *Fasoolyeh* is a green bean stew, *biseela* is made of peas, *batatas* of potato, while *bamiya* is okra. Stews are usually served on *ruz* (rice) or, more rarely, *makarone* (macaroni).

In Yemen the national dish is *salta*, a meaty (often chicken) stew with vegetables topped with fenugreek.

Other Dishes Besides straightforward meat platters and occasional stews, you may see the following on local menus:

daoud pasha – meat balls with pine nuts and tomato sauce
fatteh – an oven-baked dish of chickpeas, minced meat or chicken, and bread soaked in tahini; particularly popular in Egypt and Syria
maqlubbeh – steamed rice topped with grilled slices of aubergine or meat, grilled tomato and pine nuts

Bedouin Dishes In Jordan, Syria and the Gulf countries, menus may feature dishes with Bedouin origins. Chief of these is *mensaf*, which consists of lamb on a bed of rice and pine nuts. In its true Bedouin form the dish would be topped with the gaping head of the animal. Most restaurants tend to skip this detail. The fat from the cooking is poured into the rice. A tangy sauce of cooked yogurt mixed with the fat is served with it.

The Weird Stuff

Felafel, shwarma, hummus and kebabs make for the staples of the somewhat monotonous diet you're likely to experience while travelling in the Middle East. After a week or two you'll be wishing for a change – just be careful though about what you wish for, because the Middle East can present culinary experiences to daunt even the most adventurous of palates. For example, should you by chance be invited to join a group of Bedouin around a big dish of *mensaf*, replete with animal head, you should know that the delicacy is the eyes, which are traditionally presented to honoured guests (but don't worry if you miss out – there are other choice bits like the tongue).

Brains *(mokh)* are big in the Middle East too, grilled, boiled or baked. Generally, all manner of offal is considered finger-lickin' good fare by most locals. You'll find kidney, heart, tripe and spleen dishes, some as grilled or fried hot starters or main courses at restaurants. Even lungs – used for cat food in the West – are a favoured ingredient in the Tekirdag area of western Turkey, and are added to *kofte* to give a spongy, tender consistency. Turks are also big tripe lovers – the stuff is so popular that whole restaurants, known as *işkembeçis* are devoted to it. A soup of tripe prepared with an egg-and-lemon sauce, garlic and vinegar is supposed to be a sure-fire cure for a hangover.

Other Middle Eastern countries compete with their own glutinous horrors. In Oman one of the most typical of traditional dishes is *harees*, made of steamed wheat and boiled meat, mixed together to form a slurry. It's often garnished *ma owaal* – with dried shark, laced with lime, chilli and onions. In southern Oman, another famed dish called *rabees* is made from boiled baby shark, stripped and washed of the gritty skin and then fried with the liver to form a rich gravy. Egypt can contribute *molokhiyya* – made by stewing the *molokhiyya* leaf in chicken stock, the resulting soup looks like green mucus. The 11th-century caliph Al-Hakim found the stuff so repulsive he had the dish banned. Still, it has its fans. You may become one of them. Personally speaking, felafel, hummus and kebabs are just fine by us.

Desserts

Pastries Middle Easterners love sugar and their desserts are assembled accordingly; the basic formula is lightweight pastry heavily drenched in honey, syrup and/or rose-water. When buying from a pastry shop you order by weight – 250g *(roba kilo)*, which is generally the smallest amount shopkeepers are prepared to weigh out, is more than enough for one person. The most common pastry types are:

asabeeh – rolled filo pastry filled with pistachio, pine and cashew nuts and honey; otherwise known as 'lady's fingers'
baklava – a generic term for any kind of layered flaky pastry with nuts, drenched in honey
barazak – flat, circular cookies sprinkled with sesame seeds
isfinjiyya – coconut slice
kunafa – shredded wheat over a creamy, sweet cheese base baked in syrup.
mushabbak – lace-work shaped pastry drenched in syrup
zalabiyya – pastries dipped in rose-water

[Continued from page 82]

that you have had enough – hold the cup out and cover it with your hand. It is good etiquette to have at least three cups, although you are unlikely to offend if you have less. Coffee is then followed by tea ad infinitum.

Western-style instant coffee is often referred to as 'Neskaf'. You'll receive a coffee sachet, cup of hot water and jug of milk.

Other Nonalcoholic Drinks Juice stalls selling delicious freshly squeezed fruit juices *(aseer)* are common throughout the region. Popular juices include lemon, orange, carrot, mango, pomegranate, rockmelon and sugarcane and you can have combinations of any or all of these. For health reasons steer clear of the stalls which add milk to their drinks.

Other traditional drinks include *ayran* (yogurt and water mixed), which is tangy, refreshing and healthy. Another favourite, served hot in the winter, cold in the summer,

is *sahlab* (*sahlep* or *salep* in Turkey). It is made up of *sahlab* powder (like tapioca), milk, coconut, sugar, raisins, chopped nuts, rose-water and a glacé cherry garnish (most cheap places will have simpler versions).

International and local brands of soft drink are sold everywhere. A tiny shop in a remote village may have little of anything at all, but the chances are it'll have a few dusty bottles of sweet, sticky Coca-Cola for sale.

Alcoholic Drinks

Many Middle Eastern countries have several locally brewed alcoholic beverages, including beer (and nonalcoholic beer), wine (red, white and rosé) and *arak*, the indigenous firewater. It is similar to Turkish *raki* and, yes, the effect is the same. It is usually mixed with water and ice and drunk accompanied by food. The best *arak* comes from Lebanon.

In larger cities, you can find imported spirits and beer. For attitudes towards alcohol in the Middle East see Society & Conduct in the Facts about the Region chapter.

The Coffee House

The coffee house (in Arabic *qahwa*, the same word as for coffee; in Persian it's *cháykhána*, or teahouse) is the great social institution of the Middle East. Or rather it is for around half the population – with few exceptions, Arabic woman do not frequent *qahwas*. There's no reason, however, why a Western woman shouldn't, especially in the less staunchly Muslim countries like Egypt, Jordan, Lebanon, Syria and Turkey.

Typically just a collection of battered chairs and tables in a sawdust-strewn room open to the street with a huge urn for boiling water in the corner, the *qahwa* is a relaxed and unfussy place to meet locals who are often curious to question any *khwaja* (foreigner) who comes and sits among them. Conversation is inevitably accompanied by the incessant clacking of slammed domino and backgammon pieces and the bubbling sound of smokers drawing hard on a *sheesha*, the cumbersome water pipe, known as a *qalyan* in Iran.

Even if you don't smoke, the tobacco (often honey soaked or fruit flavoured), placed beneath a burning ember, is remarkably mild, not to say fragrant.

Favourites Although coffee houses are typically humble affairs, some shine, whether because of the coffee house itself (several are in converted *hammams*) or the location. Following are a few worth pencilling into any itinerary.

Chubi and Kháju Bridge teahouses Tucked between the pillars of bridges spanning the Záyande River in Esfahán, Iran
Çorlulu Ali Paşa Medresesi Splendid open-air coffee house in the courtyard of an old Quranic teaching school, off Divan Yolu on the edge of İstanbul's Grand Bazaar
Fishawi's Egypt's oldest and most atmospheric coffee house, its rickety tables and chairs fill an alley in Cairo's Khan al-Khalili bazaar
Hammam Vakil Occupying a converted *hammam* at the heart of the souq in Shiráz, Iran
An-Nafura One of two incredibly picturesque old coffee houses that lie in the shadow of the eastern wall of the Umayyad Mosque in Damascus, Syria

That Special Something

For the connoisseur of kitsch the Middle East is an absolute dream. How about one of the following:

Blinking Jesus There's a lot of kitsch available at Christian sites in Israel, but it's perhaps best represented by the 3-D postcards portraying a very Swedish-looking Jesus whose eyes open and close, depending on the angle of view.

Ephesus Clock A plastic version of a Roman gate with arch stones for nine o'clock through to three o'clock. However, the time (in the open portal) between three and nine o'clock is anybody's guess.

Inflatable Arafat Just put your lips to the back of his head and blow for a life-size, pear-shaped, air-filled bust of everybody's favourite *keffiyeh*-wearing world leader. Gathering dust on shelves in Gaza City.

King Tut Galabiyya Perfect for lounging around the house, a short-sleeved, brightly coloured robe that is usually too short and festooned with a giant iron-on reproduction of the famous funerary mask.

King Tut Hologram Lamp White plaster bust of the famous boy-king that appears to float like a hologram when plugged in. Available in Cairo's Khan al-Khalili for a mere US$50.

Mother-of-Pearl Telephone A real telephone, but in a wooden casing with inlaid mother-of-pearl (actually plastic) patterning. Not only is it hideous but it's about the shape and size of a typewriter. Available in the Souq al-Hamidiyya, Damascus.

Now-you-see-him-now-you-don't Khomeini Plate A plate which you tilt one way to get a stern-looking Āyatollāh, then tilt another way for a cheery prime minister Khatami. Available at the Shrine of Khomeini, south of Tehrān.

Priapus from Ephesus A small replica of the (in)famous, generously endowed statue on display at the museum here. Attach to the wall for a splendid coat hook.

Pyramid Paperweight A clear resin pyramid with a golden sphinx inside. When you shake it golden 'snow' rains down. Or maybe it's acid rain. Available in Egypt anywhere tourists congregate.

SHOPPING

One of the highlights of the Middle East is the covered souqs and bazaars where anything can be found if you look long and hard enough. Nothing beats the excitement of the expedition up and down the back alleyways of the bazaars, past pungent barrels of basil and cloves from the spice stalls through to medieval caravanserais. Take your sense of humour and curiosity with you, and if you want to buy something, be prepared to bargain – see Bargaining earlier in this chapter.

The list of things to buy varies from country to country (see the individual country chapters), but includes: handicrafts; *kilims* (rugs) and carpets; pearls, silver and gold; cotton clothing, including *keffiyeh* (headscarves), *galabiyyas* (long, loose robes worn by men), caftans and embroidered dresses; Bedouin woven bags; decorative daggers and swords; copperware and brassware; olive and cedar woodcarvings; bottles of coloured sand; *kohl* (black eyeliner); silk scarves; inlaid backgammon boards and jewellery boxes; water pipes; embroidered tablecloths and cushion covers; leather and suede; and frankincense and incense.

In addition there's heaps of tacky souvenirs and kitsch, from Khomeini watches to hieroglyphic drawings – see the boxed text 'That Special Something'.

At the other extreme are the duty-free shops of the UAE airports, reputed to be among the largest and cheapest in the world, where you'll find the latest in electronic goods and hi-tech gadgets.

Getting There & Away

This chapter tells you how to reach the Middle East by air, land and sea from other parts of the world, and outlines the routes for onward travel from the region. For details of travel once you are in the region between one country and its neighbours see the Getting There & Away section in the relevant country chapter.

AIR

Airports in the Middle East of most use to tourists and with frequent flights to/from other parts of the world are Cairo, İstanbul, Tel Aviv and Dubai. The first three are the region's big tourism hubs, while Dubai is a major link in intercontinental routes between Europe and Southeast Asia and Australasia. Outside of these four, most of the Middle East is still seen primarily as a business destination, a fact reflected in the expense of flying there.

What this means in practice is that when booking a flight to the Middle East, you shouldn't automatically aim for the airport nearest to where you are going. For instance, your destination might be Jordan, but you may find tickets to Tel Aviv significantly cheaper, even taking into account the cost of the overland trip to Amman.

Also, look out for cheap charter flight packages from Western Europe to destinations in Turkey, Egypt and Israel. Some of the flight-plus-accommodation packages offered by travel agencies can work out to be cheaper than a standard flight, although often the dates can be very restrictive.

Bizarrely, it can also often be cheaper to take a transcontinental flight involving a change of planes or a transit stop in the Middle East than to buy a ticket just to that place. This can be true even for tickets sold through the same travel agency and with the same airline. For example, a London-Karachi ticket via Dubai may cost less than the cheapest available London-Dubai ticket. The catch is that the first ticket may not allow a stopover in Dubai, may restrict it to the return leg or may only allow it for an extra charge.

The UK

You can get to the Middle East on direct flights from almost any European city of

any size. However, London has the greatest number of flight options, closely followed by Frankfurt.

Fares from London are usually cheaper than from other European cities. The real bargains used to be with the Eastern European airlines, but for the last few years the best deals have been with Olympic Airways, Air France and Alitalia. All of these involve changes of plane. For the past few years fares to the region have remained fairly steady and the cheapest return fares you can expect to find (including all taxes) are around UK£220 to İstanbul, UK£230 to Cairo or Tel Aviv and UK£280 to Damascus.

Although publications like London's weekly *Time Out* and the travel pages of the national Sunday papers are full of ads for cheap flights, when you make the call it's rare to be offered a price that's anywhere near as attractive as the one that's quoted. As far as Middle East flights are concerned there are few dedicated specialists and the best bet is to call Trailfinders and STA Travel.

STA Travel (☎ 020-7361 6142, W www.statravel .co.uk) 74–88 Old Brompton Rd, London SW7; also has branches in Bristol, Manchester and most big university cities

Trailfinders (☎ 020-7938 3939, ⓦ www.trailfind ers.com) 42–48 Earl's Court Rd, London W8; also has branches in Bristol, Manchester and other big cities

If you're looking to fly into Egypt then it's also worth calling **Soliman Travel** (☎ 020-7244 6855; ⓦ www.solimantravel.com; 113 Earl's Court Rd, London SW5), a reputable Egypt specialist that often manages to undercut the competition, particularly on services to places like Sharm el-Sheikh in Sinai and Aswan in Upper Egypt.

The USA & Canada

There are more flights from the USA than from Canada, but still not that many. Royal Jordanian flies New York–Amman five times a week and Chicago-Amman twice weekly. EgyptAir flies between New York and Cairo four times a week and Los Angeles and Cairo once a week. During the high season Egypt-Air offers one extra flight per week from New York and Los Angeles. Saudia services operate to/from Jeddah and Riyadh, linking with both New York and Washington. Kuwait Airways flies between New York and Kuwait City three times per week.

From Montreal and Toronto, El Al flies twice a week to Tel Aviv.

As well as these direct flights there are connections with changes for other Middle Eastern airports from various cities in North America. The cheapest way to get from North America to the Middle East by air might be to fly to London and buy a ticket from a bucket shop there. But this would depend on the fare to London and the time you would have to spend in London waiting for a flight out.

Discount travel agents can be found through the *Yellow Pages* or the major daily newspapers. The *New York Times*, *Los Angeles Times*, *Chicago Tribune* and *San Francisco Examiner* all produce weekly travel sections filled with travel agents' ads. **Council Travel** (head office ☎ 800-226 8624; ⓦ www.ciee.org; 205 E 42 St, New York, NY 10017), America's largest student travel organisation, has around 60 offices in the USA. Call the head office for the office nearest you or visit its website. **STA Travel** (☎ 800-777 0112; ⓦ www.statravel.com) has offices in Boston, Chicago, Miami, New York, Philadelphia, San Francisco and other major

cities. Call the toll-free 800 number for office locations or visit its website.

In Canada, the *Toronto Star*, Toronto's *Globe & Mail*, the *Montreal Gazette* and *Vancouver Sun* carry travel agents' ads and are a good place to look for cheap fares. **Travel CUTS** (☎ 800-667 2887; ⓦ www.travelcuts.com) is Canada's national student travel agency and has offices in all major cities.

Australia & New Zealand

There are no longer tight constraints on ticket discounting in Australia, but for Australians and New Zealanders there are still few route options to the Middle East. EgyptAir has a regular service from Sydney via Southeast Asia to Cairo, from where there are connections to almost all other Middle Eastern destinations. However, the aircraft and in-flight service are much better with Gulf Air and Emirates, both of which fly out of Sydney and Melbourne to Abu Dhabi, Bahrain and Dubai, with connections onward from there to most other Middle Eastern capitals. Gulf Air's round-the-world (RTW) fare could be good value if you also want to visit London and stop over in Asia.

If you're heading for Tel Aviv then Qantas Airways and El Al via Asia are the best. Other options include Alitalia via Milan, Lufthansa Airlines via Frankfurt or KLM-Royal Dutch Airlines via Amsterdam.

In both Australia and New Zealand, STA Travel and Flight Centres International are big dealers in cheap air fares. Check the travel agents' ads in the *Yellow Pages* and ring around.

On From the Middle East by Air

Europe/USA/Australasia Buying cheap air tickets in the Middle East isn't easy. Usually the best deal you can get is an airline's official excursion fare and no discount on single tickets unless you qualify for a youth or student fare. Some travel agencies in the Middle East will knock the price down by up to 10% if you're persistent, but may then tie you into fixed dates or flying with a less popular airline.

The nearest thing you'll find to a discount-ticket market in the Middle East is offered by some travel agencies in Israel, particularly in Tel Aviv, and in İstanbul, especially in Sultanahmet.

As well as discounts on tickets to Western Europe and North America, the İstanbul agencies often have cheap deals on flights to places like Moscow, Mumbai /Delhi, Singapore/Bangkok and the USA.

Africa The widest choice of African destinations is offered by EgyptAir, but despite the proximity, there is nothing cheap about flying from the Middle East into Africa. In fact, for most African capitals a ticket bought in London will be cheaper than one bought in the Middle East. The best bet is to buy your African ticket with a stopover in the Middle East.

As an idea of prices, Cairo to Addis Ababa (Ethiopian Airlines and EgyptAir) is US$580/824 one way/return; Nairobi (Kenya Airways) is US$622 one way; and Khartoum (EgyptAir and Sudan Airways) is US$394/480 one way/return.

Central Asia & the Caucasus There are a small but rapidly growing number of flights from the Middle East to Central Asian and Caucasus destinations. There are regular flights between İstanbul and Almaty (Turkish Airlines, US$180 one way, thrice weekly), Bishkek (Kyrgyzstan Airlines, US$280 one way, twice weekly), Baku (Turkish Airlines, US$240 one way, thrice weekly) and Tashkent (Uzbekistan Airways, US$510 one way, twice weekly). There are also daily İstanbul-Ashghabat flights (Turkmenistan Airlines, US$250 one way).

From Iran there are return flights (on Iran Air or Iran Asseman) from Tehrān to Almaty (US$280), Ashghabat (US$100), Bishkek (US$220), Dushanbe (US$160) and Tashkent (US$205). From Mashhad there are flights to Ashghabat (US$85 one way), Bishkek (US$220 one way) and Dushanbe (US$160 one way).

From Tel Aviv, Uzbekistan Airways flies to Tashkent twice a week for US$300 one way. There are also Uzbekistan Airways flights connecting Tashkent with Bahrain, Sharjah and Jeddah.

LAND

If you are travelling independently overland to the Middle East – whether hitching, cycling, driving your own car or riding by train or by bus – you can approach the region from three main directions:

From the West (Europe) Includes routes through Greece by bus, train and car; through Bulgaria by bus, train and car; by direct bus to İstanbul from many Western European cities or by train to İstanbul via Bucharest or Budapest; or via the Caucasus into eastern Turkey or northwestern Iran.

From the East (The Caucasus, Central Asia and Pakistan) Including by bus or train through Turkmenistan; or by train, bus, motorcycle or car through Pakistan.

From the South (Africa) Includes routes through Sudan and Chad, or across North Africa via Tunisia into Libya.

Europe

At the time of writing there were no direct trains between Western Europe and Turkey. Instead one train a day heads from İstanbul to Bucharest (17 hours) and then onto Budapest (31 hours), with connections to elsewhere in Europe. There have been reports of long delays and hassle, especially of women, at the Bulgarian border.

Despite the romantic appeal of train journeys, getting to Turkey overland is usually cheaper and faster by bus. Several Turkish bus lines, including Ulusoy, Varan and Bosfor, offer reliable and quite comfortable services between İstanbul and major European cities like Frankfurt, Munich and Vienna for around US$70 one way. These services travel via Greece and the ferry to Italy, thereby avoiding any hassle at the Bulgarian border.

Greece A bus to İstanbul departs from Athens' Peloponnese train station at 7pm daily, except Wednesday. The journey costs 17,000dr (US$58) and takes about 22 hours (slightly less than the train and a somewhat more pleasant prospect). Try to book your seat a day ahead. You can also pick up the bus in Thessaloniki (US$37) from the train-station forecourt at 2.30am (except Thursday) and at Alexandroupolis (US$14) at 8.30am (again, except Thursday).

Alternatively, you can make your own way to Alexandroupolis and take a service from the intercity bus station to the border town of Kipi (US$2.40, thrice daily). You can't walk across the border but it's easy enough to hitch (you may be lucky and get a lift all the way to İstanbul). Otherwise, take a bus to İpsala (5km east beyond the border) or Keşan (30km east beyond the border), from where there are many buses to the capital.

Greece's sole rail link with Turkey is the daily Thessaloniki-İstanbul service. The train leaves İstanbul late in the evening, arriving in Thessaloniki late the next afternoon; in the reverse direction, it leaves Thessaloniki at 10.20pm. However, the timetable is subject to seasonal changes so don't count on these times. Although the 1400km trip is supposed to take 16 hours, delays of more than five or six hours at the border are common, especially on the eastbound leg, and the train can get uncomfortably crowded and hot. Only 2nd-class seats are available (US$38).

For motorists/bikers the two border posts between Greece and Turkey are at Kastanies and Kipi. If you're lucky you may get through in an hour or two.

Bulgaria There are regular daily buses from Sofia to İstanbul (US$25). They most likely also pick up in Plovdiv and Svilengrad, transiting the border post at Kapıkule, itself accessible by train from İstanbul or by bus from Edirne.

The *Balkan Express* runs from Hungary (Budapest) via Bulgaria (Sofia) to İstanbul (US$37, 12 hours). The train leaves Sofia at 8.40pm. In the reverse direction, it departs İstanbul's Sirkeci station at 10.20pm.

Bulgaria's main road-crossing point with Turkey, which is open 24 hours, is at Kapitan-Andreevo, on the E5 road from Svilengrad; over the fence lies the Turkish border post of Kapıkule, 18km west of Edirne. The second is at Malko Târnovo, 92km south of Burgas. Motorists in transit through Bulgaria may only be allowed to cross at Kapitan-Andreevo, depending on current regulations.

If you plan on leaving the Middle East via Bulgaria, nationals of the USA and the EU are admitted without a visa for stays of less than 30 days. Travellers of other nationalities (including Aussies, Kiwis and Canadians) need a transit visa, which is issued at the border for US$68.

The Caucasus

Georgia Daily buses run from Trabzon in Turkey to Batumi and Tbilisi (Tflis) via the Sarp border crossing. Alternatively, you can take local transport from Hopa to the border at Sarp, walk across and then hope to find a bus or taxi onto Batumi. Obtain a Georgian visa in advance at the consulate in Trabzon (☎ 0462-326 2226, fax 326 2296; Gazipaşa

Caddesi 20), which costs US$20/25 for 15/30 days. A certain amount of extortion seems to be a fact of life at this border, especially when coming back into Turkey.

Armenia In Turkey, the train line from Ankara to Erzurum runs as far as Kars but at the time of writing the Turkish-Armenian border was closed to foreign travellers.

The border between Armenia and Iran is open. The crossing is at Noghdooz (near Jolfā in northwestern Iran). You could make your own way by public transport, but there are also direct daily buses to Yerevan from Tehrān's Western bus terminal and from Tabriz's bus terminal. Armenian visas are issued at the border, but not Iranian ones.

Azerbaijan Some of the buses from Trabzon to Tbilisi continue to Baku (US$75, plus a US$10 'tip' payable on the bus if you're going to Tbilisi, US$25 for Baku). It's a fairly gruelling journey with a three- to four-hour delay at Sarp on the border with Turkey and Georgia – mainly because the Georgians and Azerbaijanis buy up and take home half of Turkey. Trabzon to Tbilisi takes the best part of 19 hours.

The border at Āstārā (Iran) and Astara (Azerbaijan) is open to foreigners. There are direct daily bus services between Tehrān's Western bus terminal (IR1000,000) and Baku, although you could just as easily make your own way from Tehrān via Rasht, or from Tabriz via Ardabil, then cross the border on foot and pick up a bus or taxi to Baku. You need to arrange your visas in advance (for the address of the Azerbaijani embassy in Tehrān see the Iran chapter).

Central Asia

The main Middle East/Central Asia border crossing is at Sarakhs (Iran) and Saraghs (Turkmenistan). It's easy to reach the border by train or bus from either side, and cross the border independently. There are also direct buses between Mashhad (Iran) and Mary (Turkmenistan), but no direct trains across the border. For more information see the Sarakhs section in the Iran chapter.

There's another crossing at Bajgiran in northern Iran, which is more convenient for the Turkmen capital Ashghabat. To get to Bajgiran, take a bus from Mashhad to Quchān (about six hours) then another bus or taxi to the border. There's also a new international train service that revives (in part) the old Silk Route. It runs between Tehrān and Almaty in Kazakhstan, via Mashhad, Sarakhs (Turkmenistan) and Tashkent (Uzbekistan). It departs Tehrān at 11pm Sunday (IR670,000, 76 hours). In the other direction the Almaty departure is at 9.30pm Thursday.

Travelling in either direction you must obtain a visa in advance.

Afghanistan

Since the demise of the Taliban (a regime not recognised by Iran) in 2002, an Afghan embassy has been established in Tehrān (see the Iran chapter for the address) and the border near Tāybād is open for travel to Herat. There are regular buses from Mashhad to Tāybād (three to four hours).

Pakistan

The only proper border crossing for foreigners is between Mirjāveh (Iran) and Taftan (Pakistan). Foreigners normally pass through this border easily unless they cross by train (in which case you may have to wait up to 10 hours for your fellow Iranian and Pakistani travellers to clear customs and immigration). It's best to catch public transport to either side of the border, cross it independently and then catch onward public transport. Alternatively there's a direct bus service between Tehrān and Lahore in Pakistan (IR400,000, 65 hours). Buses depart from the Western and Central bus terminals in Tehran (where you can buy tickets) on Monday.

Africa

Travel between Africa and the Middle East is extremely problematic at the time of writing. Although the Nile ferry connecting Aswan in Egypt to Wadi Halfa in Sudan began running again in 1998, Sudan is still unsafe for travel. Most East African overlanders now skip Sudan by flying from Egypt down to Addis Ababa in Ethiopia, although the current clashes on the Eritrean-Ethiopian border also place a big question mark over the validity of this option. See later in this chapter for details of Red Sea sailings.

SEA & RIVER

The Mediterranean routes have been popular with Western travellers for many years and are fairly well publicised. However, it's not always easy to get information on many of the other services to the Middle East as the usual travel trade publications tend to ignore their existence. Your best bet is to get in touch with the carrier or its nearest agent some time in advance, and not to take too seriously what other sources tell you. This advice is particularly important if your itinerary depends on catching a particular ferry, or if you intend to ship your vehicle on one.

You're unlikely to regret taking an adequate supply of food and drink with you on any of these ships; even if it is available on board you're pretty stuck if it doesn't agree with you or your budget. Many people may find deck class on some of the longer sailings, such as the eight-day Karachi-Jeddah run, a little too much to bear.

As well as the services listed below, some cruise liners call at Middle Eastern ports such as Aden, Suez, Alexandria or Muscat, but these are outside the scope of this book. A good travel agent should be able to tell you what's available this season.

Unless stated otherwise, all services run in both directions and all fares quoted below are single. A slight discount may apply on return tickets as well as student, youth or child fares on some lines. Schedules tend to change at least annually according to demand; fares, too, often fluctuate according to season, especially on the Mediterranean routes.

Although vehicles can be shipped on most of the following routes, bookings for them may have to be made some time in advance. The charge usually depends on the length or volume of the vehicle and should be checked with the carrier. As a rule motorcycles cost almost nothing to ship and bicycles are free.

Between Greece, Cyprus & Israel

Until 2001, twice-weekly car and passenger ferry services connected Haifa and Piraeus (the port for Athens), with stops in Rhodes or Crete and at Limassol (Cyprus). However, a question mark hangs over services because of the present conflict in Israel & the Palestinian Territories. At the time of writing the main passenger ferry operator **Poseidon Line** (☎ 01-429 2046, fax 429 2041; W www .greekislands.gr/greece.htm; Akti Miaouli 35-39, Piraeus 18536, Greece) intends limiting its Piraeus-Rhodes-Limassol-Haifa service to July and August, and then only if it's certain there's a tourist demand.

Currently, the only confirmed car and passenger service is with **Salamis Lines** (☎ 01-429 4325, fax 429 4557; W www.viamare .com/salamis/salprc.htm; Fillelinon 9, Piraeus 18536, Greece), but it's mainly a cargo run.

It departs Haifa at 8pm Monday and Saturday and arrives in Limassol (US$145/166 /71 passengers/cars/motorcycles) at 6am on Tuesday and Sunday mornings; and in Piraeus (US$241/248/106) at 6am Thursday and Monday. From Piraeus, it departs at 8pm Monday and Thursday; departs Limassol at 8pm Saturday and Wednesday and arrives in Haifa at 6.30am Sunday and Thursday. Fares include port taxes, war-risk taxes and all breakfasts and dinners; return fares are about 20% less than two one-way fares.

In Israel, book through **Rosenfeld Shipping** (☎ 04-861 3613, fax 853 7002; e haifa@rosenfeld.net; W www.rosenfeld .net; 104 Ha'Atzma'ut St, Haifa). Tickets are also available through **IsraWorld Travel** (☎ 03-522 7099; 66 Ben Yehuda St, Tel Aviv) and **Allalouf Dolphin Shipping** (☎ 03-524 7899; 5 Bograshov St, Tel Aviv).

Between Italy, Greece & Turkey

Turkish Maritime Lines (TML; ☎ 464 8864, fax 464 7834) runs car ferries from İzmir to Venice weekly from May to mid-October. Fares start at US$160 one way with reclining seat; mid-price cabins are priced from US$340 per person. In summer TML also offers ferry services four times a week from Brindisi. Poseidon Lines also runs summer ferries from Bari (in Italy) to İzmir (Turkey).

Private ferries link Turkey's Aegean coast and the Greek islands, which are in turn linked by air or boat to Athens. Services are usually daily in summer, several times a week in spring and autumn and perhaps just once a week in winter.

In summer, you will find daily boats connecting Lesbos and Ayvalık, Lesbos and Dikili, Chios and Çeşme, Samos and Kuşadası, Kos and Bodrum, Rhodes and Marmaris, Rhodes and Bodrum, Rhodes and Fethiye, and Kastellorizo and Kaş.

The cheapest and most frequent ferries are Samos-Kuşadası and Rhodes-Marmaris; the most expensive and trying Lesbos-Ayvalık. For more details see the Ayvalık, İzmir, Kuşadası, Bodrum and Marmaris sections in the Turkey chapter.

Between Cyprus & Turkey

Daily ferries and hydrofoils operate from Taşucu (near Silifke) to Girne in Turkish Northern Cyprus. **Fergün Express** (☎ 0324-741 2323, fax 741 2802) offers daily hydrofoils and five-times-weekly car ferries in each direction. **Akgünler** (☎ 0324-741 4385, fax 741 4324) also operates daily car ferries and hydrofoils. The one-way fare for a car is around US$44, while passengers pay around US$14 one way on the ferry and US$19 on the hydrofoil. Both companies also operate less regularly from Alanya to Girne.

If you have a multiple-entry visa for Turkey you should be able to cross over to Northern Cyprus and back again without buying a new one. However, if your visa has expired, you should anticipate long queues at immigration.

Between Russia & Turkey

Karden Line runs ferries between Trabzon and Sochi in Russia, departing from Trabzon on Monday and Thursday at 6pm and returning from Sochi on Tuesday and Friday at 6pm. Cabin tickets (US$60) are available in Trabzon from **Navi Tour** (☎ 462-326 4484; İskele Caddesi, Belediye Duükkanları). At the time of writing most people had to get a visa from a Russian consulate in their home country to use this service, but that may change.

Between Azerbaijan & Iran

There are no passenger services across the Caspian between Azerbaijan and Iran.

Between Sudan & Egypt

A boat leaves Aswan every Monday at around 3pm, arriving in Wadi Halfa, Sudan, at about 8am Tuesday morning. You should make sure you're at the port at the High Dam by noon.

You can travel 1st or 2nd class, at a cost of E£142/88.50 and tickets are bought at **Nile Valley Navigation Company** (☎ 097-303 348; open 8am-2.30pm Sat-Thur), next to the tourist office, one street in from the Corniche in Aswan. Note that the office will not sell you a ticket unless you've got a Sudanese visa stamp in your passport. Sudanese immigration officers may also ask you for a yellow fever certificate.

If you want to take a vehicle into Sudan, the Nile Valley Navigation Company also has a cargo ferry that will carry up to five or six cars. However, there are no fixed departures and you have to pay for the entire boat, a whopping E£8000.

ORGANISED TOURS

There are three main options for letting somebody else take the strain of organising your trip to the Middle East: high-street package tours, specialist tours and overland tours.

Package tours are those offered by virtually every high-street travel agency, serving up a couple of weeks on a beach under the sun. Middle East destinations include Turkey's Mediterranean coast, Eilat in Israel and Egypt's Sinai and Red Sea coasts. Buying into one of these deals is often the cheapest way of getting a holiday, but don't expect to see much beyond your resort. Check with any big mainstream tour operators for their current deals.

Specialist tours offer a similar package of flights, connections and accommodation, but are geared toward sightseeing. They typically involve one to three weeks of travel around a single country, or a combination of countries taking in all the highlights. On an overland tour you share a truck with a bunch of other travellers taking five or six weeks to meander between (typically) Cairo and İstanbul visiting the highlights of countries in between.

Advantages of these sorts of trip are that many of the time-consuming hassles like waiting around for public transport and finding decent accommodation each night are taken care of, maximising time for exploring and sightseeing. There's also the security that comes with being in a large group, which allows for things like camping out in the desert or exploring off the beaten track, activities that might be unsafe for individuals or couples. Disadvantages include a fairly fixed itinerary and the possibility of having to spend large amounts of time with a bunch of other people, not all of whom you will necessarily get along with.

Specialist Tours

The UK The companies listed below offer a miscellany of tours ranging from the relatively mainstream (luxury Nile cruises) to the cutting edge (trekking in Iran). This list is by no means exhaustive and it pays to do some research yourself, checking travel magazines and travel supplements in the national newspapers.

Caravanserai Tours (☎ 020-8855 6373, fax 8855 6370, e info@caravanserai-tours.com, w www.caravanserai-tours.com) 1–3 Love Lane, Woolwich, London SE18 6QT. A specialist in Iran and Libya organising tailor-made and small-group tours.

Crusader Travel (☎ 020-8744 0474, fax 8744 0574, e info@crusadertravel.com, w www.crusadertravel.com) 57 Church St, Twickenham TW1 3NR. A diverse package of tours and adventure activities including diving holidays based out of Eilat or Egypt's Sinai and Red Sea coast resorts, plus lots of good stuff in Turkey including rafting, sea kayaking and mountain biking along Turkey's Mediterranean coast.

Exodus (☎ 020-8675 5550, fax 8673 0859, e sales@exodus.co.uk, w www.exodus.co.uk) 9 Weir Rd, London SW12 0LT. Lots of choice including: eight days sea kayaking, mountain biking and canyoning on Turkey's Lycian coast (UK£515 to UK£569); a 15-day highlights of Turkey trip (UK£679 to UK£759); nine days on the Nile by felucca (UK£559 to UK£679); one week in either Lebanon or Syria, or both combined; 16 days in Persia; or the 'Middle East Encompassed' – Lebanon, Syria, Jordan and Egypt in 16 days (UK£1095 to UK£1195).

Explore Worldwide (☎ 01252-760 000, fax 760 001, e info@exploreworldwide.com, w www.exploreworldwide.com) 1 Fredrick St, Aldershot, Hampshire GU11 1LQ. Small group exploratory holidays with titles like 'Lawrence's Arabia', 'Crusader Castles & Desert Cities' and 'Spice Trails of Petra' taking in one or more of Egypt, Israel, Iran, Jordan, Lebanon, Syria, Turkey and Yemen. More unusually, Explore Worldwide also offers trips to the UAE and Oman's Musandam Peninsula (including a three-day dhow cruise) and a 14-day exploration of Saudi Arabia involving desert camping.

The Imaginative Traveller (☎ 020-8742 8612, fax 8742 3045, w www.imaginative-traveller.com) 14 Barley Mow Passage, Chiswick, London W4 4PH. Highly professional, established outfit with a vast range of tours offered to destinations including Egypt (25 different options for this country alone), Iran, Israel & the Palestine Territories, Jordan, Syria and Turkey. Countries can be visited singly or as part of a combined multi-country trip.

Magic Carpet Travel (☎ 01344-622 832, fax 626 940, e info@magiccarpettravel.co.uk, w www.magiccarpettravel.co.uk) 1 Field House Close, Ascot, Berkshire SL5 9LT. Iran specialist offering several escorted tours from eight to 17 days with some specialist options including one in search of the 'perfect carpet' and another timed to coincide with the annual rose-petal harvest.

On The Go (☎ 020-7371 1113, fax 7471 6414, w www.onthegotours.com) 70 North End Rd, West Kensington, London W14 9EP. Egypt and Turkey specialists with a wide variety of tours including city stays, Nile cruising, Red Sea diving and a five-week İstanbul to Cairo overland trip.

Oonas Divers (☎ 01323-648 924, fax 738 356, w www.oonasdivers.com) 23 Enys Rd, Eastbourne BN21 2 DG. Offers diving tours from its base in Sinai, and diving safaris from Egypt's southern Red Sea coast, all at reasonable prices.

Travelbag Adventures (☎ 01420-541 007, fax 541 022, w www.travelbag-adventures.com) 15 Turk St, Alton, Hampshire GU34 1AG. Small-group 'adventure' tours with structured itineraries to Egypt, Iran, Jordan Lebanon and Turkey. Also 'combination tours' of two or more countries, for example 'Aleppo to Aqaba' in 16 days covering the best of Jordan and Syria.

Wind, Sand & Stars (☎ 020-7433 3684, fax 7431 3247, e office@windsandandstars.co.uk) 2 Arkwright Rd, London NW3 6AD. Specialises in walking and climbing tours in Sinai.

Australia In Australia most of the companies act as agents for the UK packages, though there are a few interesting home-grown outfits:

Adventure World (☎ 1800-133 322, 02-9956 7766, fax 9956 7707) 73 Walker St, North Sydney, NSW 2060. Also in Adelaide, Brisbane, Melbourne and Perth. Agents for the UK's Explore Worldwide and Exodus.

Insight International (☎ 02-9512 0767, fax 9438 5209) Suite 201, 39–41 Chandos St, St Leonards NSW 2065. Three- to 15-day packages, including a grand Jordan, Israel and Sinai tour and Nile cruises.

Passport Travel (☎ 03-9867 3888, fax 9867 1055, w www.travelcentre.com.au) Suite 11a, 401 St Kilda Rd, Melbourne, Vic 3004. Middle East specialist with no packages, no brochures; instead Passport Travel assists in arranging itineraries for individuals or groups.

Peregrine (☎ 03-663 8611, fax 663 8618) 258 Lonsdale St, Melbourne, Vic 3000. Also in Adelaide, Brisbane, Perth and Sydney. Agents for the UK's Dragoman and The Imaginative Traveller.

Travelbag Adventures (☎ freecall 1800 815 442, fax 03-9642 5838, e adventures@sundowners .com.au) Suite 15, Lonsdale Court, 600 Lonsdale St, Melbourne, Vic 3000. Agents for the UK's Travelbag Adventures – see earlier.

Ya'lla (☎ 03-9510 2844, fax 9510 8425, e yal lamel@yallatours.com.au) West Tower, 608 St Kilda Rd, Melbourne, Vic 3000. Wide variety of pick 'n' mix package tours and private arrangement tours in Egypt, Israel, Jordan, Lebanon, Syria and Turkey.

The USA & Canada The Middle East is badly served in the USA and Canada, with very few options other than expensive, top-end packages. The few exceptions include:

Adventure Center (☎ 1800-227 8747, fax 510-654 4200, e tripinfo@adventure-center.com) 1311 63rd St, Suite 200, Emeryville, CA 94608. Agents for the UK's Dragoman, Encounter Overland and Explore Worldwide.

Cross Cultural Adventurers (☎ 703-237 0100, fax 237 2558) Box 3285, Arlington, VA 22203

Himalayan Travel (☎ 203-359 3711) Stamford. Agents for The Imaginative Traveller.

Wilderness Travel (☎ 800-368 2794, fax 510-558 2489) 1102 Ninth St, Berkeley, CA 94710

Overland Tours

For people with time to indulge in six, eight or more weeks of holiday, especially those for whom lone travel doesn't appeal, these trips are ideal. You travel in a specially adapted 'overland truck' with anywhere between 16 and 24 other passengers and your group leader cum driver/navigator/mechanic/nurse/guide /fixer/entertainer – much of the success of your trip rests on this guy's shoulders. Accommodation is usually a mix of camping and budget hotels. Food is bought along the way and the group cooks and eats together. You are very much expected to muck in; cooking and shopping is done on a rota and everyone is expected to lend a hand when it comes to digging the truck out of sand.

Travelling in such a self-contained bubble, the success of the trip very much depends on the group chemistry. It could be one long party on wheels or six endless weeks of grin and bear it. Significantly, one group leader we spoke to said that the thing that most overlanders remembered most about the trips was the people they were with.

Companies & Routes The overland tour market is dominated by British companies, although passengers come from all over the world. The standard route is İstanbul to Cairo, but usually by-passing Lebanon and Israel & the Palestinian Territories. Note that not all the companies in the following list do dedicated Middle East trips; some only include the region as part of a longer 12- or 18-week Asia or Africa route, say from London to Kathmandu or London to Cape Town. A few of the companies also do short overland trips of three or four weeks, which make a good taster for first-timers.

Something you need to inquire about when considering an overland tour is what exactly the price includes. Does it include visa fees? Site admission fees? Food? Some companies do, some companies don't and you need to be aware of what you're paying for when you compare price with price.

Dragoman (☎ 01728-862 222, fax 861 127, e info@dragoman.co.uk, w www.dragoman.com) 2002 Camp Green, Debenham, Stowmarket, Suffolk IP14 6LA. İstanbul to Cairo (or vice versa) through Turkey, Syria, Jordan and Egypt in from four to 6½ weeks (UK£810 to UK£1300); Tunis to İstanbul through Tunisia, Libya, Egypt, Jordan, Syria and Turkey in nine weeks (UK£2170); plus a number of combination trips incorporating Central Asia, India and Pakistan.

Economic Expeditions (☎ 020-8995 7707, fax 8742 7707, e info@economicexpeditions.com, w www.economicexpeditions.com) 29 Cunnington St, Chiswick, London W4 5ER. İstanbul to Cairo – or vice versa – in five weeks for £380, plus £140 kitty.

Exodus (☎ 020-8675 5550, fax 8673 0859, e sales@exodus.co.uk, w www.exodus.co.uk) 9 Weir Rd, London SW12 0LT. Trips include a 'Middle East Explorer' (seven weeks through Turkey, Syria, Jordan and Egypt) for a basic UK£1190, or the same countries plus Iran, Pakistan (UK£1690, 11 weeks); plus India, Nepal (UK£2440, 16 weeks).

Kumuka (☎ freephone 0800 068 8855, fax 020-7937 6664, e enquiries@kumuka.co.uk, w www.kumuka.co.uk) 40 Earl's Court Rd, London W8 6EJ. Masses of routes offered including dedicated explorations of Egypt, Jordan or Syria. The basic İstanbul to Cairo route, or vice versa, is done as a 35-day (UK£935) or a 21-day (UK£595) trip.

Oasis Overland (☎ 01258-471 155, fax 471 166, e enquiries@oasisoverland.co.uk, w www.oasisoverland.co.uk) 5 Nicholsons Cottages, Hinton St Mary, Dorset DT10 1NF. 'Egypt Encompassed' in 10 (UK£200) or 14 (UK£240) days; or Turkey, Syria, Jordan and Egypt in 21 (UK£390) or 35 (UK£490) days.

Worldwide Adventure Travel (☎ 020-7370 4555, fax 7835 1829, e atc@topdecktravel.co.uk, w www.topdecktravel.co.uk) 125 Earl's Court Rd, London SW5 9RH. İstanbul to Cairo in 28 days for UK£375, plus combination trips with Asian destinations.

In North America and Australasia, overland companies are represented by specialist travel agencies – see Specialist Tours earlier in this chapter and check the advertisements in travel magazines and weekend metropolitan papers.

Getting Around the Region

This chapter is a directory that should be used for general planning. If you want to travel, for instance, between Turkey and Israel, this chapter will give you an overview of the options: air, land or sea, train versus bus, and so on. So, if you decide to go by bus from İstanbul to Damascus, from Damascus to Amman, and Amman to Jerusalem you should begin by going to the Getting There & Away section of Turkey for further details on buses to Syria. This same section will tell where the border crossing points are. Once in Syria, consult that chapter's Getting There & Away section for the best way to continue on to Amman, Jordan. Simple.

AIR

With no regional rail network to speak of and distances that make the bus a discomforting test of endurance, flying is certainly the most user-friendly method of transport in the Middle East. Tickets are more flexible than buses or trains, schedules more rigidly adhered to, refunds easier to get and information more readily available.

Flying isn't an option for getting to or from Iraq, nor is flying possible between Israel and most other Middle Eastern countries, except for Egypt, Jordan and Turkey. But, these exceptions aside, almost every Middle Eastern capital is linked to each of the others.

Flights are usually operated by state airlines, most of which are reasonable (if often overpriced) and some of which, such as Emirates and Gulf Air, are truly excellent. If you're in a capital city, it's usually worth buying your ticket through a reputable travel agency. It can provide you with all the available choices without you having to visit several different airline offices. The price you pay will usually be the same.

Travel agency addresses are found in the Information sections of individual cities.

Air Passes

At the time of writing, **Emirates** (W *www.ekgroup.com*) has something called the Arabian Airpass that allows cut-price travel around the Middle East. To qualify you need to buy a flight to Dubai and then onward flights (a minimum of two, maximum of six) to cities such as Cairo, Amman, Damascus and Muscat. These are available from US$40.

BUS

Bus is the universal mode of transport in the Middle East. Throughout most of the region buses will take you to almost anywhere of any size; on many routes there may be no other form of public transport. The exception is the Gulf States, where car ownership levels are so high that little demand for public bus services exists. It's not too difficult to get between the main towns in Saudi Arabia and Oman by bus, but Bahrain, Kuwait, the UAE and Qatar have few, if any, domestic services.

Most Middle Eastern countries can be reached by direct international bus from other parts of the region:

Aleppo (Syria) Several buses daily to İstanbul (US$20, 22 hours) via Ankara; and numerous daily buses to Beirut (US$6.50, six to seven hours).

Amman (Jordan) Two direct buses daily to Damascus (US$6.50, seven hours); daily direct buses to King Hussein Bridge for Israel (US$8.50, 45 minutes); daily direct buses to Riyadh, Dammam and Jeddah in Saudi Arabia and beyond (US$45, all up to 24 hours depending on destination); and daily direct buses to Baghdad in Iraq (US$17, 14 hours).

Ankara (Turkey) One daily bus to Tehrān (US$30, 28 hours); two daily buses to Aleppo (US$25, 10 hours); two daily buses to Damascus (US$30, 14 hours).

Baghdad (Iraq) Two daily buses to Amman (US$20, 14 hours); Iraq's other borders still remain closed to tourists.

Beirut (Lebanon) Frequent direct buses daily to Damascus (US$4, four hours) and Aleppo (US$6.50, six to seven hours).

Cairo (Egypt) Indirect services via Sinai to Jerusalem/Tel Aviv (US$35, 10 hours or more); daily bus-ferry combination services to Amman (US$80, 16 hours); one bus weekly to Jeddah via the Red Sea ferry from Port Suez (US$140, 52 hours).

Damascus (Syria) Two buses daily to Amman (US$6, six or seven hours); several daily departures for İstanbul (US$32, 30 hours) via Ankara (US$26); hourly buses to Beirut (US$4, four hours); and one departure weekly to Cairo (US$43, 30 hours).

Dubai (UAE) Twice daily buses to Muscat (US$20, five hours); and twice weekly buses to Damascus and Amman via Saudi Arabia (US$80, 36 hours).

İstanbul (Turkey) One daily bus to Tehrān (US$40, 35 hours); two buses a day to Aleppo (US$34, 16½ hours); two buses a day to Damascus (US$37, 20 hours).

Jeddah (Saudi Arabia) Direct buses operate several times per week from İstanbul via Ankara, Damascus and Amman. Several Turkish companies compete with Saudi Arabia's national bus company Saptco on the route. The Saudi buses tend to be newer and better maintained. For northbound travel you should visit the main bus terminals in Riyadh or Jeddah to check schedules and fares, as these change frequently. You should be aware that around pilgrimage time buses to and from Jeddah are sold out well in advance.

Muscat (Oman) Twice daily buses to Dubai (US$20, five hours).

Tehrān (Iran) Several buses daily to Ankara and İstanbul (IR69,000/81,000/115,000 for buses with 32/29/22 seats); and several buses weekly to Damascus.

For further details of these services see the Getting There & Away sections of the relevant cities.

Even in those countries without any international bus services it's usually possible to get to at least one neighbouring country by using domestic services, making your own way across the border and picking up another domestic service or taxi in the next country. This method is usually cheaper and it avoids one of the big problems of international services: waiting for the vehicle to clear customs at each border. This can mean delays of several hours. However, if you are planning on using domestic buses make sure you know that there will be onward transport on the other side of the border.

It's always advisable to book bus seats in advance at the bus station; the bus station is usually the only ticket outlet and source of reliable information about current services. That said, trying to find information can be frustrating if you don't speak the language.

The cost and comfort of bus travel vary enormously throughout the region, and further details are given in the individual country chapters. One most typical nuisance, however, is the Middle Eastern bus drivers' fondness for loud videos (a fondness presumably shared by local passengers); sleep is almost always impossible. Another potential source of discomfort is that in most Middle Eastern countries the concept of a 'no-smoking bus' doesn't yet exist.

TRAIN

No Middle Eastern country has an extensive railway network and there are few international services. Most railway lines in the region were built primarily for strategic or economic reasons, and many are either no longer in use or only carry freight. However, where there is a choice (such as in Iran and Egypt) the trains are usually much more comfortable than the buses and compare favourably in price. On the other hand, they are less frequent and usually slower, while many stations are some distance out of the town centres they serve. In general, tickets are only sold at the station and reservations are either compulsory or recommended.

The only functioning international passenger services within the region are:

Amman-Damascus/Damascus-Amman A twice weekly train connects the capitals of Jordan and Syria. It's a slow diesel train with ancient carriages – see the Amman and Damascus Getting There & Away sections for further details.

Damascus & Aleppo-İstanbul/İstanbul-Aleppo & Damascus There is a once-weekly service between these two cities – see the Syria and Turkey Getting There & Away sections for further details.

Tehrān-Damascus/Damascus-Tehrān The Tehrān-İstanbul train splits at Van and carriages divert to Damascus – see the Iran and Turkey Getting There & Away sections for further details.

Tehrān-İstanbul/İstanbul-Tehrān This is a weekly train running via Sero, the border and Ankara.

TAXI

In the West, taxis are usually an avoidable luxury. In the Middle East they are often neither. Many cities, especially in the Gulf States, have no other form of urban public transport, while there are also many rural routes that are only feasible in a taxi or private vehicle.

The way in which taxis operate varies widely from country to country, and often even from place to place within a country. So does the expense of using them. Different types of taxi are painted or marked in different ways, or known by different names, but often, local people talking to foreigners in English will just use the blanket term 'taxi'. If you want to save money, it's important to know which is which.

Details of local peculiarities are given in the Getting Around sections of the country chapters.

Regular Taxi

The regular taxi (also known as agency taxi, telephone taxi, private taxi or, in Israel, special taxi) are found in almost every Middle Eastern town or city. In some places there's no other public transport, but in most, regular taxis exist alongside less expensive means of getting around (although these usually shut down overnight). They are primarily of use for transport within towns or on short rural trips, but in some countries hiring them for excursions of several hours is still cheap. They are also often the only way of reaching airports or seaports.

For details see the individual country chapters.

Shared Taxi

A compromise between the convenience of a regular taxi and the economy of a bus, the shared taxi picks up and drops off passengers at points along its route and runs to no particular schedule (although in most places to a fixed route). It's known by different names – collect, collective or service taxi in English, *servees* in Arabic, *sherut* in Hebrew, *dolmuş* in Turkish and just *tāksī* in Persian. Most shared taxis take up to four or five passengers, but some seat up to about 12 and are indistinguishable for most purposes from minibuses.

Shared taxis are much cheaper than private taxis and, once you get the hang of them, can be just as convenient. They are dearer than buses, but more frequent and usually faster, because they don't stop so often or for so long. They also tend to operate for longer hours than buses. They can be used for urban, intercity or rural transport, but not necessarily all three in a particular place.

Fixed-route taxis wait at the point of departure until full or nearly full. Usually they pick up or drop off passengers anywhere en route, but in some places they have fixed halts or stations. Sometimes each service is allocated a number, which may be indicated on the vehicle. Generally, a flat fare applies for each route, but sometimes it's possible to pay a partial fare.

Shared taxis without routes are supreme examples of market forces at work. If the price is right you'll quickly find a taxi willing to take you almost anywhere, but if you're prepared to wait a while, or to do your journey in stages, you can get around

for almost nothing. Fares depend largely on time and distance, but can also vary slightly according to demand.

Beware of boarding an empty one, as the driver may assume you want to hire the vehicle for your exclusive use and charge you accordingly. It's advisable to watch what other passengers pay and to hand over your fare in front of them. Passengers are expected to know where they are getting off. 'Thank you' in the local language is the usual cue for the driver to stop. Make it clear to the driver or other passengers if you want to be told when you reach your destination.

CAR & MOTORCYCLE

The advantages of having your own vehicle are obvious. You aren't tied to schedules, you can choose your own company, set your own pace, take the scenic route, declare your vehicle a smoking or no-smoking zone and you won't be at the mercy of dishonest taxi drivers or have to fight for a place on a bus. And you can avoid all the hassles that go with carrying your world on your back.

But for the vast majority of short-term visitors to the Middle East the advantages of being attached to one vehicle are far outweighed by the disadvantages. The main problem isn't the expense of obtaining a *carnet de passage* (see under Carnets later). It's not the often hair-raising driving found on Middle Eastern roads. Nor is it the variable quality of the roads themselves or the sheer distance between places of interest. Nor is it even the millstone-around-the-neck worry of serious accident, breakdown or theft.

The one overwhelming obstacle that puts all these difficulties into the shade is simply establishing a feasible route through the Middle East. This can be hard enough if you're relying on public transport, but at least there's nearly always the alternative of flying if a particular overland route proves too difficult or dangerous. This is hardly an option if you have a car with you, and air freighting even a motorcycle isn't cheap. Selling or dumping a temporarily imported vehicle in the Middle East is more or less ruled out by customs regulations. It's at least theoretically possible to have it put under customs seal in one country and to return for it later, but this is a hassle to arrange, requires backtracking and somewhat negates the point of bringing a vehicle in the first place. Car ferries can get around some of these problems, but shipping a car isn't cheap, often requires an advance booking and won't help you out in every eventuality.

Overland access from Europe being restricted, it's hard to think of a route through the Middle East that would justify the expense and hassle of bringing a car and getting it out again. Even in the Gulf States, it would make more sense for short-term visitors to rent a car locally. For long-term residents it would probably be cheaper and more straightforward to buy one there and sell it before leaving.

Motorcycles are rare sights on most of the Arabian Peninsula; elsewhere in the region they are fairly popular as a means of racing around in urban areas, but little used as long-distance transport. If you do decide to motorcycle through the Middle East, try to take one of the more popular Japanese models if you want to stand any chance of finding spare parts. Even then, make sure it's in very good shape before setting out. Motorcycles can be shipped or, often, loaded as luggage onto trains.

Even if you do work out a feasible route that justifies taking your own vehicle, you'll face mountains of paperwork and red tape before you leave home. The documents usually take a month or more to obtain, and just finding out the current regulations can be difficult. It's best to get in touch with your automobile association (eg, AA or RAC in the UK) at least three months in advance. Note that the following rules and conventions may not apply if you stay more than three months in any one country, or if you're going for any purpose other than tourism.

Carnets

A carnet de passage is a booklet that is stamped on arrival at and departure from a country to ensure that you export the vehicle again after you've imported it. It can be issued by a motoring organisation in the country where the vehicle is registered. The situation on carnets alters frequently, but many Middle Eastern countries require them.

The sting in the tail with a carnet is that you have to lodge a deposit to secure it. If you default on the carnet – that is, you if don't have an export stamp to match the import one – then the country in question can claim your deposit, which can be up to 300% of the new value of the vehicle. You can get around this problem with bank guarantees or carnet insurance, but you still have to fork out in the end if you default.

Should the worst occur and your vehicle is irretrievably damaged in an accident or catastrophic breakdown, you'll have to argue it out with customs officials. Having a vehicle stolen can be even worse, as you may be suspected of having sold it.

Other Documents

An International Driving Permit (IDP) is compulsory for foreign drivers and motorcyclists in Bahrain, Egypt, Iran, Iraq, Saudi Arabia and Syria. Most foreign licences are acceptable in the other Gulf States, Israel, Lebanon and Turkey, and for foreign-registered vehicles in Jordan. However, even in these places an IDP is recommended.

For the vehicle you'll need the registration documents. Check with your insurer whether you're covered for the countries you intend to visit and whether third-party cover is included. You'll also need a green card, issued by insurers. Insurance for some countries is only obtainable at the border.

Breakdowns & Spare Parts

Mechanical failure can be a problem as spare parts – or at least official ones – are often unobtainable. Fear not: ingenuity often compensates for factory parts.

Generally, Land Rovers, Volkswagens, Range Rovers, Mercedes and Chevrolets are the cars for which spare parts are most likely to be available, although in recent years Japan has been a particularly vigorous exporter of vehicles to the Middle East. In more anti-Western countries, such as Iran, Syria and Iraq, spare parts for US vehicles may be very hard to find. One tip is to ask your vehicle manufacturer for a list of any authorised service centres it has in the countries you plan to visit. The length of this is likely to be a pretty good reflection of how easy it is to get spare parts on your travels.

Road Rules & Conditions

One of your enduring memories of the Middle East will undoubtedly be the driving standards. With the partial exception of Oman, the driving is appalling by Western norms. Fatalism rules supreme. Many regulations are, in practice, purely cautionary.

Car horns, used at the slightest provocation, take the place of caution and courtesy. At least theoretically, driving throughout the region is on the right, although many motorcyclists consider themselves exempt from this convention. You're unlikely even to know what the speed limit is on a particular road, let alone to be forced to keep to it. As a rule only non-Middle Easterners wear motorcycle helmets or car safety belts in most countries of the region.

The main roads are good or at least reasonable in most parts of the Middle East, but there are plenty of unsurfaced roads and the international roads are generally narrow and crowded.

Remember that an accident in the more remote parts of the region isn't always handled by your friendly insurance company. 'An eye for an eye' is likely to be the guiding principle of the other party and their relatives, whether you're in the wrong or not. Don't hang around to ask questions or gawp. Of course we're not saying that you shouldn't report an accident, but it may be more prudent to head for the nearest police station than to wait at the scene. Except in well-lit urban areas, try to avoid driving at night, as you may find your vehicle is the only thing on the road with lights.

A warning triangle is required for vehicles (except motorcycles) in most Middle Eastern countries; in Turkey two triangles and a first-aid kit are compulsory.

Petrol
Usually two grades are available; if in doubt get the more expensive one. Petrol stations are few and far between on many desert roads. Away from the main towns, it's advisable to fill up whenever you get the chance. Locally produced maps often indicate the locations of petrol stations. Diesel isn't readily available in every Middle Eastern country, nor is unleaded petrol.

Rental
In most large Middle Eastern cities it's fairly easy, if rarely cheap, to rent a vehicle. Some agencies can arrange vans, minibuses and buses for groups, but most deal only in cars; extremely few rent out motorcycles or bicycles. Before hiring a self-drive vehicle, ask yourself seriously how well you think you can cope with the local driving conditions and whether you know your way around well enough to make good use of one. Also compare the cost with that of hiring a taxi for the same period.

BICYCLE
While on the road researching this book we encountered maybe a half dozen touring cyclists, ranging from a bloke concentrating on exploring Sinai by bike to a young Welsh guy who was cycling through Turkey, Syria, Jordan, Saudi Arabia and Iran as part of a mammoth, two-year, round-the-world expedition. The ambitions of the rest of the cyclists fell somewhere in-between. It's clear, then, that although the numbers doing it are small, cycling round the Middle East is a viable proposition.

Most of the people we spoke to reckoned that the most enjoyable cycling was in Turkey and Syria (this is backed up by readers' letters). Although hilly, the scenery in Turkey is particularly fine and accommodation is fairly easy to come by even in the smallest villages. This is definitely not the case elsewhere, and in Syria in particular you have to expect to spend the odd night in a tent. That said, cyclists in Syria frequently receive invitations from people along the way to come home, meet the family, eat and stay over. In Turkey if you get tired of pedalling it's also no problem to have your bike transported in the luggage hold of their big modern buses. A couple writing in the guestbook at the Al-Haramein Hotel in Damascus (a good source of cycling information) reported that their tandem was accommodated without them having to remove the panniers. And there's no charge for this.

By far the major difficulty cited by all cyclists was the heat. This is at its worst from June to August and cycling in these summer months is definitely not recommended. May to mid-June and September through October are the best times for two-wheel touring of this region. Even then, most cyclists found it necessary to make an early morning start and have done with most of the pedalling by early afternoon.

Although one or two of the cyclists had been a little worried beforehand at the thought of being stuck for spares on the road, there are bicycle repair shops in most major towns and the locals are excellent 'bush mechanics'.

The positive aspects are that cyclists are given fantastic welcomes – a trademark of the Middle East – showered with food and drink, and, as mentioned above, sometimes offered free accommodation. Even the police are helpful and friendly. There are a couple of exceptions – along Jordan's King's Highway and in Sinai kids throw stones at cyclists (maybe because of the cycling shorts, we don't know) – but these are minor blips of annoyance.

Practicalities

Carry a couple of extra chain links, a chain breaker, spokes, a spoke key, two inner tubes, tyre levers and a repair kit, a flathead and Phillips-head screwdriver, and Allen keys and spanners to fit all the bolts on your bike. Check the bolts daily and carry spares. Fit as many water bottles to your bike as you can – it gets hot. Make sure the bike's gearing will get you over the hills, and confine your panniers to 15kg maximum. In your panniers include a two-person tent (weighing about 1.8kg) that can also accommodate the bike where security is a concern; a sleeping bag rated to 0°C and a Therm-a-Rest; small camping stove with gas canisters; cooking pot; utensils; Katadyn water filter (two microns) and Maglite. Wear cycling shorts with a chamois bum and cleated cycling shoes. Don't fill the panniers with food as it is plentiful and fresh along the route.

Contacts

If you are considering cycling the Middle East, but have a few pressing questions that first need answering, one place to go is the Thorn Tree on Lonely Planet's website (W www.lonelyplanet.com). Post your query on the Activities branch and there's a strong likelihood somebody will respond with the information that you're looking for.

Alternatively, you could contact the **Cyclists' Touring Club** *(CTC; ☎ 01483-417 217, fax 426 994; e cycling@ctc.org.uk; W www .ctc.org.uk)*, a UK-based organisation which, among other things, produces information sheets on cycling in different parts of the world and has a useful website. Last time we checked there was definitely a dossier on Egypt and by now there may also be sheets on other Middle Eastern countries. The club also publishes a good glossy, bi-monthly

magazine that always carries one or two travel-type cycling pieces.

HITCHING

Although many travellers hitchhike, it is not a totally safe way of getting around. There is no part of the Middle East where hitching can be recommended for unaccompanied women travellers. Just because we explain how hitching works doesn't mean we recommend you do it.

Hitching as commonly understood in the West hardly exists in the Middle East (except Israel). Although in most countries you'll often see people standing by the road hoping for a lift, they will nearly always expect (and be expected) to offer to pay. Hitching in the Middle Eastern sense is not so much an alternative to the public transport system as an extension of it. The going rate is usually roughly the equivalent of the bus or shared taxi fare, but may be more if a driver takes you to an address or place off their route. You may well be offered free lifts from time to time, but you won't get very far if you set out deliberately to avoid paying for transport.

Hitching is not illegal in any Middle Eastern country and in many places it is extremely common. However, while it's quite normal for Middle Easterners, Asians and Africans, it isn't something Westerners are expected to do. In many Middle Eastern countries, Westerners who try to set a precedent of any kind often attract considerable attention. While this can work to your advantage, it can also lead to suspicion from the local police.

Throughout the Middle East a raised thumb is a vaguely obscene gesture. A common way of signalling that you want a lift is to extend your right hand, palm down.

BOAT

Practicality is the essence of Middle East ferry services, not luxury. Even in 1st class you shouldn't expect your voyage to be a pleasure cruise, while deck class often means just that. In summer, conditions may be a little too hot for many people. While food and drink of some sort may be available on board, many passengers prefer to take their own. Vehicles can be shipped on all the following services, but advance arrangements may have to be made.

For the latest information, get in touch with the head office or local agent of the respective company some time in advance.

Red Sea

The Amman-based Arab Bridge Maritime Company sails at least once daily between Nuweiba in Sinai and Aqaba. The journey takes three hours or so. There is also a catamaran plying the same route, which does the journey in one hour. See the Egypt and Jordan chapters for more details.

The Alexandria-based Misr Edco Shipping Company and four Saudi companies sail between Jeddah and Suez. The journey takes about 36 hours direct, about 72 via Aqaba. Buy tickets and check timetables and routes directly from the shipping company or its agent rather than through a travel agency if you don't want to be given misleading information (see the Shipping Line Addresses list in the Sea & River section of the regional Getting There & Away chap-

ter). Misr Edco sails about twice weekly between Port Safaga (Egypt) and Jeddah.

The Gulf & Sea of Oman

If you want to visit the Gulf States, but don't want to fly and can't get into Saudi Arabia, you can always sail. The shortest sailing, across the Strait of Hormuz between Bandar-e Abbās and Sharjah, takes 12 hours. Fares start at around US$50 in 3rd (deck) class. There are other less-frequent services linking Bushehr and Bahrain, Bushehr and Kuwait, Bandar-e Abbās and Muscat, Bandar-e Abbās and Doha and Chābahār and Muscat. These only have 1st-class (cabin) accommodation, but are much cheaper than the equivalent airfare. Most are overnight journeys. All these ships are operated by Valfajre-8 Shipping Company, owned by Islamic Republic of Iran Shipping Lines (IRISL; see the introductory Getting There & Away section of the Iran chapter). Outside the region tickets can be obtained through IRISL in London.

Bahrain

بحرين

The only island-state in the Arab world, this tiny country (about the size of Singapore, but with a fraction of its population) is unique in several ways, not least because Arabs and foreign expatriates mix more easily here than anywhere else in the region. Bahrain is the easiest of the Gulf States to visit, though anyone visiting an Arab country for the first time should still be prepared for a little culture shock. While it is one of the most liberal countries in the Gulf, it is still, by Western standards, a very conservative place.

Facts about Bahrain

HISTORY

Bahrain occupies a strategic position on the great trade routes of antiquity, with good harbours and abundant fresh water, and its people have always been natural merchants. As far back as the 3rd millennium BC this island was the seat of Dilmun, one of the great trading empires of the ancient world.

From 2200 BC to 1600 BC Dilmun controlled a large section of the western shore of the Gulf. At times its power probably extended as far north as modern Kuwait and as far inland as the Al-Hasa Oasis in eastern Saudi Arabia. Between 1600 BC and 1000 BC, Dilmun fell into decline and by about 600 BC it had been fully absorbed by Babylon.

From the 9th to the 11th century AD, Bahrain was part of the Umayyad and, later, Abbasid empires. It was once again on the trade routes between Mesopotamia and the Indian subcontinent, and as one of the Gulf's main pearling ports clearly had economic value. The Portuguese recognised Bahrain's value and in the early 1500s invaded the island, setting themselves up as military rulers in the Bahrain Fort. However, by 1602 the country's rule changed hands again when the Persians ousted the Portuguese.

It was not until the mid-18th century that the Al-Khalifa, the family that now rules Bahrain, first arrived in the area. They initially settled at Al-Zubara, on the north-western edge of the Qatar peninsula, and

The State of Bahrain

Population: 645,000
Area: 692 sq km
Capital: Manama
Head of State: King Hamad bin Isa al-Khalifa
Official Language: Arabic
Currency: Bahraini dinar (BD)

- Best Dining – sampling traditional home-made Bahraini food at the Craft Centre Café
- Best Nightlife – enjoying a show at one of the many nightclubs in Manama
- Best Walk – taking a late afternoon walk along the Marina Corniche
- Best View – watching the sunset from the tower on the causeway near the Saudi Arabia border
- Best Activity – diving for pearls in Bahrain's shallow waters

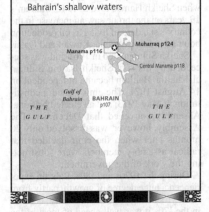

involved themselves in the region's lucrative pearling trade. They drove the Persians out of Bahrain in about 1782. Three years later, however, the Al-Khalifa were driven out by an Omani invasion and they did not return until 1820.

Bahrain was the first place on the Arabian side of the Gulf where oil was discovered. The discovery couldn't have come at a better time for Bahrain as it roughly coincided with the collapse of the world pearl market. Until that time pearling had been the mainstay of Bahrain's economy.

What to See

With just one week in Bahrain, wander around the **Bahrain National Museum** with its reconstructed burial mound and exhibits dating back 4000 years, visit the **Beit al-Quran** to view ancient Quranic manuscripts and other Islamic calligraphy and then take a guided tour of the beautiful **Al-Fatih Mosque**.

Set out early to take in sunrise at the **Bahrain Fort**, before imagining the rituals once offered to Enki, the God of Wisdom and Sweet Waters Under the Earth at the **Barbar Temple**. Kick the dust at the bleak and deserted ancient settlement of **Sar**, appreciate the quiet green oasis of **Al-Jasra** and then head on over to **A'ali** to visit traditional potters and view the sunset among the mysterious, towering burial mounds. Visit **Al-Khamis Mosque**, outside Manama, one of the oldest mosques in the Arab World; lunch on home-made Bahraini cuisine at Bahrain's **Craft Centre**; try to find as many traditional Bahraini doors as you can wandering through the narrow, twisted streets of **Muharraq** before stumbling upon the smooth, gypsum walls of **Beit Seyadi and Mosque**. Shop for gold and traditional embroidered Bahraini dresses in **Manama's souq** and take a break with a *sheesha* and Arabic coffee at one of the nearby coffee houses.

With two weeks you can learn about the history of pearl diving and go **diving** for pearls in Bahrain's oyster-filled waters and spend a couple of days watching wildlife on the **Hawar Islands**.

Bahrain's drive for modernisation began under Sheikh Hamad bin Ali and grew under his son, Sheikh Sulman, who came to power when Sheikh Hamad died in 1942. Sulman's 19 years on the throne saw an increase in the country's standard of living as oil production boomed in Saudi Arabia, Kuwait and Qatar.

Sheikh Sulman died in 1961 and was succeeded by his son, Sheikh Isa bin Sulman al-Khalifa. Bahrain became independent on 14 August 1971. The emir issued a constitution in May 1973, and an elected National Assembly convened that December. The Assembly, however, was dissolved only 20 months later when the emir decided that radical assembly members were 'obstructing the work of the government'.

During the 1970s and '80s, Bahrain experienced a huge degree of growth, partly from the skyrocketing price of oil, but also because in the '70s it was well ahead of most of the Gulf in terms of infrastructure. However, when the oil ran out and the economy started to falter, other cracks began to surface.

In the last decade of the 20th century the country was rocked by sporadic waves of unrest. The troubles began in 1994 when riots erupted after the emir refused to accept a large petition calling for greater democracy. There was more unrest in April 1995, and again in the spring of 1996, when bombs exploded at both the Diplomat and Meridien hotels. In 1997, a series of arson attacks were perpetrated by unemployed local Bahrainis, angry that jobs were being taken by workers from Asia.

On 6 March 1999, Sheikh Isa bin Sulman died and was replaced by his son, Sheikh Hamad bin Isa al-Khalifa. Upon his accession, Sheikh Hamad pledged to introduce a fully elected parliament, hold municipal elections and set up a constitutional monarchy. He also released political prisoners, allowed exiles to return and declared all nationals equal. As a result, the violence of the previous years came to a halt.

Bahrain Today

Bahrain is a much happier country today than it was even just a few years ago and this is largely due to the reforms implemented by Sheikh Hamad. In 2001 a national charter for constitutional reforms was endorsed by the country's first ever national referendum and a year later, on February 14, Bahrain was declared a constitutional monarchy and Sheikh Hamad its king. Under this new charter, both men and women are eligible to vote and stand for office and a system of financial controls and administration will be created to ensure transparency in government finances. A new national anthem has also been announced, and Bahrain's white-and-red flag will be replaced by a new design of five triangles representing the five pillars of Islam. The king will also have his own flag: a golden crown added to the new Bahraini flag.

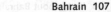

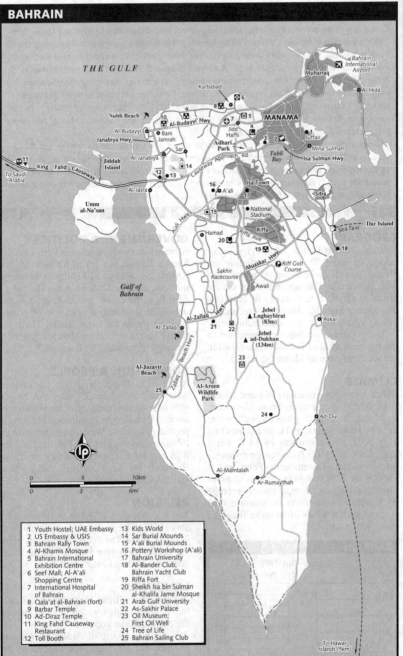

BAHRAIN

THE GULF

Bahrain International Airport

Muharraq

Al-Hidd

Karbabad

Subh Beach

Al-Budayyi' Hwy

MANAMA

Al-Budayyi

Bani Jamrah

Jidd Haffs

Juffair

Janabiya Hwy

Sar

Adhari Park

Mina Sulman

Al-Janabiya

Isa Sulman Hwy

Jiddah Island

Tubli Bay

King Fahd Causeway

Causeway Approach Rd

To Saudi Arabia

Al-Jasra

A'ali

Isa Town

Sitra

Umm al-Na'san

Dar Island

Sea Taxi

National Stadium

Gulf of Bahrain

Hamad

Riffa Ave

Riffa

Al-Zallaq

Muaskar Hwy

Riff Golf Course

Al-Zallaq

Sakhir Racecourse

Awali

Beach Hwy

Jebel Lughaybirat (83m)

Askar

Zallaq Hwy

Jebel ad-Dukhan (134m)

Al-Jazayir Beach

Al-Areen Wildlife Park

Ad-Dur

Al-Mamtalah

Ar-Rumaythah

0   5   10km
0   3   6mi

To Hawar Islands (5km)

1 Youth Hostel; UAE Embassy	13 Kids World
2 US Embassy & USIS	14 Sar Burial Mounds
3 Bahrain Rally Town	15 A'ali Burial Mounds
4 Al-Khamis Mosque	16 Pottery Workshop (A'ali)
5 Bahrain International Exhibition Centre	17 Bahrain University
6 Seef Mall; Al-A'ali Shopping Centre	18 Al-Bander Club; Bahrain Yacht Club
7 International Hospital of Bahrain	19 Riffa Fort
8 Qala'at al-Bahrain (fort)	20 Sheikh Isa bin Sulman al-Khalifa Jame Mosque
9 Barbar Temple	21 Arab Gulf University
10 Ad-Diraz Temple	22 As-Sakhir Palace
11 King Fahd Causeway Restaurant	23 Oil Museum; First Oil Well
12 Toll Booth	24 Tree of Life
	25 Bahrain Sailing Club

The Hawar Island Dispute

Ownership of the potentially oil-rich Hawar Islands was long disputed by Bahrain and Qatar. In the 1930s a bitter fight between the two ruling families led to Britain stepping in and awarding the islands to Bahrain. But this didn't settle long-running resentments. While Qatar claimed sovereignty over the islands, which lie close to its coast, Bahrain claimed the strip of Qatari coast known as Al-Zubara. As late as 1986 the two countries were brought close to war over the territorial dispute and more recently the stand off has kept relations strained. Bahrain and Qatar took their fight to the International Court of Justice in The Hague, and in March 2001, the court awarded Hawar to its current owner, Bahrain. However, it rejected its claim to Al-Zubara, and handed control of two minor islands, Janan and Hadd Janan to Qatar.

Despite the tense relations between the two countries, the dispute had its positive aspect, particularly in the eyes of environmentalists: the undeveloped and uninhabited islands are an important breeding ground for many species of migratory birds, and the surrounding waters are rich with marine life such as dugongs and turtles. Immediately after the court ruling, Bahrain invited international oil companies to drill for oil in the Hawar Islands.

GEOGRAPHY

Bahrain (706 sq km) is a low-lying archipelago of about 33 islands, including the Hawar Islands (ownership of which was long disputed by Bahrain and Qatar; see boxed text) and a few specks of sand that disappear at high tide. Bahrain Island (about 586 sq km) is the largest in the archipelego.

The population is higly concentrated in the northern third of Bahrain Island, and in the southern edge of Muharraq Island.

CLIMATE

Bahrain can get extremely hot and humid from June to September. From November to March it is quite pleasant with warm days and cool nights, and temperatures that vary between a minimum of 14°C and a maximum of 24°C. The average temperature in winter (December to February) is 18°C with 77% humidity, and in summer (June to August) temperatures average 35°C with 59% humidity. In summer, dust storms and hot winds often make life even more uncomfortable.

GOVERNMENT & POLITICS

Bahrain is a constitutional monarchy ruled by Sheikh Hamad bin Isa al-Khalifa. Sheikh Khalifa bin Sulman al-Khalifa is the prime minister, and Sheikh Sulman bin Hamad al-Khalifa is the crown prince. Bahrain is the only Gulf state with a strict rule of primogeniture within the royal family. The royal family has its opponents, but it's generally tolerated (even liked) by Bahrainis.

POPULATION & PEOPLE

About 645,000 people live in Bahrain, of which half are under 25 years old. Nearly 40% of residents (and 60% of the workforce) are non-Bahrainis or expatriates. Manama is populated by more Western businesspeople, Filipino shop workers and Pakistani and Indian shop owners than Bahrainis themselves. Bahrainis are Arabs, though many are at least partially of Persian ancestry.

RELIGION

The state religion of Islam is followed by about 85% of the population, of which about 70% are Shiite. The Sunni minority includes the royal family (see Religion in the Facts about the Middle East chapter).

LANGUAGE

Arabic is the official language of Bahrain, but English is also widely spoken among the cosmopolitan population.

For a list of useful Arabic words and phrases, see the Language chapter at the back of this book.

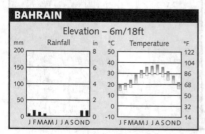

BAHRAIN

Elevation – 6m/18ft

Rainfall (mm/in) and Temperature (°C/°F) — J F M A M J J A S O N D

Facts for the Visitor

WHEN TO GO

The best time to visit Bahrain is between November and February, when it's not too hot. Avoid visiting during Ramadan, when things slow down significantly, and during Muslim festivals when merrymakers (both Arab and foreign) from Saudi Arabia and Kuwait visit and hotel rooms become difficult to find.

VISAS & DOCUMENTS
Visas

Most nationalities need a visa, which can most conveniently be obtained at the border with Saudi Arabia or at Bahrain's international airport. Visas are generally valid for up to two weeks, but extensions are possible (see below). A two-week visa on arrival costs BD5 for citizens of Australia, Canada, the EEC, New Zealand and the UK. US citizens are charged BD10/15 for a visa for three days/one week. There is a foreign-exchange office next to the immigration counter at the airport and at the border with Saudi Arabia.

US residents and Canadians can obtain a five-year multiple-entry visa at a Bahraini embassy or consulate for around about US$50 (US$55 for UK citizens). Most other nationalities can get an (extendable) visa from a Bahrain embassy or consulate, but it's easier to get a visa on arrival, as described above. For addresses of Bahraini embassies in the Middle East see the relevant country chapters.

If you're transiting through Bahrain, and travelling on to Saudi Arabia by land (and can prove it), the visa fee on arrival for all nationalities is BD2.

For details of visas for other Middle Eastern countries, see the 'Visas at a Glance' table under Visas & Documents in the Regional Facts for the Visitor chapter.

Visa Extensions These are available in Manama at the **General Directorate of Immigration & Passports** (☎ *535 111; Sheikh Hamad Causeway*). You must first find a sponsor – a Bahraini friend, or your hotel will oblige. Then fill out a form, and provide the directorate with your passport and one passport-size photo. Extensions cost BD15 for one week and BD25 for more

than one week up to one month; they will take up to a week to process.

To avoid this, your hotel (if you're staying at a good one) can sponsor your extension and deal with the directorate for a fee of about BD5. Foreigners overstaying their visas are fined BD10 per day.

Other Documents

No other special documents are needed to enter or move about Bahrain. Health certificates are not required, unless you're coming from an area of endemic yellow fever, cholera etc. If you plan to rent a car, you need an International Driving Permit. An International Student Card is next to worthless in Bahrain.

EMBASSIES & CONSULATES
Bahraini Embassies & Consulates

Following are the Bahraini embassies and consulates in major cities around the world. For addresses of Bahraini embassies in neighbouring Middle Eastern countries, see the relevant chapter.

Canada
  Consulate: (☎ 450-931 7444, fax 931 5988)
  Rene, Levesque West Montreal, Quebec
  H3H IR4
France
  Embassy: (☎ 01 45 53 01 19, fax 01 47 20 55
  75) 15 Ave Raymond Poincar, 75116 Paris
Germany
  Embassy: (☎ 228-957, 6100 fax 957 6190)
  Plittersdorfet Str 91 53173 Bonn
UK
  Embassy: (☎ 020-7370 5132, fax 7370 7773)
  98 Gloucester Rd, London SW74 AU
USA
  Embassy: (☎ 202-342 0741, fax 362 2192)
  3502 International Drive, NW Washington
  DC 20008

Embassies in Bahrain

The nearest embassies representing Australia, Canada and Ireland are in Riyadh, Saudi Arabia. Most of the embassies are in the 'diplomatic area' in Manama, between King Faisal Hwy and Sheikh Hamad Causeway. Opening hours are generally from around 8am or 8.30am to somewhere between noon and 2pm. The Saudi embassy is only open from 9am to 11am. All embassies and consulates are closed on Thursday and Friday.

France (☎ 298 660, fax 298 637) Al-Fatih Hwy
Germany (☎ 530 210, fax 536 282) Al-Hassaa
  Bldg, Sheikh Hamad Causeway
Kuwait (☎ 534 040, fax 533 579) King Faisal Hwy
Netherlands (☎ 713 162, fax 212 295) ABN
  Bldg, Al-Furdah Ave; handles Benelux countries
Oman (☎ 293 663, fax 293 540) Al-Fatih Hwy
Saudi Arabia (☎ 537 722, fax 533 261) King
  Faisal Hwy
UAE (☎ 723 737, fax 727 343) Juffair
UK (☎ 534 404, fax 536 109) Government Ave
USA (☎ 273 300, fax 272 594) Just off Sheikh
  Isa bin Sulman Hwy, Al-Zinj

CUSTOMS

Foreigners (but only non-Muslims) can import 1L of wine or spirits, or six cans of beer duty free. All passengers are allowed to bring in 200 cigarettes or 50 cigars, as well as 250g of loose tobacco and eight ounces (227ml) of perfume.

Visitors fill out a disembarkation card on arrival, which they must keep and return to the immigration authorities on departure.

MONEY
Currency

The currency is the Bahraini dinar (BD). One dinar is divided into 1000 fils. There are 500 fil and 1, 5, 10 and 20 dinar notes. Coins are 5, 10, 25, 50 and 100 fils. The Bahraini dinar is a convertible currency and there are no restrictions on its import or export. You may be offered some Saudi riyals as change, at the rate of BD1 to 10SR, but unless you're going to Saudi, insist on change in Bahraini dinars.

Exchange Rates

The dinar is pegged to the US dollar and rarely fluctuates. The rates below were current when this book went to print.

country	unit		dinar
Australia	A$1	=	BD0.206
Canada	C$1	=	BD0.208
euro zone	€1	=	BD0.368
Japan	¥100	=	BD0.309
Kuwait	KD1	=	BD1.247
New Zealand	NZ$1	=	BD0.177
Oman	Omr1	=	BD0.979
Qatar	QR1	=	BD0.103
Saudi Arabia	SR1	=	BD0.100
UAE	Dhr1	=	BD0.102
UK	UK£1	=	BD0.583
USA	US$1	=	BD0.376

Exchanging Money

Money (both cash and travellers cheques) can be changed at any bank or money-changing office. There's little to choose between banks and moneychangers in terms of exchange rates (as little as BD0.01 per US dollar usually), and it's rare for either to charge a commission – although it's always wise to check first. The main difference is that banking hours are restricted to 7.30am to noon Saturday to Wednesday, and 11am on Thursday, whereas moneychangers keep longer hours.

Currencies for other Gulf States are easy to buy and sell.

ATMs & Credit Cards Major credit cards are widely accepted throughout Bahrain. If you have your PIN number it's also very easy to obtain money from ATMs. Most banks have ATMs that accept Visa, Cirrus and MasterCard cards, while the Bank of Bahrain & Kuwait (BBK) has ATMs that take Visa, MasterCard, Cirrus, Maestro and AmEx cards.

Costs

If you stay in budget hotels, walk a lot, don't drink alcohol and eat in cheap restaurants, it's possible to get by on US$31/40 per person per day travelling as a single/double, but US$32/26 is more realistic. However for the average-budget traveller with costs such as car/taxi hire, admissions and entertainment, tours and the odd upmarket meal, a more realistic budget would be around US$95/110.

See the Accommodation and Getting Around sections later in this chapter for more information on costs.

Tipping & Bargaining

A service charge is added to some bills in Bahrain, but it generally goes to the shop, not the staff. An appropriate tip for good service would be around 10%.

Bargaining in the souqs and in most shops is acceptable and asking for a discount is even expected.

POST & COMMUNICATIONS
Post

Postcards cost 200/250 fils to Europe/North America and Australasia. Letters cost 200/250 fils per 10g. Parcels cost a standard minimum of BD3 for the first 500g to all Western countries, and BD1/1.500 for every extra 500g.

Mail to and from Europe and North America takes about one week; allow 10 days to and from Australia.

The main post office is in Manama, and there are smaller post offices in major residential areas around the country, and at the airport.

Most major international express mail and package companies have offices in Manama.

Telephone

The country code for Bahrain is ☎ 973, followed by the local number. There are no area or city codes. The international access code (to call abroad from Bahrain) is ☎ 00.

Bahrain's excellent telecommunications system is run by the government monopoly, Bahrain Telecommunications Company (Batelco). Virtually every country can be dialled direct from most payphones, and some specially marked booths also accept Visa and MasterCard. International calls from Bahrain cost BD0.350 per minute to Europe, Australia and North America. Rates are reduced to BD0.300 between 7pm and 7am every day, as well as all day Friday and on public holidays. There are several help lines with English-speaking operators including local directory assistance (☎ 181), international directory assistance (☎ 191) and the international call operator (☎ 151).

Bahrain is linked to over 100 countries through the Home Country Direct Dial service. Refer to the front of the (English-language) Bahrain telephone book for details, or ring the special inquiries number (☎ 100).

Local calls anywhere within Bahrain cost 50 fils for three minutes. Blue payphones take coins with a maximum speaking time of six minutes (100fils). Red payphones take phonecards, which are widely available in denominations of BD1, BD2, BD3.5, BD6.5 and BD15.

Mobiles Bahrain's mobile phone network runs on the GSM system through Batelco. Mobile phones can be rented through Batelco by the day/week/month for BD5/28/90. Visitors can also purchase sim cards for BD20 by

presenting their passports at the Batelco office. Recharge cards come in denominations of BD3, BD5 and BD10.

Fax

Fax services are available at most mid-range and top-end hotels, and at the Batelco building in Manama.

Email & Internet Access

The only ISP is Batelco and is called 'Inet'. (W www.inet.com.bh). If you have your own modem and access to a phone line, prepaid dial-up cards (Inet Pre-paid) are available from the Batelco office in Government Avenue and come in denominations of BD3 (200 minutes), BD8 (533 minutes) and BD12 (800 minutes).

Another service also suitable for travellers is Inet900. Dialling ☎ 900 400 will log you onto the Net for around 20 fils per minute.

There are several Internet centres in Manama – see the Manama section later in this chapter for more details.

DIGITAL RESOURCES

For a comprehensive list of Middle East/Arab world websites see Digital Resources in the Regional Facts for the Visitor chapter; otherwise some useful Bahrain-specific websites include:

Al-Reem Tours A 'green' site, which promotes Bahrain's wildlife as well as highlighting some of the environmental problems the island is facing and how these are being addressed
W www.alreem.com
Bahrain Tourism Official government site with information on hotels and tourism
W www.bahraintourism.com
Gulf Daily News One of Bahrain's English language dailies
W www.gulf-daily-news.com

BOOKS

In addition to this book, Lonely Planet also publishes a detailed country guide, *Bahrain, Kuwait & Qatar*.

Otherwise, the most interesting and up-to-date of available books are *Bahrain Island Heritage* by Shirley Kay and *Resident in Bahrain* by Parween Abdul Rahman and Charles Walsham, which is particularly useful for businesspeople.

Possibly the single best book on Bahrain is *Looking for Dilmun* by Geoffrey Bibby, which provides a fascinating picture of life in Bahrain in the 1950s and '60s.

Archaeology and history buffs might also be interested in *Bahrain Through the Ages: The Archaeology* and *Bahrain Through the Ages: The History* by Sheikh Haya Ali al-Khalifa and Michael Rice. Both are available in Bahrain, but are bulky and expensive at about BD22.

More general Middle East titles, some of which contain coverage of Bahrain, are listed in the Books section in the Regional Facts for the Visitor chapter.

NEWSPAPERS & MAGAZINES

The *Gulf Daily News* and the less interesting broadsheet, *Bahrain Tribune*, are both English-language dailies with good international news and sports coverage. They each cost 200 fils. The former contains a good classifieds section and a useful 'What's On' column. The monthly *Bahrain This Month* magazine (BD1) is also an excellent information source for entertainment, sports and local events. Also worth picking up is the annual *Visitor's Complete Guide to Bahrain* (BD2).

International newspapers and magazines are available in all major hotels and book-shops the day after publication.

RADIO & TV

Radio Bahrain broadcasts in English 24 hours a day on several FM and MW frequencies, the main one being 96.5 FM. FM and MW radio stations established for US forces based in the Gulf are also easy to pick up, as are Voice of America, the BBC World Service, and other European services on short wave.

Bahrain Television broadcasts Channel 55 in English (from late afternoon), and the BBC World Service is shown in English on Channel 57. Most satellite programmes, such as CNN and MTV, are available in top-end hotels. All radio and television programmes are listed in the two English-language dailies, and in *Bahrain this Month*.

PHOTOGRAPHY & VIDEO

Plenty of shops in Manama, and elsewhere around Bahrain, sell popular brands of print film and video cassettes, though slide film is a little more difficult to find. A roll of 24/36 colour print film costs about BD1.5/2. Colour print film can be developed in many

places, often in less than 30 minutes, for 500 fils for developing, plus 100 fils per print. Slide developing is more expensive and can take up to two days. Many photo shops around central Manama can also take passport photos for about BD2 (for four).

LAUNDRY

The best way to get your clothes cleaned is through your hotel, or at one of the numerous small laundries around central Manama. A small Indian or Pakistani-run laundry charges about 200 fils for a shirt, skirt or trousers.

HEALTH

Bahrain has a highly developed health-care system, and while treatment is not free, by Western standards it is moderately priced. If you're staying in a mid-range or top-end hotel, there should be a doctor on call to deal with minor ailments. A list of good hospitals is included in the Manama section later in this chapter. There are plenty of well-stocked pharmacies in all residential areas and the English-language dailies list those that are open 24 hours.

For more general health information see the Health section in the Regional Facts for the Visitor chapter.

WOMEN TRAVELLERS

Bahrain is fairly liberal compared to some of the other Gulf countries, so generally speaking women travellers should have no problems. However, Bahrain is still conservative by Western standards so it's important to remember that modest dress and behaviour will help to avoid any unwanted attention.

When choosing accommodation, stay clear of budget hotels and always check at mid-range hotels to see if there is a separate floor for women and/or families (see the Accommodation section for further information regarding this).

When eating out unaccompanied, avoid traditional coffee houses, which are usually the domain of men.

DANGERS & ANNOYANCES

Bahrain is an extremely safe place to visit. Travellers should note, however, that the country has one of the highest pedestrian fatality rates in the region and so should take care when crossing Manama's busy streets.

BUSINESS HOURS

Most shops and offices are generally open from around 7am to 2pm and 4pm to 8pm Saturday to Wednesday. Western-style shopping complexes are usually open from around 9am to 9pm Saturday to Thursday and from 10am to 9pm Friday.

PUBLIC HOLIDAYS

In addition to the main Islamic holidays described in Public Holidays & Special Events in the Regional Facts for the Visitor chapter, Bahrain observes the following public holidays:

New Year's Day 1 January

Ashura 10th day of Muharram (month in the Hejira calendar; date changeable) – Ashura marks the death of Hussein, grandson of the Prophet. Processions led by men flagellating themselves take place in many of the country's predominantly Shiite areas.

National Day 16 December

SPECIAL EVENTS
Bahrain Film Festival

This is held every March/April at the Bahrain Cinema Club in Juffair, and features Arab and foreign films. All films are subtitled in English. For film lists and screening times check the English dailies or call the **Bahrain Cinema Club** (☎ 725 959).

ACTIVITIES
Pearl Diving

Pearl diving in Bahrain has been a tradition, and was once a lucrative business, for centuries. While the industry may be long finished, the oysters have continued to grow, uncollected on the shallow sea beds. If you're interested in learning about pearls and even diving for them, **Aquatique** (☎ 271 780; **e** luludive@batelco.com.bh; **w** www.pearl dive.com; Sheikh Isa Ave) runs a very informative pearl-diving course. It covers everything from the history of the pearl to what sort of oysters are likely to contain pearls and ends with a dive trip to one of Bahrain's abandoned pearl beds.

ACCOMMODATION

Bahrain has a glut of four- and five-star hotels, which often have discounts – ask at the hotel reception desk or check the English dailies for current specials. However, true budget accommodation can be problematic. Bahrain has just one youth hostel, which is in the suburb of Juffair, southeast of central Manama (see the Manama section later for more details). Otherwise, cheap hotel rooms (which generally come with air-con, private bathroom and TV) typically costing BD8/12 for singles/doubles, often also operate as brothels for the (mainly) Saudi male visitors to the island and are therefore not suitable for women or families. The same is also true of many of the mid-range hotels, although some of these places do at least have a floor specially reserved for women and/or families.

FOOD

Bahraini cuisine is pretty much the same as the other Gulf States (see the Food section in the Regional Facts for the Visitor chapter). *Makboos* (rice and spices) with chicken, lamb or fish, can usually be found on the menus at Arabic-style restaurants around town. Other local dishes such as the spicy bean soups, *nekheh, bajelah* and *loobah*, as well as the very sweet desserts like *akil* (cardamom cake); *rangena* (coconut cake); *khabees* (dates, dates and more dates) and *balaleet* (sweet vermicelli with cardamom) can all be sampled at the Craft Centre Café in Manama.

Beyond local fare, Bahrain also has a plethora of restaurants serving a wide range of international cuisines. There are also plenty of fast-food outlets, which serve everything from burgers to shwarma, in shopping centres and the main streets of Manama. Anyone staying a while should, pick up the *Bahrain Restaurant Guide* (BD1). This excellent booklet highlights the best of the 2000 or so restaurants throughout the country and is updated every year.

DRINKS

Nonalcoholic drinks consist of soft drinks, delicious fruit juice, and milk shakes. Alcohol is widely available, but expensive – a can of beer costs upwards of 900 fils, and spirits start at BD1.200 a shot.

Modern cafés can be found throughout Manama, though any place called a 'coffee shop' in all but the top-end hotels is usually a bar, often dark, dingy and uninviting.

SPECTATOR SPORTS

Soccer (football) is the major sport played in Bahrain. Games are held at the immense

National Stadium, and at smaller grounds in the residential areas of Muharraq, Riffa and Isa Town. Also popular among locals are volleyball, badminton, basketball, cricket and handball.

The Equestrian & Horse Racing Club holds races every Friday between October and March at the **Sakhir Racecourse** (☎ 440 330) near Awali. The **Bahrain Motor Club** (☎ 612 338) organises popular motor racing and go-kart rallies, and in the Riffa Valley, the 18-hole **Riffa Golf Course** (☎ 750 777) has been carved out of the desert.

SHOPPING

Bahrain's specialities – pearls and gold – are good value, but shoppers should know something about quality and price. Locally produced items include pottery from A'ali, hand-woven cloth from Bani Jamrah and textiles from Al-Jasra. Bahrain also has many art galleries and craft centres selling quality, locally produced contemporary art. For more information, refer to the relevant sections in the Around Bahrain Island section later. Bahrain is also one of the best places in the Gulf to look for Persian carpets.

Getting There & Away

Refer to the Getting There & Away chapter at the beginning of this book for information about international travel to and from Bahrain and the region in general.

AIR

Bahrain is a part-owner of Gulf Air, which regularly flies between Bahrain and London, Frankfurt, Amsterdam, Rome and Paris. Gulf Air also flies frequently to major cities on the subcontinent, and three times a week to Melbourne and Sydney in Australia. Other regional airlines, such as Saudia, Kuwait Airways and Royal Jordanian, also fly to and from Bahrain, and have connections to Europe and North America. There are rarely any special deals or cheap periods for flights to Bahrain, but *from* Bahrain there are occasionally special deals to Europe, and more often to places in the Middle East like the UAE and Oman. Check the windows of the travel agents in the souq for the latest offers.

Departure Tax

The departure tax is BD3. You can pay this at the airport, or sometimes at the travel agency or airline office when you buy your ticket in Bahrain.

LAND

The only land border is with Saudi Arabia, across the incredible King Fahd Causeway (see the Around Bahrain Island section later in this chapter for details). Bahrain is, therefore, often used as a transit point for international travel to and from eastern Saudi.

Most tourists won't have a car, or be allowed to drive between Saudi and Bahrain in a rental car, nor have a Saudi visa long enough to enjoy a leisurely drive to/from Bahrain, so this border is normally only crossed by foreigners using the Saudi-Bahrain bus service.

Bus

Saudi Bahraini Transport Co (Sabtco; ☎ 263 244, fax 244 297) runs a bus service between Manama and Khobar and Dammam in Saudi Arabia. Buses leave six times a day between 8am and 8.30pm daily, and cost BD5 one way. From Dammam there are regular connections on to Riyadh (Saudi) and Doha (Qatar).

From Manama, Sabtco also has daily buses as far as Amman (Jordan) and Damascus (Syria) for BD17.5; Abu Dhabi, Dubai and Sharjah (UAE), all for about BD19; and Kuwait BD13. All departures are from the international bus station in Manama, where the Sabtco office is located.

Car & Motorcycle

To get on the causeway to Saudi Arabia, all drivers (and passengers in taxis) must pay a toll of BD2, regardless of whether they're travelling to Saudi or just as far as the border. The toll booth is on the western side of the intersection between the appropriately named Causeway Approach Rd and Janabiya Hwy.

Anyone crossing the border from Bahrain to Saudi will be given a customs form to complete, and drivers entering Bahrain from Saudi must purchase temporary Bahraini insurance and sign a personal guarantee.

SEA

The **Valfajre Shipping Company** operates a fortnightly ferry service between Manama and the Iranian port of Bushehr. A one-way /return fare, including two meals, costs BD31 /46. The ship departs Manama from the Mina Sulman port and the agent in Bahrain is **International Agencies Company** (☎ *727 114*).

UCO Travels (☎ *700 244*) has a direct weekly service to the Iraqi port of Um Qassar. A return seat will cost BD53 and an economy cabin BD89. The ship leaves Mina Sulman port at 9am every Sunday.

Getting Around

BUS
Bahrain has a good public bus system linking most of the major towns and residential areas. The fare is 50 fils per trip. Buses run about every 40 minutes between 6am and 9pm from the **Manama bus station** (*Government Ave*), and there are user-friendly bus terminals in Isa Town, Muharraq and Riffa. A few private buses and minibuses are starting to ply the main routes and cost about 100 fils per trip.

TAXI
Taxis in Bahrain have meters, but foreigners have to be very persistent before drivers will use them. The flag fall is 800 fils, which will take you 1.5km. Thereafter the meter ticks over in 100 fils increments every 1km. Fares officially increase by 50% between 10pm and about 6am. It's rare that taxis will even consider using the meter for long-term hire so expect to negotiate an hourly rate (a charge of BD6 to 7 per hour is reasonable). However, if you're visiting more than one tourist attraction a fair distance from town, it's probably cheaper to rent a car than charter a taxi.

CAR & MOTORCYCLE
If you're driving around Bahrain, buy a good road map (not usually provided in rental cars, but available in bookshops in Manama). Some roads further south of the Tree of Life are off limits.

Speed limits and the wearing of seat belts are rigorously enforced in Bahrain, and drink driving laws are also strict. Driving is on the right-hand side. Speed limits are 60km/h in towns; 80km/h in outer limits of suburbs; and 100km/h on highways. Petrol costs 80 fils per litre for lower grade *jayyid* and 100 fils for premium *mumtaz*. Petrol

stations are well-signposted and common, especially along the highways.

Rental
Oscar Rent-a-Car is the cheapest of the reliable rental agencies (BD9 per day for a small sedan). It has offices in Manama and at the airport, as do the major international car-rental agencies. The major companies charge from BD12/72 for one day/week for the smallest four-door sedan.

Avis	☎ 531 144
Budget	☎ 534 100
Europcar	☎ 692 999
Hertz	☎ 321 287
Oscar Rent-a-Car	☎ 291 591

Rates exclude petrol, but include unlimited mileage and insurance. To avoid the excess of BD200 to BD300 in the case of an accident, it's probably wise to pay the extra BD2 waiver per day. Rates are for a minimum of 24 hours. Companies normally only accept drivers over 21 years old (over 25 for more expensive models), and foreigners must have an International Driving Permit. There is nowhere to rent a motorcycle.

ORGANISED TOURS
One of the best tour agencies is the friendly **Al Badr Travels** (☎ *710 077*; e *sales@albader .com;* w *www.albader.com; shop 12, bldg 129 Osama Bin Zeid St, Adliya*). It offers the usual sightseeing trips around Manama and the island, as well as dhow and fishing trips. Also try the smaller **Ghadeer Tours** (☎ *412 571*, *fax 414 571;* e *muhanna@batelco.com.bh*), which offers similar package tours for a minimum of two people.

If you're interested in eco-tourism, **Al-Reem Tours** (☎ *710 868*; e *saeed@alreem .com;* w *www.alreem.com*) is a unique company specialising in environmental tours. It runs daily bird-watching and wildlife trips to the remote Hawar Islands and mainland desert, and also has a special six-day bird-watching package.

Manama   منامة

Manama is the very new capital of a very old place – many of the hotels and official buildings along Government Ave sit on reclaimed

BAHRAIN

MANAMA

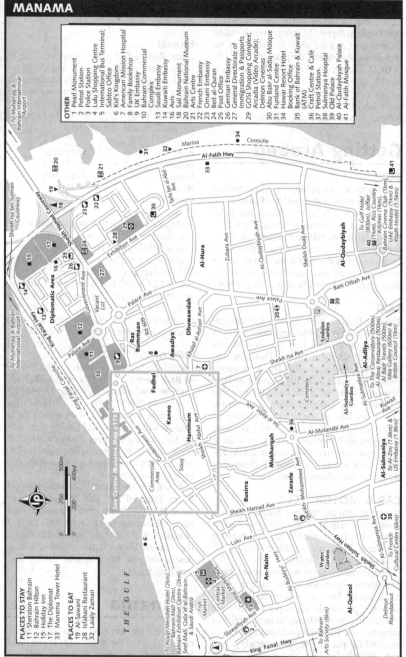

PLACES TO STAY
11 Sheraton Bahrain
12 Bahrain Hilton
15 Holiday Inn
17 The Diplomat
33 Manama Tower Hotel

PLACES TO EAT
19 Al-Sawani
28 Isfahani Restaurant
32 Laialy Zaman

OTHER
1 Pearl Monument
2 Petrol Station
3 Police Station
4 Lulu Shopping Centre
5 International Bus Terminal;
   Sabtco Office
6 Kid's Kingdom
7 American Mission Hospital
8 Family Bookshop
9 UK Embassy
10 Bahrain Commercial
   Complex
13 Saudi Embassy
14 Kuwaiti Embassy
16 Avis
18 Sail Monument
20 Bahrain National Museum
21 Arts Centre
22 French Embassy
23 Omani Embassy
24 Beit al-Quran
25 Post Office
26 German Embassy
27 General Directorate of
   Immigration & Passports
29 GOSI Shopping Complex;
   Arcadia (Video Arcade);
   Delmon Cinemas
30 Abu Bakr al-Sadiq Mosque
31 Funland Centre
34 Hawar Resort Hotel
   Booking Office
35 Bank of Bahrain & Kuwait
   (ATM)
36 Craft Centre & Café
37 Petrol Station
38 Sulmaniya Hospital
39 Old Palace
40 Al-Qudaybiyah Palace
41 Al-Fatih Mosque

land. But don't be fooled – only a few blocks inland from the shiny new hotels are sections of the city that have changed little in the last 52 years. Manama means 'Sleeping Place', and in many ways the moniker is still quite appropriate.

History
The ancient capital of Bahrain was known as the Bilad Al-Qadim (old town) and was located not far from the Al-Khamis Mosque and close to some of the island's best springs.

The capital moved to Manama in the 15th century.

Orientation
Manama's main road is Government Ave. Bab al-Bahrain, and the small roundabout in front of it, is a hub of activity, and the gateway to the souq is to the south.

Information
Tourist Offices The **Tourist Department** (☎ 231 375), in the Bab al-Bahrain Building, has a variety of brochures available on Bahrain's tourist sights, as well as a souvenir shop, which sells a dusty collection of cards, books and trinkets.

Money There are several banks along the side street that runs from the main post office to the car parks in front of the Regency Inter-Continental hotel. There are also a number of banks and moneychangers on Government Ave between the main post office and the Delmon International Hotel. There are ATMs at most banks, and **American Express** (AmEx; ☎ 228 822, fax 224 040; ABN bldg, Al-Furdah Ave) can help with currency exchange.

Post The **main post office** (open 7am-7.30pm Sat-Thur) has poste restante facilities. AmEx cardholders can also receive mail at the AmEx office.

Telephone There are telephone booths and payphones for local and international calls all over the city. International calls can also be made at the Batelco building in Manama.

Email & Internet Access There are Internet centres scattered around Manama. One of the most central is the **Internet Plus Services centre** (☎ 717 090; 1st floor Batelco bldg, Government Ave). At 500 fils per hour it has the cheapest rates in town. The **Idea Gallery** (☎ 714 828; W www.ideagal.com; Al-Adliya district) charges BD1 per hour.

Bookshops Al-Hilal bookshops, in the Bahrain Sheraton Complex, can be found in many top-end hotels and upmarket shopping centres, and in the souq. **Books Plus** (Seef Mall) has a wide range of books, including some Lonely Planet titles.

Cultural Centres Bahrain's main cultural centres are:

Alliance Française de Bahrain (☎ 683 295) Isa Town, off the 16th December Hwy
British Council (☎ 261 555) Ahmed Mansour al-Ali Bldg, Sheikh Isa bin Sulman Hwy
USIS (☎ 273 300) US embassy; has a library (open to all)

Medical Services Medical treatment is relatively easy to obtain in Bahrain. The **American Mission Hospital** (☎ 253 447; Isa al-Khebir Ave) is the oldest, and smallest, but is well-equipped. Other good hospitals include the **International Hospital of Bahrain** (☎ 591 666), just off Budayyi' Highway, and the **Sulmaniya Hospital** (☎ 255 555; Sulmaniya Ave).

Bahrain National Museum
This museum (☎ 292977; Al-Fatih Hwy; admission 500 fils; open 7am-2pm Sat, Sun & Tues, 8am-2pm & 4pm-8pm Wed & Thur, 3pm-8pm Fri) is by far the most popular tourist attraction in Bahrain. The collection is very well labelled and signposted in English. Free films are sometimes shown in the small auditorium, exhibitions of art and sculpture in the foyer, and there is a museum shop and a small cafeteria.

Museum of Pearl Diving
This museum (Government Ave; admission 300 fils; open 8am-noon Sat-Wed, 9am-6pm Thur) was originally built in 1937 to house the Ministry of Justice & Islamic Affairs. The rooms surrounding the courtyard contain displays on Bahrain's pearl diving and seafaring heritage, exhibits of antique weapons, traditional games, medicine, costumes and musical instruments as well as the various uses of the date palm. Upstairs

BAHRAIN

CENTRAL MANAMA

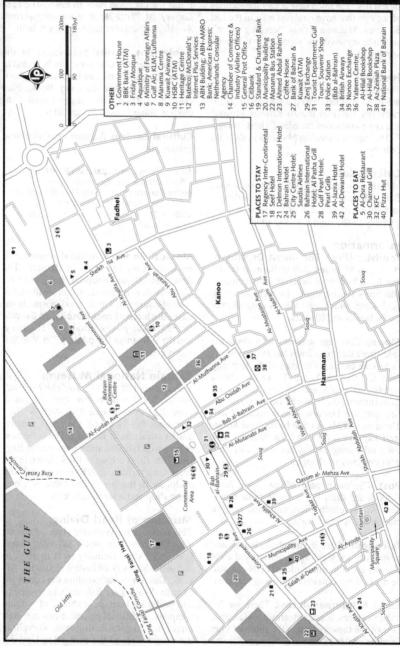

200m
180yd

100
90

0

OTHER
1 Government House
2 BBK Bank (ATM)
3 Friday Mosque
4 Aquatique
5 Ministry of Foreign Affairs
6 Gulf Air; KLM; Lufthansa
7 Kuwait Airways
8 Manama Centre
9 HSBC (ATM)
10 HSBC (ATM)
11 Heritage Centre
12 Batelco; McDonald's;
   Internet Plus Services
13 ABN Building; ABN-AMRO
   Bank; American Express;
   Netherlands Consular
   Agency
14 Chamber of Commerce &
   Industry (Airline Offices)
15 General Post Office
16 Citibank
17 Standard & Chartered Bank
20 Municipality Building
22 Manama Bus Station
23 Ahmed Abdul Rahim's
   Coffee House
27 Bank of Bahrain &
   Kuwait (ATM)
29 Zenj Exchange
31 Tourist Department; Gulf
   Tours; Souvenir Shop
33 Police Station
   (Bab al-Bahrain)
34 British Airways
35 Noron Exchange
36 Yateen Centre
37 Al-Hilal Bookshop
38 Az-Zeinah Plaza
41 National Bank of Bahrain

PLACES TO STAY
17 Regency Inter-Continental
18 Seef Hotel
19 Delmon International Hotel
21 Bahrain Hotel
25 CityCentre Hotel;
   Saudia Airlines
26 Bahrain International
   Hotel; Al Pasha Grill
28 Gulf Pearl Hotel;
   Pearl Grills
39 Al-Jazira Hotel
42 Al-Dewania Hotel

PLACES TO EAT
5 Al-Osra Restaurant
30 Charcoal Grill
32 KFC
40 Pizza Hut

Fadhel

Kanoo

Hammam

Souq

Souq

Souq

Souq

Bahrain
Commercial
Centre

Commercial
Area

Commercial
Area

THE GULF

King Faisal Corniche

King Faisal HWY

Old Jetty

Sheikh Isa Ave

Al-Khalifa Ave

Abu Huraiba Ave

Government Ave

Al-Furdah Ave

Al-Muthanna Ave

Al-Muatasim Ave

Al-Hadrami Ave

Abu Osaidh Ave

Bab al-Bahrain Ave

Al-Mutanabi Ave

Al-Mutanabi Ave

Bab al-Bahrain Ave

Al-Khalifa Ave

Tujjar Ave

Wali al-Ahed Ave

Sheikh Abdullah Ave

Qassim al- Mehza Ave

Municipality Ave

Al-Ayoob

Salah al-Deen

Al-Khalifa Ave

Municipality
Square

Fountain

houses a collection of photographs of state occasions and of numerous Arab and foreign dignitaries from Bahrain throughout the 20th century. Photography is prohibited.

Friday Mosque

The Friday mosque, built in 1938, is easily identifiable by its colourful, mosaic minaret, the mosque's most interesting architectural feature. The juxtaposition of the mosque with the tall, modern Bahrain Tower nearby provides a perfect reflection (literally) of old and new Manama.

Bab al-Bahrain

The 'Gateway to Bahrain' was built by the British in 1945 and restored in 1986 to give it more of an Islamic look. The small square in front of the *bab* was once the terminus of the customs pier (which provides some idea of the extent of land reclamation in the area). The building now houses the Tourist Department and a souvenir shop.

Beit al-Quran

The Beit al-Quran (*House of the Quran; ☎ 290101; admission by donation; open 9am-noon & 4pm-6pm Sat-Wed, 9am-noon Thur*), off Exhibition Ave, was opened in 1990 as a museum and research centre. The museum's centrepiece is a large and striking collection of Qurans, manuscripts and woodcarvings. Everything is well labelled in English, and the museum is a good introduction to Islam in general, and Islamic calligraphy in particular. Visitors should dress conservatively. The main entrance is on the southern side. The museum has an excellent but pricey craft and bookshop in the foyer.

Al-Fatih Mosque

Al-Fatih Mosque (*Al-Fatih Hwy; open to non-Muslims 9am-2pm Sat-Wed*) is the largest building in the country (about 6300 sq m), and capable of holding up to 7000 worshippers. Visitors should check in at the small library immediately to the right inside the main door. Women will be given, and are expected to wear, an *abeyya* (a black cloak) and head scarf while inside the prayer hall. Wearing shorts is prohibited.

Places to Stay – Budget

Hostels Bahrain's **Youth Hostel** (*☎ 727 170; No 1105 Rd 4225, Juffair; dorm beds YHA members/nonmembers BD1/2)* is spartan and a little run down, but great value if you're looking for a cheap bed. Toilets and showers are in a separate building, and kitchen facilities are available. The hostel is in the suburb of Juffair, southeast of Manama, but signposted in English from Al-Fatih Hwy, and easy enough to reach by taxi or bus No 3 from the city centre.

Hotels All of the following hotels have air-con, TV (but not satellite) and an attached bathroom with hot water.

Al-Dewania Hotel (*☎ 263 300, fax 259 709; singles/doubles BD10/15)* is down a tiny lane off Sheikh Abdulla Ave. It's quiet, central and has friendly staff. The rooms are tiny, but clean and well furnished.

Seef Hotel (*☎ 224 557, fax 593 363; singles/doubles BD8/12)*, just north of Government Ave, is quiet, but the rooms are small and poorly furnished. Rates are negotiable, but get one with a view and sea breezes.

Bahrain Hotel (*☎ 227 478, fax 213 509; Al-Khalifa Ave; singles/doubles BD9/13)* is an old-style building at the western end of the city centre. It's quiet, and the pleasant rooms – although many lack windows – are reasonably priced.

Places to Stay – Mid-Range

Al-Jazira Hotel (*☎ 211 810, fax 210 726; Al-Khalifa Ave; singles/doubles BD18/24)* is good value, and better than most in the area. It has bright, well-furnished and reasonably priced rooms, and the staff are friendly.

Gulf Pearl Hotel (*☎ 213 877, fax 213 943; Government Ave; singles/doubles BD30/40)* has been recently renovated and is charging accordingly. The rooms are clean and well furnished, and the bathrooms huge. The 6th floor is supposedly reserved for women and families, but this is also the floor where the main bars and discos are housed, and the hotel also has several of its own 'in house entertainers' visibly available.

Manama Tower Hotel (*☎ 295 111, fax 294 200; e mantow@batelco.com.bh; Al-Fatih Hwy; singles/doubles BD30/35)* is a fair way out of town but is still good value. Many of the large, clean rooms have sea views and all come with tea- and coffee-making facilities.

Delmon International Hotel (*☎ 224 000, fax 224 107; e delmonbn@batelco.com.bh; Government Ave; singles/doubles from BD22*

/28) is a friendly hotel in a quiet, leafy part of town. The 2nd floor is reserved exclusively for women and families and the rooms are cosy and well furnished. It's by far one of the more reputable hotels in this range and is excellent value. The **restaurant** downstairs also does a tasty buffet for breakfast (BD3), lunch and dinner (BD3.900).

Bahrain International Hotel *(☎ 211 313, fax 211 947; e bihhotel@batelco.com.bh; Government Ave; singles/doubles BD25/30)* is central and boasts large, well-appointed rooms and a health club. Certain floors are reserved for women and families.

City Centre Hotel *(☎ 229 979, fax 224 421; e cchotel@batelco.com.bh; Government Ave; singles/doubles BD19/25)* is a comfortable 'family' hotel in the centre of town, so is often full. Great coffee is served downstairs at **Costa Coffee**, and the **shwarma bar** next door has fresh juices and tasty shwarma.

Places to Stay – Top End
All Bahrain's top-end hotels (except the Royal Meridien) operate under a strict price cartel and charge the same rates of singles/doubles BD48/53 with weekend rates at BD40/45.

The Diplomat *(☎ 531 666, fax 530 843; w www.diplomatrdsas.com.bh; Sheikh Hamad Causeway)*, across from the museum, is one of the better located hotels, and many rooms have great views.

Regency Inter-Continental *(☎ 227 777, fax 229 929; e bahrain@interconti.com; King Faisal Hwy)* is convenient and popular.

Sheraton Bahrain *(☎ 533 533, fax 534 069; Palace Ave)* is a favourite among business people.

Bahrain Hilton *(☎ 523 523, fax 532 071; Palace Ave)* was the first five-star hotel in Bahrain and is now looking a bit faded.

Holiday Inn *(☎ 532 122, fax 530 154; e holin@batelco.com.bh; King Faisal Hwy)* is in the diplomatic area and close to the airport.

Le Royal Meridien *(☎ 588 000, fax 580 333; e meribah@batelco.com.bh; w www .meridien.com.bh; Al-Seef; singles/doubles from BD108/120)* is Bahrain's most luxurious (and expensive) hotel. It boasts its own private beach and secluded island.

Places to Eat
Fast-Food Outlets Western fast-food joints, such as **Pizza Hut**, **McDonald's** and **KFC** can be found throughout Manama. Cheaper, and healthier, are the **fruit juice stands** and **sandwich shops** around the souq where a small but tasty sandwich or burger costs about 500 fils, and delicious fruit juices and milk shakes cost from 200 fils.

Restaurants From freshly made shwarma juices to fine gourmet dining, homemade traditional Bahraini cuisine to fast-food burgers, Bahrain has it all.

Charcoal Grill *(Bab al-Bahrain; mains BD1.200-1.600)* has tasty kebabs with salad for BD1.200 plus, and curries for about BD1.600, but it's a little pricey because of the excellent location.

Al-Osra Restaurant *(☎ 240 098; Government Ave; open 7am-1am)* is one of the best. It has over 100 dishes, including spicy curries (from 800 fils), excellent sandwiches and burgers (about 400 fils), and cooked breakfasts (from 600 fils).

Laialy Zaman *(☎ 293 097; Marina Corniche; snacks under BD1, mains BD1.500)* is one of the few places to take advantage of the local sea views and sea breezes. Yet prices are surprisingly reasonable. It's near the Funland Centre, but not signposted in English.

Al-Sawani *(☎ 290 797; mains BD6-10; open noon-3.30pm & 7.30pm-midnight)*, next to the National Museum, is an upmarket restaurant specialising in Arabic cuisine. Its location overlooking the sea and its traditional and elaborately styled building make it well worth a visit.

Craft Centre Café *(☎ 253 554; open 8am-1pm; Mukharqah; breakfast buffet BD2)* is an excellent place to try traditional (and homemade) Bahraini food. Situated in the quiet leafy courtyard of the Craft Centre, the café is decorated with owner Muneera al-Jalahma's unusual artwork and serves a deliciously filling 'Bahraini breakfast' buffet prepared by Bahraini women in their homes.

Al-Abraj Restaurant *(☎ 714 222; Adliya; mezze from 500 fils; mains BD1-3)* is a popular restaurant that serves everything from felafel sandwiches and Iranian stews to sizzling steaks.

Isfahani Restaurant *(☎ 290 027; Exhibition Ave; mains BD1-4)* is a tasty and cheap place to try good Iranian food.

The Conservatory *(☎ 712 917; Adliya; snacks from BD1)* is Bahrain's oldest tearoom and a good place to go for morning or afternoon tea.

Self-Catering Dozens of grocery stores ('cold stores') are dotted around the residential areas, and are usually open from about 7am to 10pm. The French franchise Geant has a monstrous store in Bahrain Mall. For fruit, spices, vegetables and meat, try the **Central Market**; for fish, go to the **Fish Market**.

Entertainment

To find out what's going on around Bahrain, check out the What's On column of the *Gulf Daily News*, the *Bahrain this Month* magazine or the *What's On in Bahrain* booklet which are available in all bookshops.

Bars, Cafés & Coffee Houses Most bars and nightclubs are attached to hotels, and many are really dingy. All top-end hotels have decent bars, and many feature 'happy hours', but prices are still high.

Conventional hotel bars include the generic **Clipper Room** *(Regency Inter-Continental)*, bizarrely thematic **Sherlock Holmes** *(Gulf Hotel)*, and the Polynesian themed **Trader Vic's** *(Le Royal Meridien)*. Currently trendy nightspots include **Savage Garden** *(Mishal Hotel, Exhibition Ave)* and **Likwid** *(City Centre Hotel)*.

Serious nightclubbers should pick up the detailed *Bahrain Restaurant Guide*, which lists recommended bars and nightclubs. Live shows are listed in the 'Showtime' section of *Bahrain This Month*, and in the English-language dailies.

One of the surprisingly few decent coffee houses in Bahrain is **Ahmed Abdul Rahim's Coffee House** *(Government Ave)*. The sign is in Arabic, but you'll find it hard to miss, with all those old men sitting on benches puffing away on their sheesha. **Laialy Zaman** (see Places to Eat earlier) is also an excellent place for views, breezes, tea or coffee and *sheesha*.

Cinema, Concerts & Theatre Delmon Cinemas *(GOSI Shopping Complex)* and Seef Cineplex *(Seef Mall)* regularly show recent Western films. Programmes are advertised in the local English-language dailies and tickets cost BD2. Special films are also shown at the **Bahrain National Museum** (Sunday evenings), **Alliance Française de**

Bahrain (usually on Wednesday evenings), and the **Bahrain Cinema Club**, off Sheikh Khalifa bin Salman Highway, Juffair (Wednesday evenings).

The **Bahrain International Exhibition Centre** often has recitals of Bahraini music. The **Beit al-Quran** features occasional Quran recitals, and **Qala'at Arad** often features traditional music on Thursday and Friday afternoons.

Shopping

Most shops in the souq are open from about 9am to 1pm and 4pm to 9pm Saturday to Thursday, and open in the evenings on Friday. Some locals prefer to shop at the modern, Western-style shopping centres, which are wonderfully air-conditioned and open all day. In Manama, the **Yateem Centre** *(Al-Muthanna Ave)* and **GOSI Shopping Complex** *(Exhibition Ave)* are new. In the suburbs, the **Seef Mall**, off Sheikh Khalifa bin Salman Highway, is the biggest and best.

Despite Bahrain's small population, the country's arts community is thriving. The **Bahrain Arts Society** *(☎ 590551; W www.ba hartsociety.org.bh; Budaiya Ave)* is just one of the many centres set up to promote local art and artists. The relaxed and friendly **Craft Centre** *(☎ 254 688; Isa al-Kebir Ave; open 8.30am-1.30pm Sat-Wed, 9am-noon Thur)*, managed entirely by Bahraini women, is home to a variety of studios and workshops, and promotes the contemporary revival of traditional crafts such as weaving, palm leaf papermaking, pottery and ironwork. All the work is for sale.

Getting There & Away

Air Bahrain International Airport is one of the busiest in the Gulf. General flight information is available by phoning ☎ 325 555.

Most airline offices are situated around the Bab al-Bahrain, in the Chamber of Commerce & Industry building, or inside the Manama Centre, which is where you'll find **Gulf Air** *(Manama Centre ☎ 335 777 • airport ☎ 338 844)*.

Getting Around

To/From the Airport The airport is on Muharraq Island, about 6km from central Manama. Bus No 1 runs from just outside the airport to the Manama bus station on Government Ave about every 40 minutes between 6am and 8.45pm. A metered taxi from central Manama to the airport should cost about BD2. For trips *from* the airport there is a BD1 surcharge, and drivers are very reluctant to use the meter.

There's an ATM for American Express cards in the transit lounge of the airport.

Taxi These are easy to find, and there are taxi stands outside the Bab al-Bahrain and many upmarket hotels. Refer to the Getting Around section earlier in this chapter for details about hiring taxis.

Around Bahrain Island

QALA'AT AL-BAHRAIN قلعة البحرين

Also known as Bahrain Fort, the site *(admission free; open daylight hours daily)* has been undergoing extensive renovation (and will be for many years to come). Despite the renovations, and the on-going archaeological dig near the main fort, the site remains open.

The site appears to have been occupied from about 2800 BC. The oldest excavated part of the site is the portion of a defensive wall from the City II period (circa 2000 BC), which indicates that this spot on the north coast of Bahrain Island was important.

The excavated remains of Cities III and IV, referred to as the Kassite and Assyrian buildings, date from 1500 to 500 BC, and include the ruins of a house with a 3m-high entrance.

The site is about 5km west of Manama and easy to reach by car. Drive along King Faisal Hwy, and its extension, Sheikh Khalifa bin Sulman Hwy, and follow the signs. Then drive along a dirt track over a low hill to the site. It is not accessible by public bus.

BARBAR TEMPLE معبد بربر

Barbar *(suggested donation BD1; open daylight hours daily)* is a complex of three 2nd and 3rd millennium BC temples, probably dedicated to Enki, the God of Wisdom and the Sweet Waters Under the Earth.

The excavated complex can be seen from a series of walkways, which provide a great overview, but it's hard to understand without a detailed map (eg in *Bahrain: A Heritage Explored* by Angela Clark) or a knowl-

edgable tour guide. There is officially no admission fee but a guide pressures visitors to sign a guest book and make a donation.

Take the Al-Budayyi' Hwy west from Manama and turn right at the sign for Barbar. If you follow this road the temple is on the right. The closest bus stop is near Ad-Diraz Temple (see the following section), about 30 minutes walk away.

AD-DIRAZ TEMPLE معبد الديراز

The Ad-Diraz Temple *(admission free; open daylight hours daily)* dates from the 2nd millennium BC, and is several centuries younger than the Barbar Temple, from which it differs significantly. The site is small, and only worth visiting if you're keen on exploring even more ruins. The turn-off for the temple is clearly signposted along Al-Budayyi' Hwy from Manama (but not if you're driving in the other direction). Bus No 5 from Manama stops near the temple.

AL-BUDAYYI' البديع

This small village marks the western edge of Bahrain Island. The beach has stunning views at sunset, and of the incredible King Fahd Causeway. The mammoth building overlooking the sea is **Sheikh Hamad's Fort House**, a private residence sadly not open to the public. Al-Budayyi' is at the end of Al-Budayyi' Hwy and is accessible by bus No 5 from Manama.

SOUQ AL-KHAMIS MOSQUE

مسجد سوق الخميس

The original mosque is believed to have been built in the early 8th century but an inscription dates the construction of most of the remains as the second half of the 11th century. Nevertheless, it is the first mosque built in Bahrain, and one of the oldest in the region.

The complex *(bus Nos 2 & 7 from Manama; admission free; open 7am-2pm Sat-Wed, 8am-noon Thur & Fri)* is about 2.5km southwest of Manama. Take the Sheikh Sulman Hwy to Al-Khamis village, the mosque is on the right side of the road.

A'ALI عالي

There are over 100,000 burial mounds in Bahrain. The most impressive are the ones often referred to as the **Royal Tombs**, near the village of A'ali. These are the largest burial mounds in Bahrain, reaching up to 15m in height and 45m in diameter. The area is not signposted and has no designated entrance and there are no explanations, but it's a great place to wander around.

A'ali village is the site of Bahrain's best-known **pottery workshop**. Pottery and ceramics are on sale at several stalls around the sleepy village, and in the souvenir shop in the Bab al-Bahrain in Manama. The village also boasts a 'traditional' **Arabic bakery**, and the **Muharraqi Gallery**, which features modern Bahraini art.

From Manama, take the Sheikh Sulman Hwy south past Isa Town, then turn west along A'ali Hwy and follow the signs to the village, pottery workshop or mounds. Buses are problematic: take Bus No 2 or 7 from Manama to Isa Town, and then bus No 9 or 15 to A'ali village.

SAR سار
Sar was the site of another settlement from the Dilmun period. Hundreds of **burial mounds** are being successfully excavated, and archaeologists are excited about their finds. When excavations are finished, there are plans to turn the site into a major tourist attraction, including a museum. Like the mounds at A'ali, the area has no designated entrance or explanations.

Although the site seems close, there is no access from the Causeway Approach Rd. Instead, go to Sar village following the signposted road heading south from Al-Budayyi' Hwy, or from Janabiya Hwy, and then follow the signs to the burial mounds. Bus No 12 goes to Sar village, from where it's about 1.5km to the burial mounds.

KING FAHD CAUSEWAY
معبر الملك فهد
The causeway connecting Saudi Arabia and Bahrain is an impressive piece of engineering. Near the bridge and border, on an island, are two tall, slender towers, one on the Bahrain side of the border, the other on the Saudi side. **King Fahd Causeway Restaurant** (open 9am-11pm daily), in the tower on the Bahraini side, offers very mediocre food, but the views from the tower are superb. All drivers (and passengers in taxis) must pay a BD2 toll per vehicle at a booth along the Causeway Approach Rd, whether going to

Saudi or not. No local public bus travels along the causeway.

AL-JASRA الجسرة
Al-Jasra House (admission 200 fils; open 8am-2pm Sun-Tues, 8am-6pm Wed & Thur, 3pm-6pm Fri) is one of several historic homes around Bahrain that have been restored to their original condition. This one is famous as the birthplace of the former emir, Sheikh Isa bin Sulman al-Khalifa.

In the residential area, which is a few hundred metres before Al-Jasra House, is the government-run **Al-Jasra Handicraft Centre** (☎ 611900; open around 8am-2pm daily). This modern, well-laid-out collection of workshops specialises in textiles, basket weaving and mirrors. It's adjacent to a stop for Bus No 12.

From the Causeway Approach Rd, look for the exit to Al-Jasra (before the toll booth), and then go past two roundabouts and the Handicraft Centre, to reach Al-Jasra House (the house is not particularly well signposted).

RIFFA FORT قلعة ريفا
The Riffa Fort (☎ 779 394; admission 200 fils; open 8am-2pm Sun-Tues, 9am-6pm Wed & Thur, 3pm-6pm Fri) majestically overlooks the Riffa Valley. Originally built in the 17th century it was completely restored in 1983. The limited captions and explanations are in Arabic, and the rooms are mostly empty, but it's interesting enough and the views over the valley are appealing.

The fort is easy to spot from several main roads, but is surprisingly hard to reach and poorly signposted. Access to the fort is only possible along Sheikh Hamood bin Sebah Ave, which is off Riffa Ave. Bus Nos 7 and 11 go past the turn-off along Riffa Ave.

AL-AREEN WILDLIFE PARK
حديقة حيوانات العرين
This interesting little (10 sq km) preserve (☎ 836 116; admission BD1; open 8am-11am daily Sept-July, also 3pm-5pm Feb-July, 2pm-4pm Sept-Jan, closed during Ramadan) is a conservation area for species indigenous to the Middle East and North Africa. After a short introductory film (in Arabic only), a small bus leaves roughly every hour for a jaunt (with commentary in Arabic and English) past some of the 240 species of birds

and mammals. Oryxes and gazelles feature heavily.

The park has peculiar opening times – it's best to call the park office, or take a look at the 'What's On' column in the *Gulf Daily News* before heading out.

From Manama, follow the signs to Riffa and then Awali along Sheikh Sulman Hwy, and then continue towards Al-Zallaq. The turn-off to the park is along the Zallaq Beach Hwy.

TREE OF LIFE شجرة الحياة
The Tree of Life is a lone tree, famous because it somehow survives in the barren desert – it's presumably fed by an underground spring. Although touted as a major tourist attraction, there isn't a great deal to

see or do here, and it's quite a distance from Manama.

The best time to visit is around dusk – but leave before it's too dark, and don't park any vehicle in a sandy area. The site is not easy to find: follow the Sheikh Sulman Hwy to Riffa, then head towards Awali (or vice-versa), and follow the signs along the Muaskar Hwy. It's best to go with a knowledgeable local, or on an organised tour.

Muharraq محرق

Just over the bridge from Bahrain Island is Muharraq Island. The attractions on the island are easy to reach on foot from the Muharraq bus station – bus Nos 2 and 7

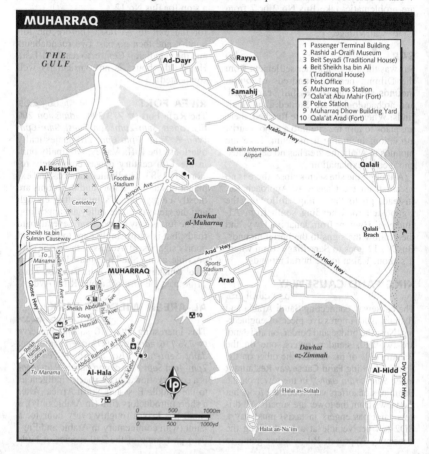

MUHARRAQ

1 Passenger Terminal Building
2 Rashid al-Oraifi Museum
3 Beit Seyadi (Traditional House)
4 Beit Sheikh Isa bin Ali
   (Traditional House)
5 Post Office
6 Muharraq Bus Station
7 Qala'at Abu Mahir (Fort)
8 Police Station
9 Muharraq Dhow Building Yard
10 Qala'at Arad (Fort)

THE GULF

Ad-Dayr   Rayya

Samahij

Aradous Hwy

Bahrain International Airport

Al-Busaytin

Avenue 20

Football Stadium

Airport Ave

Cemetery

Sheikh Isa bin Sulman Causeway

Dawhat al-Muharraq

Qalali

Qalali Beach

To Manama

Sheikh Sulman Ave

Ghose Hwy

MUHARRAQ

Arad Hwy

Sports Stadium

Al-Hidd Hwy

3   Sheikh

4   Sheikh Isa Ave

Sheikh Abdullah Ave

Abdul Rahman al-Fadel Ave

Sheikh Souq

5   Sheikh Hamad

6

Sheikh Hamad Causeway

To Manama

Al-Hala

Khalifa al-Kebir Ave

8

9

7

Arad

10

Dawhat az-Zimmah

Halat as-Sultah

Al-Hidd

Dry Dock Hwy

Halat an-Na'im

0   500   1000m
0   500   1000yd

travel between the bus stations in Muharraq and Manama at least every hour. Alternatively, charter a taxi to one place, and walk to one or more of the other attractions.

BEIT SHEIKH ISA BIN ALI & BEIT SEYADI

بيت الشيخ عسى بن علي و بيت سيادي

These two traditional houses offer a fascinating look at pre-oil life in Bahrain. **Beit Sheikh Isa bin Ali** (admission free; open 9am-2pm Sat-Wed, 9.30am-5pm Thur), which was being renovated at the time of research, was built around 1800. While the rooms are bare, the different sections of the house are well captioned in English.

Beit Seyadi (admission free; open 2pm-6pm Sat-Thur) is a smaller house of similar age but the restoration work is not quite as advanced. It's still worth a look, however. An old mosque is attached to the house.

From Manama take the Sheikh Hamad Causeway and look for the signs at the roundabout on the corner of Sheikh Sulman and Sheikh Abdulla avenues. To avoid getting lost, ask for directions if you're walking between the two houses.

QALA'AT ABU MAHIR

قلعة ابو ماهر

Qala'at Abu Mahir dates back to the 16th century, though it has been rebuilt several times since. It consists of a single watchtower with a narrow building attached to its landward side, but the building is not particularly impressive. The fort is in the grounds of the Muharraq coastguard station, so access is usually limited, but if you present yourself at the gate on a weekday (Saturday to Wednesday) morning and ask nicely they may let you in. From Manama, take the Sheikh Hamad Causeway, and turn right along Khalifa al-Khebir Ave.

QALA'AT ARAD

قلعة عراد

Qala'at Arad (☎ 672 278; Arad Fort; admission free; open 8am-2pm Sun-Tues, 9am-6pm Wed & Thur, 3pm-6pm Fri) was built in the early 15th century by the Portuguese. Although parts have been beautifully restored, there is little to see inside except an old well. Still, the location overlooking the bay is superb. During late afternoon on Thursday and

Friday the fort hosts a craft market with children's rides and traditional bands. Check *Bahrain this Month* for details.

From Manama, take the Sheikh Hamad Causeway, and follow the signs along Khalifa al-Khebir Ave and Arad Hwy.

RASHID AL-ORAIFI MUSEUM

متحفراشد العريفي

This private art gallery (☎ 335 616; admission BD1; open 8am-noon & 4pm-8pm Sat-Thur, 8am-noon Fri) is dedicated to the work of its artist/owner, most of which is based on Dilmun-related themes. From Manama, take the Sheikh Isa bin Sulman Causeway, and follow the signs along Airport Ave.

Other Islands

HAWAR ISLANDS

جزيرة حوار

The 16 islands known collectively as the Hawar Islands are very close to Qatar. The islands are home to a large number of flamingos and cormorants, about 2000 Bahraini troops and the **Hawar Resort Hotel** (☎ 849 111, fax 849 100, city office ☎ 290 377, fax 292 659; e hawar@batelco.com.bh; singles/doubles BD19/32). In winter, the resort runs comparatively cheap overnight packages, including transport, accommodation and meals. The resort also arranges day trips (BD10 per person, including lunch). Accommodation and day trips can be booked at its city office located along the Marina Corniche in Manama.

For more information on the Hawar Islands, see the boxed text 'The Hawar Island Dispute' earlier in this chapter.

DAR ISLAND

جزر الدار

Just off the coast south of Sitra, Dar Island is more accessible than the Hawar Islands. The main attraction is the sandy beach, but water sports are available, and there is an expensive **restaurant** and **bar**.

Transport to Dar Island can be haphazard. Go to the boat terminal in Sitra and ask for a sea taxi or ring the special number listed at the telephone box clearly indicated in the terminal. Sea taxis operate every day and leave when required anytime between 9am and sunset. The trip will cost BD2.5 return.

Egypt

مصر

Birthplace of one of the greatest civilisations the world has known, modern Egypt still retains the glory of the pharaohs in the extraordinary monuments they left behind and which dot the entire country. The centuries following the long era of Pharaonic rule brought Greeks, Romans, Arabs, Turks and Europeans – to mention only the main players – to the seat of power, and they all left their mark.

Modern Cairo, the over-bloated capital and the African continent's largest city is a chaotic collision of the Arab world, Africa and the remnants of 19th-century colonialism. Through it all flows the Nile, without which Egypt could not exist. On either side of the Nile lie harsh deserts, occasionally softened by pockets of life in the oases. Southeast of the famous Suez Canal stretches Sinai, a region of awesome beauty and a place of refuge and conflict for thousands of years. An unparalleled paradise off the Red Sea coast combines with the natural and architectural marvels on land to make this a fascinating destination.

Facts about Egypt

HISTORY

About 5000 years ago an Egyptian pharaoh named Menes unified Upper and Lower Egypt for the first time. For centuries beforehand, communities had been developing along the Nile. The small kingdoms eventually developed into two important states, one covering the valley as far as the Delta, the other consisting of the Delta itself. The unification of these two states, by Menes in about 3100 BC, set the scene for the greatest era of ancient Egyptian civilisation.

Little is known of the immediate successors of Menes except that, attributed with divine ancestry, they promoted the development of a highly stratified society, patronised the arts and built many temples and public works. In the 27th century BC, Egypt's pyramids began to appear. The Pharaoh Zoser and his chief architect, Imhotep, built what may have been the first, the Step Pyramid at Saqqara. Zoser ruled from the nearby capital of Memphis.

Arab Republic of Egypt

Population: 66 million approx
Area: 997,738 sq km
Capital: Cairo
Head of State: President Hosni Mubarak
Official Language: Arabic
Currency: Egyptian pound (E£)

- Best Dining – feasting on grilled fish at an open-air restaurant in Alexandria
- Best Nightlife – counting the stars while soaking in a Western Desert hot spring
- Best Walk – getting lost in the medieval backstreets of Islamic Cairo
- Best View – watching the sunrise from the top of Mount Sinai
- Best Activity – diving among the underwater wonders off Sinai's coast

---

For the next three dynasties and 500 years (a period called the Old Kingdom) the power of Egypt's pharaohs and the size and scale of their pyramids and temples greatly increased. The size of such buildings symbolised the pharaoh's importance and power over his people. The last three pharaohs of the 4th dynasty, Khufu (Cheops), Khafre (Chephren) and Menkaure (Mycerinus), built the three Great Pyramids of Giza.

By the beginning of the 5th dynasty (about 2494–2345 BC) it is clear that the pharaohs had ceded some of their power to a rising class of nobles. In the following centuries Egypt broke down into several squabbling principalities. The rise of Thebes (Luxor)

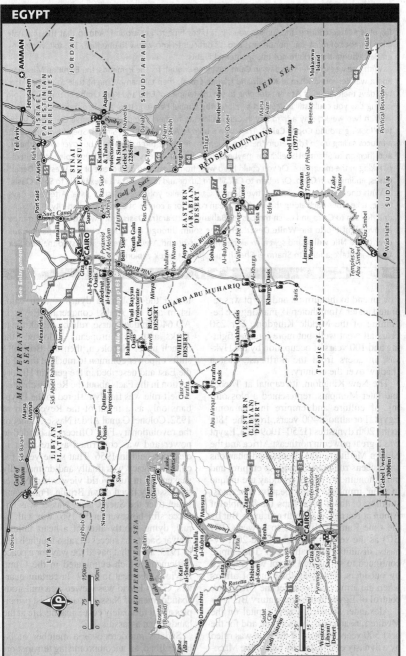

EGYPT

EGYPT

See Enlargement

See Nile Valley Map p163

What to See

Egypt is a large country and, unless you fly, it takes time to get around. Add to that the unparalleled number of must-see monuments and it's difficult to know how to prioritise. The following itineraries assume that you're not taking internal flights.

With one week, spend two days in **Cairo** (just time enough for the **Pyramids**, the **Egyptian Museum**, and a wander round **Khan al-Khalili** and **Islamic Cairo**), then take an overnight train to **Luxor**. After two days there, head to **Aswan**, stopping to see the temples of **Edfu** and **Kom Ombo** en route. The following day you could still squeeze in a visit to **Abu Simbel** before getting a train or bus back to Cairo.

With two weeks, stay a third day in Cairo (allowing further exploration of Islamic Cairo and some time looking around **Coptic Cairo**). Then take a train to Aswan and Abu Simbel. Spend two nights on a **felucca** sailing up to Edfu. From there go to Luxor for two or three days, then bus over to **Hurghada**, and then on to **Sharm el-Sheikh** (or maybe **Dahab**) by bus or ferry for a few days exploring the reefs or hiking in the mountains. Or you could head west from Luxor and do a circuit of the **Western Desert oases**, ending up in Cairo. Or return to Cairo from Luxor and head west via **Alexandria** to **Siwa Oasis**.

With one month, after four or five days in Cairo, make your way west to Siwa. After two days there, take a bus back along the Mediterranean coast for a couple of days in the port city of Alexandria. Return to Cairo and catch the bus for **Bahariyya** or **Farafra Oasis**, from where you can arrange an overnight trip to the **White Desert**. Heading south through the oases you can then take a bus over to the **Nile valley** and split a week between Luxor and Aswan. Then head east to the **Red Sea Coast** and take a ferry to Sharm el-Sheikh and spend a week exploring **Sinai**.

---

saw an end to the turmoil and Egypt was reunited under Montuhotep II, marking the beginning of the Middle Kingdom. For 250 years all went well, but more internal fighting and 100 years of occupation by the Hyksos, invaders from the northeast, cast a shadow over the country.

The New Kingdom, its capital at Thebes and later Memphis, represented a blossoming of culture and empire in Pharaonic Egypt. For almost 400 years, from the 18th to the 20th dynasties (1550–1069 BC), Egypt was a great power in northeast Africa and the eastern Mediterranean. Renowned pharaohs and queens ruled an expanding empire, and built monuments that even today are unique in their immensity and beauty. The most startling of them is perhaps the Temple of Amun at Karnak, just north of Luxor. But by the time Ramses III came to power (1184 BC) as the second pharaoh of the 20th dynasty, disunity had again set in. The empire continued to shrink and Egypt was attacked by outsiders. This was the state of affairs when the army of Alexander the Great took control of Egypt in the 4th century BC.

Alexander founded a new capital on the Mediterranean coast, Alexandria, and for the next 300 years the land of the Nile was ruled by a dynasty established by one of the Macedonian's generals, Ptolemy. Romans followed the Ptolemaic dynasty, then came Islam and the Arabs, conquering Egypt in AD 640. In due course, rule by the Ottoman Turks and the Europeans followed (the French under Napoleon, then the British) – shifts of power common to much of the Middle East and described in the general History section in the Facts about the Region chapter.

Self rule was finally restored to the Egyptians only as a result of the Revolution of 1952. Colonel Gamal Abdel Nasser, leader of the revolutionary Free Officers, ascended to power and was confirmed as president in elections held in 1956. That same year, the colonial legacy was finally and dramatically shaken off in full world view when Nasser successfully faced down Britain, France and Israel over the Suez Canal. Nasser was unsuccessful, however, in the 1967 war with Israel, dying shortly after of a heart failure. Anwar Sadat, his successor, also fought Israel in 1973, a war that paved the way for a peace settlement, which culminated in the Camp David Agreement in 1979. In certain quarters, Camp David was viewed as a traitorous abandonment of Nasser's pan-Arabist principles and it ultimately cost Sadat his life at the hands of an assassin.

Sadat's murderer was a member of Islamic Jihad, an uncompromising terrorist organisation that aimed to establish an Islamic state in Egypt. Mass round-ups of Islamists were immediately carried out on the orders of Sadat's successor Hosni Mubarak, a former air force general and vice president.

Mubarak was able to rehabilitate Egypt in the eyes of the Arab world, without abandoning the treaty with Israel. And for almost a decade he managed to keep the lid on the Islamist extremists.

But in the early 1990s the lid blew off. During the 1980s discontent had been brewing among the poorer sections of society. Government promises had failed to keep up with the population explosion, and a generation of youths were finding themselves without jobs and living in squalid, overcrowded housing with little or no hope for the future. With a repressive political system that allowed little chance to legitimately voice opposition, the only hope lay with the Islamic parties and extreme action.

There were frequent attempts on the life of the president and his ministers and frequent clashes with the security forces. The government responded with a heavy-handed crackdown, arresting thousands. By the mid-1990s, the violence had receded from the capital, retreating to the religious heartland of middle Egypt. However, with tragic irony, weeks after the government declared its victory over the extremists in 1997, terrorists carried out their bloodiest attack ever with the massacre of 58 holidaymakers at the Temple of Hatshepsut in Luxor.

Egypt Today

The 1997 attacks destroyed grassroots support for militant groups and the main terrorist organisation, the Gama'a al-Islamiyya, declared a cease-fire the following year. Since then, there has been no reported violence. But while domestic security is no longer the problem it was in the 1990s, Egypt is in the midst of a serious economic crisis. The once stable Egyptian pound lost a quarter of its value in 2000 and 2001, even though foreign currency earnings from tourism were their highest ever. Fallout from the September 11th terrorist attacks in the US hit this vital source of income in late 2001 and exacerbated the already precarious state of the economy.

Although Egypt is stable politically, President Mubarak is in his seventies and has no obvious successor, raising fears of a

power struggle upon his death. Add to this the ever-yawning gap between the sunny world of tourism posters and the reality of life in crowded slums for the majority of Egyptians, and the threat of upheaval continues to hang over the country.

GEOGRAPHY

For most Egyptians the fertile Nile Valley is Egypt. The world's longest river, the Nile emerges from two separate sources, Lake Victoria, in Uganda, and Lake Tana, in Ethiopia, which merge near Khartoum, Sudan. In all, it cuts through an incredible 6680km swathe of Africa before splitting again as it forms a Delta in Northern Egypt and then flows into the Mediterranean. Taming the Nile through sophisticated irrigation techniques was the great achievement of the ancient Egyptians; the river has remained the lifeblood of the country ever since.

To the east of the farmland in the valley is the Eastern (Arabian) Desert – a barren plateau bounded on its eastern edge by a high ridge of mountains. To the west is the Western (Libyan) Desert – a plateau punctuated by bizarre geological formations, huge dune fields and luxuriant oases.

The terrain in Sinai, the peninsula that links Africa and Asia, slopes from the high mountain ridges, which include Gebel Musa (Mt Sinai) and Gebel Katherine (Mt St Katherine; the highest in Egypt at 2642m), in the south to desert coastal plains and lagoons in the north.

CLIMATE

Egypt's climate is easy to summarise. Most of the year, except for the winter months of December, January and February, it is hot and dry. Temperatures increase as you travel south from Alexandria. Alexandria receives the most rain – approximately 190mm a year

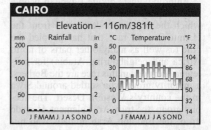

CAIRO

Elevation – 116m/381ft

– while in Aswan, in the far south, any rain at all is rare.

Summer temperatures range from 31°C (87°F) on the Mediterranean coast to a scorching 50°C (122°F) in Aswan. At night in winter the temperatures sometimes plummet to as low as 8°C, even in the south of the country. In the mountains of Sinai, night-time temperatures in winter can even fall well below zero.

GOVERNMENT & POLITICS

The bulk of power is concentrated in the hands of the president (present incumbent, Mohammed Hosni Mubarak), who is nominated by the People's Assembly and elected by popular referendum for a period of six years. This term can be renewed at least once, although, at the time of writing, Mubarak was well into his fourth consecutive term. There is no question of him failing to secure further time in office. Mubarak himself admits democracy in Egypt is 'limited' and there are no serious opposition parties to the ruling National Democratic Party (NDP).

In the last elections, held in 2001, most seats were contested by 'independents' from within the NDP. Upon winning their seats, the vast majority pledged their allegiance to the party again.

The president appoints vice presidents and ministers, as well as 10 members of the 454-member People's Assembly and 70 of the 210-member Majlis ash-Shura (Advisory Council).

POPULATION & PEOPLE

Egypt is the most populous country in the Arab world and has the second highest population in Africa (the African country with the highest population is Nigeria). The population was counted at 61.5 million during the last census in 1996. It is thought to have reached 66 million by the year 2001.

Anthropologists divide Egyptian people very roughly into three racial groups, of which the biggest is descended from the Hamito-Semitic race that has peopled the Nile (as well as many other parts of north Africa and neighbouring Arabia) for millennia. Included in this race are the Berbers, a minority group who settled around Siwa in the country's Western Desert. The second group, the truly Arab element, is made up of the Bedouin Arab nomads who mi-

Boys, Girls & the Veil

The most visible sign of the return to 'traditional values' that swept not just Egypt but much of the region in the 1990s was the huge number of women adopting more conservative dress and wearing the *hegab*, or headscarf. It remains one of the most striking symbols of the difference between Islamic and non-Islamic culture. But, as with the whole issue of women in the Middle East, it's all far more complex than first meets the eye.

For every woman who adopts the *hegab* for religious reasons, there are others who wear it because it allows them to walk around more freely – not many men would dare hassle a *muhaggaba* (the term for a girl/woman who keeps her hair covered with a scarf). By wearing the *hegab* perhaps some women feel they don't have to worry about fashion, because it *is* the fashion – check out the different styles of wearing a headscarf.

grated from Arabia and who also live in desert areas, particularly Sinai. The third group is the Nubians, who inhabit the Aswan area.

RELIGION

About 90% of Egypt's population are Muslims; most of the rest are Coptic Christians. Generally speaking the two communities enjoy a more or less easy coexistence. Though Western newspapers from time to time run stories claiming that Copts are a persecuted minority, virtually all prominent Christians in Egypt insist they are neither persecuted nor a minority.

LANGUAGE

Arabic is the official language of Egypt. The dialect here varies markedly from that spoken elsewhere in the Arab world (see the Language chapter at the back of this book), but because of Cairo's traditional status as the cultural capital of the Arab world and its correspondingly voluminous output of film, TV and song, most Arabic speakers understand Egyptian Arabic.

English is widely spoken in towns, cities and tourist centres, while Egypt's hawkers and touts are renowned for their knowledge of languages.

Facts for the Visitor

WHEN TO GO

The best time to go to Egypt depends on where you want to go. June to August is unbearable in Upper Egypt with daytime temperatures soaring to 40°C or more. Summer in Cairo is almost as hot, and the combination of heat, dust, pollution, noise and crush makes walking the city streets a real test of endurance. But then a scorching sun might be exactly what's wanted for a week or two of slow roasting on the beaches of southern Sinai.

For visiting Upper Egypt, winter is easily the most comfortable time – though hotel rates are at a premium. In Cairo from December to February skies are often overcast and evenings can be colder than you'd think, while up on the Mediterranean coast, Alexandria is subject to frequent downpours resulting in flooded and muddy streets.

The happiest compromise for an all-Egypt trip is to visit in spring (March to May) or autumn (October and November).

VISAS & DOCUMENTS
Visas

All foreigners entering Egypt, except nationals of Malta, South Africa, Zimbabwe and Arab countries, must obtain a visa. You can get this in advance from the Egyptian embassy or consulate in your home country.

Processing times for visa applications vary. In the USA and the UK, processing takes about 24 to 48 hours if you drop your application off in person, or anything from 10 days to six weeks if you send it by mail. Costs vary according to your nationality and the country in which you apply. As an example, in the UK a single-entry tourist visa for most Western applicants costs UK£15 (about US$22).

Alternatively, while travelling in the Middle East you can obtain your visa at an Egyptian embassy in any capital city; see the relevant country chapter for the address.

The most convenient option, however, is to get your visa on arrival at the airport or port. At Cairo airport the entire process takes only a few minutes and costs US$15/UK£12. If you are travelling overland you can get a visa at the port in Aqaba, Jordan before getting the ferry to Nuweiba, but if you are coming from Israel, you *cannot* get a visa at the border. Instead, you have to get the visa beforehand at either the embassy in Tel Aviv or the consulate in Eilat (see the Israel & the Palestinian Territories chapter for addresses).

A single-entry visa is valid for three months and entitles the holder to stay in Egypt for one month. Multiple-entry visas (for three visits) are also available, but although good for presentation for six months, they still only entitle the bearer to a total of one month in the country.

For details of visas for other Middle Eastern countries, see the 'Visas at a Glance' table under Visas & Documents in the Regional Facts for the Visitor chapter.

Sinai Entry Stamps It is not necessary to get a full visa if your visit is confined to the area of Sinai between Sharm el-Sheikh and Taba (on the Israeli border), including St Katherine's Monastery. Instead you are issued with an entry stamp, free of charge, allowing you a 14-day stay. Points of entry where such visa-free stamps are issued are Taba, Nuweiba (port) and Sharm el-Sheikh (airport or port).

Visa Extensions & Re-Entry Visas Extensions of your visa can easily be obtained for anything up to 12 months and cost E£8.20. If you do not have a multiple-entry visa, it is also possible to get a re-entry visa, valid to the expiry date of your visa and any extensions, at most passport offices. A single/multiple re-entry visa costs E£10/14.

Travel Permits

Military permits issued by either the Ministry of Interior or Border Police are needed to travel in the Eastern Desert south of Shams Allam (50km south of Marsa Allam), on or around Lake Nasser, off-road in the Western Desert and on the road between the oases of Bahariyya and Siwa. These can be obtained through a safari company or travel agency at least a fortnight in advance of the trip. See the introductory Getting There & Away chapter for travel agencies specialising in adventure travel or the Activities section later in this chapter for some local safari companies.

Permits to travel between Siwa and Bahariyya are given at the military intelligence offices in each town. Your best bet is to head to each town's tourist office for help.

Other Documents

It is well worth having a student card as it entitles you to a 50% discount on admission to almost all of the antiquities and museums, as well as reductions on train travel. Travellers have reported using a wide range of other cards to get student discounts for museum entry and transport, from HI cards to Eurail cards.

An International Driving Permit is required if you want to drive a car in Egypt.

EMBASSIES & CONSULATES
Egyptian Embassies & Consulates

Following are the Egyptian embassies and consulates in some major cities around the world. For addresses of Egyptian embassies in neighbouring Middle Eastern countries, see the relevant chapter.

Australia (☎ 02-6273 4437/8) 1 Darwin Ave, Yarralumla, Canberra 2600
  Consulate in Melbourne: (☎ 03-9654 8869/8634) 9th floor, 124 Exhibition St, 3000
  Consulate in Sydney: (☎ 02-9362 3388) 335 New South Head Rd, Double Bay, 2028
Canada (☎ 613-234 4931/35/58) 454 Laurier Ave East, Ottawa, Ontario K1N 6R3
  Consulate in Quebec: (☎ 514-866 8455) 1 Place Sainte Marie, 2617 Montreal, H3B 4S3
France (☎ 01 47 23 06 43, 01 53 67 88 30) 56 Ave de Lena, 75116 Paris
  Consulate in Paris: (☎ 01 45 00 49 52, 01 45 00 77 10) 58 Ave Foch, 75116
  Consulate in Marseilles: (☎ 91 25 04 04) 166 Ave d'Hambourg, 13008
Germany (☎ 228-956 8311/23) Kronprinzen-strasse 2, Bad Godesberg, 53173 Bonn
  Embassy in Berlin: (☎ 30-477 1048) Wald-strasse 15, 13156
  Consulate in Frankfurt-am-Main: (☎ 69-590557/8) Eysseneckstrasse 34, 60322
Ireland (☎ 1-660 6566) 12 Clyde Rd, Dublin 4
Netherlands (☎ 70-354 2000) Badhuisweg 92, 2587 CL, The Hague
Sudan (☎ 11-778741, fax 778741) Sharia al-Gama'a, Al-Mogran, Khartoum
  Consulate in Khartoum: (☎ 11-772191) Sharia al-Gomhurriya
UK (☎ 020-7499 2401) 26 South St, Mayfair, London W1
  Consulate in London: (☎ 020-7235 9777/19) 2 Lowndes St, SW1
USA (☎ 202-895 5400) 3521 International Court NW, Washington DC 20008
  Consulate in New York City: (☎ 212-759 7120/1/2) 1110 2nd Ave, NY 10022

  Consulate in San Francisco: (☎ 415-346 9700/2) 3001 Pacific Ave, CA 94115
  Consulate in Houston: (☎ 713-961 4915/6) Suite 2180, 1990 Post Oak Blvd, TX 77056
  Consulate in Chicago: (☎ 312-828 9162/64/67) Suite 1900, 500 N Michigan Ave, IL 60611

Embassies & Consulates in Egypt

Most foreign embassies and consulates are open from around 8am to 3pm Sunday to Thursday.

Australia (☎ 02-575 0444, fax 578 1638) World Trade Centre, 11th floor, 1191 Corniche el-Nil, Cairo
Bahrain (☎ 02-735 9996, fax 736 6609) 15 Sharia Brazil, Zamalek, Cairo
Canada (☎ 02-794 3110, fax 796 3548) 5 Al-Saraya al-Kubra, Garden City, Cairo
France (☎ 02-570 3916, fax 571 0276) 29 Sharia al-Giza, Giza
  Consulate in Cairo: (☎ 02-393 4645) 5 Sharia Fadl (off Talaat Harb)
  Consulate in Alexandria: (☎ 02-482 7950) 2 Midan Orabi, Mansheyya
Germany (☎ 02-736 0015, fax 736 0530) 8 Hassan Sabry, Zamalek, Cairo
  Consulate in Alexandria: (☎ 02-545 7025) 5 Sharia Mena, Rushdy
Iran (☎ 02-748 6400, fax 748 6495) 12 Sharia Rifa'a, off Midan al-Misaha, Dokki, Cairo
Iraq (☎ 02-337 6188, fax 760-9766) 1 Sharia Abdel Moneim Riad, Mohandiseen, Cairo
Israel (☎ 02-361 0528, fax 361 0414) 18th floor, 6 Ibn al-Malek, Giza
  Consulate in Alexandria: (☎ 03-586 0492) 207 Sharia Abdel Salem Aref
Jordan (☎ 02-748 5566, fax 760 1027) 6 Al-Shaheed Basem al-Khatib, Doqqi, Cairo
Kuwait (☎ 02-760 2261, fax 760 2657) 12 Sharia Nabil al-Waqqad, Dokki, Cairo
Lebanon (☎ 02-738 2823) 22 Mansour Mo-hammed St, Zamalek, Cairo
Libya (☎ 02-735 1864, fax 735 0072) 7 Sharia Salah ad-Din, Zamalek, Cairo
Netherlands (☎ 02-735 1936, fax 736 5249) 18 Hassan Sabry, Zamalek, Cairo
  Consulate in Alexandria: (☎ 03-482 9044) 3rd floor, 18 Tariq al-Horeyya
New Zealand (☎ 02-575 5326) 4th floor, 2 Talaat Harb, Cairo
Oman (☎ 02-303 5942, fax 303 6464) 52 el-Hegaz St, Mohandiseen, Cairo
Qatar (☎ 02-760-4693, fax 760-3618) 25 Sharia al-Kurum, Dokki, Cairo
Saudi Arabia (☎ 02-349 0757, fax 349 3495) 2 Ahmed Nessim, Giza
  Consulate in Alexandria: (☎ 03-482 9911) 9 Sharia Batalsa

Consulate in Suez: (☎ 062-222 461) Port Tawfiq (around the corner from the tourist office)

Sudan (☎ 02-794 5043, fax 354 2693) 4 Sharia al-Ibrahimy, Garden City, Cairo

Consulate in Cairo: (☎ 02-794 9661) 1 Mohammed Fahmy as-Said, Garden City

Syria (☎ 02-337 7020, fax 335 8232) 18 Abdel Rahim Sabry, Doqqi, Cairo

Turkey (☎ 02-796 3318) 25 Sharia al-Falaky, Downtown, Cairo

UAE (☎ 02-568 2262, fax 570 0844) 4 Sharia Ibn Sina, Giza

UK (☎ 02-794 0850, fax 794 0959) 7 Ahmed Ragheb, Garden City, Cairo

Consulate in Alexandria: (☎ 03-546 7001) 3 Sharia Mena, Rushdy

USA (☎ 02-795 7371, fax 797 3200) 5 Sharia Latin America, Garden City, Cairo

Yemen (☎ 02-761 4224/6) 28 Sharia Amin al-Rafi'i, Doqqi, Cairo

CUSTOMS

The duty-free limit on arrival is 1L of alcohol, 1L of perfume, 200 cigarettes and 25 cigars. On top of that, you can buy another 3L of alcohol (4L in Alexandria) plus a wide range of other duty-free articles within the next 24 hours at branches of the Egypt Free Shops company, which can be found scattered around the country.

MONEY
Currency

The official currency is the Egyptian pound (E£) – in Arabic, a *guinay*. One pound consists of 100 piastres (pt). There are notes in denominations of 10pt, 25pt and 50pt and one, five, 10, 20, 50, 100 and E£200 (the last is new and rarely seen). Coins in circulation are for denominations of 10, 20 and 25pt.

Prices can be written with or without a decimal point. For example, E£3.35 can also be written as 335pt.

Exchange Rates

Egypt's previously solid exchange rate of about E£3.5 to the US dollar suddenly became unstable in 2001, reaching E£4.6 to the dollar by the end of that year – bad news for the Egyptian economy but good news for visitors.

As a result of ongoing economic problems, the exchange rate could have changed again by the time you read this, but these were the rates for a range of currencies when this book went to print:

country	unit		Egyptian pounds
Australia	A$1	=	E£2.53
Canada	C$1	=	E£2.09
euro zone	€1	=	E£4.48
Israel	1NIS	=	E£0.95
Japan	¥100	=	E£3.71
Jordan	JD1	=	E£6.47
New Zealand	NZ$1	=	E£2.15
UK	UK£1	=	E£7.10
USA	US$1	=	E£4.58

Exchanging Money

Money can be officially changed at commercial banks, foreign exchange (forex) bureaus and some hotels. Rates don't tend to vary much but forex bureaus generally offer marginally better rates than the banks and they usually don't charge a commission fee.

Look at the money you're given when exchanging and don't accept any badly defaced, shabby or torn notes as you'll have great difficulty off-loading them.

There is no problem cashing well known brands of travellers cheques at major banks, like Banque Masr or National Bank of Egypt, and at AmEx (American Express) and Thomas Cook offices, but many forex bureaus don't take them. Most banks charge a small commission of 50pt per cheque plus E£2 or E£3 for stamps. Ask beforehand as it can vary, and remember that you must have your passport with you to cash travellers cheques.

Keep in mind that while you can, theoretically, exchange Egyptian money back into other currencies, there is a currency crisis so dollars and other hard currencies can be hard to find. Towards the end of your stay, limit the amount of money you change so that you are not left with extra Egyptian pounds.

ATMs These have spread rapidly throughout the country; as well as in Cairo you'll find them in Alexandria, Luxor, Aswan, Hurghada and Sharm el-Sheikh. However, outside these tourist towns they are rare or nonexistent. ATMs are run by a number of different banks and not all are compatible with credit cards issued outside Egypt. In general, those belonging to Banque Masr, CIB, Egyptian American Bank (EAB) and HSBC will accept Visa and MasterCard and any Cirrus- or Plus-compatible cards.

Credit Cards These have become widely acceptable in Egypt over recent years, but keep in mind that they won't work in budget hotels and restaurants, nor in remote areas like Siwa and the Western Oases. Keep your receipts to check against your statement when you get home; there have been cases of shopkeepers adding extra zeroes to the bill. Visa and MasterCard can be used for cash advances at Banque Masr and the National Bank of Egypt, as well as at Thomas Cook offices. To report lost cards in Egypt, call: AmEx (☎ 02-570 3411); MasterCard and Visa (☎ 02-796-2933/4872); or Diners Club (☎ 02-333 2638).

International Transfers Western Union, the international money transfer specialist, operates jointly in Egypt with Masr America International Bank and IBA business centres. You can receive money from any branch but can only send money from the Downtown, Garden City and Heliopolis branches in Cairo. The opening hours are the same as those of banks. For more information call the Western Union hotline: ☎ 02-795-5023.

It is also possible to have money wired to you through AmEx. The service operates through most of its branches and can be used even if you don't have an AmEx card. The charge is about US$80 per US$1000, payable in the country from which the money is sent.

Costs
By international standards Egypt is still fairly cheap and, thanks to the crumbling currency, it's getting cheaper for travellers. It is possible to get by on US$15 a day or maybe less if you are willing to stick to the cheapest hotels (you can get a bed for as little as E£7 – US$2), eat street-food snacks like *fuul* or *ta'amiyya*, and limit the number of admission-charging sites you visit. A complete visit to the Pyramids will cost E£90 (US$19) in admission charges, and if you want to see the mummies at the Egyptian Museum, the combined fee is E£60 (US$13).

Tipping & Bargaining
Bargaining is a part of everyday life in Egypt and people haggle for everything from hotel rooms to clothes. There are rare instances where it's not worth wasting your breath (supermarkets, for example), but in any tourist-type shop, even marked prices can be fair game.

Tipping, called baksheesh, is another fact of life in Egypt. Salaries are extremely low and are supplemented by tips. In hotels and restaurants the 12% service charge goes into the till; an additional tip is expected for the waiter. A guard who shows you something off the track at an archaeological site should be given a pound or two. Baksheesh is not necessary when asking for directions.

Remember to carry plenty of small change with you at all times. It's good to keep it separate from larger bills; flashing a wad of large denominations will mean demands for greater baksheesh.

POST & COMMUNICATIONS
Post
Post offices are generally open from 8.30am to 3pm Saturday to Thursday. Postcards and letters up to 15g cost 80pt to most countries and take four or five days to get to Europe and a week to 10 days to the USA and Australia. Stamps are available at post offices, and some souvenir kiosks, shops, newsstands and the reception desks of major hotels. If you use post boxes, blue is international airmail, red is internal mail and green is internal express mail.

Letters usually take a week to arrive from Europe, and a week to 10 days from the USA or Australia. Poste restante in Egypt functions remarkably well and is generally free (though in Alexandria there's a small fee to collect letters).

Larger post offices also offer Express Mail Service (EMS) for letters of up to 500g. An express letter to the UK costs E£57.50 and arrival is guaranteed in two days. Packages weighing between 500g and 1kg cost E£75.70 to the UK.

In addition to EMS, Federal Express, DHL, TNT Skypack and various other courier services work in Egypt.

Telephone
The country code for Egypt is ☎ 20, followed by the local area code (minus the zero), then the subscriber number. Local area codes are given at the start of each city or town section. The international access code (to call abroad from Egypt) is ☎ 00.

Two companies sell cardphones in Egypt. Menatel has yellow-and-green booths, while

Nile Tel's are red and blue. Cards are sold at shops and kiosks and come in units of E£5, E£10 and E£20 (the E£5 card will only work for local and national calls). Rates to Europe average E£4.20 for the first minute, E£3.90 thereafter.

Alternatively, there are the old telephone offices, known as *centrales*, where you can book a call at the desk, which must be paid for in advance (there is a three-minute minimum). The operator directs you to a booth when a connection is made. There are different rates for day (8am to 8pm) and night (8pm to 8am) calls, but using a *centrale* is no cheaper than using a cardphone and a great deal more hassle.

Collect (reverse charge) calls can be made from Egypt, but only to countries that have set up Home Country Direct phones. At the time of writing the service was only offered by a few places, all in Cairo. They include the Marriott and Semiramis Inter-Continental hotels.

International Phonecards The following cards can be accessed through these Cairo numbers: AT&T ☎ 02-510 0200; MCI ☎ 02-755 5770; and Global One & Sprint ☎ 02-796 4777.

Mobiles Egypt's mobile-phone network runs on the GSM system, like Europe. If your phone works on GSM and your account allows you to roam, you can use it in Egypt.

There are two mobile phone companies in Egypt: **Mobinil** *(☎ 02-302 8004/7, 575 7100)* and **Click Vodaphone** *(☎ 02-336 4591)*. Getting a permanent line is tricky without a work permit; however, temporary lines can be rented from both companies. A line through Mobinil's rental service, called Allo Hallo, costs about E£50. Good for a maximum of 20 days, it includes E£10 phone credit.

Click does not at present have a cheap short-term rental, although this may change.

Fax
Fax machines are available for sending and receiving documents at the main *centrales* in the big cities, at most three to five-star hotels, and also at some of the smaller hotels. From a telephone office, a one-page fax to the UK or USA costs about E£14, and E£20 to Australia. Hotel rates are quite a bit

more, usually more than E£35 per page. Faxes can be received at telephone *centrales* for E£6 per page, or at an EMS office for E£5.50 per page.

Email & Internet Access
Egypt has taken to the Internet in a big way and there are cybercafés throughout the country – for addresses see the relevant city sections.

If you have brought your own laptop you may have problems plugging your modem into the phone socket in hotel rooms because there's a whole variety of nonstandard sockets in use and, in some cases, the phone cable is wired straight into the wall. Even when you can plug your machine in, the hotel's phone system may not let you connect.

If you do manage to overcome the hardware difficulties, there are plenty of dial-up options. Egypt has a plethora of ISPs and most now have country-wide access numbers beginning with the 07 code that can be dialled up without an account. The service is paid for through the cost of the call. If you want your own account, with an email address and unlimited online time, expect to spend somewhere in the region of E£30 to E£45 per month, and as little as E£100 for a year. Some reliable ISPs include **Internet Egypt** *(☎ 02-796 2882, freenet ☎ 0707 7777; w brainy1.ie-eg.com)*, **Soficom Communications** *(☎ 02-738 1954, free dialup ☎ 0777 3777; w www.soficom.com.eg)* and **Link Egypt** *(☎ 02-336 7711, freenet ☎ 0777 0777; w www.link.net)*.

DIGITAL RESOURCES
For a comprehensive list of Middle East/Arab world websites see the Regional Facts for the Visitor chapter; otherwise some useful Egypt-specific websites include:

Al-Ahram Weekly Electronic version of the weekly English-language newspaper. Almost all of the paper is on line and the archives are searchable and free.
 w www.ahram.org.eg/weekly
Alexandria 2000 The name may be out of date but this extensive site keeps up with developments in Egypt's second city.
 w www.alexandria2000.com
Egypt: The Complete Guide The official site of Egypt's Ministry of Tourism is surprisingly good, although some of the statistics are out of date.
 w www.touregypt.net

KV5 Professor Kent Week's fascinating website focuses on the monuments of Thebes (Luxor's West Bank), particularly the Valley of the Kings. It's filled with 3-D tomb plans, history and updates on archaeological developments in the area.
ⓦ www.kv5.com

The Plateau The official website of Dr Zahi Hawass, Undersecretary of State for the Giza Plateau – ie the man who looks after the Pyramids. It's the best place to go for news of recent discoveries at Pharaonic sites in and around Cairo.
ⓦ www.guardians.net/hawass/index.htm

Red Sea Guide & Search Engine All you need to know about travel on Egypt's Red Sea.
ⓦ www.red-sea.co

Yallabina Lively site devoted to what's on in and around Cairo. Updated regularly.
ⓦ www.yallabina.com

BOOKS

More general Middle East titles, some of which contain coverage of Egypt, are listed in the Books section in the Regional Facts for the Visitor chapter.

Lonely Planet

Lonely Planet also publishes a detailed country guide, *Egypt*, and a separate 256-page city guide, *Cairo*, complete with colour maps. Other products that might be of use include LP's *Egyptian Arabic Phrasebook*, the diving guide, *Diving & Snorkeling Red Sea* and our pocket-sized, colour *Cairo City Map*.

Guidebooks

There are numerous locally produced guidebooks covering almost every square inch of Egypt. Look out for the following. *Islamic Monuments in Cairo*, by Caroline Williams, is a look at the most significant Islamic monuments in the city. Further a field, *Mount Sinai*, by Joseph Hobbs, takes a fascinating look at the history, ecology and politics of the sacred mountain. *A Guide to the Nubian Monuments on Lake Nasser*, by Jocelyn Gohary, is a comprehensive guide to the tombs and temples on the shores of Lake Nasser. *Siwa Oasis*, by Ahmed Fakhry, is an exhaustive look at the history and archaeology of Egypt's most beautiful oasis. *The Western Desert of Egypt*, by Cassandra Vivien, is an excellent guide to the geography, history and culture of the Western Desert.

Travel

Recommended travel literature includes *In An Antique Land*, by Amitav Ghosh, which is a wonderfully observed account of the author's stay in a Delta village. Mixing ancient and modern is *The Pharaoh's Shadow* by Anthony Sattin, which recounts his travels in search of Pharaonic traditions surviving in Egypt of today. From past years *Flaubert in Egypt* reprints extracts from diaries the French author kept when he visited the country for a few months in 1849. *A Thousand Miles Up the Nile*, by Amelia Edwards, gives a good idea of travel in Egypt before air-con buses and air travel.

History & Politics

Of the forests and forests of volumes on ancient Egypt, *The Complete Pyramids*, by Mark Lehner, and its companion volume, *The Complete Valley of the Kings*, by Nicholas Reeves & Richard H Wilkinson, are two superb compendiums of Pharaonic information. *The Mummy in Ancient Egypt*, by Selima Ikram and Adrian Dodson, is a fascinating look at mummies and mummification by two world authorities on the subject. *Alexandria Rediscovered*, by Jean-Yves Empreur, is an excellent and beautifully illustrated exploration of Graeco-Roman Alexandria. *The Lost Tomb*, by Kent Weeks, is a vivid description of the author's discovery of KV5, the largest Egyptian tomb ever found. *Cairo: The City Victorious*, by Max Rodenbeck, is an entertaining and prodigiously researched anecdotal meander through 5000 years of history. *No God but God: Egypt and the Triumph of Islam*, by Geneive Abdo, is one of the best books on the Islamist movement in recent years.

General

Egypt: Moulids, Saints and Sufis, by Nicholas Biegman, is the best non-academic account of this deeply Egyptian subculture. *The Hidden Face of Eve*, by Egypt's most famous feminist, Nawal el-Saadawi, remains a seminal, if polemical, examination of the issues facing Arab women. *Veiled Sentiments: Honour and Poetry in a Bedouin Society*, by Lila Abu Lughod, is a fascinating study of the Awlad Ali tribe in the Western Desert and how its members speak their minds through poetry.

There are hundreds of novels set in Egypt. Some of the best would include the *City of the Horizon* trilogy, by Anton Gill, which are entertaining mysteries set in the turmoil of post-Akhenaten Egypt. *The English Patient*, by Michael Ondaatje, has an impressionistic view of Egypt (and history), but it's brilliant nonetheless. *The Map of Love*, by Ahdaf Soueif, is the Booker-prize-short-listed historical novel that jumps between love stories set against the backdrop of contemporary and colonial Egypt. *Ramses: The Son of Light*, by Christian Jacq, is the first of a trashy, but immensely popular, five-volume series on the life of the famous pharaoh.

NEWSPAPERS & MAGAZINES
Egyptian Gazette is Egypt's awful daily English-language newspaper. *Al-Ahram Weekly* and *Middle East Times* both appear every Thursday and do a much better job of keeping English-readers informed of what's going on. The *Cairo Times* also comes out on Thursday and contains mainly hard news and analysis, but there are good cultural features and a lively 'around town' section. *Egypt Today* is an ad-saturated general-interest glossy with excellent listings.

An extremely broad range of Western newspapers and magazines are sold at hotel bookshops and street-side newsstands. Papers are just a day old and monthly magazines usually make it within a week of their home publication dates, but you can expect to pay up to twice the cover price.

RADIO & TV
FM95 broadcasts news in English on 557 kHz at 7.30am, 2.30pm and 8pm daily. This is the European-language station and, in addition to English-language programmes, it has programmes in French, German, Italian, and Greek. BBC and Voice of America (VOA) broadcasts can be picked up on medium wave at various times of the morning and evening, although reception is poor in Cairo. The BBC can be heard on 1320 kHz, and VOA on 1290 kHz.

Egyptian TV is a state-controlled mixture of soap operas, news, educational programmes and subtitled trash from around the world, none of which is inspiring, even if you speak Arabic. No surprise then that many hotels provide guests with satellite TV. The only state-run non-Arabic station is Nile TV, broadcasting news and current affairs exclusively in English and French from 7am each day until past midnight.

There's also a nightly English-language news bulletin on Channel Two at 8pm.

PHOTOGRAPHY & VIDEO
Film generally costs as much as, if not more than, it does in the West; for example, Kodacolor 100/200 (36 exposures) costs about E£22, while for Kodachrome 100 slide film, you'll pay E£24 (36 exposures). Make sure you check the expiry date and don't buy from shops that store film in direct sunlight. Colour print processing costs from E£2 to E£5 depending on whether it's a one hour or overnight service, plus from 50pt to 135pt per print depending on print size. Many Kodak and Fuji shops, particularly in Cairo, also have scanners and will make a diskette of five photos for E£10.

LAUNDRY
There are a few self-service laundries around Cairo, but virtually none elsewhere. Another option is to take your clothes to one of Egypt's many 'hole-in-the-wall' laundries where they wash and iron your clothes by hand. Prices vary wildly but average about E£1 for washing and ironing a shirt, more for larger items.

TOILETS
Public toilets, when they can be found, are bad news: fly-infested, dirty and smelly. Some toilets are still of the 'squat over a hole in a little room' variety. Only in mid-range and top-end hotels will toilet paper be provided; most toilets come equipped with a water squirter for washing yourself when you're finished.

In cities it's a good idea to make a mental note of all Western-style, fast-food joints, like McDonald's and KFC, and of the five-star hotels, as these are the places where you'll find the most sanitary facilities.

HEALTH
There are a few health hazards you should be aware of in Egypt. The 'Curse of the pharaohs', AKA diarrhoea, has been plaguing travellers to Egypt since mass tourism began here in the 19th century. Drink water from sealed mineral water bottles and avoid salads and uncooked vegetables. If you do get ill, remember to drink plenty of fluids.

More seriously, there is a very high incidence of hepatitis C among Egyptians. Barbers' razors, as well as syringes and needles, spread the disease.

Bilharzia, also known as schistosomiasis, is a debilitating disease carried in fresh water by minute snails. It is endemic in Egypt's Nile Valley and Delta. The worms enter through the skin and attach themselves to your intestines or bladder. The infection often causes no symptoms until the disease is established (several months to years after exposure) and damage to internal organs is irreversible. To be safe, do not drink, wash, paddle or even stand in the Nile or any other water except swimming pools, the ocean or oasis pools in the Western Desert Oases. A blood test is the most reliable way to diagnose the disease, but the test will not show positive until a number of weeks after exposure.

For more-general health information see the Health section in the Regional Facts for the Visitor chapter.

Doctors, Dentists & Hospitals

Hospitals in Egypt range from the glitzy to the Dickensian, depending on whether they're private or public, in the city or the country. In general, avoid any state hospital or clinic. It is best to inquire at your embassy for a list of recommended doctors and dentists. Remember that doctors and hospitals usually expect immediate cash payment for their services.

Pharmacies in Egypt are surprisingly good and almost anything can be obtained without a prescription. Many medicines are produced in Egypt under licence and are far cheaper than in other countries.

WOMEN TRAVELLERS

An entire book could be written from the comments and stories of women travelling in Egypt. Egypt is a conservative society and a woman's sexuality is, by and large, controlled by her family. Not only are Western women outside these strictures but, thanks to a steady diet of Western films and soap operas, they are perceived as sexually voracious and available. Unfortunately, the behaviour of some tourists reinforces prejudices still more.

As a result, while the country is in general safe for women, hassle is more or less constant. Sometimes it is in the form of hissing or barely audible whispers; usually it is a lewd phrase. Very occasionally there is phys-

ical harassment. Rape is rare. Commonsense tips to avoid problems include wearing a wedding ring, dressing conservatively (ie, no shorts, tank tops or above-the-knee skirts except in beach resorts), ignoring verbal comments, trying to sit beside women on public transport and avoiding eye-contact with men unless you know them. Take care not to get yourself into a situation of close proximity with men and stay alert in large crowds.

A couple of useful Arabic phrases for getting rid of unwanted attentions are: *la tilmasni* ('don't touch me'); *ihtirim nafsak* ('behave yourself'); or *haasib eedak* ('watch your hand'). Swearing at would-be Romeos will only make matters worse.

For more tips on avoiding or dealing with harassment from males see the Women Travellers section in the Regional Facts for the Visitor chapter.

GAY & LESBIAN TRAVELLERS

Egypt is an extremely conservative society that condemns homosexuality, but a strange double-think goes on whereby an Egyptian man can indulge in same-sex intercourse, but not consider himself gay because only the passive partner is queer. But while homosexuality is not actually illegal according to Egypt's penal code, 52 Egyptian men were arrested in 2001 and charged with debauchery and contempt of religion, thinly veiled legalese for being gay. Since then Egyptian gays have become more circumspect and the few gay hangouts have emptied. There are no national support groups or gay information lines in Egypt, but w www.gayegypt.com is a good source of up to date information on the situation.

BUSINESS HOURS

Banking hours are from 8am or 8.30am to 2pm Sunday to Thursday. Many banks in Cairo and other cities open again from 5 or 6pm for two or three hours, largely for foreign exchange transactions. Some also open on Friday and Saturday for the same purpose. During Ramadan banks are open from 10am to 1.30pm. Government offices generally open from 8am to 2pm Sunday to Thursday, but tourist offices are generally open longer.

Shops are generally open from 9am to 2pm and from 5pm to 10pm or even later during the summer. In the winter they tend to open from 10am to 7pm. Ramadan hours are 9.30am until about 3pm and 8pm until 10 or 11pm. Most large shops tend to close on Sunday.

PUBLIC HOLIDAYS

In addition to the main Islamic holidays described in the Regional Facts for the Visitor chapter, Egypt celebrates the following public holidays:

January
New Year's Day 1 January – official national holiday, but many businesses stay open
Coptic Christmas 7 January – a fairly low key affair; only Coptic businesses are closed for the day

March/April
Easter – the most important date on the Coptic calendar
Sham an-Nessim 1st Monday after Coptic Easter – Coptic holiday with Pharaonic origins (it literally means 'the smell of the breeze'), celebrated by all Egyptians with family picnics and outings
Sinai Liberation Day 25 April – official national holiday, which celebrates Israel's return of Sinai in 1982

May
May Day 1 May – official national holiday

July
Revolution Day 23 July – official national holiday commemorating the 1952 coup when the Free Officers seized power from the puppet monarchy

October
National Day 6 October – celebrates Egyptian successes during the 1973 war with Israel

SPECIAL EVENTS

There aren't very many events on the cultural calendar, and those that are don't always take place or else are singularly underwhelming:

January
Book Fair Held at the Cairo Exhibition Ground over two weeks, one of the city's most important cultural events drawing huge crowds

February
Ascension of Ramses II February 22 – One of the two dates each year when the sun penetrates the inner sanctuary of the temple at Abu Simbel and illuminates the gods within
International Fishing Tournament Held in Hurghada on the Red Sea
Luxor Marathon Competitors race around the monuments on Luxor's West Bank

March
Nitaq Festival Sometimes held in February, an excellent arts festival centred on Downtown Cairo with two weeks of exhibitions, theatre, poetry and music at galleries, cafés and a variety of other venues

April
South Sinai Camel Festival First held in 1999, when some 250 camels representing 17 different Bedouin tribes were present to take part in races

June
Al-Ahram Squash Tournament International competitors play in glass courts beside the Pyramids

July
International Festival of Oriental Dance Egypt's famous belly-dance gurus give showcase performances and lessons to international attendees

August
Tourism & Shopping Festival A countrywide promotion of Egyptian products with participating shops offering discounts

September
Alexandria Film Festival A very modest international film festival
Experimental Theatre Festival Ten days of performances in Cairo by international theatre troupes

October
Alexandrias of the World Festival A four-day celebration attended by delegations from the more than 40 Alexandrias around the world
Birth of Ramses 22 October – The second time in the year that the sun's rays penetrate the temple at Abu Simbel
Rally of Egypt An 11-day 4WD and motorcycle race through the desert, beginning and ending at the Pyramids

November
Arabic Music Festival A 10-day festival of classical, traditional and orchestral Arabic music held at the Cairo Opera House

December
Cairo International Film Festival A 14-day festival in which Cairenes get a rare chance to see uncensored films

ACTIVITIES

As the mantra in most tourism advertisements for Egypt says, the country is 'more than just monuments'. There are plenty of non-archaeological pursuits on offer.

EGYPT

Desert Safaris

A growth industry in Egypt, safari companies offer trips in 4WD, on camels or on foot. You can choose between the vast expanses of the Western Desert, the high desert mountains of Sinai or the rocky peaks of the Eastern Desert.

Abanoub Travel (☎ 062 250 201, fax 520 206) Started by a doctor who fell in love with Sinai, this Nuweiba-based company runs camel treks and jeep tours throughout Sinai.

Amr Shannon (☎ 02-519 6894, e ashannon@internetegypt .com) An artist and environmentalist, Shannon has been leading individuals and groups through Egypt's deserts for more than 20 years.

Badawiyya (☎ 02-345 8524, e badawya@link .com.eg) Based in Farafra, Badawiyya leads highly recommended jeep and walking tours of the Western Desert and further a field.

Khalifa Expedition (☎ 011-802 542, e info@khalifa-exp.com) Bahariyya-based operator that runs camel and jeep tours. If meditation's your thing, it does special tours for that too.

Diving

For many visitors to Egypt, the country's underwater treasures far outweigh the brilliance of its historical monuments. Some of the best diving in the world can be found here along Sinai's Gulf of Aqaba coast and on the Red Sea, south of Hurghada. If you don't like heading down into the depths, snorkelling is almost as good. Most reefs are only a few metres from the shoreline, and in some cases you don't have to go out of your depth to find yourself amid a teeming school of fish. See the Hurghada (Red Sea Coast) and Sharm el-Sheikh, Dahab and Nuweiba (all in Sinai) sections for more details.

Fishing

Apart from Hurghada's annual International Fishing Tournament – contact the **Egyptian Federation for Fishing** (☎ 02-395 3953) – the most exciting fishing opportunities in Egypt are on Lake Nasser, where Nile Perch grow to enormous proportions (more than 100kg). Two safari companies operate on the lake, and both come highly recommended: **African Angler** (☎ 097-316 052) and **Wild Nuba** (☎ 097-309 191; e wildnuba@yahoo.com).

Golf

Strange, but true: Egypt is largely desert and has limited water resources, but is scrambling to build golf courses and attract the big-money golf crowds. If you find that hitting a golf ball outweighs the questionable environmental ethics, there are a number of golf courses around Cairo, such as the **Mövenpick Jolie Ville Golf Resort** (Sharm el-Sheikh), and at the resorts of **El-Gouna** and **Soma Bay** on the Red Sea. Visit w www.touregypt.net for further details.

Horse Riding

Horse riding is possible at the Pyramids in Cairo, on Luxor's West Bank and at some Red Sea and Sinai resorts.

Unfortunately, not all of the horses are properly looked after. Try to encourage better care of horses by checking the animal before you ride. If the horse is too thin or lame, or if it has diarrhoea, respiratory problems (such as a cough) or any obvious wounds, ask for another.

Windsurfing

The Red Sea has strong steady winds for most of the year, making it an ideal place to windsurf. There are a number of windsurfing centres on the Red Sea and Sinai coasts, some of which also offer kite surfing.

Moon Beach (☎/fax 02-336 5103 or 069-401-500) in Ras Sudr is a mecca for British windsurfers. A number of hotels in the Sinai town of Dahab and in Safaga on the Red Sea also offer windsurfing.

COURSES
Language

Several institutions in Cairo offer Arabic courses. The full-blown option is to sign up at the **Arabic Language Institute** (☎ 02-797 5055, fax 795 7565; e alu@aucegypt.edu), a department of the American University in Cairo, PO Box 2511, Cairo 11511. It offers intensive instruction in Arabic language at elementary, intermediate and advanced levels with courses lasting one year. The institute also offers summer programmes.

The Arabic Department at the **British Council** (☎ 02-347 6118, fax 301 8348; w www.britishcouncil.org.eg; 192 Sharia el-Nil, Agouza, Cairo) also offers colloquial and classical courses spread over six or 12 weeks. It also offers intensive summer programmes.

The third and cheapest option is to study at one of the two **International Language Institutes** (ILI; ☎ 02-746 3087, fax 303 5624;

e ili@starnet.com.e; 4 Sharia Mahmoud Azmy, Sahafayeen, Mohandiseen • ☎ 02-291 9295, fax 418 7273; e ili@idsc.net.eg; 2 Sharia Mohammed Bayoumi, Heliopolis).

Diving

Egypt is one of the cheapest places in the world to get a diving qualification. Clubs offer a variety of certifications: PADI, NAUII, SSI and CMAS are taught here, although PADI is the most popular. Prices vary but not greatly. PADI open-water diving courses, which usually take five days, cost between US$250 and US$350.

Most well-established clubs on the Red Sea coast also offer a variety of more advanced courses, including professional-level courses or training in technical diving. See the Red Sea Coast and Sinai sections for listings of dive clubs.

ACCOMMODATION

Officially, camping is allowed at only a few places around Egypt and facilities are rudimentary. There are a few private hotels around the country that also allow campers to set up in their backyard.

Egypt has 15 hostels recognised by Hostelling International (HI). Having an HI card is

Warning

On arrival at the airport, if you're not with a group, you may be approached by a man or woman with an official-looking badge that says 'Egyptian Chamber of Tourism' or something similar. These people are not government tourism officials, they are hotel touts. These touts will tell you that the hotel you're heading for is closed/horrible/very expensive and suggest a 'better' place, for which they earn a commission, which will then be added to your bill. Many taxi drivers will also try it on too.

Do not be swayed by anyone who tries to dissuade you from going to the hotel of your choice. Hotels do not open and close with any great frequency in Cairo, and if it's listed in this book it is very unlikely to have gone out of business by the time you arrive. Some taxi drivers will stall by telling you that they don't know where your hotel is. In that case tell them to let you out at Midan Tahrir (or the Nile Hilton) and from there it's a short walk to almost all the budget hotels.

not absolutely necessary as nonmembers are admitted, but a card will save you between E£2 and E£4, depending on the hostel.

Budget accommodation is comprised of two-, one- and no-star hotels. Often the ratings mean nothing at all, as a hotel without a star can be as good as a two-star hotel, only cheaper. Generally, the prices quoted include any charges and quite often (basic) breakfast.

Mid-range hotel options are more limited and even more variable than either budget and five-star accommodation, particularly in Cairo and Alexandria. Some are little better than budget hotels, but charge extra for a non-functioning fridge and unconnected TV. Prices can range from E£60 to E£150 and extras can notch the bill up still further.

Five-star chains are everywhere in Egypt. Prices start at around US$100 per night.

FOOD

Egypt's cuisine may not rival that of Lebanon or Morocco, but it is possible to eat well (and cheaply). If you are on a budget, you are likely to find the lack of variety tiresome. Having said that, street food isn't bad. Its most ubiquitous elements are *fuul* and *ta'amiyya*. *Fuul* is mashed fava beans, usually ladled into a piece of *shaamy* bread (like pitta), which sells for about 50pt. *Ta'amiyya* is a slightly larger, flatter version of the balls that are known elsewhere in the Middle East as felafel, only *ta'amiyya* is made with mashed fava-beans instead of chick-peas. A *ta'amiyya* sandwich costs about 50pt and two make a substantial snack.

After *fuul* and *ta'amiyya*, running close behind in national affections is *kushari*, a mix of noodles, rice, black lentils, fried onions and tomato sauce. You can recognise *kushari* joints by the great tureens of noodles and rice in their windows. You'll also see plenty of shwarma (see the Middle Eastern Cuisine special section in the Regional Facts for the Visitor chapter), but it's rarely good in Egypt.

Fiteer, a kind of pizza made with filo pastry, is another common street-type food. Toppings typically include egg, cheese and chopped tomato, but avoid the meat, which is usually poor quality.

The Levantine practice of dining on mezze has filtered through to Egypt, but in cheaper restaurants there is not much variety.

EGYPT

Main meals tend to be grilled meat with accompanying rice and bread. Expect lots of kebabs, *kofta*, lamb, chicken and pigeon.

Finally, mention must be made of *moloukhia*, a green leaf added to broth to form a slimy green soup that is either passionately loved or utterly hated. Our authors stand on both sides of the *moloukhia* divide, so you'll have to try it for yourself.

DRINKS

As in the rest of the Middle East, *shai* and *ahwa* – tea and coffee – are both served strong and sugary. If you want to avoid caffeine, most coffee houses serve *yansoon* (anis) or *karkadey* (hibiscus, served either hot or cold, depending on the season). On practically every street in every town throughout Egypt there is a juice stand where you can get a drink squeezed out of just about any fruit or vegetable in season.

Beer drinkers now have a choice of brew in Egypt. Stella, a lager, is the long-time staple of Egypt's bars, but privatisation in the late 1990s added Stella Premium and Stella Meister to the range, as well as adding competition in the form of Sakkara and Sakkara Gold (also lagers).

Egyptian wine has improved of late. There are two reds, two whites and a rosé, all of which are perfectly fine, even if they will not satisfy connoisseurs.

Locally brewed spirits should be avoided (they have been responsible for blindness and even death).

ENTERTAINMENT

The *ahwa*, or coffee house, forms the nexus of most urban neighbourhoods and is the centre of village life. This is where men go to smoke *sheesha* (water pipes), drink tea and coffee, watch the game or simply chat. But if you are a woman or want some alcohol, you may want to go elsewhere. Nightlife in Cairo and (to a lesser extent) Alexandria is fairly varied, with a variety of bars and restaurants. Evenings start late, especially in summer.

Egypt is not exactly a clubbing destination and, with the possible exception of some venues in Sharm el-Sheikh and Hurghada, and one or two African discos in Cairo, DJs play uninspiring music.

Live contemporary music is limited in the capital, with the honourable exception of the

Cairo Jazz Club (☎ *02-345 9939; 197 26th July St, Agouza; shows start 9pm or later*). But if classical is your thing, **Cairo Opera House** (☎ *02-738 0598; Opera House Grounds, Gezira*) is the country's premier performing arts venue. Further a field, around Luxor and Aswan you can sometimes catch authentic local music and traditional dancing.

SPECTATOR SPORTS

Football is king in Egypt. In conversation with any Egyptian male, premier teams Zamalek and Al-Ahly arouse greater passions than almost any other subject. Demand for tickets makes them hard to get. The season begins in September and continues until May. The big matches are held in the **Cairo Stadium** (*Medinat Nasr; tickets from the box office only E£10-30*).

SHOPPING

Egypt is both a budget souvenir and a kitsch-shopper's paradise. Tourists with shelf space to fill back home can indulge in an orgy of alabaster pyramids, onyx Pharaonic cats, sawdust stuffed camels, and the ubiquitous painted papyrus. Hieroglyphic drawings of pharaohs, gods and goddesses embellish and blemish everything from leather wallets to engraved brass tables. Every town and village in Egypt has a small souq, but there's no doubt that the best is Cairo's great **Khan al-Khalili** bazaar (although you will have to be prepared to bargain hard). Cairo has a small number of boutiques that showcase some more tasteful Egyptian crafts, including traditionally inspired cotton jewellery, hand-loomed cotton and pottery.

Getting There & Away

See the Getting There & Away chapter at the beginning of this book for information about international travel to and from Egypt and the region in general.

AIR

Egypt has a handful of airports, but only six are international ports of entry: Cairo, Alexandria and, increasingly gaining status, the 'international' airports at Luxor, Aswan,

Hurghada and Sharm el-Sheikh. Most air travellers enter Egypt through Cairo. The other airports (Alexandria excepted) tend to be used for charter and package-deal flights only.

Egypt's international and national carrier is EgyptAir. It's not particularly good and fares are not cheap. All the major European airlines fly directly into Cairo and, more often than not, one of them will have some kind of discounted deal on offer at the time you are looking around. Try a couple of the travel agents mentioned in the regional Getting There & Away chapter and find out what they come up with. For shorter trips, it's worth looking into packages or combined air fare and hotel deals offered by many high-street travel agents.

Air tickets bought in Egypt are subject to some hefty government taxes, which make them extremely expensive. Always fly in on a return or onward ticket. If you do have to buy a ticket in Cairo, see Travel Agencies in the Cairo city section later in this chapter for addresses.

Departure Tax

If you are leaving Egypt by air then your departure tax is already prepaid, factored in to the cost of your ticket.

LAND

Egypt has land borders with Israel & the Palestinian Territories, Libya and Sudan, but for the latter there is no open crossing point. The only way to travel between Egypt and Sudan is to fly or take the Wadi Halfa ferry (see under Sea later in this section).

Israel & the Palestinian Territories

There are usually two ways to do this: if you want to go from Cairo directly to Tel Aviv or Jerusalem you go via Rafah; but, if you want to spend time in Sinai en route, you can also go via Taba.

At the time of writing the Rafah route (which passes via the Gaza Strip) was unsafe and no direct buses were running. Check with **Mazada Tours** (☎ 02-623 5777; 9 Koresh St, Jerusalem • ☎ 03-344 4454; 141 Ibn Gvirol, Tel Aviv) or with **Travco** (☎ 02-735 4650; 13 Sharia Mahmoud Azmy, Zamalek, Cairo) to see if there has been any change in the situation.

Taba This crossing is reached by one of three daily buses from Cairo (E£50 or E£70 depending on the bus; 8½ hours), or from any of the Sinai resorts. Once at Taba you can walk across the border (which is open 24 hours) into Israel. Immigration formalities are straightforward, but there is an Egyptian departure tax of E£7. Once you've crossed the border you can take a taxi (20NIS) or bus (4NIS; running 7am until 9pm) to Eilat (4km from the border) from where there are frequent buses onward to Jerusalem and Tel Aviv. Keep in mind that buses do not run between Friday evening and sundown Saturday, the Jewish holy day of Shabbat.

Coming from Israel to Egypt you must have a visa in advance unless your visit is limited to eastern Sinai (see the Visas & Documents section for details). There is a 67NIS Israeli departure tax to be paid plus an Egyptian entry tax of E£17.

SEA

There are no passenger boats operating between Egyptian ports and any ports in Europe at present. Neither are there currently any scheduled sailings between Egypt and Port Sudan in Sudan. However, it is possible to sail between Aswan in Upper Egypt and Sudan via Wadi Halfa – for details see the regional Getting There & Away chapter at the front of this book.

You can get a boat from Jeddah, but your transit visa for Saudi Arabia will only be issued if you ensure that it leaves the same day that you arrive from Suez. For more information call **MenaTours** (☎ 062-228 821; Sharia al-Marwa, Port Tawfiq, Suez).

Jordan

There's a sea link between Egypt and Aqaba in Jordan via Nuweiba in Sinai. A high-speed ferry leaves Nuweiba at 3pm and takes one hour. One-way tickets cost US$45 for adults, US$22.50 for five- to 12-year olds and US$11.25 for three- to five-year olds. Children under three travel free. You must be at the port at least two hours before departure. A slower car ferry takes three to four hours to make the trip and leaves each day at noon. Tickets cost US$32 for foot passengers and US$150 and up for cars, depending on the size of the engine. Foot passengers should be there at least two hours before departure. If you have a car allow at least four hours for customs procedures.

Tickets must be paid for in dollars and can be bought at the office of **Damanhour Shipping** (☎ 069-529 309) beside the port entrance. Tickets for the high-speed ferry are also on sale at the **Coral Bay Hilton** (☎ 069-520 320; Nuweiba). Jordanian visas can be bought on the boat to Aqaba if you have a European Union, US, Canadian, Australian or New Zealand passport. Otherwise you will need to get your visa in advance.

You can buy a ferry/bus combination ticket from Cairo or Alexandria through to Aqaba or even on to Amman. From Cairo's Sinai terminal the trip to Amman costs E£311, plus E£50.

Saudi Arabia & Kuwait

There are regular ferries between Jeddah and Suez (about 36 hours). Several lines compete on the route and fares can vary from one agent to another but, generally, tickets range from around E£145 for deck class to E£300 for 1st class. Most of the ferries on the route also carry cars. Getting a berth during the haj (pilgrimage to Mecca) is virtually impossible. You can get information and buy tickets at **Telestar** (☎ 062-326 25; Port Tawfiq, Suez) or **Mena Tours** (☎ 062-228 821; Port Tawfiq, Suez).

There is a daily fast ferry between Hurghada on the Red Sea coast, and Duba in Saudi Arabia (three hours). Tickets (E£180, or US$100 to US$200 per car) can be booked with **AmcoTours** (☎ 065-447 571; Hurghada).

Another ferry goes to Duba from Safaga on the Red Sea coast. It takes about seven hours, depending on the weather. For information and reservations call the **Salam Mar-**itime Transport Office (☎ 065-252 315/6; Main Hurghada-Safaga road, Safaga).

You can purchase tickets through to many destinations in the Gulf, either at Cairo's Turgoman garage or at the Sidi Gaber bus station in Alexandria.

Getting Around

AIR

EgyptAir is the main domestic carrier. Air Sinai, which to all intents and purposes is EgyptAir by another name, is virtually the only other operator. Fares are expensive and probably out of the range of most budget travellers (see the table).

During the high season (October to April), many flights are full so it's wise to book as far in advance as you can.

BUS

Buses service just about every city, town and village in Egypt. Deluxe buses travel between some of the main towns such as Cairo and Alexandria and around Sinai. These services are good with comfortable seats and air-con. The bulk of buses running south of Cairo along the Nile tend to be more basic.

Often the prices of tickets for buses on the same route will vary according to whether or not they have air-con and video, how old the bus is and how long it takes to make the journey – the more you pay, the more comfort you travel in and the quicker you get there.

Tickets can be bought at the bus stations or often on the bus. Hang on to your ticket until you get off, as inspectors almost always

Sample Domestic Air Fares

from	to	one way (E£)	return (E£)
Aswan	Abu Simbel	341	675
Cairo	Abu Simbel	991	1273
	Alexandria	248	442
	Aswan	759	953
	Hurghada	573	789
	Luxor	554	698
	Sharm el-Sheikh	573	789
Luxor	Aswan	248	489
	Sharm el-Sheikh	480	953

board the bus to check fares. There are no student discounts on bus fares.

TRAIN

Although trains travel along more than 5000km of track to almost every major city and town in Egypt, the system is badly in need of modernisation and most services are grimy and battered and a poor second option to the deluxe bus. The exceptions are some of the trains to Alexandria and the tourist trains down to Luxor and Aswan – on these routes the train is the preferred option rather than the bus.

Students with an ISIC card can get discounts of about 33% on all fares except the wagon-lit services to Aswan and Luxor.

SERVICE TAXI

Travelling by 'ser-vees' is one of the fastest ways to get from city to city. Service taxis are generally big Peugeot 504 cars that run intercity routes. Drivers congregate near bus and train stations and tout for passengers by shouting their destination. When the car's full, it's off. A driver won't leave before his car is full unless you and/or the other passengers want to pay more money. Service-taxi fares are usually cheaper than those for either bus or train and there are no set departure times, you just turn up and find a car.

CAR & MOTORCYCLE

Driving in Cairo is a crazy affair, but in other parts of the country, at least in daylight, it isn't so bad. You should avoid intercity driving at night. Driving is on the right-hand side. Petrol is readily available. Normal, or *tamaneen*, costs 90pt a litre but is tough on the engine. Better is the higher-octane super, or *tisa'een*, at E£1 a litre. Lead-free was introduced in 1995, but with only a handful of pumps in Cairo (mainly in Mohandiseen, Zamalek and Ma'adi) and Alexandria, there might be a queue. When travelling out of Cairo, remember that petrol stations are not always that plentiful; when you see one, fill up.

Speed traps are a recent innovation on Egyptian roads. If you are caught speeding your driving licence is confiscated and you must pick it up (and also pay a fine) at the nearest traffic police station several days later, which is obviously a major hassle.

Rental

Several car-rental agencies have offices in Egypt including Avis, Hertz and Budget. Their rates match international charges and finding a cheap deal with local dealers is virtually impossible. No matter who you go with, make sure you read the fine print.

An International Driving Permit is required and you can be liable for a heavy fine if you're caught renting a car without one. Drivers should be over the age of 25.

As an indication of prices, for a small car like a Suzuki Swift you'll be looking at about US$47, unlimited mileage. For a Toyota Corolla it's about US$75. These prices generally include insurance, but check this before signing.

Some companies, such as Europcar, offer the option of one-way rentals from, for example, Cairo to Sharm el-Sheikh.

ORGANISED TOURS

Travel agencies and many hotels offer tours around archaeological sites and points of interest (for desert safaris, see the Activities section, earlier in this chapter). These can be worthwhile simply because they save you the hassle of arranging transport. Reputable agencies such as AmEx and Thomas Cook have well-trained guides. At the other end of the scale, you may find yourself in an overcrowded minibus with an ill-informed guide, or visiting trinket shops, whether or not you want to buy. Check itineraries carefully and don't be bullied into a tour you don't like.

Cairo القاهرة

☎ 02

Few other countries can be so dominated by their capital: Cairo is Egypt. Both of them are known by the same name, Masr, and for Egyptians, to speak of one is to speak of the other at the same time. The city's stature spreads beyond borders – to millions of Arabic speakers, Cairo is the semi-mythical capital of the Arab world. The so-called 'Mother of the World', Cairo nurtures around 16 million Egyptians, Arabs, Africans and sundry international hangers-on. She's overburdened with one of the world's highest densities of people per square kilometre, which makes for a seething compress of people,

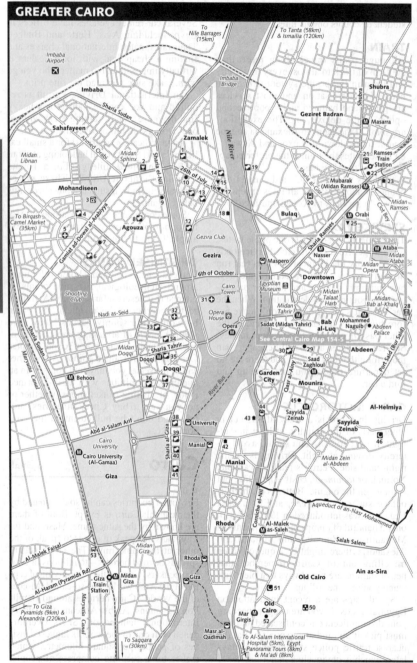

GREATER CAIRO

EGYPT

To
Nile Barrages
(15km)

To Tanta (58km)
& Ismailia (120km)

Imbaba
Airport

Imbaba
Bridge

Imbaba

Shubra

Sharia Sudan

Geziret Badran

Masarra

Sahafayeen

Zamalek

Nile River

21 Ramses
Train
Station

Midan
Libnan

1

22

26th of July

14

19

Mubarak
(Midan Ramses)

23

Midan
Sphinx

10

15

Midan
Ramses

Mohandiseen

11

13

16

17

20

Bulaq

3

9

12

18

Orabi

25

Agouza

8

26

Gezira Club

Ataba

Midan
Ataba

To Birqash
Camel Market
(35km)

4

Maspero

Nasser

Midan
Opera

5

Gezira

Downtown

7

6

6th of October

Egyptian
Museum

Cairo
Tower

31

Midan
Talaat
Harb

Midan
Bab al-Khalq

28

Shooting
Club

Nadi as-Seid

Opera
House

32

Midan
Tahrir

Abdeen
Palace

33

Opera

Sadat (Midan Tahrir)

Bab
al-Luq

Mohammed
Naguib

34

See Central Cairo Map 154-5

Midan
Doqqi

Sharia Tahrir

30

29

Abdeen

Doqqi

35

Saad
Zaghloul

Behoos

36

Garden
City

Mounira

37

Al-Helmiya

44

45

Abd al-Salam Arif

38

43

Sayyida
Zeinab

Sayyida
Zeinab

Cairo
University

39

University

46

Cairo University
(Al-Gamaa)

40

Manial

42

Midan Zein
al-Abdeen

Giza

41

Manial

Rhoda

Aqueduct of an-Nasr Mohammed

Al-Malek
as-Saleh

To Giza
Pyramids (9km) &
Alexandria (220km)

Salah Salem

Al-Malek Faisal

53

Midan
Giza

Rhoda

Ain as-Sira

Giza Train
Station

Midan
Giza

Old Cairo

51

Al-Haram (Pyramids Rd)

Giza

Old
Cairo

50

Mar
Girgis

52

Masr al-
Qadimah

To Saqqara
(30km)

To Al-Salam International
Hospital (5km), Egypt
Panorama Tours (8km)
& Ma'adi (8km)

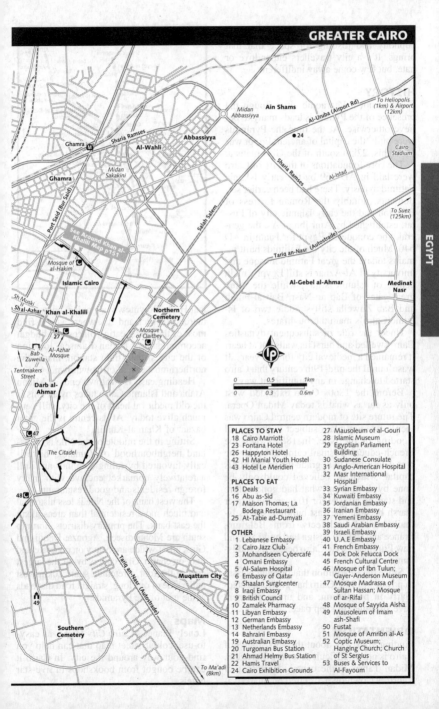

GREATER CAIRO

EGYPT

PLACES TO STAY
18 Cairo Marriott
23 Fontana Hotel
26 Happyton Hotel
42 HI Manial Youth Hostel
43 Hotel Le Meridien

PLACES TO EAT
15 Deals
16 Abu as-Sid
17 Maison Thomas; La Bodega Restaurant
25 At-Tabie ad-Dumyati

OTHER
1 Lebanese Embassy
2 Cairo Jazz Club
3 Mohandiseen Cybercafé
4 Omani Embassy
5 Al-Salam Hospital
6 Embassy of Qatar
7 Shaalan Surgicenter
8 Iraqi Embassy
9 British Council
10 Zamalek Pharmacy
11 Libyan Embassy
12 German Embassy
13 Netherlands Embassy
14 Bahraini Embassy
19 Australian Embassy
20 Turgoman Bus Station
21 Ahmad Helmy Bus Station
22 Hamis Travel
24 Cairo Exhibition Grounds

27 Mausoleum of al-Gouri
28 Islamic Museum
29 Egyptian Parliament Building
30 Sudanese Consulate
31 Anglo-American Hospital
32 Masr International Hospital
33 Syrian Embassy
34 Kuwaiti Embassy
35 Jordanian Embassy
36 Iranian Embassy
37 Yemeni Embassy
38 Saudi Arabian Embassy
39 Israeli Embassy
40 U.A.E Embassy
41 French Embassy
44 Dok Dok Felucca Dock
45 French Cultural Centre
46 Mosque of Ibn Tulun; Gayer-Anderson Museum
47 Mosque Madrassa of Sultan Hassan; Mosque of ar-Rifai
48 Mosque of Sayyida Aisha
49 Mausoleum of Imam ash-Shafi
50 Fustat
51 Mosque of Amribn al-As
52 Coptic Museum; Hanging Church; Church of St Sergius
53 Buses & Services to Al-Fayoum

buildings and traffic and all the attendant ca-
cophony and jostling for space that that
brings. It's a city travellers either love or
hate, but few come away indifferent.

HISTORY

Cairo is not a Pharaonic city, though the
presence of the Pyramids leads many to believe otherwise. At the time the Pyramids
were built, the capital of ancient Egypt was
Memphis, 22km south of the Giza plateau.

The core foundations of the city of Cairo
were laid in AD 969 by the early Islamic
Fatimid dynasty. There had been earlier settlements, notably the Roman fortress of
Babylon and the early Islamic city of Fustat, established by Amr ibn al-As, the general who conquered Egypt for Islam in AD
640. Much of the city the Fatimids built remains today: the great Fatimid mosque and
university of Al-Azhar is still Egypt's main
centre of Islamic study, while the three
great gates of Bab an-Nasr, Bab al-Futuh
and Bab Zuweila still straddle two of Islamic Cairo's main thoroughfares.

Under the rule of subsequent dynasties
Cairo swelled and burst its walls but at heart
it remained a medieval city for 900 years. It
wasn't until the mid-19th century that Cairo
started to change in any significant way.

Before the 1860s Cairo extended west
only as far as what is today Midan Opera.
The future site of modern central Cairo was
then a swampy plain subject to the annual
flooding of the Nile. In 1863, when the
French-educated Ismail came to power, he
was determined to upgrade the image of his
capital, which he believed could only be
done by dismissing what had gone before
and starting afresh. For 10 years the former
marsh became one vast building site as Ismail invited architects from Belgium,
France and Italy to design and build a brand
new European-style Cairo beside the old Islamic city.

Since the Revolution that brought Nasser
to power in 1952, Cairo has grown spectacularly in population, and urban planners
have struggled to keep pace.

ORIENTATION

Finding your way about the vast sprawl of
Cairo is not as difficult as it may first seem.
Midan Tahrir is the centre. Northeast of
Tahrir is Downtown. Centred on Sharia Ta-

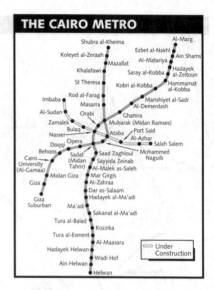

THE CAIRO METRO

laat Harb, Downtown is a noisy, busy commercial district and it's where you'll find
most of the cheap eating places and budget
accommodation. Midan Ramses, location
of the city's main train station, marks the
northernmost extent of Downtown.

Heading east, Downtown ends at Midan
Ataba and Islamic Cairo takes over. This is
the old medieval heart of the city, still very
much alive today. At its centre is the great
bazaar of Khan al-Khalili.

Sitting in the middle of the Nile is the island neighbourhood of Zamalek, historically favoured by ruling colonials and still
a relatively upmarket enclave with many
foreign residents and good restaurants.

The west bank of the Nile is less historical
and much more residential than areas along
the east bank. The primary districts, north to
south are Mohandiseen, Agouza, Doqqi and
Giza, all of which are heavy on concrete and
light on charm. Giza covers by far the largest
area of the four, stretching some 20km west
either side of one long, straight road that ends
at the foot of the Pyramids.

Maps

Lonely Planet's *Cairo City Map* is an easy-
to-use, colour street map that can help you
find your way around the city. In Cairo it
can be bought from bookshops in five-star
hotels.

INFORMATION

Visas

All visa business is carried out at the **Mogamma** *(Midan Tahrir)*, a 14-storey Egypto-Stalinist monolith. Foreigners go up to the 1st floor, pass through the door on the right then circle around to the left and straight down the corridor ahead. Go to window No 42 to collect a form and you'll be told where to go next. It's open 8am to 2pm Saturday to Thursday.

Tourist & Tourist Police Offices

Cairo's main **tourist office** *(☎ 391 3454; 5 Sharia Adly; open 8.30am-8pm daily, 9am-5pm during Ramadan)* is close to Midan Opera.

The **tourist police office** *(☎ 390 6028)* is on the 1st floor of a building in the alley just left of the tourist office.

Money

There are banks and forex bureaus all over town but the **Banque Masr** *(Nile Hilton & Helnan Shepheard's Hotels)* are open 24 hours. Otherwise the city's foreign exchange bureaus tend to close at 8pm. There are ATMs throughout the city, including at most branches of **HSBC**, **Banque Masr**, **Egyptian American Bank (EAB)** and **Commercial International Bank (CIB)**, as well as in the foyers of most five-star hotels.

Other useful offices are **AmEx** *(☎ 574 7991; 15 Qasr el-Nil, Downtown)* and the most central branch of **Thomas Cook** *(☎ 574 3776; 17 Mahmoud Bassiouni, Downtown)*.

Post & Telephone

Postal services are available at Cairo's **main post office** *(Midan Ataba; open 7am-7pm Sat-Thur, 7am-noon Fri & public holidays)*. The **poste restante office** *(open 8am-6pm Sat-Thur, 10am-noon Fri & holidays)* is down the side street to the right of the main entrance, through the last door (opposite the EMS office).

In Cairo there are also several **telephone centrales** *(northern side of Midan Tahrir, central Cairo & Sharia Mohammed Mahmoud, Bab al-Luq)*, and all have a few cardphones.

Email & Internet Access

The number of Internet cafés in Cairo has multiplied rapidly over recent years and they can be found all over the city, includ-ing in some of the budget hotels (including the Berlin, New Sun and Hotel Venice). Some of the more well-established and well-located Internet cafés include:

4U Internet Café *(☎ 575 9304)* 1st floor, 8 Midan Talaat Harb, Downtown; open 9am to 10pm daily; E£8 per hour

InternetEgypt *(☎ 796 2882)* 6th floor, 2 Midan Simon Bolivar, Garden City; E£10 per hour; open 9am to 10pm Saturday to Thursday, 3pm to 10pm Friday

Mohandiseen Cybercafé *(☎ 305 0493)* on a side street off Sharia Gamiat ad-Dowal al-Arabiyya, between McDonald's and Arby's; E£12 per hour; open 10am to midnight daily

Nile Hilton Cybercafé *(☎ 578 0444 ext 758)* in the basement of the Nile Hilton mall; E£12 per hour; open 10am to midnight daily (closed noon to 2pm Friday)

St@rnet Cyber Café *(☎ 391 0151)* in the basement of the Al-Bustan Centre, Sharia al-Bustan, Downtown; E£10 per hour; open 10.30am to 10.30pm daily

Travel Agencies

Hamis Travel *(☎ 575 2757, fax 574 2976; e hamis@hamis.com.eg; Ramses train station)*, with offices on the 1st floor in the annex just south of the main booking hall at Ramses train station, is a good place for tours of Cairo and trips down to Luxor and Aswan. Otherwise, one of the most reputable agencies in town is **Egypt Panorama Tours** *(☎ 358 5880, fax 359 1199; e ept@link.net; 4 Rd 79, Ma'adi)*, although it tends to specialise in four- and five-star hotels and cruise ships. Agents will take bookings over the phone and courier the tickets to you.

The official Egyptian government travel agency is **Masr Travel** *(☎ 393 0168, fax 392 4440; 7 Sharia Talaat Harb, Downtown)*.

Bookshops

The **American University in Cairo (AUC) bookshop** *(☎ 02-794 2964; Sharia Muhammed Mahmoud, Downtown; open 9am-4pm Sun-Thur, 10am-3pm Sat)* has stacks of material on the politics, sociology and history of Cairo, Egypt and the Middle East, but it also has plenty of guidebooks and some fiction.

Other bookshops with very good selections of books about Cairo and Egypt are **Lehnert & Landrock** *(44 Sharia Sherif; open 9.30am-2pm & 4pm-7.30pm Mon-Fri & on Sat morning)*, which is also very good for maps,

EGYPT

and **Livres de France** (☎ *393 551236; Sharia Qasr el-Nil; open 10am-8pm, Mon-Sat).*

Cultural Centres
France (☎ 794 7679) 1 Madrassat al-Huquq al-Fransiyya, Mounira; open 9am-9pm Sun-Thur
UK (☎ 303 1514) British Council, 192 Sharia el-Nil, Agouza; open 9am-2pm & 3pm-8pm Mon-Thur, 9am-3pm Fri & Sat
USA (☎ 797 3469) American Studies Library, US Embassy, 5 Latin America, Garden City; open 10am-7pm Mon & Wed, 10am-4pm the rest of the week (closed Sat)

Film & Photography
There are any number of Kodak and Fuji photo centres in Cairo. One Downtown place recommended for quality and price is the **Photo Centre** *(☎ 392 0031; 3 Sharia Mahrany),* on a backstreet off Sherifeen, which itself is a side street off Qasr el-Nil. There's also a large **Kodak Express** *(Sharia Adly, Downtown)* between sharias Sherif and Mohammed Farid.

Medical Services
Many of Cairo's hospitals have antiquated equipment and a cavalier attitude to hygiene, but there are some exceptions:

Anglo-American Hospital (☎ 735 6162/3/4/5)
   Sharia Hadayek al-Zuhreyya, to the west of Cairo Tower, Gezira

Masr International Hospital (☎ 335 3345) 12 Sharia al-Saraya, near Midan Fini, Doqqi
As-Salam International Hospital (☎ 524 0250) Corniche el-Nil, Ma'adi
Shaalan Surgical Centre (☎ 748 5479) 19 Sharia Abd al-Hamid Lutfy, Mohandiseen

There is no shortage of pharmacies in Cairo and almost anything can be obtained without a prescription. Pharmacies that operate 24 hours include **Isaaf** *(☎ 574 3369; cnr sharias Ramses & 26th of July, Downtown),* and **Zamalek Pharmacy** *(☎ 736 6424; 3 Sharia Shagaret ad-Durr, Zamalek).*

EGYPTIAN MUSEUM
More than 100,000 relics and antiquities from almost every period of ancient Egyptian history are housed in the Egyptian Museum. To put that in perspective, if you spent only one minute at each exhibit it would take more than nine months to see everything. In 2001 the government announced the construction of a new museum close to the Pyramids in Giza, but it'll be a few more years until it is complete.

Admission to the museum is E£20 (E£10 for students). Access to the Royal Mummy Room costs an additional E£40 (E£20 for students); tickets for this are bought at the 1st floor entrance to the room.

The museum is open from 9am to 4.45pm daily.

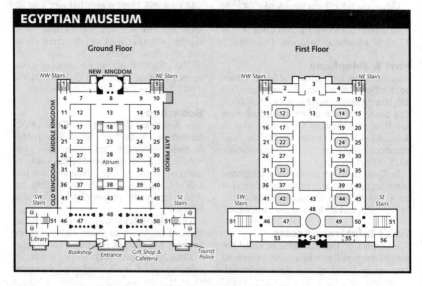

Ground Floor

Rooms 32, 37 & 42 – Old Kingdom Rooms Room 42 holds what some consider to be the museum's masterpiece – a larger-than-life-size statue of Khafre (Chephren), builder of the second Pyramid at Giza. Room 32 is dominated by the double statue of Rahotep and Nofret. The simple lines of this limestone sculpture make the figures seem almost contemporary, despite having been around for a staggering 4600 years. Also in here are the panels known as the Meidum Geese, part of a frieze that originates from a mud-brick mastaba at Meidum, near Al-Fayoum (to this day, the lakes there are still host to a great variety of bird life). Room 37 contains the tomb of Queen Hetepheres, mother of Khufu (Cheops), builder of the Great Pyramid at Giza.

Room 3 – Amarna Room This room is devoted to Akhenaten (1352-1336 BC), the 'heretic pharaoh' who set up ancient Egypt's first and last monotheistic faith. Compare the bulbous bellies, hips and thighs, the elongated heads and thick, Mick Jagger-like lips of these statues with the sleek, hard-edged norm of typical Pharaonic sculpture. Also very striking is the delicate, but unfinished, head of Nefertiti, wife of Akhenaten.

First Floor

Room 4 – Jewellery Room This is one of the museum's newer galleries, with stunning ancient jewellery from throughout Egypt. It contains crowns, diadems, daggers, belts and beadwork, as well as everyday jewellery, spanning the millennia of ancient Egypt.

Room 2 – Royal Tombs of Tanis This is a glittering collection of gold- and silver-encrusted amulets, gold funerary masks, daggers, bracelets, collars, gold sandals and finger and toe coverings from five intact New Kingdom tombs found in the Delta site of Tanis.

Tutankhamun Galleries Without doubt, the exhibit that outshines everything else in the museum is the treasure of this young and comparatively insignificant pharaoh who ruled for only nine years. About 1700 items are spread throughout a series of rooms. Room three contains an astonishing death mask made of solid gold, while rooms seven and eight house the four gilded shrines that fitted inside each other and held the gold sarcophagus of Tutankhamun at their centre.

Room 56 – Royal Mummy Room This darkened gallery houses the bodies of 11 of Egypt's most illustrious pharaohs and queens, who ruled Egypt between 1552 and 1069 BC, including Ramses II.

ISLAMIC CAIRO مصر الاسلامية

The term Islamic Cairo is a bit of a misnomer, as the area is no more or less Islamic than most other parts of the city, but maybe the profusion of minarets on the skyline gives the impression of piety.

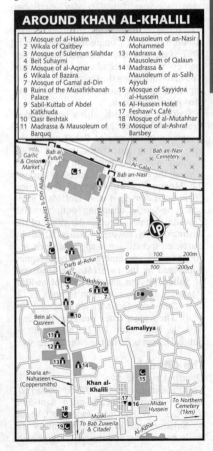

AROUND KHAN AL-KHALILI

1 Mosque of al-Hakim
2 Wikala of Qaitbey
3 Mosque of Suleiman Silahdar
4 Beit Suhaymi
5 Mosque of al-Aqmar
6 Wikala of Bazara
7 Mosque of Gamal ad-Din
8 Ruins of the Musafirkhanah Palace
9 Sabil-Kuttab of Abdel Katkhuda
10 Qasr Beshtak
11 Madrassa & Mausoleum of Barquq
12 Mausoleum of an-Nasir Mohammed
13 Madrassa & Mausoleum of Qalaun
14 Madrassa & Mausoleum of as-Salih Ayyub
15 Mosque of Sayyidna al-Hussein
16 Al-Hussein Hotel
17 Feshawi's Café
18 Mosque of al-Mutahhar
19 Mosque of al-Ashraf Barsbey

The best place to start exploring is the area around the great bazaar, **Khan al-Khalili**. It's very easy to find from central Cairo. From Midan Ataba walk straight along Sharia al-Azhar or Muski. Alternatively, it's a short taxi ride – ask for 'Al-Hussein', which is the name of both the midan and the mosque at the mouth of the bazaar. The fare should be no more than E£5 from Downtown. Before diving into the bazaar, it is worth taking time out to visit one of Cairo's most historic institutions, **Al-Azhar** *(admission free; open 24 hrs daily)*, not only one of Cairo's earliest mosques, but also the world's oldest surviving university.

One of the best walks in Cairo is north from Khan al-Khalili up towards the old **northern wall** and **gates** *(admission E£6; open 8am-5pm daily Oct-May, 8am-6pm June-Sept)*. The square-towered **Bab an-Nasr** (Gate of Victory) and the rounded **Bab al-Futuh** (Gate of Conquests) were built in 1087 as the two main northern entrances to the new walled Fatimid city of Al-Qahira. You can walk along the top of the walls and explore inside the gates via the roof of the Mosque of al-Hakim.

South of Khan al-Khalili a busy market street runs down to the twin minarets of the recently restored gate of **Bab Zuweila**, the sole surviving gate from the old city's southern wall. The view from the minarets is about the best in Cairo; access is through the **Mosque of al-Mu'ayyad** *(admission E£12; open 8am-5pm daily Oct-May, 8am-6pm June-Sept)*. Continuing south from Bab Zuweila, you pass through the **street of the tentmakers**, a covered bazaar filled by craftsmen specialising in appliqué work, and 500m further you emerge in a large square dominated by the twin **Mosque-Madrassa of Sultan Hassan** and **Mosque of ar-Rifai** *(Midan al-Qala'a; admission to both, E£12; open 8am-5pm Oct-May, 8am-6pm June-Sept)*. The former dates from the 14th century, the latter from 1912. The interior of Sultan Hassan is by far the more impressive.

The Citadel
Overlooking the two grand mosques is Cairo's Citadel *(☎ 512 1735; Midan al-Qala'a; admission E£20; open 8am-5pm daily Oct-May, 8am-6pm June-Sept)*, begun by Saladin back in the 12th century. Its walls encircle an assortment of three very different mosques, several palaces housing some fairly indifferent museums, and a couple of terraces with fine views over the city.

Mosque of ibn Tulun
Also not to be missed is the **Mosque of ibn Tulun** *(Sharia Ibn Tulun; admission E£6; open 8am-6pm daily)* 800m southwest of the Citadel. It's quite unlike any other mosque in Cairo mainly because the inspiration is almost entirely Iraqi – the closest things to it are the ancient mosques of Samarra. Right next door to Ibn Tulun is the **Gayer-Anderson Museum** *(Sharia Ibn Tulun; admission E£16; open 8am-4pm daily)*, two 16th-century houses restored and furnished by a British major between 1935 and 1942. The attraction of the museum is not the exhibits themselves but the houses, their puzzle of rooms and the lavish decor. The place is well worth a visit.

OLD CAIRO   مصر القاديمة
Once known as Babylon, this part of Cairo predates the coming of Islam and remains to this day the seat of the Coptic Christian community. There is a **Coptic museum** *(☎ 363 9742; Sharia Mar Girgis; admission E£16; open 9am-5pm daily)* with mosaics, manuscripts, tapestries and Christian artwork. **Al-Muallaqa**, or Hanging Church *(Sharia Mar Girgis; admission free; mass 8am-11am Fri, 7am-10am Sun)*, is the centre of Coptic worship. Among the other churches and monasteries here, **St Sergius** *(admission free; open 8am-4pm daily)* is supposed to mark one of the resting places of the Holy Family on its flight from King Herod. The easiest way to get here from Midan Tahrir is by Metro (50pt). Get out at the Mar Girgis station.

FELUCCA RIDES
You can hire a felucca for about E£20 an hour from the Corniche by the Semiramis Intercontinental. However, the best place is about 800m to the south at the Dok Dok landing stage, just short of the bridge over to Le Meridien hotel.

PLACES TO STAY – BUDGET
Camping
Motel Salma *(☎ 384 9152, fax 385 1010; camping with own tent or camper van per person E£7)* is next to the Wissa Wassef Art Centre at Harraniyya, south of Giza. Although inconvenient, in that it's miles from

anywhere, it does have views of the Pyramids from the back of the site. Overland tour companies occasionally stop here.

Hostels
HI Manial Youth Hostel *(☎ 364 0729; fax 398 4107; 135 Abdel Aziz el-Saud, Manial; beds in 6-bed dorms HI members/non-members E£8/12, in 3-bed dorms E£12/16)* is in reasonable nick with clean toilets, although the beds are nothing great. There are no rooms for couples or families and there's an 11pm curfew.

Hotels & Pensions
The inexpensive hotels and pensions are concentrated Downtown, mainly on and around Sharia Talaat Harb.

Sultan Hotel I-III *(☎ 577 2258; 4 Tawfiqqiya Souq, Downtown)*, **Safary Hotel** *(☎ 575 0752)* and **Hotel Venice** *(☎ 574 1171)* all occupy the same building on a colourful market street. Beds start at E£9 on the 1st floor (Sultan I) and drop to E£6 on the 5th floor (Sultan III and Safary), probably because there's no lift. All offer grubby, cramped dorms and overburdened facilities, yet remain popular because of their rock-bottom prices. Hotel Venice, with a couple of grubby private rooms is marginally better. These places are only recommended to those on the tightest of budgets.

The **Dahab Hotel** *(☎ 579 9104; 26 Mahmoud Bassiouni, Downtown; dorm beds E£12, doubles E£35)* was designed to re-create the feel of a Sinai beach camp with its collection of whitewashed huts on the rooftop. The Dahab has cushioned com munal spaces open to the sky and Bob Marley on the cassette deck. Dorm beds use shared showers; doubles come with private shower.

The reception to **Hotel Minerva** *(☎ 392 0600/1/2; 39 Talaat Harb, Downtown; singles/doubles E£18/28, doubles with shower E£32)* is on the ground floor down the alley opposite the Al'Américaine café. The hotel itself occupies the 6th and 7th floors. The not-so-obvious location means it is often overlooked, but the rooms are kept clean, as are the communal showers and toilets, and it's good value.

Ismailia House Hotel *(☎ 356 3122; 1 Midan Tahrir, 8th floor, Downtown; singles/doubles/triples E£25/40/56, doubles with*

shower E£45)* is popular despite its very dingy rooms and grubby bathrooms. If you can stand the grime, there are great views over the midan.

Despite the good location, just off Midan Tahrir, the **New Sun Hotel** *(☎ 578 1786; e newsunhotel@yahoo.com; 9th floor, 2 Talaat Harb, Downtown; quads per person E£15; singles/doubles E£25/40)* has no views. But its dingy rooms are decent-sized, and the bathrooms are spotless.

Magic Hotel *(☎ 579 5918; 3rd floor, 10 Sharia al-Bustan, Downtown; singles/doubles with fans E£27/43)* is slightly better run than its two former sister establishments, the Sun and Ismailia House. The bedrooms and bathrooms are that little bit cleaner, and the place has a cosier, less traveller-worn feel.

Pension Roma *(☎ 391 1088, fax 579 6243; 6th floor, 169 Mohammed Farid, Downtown; singles/doubles/triples E£35/55/70, with private shower E£40/60/75)* is the city's most charming budget hotel, long popular for its old-world elegance. Reservations are necessary.

Berlin Hotel *(☎/fax 395 7502; e berlinhotel cairo@hotmail.com; 4th floor, 2 Shawarby; singles/doubles/triples E£77/96 /115)* is just off Qasr el-Nil. It's a bit more pricey than most other budget options, but in our opinion well worth it for clean air-con rooms, each with their own shower.

PLACES TO STAY – MID-RANGE
The **Windsor Hotel** *(☎ 591 5277, fax 592 1621; 19 Sharia Alfy, Downtown; singles E£85-105, doubles E£105-150)* was the British Officers' Club before 1952 and retains a colonial air. Former Monty Python member, Michael Palin, stayed here while filming the BBC series *Around the World in 80 Days*. There's a wide variety of rooms.

Fontana Hotel *(☎ 592 2321, fax 592 2145; Midan Ramses; singles/doubles E£60/87)* is on the northeastern corner of Midan Ramses, high above the traffic and fumes. It has clean rooms and a pleasant rooftop café/bar.

Happyton Hotel *(☎/fax 592 8671/00; 10 Ali al-Kassar; singles/doubles E£40/52)* is tucked away down a quiet backstreet off Emad ad-Din (behind Karim Cinema). It's a relaxed, good value-for-money option with its own restaurant and a small, open-air rooftop bar. Rooms have air-con.

EGYPT

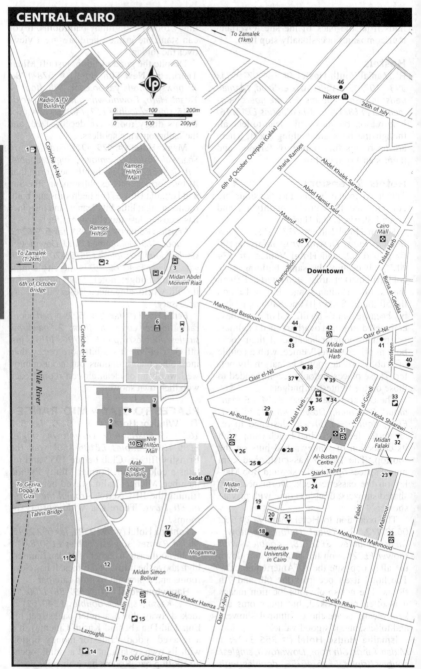

CENTRAL CAIRO

To Zamalek (1km)

Radio & TV Building

Nasser M

26th of July

Corniche el-Nil

Ramses Hilton Mall

6th of October Overpass (Galaa)

Sharia Ramses

Abdel Khalek Sarwat

Abdel Hamid Said

To Zamalek (1:2km)

Ramses Hilton

Maaruf

Cairo Mall

Talaat Harb

45

2

4

3

Midan Abdel Moniem Riad

Downtown

Champollion

Mahmoud Bassiouni

Qasr el-Nil

6th of October Bridge

Corniche el-Nil

6

5

44

43

42

Midan Talaat Harb

41

Bursa al-Gedida

Sheriffeen

40

Qasr el-Nil

38

37

39

Nile River

7

8

9

36

35

34

33

Al-Bustan

Talaat Harb

Yousef al-Guindi

Hoda Shaarawi

Midan Falaki

32

29

10

Nile Hilton Mall

Arab League Building

30

31

Al-Bustan Centre

28

27

26

25

23

To Gezira, Doqqi & Giza

Tahrir Bridge

Sadat M

Midan Tahrir

Sharia Tahrir

24

17

Mogamma

19

20

21

Falaki

Mansour

11

12

18

American University in Cairo

Mohammed Mahmoud

22

13

Midan Simon Bolivar

Abdel Khader Hamza

Qasr al-Ainy

Sheikh Rihan

16

Latin America

Lazoughli

15

14

To Old Cairo (3km)

EGYPT

0   100   200m
0   100   200yd

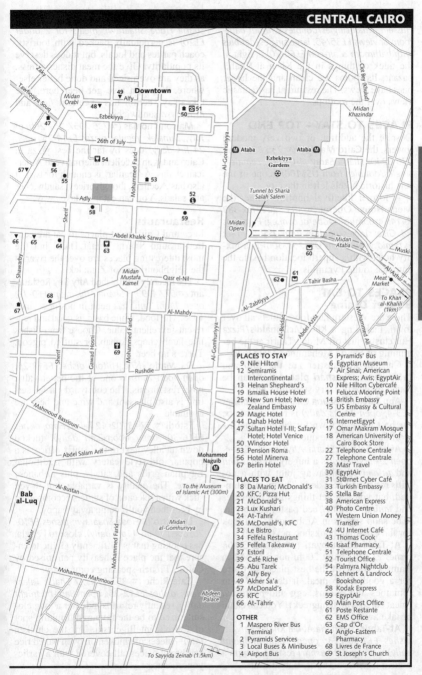

CENTRAL CAIRO

EGYPT

PLACES TO STAY
9 Nile Hilton
12 Semiramis Intercontinental
13 Helnan Shepheard's
19 Ismailia House Hotel
25 New Sun Hotel; New Zealand Embassy
29 Magic Hotel
44 Dahab Hotel
47 Sultan Hotel I-III; Safary Hotel; Hotel Venice
50 Windsor Hotel
53 Pension Roma
56 Hotel Minerva
67 Berlin Hotel

PLACES TO EAT
8 Da Mario; McDonald's
20 KFC; Pizza Hut
21 McDonald's
23 Lux Kushari
24 At-Tahrir
26 McDonald's, KFC
32 Le Bistro
34 Felfela Restaurant
35 Felfela Takeaway
37 Estoril
39 Café Riche
45 Abu Tarek
48 Alfy Bey
49 Akher Sa'a
57 McDonald's
65 KFC
66 At-Tahrir

OTHER
1 Maspero River Bus Terminal
2 Pyramids Services
3 Local Buses & Minibuses
4 Airport Bus
5 Pyramids' Bus
6 Egyptian Museum
7 Air Sinai; American Express; Avis; EgyptAir
10 Nile Hilton Cybercafé
11 Felucca Mooring Point
14 British Embassy
15 US Embassy & Cultural Centre
16 InternetEgypt
17 Omar Makram Mosque
18 American University of Cairo Book Store
22 Telephone Centrale
27 Telephone Centrale
28 Masr Travel
30 EgyptAir
31 St@rnet Cyber Café
33 Turkish Embassy
38 American Express
40 Photo Centre
41 Western Union Money Transfer
42 4U Internet Café
43 Thomas Cook
46 Isaaf Pharmacy
51 Telephone Centrale
52 Tourist Office
54 Palmyra Nightclub
55 Lehnert & Landrock Bookshop
58 Kodak Express
59 EgyptAir
60 Main Post Office
61 Poste Restante
62 EMS Office
63 Cap d'Or
64 Anglo-Eastern Pharmacy
68 Livres de France
69 St Joseph's Church

Al-Hussein Hotel (☎ 591 8089; Midan Hussein; small singles/doubles without bathroom or views E£35/45, large singles/doubles with bathroom & air-con E£60/70) is right in the thick of things in the Khan al-Khalili bazaar. Its rooms are clean and the larger ones have views. The restaurant has fantastic views over the rooftops.

PLACES TO STAY – TOP END
Despite the addition of two very modern towers, the **Cairo Marriott** (☎ 735 8888, fax 375 8240; Sharia Saray al-Gezira, Zamalek; singles/doubles from US$100) is one of the few historic hotels left in the city.

A former khedival hunting lodge, the **Mena House Oberoi** (☎ 383 3222, fax 383 7414; e obmhofc@oberoi.com.eg; Pyramids Rd, Giza; singles/doubles from US$150/180; Pyramid views from US$250/300) is a luxury hotel with a superb location beside the entrance to the Pyramids.

PLACES TO EAT
Budget Dining
There are Western fast-food outlets all over town, including a **KFC/McDonald's/Pizza Hut cluster** just off Midan Tahrir at the beginning of Sharia Mohammed Mahmoud.

Cheaper and tastier are the *fuul* and *ta'amiyya* or *kushari* places that can be found on nearly every street in Cairo.

Abu Tarek (40 Sharia Champollion; dishes E£3-4; open 24 hrs daily) is reckoned to be *the* best place in town for *kushari* and it's worth the wait in the queue.

Akher Sa'a (8 Sharia Alfy; meals E£3-4; open 24 hrs daily) is a hugely popular *fuul* and *ta'amiyya* takeaway joint with a no-frills restaurant next door. The menu is limited, but you can get things like omelettes and *tahina* (sesame-seed paste) and bread. (The shop sign is in Arabic only, but look for the Christian bookshop next door.)

At-Tabie ad-Dumyati (31 Sharia Orabi; dishes E£3-8), about 200m north of Midan Ramses, is one of the best places in Cairo for a good cheap meal. It does *fuul* with tomatoes and onions, egg and *pasturma* (meat cured with fenugreek). You can eat in or take away.

At-Tahrir (19 Sharia Abdel Khalek Sarwat, dishes E£1.50-E£3; open 10am-midnight daily) is a popular *kushari* restaurant with a branch on Sharia Tahrir, Bab al-Luq.

Felfela Restaurant (☎ 392 2751; 15 Sharia Hoda Shaarawi; meals for 2 under E£20) is perpetually packed with tourists, coach parties and locals, but it does deserve its popularity. Give the meat dishes a miss, as they are overpriced and done better elsewhere. You can also get beer here. The takeaway section has excellent *fuul* and *ta'amiyya* sandwiches.

Maison Thomas (☎ 735 7057; 157 26th of July, Zamalek; regular pizzas E£14-25; open 24 hrs daily) does by far the best pizza in Cairo and is an excellent alternative to American chains. A 'regular' is enough for two. It also has excellent, though pricey, sandwiches and salads. You can eat in or take away.

Restaurants
In central Cairo most places to eat are centred around Sharia Talaat Harb, but the most interesting places are over the river in the neighbourhood of Zamalek.

The recently refurbished **Alfy Bey Restaurant** (☎ 577 4999; 3 Sharia Alfy; mains E£9-16; open 11am-1am) has been in business since 1938. The food, while basic, is good and represents excellent value. Choose from dishes like lamb chops, kebab, or stuffed pigeon. There's no beer.

Da Mario (Nile Hilton; dishes E£18-25; open noon-2am) is one of the better value hotel restaurants. The courtyard garden setting is also pleasant and wine and beer are available.

Estoril (☎ 574 3102; 12 Talaat Harb; dishes E£16-30; open noon-2am daily), tucked down an alley next to the AmEx office, is a popular old-style eatery with traditional Egyptian grills and salads, plus Lebanese mezze. The quality is variable, but if you stick with a selection of starters accompanied by beer then you'll come away happy.

Le Bistro (8 Hoda Shaarawi; dishes E£10-20; open 11am-11pm daily), close to Felfela, has cooking that is sufficiently Gallic to ensure that the place is heavily patronised by Cairo's French-speaking community.

Café Riche (☎ 392 9793; 7 Sharia Talaat Harb; dishes E£12-25; open 8am-midnight daily), recently refurbished after a long closure, used to be the favoured drinking spot of Cairo's intelligentsia. Try the chicken *fatta* – pieces of chicken on oven baked rice and bread pieces, all covered with a garlic-yogurt sauce.

La Bodega (☎ *736 6761; 157 Sharia 26th July, Zamalek; mains E£30-50; open 7am-1am daily*), one of Cairo's best upmarket restaurants, promotes itself as a bistro, but is slightly more grand. Frescoed walls, a chilled-out lounge, consistently good food and an eclectic menu make it a favourite for wealthy Cairenes and foreign residents.

A sumptuous orientalist fantasy of a restaurant, **Abu as-Sid** (☎ *735 9640; 157 Sharia 26th July, Zamalek; dishes E£24-50; open noon-2am daily*) serves traditional Egyptian food to wannabe pashas amid hanging lamps, large cushions and brass tables. Reservations are necessary.

ENTERTAINMENT
Music & Dance
The **Mausoleum of al-Ghouri** (*admission free; open from 8pm Wed & Sat night, 8.30pm in winter*) in Islamic Cairo has displays of Sufi dancing; it's advisable to come early, especially in winter, as the small auditorium can get quite crowded.

The best belly-dancers perform at Cairo's five-star hotels, such as the Meridien and the Semiramis Intercontinental, with tickets starting at E£150 a pop. Performances begin late (around 1am). By contrast, **Palmyra** (*off 26th of July, Downtown; admission E£3; open from 8pm, performances begin around 11pm*) is a wonderfully sleazy belly-dance place (a Stella costs E£12).

For live music try the **Cairo Jazz Club** (☎ *345 9939; 197 Sharia 26th July, Agouza*).

Bars, Cafés & Coffee Houses
There are also several local bars Downtown. The best are the **Cap d'Or** (*Abdel Khalek Sarwat*), probably the most salubrious of the lot, and the **Stella Bar** (*cnr Hoda Shaarawi & Talaat Harb*), which is used to foreigners.

All the large hotels have Western-style bars, as do many of the restaurants listed in Places to Eat (try La Bodega, Estoril and Café Riche). In addition, you could try **Deals** (☎ *736 0502; 2 Maahad al-Swissry, Zamalek; open until 2am daily*), a small basement bar that gets packed with young Cairenes and foreigners. Also, the **Windsor Bar** at the Windsor Hotel has an old-world charm that makes it a pleasant place to sit.

For real night owls, **Fishawi's** (*Khan al-Khalili; open 24 hrs daily*) is one of Cairo's oldest and most famous coffee houses. It's a few steps off Midan Hussein.

GETTING THERE & AWAY
Air
EgyptAir (☎ *390 0999; 6 Sharia Adly • ☎ 393 2836; cnr Talaat Harb & Sharia al-Bustan • ☎ 579 3048; Nile Hilton*) has a number of offices. The main sales office is on Sharia Adly; the Hilton office is in the garden courtyard.

Bus
The main station is the **Turgoman bus station** (*Sharia al-Gisr*), 1km northwest of the intersection of sharias Galaa and 26th of July. It's in an awkward location in that it's too far to walk to from central Cairo: the only way to get there is by taxi (E£3 from Downtown). From the bus station **West Delta Bus Co** and **Superjet** buses go every 30 minutes to Alexandria (E£16 to E£20, 2½ hours). West Delta Bus Co also has three services a day to Marsa Matruh (E£28 to E£36, five hours).

Superjet has three Hurghada services a day (E£50, 6½ hours), while **Upper Egypt Travel** has at least nine (E£40 to E£55, 6½ hours), some of which go on to Safaga (E£35 to E£50, eight hours), Al-Quseir (E£40 to E£55, eight hours) and Marsa Alam (E£55 to E£65, 12 hours).

Upper Egypt Travel has luxury buses from Turgoman to Luxor (E£60, 10 to 11 hours) departing daily at 8.30pm, and to Aswan (E£60, 12 hours) departing at 5pm.

East Delta Bus Co has frequent buses to Ismailia (E£7, 2½ hours) and to Suez (E£7, 1½ to two hours).

Sinai Buses East Delta Bus Co has buses from Turgoman to all Sinai destinations. There are frequent services to Sharm el-Sheikh (E£50 to E£60, seven hours), a few of which go on to Dahab (E£62 to E£68, nine hours). Superjet also has four buses to Sharm el-Sheikh (E£55, seven hours). There are three daily buses to Nuweiba (E£53 to E£58, eight hours) and Taba (E£53 to E£74, 8½ hours). The only daily service to St Katherine's Monastery leaves at 10.30am (E£37, 7½ hours).

Western Oases Buses All Western Oases buses go from Turgoman. Note that to get to Siwa you must take a bus to Alexandria or

Marsa Matruh, and then another onwards. There are three buses a day to Bahariyya (Bawiti; E£12.50 to E£15, five hours), two of which go on to Farafra (E£25 to E£30, eight hours). To Dakhla (Mut; E£30 to E£35, 10 to 12 hours) there are four daily buses, two via Bahariyya and Farafra, two via Asyut and Al-Kharga. Three daily buses go to Kharga (E£30 to E£35, 10 hours) via Asyut.

Israel & the Palestinian Territories For details on buses to Tel Aviv and Jerusalem, see the introductory Getting There & Away chapter.

Train
Ramses station (Mahattat Ramses; Midan Ramses) is Cairo's main train station. The daily wagon-lit sleeper for Upper Egypt departs Cairo at 7.45pm each evening, arriving in Luxor at 5.10am the next morning and Aswan at 9.30am. Dinner and breakfast are included in the fare of E£335/670 one way/return. The **wagon-lit booking office** (☎ 574 9474, fax 574 9074) is just south of the main station building, across the car park – follow the blue on yellow signs that read 'Res. Office'.

Aside from the wagon-lit train, foreigners can only travel on the No 980, departing Cairo daily at 7.30am, and the No 996, leaving at 10pm. First/2nd class fares on the night train are E£60/36 to Luxor, while to Aswan they're E£73/42. Students pay two-thirds of the full fare.

Tickets can be bought from the ticket office beside platform 11, which is on the other side of the tracks from the main hall. You must buy your tickets at least a couple of days in advance.

The best trains running between Cairo and Alexandria are the *Turbini*, which take 2½ hours. They depart from Cairo at 8am, 2pm and 7pm, and tickets for 1st/2nd class air-con cost E£30/22. The next best trains are the *Espani*, the 'Spanish' services, which cost the same as the Turbini and leave at 9am, noon, 5pm and 10.30pm.

Service Taxi
Most service taxis depart from taxi stands around Ramses train station and Midan Ulali. They depart for Alexandria (E£10, three hours), Ismailia (E£5, one to two hours), Port

Said (E£8, two to three hours), Al-Arish (E£12, five hours) and Rafah (E£15, six hours).

GETTING AROUND
To/From the Airport
Bus No 356, the airport service, runs at 20-minute intervals from 5.45am to 11pm between Midan Abdel Moniem Riad (behind the Egyptian Museum) in central Cairo and bus stations II and I at the airport (E£2, plus E£1 per large luggage item, 40 minutes to one hour depending on traffic). To find the buses at either terminal, head out into the car park and you'll spot the stand, if not a waiting bus.

If you decide to grab a black and white taxi, then the going rate to central Cairo is around E£25 to E£30. Limousines cost anything from E£50 to E£85.

Bus & Minibus
Cairo's main local bus and minibus stations are at Midan Abdel Moniem Riad. From there, services leave for just about everywhere in the city.

Microbus
Destinations are not marked in any language, so microbuses are hard to use unless you are familiar with their routes. Position yourself beside the road that leads where you want to go and when a microbus passes, yell out your destination – if it's going where you want to go and there are seats free it'll stop.

Metro
The Metro system is startlingly efficient, and the stations are cleaner than any other public places in Cairo. It's also surprisingly inexpensive and, outside rush hours, not too crowded either. You are most likely to use the Metro if you're going down to Old Cairo (served by a station called Mar Girgis). A short-hop ticket (up to nine stations) costs 30pt (see The Cairo Metro map, earlier).

Taxi
If a destination is too far to walk, the easiest way of getting there is to take a taxi. They're cheap enough to make buses, with their attendant hassles, redundant. Use the following table as a rough guide as to what you should be paying for a taxi ride around Cairo.

Taxi Fares		
from	to	fare (E£)
Downtown	Airport	25-30
	Heliopolis	15
	Khan al-Khalili	5
	Zamalek	4
Midan Tahrir	The Citadel	5
	Midan Ramses	2
	The Pyramids	20

River Bus

The river-bus terminal is at Maspero, on the Corniche in front of the big round TV building. From there, boats depart every 15 minutes for Masr al-Qadima (Old Cairo). The trip takes 50 minutes and the fare is 50pt.

Around Cairo

MEMPHIS & SAQQARA
ممفيس سقارة

There's little left of the former Pharaonic capital of Memphis, 24km south of Cairo, but the **museum** (admission E£14; admission to entire North Saqqara area E£20; open 7.30am-4pm, to 5pm daily in summer) contains a fairly impressive statue of Ramses II.

A few kilometres away is Saqqara, a vast site strewn with pyramids, temples and tombs. A massive necropolis covering 7km of desert on the edge of the cultivation, deceased pharaohs and their families, administrators, generals and sacred animals were interred here. The star attraction is the **Step Pyramid of Zoser**, the world's oldest stone monument and the first decent attempt at a pyramid. Surrounding it is Zoser's pyramid complex, which includes a huge court, shrines and the **serdab**, a small building with small holes through which to peer at a statue of the pharaoh. Other attractions are the **Pyramid and Causeway of Unas**, with the earliest decorated royal burial chamber, and the **Serapeum**, where sacred Apis bulls were buried in massive granite sarcophagi.

It's possible to hire a horse or camel at the Pyramids of Giza to head down to Saqqara, but you'll spend much of the day in the saddle. You really need a full day to get even a superficial view of the area, and transport to get around the Saqqara site is essential.

Getting There & Away

A taxi from central Cairo will cost about E£100 shared among a maximum of seven people. This is the best way for those on a tight budget to get to and around Saqqara. Stipulate the sights you want to see and how long you want to be out, and bargain hard.

BIRQASH CAMEL MARKET
سوق الجمال برقاش

Until 1995 Egypt's largest **souq al-gamaal** (camel market; admission E£3) was among run-down tenements in Imbaba, one of Cairo's western suburbs. The city's growing population forced its relocation to Birqash, 35km northwest of Cairo, on the edge of the Western Desert.

The market is an easy half-day trip from Cairo, but like all of Egypt's animal markets, it's not for animal lovers or the faint-hearted. Hundreds of camels are sold here every day, most having been brought up the 40 Days Road from western Sudan. The market is most lively on Friday and Monday mornings from about 7am to 9am. It's an extra E£2 to bring a camera and E£15 for a video.

For some background on the camel trade see the boxed text 'From Caravans to Kebabs' later in this chapter.

Getting There & Away

The cheapest way to get to the market is to take a taxi (E£5) to the site of the old camel market at Imbaba, from where microbuses (E£1) shuttle back and forth to Birqash.

Alternatively, on Friday only, the New Sun Hotel (see Places to Stay under Cairo earlier) organises a minibus tour to the souq, leaving from the hotel at 7am and returning at about noon. The charge is E£20 per person (minimum five people); you must book a day or two in advance.

The final option is to hire a taxi to take you all the way there and back. Depending on your bargaining skills, you'll be looking at around E£70; make sure to negotiate waiting time.

AL-FAYOUM OASIS
الفيوم
☎ 084

Some 100km southwest of Cairo, Al-Fayoum is a large, irrigated oasis about 70km wide and 60km long.

[Continued on page 162]

EGYPT

THE PYRAMIDS

'It is through deeds such as these that men go up to the gods or that gods come down to men.' That was the comment of the Greek historian Philo on the Pyramids. He wrote that during an era that we tag 'ancient' – the world of 'ancient Greece'. Yet when Philo penned his comment the Pyramids were already almost 3000 years old. We are closer in time to Philo than he to the Pyramids.

To this day the Pyramids remain the oldest, largest and most accurate stone structures ever made. In 5000 years nothing built has ever equalled them. It's unlikely that anything ever will.

The **Pyramid chambers** are open from 8.30am to 4pm daily, but the site itself is open from about 7am to 7.30pm daily. There's an admission fee of E£20 for the plateau, and then the same again to enter each of the Pyramids. Note that the Pyramids are closed on a rotating basis, and only two are open for the public to clamber inside at any one time. This is to allow for necessary periodic restoration work.

Great Pyramid of Khufu (Cheops)

The oldest at Giza and the largest in Egypt, the Great Pyramid of Khufu stood 146.5m high when it was completed around 2600 BC. Although there is not much to see inside the pyramid, the experience of climbing through such an ancient structure is unforgettable, though completely impossible if you suffer from even the tiniest degree of claustrophobia.

Along the eastern and southern sides of the pyramid are five long pits which once contained the pharaoh's funerary barques. One of

Inset: The Sphinx at Giza
(Photo by Chris Mellor)

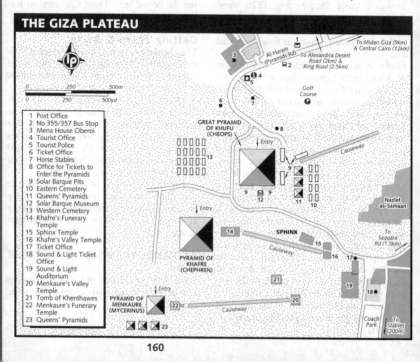

THE GIZA PLATEAU

0   250   500m
0   250   500yd

1 Post Office
2 No 355/357 Bus Stop
3 Mena House Oberoi
4 Tourist Office
5 Tourist Police
6 Ticket Office
7 Horse Stables
8 Office for Tickets to
   Enter the Pyramids
9 Solar Barque Pits
10 Eastern Cemetery
11 Queens' Pyramids
12 Solar Barque Museum
13 Western Cemetery
14 Khafre's Funerary
   Temple
15 Sphinx Temple
16 Khafre's Valley Temple
17 Ticket Office
18 Sound & Light Ticket
   Office
19 Sound & Light
   Auditorium
20 Menkaure's Valley
   Temple
21 Tomb of Khenthawes
22 Menkaure's Funerary
   Temple
23 Queens' Pyramids

To Midan Giza (9km)
& Central Cairo (12km)

Al-Haram
(Pyramids Rd) To Alexandria Desert
Road (2km) &
Ring Road (2.5km)

Golf
Course

GREAT PYRAMID
OF KHUFU
(CHEOPS)

Entry

Causeway

Nazlet
as-Samaan

To
Saqqara
Rd (1.5km)

Entry

PYRAMID OF
KHAFRE
(CHEPHREN)

SPHINX

Causeway

Entry

PYRAMID OF
MENKAURE
(MYCERINUS)

Causeway

Coach
Park

To
Stables
(200m)

FLORENCE MASON

these ancient wooden vessels, possibly the oldest boat in existence, was unearthed in 1954. It was restored and a glass **museum** was built over it to protect it from damage from the elements. Entry costs E£20.

Pyramid of Khafre (Chephren)

Southwest of the Great Pyramid, and with almost the same dimensions, is the Pyramid of Khafre. At first it seems larger than that of Khufu, his father, because it stands on higher ground and its peak still has part of the original limestone casing which once covered the entire structure. Among the most interesting features of this pyramid are the substantial remains of Khafre's mortuary temple outside to the east.

Pyramid of Menkaure (Mycerinus)

At a height of 62m (originally 66.5m), this is the smallest of the three Pyramids. Extensive damage was done to the exterior by a 16th-century caliph who wanted to demolish all the Pyramids.

The Sphinx

Known in Arabic as Abu al-Hol (Father of Terror), the Sphinx is carved almost entirely from one huge piece of limestone left over from the carving of the stones for Khufu's Pyramid. It is not known when it was carved, but one theory is that it was Khafre who thought of shaping the rock into a lion's body with a god's face, wearing the royal headdress of Egypt. Another theory is that it is the likeness of Khafre himself that has been staring out over the desert sands for so many centuries.

Getting There & Away

Bus 355/357 has air-con and runs from Heliopolis to the Pyramids via Midan Tahrir every 20 minutes. It picks up beside the Egyptian Museum (look for the crowd waiting) and costs E£2. Microbuses leave from the Midan Abdel Moniem Riad station and drop you off about 500m short of the Mena House Oberoi hotel for 25pt.

Expect to pay about E£20 one way for a taxi.

Top: In awe of one of the Seven Wonders of the World, Giza

[Continued from page 159]

There's not an awful lot to see in the main town, Medinat al-Fayoum, but you can explore such features of the oasis as the salty lake of **Birket Qarun**, the Ptolemaic temple known as **Qasr Qarun**, the springs of **Ain as-Siliyiin**, the **Hawara, Lahun** and **Meidum Pyramids**, or the **Museum of Kom Aushim** (☎ 501 825; Cairo road, Karanis; admission E£6; open 8am-4pm daily) on the road to Cairo. South of the oasis is **Wadi Rayyan**, three protected lakes in the midst of dunes that have become a major nesting area for migratory birds.

It is possible to camp in the grounds of the Museum of Kom Aushim for E£4, or at the lake; get a permit from the tourist police. Otherwise, the **Palace Hotel** (☎ 351 222; singles/doubles E£20/35, with bathroom E£30/45) on the canal in the town centre has good, clean rooms, the price of which includes breakfast. Out on Birket Qarun is the **Auberge du Lac** (☎ 700 002, fax 700 730; singles/doubles E£90/125), a four-star hotel that was originally King Farouk's hunting lodge.

Getting There & Away
There are regular buses between Medinat al-Fayoum, east of the town centre, and Cairo's **Ahmed Helmy station** (behind Midan Ramses; E£4, three hours). Service taxis also run to both these destinations. Birket Qarun can be reached by service taxi from Medinat al-Fayoum, but the trip is long and convoluted. Better to take a private taxi from the town (about E£20).

Nile Valley   وادى النيل

MINYA   المنيا
☎ 086
Because so many of the 'troubles' during the 1990s were based in the countryside around here, Minya has a preponderance of police and armoured personnel carriers (see the boxed text 'Troubles in the Nile Valley' later). Even with this, it remains a pleasant town with a long Corniche along the Nile and some great, if shabby, early 20th-century buildings testifying to its former prosperity as a centre of the cotton industry. While you can usually (but not always) wander the town rel-

atively freely, the police will want to accompany you to monuments in the countryside.

Information
There are two **tourist offices**, one on the **Corniche** (☎ 343 500) and one at the **train station** (☎ 342 044). Both are open 8.30am to 8pm. There is an ATM at the **National Bank** (cnr Corniche & Sharia al-Gomhuriyya) and a **Western Union** (☎ 364 905; Sharia Al-Gomhuriyya) for cash advances.

There's a **post office** (off Corniche, a block south of Sharia Port Said; open 8am-2pm Sat-Thur), and a **telephone centrale** (train station) that sells phonecards.

Things to See
About 7km southeast of the town, near the ferry landing on the east bank, is a large Muslim and Christian cemetery called **Za-wiyyet al-Mayyiteen** (Place of the Dead). The cemetery is said to be one of the largest in the world.

About 20km south of Minya, on the east bank, **Beni Hasan** (admission E£12; open 7am-5pm daily) is a necropolis with more than 30 distinctive Middle Kingdom tombs carved into a limestone cliff, though only four are on view. Look for the wall paintings of wrestlers and dancing girls in the **Tomb of Baqet**. To get there from Minya, you have to take a private taxi (about E£40, 20 minutes) and a phalanx of policemen.

Places to Stay & Eat
Palace Hotel (☎ 324 071; Midan Tahrir; singles/doubles E£15/20, with bathroom E£25/35) is worth a look-in even if you don't intend staying. High ceilings, hand-painted murals and a time-warp atmosphere almost make up for its worn furniture and shambolic bathrooms.

Hotel Seety (☎ 363 930; 71 Saad Zaghloul; singles/doubles/triples E£12/15/18) is half a block south of the train station and despite its run-down appearance, has reasonably clean, comfortable rooms with bathrooms.

Recently upgraded, **Akhenaten Hotel** (☎ 365 917/8; Corniche; singles/doubles E£33.10/42.50) has 48 rooms with air-con, satellite TV, fridges and, in some cases, great views of the Nile.

Nefertiti & Aton (☎ 331 515, fax 326 467; El-Corniche; singles/doubles US$51/61) The best hotel in town, this is also known locally as the 'Etap' and is about 1km north of the town centre. It's a good four-star hotel with rooms facing the Nile. Prices do not include taxes. It also has three restaurants and two bars.

There are a lot of the usual cheap *fuul* and *ta'amiyya* stands scattered around Midan al-Mahatta, Midan Tahrir and along the market street stretching south off the latter. Other than the following, most of the restaurants are at the hotels.

Cafeteria Ali Baba (*Corniche; dishes E£3-10*), just north of Sharia Port Said, serves a satisfying meal of the usual favourites – kebabs or another meat dish, salad, *tahina* and a soft drink.

Restaurant Afendina (*Midan Tahrir; meals E£1-10*) is a thriving shwarma/roast chicken restaurant that offers salads, *ta'amiyya* and other staples.

Getting There & Away

At present, the police insist that foreigners travel only by train, not bus. The trip to and from Cairo (four hours) costs E£27 to E£31 in 1st class or E£16 to E£20 in 2nd class. Trains heading south depart frequently, with the fastest trains leaving Minya between about 11pm and 1am.

There are 1st class/2nd class with air-con/ 2nd class without air-con services to Asyut (E£13/8/3.40, one hour), Sohag (E£21/13/ 5.80, three hours), Qena (E£31/19/9, three to four hours), Luxor (E£44/28/12, four to five hours) and Aswan (E£56/34/15, eight to nine hours).

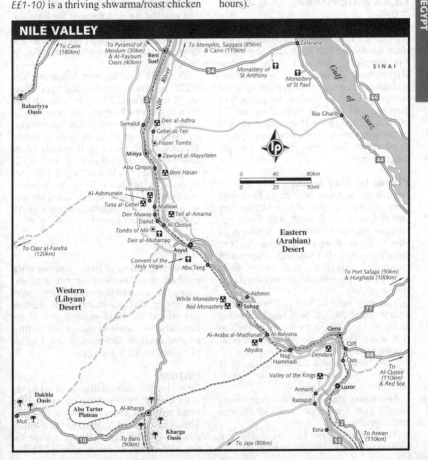

NILE VALLEY

Troubles in the Nile Valley

Throughout the 1990s Islamist violence plagued Cairo and Upper Egypt. Massive police action kept the terrorist groups from operating freely, but was unable to wipe them out all together. In the area between Minya and Qena in Upper Egypt, the often brutal policing fuelled resentment against the government and the conflict took on the aspects of a traditional feud, with police and militants as opposing 'families'. Tourists who ventured here in the early and mid-1990s were often caught up in this violence, but it was in the supposedly safe area of Luxor that militants were able to pull off their most brutal attack, when they massacred 58 tourists at the Temple of Hatshepsut in 1997.

In the aftermath of the attack, the police visibly tightened their protection of tourists throughout the country. There have been no known militant attacks since the Hatshepsut massacre and in February 2001 the American Embassy in Cairo lifted its travel advisory to the previously off-limits area between Minya and Qena. Independent travel there is now safe, but travel by road or visits to ancient sites still involve a heavily armed police escort.

QENA & DENDARA   قنا و دندرة
☎ 096

Qena has little going for it other than its proximity to the **Temple of Hathor** (Dendara; admission E£12; open 7am-6pm daily). The temple is dedicated to the goddess Hathor, and, although built by the Ptolemaic dynasty, retains the Egyptian style and serves their beliefs. Hathor, the goddess of pleasure and love, is figured on the 24 columns of the Outer Hypostyle Hall, and on the walls are scenes of Roman emperors as pharaohs. The views from the roof are magnificent.

Places to Stay & Eat

At present the police discourage foreigners from staying in Qena and insist that they stay in Luxor, 60km south, a far better option for everyone concerned. If you must stay in Qena, **Happyland Camp** is 100m from the temple. It's basically a hotel with overpriced beds. If the police relax, there may be the possibility of camping in its messy garden.

The only other choice in town is **New Palace Hotel** (☎ 332 509; singles/doubles E£26/35), just behind the Mobil petrol station, and a few cheap dives along Sharia al-Gomhuriyya.

Café Nasr (Sharia Gomhuriyya; dishes E£2.50-6) is a workers' café with reasonable, cheap food and tea.

Restaurant Hamdi (Sharia Luxor; meals around E£8) serves full meals of chicken and vegetables.

There are several kushari, kofta and ta'amiyya places along the main street.

Getting There & Away

The **bus station** is in front of the train station. However, buses not originating or terminating here pass along the main road and drop (and might pick up) passengers at the bridge over the canal.

There are two **Superjet** buses to Cairo (E£25, eight hours) at 7am and 8pm. There are 11 to Aswan (E£7, three to four hours) from 6.30am to 7.45pm, and most stop in Luxor (E£2, one hour). A few other Superjet buses only go as far as Edfu or Luxor. There are nine buses to Hurghada (three hours) and six of them go on to Suez (E£22 to E£38, nine to 10 hours). Superjet also has services to Hurghada (E£18, three hours) and Suez (E£41, six hours). There are also services to coastal destinations such as Al-Quseir (E£7, four hours).

LUXOR   الأقصر
☎ 095

The sheer grandeur of Luxor's monumental architecture and its excellent state of preservation, have made this village-city one of Egypt's greatest tourist attractions. Built on and around the 4000-year-old site of ancient Thebes, Luxor is one of the world's greatest open-air museums, a time capsule of a glorious, long-gone era.

History

Following the collapse of centralised power at the end of the Old Kingdom period, the small village of Thebes, under the 11th and 12th dynasty pharaohs, emerged as the main power in Upper Egypt. Rising against the northern capital of Heracleopolis, Thebes reunited the country under its political, religious and administrative control and ushered in the Middle Kingdom period. The strength of its government also enabled it to re-establish control after a second period of decline, liberate the country from foreign rule and bring in the New Kingdom dynasties.

At the height of their glory and opulence, from 1550 to 1069 BC, all the New Kingdom pharaohs (with the exception of Akhenaten, who moved to Tell al-Amarna) made Thebes their permanent residence. The city had a population of nearly one million and the architectural activity was astounding.

Orientation

What most visitors today know as Luxor is actually three separate areas: the town of Luxor itself on the east bank of the Nile; the village of Karnak, 2km to the northeast; and the monuments and necropolis of ancient Thebes on the west bank of the Nile.

In Luxor town there are only three main thoroughfares: Sharia al-Mahatta, Sharia al-Karnak and the Corniche el-Nil. Another road you may want to know if you're looking for cheap accommodation is Sharia Televizyon, where there are many budget places.

Information

Visa Extensions The **passport office** (☎ 380 885; open 8am-2pm Sat-Thur) is almost opposite Isis Hotel, south of the town centre.

Tourist Offices The **tourist police** & **tourist office** (☎ 372 215, 373 294; Corniche el-Nil; open 8am-8pm Sat-Thur, 8am-1pm Fri) is in the Tourist Bazaar, next to New Winter Palace Hotel. Travellers can leave messages on a notice board next to the main information counter. There is another tourist office at the train station that is supposedly open the same hours, and a third at the airport that is open from 8am to 8pm daily.

Money The **Bank of Alexandria** (Corniche el-Nil) has a branch a little way up from the Hotel Mercure. **Banque Masr** (Sharia Nefertiti) is around the corner from the Mercure, and the **National Bank of Egypt** (Corniche el-Nil) is near the Old Winter Palace. There are also a growing number of ATMs. In ad-

dition, **Egyptian Exchange Company** (☎ 388 257, Sharia Karnak) is open from 8am to 11pm daily.

AmEx (☎ 378 333) and **Thomas Cook** (☎ 372 196) both have offices at the Old Winter Palace Hotel.

Post & Telephone The main post office (Sharia al-Mahatta) also has a branch office in the Tourist Bazaar. The central **telephone centrale** (Sharia al-Karnak; open 24 hrs) has another branch (open 8am-10pm) below the resplendent Old Winter Palace Hotel entrance and a third (open 8am to 8pm) at the train station.

Email & Internet Services Internet cafés spring up almost daily in Luxor and prices average E£12 per hour. The following are the most reliable:

Aboudi (☎ 327 390) Corniche el-Nil • (☎ 365 419) Sharia Karnak. Both branches are open 9am to 10pm and charge E£3 for 15 minutes.
Internet Business Centre (☎ 311 205) West Bank. Open 8.30am to midnight. This is the cheapest option on the West Bank at E£12 per hour.
Mantel Computer & Internet (☎ 374 015) Off Sharia Medina al-Manawara. Open 8.30am to 1pm, this place is convenient for budget hotels.
Rainbow Internet (☎ 378 983) Sharia Yousef Hassan. Open 9am to 11pm. This place has the cheapest rates in town at E£6 per hour.

Where First?

With so many tombs and temples on show, the challenge in Luxor is what to miss. Our highlights, all of which could – at a push – be seen in a day, might make it easier:

Karnak The temple to see – the only place in the world where you can lose yourself in a stone papyrus forest
Valley of the Kings Filled with the tombs in which ancient Egypt's rulers tried to confound both thieves and mortality as they embarked on their voyage to the afterlife
Temple of Hatshepsut The most dramatic temple in Thebes, carved into a mountain and dedicated to one of ancient Egypt's few ruling queens
Tomb of Nefertari Spectacular and colourful reliefs that show how Theban tombs looked before time and the breath of thousands of tourists dulled them

EGYPT

LUXOR – EAST BANK

Fields

Fields

To Temple of Karnak (2km)
Karnak Hotel (2.6km)

To Temple of Mut
(300m), Avenue
of Sphinxes (500m),
Temple of Amun
(950m), Temple of
Karnak (1.2km),
Airport (7km), Hegaza
(20km), Esna (55km)
& Qena (62km)

To New Gurna (1.4km) &
West Bank Monuments

Nile River

Local Ferry

Corniche el-Nil

Sharia al-Karnak

Sharia Nefertiti

Hotel Mercure

Souqs

Souqs

Souqs

Avenue of Sphinxes

Haret es-Sahabi

Sharia Yousef Hassan

Midan Hassan

Entrance to Luxor Temple

See Luxor – West Bank Map p168

Sharia al-Behr

Sharia al-Karnak

El-Corniche

Novotel

Sharia al-Mahatta

Sharia Cleopatra

Sharia Ramses

Sharia Mohammed Farid

Midan al-Mahatta

Midan Salah ad-Din

Sharia Ahmed Orabi

Sharia Abdel Moneim al-Adasi

Sharia Ahmed Orabi

Sharia Mohammed Farid

Sharia Salah ad-Din

Sharia Ahad

Sharia Badr

Sharia Shamouz

Sharia Kawkeb

Sharia Qamr

Sharia Medina al-Manawara

Sharia Televizyon

Sharia Khalid Ibn al-Walid

Train Station

To Kings Head Pub (300m),
Passport Office (550m) &
Bridge (7km)

0   250   500m
0   250   500yd

PLACES TO STAY
1 Rezeiky Camp
3 Youth Hostel
4 YMCA Camping Ground
10 Emilio Hotel
12 Mina Palace Hotel
19 Nefertiti Hotel
25 Saint Mina Hotel
27 Anglo Hotel; Salt
& Bread Cafeteria
28 New Radwan Hotel
32 Luxor Wena Hotel
34 Mercure Inn; Dawar
al-Umda Restaurant
36 Old Winter Palace;
Telephone Centre; Thomas
Cook, EgyptAir, American
Express; Masr Travel
38 Sherif Hotel
41 Grand Hotel
42 Atlas Hotel
43 Fontana Hotel
46 Happy Land Hotel
47 St Joseph Hotel

PLACES TO EAT
11 Jamboree Restaurant
15 Chez Omar
18 Amoun Restaurant;
Al-Hussein Restaurant
29 Abu Ashraf
31 Ali Baba Cafe
39 Sayyida Zeinab
44 Mish Mish

OTHER
2 General Hospital
5 Service Taxi Station
6 Luxor Museum
7 Bank of Alexandria
8 Banque Masr
9 Telephone Centrale
13 Mummification Museum
14 Police
16 Rainbow Internet
17 Aboudi Internet Cafe
20 Egyptian Exchange
Company
21 Luxor Temple
22 Bus Station
23 Mosque of Abu al-Haggag
24 Bakery
26 Fuel Station
30 Main Post Office
33 Taxis
35 Tourist Bazaar (Tourist
Police, Tourist Office,
Aboudi Bookshop &
Internet Cafe & Post Office)
37 National Bank of Egypt
(ATM)
40 Banque Misr (ATM)
45 Mantel Computer &
Internet
48 Al-Azhar Internet Cafe

EGYPT

Museums

About halfway between the Luxor and Karnak temples, **Luxor Museum** (Corniche el-Nil; admission E£30; open 9am-1pm & 4pm-9pm daily Oct-Apr, 9am-1pm & 5pm-10pm May-Sept) has a small but well-chosen collection of relics from the Theban temples and necropolis. The displays include pottery, jewellery, furniture, statues and stellae.

Down the steps just opposite Mina Palace Hotel is the small but fascinating **Mummification Museum** (Corniche el-Nil; admission E£20; open 9am-1pm & 4pm-9pm daily Oct-Apr, 9am-1pm & 5pm-10pm May-Sept). It has well-presented displays telling you everything you ever wanted to know about mummies and mummification. The mummy of a 21st dynasty official, Maserharti, as well as a host of mummified animals and the gruesome tools of the trade are all on display.

Luxor Temple

Largely built by the New Kingdom Pharaoh Amenhotep III, on the site of an older sanctuary dedicated to the Theban triad, Luxor Temple (admission E£20; open 6am-9pm daily Oct-Apr, 6am-10pm daily May-Sept) is a strikingly graceful piece of architecture close to the banks of the Nile. It was added to over the centuries by Tutankhamun, Ramses II, Nectanebo, Alexander the Great and various Romans. In the 13th century, the Arabs built a mosque in one of the interior courts.

Temples of Karnak

Karnak (admission E£20; open 6am-5.30pm daily Oct-Apr, 6am-6.30pm daily May-Sept) is possibly one of the most overwhelming monuments of the Pharaonic legacy; work was carried out here for more than 1500 years. Most was done in the New Kingdom period, although the original sanctuary of the main enclosure, the **Great Temple of Amun**, was built under the Middle Kingdom. The entire site covers an area of 1.2 sq km.

A **sphinx-lined path** that once went to the Nile takes you to the massive **1st Pylon**, from where you end up in the **Great Court**. To the left is the **Temple of Seti II**, dedicated to the triad of Theban gods – Amun, Mut and Khons. In the centre of the court is one remaining column of the **Kiosk of Taharqa**, a 25th dynasty Ethiopian pharaoh.

Beyond the 2nd Pylon is the unforgettable **Great Hypostyle Hall**. Built by Amenhotep III, Seti I and Ramses II, it covers 6000 sq metres.

There is a kitsch **sound-and-light show** (E£33) here every evening, with three or four performances in a variety of languages. Check with the tourist office for the schedule or see w www.sound-light.egypt.com.

Microbuses make the short run to the temples from the centre of Luxor for 50pt.

West Bank

The West Bank of Luxor was the necropolis of ancient Thebes, a vast city of the dead

EGYPT

West Bank Sites	
site	admission (E£)
1 Valley of the Kings (three tombs only)	20
2 Tomb of Tutankhamun	40
3 Deir al-Bahri (Temple of Hatshepsut)	12
4 Medinat Habu (Temple of Ramses III)	12
5 Ramesseum	12
6 Assasif Tombs (Kheruef & Ankhor)	12
7 Tombs of the Nobles (Menna & Nakht)	12
8 Tombs of the Nobles (Sennofer & Rekhmire)	12
9 Tombs of the Nobles (Ramose, Userhet & Khaemhet)	12
10 Deir al-Medina Temple and Tombs	12
11 Valley of the Queens (excluding Tomb of Nefertari)	12
12 Tomb of Queen Nefertari	100
13 Temple of Seti I	12
14 Assasif Tombs (Tomb of Pabasa)	12
15 Tomb of Peshedu (Deir al-Medina)	10
16 Tomb of Ay (Western Valley)	10
17 Tombs of the Nobles (Neferronpet, Dhutmosi & Nefersekheru)	12
18 Tombs of the Nobles (Khonsu, Userhet & Benia)	12

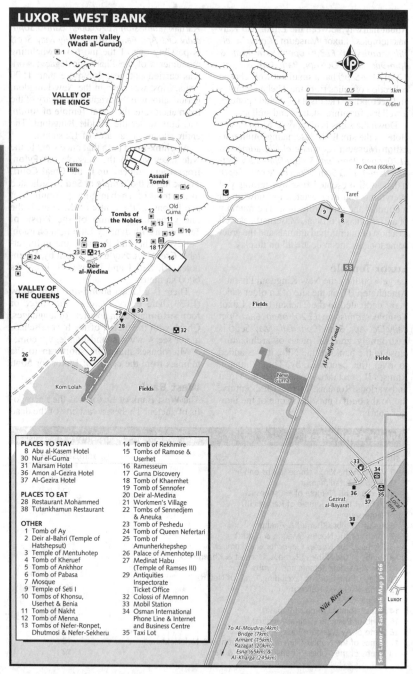

LUXOR – WEST BANK

0   0.5   1km
0   0.3   0.6mi

PLACES TO STAY
8 Abu al-Kasem Hotel
30 Nur el-Gurna
31 Marsam Hotel
36 Amon al-Gezira Hotel
37 Al-Gezira Hotel

PLACES TO EAT
28 Restaurant Mohammed
38 Tutankhamun Restaurant

OTHER
1 Tomb of Ay
2 Deir al-Bahri (Temple of Hatshepsut)
3 Temple of Mentuhotep
4 Tomb of Kherue
5 Tomb of Ankhhor
6 Tomb of Pabasa
7 Mosque
9 Temple of Seti I
10 Tombs of Khonsu, Userhet & Benia
11 Tomb of Nakht
12 Tomb of Menna
13 Tombs of Nefer-Ronpet, Dhutmosi & Nefer-Sekheru
14 Tomb of Rekhmire
15 Tombs of Ramose & Userhet
16 Ramesseum
17 Gurna Discovery
18 Tomb of Khaemhet
19 Tomb of Sennofer
20 Deir al-Medina
21 Workmen's Village
22 Tombs of Sennedjem & Aneuka
23 Tomb of Peshedu
24 Tomb of Queen Nefertari
25 Tomb of Amunherkhepshep
26 Palace of Amenhotep III
27 Medinat Habu (Temple of Ramses III)
29 Antiquities Inspectorate Ticket Office
32 Colossi of Memnon
33 Mobil Station
34 Osman International Phone Line & Internet and Business Centre
35 Taxi Lot

where magnificent temples were raised to honour the cults of pharaohs entombed in the nearby cliffs, and where queens, royal children, nobles, priests, artisans and even workers built tombs that ranged, in the quality of their design and decor, from the spectacular, such as the **Tomb of Queen Nefertari**, to the ordinary.

As an idea of distances, from the local ferry landing it is 3km straight ahead to the ticket office, past the **Colossi of Memnon**, 4km to the **Valley of the Queens** and 8km to the **Valley of the Kings**.

To see everything would cost about US$65 (without student card) and take a lot of time. With the exception of **Tutankhamun's tomb** in the Valley of the Kings, you cannot pay for admission at the sites, and individual tickets are required for each tomb, temple or group of sites, so you need to know exactly what you want to see before you set off. Tickets are valid only for the day of purchase and no refunds are given. Students pay half price. The ticket office is open from 6am to 4pm (to 5pm from June to September). All monuments are open from 7am to 5pm daily October to May (6am to 7pm June to September).

Colossi of Memnon These 18m-high statues are all that remain of a temple built by Amenhotep III. The Greeks believed that they were statues of Memnon, slain by Achilles in the Trojan War.

Temple of Seti I This pharaoh expanded the Egyptian empire to include Cyprus and parts of Mesopotamia. The temple is seldom visited, but well worth a look.

Valley of the Kings Once called the Gates of the Kings, or the Place of Truth, the valley is dominated by a barren mountain called **Al-Qurn** (The Horn). The tombs were designed to resemble the underworld, with a long, inclined rock-hewn corridor descending into either an antechamber or a series of sometimes pillared halls and ending in the burial chamber. More than 60 tombs have been excavated in the valley, although not all belong to pharaohs.

Some are closed for restoration work. **Tomb of Tutankhamun**, discovered in 1922 by Howard Carter and far from being the most interesting, requires a separate ticket. The Tomb of Ay in the Western Valley also

has a separate admission. Much better are the tombs of **Ramses VI**, **Queen Tawosret/ Sethnakht**, **Tuthmosis III** and **Siptah**.

Deir al-Bahri (Funerary Temple of Hatshepsut) Rising out of the desert plain in a series of terraces, the Funerary Temple of Queen Hatshepsut (Deir al-Bahri in Arabic), merges with the sheer limestone cliffs of the eastern face of the Theban mountain. It was desecrated and vandalised by her bitter successor, Tuthmosis III.

Assasif Tombs Three of these 18th dynasty tombs are open to the public. Like the Tombs of the Nobles further south, the artwork concentrates on events from everyday life such as fishing and hunting.

Tombs of the Nobles There are at least 12 tombs in this group worth visiting; the most colourful are those of **Ramose**, **Rekhmire** and **Nakht**. Tickets are sold for groups of two or three tombs.

Gurna Discovery This is a small, permanent exhibition of 19th-century **drawings of Gurna** by British artist Robert Hay. It documents over a century of history in this village that was once a haven of tomb robbers and now slated for demolition.

Ramesseum Ramses II was keen to leave behind him monuments to his greatness, and his funerary temple was to be the masterpiece. Sadly, it lies mostly in ruins, and the shattered remains of a giant statue of the pharaoh inspired the English poet Shelley to write 'Ozymandias' in the 19th century, ridiculing his aspiration to immortality.

Deir al-Medina This small Ptolemaic temple dedicated to the goddesses Hathor and Maat was later occupied by Christian monks – hence its name, literally 'the monastery of the city'. Near the temple are the tombs of some of the workers and artists who created the royal tombs.

Valley of the Queens Only five of the more than 70 tombs are open here. They belong to queens and other royal family members from the 19th and 20th dynasties. The crowning glory is the **Tomb of Nefertari**, whose stunning wall paintings are hailed as the finest in Egypt. Visitors are permitted to stay for 10 minutes only.

Medinat Habu The temple complex of Medinat Habu is dominated by the enormous Funerary Temple of Ramses III, inspired by the temple of his father, Ramses II. The largest temple after Karnak, it has a stunning mountain backdrop and some fascinating reliefs.

Places to Stay

Perhaps more than at any tourist destination in Egypt, the cost of accommodation in Luxor fluctuates seasonally. Some hotels drop their charges by 50% in the low season, although others don't bother altering them at all.

Try to avoid the squawking hotel touts who pounce on travellers as they get off the train/bus – they get a 25% to 40% commission for bringing you in, which ends up being factored into your bill.

Camping The **YMCA** (☎ 372 425; Sharia al-Karnak; camping per night E£4) has camping ground fees, which include the use of its 20 showers.

Rezeiky Camp (☎ 381 334, fax 381 400; tents per person E£10, vehicle E£10, hotel singles/doubles E£30/50) is where fees give access to a swimming pool and showers. There are also air-con motel-style rooms and an Internet café (50pt per minute). It's popular with overland groups.

Hostels The **Youth Hostel** (☎ 372 139; beds members/nonmembers E£10.10/11.10) is in a street just off Sharia al-Karnak. The slightly dingy rooms each have at least three beds. Breakfast is E£2.50 extra.

Hotels – South of Sharia al-Mahatta The closest place to the train station is the **Anglo Hotel** (☎/fax 381 679; singles/doubles E£20/25; doubles with bathroom & air-con

E£35). It's fairly clean and the management is friendly, but the proximity of the trains mean it can be noisy.

Grand Hotel (☎ 382 905; singles/doubles E£6/12, with air-con E£10/15), off Sharia Mohammed Farid, is clean and welcoming, has a small rooftop terrace with great views and decent shared bathrooms.

Atlas Hotel (☎ 373 514; rooms per person E£8), off Sharia Ahmed Orabi, has rooms with bathroom, some also with air-con. It's not a bad place and with 40 rooms it's rarely full. It charges E£2 for breakfast.

Fontana Hotel (☎ 380 663; bed in dorm E£7, singles/doubles with air-con & private bathroom E£15/30) is one of the best budget deals in Luxor. It has spotlessly clean rooms, a kitchen (of sorts), a rooftop terrace and washing machine for guests to use.

Sherif Hotel (☎ 370 757; Sharia Badr; doubles with shared bathroom & fan E£15, with air-con E£20) is a homey place run by a schoolteacher. It has 15 rooms, six with their own bathroom and four with air-con. It's a good deal and convenient.

Happy Land Hotel (☎ 371 828; e happy landluxor@hotmail.com; Sharia Qamr; dorm beds with fan E£8, singles/doubles with bathroom E£25/30) is where you see the fierce competition among budget hotels in Luxor at work. The rooms are spotless and breakfast, toilet paper, soap and mosquito coils are provided. It's about a 10-minute walk from the train station.

A three-star hotel with two-star prices, the **New Radwan Hotel** (☎ 385 502, fax 385 501; Sharia Abdel Moneim al-Adasi; singles/doubles E£55/70) is central with clean air-con rooms, a rooftop terrace, garden restaurant and bar.

St Joseph (☎/fax 381 707, fax 381 727; off Sharia Khalid Ibn al-Walid; singles/doubles US$30/40) is a popular, well-run, three-star hotel with a basement bar and small rooftop pool.

Although the **Mina Palace Hotel** (☎ 372 074; Corniche el-Nil; singles/doubles with air-con & private bathrooms E£60/80) could use a coat of paint, the Nile views are great. Ask for a corner room with two balconies – one looking towards Luxor Temple and the other over the Nile.

Old Winter Palace Hotel (☎ 380 422, fax 374 087, Corniche el-Nil; singles/doubles starting at US$270/304) is a monument in its own right. It's a Victorian pile, overlooking the Nile, built to attract the aristocracy of 19th-century Europe. The new addition next door is less inspiring, but cheaper.

Hotels – North of Sharia al-Mahatta
The small, friendly **Saint Mina Hotel** (☎ 375 409; off Sharia Ramses; singles/doubles E£25/45, with bathroom E£25/35) is an excellent deal. It's as good as some of the places that charge double the price.

Nefertiti Hotel (☎ 372 386; off Sharia al-Karnak; singles/doubles E£20/30) is a reasonably priced hotel with clean, air-con rooms and a roof terrace, well located on the edge of the souq.

Emilio Hotel (☎ 373 570, fax 370 000; Sharia Yousef Hassan; singles/doubles US$50/55) is a popular mid-range hotel with 48 air-con rooms and a rooftop pool.

Karnak Hotel (☎ 376 155; Sharia el-Nil; singles/doubles US$35/45) is a five-storey place about 3km north of the town centre, opposite the Luxor Hilton. If you want to be out of the bustle of Luxor, but stay on the east bank, this is a great place to be. Rates include breakfast and they go down by 20% in the summer.

Hotels – West Bank
A former archaeological mission and artists' colony, **Marsam Hotel** (Ali Abd al-Rasul Hotel, Sheikh Ali Hotel; ☎ 372 403; e marsam@africamail.com; singles/doubles E£25/50) is a West Bank institution. It has simple but clean rooms that come with breakfast.

Abu al-Kasem Hotel (☎ 310 319; Sharia Wadi al-Melouk; singles/doubles E£35/50) is near the Temple of Seti I. It has 20 dusty rooms with fans and bathrooms. Although it's basically clean, it's looking a bit scruffy these days. The best rooms overlook the mountains and there's a great view from the roof.

Nur al-Gurna (☎ 311 430; Gurna; singles/doubles E£40/60, suites E£100) is a traditional, mud-brick house, built around a palm grove, with spacious rooms and a restaurant serving local food. It comes highly recommended.

Amon al-Gezira Hotel (☎ 310 912; Al-Gezira; doubles E£60-70) is a small, spotlessly clean, family-run hotel with air-con. Five of the nine rooms have their own bathrooms; there is a terrace on each floor as well as a great roof terrace and garden.

At the **Al-Gezira Hotel** (☎/fax 310 034; Al-Gezira; singles/doubles E£40/60) the best rooms overlook the Nile and all have their own bathrooms and either air-con or ceiling fan. There is also a very pleasant rooftop restaurant overlooking the Nile where you can eat a filling Egyptian meal for around E£20. Beer is available. To get to the hotel take the small track that goes beside the bicycle hire and video rental shop just up from the local ferry landing.

The palatial, 54-room **Al-Moudira** (mobile ☎ 012-325 1307; Daba'iyya; rooms US$120-250), built to resemble a Syrian courtyard house, is secluded, exclusive and beautiful.

Places to Eat
Budget Dining Sharia al-Mahatta has a number of good sandwich stands and other cheap-eat possibilities, as well as a few juice stands at its Luxor Temple end. The other cheap eats area is Sharia Televizyon, which is where you'll find **Sayyida Zeinab** (Sharia Televizyon), one of Luxor's best kushari joints.

Salt & Bread Cafeteria (Midan al-Mahatta; meals about E£5), across from the train station, serves cheap meals. It offers a wide range of mains, including kebab, pigeon and chicken.

Abu Ashraf (Sharia al-Mahatta; dishes E£2-9) is a popular restaurant and takeaway with shwarma, roasted chicken and kushari.

Al-Hussein and **Amoun Restaurants** (Sharia al-Karnak; mains E£7-38) are two popular, adjoining restaurants that are very similar, but in fierce competition. Amoun is marginally more popular than Al-Hussein, but both serve good pizzas and basic meals.

Ali Baba Café (cnr Sharia Mohammed Farid & Sharia al-Karnak) is popular with locals and tourists. Although part of Luxor Wena Hotel, it has its own street entrance and has reasonably priced mezze and meals such as shish kebab and shish tawouk (chicken on skewers).

Mish Mish Restaurant (Sharia Televizyon; meals under E£10) serves good basic meals. Try the Mish Mish salad, a mixed platter with hummus and cold meats, enough to constitute a light meal, for E£6.

The friendly **Chez Omar** (mobile ☎ 012-282 0282; Midan Hassan; mains E£6-15), in a small oases of green, is a pleasant lunch spot with good basic Egyptian dishes, salads and french fries.

Restaurants The British-style **Kings Head Pub** (☎ 371 249; Sharia Khalid ibn al-Walid; mains E£10-30; open 24 hours) continues to be one of Luxor's most popular bars/eateries. It's a laid-back place to spend an afternoon catching up on foreign newspapers or tucking into toasted sandwiches and chips.

Jamboree Restaurant (mobile ☎ 010-146 1712; Sharia al-Montazah; mains from E£22-35) is a new British-run restaurant that has been recommended by many readers. It serves a mix of Egyptian and international fare in air-con comfort or on its small rooftop terrace.

Dawar al-Umda (☎ 373 321; Sharia Karnak; meals E£16-20) is a pleasant outdoor restaurant in the garden of the Mercure Inn that serves Egyptian specialities. There is often a belly-dancer or folkloric show during the winter high season.

Tutankhamun Restaurant (☎ 310 118; meals E£10-15), just north of the ferry dock on the West Bank, is run by a cook who once worked on one of the French archaeological missions in Luxor. He serves up excellent stews and other dishes.

Nur al-Gurna (☎ 311 430, Gurna; meals E£15-25) serves Egyptian specialities in a pleasant courtyard or cool room, depending on the season. No beer is available.

Restaurant Mohammed (☎ 311 014; Gurna; meals E£8-20) is a small, laid-back restaurant in owner Mohammed Abdel Lahi's mud-brick house, just along from the antiquities ticket office. You can get good, basic Egyptian food, as well as standard chicken and french-fry platters. Stella is available for E£7.

Getting There & Away

Air The EgyptAir office (☎ 380 580; Corniche el-Nil) is next to AmEx. There are connections with Cairo, Aswan, Sharm el-Sheikh and Abu Simbel. A one-way Luxor-Cairo ticket costs E£554 and there are frequent daily departures. Aswan (daily flights) costs E£248 one way; Sharm el-Sheikh (three flights per week) is E£480 one way. Flights to Abu Simbel operate only in the high season, when there are several departures a day via Aswan costing E£950 return.

Bus The bus station (Sharia al-Karnak) is behind Luxor Temple. There is only one daily departure to Cairo and it leaves at 7pm (E£60, 10 to 11 hours). Seven buses leave for Aswan (E£9.50, four to five hours) between 6.30am and 8pm, but only the last one has air-con. They all stop en route in Esna (E£3, 45 minutes) and Edfu (E£4.50, two hours). To Hurghada (E£21 to E£22, five hours) there are several daily buses, all of which go on to Suez (E£31 to E£42, eight to nine hours). There are 10 buses daily to Qena, but you may not be allowed to take them because of the jittery police. For the Sinai, there's just the one daily bus for Dahab at 5pm daily (E£95, 14 to 16 hours).

Train The only sleeper to Cairo (E£335, 10 hours) is the wagon-lit train that departs daily at 9pm. The only other Cairo trains that foreigners are allowed to take depart at 8.15am (1st/2nd class fares E£56/31); 8.50pm (E£60/33) and 11.10pm (E£60/36). Student discounts are available on all these services.

First/2nd-class tickets to Aswan (four hours) cost E£27/18 on the 7.30am train and E£22/14 on the 5.40pm service (three hours).

Service Taxi The service taxi station is on a street off Sharia al-Karnak, a couple of blocks inland from the Luxor Museum, but because of police restrictions you will have to take an entire car and go in convoy, which means paying about E£250 for Hurghada and E£120 for Aswan. Be at the taxi stand 30 minutes before the convoy is due to leave. Check with the tourist office for the latest convoy schedule.

Getting Around

To/From the Airport Luxor airport is 7km east of town and no taxi will take you there for less than E£20 – and will usually ask for more. There are no buses to and from the airport into town.

Motorcycle A few hotels have started renting out motorcycles for about E£40 to E£60 per day. If you are interested, hunt around a bit and check the condition of the bikes carefully.

Bicycle Luxor is bursting with bicycle rental shops and almost all hotels have bikes too. Prices range from E£6 to E£15 per day.

Hantour For about E£20 per hour you can get around town by *hantour* (horse and carriage). Rates are, of course, subject to haggling, squabbling and, occasionally, screaming.

ESNA أسنا
The hypostyle hall, with its 24 columns still supporting a roof, is all that remains of the **Temple of Khnum** *(admission adult/student E£8/4; open 6am-6.30pm daily May-Sept, to 5.30pm Oct-Apr)*, constructed by Egypt's Ptolemaic rulers.

Getting There & Away
Buses from Luxor cost E£2, but these days the police often require you to go in convoy, forcing you to hire a private taxi or go with a tour.

EDFU أدفو
The attraction in this town 53km south of Esna is the Greek-built **Temple of Horus** *(adult/student E£20/10; open 7am-4pm Oct-Apr, 7am-5pm daily May-Sept)*, the falcon-headed son of Osiris. It took about 200 years to complete. Its well-preserved state has boosted knowledge about the Pharaonic architecture it imitates.

There is one cheap hotel in Edfu, near the temple, and a couple of small places to eat at off the square.

Getting There & Away
There are frequent connections to Edfu from Luxor and Aswan, but unless you take trains, you will have to travel by taxis or buses in convoys. Buses to Luxor are E£5 and to Aswan E£2.50. There is also an 8am daily bus to Marsa Alam (E£8) on the Red Sea coast.

KOM OMBO كوم أمبو
The dual **Temple of Sobek & Haroeris** *(adult/student E£10/5; open 8am-4pm)* is dedicated to the local crocodile-god and the falcon-headed sky-god, respectively. This beautiful temple stands on a promontory at a bend in the Nile near the village of Kom Ombo. In ancient times sacred crocodiles basked in the sun on the river bank here.

Getting There & Away
Kom Ombo is an easy day trip from Aswan. However, if you don't take the train, you will be constrained by police regulations and forced to go by private taxi or bus in a convoy.

DARAW ضراوه
This small town is famous for its **camel market**, where thousands of camels from Sudan are bought and sold. Although Sunday is actually the best day to visit, the tourist office in Aswan arranges trips for tourists on Tuesday (see the boxed text).

Getting There & Away
Apart from taking the train, the only way to reach Daraw these days is in an organised tour or private taxi. In both cases you will be accompanied by a police escort.

From Caravans to Kebabs

For hundreds of years camels from Sudan have been brought to Egypt in large caravans along the Darb al-Arba'een (the 40 Days Road), the treacherous desert route thought to have been named after the number of days it took to journey from Sudan's Darfur province to southern Egypt.

In the centuries following their introduction into the region – thought to have been by the Persians in the 6th century BC – the camels brought slaves, ostrich feathers, precious stones, animal skins and other goods to Egypt, where they were used by the country's Pharaonic overlords or, in later times, distributed to the great empires in Greece, Persia, Rome and Europe. But by the 18th and 19th centuries the gradual introduction of steamers and trains in Egypt and Sudan meant that camels were no longer the most efficient way to get goods from south to north. The establishment of air links between the two countries this century seemed to seal the fate of the caravans as relics of a bygone age.

But the camels have continued to come and are sold at a weekly market at Daraw, near Kom Ombo, and also at Birqash on the outskirts of Cairo. Now, however, they themselves are often the cargo. Some are used for agricultural work, others are exported to other Middle Eastern countries, but many – if not most – are destined for the dinner tables of poor Egyptians.

ASWAN
أسوان

☎ 097

Over the centuries Aswan, Egypt's southernmost city, has been a garrison town, the gateway to Africa, a prosperous marketplace at the crossroads of the ancient caravan routes and, more recently, a popular winter resort.

It is the most attractive of the Nile towns: a drink on the terrace of the Old Cataract Hotel overlooking the river, Elephantine Island and the flocks of felucca sails on the Nile will seduce even the most spectacle-weary traveller.

Orientation

There are only three main avenues; most of the city runs parallel to the Nile. The train station is at the northern end of town, three blocks east of the river and the Corniche el-Nil, along which you'll find most of the public utilities and better hotels and restaurants.

Information

Tourist Office There is a tourist office (☎ 312 811; Midan al-Mahatta; open 8.30am-2pm & 6pm-8pm Sat-Thur, 10am-2pm & 6pm-8pm Fri) next to the train station and another (☎ 323 297; open same hours) one block in from the West Bank ferry landing on a side street.

Money The main banks all have branches on the Corniche el-Nil. **Banque Masr** and the **Banque du Caire** will issue cash advances on Visa and MasterCard. There are ATMs at the Banque Masr and the **National Bank of Egypt**. The **Bank of Alexandria** accepts Eurocheques. Banque Masr also has a **foreign-exchange booth** (open 8am-3pm & 5pm-8pm) next to its main building. **AmEx** (☎ 306 983; Corniche el-Nil) and **Thomas Cook** (☎ 304 011; Corniche el-Nil) also have offices here.

Post & Telephone The **main post office** (Corniche el-Nil; open 8am-2pm Sat-Thur) is next to the municipal swimming pool. However, poste restante must be collected from the **smaller post office** (cnr sharias Abtal at-Tahrir & Salah ad-Din; open 8am-2pm Sat-Thur).

International telephone calls can be made from the **telephone centrale** (Corniche el-Nil;

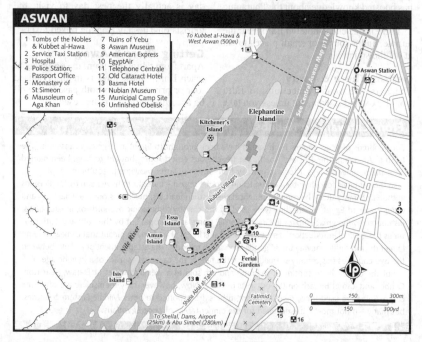

ASWAN

1 Tombs of the Nobles & Kubbet al-Hawa
2 Service Taxi Station
3 Hospital
4 Police Station; Passport Office
5 Monastery of St Simeon
6 Mausoleum of Aga Khan
7 Ruins of Yebu
8 Aswan Museum
9 American Express
10 EgyptAir
11 Telephone Centrale
12 Old Cataract Hotel
13 Basma Hotel
14 Nubian Museum
15 Municipal Camp Site
16 Unfinished Obelisk

To Kubbet al-Hawa & West Aswan (500m)

See Central Aswan Map p176

Aswan Station

Elephantine Island

Kitchener's Island

Nubian Villages

Essa Island

Amun Island

Isis Island

Nile River

Shaira Abtal at-Tahir

Ferial Gardens

Fatimid Cemetery

To Shellal, Dams, Airport (25km) & Abu Simbel (280km)

0   150   300m
0   150   300yd

open 8am-10pm) towards the southern end of town, just past the EgyptAir office. There are cardphones here (and usually stocks of cards).

Email & Internet Access There is a small but growing number of Internet cafés in Aswan:

Aswanet Internet Café (☎ 317 332) Keylany Hotel; E£10 per hour; open 9am to midnight. This is the best place in town, with lots of terminals and fast connections.

Cleopatra Hotel (☎ 314 003) Sharia as-Souq; E£20 per hour; open 8am to midnight. There's a single terminal in the lobby here.

Rowing Club Corniche el-Nil; E£15 per hour; open 9am to 11pm. This place is conveniently located in the centre of town.

There are also terminals at some of the budget hotels, such as the Rosewan and the Nubian Oasis.

East Bank
Nubian Museum A fascinating museum *(admission E£20; open 9am-1pm & 5pm-9pm)* showcasing the history, art and culture of Nubia from prehistoric times down to the present, the collection is housed in a well-designed modern building, loosely based on traditional Nubian architecture. The museum entrance is opposite Basma Hotel, about a 10-minute walk from the EgyptAir office.

Unfinished Obelisk This huge discarded obelisk *(admission E£12; open 8am-5pm Oct-May, 8am-6pm June-Sept)* lies southeast of the Fatimid Cemetery, on the edge of the northern granite quarries that supplied the ancient Egyptians with most of the hard stone used in pyramids and temples. Three sides of the shaft, which is nearly 42m long, were completed except for the inscriptions and it would have been the largest single piece of stone ever handled if a flaw had not appeared in the granite. Private taxis will charge about E£5 to take you to the site.

The River Nile
Feluccas & Ferries The river is at its most picturesque in Aswan and no visit would be complete without at least an hour spent sailing around the islands in a felucca. The official government price for hiring a felucca capable of seating one to eight people is

E£15 per hour, but with a bit of bargaining you should be able to hire a boat for three or four hours for about E£40.

Elephantine Island Once the core of what is now Aswan, the island is characterised by its huge grey boulders. Excavations of the ancient town of Yebu, now turned into an open-air museum, have revealed tombs, temples, fortifications and a Nilometer at the southern end of the island. There is also the small **Aswan Museum** *(admission E£10; open 8am-5pm Sun-Thur Oct-May, 8am-6pm Sun-Thur June-Sept).*

Kitchener's Island Lord Kitchener turned this island *(admission E£5; open daily 8.30am-5pm)* into a verdant garden, which it remains. You have to hire a boat to get there.

West Bank
Mausoleum of Aga Khan The elaborate resting place of the Aga Khan is modelled on Fatimid tombs in Cairo. Unfortunately, it's currently closed to the public.

Monastery of St Simeon This well-preserved, 6th-century mud-brick Coptic Christian monastery *(admission E£12; open 7am-5pm daily)* is a half-hour hike or short camel ride from the felucca dock near the Mausoleum of Aga Khan.

Tombs of the Nobles A few of these Old and Middle Kingdom tombs *(admission E£12; open 8am-4pm Oct-Apr, 8am-5pm May-Sept)* of local dignitaries are well-worth exploring.

Places to Stay
Camping The municipal camping ground *(behind Fatimid Cemetery; camping per person E£3, per car/motorcycle E£5/2)*, next to the unfinished obelisk, is an official facility with very basic, often filthy bathrooms.

Hostels You'll find the **Youth Hostel** *(☎ 302 235; Sharia Abtal at-Tahrir; dorm beds members/nonmembers E£7.60/8.60)* near the train station at the side entrance of the governorate-run hostel, which, just to confuse you, also calls itself a youth hostel.

Hotels – North of the Train Station Popular with budget travellers, **Rosewan Hotel**

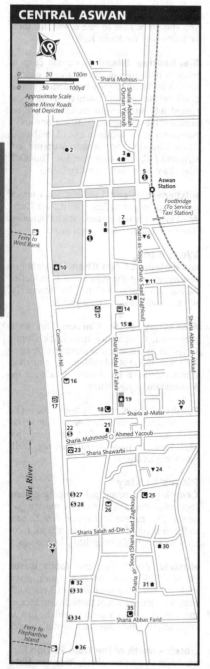

CENTRAL ASWAN

(☎ 304 497; e rosewan20@hotmail.com; singles/doubles/triples E£12/22/31) has fairly clean, rather cramped rooms with shower/toilet combinations.

The new **Queen Hotel** (☎ 326 069; Sharia Atlas; singles/doubles E£30/45, with air-con E£35/50), with spotlessly clean rooms, is close to the station, but far enough away to avoid the noise.

Although it's out of the centre, the **New Abu Simbel Hotel** (☎ 306 096; Sharia Abtal at-Tahrir; singles/doubles E£30/35) has friendly staff and a pleasant garden where you can relax with a cold beer. The screened rooms with private bathroom and air-con, are good value.

Hotels – South of the Train Station
The **Marwa Hotel** (off Sharia Abtral at-Tahrir; dorm beds E£5) is entered from an alley off Sharia Abtal at-Tahrir. Its rooms are simple and a little cramped, but the beds in a share room of three or four beds are fairly popular. A few rooms have air-con, for which you pay E£2 more.

Despite the often pushy staff, the **Nubian Oasis Hotel** (☎ 312 126; fax 312 124, Sharia as-Souq; singles/doubles E£20/35) is a popular travellers' haunt with clean, air-con rooms, a large lounge area and a rooftop garden where beer is served. It also has a computer terminal for Internet use.

Hotel Orabi (☎/fax 317 578; doubles with/without air-con E£20/25) is a friendly hotel on a quiet side street, just off the souq. Rooms are comfortable and the communal bathrooms are clean.

Keylany Hotel (☎/fax 317 332; e mo hamed@aswanet.com.eg; doubles with fan/air-con E£30/35) is an excellent budget option. Its 21 rooms have ceiling fans, pine furniture and their own spotless bathrooms.

Reached through an alleyway, **Memnon Hotel** (☎ 300 483; Corniche el-Nil; singles/doubles with fans E£45/50), above the National Bank of Egypt, has clean air-con rooms, many overlooking the Nile. There's a small pool on the roof.

Happi Hotel (☎/fax 314 115, fax 307 572; Sharia Abtal at-Tahrir; singles/doubles E£55/75) is a good lower-mid-range hotel with 64 clean, air-con rooms and friendly staff. Ask for a room with a Nile view.

Cleopatra Hotel (☎ 314 003, fax 314 002; Sharia as-Souq; singles/doubles US$48/62) is one of Aswan's few real mid-range hotels, with a central location and clean, air-con rooms. There's also a small, rooftop pool here.

The friendly, four-star **Basma Hotel** (☎ *310 901; fax 310 907, Sharia Abtal at-Tahrir; singles/doubles US$103/141)*, opposite the Nubian Museum, has a nice garden and pool, and some good Nile views. Prices are often negotiable.

The world-famous **Old Cataract Hotel** (☎ *316 002, fax 316 011; Sharia Abtal at-Tahrir; rooms start at US$175)* is where Agatha Christie wrote and where presidents and potentates have watched the Nile flow by. There are fabulous views and great Moorish architecture, but service that doesn't match the prices. Even if your budget doesn't allow you to stay here, try to come for a walk through the gardens or a drink on the terrace.

Places to Eat

The small **Medina Restaurant** *(Sharia as-Souq; dishes E£4.50-12)* is recommended for its *kofta* and kebab deals. It also serves a vegetarian meal for E£4.50.

Al-Sayyida Nefissa *(Off Sharia as-Souq; dishes E£2-11)* is tucked away in a side alley in the heart of the souq serving good-value, filling Egyptian meals.

A local institution, **Al-Masry Restaurant** (☎ *302 576; Sharia al-Matar; meals around E£16)* serves kebabs and *kofta* only, but the meat is excellent and comes with bread, salad and tahina.

Aswan Moon Restaurant (☎ *316 108, Corniche el-Nil; meals E£7-35)* is a very popular, Nile-side restaurant frequented by both foreigners and locals. It's a good place to nurse a beer, linger over a filling meal and watch the boats go by.

Chef Khalil (☎ *310 142, Sharia as-Souq; meals E£8-50)*, a tiny but popular restaurant, sells fish from Lake Nasser and the Red Sea by weight and serves it with salads, rice or french fries.

Getting There & Away

Air There are daily flights with **EgyptAir** (☎ *315 000; Corniche el-Nil)* between Aswan and Cairo (E£759 one way, 1¼ hours). The one-way hop to Luxor is E£248 (30 minutes). The return flight from Aswan to Abu Simbel costs E£675.

Bus The **bus station** *(Sharia Abtal at-Tahrir)* is in the middle of town. In their zeal to 'protect' foreigners, some policemen have been forbidding foreigners even from taking buses out of Aswan. Should this change, there is a daily bus to Cairo (E£60, 12 hours), and hourly buses to Luxor (E£6.50, four to five hours) via Kom Ombo, Edfu and Esna. There are also six buses going through to Hurghada (E£35 to E£40 seven hours) and a daily bus for Marsa Alam (E£12, five hours).

Train The wagon-lit train (No 85) costs E£335 one way to Cairo and departs at 3pm. Express train Nos 981 and 997 to Cairo leave at 5am and 8pm. The 1st/2nd class fare is E£69/38; student discounts are available. Tickets for the train to Luxor (four hours) cost E£16/11 in 1st/2nd-class on the morning service, and a few pounds more on the evening train. Both trains also stop at Kom Ombo and Edfu.

Service Taxi At the time of writing the police in Aswan were forbidding foreigners from taking service taxis, often turning them back at the checkpoint just north of town. As with all such directives, people do get around the rules, but in general it's better to take the bus or train, or else get a group of people together and hire a private taxi.

Felucca Aswan is the best place to arrange overnight felucca trips because even if the winds fail, the Nile's strong currents will propel you north. The most popular trips are to Kom Ombo (one night, two days) or Edfu (three days, two nights), but some people go on to Luxor (four days, three nights).

Officially, feluccas can carry a minimum of six passengers and a maximum of eight, for the following prices: E£25 per person to Kom Ombo, E£45 to Edfu, E£60 to Luxor. On top of this you must add E£5 for police registration, plus there's the cost of food supplies.

Boat to Sudan See the introductory Getting There & Away section to this chapter.

Getting Around

To/From the Airport The airport is about 25km southwest of town and the taxi fare is around E£20.

Taxi A taxi tour that includes the Temple of Philae, High Dam and unfinished obelisk near the Fatimid Cemetery costs around E£40 for five to six people.

Bicycle There are a few places at the train station end of Sharia as-Souq where you can hire bicycles for about E£5 a day – try around the Marwa and Ramses hotels.

AROUND ASWAN
Temple of Philae   معبد فيله
South of Aswan and relocated to another island to save it from being flooded in the 1960s (see the following High Dam section), the Temple of Philae (admission E£20; open 8am-4pm Oct-May, 7am-5pm daily June-Sept) was dedicated to Isis, who found the heart of her slain brother, Osiris, on Philae Island (now submerged). Most of the temple was built by the Ptolemaic dynasty and Romans, and early Christians turned the hypostyle hall into a chapel. It is possible to organise taxi trips to the boat landing at Shellal south of the Old Dam, or you can walk if you can get a lift to the dam.

Tickets are purchased from the small office before the boat landing at Shellal. The boat costs E£20 (E£22 at night; maximum eight people) for the return trip.

A **sound-and-light show** (E£33) is held at the temple – there are usually three performances a night. The tourist office can give you the latest schedule.

High Dam   السد العالي
The controversial Sadd al-Ali, the High Dam, 17km south of Aswan, is 3.6km across, 980m wide at its base and 111m high at its highest point. About 35,000 people helped build this enormous structure and 451 of them died during its construction. When it was completed in 1971 the water that collected behind it became Lake Nasser, the world's largest artificial lake. In creating the lake, a number of Pharaonic monuments had to be rescued in a US$40 million Unesco effort – they were taken to pieces and rebuilt at new sites above the risen water line.

Most people get to the High Dam as part of an organised trip to sites around Aswan but many are disappointed by the visit, expecting more spectacular views.

The silt-rich waters of Lake Nasser teem with fish and fishing on the lake is growing in popularity. See the Activities section at the beginning of this chapter for more information about fishing safaris.

ABU SIMBEL   أبو سمبل
☎ 097
Carved out of a mountainside and the single most photogenic of all Egypt's monuments, Ramses II's **Great Temple of Abu Simbel** (adult/student E£36/18, including mandatory guide; open 8am-5pm Oct-May, 8am-6pm May-Sept) was one of the monuments moved out of the way of the rising waters of Lake Nasser in the 1960s. The temple was dedicated to the gods Ra-Harakhty, Amun, Ptah and the deified pharaoh himself. Guarding the entrance, the four famous colossal statues of Ramses II sit majestically, each more than 20m tall, with smaller statues of the pharaoh's mother, Queen Tuya, his wife Nefertari and some of their children.

The other temple at the Abu Simbel complex is the rock-cut **Temple of Hathor**.

Sound-and-light shows (E£50 per person plus E£5 tax) are performed here each night. The tourist office in Aswan has the latest schedule.

Places to Stay
The long-standing, four-star **Nefertari Hotel** (☎ 400 508/9; singles/doubles US$70/80) is about 400m from the temples, overlooking Lake Nasser. Prices include breakfast but not taxes.

Abu Simbel Village (☎/fax 400 092; singles/doubles US$35/40) is the cheapest option in town. All rooms have bathrooms and air-con.

Getting There & Away
The road to Abu Simbel reopened to foreigners in 2001, but travel on it has to be made in convoy. Check with the tourist office in Aswan for the latest convoy times. EgyptAir has several flights to Abu Simbel each day (see the Aswan Getting There & Away section).

Western Oases   الوحات الغربية

The five main oases of the Western Desert are attracting a growing number of travellers, but still remain off the main tourist trail. The government has dubbed the string of oases the New Valley Province and hopes to develop the area, and so create new possibilities for an exploding population. Asphalt roads link all the oases now, four of them in a long loop from Asyut around to Cairo. Siwa, out near the Libyan frontier, is linked by road to Bahariyya, but permits are needed to use it. The easiest access is via Marsa Matruh on the Mediterranean coast.

KHARGA OASIS الواحات الخرجة
☎ 092

About 235km south of Asyut is the largest of the oases, Kharga. The town, Al-Kharga, is the administrative centre of the New Valley governorate, which also includes the Dakhla and Farafra Oases. The town is of no interest, but to the north you'll find the **Temple of Hibis**, built to the god Amun by the Persian Emperor Darius I. To the east are the remains of the **Temple of An-Nadura**, built by the Romans. Just north of the Temple of Hibis is the Coptic **Necropolis of Al-Bagawat**, dating as far back as the 4th century. South of the town are the Roman fortified temples of **Qasr al-Ghueita** and **Qasr az-Zayyan**.

Places to Stay & Eat
You can **camp** (E£7 per person) in the grounds of the Kharga Oasis Hotel and use the toilet and shower inside.

Convenient for buses and service taxis, **Dar al-Bayda Hotel** (☎ 921 717; Midan Sho'ala; singles/doubles E£15/22) has clean, but noisy rooms, most with fans. Breakfast is E£5 extra.

Hamad Allah Hotel (☎ 920 638, fax 925 017; singles/doubles E£31/53, with air-con E£45/75.25) is popular with overland tour groups. Rooms come with bathroom, fridge, TV and breakfast. Set lunch (E£17) and dinner (E£19) are available and there's a bar.

Kharga Oasis Hotel (☎ 921 500; Midan Nasser; singles/doubles E£65/87) is a modern homage to concrete and a favoured watering hole for thirsty desert travellers. It has a nice, palm-filled garden and serves beer. Prices include breakfast and taxes. The restaurant has lunches for E£21 and dinners for E£24.

Restaurants are few and far between in Kharga and the best places to eat are the hotels. Otherwise, try **Al-Ahram** at the front of the Waha Hotel, which sells chicken and vegetable dishes.

Getting There & Away
EgyptAir (☎ 920 838) flies from Cairo to Al-Kharga and back again on Sunday and Wednesday; the fare is E£619 one way.

Three buses leave Al-Kharga daily for Cairo (E£25 to E£E£35, seven to eight hours) via Asyut, and there are several buses from Al-Kharga to Asyut (E£7 to E£8, three to four hours).

Buses to Dakhla (E£5 to E£7, three hours) leave at 7am, noon and 2.30pm and there's a bus to Luxor each Friday, Sunday and Tuesday at 7.30am.

A service taxi to Dakhla takes three hours and costs E£7.

There's also a train from Al-Kharga to Luxor every Friday at 7am. The trip takes about seven hours and tickets (3rd class only) cost E£9.80 (students E£4.90).

DAKHLA OASIS الواحات الدخلة
☎ 092

Located 190km west of Kharga, Dakhla was created from more than 600 natural springs and ponds and has been lived in continuously since prehistoric times. It contains two small towns, Mut and Al-Qasr. Mut is the bigger and has most of the hotels and public utilities. There are government-run **hot springs** 3km to its north. Another 30km brings you to the remarkable medieval mud-brick town of **Al-Qasr**. Watch out for the 12th-century minaret.

Places to Stay
It's possible to **camp** near the dunes west of Mut or in Al-Qasr, on a desert plateau just north of town, but you should check with the **tourist office** (☎ 821 686; Sharia as-Sawra al-Khadra) first.

Al-Qasr Hotel (☎ 876 013; Al-Qasr; beds E£7) is conveniently located on the main road near the entry to the old town. The friendly Al-Qasr has four big, screened rooms with narrow balconies; breakfast is E£2 extra. Shared bathrooms are clean and, contrary to the norm, have hot water only.

Anwar Paradise Hotel (☎ 820 070; Sharia Basateen, Mut; singles/doubles E£20/40) is a new hotel above the successful restaurant of the same name. Rooms and attached bathrooms are spotless.

Nasser's Hotel (Sheikh Waley, rooms per person E£10) is a good cheap option. This five-bedroom, mud-brick house is on the edge of Sheikh Waley, a village about 5km east of Mut on the road to Kharga Oasis (or 20 minutes by bicycle from Mut).

Bedouin Camp (☎ 830 604/5; rooms per person E£15) is on a desert hilltop near the small village of Al-Dohous, 7km north of Mut. Run by Bedouin, the camp has eight reed huts and three mud-brick rooms that are simple, very clean and quiet, and have great views. Rates include breakfast.

Mebarez Hotel (☎/fax 821 524; singles/ doubles E£28/42, with bathroom & air-con E£44/58) is a four-storey hotel on the main road to Al-Qasr that's popular with groups.

Places to Eat

Ahmed Hamdy's Restaurant (☎ 820 767; Sharia as-Sawra al-Khadra; dishes E£3-15) is popular with travellers and serves hearty chicken and kebab meals, plus beer and excellent, freshly squeezed lime juices.

Abu Mohammed Restaurant (Sharia as-Sawra al-Khadra; meals E£8-10) is an excellent little restaurant with what seems to be unending servings of good-value soups, vegetables, rice, kebab, salads, sweets and nonalcoholic Stella. All emerge from a pristine kitchen.

Anwar Paradise Restaurant (☎ 820 070; Sharia Basateen; dishes E£2-15), very popular with locals, looks out over a small square and serves substantial meals as well as *fuul* and *ta'amiyya* sandwiches.

Getting There & Away

At the time of writing, EgyptAir had suspended its flights to Dakhla.

Bus services to Cairo (E£30 to E£45, eight to 10 hours) via Kharga oasis (E£8) and Asyut (E£15, five hours) leave every day at 6am, 7am and 9pm. You can also go to Cairo via Farafra and Bahariyya Oases at 6am for E£35 (six to eight hours). Service taxis leave from the bus station on Sharia as-Sawra al-Khadra and cost E£7 to Al-Kharga and E£10 to either Farafra Oasis or Asyut. There are also microbuses to Farafra Oasis for E£10.

FARAFRA OASIS　　واحة فرافرا
☎ 019

About 300km northwest of Dakhla, Farafra is the smallest and most untouched of the oases. There is really nothing much to see here, except for palms and fruit trees bear-

ing everything from dates to apricots. About 45km north of town is the stunning **White Desert**, to which you can organise excursions from the town.

Places to Stay & Eat

There are only two places to stay in town. Both can arrange desert safaris.

Tastefully designed in mud-brick, the **Al-Badawiyya Safari & Hotel** (☎ 02-345 85 24; E£10; doubles without/with bathroom E£30/E£60; with bathroom & half-board E£160) is starting to show its age, but remains something of a desert institution. The rooms come in different styles – the more expensive ones have a sitting area and TV. The food here is fresh and good.

Aquasun Resort (mobile ☎ 010-667 8099; singles/doubles E£65/100) is a new, mud-brick hotel built around a garden adjacent to a hot spring. The sulphurous waters go straight into the hotel's small pool.

Food is limited to meals at the hotels or **Hussein** (dishes E£3-10), on the main road, which is the only real restaurant in town. Even here most of the pots are empty by 7pm, so come early.

Getting There & Away

There are buses to Cairo (E£25 to E£30, seven to nine hours) via Bahariyya (E£10, 2½ hours) every day at 6am and noon. Two more go from Farafra to Dakhla (E£15, three to four hours): the first leaves between 1pm and 2pm and the other between 1am and 2am. Buses are caught from the Al-Tamawy Cafeteria, the petrol station or in front of Al-Badawiyya Hotel. Tickets are issued on board.

Microbuses to Dakhla leave from in front of the Al-Tamawy Cafeteria whenever they have a full load and a seat costs E£10. These don't stop at the other petrol station or the hotel.

BAHARIYYA OASIS　　الواحة البحرية
☎ 011

About 185km northeast of Farafra and 330km southeast of Cairo is the oasis of Bahariyya. Buses will bring you to **Bawiti**, the main village. The attractions include the **Temple of Alexander**, 26th-dynasty tombs at **Qarat Qasr Salim**, Graeco-Roman **Golden Mummies** on show at the **antiquities inspectorate** (just south of the main road, Bawiti;

admission to all local antiquities sites E£30; open 8am-2pm daily).

The oasis is also famous for its hot and cold **springs**. One of the best hot springs, Bir al-Ghaba, is accessible only by 4WD. Ask at the Alpenblick Hotel in Bawati, which has a camp site there.

Places to Stay & Eat

The government-run **Paradise Hotel** *(☎ 552 600; triples per person E£3.50)*, in the centre of town, has been renovated, although it remains quite basic. There are six rooms with three beds. Breakfast on the small vine-covered terrace is an extra E£1.50.

Ahmed's Safari Camp *(☎/fax 552 090; beds on roof E£3, hut beds E£4, dorm beds E£5, doubles with bathroom per person E£25)* is a popular travellers' haunt about 4km west of the centre. It has a wide variety of rooms and also rents bikes and runs desert safaris.

Al-Beshmo Lodge *(☎/fax 552 177; Bawiti; singles/doubles US$28/32)* is a comfortable, 20-room hotel on the edge of palm groves beside the Al-Beshmo spring. It's one of the more tasteful options in town.

The Alpenblick Hotel *(☎ 552 184)* has 15 huts with mattresses out at Bir al-Ghaba. The enclosure is watched by a warden, who will also help out with tea and firewood. It costs E£10 a night and is very peaceful, but you must bring your own food.

Unless you make your own meals, your food will be limited to the hotels or the town's one restaurant, **Popular Restaurant** *(Bawiti; meals around E£12)*, also known as Bayoumi's, which serves a selection of dishes like chicken, soup, rice and vegetables. It's also open for breakfast.

Getting There & Away

There are three daily buses to Cairo (E£12.50 to E£15). The 7am and 3pm services originate from Farafra and times can vary.

Heading to Farafra (E£10, two hours) you can pick up one of the buses from Cairo, which are supposed to leave Bahariyya at 11.30am, 1pm and 7.30pm.

There's supposedly a service taxi going to Sayyida Zeinab in Cairo between 3pm and 4pm daily, but don't count on it. Ask at the Popular Restaurant. A service taxi to Farafra (and they're not very frequent) will also cost E£11. Microbuses to either place cost about the same, but are more frequent.

They can be caught opposite the police intelligence office on the main road or, again, ask at the Popular Restaurant.

If you want to get a taxi to Siwa, expect to pay at least E£550.

SIWA OASIS واحة سيوه
☎ 046

The lush and productive Western Desert oasis of Siwa, famous throughout the country for its dates and olives, is 300km southwest of Marsa Matruh and 550km west of Cairo, near the Libyan border. There are no banks here so bring all the money you'll need.

Things to See & Do

Apart from date palms, there are a couple of **springs** where you can swim, the remains of the **temple of Amun** some Graeco-Roman **tombs** and a small **museum** of local traditions. The town centre is marked by the remnants of the medieval, mud-brick **fortress of Shali**. At the edge of town are the towering dunes of the **Great Sand Sea**. Several shops around town sell local crafts such as basket ware and jewellery.

Places to Stay

Palm Trees Hotel *(☎ 460 2204; doubles with/without private bathroom E£12/10)*, just off the main square, is a popular place to stay. Its clean rooms have fans and screened windows, and there's a shady, palm-filled garden.

Yousef Hotel *(☎ 460 2162; beds E£5)* is smack in the centre of town and run by the amiable Yousef. Some of the rooms are tiny, but everything is clean, the beds are comfortable, and the showers steaming with hot water. Prices are without breakfast.

At the **Cleopatra Hotel** *(☎ 460 2148; singles/doubles E£10/13, with bathroom E£13/18, chalet singles/doubles E£34/54)* the chalets have ceiling fans and simple wooden furniture, and are better than the shabby regular rooms. None of the prices include breakfast. It's directly south of the main square.

Shali Lodge *(☎ 460 1299, fax 460 1799; singles/doubles E£150/200)* is a tiny but beautiful mud-brick hotel in a lush palm grove a couple of hundred metres from the main square. It is highly recommended. Reservations are necessary.

EGYPT

Adrére Amellal (☎ 02-735 0052, fax 736 3331; doubles US$350 full board), outside the town, at Sidi Jaafar, is Egypt's most famous 'ecolodge'. Here the fortunate guests eat gourmet food under the stars, soak in their private Roman spring and gaze out over the Great Sand Sea. If you want something special and money is no object, this is it.

Places to Eat
Abdu Restaurant (dishes E£5-15), across the road from Yousef Hotel, is an ever-popular restaurant and hangout. It serves a wide range of traditional dishes, vegetable stews, couscous and roasted chickens. Service is slow.

Alexander Restaurant (dishes E£5-15), just along the street from the Yousef Hotel, is another popular budget hangout and has a good selection of vegetarian dishes.

Kenooz Siwa (☎ 460 1299; Shali Lodge; dishes E£3-20), on a rooftop among the palms next to Shali Lodge, is the best restaurant in town. It serves up simple but good stews, chicken and salad, or you can lean back on cushions, smoke a *sheesha* (water pipe) and sip tea.

There are several places dotted around the square where you can have a *sheesha* or a cup of coffee and play some backgammon. **Bakri's Café** (also known as the Sohag Rest House) next to Abdu Restaurant is one of the most popular.

Getting There & Away
There are three daily buses to Alexandria (E£27, eight hours), stopping at Marsa Matruh (E£12, four hours). You'll need to book ahead at the ticket kiosk in the main square. There is an additional daily service to Marsa Matruh only at 2pm that costs E£10; no bookings are taken.

Although there is a road linking the oases of Siwa and Bahariyya, no public transport travels along it. Some 4WD owners in town will take you if you can manage the E£550 they're charging. To get a permit to drive to Bahariyya, contact the tourist office.

Alexandria & the Mediterranean Coast

ALEXANDRIA   الاسكندرية
☎ 03

Alexandria (Iskendariyya) is often said to be the greatest historical city with the least to show. It was founded by Alexander the Great, yet bears no trace of him; it was the site of one of the wonders of the ancient world, but there's not a single notable monument in the city today; it was ruled by Cleopatra (see the boxed text) and was a rival of Rome, yet it's now an overcrowded provincial city short on prestige.

The reality of modern-day Alexandria is a grubby compress of apartment blocks jostling at the seafront. First-time visitors can't help but be disappointed. But to judge Alexandria on first appearances is to sell the city short. It's a city of nuances and shades, with plenty to be discovered if you're prepared to invest the time.

History
Established in 332 BC by Alexander the Great, the city became a major trade centre and focal point of learning for the entire

---

Cleopatra

Cleopatra (69–30 BC), the seventh queen of her lineage to bear that name, belonged to the Ptolemaic dynasty. In 51 BC at the age of 18 she became coregent alongside her 10-year-old brother Ptolemy XIII. The siblings fought but thanks to an alliance with Julius Caesar, to whom she bore a child, Cleopatra prevailed. Following the assassination of Caesar, the young queen found herself a new protector and husband in Roman general Marc Antony. But the union was not popular in Rome, especially with Caesar's nephew Octavian, whose sister was already married to Antony. Battle ensued and the Egyptian fleet was defeated at Actium in 31 BC by the superior forces of Octavian (who later became Emperor Augustus). As the victorious Roman fleet sailed towards Egypt, Cleopatra, rather than face capture and believing Marc Antony to be dead, reputedly put an asp to her breast. So ended the Ptolemaic dynasty.

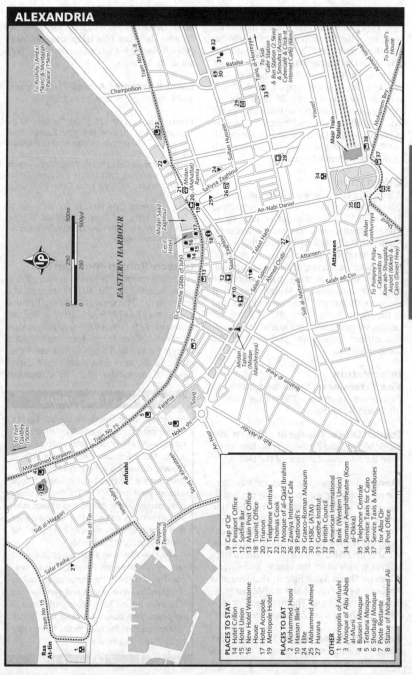

ALEXANDRIA

EGYPT

EASTERN HARBOUR

PLACES TO STAY
14 Hotel Crillon
15 Hotel Union
16 New Hotel Welcome House
17 Hotel Acropole
19 Metropole Hotel

PLACES TO EAT
2 Mohammed Hosni
10 Hassan Bleik
24 Elite
25 Mohammed Ahmed
27 Havana

OTHER
1 Necropolis of Anfushi
3 Mosque of Abu Abbas al-Mursi
4 Busseiri Mosque
5 Terbana Mosque
6 Shorbagi Mosque
7 Poste Restante
8 Statue of Mohammed Ali
9 Cap d'Or
11 Passport Office
12 Spitfire Bar
13 Main Post Office
18 Tourist Office
20 Trianon
21 Telephone Centrale
22 Thomas Cook
23 Mosque of al-Qaid Ibrahim
26 Zawiya Internet Cafe
28 Graeco-Roman Museum
29 Pastroudi's
30 HSBC (ATM)
31 Goethe Institut
32 British Council
33 American International Bank (Western Union)
34 Roman Amphitheatre (Kom al-Dikka)
35 Telephone Centrale
36 Service Taxis for Cairo
37 Service Taxis & Minibuses for Abu Qir
38 Post Office

Mediterranean world. Its ancient library held 500,000 volumes and the Pharos lighthouse was one of the Seven Wonders of the World (see the boxed text 'The Pharos of Alexandria'). Alexandria continued as the capital of Egypt under the Romans and their eastern offshoot, the Byzantine empire. From the 4th century onwards the city declined into insignificance. Napoleon's arrival and Alexandria's subsequent redevelopment as a major port attracted people from all over the world, but the 1952 Revolution put an end to much of the city's pluralistic charm.

Orientation

Alexandria is a true waterfront city, nearly 20km long from east to west and only about 3km wide. The focal point of the city is Midan Ramla, also known as Mahattat Ramla (Ramla station) because this is the central terminus for the city's tram lines. Immediately adjacent is Midan Saad Zaghloul, a large square running back from the seafront and joining Midan Ramla at the corner. Around these two midans, and in the streets to the south and west, are the central shopping area, the tourist office, airline offices, restaurants and most of the cheaper hotels.

Information

Visa Extensions The passport office *(28 Talaat Harb; open 8am-1.30pm Sat-Thur)* is off Sharia Salah Salem.

Tourist Office The tourist office *(☎ 807 9885; Midan Saad Zaghloul; open 8am-6pm)* is on the southwest corner of the midan.

Money For changing cash or travellers cheques, the simplest option is to use one of the many exchange bureaus on the side streets between Midan Ramla and the Corniche. There are also dozens of currency exchange offices along Talaat Harb. There is an ATM at the **HSBC** *(47 Sultan Hussein)*, a five-minute walk east of the centre, and several others on Sharia Salah Salem. There are also **AmEx** *(☎ 541 0177; 34 Sharia al-Moaskar ar-Romani, Rushdy)* and **Thomas Cook** *(☎ 484 7830; 15 Sharia Saad Zaghloul)* offices here.

Post, Telephone & Fax The **main post office** is a small office just east of Midan Orabi. To pick up poste restante you must go to the mail sorting centre one block west of Midan Orabi and a block north of Midan Tahrir. There are two **telephone** *centrales (Midan Ramla • Midan Gomhuriyya)*; both are open 24 hours.

Email & Internet Access There are several Internet cafés in Alexandria:

Access Cybercafé (☎ 425 5766) 1st floor of the shopping mall beside the new Zahran Mall, Smouha. E£10 per hour. Open 9am to midnight daily.
Click-It Internet Café (☎ 311 7520) Ground floor of the shopping mall beside the new Zahran Mall, Smouha. E£12 per hour. Open 10.30am to 1am daily.
Zawiya Internet Café (☎ 484 8014) Sharia Dr Hassan Fadaly, off Safiyya Zaghloul. E£5 per hour. Open 10am to 1am Saturday to Thursday, 2pm to 1am Friday.

Graeco-Roman Museum

Ancient Alexandria is almost as intangible to us as Atlantis, but the 40,000 artefacts collected in the 24 rooms of this excellent museum *(☎ 483 6434; 5 Al-Mathaf ar-Romani; admission E£16; open 9am-4pm daily, closed 11.30am-1.30pm Fri)* go some way towards bringing it to life. Things to look out for include, in the very first room, three carved heads of Alexander (the city's founder),

The Pharos of Alexandria

According to classical accounts, Egypt's Mediterranean coast was notoriously treacherous, with hidden rocks and sandbanks and a flat, featureless shoreline offering little in the way of navigational aids. So Ptolemy I ordered a great tower to be built, one that took a dozen years to complete. The finished structure, inaugurated in 283 BC was of such massive proportions and of such a unique nature that ancient scholars regarded it as one of the Seven Wonders of the World.

The tower became a lighthouse in the 1st century AD, when the Romans added a beacon. For 17 centuries the Pharos guided sailors, withstanding winds, floods and even the odd tidal wave. But in 1303 a violent earthquake finally brought it down. A century later, Sultan Qaitbey quarried the ruins for the fortress that he built on the same site.

while in room No 18 the fourth cabinet on the left contains several small terracotta lanterns in the form of the ancient Pharos lighthouse.

Roman Amphitheatre (Kom al-Dikka)

The 13 white marble terraces of the only Roman theatre *(Sharia Yousef; adult/student E£6/3; open 9am-4pm daily)* in Egypt were discovered in 1964. The theatre is at the northern end of the square with the train station.

Catacombs of Kom ash-Shuqqafa

Dating back to the 2nd century AD, the tombs *(Carmous; admission E£12; open 8.30am-4pm daily)* of Kom ash-Shuqqafa held about 300 corpses. They are in the southwest of the city, not far from the famed, misnamed and disappointing **Pompey's Pillar**.

Fort Qaitbey

The Mamluk sultan Qaitbey built a fortress *(admission E£20; open 9am-4pm daily)* on the foundations of the destroyed Pharos lighthouse in 1480. In the 19th century Mohammed Ali expanded its defences, but it was badly damaged during British bombardments in 1882. Take tram No 15 from Mahattat Ramla.

Montazah Palace

Once the summer residence of the royal family, Montazah Palace, at the eastern extremity of the city, is now reserved for the president, but the **gardens** *(admission E£4; open 8am-10pm June-Sept, to 8pm Oct-May)* are still a pleasant place to wander around. Bus No 260 from Midan Orabi passes the gardens on its way to Abu Qir, as does bus No 250 from Masr train station.

Places to Stay

New Hotel Welcome House *(☎ 480 6402; 8 Sharia Gamal ad-Din Yassin; doubles E£25)* is the best of three otherwise grotty hostels occupying the top two floors of the same building. Rooms vary in quality, but some attempt has been made to look after them.

Hotel Acropole *(☎ 480 5980; 4th floor, 1 Gamal ad-Din Yassin; singles E£15-20, doubles E£25-35)* has some rooms with great views over Midan Saad Zaghloul. Though many of the rooms are very shabby, the place has a pleasant rambling, chaotic appeal.

Hotel Union *(☎ 480 7312, fax 480 7350; 5th floor, 164 Sharia 26th of July; singles/ doubles E£35/50, with bathroom E£45/60)* offers great value with three-star accommodation at more or less budget rates. Most of the spotlessly clean rooms have harbour views. Breakfast is E£8 extra. Reservations are recommended.

Hotel Crillon *(☎ 480 0330; 5 Sharia Adib Ishaq, 4th floor; doubles with shower E£53, with bathroom E£67)*, two blocks back from Midan Saad Zaghloul, runs a close second to the Union in the cleanliness stakes – and most rooms have balconies with harbour views. Reservations are a must.

Metropole Hotel *(☎ 484 0910, fax 482 2040; 52 Sharia Saad Zaghloul; singles/ doubles from US$100/120)* is an excellent, central, four-star hotel with the high ceilings and ornate cornices that hint at Alexandria's early 20th-century heyday. Try to get rooms overlooking the harbour.

Places to Eat

The place for cheap eating is around the area where Sharia Safiyya Zaghloul meets Midan Ramla, and along Sharia Shakor Pasha, one street over to the west. There are plenty of little *fuul* and *ta'amiyya* places here as well as sandwich shops and the odd *kushari* joint.

Mohammed Ahmed *(317 Sharia Shakor Pasha; dishes E£2-10)*, one of best *fuul* places in town, also serves *ta'amiyya*, omelettes and fried cheese. The food's a bit greasy, but Alexandrians swear by it and the place is always packed.

Hassan Bleik *(18 Sharia Saad Zaghloul; dishes E£6-20; open noon-6pm)* Located next to Sofianopoulo Coffee Store, this is a venerable Lebanese restaurant. Never mind the grubby tablecloths, it has an excellent menu of traditional Levantine dishes.

Havana *(☎ 483 0661; cnr Sharia Ahmed Orabi & Sidi al-Metwali, Attareen; dishes E£5-20)* is primarily a bar (see the following Entertainment section), but also serves great food. The fried calamari is superb and the pizzas are also highly recommended.

Elite *(☎ 482 3592; 43 Sharia Safiyya Zaghloul; dishes E£4.50-30)* is another of those Alexandrian time-warps: it faintly resembles an old US diner and seems sealed in a

1950s bubble. The menu is displayed outside, beside the door, and contains meals from spaghetti bolognaise to grilled meats.

Some of Alexandria's best restaurants for straightforward, good-value, street-side dining can be found in the Anfushi district, south of Fort Qaitbey, particularly along Sharia Safar Pasha. There are at least half a dozen restaurants specialising in grilled meats and fish – we recommend **Mohammed Hosni** *(48 Sharia Safar Pasha; 2-course meals E£16-24).*

Entertainment

Our vote for the best bar in Egypt goes to the **Havana**. It's run by Nagy, whose father bought the place from a departing Greek in the 1950s. Since that time some of the details may have changed a little, but a cosmopolitan, *laissez-faire* air still prevails at its six tables.

Cap d'Or *(4 Sharia Adib)*, almost as good as the Havana, has the feel of an Andalusian tapas bar. Plenty of people come here to eat calamari, shrimp or fish, all of which are excellent, but it's an equally fine place just to pull up a stool and settle in for a Stella.

Spitfire Bar *(7 rue de l'Ancienne Bourse)* has a reputation as a sailors' bar and feels almost like a Bangkok bar – but without the women of course.

Alexandria has a great café scene.

Pastroudi's *(39 Tariq al-Horreyya)* was founded by Greeks in 1923 and immortalised in Lawrence Durrell's *The Alexandria Quartet*. It's beside the Amir Cinema.

Trianon *(Midan Ramla)* was a favourite of the Alexandrian-Greek poet Cavafy, who worked in offices above it. It's still immensely popular and a good place for a continental-style breakfast.

Getting There & Away

Air There are direct international flights from Alexandria to Athens (Olympic Airways) and Frankfurt (Lufthansa), and to Saudi Arabia and Dubai (EgyptAir).

Air travel to Alexandria from within Egypt is expensive; the one-way fare for the 40-minute flight from Cairo is E£248.

Bus Long-distance buses all go from one garage behind Sidi Gaber train station; minibus No 1 from outside the Cecil Hotel connects it with the city centre.

From here **Superjet** has buses to Cairo (E£20 to E£31, 2½ hours) every 30 minutes from 5am to 10pm. **West Delta Bus Co** services are cheaper (E£16 to E£25), and leave with the same frequency.

West Delta Bus Co has frequent buses to Marsa Matruh (E£15 to E£23), almost all of which go on to Sallum (E£23, nine hours). The 8.30am, 11am and 2pm buses go to Siwa (E£30, nine hours).

There's one Superjet service a day at 6.30pm from Alexandria to Sharm el-Sheikh (E£77, seven hours). There's also one Superjet bus daily to Port Said (E£22, four hours) and one to Hurghada (E£75, nine hours) at 8pm. West Delta Bus Co has four services a day to Port Said (E£17 to E£20), two to Ismailia (E£17) at 7am and 2.30pm, and two to Suez (E£20) at 6.30am and 2.30pm. The **Upper Egypt Bus Company** also has a Hurghada (E£55, nine hours) bus departing at 6.30pm daily.

Train Alexandria's main train terminal is **Masr Station** *(Mahattat Masr)*, although Sidi Gaber, which serves the populous eastern suburbs, is almost as busy. Cairo-bound trains leave from here at least hourly, from about 5am to 10pm (there's also one at 3.25am), stopping five minutes later at Sidi Gaber station. The best trains, the Turbini and Espani trains, depart Mahattat Masr at 7am, 8am, 2pm, 3pm, 7pm, 7.30pm and 10.15pm. Tickets in 1st/2nd class air-con cost E£22/17 (three hours).

Service Taxi The service taxi station is across the midan from the Masr train station. The fares are between E£8 and E£10 to Cairo (three hours) or Marsa Matruh.

Getting Around

To/From the Airport The airport *(☎ 427 1036)* has been temporarily relocated to Burg al-Arab, 60km west of the city. To get there take bus No 555 from in front of the Cecil Hotel. A taxi should cost no more than E£30. Should the old airport re-open, you can take bus No 203 from Midan Ramla or No 703 from Midan Orabi. A taxi should cost no more than E£10.

Bus & Minibus As a visitor to Alexandria, you won't use the buses at all – the trams are a much better way of getting around.

Tram Midan Ramla is the main tram station and from here lime-yellow-coloured trams (20pt) go west and blue ones go east.

Taxi A short trip, say from Midan Ramla to Masr train station, will cost E£2, while between E£3 and E£4 is reasonable for a trip to the eastern beaches.

EL ALAMEIN العلمين
☎ 03

The beginning of General Montgomery's offensive on 23 October 1942 ruined forever Field Marshall Rommel's hopes of pushing his Afrika Korps through to the Suez Canal. Within two weeks he was on the run, and El Alamein, 105km west of Alexandria, went down as the first great turning point of WWII. Today, a **war museum** and the Commonwealth, German and Italian **war cemeteries** mark the scene of one of the biggest tank battles in history.

If you have to stay overnight, **Al-Amana Hotel** (☎ 493 8324; rooms with/without bathroom E£30/20) is the best of a bad lot, with simple double rooms that are nothing special – but a damn sight better than rooms in the rest house down the road. It also has a small cafeteria where you can get chicken and rice meals, omelettes and *fuul* as well as drinks and biscuits.

Getting There & Away
Catch any of the Marsa Matruh buses from Sidi Gaber in Alexandria. Alternatively, service taxis leave from the taxi stand in front of Alexandria's train station and cost about E£6.

MARSA MATRUH مرسى مطروح
☎ 046

The large waterfront town of Marsa Matruh, built around a charming bay of clear, Mediterranean waters and clean, white, sandy beaches, is a popular summer destination with Egyptians. Away from the sand, the town itself, with a population of about 80,000, is dull and very unattractive. Outside the summer season, it's also completely dead, with most of the hotels and restaurants closing down over winter.

There are really only two streets in Marsa Matruh that you need to know: the Corniche, which runs all the way around the waterfront, and Sharia Iskendariyya, which

runs perpendicular to the Corniche, towards the hill behind the town. The **tourist office** (☎ 493 1841; open 8.30am-6pm daily, to 9pm in summer) is on the ground floor of the governorate building one block west of Sharia Iskendariyya on the corner of the Corniche.

You can change cash and travellers cheques at the **National Bank of Egypt**, a few blocks west of Sharia Iskendariyya and south of the Corniche, or there are several exchange bureaus on Sharia al-Galaa.

The **main post office** (Sharia ash-Shaata; open 8.30am-3pm Sun-Thur) is one block south of the Corniche and two blocks east of Sharia Iskendariyya. The **telephone** *centrale* (open 24 hrs) is across the street.

Things to See & Do
Set in the caves Rommel used as his headquarters during part of the El Alamein campaign is the rather poor **Rommel Museum**, which contains a few photos, a bust of the Desert Fox, some ageing German, Italian and British military maps and what is purported to be his greatcoat. The museum is about 3km east of the town centre, out by the beach of the same name.

Cleopatra's Beach and **Shaata al-Gharam** (Lovers' Beach), which are about 14km and 17km respectively west of town, are good, but best of all is **Agiba Beach**, about 24km west of Marsa Matruh. It is a small but spectacular beach, accessible only by a path leading down from the cliff top.

Places to Stay
The more expensive hotels are along the Corniche. Others are dotted around the town, most of them not too far from Sharia Iskendariyya.

Although there are no official camp sites, it may be possible to pitch a tent along the beach or at Rommel's Beach – check with the tourist office.

Located a couple of blocks south of Awam Mosque, the **Youth Hostel** (☎ 493 2331; bunk beds E£9) is just about OK. You get a comfortable enough bunk bed in a cramped room of six or eight. Prices are for members, but there seems to be no problem if nonmembers stay.

Ghazala Hotel (☎ 493 3519; Sharia Alam ar-Rum; beds E£10) is the most popular backpackers' stop. The entrance is sandwiched between some shops and is easily overlooked. Beds are basic but clean. Most rooms have balconies (but no view to speak of) and the shared toilet/shower combinations are clean, if lacking in hot water.

Rommel House Hotel (☎ 493 5466, fax 493 2485; Sharia al-Galaa; singles/doubles June-Sept E£70/117, Oct-May E£43/63), east of Sharia Iskendariyya, has comfortable rooms with bathroom, TV, fridge. Summer prices include obligatory half-board.

Hotel Beau Site (☎ 493 8555, fax 493 3319; Corniche; singles/doubles half-board June-Sept E£487/688, Oct-May E£243/344) is easily Matruh's most attractive option – if you have the money. The 'luxury' rooms on the beach drop to about half price in winter. There are some tiny rooms available above the disco with great balconies for substantially cheaper rates, and there is a computer terminal for Internet use.

Places to Eat
Asmak Hammo al-Temsah and **Abdu Kofta Restaurant** (Sharia Tahrir), just off Sharia Iskendariyya, are good options. Hammo al-Temsah will slap a fish on its outdoor grill and bring it to you in the Abdu Kofta Restaurant next door, where you can eat it with dips, bread, salad and rice. There's also a good takeaway called **Abu Rabie** (Sharia Iskendariyya) at the train station end of the street; it does fuul, ta'amiyya, salads and good gambary (shrimp) or calamari sandwiches for about E£1.25 each.

Beau Site Restaurant, in the hotel of the same name, is also good, but beware of the prices.

Getting There & Away
Bus Marsa Matruh's **bus station** is 2km out of town on the main coastal highway. From here **Superjet** has two services a day, one to Alexandria (E£24, around four hours) at 2.30pm and one to Cairo (E£37, five hours) at 3pm. **West Delta Bus Co** has frequent daily buses to Alexandria (E£15 to E£23, four hours) and to Cairo at 7.30am, noon, 3.30pm and 6pm (E£28 to E£36, five hours).

There are buses to Siwa (E£12, four hours) at 7.30am, 1.30pm, 4pm and 7.30pm.

Buses travelling to Sallum (E£10, four hours), on the Libyan border, depart throughout the day.

Train Don't do it. Even the station master at Marsa Matruh says that the trains are 'horrible'.

Service Taxi The **service taxi stand** is next to the bus station. Service taxis to Siwa cost E£10, if there are enough people going. Other fares include Sallum for E£10, Alexandria E£10 and Cairo E£15.

SALLUM السلوم
☎ 046
About 214km west of Marsa Matruh, Sallum (pronounced sa**loom**) is in the proverbial middle of nowhere. The water is crystal clear but is spoiled by the rubbish on the beach. Head east for a while and you can pick yourself out some secluded stretch of sand. At the eastern entrance to the town is a WWII Commonwealth war cemetery, a somewhat more modest version of the El Alamein cemetery.

The accommodation in town is dire and you should plan to avoid having to stay overnight.

Getting There & Away
Buses for Marsa Matruh (E£10, four hours) depart three times a day and at least one of these goes straight on through to Alexandria (E£23, nine hours). A service taxi to Marsa Matruh will cost about E£10.

Libya The border crossing point of Amsaad, just north of the Halfaya Pass, is 12km west of Sallum. Service taxis run up the mountain between the town and the Egyptian side of the crossing for E£2 to E£3. Once through passport control and customs on both sides (you walk through), you can get a Libyan service taxi on to Al-Burdi for about LD1. From there you can get buses on to Tobruk and Benghazi. Note that Libyan visas are not issued at the border.

Suez Canal قناة السويس

The Suez Canal, one of the greatest feats of modern engineering, links the Mediterranean with the northern end of the Red Sea. Opened in 1869 the canal severed Asia from Africa, and is now an important source of revenue for Egypt in the form of fees charged for its use by the world's tankers.

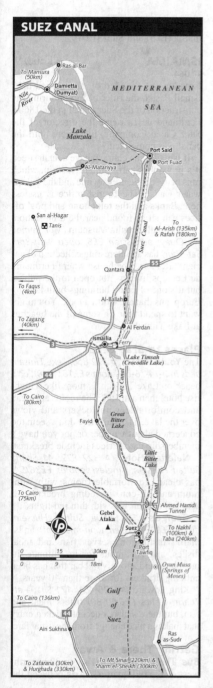

SUEZ CANAL

To Mansura (50km)
Ras al-Bar
Damietta (Dumyat)
Nile River
MEDITERRANEAN SEA
Lake Manzala
Al-Matariyya
Port Said
Port Fuad
San al-Hagar
Tanis
Suez Canal
To Al-Arish (135km) & Rafah (180km)
Qantara
To Faqus (4km)
Al-Ballah
To Zagazig (40km)
Al Ferdan
Ismailia
Ferry
Lake Timsah (Crocodile Lake)
Suez Canal
To Cairo (80km)
Fayid
Great Bitter Lake
Little Bitter Lake
To Cairo (75km)
Suez Canal
Ahmed Hamdi Tunnel
Gebel Ataka
Suez
To Nakhl (100km) & Taba (240km)
Port Tawfiq
0   15   30km
0   9   18mi
Oyun Musa (Springs of Moses)
Gulf of Suez
To Cairo (136km)
Ain Sukhna
Ras as-Sudr
To Zafarana (30km) & Hurghada (330km)
To Mt Sinai (220km) & Sharm el-Sheikh (300km)

The three principal cities along the canal are not top-of-the-list tourist attractions, but Port Said and, to a lesser extent Ismailia, have some fine examples of late 19th- and early 20th-century, colonial-style architecture well-worth checking out.

PORT SAID   بور سعيد
☎ 066

A city of 400,000 people Port Said was founded in 1859 and was a duty-free zone until 2001, although at the time of writing its duty-free status was being debated. It is effectively built on an island, connected to the mainland by a bridge to the south and a causeway to the west.

The **tourist office** (☎ 235 289; 8 Sharia Palestine; open 9am-1.30pm & 3pm-8pm Sat-Thur) has maps and information about the Suez Canal and the port.

There are a number of **banks** on Sharia al-Gomhuriyya and the **main post office** is opposite Ferial Gardens, one block north.

There are two **telephone** centrales (open 24 hrs): one is on Sharia Palestine two blocks northwest of the tourist office; the other is behind the governorate building.

Things to See & Do

If you've ever seen a picture of Port Said, it was probably of the striking green domes of **Suez Canal House**, which was built in time for the inauguration of the canal in 1869, but is now off-limits to visitors.

At the top end of Sharia Palestine, the **National Museum** (Sharia Palestine; admission E£6; open 9am-4pm daily) houses a varied collection.

The small **Military Museum** (Sharia 23rd of July; admission E£12; open 9am-4pm Sat-Thur, 9am-11am & 1pm-4pm Fri) has some interesting relics from the 1956 Anglo-French War and the 1967 and 1973 wars with Israel, as well as a small display of ancient Pharaonic and Islamic conflicts.

Places to Stay

The **Youth Hostel** (☎ 228 702; Sharia 23rd of July; beds in 20-bed dorm for members/ nonmembers E£3.25/4.25) is the cheapest option in town and is OK, but it's in a highly inconvenient location near the stadium.

Akri Palace Hotel (☎ 221 013; 24 Sharia al-Gomhuriyya; singles/doubles E£20/25, doubles with bathroom E£37) is a reasonably

EGYPT

clean, Greek-owned place with a bit of old Port Said charm.

Mereland Hotel *(☎ 227 020; singles/doubles E£15/20, with private bathroom E£24/35)* is two blocks northwest of the Akri in a lane between Sharia Saad Zaghloul and Sharia an-Nahda. It offers big, clean rooms and the communal bathrooms are decent. Breakfast is extra.

Hotel de la Poste *(☎ 224 048; 42 Sharia al-Gomhuriyya; singles/doubles with bathroom & balcony US$10/12, other singles/doubles US$8/12)* is housed in an old building with fading elegance that the management has attempted to salvage through careful renovation. Some rooms have TV and fridge. Prices are without breakfast.

Places to Eat

Not surprisingly, there are plenty of seafood restaurants in Port Said.

Galal *(cnr sharias al-Gomhuriyya & Gaberti; dishes E£12-24)* is one of the city's cheapest restaurants and a local favourite serving calamari and fish with Greek mezze. Beer is served, but not at the outdoor tables.

Pizza Pino *(☎ 239 949; Sharia al-Gomhuriyya; dishes E£12-30)*, Port Said's version of Pizza Express, serves pizza and pasta in nonplastic surroundings.

Getting There & Away

Bus There are **Superjet** buses to Cairo (E£15, three hours) 11 times a day from in front of the train station, but note that the last bus departs at 6pm. There's also a bus to Alexandria (E£22, four hours) at 4.30pm.

West Delta Bus Co leaves from a bus station near Ferial Gardens (also known as the 'Lux terminal'); buses to Cairo depart hourly between 6am and 6pm, with fares from E£13.50 to E£16, and there are four buses to Alexandria (E£17 to E£23). Buses to Ismailia (E£5) depart hourly between 6am and 6pm. Buses to Suez (E£7.50, 2¼ hours) depart at 6am, 10am, 1pm and 4pm.

Train There are four trains a day to Cairo, but this is an extremely slow and uncomfortable way to travel.

Service Taxi These leave from a garage 2km west of the town centre. Ask a taxi to take you to the *mahattat servees*. Fares include: Cairo (E£10), Qantara (E£3.50), Ismailia (E£5) and Suez (E£6).

ISMAILIA الاسماعيلية
☎ 064

Ismailia was founded by and named after Ismail Pasha, the ruler of Egypt during the construction of the Suez Canal in the 1860s. Ferdinand de Lesseps, the director of the Suez Canal Company, lived here until the canal was completed.

If Ismailia can claim to have a main street, it's probably Sharia Sultan Hussein, which runs between the railway line and the Sweetwater Canal. The **tourist office** is useless here. **Banks** and the **telephone** and **post offices** can all be found near the train station.

The small **Ismailia Museum** *(Mohammed Ali Quay; admission E£6; open 9am-3pm Sat-Thur)* has an interesting collection of ancient artefacts. The house where Ferdinand de Lesseps lived is not open to the public, but it's one of many buildings built here by Europeans that are worth a look. You might want to spend time on some of the **beaches** at Lake Timsah.

Places to Stay & Eat

The **Youth Hostel** *(☎ 322 850; Lake Timsah; beds in 2-/4-/6-bed dorms E£18/15/8)*, on a beach on Lake Timsah, is more like a high-rise hotel than a hostel. The rooms are clean and comfortable with lockers and views over the lake. The staff here don't seem too concerned about whether or not you have a membership card. Prices include breakfast.

Nefertari Hotel *(☎ 322 822; 41 Sharia Sultan Hussein; singles/doubles E£36/54)* has clean, comfortable rooms with bathroom and air-con, including breakfast. It also has a small bar with dim red lights.

George's *(11 Sharia Sultan Hussein; dishes E£12-40; open noon-midnight)*, an Ismailia institution, serves fish and meat dishes, and is famous for its intimate atmosphere and a lovely old bar that has been enticing drinkers for more than 40 years.

King Edward *(☎ 325 451; 171 Sharia at-Tahrir; dishes E£6.50-30)* offers meat and fish, but there's also a decent chicken curry that makes a nice change from the usual fare.

Getting There & Away

Bus The **bus station** is some 3km northwest of the old quarter. Taxis between the station and the town centre cost about E£3. **West Delta Bus Co** has frequent departures to Cairo (E£7, 2½ hours) and two buses to Alexandria (E£17, three hours). The **East Delta Bus Co** also has frequent buses to Cairo for E£7. East Delta Bus Co buses to Port Said (E£4, one to two hours) leave every 30 to 45 minutes, and to Suez (E£3.50, one hour) every 15 to 20 minutes. Buses to Sinai also leave from here. There are buses every hour or so to Al-Arish (E£7 to E£9, three hours) from 8am to 5pm. There are buses to Sharm el-Sheikh (E£25, four to six hours) at 6.30am, noon, 2.30pm, 3.30pm, 9pm, 10pm, 11pm and midnight.

Train There are about 10 trains a day to both Cairo and Port Said, but the service is slow and uncomfortable and no cheaper than the bus.

Service Taxi These depart from the **service taxi stand** across the road from the East Delta Bus Co station. Destinations include Suez (E£3), Port Said (E£3.50), Cairo (E£5) and Al-Arish (E£7).

SUEZ
السويس

☎ 062

Suez, which sprawls around from the entrance of the canal at Port Tawfiq south along the western side of the gulf, suffered badly in the 1967 and 1973 wars. It is above all a transit point for tankers, pilgrims to Mecca and people travelling between Sinai and the rest of the country. It's a good place to watch the passing tankers.

There's a **tourist office** *(Port Tawfiq)*, **main post office** *(Sharia Hoda Shaarawi)* and **telephone** *centrale (Sharia Saad Zaghloul)*. Most **banks** have branches around town.

Places to Stay & Eat

The **Youth Hostel** *(☎ 221 945; beds members/ nonmembers E£5/6)* is inconveniently located on the main road heading west out of Suez. It may be cheap, but it's grungy and a long way from anything.

In the centre of Suez, there's a handful of cheapies clustered around Sharia as-Salam, known locally as Sharia ag-Geish and Sharia at-Tahrir. About the best of a pretty bad bunch is **Sina Hotel** *(Sharia Banque Masr; singles/doubles E£23/34)*, which has basic, reasonably clean rooms with fans.

Arafat Hotel *(☎ 338 355; Sharia Arafat; singles/doubles E£15/22, with bathroom E£24/ 30)* is the only budget option in the vicinity of Port Tawfiq, and fortunately it's not too bad. Rooms are clean and there are snacks and toiletries on sale in the lobby.

Red Sea Hotel *(☎ 334 302, fax 334 301; 13 Sharia Riad, Port Tawfiq; singles/doubles US$42/50)* is Suez's premier establishment. Its 81 rooms have TV, bathroom, phone and air-con and are comfortable and clean. Rates don't include breakfast and tax. It has a 6th-floor **restaurant** with a great panoramic view of the canal; meals cost between E£12 and E£33.

For the cheap old favourites like *ta'amiyya* and shwarma, wander around the streets bounded by Sharia Talaat Harb, Sharia Abdel as-Sarawat, Sharia Banque Masr and Sharia Khedr.

Fish Restaurant *(Sharia as-Salaam; dishes E£25-40; open to 2am)* sells the day's catch by weight and then cooks it according to your preference.

Getting There & Away

Bus Those of the **East Delta Bus Co** leave from the **Arba'een bus station** *(Sharia al-Faarz)*, not far from the centre of town. Buses to Cairo (E£6/7, 1½ hours) leave every 30 minutes from 6am to 8pm. Buses to Ismailia (E£3, one hour) depart every 15 to 20 minutes. There are three buses directly to Port Said (E£7.50, 2¼ hours) at 7am, 9am and 3.30pm, and two to Alexandria (E£20, three to four hours) at 7am and 2.30pm.

East Delta Bus Co has five nonstop buses to Sharm el-Sheikh (E£26 to E£35, 5½ hours) along the direct route down the Gulf of Suez. They go on to Dahab (E£30 to E£40, 6½ hours) and Nuweiba (E£35 to E£45, 5½ hours). A bus leaves for St Katherine's Monastery (E£17, five hours) via Wadi Feran at 11am.

Minibuses sometimes run to destinations in Sinai too – you'll be looking at about E£15 per person to St Katherine's Monastery, E£20 to Sharm el-Sheikh or Nuweiba and E£35 to Dahab. Ask around at the bus station for more details.

For buses to the Red Sea coast, Luxor and Aswan, you must go to **Upper Egypt Bus Company station** about 3km north of town, just before the train station. There are buses heading to Hurghada (E£25 to E£35, four to five hours) almost every hour. Most of these go on to Qena (E£26/30, nine to 10 hours).

There are six buses a day to Luxor (E£35 to E£37, 10 hours), three of which continue to Aswan (E£40 to E£45, 14 hours).

Train Only a masochist would want to travel to or from Suez by train. The **train station** is 2km west of the Arba'een bus station; a microbus shuttles between them for 25pt. Six Cairo-bound trains depart daily (E£2.60/1.05 for 2nd/3rd class, 2¼ hours) and only make it as far as Ain Shams, 10km northeast of central Cairo.

Service Taxi Service taxis depart from near the bus station to many areas serviced by buses and trains. Destinations include Cairo (E£5), Ismailia (E£3), Port Said (E£6) and Hurghada (E£20). The only place in Sinai served by service taxi is Al-Tor (E£10).

Red Sea Coast

ساحل البحر الاحمر

Egypt's Red Sea coast stretches for more than 800km from Suez in the north to the village of Bir Shalatein near the disputed border with Sudan in the south. Famed for its brilliant turquoise waters, splendid coral and exotic creatures of the deep, the Red Sea attracts more than 200,000 tourists annually. It's Egypt's most rapidly developing area, with more hotels and resorts constructed here in the last few years than anywhere else in the country. Unfortunately, much of the development during the freewheeling boom of the last decade has gone unchecked, resulting in massive environmental damage.

HURGHADA   الغردقة
☎ 065

Little more than a decade and a half ago Hurghada (an anglicised version of it's Arabic name *al-Gharadaka*) had two hotels separated by nothing more than virgin beach. A once-isolated and modest fishing village, it's now home to more than 35,000 people and packed with more than 100 resorts and hotels catering to sun-seekers and diving enthusiasts on package tours from all over the world. But the crystal-clear waters and fascinating reefs that made Hurghada Egypt's most popular resort town have suffered massive damage,

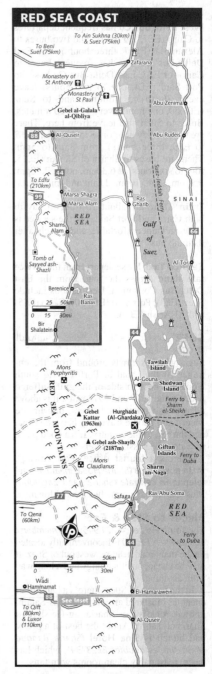

so divers have to travel to reefs. If you're not into beach resorts (or chunks of concrete, iron rods and empty oil drums – the results of the ongoing construction boom) then this ever-developing resort town has little to offer.

Orientation

The main town area, called **Ad-Dahar**, where virtually all budget hotels and most of the locals live, is at the northern end of the stretch of resorts that makes up the whole area. The main road through Ad-Dahar is Sharia an-Nasr, which also links Hurghada to Safaga and Suez. A few kilometres down the coast is **Sigala**, the rapidly growing part of town. Boats to Sharm el-Sheikh leave from here. South of Sigala, a road winds 15km down along the coast through the **'resort strip'**.

Information

Hurghada's **tourist office** (☎ 444 421; open 8.30am-8pm Sat-Thur) is a marble building south of Sigala on the main road leading to the resort strip.

In Ad-Dahar, branches of **Banque Masr**, the **National Bank of Egypt** (with an ATM machine) and the **Bank of Alexandria** are dotted along Sharia an-Nasr. There are also banks with ATMs along the resort strip. The **main post office** (Sharia an-Nasr) is towards the southern end of Ad-Dahar. The 24-hour **telephone centrale** is further north-west along the same road. Opposite the telephone centrale is a **fax booth** (fax 544 581; open 8am-2pm & 8pm-10pm Sat-Thur). There is another 24-hour centrale on Sharia Sheraton in Sigala.

Email & Internet Access Hurghada has at least three ISPs and plenty of Internet cafés. Some of the best include:

Caspar Internet Café (☎ 442 375) Sharia Sheraton, Resort Strip; (☎ 540 870) Corniche, Ad-Dahar; E£12 per hour
Down Town Internet Café (☎ 548 777) Sharia an-Nasr, Ad-Dahar; E£12 per hour
Elbess Bookshop Internet Café (☎ 540 748) Sharia Sayyed al-Qorayem, Ad-Dahar; E£15 per hour
Hotline (☎ 446 512) Sharia Sheraton, Resort Strip; E£8 per hour

Beaches

There are two **public beaches**, one in Ad-Dahar and another in Sigala. The Ad-Dahar beach was being cleaned up at the time of writing. The beach in Sigala is next to Al-Sakia restaurant and has clean sand and sunshades. Admission is E£3.50. Better, but slightly more expensive is the **Shellghada Beach** (Sharia Sheraton; admission E£10). **The Chill** (Sharia Sheraton; admission E£30) is a beachfront bar/restaurant where you can loll all day on hammocks or lie in the sun. Your only other option close to town is to pay to use one of the beaches at the resorts, where admission ranges from about E£25 to E£70.

Snorkelling

Hurghada is crawling with dive clubs and agents for snorkelling trips. Some of the reputable dive clubs take snorkellers out to better sites, and by going with one of them, you're almost assured of reef-protection practices being put into action.

Diving trips of one day or more are big business here. There are dozens of dive centres in town, many attached to the big resort hotels. Almost all have multilingual staff and their own customised, live-aboard boats for diving safaris. **Red Sea Diving Center** (☎ 442 960; e wrkneip@intouch.com) is one of the most reputable. Also good is the **Aquanaut Red Sea** (☎ 549 981; e info@aquanaut.net).

Places to Stay

With almost every major hotel chain represented in Hurghada's resort strip, it's not hard to find a four- or five-star hotel. Finding budget accommodation is more difficult.

The newly built **Youth Hostel** (☎ 544 989; Coastal Highway; E£23.10 per person in 4-bed room, E£28 per person in family room, nonmembers add E£1) is 5km north of Ad-Dahar, which is inconvenient without a vehicle. Still, the rooms are spacious and there is a beach. Lunch costs E£10 and dinner E£14.

Ad-Dahar The **Happy House** (☎ 549 611; Main Square; singles/doubles without bathroom E£30/40, doubles with bathroom E£50) is a humble but spotlessly clean pension, conveniently located on the edge of Ad-Dahar's souq. The price includes breakfast.

St George's Hotel (☎ 548 246; off Sharia Sheikh Sebak; singles/doubles E£20/30, with bathroom E£25/35) is a pleasant, family-run place with dark but very clean rooms. Breakfast is not included in the price.

HURGHADA

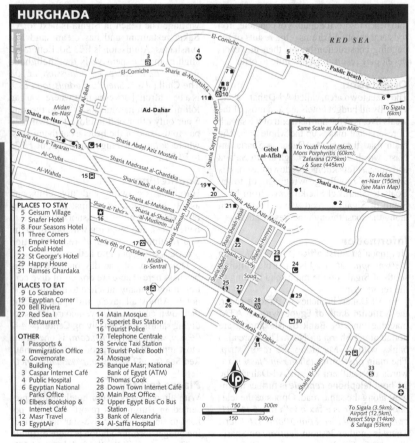

See Inset

El-Corniche

RED SEA

El-Corniche · Sharia al-Mustasha

Public Beach

Midan
en-Nasr

Sharia an-Nasr

Ad-Dahar

Sharia al-Baht

Sharia Madrasat al-Ghardaka

To Sigala
(6km)

Sharia Masr li-Tayaran

Al-Oruba

Al-Wahda

Sharia Abdel Aziz Mustafa

Sharia Sayyed al-Qorayem

Same Scale as Main Map

Gebel
al-Afish

To Youth Hostel (5km),
Mons Porphyritis (60km),
Zafarana (275km)
& Suez (445km)

To Midan
en-Nasr (150m)
(see Main Map)

Sharia an-Nasr

Sharia Nadi al-Rahalat

Sharia al-Mahkama

Sharia at-Tahrir

Sharia al-Shuban
al-Muslimin

Sharia 6th of October

Midan
is-Sentral

Sharia 23-July

Sharia Sheikh Sebak

Sharia al-Horreya

Sharia Soliman Mazhar

Sharia Abdel
Hasan

Souq

Sharia an-Nasr

Sharia Arab al-Dahar

Sharia El-Salam

To Sigala (3.5km),
Airport (12.5km),
Resort Strip (14km)
& Safaga (53km)

PLACES TO STAY
5 Geisum Village
7 Snafer Hotel
8 Four Seasons Hotel
11 Three Corners
   Empire Hotel
21 Gobal Hotel
22 St George's Hotel
29 Happy House
31 Ramses Ghardaka

PLACES TO EAT
1 Lo Scarabeo
19 Egyptian Corner
20 Bell Riviera
27 Red Sea I
   Restaurant

OTHER
1 Passports &
  Immigration Office
2 Governorate
  Building
3 Caspar Internet Café
4 Public Hospital
6 Egyptian National
  Parks Office
10 Elbess Bookshop &
   Internet Café
12 Masr Travel
13 EgyptAir

14 Main Mosque
15 Superjet Bus Station
16 Tourist Police
17 Telephone Centrale
18 Service Taxi Station
23 Tourist Police Booth
24 Mosque
25 Banque Masr; National
   Bank of Egypt (ATM)
26 Thomas Cook
28 Down Town Internet Café
30 Main Post Office
32 Upper Egypt Bus Co Bus
   Station
33 Bank of Alexandria
34 Al-Saffa Hospital

0   150   300m
0   150   300yd

Gobal Hotel (☎ 546 623; *Sharia Sheikh Sebak; singles/doubles E£15/25)*, the cheapest option in the area, has rooms that tend to be a little on the shabby side. It's also frequented by Egyptian men, so should be avoided by solo women travellers. Prices include breakfast.

Ramses Ghardaka (☎ 548 941; *Sharia Arab; singles/doubles E£45/55, with air-con E£55/65)* is inconveniently located, but has very clean rooms with telephone and fridge. Prices include breakfast.

Small and friendly, the **Four Seasons** (☎ 549 260; *off Sharia Sayyed al-Qorayem; doubles E£35)* has some newly renovated rooms with balconies and air-con. For E£5 you can also use the beach at Geisum Village hotel.

Snafer Hotel (☎ 540 260, fax 545 456; *off Sharia Sayyed al-Qorayem; doubles with fan/air-con E£45/55)*, a friendly place close to the beach in ad-Dahar, has big, bright rooms, some with sea views. A good deal for the price, which includes breakfast.

Three Corners Empire Hotel (☎ 549 200, fax 549 213; e info@threecorners.com; *Sharia Sayyed al-Qorayem; singles/doubles US$38/56)* is a large block just up from the beach. It may be impersonal but has good, clean, air-con rooms, several restaurants and a deal for beach use with the nearby Three Corners Village.

Geisum Village (☎ 548 048, fax 547 995; *El-Corniche; half-board singles/doubles E£90/155)* is the cheapest of Ad-Dahar's beach places and, if you don't mind the 'pack-em-in' holiday-village scene, is a good deal.

Sigala There's a bewildering array of mid-range and expensive hotels in Sigala, but few cheaper options.

White House Hotel *(☎ 443 688, fax 442 085; Sharia Sheraton; singles E£35-48, doubles E£55-65)* has friendly staff and all rooms have air-con. Prices include breakfast and free access to the beach at Giftun Village on the resort strip.

New Star Hotel *(☎ 442 588; Sharia Sheraton; singles/doubles E£25/40)*, just down the road from the White House, has stuffy rooms with air-con.

Places to Eat

Ad-Dahar Don't confuse **Bell Riviera** *(Sharia Abdel Aziz Mustafa; dishes E£3-10)* with its more expensive sister restaurant with the similar name across the road. It has excellent lentil soup for E£3, spaghetti for E£3.50, pizzas for between E£7 and E£10 and calamari for E£9. You can also get breakfast for E£4. Avoid the toilets.

Egyptian Corner *(dishes E£4-8)* is a tiny place next to Bell Riviera. It's popular with travellers and has a tiny menu that includes a E£5 breakfast, spaghetti bolognaise for E£4 and simple meals like chicken for E£8.

Red Sea I Restaurant *(☎ 547 704; mains E£15-40)*, on a street off Sharia an-Nasr, is popular with package tourists wanting a night away from their resorts. With a wide selection of seafood, plus Egyptian dishes and pizza, you can tailor the menu to fit most budgets.

Lo Scarabeo *(mobile ☎ 0122-364 6027; Sharia Sayyed el-Qorayem; dishes E£10-30)* is a good, Italian-run pizzeria and pasta restaurant that also serves huge (safe) salads. You can eat on the terrace or inside.

Sigala The basic, no-frills **Abu Khadigah** *(☎ 443 768; Sharia Sheraton; meals E£6-10)* attracts local workers and businessmen for its famously good Egyptian food.

Al-Masry *(☎ 443 398; off Sharia Sheraton; dishes E£1.50-48)* is another good, Egyptian restaurant with home-style cooking. Look for the sign at the beginning of Sharia Sheraton, just off Midan Sigala.

Joker *(☎ 543 146; Midan Sigala; mains E£8-60)* is an excellent, no-nonsense fish

restaurant overlooking the midan. It's popular with locals and tourists. Fish is priced by weight.

Rossi Pizza *(☎ 446 012; Sharia Sheraton; meals E£9-35)* is a good pizza and pasta restaurant with a popular bar attached.

As the name suggests, **The Chill** *(mobile ☎ 012-382 0694; Sharia Sheraton; meals E£18-20)* is a laid-back bar/restaurant with lounge music and tables in a beachfront tent. The small menu changes daily and features an interesting mix of international dishes.

Getting There & Away

Air There are daily **EgyptAir** *(☎ 546 788; Midan an-Nasr • ☎ 447 503; Resort Strip)* flights between Hurghada and Cairo (E£573 one way), plus three flights per week to Sharm el-Sheikh (E£330 one way).

Bus Two bus companies operate services from Hurghada. **Superjet** has its bus station is near the main mosque in Ad-Dahar from where there are three buses a day to Cairo (E£50, six hours) and a daily bus to Alexandria (E£75, nine hours). The **Upper Egypt Bus Company** bus station is at the southern end of Ad-Dahar. Buses run every couple of hours to Cairo (E£40 to E£55, six hours). A couple of these set down in Suez as well. There are eight daily services to Luxor (E£21 to E£22, five hours), all of which go on to Aswan (E£35 to E£40, seven to eight hours). There are several daily buses to Marsa Alam (E£20, three to four hours) via Safaga (E£6, 45 minutes) and Al-Quseir (E£12 to E£15, two to three hours).

Service Taxi The service taxi station is near the telephone *centrale* in Ad-Dahar. Taxis go to Cairo for E£30 per person (six hours). Others go to Safaga (E£3, 45 minutes) Al-Quseir (E£7, two hours), Marsa Alam (E£15, four hours) and Suez (E£20, 3½ hours). They don't take foreigners to Luxor or Aswan except on a private basis with a police convoy. If you bargain hard it'll cost about E£200 for a car that seats seven people.

Boat A luxury high speed ferry operated by **Travco** *(☎ 445 037, 443 231; US$40 or E£100 per person; vehicles E£150-200, depending on engine size; 1½ hours)* plies the waters of the Red Sea between Hurghada and Sharm el-Sheikh, departing at 5am each Monday and Tuesday and at 8am each Thursday and Saturday from the old port in Sigala. The trip can take longer when seas are rough. Be there at least 30 minutes beforehand.

There is also a daily 'flying boat' from Hurghada to Duba, Saudi Arabia (E£180 or US$100 to US$200 per vehicle). Departures are at noon but you must be at the port at least three hours in advance. For more information, call **Amco Tours** (☎ 447 571).

AL-QUSEIR القصير
☎ 065

Until the 10th century Al-Quseir was one of the most important exit points for pilgrims travelling to Mecca and later it was an important entrepot for Indian spices destined for Europe. There's not much to do but admire the **historic buildings** in this medieval port town. Some of the **beaches** out of town are worth exploring on a hire bicycle.

Places to Stay & Eat
The only choice for travellers on a tight budget, the **Sea Princess Hotel** (☎ 331 880; Sharia al-Gomhuriyya; singles/doubles E£15/20) is about to have a much-needed revamp. Rooms have fans and are small and cabin-like; tax is not included. The people here can cook you up something, too.

Al-Quseir Hotel (☎/fax 332 30; Sharia Port Said; singles/doubles with fan E£60/90; with air-con E£80/120) is a tiny gem of a hotel consisting of only six rooms in a renovated 1920s merchant's house. With high-ceilings, wooden lattice work on the windows and spotless bathrooms, it is high on both charm and comfort.

Food wise, the options are very limited. Apart from the hotels, there are a few ta'amiyya and fish joints around town and the bus station.

Getting There & Away
Bus There are four buses that go all the way through to Cairo (E£40 to E£55, 11 hours) via Hurghada (E£12 to E£15). There are three buses south to Marsa Alam (E£5, two hours) at 11.30am and 1pm and four buses daily to Qena (E£5 to E£10, four hours).

Service Taxi The **service taxi station** is at the southern end of town. The officially prescribed fares are: Cairo E£40, Suez E£25,

Qena E£15 and Hurghada E£7. As in Hurghada you have to hire the entire taxi for the trip to Luxor. Drivers ask for about E£250, but if you're lucky you may be able to bargain them down.

Getting Around
There is a no-name **bike shop** virtually opposite the service taxi station. The owner wants E£15 for a day's bike rental, but this can be bargained down.

MARSA ALAM مرسى علم
Marsa Alam is a fishing village 132km south of Al-Quseir. A road also connects the village with Edfu, 230km across the desert to the west. There are some quiet beaches around and a growing number of resorts. There is also some excellent diving.

Coral Cove Beach Safari Camp (☎ 02-764 7970; tents per person with half-board E£55) is a small camp site about 7km north of town, with semipermanent tents and a communal shower block.

Red Sea Diving Safari (☎ 02-337 1833, fax 749 4219; W www.redseadivingsafari.com; doubles full-board in tents/huts/stone chalets US$35/44/55 per person) Although designed for divers, non divers are also welcome at this spotlessly clean camp. The same outfit runs other camps further south and is one of Egypt's most reputable scuba outfits.

Getting There & Away
The new airport in Marsa Alam currently only receives charters from abroad.

The bus to Aswan (E£10.50, three hours) via Edfu (E£9) leaves from the cafés at the junction at about 7am. There are three buses a day to Al-Quseir (E£5, 1½ hours).

Sinai سينا

It was in Sinai, on Mt Sinai, that Moses received the Ten Commandments, but over the centuries the sixth has been broken here with monotonous regularity. Armies have crossed backwards and forwards, most recently from Israel, which occupied the peninsula from 1967 until 1982, when, under the Camp David Agreement, it agreed to pull out.

The area is populated mainly by Bedouin, although Egyptians are settling here, mostly to take full advantage of the tourist trade.

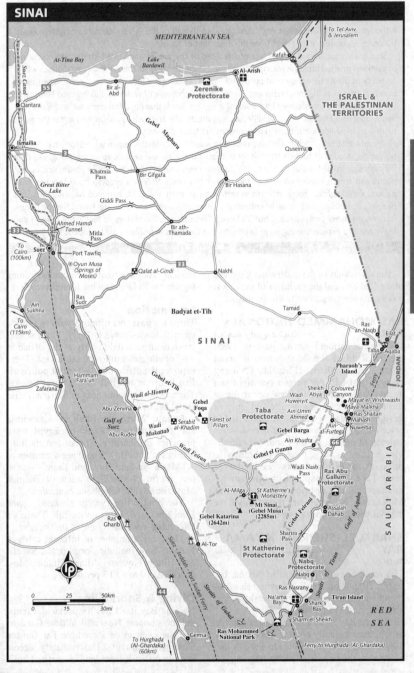

Footprints in the Sand Only, Please

Although much of Sinai is hot dry desert, it is not devoid of life. A very delicate ecosystem exists; however, it's under direct threat from the onslaught of tourism.

Sinai is a unique land of craggy mountains sliced by dry, gravel wadis in which the odd acacia tree or clump of gnarled tamarisk manages to survive. On the edge of all this are the coastal dunes where a variety of plants tenuously hold onto life in loose, sandy soil. Once every few years, when storm clouds gather over the mountains and dump colossal amounts of water on this parched landscape, the entire scene is transformed into a sea of greenery. Seeds that have lain dormant in the soil suddenly burst into life. For Sinai's wildlife, such as the gazelle and rock hyrax (as well as for the goats herded by local Bedouin), these rare occasions are times of plenty.

Up until relatively recently, the only people to wander through this region were Bedouin on camel; nowadays, groups of tourists looking for outback adventure and pristine spots are ploughing their way through in 4WD vehicles and quads (four-wheeled motorcycles) that churn up the soil, uproot plants and create erosion. Aware of the danger this poses to Sinai's ecosystem, authorities have banned vehicles from going off-road in certain areas, such as Ras Mohammed National Park, but banning something and actually enforcing it in areas as vast as these are two different things. Rangers do patrol protectorates, but it's largely up to tourists themselves to follow the rules. If you really want to explore the region in depth, do it in the age-old fashion – go by foot or hire a camel.

The splendours of the underwater kingdom of the Red Sea and the grandeur of the desert mountains are attractions not to be missed.

RAS MOHAMMED NATIONAL PARK محمية رأس محمد

Declared a national marine park in 1988, the headland of Ras Mohammed is about 30km west of Sharm el-Sheikh. Camping permits cost E£5 per person per night and are available from the visitors' centre inside the park, but camping is allowed only in designated areas. Vehicles are permitted to enter (US$5 per person), but access is restricted to certain regions and, for conservation reasons, it's totally forbidden to drive off the official tracks (see the boxed text). Take your passport with you, and remember that it is not possible to go to Ras Mohammed National Park if you only have a Sinai permit in your passport.

SHARM EL-SHEIKH & NA'AMA BAY شرم الشيخ و خليج نعمة
☎ 069

The south coast of the Gulf of Aqaba, between Tiran Island in the strait and Ras Mohammed, features some of the world's most amazing underwater scenery.

Na'ama Bay is a throbbing resort that has grown from virtually nothing since the early 1980s, while Sharm el-Sheikh, initially developed by the Israelis, is a long-standing settlement. They are 6km apart, but are joining together with fast-growing urban sprawl.

Information

There's a **passport office** (Sharm el-Sheikh; open 9.30am-2pm Sat-Thur), but visa extensions are available only at the office in Al-Tor some 80km to the northwest. There is no tourist office but the **tourist police office** is up on the hill in Sharm el-Sheikh. There is also a booth next to Marina Sharm Hotel in Na'ama Bay.

Banque Masr, the **Bank of Alexandria** and the **National Bank of Egypt** have branches in Sharm el-Sheikh (on the hill) and in Na'ama Bay. There are a number of ATMs in Na'ama Bay: and there's one at the Sharm el-Sheikh branch of Banque Masr (beside the telephone *centrale*).

The **post office** (Sharm el-Sheikh; open 8am-3pm Sat-Thur) is on the hill. There's a **telephone** *centrale* (open 24 hrs) nearby.

There are a number of **Internet cafés** in Na'ama Bay, including ones in the Sanafir and Hilton Fayrouz Village Hotels. Most charge E£10 to E£15 per hour.

Diving & Snorkelling

Na'ama Bay itself has unspectacular reefs, but the stunning **Near** and **Middle Gardens** and the even more incredible **Far Garden** have colourful reefs. Unfortunately, access is quite difficult from land because of hotel construction. Some of the most spectacular diving is off **Ras Mohammed** and in the **Straits of Tiran**. There is also good snorkelling at most of the popular coastal dive sites, including **Ras um Sid** near the lighthouse at Sharm. The deep drop-offs and strong cross currents at Ras Mohammed are not ideal for snorkelling. There are several **wrecks**, including the prized *Thistlegorm*.

Any of the dive clubs and schools can give you a full rundown of the possibilities. Among the better and more established are **Aquamarine Diving Centre** (☎ 600 276), **African Divers** (☎ 660 307), **Camel Dive Club** (☎ 600 700), **Oonas Diving Centre** (☎ 600 581) and **Red Sea Diving College** (☎ 600 313). There's a modern decompression chamber just outside Sharm el-Sheikh.

Places to Stay

Sharm el-Sheikh Up on the hill, the **Youth Hostel** (☎/fax 660 317; beds in 8-bed dorm members/nonmembers E£18.60/ 19.60; open 6.30am-9am & 2pm-10pm) is the cheapest, but by no means the best, place to stay in an area geared to tourists with comparatively fat wallets. Beds are in fairly standard dorms and come with breakfast. They don't seem overly fussed about membership cards.

Al-Kheima Camp (☎ 660 167, fax 660 166; hut singles/doubles E£40/55, room singles/ doubles E£125/140), the first place you pass on your way from the port, has bamboo huts and air-con rooms. However, it's inconveniently located and the desert behind is strewn with garbage. Breakfast is E£8.

Clifftop Hotel (☎ 660 251; singles/doubles US$35/45), up the hill from the beach, is one of Sharm's original hotels and is showing its age. However, reasonably priced rooms have TV, air-con, fridge, phone and bathroom, and the price includes breakfast. You also get to use the beach at Marina Sharm Hotel.

The 88-room **Amar Sinai** (☎ 662 222, fax 660 233; singles/doubles US$30/44), in the middle of a new subdivision above Ras Um Sid, has friendly staff, nice architecture, a pool and an Internet café.

Palermo Resort (☎ 661 561; singles/doubles US$25/31) is another three-star hotel with breakfast included. It has a large pool and a section of beach at nearby Ras Um Sid.

Na'ama Bay A popular budget option with a good atmosphere is **Pigeon House** (☎ 600 996, fax 600 965; main road, Na'ama Bay; hut singles/doubles/triples E£38/56/76, rooms E£65/85/105, with air-con & bathroom E£120/170/205). It's often fully booked, so reserve ahead. Guests get a 10% discount at the Anemone Dive Centre.

Although no longer the peaceful hangout it once was, **Sanafir Hotel** (☎ 600 197/8, fax 600 196; 'superior' air-con singles/doubles low season E£131/180, high season E£162/ 243) is a Na'ama Bay institution. It's home to one of Sharm's best nightclubs (Bus Stop) as well as a number of popular restaurants. There is a pool and guests get a beach pass.

Reasonably-priced (for Sharm), the four-star **Kahramana** (☎ 601 071, fax 601 076; singles/doubles US$70/95) offers the usual amenities and is set in the heart of Na'ama Bay. Deals are usually available if you book in advance.

Oasis Hotel (☎/fax 601 602; singles/ doubles with air-con & shared bathroom E£100/150, concrete & reed huts E£45/65), despite the (relatively) decent prices, doesn't have the ambience of the Pigeon House, although the rooms are reasonable. Rates include breakfast.

Gafy Land Resort (☎/fax 600 210; singles/ doubles US$52/74) is the cheapest hotel with beach frontage in Na'ama Bay. While less-than-inspiring (it is run by the American Days Inn chain) its rooms have all the amenities at a fraction of the usual price.

Places to Eat

Sharm el-Sheikh There are a couple of small restaurants/cafés in the shopping bazaar behind the bus station.

Sinai Star (☎ 660 323; meals E£12-14) is a popular restaurant serving some excellent fish meals.

The tiny **Safsafa Restaurant** (☎ 660 474; meals E£10-45), in the old Sharm 'mall', specialises in fish and is a favourite of local residents.

Al-Dahan Restaurant (☎ 660 840; meals E£-50) is a small 'oriental' restaurant, in the jumble of streets known as the 'souq'. It serves good Egyptian/Middle Eastern food, with an emphasis on mezze and meat.

Al-Fanar (☎ 662 618; Ras Um Sid; meals E£30-55), at the base of the lighthouse, is an open-air Bedouin-style restaurant with sunken alcoves and not-so-cheap prices. But the view of the sea is marvellous, the food is good and you can get a variety of cold beers.

Na'ama Bay One of the cheapest restaurants in Na'ama Bay, **Tam Tam Oriental Café** (*☎ 600 150; dishes E£3-20*) is deservedly popular. Jutting out onto the boardwalk, it's a laid-back place where you can delve into a range of Egyptian fare, including mezzes, or have a *sheesha* (E£3.50).

La Rustichella Restaurant (*mobile ☎ 010-116 0692; meals E£30-55*) is opposite Pizza Hut at the southwestern end of Na'ama Bay. It's an excellent Italian restaurant that's popular with Sharm's resident Italian community, who praise its home-style cooking. Fish dishes are especially good.

Mashy Café (*☎ 600 197; dishes E£4-45*) is a popular Lebanese restaurant on the sidewalk in front of the Sanafir Hotel, with a wide selection of mezze and meat dishes. There's also a racy belly-dancing show in the evenings.

Oddly, the bland, American chain restaurant **Hard Rock Café** (*☎ 602 665; dishes E£20-25*) is immensely popular in Sharm. It becomes a throbbing disco late at night.

The usual fast-food outlets are also represented here: **McDonald's**, **KFC** and **Pizza Hut** are all on or close to the street that runs in front of the Sanafir Hotel.

Getting There & Away
Air There are daily **EgyptAir** (*☎ 661 056; Sharm el-Sheikh at beginning of road to Na'ama Bay*) flights to Cairo (E£573 one way) and three times a week to Hurghada (E£330). On Saturday and Thursday there are also flights to Luxor (E£ 480).

Bus The **bus station** is behind the Mobil Station halfway between Na'ama Bay and Sharm el-Sheikh. **East Delta Bus Co** has several daily services to Cairo (E£50 to E£60, seven hours), starting at 7.30am and ending at midnight. **Superjet** has four daily buses to Cairo (E£55) leaving from its bus station next to East Delta Bus Co.

It is cheaper, but more time-consuming, to get a bus to Suez and then another bus or service taxi from there to Cairo. Buses to Suez (E£26 to E£35, 5½ hours) depart almost every hour throughout the day.

Nine daily buses go to Dahab (E£10, 1½ hours), four of which go on to Nuweiba

(E£25, 2½); the 9am bus then continues all the way to Taba (E£35, three to four hours). To get to St Katherine's Monastery you have to go to Dahab and change.

Boat A high-speed, air-con ferry operated by **Travco** (*☎ 660 764*) travels between Sharm and Hurghada in 1½ hours (although some travellers have said that it can take much longer). The boat departs at 6pm on Monday, Thursday and Saturday. Tickets cost US$40 (vehicles start at E£175). For more information contact the Travco office.

DAHAB   دهب
☎ 069
The village beach resort of Dahab (literally, 'gold') is 85km north of Sharm el-Sheikh on the Gulf of Aqaba. There are two parts to Dahab: in the new part, referred to by locals as Dahab City, are the more-expensive hotels and bus station. The other part of Dahab, named Assalah, was a Bedouin village, about 2.5km north of town. It now has more budget travellers and Egyptian entrepreneurs than Bedouin in residence.

Information
The **National Bank of Egypt** (*Novotel Holiday Village; open from 9.30am-12.30pm & 6.30pm-8.30pm*) has another branch, with an ATM, near the bus station. **Banque de Caire** (*open 9am-2pm & 6pm-9pm Sat-Thur, 9am-11am & 6pm-9pm Fri*) has a branch opposite the Christina Residence on the main road in Assalah.

The **post office** and **telephone office** (*open 24 hrs*) are opposite the bus station in Dahab City. The latter has a cardphone. There are also two cardphones in Assalah: one at the Oxford supermarket and the other at the papyrus shop in the heart of the bazaar, both of which sell phonecards.

There is a plethora of **Internet cafés** in Dahab. Most are on the strip in Assalah and charge E£10 per hour, with a minimum of E£3. One of the best is the **White Hawk Internet Café**. Nearby is **Rasta Business Centre**. Opposite Nesima Resort on the main road in Assalah is **Shark's Bay Internet**, which only charges E£8 per hour.

Activities
After loafing around, diving is the most popular activity in Dahab. The town's various

dive clubs all offer a full range of diving possibilities, including camel/dive safaris. However, you should choose your club carefully because some places have lousy reputations when it comes to safety standards. Among the best are **Inmo**, **Nesima**, **Orca** and **Fantasea**.

Snorkellers tend to head for Eel Garden, just north of town. You can hire snorkelling gear from places along the waterfront.

In the morning, camel drivers and their charges congregate along the waterfront to organise camel trips to the dry interior of Sinai. Prices for a day trip, including food, start at E£70.

Places to Stay

Most, if not all, budget travellers head straight for Assalah. There's a plethora of so-called camps, which are basically compounds with simple stone and cement huts of two or three mattresses, generally costing E£6 to E£10 per person. Many of the camps are introducing proper rooms with private bathrooms, but these are considerably more expensive than the huts. Prices are always negotiable. **Auski**, **Bishbishi**, **Penguin** and **Mirage Village** are all good camps.

Christina Residence *(☎ 640 390, fax 640 296; singles/doubles E£70/85)* is a small Swiss-run hotel back from the beach. The spotless rooms have fans and bathrooms. The same management runs the slightly more expensive **Christina Beach Palace** on the beach in front.

Nesima Resort *(☎ 640 320, fax 640 321; singles/doubles US$45/55)* is an upmarket hotel, with a popular restaurant and rooftop bar. It's close to the action, but quieter than the rest of Assalah. Domed air-con rooms, good food and a beachfront pool make this one of the better places in town.

Close to Dahab City are a few upmarket hotels.

Places to Eat

There is a string of places to eat along the waterfront in Assalah. They serve breakfast, lunch and dinner, and most seem to have identical menus hanging up out the front – a meal will generally cost you between E£6 and E£15.

The British-run **Jays Restaurant** *(mobile ☎ 012-335 3377; dishes E£4-6)* is a perennial favourite that serves the usual mixture of Egyptian and Western fare at very cheap prices. Diners sit on cushions and eat off low tables. No alcohol is served.

Tota, a ship-shape place in the heart of Assalah, has the best Italian cuisine on the strip. **Tratoria Pizzeria**, next door, does arguably better pizzas. Both serve alcohol.

North of the strip, **Lakhbatita** *(mobile ☎ 010-196 4120; dishes E£8-30)* is a quirky, beachfront place decorated with old Egyptian furniture. The menu mixes traditional Egyptian with Asian and European-influenced food. No alcohol is served.

Getting There & Away

Bus The bus station is in Dahab City. The most regular connection is to Sharm el-Sheikh (E£10, 1½ hours) with buses at 8.30am, 10am, 1pm, 2.30pm, 9pm and 10pm. There are six daily buses to Nuweiba (E£10, one hour). The 9.30am and 10.30am services go on to Taba (E£20). There's a 9.30am bus to St Katherine's Monastery (E£15, 1½). Buses to Cairo (E£62 to E£69, nine hours) leave at 8.30am, 1pm, 2pm and at 10pm. Buses for Suez (E£30 to E£40, 6½ hours) depart at 8.15am, 10am and 9pm.

Service Taxi As a rule, service taxis are much more expensive than buses – they know you're only using them because the bus times don't suit.

ST KATHERINE'S MONASTERY دير القديسة كاترينا
☎ 069

There are 22 Greek Orthodox monks living in this ancient monastery at the foot of Mt Sinai. The monastic order was founded in the 4th century AD by the Byzantine empress Helena, who had a small chapel built beside what was believed to be the burning bush from which God spoke to Moses. The chapel is dedicated to St Katherine, the legendary martyr of Alexandria, who was tortured on a spiked wheel and then beheaded for her Christianity.

In the 6th century Emperor Justinian ordered the building of a fortress with a basilica and a monastery as well as the original chapel. It served as a secure home for the monks of St Katherine's and as a refuge for the Christians of southern Sinai. St Katherine's is open to visitors from 9am to noon daily except Friday, Sunday and holidays.

St Katherine Protectorate is a 4350-sq-km area that encompasses Mount Sinai and the monastery. You can organise to hike through it with Bedouin guides. Check the protectorate website for more information: **w** www.stkparks.gov.eg.

Information

In the village of **Al-Milga**, about 3.5km from the monastery, there's a post office, phone exchange, bank and variety of shops and cafés. **Banque Masr** *(open 9am-2pm & 6pm-9pm)* here will change cash or travellers cheques and may give a cash advance on Visa and MasterCard.

Mt Sinai خبل سيناء

At a height of 2285m Mt Sinai (Gebel Musa is the local name) towers over St Katherine's Monastery. It is revered as the place Moses received the Ten Commandments from God. It is easy to climb – you can take the gentle camel trail or the 3750 Steps of Repentance, carved out by a monk. It takes two to three hours, and most people either stay overnight or climb up in time for sunrise – bring a torch (flashlight). It gets freezing cold in winter.

Places to Stay & Eat

The rooms at the **Monastery Hostel** *(☎ 470 353, fax 470 343; beds in 5-bed dorm US$20, singles/doubles US$35/50, all half-board)*, inside the monastery walls, have their own bathrooms and simple but comfortable beds with plenty of blankets for cold mountain nights. There's also a reasonable restaurant that serves beer and wine. You can sometimes leave baggage here while you hike up Mount Sinai.

Fox of the Desert Camp *(☎ 470 344, fax 470 034; E£10 per person in room or tent; E£5 per person camping)*, a new camp run by local Bedouin, is the cheapest option in town. About 200m from the main roundabout it has simple but clean facilities and a relaxed atmosphere.

The three-star **Daniela Village** *(☎/fax 470 379; singles/doubles US$44/56)* has comfortable rooms in stone bungalows, a restaurant and one of the only bars in town.

In Al-Milga there's a **bakery** opposite the mosque and a couple of well-stocked **supermarkets** in the shopping arcade. Just behind the bakery are a few small restaurants,

the most reasonable of which is **Kafeteria Ikhlas**; try its chicken meal with soup for E£12. Just by the bus stop **Katrien Rest House** (though there's no accommodation) is open for lunch only and serves a filling chicken, rice and vegetable meal inside or on the veranda.

Getting There & Away

Bus These leave from the square in front of the mosque in Al-Milga. There is a bus to Cairo (E£37, seven hours) at 6am and another at 1pm that goes via Dahab (E£10), Nuweiba (E£15) and Taba (E£20) before heading to Cairo via Nakhl. Change at Dahab to get to Sharm el-Sheikh.

Service Taxi These travel in and out of the village irregularly and infrequently. At the monastery taxis often wait for people coming down from Mt Sinai in the early afternoon. Count on between E£10 and E£20 per person to Dahab or Nuweiba.

NUWEIBA نويبع
☎ 069

Strung out over several kilometres, with no real centre and little ambience, Nuweiba is not Sinai's most beautiful spot, although the sandy beaches are nice. It is divided into three parts. To the south is the port with a major bus station, banks and fairly awful hotels. A few kilometres further north is Nuweiba City, where the tourist resort hotels and one of the area's two dive centres are located, as well as a couple of good places to eat. Tarabin, which models itself on Dahab's Assalah traveller colony, is a further 2km out, draped along the northern end of Nuweiba's calm bay. Since the Palestinian *intifada* (uprising) broke out in September 2000, tourism here has been negligible and many of the smaller hotels are closing down.

Information

The **post** and **telephone offices** are near the hospital on the exit road from Nuweiba City. There's another post office as well as two banks on the road leading into the port. The **Banque Masr** at the port has an ATM. There's a **National Egyptian Bank** at the Helnan Nuweiba Hotel, Nuweiba City. There is Internet access at the **Mondial Supermarket** in Tarabin, the **City Internet**

Café in Nuweiba City and at **Habiba Camp**, just south of the Helnan.

Activities

Once again, underwater delights are the feature attraction and scuba diving and snorkelling the prime activities. **Diving Camp Nuweiba** (☎ 500 402) is in the Helnan Nuweiba Hotel camping area and **Emperor Divers** (☎ 520 321) operates out of the Nuweiba Coral Hilton Resort.

Nuweiba is the place to organise jeep and camel treks to sights such as **Coloured Canyon**, **Khudra Oasis**, **Ain Umm Ahmed** and Ain al-Furtaga. Try your luck with the Bedouin people of Tarabin or head up to the camps at Mahash or Ras Shaitan, further up the coast.

At the Bedouin village of **Mizena**, 1km south of Nuweiba port, you can swim with a dolphin that lives in the bay there. The village elders charge visitors E£10 to swim and E£10 for a mask and snorkel.

Places to Stay

Nuweiba Port Unless you've got money for the Hilton, don't stay here.

The large, beachfront **Nuweiba Hilton Coral Resort** (☎ 520 320, fax 520 327; singles/doubles from US$125/160) has good water sports, lush gardens and the amenities you'd expect of a Hilton. Rates include taxes and breakfast.

Nuweiba City With your own tent, you can camp at **Helnan Nuweiba Hotel** (E£10) and **City Beach Village** (E£7).

Sun Beach Camp (☎ 500 163; huts E£10 per person) and the relaxing **Small Duna** (☎ 500 198; beds in huts E£10) are quiet camps in the sands for refugees from Tarabin.

The reasonable, four-star **Helnan Nuweiba Hotel** (☎ 500 401, fax 500 407; singles/doubles from US$50/65) caters mainly to package tourists or middle-class Cairenes. Rooms come with breakfast, but don't include taxes. Its **Holiday Camp** (singles/doubles E£50/70), next door, has cheaper but scruffy cabins, which also include breakfast in the price.

Habiba Camp (☎ 500 770, fax 500 565; double bungalow rooms E£120; singles/doubles in cabins E£40/80, singles/doubles in huts E£30/60) is a laid-back, beachfront camp that is transforming itself into a hotel. It also

has a Bedouin-style **restaurant** that serves groups on day trips to Nuweiba from Sharm el-Sheikh.

City Beach Village (☎ 500 307; double huts E£30, singles/doubles with bathroom & air-con E£50/70), halfway between Nuweiba City and Tarabin, is not a bad option if you just want to sit all day on a tranquil beach.

Tarabin As Tarabin develops along Dahab lines, the choice of accommodation is becoming wider. You can get a mattress in a bamboo or concrete hut at one of the camps for E£6, and there are a couple of hotels.

Places to Eat

Apart from the hotels and camps, there's not much to speak of at the port or in Tarabin. In Nuweiba City **Dr Shishkebab** is excellent, while **Hamido**, opposite the Helnan, offers excellent fish meals and mezze.

Getting There & Away

Bus Buses going to or from Taba stop at Helnan Nuweiba Hotel and Dr Shishkebab in Nuweiba City. They usually also call in at the port, but do not stop at Tarabin.

Buses generally meet incoming ferries. There are three daily buses to Cairo (E£53 to E£58, seven to eight hours) via Taba (E£10, one hour). They stop at the Helnan Nuweiba Hotel as well as at the bus station near the port. Buses to Sharm el-Sheikh (E£20, two to three hours) via Dahab (E£10) leave at 6.30am and 4pm; to Taba at 6am (E£10) and noon (E£19); and to Suez at 6am (E£25; six hours via Nakhl).

Service Taxi There is a big **service taxi station** by the port. If you can find a full car it costs E£12 to Dahab, E£25 to Sharm and St Katherine and E£60 to Cairo.

Boat For information about ferries and speedboats to Aqaba in Jordan, see the introductory Getting There & Away section to this chapter.

TABA   طابا
☎ 069

This busy crossing into Israel is open 24 hours. There is a small **post and telephone office** in the 'town', along with a hospital, bakery and an **EgyptAir** office (often closed). You can change money at booths of **Banque** du Caire (unreliable opening hours) and Banque Masr *(open 24 hrs)*, both 100m before the border, or at the Taba Hilton Hotel.

Getting There & Away

Air There is an EgyptAir (☎ 530 155) flight between Cairo and Ras an-Naqb airport (which is 38km from Taba) each Monday for the satanic fare of E£666 one way.

Bus Several buses, operated by East Delta Bus Co, run from Taba. The 7am service goes on to St Katherine's Monastery (E£25, three to four hours) and then Suez (E£45). Buses to Cairo (E£53 to E£74) leave at 7.30am, 9am and 2pm. Sharm el-Sheikh (E£25) buses leave at 8.30am, 1pm and 3pm, stopping at Nuweiba (E£10) and Dahab (E£20).

Service Taxi A taxi (up to seven people) to Nuweiba costs E£10 per person, to Dahab E£25, to Sharm el-Sheikh E£40 and to Cairo E£50 to E£60 per person. If the border is busy you shouldn't have to wait too long for the vehicle to fill up; if business is slack you may end up paying considerably more.

AL-ARISH   العريش
☎ 068

Al-Arish is the capital of the north Sinai governorate and has a population of about 40,000. The palm-fringed **beaches** and comparatively unspoiled nature make it a pleasant place for a swim.

Every Thursday, a **souq** is held in the oldest part of town and Bedouin come in from the desert to trade silver, beadwork and embroidered dresses. There's also the **Sinai Heritage Museum** on the outskirts of town along the coastal road to Rafah. Otherwise, the beaches are main attraction. The parade of palms, fine white sand and clean water makes this one of the nicer Mediterranean spots in Egypt.

Places to Stay

Moon Light Hotel (☎ 341 362; *Sharia Fuad Zikry; singles/doubles E£15/30*) is one of

only two hotels on the beach. It has newly renovated rooms, but basic facilities.

Virtually on the beach, **Green Land Beach Hotel** (☎ 360 601; *Sharia Fuad Zikry; singles/doubles E£40/60*) is one of the better deals in town. Rooms are clean and comfortable, and most have terraces. Breakfast is extra.

Egoth Oberoi (☎ 351 321, fax 352 352; *Sharia Fuad Zikry; singles/doubles US$103/128*) is the only five-star hotel in North Sinai and has the only bar in town. All rooms have sea views, balconies and the usual amenities.

Places to Eat

There's not a huge range of places to eat in Al-Arish outside of the hotels.

About the best budget restaurant in town, **Aziz Restaurant** (*Sharia Tahrir; dishes E£2-10*) has good meals of *fuul* and *ta'amiyya* as well as grilled chicken, *kofta* (grilled mince meat on a skewer), rice and spaghetti. It's also open for breakfast.

Sabry (*Sharia Tahrir; dishes 50pt-E£3*) is the best *ta'amiyya* place in town.

Maxim (☎ 340 850; *dishes E£25-40; open summer only*), tucked in amongst the palms, is an upmarket place that specialises in fish dishes.

Getting There & Away

Bus Buses for Cairo (five hours) leave Al-Arish at 7am (E£25.50) and 4pm (E£21.25). There is a bus via Qantara (E£5) to Ismailia (E£7, three hours) every hour until 3pm. For Suez, you have to go to Ismailia and take another bus from there. At 7am, 10.30am and 3pm there are buses to Rafah (E£2, ½ hour). The bus bypasses Rafah town and takes you directly to the Egyptian border post, where you can disembark with your bags to go through passport control.

Service Taxi A cheaper alternative to the expensive Sinai buses to Cairo is a service taxi, which costs about E£20 per person.

Iran

ایران

Persia, called Iran since 1934, has long fascinated and daunted travellers. From the outside it inspires images of the exotic and mysterious, but also an element of danger. The latter is a slightly misguided perception. Put aside media images of fervent anti-Western marches and secret police – Iran is a remarkably safe, stable and hospitable country to visit.

Having recovered from the excesses of the Islamic Revolution, and the aftermath of the Iran-Iraq War, Iran is one of the most fascinating, welcoming and inexpensive countries in the Middle East, and many parts of it are yet to be 'discovered' by travellers. Although getting a visa is no formality, the doors are certainly open, tourism is gradually being developed, and most foreigners – including Americans – are treated warmly and with great interest by the Iranian people.

The main attractions are history and culture: days can be spent exploring age-old bazaars, chatting over tea in traditional teahouses, shopping for carpets, visiting enormous blue-tiled mosques, shrines and ruins of ancient cities, and simply meeting ordinary Iranians. There is also some good trekking and skiing in the northern mountains. Iran is one of the largest countries in the Middle East but transport is excellent and cheap enough to allow you to combine flying with bus and train travel.

It's still a religiously conservative country and the pace of political reform is slow, but few travellers leave without a sense of wonder and respect for the people and places of modern-day Persia.

Facts about Iran

HISTORY
Persian history is riddled with invaders and shifting dynasties. In the 6th century BC Cyrus the Great emerged as the first notable Persian ruler, founding the Achaemenid empire (558–330 BC), and his successors, Darius I and Xerxes, expanded their rule all the way to India in the east and the Aegean Sea in the west. Xerxes' defeat by the Greeks at Marathon marked the end of the great Achaemenid period of Persian history,

---

The Islamic Republic of Iran

Area: 1,648,195 sq km
Population: 75 million
Capital: Tehrān
Head of State: Āyatollāh Ali Khamenei is the 'supreme leader'; the elected president is Hojjat-ol-Eslām Seyed Mohammed Khatami
Official Language: Farsi (Persian)
Currency: Iranian rial (IR)

- Best Dining – being invited into an Iranian home; failing that, eating at the former bathhouses in Shirāz, Yazd and Kāshān

- Best Nightlife – puffing on a *qalyan* (water pipe) and enjoying a pot of tea in one of Esfahān's many wonderful teahouses

- Best Walk – wandering through the ancient bazaars in Esfahān, Kermān, Shirāz or Tabriz

- Best View – looking over the ancient city of Arg-e-Bam from its citadel at sunset

- Best Activity – hiking in the hills around Māsuleh, near Rasht

---

and in the 4th century BC, Alexander the Great invaded Persia.

After Alexander's death his empire split, with Persia being controlled by the Macedonian Seleucids who gradually introduced a Hellenistic culture. The Parthians, under king Mithridates, took over in the 2nd century BC and in turn were replaced by the Sassanians, a local dynasty from the Fars province.

The Sassanians controlled Persia from AD 224–638 but suffered continuing conflict with the Roman and, later, the Byzantine empires. Weakened by this scrapping, the Zoroastrian Persians fell easy prey to the spread of Islam and the Arabs. Arabs maintained control over Persia for nearly 600 years but were gradually supplanted by the Turkish Seljuk dynasty, which heralded a new era of Persian art, literature and science, marked by such thinkers as the mathematician-poet Omar Khayyām. Then in 1194 the Seljuk era abruptly collapsed when the Mongol Genghis Khan swept in and commenced a cold-blooded devastation that was to last for two centuries.

Beginning in 1502, the Safavid era heralded a great Persian renaissance. Under Shāh Abbās I (1587–1629) foreign influences were again purged from the country, and the architectural miracles he later presided over in Esfahān have left a permanent reminder of this period. The decline of the Safavids following Shāh Abbās I's death was hastened by an invasion from Afghanistan, and in 1736, Nāder Shāh, a tribal leader from the northeast, overthrew the impotent Safavids and proceeded to throw out Afghans, Russians and Turks in all directions. It was a relief to all, both within Persia and without, when he was assassinated in 1747.

The following Zand and Qajar periods were not notable except for a brief reign of glory under Karim Khān-e Zand at Shiraz. In 1926 Rezā Khān Pahlavi, a Cossack officer in the imperial army, founded the

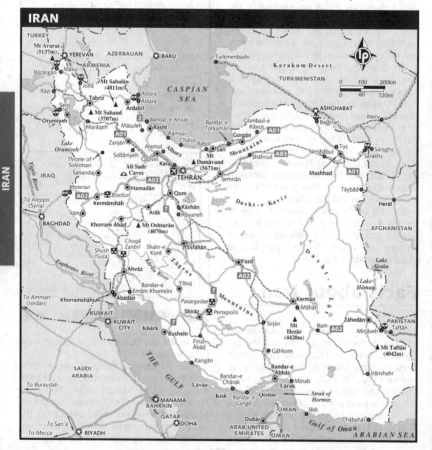

IRAN

What to See

What you choose to see in Iran – and in what order – will depend on how you're travelling. For overland travellers there's a fairly standard route that crosses the country from northwest to southeast. Assuming you're coming from Turkey your first stop will be **Tabriz**, a city with a Turkish influence and Iran's oldest bazaar. From there, travel across to the Caspian Sea coast and spend a night or two in the beautiful hill village of **Māsuleh**, where you can go hiking in the surrounding forest. Alternatively, head for the romantic **Castles of the Assassins** near Qazvin – another good area for hiking. The capital, **Tehrān**, is for many travellers merely a transport hub, but it's worth a couple of days to explore its museums or as a base for trips to the **Alborz Mountains**.

From Tehrān, journey by train to **Esfahān**, the undisputed highlight of Iran with its stunning blue-tiled architecture and teahouses built into the pillars of bridges. After a few days in Esfahān (with a possible side trip to **Kāshān** and the historic village of **Abyaneh**), continue on to **Shirāz** and spend a day exploring the ancient ruins of **Persepolis**. From there, cut across to **Yazd**, with its remarkable old city, then make the long desert crossing to **Bam**, an oasis town with a superb mud-walled citadel. If you have more time, you could break the journey at **Kermān**.

If you're not travelling overland and fly into Tehrān, you could cover the Tehrān-Bam part of this route, then fly back to Tehrān from Kermān. Since flying is cheap in Iran, you could easily add a trip to **Mashhad** to visit the **Holy Shrine of Emām Reza** or (in winter) fly down to **Kish Island** in the Persian Gulf.

Pahlavi dynasty. Foreign influence – and oil – soon became an important element in Iran's story. During WWII, Iran was officially neutral, but Rezā Khān was exiled to South Africa because he was thought to be too friendly with the Axis powers. His 22-year-old son, Mohammed Rezā, succeeded him. The government of Mohammed Rezā was repressive, but Iran was rapidly modernised. Illiteracy was reduced, women emancipated, land holdings redistributed, health services improved and a major industrialisation programme embarked upon. The 1974 oil price revolution became the *shāh*'s undoing: he allowed US arms merchants to persuade him to squander Iran's vast new wealth on huge arsenals of useless weapons. The flood of petrodollars lined the pockets of a select few, while galloping inflation left the majority worse off than before.

Since the early days of the Pahlavi era there had been a smouldering resistance that occasionally flared into violence. Students wanted faster reform, devout Muslims wanted reforms rolled back, and everybody attacked the Pahlavis' conspicuous consumption. As the economy went from bad to worse, the growing opposition made its presence felt with sabotage and massive street demonstrations. The *shāh* introduced martial law, and hundreds of demonstrators

were killed in street battles in Tehrān. The *shāh* finally fled the country in January 1979, and died a year later.

Exiled cleric Āyatollāh Khomeini returned to Iran on 1 February 1979 to be greeted by adoring millions. His fiery brew of nationalism and Muslim fundamentalism had been at the forefront of the revolt, but few outside Iran realised how much deep-rooted support he had and how strongly he reflected the beliefs and ideals of millions of his people (see the boxed text 'Āyatollāh Khomeini' later).

Khomeini achieved his goal of establishing a clergy-dominated Islamic Republic (the first true Islamic state in modern times) with brutal efficiency. Opposition disappeared, executions took place after meaningless trials and minor officials took the law into their own hands.

In 1980, Saddam Hussein made an opportunistic land grab in southwest Iran, taking advantage of Iran's domestic chaos, on the pretext that the oil-rich province of Khuzestān was historically part of Iraq. Although Iraq was better equipped, Iran drew on a larger population and a fanaticism fanned by the rhetoric of the *mullahs* (Muslim clergy). For the first time since WWI the world witnessed the hideous spectre of trench warfare and poison gas. A cease-fire was finally negotiated in mid-1988, with neither side having achieved its objectives.

IRAN

Āyatollāh Khomeini

The Āyatollāh Khomeini, the architect of the Islamic Republic, still looms large in public life in Iran. His face can be seen on billboards and photographs everywhere and every town has a major street or main square named after him. Born in the small village of Khomein in central Iran, Seyed Ruhollāh Musavi Khomeini followed in the family tradition by studying theology, philosophy and law in the holy city of Qom. He first came to public attention in 1962 when he opposed the *shāh's* plans to reduce the clergy's property rights and emancipate women. His outspoken opposition earned him exile in Turkey before he was shunted off to Iraq and then, in 1978, to France. There, he was accessible to the Western press, and, ironically, it was in Europe that his cause was boosted by the media at a time when he was little known even in his home country. After the *shāh* fled in 1979, Āyatollāh Khomeini returned to a tumultuous welcome, and took control of the country. When he died in 1989 an unprecedented 10 million mourners attended his funeral.

Iran Today

Khomeini died in 1989, leaving an uncertain legacy to the country he had dominated for a decade. Āyatollāh Ali Khamenei was appointed his successor as Iran's spiritual leader, but inherited little of his predecessor's popular appeal or political power.

In 1997, the moderate Hojjat-ol-Eslām Seyed Mohammed Khatami easily beat another candidate (who was backed by the Iranian parliament) to become president. Khatami attracted a large vote from women and youth, both hoping he could change the more stern impositions of the Islamic Republic.

However, liberalisation and reform have been slow since Khatami came to power, because hardline factions, dedicated to the Islamic Revolution, control the corridors of power within the government. Most Iranians agree that the nation's power base is still in Qom. The reforms have suffered many setbacks. During 2000 more than 30 reformist newspapers were shut down and their editors jailed. However, Khatami was overwhelmingly returned for a second term in 2001, but since he can only govern for two terms (of four years each), many Iranians are concerned about the lack of a suitable successor. Rising unemployment (and an increasing youthful population looking for work) is just one of the problems facing an isolated Iran in the new millennium.

Although Iran gave tacit support to the USA's attack on the Taliban (a regime it did not recognise), US President George W Bush's 'Axis of Evil' speech, linking Iran with global terrorism, and the US support for Israel continues to freeze political and economic relations between the two countries.

GEOGRAPHY

Iran covers 1,648,195 sq km, with the two great deserts, Dasht-e Kavir and Dasht-e Lut, occupying most of the northeast and east of the central plain. There are three dominant mountain ranges: the volcanic Sabalān and Tālesh ranges in the northwest; the vast, ancient and virtually insurmountable Zāgros range in the central west; and the Alborz range, between Tehrān and the Caspian Sea, home to Iran's highest peak, Mt Damāvand (5671m).

Most Iranian rivers drain into the Gulf, the Caspian Sea, or one of a number of salty and swampy lakes, such as Orumiye, Iran's largest lake.

CLIMATE

Iran is hot and dry in summer and cold and dry in winter. North of the Alborz Mountains, rainfall is heavy, but the rest of Iran experiences little precipitation. Summer (June-August) can get very hot down south: in the desert and along the Gulf coast, debilitating humidity and summer temperatures over 40°C are common. In mid-winter (December-February), places such as Tehrān, Mashhad and Tabriz are usually cold, and snow is common in the higher regions of the west and southeast.

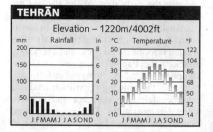

IRAN

GOVERNMENT & POLITICS

After the Islamic Revolution in 1979, some 98% of the population apparently voted in support of a unique form of Islamic government, with three levels of political power. The parliament, called the Majlis, is elected by the Iranian people every four years, though the candidates are carefully vetted. It is dominated by the *velayat-e faqih*, or supreme leader – currently Āyatollāh Ali Khamenei. The Majlis approves (but does not instigate) laws and economic decisions.

The second level of power, the Council of the Guardians, 'safeguards the Islamic Ordinances and Constitution', and comprises 12 Islamic jurists and religious experts, all selected by the supreme leader.

Thirdly, the president manages a cabinet, although final control always rests with the Majlis. The president is elected every four years (and only allowed two terms).

POPULATION & PEOPLE

Iran's population is around 75 million – and rising fast. More than 60% of inhabitants can be classified as Persians, descendants of the Aryans who first settled in the central plateau of Iran in about 2000 BC. About 25% of the population are Azerbaijanis, who live in the northwesternmost region of Iran. Turkmen (2%) are a fierce nomadic race of horse people and warriors who inhabit Iran's far northeast.

Other inhabitants include: the Lors (2%) – thought to be part Persian, part Arab – a semi-nomadic people who live in the western mountains south of Kermānshāh; Kurds (5%) who mostly inhabit the western mountains between Orumiye and Kermānshāh; and Arabs (4%) who mostly live on the south coast and Gulf islands, and in Khuzestān.

More than 300,000 nomads still roam the plains and mountains. The Baluchis are semi-nomadic and inhabit Baluchestān, a formerly semi-autonomous territory now divided between Iran and Pakistan. The Qashghārs of southwest Iran are traditionally wandering herds-people.

RELIGION

Most Iranians belong to the Shiite branch of Islam. Less than 8% of the population (Kurds, Baluchis, Turkmen and about half the Arabs) are Sunni. (For an explanation of the terms Shiite and Sunni, see Religion in the Facts about the Region chapter.) The official figures for minorities – Christians (0.7%), Jews (0.3%) and Zoroastrians (0.1%) – are probably underestimates as many followers of minority faiths call themselves Muslims in official documents.

Most Iranian Christians are Armenians, predominantly members of the Gregorian Church; the rest are mainly Assyrians. Iran is a centre of Zoroastrianism, and followers are found mainly in Yazd, Tehrān and Kermān.

Baha'i, a religion founded in Iran which regards itself as 'pure Islam', is followed by about 300,000 Iranians. The religion is not recognised by the Iranian authorities, however, and many followers have been persecuted or forced to keep a very low profile or have emigrated.

LANGUAGE

Although the vast majority of Iranians speak the national language, Farsi (Persian), it's the mother tongue of only about 60% of the population. The most important minority languages are Azerbaijani, Kurdish, Arabic, Baluchi and Lori.

English is understood by many educated middle-class men and women in the major cities, university students, most employees of mid-range and top-end hotels and restaurants, and most staff in travel agencies and tourist offices.

However, if you're travelling independently and using budget accommodation and restaurants, you cannot rely entirely on English. The Language chapter at the back of this book lists some important Farsi words and phrases.

Facts for the Visitor

WHEN TO GO

The best times to visit Iran are mid-April to early June, and late September to early November. Winter is definitely the best time to visit the southern coast and the Gulf islands. Some prefer not to visit during Ramazān (Ramadan), though it won't affect your travels too much. For about 10 days before and after the Iranian New Year (which starts on about 21 March), transport and accommodation are at a premium and may be heavily booked, and tourist sites are crowded with holidaying Iranians.

VISAS & DOCUMENTS
Visas
Visitors from Slovenia, the Former Yugoslav Republic of Macedonia and Turkey can get a three-month tourist visa on arrival. Japanese travellers can get a three-month tourist visa at any Iranian consulate/embassy without a problem. Everyone else must apply for a tourist or transit visa prior to arrival, and for most nationalities getting one is a hassle. Australians, New Zealanders, Canadians, Germans and citizens of some other European countries shouldn't have a problem applying through the embassy in their home country; citizens of the UK and USA will have to jump through hoops. The most frustrating part is that there don't seem to be any hard and fast rules – but if all else fails, contact a travel agent in Iran (see Organised Tours under Getting Around later).

If you want to travel independently, the best general advice is to apply for a one-month tourist visa (extendable) in your home country if you're flying into Iran, or a five- to 10-day transit visa (extendable) along the way if you're travelling overland to Iran. If you can only get a short transit visa, don't worry – getting an extension inside Iran is far easier than obtaining any sort of visa in the first place.

The Internet is the best place to begin your visa application as Iranian embassies and consulates in many countries have their own websites (see Embassies & Consulates later). When applying for a visa, you must complete two or three application forms (in English); provide up to four passport-sized photos – complete with the *hejab* (head covering) for women – and pay a fee, which varies according to nationality but is generally the equivalent of US$50.

If you have an Israeli stamp in your passport or any other evidence of a visit to Israel, you will be refused a visa and denied entry into the country.

For details of visas for other Middle Eastern countries, see the 'Visas at a Glance' table under Visas & Documents in the Regional Facts for the Visitor chapter.

Transit Visas A transit visa is valid for five or 10 days and is extendable. This visa is normally requested by, and given to, foreigners who are travelling overland into and out of Iran. Transit visas are normally valid for three months, ie, you must enter Iran within three months of the date of visa issue. Good places to apply for a transit visa include İstanbul and Erzurum in Turkey, Islamabad in Pakistan and Delhi in India. You generally need to provide a letter of introduction from your embassy (easy to get but often expensive) when applying for a transit visa outside your home country.

Tourist Visas Tourist (and business) visas are usually for one month (valid for three months from the date of issue) and can also be extended.

Regulations about whether you need a sponsor in Iran for a tourist visa differ from one embassy/consulate to another. If you're arranging your tourist visa through a relative, travel agency or business contact in Iran, they will need your full personal and passport details and a brief itinerary. A week or so later, your sponsor will send you an authorisation number from the Ministry of Foreign Affairs in Tehrān, which you then use to collect your visa from the relevant embassy.

If you're having difficulty getting a visa and don't have a sponsor, contact a travel agency in Iran (see Organised Tours in the Getting Around section later), or a visa service agency in your home country. These agencies may charge US$50 (or more) for their services (on top of the visa fee), but you're usually under no obligation to take any of their tours.

Going in through the 'back door' – Kish Island – is an option. Kish, in the Gulf, is Iran's favourite duty-free shopping destination and is also a visa-free port, popular with people hopping over from the UAE. There is a daily flight from Dubai to Kish (US$110) and your passport is stamped on arrival for a stay of up to 14 days. From there, head to the Ministry of Foreign Affairs, which claims to issue 30-day tourist visas to most foreign nationals within two working days. Then you can easily get to the mainland by boat or air.

Visa Extensions Extensions of up to two weeks each are usually no hassle, but don't expect extensions totalling more than one month.

You can normally only apply for an extension two or three days before a transit visa is due to expire, and a week before a tourist visa expires. The best places to get extensions are Esfahān, Shirāz, Kermān, Yazd, Tehrān, Tabriz and Zāhedān. The problem with the latter two is that if you've just entered Iran (via Turkey or Pakistan), officials probably won't be interested in issuing you with a visa extension straight away. The locations of the visa offices are provided in the relevant sections.

To get an extension arrive early (most offices close at 1pm), then obtain and fill out the visa extension form. You'll then be directed to a branch of Bank Melli where you pay IR10,000 and receive a receipt. A further IR2500 is payable at the visa office. You also need to provide one or two photocopies of your passport and original Iranian visa, and two passport-sized photos (women must be photographed in a *hejab*). Once accepted, you can normally collect your passport the next day, though in some places such as Tabriz, Esfahān and Shirāz, the extension is issued on the spot.

Driving Licence & Permits
To drive around Iran you must have an International Driving Permit. If you're bringing in a vehicle, get a *carnet de passage* from the relevant international automobile organisation in your country.

Student & Youth Cards
A valid ISIC (International Student Identity Card) is gold in Iran if you plan to do a lot of sightseeing. With it you can get a 50% discount on the high entrance fees at most (but not all) tourist sites – Persepolis is an exception, as are most of Esfahān's sights. Sometimes it just depends on who's behind the ticket counter, so always ask '*Danesh taktfief?*' ('Student discount?') and be persistent.

EMBASSIES & CONSULATES
Iranian Embassies & Consulates
Following are the Iranian embassies and consulates in major cities around the world. For addresses of Iranian embassies in neighbouring Middle Eastern countries see the relevant country chapter.

Australia (☎ 02-6290 2421, fax 6290 2431, W www.embassyiran.org.au) 25 Culgoa Crt, O'Malley, ACT 2606
Canada (☎ 613-235 4726, fax 232 5712, W www.salamiran.org) 245 Metcalfe St, Ottawa, Ontario, K2P 2K2

France (☎ 01 47 20 30 95, fax 01 40 70 01 57, W www.ambassadeiran.com) 4 Ave d'Iena, 75016, Paris
Germany (☎ 228-816 110, fax 376 154, W www.iranembassy.de) Godesberger Allee 133–137, 5300, Bonn
Consulate: (☎ 69-560 0070, fax 560 0071, W www.iranconsulate.com) Guiollettstrasse 56, 6000 Frankfurt
Ireland (☎ 01-885 881, fax 834 246) 72 Mount Merrion Ave, Blackrock, Dublin
Netherlands (☎ 70-354 8483) Duinweg 24, The Hague 2585 JX
New Zealand (☎ 04-386 2983, fax 386 3065) The Terrace, Wellington
UK (☎ 020-7225 3000, fax 7589 4440) 16 Princes Gate, London SW7 1PT
Consulate: (☎ 020-7937 5225, visa info line ☎ 0906-802 0222, fax 7938 1615, W www.iran-embassy.org.uk) 50 Kensington Crt, London
USA (☎ 202-9654 990, W www.daftar.org) Iranian Interests Section at the Embassy of Pakistan, 2209 Wisconsin Ave NW, Washington, 20007

Embassies in Iran
The embassies listed below are all in Tehrān. Most are open from around 8am or 9am to 2pm or 3pm Sunday to Thursday.

Afghanistan (☎ 873 5040, fax 873 5600) 4th Alley, Pakistan St, Shahid Beheshti Ave
Azerbaijan (☎ 750 2724) 10 Malek St, Shariati Ave
Australia (☎ 872 4457, fax 872 0484, W www.iran.embassy.gov.au) No 13, 23rd St Khalid Eslambuli Ave
Bahrain (☎ 877 5365, fax 877 9112, e bahmanama@neda.net) 248 Zoubin St, Africa Ave
Canada (☎ 873 2623, fax 873 3202) 57 Shahid Sarafraz St
Egypt (☎ 224 2268, fax 224 2299, e egysee@ mail.neda.net.ir) Interest Section, 6–8 Rezaeei Alley, Ater Pol-e-Roumi, Shariati Ave
France (☎ 670 6005, fax 670 6544) 85 Nofl-Loshāto St
Germany (☎ 311 4111, fax 311 9883) 324 Ferdosi St
Iraq (☎ 221 1154, fax 223 3902) 17 Karamian Alley, Pole Roomi, Dr Shariati Ave
Ireland (☎/fax 222 2731) 10 Razan Shomali, Mir Damad
Jordan (☎ 204 1432) No 6, 2nd St, Mahmodyeh Ave
Kuwait (☎ 878 5997, fax 878 8257) 323/2 Vahid Dastgerdi St, Africa Ave
Lebanon (☎ 890 8451, fax 890 7345) 31 Shahid Kalantari St, Sepahbod Gharani Ave

IRAN

Netherlands (☎ 256 7005, fax 256 6990) 33 East Lane, Kamasaie St
New Zealand (☎ 280 0289, fax 283 1673) 34 Sosan St, North Golestan Complex, Niavaran
Oman (☎ 205 6831, fax 204 4672) 12 Tandis Alley, Africa Ave
Qatar (☎ 205 1255, fax 205 6023) 4 Golazin St, Africa Ave
Syrian Arab Republic (☎ 205 9031, fax 205 9409, e syrembir@neda.net.ir) 22 Arash St, Africa Ave
Turkey (☎ 311 5299, fax 311 7928) 337 Ferdosi Ave
UAE (☎ 878 1333, fax 878 9084, e emaratemb@mail.dci.co.ir) 355 Vahid Dastjerdi St, Valiasr Ave
UK (☎ 670 5011, fax 670 8021) 198 Ferdosi St
USA (☎ 878 2964, fax 877 3265) US Interests Section in the Swiss embassy, 59 West Farzan St
Yemen (☎ 201 5622, fax 205 8005, e yem .emb.ir@neda.net) 17 Giti St, Golestan Blvd, Africa Ave

CUSTOMS

You may bring into Iran duty-free 200 cigarettes, 200 cigars or 200g of tobacco, and a 'reasonable quantity' of perfume. But strictly no alcohol. Baggage checks on Western tourists are rare these days, but don't risk bringing in magazines that may promote 'moral outrage'.

You may officially take out Iranian handicrafts up to the value of IR150,000; one or two Persian carpets or rugs up to 6 sq metres in total (there is no limit on *kilims* – flat woven mats); and 150g of gold and 3kg of silver (without gemstones). If you want to exceed the stated values, or quantities, you officially need an export permit from the local customs office. However, foreigners are normally given some leeway in this and allowed to go home with a reasonable amount of souvenirs. Visitors must not take out more than IR500,000 or US$3000 in cash.

On arrival, you have to fill out a disembarkation card, and, possibly, a customs declaration, which you must keep and then return to customs and immigration when you leave. Not holding on to your disembarkation card is more trouble than it's worth.

MONEY
Currency

The official unit of currency is the rial (IR), but in conversation Iranians almost always refer to the *tomān*, a unit of 10 rials. It is essential when asking the price of everything from a taxi fare to a hotel room to think in *tomāns* – that way you won't find yourself in a situation where the vendor is demanding 10 times more than you thought you had agreed on. Often the unit of currency is omitted when discussing prices, so be aware and don't assume you are deliberately being ripped off. There are coins for 250, 100 and 50 rials, and notes for 10,000, 5000, 1000, 500 and 200 rials. In mid-2002 the government announced that it would be printing IR20,000 and IR50,000 notes.

Exchange Rates
Exchange rates at the time of writing include:

country	unit		Iranian rial
Australia	A$1	=	IR949
Canada	C$1	=	IR1,119
euro zone	€1	=	IR7000
Japan	¥100	=	IR1,469
New Zealand	NZ$1	=	IR813
UK	1£UK	=	IR11,000
USA	US$1	=	IR7700

Exchanging Money
The 'official' exchange rates set by Interbank are virtually meaningless and apply only to export business. At the time of writing the government had fixed the internal rate of exchange at IR7700 to US$1.

The US dollar is still the preferred currency for exchange in Iran, but you will also be able to change euros, pound sterling and some other currencies at exchange offices and some banks. The days of the Iranian black market – where the difference between the bank and street rates was significant – are over, but you still find black marketeers willing and able to change money for you. The speed of the transaction is the only advantage, and you may end up being short changed.

Don't bring any types of travellers cheques. Few banks will exchange travellers cheques and the ones that do ask 10% commission. AmEx travellers cheques are not accepted anywhere because of the US trade embargo.

ATMs & Credit Cards While there are ATMs in Iran, none are linked to international banking networks so they're of no use to travellers.

Credit cards are similarly of no use in Iran. Visa and AmEx are both blacklisted and completely worthless, and during our research trip MasterCard went the same way (prior to that Bank Melli routinely gave cash advances on MasterCard, provided it wasn't issued in the USA).

Some well-connected carpet shops or major travel agencies that specialise in international tourism might accept MasterCard, but don't count on it. Airlines offices, restaurants and practically all hotels take cash only.

Costs

Iran is an extremely cheap country for travellers, although accommodation and entrance to tourist sights can seem disproportionately expensive because of higher charges for foreigners (see Dual Pricing).

The cheapest hotels or *mosāferkhunes* cost from about IR25,000/40,000 (US$3/5) for singles/doubles.

Meals start at as little as IR2000 (US$0.25) for Iranian hamburgers (sandwiches), about IR8000 (US$1) for *chelo kebab*, but up to IR25,000 (US$3) at better restaurants, IR600 (US$0.08) for a soft drink and IR1000 (US$0.12) for a pot of tea (IR2000 in better teahouses).

Transport is dirt cheap, with long-distance bus travel about IR2000 (US$0.25) for each hour. So on a tight budget you could get by on about IR80,000 (US$10) per person per day travelling as a couple. This would still allow admission to some tourist attractions and an occasional restaurant meal.

You may not always be able to find that dirt cheap hotel though (and if you do they might not let you in), so allow at least IR120,000 (US$15) per person, and add to this extra money for internal flights (very cheap), long-distance taxis, souvenirs and the occasional splurge on a good hotel or restaurant. With say, US$25 a day, you can travel quite comfortably in Iran.

Dual Pricing An unfortunate aspect of travelling in Iran is dual pricing, where foreigners are officially charged much more than the locals, mainly for admission to tourist attractions and for all but the cheapest hotels. Because almost all tourist sights, even mosques, cost between IR20,000 and IR30,000 (US$2.50 to US$3.50) to visit, a day spent touring the attractions of, say, Esfahān or Shirāz, can easily blow your budget. It's even more galling in a town like Hamadān where the sights are of relatively minor interest. The result is that most budget travellers will be very selective about which mosques, museums and gardens they choose to visit. If you have a student card (ISIC), always ask if there's a discount available.

Tipping & Bargaining

Tipping is not expected in Iran, but it's usual to round up a bill or add on 10% at good restaurants. You'll also be expected to offer a small tip to anyone who guides you or opens a door that is usually closed, but Iran doesn't have the baksheesh mentality of much of the Arab world.

Fares in private taxis are always negotiable, but not in any other form of transport (including a shared taxi) because their prices are set by the government.

Rates in some hotels are open to negotiation, but a surprising number of places refuse to bargain at all – even when they're not busy.

Prices in restaurants are set; food in bazaars (but not in shops) is sometimes negotiable, but so cheap that it's hardly worth the effort. Everything else is definitely negotiable, particularly handicrafts.

POST & COMMUNICATIONS
Post

The Iranian international postal service is generally reliable and reasonably swift; the domestic service is reliable, but slow.

Postcards by air mail to Europe, North America and Australasia cost IR500; letters are IR2000. Sending parcels can be expensive. As a guide, a 1kg package using normal parcel post costs IR47,650 to Australasia or North America, and IR43,650 to the UK and Europe. Using EMS (registered express post) the same parcel to Australasia or North America costs IR140,000. Carpets cannot be sent through the post, but *kilims* can.

You can receive mail, including parcels, at the head post office in any major city; the most reliable poste restante services are at the post office at Emām Khomeini Square in Tehrān and at the head post offices in Shirāz and Esfahān. Poste restante mail is normally held indefinitely, despite requests for it to be forwarded.

Telephone

The country code for Iran is ☎ 98, followed by the local area code (minus the zero), then the subscriber number. Local area codes are given at the start of each city or town section. The international access code (to call abroad from Iran) is ☎ 98.

Making telephone calls within Iran, and overseas, is easy. A growing number of modern cardphones are replacing the old coin phones (which are only good for local calls); there are rows of them outside telephone and post offices.

You can buy a *kard telefon* from a newsstand or any telephone office, and use it to make local or long-distance calls in Iran, but not international calls. Local calls are almost free in Iran so your hotel should let you make them for nothing.

International calls can be made at a *markaz-e telefon* (telephone office), or from a private telephone office in any town. International calls are charged a minimum period of three minutes, then per subsequent minute.

The cost per minute from the Tehrān phone office is IR3000 to Europe and Australasia, and IR4000 to North America. Private phone offices charge IR5000 to IR6000 per minute.

Easily the cheapest and quickest way to make an international call is through an Internet Service Provider (ISP) with a service such as Phone2phone or Telnet, and the connections are usually surprising clear.

Most dedicated Internet cafés in major cities have this service and it costs between IR1000 and IR1500 per minute to Europe or Australasia, slightly more to North America.

Mobiles Although mobile phones are common in Iran, it's expensive and impractical to get hooked up to the network short term.

Fax

Faxes can be sent from phone and post offices in provincial capitals and mid-range and top-end hotels, though this is not cheap.

Email & Internet Access

Iran is no longer a cyber wasteland. The government has always been wary of the Internet and the difficulty in controlling its use, which led to a crackdown on more than 400 'illegal' Internet cafés in 2001. However, legitimate Internet businesses are now on the increase and you'll find Internet cafés with fast connections in most major cities.

They're often referred to as 'Coffee Net', which is probably a corruption of 'café net' because the chances of getting a cup of coffee are about equal to the chances of getting a stiff whisky. Costs range from IR7500 an hour to IR20,000 an hour.

DIGITAL RESOURCES

For a comprehensive list of Middle East/ Arab world websites, see the Regional Facts for the Visitor chapter. Some Iran-specific websites include the following:

Iran Mania This search engine provides links to just about every subject you could ever pursue in Iran, from art and literature to the Iranian Yellow Pages.
Ⓦ www.iranmania.com

Iran Touring & Tourism Organisation A useful summary of facts and figures about Iran and its various regions. Includes features about tourist attractions and accommodation search engine.
Ⓦ www.itto.org

Net Iran This website provides a useful rundown of facts and figures about Iran, covering politics, law and government structure. There are also links to English-language media sites.
Ⓦ www.netiran.com

Payvand This site provides some good links to Iranian information sites and links to Persian writing facilities.
Ⓦ www.payvand.com

BOOKS

As well as this book, Lonely Planet publishes a comprehensive country guide, *Iran*. In LP's travel literature series 'Journeys' there's *Black on Black: Iran Revisited* by Ana Briongos.

Otherwise, one of the classics is *The Road to Oxiana*, by Robert Byron, widely acknowledged as one of the great travel books of its era. Although Byron has a scholarly preoccupation with Islamic architecture, the book is lively and worth bringing.

Many books have been written about personal experiences before, during or after the Islamic Revolution (1979). *Out of Iran*, by Sousan Āzādi, is a revealing, though one-sided, autobiography of the western Iranian elite who stayed in Iran after the revolution.

Lifting the Veil (first published as *Behind Iranian Lines*) by John Simpson & Tira Shubart is one of the best accounts of life after the Islamic Revolution.

One of the few authentic travel narratives is *Danziger's Travels: Beyond Forbidden Frontiers*, by Nick Danziger, who travelled throughout the region in the mid-1980s with no regard for tiresome formalities like visas. The fearless Freya Stark wrote several accounts of her travels around Iran in the 1930s, including *Valleys of the Assassins*.

More general Middle East titles, some of which cover Iran, are listed in the Books section in the Regional Facts for the Visitor chapter.

NEWSPAPERS & MAGAZINES

If you ignore, or at least appreciate, the extreme bias against the USA and Israel, the English-language daily newspapers printed in Tehrān are not too bad. They can be hard to find among the dozens of Farsi newspapers and many newsstands don't stock them. *Iran Daily* (w www.iran-daily.com) is easy to read and carries some international news beyond the immediate region; *Iran News* toes the official line, but also has a good world news section and some handy classifieds; the *Tehrān Times* (w www.tehrantimes.com) is generally a good read.

In a few major cities, the latest issues of *Time* and *Newsweek* (appropriately censored) are sometimes available, but cost up to IR25,000.

RADIO & TV

All Iranian radio and TV stations are heavily controlled by the state. Most of the numerous radio stations are based in Tehrān, and relayed to each province. The BBC World Service, most European international radio services and Voice of America can be picked up in most parts of Iran with a world band radio.

Iranian TV is of little interest to travellers since none of it is in English, and it's so boring most Iranians don't bother watching it either. International satellite stations, such as MTV and CNN, are only available at top-end hotels and in a growing number of homes.

PHOTOGRAPHY & VIDEO

Most towns have at least one photographic shop for film and/or developing, though the range of available film and camera equipment is limited (except in Tehrān, Esfahān and Mashhad). Despite signs for Fuji and Kodak that you might see in shop windows, the majority of film available is the cheap Konica brand. A roll of 100ASA 36 print film costs about IR12,500 and processing costs around IR40,000. Slide film costs IR25,000 for cheaper brands, IR35,000 for Kodak Ektachrome, but it's not widely available – if you value your photos enough to use slide film you should bring a supply with you.

Bring your own video cassettes, along with spare batteries.

LAUNDRY

There are reliable laundry services in most cities but no do-it-yourself laundrettes. Many hotels also have a laundry service for guests. Washing detergent and soaps are widely available, but it's very cheap to have your laundry done for you.

TOILETS

Toilets are either the European sit-down type, or (more commonly) the Middle Eastern squat kind. Public toilets will almost always be the latter, but even a US$40 hotel room may still have a hole in the ground, so always be prepared for this. Toilet paper is only reliably provided in top-end hotels, but is available in most grocery shops in major cities.

HEALTH

No compulsory vaccinations are required before visiting Iran. Malaria is rare, though there is a slight risk in south and southeastern Iran during summer.

If you're mildly sick, seek advice from someone at your hotel, or an Iranian friend. They should be able to find a reputable doctor who speaks English and will hopefully come to your hotel. If your situation is more serious, your embassy should be able to recommend a reputable doctor and/or hospital and possibly arrange everything.

The standard of medical facilities varies greatly. The best place to get ill or injured is Tehrān, which has a disproportionate number of doctors and medical establishments. Doctors' surgeries and pharmacies (drug stores) are often clustered around major hospitals; surgeries often have signs outside

The Big Cover Up

From the moment you enter Iran, you are legally obliged to observe its rigid dress code, although it has eased in recent years and you'll notice young Iranian women in Tehrān and Esfahān showing more hairline and wearing more colourful clothing than at any time since the Islamic Revolution. You will be reprimanded for any serious lapses, though foreigners are unlikely to get into big trouble. The dress code is more strictly enforced during Ramazān, when Iranians avoid wearing red and other loud colours. Black is usually worn during the mourning month of Moharram.

Females older than seven must wear the *hejab* (modest dress) whenever in the actual or potential sight of any man who isn't a close relative. All parts of the body, except hands, feet and the face above the neckline and below the hairline, should be covered, and the shape of the body must be disguised. The outfit commonly associated with Iranian women is the *chador*, a tent-like cloak (normally black), draped loosely over the head, legs and arms. However, it's not necessary – nor advisable – to go this far: the standard dress for many Iranian women is a full-length skirt, or trousers (jeans will do), worn beneath a loose-fitting, below-the-knees black or dark blue coat, known as a *roupush*. Hair is hidden beneath a large, plain headscarf (although it's acceptable to allow a very modest fringe to show).

Foreign woman visiting Iran can wear a baggy shirt, or loose-fitting jacket, which comes down to at least their mid-thighs, over a long, loose, ankle-length skirt or jeans – plus socks and a headscarf. In Iran, foreign women can easily buy a *roupush*, which allows the freedom of wearing just a light vest or bra only underneath – a lot cooler in summer.

Men have it a lot easier, though they must wear full trousers; shorts are only acceptable when swimming and playing sport and three-quarter pants are frowned upon. Short-sleeve shirts are normally acceptable, except when visiting particularly holy places. During Ramazān, it's recommended that you stick to long sleeves.

their building with the doctor's name and specialty in English.

For more general health information see the Health section in the Regional Facts for the Visitor chapter.

WOMEN TRAVELLERS

Although women travellers have the hassle of staying covered up – see the boxed text 'The Big Cover Up' – most women find that the sexual harassment and constant come-ons from the local males that are common in other Middle Eastern countries are largely absent in Iran.

By comparison, women enjoy considerably more independence in Iran than elsewhere in the Middle East. One welcome consequence of this is that female visitors will find it quite easy to meet and chat with Iranian women, particularly in large cities such as Esfahān, Shirāz and Tehrān where educational standards are higher.

Unwanted attention does occur, though, especially in remote or untouristed areas, and some women will feel more comfortable travelling with a male companion or in a group.

DANGERS & ANNOYANCES

Open hostility towards Western visitors is extremely rare. In fact, many travellers regard Iran as one of the safest and most hospitable countries in the world. There are a number of police forces, but as long as you behave yourself, dress appropriately and don't point your camera at anything you shouldn't, you will normally receive nothing but a smile, and a helping hand if you need it. The notorious *komite* (religious police) have vanished from the streets. If you're arrested, or taken away for questioning, demand identification, insist on telephoning your embassy, and find an interpreter if you don't speak Farsi.

A few travellers have been stopped in the street by bogus plainclothes policemen. *Never* show or give any important documents or money to any policeman in the street; always insist on going to the police station, or claim that your passport and valuables are at your hotel.

Iran is no stranger to political crises, and huge government-organised marches are sometimes held in major cities. However, you should always stay well clear of all political marches and gatherings.

BUSINESS HOURS

Few places have uniform opening and closing times, but most businesses close early on Thursday and all day Friday. Most government offices open from 8am to 2pm Saturday to Wednesday, and close at noon on Thursday. Many shops and businesses close during the afternoon for a 'siesta' (from about 1pm to 3pm or 4pm), and open again in the evenings.

PUBLIC HOLIDAYS

In addition to the main Islamic holidays described in the Regional Facts for the Visitor chapter Iran observes the following national holidays:

Qhadir-e Khom 18 Zu-l-Hejje (changeable) – the day that the Prophet Mohammed appointed Emām Ali as his successor

Ashura 9 & 10 Moharram (changeable) – anniversary of the martyrdom of Hussein, the third *emām* of the Shiites; marked with religious dramas (passion plays) and noisy, chain-flailing street parades

Arba'een 20 & 21 Safar (changeable) – the 40th day after 9 & 10 Moharram (see Ashura earlier)

Anniversary of Khomeini's Rise to Power 11 February (22 Bahman)

Oil Nationalisation Day 20 March (29 Esfand)

No Ruz around 21–24 March (1–4 Farvardin) – Iranian New Year (see the boxed text)

Islamic Republic Day 1 April (12 Farvardin) – anniversary of the establishment of the Islamic Republic of Iran in 1979

Sizdah Bedar 2 April (13 Farvardin) – 13th day after the Iranian New Year, when most Iranians leave their houses for the day

Death of Emām Khomeini 4 June (14 Khordād) – particularly chaotic in Tehrān and Qom

Arrest of Emām Khomeini 5 June (15 Khordād)

Anniversary of Dr Seyed Beheshti 28 June (7 Tir) – commemorates the 1980 bomb blast at a meeting of the Islamic Republic Party that killed Dr Beheshti and several others

Day of the Martyrs of the Revolution 8 September (17 Shahrvar)

ACTIVITIES

Most travellers visit Iran for its culture and architecture, but **hiking** and **skiing** in the mountains are popular activities. There are reasonably easy trails in the Alborz Mountains north of Tehrān and in the Caspian Region around places such as Rasht and Rāmsar. For the more adventurous, Mt Damāvand can be climbed in three days.

No Ruz

The Iranian New Year, or No Ruz, is the main annual holiday and a huge family celebration. Starting on about the spring equinox (around 21 March), Iranians traditionally return to their home villages and towns to celebrate with friends and relatives. It can be very difficult to find hotel accommodation about 10 days before and after the Iranian New Year, and all forms of public transport are very heavily booked. Both hotel and transport costs rise by about 30% as a matter of course. Most businesses (but not hotels), including many restaurants, will close for about five days after the start of the New Year. This is generally not a good time to travel around Iran. The 13th day of the Iranian New Year is when families traditionally leave their homes and picnic out in the open.

There is also **diving** on Kish Island in the Gulf.

ACCOMMODATION

Because of the lack of tourism, Iran doesn't have many backpacker-style guesthouses, but there's no shortage of beds. In Iran our term 'budget hotel' encompasses the *mosāfer-khune* (a very basic guesthouse, literally 'traveller's house'), the odd backpacker lodge and one- and two-star hotels, all of which are reasonably priced.

'Mid-range' is two- and three-star hotels and 'top end' is four- and five-star hotels. There are also 'home stays' (a room in someone's home) and 'suites' (fully equipped apartments), mainly in the Caspian provinces.

The very cheapest places have shared shower and toilet facilities, which are rarely clean by Western standards. Some *mosāfer-khunes* don't have a shower on the premises at all – guests are expected to use a local *hammam* (bathhouse), or stay dirty. From about IR50,000 to IR80,000 you should get a room with private bathroom (and hot water), and a fan and central heating.

Most mid-range hotels, and all top-end places will charge foreigners much more than Iranians. Some mid-range hotels are open to negotiation outside peak times and although many quote prices in US dollars they accept (and usually prefer) rials. All guests (Iranian and foreign) must fill out a registration form, and hotel management will usually want to keep your passport during your stay, ostensibly because a police/security officer may come at any time and ask to see it. Check-out is usually at 2pm.

Some *mosāferkhunes* will not accept foreigners due to local police regulations. You can get around this by obtaining a special permit from the local police station allowing you to stay at any *mosāferkhune* in that town/city. The permit is usually not worth the hassle because there's always going to be a *mosāferkhune* somewhere that *will* accept foreigners.

Camping is not really viable. There are only a handful of inconveniently located camp sites, and authorities don't like anyone – least of all foreigners – pitching tents in the countryside except nomads.

FOOD

Iranian food varies considerably from the Middle Eastern norm, but you'll soon discover that the main dish on most restaurant menus is the *kebab*, in all its many forms. The diet is heavily based on rice, bread, fresh vegetables, herbs and fruit. Rice in general is called *berenj*.

Chelo is boiled and steamed rice and is often the base for meals such as *chelo morgh* (chicken and rice). Rice cooked with other ingredients, such as nuts and spices, is called *polo*. Saffron is frequently used to flavour and colour the rice.

Iranian bread, known generally as *nun*, is served with every meal. *Lavāsh* is the cheapest and least appetising – a flat, thin cardboard-type bread; *sangak* is thicker, oval-shaped and pulpy, and baked on a bed of stones to give it its characteristic dimpled look; *taftun* is crisp, thick and oval-shaped, with a characteristic ribbed surface; and *barbari* is crisp and salty, with a glazed and finely latticed crust.

Māst is similar to Greek or Turkish yogurt. It's commonly used as a cooking ingredient, often mixed with rice, and comes with diced cucumber or other vegetables, fresh herbs and spices.

Sup (Iranian soup) is thick and filling. Even thicker is *āsh*, more of a pottage or broth; thicker still is *ābgusht* (also called *dizi*), which is commonly served as a main dish and is often found on the menu at teahouses. *Khoresht* is the name for any kind of thick meaty stew with vegetables and chopped nuts. It's a tasty alternative to ubiquitous kebabs. One popular dish to look out for is *fesenjān*, a stew of duck, goose or chicken in a rich sauce of pomegranate juice and chopped walnuts.

The main dish in restaurants is the *kebab*, a long thin strip of meat or mince served as *chelo kebab* (with a mound of rice), or with bread and grilled tomatoes. There are several varieties: *fille kebab* is made from chunks of lamb; *kebab-e makhsus* (special kebab) is a larger strip of decent meat; *kebab-e barg* is thinner and varies in quality; *kebab-e kubide* (ground kebab) is made of minced meat and is the cheapest; while *juje kebab* is chicken fillets.

Turkish kebabs, where the meat is cooked on a vertical spit and shaved off in thin slices, are a popular form of takeaway food, as are felafel rolls. Western-style pizza and hamburger restaurants are also very common in the big cities.

The main vegetarian alternative to all these kebabs is soup and salad, often part of a meal in any decent restaurant anyway. Vegetarians can easily buy their own food at the market: nuts, fruits and vegetables, such as cucumbers, tomatoes and pickles, are commonly available and cheap. There is also plenty of fresh bread, as well as cheese and eggs.

Sweet Stuff

Another important Iranian institution is sweets. Most cities or provinces have their own particular type of sweet, usually available from shops in the bazaar. Probably the best known is *gaz*, a type of nougat with pistachio, from Esfahān.

In Shirāz try *koloche masqati*, a combination biscuit and jelly sweet; in Yazd look out for *pashmak*, spun sugar that tastes like sweet cotton wool; in Kermān and Bam *kolompeh* (date cookies) are unbeatable; in Qom you can't miss the tins of *sohun*, a delicious pistachio brittle.

DRINKS

The national drink is undoubtedly *chāy* (tea), served hot, black and strong, and traditionally in a small glass cup; tea bags are a depressingly common alternative to green tea leaves these days, but not in genuine teahouses.

Only upmarket hotel restaurants offer milk with tea (or coffee).

Qahve (Iranian coffee) is the same as Turkish coffee, served strong, black and sweet. 'Nescafé' is the generic term for powdered coffee, served from sachets with powdered milk and sugar.

All sorts of delicious, fresh fruit juices and shakes are available from street-side stands lined with blenders and festooned with melons, bananas and oranges. Tap water varies widely in quality, while generally safe to drink, it's becoming less palatable, mainly due to ongoing droughts affecting the water supply. Bottled mineral water is available just about everywhere. All sorts of soft drinks (sodas) are available, including locally bottled versions of Coca-Cola and Fanta, and they come virtually as a standard accompaniment with any restaurant meal.

Dugh is made of churned sour milk or yogurt, mixed with either sparkling or still water and often flavoured with mint and other ground herbs – definitely an acquired taste. *Mā'-osh-sha'r* ('Iranian beer'), often labelled as 'nonalcoholic malt beverage', tastes awful, vaguely like flat beer.

Persian Carpets

Persian carpets (or rugs) are more than just a floor-covering to an Iranian: they are a display of wealth, an investment, an integral part of religious and cultural festivals, and used in everyday life (eg, as a prayer mat).

Types of Carpet Persian carpets often come in three sizes: the *mian farsh* is up to 3m long and up to 2.5m wide; the *kellegi* is about 3.5m long and nearly 2m wide; and the *kenareh* is up to 3m long and 1m wide.

A kilim is a double-sided flat-woven mat, without knots, which is thinner and softer than knotted carpets. They are popular as prayer mats and wall-hangings.

Making Carpets Most handmade carpets are made from wool. The wool is spun, and then rinsed, washed and dried. It's then dyed, either with natural dye or chemicals. Nomadic carpet weavers often use high-grade wool, and create unique designs, but they use unsophisticated horizontal looms so the carpets are often less refined. In villages, small workshops use upright looms, which create carpets with more variety, but the designs are often uninspiring. City factories usually mass-produce carpets of monotonous design and variable quality.

Carpets are made with Persian knots, which loop around one horizontal thread, and under the next; or Turkish knots, looped around two horizontal threads, with the yarn lifted between them. But the difference is not obvious to the layman (or tourist).

The higher number of knots per sq cm, the better the quality – and, of course, the higher the price. A normal carpet has up to 30 knots per sq cm; a medium-grade piece 30 to 50 knots; and a fine one, 50 knots or more. A nomadic weaver can tie around 8000 knots each day; a weaver in a factory about 12,000 knots.

Buying Carpets If you don't know much about Persian carpets take a trustworthy and knowledgeable Iranian friend with you when shopping. You might be able to pick up a bargain in Iran, but dealers in Western countries often sell Persian carpets for little more than you'd pay in Iran (plus postage), and you're less likely to be ripped off by your local warehouse dealer than a savvy Iranian bazaar merchant. Unless you're an expert, never buy a carpet as an investment.

Before buying anything, lie the carpet on the floor and check for any bumps or imperfections. Small bumps will usually flatten out with wear, but large bumps will remain. To check that a carpet is handmade, turn it over. The pattern will be distinct on the underside – the more distinct the better the quality.

Taking them Home Shipping a carpet/rug home adds about one-third more to the cost. Currently, each foreigner can take out of Iran one Persian carpet or two small Persian rugs totalling six sq metres. Carpets cannot be sent overseas through the post office.

Alcohol is strictly prohibited and officially unavailable in Iran.

SPECTATOR SPORTS

Football (soccer) is the major sport. The national competition lasts from about October to June, and games are played throughout the country on Thursday and Friday. In Tehrān major matches are played at Āzādi Stadium.

Iran has a decent international side that qualified for the 1998 World Cup, and several Iranians play in major European football leagues.

Second in popularity is wrestling, which you can sometimes witness (if you ask around) at a *zurkane*, or wrestling ground – usually a sunken, circular pit. In Sistān va Baluchestān province, traditional camel races are sometimes organised.

SHOPPING

Iran is a buyers' market for souvenirs. Thanks largely to the shortage of tourists, mass production is not common, prices are reasonable and the quality is generally high. Naturally, the bazaar is the best place to start looking, but in Esfahān, Shirāz and any place where foreign tourists are more common, it's harder to get a good price.

Souvenirs and handicrafts include ceramics, hand-beaten bronze ware and copperware, inlaid boxes, tea-sets, *qalyans* (water pipes), jewellery, spices, silk products, glassware, miniatures and, of course, carpets and rugs (see the boxed text 'Persian Carpets').

If you don't like bargaining, and don't have time to look around, the government-run Iran Handicrafts Organisation has stores in most provincial capitals.

General Export Restrictions

Officially, you need permission to export anything 'antique' (ie, more than 50 years old), including handicrafts, gemstones, coins and manuscripts. To send home by mail a few books (whether old or new, Islamic or not), get permission from the Ministry of Culture & Islamic Guidance in Tehrān.

If you're worried about whether an expensive item will be confiscated, contact the *edāre-ye gomrok* (local customs office) before buying anything, or place it carefully in your hand luggage, which is rarely searched on departure.

Getting There & Away

AIR

Iran's main international airport is in the western suburbs of Tehrān, though a new airport is taking shape about 45km south of the city. There are also some international flights to airports at Shirāz, Tabriz and Mashhad, usually from elsewhere in the Middle East.

The national carrier is Iran Air (**w** www.iranair.com), with a few smaller Iranian airlines, such as Iran Asseman, also offering a handful of international flights. Iran Air has a vast network of direct flights between Tehrān and Europe and Asia, the Middle East and Central Asian republics.

Female passengers must wear the *hejab* and no alcohol is served. Iran is also reasonably well covered by other regional airlines like Gulf Air, Emirates and Kuwait Airways.

Buying Tickets in Iran

There are no particularly cheap flights from Iran, and flights are no cheaper at travel agencies than airline offices.

On Iran Air, a one-way flight from Tehrān to London (also good for connections to the USA) will cost somewhere in the order of US$735; to Frankfurt, Amsterdam, Paris, Berlin (for connections elsewhere in Europe) US$633, Dubai US$156, Damascus US$202, Rome US$564, Athens US$433; and to Kuala Lumpur (for connections to Australia) US$602.

Departure Tax

The tax for all international flights is IR70,000, which is included in the price of most tickets. Check with the airline when you book your ticket or confirm your reservation.

LAND

Iran shares a border with seven countries, but most travellers enter or exit overland via Turkey or Pakistan.

The border crossings into the Central Asian Republics to the north are open, as is Afghanistan – but not Iraq. For details of travel between Iran and Afghanistan, Armenia, Azerbaijan, Pakistan and Turkmenistan see the Getting There & Away chapter earlier in this book.

Turkey

Road There are two border crossings. The easiest and most popular is at Bāzārgān/Gurbulak, reached via Tabriz. Most long-distance buses between Tehrān and İstanbul use this route, but it is far quicker to catch a bus, minibus or shared taxi to either border, cross the border independently, and then catch onward transport rather than wait for the rest of the bus to clear customs and immigration.

Further south, Sero (Iran)-Yüksekova (Turkey) is becoming a useful alternative for travellers heading from Van to Orumiye or vice versa. This crossing is relatively safe now, and there are daily buses from Orumiye to İstanbul via Van.

Train There are now international trains from Tehrān to İstanbul and Damascus. The Tehrān-İstanbul train via Sero border and Ankara (IR350,000, about 66 hours) departs every Monday at 6.35pm (return train departs İstanbul on Thursday at 6.35pm). For Damascus, you catch the same train, which then splits at Van in Turkey (IR340,000, about 65 hours).

SEA

Kuwait & the UAE

Passenger ferries sail across the Gulf from Bushehr, Bandar-e Abbās and Bandar-e Lenge to Kuwait and the UAE. The ferries are operated by the **Valfajre-8 Shipping Company** (☎ 889 2933, fax 892 409; cnr Shahid Āzādi & Karim Khān-e Zand, Tehrān).

Services include Bandar-e Abbās to Dubai (IR450,000, five hours) leaving every Tuesday, and from Bandar-e Abbās to Sharjah (IR320,000, 12 hours) on Monday, Wednesday and Saturday.

Getting Around

AIR

Iran is one of the cheapest countries in the world for domestic flights, although fares have crept up in the last few years. A 40-minute flight from Tehrān to Esfahān costs around US$15. You can usually get on the flight you want, even on the day of travel (except during the Iranian New Year). Domestic flights are more expensive if pre-booked from overseas, so allow yourself the flexibility and book flights as you need them.

The main domestic airline, Iran Air, has regular services to just about anywhere you want to go. The airline is reliable, safe (now that it's phasing out the disastrous Russian Tupolov planes), efficient and fully computerised. Ask for the useful pocket-sized timetable from an Iran Air office. Other smaller airlines, such as Iran Asseman, Caspian Airlines and Kish Airlines, have more-limited and erratic schedules, but are certainly useful for specific destinations (eg, Kish Airlines flies more regularly to Kish than Iran Air does). Fares for domestic flights are the same whether booked at a travel agent or directly at the airline office.

Iran Air services from Tehrān include:

to/from	one-way fare (IR)	duration (hrs)
Ahvāz	151,000	1½
Bam	248,000	2
Bandar-e Abbās	275,000	2
Esfahān	117,000	¾
Kermān	208,000	1½
Mashhad	197,000	1½
Rasht	117,000	¾
Shirāz	180,000	1½
Tabriz	147,000	1
Yazd	144,000	1

BUS & MINIBUS

Iran is extremely well covered by bus and minibus – fares are very cheap and services are frequent. Most buses are comfortable, with individual cushioned seats, and standing is not normally allowed.

The best companies, with the most extensive networks, are TBT and Cooperative Bus Company No 1, while Sayro Safar has the most modern fleet (mostly air-con Volvos).

There's rarely any need to book ahead – it's just a matter of asking around at the bus company offices in the terminal and getting on the next bus going your way. From one major city to another, say Shirāz to Esfahān, a bus from one company or another leaves every 15 minutes or so, but departures are much less frequent in more remote places, and between smaller towns.

The standard class of long-distance bus is sometimes called 'lux', while the more comfortable air-con buses with reclining seats and onboard videos are called 'super' or more commonly 'Volvo'. The latter is considerably more expensive and you'll only really notice the difference on long overnight trips or day trips in the height of summer when the air-con really is worth having. Don't count on averaging more than 80km/h on most routes – although the roads are good, all buses are speed limited and must make regular stops at police checkpoints to show their trip log.

Minibuses are often used for shorter distances and between less-populated places. They may be faster than buses, but they are always cramped and less comfortable.

TRAIN

Tehrān is the usual starting or finishing point for train. There are services from Tehrān to Tabriz, Ahvāz, Esfahān, Bandare Abbās, Kermān and Mashhad, but Iran is not nearly as well covered by train as it is by bus and plane. However, trains are comfortable, efficient, reasonably fast, and so cheap that you'd be mad not to go 1st class on an overnight trip. The old-style compartments are a good place to meet Iranians.

Most trains have two classes, some have three, although the Tehrān-Esfahān overnight express has only one. It's always worth paying a little more for 1st-class compartments, but if you buy a ticket from any town along a route (ie, not at the starting or finishing point), you may only be able to get a 2nd-class ticket. On trains that travel overnight, 1st class has sleeper compartment with four or six bunks and bedding provided.

LONG-DISTANCE TAXI

Shared taxis *(savari)* are normally available between any major town less than four hours away by car. This form of transport is more common in western Iran and the Caspian provinces, rather than the sparsely populated central desert areas.

Speed is the main advantage, because shared taxis are generally less comfortable than the bus since they invariably squeeze five people in, with two in the front seat. Shared taxis cost about three times more than the bus, but are still very cheap.

If you wish to speed up a departure, or crave a little extra comfort, pay for an empty seat or simply charter the vehicle (which should cost no more than five times

the single shared-taxi fare). Shared taxis normally leave from inside, or just outside, the relevant bus terminal, or from a designated point (usually a roundabout) on the outskirts of town.

In towns, shared taxis are used for short trips, constantly plying set routes between designated points for between IR200 and IR2000. Avoid getting in an empty shared taxi – the driver may assume you want to charter it.

CAR & MOTORCYCLE

Driving your own vehicle gives you flexibility, but distances across Iran are great, the countryside is often boring, and the traffic is truly horrendous. Road surfaces throughout Iran are generally good, but the roads are poor or unpaved in remote desert and mountainous regions. Never drive off the main road near the Pakistani, Iraqi or Afghani borders.

In theory, the rule of the road is to drive on the right. Leaded petrol currently costs IR500 per litre (very cheap, but it has doubled in price in the past three years). Diesel is even cheaper, but travellers transiting through Iran in diesel vehicles have reported being hit with a hefty 'fuel tax' at the border. Petrol stations are open every day, and the outskirts of every city, town and village has filthy shops where you can arrange repairs.

The main automobile organisation is the **Touring & Automobile Club of the Islamic Republic of Iran** (☎ 895 8096, fax 896 6800; *12 Shahid Arabali, Khorramshahr Ave, Tehrān*). If you are driving, carry a good map, preferably in Farsi and English.

Rental

Although it is possible to rent your own car in Tehrān (check the *Tehrān Times* for advertisements), car rental in Iran generally means with a driver. You can hire a taxi with a driver for about IR250,000 per day, and the driver can cope with the appalling traffic and navigation.

ORGANISED TOURS

A growing number of tour and travel agencies in Iran offer tours for foreigners around Iran and these can usually be arranged over the Internet. Services range from simply booking accommodation and transport to fully organised and catered tours. Expect to pay around US$100 per person per day for the latter. These trips are rarely scheduled, but are customised for groups and (less commonly) individuals. Many travellers, particularly from the USA and UK, use Iran-based agencies at least as a starting point to facilitate or speed up the visa process – travel agents can organise your visa surprisingly easily and this is included in the cost of a tour.

The following is a selection of reputable operators.

Arg-e-Jadid Travel Co (☎ 881 1072, fax 882 6112, e atc@neda.net) 296 Ostad Mottahari Ave, Tehrān

Caravan Sahra Co (☎ 884 8672, fax 884 8671, w www.caravansahra.com) 29 Ghaem Magham-e Farahani; also has an office in the Laleh International Hotel; both are in Tehrān

Iran Touring & Tourism Organisation (☎ 655 687, fax 656 800, w www.itto.org) 154 Bolvār-e Keshāvarz, Tehrān

Pars Tourist Travel Agency (☎ 0711-222 3163, w www.key2persia.com) Zand Ave, Shirāz

Tehrān تهران

☎ 021

Iran is not blessed with one of the world's loveliest capitals. It suffers from pollution, chronic overcrowding and a lack of any responsible planning, so don't expect an exotic crossroads steeped in oriental splendour. However, Tehrān is the economic heart of Iran and the vacuum that draws in people from all over the country. It has the finest museums in Iran, good hotels and restaurants and it's very easy to day trip into the Alborz Mountains.

Give the capital a chance – at least a couple of days spent exploring Tehrān is an essential part of the Iran experience.

ORIENTATION

Tehrān is so vast that getting hopelessly lost at least once is on the cards, but thankfully about 90% of the streets that you're likely to use are marked in English and the development of the Metro is making it easier to get around. If you need landmarks, the Alborz Mountains are usually visible through the haze to the north, and the huge telephone office at Emām Khomeini Square dominates inner southern Tehrān.

If you're using public transport, get to know the names and locations of the main squares as soon you can (vital for shared taxi navigation), and if you're staying a while, pick up the *Tourist Guide to Tehrān* map from Gita Shenasi.

INFORMATION
Visa Extensions

Tehrān is probably the worst place to obtain a visa extension in Iran, mainly because the office is always so busy and you may have to wait several days. If your visa is on its last legs, head to the **Department of Alien Affairs** (☎ 890 4560; Khalantar St; open 7.45am-1.30pm Sat-Wed, 7.45am-11am Thur), just off Nejātollāh St.

Tourist Offices

There is no genuine tourist office in Tehrān. The government-owned **Iran Touring & Tourism Organisation** (ITTO; ☎ 655 687; 154 Keshavarz Blvd) is primarily a tour operator, but can be of help. The information booths at the train station and both airport terminals have English-speaking staff but they are of little use for general information.

Money

If you arrive by air, change some money at the bank in the airport – the rates are only marginally lower than in the city. Most of the banks along Ferdosi St, and around Ferdosi Square, change cash but won't touch travellers cheques.

It's quicker to use official moneychangers, of which there are still a few along Ferdosi St (including one about 100m up from Bank Melli).

There are also plenty of moneychangers hanging around Ferdosi St waving wads of rials. Provided you're careful it doesn't hurt to use them, but you risk being ripped off by sleight-of-hand tricks so count your money carefully.

Post & Communications

The main post office (with poste restante) is along Emām Khomeini St just west of the square. The huge telephone office is on Emām Khomeini Square, but the public entrance is a small office (open 24 hours) tucked around on Naser Khosro St. Other post offices and telephone offices are located around major squares in the city.

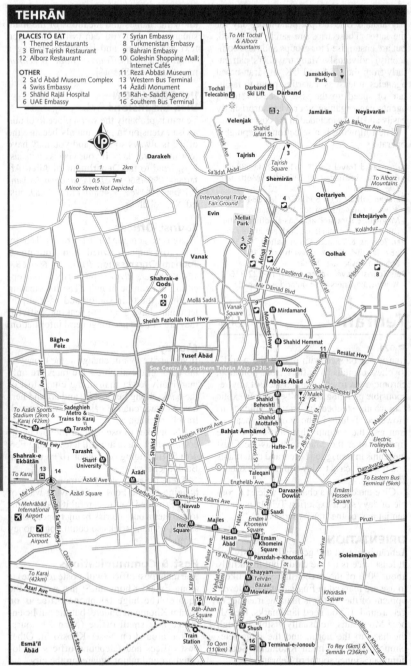

TEHRĀN

PLACES TO EAT		7 Syrian Embassy
1 Themed Restaurants		8 Turkmenistan Embassy
3 Elma Tajrish Restaurant		9 Bahrain Embassy
12 Alborz Restaurant		10 Goleshin Shopping Mall;
		Internet Cafés
OTHER		11 Rezā Abbāsi Museum
2 Sa'd Ābād Museum Complex		13 Western Bus Terminal
4 Swiss Embassy		14 Āzādi Monument
5 Shāhid Rajāi Hospital		15 Rah-e-Saadt Agency
6 UAE Embassy		16 Southern Bus Terminal

To Mt Tochāl & Alborz Mountains

Jamshidiyeh Park

Tochāl Telecabin

Darband Ski Lift

Darband

Jamārān Neyāvarān

Velenjak

Shahid Jafari St

Tajrish

Tajrish Square

Shemirān

Shahid Bāhonar Ave

Darakeh

Sa'ādat Ābād

To Alborz Mountains

Darakeh

Qeitariyeh

International Trade Fair Ground

Evin

Mellat Park

Eshtejāriyeh

Kolāhduz

Vanak

Afriqā Hwy

Vahid Dastjerdi Ave

Doktor Ali Shari'ati

Qolhak

Pāsdārān Ave

Shahrak-e Qods

Mollā Sadrā

Mir Dāmād Blvd

Vanak Square

Mirdamand

Sheikh Fazlollāh Nuri Hwy

Bāgh-e Feiz

Modarres Hwy

Shahid Hemmat

Resālat Hwy

Yusef Ābād

See Central & Southern Tehrān Map p228-9

Mosalla

Abbās Ābād

Shahid Beheshti Ave

Shahid Chamrān Hwy

Shahid Beheshti

Malek St

To Āzādi Sports Stadium (2km) & Karaj (42km)

Sadeghieh Metro & Trains to Karaj

Tarasht

Dr Hossein Fātemi Ave

Shahid Mottafeh

Bahjat Ābmāmd

Ferdosi St

Hafte-Tir

Madani

Electric Trolleybus Line

Tehrān Karaj Fwy

Tarasht

Sharif University

Āzādi

Dr Ali-ye Shari'ati St

Damavand

Shahrak-e Ekbātān

Āzādi Ave

Āzarbāyān

Talaqani

Enghelāb Ave

Darvazeh Dowlat

To Eastern Bus Terminal (5km)

Merāj

Āzādi Square

Jomhuri-ye Eslāmi Ave

Navvab

Saadi

Emām Hossein Square

Piruzi

Mehrābād International Airport

Ayatollāh Saidi Hwy

Saadi St

Hāfez St

Emām Khomeini Square

Domestic Airport

Qazvin

Hor Square

Majles

Hasan Ābād

Emām Khomeini Square

Panzdah-e-Khordad

Soleimāniyeh

To Karaj (42km)

Vāllasr Ave

Vahrde-e Eslāmi

15 Khordād Ave

Khorāsān Square

Āzari Ave

Kargar

Khayyām

Tehrān Bazaar

Mowlavi

17 Shahrivar

Mostafa Khomeini St

Esmā'il Ābād

Jaddeh-ye Sāveh

Molavi

Rāh-Āhan Square

Shush

Khayyām

Takhti

Khavābān-e Khāhrāzān

Train Station

To Qom (110km)

Shush

Terminal-e-Jonoub

To Rey (6km) & Semnān (236km)

0   0.5   1mi
0   1   2km
Minor Streets Not Depicted

IRAN

Internet phone calls can be made from various Internet cafés.

Email & Internet Access

Internet cafés are popping up again after a government crackdown in 2001. In south Tehrān, near the Glass & Ceramics Museum, there is **Ahov@n Computer** (☎ 676 0601; No 117 30 TIR St), with access for IR15,000 per hour, and **Persian Computer** (☎ 672 5899; No 290 30 TIR St; open 8am-midnight daily), with access for IR18,000 per hour. Both offer cheap international phone calls.

There are many more Internet cafés in central and northern Tehrān, including two at the Goleshin Shopping Centre, two opposite the Carpet Museum, and there's Internet access at the international airport.

Bookshops

There are several bookshops around the city, including **Gulestan Bookshop** (Manucheri St) and **Argentin Bookshop**, just off Ārzhāntin Square, and there are good (but expensive) bookshops inside most top-end hotels.

The tiny **Ferdosi Bookstand**, which is on the footpath on Ferdosi St, sells battered, second-hand English-language novels, and pre-revolutionary books in major European languages.

Medical Services

The best place to find a reputable doctor is along streets such as Valiasr Ave, Keshāvarz Blvd and Tāleghāni St, and near major hospitals. Clean, reputable hospitals include **Emām Khomeini Hospital** (☎ 938 081), **Pārs Hospital** (☎ 650 051) and **Tehrān Clinic** (☎ 872 8113).

Your embassy in Tehrān should also be able to recommend a doctor and hospital.

MUSEUMS

Tehrān has an outstanding selection of museums, although visiting them all is an expensive business. The best of the museums are in southern Tehrān and can be visited in a couple of days.

If you're pushed for time, stick to the Golestān Palace, National Jewels Museum, Carpet Museum, National Museum of Iran and Malek Museum. Most of Tehrān's museums are closed on Monday.

Golestān Palace & Gardens

This wonderful complex (☎ 311 8335; open 9am-2pm daily) includes seven buildings open to the public and set around a formal garden. You can wander around the gardens and admire the painted tile work for free, otherwise each museum costs IR10,000.

The most interesting are: the **Ethnographical Museum**, with a colourful exhibition of wax dummies wearing ethnic costumes and holding traditional cooking and musical implements; **Ivan-e Takht-e Marmar** (Marble Throne Verandah), a ceremonial hall containing an alabaster throne; **Negar Khane**, a gallery with a fine collection of Qajar artworks; and the **Shams-Al Ermarat**, a palace with furniture collected by the shāhs.

There's a basement **teahouse** in the southeast of the complex for refreshments, as well as a bookshop.

National Jewels Museum

If you only visit one museum in Tehrān, this should be it – for the sheer indulgence of it all! The museum (☎ 311 2369; admission IR30,000; open 2pm-4.30pm Sat-Tues) has more jewels on display than you are ever likely to see in one place again. Rubies, emeralds, diamonds, pearls and spinels are encrusted to everything from crowns and sceptres to cloaks, jewellery boxes and swords. Among the impressive displays is a world globe with rubies forming the countries and emeralds the oceans, and the famous Peacock Throne. It's in the heavily alarmed and guarded vault in the basement of Bank Melli. Look for the huge black gates, and a couple of machine-gun-toting guards.

National Museum of Iran

This museum (☎ 670 2061; admission IR60,000; open 9am-5pm Tues-Sun) houses a surprisingly small but fascinating collection from some of Iran's most famous archaeological sites, including Persepolis and Shush.

From Persepolis, there's a 6th-century BC audience hall relief of Darius I, a frieze of glazed tiles, a famous trilingual Darius I inscription and a carved staircase.

An intriguing exhibit is the grizzly 'salt man', a remarkably intact skull with white hair and beard, plus a leather boot with the foot still in it. The remains are thought to date from the 3rd or 4th century and were naturally preserved in salt.

Not everything is labelled in English and there are no English-speaking guides, which makes the admission seem a bit steep, although it also gets you into the Museum of the Islamic Period.

Museum of the Islamic Period

This museum (☎ 670 2655; open 9am-5pm) is next to, and included on the same ticket as, the National Museum of Iran. It features two floors of exhibits of carpets, textiles, ceramics, pottery, silks, portraits from the Mongol period (1220–1380), and excellent examples of stucco work from various mosques throughout the country. There's a good bookshop on the second floor and English speaking guides are usually available.

Malek Museum & Library

This museum (☎ 672 6653; admission IR10,000; open 8.30am-1.30pm Mon-Sat) houses the impressive private collection of the late Hussein Agha Malek, including carpets, coins and stamps, furniture and paintings by well-known Iranian artist Kamal ol-Molk.

Glass & Ceramics Museum

This is one of the more impressive museums (☎ 670 8153; admission IR25,000; open 9am-5pm Tues-Sun), not only for the exhibits but for the building itself, an interesting example from the Qajar period (1779–1921).

Although the exhibits are not stunning, the pieces are beautifully displayed in modern, individually lit cases and most are labelled in English.

Carpet Museum

The modern Carpet Museum (☎ 657 707; admission IR20,000; open 9am-6pm Tues-Sun) contains more than 100 high-quality pieces from all over Iran, from the 18th century to the present, and is a must if you're interested in Persian rugs. There's a decent café inside.

Museum of Contemporary Art

This museum (☎ 653 445; admission IR2000; open 9am-6pm Sat-Thur, 2pm-6pm Fri), near the Carpet Museum, contains interesting paintings from modern Iranian artists,

as well as temporary exhibitions featuring Iranian and foreign photographers and calligraphers.

Rezā Abbāsi Museum

This often-ignored museum (☎ 863 001; admission IR25,000; open 9am-5pm Sat) contains fine examples of Islamic painting and calligraphy from ancient Qurans, and galleries with delicate pottery and exquisite jewellery from several dynasties. It's not signposted in English, and a little hard to find so if in doubt, ask.

Sa'd Ābād Museum Complex

In the pretty and extensive grounds of the former shāh's summer residence, this complex (☎ 228 2074; grounds open 8am-6pm daily) consists of several small museums. These include the **National Palace (White) Museum**, the last shāh's palace (with 54 rooms); the interesting **Military Museum**, with a collection of armoury; the enormous **Green (Shahvand) Palace**, with its collection of carpets, furniture and other oddments; and the **Museum of Fine Arts**, with some charming Persian oil paintings.

The grounds are open daily but the museums have slightly different opening times and separate entrance fees – IR25,000 or IR30,000 each! Take a shared (or private) taxi from Tajrish Square, or walk about 1.5km from Tajrish, along Shahid Ja'afar.

OTHER MUSEUMS

The **Telephone, Post & Telegraph Ministry Museum** (admission free; open 8am-4pm Sat-Thur), just off Emām Khomeini St, has a huge collection of stamps including the famous anti-American stamps and sets commemorating the death of Āyatollāh Khomeini and the Iran-Iraq War.

13 Aban Museum (admission IR1000; open 8am-7pm daily), right on the corner of Emām Khomeini Square and Ferdosi St, houses an unusual collection of sculptures by Ali Akbar-e San'ati.

MOSQUES

There are surprisingly few mosques and mausoleums worth visiting in Tehrān. The 18th-century **Emām Khomeini Mosque**, in the bazaar area, is a working mosque, one of the largest and busiest in Tehrān. The **Sepahsālār Mosque & Madrassa** is Tehrān's largest and most important Islamic building. It was built between 1878 and 1890, after the golden age of Persian architecture had passed, so it's ungainly and gaudy, but the eight minarets are impressive, and the poetry, inscribed in several ancient scripts in the tiling, is famous.

US DEN OF ESPIONAGE
The only indication that this vast complex was once the US embassy is a single faded symbol of the bald eagle on one of the entrances and the anti-American slogans daubed along the outer wall. Now called the US Den of Espionage, and used by the military, the building is closed to visitors, but there are fascinating **murals** on the southern walls.

Be very discreet about taking any photos in the area. Taleqani Metro stop is right outside.

PLACES TO STAY – BUDGET
Most cheap places are within a 1km radius of Emām Khomeini Square. This is certainly the most convenient area for travellers to base themselves since it's reasonably central to the museums, the bazaar and even the train station, but it's also the noisiest and grubbiest part of the city.

Hotel Shams (☎ 390 0446; Marvi Bazar Alley; singles/doubles IR20,000/30,000) is a cheap, reasonably friendly option in a busy part of the bazaar.

Hotel Mashhad (☎ 311 3062; e mashhad hotel@yahoo.com; 416 Amir Kabir St; dorm beds/singles/doubles IR25,000/30,000/50,000 is the best, genuinely cheap, place for travellers in Tehrān. Rooms are small but spotless (with shared bathroom) and the friendly manager has set the place up with travellers in mind. Internet access is available here. Don't get this confused with the mid-range Hotel Mashhad on Shahid Mofatteh St.

Hotel Tehrān Gol (☎ 311 3477; 582 Amir Kabir St; singles/doubles/triples IR40,000/60,000/70,000) is more your typical Iranian hotel and cleaner than some. Most rooms have shared bathroom while larger rooms have a shower inside but no toilet.

Hotel Arman (☎ 311 2323; fax 392 0600; Ekbātān St; singles/doubles US$10/12) is a step up in quality. Clean rooms have attached bathroom with Western toilet, TV

and fridge. It's in an alley just off the main road, and breakfast is included.

Asia Hotel (☎ 311 8551, fax 392 3872; Mellat St; singles/doubles US$10/15, doubles with bathroom US$20) is a friendly, family-run place accustomed to travellers. It's very clean – bordering on sterile – though the rooms are quite plain.

Hotel Naderi (☎ 670 1872, fax 672 0791; Jomhuri (Naderi) Ave; singles/doubles US$10/20) is easily the best value in the upper budget range. It's well located and welcoming, and the clean, furnished rooms are large with private bathroom. There's a superb coffee shop next door.

PLACES TO STAY – MID-RANGE
Set back off Amir Kabir St, **Hotel Khayyam** (☎ 311 3757; e hotelkhayyam@hotmail.com; 3 Navidy St; singles/doubles US$20/40) is popular with travellers but is well overpriced these days. Rooms are small (with squat toilet).

Ferdosi Grand Hotel (☎ 671 9991, fax 671 1449; 24 Mesri; singles/doubles US$40/55) is an old favourite. It's very central, plush and stylish in an Oriental old-world sort of way. There's a good restaurant and coffee shop here.

Atlas Hotel (☎ 890 0286, fax 880 0407; Tāleqāni St; singles/doubles US$35/52) is a good choice and well situated if you want to be out of southern Tehrān. The rooms are quiet and clean with large bathrooms and some have balconies or views over a courtyard. There's a good restaurant here and breakfast is included in the price.

Omid Hotel (☎/fax 641 4564; e info@omid_hotel.com; East Nosrat St; singles/doubles US$38/58), just off Kārgar Ave, is in a pleasant, quiet location near Tehrān University. The staff are friendly, the rooms spacious and modern – there are also suite rooms with kitchen for US$70. There's a restaurant, and rates include breakfast.

PLACES TO STAY – TOP END
Most of the four- and five-star hotels in Tehrān are hopelessly inconvenient to the rest of the city, and ludicrously overpriced.

Laleh International Hotel (☎ 896 5021, fax 896 5517; Dr Hosein Fātemi; singles/doubles US$99/112 plus 15% tax) is one of the few top-end places in the city centre, and is also one of the best. It has comfortable rooms, a

IRAN

CENTRAL & SOUTHERN TEHRĀN

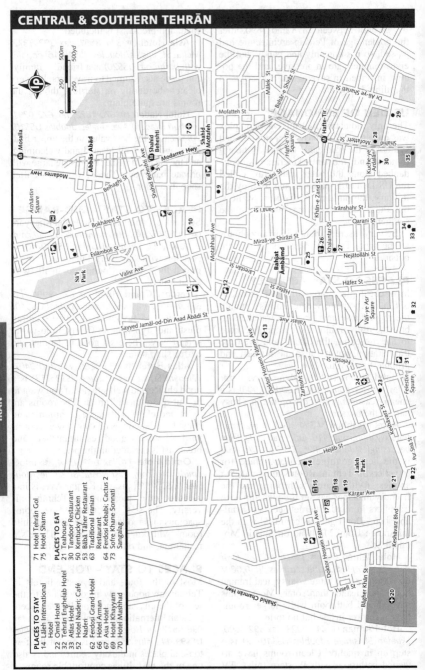

PLACES TO STAY
14 Laleh International Hotel
22 Omid Hotel
32 Tehrān Enghelab Hotel
33 Atlas Hotel
52 Hotel Naderi; Café Naderi
62 Ferdosi Grand Hotel
66 Hotel Arman
67 Asia Hotel
69 Hotel Khayyam
70 Hotel Mashhad
71 Hotel Tehrān Gol
75 Hotel Shams

PLACES TO EAT
21 Teahouse
30 Tandoor Restaurant
50 Kentucky Chicken
53 Bābā Tāher Restaurant
63 Traditional Iranian Restaurant
64 Ferdosi Kebabi; Cactus 2
73 Sofre Khane Sonnati Sangalag

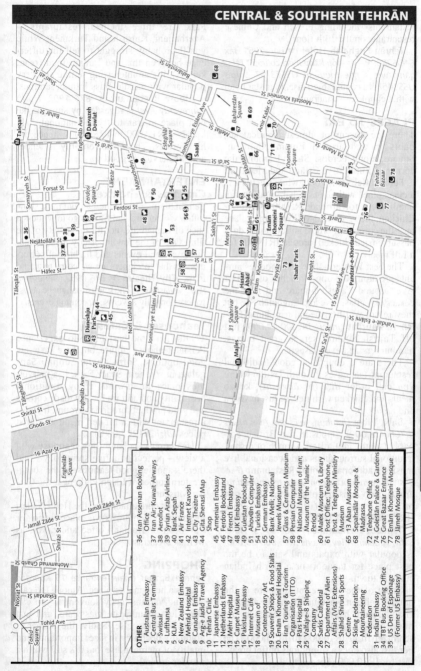

CENTRAL & SOUTHERN TEHRĀN

IRAN

OTHER
1 Australian Embassy
2 Central Bus Terminal
3 Swissair
4 Lufthansa
5 KLM
6 New Zealand Embassy
7 Mehhād Hospital
8 Canadian Embassy
9 Arg-e Jadid Travel Agency
10 Tehrān Clinic
11 Japanese Embassy
12 Netherlands Embassy
13 Mehr Hospital
16 Pakistan Embassy
17 Internet Café
18 Museum of
   Contemporary Art
19 Souvenir Shops & Food Stalls
20 Emām Khomeini Hospital
23 Iran Touring & Tourism
   Organisation (ITTO)
24 Pārs Hospital
25 Valfare-8 Shipping
   Company
26 Sarkis Cathedral
27 Department of Alien
   Affairs (Visa Extensions)
28 Shahid Shirudi Sports
   Centre
29 Skiing Federation;
   Mountaineering
   Federation
31 Indian Embassy
34 TBT Bus Booking Office
35 US Den of Espionage
   (Former US Embassy)

36 Iran Asseman Booking
   Office
37 Iran Air Kuwait Airways
38 Aeroflot
39 Syrian Arab Airlines
40 Bank Sepah
41 Air France
42 Internet Kavosh
43 City Theatre
44 Gita Shenasi Map
   Shop
45 Armenian Embassy
46 Ferdosi Bookstand
47 French Embassy
48 UK Embassy
49 Gulestan Bookshop
51 Ahovân Computer
54 Turkish Embassy
55 German Embassy
56 Bank Melli; National
   Jewels Museum
57 Glass & Ceramics Museum
58 Persian Computer
59 National Museum of Iran;
   Museum of the Islamic
   Period
60 Malek Museum & Library
61 Post Office; Telephone,
   Telegraph Ministry
   Museum
65 13 Aban Museum
68 Sepahsâlâr Mosque &
   Madrassa
72 Telephone Office
74 Golestān Palace & Gardens
76 Great Bazaar Entrance
77 Emām Khomeini Mosque
78 Jāmeh Mosque

coffee shop, business centre and three restaurants (including French and Chinese restaurants on the 13th floor).

Tehrān Enghelab Hotel (☎ 646 7251, fax 646 6285; e eng-hotel@mail.dci.co.ir; 50 Tāleqāni Ave; singles/doubles US$73/97, suites US$145) is a central, high-rise, four-star hotel with a couple of restaurants.

PLACES TO EAT

There are dozens of almost identical **kebabis** in and around Emām Khomeini Square, along Ferdosi St, and around the corner of Jomhuri-ye Eslāmi and Mellat St.

Ferdosi Kebabi is good, while **Cactus 2** is a clean place with doner kebabs and Iranian hamburgers for around IR5000. **Kentucky Chicken**, the green-and-yellow striped place near the corner of Ferdosi and Jomhuri, does passable fried chicken (around IR18,000 for a full meal).

The best Western-style fast-food restaurants are along the upper reaches of Valiasr Ave, around Tajrish Square and near the corner of Valiasr Ave and Enghelāb Sts, but they're not worth a special trip. **Elma Tajrish Restaurant** (meals IR5000-14,000) just off Tajrish Square, serves great pizzas, hamburgers and even lasagne.

There are a couple of good traditional restaurant-teahouses in south Tehrān where you can order dizi (or ābgusht), kebab meals and chicken with rice, or just have tea and a qalyan.

Bābā Tāher (Jomhuri-ye Eslami Ave; meals IR7000-18,000), opposite the British embassy (south side), offers a range of dishes, traditional surroundings and occasional live music. **Traditional Iranian Restaurant** (Ferdosi St; open lunch noon-3pm, teahouse until 7pm) is a no-nonsense place in the cheap part of town serving dizi (IR6000) and kebabs (IR11,000 to IR18,000).

Tandoor Restaurant (☎ 882 5705; Hotel Safir, Ardalān Alley; mains IR15,000-25,000) is popular with expats and said to be the best place for tandoori or a North Indian curry in town.

Some of the best restaurants are in the hotels. **Zeitoon Restaurant**, in the Ferdosi Grand Hotel, has a menu in English and huge meals, such as trout and chicken schnitzel from IR16,000 to IR33,000. The Ferdosi also does a sumptuous buffet breakfast for IR30,000 (but worth it).

In the far north of the city at Jamshidiye Park are three themed **restaurants** – Azerbaijani, Kurdish and Turkmen. While you'll probably struggle to tell the difference between this and Iranian food (read: kebabs), it's an interesting setting and very popular with middle-class Iranian families.

Alborz Restaurant (☎ 876 1907; North Sohrevardy Ave) is regarded by some as the best place in Iran to try the national dish, kebabs (IR12,000 to IR51,000), hence the high prices. The meat certainly is tender and the service is good.

ENTERTAINMENT
Cinemas & Theatres

Tehrān has plenty of cinemas, but most show (often violent) Iranian films – go to witness a slice of Iranian life, not for the quality of the film. One of the few inner-city theatres featuring cultural events and traditional performances that foreigners are welcome to attend is the **City Theatre** (☎ 646 0952; Daneshjoo Park, Valiasr Ave). The English-language newspapers normally advertise upcoming events.

Teahouses & Cafés

Tehrān isn't the best place to experience Persian teahouse culture, but there are a few good options. **Sofre Khane Sonnati Sangalag**, in southern Shahr Park, is a marvellous place to unwind, enjoy traditional hospitality and admire locally made carpets and gold products around the room. It's also a restaurant with a limited menu at tourist prices (dizi at IR25,000!).

Head up to Darband for a **teahouse** with a view – perfect on a fine spring day – and there's another good **teahouse** in the southwestern corner of Laleh Park, near the Carpet Museum.

Café Naderi, attached to the Hotel Naderi in southern Tehrān, is the place to go for European or Iranian coffee and cakes, as well as breakfast.

SHOPPING

Tehrān Bazaar (main entrance 15 Khordād Ave) is a huge marketplace. Among the carpets and various tacky souvenirs, you can also pick up intricate glassware, and just about anything else. Sadly, the bazaar is gradually declining in size, importance and quality of merchandise, but it's still worth a wander around.

Other good shopping strips are the endless Valiasr Ave, and Jomhuri-ye Eslami Ave. Shops selling particular goods are always clustered together.

GETTING THERE & AWAY
The Getting There & Away chapter at the beginning of this book has details about international air and bus services to/from Tehrān.

Air
Iran Air flies every day between Tehrān and most cities and larger towns in Iran (see the Getting Around section earlier in this chapter for a list of fares). Services are less frequent on the smaller airlines, such as Iran Asseman and Kish Airlines.

Most international airline offices (and many travel agencies) are along, or very near, Nejātollāh St, but it's easier to purchase a ticket on a domestic flight at any reputable travel agency. **Iran Air** has three offices: one office (☎ 882 6532; Ferdosi Square) handles domestic flights only; there is a main office (☎ 911 2650 for reservations; Tāleqāni St) for domestic flights; and there is an office (☎ 911 2591, 600 1191 for reservations; Nejātollāh St) for international flights.

Bus
There are four bus terminals at far-flung corners of the city, but, in practice, travellers should only need to use the Western Bus Terminal and Southern Bus Terminal. Tickets can be pre-booked at the **TBT office** (Qarani St) or at the **Union of Countries Travelling Companies**, at the Central Bus Terminal, but there are so many buses going to every possible destination that you really just need to turn up at the appropriate terminal and ask around at the many bus company offices.

The **Western Bus Terminal** caters for all places west of Tehrān, and anywhere along the Caspian Sea west of, and including, Chālus. Services include Rasht (IR10,000, eight hours), Rāmsar (IR1800, six hours), Chālus (IR15,000, about five hours), Tabriz (IR17,000, nine hours), Qazvin (IR4000, three hours), Hamadān (IR10,000, about six hours), Kermānshāh (IR17,000, about eight hours). International buses to Turkey, Armenia and Azerbaijan also leave from here. To get to the terminal, take a shared taxi to

Āzādi Square, from where it's a 10-minute walk. Alternatively, take the Metro to Sharif University or Sadeghieh and a taxi from there.

The **Southern Bus Terminal** has buses to the south and east of Tehrān, including Mashhad (IR28,000, about 14 hours), Esfahān (IR15,700, seven hours), Shirāz (IR30,000, 16 hours), Yazd (IR23,000, 14 hours), Kermān (IR30,500, 18 hours), Bam (IR37,000, 20 hours) and Bandar-e Abbās (IR47,000, 20 hours). There's a Metro stop here (Terminal-e-Jonoub), so it's easily reached from Emām Khomeini Square.

The small **Eastern Bus Terminal** has buses to anywhere east, and anywhere along the Caspian Sea east of Chālus. Take a shared taxi to Emām Hussein Square, and the electric trolleybus (or another shared taxi) from there.

The **Central Bus Terminal** (Sayro Safar Iran; Ārzhāntin Square) has buses to Esfahān, Kermān, Mashhad, Rasht, Shirāz and Yazd, but the Southern Bus Terminal is better for all these destinations.

Train
All train services around the country start and finish at the impressive train station in southern Tehrān. Destinations, and times of arrivals and departures, are helpfully listed in English on a huge board at the entrance, and the knowledgeable staff at the **information booth** (☎ 556 114; open 7am-9pm) speak English.

There are daily services between Tehrān and Ahvāz (IR38,400/33,000 in 1st/2nd class), Gorgān (IR27,700/10,700), Tabriz (IR39,900/21,600), Esfahān (IR22,500 1st class only), Mashhad (IR49,700/25,700), Bandar-e Abbās (IR66,100 1st class only), Yazd (IR26,000 1st class only) and Kermān (IR45,200/27,100).

Tickets can only be bought at the station on the day of travel. If you want to book in advance, go to **Rah-e-Saadt Agency** (☎ 538 2939; 270 Moktari, Valisar Ave) about 200m north of the station.

The train station is about 1.5km west of the Shush Metro stop; or take any bus heading down Valiasr St.

Shared Taxi
Most towns within about three hours by car from Tehrān are linked by shared taxi.

Shared taxis leave from specially designated sections inside, or just outside, the
appropriate bus terminals. For instance,
shared taxis to Rasht leave from the Western Bus Terminal (or from nearby Āzādi
Square) and shared taxis to Qom leave from
the Southern Bus Terminal.

GETTING AROUND
To/From the Airport

If you're arriving in Tehrān for the first
time, it's wise to pay for a private taxi to
your hotel. Avoid the taxi drivers who huddle immediately outside the domestic and
international terminals, and walk for about
two minutes out of the main gate and catch
a chartered taxi (about IR30,000), or shared
taxi, to the city. From the domestic terminal
you could catch a bus to Vanak Square or
to the train station.

You can also take the Metro out as far as
Sadeghieh near Āzādi Square and get a bus
or shared taxi the short distance from there.

Bus

Extensive bus services cover virtually all of
Tehrān. They're often crowded, but cheap –
IR200 to IR400 across most of central
Tehrān – and since there are dedicated bus
lanes, they can be faster than a taxi during
heavy traffic. Some useful routes include:
No 126 between Tajrish Square and
Ārzhāntin Square; No 127 between Tajrish
Square and Valiasr Square; and Nos 128
and 144 between Valiasr Square and Emām
Khomeini Square. You buy tickets in strips
of 10 (IR1000 for a strip) at ticket boxes
near major buses stops.

Taxi

Shared taxis travel every nano-second along
the main roads, linking the main squares:
Emām Khomeini, Vanak, Valiasr, Tajrish,
Ārzhāntin, Āzādi, Ferdosi, Enghelāb, Haft-
e Tir, Rāh Āhan and Emām Hussein. Any
taxi can be chartered for a private trip but
you'll have to negotiate a fare and Tehrān
is the hardest place in Iran to get a reasonable price.

Metro

The long-awaited Metro (**w** www.tehra
metro.com) is up and running but it's an
ongoing project that will become progressively more useful as more stops open up.

It's amazing how modern, clean and orderly
it is after the chaos above ground. Line 1,
running north-south is already quite handy
for travellers. There's a stop at the Southern
Bus Terminal and stops near the bazaar before reaching Emām Khomeini Square, then
continuing up to Mirdamand, near Vanak
Square. Eventually it will go all the way up
to Tajrish Square. Line 2 runs west from
Emām Khomeini Square to Sadeghieh (also
called Tehrān stop), near the Western Bus
Terminal. A single trip on either line costs
IR500.

Around Tehrān

TOCHAL & DARBAND
توچال دربند

To get a complete picture of Tehrān and its
people, you need to venture into the affluent,
leafy northern suburbs at the very foot of the
Alborz Mountains – a perfect antidote to
busy, working-class southern Tehrān. From
Tajrish Square you can take a minibus to the
Tochal telecabin, an enclosed cable car
which takes you up part of Mt Tochal
(3957m). It operates from 8am to 2pm daily
(until 5pm Thursday and Friday) and costs
IR20,000 to the first station and IR28,000 to
the top, where there's a restaurant. Skiing is
possible here in winter and at any time of
year the views of Tehrān make it worth the
effort.

At **Darband**, reached by shared taxi from
Tajrish Square, there's a smaller chairlift
(IR3000) and popular walking trails up into
the mountains. The scenery here is better than
at Tochal and Darband village has something
of a carnival atmosphere with food and drink
stalls, teahouses and shops. Both Tochal and
Darband get very crowded on a Friday, but
are peaceful for most of the week.

REY
ری

Swallowed up by the urban sprawl of
Tehrān, Rey boasts the lovely **Mausoleum
of Shah-e Abdal-Azim**, which contains a
shrine to the brother of Emām Rezā (of
Mashhad fame); **Tabarak Fortress**, on a
nearby hill; the 12th-century **Toghoral Tomb
Tower** in the town centre; and the **Cheshmeh
Ali** mineral springs. From Tehrān, minibuses
and shared taxis leave from the Southern
Bus Terminal.

MT DAMĀVAND کوه دماوند

This magnificent conical volcano (5671m) is the highest in the country. It's possible to climb in three days, starting from the pretty village of **Reyneh**, but if you intend to go mountain climbing, first contact the **Mountaineering Federation of Iran** (☎ 021-883 9928, fax 830 6641; e irmountfed@neda.net; 15 Varzandeh, Moffateh Ave, Tehrān). Even if you're not a mountain climber, there are plenty of gentle hiking trails in the area.

THE HOLY SHRINE OF EMĀM KHOMEINI حرم قم

The resting place of His Holiness Emām Khomeini (admission free; open daily), about 35km south of Tehrān on the main road to Qom, is destined to become one of the largest Islamic complexes in the world. There are shops and restaurants, and eventually a university campus will be established here. The shrine itself is in the aircraft hangar-sized main building, which is invariably packed with Iranians, though foreigners are welcome to enter. The shrine is easily reached by taking a Qom-bound bus, minibus or shared taxi from the Southern Bus Terminal in Tehrān.

BEHESHT-E ZAHRĀ بهشت زهرا

The main military cemetery for those who died in the Iran-Iraq War is an extraordinary, but eerie, place. It can easily be combined with a trip to the holy shrine of Emām Khomeini. The cemetery is about 500m east from the back of the shrine, past a huge civilian cemetery and over the main road.

Central Iran

The dry and dusty plain of central Iran is relatively sparsely populated, especially in the east where the two great deserts of Iran meet. However, this part of the country contains arguably Iran's three most interesting cities – Esfahān, Shirāz and Yazd – and is a must for any traveller.

QOM قم
☎ 0251

Qom is a conservative but fascinating city. It is the training ground for many of Iran's mullahs (Muslim clergy), the heartland of the Islamic Republic and the unofficial political power centre of the nation. The main attraction of this holy city is **Hazrat-e Masumeh**, the tomb of Fatima (sister of Emām Rezā), who died and was buried here in the 9th century. This extensive complex was built under Shāh Abbās I, and the other Safavid rulers, all anxious to establish their Shiite credentials. Non-Muslims are not permitted to enter the shrine itself but you can enter the courtyards from several entrances and observe the passing parade of pilgrims, mullahs and Shiite devotees. Be discreet if taking photographs.

There is a huddle of cheap guesthouses directly opposite the (dry) river from the shrine complex, and most welcome foreigners. **Etminan Hotel** (☎ 660 9640; Haramnema Lane; singles/doubles IR50,000/60,000) is one of the better places with tidy rooms with attached bathroom. **Safa Hotel** (☎ 661 7370; Emām Musa Sadr Blvd; singles/doubles for IR29,000/42,000), in the next lane south, has slightly more spartan rooms with shared bathroom.

Buses, minibuses and shared taxis regularly travel from Tehrān's Southern Bus Terminal to Qom (110km), and it can easily be visited as a day trip or on the way to Kāshān. The main bus terminal is way out of town, but it's usually possible to pick up buses and shared taxis to Tehrān, Esfahān and Kāshān from the city centre.

KĀSHĀN کاشان
☎ 0361

Kāshān is an attractive oasis town with a surprising number of things to see and is well worth a stop between Tehrān and Esfahān. The centre of town is the stretch of Mohtasham between Emām Khomeini Square and Kamāl-ol-Molk Square, about 700m to the south, though most of the attractions are southeast in the old part of town.

Things to See

The main reason to visit Kāshān is to see the beautifully restored traditional houses clustered around the old city just off Alavi St in the southeast of town. There are three main houses, all within walking distance of each other.

Khan-e-Borujerdi (adult/student IR20,000/ 10,000; open 8am-6pm daily), once the home of a wealthy handicrafts merchant, contains charming wall paintings and a lovely courtyard flanked by summer and winter houses. **Khan-e-Tabatabai** (*adult/student IR20,000/10,000; open 8am-6pm daily*) was the home of a carpet merchant and is famous for its carved reliefs and mirror and stained-glass work. The entrance is adjacent to the mosque.

Khan-e-Abbasi (*adult/student IR20,000/ 10,000; open 8am-6pm daily*) was still being restored at the time of writing, but its two-storey courtyards and fine stained-glass windows are exceptional.

The revered Shāh Abbās I would be disappointed with his unimpressive mausoleum, **Zeyārat-e Habb ibn-e Musā**, about 100m north of Emām Khomeini Square.

Places to Stay & Eat
On Motahhari Square, **Golestan Inn** (☎ 446 793; Abazar St; doubles/triples IR70,000/ 100,000) has basic, clean rooms with shared bathroom and is handy for the bazaar, the north end of which starts about 50m away.

Sayyah Hotel (☎ 444 535; Abazar St; singles/doubles US$15/20, with bathroom US$20/25), about 100m west of Emām Khomeini Square, is the best mid-range option. It has clean, pleasant rooms, courtyard parking and a decent **restaurant** (breakfast is included).

Dellpazir Restaurant (*Āyatollāh Kāshāni St*) is a fine restaurant run by an English lady and her Iranian husband. Dishes include *fesenjān*, various other stews and marinated chicken.

Soltan Amir Ahmad Hammam (*Alavi St*) is a beautifully restored hammam-turned-restaurant close to the traditional houses.

Getting There & Away
Kāshān is well connected by bus, minibus and shared taxi to Esfahān, Qom and Tehrān; many services leave from 15 Khordād Square, about 600m west of Emām Khomeini Square. Daily express trains pass through between Tehrān and Esfahān or Kermān.

AROUND KĀSHĀN
Fin Gardens   ناغات فین
About 8km southwest of Kāshān, these beautiful gardens (*admission IR30,000; open 8am-6pm daily*) have buildings from the Safavid (1502–1722) and Qajar (1779–1921) periods, as well as pools, natural springs, orchards and a charming **teahouse**. The gardens are fa-

mous as the site of the murder of Mirza Taghi Khan – commonly known as Amir Kabir – in 1851. Although attractive, the gardens aren't worth a special trip, especially if you've visited formal gardens in Shirāz. On the way, visit the delightful **Shrine of Ibrahim** (*admission free*), with its exquisite tile work and pretty courtyard.

Abyaneh   ابیانه
Nestled in a mountain valley 82km south of Kāshān, this ancient, mud-walled village is well worth a side trip. Recognised for its antiquity and uniqueness by Unesco, most of the original structures date back to the Safavid period (1502–1722). Villagers still wear distinctive clothing, including colourful floral headscarves for the women.

Abyaneh Motel (☎ 0362436-3441; dorm beds US$12) is the only place to stay and it also serves meals. It was only half-built when we visited, but going by the cost of the (admittedly cosy) dorm beds, the rooms will be expensive.

Although possible to get there by bus from Kāshān, Abyaneh is 40km off the main highway, so you may have a long wait by the roadside. You can charter a taxi for a full day from Kāshān or even Esfahān for around IR150,000.

ESFAHĀN   اصفهان
☎ 0311
Of all Iran's cities, don't miss Esfahān. The cool, blue tiles of its Islamic buildings, and the city's majestic bridges, contrast perfectly with the hot, dry Iranian countryside around it. The architecture is superb and there's a relaxed atmosphere compared with other Iranian towns. It's a city in which to walk, get lost in the bazaar, shop for handicrafts, doze in beautiful gardens, and meet people.

Esfahān had long been an important trading centre, but it reached its peak when Shāh Abbās came to power in 1587. He set out to make Esfahān a great city, and the famous half-rhyme *Esfahān nesf-e jahān* ('Esfahān is half the world') was coined at this time to express its grandeur.

Information
Visa Extensions Esfahān is a good place to get a visa extension. The **Foreign Affairs Branch** (☎ 668 8166) is about 2km south of

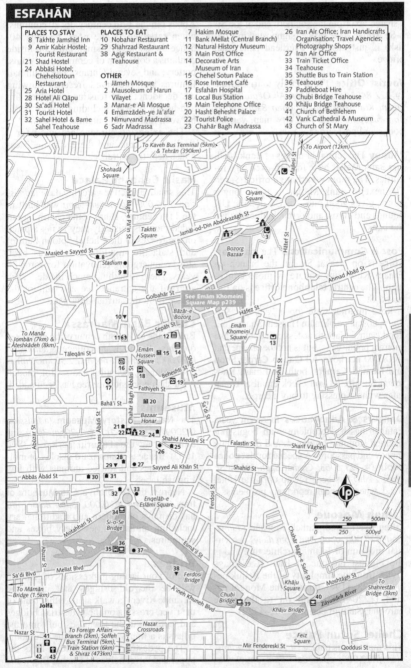

ESFAHĀN

PLACES TO STAY
8 Takhte Jamshid Inn
9 Amir Kabir Hostel;
   Tourist Restaurant
21 Shad Hostel
24 Abbāsi Hotel;
   Chehelsotoun
   Restaurant
25 Aria Hotel
28 Hotel Ali Qāpu
30 Sa'adi Hotel
31 Tourist Hotel
32 Sahel Hotel & Bame
   Sahel Teahouse

PLACES TO EAT
10 Nobahar Restaurant
29 Shahrzad Restaurant
38 Agig Restaurant &
   Teahouse

OTHER
1 Jāmeh Mosque
2 Mausoleum of Harun
   Vilayet
3 Manar-e Ali Mosque
4 Emāmzādeh-ye Ja'afar
5 Nimurvand Madrassa
6 Sadr Madrassa

7 Hakim Mosque
11 Bank Mellat (Central Branch)
12 Natural History Museum
13 Main Post Office
14 Decorative Arts
   Museum of Iran
15 Chehel Sotun Palace
16 Rose Internet Café
17 Esfahān Hospital
18 Local Bus Station
19 Main Telephone Office
20 Hasht Behesht Palace
22 Tourist Police
23 Chahār Bagh Madrassa

26 Iran Air Office; Iran Handicrafts
   Organisation; Travel Agencies;
   Photography Shops
27 Iran Air Office
33 Train Ticket Office
34 Teahouse
35 Shuttle Bus to Train Station
36 Teahouse
37 Paddleboat Hire
39 Chubi Bridge Teahouse
40 Khāju Bridge Teahouse
41 Church of Bethlehem
42 Vank Cathedral & Museum
43 Church of St Mary

IRAN

the river, opposite Esfahān University. Take a shared taxi from the southern end of the Si-o-Se Bridge – the office (signposted in English) is just past the overhead pedestrian bridge.

Tourist Office The friendly tourist office (☎ 222 8491; ground floor, Ali Qāpu Palace, Emām Khomeini Square; open 8am-1pm & 3pm-5.30pm) has a free city map, various books and postcards for sale.

Money The central branches of **Bank Melli** and **Bank Mellat** have foreign-exchange facilities. The **money-exchange office** (Sepāh St), next to Bank Mellat, is open longer hours, gives good rates for US dollars, UK pounds and euros, and is much quicker than the banks.

Post & Communications The main post office is on Neshāt St, but the branch on Emām Khomeini Square is more convenient. The central **telephone office** is on Beheshti St.

Rose Internet Café (open 9am-9pm Sat-Thur), upstairs on Emām Hussein Square, is a good central place to access email and make Internet phone calls, but is not the cheapest at IR18,000 per hour. **Ali Qapoo Carpet Shop** and **Nomad Carpets**, both on Emām Khomeini Square, let you check email at cheap rates without pressure to buy a carpet.

Dangers & Annoyances In recent years Esfahān has had problems with bogus policemen stopping foreigners and demanding money and passports. A special **tourist police booth** (☎ 221 5953; Chahār Bāgh Abbāsi St; open 24 hr) has been set up opposite Hotel Shad, where you can report any problems.

Jāmeh Mosque

Often overlooked, Jāmeh Mosque (admission IR25,000; open 7am-7pm daily) is a virtual museum of Islamic architecture and is the biggest mosque in Iran. It displays styles from the simplicity of the Seljuk period (1038–1194), through the Mongol period (1220–1380) and on to the more baroque, Safavid period (1502–1722).

Chehel Sotun Palace

This marvellous palace (☎ 222 2484; admission IR20,000; open 8am-5pm daily) was constructed as a reception hall by Shāh Abbās I in the 17th century. Its 20 columns, when reflected in the pool, become 40, hence the name. The small museum inside contains a collection of ceramics, old coins, pottery, and several Qurans. The main hall features well-preserved frescoes showing the decadence and feasting of palace life and horror of war, including a gory battle between Shāh Abbās and the Uzbeks.

The extensive gardens are good for a stroll or a picnic, and there's a small teahouse near the entrance.

Hasht Behesht Palace

This small, attractive garden palace (admission IR20,000; open 8am-6pm) was built in the 11th century. It has some charming but faded mosaics (visually they're not a patch on the friezes in the Chehel Sotoun Palace) and stalactite mouldings, and has been slowly undergoing renovation for some 20 years. There is nothing much inside – save yourself the entrance fee and admire the palace from the surrounding park.

Chahār Bāgh Madrassa

Built in the early 18th century, the courtyard of this theological college (admission IR20,000; open 8am-noon & 2.30pm-7pm) is extraordinarily beautiful and restful, though it's a shame an entrance fee has been added.

Museums

The **Natural History Museum** (admission IR2000; open 9am-1pm & 2.30pm-7pm) was built during the Timurid period (1380–1502). Inside is a haphazard display of molluscs, stones and stuffed animals with few English labels.

Nearby, the **Decorative Arts Museum of Iran** (admission IR20,000; open 8am-1pm) has displays of modern and traditional art, including miniatures, jewellery boxes and sculptures.

Bridges

One of your lasting impressions of Esfahān will be the old bridges that cross the Zāyande River – a walk along either bank of the river, crossing on the pedestrian bridges and stopping in the teahouses built into the pillars is a fine way to spend the afternoon.

The pedestrian **Si-o-Se Bridge** links the upper and lower halves of Chahār Bāgh, and was named because it has 33 arches. It was built in 1602 and has simple teahouses at either end. **Chubi Bridge** was built by Shāh Abbās II, primarily to help irrigate palace gardens in the area.

Khāju Bridge doubles as a dam, and if you look hard you can still see the original 17th-century paintings and tiles. On hot summer days, Iranians lounge around under the cool arches here, making this a great place to meet people.

Shahrestān Bridge is the oldest – most of its present stone and brick structure is believed to date from the 12th century – but it's a good 3km walk from Khāju.

Jolfā

The Armenian quarter of Jolfā dates from the time of Shāh Abbās I. The 17th-century **Vank Cathedral** (admission IR30,000; open 8am-noon & 2pm-5pm Mon-Sat) is the historic focal point of the Armenian church in Iran. The exterior of the church is a little dull, but the interior is richly decorated, and shows a fascinating mixture of styles – Islamic and Christian, with a domed ceiling. The attached **museum** (open 8am-noon & 2pm-5pm Mon-Sat) contains over 700 handwritten books, and other ethnological displays relating to Armenian culture and religion, including a moving pictorial display on the Armenian genocide in Turkey.

Jombān Minaret

In Kaladyn, about 7km west of the city centre, is the tomb of Abu Abdollah, known as the Shaking Minarets because if you lean hard against one minaret it will start to sway back and forth – and so will its twin. If it's crowded you won't be able to climb the minaret, but an attendant will shake it so you can see the effect – which could also be seen from outside the gates. This is definitely an attraction you could skip to save the admission fee (IR20,000).

Places to Stay – Budget

Still the most popular choice for travellers, **Amir Kabir Hostel** (☎/fax 222 7273; e mr_ziaee@hotmail.com; Chahār Bāgh Abbāsi St; dorm beds IR25,000, singles/doubles/triples IR35,000/55,000/75,000) is the best-value budget place. The rooms, all with shared bathroom, are nothing special (the singles are minuscule) but the central courtyard is a great place for meeting travellers and the Ziaee brothers who own the place are friendly and helpful.

Shad Hostel (☎ 233 6883; Chahār Bāgh Abbāsi St; twins/triples IR48,000/64,000) is friendly and another good, central option. There is no single rate and it packs the beds into some of the rooms. All rooms have shared bathroom.

Takhte Jamshid Inn (☎ 233 2216; Masjed-e-Sayyed St; singles/doubles IR40,000/70,000) is in a quieter location west of Takhti Square. The reasonably clean rooms have a shared bathroom.

Sa'adi Hotel (☎ 233 6363; Abbās Ābād St; doubles/triples IR100,000/160,000) is in a good location down a relatively quiet street off Chahār Bāgh-e Abbāsi. It has large, comfortable rooms with attached bathroom.

Places to Stay – Mid-Range & Top End

There are a couple of places at the low end of mid-range. **Sahel Hotel** (☎ 233 4585; Enghelāb-e Eslāmi Square; singles/doubles US$15/20) is in a busy but very convenient part of town, close to the river. The rooms, with attached bathroom, are clean and good value (breakfast is included), and there's a traditional teahouse on the 1st floor, overlooking the square.

Aria Hotel (☎ 222 7224; Amadegah St; singles/doubles US$15/20) is in a good, quiet location. Rooms have private bathroom and sometimes a balcony but they are not particularly clean. Rates, however, do include breakfast.

Tourist Hotel (☎ 236 7605, fax 233 8688; Abbās Ābād St; singles/doubles US$30/45) is a relatively new and spotless hotel in a good location, however, it had just increased its prices when we visited, making it a little overpriced.

Abbāsi Hotel (☎ 222 6010, fax 222 6006; w www.abbasihotel.com; Amadegah St; singles/doubles US$96/144), luxuriously created in the shell of an old caravanserai, is undoubtedly the most romantic place to stay in the whole of Esfahān. Most of the rooms (which in themselves are not luxurious) have balconies opening onto the wonderful courtyard, like a miniature Emām Khomeini Square.

[Continued on page 240]

IRAN

EMĀM KHOMEINI SQUARE

Still sometimes known as Meidun-e Naghsh-e Jahān, this huge square is one of the largest in the world (about 500m by 160m) and the centrepiece of Esfahān. Built in 1612, it is a majestic example of town planning. Visitors can buy an ice cream, stop at a teahouse, take a ride on a horse and buggy around the square, go shopping at the dozens of souvenir shops or just watch Esfahānis go about their business. Open-air prayer services are held here on Friday and religious holidays, and the square is often beautifully illuminated at night.

Emām Mosque

This magnificent building is one of the most stunning in Iran. It is completely covered, inside and out, with the pale blue and yellow tiles that are an Esfahāni trademark. The mosque was built over a period of 26 years by an impatient Shāh Abbās I, and eventually completed in 1638.

The main dome (54m high) is double-layered, and though the entrance, flanked with its twin minarets (both 42m high), faces the square, the mosque itself is angled towards Mecca. The tiles of the mosque take on a different hue according to the light conditions, and the magnificent portal (about 30m tall), is a supreme example of architectural styles from the Safavid period (1502–1722). Through a short corridor, a hallway leads into an inner courtyard, surrounded by four *eivāns* (rectangular halls). Three lead into vaulted sanctuaries; the largest to the south. In the east sanctuary, a few black paving stones under the dome create seven clear echoes when stamped upon. To the east and the west of the mosque, there are two madrassas (theological schools).

The mosque is open to visitors from 8am to 5.30pm daily (admission IR25,000), but closed 12-12.30pm and on Friday morning for prayers.

Ali Qāpu Palace

This six-storey palace *(open 8am-5.30pm daily; admission IR20,000)* was built in the 18th century as a functioning seat of government. Many of the murals and mosaics which once decorated the many small rooms, corridors and stairways have been destroyed, but the fretwork stalactites on the top floor, chiselled out in the shapes of musical instruments, are beautiful. The palace is almost completely devoid of any furniture, but the views of the square from the top floor are superb.

Sheikh Lotfollāh Mosque

This small mosque was also built during the time of Shāh Abbās I, and dedicated to his father-in-law, Sheikh Lotfollāh, a holy preacher.

PAUL HARDING

Inset: View of the Sheikh Lotfollāh Mosque through the latticework in the Ali Qāpu Palace (Photo by Phil Weymouth)

Left: Covered entirely in blue tiles, the magnificent Emām Mosque

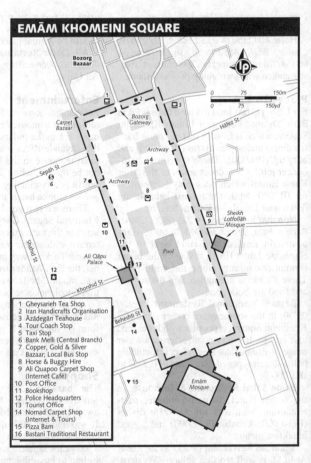

EMĀM KHOMEINI SQUARE

Bozorg Bazaar

Bozorg Gateway

Carpet Bazaar

Hāfez St

Archway

Sepāh St

Archway

Sheikh Lotfollāh Mosque

Shahid St

Pool

Ali Qāpu Palace

Khorshid St

Beheshti St

Emām Mosque

1 Gheysarieh Tea Shop
2 Iran Handicrafts Organisation
3 Āzādegān Teahouse
4 Tour Coach Stop
5 Taxi Stop
6 Bank Melli (Central Branch)
7 Copper, Gold & Silver Bazaar; Local Bus Stop
8 Horse & Buggy Hire
9 Ali Quapoo Carpet Shop (Internet Café)
10 Post Office
11 Bookshop
12 Police Headquarters
13 Tourist Office
14 Nomad Carpet Shop (Internet & Tours)
15 Pizza Bam
16 Bastani Traditional Restaurant

This beautifully proportioned and decorated 17th century mosque, which boasts some of the best mosaics from the era, took nearly 20 years to complete. The mosque is unusual because there is no minaret or courtyard.

The pale tiles of the dome change colour, from cream to pink, depending on the light conditions. The figure painted in the middle of the floor under the dome is a peacock; at certain times of the day the sunlight enhances the peacock's tail. The mosque was once called the 'Women's Mosque', because there is apparently a tunnel between this mosque and the Ali Qāpu Palace, which allowed women from the old dynasties to attend prayers without being seen in public. The mosque is open the same hours and has the same admission fee as the Emām Mosque.

[Continued from page 237]

Hotel Ali Qapu (☎ *233 1282, fax 233 9519; Chahār Bāgh Abbāsi St; singles/doubles US$54/78)* is a cheaper but less ambient, five-star choice with swimming pool and sauna.

Places to Eat

For US-style fast food it's hard to beat **Pizza Bam** *(Ostandari St)*, near Emām Khomeini Square, which is usually full of young Iranian diners and serves pizzas (IR15,000) and burgers (IR6000). There's a small **hamburger joint** a few doors south of the Amir Kabir Hostel which does tasty felafel rolls for IR2000, while the busiest **kebabis** are down near Enqelab-e Eslāmi Square.

Nobahar Restaurant (☎ *221 0800; Chahār Bāgh-e Pā'n; dishes IR8000-18,000)*, signposted in English and right next to the Naghsh-e Jahan Hotel, is one of the better Iranian restaurants along the main road. There's a menu in English, and the service and food are both good.

Bastani Traditional Restaurant (☎ *220 0374)*, in the southeastern corner of Emām Khomeini Square, is popular with lunchtime tour groups. It's very good, offering a wider range of dishes than most places, including half a dozen types of *khoresht* (IR12,000 to IR15,000).

Bame Sahel Restaurant & Teahouse, in the Sahel Hotel, is part-teahouse, part-restaurant, with *dizi* and *khoresht* dishes (IR10,000), kebabs (IR11,000) and a good breakfast menu.

Shahrzad Restaurant (☎ *233 9109; Abbās Ābād St)* is well worth a splurge. Western-style meals, such as a trout or schnitzel, cost about IR20,000; kebab-type meals are about IR15,000 to IR24,000, and you can get dishes such as *fesenjān* (IR19,000). The service is excellent and it's open from 11am to 10.30pm daily.

Chehelsotoun Restaurant, in the Abbāsi Hotel, is the last word in luxurious dining and the prices are reasonable considering the elegant surroundings – most dishes are under IR30,000.

Tourist Restaurant, next to and run by the brothers at Amir Kabir Hotel, was due to open just after we visited and should be a breath of fresh air on the dining scene – not a kebab in sight! The menu is vegetarian with traditional Iranian dishes and fruit drinks, vegetarian pizza, salads and fruit salad. The decor is traditional and this should be a great place to meet travellers.

Ali Qapu Restaurant *(buffet breakfast IR23,500; open 6.30am-10am)* is in the Hotel Ali Qapu.

Entertainment

Esfahān has some of the finest and most atmospheric teahouses in Iran. The most famous are in the pillars of bridges spanning the Zāyande River – the tiny, richly decorated teahouse in the **Chubi Bridge** should not be missed, while the **Khāju Bridge teahouse** is a fascinating local hangout where *qalyan* smoke hangs thick in the air.

There are two good teahouses on Emām Khomeini Square. **Gheysarieh Tea Shop**, upstairs at the far northern end has an outdoor terrace with superb views of the mammoth square. Tucked away in the northeastern corner, the busy **Azādegān Teahouse** is adorned with statues, bells, weapons, ceramics and traditional teahouse memorabilia.

The newest teahouse in Esfahān is **Agig Restaurant & Teahouse**, built out on a platform on the river. If you ignore the family dining areas and head backstage to the smoking area, it's also quite atmospheric.

Shopping

The **bazaar**, linking Emām Khomeini Square with Jāmeh Mosque, about 2km away, is one of Esfahān's many highlights. It was mostly built during the early 16th century, though some of it dates back almost 1300 years. Esfahān is one of the best places in Iran to buy miniatures (painted on camel bone), picture-frames, carvings, inlaid boxes and hand-painted enamel plates and vases. It's well worth browsing the many shops lined along the main square, but you may find prices lower further into the bazaar.

Esfahān is also famous for its carpets, but here you'll find dealers selling carpets from all over the country. The main carpet bazaar is in the northwestern corner of the square.

Getting There & Away

Air The central office of **Iran Air** (☎ *222 8200)* is in a shopping complex opposite Abbāsi Hotel; there's another office (☎ *222 7778; Chahār Bāgh Abbāsi St)* around the corner. Iran Air flies to Tehrān (IR117,000, once a day), Shirāz (IR117,000, once daily),

Ahvāz (IR117,000, six weekly), Mashhad (IR217,000, five weekly), Bandar-e Abbās (IR207,000, four weekly), Kermān (IR153,000, twice weekly), Bushehr (IR150,000, twice weekly) and Zāhedān (IR234,000, twice a week).

Bus There are two major bus terminals – **Soffeh**, about 5km south of the river, and **Kaveh**, about the same distance north. However, every bus you'll need departs from the Kaveh bus terminal, which is more convenient for the hotels along Chahār Bāgh Abbāsi St. Buses depart regularly for Tehrān (IR17,000/29,000 ordinary/deluxe, seven hours); Shirāz (IR15,000/29,000, eight hours); Yazd (IR10,400/17,000, five hours); Hamadān (IR13,000/20,000, seven hours); Kermānshāh (IR18,000/35,000, nine hours); Kermān (IR19,000, 12 hours); and Kāshān (IR6000, four hours). City buses and shared taxis pass by regularly on the main road outside the terminal.

Train There trains from Esfahān to Tehrān (eight to 10 hours, twice a day at 11.40am and 10.40pm). The evening service is an overnight express (IR22,400 1st class only). There are also trains heading south to Bandar-e Abbās (IR47,950, thrice a week) via Yazd.

To book a ticket or check times, head for the convenient **train ticket office** (☎ 668 6753; Enqelāb-e Eslāmi Square; open 8am-1pm & 2pm-4pm Sat-Thur, 8am-noon Fri). It's not marked in English, but you can't miss the blue train insignia. The train station is about 6km south of town but if you have a pre-booked ticket you can catch a shuttle bus (IR1000) from outside the Kowsar International Hotel at the southern end of Si-o-Se Bridge – tee this up with the ticket office.

Getting Around

The airport is about 12km from the city centre. To get there catch a shared taxi from Takhti Square and another from Qods or Lale Squares. To charter a taxi in either direction costs around IR20,000.

A useful local bus service runs up and down Chahār Bāgh Abbāsi St, delivering you pretty much anywhere you need to go between Kaveh bus terminal and Si-o-Se Bridge (IR200 to IR500).

SHIRĀZ
شيراز
☎ 0711

Shirāz was one of the most important cities in the medieval Islamic world, and was the Iranian capital during the Zand period (1747–79), when many of its most beautiful buildings were built or restored. Through its many artists and scholars, Shirāz has been synonymous with learning, poetry, roses and, at one time, red wine.

Shirāz is a relaxed and cultured city, with wide tree-lined avenues, and enough monuments, gardens and mosques to keep most visitors happy for several days. It's also the base for visiting Persepolis – making this one of Iran's most visited cities.

Orientation & Information

Most of the things to see, and many of the tourist facilities, are along, or near Karim Khān-e Zand Blvd – simply called 'Zand'. The city centre is Shohadā Square, still widely known as Shahrdāri Square.

Visa Extensions Along with Esfahān, Shirāz is the best place in Iran to get a visa extension. The **Aliens Bureau** (☎ 726 2214; Modarres Blvd) is just south of Valiasr Square. Extensions of one or two weeks are given within 24 hours.

Tourist Offices There are three tourist offices in progressive-thinking Shirāz. The most convenient is a **booth** (☎ 224 1985) in the pedestrianised section of Zand outside the citadel. The other offices are at the Carandish Bus Terminal and out at the airport, and there's an information office at Persepolis.

Money The central branches of **Bank Melli** and **Bank Saderat** will change money. It's quicker and easier to change cash at one of the exchange offices on Zand, such as **Chantoosie** (open 7am-10pm daily).

Post & Communications The well-organised **post office** is easy to find along a laneway off 22 Bahman St, while the main **telephone office** is around the corner on 22 Bahman St itself.

The best place to access the Internet is **Pars Tourist Travel Agency**, on Zand, although there are a couple of other Internet cafés along here.

IRAN

SHIRĀZ

PLACES TO STAY
10 Aryo Barzan Hotel
      & Apadana
      Restaurant
11 Shirāz Eram Hotel;
      Sarve Naz Restaurant
14 Kowsar Hotel
15 Kowsar Hotel
24 Esteghlāl Hotel
25 Zand Hotel
26 Darya Hotel

PLACES TO EAT
13 110 Hamburgers
16 Roodaki Hotel
20 Burger Pizza Fars
33 Shazeh Restaurant
34 Hammam Vakil

OTHER
1   Gahvarch-Deed
2   Qurān Gateway
3   Hāfez Hospital
4   Iran Asseman Office
5   Gulf Air Office
6   Dr Faqihi Hospital
7   Iran Air Office
8   Mausoleum of Hāfez; Teahouse
9   Emāmzādeh-ye Ali Ebn-e Hamze
12 Church of St Simon the Zealot
      (Kelisā-ye Moqaddas-e
      Sham'un-e Ghayur
17 Cinemas
18 Bank Sāderat (Central Branch)
19 Pars Tourist Travel Agency;
      Chahtoosi Exchange; Bus
      Co-operative No 1 Office
21 Stop for Bus No 2
22 Police Headquarters
23 Internet
27 Pārs Museum
28 Tourist Information Booth
29 Arg-e Karim Khāni
30 Main Telephone Office
31 Main Post Office
32 Bank Melli (Central Branch)
35 Vakil Mosque (Regent's Mosque)
36 Serai Mushi
37 Carandish Bus/Minibus Terminal
38 Aliens Bureau (Visa Extensions)
39 Nasir ol-Molk Mosque
40 Khān Madrassa
41 Mausoleum of Sayyed Mir
      Mohammed
42 Jāme-ye Atigh Mosque
43 Mausoleum of Shāh-e Cherāgh
44 Martyr's Mosque (Masjed-ye
      Shohadā)
45 Armenian Church (Kelisā-ye
      Āramāneh)

Arg-e Karim Khān

Dominating the city centre is a very well-preserved **citadel** *(admission IR20,000; open 7am-6pm daily)* with four circular towers. During the Zand period, the citadel was part of a royal courtyard that Karim Khān planned to rival that of Esfahān. However, the citadel is more impressive from the outside – there is little to see inside, except for the courtyard and an only partially restored bathhouse.

Opposite the citadel, the small **Pārs Museum** was closed for restoration at the time of writing. It normally contains an exhibition relating to the life of Karim Khān.

Vakil Mosque

The 'Regent's Mosque' has two vast *eivāns* (rectangular halls opening on to courtyards) to the north and south, and a magnificent inner courtyard surrounded by beautifully tiled alcoves and porches. Although the structure of the mosque dates from 1773, most of the tiling, with its predominantly floral motifs, was added in the early Qajar era (about 1820).

The best time for a look is during noon prayers (from about noon to 1.30pm), although you may be refused entry. At other times admission is IR15,000.

Mausoleum Shāh-e Cherāgh

The tomb of the 'King of the Lamp' houses the remains of Sayyed Mir Ahmad (another brother of Emām Rezā of Mashhad fame) who died, or was killed, in Shirāz in 835. A mausoleum *(admission free; open 7am-10pm daily)* was originally erected over the grave in the mid-14th century, and it's now an important Shiite place of pilgrimage (the third most important after Mashhad and Qom). The intricate mirror tiling inside the shrine is dazzling. At the mausoleum there is a separate entrance for men and women. Women must wear a *chador* (available from a desk at the entrance).

Khān Madrassa

This theological college was built in 1615 and is the only remaining example of Safavid architecture in Shirāz. The mullahs' training college (still in use today) has a fine, stone-walled inner courtyard set around a small garden. There's no entrance fee but the caretaker will demand a tip.

Mausoleum of Hāfez

The tomb *(admission IR20,000; open 7am-10pm daily)* of the celebrated poet Hāfez is surrounded by a charming garden and flanked by two pools. The marble tombstone, engraved with a long verse from the poet's works, was placed here, inside a small shrine, by Karim Khān in 1773. In 1935, the octagonal pavilion was erected above it.

There is a wonderfully atmospheric **teahouse** in a private, walled garden inside the grounds, and there's a library and bookshop nearby. The tomb is floodlit at night and early evening is a good time to stroll around with the locals. Take a shared taxi from Shohadā Square, or take bus No 2.

Mausoleum of Sa'di

The tomb *(admission IR20,000)* of another famous local poet, Sa'di, is tranquil, but not as impressive as Hāfez's. The plain marble tomb, which dates from the 1860s, is in an octagonal stone colonnade, inscribed with various verses from Sa'di. The grounds, about 5km southeast of the centre, are open daily during daylight hours.

A small, underground **teahouse** is located around a fish pond inside the complex. Take a shared taxi from Shohadā Square, and another from Valiasr Square.

Formal Gardens

Apart from those surrounding the mausoleums of Hāfez and Sa'di, Shirāz has several formal gardens, though at IR30,000 admission, seeing one is probably enough.

Famous for its cypress trees, **Eram Garden** *(Garden of Paradise; admission IR30,000; open daylight hours daily)* is the most famous of the gardens in Shirāz. Alongside a pretty pool is the charming 19th-century **Eram Palace**, though it's not open to visitors. Take any shared taxi along Zand heading towards the university.

Picturesque **Afif Ābād Garden** *(admission IR30,000; open 5pm-8pm daily)* contains the **Afif Ābād Palace**, once owned by the *shāh*. Built in 1863 and influenced by the Qajar style of architecture, the lower floor of the palace is now an interesting military museum. The gardens are a fair way from the city centre, so it's best to charter a taxi.

Naranjestān Gardens *(admission IR30,000; open 7.30am-6pm daily)*, east of the bazaar, features a pavilion that was once used as a governor's residence during the Qajar period.

Quran Gateway

Mir Ali, grandson of Emām Musā Kazem, is buried at this impressive site. There are great views over the city, several short walks in the hills, and two charming **teahouses** set high above the road. It's particularly pleasant in the evening.

Organised Tours

Pars Tourist Travel Agency (☎ 222 3163, fax 222 9693; ⓦ www.key2persia.com; Karim Khān-e Zand Blvd) has dozens of tours throughout Fārs province, and offers the best value group tours to Persepolis (US$5, once a day). If you want to charter a driver and guide, expect to pay US$10.

Places to Stay – Budget

Piruzi St has several budget hotels, although some won't accept foreigners. **Darya Hotel** (☎ 222 1778; Piruzi St; singles/doubles IR50,000/60,000) is a bit unkempt and whiffy but it has a range of rooms (with shower inside but shared toilet), and a manager who speaks English.

Esteghlal Hotel (☎ 222 5383; Dehnadi St; doubles/triples/quads IR50,000/60,000/ 70,000, with shower IR55,000/65,000/80,000) is accustomed to foreigners and prices are posted on the front desk. The rooms with bathroom have shower only – toilets are shared.

Zand Hotel (☎ 222 2949; ⓔ alvanch@ yahoo.com; Dehnadi St; doubles/triples/quads IR57,000/66,500/76,500), across the road, is a good option for overlanders with a vehicle as there's secure parking in the courtyard and guests can use the kitchen. Rooms are OK in the cleanliness department and have attached bathroom. In quiet times you can negotiate a single rate of around IR30,000.

Anvari Hotel (☎ 233 8041; Anvari St; singles/doubles/triples IR50,000/70,000/ 100,000) is the best in the upper budget range. Staff are friendly, and the presentable rooms have attached bathroom.

Places to Stay – Mid-Range & Top End

Shirāz Eram Hotel (☎ 230 0814, fax 233 7201; Karim Khān-e Zand Blvd; singles/doubles US$25/35) has large, well-furnished rooms with a fridge, sunny bathroom and enormous beds. Rates include breakfast. There's a good restaurant upstairs and a 24-hour coffee shop.

Kowsar Hotel (☎ 233 5724, fax 233 3117; Karim Khān-e Zand Blvd; singles/doubles/ triples US$20/30/37) has comfortable rooms, with a fridge and satellite TV, underground parking and attentive staff, but is a little outclassed by other places in Shirāz.

Places to Eat

Zand is lined with plenty of cheap kebabis and hamburger joints, including **Burger Pizza Fars** (cnr Zand & Sa'di Sts). The trendy **110 Hamburgers** (Anvari St) is another good bet.

Shirāz has some great restaurants, many of them with the word 'traditional' in the title and often with a traditionally attired doorman hovering at the entrance.

Roodaki Traditional Restaurant (☎ 222 9594; Roodaki St), downstairs from the Roodaki Hotel, is central and a good bet for meat, chicken and fish kebabs and has a salad bar.

Sharzeh Restaurant (☎ 224 1963; dishes IR10,000-21,000), down the lane leading to Vakil Mosque, is a recommended basement restaurant with live music in the evenings. As well as kebabs it serves kalam polo, a Shirāzi speciality of meatballs with rice and cabbage.

Nearby, the superb **Hammam Vakil** (☎ 2226 4467) is a restored bathhouse alongside the Vakil Mosque, now operating as one of the most ambient teahouses in Iran. As well as tea and the qalyan, you can order dizi and other light dishes, and watch the bread being baked fresh in a stone oven on the premises.

Hotel restaurants include the elegant **Sarve Naz Restaurant** (1st floor, Shirāz Eram Hotel), with Western-style dishes such as schnitzel and attempts at steak; and the more modern **Apadana Restaurant**, at the Aryo Barzan Hotel, which also has a good buffet breakfast.

Yord Restaurant (☎ 625 6774), about 8km northwest of the city centre, is a theme restaurant based on a Qashgar nomad camp. It's authentic in that it's run by a Qashgar family and is basically a large tent furnished with traditional Gabeh carpets and decorations, and offering traditional food. Even the location is a world away from Shirāz and you'll need help to find it – charter a taxi (IR8000 an hour) and ask for the Dinakan neighbourhood, or ask directions at Pars Tourist Travel Agency on Zand.

Shopping

The **Vakil Bazaar** was constructed by Karim Khān as part of a plan to make Shirāz into a great trading centre. The vaulted brick ceilings ensure that the interior is cool in the summer and warm in the winter. It's one of the finest bazaars in Iran, and houses a few **teahouses** as well as the **Serai Mushi**, a pleasant courtyard and two-storey *caravanserai*. Shirāz is a good place to buy printed fabrics, tea sets and *qalyan* pipes made from copper and bronze.

Getting There & Away

Air There are **Iran Air** (☎ 56061) flights to Tehrān (IR180,000, one a day), Esfahān (IR117,000, one a day), Bandar-e Abbās (IR133,000, four flights a week), Mashhad (IR246,000, six a week), Ahvāz (IR131,000, one a week) and Bushehr (IR117,000, one a week).

Bus & Minibus The main bus/minibus terminal is the **Carandish Bus Terminal**. Bus Company No 1 (for Tehrān, Esfahān and Bandar-e Abbās) has an office on Zand. Buses and minibuses leave regularly for Bandar-e Abbās (IR21,000, 10 hours); Bushehr (IR10,000, five hours); Esfahān (IR16,000, eight hours); Kermān (10,800, eight hours); Tehrān (IR29,000/50,000 ordinary/deluxe, 16 hours); Yazd (IR14,000, around seven hours), Ahvāz (IR20,000) and Kermānshāh (IR35,000).

Minibuses to Marvdasht (for Persepolis) leave every 15 minutes or so from behind the main terminal (IR2000).

Getting Around

To/From the Airport Bus No 10 travels between the airport and a stop behind the Citadel of Karim Khān. Shared taxis for the airport leave irregularly from Valiasr Square. There's a taxi booth outside the arrivals terminal (IR10,000 for a private taxi), or there are plenty of shared taxis.

Bicycle Shirāz is one of the few places in Iran where it's easy to hire a bicycle and the traffic is certainly manageable. **Pars Tourist Travel Agency** hires out decent mountain bikes for IR10,000 an hour and also has guided bike tours of the major sites for IR55,000/80,000 a half/full day.

AROUND SHIRĀZ
Naghsh-e Rostam نقش رستم

Hewn out of a cliff, the four tombs of Naghsh-e Rostam are believed to be those of Darius I, Artaxerxes, Xerxes I and Darius II (from left to right). There are also eight **reliefs** from later in the Sassanian period (AD 224–637) depicting scenes of imperial conquests and royal investitures, and what is probably a **fire temple** from the Achaemenid period (559–330 BC). The best time for photos is before mid-afternoon.

If you want, or need, to avoid paying the entrance fee (IR20,000), you can see most of the tombs from outside the fence. Naghsh-e Rostam is 6km along the road north from Persepolis. If you charter a taxi to Persepolis, this site can be visited along the way.

Pasargadae پاسارگاد

Begun under Cyrus (Kouroush) the Great in about 546 BC, the city of Pasargadae *(admission IR20,000; open 7.30am-8pm daily)* was superseded by Persepolis soon after Cyrus' death. It's nowhere near as visually stimulating as Persepolis, and what remains is widely scattered.

The first structure you'll see is the six-tiered **Tomb of Cyrus**, one of the best preserved of the remains. Within walking distance of the tomb are the insubstantial remains of three **Achaemenid Palaces**; and the ruins of a tower on a plinth, known as the **Prison of Solomon**.

Pasargadae is 130km north of Shirāz. The best option is to charter a taxi (or take an organised tour) and combine it with a visit to Persepolis.

Firuz Ābād فیروز آباد

The remains of the old cities of Firuz and Gur, dating back to the Sassanian period (AD 224–637), are often ignored. About 6km before Firuz, on the road from Shirāz, an abandoned chairlift leads to the ruins of the three-storey **Doktar Palace**.

About 2km further towards Firuz, an unsignposted, rocky trail leads to the **Ardeshir Fire Temple**.

There's at least one bus and several mini-buses every day between Shirāz and Firuz.

YAZD یزد
☎ 0351

Yazd comes as a pleasant surprise to many travellers. Wedged between the northern Dasht-e Kavr desert, and the southern Dasht-e Lut, Yazd boasts the best old – and still inhabited – city in Iran. Yazd was an important centre for the pre-Islamic religion, Zoroastrianism, and the region still has the largest Zoroastrian population in the country.

Information
You can arrange visa extensions at the unsignposted office directly opposite the bus terminal. The easiest place to change money is **Amin Money Exchange** *(Emām Khomeini St)* or upstairs at the busy central branch of **Bank Melli** *(Shohadā Crossing)* opposite the clock tower. The main post office is next to Bank Melli.

Y@zd Internet Café *(☎ 622 3832)* is friendly and relaxed and the guys that run the place are extremely knowledgeable. They also run excellent tours to Chak Chak, offer desert safaris, and hire out bicycles. **Isatis Internet Café** *(☎ 623 1425; open 9am-9.30pm)*, opposite the Āteshkade, is another good place with a fast, fixed wireless connection. Access here cost IR15,000 per hour.

[Continued on page 249]

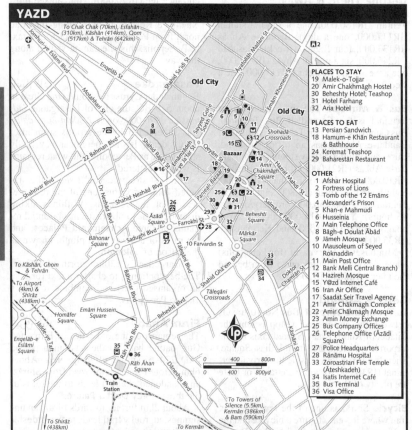

YAZD

To Chak Chak (70km), Esfahān (310km), Kāshān (414km), Qom (517km) & Tehrān (642km)

Old City

Old City

Bazaar

Shohadā Crossing

Amir Chakmāgh Square

Beheshti Square

Mārkār Square

Āzādi Square

Bāhonar Square

Farrokhi St

10 Farvardin St

To Kāshān, Ghom & Tehrān

To Airport (4km) & Shirāz (438km)

Homāfer Square

Emām Hussein Square

Enqelāb-e Eslāmi Square

Rāh Āhan Square

Train Station

To Shirāz (438km)

Tāleqāni Crossroads

To Towers of Silence (5.5km), Kermān (386km) & Bam (590km)

To Kermān

0   400   800m
0   400   800yd

PLACES TO STAY
19 Malek-o-Tojjar
20 Amir Chakhmāgh Hostel
30 Beheshty Hotel; Teashop
31 Hotel Farhang
32 Aria Hotel

PLACES TO EAT
13 Persian Sandwich
18 Hamum-e Khān Restaurant & Bathhouse
24 Keremat Teashop
29 Baharestān Restaurant

OTHER
1 Afshar Hospital
2 Fortress of Lions
3 Tomb of the 12 Emāms
4 Alexander's Prison
5 Khan-e Mahmudi
6 Husseinia
7 Main Telephone Office
8 Bāgh-e Doulat Ābād
9 Jāmeh Mosque
10 Mausoleum of Seyed Roknaddin
11 Main Post Office
12 Bank Melli Central Branch)
14 Hazireh Mosque
15 Y@zd Internet Café
16 Iran Air Office
17 Saadat Seir Travel Agency
21 Amir Chākmagh Complex
22 Amir Chākmagh Mosque
23 Amin Money Exchange
25 Bus Company Offices
26 Telephone Office (Āzādi Square)
27 Police Headquarters
28 Rānāmu Hospital
33 Zoroastrian Fire Temple (Āteshkadeh)
34 Isatis Internet Café
35 Bus Terminal
36 Visa Office

IRAN

PERSEPOLIS (TAKHT-E JAMSHID)

In about 512 BC, the Persian king Darius I (the Great) began constructing this massive and magnificent palace complex as a spring capital. It was completed by a host of subsequent kings over the next 200 years.

The original name was Pārsā, but the Greeks, who invaded and destroyed the city in 331 BC, bestowed upon it the name Persepolis.

The Site

At the top of the grand entrance stairway is **Xerxes' Gateway**, with three separate doors and a hallway. It once covered an area of more than 600 sq metres. The remaining doors are still covered with inscriptions and carvings in the ancient Elamite language. To the east, near the **Unfinished Gate**, are some double-headed eagle capitals which once topped the columns in the Apadana Palace.

The southern door of Xerxes' Gateway leads to the immense **Apadana Palace**, where the kings received visitors. Inside, the **Court of Apadana** was built from stone somehow excavated from nearby mountains. The roof of the **Central Hall of Apadana Palace** was supported by 36 stone columns, each 20m high. The stairways are decorated with superb reliefs, each representing ancient nationalities.

Behind the central hall, and connected by another stairway, is the **Palace of Darius I**. Once the private residence of Darius I, it was filled with statues covered with jewels, but only the carvings along the staircase remain.

The **Palace of 100 Columns** was probably one of the largest buildings constructed during the Achaemenid period (559–330 BC), and contained 100 columns about 14m high, each with reliefs showing Darius struggling with evil spirits. **Darius' Treasury** was a large collection of rooms housing the wealth of the city. Overlooking all of this are the **Tomb of Artaxerxes II**, and the larger **Tomb of Artaxerxes III**, which are both carved into the rock face of the mountains that overshadow the site.

The small **Persepolis Museum** contains some ceramics, carvings, cloth and coins, with captions in English.

There's a very impressive sound-and-light show on Thursday and Friday evenings from March to September (and daily during No Ruz), beginning around 8.30pm, but it's in Farsi only – check that it's definitely on before heading out for it.

Admission to the site is IR50,000 (IR30,000 plus IR20,000 for the museum; no student discount). It's open from 7am to sunset.

Inset: Detail of one of the three Achaemenian kings of Persepolis (Photo by Phil Weymouth)

Right: A lion devouring a bull is a recurrent image among the ruins

PERSEPOLIS (TAKHT-E JAMSHID)

1 Entrance	11 Apadana Staircase
2 Grand Stairway	12 Central Hall of Apadana Palace
3 Xerxes' Gateway (Gate of	13 Central Palace Stairway
All Nations)	14 Central Palace (Xerxes' Hall
4 Northern Staircase to	of Audience)
Apadana Palace	15 Palace of Darius I
5 Court of Apadana	(Tachara Palace)
6 Unfinished Gate	16 Palace of Artaxerxes III
7 Hall of 32 Columns	17 Xerxes' Palace
8 Garrison	18 Perseplois Museum
9 Tomb of Artaxerxes II	19 Darius' Treasury
10 Palace of 100 Columns	20 Tomb of Artaxerxes III

To Ticket Booth & Information Office (75m)

Getting There & Away

By public transport, catch a minibus from the back of the Carandish Bus Terminal in Shirāz to Marvdasht, and then take a shared taxi to Persepolis (14km). Alternatively, catch a Shirāz-Esfahān bus and ask to be let off at the Persepolis (Takht-e Jamshid) junction; from there it's a 4km walk, or look for a shared taxi. Chartering a taxi from Shirāz costs about IR100,000 with two hours waiting time.

[Continued from page 246]

Old City

According to Unesco, Yazd is one of the oldest towns in the world. Every visitor should spend a few hours getting completely lost in this living museum. Look for the tall *bādgirs* (wind-towers) on rooftops, designed to catch even the lightest breeze and funnel it to underground living rooms. Ask locals to direct you to one of the restored traditional houses, notably **Khan-e-Mahmudi** (also called Khan-e-Lari). The twin minarets of the Jāmeh Mosque serve as a vital landmark when you get lost.

Mosques & Shrines

Yazd has dozens of mosques. The magnificent 14th-century **Jāmeh Mosque** dominates the old city. It has a remarkably high, tiled entrance portal, flanked with two magnificent minarets and adorned with an inscription from the 15th century. The beautiful mosaics covering the dome, and on the *mehrāb* (the niche indicating the direction of Mecca), are also quite special. The area immediately in front of the mosque is being excavated to reveal an underground *hammam*.

Nearby, the **Mausoleum of Seyed Roknaddin** is easily recognised by the beautiful, tile-adorned dome. The interior is still being restored. The 11th-century **Tomb of the 12 Emāms** has fine inscriptions inside. Next door is **Alexander's Prison**, allegedly built by Alexander the Great. One ticket (IR10,000) gives entry to both.

The impressive twin-minareted entrance to the **Amir Chakmāgh Complex** – one of the most recognisable images in Iran – is not actually a mosque, but leads to a **bazaar** and the **Takyeh Mosque**.

Zoroastrian Sites

The **Zoroastrian Fire Temple** (*Āteshkade; open 7am-11am & 5pm-7pm daily*) attracts followers from around the world. The sacred flame has apparently been burning since about AD 470, and was transferred from its original site in 1940. Another flame burns at the **Fortress of Lions** at the northern end of Emām Khomeini St.

In the hills about 7km south of Yazd, the **Towers of Silence** were once used as burial towers where the corpses were picked clean by vultures. The best way to get there is to charter a taxi (around IR12,000).

Places to Stay

Amir Chagmagh Hostel (*☎ 669 823; singles/doubles/triples IR35,000/50,000/75,000*) is the pick of the budget hotels for the location alone – overlooking Amir Chakmāgh Square. The rooms are nothing special and the showers are a bit grimy, but it's reasonable value.

Aria Hotel (*☎ 626 0411; 10 Farvadin; singles/doubles IR50,000/70,000, doubles with shower IR80,000*) has long been one of the more popular budget places in Yazd, but it's not doing much to enhance its reputation. Most of the rooms are clean but very tiny; some have private shower, but all have shared toilets. There's a central courtyard.

Beheshty Hotel (*☎ 24717; Emām Khomeini St; singles/doubles/triples IR40,000/70,000/100,000*) is in a good location just off Beheshty Square and was getting a bit of a touch-up when we visited. Most of the rooms have attached bathroom.

Hotel Farhang (*☎ 665 011, fax 660 725; Emām Khomeini St; singles/doubles IR120,000/150,000*) is also centrally located. It has large threadbare rooms.

Malek-o-Tojjar (*☎ 626 1479, fax 626 1679; e info@malekhotel.com; Panjeali Bazaar; dorm beds/singles/doubles US$5/35/45*) is the best choice in Yazd and one of the most atmospheric hotels in Iran. It's not fancy but it's certainly historic – a 200-year-old, merchant's home buried in the heart of the bazaar. Low ceilings and medieval doorways are contrasted by modern bathrooms, TV and fridge, and there's a lovely central courtyard. There's also a four-bed room for US$55. If you arrive by taxi, ask to be let off at the entrance to Panjeali Bazaar on Qeyām St – it's about 100m further.

Places to Eat

Beheshti Square and Emām Khomeini St are lined with fast-food places and kebabis. **Persian Sandwich** (*Amir Chakbaq*) is a good choice, and just around the corner on Emām Khomeini St there's a great little **felafel stand** churning out delicious felafels for only IR800.

There are also quite a few clean and bright pizza places that are more Western in style, but still Iranian in price, and stay open late. **Tourist Pizza** (*Emām Khomeini St*) is easy to spot with the neon hamburger flashing at the top. A 'special pizza' is IR10,500.

For a tasty breakfast, tea and *qalyan*, try the rustic **Keremat Teashop** *(Emām Khomeini St)* near Hotel Farhang. The entrance is not marked in English, but there's a red and yellow sign above the door.

Baharestan Restaurant *(Beheshti Square)* is a more traditional Iranian budget restaurant with cheap kebabs, salads and soups.

The best restaurant in Yazd, and also a great place to while away the afternoon over a pot of tea, is **Hamun-e-Khan**. This beautifully restored underground bathhouse in the heart of the old city has cool tiles, pools and fountains and traditional furniture. The food and service are good although it's not cheap – around IR40,000 for a full meal and drinks. Try the local meatballs (IR19,000). The restaurant is in the southwestern corner of a large courtyard just south of Qeyam St.

Shopping

All sorts of beautiful material woven from a silk called *tirma* is made in Yazd province, and can be bought in the **bazaar**. Yazd is also famous for intricate glassware and leather bags.

Getting There & Away

Air There are flights by **Iran Air** *(☎ 20348)* to Tehrān (IR144,000, once a day) and Mashhad (IR183,000, twice a week).

Bus & Minibus Many bus companies have convenient offices along Emām Khomeini St. Buses leave from the bus terminal, accessible by shared taxi from Beheshti Square and Āzādi Square. Yazd is well-connected to all major cities, including Tehrān (IR22,400, 10 hours), Esfahān (IR10,400, five hours), Kermān (IR9600, five hours), Shirāz (IR14,900, seven hours), Bandar-e Abbās (IR25,500, 11 hours), Bam (IR20,000, eight hours) and Mashhad (IR36,700, 16 hours).

Train Two trains pass through Yazd on the way two and from Tehrān – one originating in Bandar-e Abbās and the other in Kermān. Tickets can be booked at the **Saadat Seir Travel Agency** *(☎ 666 599, fax 666 599)*. The train station is south of town near the bus terminal.

AROUND YAZD
Chak Chak   چک چک

About 70km northwest of Yazd, Chak Chak is the most important Zoroastrian shrine in Iran. The fire temple, perched on a cliffside, is in a spectacular setting, but it's in the middle of nowhere and you may need permission from the authorities at the *āteshkade* (fire temple) in Yazd before entering. The best way to visit is with a guide on a tour organised by the Y@zd Internet Café (see Information under Yazd) for IR120,000. To charter a taxi costs about IR100,000.

Eastern Iran

For most travellers, eastern Iran consists of two distinct parts: the road from Tehrān to the holy city of Mashhad and the Turkmenistan border in the north; and the road to Pakistan via Kermān, Bam and Zāhedān in the south. Although the desert terrain may be familiar, this part of the country is different from central Iran, less developed certainly but also steeped in archaeological and historical interest.

Although Afghanistan is considered relatively safe since the ousting of the Taliban, the smuggling of drugs and other illegal goods through Iran from Afghanistan and Pakistan still creates a certain amount of tension in many border areas in eastern Iran. You should be extremely careful when travelling overland anywhere near the border area.

TEHRĀN TO MASHHAD

Flying or taking the overnight train at least one way to Mashhad is a good idea, but if you decide to go by road there are a few interesting stops along the way.

Semnān   سمنان

This ancient town, which probably dates back to the Sassanian period (AD 224–637), is dominated by the 15th-century **Jāmeh Mosque**, with its impressive entrance portal, interesting stucco and 21m-high minaret. About 200m east of the Jāmeh Mosque, **Emām Khomeini Mosque** has a very attractive entrance portal.

Hotel Kormesh, next to the park on Emām Square, is the best hotel in town with doubles for IR30,000.

The bus terminal is about 3km west of the bazaar.

Shāhrud شاهرود

Shāhrud is a pleasant place to break up the long overland journey between Tehrān and Mashhad and is also easily reached from Gorgān or Gonbad in the Caspian region. Only 7km from Shāhrud, the pretty village of **Bastām** has a beautiful mosque, possibly dating from the 11th century.

New Islami Hotel (☎ 222 2335; Shohadā St; doubles IR30,000), a few doors east of Jomhur-ye Eslāmi Square, is the cheapest place around. It has courtyard parking and basic rooms, but no showers.

Hotel Rezā (☎ 222 5711; 22 Bahman St; doubles IR200,000), on the main drag about 300m south of Āzādi Square, has tidy rooms with attached bathroom, and a restaurant.

The bus/minibus terminal is about 5km south of Jomhuri-ye Eslāmi Square, but you can book tickets at bus agents around the square. Buses go to Tehrān (IR13,000), Mashhad (IR14,500), Gorgān (IR8900) and Sāri (IR12,300).

Neishābur نیشابور

Neishābur, 114km west of Mashhad, is the home town of the famous poet Omar Khayyām (see Literature in the Facts about the Region chapter). The **Mausoleum of Omar Khayyām** is unimpressive but the gardens surrounding it are attractive. The grounds also contain the fine 16th-century **Mausoleum of Mohammed Mahrugh** (IR25,000). In the town centre, a partially restored Silk Road **caravanserai** dating from Safavid times houses a small museum.

Neishābur can be visited as a day trip from Mashhad, but the **Tourist Hotel** (☎ 0551-33445; singles/doubles US$20/30), in the centre of town, is a reliable option if you want to spend the night here, and it has a very good **restaurant**.

Several minibuses leave every morning from the Mashhad bus terminal (IR5000, 2½ hours) or hop on any bus heading towards Semnān. If you charter a taxi it's easy to combine Neishābur with a trip to the charming, 17th-century **Qadamgāh Mausoleum**, just off the main Mashhad-Neishābur road, as well as the ruins of the 15th-century **Mosallāye Torāq** and minaret and dome at **Sang Bast**.

MASHHAD مشهد
☎ 051

Mashhad (The Place of Martyrdom) is extremely sacred to Shiites as the place where the eighth Emām and direct descendant of the Prophet Mohammed, Emām Rezā, died in 817. The story spread that Emām Rezā had been poisoned, so his tomb became a major Shiite pilgrimage site. At the time of Iranian New Year (about 21 March), and the height of the pilgrimage season (mid-June to late July), Mashhad almost bursts: more than 15 million pilgrims visit Mashhad each year.

Although the Khorāsān province, of which Mashhad is the capital, is a far-flung corner of Iran, there are a few additional attractions within easy reach of Mashhad, and the city is a natural staging post if you're travelling to/from Turkmenistan.

Information

Although not the best place in Iran to apply for a visa extension, it is possible to get one here within 24 hours from the **Aliens Office** near Rāhnamā Square in the northwest of the city.

The best place for information regarding the Holy Shrine is at the **International Relations Office** (☎ 221 3474) in the shrine complex (see the following section).

The central branch of **Bank Melli** will change money, as will the **Sepehri Exchange Office**.

Internet access is available for IR8000 an hour at the convenient **Khayyam Coffee Net** (Emām Rezā Ave; open 9am-1am). You can also make international calls here at much cheaper rates than the telephone office.

Adibian Travel & Tours (☎ 859 8151, fax 8542 2373; W www.adibiantours.com; 56 Pasdaran Ave) is an excellent travel agency that can arrange local guides, trips to Neishābur and further afield and book transport.

Āstān-e Ghods-e Razav

The Holy Shrine of Emām Rezā, and the surrounding buildings, are known collectively as the Āstān-e Ghods-e Razav (open 7am-5pm daily, closed to non-Muslims Fri) and comprise one of the marvels of the Islamic world. The original tomb chamber of Emām Rezā was built in the early 9th century, but later destroyed, restored and destroyed again. The present structure in the centre of the

IRAN

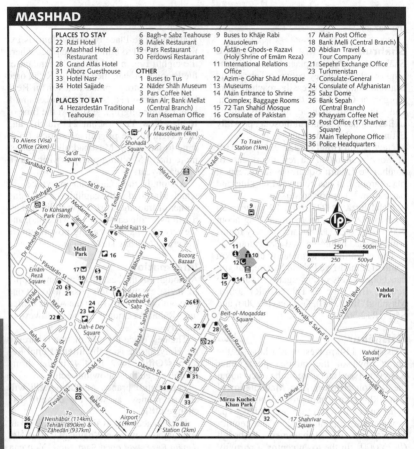

MASHHAD

PLACES TO STAY
22 Rāzi Hotel
27 Mashhad Hotel &
     Restaurant
28 Grand Atlas Hotel
31 Alborz Guesthouse
33 Hotel Nasr
34 Hotel Sajjade

PLACES TO EAT
4 Hezardestān Traditional
    Teahouse

6 Bagh-e Sabz Teahouse
8 Malek Restaurant
19 Pars Restaurant
30 Ferdowsi Restaurant

OTHER
1 Buses to Tus
2 Nāder Shāh Museum
3 Pars Coffee Net
5 Iran Air; Bank Mellat
    (Central Branch)
7 Iran Asseman Office

9 Buses to Khāje Rabi
    Mausoleum
10 Āstān-e Ghods-e Razavi
     (Holy Shrine of Emām Reza)
11 International Relations
     Office
12 Azim-e Gohar Shād Mosque
13 Museums
14 Main Entrance to Shrine
     Complex; Baggage Rooms
15 72 Tan Shahid Mosque
16 Consulate of Pakistan

17 Main Post Office
18 Bank Melli (Central Branch)
20 Abidian Travel &
     Tour Company
21 Sepehri Exchange Office
23 Turkmenistan
     Consulate-General
24 Consulate of Afghanistan
25 Sabz Dome
26 Bank Sepah
     (Central Branch)
29 Khayyam Coffee Net
32 Post Office (17 Sharīvar
     Square)
35 Main Telephone Office
36 Police Headquarters

complex was built under the orders of Shāh Abbās I at the beginning of the 17th century.

As well as the shrine, the complex contains two mosques, museums, 12 lofty *eivāns* or halls (two of them coated entirely with gold), six theological colleges, several libraries, a post office and a bookshop. The remarkable **Azim-e Gohar Shād Mosque** has a 50m blue dome and cavernous golden portal.

To one side of the main Emām Khomeini Courtyard are three museums. The three-storey **Central Museum** (*admission IR3000; open 8am-4pm*) houses an eccentric collection including Olympic medals, stamps, paintings, shells, a huge 800-year-old wooden door and a one tonne stone drinking vessel made in the 12th century. The at-

tached **Quran Museum** has a collection of more than 100 hand-inscribed Qurans, and the **Carpet Museum** (*admission IR2000; open 8am-1pm*) has a small collection of carpets dating back 500 years.

The Holy Shrine itself is strictly closed to non-Muslims, and several other parts of the complex are off-limits. If you're not with a guide, report first to the friendly **International Relations Office** in the far west of the complex, where you register your presence and see a short film. Please dress extremely conservatively, and avoid large religious gatherings and the main pilgrimage season.

The complex is open daily until late in the evening. Perpetual renovations to the perimeter – which started in 1983 – will continue for some time to come. The main entrances are at the end of Emām Rezā Ave and Shirāzi St. Bags and cameras are not permitted inside.

Places to Stay

There is a vast range of hotels in Mashhad. All cater for pilgrims, so most are within a few minutes' walk of the shrine complex, and some will not accept foreigners at any time. In the off-season (outside No Ruz and the June-September pilgrimage season), the prices of mid-range hotels are negotiable.

Hotel Nasr *(☎ 859 7943; Onsure St; singles/doubles IR35,000/45,000)* is down a side street off Emām Reza Ave and is good value for rooms with bathroom.

Alborz Guesthouse *(☎ 851 1877; Emām Rezā Ave; doubles IR20,000)* has shared bathrooms and is a bit of a dive, but it's in a good location and very cheap.

Hotel Sajjade *(☎ 854 5238; Emām Reza Ave; apartment rooms IR80,000)* is central and has rooms with bathroom, lounge furniture and a nifty little urn for making your own tea. A four-bed room costs IR130,000.

Razi Hotel *(☎ 854 5333; Rāzi St; singles/doubles US$10/20)* is a good, mid-range choice and nicely located away from the chaos, but within walking distance of the shrine and bazaars. There's a restaurant downstairs and breakfast is included.

Grand Atlas Hotel *(☎ 854 5061, fax 854 7800; Moggadas Square; singles/doubles IR160,000/240,000)* is a remarkably good-value, four-star hotel for its position, virtually overlooking the shrine.

Places to Eat

There are plenty of cheap eating houses around the shrine complex, especially along Emām Rezā Ave, and many of them serve hearty *dizi*. **Ferdowsi Restaurant**, down a set of stairs, is a good choice.

Hezardastan Traditional Teahouse *(☎ 222 2943)* is the most atmospheric place to relax with a pot of tea, water pipe or a bowl of dizi. It's below ground, about halfway along Jannat Mall. Another good teahouse, frequented mainly by young Iranian men, is **Bagh-e Sabz** *(1st floor, cnr Emām Khomeini & Shahid Raja'i Sts)*. Traditional live music is occasionally performed here.

Malek Restaurant *(Andarzgu St; dishes IR12,000)* is a clean, friendly restaurant with dishes such as chicken kebab.

Pars Restaurant *(cnr Emām Khomeini & Pāsdārān Sts)* is another standard restaurant serving tasty Iranian food.

Some of the best restaurants are in the mid-range hotels. **Mashhad Hotel** *(☎ 222 2666, fax 222 6767; Emām Rezā Ave)* has Iranian meals (around IR20,000), and an excellent buffet breakfast (IR13,000).

Shopping

Mashhad has several bazaars, including the 700m long **Rezā Bazaar**. The city is famous for turquoise (but beware of fakes), saffron and rugs.

Getting There & Away

Air There are many **Iran Air** *(☎ 55468)* flights a day to Tehrān (IR197,000); daily to Esfahān (IR217,000) and Shirāz (IR246,000); and less often to Ahvāz, Bandar-e Abbās, Rasht, Tabriz, Yazd (IR183,000) and Zāhedān (IR199,000). **Iran Asseman** *(☎ 58 200)*, also links Mashhad with Tehrān and Esfahān, and **Mahan Airlines** *(☎ 221 9294)* flies to Kermān.

Bus Mashhad is a long way from virtually anywhere if you're travelling by bus. The bus terminal is about 2km south of the Holy Shrine (reached by shared taxi or bus along Emām Rezā Ave), and from here a plethora of buses go to every major city and regional town. Long-distance routes include: Shāhrud (IR15,000, 10 hours), Tehrān (IR29,500, 14 hours), Yazd (IR41,000, 16 hours), Esfahān (IR43,500, around 22 hours) and Zāhedān (IR40,000, 15 hours).

Train There are seven trains a day between Tehrān and Mashhad, including overnight services (around 13 hours). Fares in sleeper compartments range from around IR38,000 to IR43,000. There's also a 'green class' sleeper, which includes dinner and breakfast, for IR88,000.

AROUND MASHHAD
Tus توس

Tus (also known as Ferdowsi) is a former regional capital. It was abandoned in the 15th century and is now better known for the **Mausoleum of Ferdosi** *(admission IR20,000; open 8am-8pm daily Apr-Oct, 8am-5pm daily Nov-Mar)*, dedicated to one of Iran's most famous poets, Haim Abulqasim Ferdosi,

IRAN

who wrote the epic *Shā-nama* (Book of Kings). Beneath the stone mausoleum (completed in 1965) is a simple marble tomb and some plaster reliefs depicting scenes from the Book of Kings. There's also a small museum in the gardens, but it was closed for renovation at the time of writing (the additional entry fee of IR30,000 is way over the top anyway).

There's no village here as such, but a café inside the gardens serves drinks and simple meals during the day. The 14th-century **Hordokieh Mausoleum**, about 1km south of Ferdosi's mausoleum, is the only remaining structure of the original city of Tus. You'll also see parts of the original city walls being excavated. Minibuses and shared taxis leave about every 30 minutes from Shohadā Square in Mashhad.

Sarakhs
سرخس

Sarakhs is on the border with Turkmenistan. (For details about crossing the border, refer to Central Asia under Land in the Getting There & Away chapter earlier in this book.) If you're going to Sarakhs, allow time to visit the vast **Sheikh Loghmān Bābā Tower** on the outskirts of town, and look out for the impressive **Rubat Sharaf Caravanserai**.

Several buses travel daily from the bus terminal in Mashhad to Sarakhs (IR5000, three hours). There's a train (also three hours) that leaves Mashhad every day at 3.30pm (but arrives when the border is closed), and leaves Sarakhs at 6.30am (before the border is open).

KERMĀN
کرمان

☎ 0341

Kermān is a pleasant desert city on the road to or from Pakistan (and Bam), with enough attractions to justify a stopover of a day or more. For many centuries, the livelihood of Kermān depended on its place along the Asian trade routes, but from about the beginning of the Safavid period (1502–1722) the city has relied more on the production of carpets – still one of the major local industries.

Information

The **Kermān Tourism Organisation** (☎ 58115; Hāfez St; open 8am-3.30pm Sat-Thur) has helpful English-speaking staff as well as a few colourful brochures.

Visa extensions can be obtained at the **Management of Foreign Affairs Office** (☎ 222 240) near the bus terminal (in the street behind the main bus company offices).

The central branch of **Bank Melli** will change money, but it's easier and quicker to change cash at your hotel or at Iran Handicrafts, near the corner of Felestin and Doktor Shari'ati Sts, which doubles as an exchange office.

There are several Internet cafés in town. On Valiasr Square, there's **Asha Internet** (open 8am-1pm & 2pm-10pm Sat-Thur), which offers access for IR12,000 per hour.

Vakil Bazaar

Kermān's 1km-long covered bazaar, running from Tohid Square to the Jāmeh Mosque, is one of the best in Iran.

The **Ganjali Khan Hammam Museum** (admission IR20,000; open 9am-6pm Sat-Thur) is an interesting, though slightly tacky, museum with a collection of wax dummies indicating the various functions of the bathhouse. You can see (and dine in) better restored bathhouses elsewhere in Iran without paying the entry fee.

Ebrahim Khan Hammam, near the Gold Bazaar, is the real thing where men (it's not open to women) can get a scrub and massage for IR20,000.

Mosques & Mausoleums

Built in 1349, the well-preserved **Jāmeh Mosque**, in the bazaar district, has four lofty *eivāns*, shimmering blue tiles and a unique clock tower. The **Emām Khomeini Mosque** was constructed in the 11th century, and includes remains of the original *mehrāb* and minaret, though much of the building has been rebuilt since. The 14th-century **Pā Manār Mosque** has fine original tile work in its portal, and the twin-domed **Mausoleum of Mushtāq Ali Shāh** is also worth a quick look.

Museums

The **Museum of the Holy Defence** (admission IR20,000; open 8am-noon & 3.30pm-6pm daily) is a new museum commemorating the eight-year Iran-Iraq War – according to some literature it introduces the 'culture of sacrifice, Jihad and martyrdom'.

There's a lot of symbolism here, although much of it won't be obvious without an

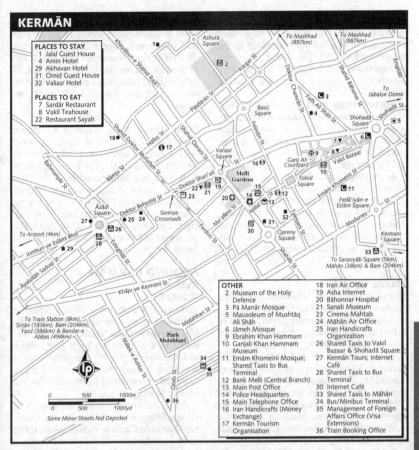

KERMĀN

PLACES TO STAY
1 Jalal Guest House
4 Amin Hotel
29 Akhavan Hotel
31 Omid Guest House
32 Valiasr Hotel

PLACES TO EAT
7 Sardār Restaurant
8 Vakil Teahouse
22 Restaurant Sayah

OTHER
2 Museum of the Holy Defence
3 Pā Manār Mosque
5 Mausoleum of Mushtāq Ali Shāh
6 Jāmeh Mosque
9 Ebrahim Khan Hammam
10 Ganjali Khan Hammam Museum
11 Emām Khomeini Mosque; Shared Taxis to Bus Terminal
12 Bank Melli (Central Branch)
13 Main Post Office
14 Police Headquarters
15 Main Telephone Office
16 Iran Handicrafts (Money Exchange)
17 Kermān Tourism Organisation
18 Iran Air Office
19 Asha Internet
20 Bāhonnar Hospital
21 Sanati Museum
23 Cinema Mahtab
24 Māhān Air Office
25 Iran Handicrafts Organization
26 Shared Taxis to Vakil Bazaar & Shohadā Square
27 Kermān Tours; Internet Café
28 Shared Taxis to Bus Terminal
30 Internet Café
33 Shared Taxis to Māhān
34 Bus/Minibus Terminal
35 Management of Foreign Affairs Office (Visa Extensions)
36 Train Booking Office

Some Minor Streets Not Depicted

0   500   1000m
0   500   1000yd

English-speaking guide. Inside is a gallery of gruesome photos, artefacts, letters and documents collected from the war and a huge animated model that puts on a show re-enacting the Val-Fajr 8, a famous battle from the war.

Outside, along with a line up of tanks and missile launchers (many captured from the Iraqis), is a battlefield complete with bunkers, minefield and sound effects recorded from the actual war. In all, it's a fascinating look at the most devastating and bloody event of Iran's recent history.

The **Sanati Museum** (Doktor Shari'ati St; admission IR2000; open 10am-5pm) contains a large collection of watercolours, oil paintings and plaster sculptures, mostly by local artist Sayyed Ali Akhbar Sanati.

Places to Stay

There are a couple of seedy *mosāferkhunes* near Tohid Square charging IR25,000, but neither have showers and would require some desperation to consider. **Valiasr Hotel** (☎ 24912; Taleqani St), next to Bank Mellat, is the better of the two.

Omid Guest House (☎ 220 571; Gharaney St; singles/doubles/triples IR35,000/50,000/ 75,000) is also close to the bazaar, but is much nicer. The 'with special parking' sign refers to the big central courtyard around which basic, but presentable rooms with shared bathroom are arranged.

Jalal Guest House (☎ 270 185, fax 274 257; 11 Emām Reza St; US$10 per person) is a genuine travellers' home stay and a great place to bed down. Jalal, a local guide, is an affable host and speaks good English and fluent German. There are three double rooms and if it's full you can sleep in the front room for US$5. The shared bathrooms are spotless and breakfast is included. Guests can use the kitchen and washing machine.

Akhavan Hotel (☎ 41411, fax 49113; e ak havanhotel@yahoo.com; Āyatollāh Sadugh; singles/doubles US$15/20) is easily the best mid-range place and is popular with tour groups. It has large, well-furnished rooms, and the managers speak good English.

Amin Hotel (☎ 221 954; e aminhotel@ yahoo.com; Doktor Chamran St; singles/doubles US$10/15, with bathroom US$15/25) is a reasonable mid-range choice close to the bazaar. Rooms are reasonably spacious, clean and have TV and fridge. Management is friendly and there's an attached restaurant (breakfast is included).

Places to Eat

The restaurant at the **Akhavan Hotel** (see Places to Stay) is the place to fill up on hearty Iranian food. It has a superb nightly buffet of fish/meat/chicken, soup, bread, salad, rice and drinks for IR25,000 per person.

Vakil Teahouse (☎ 225 989) inside the bazaar is a glorious, restored subterranean bathhouse with elegant brickwork. It's so popular that there's an admission fee (IR5000) just to get in, and you order at the front desk. It's a great place for tea and the hubble-bubble, but you can also get meals such as dizi (IR8000) from noon to 3pm.

Restaurant Sayah (☎ 269 822), in the grounds of the Sanati Museum, has traditional decor and furniture and live music every night. Quality food includes kebabs from IR10,000 to IR30,000, a salad bar, schnitzel and desserts.

Sardār Restaurant, just north of the bazaar, is another traditional teahouse, but much more a local hangout. As well as a range of drinks, there are meals from IR12,000 to IR19,000 and a semi-open-air courtyard. It's a bit hard to find from the bazaar, but locals can direct you.

Getting There & Away

Air There are flights on **Iran Air** (☎ 57770) daily to Tehrān (IR208,000); and others, less often, to Esfahān (IR117,000) and to Mashhad (IR197,000).

Bus & Minibus From the orderly terminal, buses and minibuses regularly go to: Bam (IR7100, three hours); Bandar-e Abbās (IR20,000, eight hours); Esfahān (IR17,400, 11 hours); Shirāz (IR16,200, eight hours); Tehrān (IR27,600, 18 hours); Yazd (IR9600, five hours); and Zāhedān (IR14,400, six hours).

Train Trains leave Kermān to Tehrān (IR45,200/27,100 1st/2nd class, 15 hours, once a day at 5pm) via Yazd (IR16,950/ 10,900), Kāshān and Qom. For train tickets, there's a handy **booking office** (☎ 251 1770; Qods St; open 7.30am-noon & 2.30pm-4.30pm daily) about 200m south of the bus terminal. Look for the stylised blue train logo. The train station itself is about 8km southwest of town – take a shared taxi from Āzādi Square.

AROUND KERMĀN
Māhān ماهان
☎ 0342622

Māhān is a pleasant town 38km southeast of Kermān. The most important building is the **Mausoleum of Shāh Ne'matollāh Vali**, dedicated to a well-known local poet, mystic and founder of the Ne'matollāh order of dervishes. It dates from the early 15th century, and is renowned for its tile work and ancient wooden doors.

About 5km up the main road through the village from the mausoleum are the charming **Shāhzāde Gardens** (admission IR20,000; open 8am-7pm daily), with a collection of pools leading to a large palace. This is one of Iran's better formal gardens, and part of the palace has been converted into a working teahouse.

Māhān is easily visited on a day (or half-day) trip from Kermān, but you could spend the night at the comfortable and clean **Māhān Inn** (☎ 2700; doubles US$25). The attached restaurant is good.

Shared taxis and minibuses travel between Āzādi Square and Fedā'yān-e Eslāmi Square in Kermān, and the mausoleum in Māhān, about every hour.

BAM بم
☎ 03447

Bam is a desert oasis in the southeastern corner of Iran, but it is well worth the long haul out here. Its incredibly well-preserved, ancient, mud-brick city is unquestionably a highlight of Iran. Bam also has a lively little bazaar and is the 'date capital' of Iran. Go for a walk in the sea of date palms that surrounds the town. You can buy a box of dates here for around IR3000. Some travellers (and tour groups) visit Bam as a long day trip from Kermān, but it's a far better option to stay overnight.

Siahate-Kavir Tours & Travel (*☎ 4806, fax 90976; e hmsiahatekavir@yahoo.com; Emām Khomeini St*), next to the Jāmeh Mosque, has Internet access, but it charges a steep IR40,000 per hour.

Arg-e-Bam

The original city of Bam (*adult/student IR30,000/15,000; opening hours 7.30am-6.30pm daily*) was probably founded in the Sassanian period (AD 224–637), but most of the remains date from the Safavid period (1502–1722). Between 9000 and 13,000 people once lived in this 6-sq-km city until it was abandoned after an invasion by the Afghans in 1722. Despite the intervening 300 years, it requires little effort to imagine what this city must have been like in its heyday as you wander through the twisting lanes.

All of the steep, narrow stairways lead to the pinnacles of the outer wall for a definitive outlook over the old and new towns. The best way to appreciate the old city initially is to climb to the outer wall and walk right around the perimeter – the city looks different from every angle and you get a great perspective on the perfectly preserved citadel.

The **inner citadel** contains a fortified 17th-century residence known as the Chahār Fasl. In the garrison, shout something and listen to the extraordinary echo – archaeologists believe this is an ancient loudspeaker system. Nearby are the 14th-century stables, which once housed 200 to 300 horses.

On the way up to the governor's residence, there are some very dark dungeons. The residence of the garrison's commander provides awesome views of the ancient town. The bazaar square, near the main entrance, was once a covered, busy market.

The main entrance is at the historic (southern) **gatehouse**. The best times to visit are early morning, when you'll proba-

BAM

1 Bamarg Restaurant
2 Palace Teahouse
3 Emāmzadeh-ye Asiri
4 Bus Co-operative No 7
5 Setar-e-Nakhl Tours & Travel
6 Gol-e-Gandom
7 Bank Melli
8 Post Office
9 Ali Amir's Guest House
10 Siahate-Kavir Tours & Travel; Jame Mosque
11 Bus Co-operative No 8
12 Bam Inn
13 Akhbar Tourist Guest House
14 Bus drop-off point
15 Main Bus Terminal

bly have the place to yourself, and late afternoon when the setting sun brings out the rich colours and contrasts. Allow two hours to look around plus time for relaxing in the excellent **Arg Persian Tea Rooms** above the gatehouse to the citadel. Crammed with antique water pipes and rugs, this atmospheric place offers not only tea, but fine coffee and superb date cookies.

Organised Tours

Siahate-Kavir Tours & Travel (*☎ 4806, fax 90976; e hmsiahatekavir@yahoo.com; Emām Khomeini St*), next to the Jāmeh Mosque, has tours of the Arg-e-Bam (IR50,000), and evening desert tours (IR200,000) which can be extended to overnight tours staying in a nomad camp (IR400,000).

Places to Stay

Bam has only a handful of hotels but is blessed with two very good family-run guesthouses.

Akhbar Tourist Guest House (☎ 5842; *Saled Jamaladin; dorm beds/singles/doubles IR25,000/30,000/60,000, doubles with bathroom US$10-15*) is one of Iran's best budget guesthouses, thanks mainly to the gregarious manager (a former English-language teacher) and his son, and the breezy courtyard where travellers can gather to talk. As well as rooms in the main part of the house there are two totally spotless doubles with Western-style bathrooms facing the garden (US$15). Wonderful home-cooked breakfasts (IR5000) and dinners (IR10,000) are available.

Ali Amir's Guest House (☎ 4481, fax 90085; *Pasdaran St; dorm beds IR25,000, singles/doubles/triples IR40,000/60,000/ 90,000*) is in a good, central location, just down a lane from Emām Khomeini Square, but it lacks a personal touch or communal areas. Clean rooms include a six-bed dormitory and the triple has attached bathroom. You can eat with the family for IR12,000.

Bam Inn (☎ 3323; *17 Shahrvar Square; doubles without/with bathroom IR216,000/ 240,000*) looks like a fall-out shelter (post explosion). It's a shell of a hotel awaiting renovations and although it's OK inside, the plain rooms are way overpriced. There's a reasonable restaurant here.

Places to Eat

Gol-e-Gandom Restaurant (☎ 4046; *Shāhid Sadoqi St*) is a bright, clean and welcoming restaurant near Emām Khomeini Square with dishes such as *khoresht* (meat stew) for IR12,000, various kebab meals and 'barberry, rice and hen' for IR15,000.

Bamarg Restaurant, opposite the entrance to the old city, has a charming garden setting, but is open for lunch only.

Palace Teahouse, down an alley off Tabatabaei St, is a marvellous teahouse in a converted underground *hammam*. It's a warren of cool, marble-tiled rooms, naturally lit by skylights, where you can relax with a pot of tea and a water pipe. It's less formal than the hammam restaurants in Yazd and Shirāz.

Getting There & Away

Iran Asseman flies between Bam and Tehrān (IR248,000, once a week). Book through **Setar-e-Nakhl Tours & Travel** (☎ 7500; *Shahid Sadoqi St*).

All buses leave Bam from the bus terminal at Arg Square, but you can buy tickets from the bus co-operative offices in town. Through buses (between Zāhedān and Kermān) pick up and drop off at Arg Square (on

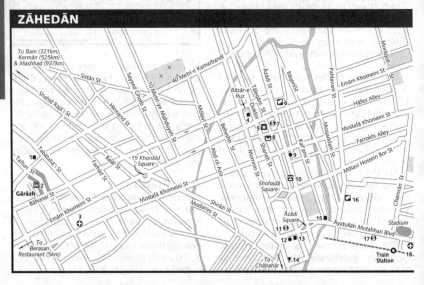

ZĀHEDĀN

the northwest side of the roundabout). A taxi from Arg Square to the town centre costs around IR4000, a shared taxi is IR1000. Ordinary buses from Bam include: Bandar-e Abbās (IR12,500, eight hours); Kermān (IR5900, three hours); Yazd (IR18,000, nine hours); Esfahān (IR30,000, 11 hours) and Zāhedān (IR9500, five hours). The bus to Zāhedān leaves at 6.30am so you can cross the border into Pakistan in one day. Bus co-operative No 8 has a daily deluxe air-con service to Tehrān (IR31,400) and Yadz (IR15,500).

ZĀHEDĀN زاهدان
☎ 0541

Zāhedān is a dusty, featureless frontier desert town not worth a visit in its own right, but since it's the nearest major town to the border with Pakistan, most overland travellers spend time here – either at the bus station or overnight.

The **Police Dept of Alien Affairs** (*1st floor, Motahhari Blvd; open 8am-2pm Sat-Wed*) handles visa extensions. The central branch of **Bank Melli**, near the bazaar, changes money, including Pakistani rupees, as does **Bank Saderat** on Āzādi Square.

There's an **Internet café** at the Esteghlal Grand Hotel.

If you do end up in Zāhedān, the **bazaar** is the most interesting part of town. It has a

definite Pakistani and Afghani flavour, with the *shalwar kamiz* being the dominant form of dress among men here.

Places to Stay
Abuzar Hotel (☎ 451 2132; *doubles IR 28,000*) is the best in the noisy bus terminal area. Rooms with shared bathroom are passably clean and there's a restaurant attached.

Hotel Momtazhirmand (☎ 322 2728; *singles/doubles IR22,000/30,000*), right in the midst of the bazaar, is a good budget choice and was a good place to meet other travellers when the overland trail was going a bit stronger. It's along the first laneway on the left off Doktor Shar'ati (look for a brown door with coloured glass panels).

Kavir Hotel (☎ 322 4010, fax 322 0059; *Kaf'ami St; singles/doubles IR80,000/110,000*) is in a quiet location and the cheapest of the 'mid range' places but its run-down, untidy rooms struggle to make that grade.

Given that Zāhedān's mid-range hotels are so mediocre, the **Esteghlal Grand Hotel** (☎ 323 8052, fax 322 2239; *Āzādi Square; singles/doubles IR360,000/520,000*) deserves a mention. It's a luxury, four-star hotel, from the lobby to the well-appointed rooms (with satellite TV), but is very good value and might be worth a splurge to make the Zāhedān experience more bearable.

Places to Eat
There are plenty of fast-food outlets in the bazaar, including **kebabis** and **barbecue chicken** places.

Elsewhere the best places to eat are hotel restaurants. The downstairs restaurant at **Saleh Hotel** (*Momnin St*), offers the standard range of chicken and fish kebabs with rice from IR10,000 to IR17,500.

If there's one good reason to stay overnight in Zāhedān, it's to dine at the **Berasan Restaurant** (☎ 0911-541 3477; *open from 6pm*), in the desert about 5km south of town. The open-air theme restaurant is modelled on a Baluchi nomadic camp with a group of individual tents in which you sit on rugs and cushions. The traditional food is good, though not cheap, with kebab meals around IR20,000 to IR25,000 and the speciality *champ* (lamb ribs) at IR35,000. You'll have to charter a taxi here (IR10,000 including waiting time).

ZĀHEDĀN

PLACES TO STAY & EAT
1 Abuzar Hotel
4 Hotel Momtazhirmand
13 Esteghlal Grand Hotel
14 Sāleh Hotel Restaurant; Kabābis
15 Kavir Hotel

OTHER
2 Bus Terminal
3 Hospital
5 Police Headquarters
6 Consulate of India
7 Bank Melli (Central Branch)
8 Main Post Office
9 Khaterat Zāhedān Travel & Tours (Iran Asseman Agency)
10 Main Telephone Office
11 Bank Saderat
12 Iran Air Office
16 Consulate of Pakistan
17 Bank Melli
18 Hospital
19 Pik-ups & Shared Taxis to Mīrjaveh
20 Police Department of Alien Affairs (Visa Office)
21 Gate to Airport

Airport ✈

Montazeri St
Motahhari Blvd
Forūdgāh Square
To Mīrjaveh (84km)
21
20
0   400   800m
0   400   800yd
Some Minor Roads Not Depicted
19

Getting There & Away

There are flights with **Iran Air** (☎ 220 811) to Tehrān (IR273,000, one flight a day), Esfahān (IR234,000, two flights a week), Kermān (IR234,000, two flights a week), Mashhad (IR199,000) and Chābahār (IR130,000). Iran Asseman also has regular flights to Tehrān; its representative is **Khaterat Zāhedān Travel & Tours** (☎ 225 001; *Āzādi St*).

The **bus terminal** is a noisy, asthma-inducing mess in the west of the city, but the bus companies have offices nearby along Taftun St, so you just have to ask around. Buses leave many times a day to Bam (IR9500, five hours), Kermān (IR14,000, six hours), Yazd (IR23,000, 14 hours), Esfahān (IR30,500/55,000 ordinary/deluxe, around 21 hours), Shirāz (IR33,500, 17 hours), Bandar-e Abbās (IR29,000, 17 hours), Mashhad (IR50,000 deluxe, 15 hours) and Tehrān (IR75,000 deluxe, 22 hours).

For transport to the Pakistan border or Mirjāveh, take a pick-up or shared taxi (around IR5000) from Forudgarh Square (also known as Mirjāveh Square), east along Āyatollāh Motahhari Blvd.

MIRJĀVEH   میرجاوه
☎ 0543322

Mirjāveh is the closest village to the border with Pakistan, although it's not necessary to come here as pick-ups and shared taxis run directly between Zāhedān and the border – see the Getting There & Away chapter earlier in this book for information about crossing the border.

Mirjaveh Tourist Inn (☎ 2486; *doubles IR70,000*) is a more pleasant alternative than most hotels in Zāhedān.

Western Iran

There is evidence of settlement in western Iran as early as the 6th millennium BC, and many of the earliest empires and kingdoms of Persia had their capitals here. Standing at the frontiers with Mesopotamia and Turkey, much of the region has been vulnerable to incursions from the west throughout its long history. During the Iran-Iraq War, border towns were bombed and, in some cases, occupied by Iraqi forces. This region extends from the border with Armenia and Azerbaijan in the north to the industrial city of Ahvāz near the Gulf and, with the exception of Tabriz, is largely ignored by travellers. However, if you have the time and energy there are several important historical and natural sites to explore.

This section begins with Bāzārgān, the overland border crossing from Turkey.

BĀZĀRGĀN   بازرگان

Bāzārgān is on the Iran-Turkey border but there's virtually no reason to stop here. For details about crossing the border see the Getting There & Away section earlier in this chapter.

The main road from Māku goes through Bāzārgān and stops at the border. The road is lined with a dozen cheap hotels and kebabis, and shared taxis regularly go to Māku and to Tabriz when there are enough passengers.

MĀKU   ماکو
☎ 04634

Many travellers stop in Māku just before, or after, crossing the border with Turkey. Everything is along one very long road, part of the main highway between Tabriz and the Turkish border.

Hotel Alvand (☎ 23491; *Emām Ave; singles/doubles IR36,000/51,000*) on the town's main square has clean rooms with shared bathroom.

Buses and shared taxis travelling to Tabriz and Orumiye leave regularly in the morning from the terminal, 3km from the town centre on the road to Tabriz. Shared taxis to Bāzārgān leave from outside Hotel Alvand.

QARA KELISĀ   قره کلیسا

The **Church of St Thaddaeus** (*admission IR20,000; open 8am-7pm daily*) is probably the most remarkable Christian monument in Iran. (It's often called Qara Kelisā, Azerbaijani for 'Black Church', but it is more accurately known as Kelisā-ye Tād – the Church of St Thaddaeus.)

The period of construction is unknown, and very little remains of the original church. It was largely rebuilt after extensive earthquake damage in the 13th century. The church has one service a year, on the feast day of St Thaddaeus (around 19 June), when Armenian pilgrims from all over Iran attend the ceremonies.

From Māku, catch any bus or shared taxi towards Bāzārgān, get off at a junction with the sign to 'Kandi Kelisa', and wait for another shared taxi. You should be able to charter a taxi from Māku for around IR25,000.

JOLFĀ
جلفا

Jolfā is near the border between Iran and Azerbaijan and Armenia, but if you're heading to Azerbaijan the proper crossing is Āstārā. For details see the Getting There & Away chapter earlier in this book.

The other reason to come to Jolfa is to visit the **Kālisā Darreh Shām** (Church of St Stephen), an impressive Armenian monastery 16km to the west. Admission to the monastery is free, except on Friday when it's IR20,000. If you take a public bus to Jolfa, you'll need official permission from the police in Tabriz to visit the monastery. If you charter a taxi all the way, permission is not required (strange, but true). The full-day tours run by **ALP Tours & Travel** (☎ 331 0340) in Tabriz are therefore good value at IR35,000 (but they only run on Friday).

The ITTO **Jolfa Tourist Inn** (☎ 0492302-2220; Emām Khomeini Blvd; doubles IR110,000) is the best of an average bunch of hotels.

ORUMIYE
ارومیه

☎ 0441

Orumiye lies to the west of the lake of the same name, and although quite remote from the rest of Iran, it's on an increasingly important trade route with Turkey, so the city is more Turkish and Azerbaijani than Persian. For travellers it's most likely a staging post for the alternative border crossing at Sero (to or from Van in Turkey).

Most facilities are on Emām Khomeini St, between Faghye Square and Enghelāb Square.

Things to See

The large **Jāmeh Mosque**, near Faghye St, has some fine plaster mouldings, and a large dome. The 12th-century **Se Dome** is notable for its stucco and stalactite decorations – take the second lane on your left along Jāmbāzān, north of the intersection with Dastgheib (about 800m southeast of Rezā Hotel).

The **Orumiye Museum** (Beheshti Faculty Ave; admission IR20,000) has a small display

but there's no labelling in English so it's hardly worth the time or money. Orumiye has Iran's largest Christian community and the Assyrian, Armenian, Nestorian and Roman Catholic communities have interesting **churches**, several of which are around Enghelāb St and the nearby Qods Square – ask locals for directions.

Places to Stay & Eat

Hotel Iran Setareh (☎ 235 4454; Janbazan Square; singles/doubles IR40,000/60,000), about 700m southeast of the bazaar, is spotlessly clean and very welcoming.

Hotel Khorram (☎ 222 5444; Emām Ave; singles/doubles IR55,000/81,500), in a quiet street directly behind the Sardar Mosque, is very good value with clean, comfortable rooms with private bathroom, and a restaurant. **Rezā Hotel** (☎ 222 6580; Besat St) also has a good restaurant.

Stalls around town sell delicious baked potatoes for IR1000.

Getting There & Away

There are flights with **Iran Air** (☎ 468 400) to Tehrān (IR160,000, twice a day).

Some bus companies have booking offices along Emām Ave. The **terminal** for buses, minibuses and shared taxis is northeast of the town centre – catch a shared taxi along Emām Khomeini St. Buses regularly go to Kermānshāh (IR24,000, 11 hours), Māku (IR7900, four hours), Tabriz (IR10,000, five hours) and Tehrān (IR31,500, 14 hours). Buses to Tabriz must take the longer route around the lake, so it's better to take a shared taxi straight across, although you'll probably wait a while for the vehicle ferry anyway. For other destinations, get connections in Tabriz or Kermānshāh.

SERO
سرو

This nondescript village is on the border with Turkey and is an alternative to the Bāzārgān border crossing. There is nowhere to stay. Shared taxis (IR5000) regularly travel between Serō and Tōhid Square in northern Orumiye.

TABRIZ
تبریز

☎ 041

Tabriz had a spell as the Persian capital during the Safavid period (1502–1722), although most of its inhabitants are now Azerbaijanis.

IRAN

For most travellers coming overland from Turkey it's their first taste of an Iranian city. From a distance it looks like an ugly sprawl of high-rise apartments, but the central bazaar area is lively and Tabriz is a good base for exploring northwestern Iran.

Information

Tabriz is a good place to get a visa extension, provided you haven't got too long left to run on your visa. Go to the police headquarters; the foreign affairs department is on the 3rd floor and is open from 7am to 1.30pm Saturday to Thursday.

The helpful **tourist office** *(☎ 68491; open 9am-1pm & 4.30pm-7.30pm Sat-Thur)* is easy to find near the entrance to the bazaar on Jomhuri St. You can change money at the

huge central branch of **Bank Melli** *(Shohadā Square)*, but it's quicker to use the exchange offices in the bazaar – ask for directions at the tourist office.

The best Internet cafés are out in the trendy Valiasr district (take a shared taxi from the bazaar). **Red Net** charges IR12,000 an hour and has international calls to Europe, USA and Australia for IR1000 per minute.

Closer to the bazaar, there's a small **Internet café** in the lane on the western side of the citadel.

Things to See

Tabriz has the largest and oldest **bazaar** in Iran. It was built more than 1000 years ago but was damaged several times by earth-

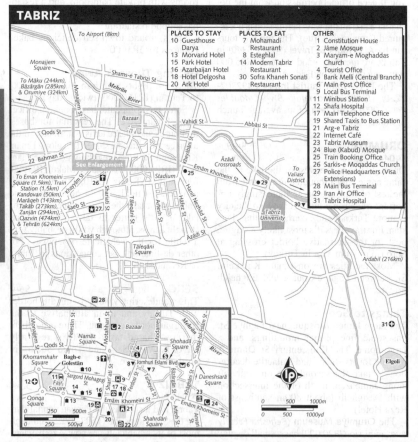

TABRIZ

PLACES TO STAY	PLACES TO EAT	OTHER
10 Guesthouse Darya	7 Mohamadi Restaurant	1 Constitution House
13 Morvarid Hotel	8 Esteghlal	2 Jāme Mosque
15 Park Hotel	14 Modern Tabriz Restaurant	3 Maryam-e Moghaddas Church
16 Azarbaijan Hotel	30 Sofra Khaneh Sonati Restaurant	4 Tourist Office
18 Hotel Delgosha		5 Bank Melli (Central Branch)
20 Ark Hotel		6 Main Post Office
		9 Local Bus Terminal
		11 Minibus Station
		12 Shafa Hospital
		17 Main Telephone Office
		19 Shared Taxis to Bus Station
		21 Arg-e Tabriz
		22 Internet Café
		23 Tabriz Museum
		24 Blue (Kabud) Mosque
		25 Train Booking Office
		26 Sarkis-e Moqaddas Church
		27 Police Headquarters (Visa Extensions)
		28 Main Bus Terminal
		29 Iran Air Office
		31 Tabriz Hospital

quakes so most of it now dates to the 15th century. The bazaar is a great place to get lost in and it has several local teahouses lined with water pipes with men attached to them. Tabriz is renowned for carpets, silverware, jewellery, silk and spices such as henna.

Although badly damaged by earthquakes, the 15th-century **Blue Mosque** *(Kabud; admission IR20,000)* is still notable for the extremely intricate tile work. Extensive restoration work is underway and the area around the mosque looks like a construction site.

Tabriz Museum *(☎ 66343; admission IR25,000; open 7am-8pm daily)* has a mildly interesting collection of exhibits from regional archaeological digs, silverware and pottery.

The very large, crumbling **Arg-e-Tabriz** (citadel), built in the early 14th century and gradually being restored, still towers over Emām Khomeini St. One of the more interesting local churches is the old, but substantially rebuilt, **Maryam-e Moghaddas Church**.

Elgoli is a large, pleasant park and a good place to get away from the city – as many locals do on summer evenings. Take a shared taxi (IR2000) from Shahrdāri Square.

Places to Stay

Tabriz is awash with cheap places to stay, many of which are happy to take foreigners. Some of the cheapest places don't have showers, while others charge extra for using the shower.

Hotel Delgosha *(☎ 555 2054; 18 Ferdosi St; singles/doubles/triples IR20,000/30,000/ 35,000)* is a relatively new place with clean, slightly cramped rooms with shared bathroom. Showers cost an extra IR3000.

Park Hotel *(☎ 555 1852; Emām Khomeini St; singles/doubles IR35,000/50,000)* has very large, old-fashioned rooms with shared bathroom.

Guesthouse Darya *(☎ 554 0008; Mohagegi St; singles/doubles/triples IR20,000/ 28,000/33,000)* is a clean, friendly place popular with Japanese travellers. Showers cost IR4000.

Morvarid Hotel *(☎ 553 1433, fax 556 0520; Fajr Square; singles/doubles/triples IR56,500/ 79,000/94,000)* is pretty good value for money. The rooms are nothing special, though they have private bathroom, fridge and that old-fashioned accessory, a black-and-white TV.

Hotel Ark *(☎ 555 1277; singles/doubles IR50,000/80,000)* is down a quite side road alongside the citadel. It's well-kept (decorated in shades of apricot) and the tidy rooms with attached bathroom are good value for this price.

Azarbaijan Hotel *(☎ 555 9051, fax 553 7477; Shar'ati St; singles/doubles IR74,000/ 102,000)*, recognisable by the violet columns on the outside, is worthy of a splurge.

Places to Eat

Tabriz' most famous dish is the cheap and hearty *ābgusht* (meat stew) and this is the best place in Iran to sample it. **Esteghlal** is one of the better proponents of *ābgusht* (IR9000), although you'll find more locals at the small **Mohamadi Restaurant** *(Tarbeyat St)*.

Modern Tabriz Restaurant *(☎ 556 7411; Emām Khomeini St)*, downstairs and signposted in English, is a bright, clean restaurant with cheque tablecloths and attentive waiters. Kebab meals with all the extras cost IR17,000 to IR30,000 and you can also get a good *ābgusht* (IR15,000) and omelette (IR12,000).

Sofra Khaneh Sonati *(☎ 332 7990; 29 Bahman Ave; dishes IR12,000-30,000)* is the place to go for fish meals, in a slightly tacky mock forest setting with ponds and a cave grotto. You sit on carpets rather than at tables and the food is very good. It's near the university.

Getting There & Away

Air There are flights with **Iran Air** *(☎ 334 9038)* to Tehrān (IR147,000, several a day) and Mashhad (IR291,000, twice a week).

Bus, Minibus & Shared Taxi The modern bus and minibus terminal is in the south of the city – take a shared taxi from the corner of Emām Khomeini and Shar'ati Sts. Buses regularly go to Jolfā (IR4800, three hours), Kermānshāh (IR25,000, 11 hours), Māku (IR6000, about four hours), Orumiye (IR8000, five hours), Ardabil (IR7800, four hours), Rasht (IR15,000, eight hours, overnight only) and Tehrān (IR16,700, nine hours). For Qazvin and Zanjān take any Tehrān-bound bus.

IRAN

Also from the bus terminal, shared taxis go to Orumiye (IR30,000), Māku and Bāzārgān (IR20,000) and Ardabil (IR20,000).

Train There are two daily express trains from Tabriz to Tehrān (IR40,000/21,600 1st/2nd class, 12 hours), both travelling overnight. Trains also travel west to Turkey (Van, Ankara and İstanbul) and to Damascus (Syria). The train station is about 5km west of the town centre, accessible by shared taxi along Emām Khomeini and 22 Bahman Sts, but there's a handy ticket booking office on the corner of Emām Khomeini and Hāfez Sts.

AROUND TABRIZ
The remarkable village of **Kandovan**, 50km southwest of Tabriz, is built around volcanic rock formations similar to Cappadocia in central Turkey, though in Kandovan many cave homes are still inhabited. Catch a minibus from Tabriz to Oshu, then a shared taxi to Kandovan; or charter a taxi from Tabriz for around IR50,000, including one hour waiting time.

Marāghe, the former capital of the Mongol dynasty (1220–1380), is famous for its four ancient brick tomb towers, and its ceramics and mosaic tiles. It's 150km southeast of Tabriz and can easily be visited as a day trip in combination with Kandovan.

ARDABIL
اردبیل

☎ 0451

If you're heading to Azerbaijan or the Caspian Sea coast from Tabriz you'll pass through Ardabil, home to the impressive **Mausoleum of Sheikh Saf-od-Din** (admission IR20,000; open 8am-8pm), founder of the Safavid dynasty. It also has an interesting **bazaar**, and the hot mineral springs at Sareiyn are 27km away.

Ojahan Inn (Emām Khomeini Square; singles/doubles IR22,000/32,000) is conveniently located on the noisy main square, and is the cheapest place around. It's clean enough, but there are no showers.

Sabalan Grand Hotel (☎ 448 081, fax 449 991; Sheiki Safi St; singles/doubles IR100,000/200,000) is in a good location close to the mausoleum and about halfway between Ali Qapu and Emām Khomeini Squares. Rooms are comfortable, though a bit overpriced, and there's a good **restaurant**.

Iran Air (☎ 224 8808) flies between Ardabil and Tehrān daily (IR125,000). There are also regular buses to Tabriz (via Bostan Abad), Rasht and Zanjan. For Āstārā, a shared taxi (IR10,000) from the bus terminal is the quickest option. The terminal is some way from the centre – a private taxi from Ali Qapu Square costs about IR3000.

ĀSTĀRĀ
آستارا

This border town is on the Caspian coast but close enough to Ardabil to be included here. It's the main border crossing point between Iran and Azerbaijan. For information about crossing the border see the Getting There & Away chapter earlier in this book.

Hotel Aras is the best of the cheap hotels around Shahrdar Square. Plenty of shared taxis and minibuses head towards Rasht, Bandar-e Anzali and Ardabil – from where there are onward connections elsewhere.

THRONE OF SOLEIMĀN
تختسلیمان

This large and remote fortified settlement (admission IR30,000; open 7am-7pm daily) is built around a small lake on a hilltop and dates from the Achaemenid (559–330 BC), Parthian (190 BC–AD 224), Sassanian (AD 224–637) and Arab (637–1050) periods. The oldest remaining structures are the ruins of a **Sassanian palace** and the substantial **fire temples**.

The top of the conical **Prison of Soleimān** mountain, about 2.5km west of the ruins, offers superb views of the countryside, village and ancient city.

To reach these impressive ruins, go to Takāb on a series of minibuses from Tabriz, via Meyāndo'āb and Shāhn Dezh; or from Zanjān by direct bus. From Takāb, take a minibus to Nosratabad village, and then walk to the ruins. Alternatively, charter a taxi from Takāb.

QAZVIN
قزوین

☎ 0281

Qazvin is a pleasant stopover, and the best base from which to visit the Mausoleum of Soltāniye and the Castles of the Assassins. Most of the life-support systems are on or near the central Āzadi Square, including the post office and major banks.

There's cheap Internet access (IR7500) and international phone calls at **Café Net**

(Khayyam St), near the corner of Danesh Alley about 75m north of Āzādi St.

The ancient **Jāmeh Mosque**, 700m south of Āzādi Square, has some features dating back to the Arab period (637–1050), including an exquisitely decorated prayer hall. About 300m further south, the 16th-century **Shrine of Hossein** is particularly beautiful, and revered by all Iranians.

Qazvin Museum (Āzādi Square; admission IR10,000; open 8am-2pm & 4pm-8pm) is housed in the striking two-storey Chehel Sotun Palace surrounded by a lovely park, both of which are more interesting than the museum itself.

Places to Stay & Eat
Qazvin has only a handful of hotels, but they're all very good value. **Hotel Iran** (☎ 228 877; Shohadā St; singles/doubles IR27,500/40,000) is the top budget place. It's central and has reasonably clean rooms with private shower (but shared toilet). The management is friendly and can arrange trips into the Alamut region.

Alborz Hotel (☎/fax 226 631; Āyatollāh Tāleghāni Ave; e hotel_alborz_q@yahoo.com; singles/doubles US$23/35) is a very modern, European-style place with semi-luxurious rooms at a reasonable price. There's Internet access and a good coffee shop.

Eghbali Restaurant (☎ 223 347; Tāleghāni Blvd), about 200m east of Āzādi Square, is a great restaurant with something more than the usual kebab fare (although there are plenty of kebabs on the menu, including a 'Bulgarian kebab'). Among the other dishes are gheymeh nasar (traditional lamb stew) and, as a starter, a bowl of pitted olives in a thick sauce.

Getting There & Away
The main bus and minibus terminal is at Gateway to Tehrān (Darvāzeh Square) and from there frequent buses go to Tehrān (IR5200, three hours), and a few buses go to Hamadān (IR9700, 3½ hours) and Kermānshāh (IR10,400, six hours). Shared taxis to Tehrān leave from outside.

For destinations east such as Zanjān (IR10,000), Tabriz (IR25,000) and also Hamadān, go to the junction of Jomhuri Blvd and Asad Abadi Blvd where you can pick up any passing bus. For Rasht, go to Enqelab Square, west of Āzādi Square.

Qazvin is on the train line between Tabriz and Tehrān, but arrival and departure times are antisocial and tickets hard to get – the bus is better. The train station is about 2km south of Āzādi Square.

AROUND QAZVIN
Alamut & the Castles of the Assassins قلعه دژهای حشیشیون
In the southern foothills of the Alborz Mountains are the historic fortresses known as the Castles of the Assassins. The castles were the heavily fortified lairs of the adherents of a bizarre religious cult, based loosely on the precepts of the Ismaili sect. There are seven castles in all though little more than rubble remains of most. While the story surrounding the castles is very romantic, the stunning views, mountain villages and opportunities for hiking are the main attractions.

The most famous castle is **Alamut**, once occupied by Hasan Sabah, founder of the Assassins, and reached by a paved road about 110km northeast from Qazvin. **Lam Besar** is the most extensive ruined site (best visited with a guide) and is only 65km from Qazvin. The best way to organise a day trip to either site is through Hotel Iran in Qazvin, which will take you up in a 4WD for around IR140,000.

It's possible to charter a taxi (or take an infrequent minibus) up into the mountains, stay in a local village and organise a guide and donkeys to explore the less-accessible sites.

Mausoleum of Soltāniye گورستان سلطانیه
The famous mausoleum of the Mongol Soltān Oljeitu Khodābande was originally built as the final resting place of Ali, the son-in-law of the Prophet Mohammed, but this never eventuated. It has one of the largest domes in the world – 48m high, and nearly 25m in diameter – and the **views** from the top are superb. The entire building and surrounding complex is undergoing extensive renovations, so much of the interior is covered by scaffolding.

The mausoleum is not far from the main road between Zanjān and Qazvin, but is much closer to Zanjān (36km). Take any bus, minibus or shared taxi between the two towns, get off at the junction and catch another shared taxi to Soltāniye village.

HAMADĀN همدان

☎ 0261

Hamadān has always been a major stop on the ancient royal road to Baghdad, and it remains an important trading and transit centre. Backed by some impressive snow-clad mountains, Hamadān is a popular retreat for Iranians and there are a few things to see in the city and nearby. The problem with sightseeing in Hamadān is that it can get just as expensive as in Esfahān or Shirāz, the difference being that the sights are nowhere near as interesting.

The centre of town is the huge Emām Khomeini Square. Bank Melli dominates the northern side of the square, and is the only place to change money (other than the bazaar).

Net Gostar Company (Bu Ali Sina Square) has Internet access.

Things to See

About 200m north of the main square, Jāmeh Mosque has 55 columns, and was built during the Qajar period (1779–1921). Also, worth a look is the Shrine of Abdollah, about 600m northwest of the main square.

The Mausoleum of Ester va Mōrdekhāy (admission IR20,000; open 8am-7pm) is the most important Jewish pilgrimage site in Iran. Jews believe that it contains the body of Esther, the Jewish wife of Xerxes I, who is credited with organising the first Jewish emigration to Persia in the 5th century.

The Avicenna Memorial (admission IR20,000; open 8am-6pm daily), built in memory of the local famous poet, Bu Ali Snā, has a library and museum.

The Museum of Natural History has an off-beat collection of stuffed animals and other exhibits, all labelled in English. It's at the end of Bolvār-e Azadegan, about 5km from the city centre – charter a taxi.

Some ruins of the ancient city can be seen around Hekmatāne Hill (admission IR20,000), which is slowly being excavated, but most items of interest have been pilfered by the National Museum of Iran in Tehrān.

Places to Stay & Eat

The cheapest hotels are around Emām Khomeini Square. Hamadān Guest House (☎ 252 7577; Ekbātan St; rooms IR50,000) is accustomed to foreigners and is the best place to park your bags. Clean rooms all have shared bathroom, and the price is the same whether for one, two or three beds. It also has a cheap restaurant/teahouse.

Ekbatan Hotel (☎ 252 4024; Shohadā St; singles/doubles IR28,000/37,500) is nearby and has very small and basic rooms with shared bathroom.

Buali Hotel (☎ 825 0788, fax 825 2824; e bu ali-hotel@hotmail.com; Buali Ave; doubles US$60), 1.2km south of the main square, is a very comfortable hotel but not outstanding for this price. Large ground-floor rooms have bathtub, satellite TV and fridge.

Restaurant Kaktoos (Bu Ali Sina Square; full meal IR25,000) is regarded as one of the better restaurants in Hamadān. It's clean and incredibly popular with locals, but the menu is standard kebabs and chicken dishes (around IR10,000).

The restaurant (dishes IR21,000-32,000) at the Buali Hotel is good for a splurge with the fare ranging from schnitzel to gulf shrimps.

Getting There & Away

The bus terminal is about 1.2km north of the main square and easily reached along Ekbātan St. Buses regularly go to Esfahān (IR15,800, about seven hours), Kermānshāh (IR7000, three hours), Khorram Ābād (IR9000, four hours), Shirāz (IR29,000, 15 hours) and Tehrān (IR12,500, five hours).

The minibus terminal is about 200m northeast of the bus terminal and has buses to Kermānshāh, Ali Sadr village, Lalejin and other local destinations. Shared taxis to Kermānshāh and Qazvin (about IR20,000 for each) gather at Sepah Square, near the bus terminal.

AROUND HAMADĀN

The village of Lalejin, 32km north of Hamadān, is famous for its pottery and turquoise glazing. You can browse the showrooms and visit workshops, although tourists get a bit of the hard sell.

The Ali Sadr Caves (☎ 0812-553 3440; admission IR20,000; open 8am-8pm daily), approximately 100km north of Hamadān, are about 40m high and contain several huge lakes with clear water up to 8m deep. The entrance fee includes a tour in a paddleboat. The caves are interesting but have only a few outstanding limestone formations and unless you're a big fan of watery caves (as many Iranian families clearly are), it's pretty hard to justify the 200km round trip from Hamadān. There are a couple of cafés in the caves themselves, and it's possible to stay overnight at the complex in a self-contained **cabin** *(doubles with bathroom & kitchen IR80,000)*.

Minibuses travel to Ali Sadr village (IR6000) from the minibus terminal in Hamadān. To charter a taxi costs about IR80,000, including waiting time.

KERMĀNSHĀH كرمانشاه
☎ 0431

Kermānshāh is the largest and busiest city in the central west, and a good place to base yourself while exploring the region.

The centre of town is the mammoth Āzādi Square. South of there (along Modarres St) you'll find the bazaar, and a long way north (along Beheshti St) is the bus terminal and Tāq-e-Bostān. The branch of Bank Melli on Modarres St (opposite the mosque) will change money.

There's Internet access for IR8000 an hour at **Nazari Computers**, opposite the local bus terminal, just off the northwest side of Āzādi Square.

Things to See
The bas-reliefs and carved alcoves at **Tāq-e Bostān** *(admission IR20,000; open 8am-sunset)* are the main attraction in Kermānshāh. They are carved into a large rock outcrop overlooking a pool and pleasant garden, and date back to the Sassanian period (AD 224–637). The figures in the large grotto are believed to represent Khosro II, a contemporary of the Prophet Mohammed, and a famous hunter. Next to it, a small arched recess carved in the 4th century shows Shāpur II and his grandson, Shāpur III. From Āzādi Square take a shared taxi to the bus terminal and another from the square near the terminal, or charter one for around IR5000.

At the other end of town, **Takieh Mo'van al Molk** *(admission IR20,000; open 8am-noon & 4pm-8pm Sat-Thur)* is used to commemorate the death of Emām Hossein, particularly during Moharram.

Places to Stay & Eat
Hotel Nabovat *(☎ 831 018; Āzādi Square; singles/doubles/triples IR35,000/55,000/85,000)* is central and the best budget option with simple but clean rooms.

Hotel Bisutun *(☎ 21230; Kāshāni St; singles/doubles US$20/30)* is an outstanding mid-range hotel for this part of the world. It looks more like an English country manor than an Iranian hotel, has a lovely big garden at the back, and the rooms are spacious and immaculate. It's about 3km south of Āzādi Square.

The best places for lunch or an early dinner are the **restaurants** around Tāq-e Bostān. There are dozens of them outside the entrance and lining the street leading up to it. Almost directly opposite the entrance is a great open-air **tea garden** where you can sit on raised platforms and relax with a pot of tea and a *qalyan*.

Getting There & Away
There are daily **Iran Air** *(☎ 849 674)* flights to Tehrān (IR125,000).

The huge bus and minibus terminals are side by side about 8km north of Āzādi Square – shared taxis to the terminal (IR1000) leave from the northeastern corner of the square. Buses regularly go to Esfahān (IR25,000, nine hours), Hamadān (IR7000, around three hours), Tabriz (IR27,000, 11 hours), Ahvāz (IR30,000), Shirāz (IR37,500) and Tehrān (IR20,000, nine hours). For Khorram Ābād, take any bus heading to Ahvāz.

AROUND KERMĀNSHĀH
Bisotun بيستون
Overlooking the main road to Hamadān, about 2km west of Bisotun village, are two eroded **Parthian bas-reliefs**. The one on the left shows King Mithradates standing before four supplicants. The one on the right depicts several scenes relating to Gotarzes II. In the cliffs, another 200m towards Kermānshāh, the vast unfinished **stone panel** was probably started in about the 7th century BC, but its intended purpose remains a mystery. At the time of writing the carvings were covered in scaffolding that didn't look like coming down anytime soon.

KHORRAM ĀBĀD خرم آباد
☎ 0661

The main reason to stop in Khorram Ābād is to visit the impressive and dominating **Falak-ol-Aflak** *(admission IR30,000; open 9am-6pm daily)*. Even if you don't go into this fortress, it's worth climbing to the main entrance for the views.

Khorram Ābād doesn't have any stand-out budget accommodation.

Hotel Karun (*☎ 25408; Shar'ati St; singles/doubles IR120,000/ 150,000*) used to be reasonably cheap but has evidently learned about dual pricing. The rooms are clean and have attached bathroom.

Hotel Shaqayeq (*☎ 432 648; Emām Hossein Square; singles/doubles US$25/37*) has a good restaurant attached where a plate of *chelo morg*, salad and drink costs IR15,000.

Iran Air flies to Tehrān (IR117,000, twice a week). You can buy tickets through **Peyman Travel Agency** (*☎ 432 222*). Buses leave from outside the relevant bus company offices along Shar'ati St. There are plenty of services to Tehrān and Ahvāz. **Bus Company 17** has a service to Kermānshāh (once a day at 2pm). It's even harder getting to Hamadān – you have to flag down a bus (or shared taxi) heading towards Tehrān and change at Borujerd. Minibuses to Andimeshk depart from south of Emām Hussein Square (IR6000).

AHVĀZ   اهواذ
☎ 0611

The main reason to drag yourself out to Ahvāz is to use it as a base or starting point for trips to Choqā Zanbil and Shush. Much of Ahvāz was devastated by unremitting Iraqi bombardments throughout the Iran-Iraq War, and has since been ruined by uncontrolled redevelopment, although the broad Karun River flowing through town is pleasant.

Hotel New Karun (*cnr Emām Khomeini & Moslem Sts; doubles IR40,000*) has simple, clean rooms with shared bathroom and a guest kitchen. There's no sign in English but it's easy to find (it's opposite Hotel Star).

Hotel Iran (*☎ 221 7201, fax 217 206; Shar'ati St; singles/doubles IR108,000/219,000*) was once reasonably good value but it's now a cheap hotel with a mid-range price tag. Rooms have attached bathroom and are reasonably comfortable.

There are two good restaurants overlooking the river on its east bank. **Restaurant Khayyām**, below Shohadā Square, has great views and good food. **Pol Restaurant**, under the Chaharom Bridge, is particularly good for fish kebabs (IR18,000).

Ahvāz is well connected by air and given its far-flung location, it can make sense to fly in one way from Tehrān and work

your way back. **Iran Air** (*☎ 365 680*) flies daily to Tehrān (IR151,000) and Esfahān (IR117,000), and less often to Mashhad and Shirāz.

The main bus terminal is about 5km west of the river. Bus services include Bushehr (IR20,300, seven hours), Esfahān (IR29,400, 14 hours), Khorram Ābād (IR16,000, six hours), Kermānshāh (IR22,000, nine hours) and Shirāz (IR17,000, 10 hours).

There are three trains a day to Tehrān (IR38,350/23,050 1st/2nd class, 16 hours).

ANDIMESHK   اندیمشک
☎ 064242

Andimeshk is much smaller than Ahvāz and a good place to base yourself while exploring the southwest region, particularly Shush and Choqā Zanbil.

Hotel Rostam (*☎ 22818; singles/doubles IR50,000/70,000*), 300m north of Beheshti Square, has quiet rooms with attached bathroom and a restaurant.

Hotel Bozorg Andimeshk (*☎ 21000, fax 29295; Azardegan Square; singles/doubles IR200,000/350,000*) is a large, mid-range place with comfortable rooms and a restaurant. Taxis to Shush and Choqā Zanbil can be arranged here (around IR60,000 for a half day).

Some bus companies in Andimeshk have direct services to Tehrān, via Khorram Ābād. For other services you'll have to hail down a bus from the roundabout along the main highway in Andimeshk.

SHUSH   شوش
Shush (Susa) was one of the great ancient cities of Iran, and one of the earliest to be explored by archaeologists. It was an important regional centre from at least the 4th millennium BC, and reached its peak in the 13th century BC and again in the 6th century BC. It must have once been as grand as Persepolis, but there's now very little left to see.

Apadana Hotel (*doubles IR100,000*) is the only tourist hotel in the village and it's close to the ancient site, although the rooms are a bit overpriced. There's a good restaurant here.

Ancient City
The city (*admission IR20,000; open 8am-6pm daily*) was built on four small mounds.

The largest mound contains the remains of the **Royal Town**, once the quarter of the court officials. Northwest of this was the **Apadana**, where Darius I built his residence and two other palaces. Two well-preserved foundation tablets found beneath the site of **Darius' Palace** record the noble ancestry of its founder. The mound labelled as the **Artisans' Town** dates from the Seleucid (331–190 BC) and Parthian (190 BC–AD 224) periods. The imposing **fort**, near the entrance, was built by the French Archaeological Service at the end of the 19th century as a necessary defence against the unpacified Arab tribes of the region, but is not currently open to the public.

CHOQĀ ZANBIL چغا ذنبيل

The well-preserved *ziggurat* (pyramidal temple) of Choqā Zanbil *(admission IR30,000)* is the best surviving example of Elamite architecture anywhere. It was built during the 13th century BC, but later sacked and then abandoned. Incredibly, this imposing landmark was lost to the world for more than 2500 years, and only rediscovered in 1935.

Originally, it had five concentric storeys but only three remain, reaching a total height of about 25m. There was originally a complex of chambers, tombs, tunnels and water channels on the lowest level, as well as two temples to Inshushinak on the south-eastern side. The ziggurat was surrounded by a paved courtyard protected behind a wall, outside of which were the living quarters of the town, as well as 11 temples. The rest of the city is not well-preserved, but there are still the remains of three simple, but well-constructed **royal palaces**.

Choqā Zanbil is well off the main highway and not accessible by public transport. A taxi from Ahvāz, with a stop at Shush, shouldn't cost more than IR120,000.

Caspian Provinces

The Caspian region, known as the Shomāl (North), has a varied terrain, with thick forests, mountains and a coastal plain up to 100km wide, and is particularly wet and densely populated. This is a popular holiday destination for Iranians, especially Tehrānis and particularly in summer when it gets quite humid. But don't come expecting pretty beaches and seaside attractions. This is essentially a forested, grey lake and the sprawl of ugly housing development stretches all the way from Rasht to Sāri.

Shared taxis, rather than buses, are the quickest and easiest way to get around the Caspian if you're hopping from town to town. Minibuses are also common.

RASHT رشت
☎ 0131

Rasht is the largest town in the Caspian region and is a popular weekend and holiday destination for Tehrānis. The city itself has little to offer travellers, but it's a transport hub and the jumping-off point for the hill village of Māsuleh and the seaside port of Bandar-e Anzali (see the Around Rasht section following).

The city centre is chaotic Shohadā Square, where you'll find the **post office** and **police headquarters** (several readers have reported success in getting visa extensions there). Emām Khomeini Blvd is the main thoroughfare, stretching southeast from Shohāda Square.

The major banks will change money, but it's quicker at **Mehra Pooya Currency Exchange**, down a lane off Emām Khomeini Blvd (near Hotel Golestan).

There's Internet access at **Rata Computer** *(Āyatollāh Ziabari Blvd)*.

Places to Stay & Eat
Carvan Hotel *(☎ 222 2613; Emām Khomeini Blvd; rooms IR50,000)* is the best of the budget hotels. It's central, clean and friendly.

Salar Excellent Hotel *(☎ 223 2407; Emām Khomeini Blvd; singles/doubles IR35,000/ 40,000, doubles with bathroom IR52,000)*, a little further along and on the other side of Emām Khomeini, is not particularly excellent but it's cheap enough.

Ordibehesht Hotel *(☎ 22210; Shohadā Square; singles/doubles US$25/30)* is a good mid-range hotel, set back from the square but easily visible. Rooms are clean and comfortable, with a certain old-fashioned charm, and there's a good **restaurant**.

Grand Father Pitza Restaurant *(A'lam-ol-Hoda St)*, southwest of Shohada, has decent pizzas as well as doner kebabs and barbecued chicken.

Kourosh Restaurant is one of several in Rasht that serve *fesenjān*. It's clean and efficient; a full meal comes to IR28,000. It's down an alley just off Sa'adi St, about 50m north of Shohadā Square.

Getting There & Away

There are daily **Iran Air** (☎ 772 4043) flights to Tehrān (IR117,000), and less regular ones to Mashhad (IR226,000) and Tabriz (IR117,000).

Buses head in all directions from the main bus terminal, accessible by shared taxi heading southeast along Emām Khomeini Blvd. Tickets are also available at bus company offices around Shohadā Square. Long-distance buses go to Tehrān (IR23,000), Tabriz (IR18,000) and Gorgān (IR15,000). For destinations east along the Caspian coast, either take a Gorgān bus or a shared taxi or minibus. Shared taxis to Qazvin, Tehrān, Rāmsar and Bandar-e Anzali leave from around Shohadā Square.

AROUND RASHT
Māsuleh   ماسوله

Māsuleh is one of the most beautiful villages in the region, with its cream-coloured houses stacked on top of one another and clinging to the hillsides. The mountains around the village are great for hiking.

Monfared Masooleh Hotel (☎ 0132-757 3250; singles/doubles US$20/30) is the only real hotel in Māsuleh and this is unfortunately reflected in the price (from No Ruz to September there's no single rate). The rooms, with attached bathroom, are quite good, but you can rent a room in a local home (often with private bathroom) for much less – around IR40,000 to IR50,000 outside peak holiday times. Ask around at any of the stalls or teahouses.

From Sabze Square in Rasht, take a shared taxi to Fuman, then another past stunning scenery to Māsuleh (around IR5000 all up). Chartering a taxi costs around IR50,000, including waiting time.

Bandar-e Anzali   بندر انزلی

Anzali is a popular resort for Iranians. The town centre is Emām Khomeini Square, just past the second bridge coming from Rasht. From the **promenade**, you can charter a boat (US$10 an hour) for trips into the 450-sq-km **Anzali Lagoon**, home to several species of water birds. There's also a busy **bazaar** full of Russian goods.

There are a couple of decent hotels on Emām Khomeini Square. **Tehrān Hotel** (☎ 22868; singles/doubles IR20,000/30,000) is the budget option but is often full. **Hotel Ancient Golsang** (☎ 0181-23910; singles/doubles IR75,000/95,000) is a friendly place with large, old-fashioned rooms with attached bathroom.

Shared taxis leave for Rasht (IR3000, 30 minutes) from around Emām Khomeini Square. Regular minibuses and shared taxis to Āstārā depart from a junction just south of the town centre.

RĀMSAR   رامسر
☎ 01942

Backed by forested hills, Rāmsar is one of the more attractive resort towns along the Caspian – just don't come here for the beaches! The main road is Motahhari, and the centre is Enghelāb Square, where Bank Melli (foreign exchange) is located.

There's Internet access in the computer shop in the shopping arcade below the Caspian Hotel.

Things to See

The **Caspian Museum** (☎ 25374; admission IR20,000; open 8.30am-2.30pm & 3.30pm-9.30pm daily) is the original marble summer palace built in 1937 for Rezā Shāh. The interior is adorned with Persian carpets, and paintings, furniture and ornaments gifted to the *shāh*, mainly from France and Italy. An English-speaking guide will lead you through the rooms.

It's possibly worth visiting the **beach** just to see what passes for a seaside resort in Iran – a depressing strip of pebbles, a forlorn fairground with a few deserted cafés and a couple of mangy ponies for hire.

Even if you have no interest in taxidermy, check out the bizarre **stuffed animal shop** along the main street.

Places to Stay & Eat

You can usually stay in a local **home** for about IR50,000. Ask at the restaurants along the main road, or just look lost for a few minutes – someone will offer you something soon enough.

Rāmsar has some of the best self-contained accommodation in the Caspian.

Safatian Suites (☎ 22917; apartments IR100,000), **Caspian Suites** (☎ 2243; apartments *IR100,000)* and **Nazia Suites** (☎ 24 588; *apartments IR120,000)* are grouped together about 50m from Enghelāb Square and all offer good value apartments with kitchen, lounge and verandas. Safatian has apartments sleeping up to eight people.

Caspian Apartment Hotel (☎ 29457, fax 22457; *Motahhari St; double suites IR150,000)*, in the town centre, is a good alternative. The rooms are comfortable with kitchen, lounge and bathroom, and the management is friendly.

Rāmsar Grand Hotel (☎ 522 3593, fax 522 5174; *singles/doubles from US$55/74)* dominates the town and is set on a splendid hillside – even if you don't stay here there's a good restaurant and coffee shop.

Golesorkh Restaurant is the best of the central restaurants on Motahhari St. It has a menu is English and a range of dishes including sturgeon, whitefish and the local *torsh kebab* (IR22,000). If you're staying in a suite, Rāmsar is the obvious place to do your own cooking. Grocery stores (some open 24 hours) line Motahhari St to fulfil your every need.

Getting There & Away
From the terminal in western Rāmsar, frequent minibuses and shared taxis go to Rasht and Chālus. To Chālus, Sāri and Gorgān, you can also catch any bus along a road one block north of Motahhari. Direct buses to Tehrān leave from a terminal about 500m north of the Rāmsar Grand Hotel.

NOSHAHR/CHĀLUS & AROUND
نوشهر چالوس
☎ 0191
The twin towns of Noshahr and Chālus are situated where the motorway from Tehrān (via Karaj) meets the coast, so they're easily reached. However, the only reason to come here is to visit nearby attractions, and although there are some outstanding midrange hotels, there's nothing for budget travellers. Noshahr is definitely the nicer of the two towns if you plan on staying, while Chālus has most of the transport connections. It's easy to commute between the two by shared taxi.

At **Namak Abrud**, about 12km west along the main road from Chālus, there's a **telecabin** *(IR20,000 return; open 10am-4pm)* to the top of Mt Medovin (1050m). It's very popular with Iranian tourists in summer – get there early to avoid not only the queues but the clouds that roll in later in the day. The telecabin is in a large park about 2km back from the highway.

The small **Sisangān National Park**, 31km east of Noshahr, is a lovely pocket of rare forest with a few walking trails. Take any transport between Chālus and Nur and get off at the sign saying 'Jungle Park'.

Places to Stay & Eat
In Noshahr, **Shalizar Restaurant & Hotel** (☎ 32090; *Āzādi Square; doubles IR100,000)* has charming, well-furnished rooms and is the best choice in this harbour town.

Two very comfortable mid-range places are opposite each other on Noshahr Blvd at the official western entrance to Noshahr. **Hotel Malek** (☎ 24107, fax 23602; *doubles IR150,000)* is extraordinarily modern by Iranian standards. The **restaurant** is equally contemporary (the only thing missing is the cocktail bar) and as well as kebabs (IR18,000 to IR35,000) you can get steaks, schnitzels, fish dishes and caviar (IR120,000).

Hotel Kourosh (☎ 24103, fax 24174; *doubles US$20)* is a big resort-style place, but the rooms aren't up to Malek's standard.

The **restaurants** in the Malek, Shalizar and Kouroush hotels are all very good.

SĀRI
ساری
☎ 0151
Sāri is a busy university town some distance back from the coast. The centre of town is Sā'at Square (Clock Square), from where streets radiate in all directions. Things to see include the 15th-century **Shrine of Yahyā** at the end of a laneway off Jomhuri Eslami (opposite Hotel Nader); the nearby **Soltān Zein-ol-Ābedn Tower**; and the **Shrine of Abbās**, about 2.5km east of Clock Square.

Places to Stay & Eat
Tavakol Hotel (☎ 324 2493; *Modarres St; doubles IR39,200)* is one of the few cheap places to accept foreigners and it has reasonable rooms with shared bathroom. There's no sign in English but it's virtually on the corner of Modarres St and Sa'at Square.

Valiasr Hotel (☎ 324 5476; *Beheshti Blvd; rooms IR50,000)* also accepts foreigners (with a bit of persistence). It's clean and rooms have a basin but shared bathroom.

Hotel Asram (*☎ 325 5090, fax 325 5092; singles/doubles US$30/45*), near the bus terminal, is a considerable jump in price and is poorly located, but it's the best mid-range hotel in town and has a good **restaurant**.

Getting There & Away

Sāri is a stopover on the regular **Iran Air** flights between Tehrān (IR117,000) and Mashhad (IR157,000).

The bus terminal is about 3km northeast of Sā'at Square (take a shared taxi along 18 Dei St) and from here there are daily services to Tehrān (IR11,900), Mashhad (IR22,400), Rasht (IR17,000) and Ardabil (IR21,000). For Gorgān, minibuses (IR4000) leave from a separate terminal, 2km east of Sā'at Square, or take a shared taxi (IR12,000) from the office opposite.

Trains to Tehrān and Gorgān depart daily. The train station is about 1km south of Sa'at Square.

GORGĀN گرگان
☎ 0171

Gorgān is a reasonable place to break up a journey between the Caspian and Mashhad. In the bazaar, **Jāmeh Mosque** has a traditional, sloping, tiled roof and an unusual minaret. About 200m west, the **Shrine of Nur** is a small polygonal tomb tower, with outer walls decorated with simple brickwork designs. **Gorgān Museum** (*admission IR20,000*), about 1km west of Shahrdāri Square, has some mildly interesting archaeological displays, but is hardly worth the admission fee.

About 6km east of Gorgān, **Nahar Khoran** is an unspoilt forest area with plenty of hiking trails.

Taslimi Hotel (*☎ 4814*), 200m south of Shahrdāri Square, is a cheap central place and has rooms with attached bathroom.

Tahmasebi Jadid Hotel (*☎ 2780; singles/doubles US$20/25*), 500m down from Emām Khomeini, is the best choice, although it's nothing special for the price. There's a restaurant here.

Getting There & Away

From the bus terminal, 2km northwest of Shahrdāri Square, buses regularly go in all directions including Tehrān (IR14,500), Mashhad (IR18,000) and Shāhrud (IR9500). Minibuses for Sāri (IR4000) leave from a

separate terminal about 3km southwest of Emām Khomeini Square. Shared taxis and minibuses also make the trip to Shāhrud, a very scenic drive which crosses the foothills of the Alborz Mountains.

The train to Tehrān (IR27,650/10,700 1st/2nd class) departs daily; the station is about 300m west of the bus terminal.

AROUND GORGĀN
Gonbad-e Kāvus کنبد کاووس

In this unexciting Turkmen town, 93km west of Gorgān, is a spectacular **tomb tower** (*admission IR10,000; open 8am-8pm*) built by Ghābus ibn-e Vashmgir. It's about 55m tall, and has a circular structure with 10 buttresses rising from the base to an 18m-high pointed dome. From Gorgān, minibuses leave about every hour from a terminal 5km north of Shahrdāri Square. It's worth the short detour if you're heading to Mashhad or along the spectacular mountain pass road to Shāhrud, but not as a special trip from Gorgān.

The Gulf

The Gulf, with a shoreline stretching from Kuwait to the Straits of Hormoz, is one of the least visited parts of Iran and is definitely best avoided in summer when it gets unbearably hot and very humid. However, it has some interesting historical and cultural influences – a unique mix of Persian and Arab – and can be used as a gateway to Iran.

BANDAR-E ABBĀS بندر عباس
☎ 0761

Bandar-e Abbās is the busiest port in Iran, and the major city along the Gulf. There's not much to see or do, but the city – known simply as Bandar by the locals – is a stepping-off point for the nearby islands. Bandar's population is a fascinating mix of Arabs and black Africans, with a large Sunni minority.

Orientation & Information

The city centre is 17 Shahrvari Square, where the **police headquarters** (for visa extensions) and **Bank Melli** are located. A better place to change money is **Morvarid Exchange**, in a small arcade just off Emām Khomeini St (a few doors from Persia Restaurant).

Internet access for IR15,000 an hour and Internet phone calls are available at **Soroush Internet** (shop 185, Zeytoon shopping mall, Emām Khomeini St).

Places to Stay

There are several cheap guesthouses around the bazaar area, although some won't accept foreigners. **Mosāferkhuneh-ye-Bazar** (Taleqani Blvd; dorm beds/doubles/triples IR11,000/27,500/44,000) is one of the best and right in the thick of things, above the bazaar on the waterfront. It's clean and as cheap as you'll find.

Hotel Hormozgan (☎ 24856; Asad Abadi St; singles/doubles IR35,000/45,000) is a little removed from the centre but a good budget option and English is spoken here.

Hotel Ghods (☎ 22344, fax 20158; Emām Khomeini St; singles/doubles IR150,000/ 200,000) is the best mid-range hotel. Rooms are enormous and very clean, and it's reasonably quiet for the central location. There's a decent **restaurant** downstairs.

Places to Eat

Sayyādān St, between Shohādā Square (in western Bandar) and the sea, has a strip of clean, modern **pizza restaurants** where you can eat well for IR12,000. **Felfely Pizza** is another place closer to the town centre; it does huge burgers for IR5000.

There are the usual line-up of **kebabis** along Emām Khomeini St, as well as several bakeries specialising in something you rarely see elsewhere in Iran – profiteroles (IR1000 each).

Persian Restaurant (Emām Khomeini St; dishes IR20,000) is a good place for chelo khoresht (stew and rice), fish with rice, and kebabs at reasonable prices.

There's a good restaurant and teahouse in **Atilar Suites No.1** (☎ 27420; Emām Khomeini St), and a pleasant open-air **teahouse** on the waterfront opposite the half-built mosque.

Getting There & Away

Bandar-e Abbās is well connected to the rest of Iran by road, rail and air, but if you're travelling overland, it's a long, hot ride. For details about international ferry services to/from Bandar-e Abbās see the Getting There & Away chapter earlier in this book.

Air Domestic airline, **Iran Air** (☎ 37170), flies to Tehrān (IR275,000, once a day), Shirāz (IR133,000, once daily), Esfahān (IR133,000) and Mashhad (IR268,000). **Iran Asseman** also flies to Tehrān and Shirāz for the same price as Iran Air. **Kish Air** flies to Kish Island (IR130,000, once a day).

Bus The bus terminal is in the far east of the city – you may need to take two shared taxis, or charter one directly (about IR8000). Buses depart regularly to all major places including: Bandar-e Lenge (IR6500, three hours), Bushehr (IR26,000, 14 hours), Bam (IR12,500, eight hours), Kermān (IR15,000, eight hours), Yazd (IR20,500, 10 hours), Shirāz (IR18,000, 10 hours) and Esfahān (IR26,000, eight hours).

Train The train to Tehrān leaves daily at 1pm (IR64,000 1st class only, 21 hours), travelling via Sirjān and Yazd (but not Esfahān). The station is in the far north of the city so you'll need to charter a taxi. There is a central **ticket office** (unsignposted in English) on the 2nd floor, one door east of the Bala Parvaz Travel Agency (almost opposite Hotel Ghods).

Boat Ferries to Hormoz (IR6000) and Qeshm (IR8500) Islands leave when full from the main jetty, opposite the bazaar. Ferries across the Gulf leave from the Shahid Bāhonar docks, about 6km west of the city centre. Tickets for international ferries to Dubai and Sharjah are available at travel agencies around the town, or direct from **Valfajre-8 Shipping Company** (☎ 559 075), between the city centre and docks.

AROUND BANDAR-E ABBĀS
Hormoz Island   جزیره هرمز

The 42-sq-km Hormoz Island is worth a quick visit, and easily accessible from Bandar-e Abbās. The only village on the island is also called Hormoz, and the rest of the island is virtually uninhabited. About 750m northeast of the jetty are the ruins of a 16th-century **Portuguese castle**. It's the most impressive colonial fortress in Iran, but is badly neglected. A wandering ticket seller demands IR20,000 to look around.

Speedboats travel between the jetty (opposite the bazaar) in Bandar-e Abbās and

Hormoz village (IR6000, 30 minutes) about every hour. There are more frequent boats in the morning.

Qeshm Island   قشم جزیره
☎ 0763

Qeshm is the largest island (1335 sq km) in the Gulf, but has little to interest travellers. The island is mountainous, dotted with villages and mangrove forests and is gradually being developed as a duty-free resort (known as the Qeshm Free Zone) to rival Kish, but it's a long way from that sort of upmarket modernisation. The main town, Qeshm, is developing fast but is still pretty much a backwater.

The highlight of the island is **Lāft**, a pretty village 58km west of Qeshm town, with wind-towers, wells and an empty **beach**.

In Qeshm town, **Qeshm Inn** (☎ 522 5558; doubles IR150,000) is pleasant, and has good rooms and an excellent **restaurant**. Like Kish, there are plenty of expensive hotels on the island.

For information about boat transport to Qeshm refer to Getting There & Away in the Bandar-e Abbās section earlier.

Mināb   میناب
☎ 0765

Surrounded by date palms and with a crumbling fortress overlooking the town, Mināb is an easy and pleasant day trip from Bandar-e Abbās – or an alternative base. The region is famous for ceramics and mosaic tiles, and the Thursday **market** here is one of the most colourful in Iran.

Sadaf Hotel (☎ 8999; singles/doubles IR60,000/80,000) is one of the better value hotels in Iran. Large, spotless rooms with TV, fridge, air-con and attached bathroom are a bargain, and there's a good restaurant downstairs. It's walking distance from the bazaar and town centre, just before the main bridge into town.

The easiest way to get to Mināb from Bandar is by shared taxi (IR10,000, 1½ hours) from a designated terminal (known locally as 'garage'), just south of Abuzar Square.

BANDAR-E LENGE   لنگه بندر
☎ 0762

Bandar-e Lenge is an infectiously lethargic place, and a pleasant overnight stop before or after visiting Kish Island. There is not much to do here except wander the bazaar or waterfront taking in the atmosphere.

Hotel Amir (☎ 22311; Enghelāb St; singles/doubles IR29,000/39,000), about 150m north of the docks, is easily the best budget choice. Clean, basic rooms have shared bathroom and the manager speaks English. The **restaurant** downstairs is the best place to eat. A dish of fish, rice, yoghurt and a soft drink comes to IR18,000.

Iran Air (☎ 24300) flies daily to Tehrān (IR265,000) via Shirāz. From the bus terminal, about 2km east of the docks, buses go to Bandar-e Abbās (IR6500, three hours) about every hour, and daily to Bushehr (IR13,000) and Shirāz (IR22,000). Shared taxis or pick-ups to Bandar-e Charāk (for boats to Kish) also leave from the bus terminal (IR12,500, one hour).

Ferries sail to Kish Island (IR60,000, four hours, twice a day at 9am and 7pm). There are also international ferries to Dubai (IR440,000, twice a week on Thursday and Saturday).

KISH ISLAND   کیش جزیره
☎ 0764

The main attraction of Kish for Iranians is duty-free shopping, which can be done in shopping malls of the sort you'll find anywhere in the world. Since each person can only take out US$80 worth of goods before duty is payable, it hardly seems worth the effort. Having been left somewhat idle since the Islamic Revolution, however, Kish is being reborn as a fashionable resort island, and upscale development is really making its mark.

An attraction for travellers may be getting a tourist visa here, since this is a visa-free port – see Visas & Documents under Facts for the Visitor earlier. The **Ministry of Foreign Affairs** (☎ 442 0734; Ferdous Villas, Ferdosi St) is almost opposite the Kish Trade Centre.

Although Kish has no real 'centre', the modern settlement is in the north east, where you'll find banks, offices, shopping malls and the **Kish Tourism Organisation** (☎ 442 2434; open 7am-2.30pm & 6pm-9pm), which has helpful, English-speaking staff and can provide a map of the island. There's Internet access (IR20,000 an hour) upstairs in Paradise I shopping centre.

Things to See & Do

A **Special Bicycle Path** has been established on Kish, circling most of the island close to the shoreline, so the obvious thing to do is hire a bike and circumnavigate. Bikes can be hired from several stalls on the beach in front of Hotel Shayyam for a hefty IR15,000 an hour. It takes a good three hours to ride around the island; with stops allow half a day.

Along the way are the limited ruins of the ancient city of **Harireh** near the fast-developing village of **Saffein**. Another local attraction is the **Greek ship**, stranded off the island's southwestern waters since 1966. Kish has several sandy **beaches**, but females must use Ladies Exclusive Beach, and men, the Men's Beach.

Kish has several **water sports** operators, mostly located on the beach in front of Hotel Shayyam. Nothing is cheap – an hour on a jet ski costs IR600,000. **Kish Diving School** (☎ 442 4355) is Iran's only PADI dive school and has boat dives from US$30 and courses for US$180.

Places to Stay & Eat

Kish has plenty of hotels, but there's no way to stay here cheaply. The tourist office has a list of places and may be able to suggest something, or make a few calls for you.

Sahar Guest House (☎ 442 2067; doubles from IR85,000) is reasonable but in a poor location south of the airport, and it's usually full anyway.

Goldis Hotel (☎ 442 2237; doubles IR200,000) is one of the best-value places on the island. It's away from the shopping malls but convenient for the port, the rooms are huge and well kept, and it has a restaurant.

In Saffein, **Asia Hotel** (☎ 443 1800; Niayesh St; doubles US$35) has comfortable suite rooms and is willing to drop to US$20 without too much bargaining.

Kish has a curious mix of Western-style, fast-food places and try-hard theme restaurants, but there are some interesting places to eat scattered around the northern and eastern parts of the island. Eating out is expensive on Kish, but watch out for blatant overcharging and ask menu prices before you order. One of the more unusual places is **Payab** (Olympic Blvd), a traditional teahouse and restaurant built in a subterranean water tunnel between the harbour and Saffein.

Venus Burger is a popular Western-style hamburger joint in the easy-to-spot Venus Mall, and there are several modern cafés in **Paradise Shopping Centre**.

Getting There & Away

There are regular **Iran Air** (☎ 22273) flights from Tehrān (IR259,000), and **Kish Airlines** (☎ 2259) flies from Tehrān (daily), Shirāz (IR117,000), Esfahān (IR191,000) and Mashhad. There are also charter flights to Kish so it's worth asking at a travel agent if the main airlines are booked up.

Ferries operated by **Valfajre-8 Shipping Company** (☎ 24655) sail daily from Bandar-e Lenge (IR60,000, four hours, twice daily at 9am and 7pm). Quicker and more frequent are the speedboats (IR30,000, one hour) from Bandar-e Chārak – an easy ride from Lenge by shared taxi (IR12,000, 1½ hours).

BUSHEHR بوشهر
☎ 0771

Set on a peninsula jutting out into the ocean, and with a crumbling old city, Bushehr is perhaps the most relaxed town along the Gulf. Bushehr's downfall is that it's almost impossible to find a cheap place to stay, and it's not really on the way to anywhere – it's a long way from the other Gulf towns and is closest by road to Shirāz. Come here only if you have the time and budget to take it in without hurrying.

The highlight is the easily explored **old city**, a living museum of traditional Bandari architecture. Although spared from the destructive effects of development, the old facades on many of the houses are falling into disrepair.

Places to Stay & Eat

Bushehr is not set up for foreign travellers on a budget and the cheap places, such as **Mosāferkhuneh Hāfez** and **Mosāferkhuneh Pārs**, both in the bazaar district, will usually only accept foreigners with special permission from the local police station. To complicate matters, when we visited the police department they simply told us to bite the bullet and stay in a hotel! You might have more luck – the police office is on Leyan St about 300m west of Engelab Square.

There are no problems staying at the **Hotel Saadi** (☎ 252 2605; Hafez St; rooms without/with bathroom IR120,000/160,000),

IRAN

also in the bazaar area, but the price is extortionate for utterly basic rooms.

Bushehr Tourist Inn *(☎ 252 4470, fax 252 2411; Valiasr St; doubles US$30)* is a government owned and managed tourist hotel with a great waterfront location. The rooms are very worn and tired-looking but it's a welcoming enough place with a decent restaurant.

There are a couple of good open-air **cafés** facing the ocean on the western side of the peninsula (along the Esplanade). They offer cheap Iranian hamburgers, drinks and ice-cream, and a good position from which to watch the sunset.

Āzādi Restaurant *(cnr Shohāda & Mo'allem Sts; dishes IR11,000-18,000)* is a tiny place

sitting alone and a little forlornly. It has a cosy atmosphere and the usual line-up of kebabs (including fish).

Getting There & Away

Iran Air *(☎ 22041)* flies daily to Tehrān (IR220,000), Esfahān (IR150,000) and Shirāz (IR117,000). Buses go to major destinations, but not particularly frequently. Services include Bandar-e Abbās (IR33,000, about 14 hours), Bandar-e Lenge (IR20,000, nine hours), Ahvāz (IR15,700, seven hours), Shirāz (IR10,000, five hours) and Esfahān (IR25,000, 16 hours).

Valfajre-8 Shipping Company *(☎ 24234)* has passenger ferries to Kuwait, Bahrain and Qatar, but none to other ports in Iran.

Iraq

العراق

Long ago in the fertile valleys between the Tigris and Euphrates rivers, a great civilisation was born. It was to leave an indelible mark on the future of the world. This land was known as Mesopotamia, from the Greek meaning 'between two rivers', and is now part of modern Iraq. It was here that human beings first began to cultivate their land and where writing was invented.

Recent history has dealt less kindly with Iraq; few countries in the region have experienced such political turbulence and, in the early years of independence, so many changes of regime.

In the mid-1970s the country began to reap considerable benefits from its huge oil reserves and Iraq's industrial infrastructure, education system, and nationwide literacy campaigns were the envy of many countries in the region.

However by the end of the 1980 to 1988 Iran-Iraq War, Iraq's economy was in tatters. Before the country had a chance to rebuild, it was plunged once again into crisis with its invasion of Kuwait, the subsequent Gulf War in 1991, and the imposition of debilitating UN economic sanctions against it.

Facts about Iraq

HISTORY

Iraq became independent in 1932 after a period of Ottoman and then British rule. On 14 July 1958, the monarchy was overthrown in a military coup and Iraq became a republic, ushering in a period of instability characterised by a series of coups and countercoups that continued throughout the 1960s.

The Arab-Israeli conflict of 1967 caused Iraq to turn to the Soviet Union for support, accusing the USA and UK of supporting Israel. On 17 July 1968, a bloodless coup by the Ba'ath Party, a secular socialist party founded in Syria in 1942, put General Ahmad Hassan al-Bakr in power.

Despite some minor border skirmishes with Iran over the question of sovereignty over the Shatt al-Arab waterway in 1969, the 1970s represented a period of relative stability for Iraq. In 1975, Iraq and Iran decided to settle their differences, and a

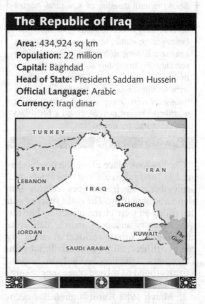

The Republic of Iraq

Area: 434,924 sq km
Population: 22 million
Capital: Baghdad
Head of State: President Saddam Hussein
Official Language: Arabic
Currency: Iraqi dinar

boundary line was drawn down the middle of the Shatt al-Arab (Iraq had been granted exclusive control of the waterway in 1937). Iran also stated that it would stop giving aid to Iraqi Kurds. By the end of 1977, Kurdish had become an official language and greater autonomy had been granted, offering hope for a lasting peace between the Kurds and Iraqi authorities, conflict between whom had been simmering since 1961 (see the boxed text 'The Kurds' later in this chapter). These factors resulted in Iraq becoming a more stable country, and the growing oil revenues brought about an unprecedented improvement in the economy.

In 1979 Saddam Hussein replaced Al-Bakr as president, the revolution in Iran took place and relations between the two countries quickly sank to an all-time low. Iraq declared that it was dissatisfied with the 1975 boundary agreement of the Shatt al-Arab and wanted a return to the exclusive control of the waterway. The Iraqi government had always been dominated by Sunni Arabs, even though Shiites form a majority of the Iraqi population, and Hussein became increasingly concerned about the threat of a Shiite revolution in his own country.

IRAQ

277

Travel Warning

Since the Iraqi invasion of Kuwait in August 1990 and the subsequent Gulf War, Iraq has been virtually closed to visitors. Western governments continue to advise their citizens against travelling to Iraq, citing the ongoing volatility in the internal security situation throughout the country. Baghdad's airport remains shut and, at the time of writing, no Iraqi visas were being issued to foreigners. It was therefore not possible to do a first-hand update of Iraq for this edition.

Clashes took place along the border during 1980 and full-scale war broke out on 22 September, with Iraqi forces entering Iran along a 500km front. The eight years of war that followed were characterised by human-wave infantry advances and the deliberate targeting of urban residential areas by enemy artillery, all for little territorial gain. The waters of the Persian Gulf also became a battleground as oil and other supply ships were destroyed.

In March 1988 Kurdish guerrillas occupied government-controlled territory in Iraqi Kurdistan, and the Iraqi government in response killed thousands of civilians, forcing many more to escape to Iran and Turkey. It is alleged that chemical weapons were used – an allegation that Iraq continues to deny.

In August 1988 the UN brokered a cease-fire between Iran and Iraq. In the eight years of war, a million lives had been lost on both sides, and the economic cost to Iraq is estimated at more than US$100 billion.

As Iraq started to emerge from the ravages of the war, relations with neighbouring Kuwait began to sour. In July 1990, Hussein accused the Kuwaitis (with some justification) of waging 'economic warfare' against Iraq by attempting to artificially hold down the price of oil, and of stealing oil from the Iraqi portion of an oilfield straddling the border.

Arab attempts to mediate a peaceful end to the dispute failed and on 2 August 1990 Iraq sent its troops and tanks into Kuwait. The UN quickly passed a series of resolutions calling on Iraq to withdraw. Instead, on 8 August, Iraq annexed the emirate as its 19th province.

Western countries, led by the USA, began to enforce a UN embargo on trade with Iraq by stopping and searching ships bound for Iraq and Jordan. In the months that followed, more than half a million troops from 27 countries flooded into Saudi Arabia as the diplomatic stand-off over Kuwait deepened. At the end of November, the USA and the UK secured a UN resolution authorising the use of force to drive Iraq out of Kuwait if Baghdad did not voluntarily pull out before 15 January 1991.

Despite frantic last-minute attempts by international leaders to broker a deal, the deadline passed, the Iraqis did not budge, and within hours a barrage of Tomahawk cruise missiles was launched against strategic targets in Baghdad and elsewhere which signalled the start of the Gulf War. Allied (mostly US) aircraft began a five-week bombing campaign over Iraq and Kuwait. In contrast, the subsequent ground offensive lasted only 100 hours. While there were relatively few casualties on the Allied side, controversy has persisted over the number of civilian and military deaths in Iraq and Kuwait: estimates range from 10,000 to more than 100,000.

A cease-fire was announced by the USA on 28 February 1991 and Iraq agreed to comply fully with all UN Security Council resolutions. The Security Council demanded full disclosure, inspection and destruction of the country's biological, chemical, ballistic and nuclear weapons stockpiles and development programmes before UN sanctions would be lifted.

The elite remnants of the Iraqi army turned their guns on Kurdish and Shiite uprisings in the north and south, causing a further mass exodus into neighbouring countries, particularly Iran and Turkey. This led the Allied forces to impose two 'no-fly' zones, in the north and south, to protect the civilian population from Iraqi air raids.

As malnutrition increased and medical care became inadequate throughout Iraq, the food for oil plan was introduced in 1996. Under this programme, Iraq was permitted to export US$2 billion of oil over a six-month period in order to buy food and medicine, although limited hard currency reserves and extensively damaged infrastructure prevented full implementation of the plan.

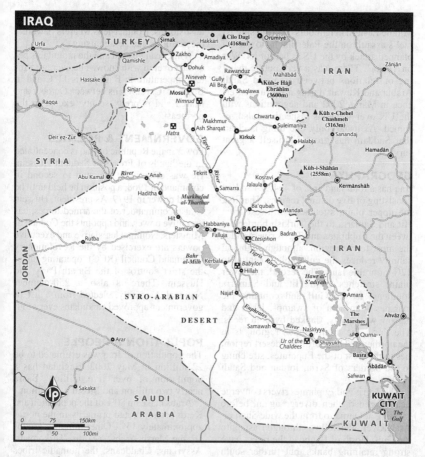

IRAQ

Iraq Today

Tensions between Iraq and the UN (principally the USA) have risen and fallen cyclically since mid-1996. In August of that year, the Iraqi army moved into an area forbidden to it by international rules, resulting in the US destruction of air defences in southern Iraq. In November 1997 and then again in January and February of the following year, Iraqi-US stand-offs threatened to spill over into open military confrontation.

In early August 1998, weapons inspectors were denied access to a number of sites and the Iraqi government announced the suspension of all cooperation until the sanctions were removed. The USA, with British backing, responded with four days of air strikes in December, drawing protests from

Russian, Chinese and Arab representatives at the UN.

While sanctions have had a crippling effect on the Iraqi people, resulting in over half a million children's deaths according to the WHO, world consensus is now that they have done little – if anything – to undermine Saddam himself or his regime. Indeed, Iraqi Airways resumed domestic flights in October 2000, a free-trade was set up with Turkey in May 2001, and oil is smuggled out to be sold on the black market.

Iraq was listed as being part of an 'axis of evil' by the US after the 11 September attacks, meaning its continuing isolation appeared almost guaranteed. However, in January 2002 Iraq finally invited a UN human rights team to visit the country, and

IRAQ

managed to rouse enough support among Middle Eastern neighbours by criticising Israel's assault on the Palestinians to avert a planned attack by the US as part of its 'War on Terror'. There was a very public thawing of relations between Iraq and Saudi Arabia and Kuwait during a Beirut conference in March 2002 and negotiations with the UN over weapons inspections also resumed. As usual, only one thing is clear: that Saddam has proved himself a great survivor.

GEOGRAPHY

Iraq has a total land area of 434,924 sq km, consisting of five distinct regions. The first, the upper plain, stretches northwest from Hit and Samarra to the Turkish border between the Euphrates and Tigris rivers and is the most fertile region, although high soil salinity reduces the cultivable potential to 12% of arable land. The second, the lower plain, stretches from Hit and Samarra southeast to the Gulf and contains the marshes – an area of swamps, lakes and narrow waterways, flanked by high reeds. The third, the mountainous region, is in the northeast. The fourth, the desert region, lies to the west of the Euphrates, stretching to the borders of Syria, Jordan and Saudi Arabia.

The Tigris and Euphrates rivers converge near Baghdad, then diverge again, before meeting at Qurna to form the wide Shatt al-Arab River, which flows through Basra into the Gulf. North of Baghdad the rivers have strong retaining banks, but further south they often flood in spring.

CLIMATE

Iraq is hot in summer (May to September); the average summer temperature in Baghdad is 34°C and in Basra 37°C; the north is slightly cooler. In the south there is high humidity and in the central plains there are dust storms. Contact-lens wearers beware – these storms can be agonising.

Winter can be cold and the mountains become covered with snow. The average winter temperature in Baghdad is 11°C and in Basra 14°C. Rain falls between October and March and is pretty scanty, except in the northeast.

GOVERNMENT & POLITICS

Power in the Republic of Iraq is concentrated in the hands of President Saddam Hussein. He was effectively elevated to second in command in 1968, a position he held until he seized power in 1979. As president, Hussein is also commander of the armed forces, has executive power, and appoints the Council of Ministers. Nominal legislative and executive powers are exercised by the Revolutionary Command Council (RCC), operating under the strict control of the Ba'ath Party and Hussein. There is also a 250-member National Assembly, elected from a list of government-approved candidates every four years.

POPULATION & PEOPLE

The population of Iraq was estimated to be 22 million in May 2002. Baghdad has a population of over five million, Basra nearly two million and Mosul 1.5 million.

Arabs make up 80% of the population and Kurds (concentrated primarily in the north) approximately 15%. Other minority groups are the Marsh Arabs, Yezidis, Turkomans, Assyrians, Chaldeans, the nomadic tribes who live in the western desert region, and the Jezira Bedouin who live in the highlands of the north.

RELIGION

The official religion is Islam. Muslims make up 95% of the population, with considerably more Shiites than Sunni. The Shiites tend to live in the south of the country, the Sunni in the central and northern districts.

The largest group of non-Muslims are Christians who belong to various sects, including Chaldeans, Assyrians, Syrian and Roman Catholics, Orthodox Armenians and Jacobites. Other religious minorities are the Yezidis, often erroneously called devil worshippers, and the Sabaeans, or Mandeans, who are followers of John the Baptist.

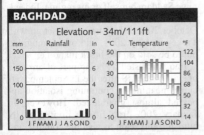

BAGHDAD

Elevation – 34m/111ft

	Rainfall			Temperature	
mm		in	°C		°F
200		8	50		122
			40		104
150		6	30		86
100		4	20		68
			10		50
50		2	0		32
0		0	-10		14
	J F M A M J J A S O N D			J F M A M J J A S O N D	

IRAQ

The Kurds

Iraq is home to over four million Kurds, the overwhelming majority of whom are Sunni Muslims and live in the northern provinces of the country. These provinces form part of the ancient Kurdish homeland of Kurdistan, which extended across the modern-day borders with Iran, Turkey and Syria. The 1961 Kurdish campaign to secure independence from Iraq laid the foundations for an uneasy relationship between the Kurds and the Iraqi state. Cycles of conflict and détente have consistently characterised this relationship ever since, as greater official recognition and freedom have been alternately offered and denied, culminating frequently in brutal repression. This process was tragically re-enacted after the 1991 Gulf War when over two million Kurds were forced to flee across the mountains to the relative safety of Turkey and Iran, countries with their own restive Kurdish populations. Under UN protection, the Kurdish Autonomous Region was set up in northern Iraq. However, ongoing Iraqi and external interference, and the often bitter rivalry between the Patriotic Union of Kurdistan (PUK) and the Kurdistan Democratic Party (KDP), ensure that these tentative moves towards autonomy remain precarious.

LANGUAGE

Arabic, the official language, is spoken by 80% of the population. The Kurds speak Kurdish, an Indo-European language. The Turkomans, who live in villages along the Baghdad to Mosul highway, speak a Turkish dialect. Persian is spoken by minorities near the Iranian border, while similar numbers speak Assyrian and Chaldean. English is quite widely spoken in urban centres.

For a list of Arabic words and phrases refer to the Language chapter at the back of this book.

Facts for the Visitor

VISAS & DOCUMENTS

At the time of writing, Iraqi embassies overseas were still not issuing visas to visitors. Some adventurous travellers have applied for visas at the Iraqi embassy in Jordan. We are not aware of anyone being granted a visa, other than journalists and aid workers.

For details of visas for other Middle Eastern countries, see the 'Visas at a Glance' table under Visas & Documents in the Regional Facts for the Visitor chapter.

EMBASSIES & CONSULATES

Following are the Iraqi embassies and consulates in major cities around the world. For addresses of Iraq's embassies in neighbouring Middle Eastern countries see the relevant chapter.

Australia (☎ 02-6286 1333) 48 Culgoa Circuit, O'Malley 2606
Canada (☎ (613) 235-4726, fax (613) 232-5712) 245 Metcalfe St, Ottawa, Ontario, K2P 2K2
France (☎ 01 45 01 51 00) 53 rue de la Faisanderie, Paris 75016
UK (☎ 020-7584 7141, 7584 7146) 22 Queen's Gate, London SW7
USA (☎ 202-483 7500) Iraqi Interests Section, c/o Embassy of Algeria, 1801 Peter St NW, Washington, DC 20036

MONEY

There are 1000 fils to the Iraqi dinar.

country	unit		Iraqi dinar
Australia	A$1	=	ID1784.05
Bahrain	BD1	=	ID8680.71
Canada	C$1	=	ID2081.91
euro zone	€1	=	ID3195.72
Japan	¥100	=	ID2745.75
Jordan	JD1	=	ID4662.29
New Zealand	NZ$1	=	ID1534.09
Qatar	Qr1	=	ID897.53
UAE	Dh1	=	ID888.56
UK	UK£1	=	ID4990.04
USA	US$1	=	ID3263.60

BOOKS

If you are interested in archaeology, there are many books available about Iraq's ancient sites. *Nineveh & its Remains* by Austen Henry Layard is particularly interesting; Layard was the pioneer as far as excavations in the Middle East are concerned. This book also gives an insight into the lives of ordinary people in Iraq in the 19th century.

Essential reading for anyone hoping to catch a glimpse of the marshes is the excellent *The Marsh Arabs* by Wilfred Thesiger, who felt a great affinity with the Marsh

Arabs and lived with them for five years in the 1950s.

Gavin Young also visited the marshes in the 1950s at the instigation of Thesiger. He returned again in the '70s to see how much the Marsh Arabs' lives had changed. *Return to the Marshes* is an account of this visit.

The Longest War by Dilip Hiro is a detailed account of the Iran-Iraq War. Hiro also published a painstaking account of the events surrounding the 1991 Gulf War. In a conflict characterised by partial media reporting on both sides, Hiro's detailed narrative, *Desert Shield to Desert Storm*, is about as objective as it gets.

FOOD & DRINKS

Food in Iraq is similar to that of other Middle Eastern countries (see the special section 'Middle Eastern Cuisine' in the Regional Facts for the Visitor chapter).

Tea, drunk sweet without milk, is the most popular hot drink, followed by thick, black coffee. Other drinks include fruit juices, soft drinks and alcohol, including locally made *arak*.

SHOPPING

Iraq is known for Bedouin and Kurdish rugs, copperware and jewellery.

Getting There & Away

AIR

Commercial flights have now been re-established between Ireland, Russia and Iraq, but since it is impossible to get a tourist visa for Iraq these services are strictly for Iraqi nationals and business people only. In any case, there are still no formal schedules, and flight details change by the week.

LAND & SEA

At the time of writing, none of the overland routes to Iraq from Jordan, Syria and Iran were open to foreigners.

The train from Istanbul to Baghdad reopened in May 2001 as part of a new free-zone agreement. However, there have been no passenger ships operating to or from Iraq since the start of the Gulf War.

Getting Around

There are international airports at Baghdad and Basra. Iraqi Airways resumed domestic passenger flights in October 2000.

Iraq has a good road network and there are buses between towns and cities, plus a rail line that connects Baghdad to Mosul and Basra. Shared taxis are used between towns and cities in the north of Iraq.

Baghdad بغداد

For many people, the name of this ancient city conjures up vivid images: starry skies, golden domes and minarets; women shrouded in black gliding through narrow streets with old houses leaning precariously towards one another; shafts of sunlight filtering through gloomy bazaars, their open shop fronts overflowing with exotic merchandise. Compared with these images, one's first impression of Baghdad can be disappointing, for it is not a city that makes an immediate impact. The old Baghdad has almost disappeared and the Iran-Iraq and Gulf Wars destroyed much of the modern city.

History

Baghdad was founded by Al-Mansur, the second caliph of the Abbasidian dynasty, in AD 762. The city he built was on the western bank of the Tigris, enclosed within a circular wall and called Medinat as-Salaam, which meant 'City of Peace'; it became known as the Round City. The caliph's palace and the grand mosque were in the centre with four roads radiating from them. The city expanded beyond the wall and was eventually joined by a bridge of boats to the eastern bank, where a district called Rusafah developed. By 946 this district had grown sufficiently large to rival the Round City.

Baghdad reached the height of its prosperity and intellectual life in the 8th and 9th centuries under the caliphs Mahdi and Haroun ar-Rashid. It was the richest city in the world, the crossroads of important trade routes to the east and west, and supplanted Damascus as the seat of power in the Islamic world. Arabic numbers, the decimal system and algebra all came into being at this time. Advances were also made in medicine, and magnificent buildings were constructed with beautiful gardens.

From the mid-9th century onwards, the Abbasid caliphate became weakened by internal conflict, and civil war between Ar-Rashid's two sons resulted in the partial destruction of the Round City. Total destruction came about when the Mongols sacked Baghdad, killed the caliph and many of the residents, and destroyed the irrigation system. In 1534 it became part of the Ottoman Empire and centuries of neglect followed.

Efforts were made to improve the city in the early years of the 20th century. The administration was reformed, hospitals and schools were built and a postal service developed, but these improvements were belated and inadequate. Baghdad's greatest developments took place when large oil revenues started to flow in after 1973. However, all developments were curtailed by the wars of the 1980s and '90s.

Orientation

The city extends along both sides of the Tigris. The eastern side is known as Rusafah and the western as Karkh. The core of the city is a 3.5km by 2km area in Rusafah, extending from Midan Muadham in the north to Midan Tahrir in the south. Sharia Rashid is the main street of this area and contains the city's financial district, and the copper, textile and gold bazaars.

Running parallel to Sharia Rashid is Sharia al-Jamouri, which has some historical mosques and government offices. South of Sharia Rashid is Sharia Sadoun, a newer commercial area. Parallel to here along the river bank is Sharia Abu Newas, which has many outdoor cafés.

Sharia Damascus in Karkh stretches from the Iraqi Museum to the international airport road. The central train station, Alawi al-Hilla bus/taxi station, Al-Muthana airport and Zawra Park are along here. Sharia Haifa, parallel to the river, is another major street in Karkh.

Since the 1950s the city has expanded enormously, and planned, middle-class neighbourhoods have sprung up between the city centre and the Army Canal. On the western bank are a number of residential areas, including affluent Mansour, which is surrounded by a race track and has trendy boutiques and fast-food restaurants. A number of embassies are in Mansour.

Museums

Baghdad has numerous excellent museums and interesting mosques. Many museums are free, others have only a nominal fee, and most are closed on Friday. In Karkh, near the Alawi al-Hilla bus/taxi station, is the large, well-organised **Iraqi Museum** (Sharia Damascus) that has a collection carefully labelled in English and Arabic that is from prehistoric, Sumerian, Babylonian, Assyrian and Abbasid times. Near Midan Rusafah, the **Baghdad Museum** houses an interesting collection of life-sized models in tableaux depicting traditional Baghdadi life.

The **Museum of Pioneer Arts** (Sharia Rashid) is worth a visit just for the wonderful old Baghdadi house in which the art collection is hung. The rooms are built around a central courtyard with a fountain in the middle. It's a peaceful retreat where you can sit and relax after the hustle and bustle of Sharia Rashid. Some of the rooms are traditionally furnished, and the guest rooms upstairs are the nicest of all.

Housed also in a large traditional Baghdadi house, the **Museum of Popular Heritage** (Sharia Haifa), on the western side of the street, has some fine examples of traditional Iraqi crafts, including woodwork, metalwork, basketwork and carpets, all tastefully displayed.

The **Saddam Art Centre** (Sharia Haifa), on the western side of the street, is a beautiful building with high ceilings, white walls and chandeliers. It was opened only in 1986 and the works in the permanent collection are mainly from the 1970s and '80s. The **Museum of Modern Art** (Midan Nafura), near the Tahrir bus station, is a bit of a letdown after the Saddam Art Centre, but it has some interesting temporary exhibitions.

Mosques

Never go into a mosque in Iraq unless you are invited. If you want to go inside one, stand at the entrance and someone will soon appear and indicate whether or not you are welcome inside. You must of course be dressed modestly and women must cover their heads.

The **Kadhimain Mosque** is the most important in Iraq after those at Kerbala and

Najaf. Inside are the shrines of the two *imams* (religious teachers) Musa al-Kadhim and Mohammed al-Jawad. The very large and elaborate mosque has gold-coated domes and minarets and was built in 1515.

The **Caliph's Mosque** is on the eastern side of Sharia al-Jamouri, between Midans Wathba and Amin. It's a new mosque with an ancient minaret that dates from 1289. Built 40 years ago, the **14th Ramadan Mosque** *(Midan Fardous, Sharia Sadoun)* has lovely arabesques and glazed wall tiles. Another attractive mosque is the **Ibn Bunnieh Mosque** in front of Alawi al-Hilla bus station. Yet another is the **Umm Attubol Mosque** on the road to the international airport. It has an unusual architectural style, very ornate and delicate, and gives the impression of being modelled in icing sugar.

The **Marjan Mosque** *(Sharia Rashid)*, on the eastern side of the street, was built in 1357, and in its early days served as the Murjaniyya School. Early 20th century, most of it was pulled down and rebuilt as a mosque. A little way down the opposite side of the road is the Murjin Khan, where the scholars used to live. It has been converted into a restaurant.

Mustansiriyya School
Opposite the Baghdad Museum, turn left at the mosque to get to the school entrance. The school was built in the reign of the 36th Abbasid caliph, Mustansir Billah, and was the most highly esteemed university of that time. It was completed in 1232 and now stands as an outstanding example of Abbasidian architecture.

Abbasid Palace
From Sharia Rashid, turn left at Midan Maidan and take the road to the right of the mosque. The palace is at the bottom of the road on the right, overlooking the Tigris. Because of its resemblance in style and structure to the Mustansiriyya School, some scholars believe it is the Sharabiyya School mentioned by old Arab historians.

Zawra Park
This vast park on Sharia Damascus, opposite Al-Muthana airport, is a little parched-looking compared with European parks, but parts of it, like the Islamic garden where fountains play, are attractive. There's a good

view of the city from the 54m-high Baghdad Tower in the park.

There is also a zoo, a swimming pool and a planetarium in the park.

Other Attractions
When it's not too hot, Baghdad is a fascinating city to explore on foot. If and when it gets onto the tourist map, the bazaars of Sharia Rashid will be where visitors go to see the 'real' Baghdad.

A far more interesting area, and one that gives a greater insight into the city, is that behind the Saddam Art Centre on Sharia Haifa. Here, you will see men in *galabiyyas* (long loose shirts), sitting in coffeehouses smoking water pipes or sitting cross-legged on the pavement selling their wares; little shops selling fresh herbs, spices or fruit and vegetables; men covered in oil mending old cars; narrow streets of old crumbling houses with overhanging balconies; and barefoot children playing in the streets. Fascinating though this area is, it is also a sad testimony to Iraq's enormous social and economic problems.

Around Baghdad

BABYLON, KERBALA & NAJAF
Ancient Babylon and the important Muslim shrines of Kerbala and Najaf all lie south of Baghdad, and it's quite possible to visit them all in a day trip from the capital.

Babylon بابل
Babylon lies 90km south of Baghdad and 10km north of Hillah, and is perhaps the most famous of Iraq's ancient sites. The ancient city reached its height during the reign of Nebuchadnezzar II (605–563 BC). With its high walls and magnificent palaces and temples it was regarded as one of the most beautiful cities in the world. It was most renowned for its Hanging Gardens, one of the Seven Wonders of the World.

All that remains of the ruins of Babylon is a huge and magnificent lion, eroded by time and the weather.

Kerbala كربلا
Kerbala is 108km southwest of Baghdad and is of great religious significance to Muslims because of the battle of Kerbala in AD 680. The battle between those who believed

the rulers of the Islamic community must be the direct descendants of Mohammed, and those who argued that virtue alone bestowed legitimacy upon leaders, led to the schism between the Sunni and Shiite sects. Hussein ibn Ali, who has become revered as leader of the Shiites, and his brother Abbas, grandsons of the Prophet Mohammed, were killed in the battle, and their shrines are contained in the two mosques here, thus making Kerbala one of the greatest pilgrimage centres in the Islamic world. Non-Muslims are not allowed to enter the shrines but, with the permission of an attendant, may be able to walk around the surrounding courtyards.

Najaf النجف

Najaf is 160km south of Baghdad, just west of the Euphrates. It was founded by Haroun ar-Rashid in AD 791. In the city centre is a mosque containing the tomb of Ali ibn Abi Talib (600–661), cousin and son-in-law of Mohammed and founder of the Shiites, thus making this mosque one of the sect's greatest shrines.

It is a great honour for Muslims to be buried in graveyards in either Kerbala or Najaf. The latter especially seems to have graveyards all over the place and it's fascinating, if a little macabre, to wander around them. Many of the graves are small shrines.

THE ARCH OF CTESIPHON سلمان بك

Little is left of the city of Ctesiphon, apart from the arch. It is 30km southeast of Baghdad, east of the Tigris. The city was built in the 2nd century BC by the Parthian Persians. The arch was part of a great banqueting hall and, apparently, is the widest single-span vault in the world. It survived the disastrous flooding of the Tigris in 1887, which destroyed much of the rest of the building.

Basra البصرة

Basra was founded by the caliph Omar in AD 637. It was originally a military base but rapidly grew into a major Islamic city. It became the focal point of Arab sea trade during the 16th century, when ships left its port for distant lands in the east. Its strategic position has made it the scene of many battles,

sometimes between the Marsh Arabs and the Turks and sometimes between invading Persians and Turks.

In 1624 Ali Pasha repulsed a Persian attack and, in the period of peace that followed, Basra became a mecca for poets, scientists and artists. The peace was shortlived; Ali Pasha's son imposed a buffalo tax upon the Marsh Arabs and the fighting and instability resumed.

Basra is Iraq's main sea port and secondlargest city, 550km southeast of Baghdad and 130km from the Gulf. There are extensive palm groves on the outskirts of the city and most of Iraq's dates are grown in and around Basra.

Orientation & Information

The city comprises three main areas – Ashar, Margil and Basra proper. Ashar is the old commercial area and includes the Corniche, which runs alongside the Shatt al-Arab River; Sharia al-Kuwait; and Sharia ath-Thawra, where banks and the old Iraqi Airlines office are found. Basra's bazaars are also here and behind them is the Ashar bus garage. The central post office is on the road to the west of the bus garage.

The Basra train station is in Margil, which also includes the port and a modern residential area to the northwest of Ashar.

Basra proper is the old residential area to the west of Ashar. Here you can see the lovely 19th-century houses called *shenashils* by the canal that flows into the Shatt al-Arab. One of these is the Basra Museum. Further along this road is the Basra bus station from where intercity buses leave.

Basra Museum

There isn't an extensive collection held at this museum – it includes objects from Sumerian, Babylonian, and Islamic eras – but it's worth coming here to see the beautiful *shenashil* houses with high, pointed windows and ornate, wooden overhanging balconies.

Not far from the museum is the derelict St Thomas Chaldean Church.

Floating Navy Museum

This museum is in Ashar at the northern corner of the Corniche. Its exhibits include guns from both sides in the Iran-Iraq War, models of ships and parts from wrecked Iranian aircraft and ships.

IRAQ

Museum for The Martyrs of the Persian Aggression

This white building has some war-wrecked vehicles in the grounds, while inside are heart-rending displays of the sufferings of the ordinary local people of Basra during the war with Iran. The museum is on the northeastern corner of Sharia Istiklal.

Basra Bazaar

Basra's bazaar in Ashar is one of the most atmospheric in Iraq, and was once home to a particularly good gold bazaar with some very fine pieces of jewellery. In parts you can see old houses with wooden facades and balconies tilting at such precarious angles that it's amazing they manage to stand at all.

Sinbad Island

Sinbad is supposed to have started his voyages from here. The island used to be attractive, with outdoor restaurants and gardens, but it suffered extensive bombing and now is a little dreary.

Nasiriyya   النصرية

Nasiriyya is 375km southeast of Baghdad, on the northern bank of the Euphrates. Most people stay here only to visit Ur of the Chaldees, but it's a pleasant, relaxed place to spend a day or two. The centre of Nasiriyya is Midan Haboby.

Nasiriyya Museum

The museum has an interesting collection from Sumerian, Assyrian, Babylonian and Abbasid times. It's on the southern side of the river, a pleasant 20-minute walk along the river bank. Walk south along Sharia Neel and turn right into the road that runs by the river; walk along here and cross over the bridge; take the first turning right and the museum is on the right.

AROUND NASIRIYYA
Ur of the Chaldees   أور الكادانية

Ur is one of the most impressive ancient sites in Iraq. It was mentioned in the Bible as being the birthplace of Abraham, and its earliest buildings date from 4000 BC. For three successive dynasties it was the capital of Sumeria, although it reached its height during the third and last dynasty (2113–2095

BC). The ziggurat is impressive and the royal tombs well preserved.

The Marshes   الأهوار

The marshes originally covered an area of approximately 10,000 sq km between the Tigris and the Euphrates, stretching from Basra in the south, Nasiriyya in the west and Kut in the north. Some parts were permanent, and others were temporary marshland, changing with the seasons.

The marshes were a world of vast expanses of water and shallow lagoons. Here it is sometimes possible to see *sarifas* (Marsh Arab dwellings) with their ornate latticework entrances. The people row *mashufs* (long, slender canoes) through the high reeds. There is archaeological evidence that life has continued here, almost unchanged, for 6000 years and the marshes are also home to many species of water birds. Sadly, much of the marshes were drained in the late 1980s and most Marsh Arabs have moved to refugee camps, mainly in Iran.

Mosul   الموصل

Mosul, 396km north of Baghdad, is Iraq's third largest city. It's also the most ethnically mixed, with Arabs, Kurds, Assyrians and Turkomans.

In Abbasid times, Mosul achieved commercial importance because of its position on the caravan route from India and Persia to the Mediterranean. Its most important export was cotton. The word 'muslin' is derived from Mosul, and cotton is still produced here today. Mosul was devastated by the Mongols in the 13th century but began to revive under the Ottomans.

The main street and commercial area is Sharia Nineveh, along which are several old houses that are fine examples of 19th-century Mosul architecture. The old part of the city is a maze of narrow streets off both sides of Sharia Nineveh, west of the bazaar.

The city centre is Midan Babatub, a huge open area with a fountain in the middle. The bazaar is between here and Sharia Nineveh. Sharia Duwasa runs south from Midan Babatub. Behind the eastern side of the square is the Babatub bus station. The central post office is on the eastern side of the station.

Mosul Museum

This museum has a large collection of finds from the successive civilisations of Iraq, from prehistoric to Islamic times, with an emphasis on finds from Nineveh to Nimrud. It's on the western side of the river.

Mosul House

This beautiful old house, built around a central courtyard, has a facade of Mosul marble. It houses life-sized models depicting traditional Mosul life. Admission is free but the museum is difficult to find and doesn't have a sign in English. Walking west along Sharia Nineveh, turn left at the crossroads before the Clock & Latin Church, take the second turning left along here, go under the arches and the house is on the right. It has a large wooden entrance.

Mosques

Believed to be the burial place of Jonah, the **Mosque of Nebi Yunus**, on the eastern side of the Tigris, is built on a mound beneath which are buried some ruins of Nineveh, but because of the sanctity of the site, excavation is impossible. A little community of mud-brick houses and narrow, winding streets has grown up around the mosque. Take a bus from the Babatub bus station towards the Ash-Shamal bus station in Nineveh (see that section, later, for details) and look out for the mosque on the right, about 3km from the Horeyya Bridge.

The **Great Nur ad-Din Mosque** was built in 1172 by Nur ad-Din Zanqi and is famed for its remarkably bent minaret, which stands 52m high and has elaborate brickwork. To get there, walk west along Sharia Nineveh and turn right at the crossroads before the Clock & Latin Church; the mosque is on the right.

Churches

Mosul has a higher proportion of Christians than any other Iraqi city. The **Clock & Latin Church** is a good place to start because it's easy to find and also sells a booklet called *The Churches of Mosul*. This booklet contains a numbered list in Arabic and English of the major churches in Mosul, and a map of sorts that will help you find them, or at least enable you to get assistance from someone. The church is on the southern side of Sharia Nineveh. Inside is lots of blue

Mosul marble, lovely brickwork in blue, brown and cream, and stained-glass windows of abstract patterns.

Many of the churches are near this one, but hidden away in the labyrinth of old Mosul's fascinating backstreets.

Other Attractions

The imposing ruins of **Bash Tapia Castle**, rising high above the Tigris on its western bank, are now the only part of Mosul's city wall still in existence. Just a few minutes away, a little further south on the river bank, are the remnants of the 13th century palace of the sultan Badr ad-Din called the **Qara Saray** (Black Palace).

Between the two ruins is the **Chaldean Catholic Church of at-Tahira**, or the Church of the Upper Monastery. The oldest part was built in AD 300 as a monastery, and in 1600 was added to and became a church. In the street running parallel to this is the Syrian Orthodox Al-Tahira Church (1210).

AROUND MOSUL
Nineveh   نينوى

The ancient city of Nineveh was the third capital of Assyria. Up until King Hammurabi's death it was a province of Babylonia, but after this time it developed as an independent kingdom. By 1400 BC it had become one of the most powerful countries in the Middle East, but by 500 BC it had been destroyed by the Medes of Northern Persia. For 200 years prior to this, however, Nineveh was the centre of the civilised world.

Nineveh is on the outskirts of Mosul, on the eastern bank of the Tigris. Its walls measured 12km in circumference and there were 15 gates, each named after an Assyrian god. Several have been reconstructed. The **Shamash gate** is just beyond the Ash-Shamal bus station. The Nergal gate is about 2km from the university and it has a small **museum** with some Assyrian reliefs and a model of the city of Khorsabad, which was the fourth capital of Assyria. To get there you must walk south from the university and then turn left just before the reconstructed walls on both sides of the road. You will see the gate just along here on the right.

Nimrud   نمرود

Nimrud, the second capital of Assyria, is 37km southeast of Mosul and one of the best preserved of Iraq's ancient sites. The city wall has an 8km circumference containing several buildings, the most impressive being King Ashurnasirpal II's palace. On either side of the entrance are two huge sculptures of human-headed lions with hawk wings. Inside are some beautiful bas-relief slabs. Two 2,800-year-old **Assyrian tombs** were discovered shortly before the Gulf War. They include large quantities of gold and jewellery from what archaeologists believe are two 9th- and 8th-century BC tombs of princesses or consorts – possibly of the court of Ashurnasirpal II. One tomb held three bronze coffins containing the remains of 13 people. In one coffin, a woman in her twenties was buried with a foetus, four children and 449 objects.

Hatra حترا

Hatra is 110km to the southwest of Mosul. Once an important city, it dates from the 1st century AD. In architecture, sculpture, metalwork and military expertise, Hatra was no less advanced than Rome. The ruins contain many fine pieces of sculpture.

Northeastern Mountains

Scenically this area contrasts starkly with the rest of the country, consisting of high mountains and fertile valleys. Much of it is in the Kurdish Autonomous Region. The Kurds are descendants of the Medes and have inhabited 'Kurdistan' since Parthian times (247 BC–AD 224; see also History in the Facts about the Region chapter).

ARBIL أربيل

Arbil, 84km heading east from Mosul, is one of the oldest continuously inhabited cities in the world, and headquarters of the Kurdish Autonomous Region. Its beginnings are buried in the mists of antiquity, but there is archaeological evidence that Neolithic peoples roamed the area 10,000 years ago.

Fortress

The modern town occupies the top of a mound formed by successive building over a long period of time. It is dominated by a fortress, behind which are three large **19th**-century Kurdish houses which, along with the fortress, have been turned into museums. The houses have ceilings decorated with floral patterns and coloured-glass windows. One has a room with an interesting collection of everyday Kurdish objects and handicrafts, another an art gallery showing works by contemporary Iraqi artists. Nearby is a large *hammam* (bathhouse), also part of the house.

Arbil Museum

The museum was opened in 1989 and has a comprehensive collection from Sumerian to Abbasidian times. From Midan Nishteman, walk away from the fortress, along the main road, cross Midan Media, and the museum is on the left.

SHAQLAWA & GULLY ALI BEG شقلاوة قلي علي بيك

The road from Arbil winds steeply upwards to Salahuddin at 1090m above sea level, and then on to Shaqlawa, 50km northeast from Arbil. This is an idyllic town surrounded by mountains and orchards where pears, apples, grapes, pomegranates, almonds and walnuts grow in profusion.

From Shaqlawa the mountain ranges begin to close in and the scenery becomes more rugged and dramatic. Gully Ali Beg, 60km from Shaqlawa, is a narrow 10km-long pass with a lovely 80m-high waterfall tumbling into it.

DOHUK دهوك

Dohuk is a small Kurdish town 73km north of Mosul. It's a pleasant place, with an interesting market, but serves mainly as a base from which to explore the surrounding mountains.

AMADIYA العمادية

Amadiya is 90km northeast of Dohuk. The road passes through scenery that, as the road unfolds, becomes more and more spectacular. It winds through several villages – firstly Zawila, then Suara Tuga, which has a wonderful view of the plain of Sarsang, then through Anshki to Sulaf, a village with waterfalls and lots of cafés where you can sit and enjoy the views. The road finally ends at Amadiya, an extremely picturesque village on a plateau 1985m above sea level, surrounded by magnificent mountains and endless green valleys.

ZAKHO زاخو

Zakho, near the Turkish border, is Iraq's most northerly town and is famous for its old, stone bridge, well preserved and still in constant use. Its age is unknown but it's reputed to have been built by a local Abbasidian ruler and is at the far side of town. The approach to Zakho is spectacular, crossing many high mountain ridges.

SINJAR سنجار

The town of Sinjar is 160km west of Mosul on the slopes of the Jebel Sinjar range in the desert, near the Syrian border. It is most renowned for being the town of the Yezidis, the so-called devil worshippers who are of Kurdish stock.

What they actually believe is that the devil is a fallen angel, bringing evil to the world, and must be appeased so he will once again take up his rightful place among the angels. The Yezidis will never say his name, Shaitan, or any similar-sounding word. Their religion contains elements of nature worship, Islam and Christianity. In October a festival is held at the shrine of Sheikh Adi, the sect's founder. Like the Kurds, the Yezidis are friendly and hospitable.

Israel & the Palestinian Territories

In most parts of the world, wise travellers normally avoid discussing either religion or politics. In Israel & the Palestinian Territories, however, these topics collide inseparably and dominate nearly everyone's concerns and daily conversations. This is Israel, Palestine, the Holy Land, and above all else, the Promised Land, and it elicits emotional responses from its citizens, residents, pilgrims, travellers and nearly everyone who experiences its lovely, historical landscapes.

A small region of disproportionate contrasts, Israel & the Palestinian Territories offer a wealth of remarkable views, adventures, climates, cultures and religions. Slightly smaller than New Jersey or Belgium, and half the size of Tasmania, the region takes in an appealing range of terrain: rugged mountains, subtropical valleys, fertile farmlands and blazing deserts.

The historical and religious perspectives found here are equally diverse. Jewish, Muslim and Christian pilgrims are drawn to it with the conviction that it's favoured by God, and in the case of the Jews, that it's the Promised Land. Unfortunately, everyone has a different idea of what constitutes an appropriate stewardship. This, combined with its strategic location, has made Israel & the Palestinian Territories the most hotly disputed bit of real estate in the modern world.

Facts about Israel & the Palestinian Territories

HISTORY

The first inhabitants of modern Israel & the Palestinian Territories were probably the Canaanites, who had migrated to the productive coastal areas from Arabia and Mesopotamia as early as the 20th century BC. (It's believed that these Canaanites were Semitic – that is, descended from Shem, the son of Noah of diluvial fame, but that seriously strains the biblical time line.) Around 2800 BC, Egypt claimed Canaan as part of its empire, and in a period of famine,

Israel & the Palestinian Territories

Area: 28,000 sq km (including the Gaza Strip and the West Bank)
Population: 6.43 million (including the Gaza Strip and the West Bank)
Capital: Jerusalem (claimed by both Israel and Palestine)
Head of State: Prime Minister Ariel Sharon, with a president, Moshe Katzav, in a largely symbolic role
Official Languages: Hebrew & Arabic
Currency: new Israeli shekel (NIS)

- Best Dining – eating at the Village Green or Lebanese Restaurant, Jerusalem, and Dr Shakshuka in Jaffa

- Best Nightlife – getting down at Tel Aviv's bars, clubs and all-night beach parties

- Best Walk – hiking from HaYoash to Taba along the Israel National Trail

- Best View – admiring the patchwork Galilee fields from the Arbel Cliffs

- Best Activity – floating on the Dead Sea

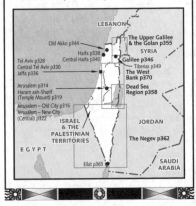

the Israelites (descendants of Israel, grandson of the patriarch Abraham) migrated to the Nile Valley for work. According to the Book of Genesis, God had promised that there, Israel would be made a great nation. After a period of prosperity in exile, the pharaoh Ramses forced the 'migrant workers' into servitude. Some time around the

13th century BC, Moses led the descendants of the Israelites for 40 years through the Sinai (as reported by the Book of Exodus) and across the Jordan River back into their Promised Land. At this point, the lands were divided between the 12 tribes of Israel – descendants of the 12 sons of Israel.

Around 1200 BC, the Semitic civilisation known as the Philistines arrived and established a coastal government between present-day Ashdod and Gaza. The Israelites, threatened by the Philistines' political superiority, consolidated their disparate tribes under one king, Saul. Upon Saul's death, some Israelites supported his son Ishbaal as successor, but the tribe of Judah supported King David, who became a local hero when he killed the Philistine Goliath and eventually conquered the city-state of Jerusalem. There, in the 10th century BC, David's son Solomon built the First Temple.

This is at least one version of history. However, the history of the region is just as much a battleground as the present-day streets of Jenin or Ramallah, and millennia-old events are constantly being requestioned, reinterpreted and fresh claims made. This is a part of the world where archaeology and scholarship have serious political implications.

Few accounts written prior to the Roman era can be considered absolute facts (see the Facts about the Region chapter for a boxed text on 'The Bible as History'), and millennia-old events are constantly being reinterpreted to fit current political agendas.

Fast-forward a few thousand years, to the modern Middle Eastern conflict between the Jews (said to be the tribe of Judah and remnants of the scattered Diaspora or 'lost tribes') and the Palestinians (who argue descent from the Philistines). Many Jews claim the right to live in the lands now known as Israel based on a historical lineage stretching back to the kingdoms of Solomon and David, and, before that, to the rule of the 12 tribes. Taken to its extreme, some Israelis claim that 'God gave Israel to the Jews', and that the land is theirs by divine right.

The Palestinian claim is based on centuries of occupancy. Whether they are descendants of the Philistines or not, Arabs were the majority inhabitants of 'Palestine' from soon after the ascendancy of Islam in the 7th century until the 20th century. Conflicts over the Palestinians' right of abode

What to See

Timeless Israel is filled with interest from north to south, and history buffs and religious pilgrims will find limitless inspiration. If you have just one week, head straight for **Jerusalem**, which is certainly one of the world's greatest cities. A highlight is the enigmatic **Old City**, which is sacred to the world's three great monotheistic religions. Here, observant Jews gather around the **Western Wall**, Muslims make pilgrimages to **Haram ash-Sharif**, and Christians find inspiration in the **Church of the Holy Sepulchre**, the **Garden Tomb** and a number of other biblical sites.

An excellent side trip from Jerusalem will take you to the shores of the **Dead Sea**, with its history, wildlife and health resorts.

Those with two weeks may want to add a visit to **Tel Aviv**, where you'll find a wilder side of Israel, with great **cafés**, excellent **nightlife** and a thriving **beach scene**. Tel Aviv's nearby historical 'suburb' of **Jaffa** provides a solid Middle Eastern counterpoint to its modern upstart neighbour. In addition, two-week visitors may want to add several of the ancient cities, such as **Akko**, **Caesarea**, **Tzippori** or **Megiddo**, or any of dozens of other historic sites in the northern part of the country. Alternatively, visit the **Sea of Galilee** or **Haifa**, which boasts the Baha'i **Shrine of the Bab** and the internationally acclaimed **Baha'i Gardens**.

Those with three or more weeks should definitely visit Haifa. Other sites of interest would include the vast expanses of the **Maktesh Ramon**, in the Negev, plus the lush mountains of the **Golan Heights** and the **coral-fringed beaches** and **desert landscapes** around **Eilat**.

date back to the rise of Zionism, which has its roots in 19th-century Europe.

In his 1896 book *Der Judenstaat*, Austrian journalist Theodore Herzl, widely regarded as the founding father of Zionism, determined that the Jews would never be accepted in Europe and had to establish their own homeland. The following year he organised the first International Zionist Congress in Basel, Switzerland, which resolved that 'the goal of Zionism is the establishment for the Jewish people of a home in Palestine'.

Waves of Jewish immigrants began making their way to Palestine, which was then a part of the Ottoman Empire. In the wake of World War I, these lands passed into the British sphere of influence (see History in the Facts about the Region chapter). The increasing numbers of Jews arriving at the ports of Haifa and Jaffa had been causing unrest among the Arabs of Palestine, sparking fighting and rioting, and Britain determined it had to take a stance. In November 1917 the British cabinet announced the Balfour Declaration, which licensed Jewish immigration into their ancient homeland, which their scriptures identified as their Promised Land.

In the 1930s Adolf Hitler came to power in Germany and after he'd murdered six million people – mostly Jewish – hundreds of thousands of survivors moved to British-controlled Palestine. Palestinian Arabs felt ever more threatened and resented having to bear the brunt of what they saw as a European problem. In February 1947 the British decided to turn the issue over to the United Nations, which voted to partition the region into Arab and Jewish states, and make Jerusalem an international city. While the Jews accepted the proposal, the Arabs rejected it outright. Britain washed its hands of the whole affair and withdrew from Palestine in 1948; the Jews declared the independent state of Israel, and war broke out. The combined armies of Egypt, Jordan and Syria invaded.

Israel emerged victorious. An armistice of 1949 delimited the Jewish state, leaving the Gaza Strip under Egyptian mandate and the West Bank under Jordanian control. Millions of Palestinians became refugees in Syria, Lebanon and Jordan and Arab governments refused any sort of dialogue with the new state. Israel's decisive victory in the Six Day War of 1967 established it as the Middle East's pre-eminent military superpower. However, early defeats in the Yom Kippur War of 1973 left the Jewish state less certain of its defences. Subsequent negotiations resulted in the 1978 Camp David Agreement, which brought peace between Egypt and Israel – for which Egypt was ostracised by the rest of the Arab world.

During the 1970s and '80s, under the spearhead of Yasser Arafat's Palestine Liberation Organization (PLO), a terrorist campaign brought the Palestinian plight to international attention. Initially, much of the world watched in horror, condemning the Palestinians for their ruthlessness, but in 1987

the *intifada* ('popular uprising') pitted stone-throwing Arab youths against well-equipped Israeli soldiers and the resulting images seen worldwide on TV news did much to resurrect international sympathy for the Palestinians.

The 1991 Gulf War between the US and Iraq brought about a renewed dialogue between factions that were desperate to score approbation from the international community. While the US bombed Iraq, it encouraged Israel, which was largely dependent on US aid, to exercise military restraint in order to maintain a shaky anti-Iraqi coalition that included Saudi Arabia. Despite Israel's nuclear capabilities, it distributed gas masks to its citizens and suffered Iraqi Scud-missile attacks on Haifa and Tel Aviv without responding.

After much coaxing from the international community, Israel agreed to attend the Madrid Peace Conference of October 1991. Israel's major sticking point was dealing with Yasser Arafat's PLO, which it considered to be a terrorist group. This was followed by nearly two years of inconclusive talks with Syria, Lebanon, Jordan and non-PLO Palestinians.

Then, in August 1993, the news broke that Israel and the PLO had been holding secret talks for some 18 months in Norway, resulting in mutual recognition. On 13 September, deputies from both sides signed a joint Declaration of Principles outlining Israeli withdrawal from Jericho and the Gaza Strip, and authorising limited autonomy for the Palestinian Authority (PA). Now, PLO leader Yasser Arafat and the Israeli prime minister Yitzhak Rabin made their (prematurely) Nobel Prize–winning handshake on the White House lawn in Washington. As a result, the Gaza Strip and most of the West Bank were handed over to PA rule, with Yasser Arafat ostensibly at the helm.

Despite the Washington show, mutual trust between Rabin and Arafat wasn't exactly solid, and there remained quite a few details to be hashed out. In May 1994 both parties signed the Cairo accord, and by 1995 Israeli troops had been withdrawn from most of the West Bank. The peace process went forward, despite the assassination of Yitzhak Rabin by a disgruntled Jewish extremist on 4 November 1995.

Attempts by the new prime minister, Shimon Peres, to carry the peace process

ISRAEL & THE PALESTINIAN TERRITORIES

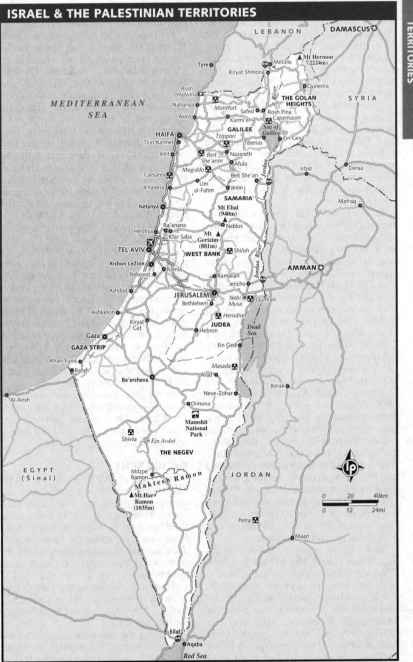

MEDITERRANEAN SEA

LEBANON

DAMASCUS

SYRIA

Tyre
Rosh HaNikra
Nahariya
Akko
HAIFA
Tirat Karmel
Atlit
Caesarea
Khadera
Netanya
Herzliya
Ra'anana
Kfar Saba
TEL AVIV
Rishon LeZion
Rehovot
Ashdod
Ashkelon
Gaza
GAZA STRIP
Khan Yunis
Rafah
Al-Arish

Kiryat Shmona
Metulla
Mt Hermon (2224m)
Quneitra
THE GOLAN HEIGHTS
Safed
Rosh Pina
Capernaum
Sea of Galilee
Ein Gev
Montfort
Karmi'el
GALILEE
Tzippori
Tiberias
Nazareth
Beit She'arim
Afula
Megiddo
Beit She'an
Um al-Fahm
Jenin
SAMARIA
Mt Ebal (940m)
Nablus
Mt Gerizim (881m)
Shiloh
WEST BANK
Ramallah
Jericho
Ramla
JERUSALEM
Bethlehem
Nebi Musa
Qumran
Herodion
JUDEA
Hebron
Dead Sea
Ein Gedi
Masada
Arad
Neve-Zohar
Dimona
Mamshit National Park
Shivta
Ein Avdat
THE NEGEV
Mitzpe Ramon
Maktesh Ramon
Mt Har Ramon (1035m)

Ein

Irbid

Deraa

Mafraq

AMMAN

JORDAN

Petra

Maan

Kiryat Gat

Be'ersheva

EGYPT (Sinai)

Kerak

Eilat
Aqaba
Red Sea

0   20   40km
0   12   24mi

forward were complicated by terrorist activities by the extremist organisation, Hamas (Harakat al-Muqaama al-Islamiya). In the May 1996 elections, Peres lost the prime ministership to Benjamin Netanyahu. Committed to tough security measures, Netanyahu decided to seek a sounder footing by subjecting Arafat to increased scrutiny.

Unfortunately, several sticky matters remained, not least of which were the status of Jerusalem and the future of the two million Palestinians in Egypt, Jordan and Lebanon. Added to that were Syria's demands for the return of the Israeli-annexed Golan Heights and the continued confrontation with Hezbollah (Party of God) in southern Lebanon.

In October 1998 US president Bill Clinton, morally encouraged by Jordan's ailing King Hussein, rekindled the peace process by encouraging further talks between Arafat and Netanyahu. The ensuing Wye River Accord called for Israel to hand over a further 13% of the West Bank to the Palestinians, and for the Palestinians to redouble their commitment to halt terrorism. In November 1998, failed terrorist attacks on an Israeli school bus and Jerusalem's Mahane Yehuda market, combined with increasing opposition from within Netanyahu's coalition government, presented new setbacks to any sort of peace-promoting dialogue.

After a landslide election victory in May 1999, Prime Minister Ehud Barak immediately set about resuscitating the faltering peace process, which was somewhat stalled during Benjamin Netanyahu's three years. In September, Barak and Arafat signed the Sharm el-Sheikh Memorandum (also called the Wye-II Agreement), outlining a timetable for a permanent resolution by 13 September 2000 – the seventh anniversary of the Oslo Accords. Arafat rejected the plan, however, and instead of a settlement, a new Palestinian *intifada* was declared.

Israeli voters, apparently fed up with the failed peace process, elected hard-liner Ariel Sharon as prime minister, to lead them into what they expected to be a coming storm. While most Israelis and Palestinians continued to support the cause of peace and the creation of a Palestinian state, from late 2000 to early 2002, tit-for-tat violence escalated, with suicide bombers targeting Israeli civilians and the Israel Defence Forces

(IDF) pummelling Palestinian targets (and civilians) on the West Bank and Gaza.

For Israel, the breaking point came on 27 March 2002, when a Palestinian suicide bomber killed 26 people and injured nearly 150 at a Seder (Passover dinner) at the Park Hotel in Netanya. At this point, both sides rejected a new Saudi peace proposal that supported the Arab nations' diplomatic recognition of Israel in exchange for a Palestinian state on the West Bank, Gaza and East Jerusalem (based on pre-1967 boundaries). In the days that followed, hopes of a negotiated settlement crumbled in the face of escalating violence. Palestinian terrorists and suicide bombers stepped up attacks on Israeli civilians and the IDF isolated Yasser Arafat in his Ramallah compound and set about routing out terrorists on the West Bank and crippling the PA.

The Bush administration in the US, still reeling from the 11 September 2001 Arab terrorist attacks on New York and the Pentagon (Virginia), frantically struggled to reconcile its Middle Eastern petroleum interests, the traditional US support of Israel, its European allies' largely Palestinian sympathies and its own worldwide jihad against terrorism. In April 2002, US secretary of state Colin Powell visited both Ariel Sharon and Yasser Arafat, but the three parties found little common ground.

At the time of writing, 'common sense' seems a lamentably uncommon commodity. Civilians continue to lose their lives and peace seems elusive. We'll all just have to wait and see how things pan out.

GEOGRAPHY

With an area of 28,000 sq km, Israel & the Palestinian Territories are geographically dominated by the Great Rift Valley (also known as the Syrian-African Rift), which stretches from Southern Turkey to Lake Kariba on the Zambia-Zimbabwe border. This tectonic spreading zone, where the Arabian and African plates are being forced apart by igneous activity, runs the length of eastern Israel, following the Hula Valley southward through the Sea of Galilee, the Jordan Valley, Dead Sea and Wadi Arava to the Red Sea at Eilat.

Between the mountain-fringed rift and the Mediterranean Sea stretches the fertile, but sandy, coastal plain where the bulk of the population and agriculture is concentrated. The lightly populated Negev, the country's southern wedge, is characterised by lonely desert mountains, plains and wadis, and punctuated by mines, military bases and desert-transforming irrigation schemes.

CLIMATE

Although climatic conditions vary between regions, the climate in Israel & the Palestinian Territories is mostly Mediterranean, with generally cool, rainy winters (November to March) and hot, dry summers (April to October); intermittent periods in March-April and October-November can go either way. The winter rainfall ranges from less than 100mm at Eilat, on the Red Sea, to over 1000mm annually on Mt Hermon. Especially in the highlands, Israeli winters can be surprisingly chilly, and on the coldest days, temperatures may drop below freezing. Even in the typically stifling summers, when daytime temperatures of 45°C aren't uncommon, in the evenings – especially in the highlands and deserts – temperatures may drop as much as 30° to 40°C below the daytime highs.

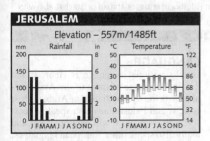

GOVERNMENT & POLITICS

Israel is a secular, parliamentary and democratic republic, headed by a largely symbolic president – a post currently held by Moshe Katzav. The Knesset, a single-chambered parliament of 120 members (known as 'MKs'), convenes in the capital, Jerusalem. The current prime minister, Ariel Sharon, leads the ruling Likud party, which won a majority in the elections of 6 February 2001.

The Palestinian leader, Yasser Arafat, was chosen by the Palestinian Liberation Organisation (PLO) to serve as the chairman of its executive committee and presi-

dent of the Palestine National Authority (PNA). He also holds the nominal title of president of the (as yet nonexistent) state of Palestine. The Palestinian legislative branch is theoretically represented by the 88-seat Palestinian Legislative Council, with 51 seats from the West Bank and 33 from Gaza, and by proclamation is democratically elected. However, any sort of official popular mandate is probably at best still several years off.

POPULATION & PEOPLE

Israel has a total population of 6.43 million. Of this number 79.3% are Jews, 14.9% are Muslims, 2.1% are Christians and 1.6% are Druze. The population of the Palestinian Territories – the West Bank and Gaza – is about three million (including nonresident refugees), most of whom are Muslim. Other groups in the Palestinian Territories include the Jewish minority living in scattered Jewish settlements.

SOCIETY & CONDUCT

As the only Jewish state, Israel and its society are unique in the Middle East – and in the world. However, it's impossible to generalise about characteristics, mainly because Jewish society is so diverse, and ranges from secular (nonreligious) to conservative ultra-Orthodox. While mainstream Israeli society is quite similar to that found in southern Europe, due care should be taken when interacting with Orthodox people – or even walking through Orthodox areas, such as the Jerusalem neighbourhood of Me'a She'arim. Women must wear modest clothing that covers their arms and legs, and outsiders should avoid these areas during Shabbat (the Jewish Sabbath observed from sundown on Friday evening to an hour after sundown on Saturday), unless invited by a local resident.

While a handshake is a common greeting in Israel, Jewish rabbis don't normally shake hands, and in Palestinian communities, men should avoid shaking hands with women.

Cultural guidelines for interacting with Arabs outlined in the Facts about the Region chapter apply to both Christian and Muslim Arabs. Israel is a special case in the region, however. In Palestinian areas, anyone who sympathises with the Israeli cause may well be considered impolite if they

Arabs & Jews

As if the dispute between Israel and the Palestinians wasn't convoluted enough, neither side represents anything like a homogenous society. Not all Israelis are Jews; not all Palestinians are Muslims.

While most Israelis are of Jewish heritage, Judaism encompasses people from a range of origins and belief systems. In addition, many non-Jewish ethnic and religious groups are also represented, including significant numbers of Muslims and Christians, as well as other racial and linguistic minorities. Among the Jews, divisions exist between secular and nonsecular; Orthodox and Reform; hawks and doves; Sephardim and Ashkenazim; and more. In short, everything is an issue to be debated in cafés and newspaper columns, on TV talk shows and at family meals.

Most Jewish Israelis are associated with one of several main cultural denominations. The **Ashkenazi** (meaning 'Germany' in classical Hebrew) Jews originated in Central and Eastern Europe, particularly Germany and Russia. Many of Israel's Ashkenazim are descended from emigrants to North and South America, South Africa and Australasia. The **Sephardic** (Sephard is the Hebrew for 'Spain') Jews, also called Oriental Jews, are descendants of those expelled from Spain and Portugal in the 15th century to various Muslim and Arabic-speaking countries, particularly Yemen. Most Yemeni Jews arrived soon after Yemen's independence, when the massive airlift 'Operation Magic Carpet' brought virtually the entire community to Israel. The Iraqi Jews arrived at around the same time, and today Israel also has Afghan, Bukharan (from Central Asia), Cochin (from India) and Iranian Jewish communities. Generally less educated than the Ashkenazim, the Sephardim are also less represented in politics and white-collar professions, and many claim that they're treated as second-class citizens.

Less numerous are the **Falashim**, Ethiopian Jews who were airlifted to Israel from their famine-struck country in two massive operations in 1985 and 1991. While their integration into Israeli society wasn't immediate, they're now accepted as full Israeli citizens.

The **Arabs**, concentrated mainly in Gaza, the West Bank, some northern cities and the Bedouin areas of the Negev, are 80% Sunni Muslim, while the remainder are Christian. According to the Israeli Bureau of Statistics, the 1998 Arab population of the Palestinian areas was about 2.9 million. However, this number does not include nonresident Palestinian refugees abroad or Israeli Arabs, who live in non-Palestinian areas and follow either Muslim or Christian traditions. At the heart of the

---

bring up political issues without first assessing their host's degree of open-mindedness. While Jewish Israelis are generally happy to openly discuss the issues, die-hard Palestinian sympathisers may want to temper any enthusiasm they may have to 'push Israel into the sea'.

RELIGION

Israel's religious scene is dominated by Judaism, which is followed to varying degrees by nearly 80% of the population. Muslims make up 15% of the total and Christians and other sects make up 5%. While all three major religions share common features, relations are at best politely cordial and at worst, famously hostile. Many Christian Arabs have left Muslim-dominated communities for other parts of Israel, particularly Nazareth and Haifa, dramatically shifting the demographic balance in those places.

LANGUAGE

Israel's national language is Hebrew, but the first language of most of the Arab population is the Syrian dialect of Arabic. Most Israelis and Palestinians also speak at least some English – or will attempt to – and many also speak other European languages, especially in the tourist centres.

Because Israelis are largely immigrant stock from the Diaspora, various other languages are also represented. Some Ashkenazim still speak Yiddish (medieval German using the Hebrew alphabet) in everyday conversation, but due to an influx of over a million Russian Jews from the former Soviet Union, Russian has now emerged as Israel's fourth major language. Interestingly, a very small number of Sephardic people still speak their traditional – but dying – language, Ladino, which is a blend of Hebrew and Spanish written in the Hebrew alphabet.

Arabs & Jews

'Palestinian problem' is the controversy over the origins of the Palestinian people. Israelis contend that they are descended from Arabs who invaded Palestine in the 7th century or from immigrants from neighbouring countries in the 19th century. Palestinians, on the other hand, claim that their ancestors settled down to a life of fishing, farming and herding along the Mediterranean coast over five millennia ago. It's likely that both claims hold some truth, and that the Palestinian people, like the Jews, are a diverse group united mainly by religion and tradition.

About 10% of Israeli Arabs are **Bedouins**, traditionally nomadic people of the Negev, who continue to live in tents and raise sheep, goats and camels. Christians in Israel are mainly represented by **Christian Arabs**, who are concentrated in Nazareth, Bethlehem, Haifa and smaller communities around Northern Israel. Most other Israeli Christians are Armenians, foreign clergy, monks, nuns and those working for Christian organisations.

Nearly 10% of Israel's non-Jewish population belongs to the **Druze** sect, which is an offshoot of Islam. Lacking both a separate language and a homeland, most of the Druze are Israeli citizens and, as with nearly all citizens, are required to perform military service. Most Israeli Druze inhabit a few villages in Galilee, on Mt Carmel and on the slopes of Mt Hermon in the Golan Heights.

The **Circassians**, an independent community of Muslims who are mostly loyal to the Israeli state, number some 4000 people in two Galilee villages. Originating in the Caucasus area of Russia, they immigrated to the Middle East in the 1890s.

The **Samaritans** (people of Samaria – the northern West Bank), numbering less than 600 people, speak Arabic but pray in Hebrew and consider themselves to be descendants of the tribes of Joseph. Until the 17th century, they claimed that their high priesthood was descended directly from Aaron through Eleazar and Phinehas.

Finally, the **Hebrew Israelite Community**, better known as the 'Black Hebrews', occupy one small enclave in the Negev town of Dimona. Mostly African-Americans, they are believed to have descended from one of the Lost Tribes of Israel. This information, they believe, was revealed in the 1960s in a vision to their Chicago founder, Ben Ami ben Israel. Although their first arrivals in 1969 drew controversy and their claims were met with scepticism from immigration authorities, the group now holds Israeli citizenship.

Most road signs appear in all three alphabets, but often with baffling transliterations – Caesarea, for example, may be rendered Qisariyya, Kesarya, Qasarya, and so on, and Safed may appear as Zefat, Zfat, Tsfat and other renditions. In other cases, signs may use Hebrew names, such as Yerushalayim for Jerusalem or Tverya for Tiberias.

Facts for the Visitor

WHEN TO GO

If possible, avoid visiting Israel during the Jewish religious holidays of Pesah (Passover, which coincides with the Christian Easter), and Rosh HaShanah, Yom Kippur and Sukkot, which fall around October (dates vary). At these times shops, businesses, cafés and restaurants close, public transport is nonexistent and accommodation prices double or triple.

VISAS & DOCUMENTS

Visas

With a few exceptions, visitors to Israel need only a passport that's valid for at least six months from the date of entry. Nationals of most Central American and African countries (but not South Africa), India, Singapore and some ex-Soviet republics also require a pre-issued visa.

Visitors who fly into Israel are normally given 90 days, but those entering through land borders with Egypt or Jordan may be granted only 30 days (which is normally readily extendible). Kibbutz and moshav volunteers must secure a volunteer's visa, which can be arranged with the assistance of the kibbutz or moshav.

Anyone who appears 'undesirable' or is suspected of looking for illegal employment may be questioned by immigration officials about the purpose of their visit and asked to provide evidence of a return ticket and sufficient funds for their intended length of stay. Those who can't comply may find themselves on the next flight home.

For details of visas for other Middle Eastern countries, see the 'Visas at a Glance' table under Visas & Documents in the Regional Facts for the Visitor chapter.

Visa Extensions To stay more than three months, visitors must apply for a visa through the **Ministry of the Interior**, which has offices in Tel Aviv (☎ 03-519 32888; *Shalom Tower*), Jerusalem (☎ 02-629 0222; *1 Schlomzion HaMalka St*), Eilat (☎ 08-637 6332; *HaTemarim Blvd*) and most other cities and towns. Join the queue by 8am or you could be waiting all day (and may even have to return the next day). You'll need 125NIS and one passport-sized photo, and you must also present evidence of sufficient funds for the extended stay. Note that overstaying your allotted time elicits a fine of 135NIS per month – this can be sorted out at Ministry of the Interior offices or Ben-Gurion airport, but not at land borders; note that overstaying in Israel will exclude you from admission to the UK.

Other Documents

A Hostelling International (HI) card is useful for obtaining discounts at official HI hostels and an ISIC card entitles bearers to a 10% student discount on Egged buses, a 20% discount on Israel State Railways aswell as reductions on admissions to most museums and archaeological sites. Having said that, many places offer student discounts only to those studying in Israel, and cards issued by individual universities may not be recognised.

The useful Green Card pass allows unlimited admission to national parks, archaeological sites and nature reserves administered by the **Israel Nature & National Parks Protection Authority** (see the boxed text 'Green Teams' later for contact details). It's available at most sites or through the Israel Nature & National Parks Protection Authority. It costs 190/210NIS for one/two people for a full year; family cards for up to two adults and three children cost 280NIS.

Drivers won't need an international driving licence, but must have their home driving licence in order to rent a car or drive a private vehicle.

EMBASSIES & CONSULATES
Israeli Embassies & Consulates

Following are the Israeli embassies and consulates in major cities around the world. For addresses of Israeli embassies in neighbouring Middle Eastern countries, see the relevant country chapters. Note: there is no Israeli embassy in Lebanon, Syria or other Middle Eastern countries.

Australia (☎ 02-6273 1309, fax 6273 4273, e israel.embassy@bigpond.com) 6 Turrana St, Yarralumla, Canberra, ACT 2600
Consulate: (☎ 02-9264 7933, fax 9290 2259, e sydney@israel.org) 37 York St, 6th floor, Sydney, NSW 2000
Canada (☎ 613-567 6450, fax 237 8865, e ottawa@israel.org) 50 O'Conner St, Suite 1005, Ottawa, Ont KIP 6L2
Consulate: (☎ 514-940 8500, fax 940 8555, e montreal@israel.org) 1155 Blvd Rene Levesque Ouest, Suite 2620, Montreal, PQ H3B 4S5
France (☎ 01 40 76 55 00, fax 40 76 55 55, e paris@israel.org) 3 rue Rabelais, F-75008 Paris
Consulate: (☎ 04-91 53 39 90, fax 91 53 39 94, e isconsulat@aol.com) 146 rue Paradis, Marseille F-13006
Germany (☎ 30-8904 5500, fax 8904 5555, e berlin@israel.org) Auguste Victoriastr 74-75, D-14193 Berlin
Ireland (☎ 01-230 9400, fax 230 9446, e dublin@israel.org) Carrisbrook House, 122 Pembroke Rd, Ballsbridge, Dublin
Netherlands (☎ 070-376 0500, fax 376 0555, e hague@israel.org) Buitenhof 47, 2513AH Den Hague
New Zealand (☎ 04-472 2362, fax 499 0632, e wellington@israel.org) Equinox House, 111 The Terrace, PO Box 2171, Wellington
UK (☎ 020-7957 9500, fax 7957 9555, e london@israel.org) 2 Palace Green, London W8 4QB
USA (☎ 202-364 5500, fax 364 5423, e ask@israelemb.org) 3514 International Drive NW, Washington DC 20008
Consulate: (☎ 212-499 5400, fax 499 5555, e newyork@israel.org) 800 Second Ave, New York NY10017; Israel has nine consulates in the USA – the listed contacts can provide details.

Embassies & Consulates in Israel

Jerusalem may be Israel's capital, but the vagaries of international politics have led most diplomatic missions to locate in Tel Aviv; some also maintain consulates in Jerusalem, Haifa and/or Eilat.

Most diplomatic missions are open in the morning from Monday to Thursday, and some for longer hours. The only Middle Eastern countries with diplomatic representation in Israel are Jordan, Egypt and Turkey. There is no Lebanese or Syrian embassy in Israel.

Australia (☎ 03-695 0451, fax 691 5223) Shderot Sha'ul HaMelekh 37, Tel Aviv 64928
Canada (☎ 03-636 3300, fax 636 3381) Rehov Nirim 3/5, Tel Aviv 67060
Egypt (☎ 03-546 4151, fax 544 1615) Rehov Basel 54, Tel Aviv 64239
  Consulate in Eilat: (☎ 08-637 6882) 68 HaAfroni St
France (☎ 03-520 8300, fax 520 8340) Tayelet Herbert Samuel 112, Tel Aviv 63572
  Consulate in Jerusalem: (☎ 02-625 9481, fax 625 9178) Rehov Paul-Émile Botta 5
  Consulate in Haifa: (☎ 04-851 3111, fax 851 3931) Rehov HaGefen 37
Germany (☎ 03-693 1313, fax 696 9217) Rehov Daniel Frisch 3, Tel Aviv 64731
Ireland (☎ 03-696 4166, fax 696 4160) Rehov Daniel Frisch 3, Tel Aviv 64731
Jordan (☎ 03-751 7722, fax 751 7712) 14 Rehov Abbe Hillel, Ramat Gan 52506
Netherlands (☎ 03-695 7377, fax 695 7370) Beit Asia, Rehov Weizmann 4, Tel Aviv 64239
Turkey (☎ 03-517 1731, fax 517 6303) Rehov Ben Yehuda 1, Migdalor Bldg 2009, Tel Aviv 63405
  Consulate in Jerusalem: (☎ 02-532 1087, fax 582 0214) Rehov Nashashibi 20
UK (☎ 03-725 1222, fax 527 1572) Rehov HaYarkon 192, Tel Aviv 63450
  Consulate in Jerusalem: (☎ 02-671 7724, fax 532 2368) Rehov Nashashibi 19, Jerusalem 97200
USA (☎ 03-519 7575, fax 510 8093) Rehov HaYarkon 71, Tel Aviv 63903
  Consulate in Jerusalem: (☎ 02-625 3288, fax 625 9270) Rehov Agron 18, Jerusalem 94190

CUSTOMS

Israel allows travellers to import duty free up to 1L of spirits and 2L of wine for each person over 17 years of age, as well as 250g of tobacco or 250 cigarettes. Animals, plants, firearms or fresh meat may not be imported at all. Any video, computer or diving equipment may need to be declared on arrival, and a deposit paid to prevent its sale in Israel (however, this regulation is rarely applied).

MONEY
Currency

The official currency is the new Israeli shekel (NIS), which is divided into 100 agorot. The Hebraically correct plural is *shekelim*, but in English, even Israelis say 'shekels'. Coins come in denominations of 10 and 50 agorot (actually marked ½ shekel) and one and five NIS, and notes in 10, 20, 50, 100 and 200NIS.

Most top-end hotels, HI hostels, car-hire companies and many airlines quote their rates and accept payment in US dollars, and paying in US dollars will save you the 17% Value Added Tax (VAT). In this chapter, we've used the denominations preferred by individual proprietors.

Exchange Rates

Below are the rates for a range of currencies when this book went to print.

country	unit		new Israeli shekel
Australia	A$1	=	2.62NIS
Canada	C$1	=	3.05NIS
euro zone	€1	=	4.72NIS
Japan	¥100	=	3.90NIS
New Zealand	NZ$1	=	2.26NIS
Singapore	S$1	=	2.71NIS
UK	UK£1	=	7.49NIS
USA	US$1	=	4.83NIS

Exchanging Money

Exchange rates vary little from place to place, but banks may charge voracious commissions and the best deals are the independent exchange bureaus dotted around every major city and town. Typically, they charge no commission at all.

After the US dollar, most popular foreign currencies are created equal, and few money-changers will refuse any foreign currency (although from the EU, you may be limited to euros and pounds sterling). Note: exchange rates on the Egyptian pound are very poor.

Banks function from 8.30am to 12.30pm and 4pm to 5.30pm on Sunday, Tuesday and Thursday, from 8.30am to 12.30pm on Monday and Wednesday, and 8.30am to 11.30am on Friday and holiday eves. Most exchange bureaus keep longer hours.

Travellers cheques may be changed at most banks, but commission charges can be as high as 20NIS, regardless of the cheque amount. A better option is to change them at a no-commission exchange bureau or an office of American Express (AmEx) or

Thomas Cook, as applicable. Eurocheques can be exchanged at post offices.

ATMs & Credit Cards Visa cards are accepted almost everywhere, and many banks are equipped with cash-dispensing ATMs, either in the foyer or on the wall outside. Bank Leumi accepts Visa and several other bank cards, but with MasterCard or a home Cirrus or Plus format ATM card, you'll have to use Bank HaPoalim. Other banks rarely accept foreign cards of any kind. Note also that banks typically won't organise over-the-counter credit-card cash advances, so be sure to memorise your PIN.

Some bank branches also have 24-hour currency-exchange ATMs that accept major international currencies; the drawback is a whopping transaction charge.

International Transfers For anyone unfortunate enough to run out of cash, the Israeli Post Office operates instant Western Union international money transfer services; the process takes about an hour. All you need is someone to send you some cash!

Costs

In a Middle Eastern context, Israel is expensive, but it's still generally cheaper for budget-conscious travellers than Europe, North America or Australasia.

Realistically, shoestring travellers can manage on 150NIS (US$32) per day, but will be happier with a bit more. While the HI hostels offer sparkling dormitory accommodation for 70NIS to 90NIS, the cheapest digs are the private hostels, where 25NIS to 70NIS will buy a decent dorm bed in a room that may have its own bathroom facilities, air-conditioning and in some cases cable TV. Eating out is another matter, and while it's possible to subsist on three felafel or shwarma pittas per day for 6NIS to 19NIS each, sit-down nosh will set you back at least 20NIS and a proper meal out will realistically cost from 40NIS to 75NIS or more (plus 10% service).

Museum and national park admissions – anywhere from 20NIS to 50NIS – are also a consideration, but this is offset by relatively inexpensive public transport. At the time of writing, city bus tickets cost 4.90NIS and an Egged bus trip between Jerusalem and Tel Aviv was just 18.80NIS.

Tipping & Bargaining

Until recently, tipping wasn't an issue in Israel, but these days, restaurant bills arrive with a 10% to 12% addition for service, or a notice that service is not included. Note that taxi drivers do not expect tips – they're usually content just to overcharge. Bargaining is only acceptable in informal souqs and markets.

Taxes & Refunds

Israel slaps Value Added Tax (VAT) on a wide range of goods but in most cases, tourists who pay in foreign currency are exempt, and others are entitled to a refund on most items purchased in shops that are registered with the Ministry of Tourism (there'll be a sign in the window or at the till). Purchases must be wrapped in sealed, partially transparent plastic, and the original invoice must be legible without opening the parcel (you can't open it at all while you remain in Israel). Claim your refund from Bank Leumi in the departure lounge at Ben-Gurion airport.

POST & COMMUNICATIONS
Post

Letters and postcards to North America and Australasia take seven to 10 days to arrive, and to Europe, a bit less. Incoming mail takes three or four days from Europe and around a week from other places. At the time of writing, small postcards to anywhere in the world cost 1.40NIS, while large postcards and airmail letters were 1.90NIS to Europe, 2.30NIS to North America and 2.80NIS to Australasia.

Although it has been made somewhat obsolete by email, poste restante still works; have correspondents write to you at Poste Restante at the main post office in the city or town where you'll pick up post. Note that the AmEx offices in Jerusalem and Tel Aviv will receive mail for card holders or travellers-cheque customers.

Telephone

The country code for Israel & the Palestinian Territories is ☎ 972, followed by the local area code (minus the zero), then the subscriber number. Local area codes are given at the start of each city or town section. The international access code (to call abroad from Israel & the Palestinian Territories) is ☎ 013 with Barak, ☎ 011 with Golden Lines and ☎ 001 with Bezeq, all of which offer comparable international rates.

Local and international calls can be made from cardphones, which are found at post offices and other public places. The best-value telephone cards are sold at post offices, but are also available from lottery kiosks, newsstands and bookshops. Standard rates (14NIS/minute) to anywhere in the country, including local calls, apply between 7am and 7pm. Between 7pm and 7am and on weekends, calls cost considerably less.

Mobiles Cellular phones are extremely popular in Israel, and most foreign providers operate here (but it may be worth checking with your provider before you leave home). In Israel, Nokia, Pelefon and Orange all offer both fixed line (local user) and pay-as-you-go services. It's difficult to get a fixed-line account without a local bank account and other credit assurances, but companies do offer phone rentals if you leave a signed credit-card slip as a guarantee of payment. Most visitors wind up using pay-as-you-go services from Orange, which can also be used outside Israel. To purchase a mobile phone in Israel costs around US$55.

Fax

At post offices, you can send a local or international fax for 12NIS for the first sheet and 5.20NIS for subsequent sheets, regardless of the destination. At most Internet cafés, you can send or receive faxes for 7NIS to 10NIS for the first page and 5NIS for each page thereafter.

Email & Internet Access

Most cities and towns have Internet cafés, which typically keep very long hours and charge anywhere from 12NIS to 30NIS per hour (see the relevant city sections for addresses). Visitors carrying laptops may want to sign up with a local ISP. A reputable option is the well-known **Netvision** (☎ 04-856 0660, fax 855 0345; e admin@netvision.net.il; w www.netvision.net.il/services).

Israeli phone networks are now 100% digital. Phone plugs look similar to those used in the UK, but they employ a different wiring polarity, so either bring an Israel-specific adaptor or buy one locally.

DIGITAL RESOURCES

For a comprehensive list of Middle East /Arab websites, see the Regional Facts for the Visitor chapter. The following sites are specific to Israel & the Palestinian Territories; in addition, lots of useful links are found throughout this chapter:

Arab Net The Palestinian page of the useful pan-Arab site
 W www.arab.net/palestine_contents.html
In Israel Handles upmarket travel bookings
 W www.inisrael.com
Israeli Government Website Provides facts, figures, news and political and historical data on Israel
 W www.mfa.gov.il
IsraWorld Travel Has lots of useful links, including information for budget conscious travellers
 W www.israworld.com
Jerusalem Post Includes breaking news and historical archives
 W www.jpost.com
Palestine Net A link to sites of Palestinian interest
 W www.palestine-net.com
Visit Palestine Includes information on visiting the Palestinian Territories
 W www.visit-palestine.com

BOOKS

As well as this book, Lonely Planet publishes a comprehensive country guide, *Israel & the Palestinian Territories*. In LP's travel-literature series, 'Journeys', is *Breaking Ranks: Turbulant Travels in the Promised Land* by Ben Black.

Otherwise, although somewhat dated by recent events, *Winner Takes All* by Stephen Brook is still the best available primer for a visit to Israel. Equally illuminating and entertaining is *Jerusalem: City of Mirrors* by Amos Elon, about the author's home city. *The Innocents Abroad* by Mark Twain, written in 1871, is still one of the best accounts of the tourist experience in the Holy Land.

The well-known novelist Amos Oz deals in Israeli history and peace efforts in his three collections of essays: *In the Land of Israel*; *The Slopes of Lebanon*; and *Israel, Palestine and Peace*. The BBC's *The Fifty Year War: Israel & the Arabs* was published to accompany the television series of the same name. This largely balanced account of the conflict was co-written by the Jewish Israeli Ahron Bregman and the Arab Jihan al-Tahri, and contains hitherto unpublished interviews with key players on both sides. *Israel: A History*, by Martin Gilbert, an authoritative account of Israeli history over the last century.

The list of popular historical novels is topped by *Exodus* by Leon Uris; *The Source* by James Michener; and *The Antagonists* (later published as *Masada*) by Ernest K Gann, all of which have enjoyed enormous international success.

For a Palestinian perspective, see Edward Said's *The Palestinian Question* and the more emotive and gritty *Gaza: Legacy of Occupation* by Dick Doughty and Mohammed al-Aydi.

The Jewish and Christian Bibles are also logical texts for anyone interested in Israel's historical significance. The Jewish Bible includes the Pentateuch (the five books of Moses), and most of the rest of the Christian Old Testament. Among the many translations of the Christian Bible, which includes the Old and New Testaments, the King James Version is the most literary and the Septuagint (the Greek version) is generally considered the most historically sound. The Catholic Bible also includes the several engaging books of the Apocrypha. Scholars may prefer the well-annotated NIV Study Bible or other popular or simplified translations.

Many of the above are available in new editions at Steimatzky bookshops around the country; you may also find them in the second-hand bookshops along Allenby St in Tel Aviv or at Sefer VeSefel bookshop in Jerusalem.

NEWSPAPERS & MAGAZINES

Those who don't read Hebrew or Arabic will be limited to the English-language daily (except Saturday) newspapers, *Ha'aretz* (W www.haaretzdaily.com) and the *Jerusalem Post* (W www.jpost.com), which present a decidedly Israeli appreciation of the news. On Friday, the *Jerusalem Post* includes an extensive 'What's On' weekend supplement. In East Jerusalem, you can pick up the weekly *Jerusalem Times*, which takes the Palestinian angle on the week's events.

For a break from all the politics, pick up the free *B&T* (AKA *The Big Orange*), which is published regularly (that is, 'whenever they want to') by IsraWorld Travel. It includes a wealth of information for travellers, and lots of comic relief. It's distributed in hostels, tourist offices and sites of

visitor interest, as well as from IsraWorld's Tel Aviv office.

Steimatzky bookshops are the best source for current editions of *Time*, *Newsweek*, the *International Herald Tribune*, the *Wall Street Journal*, the *Economist* and so on.

RADIO & TV

For news in English, tune in at 7am or 7pm daily to 100.7 FM in Tel Aviv, 98.4 FM in Jerusalem, 97.2 FM in Haifa or 102.8 FM in Galilee, or at 1.30pm to 88.2 FM in Jerusalem and Tel Aviv, 93.7 FM in Haifa or 94.4 FM in Galilee. The short-wave BBC World Service (1323 kHz) broadcasts news in English on the hour every hour, with a full-hour news programme at 3pm and 11pm daily. The Voice of America broadcasts on 1260 kHz.

Israel's own state TV channels feature heaps of English-language programming with Hebrew subtitles. These are supplemented by the Arabic-language Jordan TV. Most private homes, nearly all hotels and many hostels and guesthouses also have cable television, which carries CNN, Sky, BBC World, Discovery, MTV and a host of other channels.

See the *Jerusalem Post* for TV and radio programme listings.

PHOTOGRAPHY & VIDEO

Whatever film or other photographic matter you may need is available in Israel, but almost certainly at higher prices than you'd pay at home. Outside the Palestinian areas, one-hour film processing and all types of film are readily available.

Avoid photographing the nuclear research facility fence line east of Dimona, where Israel's nuclear weapons are concentrated.

LAUNDRY

Nearly all hostels, guesthouses, B&Bs and hotels have laundry facilities or offer laundry services, and coin-operated laundrettes are found in most cities and towns. Expect to pay around 10NIS to wash and the same to achieve a wearable degree of dryness.

TOILETS

Most Israeli towns have clean (and often free) public toilets in such prominent places as town squares, pedestrian underpasses, and bus and railway stations. Alternatively, buy a Coke at a McDonald's or Burger King, where you'll normally have access to sparkling facilities. In an emergency, do as the Israelis do and just ask at any restaurant – most Israelis are sympathetic to such plights and will normally let you use the facilities without expecting you to buy anything.

HEALTH

While Israel & the Palestinian Territories present few serious health risks, the health services there are among the best in the Middle East, and in Jerusalem the **Hadassah hospitals** (☎ 02-677 7111) offer some of the world's finest medical care. In Tel Aviv, the **Physicians for Human Rights** (☎ 03-687 3718, fax 687 3029; 30 Levander St; open Sun, Tue & Wed from 8am-5pm) provide free medical assistance for visitors who aren't covered by health insurance.

WOMEN TRAVELLERS

By European standards, Israeli men aren't known for their gentlemanly conduct, but they rarely harass women and Israel's Jewish areas are surely the safest parts of the Middle East for women travellers. In most of Israel, women will have few problems travelling alone or with other women (although, given the Israelis' tendency to travel in enormous groups, they may look askance at anyone travelling without a companion).

Unfortunately, the same can't be said for the Arab areas, particularly the Muslim Quarter of Jerusalem's Old City, the Mount of Olives and the Kidron Valley, and, to a lesser extent, Nazareth and Akko. The West Bank and Gaza are also potentially risky, and even if the violence ends, women may be well advised not to visit these areas alone.

When visiting Orthodox Jewish neighbourhoods or Palestinian areas, women should dress modestly, avoid tight-fitting clothing and take care to cover their arms and legs.

GAY & LESBIAN TRAVELLERS

Undoubtedly, freewheeling Tel Aviv is the gay capital of Israel, and nearly all of those bars and nightspots that don't specifically cater to gays are at least gay-friendly. Jerusalem, Haifa and Eilat also have gay-oriented entertainment venues. For details, see the coverage for those cities in this chapter or contact the **Gay Hotline** (☎ 03-516 7234; operates 7.30pm-10.30pm Sun, Tues &

Thur) in Tel Aviv or the **Jerusalem Infoline** (☎ 02-537 3906; operates 8pm-10pm Tues) in Jerusalem. Alternatively, visit the gay website ⓦ www.globalgay.co.il, or the lesbian website ⓦ www.aquanet.co.il/vip/klaf.

Several local organisations may also be useful: **Association of Gay Men, Lesbians, Bisexuals & Transgenders** (Agudah; ☎ 03-516 7234; 18 Nahalat Binyamin; open Sun, Tues & Thur 10.30am-4pm), **Jerusalem Open House** (Joh; ☎ 02-625 3191, fax 625 3192; ⓔ joh@gay.org.il; ⓦ www.gay.org.il/joh; 7 Ben Yehuda St, Jerusalem; open 10am-5pm Mon-Wed, 10am-11pm Sun & Thur) and the lesbian organisation **KLAF** (☎ 03-516 5606; ⓦ www.aquanet.co.il/vip/klaf; 22 Lilienblum St, Tel Aviv; open Mon & Wed 11am-4pm).

DISABLED TRAVELLERS

Many hotels, a couple of hostels and most public institutions provide ramps, accessible toilets and other conveniences for those with limited mobility. For blind visitors, both the Tower of David Museum and the Mormon-run Center for Middle Eastern Studies in Jerusalem have raised historical relief models of Jerusalem.

For information on accessible facilities, contact **Access Israel** (☎ 04-632 0748, 054-287702; ⓦ www.access-israel.com). **The Yad Sarah Organisation** (☎ 02-624 4242; 43 HaNevi'im St; open 9am-7pm Sun-Thur, 9am-noon Fri) in Jerusalem loans wheelchairs, crutches and other mobility aids free of charge (a deposit is required). You may also want to look for the guidebook Access in Israel & the Palestinian Authority by Gordon Couch (ⓔ gordon.couch@virgin.net; 39 Bradley Gardens, West Ealing, London W13 8HE, UK), which provides the low-down for travellers with mobility restrictions.

DANGERS & ANNOYANCES
Theft

Theft is as much a problem in Israel as it is in any other developed, Western country, so take the usual precautions: don't leave valuables in your room or vehicle and use a money belt, pouch, internal pockets or a leather wallet attached to your belt. Also keep a separate record of your passport, credit-card and travellers-cheque numbers.

In hostels, it's wise to check your most valuable belongings into the desk safe. On intercity buses, it's fine to stow large bags in the luggage hold, but keep valuables with you inside. Crowded tourist spots and markets are obvious haunts for pickpockets, so stay aware of what's happening around you.

Terrorism & Military Action

At the time of research and writing, violence in Israel & the Palestinian Territories was a fact of life. Suicide bombers were launching frequent attacks on Israeli civilians, police and military personnel, and the IDF was retaliating by attacking Palestinian Authority targets with increasing force. The situation could erupt into all-out war at any time, so stay apprised of the current situation – read the papers and tune in to news broadcasts in order to know which areas are best avoided at any particular time.

In short, while terrorists may strike anywhere in the country at any time, visitors aren't at great risk and nearly everyone who avoids the West Bank, Gaza and a few vulnerable Jerusalem neighbourhoods (such as Gilo) should have few worries regarding their personal safety.

Having said that, both local and inter-city buses are also frequent targets, and although most Israelis use them daily without incident, vigilance is always necessary. If you notice suspicious behaviour on the part of any fellow passenger, or anyone who appears to be oddly bulky around the middle, immediately report the situation to the bus driver.

Security Measures

When it comes to security, travellers won't be able to ignore Israel's justifiably paranoid – but almost universally welcomed – measures. Suspiciously parked vehicles are towed and/or destroyed by police; abandoned parcels and packages are blown up; streets, markets and public facilities are spontaneously closed at the vaguest rumour of a threat; and people and their belongings are frequently subjected to official scrutiny. When entering bus or rail terminals, airports, shopping malls, supermarkets, museums, US fast-food outlets, parking garages, government buildings and any place else that might conceivably be a terrorist target, your bags will be searched – and in some cases X-rayed. You will also be checked with a metal detector or body search.

Along the highways – especially along the 'safe' West Bank highways (eg, the Jeri-

cho road and the Jordan Valley highway) – you'll also encounter police and army roadblocks where you may be questioned about your itinerary and purpose of travel. Similarly, those leaving the country from Ben-Gurion airport are likely to be grilled about their stay and have their luggage thoroughly scrutinised. As annoying as they may be, such measures have thwarted countless terrorist attacks and until the situation improves, things aren't likely to be relaxed.

EMERGENCIES

Throughout Israel & the Palestinian Territories, the phone number for police is ☎ 100, for first aid ☎ 101 and for fire, ☎ 102.

BUSINESS HOURS

Israeli shopping hours are 8am to 1pm and 4pm to 7pm (or later) Sunday to Thursday, and 8am to 2pm Friday, with some places opening after sundown on Saturday.

Above all else, bear in mind that in most parts of the country, things grind to a halt during Shabbat, the Jewish Sabbath, which starts at sundown on Friday and ends one hour after sundown on Saturday. In Jerusalem and most other parts of the country, businesses close down around 2pm on Friday, buses stop running and you'd be hard pressed to even find something to eat. On Friday mornings, do as the Israelis do and pick up enough supplies to last until Saturday evening, when the country kicks back into action with a great post-Shabbat rush.

In largely secular Tel Aviv, most shops and offices close at around 2pm on Friday afternoon, but at the same time, street markets and cafés spring to life. In fact, Friday is the biggest night out of the week.

In predominantly Muslim areas – East Jerusalem, the Gaza Strip and the West Bank – businesses are closed all day Friday but remain open on Saturday. Christian-owned businesses (concentrated in Nazareth and the Armenian and Christian Quarters of Jerusalem's Old City) are closed on Sunday.

PUBLIC HOLIDAYS

Dates of Jewish holidays may vary from year to year, as they're based on the Jewish lunar calendar. **About.com** (🄦 *www.judaism.about .com/religion/judaism/library/holidays/bl_ho lidays.htm*) presents a current calendar of

Jewish holidays complete with links to historical overviews and related discussion forums. For a list of Islamic holidays, see the Regional Facts for the Visitor chapter. Jews and Christians observe the following holidays:

January
Eastern Orthodox Christmas 5-6 January
Armenian Christmas 19 January
Tu BiShvat (Arbour Day)

February
Black Hebrew Day of Appreciation & Love

March/April
Purim The Feast of Lots commemorates the Persian Queen Esther's deliverance of her Jewish subjects from the despicable secular politician, Haman. It's marked, carnival-like, by well-dressed parents who take to the streets with their Batmen, Madonnas and Power Rangers. Later, the older folk transform into kings, fairies and gangsters to enjoy an evening of revelry. This is the time for the typically nondrinking Israelis to atone; according to tradition they get so plastered that they can't distinguish between 'bless Mordechai' and 'curse Haman'.

Good Friday This is a Christian holiday commemorating the crucifixion of Jesus.

Easter Sunday Celebrated first by the Roman Catholics and Protestants and about two weeks later by the Armenian and Eastern Orthodox churches, Easter commemorates the resurrection of Jesus on the third day after the crucifixion. When times are calm, Catholic pilgrims throng the Via Dolorosa and Church of the Holy Sepulchre in the Old City, while many Protestants gather at the Garden Tomb for religious services.

Pesah The Feast of Passover celebrates the exodus of the Children of Israel from Egypt, led by Moses. On the first and last days of this weeklong festival, most businesses (including shops and markets) are closed and public transport shuts down; on other days of the festival, businesses may open for limited hours. Passover dinner, or Seder, consists of several prescribed dishes, each commemorating a different event, and during the entire period, bread is replaced with matzo, an unleavened wafer up to 1m in diameter.

Omer (Pesah to Shevuot) This is a Lent-like period solemnly commemorating the various trials of the Jewish people.

Soldiers Memorial Day This day commemorates fallen soldiers in various Israeli conflicts.

The Armenian Holocaust Memorial Day 24 April

Mimouna – This is a North African Jewish festival.

Eastern Orthodox & Armenian Good Friday This holiday takes place two weeks after the Protestant and Catholic Good Friday.

Eastern Orthodox & Armenian Easter This falls two weeks after the Protestant and Catholic Easter.

May
Yom HaSho'ah On Holocaust Day (22nd day of Omer) sirens sound periodically throughout the day signalling two minutes of silence in memory of the six million victims of the Nazi Holocaust.

Lag B'Omer Picnics, sports matches and bonfires and a permissible feast on the 33rd day of Omer commemorate the 2nd-century break in the plague that killed Rabbi Akiva's students (in some years, it may fall in late April).

Yom HaAtzma'ut This day commemorates 14 May 1948, when Israel became an independent state. The day before, Yom Hazikaron, is a memorial day dedicated to soldiers lost in Israel's various conflicts.

June
Liberation of Jerusalem Day (4 June) This is a commemoration of the reunification of Jerusalem in June 1967.

Shevuot (Pentecost) Seven weeks after Pesah, this day celebrates the delivery of the Torah to Moses on Mt Sinai.

August
Tish'a BeAv This is a commemoration of the 'Destruction of the Temples'.

September
Rosh HaShanah This is the 'head of the Year' (Jewish New Year) and prayer services begin on the eve of the holiday

October
Yom Kippur Known as the Day of Atonement, Yom Kippur ends the 10 days of penitence which begin on Rosh HaShanah. The observant spend 25 hours in prayer and contemplation, confessing sins, and abstaining from food, drink, sex, cosmetics (including soap and toothpaste) and animal products.

Sukkot On Sukkot (Tabernacles Festival) people erect home-made *sukkotim* (shelters) in commemoration of the 40 years which the ancient Israelites spent in the wilderness after the Exodus. The *sukkotim* walls are constructed of plywood with a roof of loose branches (so the sky is visible from inside); these sit on apartment balconies, gardens and even in hotels and restaurants.

Simhat Torah This falls seven days after Sukkot.

Yitzhak Rabin Memorial Day This day honours the assassinated Prime Minister, Yitzak Rabin.

December
Hanukkah Also called the Festival of Lights, Hanukkah celebrates the re-dedication of the Temple after the triumphant Maccabean revolt against the Seleucids. Each night for a week, families light a candle on a menorah (an eight-branched candelabrum) and hang a Hanukkah lamp in the window or outside the door.

Christmas Commemorating the humble birth of Jesus in Bethlehem, Christmas is celebrated by Catholics and Protestants on 25 December, while the Eastern Orthodox churches celebrate it on 7 January and the Armenians on 19 January. When things are calm on the West Bank, the event to attend is the Christmas Eve (24 December) midnight mass on Bethlehem's Manger Square outside the Church of the Nativity. Note that space inside the church is reserved for observant Catholics who hold tickets (distributed free at the Christian Information Centre in Jerusalem's Old City).

SPECIAL EVENTS

The specific dates of Jewish festivals may vary from year to year. For the latest dates, ask at tourist offices.

March
International Poets Festival (Jerusalem)
International Judaica Fair (Jerusalem)
Boombamela Festival (Netzanim Beach, Ashkelon) – very popular and lots of fun!
Haifa International Youth Theatre (Haifa)

April
Ein Gev Music Festival (Ein Gev, Galilee)

May
Shantipi New Age Festival (Kibbuts Lehavot Haviva, Pardesh Hanna) – a gathering in the spirit of Glastonbury
Jacob's Ladder Anglo-Saxon Folk Music Festival (Sea of Galilee) – draws artists from around the world
Abu Ghosh Vocal Music Festival (Abu Ghosh, near Jerusalem)
Jerusalem International Book Fair (Jerusalem)
Tribal Dance Experience (Barkai Forest)
Israel Festival (Jerusalem)

July
Karmi'el Dance Festival (Karmi'el)
Cherry Festival (the Golan Heights)
Oriental Soul Music Festival (Sea of Galilee)
Kol Israel Music Days (Kfar Blum, Upper Galilee)
Dead Sea Water Festival (Dead Sea)
Jerusalem Film Festival (Jerusalem)
International Street Theatre (Bat Yam)
August
Klezmer Dance Festival (Safed)
Red Sea Jazz Festival (Eilat)
Full Moon Desert Festival (Negev)

September
Bereshet Festival (Meggido Forest) – a Bohemian gathering in the spiritual Megiddo Forest, with lots of live music
Wigstock (Independence Park, Tel Aviv) – Tel Aviv's answer to a gay Woodstock

October
Fringe Theatre Festival (Akko)
Haifa International Film Festival (Haifa)
Love Parade (Tel Aviv)
Jerusalem Marathon (Jerusalem)

December
International Christmas Choir Assembly (Nazareth)

ACTIVITIES
Hiking

With its range of terrain, Israel offers a wealth of superb hiking opportunities. The most popular venues include Maktesh Ramon, the Wilderness of Zin, Ein Gedi, the Eilat Mountains and the Golan Heights. For guidelines and detailed route information, visit the Society for the Protection of Nature in Israel (SPNI) in Jerusalem or Tel Aviv, or any of its field schools around the country (see the boxed text 'Green Teams' for contact details). The SPNI also sells detailed sectional hiking maps for 60NIS each, but only the Eilat Mountains map is available in English.

Long-distance hikers may want to attempt all or part of the Israel National Trail, which rambles for over 1200km through Israel's least-populated and most scenic areas, from Tel Dan in the north to Taba in the south. This remarkably varied and beautiful route is marked with red, white and blue blazes.

Water Sports

Despite its subtropical climate, Eilat's beaches are rather overrated, but the beaches at Bat Yam, Tel Aviv, Netanya, Dor, Carmel (near Haifa), and most intervening areas are excellent. These, along with the Sea of Galilee, all offer ample opportunities to swim, windsurf and sail, while the Dead Sea provides a unique and therapeutic 'floating' experience, and the water-sports capital of Eilat offers everything from parasailing to water-skiing.

While many privately-owned beaches along the Sea of Galilee, the Dead Sea and the Mediterranean and Red Sea coasts charge admission fees (or are restricted for military reasons), some remote, marginal and/or undeveloped beaches are accessible to the public free of charge.

Along the Mediterranean coast, it's also fun to watch the kite surfers, who tackle the breakers and launch themselves into the air while attached to a large kite-like chute; those who want to have a go can rent a kite on several popular beaches.

Eilat is Israel's major scuba-diving and snorkelling venue (see Eilat in the Negev section later in this chapter), but if you're headed for the world-class reefs of Sinai, it's hardly worth a stop. An alternative is to dive amid the underwater ruins of Herod's city at Caesarea; contact the **Diving Centre** (☎ 04-636 1787) inside Caesarea National Park.

COURSES

Some Israeli universities operate overseas programmes for students of Hebrew, Arabic and Middle Eastern studies. Participants don't necessarily need to speak Hebrew, but may be required to study it as part of their curriculum. Bir Zeit University on the West Bank runs both beginners and advanced courses in Arabic language and literature for US$650 per course. For full details check out the website, **W** www.birzeit.edu/pas/.

Travellers wishing to learn Hebrew will probably want to look for an *ulpan* – a language school catering mainly to new Jewish immigrants – but will have to find one that also welcomes nonimmigrant students. Courses for beginners are divided into *Aleph*, *Bet* and *Gimmel* levels, and most programmes present all three over a five-month period, with classes two or three nights a week. A good choice is the relaxed **Gordon Ulpan** (☎ 03-522 3095; *LaSalle 7, Tel Aviv*), which offers three- to five-month programmes for around 800NIS; it also runs more intensive full-time programmes.

For those who prefer not to study too hard, there are also kibbutz *ulpanim*, where you can take-on study in a rural atmosphere and work at the same time. The website **W** www .kibbutzprogramcenter.org/kibulpan.htm is a good source of information.

WORK

While it isn't difficult to find casual work in Israel, to work legally you'll need a work permit from the Ministry of the Interior and they aren't easy to get. Unfortunately, unscrupulous employers often take advantage of illegal workers, assuming the workers have no recourse. They're wrong. The *pro bono publico* service **Kav l'Oved** (☎ 03-688 3766, fax 688 3537; *17 Il Peretz St, 3rd floor, Tel Aviv; open 9.30am-4.30pm Sun, Tue & Wed, noon-*

Green Teams

The **Society for the Protection of Nature in Israel** (*SPNI;* **W** *www.teva.org.il*), which is charged with the conservation and protection of antiquities, wildlife and the environment, is an excellent source of information for travellers. At the main offices in Tel Aviv and Jerusalem you'll find outdoor shops selling a range of nature and wildlife publications. The Tel Aviv shop also stocks camping and outdoor equipment.

The SPNI also runs field trips and tours, and operates 10 field schools, where enthusiastic specialists can provide information on local hikes, natural sites, indigenous wildlife and accommodation. For a complete list of addresses, contact either of the two main offices:

SPNI Jerusalem (☎ 02-624 4605, fax 625 4953, **e** tourism@spni.org.il) 13 Heleni HaMalka St, PO Box 930, Jerusalem 96101
SPNI Tel Aviv (☎ 03-638 8674, fax 688 3940, **e** tourism@spni.org.il) 4 Hashfela St, Tel Aviv 66183

The network of managed forests in Israel & the Palestinian Territories is overseen by the government-sponsored **Kakal**, which has brought lush greenery to formerly brown and stony areas. The numerous national parks and archaeological sites are managed by **Israel Nature & National Parks Protection Authority** (☎ 02-500 5444; **W** *www.parks.org.il; Am Ve'olamo St, Givat Shaul, Jerusalem 95463*).

6pm Thur, 10am-2pm Fri) provides legal services on behalf of workers – legal or not – who have not been paid by their employers.

In good times, eager international volunteers descend on Israel for a stint on a kibbutz or moshav, many nurturing visions of participating in a communal society. After a short stint, however, quite a few are disappointed with what they encounter, and Tel Aviv hostels are crowded with dropouts who found things less utopian than anticipated. Before committing yourself to a volunteer program, be sure to balance agency propaganda with testimonials from previous volunteers to get a realistic idea of what to expect. Note that kibbutz volunteers must be between the ages of 18 and 32 and moshav volunteers 20 to 35.

Kibbutz Volunteer Work

Even those who are unfamiliar with Israel have probably heard of its kibbutz programme. By definition, a kibbutz (plural kibbutzim) is a communal farm or other rural project staffed by volunteers, who trade their labour for food, lodging and a small stipend.

Some volunteers organize a kibbutz stay through a kibbutz representative office in their own country, and sign up either for a group (of about 15 volunteers) or opt to volunteer on an individual basis. After collecting a basic registration fee (around US$50), the kibbutz representative will arrange flights and visas (individuals may make their own travel arrangements, which is generally cheaper). For information, contact one of the following offices:

Australia
  Melbourne: **Kibbutz Program Desk** (☎ 03-9272 5688, fax 9272 5640) 306 Hawthorn Rd, Caulfield South, Victoria 3162
  Sydney: **Kibbutz Program Centre** (☎ 02-9360 2368, fax 9380 5124) 140 Darlinghurst Rd, Darlinghurst, NSW 2010
Canada
  Montreal: **Kibbutz Aliyah Desk** (☎ 514-486 9526, fax 483 6392) 1 Carre Cumming Square, Suite 206, Montreal, PQ H3X 2H9
  Ontario: **Kibbutz Aliyah Desk** (☎ 416-633 4766, fax 633 2758) 3995 Bathurst St, Suite 100, North York, Ont M3H 5V3
  Vancouver: **Kibbutz Aliyah Desk** (☎ 604-257 5141, fax 257 5110) 950 W 41st Ave, Vancouver, BC V5Z 2N7
New Zealand
  Kibbutz Program Desk (☎ 04-384 4229, fax 384 2159) 80 Webb St, Wellington
UK
  Kibbutz Representatives (☎ 0181-458 9235, fax 455 7930) 1A Accommodation Rd, London NW11 8ED
USA
  Florida: **Israel Aliyah Centre** (☎ 305-573 7631, fax 573 1870) 4200 Biscayne Blvd, Miami, FL 33137
  New York: **Kibbutz Program Centre** (☎ 800-247 7852, fax 212-318 6134, e kibbutzdsk@aol.com, w www.kibbutzprogramcenter.org) 633 3rd Ave, 21st Floor, New York, NY 10017

Alternatively, would-be volunteers can apply in person at the kibbutz agents in Tel Aviv. Your chances of success will increase dramatically if you can convince the officials that you're not a drug-crazed, beer-guzzling layabout.

IsraWorld Travel (☎ 03-522 7099, fax 523 0319) 66 Ben Yehuda St; open 9am-6pm Sunday-Thursday, 9am-2pm Fri
Kibbutz Program Centre (☎ 03-527 8874) 18 Frishman St, corner of Ben Yehuda St; open 8am-2pm Sunday-Thursday
Meira's (☎ 03-523 7369, fax 524 3811) 73 Ben Yehuda St, entrance behind the restaurant; open 9.30am-3pm Sunday-Thurday

Moshav Volunteer Work

On a moshav, which is a community of small, individually worked farms, the work is typically more strenuous and more interesting than on a kibbutz. It also pays better and allows more privacy and independence. Volunteers must take out a health-insurance policy that includes hospital coverage. Those who appear to be hard-working, punctual and well-behaved will probably find work almost immediately.

The easiest place to apply is the **Moshav Main Office** (☎ 03-625 6333; 19 Leonardo da Vinci St, Tel Aviv; open Sun-9am-noon Thur); you can also try IsraWorld and Meira's (see Kibbutz Volunteer Work earlier in this section for contact details).

ACCOMMODATION

Camping

Camping grounds with all the usual amenities are found all over Israel, but they don't offer the sort of cheap alternative most people would expect; in fact, hostels cost only a bit more. On a few public beaches, you can pitch a tent free of charge, but not on the Dead Sea shore, much of the Sea of Galilee, the Mediterranean coast north of Nahariya, most of the Red Sea coast or the Gaza Strip. Note that theft is a big problem on beaches, particularly around Eilat, Tel Aviv and Haifa. Wilderness camping is possible in many places along major hiking tracks (except in national parks), but water may not be available, especially in the Negev region.

Hostels

Israel has an extensive network of roughly 30 official HI hostels (several are currently closed due to the strife), all of which are clean and well appointed. In most cities and towns, however, private hostels charge a third to half the prices of the official hostels and they're generally more amenable for socialising – but also louder. For more on HI hostels, contact the **Israel Youth Hostels Association**

(☎ 02-655 8405, fax 655 8432; ⓔ iyhtb@iyha
.org.il; ⓦ www.iyha.org.il; Binyanei Ha'Umah
Conference Centre, 6th floor, PO Box 6001,
Jerusalem 91060; open 8.30am-3pm Sun-Thur,
9am-noon Fri).

Kibbutz Guesthouses

In a bid to diversify their income, quite a
few kibbutzim have turned to the guesthouse
concept. They fit mostly into the mid-range
category and facilities may include swimming pools, beach access, and renowned
dining and guest activities. The **Kibbutz Hotels Reservations Office** (☎ 03-524 6161,
fax 527 8088; 90 Ben Yehuda St, PO Box
3194, Tel Aviv 61031) publishes a booklet
listing all of its hotels, restaurants and camp
sites, with prices, amenities and a map. Alternatively, call up the website, ⓦ www
.kibbutzimmer.co.il, which accesses kibbutz
accommodation all over the country.

B&Bs

All over Israel you'll find accommodation
in private homes, ranging mostly from
US$25 to US$70 for a single or double. Facilities vary from simple rooms with shared
facilities to self-contained studio apartments with kitchenettes and cable television. They're typically very friendly and
what's more, many places include a hearty
Israeli breakfast. You'll find them by looking for signs posted in the street or check
the website of the **Home Accommodation
Association** (ⓦ www.bnb.co.il).

Hotels

Israel has a disproportionately high number
of expensive big-chain hotels. Prices are
comparable to those at similar places
worldwide, and the facilities and service are
top class. However, many mid-range establishments offer equal (or better!) facilities
for considerably lower prices.

FOOD

Excellent fare can be found in Israel – you
just have to look for it, and it helps to have
local contacts to provide recommendations.

In the street markets and supermarkets,
you can choose from an appealing range of
quality fruit and vegetables – they're normally fresh from the kibbutz. Alternatively,
follow the locals to the pervasive felafel and
shwarma stands; for a 6NIS-to-19NIS filled

pitta, you'll also be able to heap on a selection of salads, pickles and sauces.

Much of the best sit-down fare varies little from that in other Middle Eastern countries – kosher and halal fare are quite similar
– and most Lebanese restaurants produce superb cuisine (especially the many variations
of hummus). On workdays, most fully
fledged restaurants offer a good-value 'business lunch', a set lunch special that typically
costs a third to half less than other options.

Certified kosher restaurants can't prepare
meat and dairy products in the same kitchen,
so they'll have either a meat format or a
dairy, fish and pasta format. Vegetarians
will find joy in the latter, which generally
focuses on vegetarian dishes. Meat-oriented
places typically include steakhouses, Chinese restaurants and traditional Ashkenazi
restaurants serving such Eastern European
fare as schnitzel, goulash, liver and gefilte
fish. In addition, sidewalk cafés and pizza
places abound, and even smaller towns will
have a McDonald's in their local high street,
bus terminal or *kanyon* (shopping mall).

DRINKS
Nonalcoholic Drinks

A real treat in Israel is the variety of juices,
which are freshly squeezed and sold in juice
bars all over the country. Coffee is generally either instant or of the gritty and syrupy
Turkish variety (*qahwa bi-hel*) with cardamom. A real treat is the delicious and
popular tea with spearmint (*shai bi-naana*).

Alcoholic Drinks

Alcohol is available everywhere, but observant Muslims don't drink at all and Jewish Israelis drink very little – that is, with the
exception of the Russian immigrants, who've
brought their vodka habits with them. Although Israelis use wine mainly for ceremonial purposes (eg, during Shabbat and Pesah),
the country now produces a range of very
nice red and white wines, including Carmel,
Golan, Barchan, Tishbi and Tzora, to name
but a few. In addition, many younger people
are catching on to the appeal of beer as a
nightlife accompaniment. The national brew-
ery produces Maccabee, Gold Star and
Nesher, which are acceptable (in descending
order), while imported Carlsberg, Guinness,
Murphy's, Heineken and Staropramen are also
quite popular. In the Palestinian Territories,

you can try the tasty but rather expensive boutique (micro) brew Taybeh.

SHOPPING

Tacky souvenirs in Israel are generally more expensive than those in neighbouring countries, but most of the stuff on offer has little more than novelty value. Worthwhile purchases may include ceramics, items of religious significance, and Palestinian embroidered clothing, as well as the Middle Eastern antiques that can be dredged up in flea markets. An excellent place for Judaica is Me'a She'arim, in Jerusalem, but you must shop around.

Getting There & Away

AIR

The main international airport is Ben-Gurion Airport in Tel Aviv, although some international charter flights may touch down at Ovda airport, outside Eilat. Israel's national carrier El Al operates flights to and from Ben-Gurion (except on Saturday), but many passengers opt for British Airways' daily connection with London Heathrow. To check on international flights, phone **Ben-Gurion Airport information** (☎ 03-972 3388).

Note that airport security is tight, especially on El Al services, and international travellers should check in at least three hours prior to their flight. In Tel Aviv, passengers can check in downtown on the day before their flight and avoid lugging baggage to the airport (see Getting There Away under Tel Aviv later in this chapter).

Fares into Israel aren't especially cheap and it's rarely an allowable stop on round-the-world itineraries. The best deals are normally available on the Internet (try w www.travelocity.com), or with a discount travel agent or consolidator. At the time of writing, the lowest return fare from New York to Tel Aviv was US$599 with LOT Polish Airlines, via Warsaw. From London Heathrow, return fares start at US$188 on Olympic Airways, via Athens, and US$255 on El Al, nonstop. From Sydney, the lowest current return fare is US$1177 on Qantas to London Heathrow, then with British Airways to Tel Aviv.

Apart from neighbouring Jordan and Egypt, which may be visited overland, Turkey is the only Middle Eastern country that may be visited from Israel, and lots of Israelis take advantage of the great airfare deals that are available between Tel Aviv and İstanbul.

Departure Tax

The departure tax of US$13 and a security tax of US$2-8 (depending on the airline) are included in ticket prices.

Buying Tickets in Israel

The **Israel Student Travel Association** (ISSTA; ☎ 521 0535, fax 521 0472; w www.issta.co.il; 128 Ben Yehuda St; open 9am-6.30pm Sun-Tues & Thur, 8.30am-1pm Wed & Fri) doesn't always offer the most competitive fares, so it's wise to shop around in Tel Aviv or Jerusalem. For one-way tickets, you can't beat **IsraWorld Travel** (☎ 03-522 7099; e info@israworld.com; 66 Ben Yehuda St, Tel Aviv). Alternatively, check around the hostels and nightspots for cut-price flight advertising.

LAND

If you're planning to visit Lebanon or Syria, do so before arriving in Israel or you can forget it. Not only are the borders with these countries closed, but having set foot in Israel will bar you from visiting them in any case (see the boxed text 'The Israeli Stamp Stigma' in the Regional Facts for the Visitor chapter).

On the other hand, Egypt and Jordan both have open land borders with Israel, and you may cross on foot or by private vehicle, but not in a taxi or rental car. Drivers and motorcyclists will need the vehicle's registration papers and proof of liability insurance, plus a driving licence from home (but not necessarily an international driving licence).

Egypt

The **Taba crossing** (☎ 08-633 6811; open 24hrs daily) is currently the only open border between Israel and Egypt. Here, travellers pay a 73NIS fee to leave Israel, plus around E£20 to enter Egypt. For safety and security reasons, the **Rafah crossing** (☎ 08-671 9314), on a 'safe' road in the Gaza Strip, is currently closed; until it closed in early 2002, the normal crossing fee was 109NIS and vehicles required a police escort.

Nearly all visitors require visas to enter Egypt, which cost 85NIS for UK, South African and Australian citizens, and 60NIS for everyone else. They're available at the **Egyptian embassy** (☎ 03-546 4151; Rehov Basel 54, Tel Aviv; open for applications 9am-11am Sun-Thur) and the **Egyptian consulate** (☎ 08-637 6882; 68 HaAfroni St, Eilat; open for applications 9am-11am Sun-Thur). Deliver your passport, application and one passport-sized photo during opening hours in the morning and pick up the visa around 2pm the same day.

Alternatively, at the Taba border you can pick up a free Sinai-only entry permit, which is valid for 14 days and allows travel between Taba and Sharm el-Sheikh, and to Mt Sinai and St Katherine's Monastery; however, it is not valid for diving at Ras Mohammed National Park near Sharm el-Sheikh.

Access to the Taba border from Eilat is on city bus No 15; walk the 1km across the border, where buses and shared taxis leave for Sinai; there are also buses to Cairo (6 to 8 hours, US$20) at 9am and 2pm daily. Alternatively, use the **Mazada Tours** (☎ 03-544 4454; 141 Ibn Gvirol St, Tel Aviv • ☎ 02-623 5777; 19 Jaffa Rd, Jerusalem) direct bus service between Tel Aviv or Jerusalem and Cairo via Taba (US$88, 14 hours) or (when it's open) Rafah (US$73, 12 hours). Buses leave Tel Aviv/Jerusalem at 9pm/7.30pm Sunday, Tuesday and Thursday. After picking up passengers in Cairo, they head back. Mazada is represented in Cairo by **Masr Travel** (☎/fax 335 5470; Cairo Sheraton).

Jordan

There are three border crossing points between Israel & the Palestinian Territories and Jordan.

The least used of the three is the **Jordan River crossing** (☎ 04-658 6422; open 6.30am-10pm Sun-Thur, 8am-8pm Fri-Sat), which is 6km east of Beit She'an in Galilee. It's not particularly convenient for anywhere.

More popular is the **Allenby/King Hussein Bridge crossing** (☎ 02-994 2626; open 8am-6pm Sun-Thur, 8am-2pm Fri-Sat), which is only 30km from Jerusalem and 40km from Amman. Traffic can be heavy here, especially between 11am and 3pm.

In the south the **Yitzhak Rabin crossing** (☎ 08-633 6811; open 6.30am-10pm Sun-Thur, 8am-8pm Fri-Sat), called Wadi Araba

by Jordanians, lies just 2km northeast of central Eilat, making it handy for day trips from Eilat to Aqaba, Petra and Wadi Rum.

Nearly all travellers require visas to enter Jordan: EU, USA, Canadian and Australasian citizens pay 66NIS for a three-month single-entry visa and 126NIS for a six-month multiple-entry visa; South Africans and Japanese pay nothing. Visas can be purchased at both the Rabin (formerly called Arava) and Jordan River border crossings (where the exit tax is 73NIS), but not at Allenby Bridge (where the exit tax is 138NIS). If you're going that way, get a visa at the **Jordanian embassy** (☎ 03-751 7722; 14 Abbe Hillel St), in the Tel Aviv suburb of Ramat Gam (take the No 66 bus from Ben Yehuda St). You can apply in the morning and pick the visa up around 2pm the same day; bring one passport-sized photo.

SEA

For details of sailings between Haifa and Piraeus (the port for Athens) see the regional Getting There & Away chapter at the front of this book.

Getting Around

AIR

Israir (☒ www.israir.co.il) flies at least once daily (including Saturday) between Ben-Gurion, Tel Aviv Sde Dov, Eilat and Haifa. **Arkia** (☒ www.arkia.co.il), which also runs international charters, operates flights connecting Jerusalem, Tel Aviv, Haifa, Eilat and other large cities. You can book through any of the following Arkia offices:

Ashdod (☎ 08-852 1212) 11 Rogosin St
Bat Yam (☎ 03-507 3366) 35 Rothschild St
Be'ersheva (☎ 08-628 7444, fax 628 7450) Promenade-Kakal 183
Eilat (☎ 08-638 4888, fax 637 3370) Red Canyon Centre
Haifa (☎ 04-861 1606, fax 867 1661) 80 HaAtzma'ut St, corner of Kiat St
Jerusalem (☎ 02-625 5888) 8 Schlomzion HaMalka St
Lod (☎ 03-977 2668) Ben-Gurion Airport
Nazareth (☎ 04-680 1990) 34, 720 St, Massui, Nazareth
Netanya (☎ 09-884 3143) 10 Stampfer St
Ra'anana (☎ 09-770 1111) 4 Ben-Gurion St, behind Yad Lebanim House
Tel Aviv (☎ 03-690 3333) 74 HaYarkon St & at Sde Dov airport

BUS

The small size and excellent road system in Israel & the Palestinian Territories combine to make bus travel the public transport of choice. The network is dominated by **Egged** (☎ *1770-225 555, 03-694 8888)*, which runs fast and modern air-con buses on both long-distance and city bus routes; call for information on schedules and prices, including city buses.

In Nazareth, East Jerusalem and the West Bank, a number of small Arab-run bus companies provide public transport on typically slow and antiquated vehicles. Fares are quite cheap and ISIC holders are entitled to a discount of about 10% on interurban fares.

Note that Egged bus schedules are affected by public holidays and usually don't run during Shabbat, while Arab buses operate daily.

TRAIN

Israel State Railways *(ISR;* Ⓦ *www.israrail .org.il)* runs a limited but convenient, efficient and inexpensive network of passenger rail services between Be'ersheva and Nahariya, and is especially recommended for travel between Tel Aviv and Haifa or Akko. ISIC holders get a 20% discount. For the latest details, see its website.

CAR & MOTORCYCLE

Good roads, beautiful scenery and short distances make Israel a great place to drive, and it presents no major problems – apart from an annoying number of traffic lights on rural routes, frequently constipated streets and highways, and the Israelis' typically lunatic driving habits.

Because buses are less frequent in the Golan Heights and the Negev areas, these places are best seen with a rental car, and those on a budget will find that sharing a vehicle can be quite economical (unless you're staying in Tel Aviv, where parking costs at least US$10 per day). Car hire companies include:

Best Car (☎ 03-524 4122) 112 HaYarkon St, Tel Aviv; (☎ 02-625 8866) 159 Jaffa Rd, Jerusalem

Eldan (☎ 03-977 340) Ben-Gurion Airport; (☎ 03-527 1166) 114 HaYarkon St, Tel Aviv; (☎ 02-625 2151) 24 HaMelekh David St, Jerusalem

With Best Car and Eldan you can hire a car with insurance and unlimited kilometres for as little as US$250 per week or US$600 per month. Just make sure your designated driver is good on both the offence and defence, and has a long fuse, especially when tackling Jerusalem or Tel Aviv.

BICYCLE

Cycle tourists should bear in mind the hot climate, winter rainfall, steep hills, and the fact that 99% of drivers in Israel & the Palestinian Territories are insane when behind the wheel and fail to recognise cyclists as legitimate road users. Having said that, a cycle trip around the Sea of Galilee in particular makes a pleasant day tour; for such purposes, several Tiberias hostels hire out bicycles for quite reasonable rates.

HITCHING

Hitching was once a common way of getting around in Israel & the Palestinian Territories, but modern problems dictate that even women soldiers are forbidden to hitch and foreign women should not hitch without male companions. The local method of soliciting a lift is to simply point an index finger at the road. Note that among locals, male Israeli soldiers are given precedence over other hitchers.

LOCAL TRANSPORT
Service Taxi

Along with its Middle Eastern neighbours, Israel is the land of the shared taxi, most commonly called the *sherut*. The Arabs call it a service taxi (pronounced 'ser-**vees**'). During Shabbat, service taxis provide the only transport on certain major intercity routes, and on the West Bank, where Egged is limited to Jewish towns, the service taxis save hours of travelling time over the typically spluttering, smoke-belching Arab buses.

Special Taxi

Drivers of 'special' (ie, nonshared) taxis are renowned for overcharging (sometimes spectacularly!) and have a reputation for rudeness and unhelpfulness. If you can't negotiate a reasonable fare – trips around central Jerusalem or Tel Aviv should run between 20NIS and 25NIS – insist that the driver use the meter, and watch your progress on a map to ensure that the shortest route is followed. Tariff 1 is applicable from 5.30am to 8.59pm and Tariff 2 from 9pm to 5.29am; by law, drivers must provide clients with a printed receipt, so if they refuse, just get out and thank them for the free ride.

Be sure to take the number of the taxi when you climb in and if you are cheated or otherwise treated badly, get the number of the driver, note the time and place, and report the incident to the **national taxi complaint line** (☎ 03-565 7199).

Note that taxi drivers are not normally tipped, but in the absence of a rip-off attempt, it's fine to refuse a shekel or two in change.

ORGANISED TOURS

Several local companies offer day tours to sites of interest around Israel. The following options operate only when demand is sufficient, so it helps to turn up with a motivated group. These are some of the more useful ones:

Ben Harim Tours (☎ 03-546 8870, fax 546 8873; e info@beinharim.co.il, w www .beinharim.co.il)

Egged Tours (☎ 03-527 1212, fax 527 2020, w www.eggedtours.com) 59 Ben Yehuda St, Tel Aviv

United Tours (☎ 03-693 3412, fax 578 5232; e united1@netvision.net.il, w www .unitedtours.co.il) 113 HaYarkon St, Tel Aviv

Jerusalem ירושלים القدس

☎ 02

Jerusalem, Israel's ancient and enigmatic capital, is certainly one of the world's most fascinating cities, as well as one of the holiest, most beautiful – and most disputed.

History

Jerusalem, originally a small Jebusite settlement, occupied the slopes of Mt Moriah, where according to the Old Testament Abraham offered his son Isaac as a sacrifice. In 997 BC, King David captured the city and made it his capital, and his son and successor, Solomon, built the great First Temple. The temple was destroyed by the Babylonian king Nebuchadnezzar in 586 BC and the Jews were exiled into the wilderness.

In 539 BC, the Babylonians gave way to the Persians under Cyrus the Great, whose benevolent rule allowed the Jews to return and reconstruct a 'Second Temple', which was completed in 515 BC. In 332 BC, however, the Persians were swept out by Alexander the Great, who was succeeded by the Greek Seleucid dynasty. After the Jewish Maccabean revolts against Hellenic rule, which lasted from 167 to 141 BC, the Seleucids collapsed. However, the resulting Jewish self-rule was short-lived and in 63 BC the emerging Roman Empire annexed the province of 'Judea'. Herod the Great was installed as the king of Judea, and launched a massive building campaign in Jerusalem, and the city was subsequently ruled by a series of procurators. It was the fifth of these, the renowned Pontius Pilate, who ordered the crucifixion of Jesus.

The swell of Jewish discontent with Roman rule escalated into the First Revolt in AD 66, resulting in the destruction of the Temple. A Second Revolt in AD 132 took the Romans four years to quell. The Jews were banished from Jerusalem and the Emperor Hadrian razed the city and rebuilt it as Aelia Capitolina, which is the basis of today's Old City.

The conversion of the Roman emperor Constantine to Christianity and the subsequent visit to Judea of the emperor's mother, St Helena, triggered the construction of churches and monasteries over 'traditional' sites of Christian significance. During this period, Christianity became the official state religion, and many local Jews and Samaritans converted. In 638 AD, however, after weathering a short-lived Persian invasion and occupation, Byzantine Jerusalem fell to a new power, Islam.

For a time all faiths were free to live and practise in the city, but in the 11th century Palestine fell to the Seljuk Turks, who stopped Christian pilgrims from visiting Jerusalem. Hence, between 1095 and 1270, Western Christians led a series of Crusades to deliver the Holy Land from 'pagan' rule. The Crusaders took Jerusalem in 1099 but lost it in 1187, to Saladin.

In 1250, the city came under the influence of the Mamluks, successors to Saladin's Ayyubid dynasty, who ruled out of Egypt. They endowed the holy city with much fine architecture and turned it into a centre of Islamic learning. In 1517 the Ottoman Turks under Selim I defeated the Mamluks in battle near Aleppo, and thereby absorbed Jerusalem into their expanding empire. The

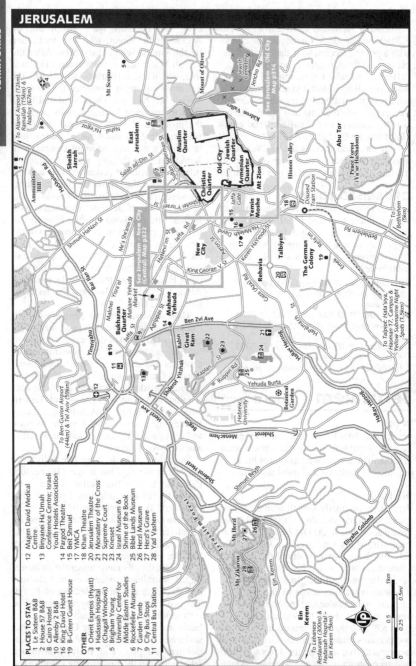

ISRAEL & THE PALESTINIAN TERRITORIES

JERUSALEM

PLACES TO STAY
1 Le Sixteen B&B
2 House 57 B&B
8 Cairo Hostel
10 Allenby 2 B&B
16 King David Hotel
19 B-Green Guest House

OTHER
3 Orient Express (Hyatt)
4 Hadassah Hospital
5 Brigham Young
  University Center for
  Middle Eastern Studies
6 Rockefeller Museum
7 Garden Tomb
9 City Bus Stops
11 Central Bus Station

12 Magen David Medical
  Centre
13 Binyanei Ha'Umah
  Conference Centre; Israeli
  Youth Hostels Association
14 Pargod Theatre
15 Beit Shmuel
17 YMCA
18 Khan Theatre
20 Jerusalem Theatre
21 Monastery of the Cross
22 Supreme Court
23 Knesset
24 Israel Museum &
  Shrine of the Book
25 Bible Lands Museum
26 Herzl Museum
27 Herzl's Grave
28 Yad Vashem

city remained under loose Turkish rule from İstanbul for 400 years. A lack of central authority from the 18th century on resulted in squabbles between landowners, and in the mid-19th century the power vacuum seemed to invite portions of the Jewish Diaspora to return to their ancestral homeland.

Subsequently, Jerusalem became a hotbed of Arab and Jewish rivalry, which intensified during the 1930s, when a large number of European Jews returned to the region to escape the Nazi Holocaust. The Ottomans rejected a British proposal to create an international enclave in the city, and when the State of Israel was proclaimed in 1948, the Arabs and Jews partitioned the city between themselves. The Arabs took control of the Old City and the Jews took the city's western areas, also known as the New City. After the Six Day War of 1967, Jerusalem was reunified under Israeli rule, but the control of Jerusalem remains a bone of contention with the Palestinians, who also claim it as their capital.

Orientation
Jerusalem is conveniently divided into three parts: the walled Old City with its four Quarters – Jewish, Muslim, Christian and Armenian; the predominantly Arab enclave of East Jerusalem; and the Israeli New City, also known as West Jerusalem. The main street in the New City is Jaffa Rd, which is open only to buses and taxis; the main shopping area (which has been sadly prone to bombings) is concentrated on King George V, Ben Yehuda and Ben Hillel Sts.

The Lionisation of Jerusalem

Currently, a city-wide project is filling the streets with the Jerusalem icon and mascot, the lion, and at least 60 of them – created by some of Israel's finest artists – now prowl the city's pavements.

The lion logo is taken from an ancient Israelite coin which bore the image of a lion. Historically, lions roamed the hills of Judea, and its association with Jerusalem is thought to stem from the likening of Judah, son of Jacob, to a lion, due to his exceptional strength and fortitude.

For a map and description, visit w www .lions.jerusalem.muni.il/.

Information
Tourist Offices The **Jerusalem Information & Tourism Centre** (☎ 625 8844; Safra Square; open 8.30am-4.30pm Sun-Thur, 8.30am- noon Fri) is in the palm-filled square near the eastern end of Jaffa Rd. The **Jaffa Gate Tourist Office** (Jaffa Gate, Old City; open 8am-2pm Sun-Fri) is especially helpful.

The **Christian Information Centre** (☎ 627 2692, fax 628 6417; Omar ibn al-Khattab Square; open 8.30am-1pm Mon-Sat), opposite the entrance to the Citadel, provides information on the city's Catholic sites.

The **Jewish Student Information Centre** (☎ 628 8338; e jseidel@jer1.co.il; 5 Beit El St), which is committed to providing young Jews with an appreciation of their heritage, organises free walking tours of Jewish sites around the Old City. Phone for the current opening hours.

Money The best deals for changing money are at the private commission-free change offices all over the New City, Old City and East Jerusalem (especially just outside Damascus Gate). Note that they close early on Friday and remain closed all day Saturday. There's an **AmEx office** (☎ 624 0830, fax 624 0950; 19 Hillel St) in the New City.

Post & Communications The **main post office** (☎ 624 4745; 23 Jaffa Rd; main section open 7am-7pm Sun-Thur, 7am-noon Fri) provides a full range of postal facilities, including poste restante.

Email & Internet Access Jerusalem has quite a few Internet cafés and nearly all hostels and guesthouses provide online services for their guests, charging anywhere from 15NIS to 30NIS per hour. In the New City, try the **Zion Square Hostel** (☎ 624 4114, fax 623 6245; 42 Jaffa Rd, Zion Square), which has a 24-hour Internet service (nonguests pay 15NIS per hour). **Strudel** (☎ 623 2101, fax 622 1445; e strudel@inter.net.il; 11 Mounbaz St) charges 24NIS per hour. In the Old City, try the well-known **Mike's Centre** (☎ 628 2486; e mikescentre@hotmail.com; 9th Station, Souq Khan az-Zeit 172; open 9am-10pm daily), which also has laundry services. Beside the main post office is **Dot Link Internet Café** (open 9.30am-2am daily), which charges 8/15NIS for a half/full hour and, for those with a lot to do, 100NIS for 10 hours.

JERUSALEM – OLD CITY

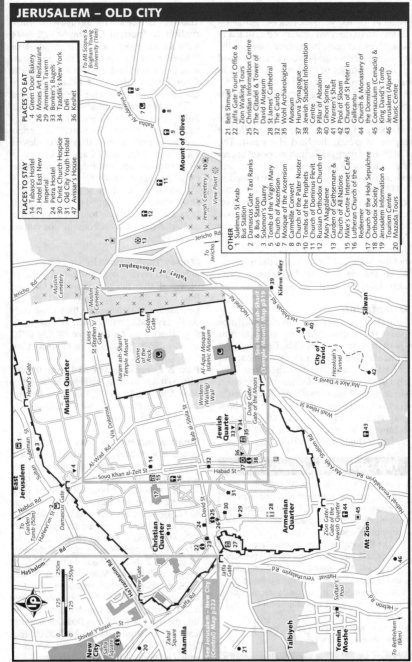

PLACES TO EAT
4 Green Door Bakery
26 Moses Art Restaurant
29 Armenian Tavern
33 Bonker's Bagels
34 Tzaddik's New York Deli
36 Keshet

PLACES TO STAY
14 Tabasco Hostel
23 Hotel East New Imperial
24 Petra Hostel
30 Christ Church Hospice
31 Old City Youth Hostel
47 Avissar's House

OTHER
1 Suleiman St Arab Bus Station
2 Damascus Gate Taxi Ranks & Bus Station
3 Solomon's Quarry
5 Tomb of the Virgin Mary
6 Church of Ascension
7 Mosque of the Ascension
8 Carmelite Convent
9 Church of the Pater Noster
10 Tombs of the Prophets
11 Church of Dominus Flevit
12 Russian Orthodox Church of Mary Magdalene
13 Garden of Gethsemane & Church of All Nations
15 Mike's Centre Internet Café
16 Lutheran Church of the Redeemer
17 Church of the Holy Sepulchre
18 Orthodox Society
19 Jerusalem Information & Tourism Centre
20 Mazada Tours
21 Beit Shmuel
22 Jaffa Gate Tourist Office & Zion Walking Tours
25 Christian Information Centre
27 The Citadel & Tower of David Museum
28 St James' Cathedral
32 The Cardo
35 Wohl Archaeological Museum
37 Hurva Synagogue
38 Jewish Student Information Centre
39 Pillar of Absalom
40 Gihon Spring
41 Warren's Shaft
42 Pool of Siloam
43 Church of St Peter in Gallicantu
44 Church & Monastery of the Dormition
45 Coenaculum (Cenacle) & King David's Tomb
46 Jerusalem (Alpert) Music Centre

Travel Agencies The student-travel agency **ISSTA** (☎ 625 7257; 31 HaNevi'im St; open 9am-6pm Sun-Tues & Thur, 9am-1pm Wed & Fri) can organise inexpensive flight tickets. **Egged Tours** (☎ 625 3454; 44A & 224 Jaffa Rd) runs whirlwind day tours to far-flung parts of Israel, while **Mazada Tours** (☎ 623 5777; 19 Jaffa Rd) operates buses to Cairo.

Bookshops There are **Steimatzky** branches at 39 Jaffa Rd, just east of Zion Square, and 7 Ben Yehuda St, but Jerusalem's finest bookshop is the creaky **Sefer VeSefel** (2 Ya'Avetz St; open 8am-8pm Sun-Thur, 8am-2.30pm Fri, end of Shabbat-11.30pm Sat), with floor-to-ceiling new and second-hand fiction and nonfiction titles. There's also an especially large selection of Judaica. Sefer VeSefel is upstairs in an alley linking Jaffa Rd with Mordechai Ben Hillel.

Medical Services In the Old City's Christian Quarter, the **Orthodox Society** (☎ 627 1958; Greek Orthodox Patriarchate Rd; open 8am-3pm Mon-Sat) operates a low-cost medical and dental clinic that welcomes travellers. Alternatively, try the **Magen David Medical Centre** (☎ 652 3133; 7 Himem Gimel St, Romema; open 24hrs daily), which is just five minutes' walk from the central bus station.

For more serious matters, Jerusalem's two **Hadassah Hospitals** (☎ 677 7111) offer some of the finest medical care in the world. One is on Mt Scopus and the other, above Ein Kerem.

Emergencies As with everywhere in Israel & the Palestinian Territories, the phone number for police in Jerusalem is ☎ 100, for first aid ☎ 101 and for fire, ☎ 102. The **central police station** (emergency ☎ 100) and lost-and-found office are near the Russian Compound in the New City. There is also a **rape crisis centre** (☎ 514 4550).

The Old City

Bound by stone ramparts, the Old City is divided into Jewish, Muslim, Christian and Armenian Quarters. Sites of interest include the Haram ash-Sharif (Temple Mount to the Jews), the site of the Dome of the Rock; the Western Wall; and the Church of the Holy Sepulchre, built over what's claimed to be the traditional site of the Crucifixion.

Walls & Gates The Old City walls are the legacy of Süleyman the Magnificent who built them between 1537 and 1542, although they've since been extensively renovated. It was once possible to walk two sections along the ramparts – from Jaffa Gate north to Lion's Gate (also called St Stephen's Gate), via New, Damascus and Herod's Gates, and Jaffa Gate south to Dung Gate (also called Gate of the Moors), via Zion Gate – but the walk is currently closed for security reasons.

There are seven open gates. The recently restored **Jaffa Gate**, so named because it was the start of the old road to Jaffa, is now the main entrance to the Old City from the New City. Moving clockwise, the 1887 **New Gate** also gives access from the New City. Down the hill, **Damascus Gate**, the most attractive and crowded of all the city gates, opens into bustling East Jerusalem. **Herod's Gate** also faces Arab East Jerusalem, and it was near here in 1099 that the Crusaders first breached Jerusalem's walls.

Lion's Gate, facing the Mount of Olives, has also been called St Stephen's gate after the first Christian martyr, who was stoned nearby. Its official name, Gate of the Moors, may reflect the fact that North African immigrants occupied the area in the 16th century. **Zion Gate** became known as the Gate of the Jewish Quarter in late medieval times and is still pocked with reminders of the fierce fighting here in the 1948 war.

Jewish Quarter Flattened during the 1948 fighting, the Jewish Quarter has been almost entirely reconstructed since its recapture by the Israelis in 1967. There are few historic monuments above ground level but the excavations during reconstruction unearthed a number of archaeological sites. The most significant is **The Cardo**, the main north-south street of the Roman Aelia Capitolina and, later, of Byzantine Jerusalem. Part of it has been restored to what may have been its original appearance, while another part has been reconstructed as a shopping arcade with expensive gift shops and galleries of Judaica. Through the arch, however, lies the Muslim Quarter, where you're back in the bustle of the Arab market.

[Continued on page 320]

HARAM ASH-SHARIF (TEMPLE MOUNT)

The gleam of the golden cupola of Haram ash-Sharif *(adult/student mosques & museum 36/24NIS; open 8am-3pm Sat-Thur; closed during prayers 11.30am-12.30pm in winter & 12.30-1.30pm in summer; during Ramadan open 7.30am-10am Sat-Thur)* identifies Jerusalem on travel posters around the world. This is the biblical Mt Moriah, where Abraham was instructed by God to sacrifice his son Isaac in a test of his faith, and the site of the ancient First and Second temples (the remnant of which, the Western (Wailing) Wall, is now Judaism's most revered site). Israeli Jews generally avoid the area and Orthodox Jews feel unworthy to approach it, lest they unwittingly tread on the Holy of Holies, which was the most sacred and powerful altar in Solomon's (the First) or Herod's (the Second) Temple. It's also the site where Muslims believe Mohammed launched himself into heaven to take his place alongside Allah.

Today, the hilltop is fringed with attractive Mamluk structures, with the Dome of the Rock in the centre and Al-Aqsa Mosque to the south.

The Dome of the Rock encloses the sacred rock upon which Abraham prepared to sacrifice his son and from which, according to Islamic tradition, the Prophet Mohammed was accepted into heaven to pray with the other saints and Allah himself. It was built between AD 688 and 691– making it one of the oldest surviving Islamic monuments in existence – under the patronage of the Umayyad caliph Abd al-Malik, to provide an impressive site for Muslims who might have been seduced by the opulence of the Christian Church of the Holy Sepulchre. His short-lived original roof was quickly melted down to pay off his debts, but it was replaced by lesser structures. An anodised alu-

Inset: The Dome of the Rock, Old Jerusalem (Photo by Russell Mountford)

Left: The Dome of the Rock, Haram ash-Sharif and the Stairs of the Scales of Souls

ANDREW BURKE

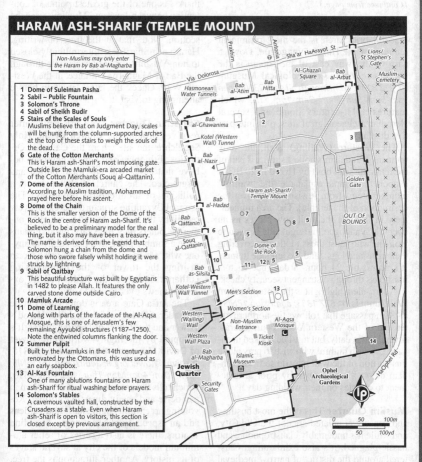

HARAM ASH-SHARIF (TEMPLE MOUNT)

Non-Muslims may only enter the Haram by Bab al-Magharba

1 Dome of Suleiman Pasha

2 Sabil – Public Fountain

3 Solomon's Throne

4 Sabil of Sheikh Budir

5 Stairs of the Scales of Souls
Muslims believe that on Judgment Day, scales will be hung from the column-supported arches at the top of these stairs to weigh the souls of the dead.

6 Gate of the Cotton Merchants
This is Haram ash-Sharif's most imposing gate. Outside lies the Mamluk-era arcaded market of the Cotton Merchants (Souq al-Qattanin).

7 Dome of the Ascension
According to Muslim tradition, Mohammed prayed here before his ascent.

8 Dome of the Chain
This is the smaller version of the Dome of the Rock, in the centre of Haram ash-Sharif. It's believed to be a preliminary model for the real thing, but it also may have been a treasury. The name is derived from the legend that Solomon hung a chain from the dome and those who swore falsely whilst holding it were struck by lightning.

9 Sabil of Qaitbay
This beautiful structure was built by Egyptians in 1482 to please Allah. It features the only carved stone dome outside Cairo.

10 Mamluk Arcade

11 Dome of Learning
Along with parts of the facade of the Al-Aqsa Mosque, this is one of Jerusalem's few remaining Ayyubid structures (1187–1250). Note the entwined columns flanking the door.

12 Summer Pulpit
Built by the Mamluks in the 14th century and renovated by the Ottomans, this was used as an early soapbox.

13 Al-Kas Fountain
One of many ablutions fountains on Haram ash-Sharif for ritual washing before prayers.

14 Solomon's Stables
A cavernous vaulted hall, constructed by the Crusaders as a stable. Even when Haram ash-Sharif is open to visitors, this section is closed except by previous arrangement.

minium roof was donated by several Gulf State governments, and rumour has it that Jordan has now financed a gold leaf veneer.

Although it's thought to be reconstructed from a 6th-century Byzantine church, Muslims believe that the al-Aqsa Mosque was constructed in the 8th century by the son of Abd al-Malik. Twice destroyed by earthquakes in its first 60 years, the modern building is a mixture of repairs and restorations. The intricately carved mihrab (prayer niche indicating the direction of Mecca) dates from the time of Saladin (Salah ad-Din).

While the Dome of the Rock serves more as a figurehead than a mosque, Al-Aqsa is a functioning house of worship, accommodating up to 5000 praying worshippers at a time.

[Continued from page 317]

At Hurva Square, east of the Cardo, a graceful brick arch is the most prominent remnant of the **Hurva Synagogue**. Down a narrow alleyway east of the square is the impressive **Wohl Archaeological Museum** (☎ *628 8141; admission to all sites 23NI; open 9am-5pm Sun-Thur, 9am-1pm Fri*), which features a 1st-century home and several Herodian archaeological sites, plus interpretive displays.

The **Western (Wailing) Wall**, the only remnant of Judaism's holiest shrine, is part of the retaining wall built by Herod in 20 BC to support the temple esplanade (the 'wailing' moniker stems from Jewish sorrow over the destruction of the temple). The area immediately in front of the wall now serves as an open-air synagogue; the right side is open to women (who must dress modestly, covering their arms and legs), and the left side to men. It's accessible 24 hours a day, but visitors must pass through a stringent security check.

A Jerusalem highlight is the **Kotel Western Wall Tunnels** (☎ *627 1333; admission 18NIS*), a 488m passage that follows the northern extension of the Western Wall. Tours operate several times daily, but must be booked in advance. Jewish faithful who wish to pray along this portion of the wall may do so from 6am-8am daily; it's also open by prior arrangement to couples on their wedding day.

Muslim Quarter This is the most bustling and densely populated area of the Old City, and while it's undeniably claustrophobic and hassle-plagued, it's also exhilarating. Clustered around the district of narrow medieval alleys are some fine examples of **Mamluk architecture**. At the Lion's/St Stephen's Gate is **St Anne's Church**, perhaps the finest example of Crusader architecture in Jerusalem.

The road leading from the Lion's/St Stephen's Gate into the heart of the Old City is known as **Via Dolorosa** ('sorrowful way') or Stations of the Cross, the route that tradition claims was taken by the condemned Jesus as he lugged his cross to Calvary. While this was probably not the actual route taken, the notion does appear to promote faith in believers and at 3pm on Fridays, the Franciscan Fathers lead a solemn procession here.

Haram ash-Sharif, or the Temple Mount, with Jerusalem's most recognizable landmarks, is one of the greatest points of contention between Jews and Muslims – see the 'Haram ash-Sharif (Temple Mount)' special section. Note that at the time of writing, Haram ash-Sharif was intermittently closed to non-Muslims, or only accessible through the Bab al-Magharba entrance, at the Western Wall. Check the latest situation before attempting to visit it.

Christian Quarter The Christian Quarter revolves around the **Church of the Holy Sepulchre**, the site where the Catholic, Orthodox, Ethiopian and Coptic churches believe that Jesus was crucified, buried and resurrected. The church itself represents a collision of architectural traditions. The original Byzantine structure was extensively rebuilt by the Crusaders and tweaked by numerous others over the years, but it remains quite a sombre place. It's open daily to anyone who's modestly dressed. It's also worth visiting the tower of the neighbouring **Lutheran Church of the Redeemer**, for excellent views over the Old City.

The Jaffa Gate area is dominated by the Crusader **Citadel**, which includes Herod's Tower and the Tower of David minaret. It's occupied by the highly worthwhile **Tower of David Museum** (☎ *626 5333, 626 5310;* e *shivuk@tower.org.il; adult/child 35/15NIS; open 10am-4pm Mon-Thur, 10am-2pm Sat*), which tells the entire history of Jerusalem in a concise and easily digestible format. Revolving art exhibits in the halls and gardens add an especially pleasant angle. For blind visitors, there is also a series of relief aluminium models of the city at several stages of its history. Another attraction is the free, clean public toilet facility just inside the Old City at Jaffa Gate.

Armenian Quarter & Mt Zion A worthwhile visit is the Armenian **St James' Cathedral** (*open for services 6.30am-7.15am & 2.45pm-3.30pm Mon-Fri, 2.30pm-3pm Sat & Sun*), which has a sensuous aura of ritual and mystery. It's open only for services. There's also the **Church of St Peter in Gallicantu** (*adult/student 6/4NIS*), which commemorates the crowing of the cock that Jesus had predicted would reveal Peter's three denials of him.

From the Armenian Quarter, Zion Gate leads out to Mt Zion, site of the **Coenaculum**

(Cenacle), traditionally held to be the site of the Last Supper. At the back of the same building is the traditional site of **King David's Tomb**, and around the corner, the **Church & Monastery of the Dormition**, where Jesus' mother Mary fell into 'eternal sleep'.

Mount of Olives, Mt Scopus & the Kidron Valley

East of the Old City, outside Lion's/St Stephen's Gate, the land drops away into the lovely Kidron Valley, then rises again up the slopes of the Mount of Olives. For Christians, this hillside holds special significance as the site where Jesus took on the sins of the world, was arrested and later ascended into heaven. Predictably, several churches have been built here, and visitors can still see the olive grove in the **Garden of Gethsemane**, and the **Tomb of the Virgin Mary**. Equally impressive is the **panorama** of the Old City from the summit – visit early in the morning for the best light.

On Mt Scopus, between the Mount of Olives and Hebrew University, is the Mormon **Brigham Young University Center for Middle Eastern Studies** (☎ 626 5621). Here, free guided tours (10am-3.30pm Tues-Fri) explain the centre's wonderful architecture and include a demonstration of the incredible pipe organ in the main assembly hall; it also shows off the best city view in all of Jerusalem. On Sunday evenings, it hosts free public concerts; a list is available on request (from e concerts@jc.byu.ac.il).

The **Kidron Valley**, between the City of David/Mt Ophel (the original Jerusalem) and the Mount of Olives, presents an enigmatic set of historical sites. At the top of the valley sits the 1st-century **Pillar of Absalom**, which is almost certainly not Absalom's tomb, as claimed. The historic **Gihon Spring**, just outside the City of David, provided water for ancient Jerusalem, and in 701 BC its waters were diverted to the city via the 500m-long **Hezekiah's Tunnel** (☎ 625 4403; open 9am-4pm Sun-Thur, 9am-2pm Fri). Those who aren't claustrophobic and don't mind getting wet can take a tour through this underground passage. The tunnel ends at the **Pool of Siloam**, where a blind man was healed after Jesus instructed him to wash in it.

Note that quite a few women (including the author) have reported unpleasant experiences while walking around the Mount of Olives and Kidron Valley, and we strongly advise women not to visit these areas alone.

East Jerusalem

The modern, blaring, fume-hazed Palestinian part of Jerusalem is characterised by small shops, businesses and ageing hotels. On Sultan Suleiman St, just outside the Old City walls, the **Rockefeller Museum** (☎ 628 2251; adult/student 26/16NIS; open 10am-5pm Sun-Thur, 10am-2pm Fri-Sat) has some impressive archaeological and architectural exhibits, although the presentation is a bit musty (your Israel Museum ticket is also good here). Opposite the Sultan Suleiman St bus station you'll find **Solomon's Quarry**, a vast cave beneath the north wall of the Old City. While there's little to see, it does offer cool refuge on a hot day.

Behind a heavy stone wall on Nablus Rd is the beautiful **Garden Tomb** (☎ 627 2745, fax 627 2742; open 2pm-5.30pm Mon-Sat), which contains a 2000-year-old stone tomb and lovely garden that are believed to have once been the property of Joseph of Arimathaea. The site also provides a view of what some claim to be the hill Golgotha (The Place of the Skull), also known as Gordon's Calvary. For the many reasons outlined on the guided tour (which is free, but badly needed donations are graciously accepted), it's believed by most Protestants to be the site of Jesus' crucifixion and resurrection. Whatever your beliefs, this peaceful place is certainly one of the highlights of Jerusalem.

The New City

The New City is roughly centred on the triangle formed by Jaffa Rd, King George V St and the pedestrianised Ben Yehuda St. However, the most colourful and bustling district is **Mahane Yehuda**, the Jewish food market. Possibly one of the world's most reluctant tourist attractions, the ultra-Orthodox Jewish district of **Me'a She'arim** is reminiscent of a *shtetl* (ghetto) in pre-Holocaust Eastern Europe. Dress conservatively, don't take photos without permission and avoid the area during Shabbat.

Museums The Holocaust museum **Yad Vashem** (☎ 644 3400; admission free; open 9am-5pm Sun-Thur, 9am-2pm Fri), on Mt Zikaron, serves as a moving memorial to the six million victims of the Nazi Holocaust. It's

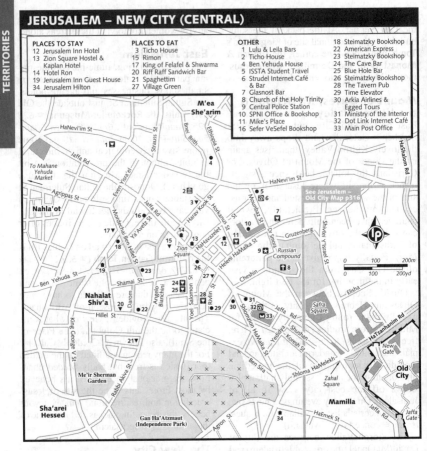

JERUSALEM – NEW CITY (CENTRAL)

PLACES TO STAY	PLACES TO EAT	OTHER	
12 Jerusalem Inn Hotel	3 Ticho House	1 Lulu & Leila Bars	18 Steimatzky Bookshop
13 Zion Square Hostel & Kaplan Hotel	15 Rimon	2 Ticho House	22 American Express
14 Hotel Ron	17 King of Felafel & Shwarma	4 Ben Yehuda House	23 Steimatzky Bookshop
19 Jerusalem Inn Guest House	20 Riff Raff Sandwich Bar	5 ISSTA Student Travel	24 The Cave Bar
34 Jerusalem Hilton	21 Spaghettim	6 Strudel Internet Café & Bar	25 Blue Hole Bar
	27 Village Green	7 Glasnost Bar	26 Steimatzky Bookshop
		8 Church of the Holy Trinity	28 The Tavern Pub
		9 Central Police Station	29 Time Elevator
		10 SPNI Office & Bookshop	30 Arkia Airlines & Egged Tours
		11 Mike's Place	31 Ministry of the Interior
		16 Sefer VeSefel Bookshop	32 Dot Link Internet Café
			33 Main Post Office

a powerful experience, and no-one should miss the Valley of the Communities, so allow at least half a day to see it all. Take bus No 13, 17, 18, 20 or 27 – and lots of tissues.

The **Bible Lands Museum** (☎ 561 1066, fax 563 8228; e biblelnd@netvision.net.il; w www.blmj.org; 25 Granot St, Givat Ram; admission 35NIS; open 9.30am-5.30pm Sun-Tues & Thur, 9.30am-9.30pm Wed in summer, 1.30pm-9.30pm Wed in winter, 9.30am-2pm Fri, 11am-3pm Sat) chronologically reveals the history of the Holy Lands with a wealth of well-displayed artefacts and background information.

The country's major museum complex is the **Israel Museum** (☎ 670 8811; adult/child 37/18NIS; open 10am-4pm Mon, Wed & Sat, 4pm-9pm Tues, 10am-9pm Thur, 10am-2pm Fri), just west of the New City. An assemblage of several major collections of national historical and artistic significance, it also includes a peaceful sculpture garden and the jar-shaped and architecturally inspiring **Shrine of the Book**. Here you'll see background displays and examples of the Dead Sea Scrolls, which were uncovered at Qumran between 1947 and 1956. Your ticket is also good for seven days to visit the Rockefeller Museum in East Jerusalem.

A cross between a museum, a theatre and a carnival ride is the **Time Elevator** (☎ 625 2227; Beit Agron, 37 Hillel St; admission 45NIS; open 1pm-5.30pm daily). Spectators are jolted around in their seats along with the on-screen action as Chaim Topol leads them through Jerusalem's equally moving history.

Organised Tours

The municipal tourist office guides free Saturday-morning city walking tours to different areas of the city each week. Meet at 10am by the entrance to the **Russian Compound** (32 Jaffa Rd).

Egged Tours (☎ 622 1999, fax 622 1717; 8 Shlomzion HaMalka St; ⓦ www.eggedtours.co.il) runs half-/full-day Jerusalem tours for 135/210NIS, and full-day tours to the Dead Sea (315NIS), the Sea of Galilee (270NIS) and the northern Mediterranean coast (315NIS). A good introduction to the city is Egged's **Route 99 Circular Line** (☎ 530 4704; 10am Sun-Thur). This coach service cruises past 36 of Jerusalem's major sites, with basic commentary that's more or less in English. It departs from HaEmek St by Jaffa Gate, but only runs once daily, which nullifies its once-very-amenable hop-on-hop-off value.

Zion Walking Tours (☎/fax 628 7866, 050-305552; Omar ibn al-Khattab Square) has its office opposite the entrance to the Citadel. Its three-hour Four Quarters walking tour of the Old City operates at 9am, 11am and 2pm daily (when there are at least four participants), and is particularly good value at 45NIS (students and seniors 41NIS). Other offerings include the Pre-Temple Period route, the Underground City of Jerusalem and Me'a She'arim.

Abu Hassan Alternative Tours (☎/fax 628 3282, 052-864205; Jerusalem Hotel; ⓦ www.jrshotel.com) organises custom tours on the West Bank (Bethlehem, Hebron, Jericho, Refugee Camps etc) and Gaza, and prices are quite reasonable – about US$25 per person – if you can muster a group.

Places to Stay – Budget

Jerusalem was once replete with hostels of all shapes and sizes, but the recent downturn in visitor numbers has caused many to close. Whether this is temporary remains to be seen, but chances are that any hostel revivals will be accompanied by changes in ownership and price structure.

In general, the Old City and East Jerusalem have always offered the cheapest options, most pleasant atmosphere and best access to sites of interest. However, these areas virtually shut down at dusk and most of the hostels impose strict curfews (most people wouldn't want to walk around the Old City or East Jerusalem at night, in any case). Those who wish to participate in the New City nightlife would probably want to pay a bit more and stay in West Jerusalem.

Old City The **Tabasco Hostel** (☎ 628 1101; ⓔ ahmedzatari@hotmail.com; Aqabat at-Takiya St; dorm beds 15-20NIS, private doubles without/with bathroom 60/100NIS), buried inside the Muslim Quarter's Souq Khan al-Zeit, surprisingly, remains open. In the past, it was almost impossible to find a bed in this clean and rather exotic choice, but now it's barely hanging on. Note that quite a few readers have complained about robbery and harassment here. Internet and email access is available for 20NIS per hour.

Petra Hostel (☎ 628 6618; Omar ibn al-Khattab Square; dorm beds/roof mattresses 25/35NIS), with a superb location near Jaffa Gate, is an airy, breezy place with a view over a major touristed area of the Old City. Housed in what was once a grand hotel, it's an old and enigmatic favourite with travellers. Those who opt for a rooftop mattress (summer only) will have a great view over the Dome of the Rock.

Old City Youth Hostel (☎ 628 8611; 1 Birkur Ha'lim St; dorm beds 60NIS), near the boundary of the Jewish, Armenian and Christian Quarters, is the only official hostel that remains open in the Old City. It's housed in a beautiful old hospital, with space for 70 guests. It's often booked by private weddings or Bar Mitzvahs, so advance reservations are required. Note that due to strict kosher rules, the kitchen is not available to guests.

Christ Church Hospice (☎ 627 7727, fax 627 7730; ⓔ christch@netvision.net.il; Jaffa Gate; dorm beds/singles/doubles 72/200/315NIS), in the Anglican compound near Jaffa Gate, enjoys a quiet and comfortable atmosphere, with friendly staff and a lovely courtyard. Attached are the Christian Heritage Centre and an Anglican church that's built in the form of a synagogue for Messianic Jews. Singles and doubles include a full breakfast and discounts are available for stays of more than two nights.

East Jerusalem There were once quite a few hostels along HaNevi'im St near Damascus Gate, but only one is now operating with any success. Given the recent strife, travellers should seek local advice before staying in this area.

Cairo Hostel (☎ 627 7216; 21 Nablus Rd; dorm beds/private rooms 20/80NIS) is one street east and just north of the parking area that serves as the Damascus Gate bus station. You're welcomed up the stairway by the Pink Panther and Skippy the Kangaroo, but it's otherwise a bit soulless. The nicest features are the large lounge with satellite TV and the free coffee and tea in the kitchen.

New City The **Zion Square Hostel** (☎ 624 4114, fax 623 6245; 42 Jaffa Rd, Zion Square; dorm bed/doubles 60/180NIS) is conveniently placed (the sign on the front says 'Hostel @') and offers both dorms and private doubles with satellite TV and shower. Everyone has access to the kitchen facilities and 24-hour Internet service (nonguests pay 15NIS per hour); all rates include breakfast. In summer the management organises day tours to Masada and Galilee.

Places to Stay – Mid-Range

Mid-range accommodation in Jerusalem – as in most of Israel – is represented by B&Bs and pleasant but simple hotels and guesthouses. For a list of B&Bs, contact the **Home Accommodation Association of Jerusalem** (☎ 645 2198; e hq@bnb.co.il; w www.bnb .co.il; PO Box 7547, Jerusalem 91074).

Old City The **Hotel East New Imperial** (☎ 628 2261, fax 627 1530; e imperial@palnet .com; Jaffa Gate; singles/doubles US$30/54) was built in 1885 on the site of Bath Shebiye, where King David supposedly saw the wife of Uriah bathing in a pool. This rambling old hotel has loads of character, and the common rooms are decorated with lovely Palestinian embroidered clothing and an incredible hand-drawn family tree. Email and Internet facilities are available for 15NIS per hour.

New City The **Allenby 2 B&B** (☎ 052 578493, fax 534 4113; e nmr@netvision.net .il; w www.bnb.co.il/allenby; Allenby Square 2, Romema; singles US$20-55, doubles US$30-70) is a clean, comfortable and friendly B&B in a historic house just two minutes' walk from the central bus station. Here you'll find several single and double rooms, some with private facilities, and a roomy self-contained apartment for up to five people. The irrepressible owner is a font of knowledge on Jerusalem and is a most delightful host.

Rates include a large and unique breakfast, cable TV in the rooms, and use of the communal kitchen. Long-term rates are available, and if there's no rooms at the hostel, staff will find you an alternative place in the same price and quality range.

B-Green Guest House (☎ 566 4220, fax 563 8505; e boaz3@barak-online.net; w www .bnb.co.il/green/index.htm; 4 Rachel Imeinu, German Colony; doubles US$50) sits in a lively neighbourhood about 20 minutes' walk or a short bus ride from the Old City. Each room has private facilities and a kitchenette, and parking is available.

Avissar's House (☎ 625 5447, fax 625 1507; e avisa_nm@netvision.net.il; 12 Hamevasser St, Yemin Moshe; singles US$60-107, doubles US$73-120) is a conveniently located B&B with a variety of suites and studio guest flats. It's one of the closest mid-range places to the Old City, but unfortunately it imposes a minimum three-night stay.

Le Sixteen B&B (☎ 532 8008, fax 581 9159; e le16@le16-bnb.co.il; w www.bnb .co.il/le16/index.htm; 16 Midbar Sinai St, Givat Hamivtar; singles US$34-45, doubles US$50-65) has five rooms, all with private facilities, cable TV and kitchenette. Rates also include breakfast. It's a bit out of the way, but it's good value and readily accessible to the main sites by convenient bus routes.

House 57 B&B (☎ 581 9944, 052-601826, fax 532 2929; e house57@netvision.net.il; w www.house57.co.il; 57 Midbar Sinai St, Givat Hamivtar; singles US$35-50, doubles US$55-70), in a nice stone house near Ammunition Hill, is another good choice. You can choose between rooms with or without private facilities, and a studio apartment; kitchen facilities are available and all rates include breakfast.

Jerusalem Inn Hotel (☎ 625 2757, fax 625 1297; e jerinn@netvision.net.il; w www .jerusaleminn.co.il; 7 Horkanus St; singles/ doubles with shared bathroom US$36/40), in the New City, features custom carpentry, masses of open space and a large lounge and bar/restaurant. It can, however, get a bit noisy at night. The affiliated **Jerusalem Inn Guest House** (☎ 625 1294, fax 625 1297; 6 Ha'Histadrut St; doubles US$50), just off pedestrianised Ben Yehuda St, offers air-conditioning, private baths and satellite TV.

Attached to the Zion Square Hostel, the **Kaplan Hotel** (☎ 624 4114, fax 623 6245;

e *jrpool@inter.net.il; 42 Jaffa Rd, Zion Square; doubles 200NIS)* has comfortable rooms with satellite TV and private facilities, plus access to cooking facilities.

Hotel Ron *(☎ 622 3122, fax 625 0707;* e *ronhotel@inter.net.il; 44 Jaffa Rd; singles/ doubles US$89/94)* has large and reasonably pleasant rooms, although those facing the front may be a little noisy.

Places to Stay – Top End
Jerusalem is top-heavy with frightfully expensive luxury hotels, most of which are in the New City.

The **Jerusalem Hilton** *(☎ 621 1111, fax 621 1000;* e *info-jerusalem@hilton.com; 7 HaMelekh David St; singles US$150-350, doubles US$200-400)* is in Mamilla, a champagne cork's arc from the Old City walls. Opened in 1997, it's now the city's most glitzy hotel.

The **King David** *(☎ 620 8888, fax 620 8882;* e *danhtls@danhotels.co.il; 23 HaMelekh David St; singles US$150-520, doubles US$198-550)*, Israel's most renowned hotel, is continuously stamped with a seal of approval by a stream of visiting kings and queens, presidents and prime ministers.

Places to Eat
Most of the fine dining places are in the New City, with a concentration of ethnic restaurants along Yoel Salomon St.

Street Food There are surprisingly few felafel places in the Old City, and even fewer are especially good. The most convenient is a stall at the bottom of the slope as you enter from Damascus Gate, in the narrow frontage between the two forking roads. As you face the felafel stall, look to your left and you'll see the street leading to the **Green Door Bakery** *(Aqabat ash-Sheikh Rihan St)*. These folks will rustle up personal-sized cheese, egg and tomato pizzas for as little as 6NIS.

You'll find the New City's greatest concentration of felafel and shwarma stands on King George V St between Jaffa Rd and Ben Yehuda St – just follow the pavement trail of tahina, salad and squashed felafel balls.

One of the most popular stands with locals is **King of Felafel & Shwarma**, at the corner of King George V and Agrippas Sts, which serves Israeli and Ethiopian food.

Old City The **Moses Art Restaurant** *(☎ 628 0975; Omar ibn al-Khattab Square)* is a friendly and informal Lebanese choice just inside Jaffa Gate in the Old City. Don't miss the excellent hummus.

Armenian Tavern *(☎ 627 3854; 79 Armenian Patriarchate Rd; meat dishes 35-45NIS; open 11am-10.30pm daily except Monday)*, in the Jaffa Gate area, attracts diners with its beautiful stone-and-tile interior and a gently splashing fountain. The strongly flavoured meat dishes are excellent, including *khaghoghi derev*, a spiced minced-meat mixture bundled in vine leaves. It's open daily, including Friday and Saturday evening, when other places are closed.

Keshet *(☎ 628 7515; Tiferet Israel; lunches 35-48NIS)* is ideal for a nice lunch on a quiet, sunny square in the Jewish Quarter. You can choose from salads, pasta, filled bagels, omelettes, quiches, blintzes and quiches.

Bonker's Bagels *(☎ 627 2590; Tiferet Israel; bagels 3-13NIS)* is a friendly little place where you can snack on the original unleavened Jewish snack with a choice of fillings.

Tzaddik's New York Deli *(☎ 627 2148;* e *tzaddiksdeli@hotmail.com; Tiferet Israel; hot dishes 20-29NIS, sandwiches 15NIS)*, a clone of a New York Deli, is best known for its attached Internet café and convenient location relative to the Western Wall.

New City The **Riff Raff Sandwich Bar** *(☎ 625 0291; 19 Hillel St; dishes 30-40NIS; open 24hrs daily)* is the place if you're craving an English breakfast (28NIS) at any time of the night or day. Alternatively, there's an enormous choice of sandwiches for 20NIS to 30NIS, as well as salads, pasta, pizza, coffee and sweets.

Rimon *(☎ 624 3712, fax 625 2199; 4 Luntz St, Zion Square; dishes 30-40NIS; open 24hrs daily)* is another 24-hour place that serves up pizza, quiche, grilled steaks and, believe it or not, Ben & Jerry's ice cream. Though lacking character, it manages to stay packed most of the time.

Ticho House *(☎ 624 4186; Ticho House Museum, 9 Harav Kook St; lunch 30-60NIS; dinner 60-70NIS; open 10am-midnight Sun-Thur, 10am-3pm Fri, 8pm-midnight Sat)*, housed in the 19th-century home of artist Anna Ticho, is a renowned bohemian café and restaurant. You can eat a late breakfast from 10am to noon, and for lunch and dinner the speciality is fish and vegetarian pasta dishes. On Tuesday at 8pm, it holds a cheese-and-wine evening (75NIS) with live jazz music, and on Saturday a string quartet accompanies a Viennese buffet (75NIS); bookings are required for both.

Village Green (☎ 625 3065; 33 Jaffa Rd; dishes 21-25NIS; open 9am-10pm Sun-Thur, 9am-3pm Fri) is a clean, kosher vegetarian place heartily recommended by many readers as the best restaurant in Israel, and we won't disagree! It serves up a range of vegetable soups, quiches, veggie burgers, pizza, stuffed vegetables, blintzes, savoury pies and lasagne dishes, all served with home-baked bread (and it has a well-stocked salad bar).

Spaghettim (☎ 623 5547; 8 Rabbi Akiva St; dishes 25-50NIS; open noon-midnight daily), off Hillel St in the New City shopping area, is among the best. The spaghetti-only menu includes 54 spaghetti incarnations, from the predictable bolognaise and carbonara to the bizarre ostrich in hunter sauce and fresh fruit sherbet sauce.

Lebanese Restaurant (☎ 643 0992; Ein Kerem Rd; dishes 30-50NIS), in Ein Kerem, is an incredible treat – a friendly, unassuming place serving some of the best Lebanese food you'll find in all of Israel & the Palestinian Territories. Don't miss the wonderful hand-pounded hummus, which is a meal in itself. Take bus No 17 from the main bus terminal to the suburb of Ein Kerem; the restaurant is 100m from the bus stop.

Self-Catering The Mahane Yehuda market (open Sun-Fri) offers Jerusalem's best-value food shopping. For the best deals, stroll in just as it's winding down for the day (5.30pm to 6.30pm Sun-Thur in winter, 7.30pm to 8.30pm Sun-Thur in summer, and 3pm to 4pm Fri), when stallholders are clearing out the day's produce.

Entertainment

Pubs, Bars & Nightclubs East Jerusalem and the Old City roll up their pavements at sundown and only a hike into the New City will provide an alternative to beer and a book in your room. Yoel Salomon and Rivlin, the two parallel main streets in Nahalat Shiv'a, in the New City, are lined with enough late-night bars and cafés to defeat even the most ardent pub-crawlers. The

Russian compound is also a safe bet for drinks and late-night dancing.

The Tavern Pub (☎ 624 4541; 16 Rivlin St), one of the city's oldest pubs, attracts an expat, bar-propping, beer-guzzling crowd. Don't miss the Polish Butterfly, which is the most intoxicating drink east of the Pecos.

The Cave Bar (☎ 625 6488; 12 Yoel Salomon St) is a homely family operation, with good, low red lighting. In the same building is the **Blue Hole**, an intimate bar with Guinness on tap. The outdoor courtyard is great on hot summer nights.

Mike's Place (☎ 052-670965; 7-9 Heleni HaMalka St), with two venues across the street from each other, is usually packed with students, expats, tourists and locals. There's live blues and rock every night of the week, and the summer block parties are legendary.

Glasnost (☎ 625 6954; 15 Heleni HaMalka St) is a Jerusalem institution, with live music on most evenings.

Strudel (☎ 623 2101; 11 Mounbaz St) is an Internet café by day and a party bar by night. At dusk, the computer-geek atmosphere is replaced by low lighting, loud music and a good long happy hour.

Pargod Theatre (☎ 625 8819; 94 Bezalel St) is great for jazz; jam sessions take place every Friday from 2.30pm to 5.30pm.

Haoman 17 (☎ 678 1658; 17 Haoman St, Talpiot; cover charge 50-80NIS), with its warehouse location, booming sound system and great lighting, is one of the ultimate clubbing venues. Serious partygoers shouldn't miss the legendary monthly After-Parties (100NIS to 200NIS; 6am to 8pm Saturday).

Hata'siya (☎ 052-635033; 5 Hata'siya St, Talpiot; 50-80NIS) is another large warehouse dance spot, with techno-beat and '80s music. The big nights are Thursday and Friday.

Orient Express (☎ 581 1334; Hyatt Regency Hotel, 32 Lehi St, Mt Scopus; 30-50NIS) is a dance venue playing hip-hop, R&B, rock and pop nightly from 11pm. There's also a quiet area for more relaxed patrons.

Campus (☎ 053-840170; 30 Haoman St) is the university students club, with three separate rooms featuring salsa, samba and '80s groove music.

There are also several gay venues:

Yellow Submarine (☎ 656 6611; 13 Rahavim St; cover charge 50-80NIS), in the Talpiot neighbourhood, is a gay-friendly live music venue that attracts a young crowd.

Lulu (☎ 537 6369; 59 HaNevi'im St; open 9pm-late Sat & Mon-Thur, 10pm-late Fri) is a small and always crowded gay and lesbian bar, with ladies only on Wednesday and men only on Saturday. In the same building, **Leila** (☎ 537 8225) hosts gay and lesbian parties every Thursday.

Music & Theatre
Free classical performances are sometimes held at the **YMCA** (☎ 569 2692; 26 HaMelekh David St); at the **Jerusalem Music Centre** (☎ 623 4347; Mishkenot Sha'ananim), on alternate Fridays; and at **Beit Shmuel** (☎ 620 3466; 6 Shema St), part of Hebrew Union College (Saturday morning).

Jerusalem Theatre (☎ 561 7167; 20 David Marcus St) has simultaneous English-language translation headsets available for certain performances. It's also home to the Jerusalem Symphony Orchestra.

Khan Theatre (☎ 671 8281; 2 David Remez Square) sometimes stages English-language performances.

Binyanei Ha'Umah Conference Centre (☎ 622 2481) is the residence of the Israel Philharmonic Orchestra.

Al-Masrah Centre for Palestine Culture & Art and **Al-Kasaba Theatre** (☎ 628 0957; Abu Obeida St), off Salah ad-Din St in East Jerusalem, stage plays, musicals, operettas and folk dancing in Arabic, often with an English synopsis.

Getting There & Away
Air Flights with **Arkia** (☎ 625 5888; 8 Shlomzion HaMalka St) depart from **Atarot airport**, north of the city, but most travellers opt to fly from Ben-Gurion, which is just a 40-minute bus ride away. See the Getting There & Away section earlier in this chapter for more information.

Bus From the sparkling **Egged central bus station** (Jaffa Rd), buses connect to all major cities and towns around Israel. Buses to Tel Aviv (18.80NIS, one hour) depart every 15 minutes; to Haifa (41NIS; 2½ hours), Tiberias (44NIS, 2½ hours) and Be'ersheva (35NIS, 90 minutes) roughly hourly; and to Eilat (62NIS, 4½ hours) four times daily. For day trips to the Dead Sea, including Ein Gedi or Masada (39NIS, two hours), be sure to leave on the first service of the day or you'll be pressed to get back the same day.

For information on buses to Egypt, see the Getting There & Away section earlier in this chapter.

Service Taxi Service taxis (sheruts) are much faster than buses, depart more frequently and cost only a few shekels more; they're also the only way to travel during Shabbat. Service taxis for Tel Aviv (20NIS per person on weekdays, 30NIS on Friday and Saturday) depart from the corner of Harav Kook St and Jaffa Rd.

Service taxis for all destinations on the West Bank and Gaza depart from the ranks opposite Damascus Gate in East Jerusalem.

Getting Around
To/From the Airport Bus No 111 departs from the central bus station for Ben-Gurion Airport (19NIS, 40 minutes) at least hourly from 6.30am to 8pm Sun-Thur, 6am to 4pm Fri, 7pm to 10pm Sat. Alternatively, **Nesher service taxis** (☎ 623 1231, 625 7227; 23 Ben Yehuda St) picks up booked passengers from their accommodation 24 hours a day (40NIS).

Bus Jerusalem is laced with a very good network of city bus routes (4.90NIS per ride). Unfortunately, they're currently changing at a rate of knots and the bus-route map distributed by the tourist office is a historical document. For the latest route information, call ☎ 530 4704.

Taxi Jerusalem special taxis suffer from the same rip-off tendencies that pervade the entire country (see Local Transport in the Getting Around section earlier in this chapter). Plan on spending 20NIS to 25NIS for trips anywhere within the central area of town.

Mediterranean Coast

The Israeli coast from Ashkelon to Rosh HaNikra is a long band of white sand backed up by a flat, fertile coastal plain interrupted intermittently by low coastal hills. Most of the growing population of Israel & the Palestinian Territories is concentrated in this area, particularly in Tel Aviv, Netanya, Haifa and a host of sprouting new suburbs and communities.

TEL AVIV

PLACES TO STAY
4 Tel Aviv Hilton
8 Carlton Hotel
9 Sheraton Moriah
10 Crowne Plaza
11 Renaissance
24 Dan Panorama

PLACES TO EAT
2 Hummus Ashkara
14 Osteria della Fiorella

25 Tel Aviv Brewhouse
29 Spaghettim

OTHER
1 MASH
3 Branch Post Office
5 Police
6 Mazada Tours (Egypt Buses)
7 Egyptian Embassy
12 Ben-Gurion's House
13 Gordon Ulpan

15 ISSTA Student Travel
16 Book Boutique
17 Gan Ha'Ir Shopping Centre
18 Arlosoroff Bus Terminal
19 Australian Embassy
20 Tel Aviv Museum of Art
21 Steinmatzky Bookshop
22 Rainbow Bar
23 Hassan Beq Mosque
26 OUT Bar
27 Great Synagogue

28 Halper's Bookshop
30 Steimatzky Bookshop
31 Rothschild Ave Food Fair
32 Main Post Office, Poste
   Restante, Police, Lost & Found
33 SPNI Office, Bookshop &
   Outdoors Shop
34 Shimon Rokakh Home &
   Nahum Gutman Museum
35 Suzanne Dellal Centre
36 Central Bus Station
37 Physicians for Human Rights

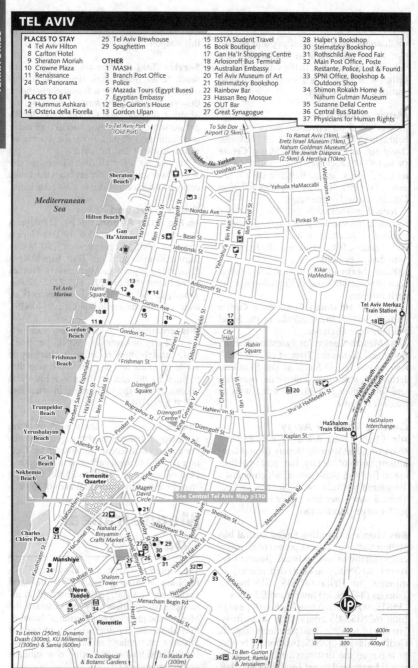

TEL AVIV   תל-אביב‏   تل أبيب
☎ 03

Tel Aviv, barely a century old, is a greatly underrated Mediterranean city that proclaims a modern, tolerant, laissez-faire attitude while thumbing its nose at Jerusalem's piety and 3000-year history. Forsaking spirituality for the stock exchange and tradition for the latest fads, this modern, secular city concerns itself with finance, commerce and, above all else, fun.

For visitors, Tel Aviv shows off an absorbing array of distinctive faces – a result of mass immigration from all over the Jewish world, along with its piles of intact cultural baggage. These days, a short walk connects the exotic orientalism of the Yemenite Quarter with the seedy cafés of Russified lower Allenby St and the Miami chic of the pastel, glass-fronted condos along the glitzy beachfront.

Orientation

Tel Aviv is a large agglomeration of suburbs sprawling across the coastal plain, but most visitors spend their time in the well-defined central district. This bustling area focuses on four roughly parallel north to south streets that follow the 6km of seafront from the Yarkon River in the north to the Yemenite Quarter (the 1930s town centre) in the south. Nearest the sand is Herbert Samuel Esplanade, while the hotel-lined HaYarkon St lies just a block inland. The next main street eastward is the backpacker-central Ben Yehuda St, while the trendy shopping zone, Dizengoff St, defines the easternmost limit of visitor interest. Allenby St, effectively a continuation of Ben Yehuda St, is lined with bars, cafés, Russian hangouts and second-hand bookshops.

Information

Tourist Offices There are currently **municipal tourist offices** at City Hall (☎ 521 8500; 69 Ibn Gvirol St) and in central Tel Aviv (☎ 516 6188; 46 Herbert Samuel St), on the corner of Geula St. At the moment, however, the best source of information is the convenient Isra-World Travel (☎ 522 7099; e info@israworld .com; w www.israworld.com; 66 Ben Yehuda St), which has an agreement with the municipal tourist office and keeps a database of all the latest happenings.

Money The best currency-exchange deals are at the private bureaus that don't charge commission, and there are plenty of them; on Saturday afternoon, try the change bureau at the foot of the Opera Tower escalator. Tel Aviv also has an **AmEx office** (☎ 524 2211, fax 523 1030; Beit El Al Bldg, cnr Ben Yehuda & Shalom Aleichem Sts; open 9am-5pm Sun-Thur).

Post & Communications The **main post office** (HaRakevet St; open 7am-6pm Sun-Thur, 7am-noon Fri) is on the corner of Yehuda HaLevi St. This is the place to pick up poste restante.

Useful Internet cafés include **Non-Stop** (☎ 522 2881; 101 Dizengoff St; open 8.30am-2am daily), charging 12NIS per hour; **Private Link** (☎ 529 9889, fax 529 9848; e private_link@hotmail.com; 78 Ben Yehuda St), charging 13NIS per hour, with branches at Ben-Gurion Airport and in the Dizengoff Centre; and **Web Stop** (☎ 620 2682, fax 629 2692; e info@webstop.co.il; 28 Bograshov St), charging 12NIS per hour. Most of these places also offer fax, printing and CD-burning services.

Travel Agencies A great source of discounted air tickets out of Israel is **IsraWorld Travel** (☎ 522 7099; e info@israworld .com; w www.israworld.com; 66 Ben Yehuda St). The student-travel agency **ISSTA** (☎ 521 0535, fax 521 0472; w www.issta.co.il; 128 Ben Yehuda St; open 9am-6.30pm Sun-Tues & Thur, 8.30am-1pm Wed & Fri) can sometimes come up with very good-value airline tickets.

Bookshops The **Steimatzky** chain has several branches: at 71 and 103 Allenby St; in the central bus station; and in the Dizengoff and Opera Tower shopping centres. The best second-hand bookshops are **Book Boutique** (☎ 527 4527; 190 Dizengoff St) and **Halper's** (☎/fax 629 9710; e halpbook@netvision .net.il; 87 Allenby St); the latter has a large selection of English-language titles.

Medical Services The **Physicians for Human Rights** (☎ 687 3718, fax 687 3029; 30 Levander St; open 8am-5pm Sun, Tues & Wed) provides free medical assistance for visitors who aren't covered by health insurance in Israel.

ISRAEL & THE PALESTINIAN TERRITORIES

Emergencies As everywhere in Israel & the Palestinian Territories, dial ☎ 100 for police, ☎ 102 for the fire brigade and ☎ 101 for an ambulance. The **Tourist Police office** (☎ 516 5382) is on the corner of Herbert Samuel Esplanade and Geula St.

Museums

The recommended **Nahum Goldman Museum of the Jewish Diaspora** (☎ 646 2020, fax 646 2134; e bhmuseum@post.tau.ac.il; w www.gh.org.il; Beit Hatefutsoth, 2 Klausner St, Matiyahu Gate, Ramat Aviv; adult/student 26/20NIS; open 10am-4pm Sun-Tues & Thur 10am-4pm, 10am-6pm Wed) has dioramas, films and displays chronicling 2500 years of Jewish culture in exile. It's on the grounds of Tel Aviv University, 1km north of

the Yarkon River. Take bus No 25 from King George V St or bus No 27 from the central bus station.

Eretz Israel Museum (☎ 641 5244; 2 Chaim Levanon St, Ramat Aviv; adult/student 27/22NIS; open 9am-3pm Sun-Thur, 10am-2pm Fri-Sat), south of the Diaspora museum, consists of 11 themed collections (glass, ceramics, folklore etc) constructed around the Tel Qasile archaeological site.

The **Tel Aviv Museum of Art** (☎ 695 7361; e info@tamuseum.com; 27 Shaul HaMelekh Ave; adult/student 27/20NIS; open 10am-4pm Mon & Wed, 10am-10pm Tues & Thur, 10am-2pm Fri, 10am-4pm Sat) is home to a superb collection of Israeli art that's especially strong on works from the late 19th- to early 20th-century.

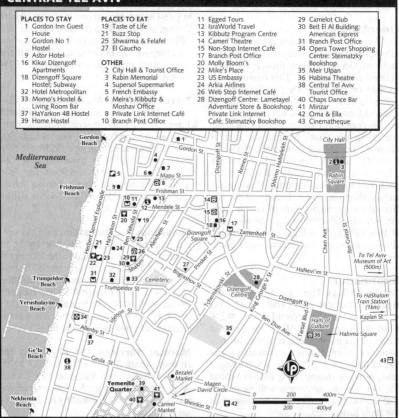

CENTRAL TEL AVIV

PLACES TO STAY
1 Gordon Inn Guest House
7 Gordon No 1 Hostel
9 Astor Hotel
16 Kikar Dizengoff Apartments
18 Dizengoff Square Hostel; Subway
32 Hotel Metropolitan
33 Momo's Hostel & Living Room Bar
37 HaYarkon 48 Hostel
39 Home Hostel

PLACES TO EAT
19 Taste of Life
21 Buzz Stop
25 Shwarma & Falafel
27 El Gaucho

OTHER
2 City Hall & Tourist Office
3 Rabin Memorial
4 Supersol Supermarket
5 French Embassy
6 Meira's Kibbutz & Moshav Office
8 Private Link Internet Café
10 Branch Post Office

11 Egged Tours
12 IsraWorld Travel
13 Kibbutz Program Centre
14 Cameri Theatre
15 Non-Stop Internet Café
17 Branch Post Office
20 Molly Bloom's
22 Mike's Place
23 US Embassy
24 Arkia Airlines
26 Web Stop Internet Café
28 Dizengoff Centre: Lametayel Adventure Store & Bookshop; Private Link Internet Café; Steimatzky Bookshop

29 Camelot Club
30 Beit El Al Building: American Express
31 Branch Post Office
34 Opera Tower Shopping Centre: Steimatzky Bookshop
35 Meir Ulpan
36 Habima Theatre
38 Central Tel Aviv Tourist Office
40 Chaps Dance Bar
41 Minzar
42 Orna & Ella
43 Cinematheque

Yemenite Quarter

The Yemenite Quarter's maze of narrow, dusty streets and crumbling buildings seems at odds with the clean-cut modernism of the rest of Tel Aviv. Imbued with an oriental flavour, the **Carmel Market** is one of the few places in the city that reminds visitors of Tel Aviv's Middle Eastern location. Push past the first few metres of knock-off brand-name clothing and trainers to reach the more aromatic and enticing stalls of fresh fruits and vegetables, hot breads and spices. Nearby **Nahalat Binyamin St** is a busy pedestrianised precinct full of fashionable cafés and arty shops. On Tuesday afternoon and Friday midday, it hosts a crafts market and fills with buskers and other street performers.

A block west of Nahalat Binyamin St is the imposing bulk of Tel Aviv's most prominent building, the **Shalom Tower** (☎ 517 7304; 9 Achad Ha'am St; admission 15NIS; open 8am-5pm Sun-Thur, 8am-1.30pm Fri). The lower levels host a shopping mall, while the top (30th) floor is an observation deck with great views over the city and beyond.

Neve Tsedek

Lovely Neve Tsedek, with its narrow streets and historic houses, is one of Tel Aviv's most upmarket and character-filled neighbourhoods. In the late 19th century it was the choice area for intellectual Jews looking for a prestigious address.

The **Suzanne Dellal Centre** (☎ 510 5656; 5 Yechieli St), a former school and cultural centre, serves as a venue for festivals, exhibits and cultural events, as well as a relaxing place to look at artistic murals and spend a sunny afternoon. On weekends, you can visit the historic 1887 **home of Shimon Rokakh** (☎ 516 2532; Rokakh St; open 10am-2pm Fri-Sat), with a video and exhibits outlining life in 19th-century Tel Aviv. On the same street is the **Nahum Gutman Museum** (☎ 516 1970; Rokakh St 21; admission adult/child 10/4NIS; open 10am-4pm Sun-Wed, 10am-7pm Thur, 10am-2pm Fri, 10am-5pm Sat), which displays 200 lively and fanciful works by the 20th-century Israeli artist.

Beaches

Tel Aviv's strand of white sand along the Mediterranean coast serves as a fashion runway for the city's beautiful people, a staging point for kite surfers, and a vast sandy court for pairs playing *matkot* (Israeli beach tennis). On summer nights the beaches become venues for impromptu concerts and discos.

Swimmers should beware of the strong undertow, not overestimate their abilities, and heed the warning flags: a black flag means swimming is forbidden; red alerts of potential risks and advises not to swim alone; and white means that the area is currently safe. Light-skinned visitors – especially those from less sunny climes – should also take the usual precautions against exposure to the sun.

Places to Stay – Budget

Tel Aviv's lively budget hostels are concentrated near the central beaches, trendy restaurants, shopping centres and nightspots. Those who prefer solitude may want to consider staying in nearby Jaffa.

Dizengoff Square Hostel (☎ 522 5184, fax 522 5181; e dizengof@trendline.co.il w www .dizengoff-hostel.co.il; 13 Ben Ami St; dorm beds 40NIS, doubles 100-155NIS) offers a range of facilities – including a kitchen, TV lounge and billiards room – plus a rooftop garden and a great central location. Rates include a continental breakfast.

Gordon No 1 Hostel (☎ 523 7807; e sleepin@inter.net.il; 84 Ben Yehuda St; dorm beds 38NIS, singles/doubles 150/172NIS) is a popular and excellent hostel in the heart of Tel Aviv. This well-organised place has a kitchen and a bright, glassy common room overlooking the city rooftops. Each of the single-sex dorms has its own bathroom facilities.

Momo's Hostel (☎ 528 7471, fax 528 0797; e momos28@hotmail.com; 28 Ben Yehuda St; dorm beds 35NIS, doubles 100-160NIS) is a colourful, amenable, character-filled place with an attached bar/café and a good central location. Rates include a light breakfast and use of the kitchen. Men and women, and travellers and long-term workers, have separate dorms and it's the only Tel Aviv hostel with free parking. In summer you can sleep on the roof for 30NIS.

HaYarkon 48 Hostel (☎ 516 8989, fax 510 3113; e info@hayarkon48.com; w www .hayarkon48.com; 48 HaYarkon St; dorm beds/doubles 42/160NIS), in a converted school, sits just two blocks from the beach and is consistently cited as Israel's poshest hostel. Guests rave about the clean kitchen, great showers, laundry facilities, free breakfast, cable-TV lounge and billiards room. Those looking for a great double may want to request room No 35. Internet access costs 13NIS per hour.

Home Hostel (☎ 517 6736; 20 Al-Sheikh St; e home1@bezeqint.net; dorm beds 30NIS, doubles 50-70NIS), in the Yemenite Quarter, is a very basic option with simple dorms and private rooms. Guests have use of the limited cooking facilities and the attached bar sells cheap beer. Rates include a simple breakfast and discounts are available to students and volunteers. When the hostel is busy, the owner organises free Saturday lunches, and even travellers staying at other hostels are invited.

Places to Stay – Mid-Range

Note that prices for these places vary according to the season; the highest rates apply mainly to the summer high season and Jewish holidays.

Kikar Dizengoff Apartments (☎ 524 1151, fax 523 5614; e neemanam@netvision.net.il; w www.hotel-apt.com; 89 Dizengoff St; singles US$60-95, doubles US$80-105, suites US$120-160) is hard to beat for price and quality. All four types of units have phones, separate data lines, cable TV, safes and kitchenettes. Overlooking pleasant Dizengoff Square, this place is within easy walking distance or a short bus ride from almost everything that's of interest to visitors. Guests have free Internet access and discounts are available to those who book through the Internet.

Gordon Inn Guest House (☎ 523 8239, fax 527 4790; e sleepin@inter.net.il; w www.sleepinisrael.com; 17 Gordon St; singles US$39-57, doubles US$49-71) is a hybrid hostel/hotel that also represents very good value. Friendly and beautifully kept, it offers a sparkling and inexpensive option; the lowest-priced private rooms have shared bathroom facilities. All rates include breakfast.

Astor Hotel (☎ 520 6666, fax 523 7247; e astor@prima.co.il; 105 HaYarkon St; singles US$105-130, doubles US$125-160) is a pleasant but soulless upper mid-range option. For a sea-view room, add US$25 to the standard rates.

Hotel Metropolitan (☎ 519 2727, fax 517 2626; e reserve@metrotlv.co.il; w www.hotel metropolitan.co.il; 11-15 Trumpeldor St; singles/doubles US$100/115) is a clean and decent

place with a terrace pool; the suites here cost about 50% more than the standard rooms.

Places to Stay – Top End

Most of Tel Aviv's top-end palaces rise just a quick shuffle from the beach, and, as with the mid-range places, rates change with the season. Generally, a good travel agent will get a better deal than you'll manage on your own.

Tel Aviv Hilton (☎ 520 2222, fax 527 2711; Gan HaAtzma'ut or Independence Park; doubles US$230-385), with its parkland setting and beach access, is one of the best choices. South of the square on HaYarkon St are the virtually indistinguishable **Sheraton Moriah** (☎ 521 6666, fax 527 1065; 155 HaYarkon St; doubles US$140-220); **Crowne Plaza** (☎ 520 1111, fax 520 1122; 145 HaYarkon St; doubles US$140-170); and **Renaissance** (☎ 521 5555, fax 521 5588; 121 HaYarkon St; doubles US$140-200).

Dan Panorama (☎ 519 0190, fax 517 1777; e danhtls@danhotels.co.il; 10 Kaufmann St; doubles US$145-230) is decent and well known, but it's a long walk from the centre of things.

Places to Eat

Street Food & Snack Bars The heaviest concentration of Middle Eastern fast food is found along the busy reaches of Ben Yehuda and Allenby Sts. Besides felafel, the cheapest eating in Tel Aviv can be found at the travellers' bars Buzz Stop, Mike's Place and MASH (see Entertainment later in this section). Their popular menus typically feature English breakfasts, grilled burgers, stir-fries and fish and chips.

The city's many cafés provide ringside seating for its continuous pavement carnival-cum-fashion show. Unfortunately, food quality takes a low priority and most locals fuel themselves on coffee, croissants and a variety of sweets and pastries. On Saturday afternoon, you can sample all sorts of fare when local restaurants set up an informal **food fair** along Rothschild Ave.

Shwarma & Felafel (46 Ben Yehuda St) is a friendly corner stand that's generally known as Tel Aviv's best Israeli fast-food place.

Restaurants The **Hummus Ashkara** (☎ 546 4547; 45 Yirmiyahu St) is where Israelis go in north Tel Aviv when they're after excellent hummus and *fuul* (fava bean paste). The sign is in Hebrew only, so look out for the Coca-Cola sign and the tables on the street.

Taste of Life (☎ *620 3151; 60 Ben Yehuda St; dishes 30-45NIS; open 9am-9pm Sun-Thur, 9am-2pm Fri)*, run by the Black Hebrew community, does vegan cuisine that includes veggie shwarma, salads, sandwiches, steamed vegetables, vegetarian hot dogs, *tamali*, *tofu-lafel*, barbecue twist burgers, cheeses, yogurts, ice cream and shakes.

El Gaucho (☎ *629 2062; 51 Pinsker St; dishes from 45NIS; open for lunch & dinner Sun-Thur)*, on the corner of Bograshov St, is a good choice if you're craving a steak. A business lunch with a starter, empanadas, a 250g steak and dessert is just 45NIS.

Spaghettim (☎ *566 4467; 18 Yavne St; open noon-1am daily)*, one block east of Allenby St, is where pasta fans should head. It's spaghetti only, but there's a choice of more than 50 sauces.

Osteria della Fiorella (☎ *524 8818; 148 Ben Yehuda St; dishes 35-45NIS; open for lunch & dinner Sun-Fri)* is a recommended option serving as close as you'll get to genuine Italian fare.

Tel Aviv Brewhouse (☎ *516 8666; 11 Rothschild Ave; dishes 25-30NIS)*, just south of the Shalom Tower, is Tel Aviv's poshest bar/restaurant. Here, yuppies sip four kinds of designer ales (9NIS to 23NIS). Try the Masters, a 6% dark ale. The food is excellent, but doesn't stray much from the usual beer accompaniments.

Self-Catering Some of the best fresh fruit and vegetables anywhere are sold at the **Carmel Market**. For one-stop shopping, try the convenient **Supersol supermarket** *(79 Ben Yehuda St; open 7am-midnight Sun, Mon & Tues, 24hrs Wed & Thur, 7am-3pm Fri)*.

Entertainment

Tel Aviv is well known for its nightlife, and the mind-boggling variety of spots can keep you crawling all night long. The funkiest café district is undoubtedly Sheinkin St, which is a great place to meet people and soak up the atmosphere.

Pubs & Bars The bars clustered around the intersection of Allenby and Lilienblum Sts, and along Sheinkin, are considered locally to be the most fashionable. Travellers' bars

remain the least expensive option for serious beer aficionados, but it's hard to keep track of what's hot, what's not and what's gone.

Buzz Stop (☎ *510 0869; 86 Herbert Samuel Esplanade; open 24hrs daily)*, at the beach beside the US Embassy, is possibly Tel Aviv's most renowned travellers' bar. Night owls and dawn watchers will appreciate the mainstream music, cheap grub, good choice of beer and the full English breakfast (which is often administered as a hangover cure).

MASH (☎ *605 1007; 275 Dizengoff St; open 11am-4am Sun-Fri, 10am-4am Sat)*, which stands for More Alcohol Served Here, is Tel Aviv's oldest travellers' bar and is also a haunt of middle-aged patrons and the long-stay community. The main draws include the music, billiards and sports on the big-screen TV.

Living Room (☎ *528 7471; 28 Ben Yehuda St)*, attached to Momo's Hostel, is often filled with travellers who come to drink and meet other travellers.

Minzar (☎ *517 3015; 58 Allenby St; open 24hrs daily)*, set back from the main street, is a bohemian-style lounge-like coffee bar that actually specialises in beer. Happy hour extends from 5pm to 10pm.

Samia (☎ *518 2382; Abulafia 5; cover charge 20NIS)*, in Florentin, is a serious, lowlight cocktail lounge where patrons remove their shoes, sit on overstuffed cushions and relax in the low lighting and ambient music.

The Rasta Pub (☎ *054-247290; 26 Shocken St)* features open mike on Thursday from 10pm and live reggae (cover charge 30NIS to 40NIS) on Friday and Saturday nights.

Mike's Place (☎ *052-670965; 86 Herbert Samuel Esplanade)*, on the beach, is the place to go for live music. Blues and rock bands play from 10.30pm every night, but the liveliest nights are Thursday, Friday and Saturday; there's no cover charge, but they do pass the tip jar around to pay the bands. There's also a good, cheap menu of grill-style meals, cocktails and, especially, beer. Happy hour lasts from 5pm to 9pm daily.

Camelot Club (☎ *528 5222; 16 Shalom Aleichem St; cover charge 40-90NIS)*, on the corner of Ben Yehuda St, and built in an acoustically sound underground cave, is Tel Aviv's most prestigious live music venue, where you'll have a chance to see local celebrities and visiting artists. The action starts cranking up nightly around 10.30pm.

Molly Bloom's (☎ 522 1558; 2 Mendele St; open 4pm-late Sat-Thur, noon-late Fri), one of only two Irish pubs in Israel (the other is The Bear in Haifa), with wooden floors and fixtures shipped in from the Emerald Isle. It attracts both locals and tourists, and is great for a draught Guinness along with a good conversation or a sports match on the TV. The decent bar menu features such Gaelic options as Irish stew and shepherd's pie. Happy hour lasts from 4pm to 8pm nightly.

Nightclubs Especially in summer, Tel Aviv's night club action rivals that of even the big European cities, and it's essential that you dress to impress. Cover charges range from 50NIS to 120NIS.

TLV Club (☎ 516 6582; Old Port, north of the centre; open midnight-late) is a multi-level complex that features local celebrities and visiting artists. The big music night is Thursday, and on Friday, it hosts Tel Aviv's wildest gay night.

KU Millennium (☎ 510 2060; 132 Salame St; open 10.30pm-late Wed, Fri & Sat) is popular for its live, big-name music.

Dynamo Dvash (☎ 683 5159; 59 Abarbanel St), which is rather low-key, features hip-hop, trance and techno-beat.

Lemon (☎ 529 0126; 17 HaNagarim St; open Fri & Sat nights), in Florentin, holds house parties every Friday and Saturday.

Gay Clubs Tel Aviv has the Middle East's most vibrant gay community, and even plays host to an annual Gay Pride Parade. Most of the nightlife is focused on Sheinkin and Nahalat Binyamin Sts, where you'll find plenty of rainbow flags, but the best gay night out in town is surely **FFF** (TLV Club) in the Old Port, north of the centre (see Nightclubs earlier in this section).

Orna & Ella (☎ 620 4753; 33 Sheinkin St; open 10am-midnight Sun-Thur, 10am-3am Fri-Sat) is a gay-friendly café/bar that attracts a fashion-conscious crowd with sweet treats in the afternoon and drinks at night.

OUT (☎ 560 2391; 45 Nahalat Binyamin St; closed Wed) features a well-stocked bar and diverse music – along with a 'beautiful' clientele. You'll find the best action after midnight on Thursday, Friday and Saturday nights.

Rainbow (22 Kikar Rambam, Nahalat Binyamin St; open nightly 8pm-late) is a predominantly lesbian café/bar that gets very friendly late at night.

Chaps Dance Bar (☎ 052-589629; 22 Rabbi Akiva St; open nightly 11pm-late) is a cruise joint with ladies only on Tuesday and live drag shows on Thursday.

Cinemas & Theatres In summer, free films are sometimes screened on the beach near Allenby St.

Cinematheque (☎ 691 7181; 1 Ha'Arba'a St; admission 35NIS; open 11am daily) is the flagship in a chain of Israeli cinemas that feature classic, retro, foreign, avant-garde, new-wave, and off-beat films. Alternatively, choose a film from the video library and pay 20NIS for a private screening. From Dizengoff St, head south on Ibn Gvirol St and fork left onto Carlibach St; the Cinematheque is visible to your left across a triangular plaza.

Cameri Theatre (☎ 523 3335; 101 Dizengoff St) hosts theatre performances in Hebrew, with simultaneous English translation on Tuesday only.

Habima Theatre (☎ 629 5555; Tarsat Blvd, Habima Square), home of Israel's national theatre company, stages performances on Thursday, with simultaneous English-language translation.

Getting There & Away

Air Most travellers fly in and out of Ben-Gurion Airport, but **Arkia** (☎ 699 2222; 11 Frishman St) also has daily (except Saturday) flights to Eilat, Haifa and Jerusalem from Sde Dov airport, north of the Yarkon River.

Travellers leaving Israel on El Al flights from Ben-Gurion Airport can pre-check their bags the day before their flight at the **Arlosoroff bus terminal** (☎ 972 3388). Those using other airlines can do the same at the **Dan Panorama Hotel** (☎ 519 0190; 10 Kaufmann St) for 20NIS.

Bus Doubling as an enormous shopping centre, the **central bus station** complex may confound you for several hours while you look for a way out. Outgoing intercity buses depart from the 6th floor, where there's also an efficient information desk. Suburban and city buses use the poorly signposted stalls on the 4th floor. Note that during Shabbat you'll have to resort to service taxis.

Buses leave for Jerusalem (18.90NIS, one hour) roughly every 10 minutes; for Haifa (21.50NIS; 90 minutes) every 15 to 20 minutes; Tiberias (37NIS, 2½ hours) once or twice hourly from 6am to 9pm; and Eilat (62NIS, five hours), more or less hourly from 6.30am to 5pm (an overnight service departs at 12.30am).

Tel Aviv's second bus station, the Arlosoroff terminal, adjoins the central train station northeast of the centre. To get there, take bus No 61, which travels along Allenby, King George V, Dizengoff and Arlosoroff Sts.

For information on buses to Egypt, see the Getting There & Away section earlier in this chapter.

Train Tel Aviv has two train stations: the main station, **Tel Aviv Merkaz** (☎ 693 7515), and the smaller **HaShalom station**. From Tel Aviv Merkaz, you can travel to Haifa (21.50NIS, one hour), via Netanya (11.50NIS, 25 minutes), more or less hourly from 6am to 8pm Sunday to Friday, and on to Akko (29.50NIS, 90 minutes) and Nahariya (33NIS, 1.75 hours). Heading south, you can travel as far as Be'ersheva (23.50NIS, 1.25 hours). To reach Tel Aviv Merkaz from the centre, take bus No 61 or 62 north from Dizengoff St to the Arlosoroff bus terminal, which is a two-minute walk from the station.

Service Taxi The service taxis outside the central bus station can get you to Jerusalem (25NIS) and Haifa (20NIS). On Saturday, they leave from HaHamashal St just east of Allenby St and charge about 20% more than the weekday fare.

Getting Around

To/From the Airport Bus No 222 (☎ 691 6256) runs hourly on the hour from the Dan Panorama hotel to s (16NIS, 45 minutes), from 6am to 11pm Sunday to Thursday, 6am to 7pm Friday, and noon to 11pm Saturday. At half-past each hour, it calls in at the Arlosoroff bus terminal (near Tel Aviv Merkaz train station). It also runs hourly in the opposite direction.

Bus Tel Aviv city buses follow an efficient network of routes. The single fare is 4.90NIS, but for 9.50NIS you can buy a *yonim* pass, which allows unlimited bus travel around Tel Aviv and its suburbs on

the day of purchase. The city centre is well covered by bus No 4, which travels from the central bus station to the Reading Terminal via Allenby, Ben Yehuda and northern Dizengoff Sts.

Taxi Tel Aviv special taxis suffer from the same rip-off tendencies that pervade the entire country (see Local Transport in the Getting Around section for the whole country). Plan on 20NIS to 25NIS for trips anywhere within the central city.

JAFFA   יפו يافا
☎ 03

After Noah was catapulted to fame in a flood of worldwide proportions, one of his sons, Japheth, headed for the coast and founded a new city that was humbly named Jaffa (Yafo in Hebrew) in his own honour. During Solomon's time, it came to prominence as a major port city, but this largely Arab town has now been superseded – and swallowed up – by its neighbouring upstart Tel Aviv.

Today, it's a quaint and mostly Christian harbour-side suburb where you'll get a taste of both the enigmatic Middle East and the fruits of the adjacent sea.

Things to See & Do

The central attraction is **Old Jaffa**, a walled city of narrow twisting alleys lined with galleries, art studios, restaurants and superfluous shops. The **Antiquities Museum of Tel Aviv-Jaffa** (*10 Mifraz Shlomo St; open 9am-2pm Sun-Tues & Thur, 9am-6pm Wed, 10am-2pm Sat*) was originally a Turkish administrative and detention centre but it now houses a collection of local archaeological discoveries.

On the grassy knoll behind the museum are the **HaPisgah Gardens**, where an amphitheatre affords a panorama of the Tel Aviv beachfront; ongoing archaeological excavations reveal Egyptian ruins dating back at least 3300 years.

From the gardens, a footbridge leads to **Kikar Kedumim** (Kedumim Square), which is ringed by restaurants, clubs and galleries but dominated by the orange-painted **St Peter's Monastery**. In an underground chamber, the well-designed **Visitors Centre** (☎ 518 2680; open 9am-10pm Sun-Thur, 9am-2pm Fri, 10am-10pm Sat) presents visitors with a six-minute video and the partially excavated remains from the Hellenistic and Roman eras.

A worthwhile stop is the **Ilana Goor Museum** (☎ 683 7676; 4 Mazal Dagim St; admission adult/child/student/senior 24/14/20/20NIS; open 10am-6pm Sun-Thur, 10am-4pm Fri), housed in an 18th-century stone hostel for Jewish pilgrims. It features the design and wooden, stone, glass, bronze and iron sculpture of its namesake and owner, Ilana Goor.

Outside the Old City, east of the landmark Ottoman **clock tower**, is a desultory market-like expanse locally known as the **flea market** or **junk market**. In fact, there are some wonderful finds here, including a range of lovely Middle Eastern antiques and paraphernalia that are just awaiting an appreciative buyer.

Normally, a free three-hour **Old Jaffa walking tour** departs from the clock tower at 9.30am Wednesday.

Places to Stay

Old Jaffa Hostel (☎ 682 2370, fax 682 2316; e ojhostel@shani.net; w www.inisrael.com/oldjaffahostel; 8 Olei Zion St, enter from Ami'ad St; dorm beds 40NIS, singles US$30-46, doubles US$34-50), in a beautiful old Turkish home, is both friendly and atmospheric. The large bar and common room, as well as the airy dorms and comfortable private rooms, are decorated with historic Arabic furniture and *objets d'art*. In summer, you can opt for a mattress in the rooftop garden (25NIS).

Places to Eat

For Israelis, Jaffa's main culinary attraction is fish, and both Mifraz Shlomo St and the port area boast numerous outdoor restaurants.

Said Abu Elafia & Sons (☎ 681 2340; 7 Yefet St; open 24hrs Mon-Sat) is a bakery that has become a legend in Israel. In addition to all sorts of breads, pastries and samosas (locally called *sambusas*), it does a spinach-and-egg pitta and a uniquely Arab pizza-like concoction which involves cracking a couple of eggs on a pitta, stirring in tomato, cheese and olives, and baking it in the oven.

Dr Shakshuka (☎ 682 2842; 3 Beit Eshal St; meals 30-40NIS) is a culinary highlight in the Tel Aviv area. Along with its eponymous *shakshuka* (a skillet concoction featuring egg, capsicum, tomato sauce and spices), the Gabso family whips up a range

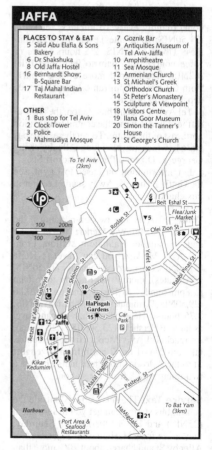

JAFFA

PLACES TO STAY & EAT	
5	Said Abu Elafia & Sons Bakery
6	Dr Shakshuka
8	Old Jaffa Hostel
16	Bernhardt Show; B-Square Bar
17	Taj Mahal Indian Restaurant

OTHER	
1	Bus stop for Tel Aviv
2	Clock Tower
3	Police
4	Mahmudiya Mosque
7	Goznik Bar
9	Antiquities Museum of Tel Aviv-Jaffa
10	Amphitheatre
11	Sea Mosque
12	Armenian Church
13	St Michael's Greek Orthodox Church
14	St Peter's Monastery
15	Sculpture & Viewpoint
18	Visitors Centre
19	Ilana Goor Museum
20	Simon the Tanner's House
21	St George's Church

of Libyan and other North African delights. For an enormous business lunch, you'll pay 59NIS, and a massive 'complete couscous' spread with couscous, bread, salads, lamb and a stuffed potato will set you back just 40NIS. Don't miss it!

Bernhardt Show (☎ 681 3898; 10 Kikar Kedumim; mains from 75NIS) is an upmarket seafood blast, serving calamari, sea trout, mullet, mussels and other *fruits-de-mer* (including lobster from 220NIS). Those on a tight budget can stick to the starters and salads, which average 35NIS to 40NIS.

Taj Mahal Indian Restaurant (Kikar Kedumim; dishes 50-60NIS) bears little resemblance to British Indian takeaways, but it enjoys a wonderful sea view and does an Indian business lunch for 40NIS.

Entertainment

In the evenings, you may want to check out the bars. **Goznik** (☎ 683 7890; 28 Olei Zion St; open 9pm-late Sat-Thur, 10pm-late Fri), with its loud pop music and free admission, and the cave-like **B-Square** (☎ 683 6507; 14 Kikar Kedumim) both provide a touch of night-time colour in Jaffa.

Getting There & Away

From the centre of Tel Aviv, it's a pleasant 2.5km seafront stroll to Old Jaffa. Alternatively, take bus No 46 from the central bus station, bus No 10 from Ben Yehuda St, bus No 18 from Dizengoff St or bus No 18 or 25 from Allenby St, and get off at the clock tower. To return to the centre, take bus No 10 from immediately north of the clock tower.

NETANYA נתניה
☎ 09

As a sun-and-sand resort, Netanya offers some 11km of the finest **free beaches** in Israel (beware of the undertow). There's also a lively pedestrianised main street lined with shops, cafés and patisseries. The **tourist office** (☎ 882 7286, fax 884 1348; open 8.30am-4pm Sun-Thur, 9am-noon Fri) is housed in a kiosk at the southwestern corner of Ha'Atzma'ut Square.

In a prime position near the beach, the budget accommodation of choice is the **Atzma'ut Hostel** (☎ 862 1315, fax 882 2562; 2 Ussishkin St, Ha'Atzma'ut Square; dorm beds 50NIS). **Hotel Orit** (☎ 861 6818; 21 Chen St; singles/doubles 150/200NIS), run by Swedish Christians, is a fairly good-value alternative. Rates include breakfast.

Getting There & Away

Buses run roughly every 15 minutes to and from Tel Aviv (10NIS, 30 minutes), and every half-hour to and from Haifa (17NIS, one hour) and Jerusalem (20NIS, 1¼ hours). To reach Caesarea, Megiddo, Nazareth or Tiberias, change buses in Khadera.

HAIFA חיפה حيفا
☎ 04

The attractive multilevel city of Haifa spills down the wooded slopes of Mt Carmel and takes in a busy industrial port area; a trendy German Colony; the landmark Baha'i Gardens; and a host of white-sand beaches, promenades and panoramic views.

While Jerusalem is swathed in historical mystique and Tel Aviv buzzes with hedonism and *joie de vivre*, Haifa, Israel's third-largest city, seems content with its lot as a student town and a solid cornerstone of the country's technological industry. Perhaps it's this air of prosperity that provides it with what appears to be Israel's most relaxed attitude, in which Jews, Christians and Muslims live and work together without the tensions that seem to pervade many other cities.

Orientation

Haifa occupies three main tiers on the slopes of Mt Carmel. New arrivals by bus, train or boat are ushered into Haifa in the Port Area, also known as Downtown. Uphill lie the busy Arab commercial district of Wadi Nisnas and the bustling Hadar district, both brimming with shops, hotels and restaurants. In the Carmel Centre district at the top of the mountain, the university, exclusive residences and trendy Carmel Centre bars and eateries benefit from the high-altitude breezes and magnificent views. The city's sprawling outskirts take in several of the country's most extensive shopping malls, including the art-oriented Castra and the vast 150-shop Grand Kanyon in Neve Sha'anan.

Information

Tourist Offices Haifa's excellent tourist office the **Haifa Tourism Development Association** (☎ 853 5605, fax 853 5610; e info@tour-haifa.co.il; w www.tour-haifa.co.il; 48 Ben-Gurion Ave; open 8am-6pm Sun-Thur, 8.30am-1pm Fri) is probably the country's most useful. It occupies a historic home in the German Colony, immediately at the foot of the Baha'i Gardens. It distributes several useful publications, including *A Guide to Haifa Tourism* and a free city map, which outlines four themed walking tours.

Money The **Bank Leumi** and **Bank Ha-Poalim** main branches are both on Jaffa Rd, and you'll find lots of change places around Hadar and other shopping districts. Informal moneychangers hang around the port area, but there's always a risk of rip-offs.

Post & Communications The **main post office** (19 HaPalyam Ave; open 8am-8pm Sun-Thur, 8am-2pm Fri) is in the port area. There are several Internet cafés around the

HAIFA

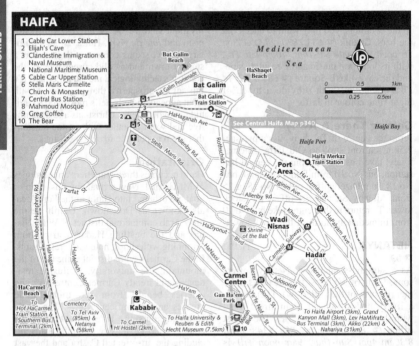

1 Cable Car Lower Station
2 Elijah's Cave
3 Clandestine Immigration & Naval Museum
4 National Maritime Museum
5 Cable Car Upper Station
6 Stella Maris Carmelite Church & Monastery
7 Central Bus Station
8 Mahmoud Mosque
9 Greg Coffee
10 The Bear

city; a popular choice in Hadar is the **Publo (Norem) B&B** (☎ 866 5656; 27-29 Nordau St), which charges 25NIS per hour.

Baha'i Gardens

The 19 immaculately kept terraces of the dizzily sloped **Baha'i Gardens** (☎ 831 3131; admission free; open 9am-5pm Sun-Thur, 9am-noon Fri, shorter hours Oct-May) are truly a wonder. Apart from the top two tiers, the gardens are accessible to the general public only on guided tours, which must be pre-booked well in advance. Baha'i pilgrims, however, can organise individual entry.

Amid the perfectly manicured gardens, fountains and walkways rises Haifa's most imposing landmark, the golden-domed **Shrine of the Bab** (open 9am-noon daily). Completed in 1953, this tomb of the Baha'i prophet, Al-Bab, integrates both European and Oriental design, and is considered one of the two most sacred sites for the world's five million Baha'is (the other is the tomb of Mizra Hussein Ali outside nearby Akko). Visitors to the shrine must remove their shoes and be modestly dressed (no shorts or bare shoulders).

Near the upper entrance to the Baha'i Gardens is the **Ursula Malbin Sculpture Garden** (Gan HaPesalim; HaZiyonut Blvd), a small park filled with 'hands-on' sculptures, where families come to relax amid the greenery.

Stella Maris Monastery & Elijah's Cave

The neo-Gothic Stella Maris Carmelite church and monastery (open 6am-1.30pm & 3pm-6pm Mon-Sat), with its wonderful painted ceiling, was originally established as a 12th-century Crusader stronghold. It was later used as a hospital for the troops of Napoleon in 1799, but was subsequently destroyed by the Turks. In 1836, it was replaced by the present structure.

The easiest access to Stella Maris is the **cable car** (one way/return 16/22NIS) that also provides access to the National Maritime Museum and the grotto known as **Elijah's Cave** (admission free), lower down the slope. Here the prophet Elijah hid from King Ahab and Queen Jezebel after slaying the 450 priests of Ba'al, as reported in 1 Kings:17-19. It now attracts pilgrims of all three monotheistic faiths, and the adjacent garden is a favoured picnic site for local Christian Arabs.

Museums

The **Haifa Art Museum** (☎ 852 3255; **w** www .haifa.gov.il; 26 Shabtai Levi St; adult/child/student/senior 33/22/22/16.50NIS; open 10am-5pm Mon & Wed-Thur, 10am-2pm & 5pm-8pm Tues, 10am-1pm Fri, 10am-2pm Sat) is three museums in one – ancient art, modern art, and music and ethnology. The same ticket (good for three days) also admits you to the following museums: **Haifa City Museum** (☎ 851 2030; 11 Ben-Gurion Ave), with a selection of historic photos; the wonderful **Tikotin Museum of Japanese Art** (☎ 838 3554; 89 HaNassi Ave) and its unique collection of Far Eastern works; and the **National Maritime Museum** (☎ 853 6622; 198 Allenby Rd), which presents the history of Mediterranean shipping.

The **Clandestine Immigration & Naval Museum** (☎ 853 6249; 204 Allenby Rd; adult/child 10/5NIS; open 8.30am-4pm Sun-Thur) commemorates Israel's naval history and the Zionists' 1930s and '40s attempts to migrate into British-blockaded Palestine.

The **Reuben & Edith Hecht Museum** (☎ 825 7773; **e** mushecht@research.haifa .ac.il; Eshkol Tower, Haifa University; admission free; open 10am-4pm Sun-Mon & Wed-Thur, 10am-7pm Tues, 10am-1pm Fri, 10am-2pm Sat) features Israeli archaeology and a collection of French Impressionist art. The museum was donated by Belgian philanthropist, Dr Reuben Hecht, who migrated to Israel in 1939.

A great place to take kids is the hands-on **National Museum of Science, Planning & Technology** (☎ 862 8111; **e** sci_muse@ netvision.net.il; **w** www.netvision.net.il/inmos; Technion Bldg, Shemaryahu Levin St, Hadar; open 9am-6pm Sun-Mon & Wed-Thur, 9am-7.30pm Tues, 10am-2pm Fri, 10am-5pm Sat).

Organised Tours

The **Haifa Tourism Development Association** (☎ 853 5605, fax 853 5610; **e** info@ tourhaifa.co.il; **w** www.tour-haifa.co.il; 48 Ben-Gurion Ave; open 8am-6pm Sun-Thur, 8.30am-1pm Fri) organises a free guided walking tour on Saturday at 10am; meet at the signposted observation point on the corner of Sha'ar HaLevenon and Ye'fe Nof Sts, in Carmel Centre.

Places to Stay

The **Port Inn** (☎ 852 4401, fax 852 1003; **e** port_inn@yahoo.com; **w** www.portinn.co.il; 34 Jaffa Rd; dorm beds 50NIS, singles/doubles US$39/50), Haifa's best budget option, is a friendly and central family-run place that's more like a hotel than a hostel. Laundry (30NIS), Internet facilities (20NIS per hour) and free parking are available, and rates include use of the kitchen and a substantial Israeli breakfast in good company.

Publo (Norem) B&B (☎ 866 5656; **e** info@ norem.israel.net; **w** www.norem.israel.net; 27-29 Nordau St; dorm beds/singles/doubles US$20/40/55), on the corner of Hayim St, is a funky sort of place right in the heart of the Hadar district. The action focuses on the pub and Internet café (25NIS per hour) downstairs. Free parking is available, but there's no guest kitchen.

St Charles Hospice (☎ 855 3705, fax 851 4919; Jaffa Rd; singles/doubles US$35/60), with a lovely garden, is owned by the Latin Patriarchate and run by the Catholic Rosary Sisters. Rooms all have fans and private showers and rates include a good breakfast. The only drawback is the 10pm curfew.

Carmel HI Hostel (☎ 853 1944, fax 853 2516; dorm beds/singles/doubles 85/162/224NIS) is inconveniently located southwest of the city. Take the hourly bus No 43 from the central bus station (via Hof HaCarmel train station) or the half-hourly bus No 44A or 3A from the Hof HaCarmel train station.

Beit Shalom Hotel (☎ 837 7481, fax 837 2443; 110 HaNassi Ave; singles/doubles US$60/84), in the Carmel district, is a basic but comfortable Lutheran 'evangelical guesthouse' (in summer there's a minimum three-night stay). Rates include breakfast, and rooms all have air-con, private bathroom and phone, but there's no TV. Dinner is available for an additional US$10. From the central bus station, take bus No 22 or 37.

Places to Eat

Around the HaNevi'im St end of HeHalutz St, you'll find a good range of excellent felafel and shwarma, as well as bakeries selling sweet pastries, doughnuts, sticky buns and other delights. The other good felafel area is Allenby Rd, around HaZiyonut Blvd. **Avraham's** (☎ 852 5029; 36 Allenby Rd) claims to be Haifa's 'King of Felafel'. Around Kikar Paris a couple of cheap places also do felafel

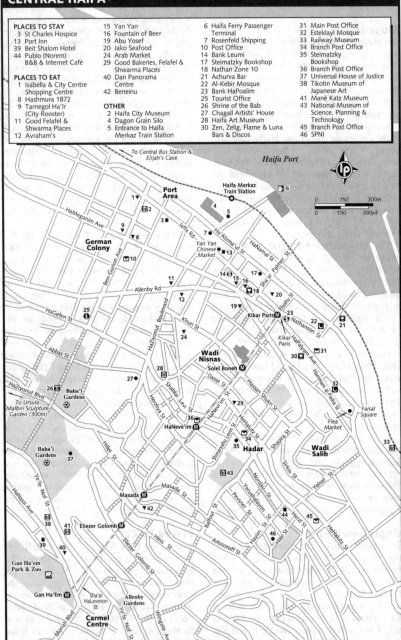

CENTRAL HAIFA

PLACES TO STAY
3 St Charles Hospice
13 Port Inn
39 Beit Shalom Hotel
44 Publo (Norem)
 B&B & Internet Café

PLACES TO EAT
1 Isabella & City Centre
 Shopping Centre
8 Hashmura 1872
9 Tarnegol Ha'Ir
 (City Rooster)
11 Good Felafel &
 Shwarma Places
12 Avraham's

15 Yan Yan
16 Fountain of Beer
19 Abu Yosef
20 Jako Seafood
24 Arab Market
29 Good Bakeries, Felafel &
 Shwarma Places
40 Dan Panorama
 Centre
42 Beneinu

OTHER
2 Haifa City Museum
4 Dagon Grain Silo
5 Entrance to Haifa
 Merkaz Train Station

6 Haifa Ferry Passenger
 Terminal
7 Rosenfeld Shipping
10 Post Office
14 Bank Leumi
17 Steimatzky Bookshop
18 Nathan Zone 10
21 Achurva Bar
22 Al-Kebir Mosque
23 Bank HaPoalim
25 Tourist Office
26 Shrine of the Bab
27 Chagall Artists' House
28 Haifa Art Museum
30 Zen, Zelig, Flame & Luna
 Bars & Discos

31 Main Post Office
32 Esteklayl Mosque
33 Railway Museum
34 Branch Post Office
35 Steimatzky
 Bookshop
36 Branch Post Office
37 Universal House of Justice
38 Tikotin Museum of
 Japanese Art
41 Mané Katz Museum
43 National Museum of
 Science, Planning &
 Technology
45 Branch Post Office
46 SPNI

and shwarma, as well as soups, hummus, grilled meat and offal. Nordau St and the rest of Hadar boast a few pleasant cafés and pastry shops, but the best coffee in town is served at **Greg Coffee** (☎ 837 1670; 3 Hayam St), high up in Carmel Centre.

Tarnegol Ha'Ir (City Rooster; ☎ 855 2151; 22 Ben-Gurion Ave; dishes 29-38NIS; open 11.30am-midnight) is the place to go for chicken; the sign is in Hebrew only, but the pictures on the front give it away. Here you'll find salads, chicken kebabs, chicken soup and chicken parts of all kinds.

Abu Yosef (☎ 866 3723; 1 HaMeganim Ave; dishes 15-25NIS) is an informal but friendly and excellent-value Middle Eastern option, where you'll find superb hummus, salads, pickles, grills and other local fare.

Yan Yan (☎ 855 7878; 28 HaMeganim Ave; main dishes 35-50NIS; open noon-11pm daily) is an exceptionally friendly place serving excellent Chinese and Vietnamese fare. The Chinese business lunch costs 39.50NIS and in the evening there's a 49NIS all-you-can-eat special.

Jako Seafood (☎ 866 8813; 12 Qehilat Saloniki St; dishes 55-65NIS; open noon-11pm Sun-Thur, noon-8pm Fri & Sat), famous for its seafood, offers excellent value. The prices are good and you can choose between a variety of fish (including salmon, bream, bass, shark, triggerfish and St Peter's fish) and seafood (calamari, crab or shrimp). For 190NIS, it will even rustle up such delicacies as snapper, grouper, sole and lobster.

Fountain of Beer (Nathanson St; dishes 25-55NIS; open noon-5pm Sun-Mon & Wed-Thur, noon-midnight Tues) is a friendly and intimate Haifa institution. The fare is typically heavy, meat-oriented Ashkenazi fare that's strong on the offal. As the name suggests, you can accompany your meal with 12 different kinds of draught beer – or just have the beer.

Beneinu (☎ 852 4155; 49 Hillel St; dishes 25-35NIS; open from 10am-1am Sun-Thur, 10.30am-5pm & 8.30pm-2am Fri, 6pm-2am Sat) is a friendly, laid-back vegetarian place with Tibetan prayer flags outside. It's popular for breakfast, lunch, dinner and late-night snacks, and does healthy breakfasts, soups, salads, crepes and hot sandwiches.

Isabella (☎ 855 2204; City Centre Shopping Centre, cnr Ben-Gurion Ave & Jaffa Rd; dishes 25-75NIS) is a relatively classy Italian-oriented place where you can find anything from simple salads to a range of pizzas and pasta, chicken, veal and steak dishes.

Hashmura 1872 (☎ 855 1872; e info@hashmura.co.il; w www.hashmura.co.il; 15 Ben-Gurion Ave; dishes 42-105NIS) is a classy and recommended splurge in the German Colony. It does a range of pasta, chicken, steak and lamb dishes, but the speciality is seafood. Shrimp, carpaccio (thinly sliced raw fish) or squid starters cost 39NIS to 55NIS, and salmon, bream or mussel mains are 72NIS to 80NIS. A glass floor reveals the extensive wine cellar in the historic 1872 basement, where there's also an atmospheric pub.

For fruit and vegetables, shop at the great little market between Ha'Atzmaut St and Jaffa Rd in the port area. If you're looking for Chinese ingredients, the same family that runs the Yan Yan has a Chinese market two doors from the Port Inn on Jaffa Rd.

Entertainment
For an evening out, locals head for the trendy bars and cafés along Moriah St and environs in Carmel Centre. Most discos are clustered around the Port area and Ha-Palyam Ave, east of Kikar Paris; these include **Zen**, **Zelig**, **Flame**, **Luna** (which has a gay night on Friday) and **Achurva** (cover charge 50NIS, discount for students; open midnight-morning Thur night). Most of the gay bars and cafés are concentrated uphill from Hadar along Hillel and Masada Sts.

The Bear (☎ 838 1703; e hagi_s@bears-pub.co.il; 135 HaNassi Ave; pub meals 25-75NIS; open 11am-3am Sun-Tues & Thur, 11am-4am Wed & Fri, 5pm-3am Sat) is one of only two Irish-style pubs in Israel, and it's a winner. The prices are far from modest, but the friendly atmosphere, 12 types of draught beer and the various bear, pelican and toucan murals are certainly endearing. For meals, you can choose between salads, sandwiches, chicken, goose, steak and seafood.

Nathan Zone 10 (☎ 051-309872; 10 Nathanson St; cover charge 50NIS; open 11pm-morning Thurs & Sat) is a weird and wonderful pub and disco housed in a historic cave-like room with a bizarre array of original artwork on the walls and ceiling. On Thursday, it caters to the Arab community; Saturday is gay night. On the first Sunday of each month, it holds an Arab cultural night with singing, theatre and poetry from 9pm until morning.

Getting There & Away

Air flights with **Arkia** (☎ 864 3371; 80 Ha'Atzma'ut St) connect Haifa airport with Eilat, Tel Aviv and Jerusalem.

Bus Haifa is currently changing its bus-transport system to accommodate a greater traffic volume. The **central bus station** (Ha-Haganah Ave) will handle city buses and connecting buses to intercity terminals at the eastern and southern ends of town. At the time of writing, most intercity buses still use the main terminal, but the southern terminal at Hof HaCarmel (adjacent to the train station of the same name) was just getting started. The eastern terminal at Lev HaMifratz won't be far behind.

During the day, buses depart every 20 minutes for Tel Aviv (21.50NIS, 90 minutes), while there's an hourly service to Jerusalem (34NIS, two hours), with extra buses at peak travel times. Heading north, buses No 271 and 272 (express) go to Nahariya (13.50NIS, 45 to 70 minutes) via Akko, and buses No 251 and 252 (express) stop at Akko (10NIS, 30 to 50 minutes).

Train Haifa has three train stations: Haifa Merkaz, near the port; Bat Galim, adjacent to the central bus station (accessible via the passage from platform 34); and Hof HaCarmel, at the new southern bus terminal. From Haifa Merkaz, trains depart roughly hourly for Tel Aviv (45NIS, 90 minutes) via Netanya (20NIS, one hour), and north to Nahariya (13.50NIS, 45 minutes) via Akko (11.50NIS, 30 minutes).

Ferry For information on travelling to and from Cyprus and Greece by ferry, see the Sea & River section in the Getting There & Away chapter.

Getting Around

Israel's only underground, the **Carmelit** (☎ 837 6861; single 4.80NIS; open 6am-10pm Sun-Thur, 6am-3pm Fri), connects Kikar Paris with Carmel Centre, via the Hadar district. Visitors can ride to the top and see the city sights on a leisurely downhill stroll.

DRUZE VILLAGES

The dusty but friendly Druze villages of **Isfiya** and **Daliyat al-Karmel**, on the slopes of Mt Carmel, have popular high-street bazaars

where you'll find inexpensive Indian clothing and trinkets. From the central bus station in Haifa, you can visit on a half-day trip on bus No 192 (10NIS, one hour), which makes three afternoon runs daily from Sunday to Friday. Alternatively, take a service taxi (10NIS, 30 minutes) from Eliyahu St, between Kikar Paris and Ha'Atzmaut St; they leave all day until about 5pm.

CAESAREA   קיסריה
☎ 04

Founded by Herod the Great, Caesarea's world-class archaeological sites stretch for around 3km along the Mediterranean coastline, and its bright, upmarket housing developments continue to attract Israel's rich and famous. The central attraction of **Caesarea National Park** (☎ 636 1358; adult/child 20/ 10NIS; open 8am-5pm daily) is the walled **Crusader city**, with its citadel and harbour. Beyond the walls to the north stretch the beachfront remains of an impressive Roman aqueduct. To the south lies a heavily reconstructed **Roman amphitheatre**, which serves as a modern-day concert venue.

Immediately south of the amphitheatre is a free beach, but heed the 'No Bathing' signs, which identify waters polluted by nearby industry.

Places to Stay & Eat

Free camping on the beach is possible, but theft is common.

Grushka B&B (☎ 638 9810, 054-799776, fax 638 0580; e gruska@netvision.net.il; w www.uniqo.com/binyamina; 28 Hameyasdim St, Binyamina; singles & doubles US$60-75, plus US$20 per child) is your best bet in the area. This friendly Dutch-and-Israeli-run B&B offers several comfortable rooms as well as a quiet cottage and a fully equipped villa for family and business groups. It's just a seven-minute walk from the Binyamina train station, and rates include cable TV, kitchen facilities, and a free shuttle to the ruins at Caesarea. Breakfast costs 25NIS.

Caesarea Garden (☎ 626 4644, fax 626 4645; e caeswine@zahav.net.il; w www.caesariacellars.co.il; dishes 35-55NIS), beside the statue garden opposite the national park citadel entrance, is a wine cellar and classy restaurant where you'll enjoy a very pleasant lunch or dinner.

Getting There & Away

From Tel Aviv or Netanya, take any bus along the coastal road towards Khadera, where you can disembark and hope to connect with bus No 76 to Caesarea. Coming from Haifa, get off at the Caesarea intersection and hike the last 3.5km to the site. Alternatively, take the train to Binyamina (☎ 638 8007) from Tel Aviv (20NIS, 45 minutes) or Haifa (16.50NIS, 30 minutes) and look for a taxi to take you the last 7km.

BEIT SHE'ARIM   בית שערים
☎ 04

A pleasant day trip from Haifa, the archaeological site of Beit She'arim, 19km southeast of Haifa, includes a network of burial caves and 2nd-century ruins. To get there, use bus No 338 from Haifa to Kiryat Tivon.

AKKO   עכו عكا
☎ 04

Few of the world's cities are as timeless as Akko, the stonewalled fortress by the sea. After enjoying a long and varied history under Alexander the Great, the Egyptians and the Romans, Akko came to prominence as the Crusader city of Acre.

During the Jewish immigration of the 1930s, it served as a hotbed of Arab hostility, and in the end the Jews left Old Akko to the Arabs and set about developing a 'new city' outside its historic walls. As a result, Akko has avoided modern development, and while the rest of Israel scrambles to package its history for tourists, Akko soldiers on as an oblivious – and genuine – remnant from the past. Akko's historic homes house families rather than artists, and in the souq and on the quays, merchants and fisher-folk carry on pretty much as they have for several thousand years.

Orientation & Information

From the bus and train stations, it's roughly a 20-minute walk to Old Akko. From the bus station, exit to the left on Derekh HaArba'a and continue one long block to the traffic lights. There, turn right (west) onto Ben Ami St. After two blocks (including the pedestrianised shopping centre), turn left onto Weizmann St and you'll see the city walls ahead. From the train station, turn left on David Remez St, then right on Herzl St; after a block, you'll come out on Derekh

HaArba'a one block north of the bus station. Turn left there and follow the bus station instructions to the Old City.

The **tourist office** (☎ 991 2171, fax 991 9418; 1 Weizmann St; open 9am-6pm Sun-Thur, 8.30am-2.30pm Fri, 9am-6pm Sat) is north of the 'Festival Garden', inside the cave-like walled compound of the Crusader citadel.

Old Akko

Through walls built by Ahmed Pasha al-Jazzar in 1799, visitors enter the predominantly Arab enclave of Old Akko. Its northwestern corner is secured by Al-Jazzar's Citadel, which was reconstructed on the foundations first laid out by the 13th-century Christian Crusaders. The fortress is now home to the **Museum of Underground Prisoners**, which is dedicated to the Jewish resistance during the British Mandate.

The **Al-Jazzar Mosque**, with its green, distinctly Turkish dome and minaret, is the dominant element on the Akko skyline. Across the street from the mosque is the entrance to the Crusaders' **Subterranean Crusader City** (☎ 995 6151; adult/child 25/18NIS; open 8.30am-4.15pm Sun-Thurs & Sat, 8.30am-2pm Fri), a haunting series of vaulted halls that lie 8m below the street level. At one time, they served as the headquarters of the crusading Knights Hospitallers. Admission also includes entry to the **Hammam al-Pasha** (Municipal Museum), housed in the 1780 bathhouse built by Al-Jazzar, which remained in use until the 1940s.

As you exit, follow the alley south into the souq, which is the Old City's main marketplace. Beyond it lies the **Khan al-Umdan**, once a grand khan (caravanserai) that served the camel trains carrying grain from the hinterlands, and above its courtyard rises an Ottoman **clock tower**. En route to the harbour, don't miss the amazing **Templar Crusader Tunnel** (adult/child 10/7NIS; open 8am-5.10pm Sat-Thur, 8am-2.30pm Sat), an underground passageway that follows a historic water conduit.

The original **sea walls** date from the 12th century, but were refurbished in the 18th century by the ubiquitous Al-Jazzar. Throughout the day and evening, **Malkat Akko** (☎ 991 0606, 050-551136) runs tourist cruises from the end of the breakwater.

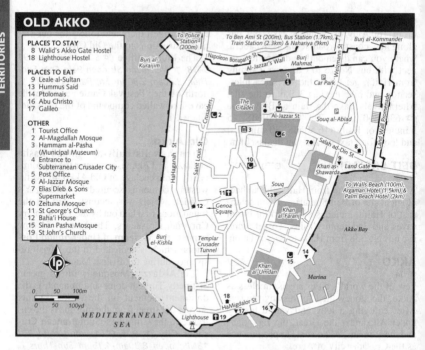

OLD AKKO

PLACES TO STAY
8   Walid's Akko Gate Hostel
18 Lighthouse Hostel

PLACES TO EAT
9   Leale al-Sultan
13 Hummus Said
14 Ptolomais
16 Abu Christo
17 Galileo

OTHER
1   Tourist Office
2   Al-Magdallah Mosque
3   Hammam al-Pasha
     (Municipal Museum)
4   Entrance to
     Subterranean Crusader City
5   Post Office
6   Al-Jazzar Mosque
7   Elias Dieb & Sons
     Supermarket
10 Zeituna Mosque
11 St George's Church
12 Baha'i House
15 Sinan Pasha Mosque
19 St John's Church

Map labels: To Police Station (200m); Burj al-Kuraijim; To Ben Ami St (200m), Bus Station (1.7km), Train Station (2.3km) & Nahariya (9km); Burj al-Kommander; Napoleon Bonaparte St; Al-Jazzar's Wall; Burj Mahmat; Car Park; The Citadel; Al-Jazzar St; Souq al-Abiad; Salah ad-Din St; Crusaders St; Saint Louis St; HaHaganah St; Khan as-Shawarda; Land Gate; Land Wall Promenade; Weizmann St; To Walls Beach (100m), Argaman Hotel (1.5km) & Palm Beach Hotel (2km); Souq; Genoa Square; Khan al-Faranj; Akko Bay; Burj el-Kishla; Templar Crusader Tunnel; Khan al-Umdan; Marina; HaMigdalor St; MEDITERRANEAN SEA; Lighthouse

Scale: 0 50 100m / 0 50 100yd

A worthwhile site just outside new Akko is the **Beit Lohamei HaGeta'ot Museum** (☎ 995 8052; admission 20NIS; open 9am-4pm Sun-Thur), which commemorates the ghetto uprisings, Jewish resistance and Allied assistance during the Nazi Holocaust. Despite the depressing theme, it presents a hopeful picture of this tragic period. From May to September, it's open two hours later.

Places to Stay
Walid's Akko Gate Hostel (☎ 991 0410, fax 981 5530; Salah ad-Din St; singles/doubles 160/200NIS) is a lovely and friendly option with all the creature comforts: private baths, fridges and cable TV. The attached restaurant does Arabic meals (from 24NIS) and in good times, the management can organise tours to the Golan Heights (170NIS), Rosh HaNikra (70NIS) and other sites around northern Israel.

Lighthouse Hostel (☎ 991 1982; fax 981 5530; 11/175 HaGana St; dorm beds 30NIS), run by the same management as Walid's Akko Gate Hostel, is housed in an old Turkish mansion with a great location near the harbour lighthouse. Guests have use of the kitchen facilities.

Argaman Hotel (☎ 991 6691, fax 991 6690; singles/doubles US$60/97), outside the Old City on Purple Beach, is a shabby complex, but it has free access to the sand and a great view of the walled city.

Palm Beach Hotel (☎ 987 7777, fax 991 0434; e palmbeach@netvision.net.il; w www .palmbeach.co.il; singles US$95/160, doubles US$124-200), adjacent to the Argaman Hotel, has much better facilities, including a pool, sauna, tennis court, health spa and water sports. Book through the Internet for a 10% discount.

Places to Eat
For cheap eating there are several **felafel places** around the junction of Salah ad-Din and Al-Jazzar Sts. In the rather trendy **Leale-al Sultan** coffee shop, inside the Khan as-Shawarda, local youths sip Turkish coffee and suck on *sheeshas* (water pipes). Self-catering supplies are available at **Elias Dieb & Sons** (Salah ad-Din St), a great little cave-like supermarket opposite Souq al-Abiad; there's no English sign.

In the souq, don't miss **Hummus Said** (*open 6am-2pm daily*), which is well known only to locals and does some of the best hummus you'll ever taste. For 12NIS, you'll get salads, pickles, pitta and a big glob of hummus with *fuul* or garlic.

The imagined romance of a moonlit meal in a scene straight out of the Arabian Nights provides a distinct advantage to the touristy eateries around the lighthouse. Most of the places here are open daily for tour-group lunches from 11am to mid-afternoon and then serve dinner until at least 10pm. Fish is the obvious choice, but despite its ready availability, you'll pay at least 40NIS for seafood dishes.

Abu Christo (☎ 991 0065; *dishes from 45NIS*) is pricey but excellent, and is probably the best of the lot.

Galileo (☎ 991 4620; *176/11 HaMigdalor St*) is an alternative, built into the sea wall almost opposite the Lighthouse Hostel.

Ptolomais (☎ 981 8280; *dishes 45-50NIS*), on the harbour, provides a more laid-back and cosy ambience. The food is filling, but generally unspectacular.

Getting There & Away

Akko's bus terminal and train station lie about a 20-minute walk from the main entrance to the Old City. From Haifa (10NIS, 30 to 50 minutes), buses No 252 and 272 depart frequently, as do the slower buses No 251 and 271. From Akko, buses No 270, 271 and 272 (express) run north to Nahariya (7NIS, 15 to 25 minutes). The most pleasant way to travel between Akko and Haifa (11.50NIS, 30 minutes) or on to Nahariya (6.50NIS, 15 minutes), however, is by train along the beachfront railway.

NAHARIYA   נהריה
☎ 04

The appeal of the quiet seaside resort of Nahariya lies solely in its lovely beaches. This is about as lethargic as Israel gets, so don't come looking for round-the-clock action. You can choose between the **Galei Galil Beach** (*admission 15NIS*) north of town or the free **Sokalov Beach** to the south. The local **tourist office** (*HaGa'aton Blvd*) is on the ground floor of the municipality building, west of the bus station.

Hotel Rosenblatt (☎ 992 0051, fax 992 8121; **e** jael@walla.co.il; 59 Weizmann St;

singles US$40-55, doubles US$60-75), on the corner of HaGa'aton Blvd, is the most economical accommodation option. In addition to a lovely green garden, there's a pool, restaurant and takeaway, and all rooms have cable TV and air-con. For vegetarian meals, check out **Kapulsky**, where the main street, HaGa'aton Blvd meets the beach.

Buses No 270, 271 and 272 (express) run roughly every 25 minutes (until 10.30pm) to Akko (7NIS, 15 to 25 minutes), with the 271 and 272 services continuing to Haifa (10.50NIS, 45 to 70 minutes).

ROSH HANIKRA   ראש הניקרה
☎ 04

Right on the Lebanese border, the wondrous sea caves at Rosh HaNikra were originally carved by nature but were enlarged by the British for a railway and by the Israelis to improve visitor access. The 10km road from Nahariya ends at the **Rosh HaNikra Tourist Centre** (☎ 985 7109) from where a cable car (*adult/child 36/28NIS; open 8.30am-4pm Sun-Thur, 8.30am-5pm Fri-Sat*) descends steeply to the caves. Alternatively, find the dim walking track that leaves the main highway about 300m south of the tourist centre; it leads through a former rail tunnel to the caves.

Places to Stay & Eat

For meals, there's only a simple **tourist café** at the top of the cable car.

Rosh HaNikra Holiday Village (☎ 982 3112, fax 952 0528; camp sites/rooms 40/165NIS per person) is housed in the old British Customs Post about 500m south of the cable car. This self-styled health spa also offers a pool, gym (40NIS) and massage (175NIS to 195NIS). Rates include breakfast, but add 40NIS for lunch and 50NIS for dinner.

Akhziv-Land (☎ 982 3219, 054-982325; camp sites per person 80NIS, dorm beds 80-100NIS) is a rustic 'lost-hippie' hideaway. It claims to be a separate state – you'll even get a passport stamp – and the rambling property takes in not only a beautiful stretch of **Akhziv Beach** (national park fee 25NIS), but also a desultory **museum** (admission 10NIS) of archaeological finds from all over Israel. Volunteer landscapers, cleaners and builders can arrange free accommodation in exchange for their work and expertise.

Getting There & Away

From Nahariya, buses No 20 and 22 run three times daily to Rosh HaNikra (7NIS, 15 minutes). Other more frequent services pass Rosh HaNikra junction, which is a 3km walk from the caves.

Galilee   הגליל

With its lush scenery and religious heritage, Galilee's green valleys, verdant forests, fertile farmland and, of course, the Sea of Galilee, provide relief from the drier lands to the south. For Christians, this is serious Bible territory: it was here that Jesus grew up, gathered his disciples, preached one of history's most enigmatic sermons, multiplied loaves and fishes, walked on water – and even turned it into wine, when necessary (see the boxed text 'Jesus Christ' later in this section).

NAZARETH   נצרת الناصرة
☎ 04

As the childhood home of Jesus, and the place where he preached, taught and worked in his father's carpentry shop, the timeless but scruffy Arab town of Nazareth is one of Christendom's most revered sites. While modern Nazareth may not fulfil everyone's expectations, it's certainly worth a visit, if only for half a day.

Orientation & Information

Most sites of pilgrim interest are concentrated on Paul VI St and El-Bishara St (also called Annunciation or Casa Nova St). On El-Bishara St, just above the Paul VI intersection, is the helpful **tourist office** (☎ 657 0555, fax 657 3078; open 8.30am-5pm Mon-Fri, 8.30am-2pm Sat).

Things to See

Nazareth's revered **Basilica of the Annunciation** (open 8.30am-11.45am & 2pm-5pm Mon-Sat) stands on the site where Catholics believe the Angel Gabriel announced to the Virgin Mary that she would bear the Son of God. Its rather bland 1969 exterior is redeemed by remnants of earlier Crusader and Byzantine churches, and the outdoor collection of 'Madonna and Child' artwork donated by Catholic communities around the world. The pieces from Southeast Asia and Eastern Europe are especially good.

At the **Sisters of Nazareth Convent** (open 8.30am-11.45am & 2pm-5pm Mon-Sat), up the street, you can see one of the best examples of an ancient stone-sealed tomb; it lies under the present courtyard and can only be viewed by appointment. The nearby **Church of St Joseph** (Al-Bishara St; open 8.30am-11.45am daily & 2pm-5pm Mon-Sat), built in 1914, occupies the traditional site of Joseph's carpentry shop, over the

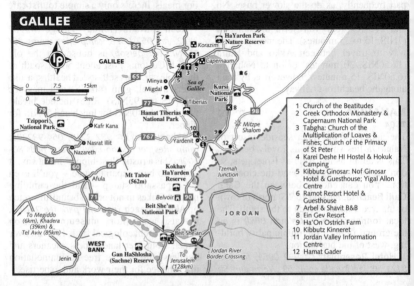

GALILEE

1 Church of the Beatitudes
2 Greek Orthodox Monastery & Capernaum National Park
3 Tabgha: Church of the Multiplication of Loaves & Fishes; Church of the Primacy of St Peter
4 Karei Deshe HI Hostel & Hokuk Camping
5 Kibbutz Ginosar: Nof Ginosar Hotel & Guesthouse; Yigal Allon Centre
6 Ramot Resort Hotel & Guesthouse
7 Arbel & Shavit B&B
8 Ein Gev Resort
9 Ha'On Ostrich Farm
10 Kibbutz Kinneret
11 Jordan Valley Information Centre
12 Hamat Gader

remains of a medieval church. In pre-Byzantine times, the underground cavern was probably used for grain storage.

The **Al-Balda al-Qadima souq**, west of upper Al-Bishara St, occupies a maze of narrow streets. In its midst sits the **Greek Catholic Church** (open 8.30am-11.45am & 2pm-5pm Mon-Sat), on the site of the synagogue where the young Jesus prayed and taught. The attractive **St Gabriel's Greek Orthodox Church** (open 8am-6pm Mon-Sat) lies about 10 minutes' walk northeast of the basilica, two blocks off Paul VI St. Across Well Square from here is **Mary's Well** (Al-Hanuq St; open 8am-6pm Mon-Sat), which the Greek Orthodox Church claims is the site of the Annunciation. Beside it at the **Cactus gift shop** is a wonderful **ancient bathhouse** (☎/fax 657 8539; adult/child 12/8NIS; open 9am-7pm Mon-Sat), privately excavated in 1993, which utilised water from Mary's Well.

Those who just can't imagine Jesus amid Nazareth's modern bustle may want to head for the worthwhile **Nazareth Village** (☎ 645 6042, fax 655 9295; e info@nazarethvillage .com; w www.nazarethvillage.com; adult/child 26/20NIS; open 9am-5pm Mon-Sat). This nonprofit project, staffed by period actors, reconstructs everyday life and commerce in Nazareth of 2000 years ago. It's a 15-minute walk due west from the basilica, just beyond Al-Wadi al-Jawani St.

Places to Stay

Sisters of Nazareth Convent (☎ 655 4304, fax 646 0741; dorm beds 36NIS, singles/doubles US$28/46), with dormitories and 30 private rooms, is by far the best accommodation in town. Kitchen facilities are available, private room rates include breakfast (US$4 otherwise), and other meals cost US$9 each. The door, marked 'Réligieuses de Nazareth', is closed for security reasons, so you'll have to ring the bell. Reception closes at 9.30pm, but if you're pre-booked (which is wise, in any case), they may wait a bit later.

Casa Nova Hospice (☎ 645 6660, fax 657 9630; El-Bishara St; singles/doubles US$39/54), opposite the basilica, caters mainly for Italian pilgrimage groups. Advance bookings are essential, as the hospice may not open during low periods. Breakfast is included in the rates.

Places to Eat

In addition to the Christian hospices, the city centre has a couple of decent places to eat.

Astoria Restaurant (☎ 657 7965; cnr Paul VI & El-Bishara Sts) is a reasonable place for hummus (14NIS), shwarma (17NIS) and inexpensive beer.

El Sheikh (☎ 656 7664; Iksal St; open 7am-2pm daily), in a street full of automobile workshops, enjoys a winning reputation for its hummus. Don't miss the wonderful felafel and shwarma stand next door, which is one of the country's best.

Mahroum's Sweets (cnr El-Bishara & Paul VI Sts) is renowned as the best place in town for baklava and other honey-soaked Arabic-style sweets and pastries.

Holy Land Restaurant (☎ 657 5415; 6168 St; set menus US$10), with exotic handmade tiles and lots of old artefacts, is housed in a cave-like 1860 building that once served as Nazareth's first sesame mill, and, during WWI, as a German and Turkish supply depot. It's friendly, but caters mainly for tour groups, so you're normally limited to a set menu.

Alternatively, pick up fresh produce from the market or check out the groceries and bakeries along Paul VI St.

Getting There & Away

There's no main bus terminal in Nazareth. Bus No 431 for Tiberias (15NIS, 45 minutes) departs hourly from the Hamishbir department store on Paul VI St; over the road, buses leave for Haifa (17NIS, 45 minutes) with about the same regularity. To Akko (15.50NIS, 45 minutes), buses stop opposite the Egged information office. For Tel Aviv (32NIS, two hours), take bus No 823 or 824. For reaching Nazareth from other towns around the country, the times, prices and frequencies are the same.

Service taxis to Tiberias leave from in front of Hamishbir department store. For Haifa and Tel Aviv, they leave from the Paz petrol station.

TZIPPORI
☎ 04

The impressive archaeological site **Tzippori (or Sepphoris) National Park** (☎ 656 8262; admission 20NIS; open 8am-5pm daily in summer, 8am-4pm daily in winter) makes a wonderful day trip. The 289m hill, Tzippori, was first settled by the Hasmoneans in the 2nd century BC, but in 63 BC it was conquered by the Roman general Pompeii and served as the Roman capital of Galilee through the reign of Herod. Today it brims with ruins, including original colonnaded roadways, an amphitheatre, a Roman villa with some lovely mosaic floors, a Crusader citadel and a haunting underground system of cisterns and aqueducts. Allow at least three hours to catch the highlights.

Buses between Nazareth and Akko stop at Tzippori Junction, about 4km from the site. From there you'll have to walk or hitch.

MEGIDDO מגידו
☎ 04

Better known as Armageddon (in Hebrew Har Megiddo, or Mt Megiddo), the site that St John predicted would host the last great battle on earth is now preserved in **Megiddo National Park** *(open 8am-5pm Sat-Thur, 8am-4pm Fri)*. Ongoing excavations here have unearthed evidence of 20 distinct historical phases dating from 10,000 to 400 BC. The most enigmatic ruins are those of the 10th-century-BC fortified city, originally built by King Solomon, and the 9th-century-BC water system, which connected the city with a natural spring. The several excellent visitor-centre models depict how it must have looked.

The site lies 2km north of Megiddo Junction, west of the Haifa road, and is best accessed on the Haifa-Afula bus. Alternatively, take the half-hourly Tel-Aviv–Tiberias bus, get off at Megiddo Junction and walk or hitch the last 2km up the hill.

BEIT SHE'AN בית שאן
☎ 04

The tidy town of Beit She'an makes a great stop along the scenic Jordan River Hwy route between Jerusalem and Tiberias, but check the latest security situation before following this route.

Bet She'an National Park *(adult/child 20/ 10NIS; open 8am-4pm daily in winter, 8am-5pm daily in summer)* features Israel's best-preserved Roman amphitheatre, as well as extensive and ongoing excavations, which so far have revealed a temple, basilica, nymphaeum, a colonnaded Roman street and 0.5 hectare of elaborate, mosaic-floored Byzantine baths. There's also a smaller amphitheatre in the town centre, and several inviting walking tracks along the lush riverfront.

Buses run frequently between Jerusalem and Tiberias, via Beit She'an, and there are also regular bus services to and from Afula.

TIBERIAS טבריה
☎ 04

As the only town beside the Sea of Galilee, Tiberias is the obvious base for visiting the lakeside beauty spots and points of interest. With its mix of natural spas and tombs of venerated sages, the town invites observant Jews to combine treatment of the body with purification of the soul, while the less observant can partake of the town's lakeside wining, dining and nightlife.

Orientation & Information
The helpful **tourist office** *(☎ 672 5666; 9 Ha-Banim St; open 9am-1pm & 2pm-4pm Sun-Thur, 8.30am-12.30pm Fri)*, in the open space labelled 'archaeological park' on the town map, provides the latest visitor information. A free city walking tour departs from the Sheraton Hotel on Saturday at 10am.

Things to See
The dignified but incongruous mid-18th-century **Al-Omri Mosque** is one of the few historic structures in Tiberias' Old Town; a second mosque, **Jama al-Bahr** (1880), now stands forlorn and abandoned. The enigmatic **St Peter's Church** *(mass 6pm Mon-Sat, 8.30pm Sun)*, on the waterfront promenade, was originally built by 12th-century Crusaders, but the present structure dates from 1870. The boat-shaped nave is a nod to St Peter's piscatorial profession.

Part of a modern waterfront development, **The Galilee Experience** *(☎ 672 3620; adult/student 35/26NIS; open 1pm-10pm Sun-Thur, 1pm-4pm Fri)* presents an hourly audiovisual programme in 12 languages, recounting the historical, geographical and political story of Galilee from Abraham to Jesus, Napoleon and Moshe Dayan.

Uphill from the centre, the **Tomb of Rabbi Moshe Ben Maimon** *(Ben Zakkai St)* is the final resting place of the Spanish physician, also known as Maimonides or Rambam, who worked in the court of the Muslim ruler Saladin. This revered rabbi, who died in 1204, was one of 12th-century Egypt's most

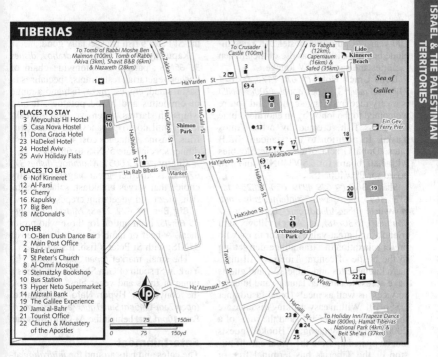

TIBERIAS

To Tomb of Rabbi Moshe Ben Maimon (100m), Tomb of Rabbi Akiva (3km), Shavit B&B (6km) & Nazareth (28km)

To Crusader Castle (100m)

To Tabgha (12km), Capernaum (16km) & Safed (35km)

Lido
Kinneret
Beach

Sea of Galilee

Ein Gev
Ferry Pier

Shimon Park

Market

Midrahov

Archaeological Park

City Walls

To Holiday Inn/Trapeze Dance Bar (800m), Hamat Tiberias National Park (4km) & Beit She'an (37km)

PLACES TO STAY
3 Meyouhas HI Hostel
5 Casa Nova Hostel
11 Dona Gracia Hotel
23 HaDekel Hotel
24 Hostel Aviv
25 Aviv Holiday Flats

PLACES TO EAT
6 Nof Kinneret
12 Al-Farsi
15 Cherry
16 Kapulsky
17 Big Ben
18 McDonald's

OTHER
1 O-Ben Dush Dance Bar
2 Main Post Office
4 Bank Leumi
7 St Peter's Church
8 Al-Omri Mosque
9 Steimatzky Bookshop
10 Bus Station
13 Hyper Neto Supermarket
14 Mizrahi Bank
19 The Galilee Experience
20 Jama al-Bahr
21 Tourist Office
22 Church & Monastery of the Apostles

0   75   150m
0   75   150yd

highly regarded sages. Legend has it that before his death in Cairo, he instructed followers to load his remains onto a camel and bury him wherever the camel expired. The beast was apparently drawn to Tiberias.

In the hills about 6km west of town, you'll find one of Israel's most incredible vistas at the lovely **Arbel Cliffs**. This lofty vantage point affords superb views of the surrounding rock as well as the Sea of Galilee below, a patchwork of fields and a distant view to the hilltop town of Safed. Unfortunately, access is difficult, as there's only one inconvenient daily bus in either direction. Prospective visitors who aren't staying in Arbel will probably have to hitch.

Organised Tours
Wooden sailing boats (☎ 672 3007, 050-217416) run sightseeing cruises on the Sea of Galilee and for pre-booked groups, provide ferry services between Tiberias, Tabgha and Ein Gev.

Places to Stay
Hostel Aviv (☎ 671 2272, fax 671 2272; Achiva St/HaNoter 2; dorm beds 30-45NIS,

doubles 120NIS, holiday flats US$50) is probably the best budget option in town. Both the dorms and private rooms have showers, fridges, air-con and cable TV, and some have private balconies with lake views. The Aviv holiday flats in the adjacent building also feature kitchenettes and private balconies, and some have Jacuzzi tubs. Breakfast costs 20NIS and top-quality bicycles can be hired for 30NIS to 40NIS per day.

HaDekel Hotel (☎/fax 672 5318, 052-417699; 1 HaGalil St; dorm beds/doubles 25/100NIS), which is a bit scruffy, offers four-bed dorms and private doubles, all with air-con, fridge and showers. Anyone can hire a top-quality bicycle here for just 30NIS per day.

Meyouhas HI Hostel (☎ 672 1775, fax 672 0372; e tiberias@ihya.org.il; 2 Jordan St; dorm beds/singles/doubles 78/160/224NIS), in a 180-year-old stone building, is one of Israel's most pleasant HI hostels. All rates include breakfast.

Casa Nova Hostel (☎ 571 2281, 051-342540, fax 671 2278; 1 HaYarden St; dorm beds/singles/doubles US$13/35/50), adjacent to St Peter's Church, is a clean and quiet 100-year-old pilgrims' hostel. All rates include breakfast as well as use of the kitchen facilities and satellite-TV lounge.

Dona Gracia Hotel *(☎ 671 7176, fax 671 7175; HaPrahim 3; singles/doubles 200/300NIS)* is a very nice mid-range option, and you're welcomed to the lobby by an enormous blue fibreglass fish, created by artist Amos Yaskil. In addition to the standard B&B rates, Dona Gracia offers singles/doubles with half board for 250/340NIS and full board for 290/400NIS.

Shavit B&B *(☎ 679 4919, 050-928257, fax 673 3695;* e *shavit52@internet-zahav.net;* w *www.members.tripod.com/~shavit/; singles/ doubles US$30/48)*, in Arbel village, is a friendly and great-value treat for those who prefer relaxation in a tranquil garden setting to the bustle of central Tiberias. All units have kitchenettes and cable TV, and guests have access to parking, laundry and Internet services, as well as meals (breakfast/dinner US$6/10). Within easy walking distance are the dramatic Arbel Cliffs and the ruins of a 2000-year-old synagogue. Booked guests can be picked up from the Arbel cut-off bus stop or the Tiberias bus terminal free of charge.

Places to Eat

With a parade of felafel and shwarma stands on HaYarden St, Tiberias is great for fans of Middle Eastern fast food. The cheapest sit-down dining is at the HaBanim St restaurants and cafés at the top end of the *midrahov* (pedestrian mall).

At the several waterfront restaurants, you can grab a table overlooking the water and perhaps even see relatives of the fish on your plate as they flit and glide through the shallows below. For a fast-food fix, check out the remarkable **McDonald's**, festooned with bougainvillea, which enjoys a leafy lake view.

Al-Farsi *(☎ 050-384348; cnr HaGalil & HaYarkon Sts; snacks 14NIS)* seems a bit aloof, but has good prices for a range of local staples, including shashlik, liver and shwarma.

Nof Kinneret *(☎ 679 2285; cnr Promenade & HaYarden St; main dishes 48-85NIS)* isn't cheap, but there's a great view over the lake and cat lovers can commune with all the stray felines that are attracted to the fishy smells. The salads are great and you can

choose between lots of grills and fish dishes; the St Peter's fish is especially good.

Kapulsky *(☎ 672 0341; Midrahov; dishes 35-65NIS)*, part of a nationwide chain of kosher vegetarian restaurants, specialises in pasta, salad, crepes, pizza, fish and a range of omelettes and baked potatoes. It also whips up starters, extensive Israeli breakfasts (until noon), Japanese sushi and stir-fries. Business lunches cost 45NIS and fish dinner specials are 59NIS to 65NIS.

Cherry *(☎ 679 0051; Midrahov; dishes 37-67NIS)* is another great vegetarian/dairy choice that serves breakfast, salads, pasta, fish, pizza and vegetarian crepes.

Big Ben *(☎ 672 2248; Midrahov; dishes 35-65NIS)* is an option for those who prefer meat. A beef or lamb business lunch costs 37NIS; with St Peter's fish, it's 44NIS.

The small **market** *(open Sun-Fri)*, off HaYarkon St south of Gan Shimon Park, sells a range of fruits and vegetables. There's also the convenient **Hyper Neto supermarket** *(open 7am-6.45pm Sun-Thur, 7am-3.30pm Fri, 8am-10pm Sat)* behind the Al-Omri Mosque.

Entertainment

The cafés and bars around the *midrahov* attract crowds on weekend evenings, especially in summer.

O-Ben Dush Dance Bar *(☎ 050-451133; open 10.30am-late Thur-Sat in summer)* features salsa, techno, rumba, samba and disco dancing.

Trapeze Dance Bar *(☎ 052-211666)*, at the Holiday Inn complex, is a popular pub, restaurant and disco.

From the Lido Kinneret Beach, **disco cruises** *(☎ 672 1538)* depart according to demand on Thursday, Friday and Saturday night; in summer, they may also operate on Tuesday. Phone to see what's on.

Getting There & Away

Egged buses *(☎ 672 9222)* depart for Tel Aviv (37NIS, 2½ hours) and Jerusalem (44NIS, three hours) at least hourly from the central bus station. There are also several daily (except Saturday) services to Haifa (24.50NIS, 90 minutes), Nazareth (18.80NIS, 45 minutes), Safed (17.80NIS, one hour), Katzrin (22.50NIS, one or two hours depending on the route taken), Beit She'an (18.80NIS, 40 minutes) and Kiryat Shmona (22.50NIS, 90 minutes).

Outside the bus station and across the grass, a few morning service taxis leave for Nazareth (20NIS, 40 minutes) and occasionally Haifa (20NIS, 40 minutes).

SEA OF GALILEE

Around 21km-long and 55km in circumference, the Sea of Galilee, fed by the Jordan River, lies 212m below sea level and is both a natural beauty site and the source of most of the water supply for Israel & the Palestinian Territories. Using Tiberias as a base, travellers can readily explore the area in a couple of days; lots of people opt to rent a bicycle and pedal around the major sites (most of which aren't accessible by bus).

Information

The **Jordan Valley Information Centre** (☎ 675 2056; open 8.30am-4pm Sun-Thur, 8.30am-2.30pm Fri-Sat), at the shopping centre in Tzemah, provides regional information and direction.

Northwestern Shore

Migdal, 6km north of Tiberias, was the birthplace of Mary Magdalene. The connection is commemorated with a tiny white-domed shrine, overgrown with vegetation, beside a fetid canal near junky Restal Beach.

On Kibbutz Ginosar is the **Yigal Allon Centre** (☎ 672 1495, fax 672 2910; e be talon@netvision.net.il; adult/child 18/14NIS), a museum devoted to the theme 'man in the Galilee'. Its most celebrated exhibit is the skeletal remains of an 8.2m fishing vessel that shrewd tour operators have dubbed 'the Jesus boat'. Discovered in 1986, it has been dated to the time of Christ's ministry.

Tabgha & Capernaum

Generally considered to be the most beautiful and serene of the Christian holy places, **Tabgha** (an Arabic rendition of the Greek *hepta pega*, or 'seven springs') is associated with three salient episodes from the New Testament.

The **Church of the Beatitudes** (open 8am-noon & 2pm-5pm), which commemorates the Sermon on the Mount, sits in a lovely garden about 100m above the lake. The Beatitudes of Jesus are commemorated in stained glass around the dome. The altar of the **Church of the Multiplication of Loaves & Fishes** (open 8.30am-5pm Mon-Sat, 9.45am-

---

Jesus Christ

What's known of the life of Yeshua ben Yusef of Nazareth – better known as Jesus Christ – was written down in the Christian Gospels in the century after his death. It's known that he was born in Bethlehem into a middle-class Jewish family resident in Nazareth. These were turbulent times; the provinces of Judea and Samaria (the present-day West Bank) had recently been conquered by the Roman Empire and political dissent among the local Jews had reached a fevered pitch.

During this period, Jewish agitators frequently delivered soapbox orations protesting Roman rule, and also derided the materialism and decadence of wealthy Jebusites. It's likely that Jesus was such a figure, and that he had his greatest influence in the last three years of his life. In Galilee, he gathered 12 followers and set about preaching to the masses in readily understood parables, performing miracles and establishing his church. While his miracles drew the attention of the people, his growing influence incurred the wrath of the authorities. On orders of the Roman governor of Judea, Pontius Pilate, Jesus was crucified at the age of 33, just outside the city of Jerusalem. According to the Gospels, he arose from the dead after three days and took leave of his followers with a promise to return.

Jesus' followers, who came to be known as Christians, accept that he was the promised Messiah of the Old Testament, while Jews maintain that their Messiah has not yet arrived. Nowadays, ethnic Jews who believe that Jesus was in fact the Messiah are known as Messianic Jews.

5pm Sun), also called the Heptapagon Church, is thought to include the rock where Jesus laid the five loaves and two fishes that multiplied to feed 5000 faithful listeners. In 1932, excavations uncovered some beautiful mosaic floors, including the ubiquitous 'loaves-and-fishes' mosaic. The wonderfully serene **Church of the Primacy of St Peter** (open 8am-noon & 2pm-5pm daily), with its lovely stained glass, was built by Franciscans in 1933 at the site called Mensa Christi. In the 4th century, a now-ruined church was constructed here to commemorate the spot where the resurrected Jesus conferred the church leadership on St Peter.

Capernaum (admission 3NIS; open 8.30am-4.15pm daily), or Kfar Nahum, was the home base of Jesus during the most influential period of his Galilean ministry. An octagonal church hovers over the ruins of a 3rd- or 4th-century synagogue that was built over his lodgings. Further east along the shoreline rises the very pink, domed **Greek Orthodox Monastery**. Just beyond it lies the tranquil **Capernaum National Park**, which has a souvenir shop, lakeside gardens and a boat terminal. **Lake cruises** (25NIS) to Tiberias, Ein Gev and Ginosar are available when there's sufficient demand.

Buses from Tiberias pass by Capernaum Junction (12NIS, 30 minutes), which is a 5km hike or hitch to any of the major sites.

The Eastern Shore

The highlight of the eastern shore of the Sea of Galilee is the **Ein Gev Resort** (see Places to Stay later in this section), with its renowned seafood restaurant. The Kibbutz Ha'On **ostrich farm** was closed at the time of research, but will probably reopen if there's an increase in tourist numbers.

Kursi National Park (☎ 673 1983; adult/child 10/5NIS; open 8am-4pm Sun-Thur, 8am-3pm Fri), designated by the Jewish Talmud as a site for idol worship, was also the place where Jesus cast a contingent of demon spirits into a herd of swine. The beautiful, recently excavated ruins feature an impressive 5th-century Byzantine era monastery.

Hamat Gader

Hamat Gader (☎ 675 1039, fax 675 2745; e office@hamat-gader.com; w www.hamat-gader.com; admission 65NIS Sun-Thur, 75NIS Fri-Sat; open 7am-10pm Mon-Sat, 7am-4pm Sun), which is actually in the Golan Heights, occupies the bottom of a deep valley split by the Jordanian border. Billboard saturation welcomes visitors to this blatantly commercial tourist trap that features Roman bathhouse ruins, hot mineral springs, beauty spas (at an extra charge), a range of ethnic restaurants, a water park, a 'wet dance floor', a parrot show, an aviary and an alligator farm.

From Tiberias, bus No 24 departs Sunday to Thursday at 8.45am and 10.30am, and Friday at 8.30am and 9.30am. On the return trip, buses leave Hamat Gader Sunday to Thursday at noon and 3pm, and Friday at noon and 1pm.

Places to Stay

If you thought camping was an alternative to paying high prices, think again. The many shoreline camping grounds are either run by kibbutzim or private resorts, and serve mainly as venues for family outings with no delusions of economy. There are a few places where you can pitch a tent free of charge, but they lack facilities, and security can be a problem. For information, check with the tourist office at Tzemah.

Hokuk Camping (☎ 671 5441; camp sites 60NIS), at Karei Deshe, is open from April to October; you may want to check out the neglected Sappir archaeological site over the road.

Karei Deshe HI Hostel (☎ 672 0601, fax 672 4818; singles/doubles 165/250NIS), in Tabgha, is a sparkling white facility set in attractive grounds with date palms, eucalyptus trees, a rocky beach and a few peacocks. Meals are available for 39NIS. To get here, take bus No 52 from Tiberias.

Nof Ginosar Hotel & Guesthouse (☎ 670 0311, 670 0300, fax 672 2991; e ginosar@netvision.net.il; w www.ginosar.co.il; singles US$50-88, doubles US$60-110), on Kibbutz Ginosar, provides comfortable lakeside accommodation flanked by gardens and a private beach. It's clearly signposted just off the main road south of Tabgha. The lower rates are for the guesthouse and the higher are for the hotel; add 50% to all rates in summer and during Jewish holidays. Rates include breakfast, and set lunches and dinners are 45NIS each. Nonguests can use the beach for 25NIS.

Ramot Resort Hotel & Guesthouse (☎ 673 2732, fax 679 3590; doubles 125-250NIS), with a great high-level view over the Sea of Galilee, is a scenic good-value option. Low-end rates are for the guesthouse and high-end rates are for the hotel. On weekends and Jewish holidays, add 50% to the normal rates.

Ein Gev (☎ 665 9800, fax 665 9818; e resort@eingev.org.il, ein_gev@eingev.org.il; w www.eingev.co.il; doubles 333-424NIS), on a working agricultural and dairy kibbutz, has 166 units with kitchenettes, air-con and cable TV. The site also features an acclaimed garden restaurant specialising in seafood.

Places to Eat

Outside of Tiberias, all meal options around the Sea of Galilee are associated with

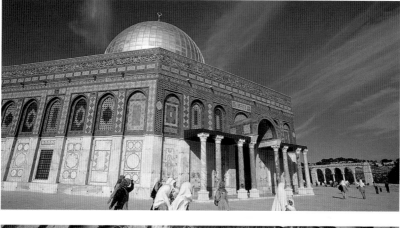

Israel & the Palestinian Territories is a Holy Land for the three great monotheistic religions. In Jerusalem, Judaism's Wailing or Western Wall (top), Islam's Dome of the Rock (middle) and Christ-ianity's Stations of the Cross all attract pilgrims from around the world.

PAUL JOHN DOYLE

MARK WEBSTER

ANDERS BLOMQVIST

Alive or Dead, the sea is never too far away. The harbour at Byblos, Lebanon, home to sea-going traditions since Phoenician times (top); the spangled depths of the Red Sea, Ras Mohammed National Park, Egypt, will enthral (middle); while the action's all on the surface of the Dead Sea, Israel (bottom).

Places to Stay. The best choice is Ein Gev – please see the prior Places to Stay entry.

Getting There & Around

All long-distance access to the Sea of Galilee is via Tiberias. Unfortunately, there's a shortage of bus services from town to other parts of the lakeshore, but the main sites along the relatively level road around the Sea of Galilee are accessible to cyclists in an easy two-day circuit. In Tiberias, anyone can rent an 18-speed mountain bike (30NIS to 40NIS per day) from the Aviv or HaDekel hostels.

SAFED   צפת صفد
☎ 04

The attractive hilltop town of Safed (also spelt Zefat, Tzfat or Tsfat) enjoys a temperate, high-altitude setting and a rich heritage of Jewish mysticism. It makes a pleasant visit on weekdays, but don't under any circumstances turn up during Shabbat, when even the birds are grounded.

Orientation & Information

Safed is spread over a single hilltop, with the bus station on the east side and the old town centre directly opposite on the west side – the hill is scored by Yerushalayim (Jerusalem) St, which makes a complete loop between the two. The **Tourist Office** (☎ 692 0961; open 8am-2pm Sun-Thur) is in the Wolfsson Community Centre.

Things to See

At the hilltop, the pleasant breeze-cooled park and viewpoint **Gan HaMetsuda** was once the site of a Crusader citadel. Central Safed's old quarters slither down from Yerushalayim St, divided by the broad, stiff stairway **Ma'alot Olei HaGardom St**. This sector was developed by the British after the 1929 riots that divided the Arab and Jewish communities.

The **Synagogue Quarter**, accessed via the stairway north of the City Hall, is a traditional Jewish neighbourhood that focuses on **Kikar HaMaganim** (Defenders' Square). Two of the synagogues are worth a visit: the **Ha'Ari Ashkenazi Synagogue** and the **Cairo Synagogue**. Prospective visitors should dress modestly; women should avoid bare ankles or shoulders and cardboard yarmulkes are available to male visitors. Photography is permitted except during Shabbat.

Since the Arab defeat in 1948, the district south of the Ma'alot Olei HaGardom St stairway has served as a deteriorating **artists colony**; currently, much of the local talent is defecting to nearby Rosh Pina. The **General Exhibition Hall** (10am-3pm Sun-Thur, 10am-2pm Fri-Sat) is housed in a white-domed Ottoman-era mosque south of the stairway.

Courses

Courses in Torah teachings, the Kabbalah and general Jewish mysticism are available at the well-known **Ascent of Safed** (☎ 692 1364, fax 692 1942; e ascent@ascent.org.il; w www.ascent.org.il). Classes are open to anyone; for an introduction to the concept, check out the websites w www.kabalaonline.org and w www.thirtysevenbooks.com.

Places to Stay

Beit Binyamin HI Hostel (☎ 697 3514, fax 692 1086; 1 Lohamei HaGeta'ot St; dorm beds/singles/doubles 89/153/224NIS) sits at the edge of town, about 2km (and a stiff slog) from the town centre. All rates include breakfast. This place is more than a little institutional, but at the time of writing it was effectively the only choice in Safed. Take bus No 6 or 7 from the central bus station.

Ascent of Safed Hostel (☎ 692 1364, fax 692 1942; e ascent@ascent.org.il; w www.ascent.org.il; dorm beds US$8-12, single & double rooms US$35) is open to Jews who are studying at Ascent of Safed.

Places to Eat

Safed's main attraction is its range of eating establishments along pedestrianised Yerushalayim St, which are accompanied by some of Israel's most inspiring views. The **fruit-and-vegetable market** operates on Wednesday; there's also a **supermarket** at the eastern end of Yerushalayim St near the Javits St steps.

California Felafel (Yerushalayim St; snacks 6-10NIS) is an excellent felafel and shwarma option; it's just below the HaPalmach St overpass.

Jerusalem Pizza (pizzas 24-44NIS) is a good pizza choice that serves up pizza by the slice for 8NIS.

Hamama (☎ 682 2606; Yerushalayim St; open 8.30am-10.30pm Sun-Thur, 8.30am-2pm Fri) is mainly a bakery that also serves up sandwiches, cakes, soup, fish, pizza, pasta and omelettes. The attached Internet café charges 20NIS per hour.

Chesimo (☎ 692 2727; *Yerushalayim St; dishes 32-63NIS)*, which was meant to be Chez Simon, is a good choice for breakfast, quiche, fish, and pasta dishes. The main attractions, however, are the sidewalk seating and the spectacular view.

Cafe Baghdad (☎ 697 4065; *61 Yerushalayim St; dishes 32-55NIS)* is a dairy and vegetarian restaurant that, as well as reasonable dinners, serves up breakfasts, blintzes, soup, salad and sandwiches. It also enjoys a great terrace view.

Restaurant HaMifgash (☎ 692 0510; *75 Yerushalayim St; dishes 35-55NIS)* is nothing flash, but it has a range of beef, lamb, chicken and fish dishes, as well as salads, kebabs and burgers.

Getting There & Away

Buses run to Haifa (28NIS, two hours) every 30 minutes until 9pm (5.45pm on Friday), and hourly to Tiberias (18.80NIS, one hour) until 7pm (4pm on Friday). Three daily buses go to Tel Aviv (44NIS, some via Haifa); once daily they go to Jerusalem (40NIS), with a change at Rosh Pina.

Upper Galilee & the Golan Heights

הגליל העליון   הגולן

The Upper Galilee is an area of lush greenery watered by runoff from the surrounding mountains. These streams flow together in the Hula Valley to form the Jordan River, which provides most of Israel's fresh water. The chain of high peaks known as the Golan Heights rises to form a tense barrier between the fertile Jordan Valley and the more arid plains of Syria, to the east.

A shortage of public transport makes the Upper Galilee and the Golan Heights more difficult to explore than the rest of Israel. Independent travellers with a vehicle should plan at least two days in the area, especially if they include hiking in the national parks and nature reserves.

Those with limited time and money may prefer a guided tour of the regional highlights, which will cost an average of US$38

per day. Hostels in Tiberias, Akko and elsewhere in northern Israel can provide information and details on the latest operators.

ROSH PINA   ראש פינה
☎ 04

It seems that many of Safed's artists are moving down the mountain and Rosh Pina has recently taken its former reputation as a laid-back bohemian colony. The 1882 **Rosh Pina Pioneer Settlement Site** (☎ 693 6603), about 1.5km up the hill west of the main road junction, was the first Jewish settlement in Galilee. Here you'll find a spotless public toilet and several historic buildings that have been renovated to serve as restaurants, galleries and pubs. You may also want to check out the bizarre **Chocolate Cafe**, which specialises in X-rated chocolate confections (a whole new twist on the sinful nature of that medium!).

Rosh Pina HI Hostel (☎ 692 1086, 051-572141, fax 697 3514; *dorm beds/rooms 50/100NIS)* is the simplest of Israel's youth hostels, with only two rooms and no private facilities.

Amburger Pub (☎ 680 1592; *meals 23-38NIS)*, which specialises in burgers and beer, is a friendly choice about two blocks downhill from the historic settlement. There's a good-value supermarket around the corner in the Rosh Pina Commercial Centre.

Rosh Pina lies on the bus routes between Tiberias, Safed and Kiryat Shmona.

HULA VALLEY
עמק החולה ושמורת הטבע
☎ 04

Thanks to a reflooding project along the upper Jordan River, the beautiful Hula Valley attracts lots of migratory birds and nesting waterfowl. The best wildlife-viewing spot is **Hula Lake** in the HaHula Reflooding Site, 12km south of Kiryat Shmona then 3km east on an unmarked side road. Here, an elevated hide overlooks ponds and wetlands that attract ducks, coots, moorhens and other waterfowl. You'll also see nutrias ploughing through the incongruous water holes.

The **Hula Nature Reserve** (☎ 693 7069; *adult/child 20/10NIS; open 8am-4pm Sat-Thur, 8am-5pm Fri, 1 hr later in summer)*, best known for its stork population, has a visitors centre that explains its eucalyptus forest and wetland environment. Free guided tours are

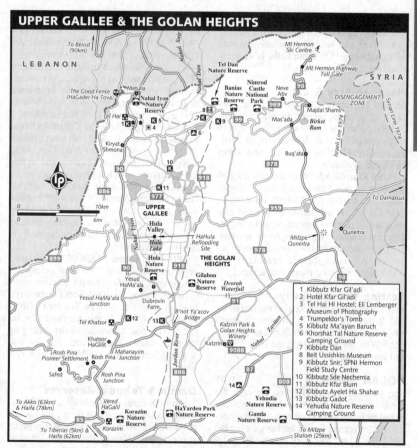

UPPER GALILEE & THE GOLAN HEIGHTS

1 Kibbutz Kfar Gil'adi
2 Hotel Kfar Gil'adi
3 Tel Hai HI Hostel; Eli Lemberger Museum of Photography
4 Trumpeldor's Tomb
5 Kibbutz Ma'ayan Baruch
6 Khorshat Tal Nature Reserve Camping Ground
7 Kibbutz Dan
8 Beit Ussishkin Museum
9 Kibbutz Snir; SPNI Hermon Field Study Centre
10 Kibbutz Sde Nechemia
11 Kibbutz Kfar Blum
12 Kibbutz Ayelet Ha Shahar
13 Kibbutz Gadot
14 Yehudia Nature Reserve Camping Ground

---

conducted between 9.30am and 1.30pm on Saturday, Sunday, Tuesday and Thursday. Buses between Rosh Pina and Kiryat Shmona will drop you at the signposted junction 2.5km west of the reserve.

Kibbutz Kfar Blum (☎ 694 8409, fax 694 8555; singles US$80-100, doubles US$100-150), with a comfortable guesthouse, lies 3km east of the main road between Kiryat Shmona and Rosh Pina.

KIRYAT SHMONA   קרית שמונה
☎ 04
Kiryat Shmona, the 'town of the eight', was named for the eight Jewish settlers killed at nearby Tel Hai in 1920. Since then, its proximity to the Lebanese border has made it a target for Hezbollah (Party of God)

attacks, resulting in more casualties. At Tel Hai, the original watchtower and stockade have been converted into a **museum**. Immediately south, a museum at **Kibbutz Kfar Gil'adi** documents the history of WWI Zionist regiments in the British Army. Also, you may want to see the **Eli Lemberger Museum of Photography** (☎ 695 0769; W www.open-museums.co.il; admission 15NIS; open 8am-4pm Sun-Thur, 10am-5pm Sat), which displays the work of many renowned Israeli and international photographers.

Above the frontier town of Metulla, you can saunter up to **The Good Fence** (HaGader Ha Tova), which proverbially makes for good neighbours. On a clear day, you can clearly see several Lebanese Christian villages, as well as Beaufort Castle to the northwest.

East of the Metulla road, **Nahal Iyon Nature Reserve** encompasses the valley of the Iyon River and several impressive waterfalls, including 18m **Tanur Falls**. It's a great place for a quick leg-stretch.

Places to Stay & Eat

Tel Hai HI Hostel (☎ 694 0043, fax 694 1743; dorm beds/singles/doubles 89/170/240NIS) offers the least expensive option in northeastern Israel & the Palestinian Territories. Breakfast is included and other meals are available.

Hotel Kfar Gil'adi (☎ 690 0000, fax 690 0069; e giladi_k@netvision.net.il; singles US$70-95, doubles US$90-130), on Kibbutz Kfar Gil'adi, is a beautifully situated getaway with a range of amenities, including indoor and outdoor swimming pools, a sauna, gym, tennis courts and organised outdoor activities. All rates include breakfast; add US$30 for a superior room with a view.

Getting There & Away

Kiryat Shmona is connected to the rest of Israel & the Palestinian Territories via buses Nos 541, 841 and 963, which run to Tiberias (22.50NIS, 90 minutes) via the Hula Valley and Rosh Pina.

GOLAN HEIGHTS   הגולן

The beautiful Golan Heights, between the Jordan River and the Syrian border, was annexed by Israel in 1981, after it forcefully occupied this former Syrian territory during the 1967 Six Day War and successfully defended it in the Yom Kippur War of 1973. Despite the conflicts, it remains a lovely area of rich agricultural developments, traditional Druze villages and wonderful national parks and nature reserves. You'll also see trenches, bomb shelters, bunkers, bombed out villages, minefields and a host of modern ruins.

Mitzpe Shalom

From the dramatic **Mitzpe Shalom** (☎ 676 1991; open 9am-5pm daily) lookout at Haruv you'll have a view across all of the Sea of Galilee, and see Tiberias spilling down the slopes in the distance.

Katzrin   קצרין
☎ 04

The planned community of Katzrin, the Golan Heights' 'capital', makes a decent if soporific regional base. Highly worthwhile is the ancient Talmudic village at **Katzrin Park** (☎ 696 2412, fax 696 2815; adult/child 27/19NIS; open 8am-5pm Sun-Thur, 8am-3pm Fri, 10am-4pm Sat), which includes the remains of a 3rd-century synagogue, two reconstructed houses and a **Talmudic Experience** audiovisual programme (admission 10NIS). This also serves as the local **tourist office**.

Another highlight is the **Golan Archaeological Museum** (☎ 696 1350; adult/student 15/12NIS; open 9am-4pm Mon-Thur, 9am-1.30pm Fri, 10.30am-1.30pm Sat), in the town centre, which features discoveries from Gamla and Katzrin Park. The laudable **Golan Heights Winery** (☎ 696 8435, fax 696 4004; open 8.30am-5pm Sun-Thur, 8.30am-1.30pm Fri), at Katzrin's western entrance, conducts tours during business hours from Sunday to Thursday.

SPNI Field School (☎ 696 2817; Daliyat St; camp site/doubles 24/275NIS) has a clean and comfortable guesthouse with air-con rooms.

Several times daily (except Saturday), buses connect Katzrin with Khatsor HaGlilit/Rosh Pina (15NIS, 30 minutes) and Tiberias (22.50NIS, one to two hours depending on the route taken). A twice-daily bus also follows the scenic route via Mas'ada to Kiryat Shmona.

Gamla & Yehudia Reserves

South of Katzrin, a large wild area presents some terrific hiking along deep canyons and past lovely, feathery waterfalls and freshwater pools. **Gamla Nature Reserve** (adult/child 20/10NIS; open 8am-4pm Sun-Thur, 8am-3pm Fri) preserves both a large natural area and the ruins of the ancient Jewish stronghold, **Gamla**, overlooking the Sea of Galilee. In a Roman siege on 12 October, in the year AD 67, three legions of the Roman army killed 4000 Jewish inhabitants; the historian Flavius Josephus reports that another 5000 leapt off the cliff face rather than submit.

Between Gamla and Katzrin lies the fantastic 66-sq-km **Yehudia Nature Reserve** (adult/child 20/10NIS), where there's a camping ground and a large network of hiking tracks. The popular five-hour Nahal Zavitan hike leads past some interesting hexagonal basalt formations, as well as canyons, waterfalls and swimmable pools. Try to ignore the fridge that someone has dumped at the foot of the Ayit waterfall.

Majdal Shams & Mas'ada

מגידל שאמס מסדה מجدل شمس

The Druze villages of Majdal Shams and
Mas'ada, on the slopes of Mt Hermon, maintain their autonomy from Israeli authority and
continue to protest the Israeli occupation of
the Golan Heights. At the **Mitzpe Quneitra**
viewpoint, 15km south of Mas'ada, you can
look across the border to the Syrian ghost
town of **Quneitra**, abandoned after the 1967
Six Day War. Along the road here, sample
the unleavened bread with goat cheese sold
by local Druze villagers at roadside stalls.

Mt Hermon

In the northeastern corner of the Golan
Heights rises 2224m Mt Hermon, the highest
peak in Israel & the Palestinian Territories,
which is shared with Syria and Lebanon.
Limited ski facilities are available from late
December to early April. To reach the ski lifts
(adult/child Sun-Fri 27/24NIS, Sat 31/26NIS),
drivers must use the Mt Hermon toll road
(30NIS per vehicle). For information, visit
the **ski centre** (☎ 698 1337), down the mountain in the tourist settlement of **Neve Ativ**,
where there are also a few places to stay.

Banias Nature Reserve & Nimrod Castle

בניאס קלעת נמרוד

One of the region's most spectacular spots,
Banias Nature Reserve *(adult/child 20/
10NIS; open 8am-4pm Sun-Thur, 8am-2pm
Fri)*, also known as the Nahal Hermon Reserve, takes in the Banias Cave sanctuary as
well as the lovely **Banias waterfall**, about
1km away. On a hill above the cave, the
grave of the prophet Elijah is marked by a
white cliffside memorial, which the Jewish
historian Josephus described as '...a temple of
white marble, hard by the fountains of Jordan...'. Less than 2km east of Banias, Israel's
best-preserved Crusader fortress rises above
its hilltop surroundings in **Nimrod Castle National Park** (☎ 050-813227; adult/child 16/
7NIS; open 8am-4pm daily). Bus No 55 from
Kiryat Shmona passes by Banias twice daily
and buses Nos 25, 26 and 36 pass by Kibbutz
Dan, 6km to the west.

Tel Dan

תל דן

East of Kiryat Shmona, an appealing forested
area of natural springs and ancient Canaanite
ruins (2700–2400 BC) are preserved in Tel

Dan Nature Reserve *(adult/child 20/10NIS;
open 8am-4pm Sun-Thur, 8am-3pm Fri)*. The
site was first settled in the 5th century BC as
the city of Leshem, but was conquered in the
12th century BC by the tribe of Dan and became the northernmost Israelite outpost.

This popular and often crowded picnic spot
is best known for its walking tracks, bubbling
waters and ancient stands of oak and ash
trees. From Kiryat Shmona, take buses No
25, 26 or 36. The adjacent **Beit Ussishkin
Museum** (☎ 694 1704; admission 10NIS; open
9am-4pm Sun-Thur, 9am-3pm Fri, 10am-4pm
Sat) features an audiovisual programme, dioramas and extensive natural-history exhibits.

Camping is available at nearby **Khorshat
Tal Nature Reserve** (☎ 694 2360; camp sites
30NIS), which also offers basic bungalows.
The **SPNI Hermon Field Study Centre**
(☎ 694 1091, fax 695 1480; doubles 275NIS),
at Kibbutz Snir, has guest cottages set on
oak-shaded lawns.

Dead Sea

ים המלח

At an elevation of 400m below sea level,
the Dead Sea shoreline is the lowest bit of
dry real estate in the world. After the obligatory float (see the special section 'The
Dead Sea'), don't miss the ruins at **Masada**,
which is probably Israel's most enigmatic
attraction. Not as well frequented by travellers, the hiking tracks and springs of **Ein
Gedi National Park** also merit exploration.

QUMRAN

קומרן قمران

☎ 02

Described as 'the most important discovery
in the history of the Jewish people', the **Dead
Sea Scrolls**, now on display at the Israel Museum in Jerusalem, were discovered at Qumran in 1947. The site includes the settlement
and caves of the Essenes, the Jewish sect that
authored the scrolls from 150 BC to AD 68,
when the Essenes were disbanded by the
Roman invaders. **Qumran National Park**
(☎ 994 2235, fax 994 2533; e qumran@
mishkei.org.il; adult/child 16/12NIS) includes
a multimedia programme, a self-service **cafeteria** *(set meals 44NIS)* and shops selling
books, souvenirs, Dead Sea mineral creams
and beauty products.

[Continued on page 360]

THE DEAD SEA

Caught in the Great Rift Valley (also called the Syrian-African Rift), the Dead Sea – which is actually an inland lake – separates the West Bank and Jordan. The falling water level of recent years is due to overuse of its sole source, the Jordan River, by farmers in Israel & the Palestinian Territories and Jordan.

No visit to Israel would be complete without a float in its mineral-rich waters, where the sheer volume of solids in the water holds bathers suspended in a salty soup. When you're choosing a bathing spot, bear in mind that the slimy residue left on your skin – the product of minerals leaching down into this low spot with no outlet – will require immediate treatment with fresh water, so look for a place with a shower. Most visitors to the Dead Sea come to swim – or rather float – at the lowest point on the Earth's surface.

The nicest places are the sandy, well-kept sites at the main hotel area, Ein Bokek, or a bit further south at Neve Zohar. Nearer to Jerusalem are the several beaches at Qumran and around Ein Gedi.

Inset: Watching the Dead Sea in Ein Bokek, Israel (Photo by Russell Mountford)

Mineral Waters

The water of the Dead Sea is laden with minerals. It is 33% solids, contains 20 times as much bromine as sea water, 15 times as much magnesium and 10 times as much iodine. Bromine, a component of many sedatives, relaxes the nerves; magnesium counteracts skin allergies and clears bronchial passages; iodine, which is essential to good health, has a beneficial effect on thyroid functions. Not surprisingly, this is all loudly proclaimed by local health-spa owners and cosmetic companies.

Healthy or not, wading into the Dead Sea may seem distinctly unhealthy if you have any exposed cuts or grazes – in fact, you'd instantly assimilate the phrase 'to rub salt into the wound'.

Similarly, swallowing even a drop of this foul-tasting brew will induce retching and may well burn your throat for half an hour. It goes without saying that if you splash this water in your eyes, you must immediately flush them with fresh water.

Getting There & Away

The road along the 90km west coast of the Dead Sea turns off the Jerusalem-Jericho highway in the north and follows the shoreline southwards to Sodom and Eilat. On weekdays, bus Nos 486 and 487 travel three times in the morning and

DEAD SEA REGION

Allenby Bridge Border Crossing

Jericho

No Border Crossing

Almog Junction

JERUSALEM

Nebi Musa

Almog

Suweimeh

Attrakzia

Kibbutz Kalia Guest House

Qumran

Kalia Beach

Neve Midbar Beach

Bethlehem

Qumran National Park

Qumran

Ein Feshka Reserve

Mar Saba

WEST BANK

Judean Desert

Monastery

Metzoke Dragot

Metzoke Dragot Junction

0   10   20km

0   6   12mi

Mineral Beach

Mineral Beach Spa

Wadi al-Mujib

Wadi David

Dead Sea

Ein Gedi National Park

Ein Gedi

Wadi Arugot

Cape Costigan

Ein Gedi Spa

Masada Sound & Light Show

Masada

To Be'ersheva (44km)

Masada Tourist Complex

Masada Junction

Arad

Lashon Peninsula

Ein Bokek

Neve Zohar

Dead Sea Works Plant

THE NEGEV

Sodom

JORDAN

Evaporation Ponds

To Dimona

Dead Sea Works

Plain of Sodom

Safi

To Eilat (164km)

Ne'ot HaKikar Reserve

JANE SWEENEY

three times in the afternoon between Jerusalem and Masada (39NIS, two hours) via Qumran (18NIS, about onehour) and Ein Gedi (30NIS,1¾ hours). Alternatively, take bus No 421 from Tel Aviv, No 384 from Be'er-sheva and Arad, or No 444 from Eilat.

To inexpensively sample the Dead Sea highlights, your best option is the exhausting 12-hour Stopwatch tour advertised in Jerusalem hostels. It departs the Old City in the wee hours of the morning and arrives at Masada in time for the desert sunrise. It then stops at Ein Gedi and allows a quick float in the Dead Sea before photo stops at Qumran and Jericho's Mount of Temptation.

Schedules are now very limited due to recent violence in the region, but tours will probably run if you have a group of three or four people.

Top: Afloat on the Dead Sea in Jordan

[Continued from page 357]

There are also a couple of beaches at Qumran. **Neve Midbar Beach** (☎ 994 2781, 054-997928, fax 994 2782; e nevem@nana .co.il; admission adult/child 20/15NIS, camp sites 35NIS per person) has a bar and a simple restaurant serving Bedouin meals (40NIS). **Kalia Beach** (☎ 994 2391, fax 994 2533; e qumran@mishkei.org.il; admission 100NIS) is more amenable, but is open only to groups of at least 10.

Kibbutz Kalia Guest House (☎ 993 6333, fax 994 2833; e kaliagh@mishkei.og.il; w www .kalia.org.il; singles US$50-70, doubles US$60-100) occupies a beautiful oasis of gardens and date palms just 1km from Qumran National Park. Rooms have cable TV, and guests can enjoy both swimming and horse riding. Rates include breakfast and other meals are available for US$7 to US$10.

EIN GEDI   שׁינגדי
☎ 08

Ein Gedi National Park (☎ 658 4285; adult/child 20/10NIS) is a paradise of dramatic canyons, freshwater springs, waterfalls, pools and lush tropical vegetation. Despite the busloads of rampaging school groups that descend on it daily, it continues to provide a haven for desert wildlife. In the winter months, hikers can enter Wadi David from 8am to 3pm and Wadi Aragot from 8am to 2pm; in summer, the trails are open one hour later. The neighbouring **Ein Gedi National Antiquities Park** (adult/child 10/5NIS; open 8am-4pm daily) includes the ruins of an ancient trapezoid synagogue with an especially inspiring mosaic floor, which was used from the 3rd to 6th centuries AD.

South of the reserve lie the **Ein Gedi spa bathing beach** (admission 50NIS), **petrol station**, **information centre** (☎ 658 4444, fax 658 4367; open 9am-4pm daily), **restaurant** and **camping ground**, and the turnoff for Kibbutz Ein Gedi. One of the nicest places to bathe is the **Mineral Beach spa complex** (☎ 994 4888, fax 994 4488; w www.dead-sea .co.il; admission 35NIS), 15km north of Ein Gedi, with its pools, mud and sulphur baths.

Places to Stay & Eat
Beit Sarah Hostel (☎ 658 4165, fax 658 4445; e eingedi@iyha.org.il; dorm beds/singles/ doubles US$17.50/38/56), 250m from the bus stop, occupies the finest setting of any Israeli hostel. Rates include breakfast and other meals are available.

SPNI Field School (☎ 658 4288, fax 658 4257; dorm beds/singles 75/130NIS, doubles 190-305NIS), perched high on the hillside, enjoys great views and is an excellent launch point for early hikes. Stay a few days and watch the magical light and changing scene over the lake. Rates include breakfast and dinner is 38NIS to 45NIS.

Kibbutz Ein Gedi (☎ 659 4222, fax 658 4328; e eb@kibbutz.co.il; singles US$122-143, doubles US$174-204) has a guesthouse surrounded by lush gardens, with a pool and hot spa. Rates include half board.

MASADA   מסדה
☎ 08
Masada, a desert mesa rising high above the Dead Sea, figures prominently in the Israeli psyche. In 150 BC, a fortress was built atop this superb natural lookout, and was refortified and improved in 43 BC by Herod the Great, who used it as a retreat. During the Jewish First Revolt against the Romans in AD 66, after the sacking and burning of Jerusalem, the Zealots fled to Masada, which became the last outpost of Jewish Resistance. Faced with imminent attack as the Romans constructed an earthen ramp to invade the fortress, 10 men were elected to slay the other men. In the end, one of these killed the rest before committing suicide himself. When the Romans stormed the fortress, they discovered 960 bodies; only seven people, who'd hidden in a water cistern, survived to relay the tale to the world.

Once a dusty outpost, Masada is now guarded by a massive **tourist complex** (☎ 559 6484, fax 559 6483; e hayil@ zahav.net.il), including a restaurant (lunches 35NIS) and a huge underground car park. The summit ruins are accessible on foot via the steep and sinuous 'Snake Path' or on the considerably more popular **cable car** (adult one way/return 41/65NIS, child one way/ return 20/31NIS). From March to October, a **Sound-and-Light show** (☎ 995 9333) is presented on the Arad side.

Places to Stay & Eat
Isaac H Taylor HI Hostel (☎ 658 4349, fax 658 4650; e massada@itha.org.il; dorm beds/singles/doubles 78/162/224NIS) by the

Masada bus stop provides air-con dorms with breakfast included. Breakfast/lunch/dinner cost 27/22/39NIS (a bit more on Saturday). Sleeping out on Masada is no longer permitted, but the hostel will let you set up a tent in its garden.

Getting There & Away

You can approach Masada from either the Dead Sea (for the youth hostel, tourist complex and summit access) or Arad (for the Sound-and-Light show). For the former, there are about eight daily Jerusalem buses (39NIS, two hours) and four Eilat buses (45NIS, 3.75 hours).

The Negev   הנגב

The Negev, Israel's sparsely inhabited southern wedge, takes in nearly half the national area but the only towns of any size are Be'ersheva, Arad, Mitzpe Ramon and Israel's subtropical toehold, Eilat. In addition to numerous military bases, this desert area supports a number of experimental agricultural projects and 75,000 semi-nomadic tent-dwelling Bedouins.

Not surprisingly, the Negev presents some of the best hiking venues in Israel & the Palestinian Territories, including the recommended Sde Boker, the Wilderness of Zin, Ein Avdat, Maktesh Ramon, Timna National Park and the Eilat Mountains. For route information and maps, visit the **SPNI field schools** at Sde Boker, Mitzpe Ramon or Eilat. Note that much of the Negev is a firing zone for the area's numerous military bases; for the latest information, phone the **army co-ordination office** (☎ 990 2294).

For Negev tourist information, contact **Negev Tourism** (☎ 658 8691, fax 658 8620; e kibbutzimmer@ramat-negev.org.il).

BE'ERSHEVA   באר שבע بئرالسبع
☎ 08

Scruffy, dusty Be'ersheva probably won't impress anyone, and although it's the Negev 'capital', the most satisfaction it's likely to offer is the view from the rear window as you leave.

The **tourist office** (☎ 646 3795, fax 627 9306; open 8am-10pm Sun-Fri), at Abraham's Well, appears to be closed even during its posted opening hours.

The **main post office** (cnr HaNessi'im & Ben Zvi Sts) is just north of the central bus station. There are plenty of banks in the adjacent **Kanyon shopping centre**. A good travel bookshop is **Memsi** (☎ 627 0695; Ben Zvi 5/8; open 8.30am-4.30pm Sun-Thur, 8am-1pm Fri), opposite the bus station.

Things to See

The much-vaunted **Bedouin market** (6am-4pm Thur) provides evidence that the Israeli Bedouin are as interested in Nike and Yves St-Laurent knock-offs as anyone in the world. You may see the odd camel, but it's definitely less a cultural than a commercial experience. While that's fair enough, it's not an especially interesting visit.

Be'ersheva's most worthwhile attraction is the **Israeli Air Force Museum** (☎ 690 6855; admission 20NIS; open 8am-5pm Sun-Thur, 8am-1pm Fri), at the Khatserim IAF base 6km west of the centre. From the central bus station take bus No 31 (8.70NIS, 10 minutes).

On Kibbutz Lahav, off the Be'ersheva to Kiryat Gat road, the Joe Allon Centre features the **Museum of Bedouin Culture** (☎ 991 3322, fax 991 9889; admission 20NIS; open 9am-4pm Sun-Thur, 9am-2pm Fri, 9am-1pm Sat). Bus No 42 runs directly to the kibbutz once daily, but immediately heads back to Be'ersheva without allowing time for a visit. Alternatively, use bus No 369 towards Tel Aviv, which will drop you at the junction 8km from the kibbutz.

Places to Stay & Eat

Beit Yatziv HI Hostel (☎ 627 7444, 627 5735; e beit_yatziv@silverbyte.com; 79 Ha'Atzma'ut St; dorm beds US$22-24, singles US$38-42.50, doubles US$56-59) isn't all that cheap, but it has a swimming pool, a garden and no curfew. Rates include breakfast and other meals cost US$11.

Poco Loco (☎ 628 2789; cnr HaNessim & Rambam Sts; dishes 25-35NIS; open 8.30am-2am daily) is a trendy café with sidewalk seating that serves recommended breakfasts, soup, salads, pizza, pasta and burgers. The full business lunch costs 45NIS.

Yitzhak's Bulgarian Restaurant (☎/fax 623 8504; 112 Keren Kayemet Le-Y'israel St; dishes 30NIS; open 9am-10.30pm Sun-Thur, 10.30am-9.30pm Sat) does meat-oriented sit-down meals. The focus is on Ashkenazi specialities: kebabs, schnitzel, liver etc.

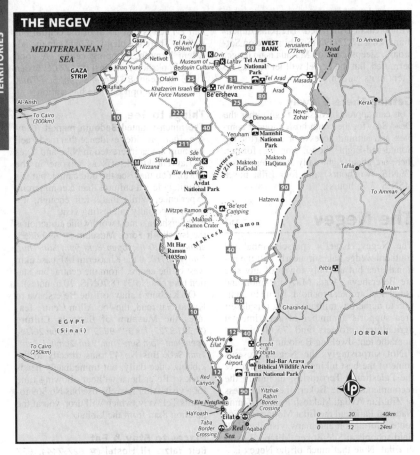

THE NEGEV

For fast food, try the **Kanyon shopping centre**, where the lower floor is given over to a range of franchises. Alternatively, the pedestrianised centre is lined with **cafés** serving grilled meats and salads, along with ice-cream parlours and snack outlets.

Getting There & Away

On business days, buses run every 20 minutes to Tel Aviv (21.50NIS, 90 minutes) and at least half-hourly to Jerusalem (35NIS, 90 minutes). For Eilat (35NIS, three hours), buses depart more or less hourly via Mitzpe Ramon (22.50NIS, 1.25 hours). To Dimona (10.50NIS, 30 minutes) and Arad (17.80NIS, 45 minutes), buses run at least half-hourly.

From Be'ersheva's central train station, adjacent to the central bus station, you can travel comfortably to Tel Aviv (23.50NIS, 90 minutes) roughly hourly on business days.

DIMONA   דימונה
☎ 08

Unless you're involved in espionage (Dimona is the site of Israel's no-longer-secret nuclear weapons facility), the main interest in this bleak desert town is the Hebrew Israelite Community (Black Hebrews). In one small enclave, this motivated and self-contained group operates its own school, and members make their own jewellery and natural-fibre clothing. Dietary restrictions are a variation on veganism, as Black Hebrews don't eat meat, dairy products, fish, eggs, or refined sugar or flour. Visitors are welcome, but the community prefers advance notice of any visit. Call ☎ 655 5400 in Dimona or contact the Taste of Life restaurant in Tel Aviv (☎ 620 3151; 60 Ben Yehuda St).

The Black Hebrews run a small **guest-house** (beds with half board 100NIS). For meals, try Frena (☎ 657 9330; snacks 18-20NIS), which serves up pizza rolls, egg-and-tuna sandwiches and various empanadas. It's on the main traffic circle beneath bright-red cigarette advertising that instructs you to 'Have a Good Time'.

From the central bus terminal, buses run frequently to and from Be'ersheva (10.50NIS, 30 minutes).

ARAD ערד
☎ 08

More appealing than Be'ersheva or Dimona is Arad, a lethargic eastern Negev community that benefits from its surrounding wealth of mineral deposits. The **Arad Visitors Centre tourist office** (☎ 995 4409; beside the Kanyon Mall; admission 20NIS; open 9am-5pm Sun-Thur, 9am-2.30pm Fri) presents an audiovisual programme about the Dead Sea and Judean Desert, and includes a museum of artefacts from Tel Arad.

Tel Arad National Park (adult/child 10/5NIS; open 8am-4pm Sun-Thur, 8am-3pm Fri), 8km west of town, includes the ruins of a Bronze Age city from the 3rd century BC. Take any bus towards Be'ersheva, get off at the Tel Arad junction and walk the final 2km to the site. On the road between Dimona and Arad lies **Mamshit National Park** (☎ 655 6478; adult/child 10/5NIS), which features a complex of extensive and impressive 1st-century Nabataean ruins.

Places to Stay & Eat
Blau-Weiss HI Hostel (☎ 995 7150, fax 995 5078; e arad@iyha.org.il; 4 HaAtad St; dorm beds/singles/doubles 73/171/247NIS) has typically comfortable rooms in a distinctly institutional atmosphere.

Lavie B&B (☎ 995 4791, 053-913149, fax 658 4249; 13 Irit St; singles/doubles 150/200NIS), with its friendly management, offers rooms with private baths and handy kitchenettes.

The place to go on weekends is the **Muza Pub** (off Yehuda St), which has been around for two decades and has enjoyed enormous popularity. Anyone in town can tell you where it is.

Getting There & Away
From the central bus terminal on Rehov Yehuda, buses run regularly to and from Be'ersheva (17.80NIS, 45 minutes).

SDE BOKER & AVDAT שדה בוקר עבדת
☎ 08

These worthwhile stops along the route between Be'ersheva and Mitzpe Ramon merit anything from a few hours to a couple of days. Jewish history buffs will appreciate David and Paula Ben-Gurion's beloved desert homestead – and their graves – at Sde Boker, and day hikers will love the incredible walk from Sde Boker into the colourful **Wilderness of Zin** passes and the bizarrely chilly desert spring, **Ein Avdat**. Note that this is a one-way hike and there's no bus stop at the end, so you'll have to hitch back to Sde Boker.

A great place to stay is the British-run **Krivine's** (☎ 653 5115, 052-712304, fax 653 2217; e krivjohn@netvision.net.il; dorm beds/singles/doubles 75/145/215NIS), which provides excellent tourist information, meals, mountain-bike rental and transport from the Sde Boker bus stop. Advance booking is essential.

Avdat National Park (☎ 658 6391; adult/child 20/10NIS), a ruins complex with Nabataean, Roman and Byzantine elements, served as a location for the film Jesus Christ Superstar and is now best known for the camel-caravan sculpture on the crest of the hill. Constructed by Nabataeans in the 2nd century BC, it served as a caravanserai along the trade route between Petra and the Mediterranean coast. Note that there's no bus stop here. For meals, try the recommended 'Nabataean' restaurant **Avdat Inn** (☎ 653 5341; meals 30-50NIS), at the park entrance.

MITZPE RAMON מצפה רמון
☎ 08

Mitzpe is Hebrew for 'watchtower', and accordingly, this small but engaging desert town enjoys an impressive vista across the dramatic **Maktesh Ramon** crater, which measures 300m deep, 8km wide and 40km long. All along this dramatic 'watchtower', you'll find far-ranging views and an extensive network of hiking routes. Pick up a Makhtesh Ramon Nature Reserve map at the Visitors Centre and set off into the desert on foot; this wild wonderland is good for days of wandering – but be sure to carry lots of water.

Information
The ammonite-shaped **Visitors Centre** (adult/child 24/12NIS; open 8am-5pm Sat-Thur, 8am-4pm Fri), perched on the crater rim, has a tourist office and presents an overview of Maktesh Ramon's intriguing natural history.

Things to See
Downhill from the Visitors Centre, the **Bio-Ramon** (☎ 658 8755, fax 658 8754; adult/child 20/10NIS; open 9am-6pm Sun-Thur, 9am-4pm Fri, 9am-5pm Sat) complex displays a collection of desert flora and fauna. East of town, the **Alpaca Farm** (☎ 658 8047; adult/child 22/18NIS; open 8.30am-4.30pm Sat-Thur) is a labour of love for its owners, who keep a variety of South American camelids (ie, llamas and alpacas) and spin wool.

Organised Tours
Lots of companies run rugged jeep tours, but they come and go with the desert wind and you may need to muster a group; see the Visitors Centre for the latest offerings. A popular choice is **Alen Gafny Desert Tours** (☎ 659 5555, 052-762777, fax 658 6273; 6 Gvanim St), where you'll pay US$55 to US$60 for a jeep tour into the crater and surrounding desert. It also organises abseiling and mountain biking.

Places to Stay
Be'erot Camping (☎ 658 6718, 050-375265; camp sites/Bedouin tent beds 15/30NIS), 20km south of town, offers camping in a wild setting (adjacent to the Bedouin Experience, a small Bedouin cultural presentation), with local tents and cuisine. Access along the rough route is by private vehicle only.

Mitzpe Ramon HI Hostel (☎ 658 8443, fax 658 8074; dorm beds/doubles 89/260NIS) is a short downhill walk from the Visitors Centre. Most rooms have a great crater view. Rates include a continental breakfast.

SPNI Field School (☎ 658 8616, fax 658 8385; e har@spni.org.il; Bedouin tents/dorm beds/doubles 25/83/275NIS) is a truly beautiful complex in a dramatic pass on the crater rim. It's an easy 2km walk from the town centre, but there are also two daily buses and booked guests can phone to see if transport is available. Room rates include breakfast.

Chez Alexis (☎ 658 8258, 056-432627; En Saharonim 7; dorm beds 60NIS) is probably the friendliest place in town, thanks to the French-Algerian owner, who speaks French, English and Hebrew. Guests have access to the kitchen facilities.

Adama (☎ 695 5190, 053-258596; Har Boker Industrial Complex; dorm beds 70NIS) is a friendly hostel and dance studio that occasionally hosts three-day metaphysical workshops (600NIS). Skilled construction volunteers are eligible for up to three weeks of free room and board.

Succah in the Desert (Succah HaMidbar; ☎ 658 6280, fax 648 6464; w www.succah .co.il; PO Box 272, Mitzpe Ramon; singles/doubles 250/400NIS Sat-Thur, 400/550NIS Fri), 7km from town on a very poor track, is the place to stay if you're intrigued by any sort of mysticism. This place may be short on creature comforts, but the point is integration with the desert, so if you can't live without modern plumbing, forget it. Advance bookings, which are essential, will avail you of free transport from Mitzpe Ramon.

Places to Eat
Hannah's Restaurant (meals 35-40NIS; open 8am-8pm daily), at the petrol station, is a standard buffet-style stop located along the Be'ersheva-Eilat bus route.

Happy Cheff (☎ 653 9111; dishes 30-50NIS; open 10am-8pm daily), in the shopping centre, specialises in salads and Thai stir-fries.

HaHavit (meals 45NIS; open 9am-2am daily), at the Visitors Centre, dishes up business lunches and set meals all day, while the pub operates until late.

Self-caterers will find joy at the **Hyper Neto** and **Supersol supermarkets**, both in the town centre.

Getting There & Away
Arrive before 6am to catch the first bus No 392 to Eilat (35.50NIS, 2½ hours). From 6am to 9.30pm, bus No 60 shuttles hourly to and from Be'ersheva (22.50NIS, one hour), via Sde Boker and Ein Avdat.

EILAT אילת

Wedged between Jordan and Egypt, and separated from the Israel of international headlines by 200km of desert, Eilat is a resort town where glitzy, ziggurat-like hotels line an artificial lagoon and glass-bottomed boats ply deteriorating coral reefs. While there's plenty of sun and heat, the beaches are coarse and cluttered, and the nicest stretch of sand is interrupted by tanker docks and loading facilities. Okay, this coastline is as tropical as Israel can manage, but Eilat's real appeal lies in its surrounding desert mountains and canyons. Divers, snorkellers, beach bums and anyone else searching for the Red Sea's magical underwater world should head posthaste for the Egyptian Sinai.

Orientation & Information

Eilat consists of a town centre, the hotel-fringed lagoon and beaches, and the 5km coastal strip between the town centre and the Egyptian border. The helpful **tourist information office** (☎ 637 4233, fax 637 6763; Ha'Arava Rd; open 8am-9pm Sun-Thur, 8am-2pm Fri, 10am-2pm Sat) is marked by the sign for the Burger King that shares the complex.

To change money, head for the many no-commission change bureaus in the town centre. The **police station** (☎ 100), at the eastern end of Hativat HaNegev Ave, is useful for reporting robberies for insurance purposes.

Internet and email access is good value at **Private-Link Internet Shop** (☎ 634 4331; W www.private-link.co.il) in the central bus station, where you'll pay 13NIS per hour.

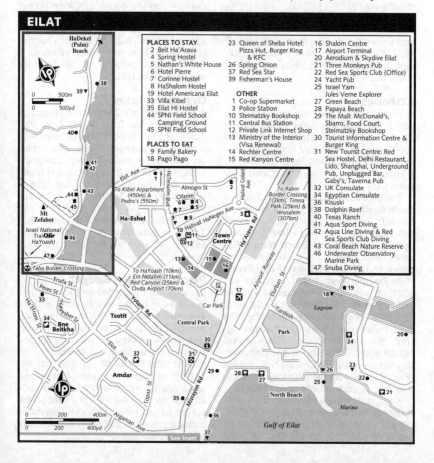

EILAT

HaDekel (Palm) Beach

0   500m
0   500yd

PLACES TO STAY
2 Beit Ha'Arava
4 Spring Hostel
5 Nathan's White House
6 Hotel Pierre
7 Corinne Hostel
8 HaShalom Hostel
19 Hotel Americana Eilat
33 Villa Kibel
35 Eilat HI Hostel
44 SPNI Field School Camping Ground
45 SPNI Field School

PLACES TO EAT
9 Family Bakery
18 Pago Pago

23 Queen of Sheba Hotel: Pizza Hut, Burger King & KFC
26 Spring Onion
37 Red Sea Star
39 Fisherman's House

OTHER
1 Co-op Supermarket
3 Police Station
10 Steimatzky Bookshop
11 Central Bus Station
12 Private Link Internet Shop
13 Ministry of the Interior (Visa Renewal)
14 Rechter Centre
15 Red Kanyon Centre

16 Shalom Centre
17 Airport Terminal
20 Aerodium & Skydive Eilat
21 Three Monkeys Pub
22 Red Sea Sports Club (Office)
24 Yacht Pub
25 Israel Yam Jules Verne Explorer
27 Green Beach
28 Papaya Beach
29 The Mall: McDonald's, Sbarro, Food Court, Steimatzky Bookshop
30 Tourist Information Centre & Burger King
31 New Tourist Centre: Red Sea Hostel, Delhi Restaurant, Lido, Shanghai, Underground Pub, Unplugged Bar, Gaby's, Taverna Pub
32 UK Consulate
34 Egyptian Consulate
36 Kisuski
38 Dolphin Reef
40 Texas Ranch
41 Aqua Sport Diving
42 Aqua Line Diving & Red Sea Sports Club Diving
43 Coral Beach Nature Reserve
46 Underwater Observatory Marine Park
47 Snuba Diving

Elot Ave
HaTmarim St
Almogin St
Ofarim
Ha-Eshel
To Kibel Arpartment (450m) & Pedro's (550m)
Hativat Golani Ave
To Rabin Border Crossing (2km), Timna Park (25km) & Jerusalem (307km)
Hativat HaNegev Ave
Ha Arava Rd
Town Centre
Mt Zefahot
Israel National Trail (Qsir HaYoash)
To HaYoash (10km), Ein Netafim (11km), Red Canyon (25km) & Ovda Airport (70km)
Taba Border Crossing
Enafa St
Peres St
Ha Eroni St
Kesher St
Tsotit
Yotam Rd
Central Park
Car Park
Airport Runway
Durban St
Tarshish
Lagoon
Park
Bne Beitkha
Elot Ave
Amdar
Mizrayim Rd
Topaz St
North Beach
Argaman Ave
Gulf of Eilat
Marina
See Inset

0   200   400m
0   200   400yd

Things to See

The **Underwater Observatory Marine Park** (☎ 636 4200, fax 637 3193; **w** www.coralworld .com; adult/child/senior 76/58/55NIS; open 8.30am-5pm Sat-Thur, 8.30am-3pm Fri) features the 'Oceanarium' mock submarine ride, tanks with sharks and rare green and hawksbill turtles (which live for 150 to 200 years!). The highlight is the magical glassed-in underwater-viewing centre, where, 4.25m below the surface, you can get in on the private life of the surrounding reef – it's like snorkelling without getting wet. The adjacent aquarium displays many of the tropical species you may have missed on the reef. For a deeper look at the underwater world and an impressive coral wall, take a budget-busting 60m dive in the **Yellow Submarine** (adult/child/senior 192/100/143NIS).

Originally built as a movie set, **Texas Ranch** (☎ 637 6663; adult/child 15/5NIS), best known for its pub, is an unimpressive Wild West town inspired by its desert backdrop. It also offers horse riding and half-day camel treks.

Activities

A popular excursion from the main hotel area is the **Israel Yam** *Jules Verne Explorer* (☎ 637 5528, 050-310090; adult/child 60/40NIS) glass-bottomed boat cruise, between the Egyptian and Jordanian borders. It lasts two hours and operates at least three times daily.

The crowded and cluttered hotel area at **North Beach** is great for a drink in the sun, but isn't especially appealing for underwater activities. For snorkelling, your best options are the **Coral Beach Nature Reserve**, with underwater trails marked by buoys, and the free **HaDekel (Palm) Beach**.

At **Dolphin Reef** (☎ 637 1846, fax 637 5921; **e** info@dolphinreef.co.il; **w** www .dolphinreef.co.il; Southern Beach; adult/child 38/28NIS; open 9am-5pm daily), on the Taba road, visitors can observe dolphin training, feed the dolphins and even snorkel (adult/child 227/204NIS) or dive (introductory dive adult/child 274/246NIS, guided dive 223NIS) with them. Diving certification courses are available from 1400NIS.

You can also dive with one of Eilat's other operators: **Red Sea Sports Club** (☎ 637 6569, fax 637 0655; **e** manta1@netvision.net.il); **Snuba** (☎ 637 2722, fax 637 6767; **e** info@ snuba.co.il; **w** www.snuba.co.il); **Aqua Line Diving** (☎ 632 6628; **e** aqualine1@hotmail .com); or **Aqua Sport** (☎ 633 4404, fax 633 3771; **e** aquaspor@isdnet.net.il; **w** www .aqua-sport.com). All charge US$54 for an introductory dive, or US$275 for six-day PADI or NAUI certification. You can rent diving equipment for around US$8 per day.

These places also rent sailboards for 35NIS to 45NIS per hour, and Red Sea Sports Club organises water-skiing (70NIS) and parasailing (120NIS). With **Kisuski** (☎ 637 2088; **e** kisoski@actcom.co.il; **w** www .kisos.co.il; Red Rock Beach), you can rent jet skis, jet boats, parasails, pedal boats, kayaks, ski tubes and other water toys.

If you want to jump out of a perfectly good aeroplane, see **Skydive Eilat** (☎ 633 2386; **e** roy@skydive.co.il; **w** www.skydive .co.il; Aerodium, North Beach; US$180 per tandem jump, US$990 for four-day accreditation course), which has its jump site north of Ovda, a one-hour drive north of town. At the in-town Aerodium, you can fly in the wind tunnel for US$30.

Organised Tours

A good choice for wilderness tours is the reputable **Desert Eco Tours** (☎ 637 4259, 052-765753, fax 637 0104; **e** erez@desertecotours .com; **w** www.desertecotours.com), which does half-day to multi-day jeep, camel and hiking tours in the Negev, Sinai and southwestern Jordan. If you're camping, plan on US$40/100 for a half/full day (plus any border taxes). A recommended private guide, who also works for Desert Eco Tours, is **Josa Wilf** (☎ 633 5201, 051-562919; **e** abundany@actcom.co.il; 1/27 Zaharon St).

Places to Stay – Budget

Camping isn't permitted on most beaches, but you can try the muddy areas near the Jordanian border and in a few select spots near the Egyptian border. Note that security is a serious problem, so only attempt it if you're really destitute and desperate.

SPNI Field School (☎ 637 2021, fax 637 1171; **e** eilat@spni.org.il; camp sites per person 25NIS, singles 140-180NIS, doubles 245-295NIS), on the Taba road, is a comfortable but institutional option with a well-appointed camping ground. It's also your best source of hiking information.

HaShalom Hostel *(☎ 637 6544, fax 637 4683; Hativat HaNegev; dorm beds/private rooms 70/280NIS)* has rooms with private showers and toilets, and communal kitchen facilities are available to guests.

Corinne Hostel *(☎ 637 1472; 127 Retamim St; dorm beds 25NIS, doubles 100-180NIS)* is Eilat's oldest hostel, and this friendly, atmospheric and highly recommended place keeps plugging along. Kitchen facilities and cable TV are available.

Nathan's White House *(☎ 637 6572, fax 637 4829; Retamim St; dorm beds 30-50NIS, doubles 100-180NIS)* is quite basic, but has air-con dorms with fridges and attached bathrooms. There's also a bar and snooker table available for guests.

Spring Hostel *(☎ 637 4660, fax 637 1543; W www.avivhostels.co.il; 126 Ofarim Lane; dorm beds 35NIS, doubles 120-160NIS)* is a comparatively large place with a more upmarket feel – but a considerably less friendly atmosphere – than other budget options. All rooms have a bathroom and shower, and rates include breakfast and use of the swimming pool, kitchen and Internet facilities (15NIS per hour).

Beit Ha'Arava *(☎ 637 4687, fax 637 1052; e aravahos@actcom.co.il; 106 Almogin St; dorm beds 30NIS, doubles 100-150NIS)*, three-minutes' walk from the bus station, includes a pleasant patio garden and Internet access (12NIS per hour). Breakfast costs an additional 12NIS to 20NIS.

Red Sea Hostel *(☎ 637 6060, fax 637 4605; dorm beds/singles/doubles 30/80/120NIS)*, a rather shabby option in the New Tourist Centre, has a kitchen and easy access to lots of nightspots. Rates rise exponentially in summer and during Jewish holidays.

Eilat HI Hostel *(☎ 637 0088, fax 637 5835; e elait@iyha.org.il; Mizrayim Rd; dorm beds 79-89NIS, singles 162-190NIS, doubles 224-390NIS)* is an immaculate but rather cold and seriously overpriced option. Rates include breakfast but there's no kitchen, TVs and fridges each cost an additional 20NIS per day and Internet access is 48NIS per hour.

Places to Stay – Mid-Range
Villa Kibel *(☎/fax 637 6911, 050-345366; e russell@eilat.ardom.co.il; W www.villaki bel.co.il; 18 Peres St; flats 160NIS)* is a friendly and quiet private home divided into a collection of comfortable holiday flats

with kitchenettes, cable TV and air-con. The same management also offers a 14-bed house for 760NIS. It tends to fill up, so bookings are highly recommended. If you have a lot of luggage, the owner will pick you up at the bus station.

Hotel Pierre *(☎ 632 6601, fax 632 6602; e pierrehotel@bezeqint.net; 123 Ofarim Alley; singles US$25-50, doubles US$30-60)* is friendly, quiet, unassuming and very French. The small-but-comfortable rooms all have fridges, phones, cable TV and air-con.

Hotel Americana Eilat *(☎ 633 3777, fax 633 4174; e info@americanahotel.co.il; singles 140-190NIS, doubles 160-220NIS)*, a colourful but stark option at the inland end of the marina, has a pool, nightclub, tennis courts and the Cave Bar, complete with fake rocks. Breakfast is an additional 30NIS per person.

Places to Eat
Fast food is the staff of life in Eilat. Most of the felafel and shwarma places are on HaTemarim Blvd near the bus station. If a sandwich is sufficient – and it probably will be given Eilat's appetite-busting temperatures – try the **Co-op supermarket** *(cnr Elot Ave & HaTemarim Blvd)*, or the one in the Shalom Centre. The **Food Court**, upstairs in The Mall, serves up pizza, steaks, empanadas, felafel, shwarma and coffee concoctions; elsewhere in the same complex, **McDonald's** and **Sbarro** also have outlets. Alternatively, head for the amazing Las Vegas clone, the **Queen of Sheba Hotel**, which has a **Pizza Hut**, **Burger King** and **KFC**.

There are a couple of good bakeries on HaTemarim Blvd, mainly between Hativat HaNegev Ave and Almogin St. Try the **Family Bakery** *(cnr Ofarim Lane & HaTemarim Blvd; open 24 hrs daily)*, with patio seating (the sign is in Hebrew and Russian only).

Fisherman's House *(☎ 637 9830; Taba road; buffets adult/child 36/18NIS; open noon-midnight daily)*, also known as Beit Dug, is the place to go with a serious appetite. For 36NIS, you'll get all-you-can-eat salads, pasta, bread, hummus and at least six types of fish. After paying, you can socialise for hours.

Spring Onion *(☎ 637 7434; dishes 30-60NIS)* is a popular dairy and vegetarian place beside the lagoon bridge in the hotel area. In addition to a great breakfast (34NIS), you'll find salads, pizza, pasta and fish dishes.

Delhi Restaurant (☎ 634 1555; dishes 45-65NIS), in the New Tourist Centre, is one of the best Indian restaurants in Israel & the Palestinian Territories. In the same complex are **Lido** (☎ 634 1666; dishes 30-65NIS), which does vegetarian meals, pizza, pasta, salad, beef, fish and other seafood; and **Shanghai** (☎ 634 1666; dishes 25-75NIS), which specialises in Chinese cuisine. In any of these places, very filling three-course business lunches cost 45NIS.

Pago Pago (☎ 637 6660; dishes 45-85NIS), on a boat in the marina, is the place to go for an atmospheric seafood dinner or grilled speciality in nice watery surroundings. It's best known for sushi combos (from 45NIS), seafood platters (66NIS to 128NIS), and fish, beef, chicken, ostrich and duck grills.

Pedro's (☎ 637 9504; main dishes 56-78NIS) is an excellent steakhouse that also serves fish, ostrich and chicken specialities. If you're after a local hangout, it's tops.

Red Sea Star (☎ 634 7777, fax 634 7171; dishes 45-75NIS; open 10am-1am daily; underwater restaurant open noon-midnight daily) is the place to go for underwater dining – that is, if you don't mind eating your fish dinner while accusing eyes glare at you through the windows. In the evening, there's a dance bar on the upstairs deck.

Entertainment

Eilat's nightlife is firmly bar-based, and the action focuses on the New Tourist Centre. This compact little area is packed with frequently changing options.

Underground Pub (☎ 637 0239; open 10am-4am daily) is the travellers favourite, with cheap pub grub and beer, easy music and nightly live entertainment.

Unplugged (☎ 632 6299; open 2pm-5am daily), next door, attracts a younger crowd with a dance-bar atmosphere.

Gaby's, up the stairs behind Unplugged, is a hole in the wall that offers a bit more peace and quiet.

Taverna (☎ 637 3406; open 24hrs daily) is a typical English pub serving up a good English breakfast, pie and mash, free pool tables and occasional films in the afternoon.

The beach bars are fashionable with Eilat's beautiful people, but there's not much between them. Try **Green Beach** (☎ 637 7032) and **Papaya Beach** (☎ 634 0804) and

think DJs and tanned, bikini-clad bods partying until sunrise.

Alternatively, try the upmarket **Yacht Pub** (☎ 636 3444; King Solomon Promenade; open 10am-3pm Wed-Sat) or the recommended **Three Monkeys Pub** (☎ 636 8888; Royal Beach Hotel; open 9pm-late daily).

Getting There & Away

Air Eilat's municipal airport (☎ 637 3553), which splits the town, may well be one of the world's most convenient airports – unfortunately, it occupies an incredibly valuable strip of land, and will eventually be shifted out into the desert. On the other hand, Eilat's charter airport **Ovda** (☎ 635 9442), 70km from town, may well be the world's least convenient.

Both Arkia and Israir fly several times daily (except Saturday) between the municipal airport and Tel Aviv (US$80).

Bus Tel Aviv (62NIS, five hours) buses depart every 90 minutes between 8am and 5pm, with an additional overnight service at 1am. The last Friday bus is at 3pm and the first Saturday bus at 11.30am; this bus also stops in Be'ersheva (51NIS, three hours). To Mitzpe Ramon (39NIS, 2½ hours), buses run more or less hourly on weekdays and at least twice on Saturday. To Jerusalem (62NIS, 4½ hours), there are four buses daily Sunday to Thursday, three on Friday and one on Saturday. Buses to Haifa (71NIS, 6½ hours) depart at 9am Sunday to Friday and 11.15pm Saturday to Thursday.

Getting Around

The town centre is walkable, but you'll need a bus for locations along the Taba road. The hourly bus No 15 connects the central bus station with the Egyptian border at Taba (4.90NIS) from 7am to 9.30pm Sunday to Thursday, 7am to 5pm Friday and 9am to 9.30pm Saturday. To reach the Rabin border crossing into Jordan, you'll have to get a taxi (25NIS). The Underground Pub in the New Tourist Centre rents bikes for 50NIS per day. You can hire a motor scooter from **Rent-a-Scooter** (☎ 633 5565) for 70/115NIS for four/24 hours.

AROUND EILAT

Hikers will want to head for the Eilat Mountains, but be sure to pick up a copy of the

SPNI *Eilat Mountains* hiking map (60NIS), which is sold at the SPNI Field School in Eilat. Any of the following places is accessible on a 38NIS to 50NIS taxi ride from Eilat.

The small spring and 30m waterfall at **Ein Netafim**, which attract wildlife with their perennial water, lie less than 1km off the main road. From here, hikers can follow the Israel National Trail to the spectacular **Shehoret Canyon**, 15km away; book a taxi to pick you up at the trailhead at the finish. Near the mouth of Shehoret Canyon lie the impressive **Amram Pillars**, also along the Israel National Trail, where there's an official camp site (no water).

An excellent six- to seven-hour day hike will take you through spectacular desert and canyon scenery along the Israel National Trail from **HaYoash to Taba**. It's a highlight of Israel & the Palestinian Territories, and in the early 1990s the Dalai Lama walked part of this route, accompanied by musician Paul Winter. Get an early start and carry at least 3L of water per person.

Further north, the 600m-long **Red Canyon**, a slot canyon 1m to 3m wide and 10m to 20m deep, is readily accessed on foot via a 1.5km walking track from the car park. It makes a great short hike.

Timna National Park

About 25km north of Eilat and accessible by public bus, **Timna National Park** (☎ 631 7850, fax 633 9403; adult/child 31/20NIS) is the site of some stunning desert landscapes, enlivened with multicoloured rock formations. It's best known as a source of copper for 5th-century-BC Egyptian miners – the park is dotted with ancient mine shafts – but it also includes a wonderland of geological phenomena. The most intriguing are the **Natural Arch**, the eroded monolith known as the **Mushroom** and the photogenic **Solomon's Pillars**. There is also a range of excellent day hikes through one of Israel's wildest desert landscapes.

Overnight **accommodation** (camping/ Bedouin tents 15/20NIS per person) is available at the artificial **Timna Lake**. For meals, try the adjacent **restaurant** (meals 45NIS; open 9am-5pm daily).

Buses between Eilat and Jerusalem pass the park turn-off, 2.5km from the park entrance. From there, it's a long walk or hitch to anything of interest.

Yotvata

At Yotvata (☎ 635 7449, fax 635 7363; e yotvata-office@yotvata.ardom.co.il), well known for its wonderful dairy and vegetables, is the **Hai-Bar Arava Biblical Wildlife Reserve** (☎ 637 6018; admission per person 40NIS plus 5NIS per car; open 8.30am-5pm Sun-Thur, 8.30am-4pm Fri-Sat), created to establish breeding groups of threatened Negev wildlife. Also on the kibbutz is the **Predator Centre** (☎ 637 6018; admission 20NIS), with a natural-history video, and an exhibition of maps, diagrams and photographs of the area's zoology, botany, archaeology and settlement history. Yotvata lies on the main bus route, 40km north of Eilat, but access to the Wildlife Reserve requires a private vehicle.

Gaza Strip & the West Bank

רצועת עזה   הגדה המערבית (יו"ש)

The Gaza Strip and the West Bank, predominantly Palestinian territories captured by Israel in 1967 during the Six Day War, have been neither annexed by Israel (as were East Jerusalem and the Golan Heights), nor granted outright autonomy. Although Gaza is well defined by razor wire and watchtowers, the pre-1967 border between Israel and the West Bank (known as the 'green line') is marked only by military checkpoints.

Since 1994 the Palestinians have existed under limited self-rule in the Gaza Strip, Hebron and Jericho. In late 1995, the IDF also withdrew from Jenin, Nablus, Bethlehem and Ramallah, releasing them to the direct control of the Palestine National Authority (PNA). In early 2002, the IDF acted with military force in these areas to thwart escalating Palestinian terrorist attacks against Israeli citizens and

WARNING

At the time of research, the West Bank and Gaza were most emphatically *not* safe for visitors. The information in this section has been only superficially updated, but this chapter remains in hope that the situation will change for the better. Seek local advice – and keep abreast of the latest news – before visiting any of the areas mentioned in this section.

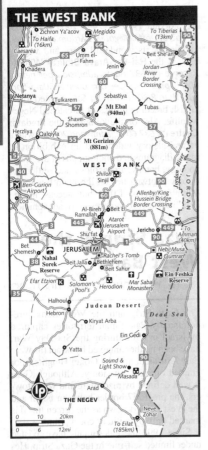

THE WEST BANK

Zichron Ya'acov Megiddo   To Tiberias (13km)
To Haifa (16km)
Caesarea   Umm el-Fahm   Beit She'an
Khadera   Jenin   Jordan River Border Crossing
Netanya   Tulkarem   Sebastiya
            Mt Ebal (940m)   Tubas
Shavei-Shomron   Nablus
Herzliya   Qalqilya   Mt Gerizim (881m)
            WEST   BANK
            Shiloh
Ben-Gurion Airport   Sinjil
Lod   Allenby/King Hussein Bridge Border Crossing
    Al-Bireh   Beit El
    Ramallah   Atarot   Jericho   To Amman (40km)
    Jerusalem Airport
Bet   Shu'fat   JERUSALEM
Shemesh   Rachel's Tomb   Nebi Musa   Qumran
    Nahal   Beit Jalla Bethlehem
    Sorek   Beit Sahur   Ein Feshka
    Reserve   Reserve
Efar Etzion   Solomon's   Mar Saba
            Pool's Herodion Monastery
Halhoul   Judean Desert   Dead Sea
Hebron   Kiryat Arba
    Yatta   Ein Gedi
            Sound & Light Show
            Masada
    Arad
    THE NEGEV
0   10   20km   Neve Zohar
0   6   12mi   To Eilat (185km)

JORDAN

the future status of the West Bank and Gaza
Strip is now in question.

GAZA   غزة
☎ 08

Historically, Gaza has been one of the most
strategically important eastern Mediterranean towns, and has long served as a staging post on the major trade routes linking
Central Asia and Persia with Arabia, Egypt
and sub-Saharan Africa. In fact, it's believed that Gaza has been captured and destroyed more than any other town in the
world – and that tradition lives on. After the
establishment of limited self-rule in 1994,
Gaza became a respectable place, but the re-
sumption of the *intifada* has brought about
renewed lawlessness, rebellion and IDF re-

taliation. Visitors are strongly advised to
stay away.

Orientation & Information
The main street, Omar al-Mukhtar St, runs for
4km from Al-Shajaria Square to the seafront.
The centre of activity is Palestine Square
(Midan Filisteen), which is 500m west of Al-
Shajaria Square on Omar al-Mukhtar St. The
coastal district, Rimal (Sand), is full of posh
villas and apartment blocks, which are home
to wealthy Palestinians and expat aid workers
– as well as Yasser Arafat and family.

The Old Town
Palestine Square holds most of the city's sites
of historical interest. The most distinguished
structure is the converted Crusader-era
church, **Jama'a al-Akbar (Great Mosque)**.
Non-Muslims may enter between prayer sessions. Along its southern wall runs the short,
vaulted **Goldsmiths' Alley**, which served as a
lively souq during the Mamluk era.

In 1799, during his Egyptian campaign,
Napoleon Bonaparte camped in Gaza and established his headquarters on Al-Wahida St
in the attractive Mamluk-era building now
called **Napoleon's Citadel**, which now serves
as a girls' school. From the citadel, head
west and take the second right to reach the
Mosque of Said Hashim, which was erected
on the grave of the Prophet Mohammed's
great-grandfather.

Places to Stay & Eat
Due to the current strife, most visitor facilities have been closed either temporarily or
permanently. Perhaps try the **Al-Amal Hotel**
(*☎ 286 1832, fax 284 1317; Omar al-Mukhtar
St; singles/doubles US$40/50*), 300m from the
coast. Alternatively, there's **Marna House**
(*☎ 282 2624, fax 282 3322; singles/doubles
US$60/70*), two blocks north of Omar al-
Mukhtar St, just west of An-Nasser St; rates
include breakfast. For meals, try the waterfront **seafood restaurants** or the **felafel and
shwarma stalls** around Palestine Square.

Getting There & Away
The only entry/exit point at the time of writing was Erez. To get there, take a service
taxi from Damascus Gate in East Jerusalem
(40NIS per person), but allow lots of time to
await other passengers. Those in more of a
hurry can pay 250NIS and leave on the spot.

Alternatively, take an Egged bus from Tel Aviv to Ashkelon and find a southbound bus to Yad Mordechai junction, where taxis (3NIS, five minutes) run the last 5km to the Erez border.

Getting Around

Because Gaza has only one 4km-long main road, you can just stand along it and hail a taxi (mostly unofficial). Up and down Omar al-Mukhtar St the fare is 1NIS, no matter where you get in or out. Off the main street, however, the fare jumps to 5NIS.

JERICHO   יריחו حيفا
☎ 02

Jericho is best known for the biblical account of Joshua, his army's seven circuits with its trumpets and the subsequently tumbling walls. Unfortunately, precious little remains of this legacy, but Jericho still claims the title of the world's oldest town. While Jericho's archaeological sites remain impressive, they're readily surpassed by the surrounding desert landscapes and the views across the Dead Sea to the mysterious Mountains of Moab.

Ancient Jericho

Ancient Jericho's main sites are best accessed on the 6km anticlockwise loop formed by Qasr Hisham St and Ein as-Sultan St. Essential stops include Hisham's Palace – the impressive ruins of a 7th-century hunting lodge, with its beautiful Byzantine mosaic floor – and the ruins of a 5th- or 6th-century synagogue. At the site of Tel Yericho, otherwise known as Tel as-Sultan, only archaeology buffs are likely to be impressed by the signposted trenches and mounds of dirt.

Mount & Monastery of Temptation (open Mon-Sat), on the other hand, is well worth the steep climb. This 12th-century Greek Orthodox monastery, rebuilt in the 19th century, clings to the rocks at the traditional site where Jesus was tempted by Satan.

Places to Stay & Eat

Tourism in Jericho is utterly dead at the moment, but if you're stuck for the night, you may want to try Hisham's Palace Hotel (☎ 992 2156; Ein as-Sultan St), which is so neglected that the carpets have started to sprout vegetation; plan on paying around 135NIS for a shabby room. New Jericho Pension

(☎ 992 2215; Sharia al-Quds; dorm beds 45NIS, singles/doubles around 130/160NIS) may be a slightly better option.

There are several cafés and felafel/shwarma joints around the main square.

Getting There & Away

At present, no buses service Jericho, but stretch-Mercedes or Peugeots depart when full from Damascus Gate in East Jerusalem and cost around 5NIS per person; they'll drop you at the town square, where you'll find most of Jericho's shops, restaurants and other businesses. You can make the return trip from Jericho's town square until around 7pm.

AROUND JERICHO

About 8km before Jericho a road leads right to Nebi Musa, a small monastic complex revered by Muslims as the tomb of Moses, with the Judean Desert as a dramatic backdrop.

Wadi Qelt is a nature reserve with a natural spring where you can swim in a pool under a waterfall and hike along an aqueduct to St George's Monastery, built into the cliff face of a canyon on the Mount of Temptation. The hike takes about four hours (there's also a cable car). The starting point is the Wadi Qelt turn-off on the Jerusalem-Jericho road (get the bus driver to drop you off here) and the finishing point is Jericho, from where you can continue sightseeing in the town or easily find transport back to Jerusalem.

BETHLEHEM   בית לחם بيت لحم
☎ 02

The Christian Arab town of Bethlehem no longer resembles the cosy Middle Eastern village portrayed on Christmas cards, but even worse, much of it has been bombed and otherwise damaged in recent conflicts. Christian visitors will probably still want to see Bethlehem, but those hoping for a spiritual experience may be disappointed by the blatant commercialism and the unheavenly host of kitsch that surfaces here. If it's all too much for you, head out to the Shepherds' Fields early in the morning, before the tour groups arrive, and gaze back at the town from a contemplative distance.

Besides the pilgrimage sites, there are also some excellent excursions to places just outside the town, such as the Mar Saba Monastery and the Herodion.

Orientation & Information

Around Manger Square, right in the centre, are the Church of the Nativity, the tourist office, police station, post office and various shops, hotels and eateries. Milk Grotto St heads off to the southeast, past the Milk Grotto Chapel, and uphill to the northeast Paul VI St leads to the museum, outdoor market and more shops and hotels. The winding Manger St, off the east side of the square, is the main street through the new town; it eventually intersects with the Jerusalem-Hebron highway opposite the Jewish shrine of Rachel's Tomb.

Things to See

The venerable **Church of the Nativity**, which is one of the world's oldest functioning churches, is built like a citadel over the cave cited by tradition as Jesus' birthplace. In April 2002, it suffered damage as 200 Palestinian troops sought sanctuary there from the IDF.

Down Milk Grotto St is **Milk Grotto Chapel**, a shrine that commemorates the lactation of the Virgin Mary. North of the square on Paul VI St, the **Bethlehem Museum** (open 10am-noon & 2.30pm-5.30pm Mon-Sat) exhibits traditional Palestinian crafts and costumes.

Revered especially by Jews – but also by Christians and Muslims – is **Rachel's Tomb** (cnr Hebron Rd & Manger St), which is housed in a small white-domed building.

Places to Stay & Eat

Accommodation in Bethlehem is limited, especially at Christmas and Easter, and it makes more sense to stay in nearby Jerusalem.

Casa Nova Hospice (☎ 274 3981, fax 274 3540; B&B/half board/full board US$20/$25/ $30), a Franciscan-run guesthouse beside the Church of the Nativity, is probably the best option, with great facilities and a good dining room.

Alexander Hotel (☎ 277 0780, fax 277 0782; singles US$40-55, doubles US$50-85) offers tastefully furnished rooms with a scenic view over the valley.

You'll find plenty of felafel and shwarma merchants around Manger Square, and the **Reem Restaurant** (Paul VI St; light dishes 15NIS), down the side street past the bakery, is inexpensive for hummus and salads.

Getting There & Away

Arab bus No 22 (3NIS, 40 minutes) runs from East Jerusalem, stopping en route at Jaffa Gate, but if you're in a hurry, take a more frequent service taxi (5NIS, 20 minutes) from outside Damascus Gate.

Alternatively, follow the pilgrims' option and walk from Jerusalem (at Christmas, there's an official procession). Unfortunately, the 2½ hour up-and-downhill trek attracts heavy traffic all the way.

AROUND BETHLEHEM

From Jerusalem, Arab bus No 21 heads west past Rachel's Tomb on the Hebron road to the pleasant Christian Arab village of **Beit Jalla**. Further along lies the summit of **Har Gillo**, with great views, and a side road leads to the attractive Salesian monastery of **Cremisan**, renowned for its wine and olive oil.

Various biblical events are associated with the **Field of Ruth** and the **Shepherds' Fields**, about 2km from Beit Sahur (1km east of Bethlehem). The ruined Byzantine monastery here was destroyed by the Persians in AD 614, and there's also a 5th-century church built over a mosaic-floored cave. From Manger St in Bethlehem, take Arab bus No 47 to Beit Sahur and walk for 20 minutes to the fields. The **Herodion**, the amazing volcano-shaped remains of the palace complex built by Herod between 24 and 15 BC, lies 8km south of Beit Sahur. Buses run infrequently from Bethlehem and your best bet is to take a taxi, walk or hitch.

Splendid architecture and a superb location combine to make the Greek Orthodox Monastery of **Mar Saba**, on the steep Kidron banks, one of the Holy Lands' most impressive structures. The interior is open only to men, but the exterior is also quite impressive. Without a private vehicle, however, you'll have to walk the 6km from the bus stop at Abu Diye (accessible on Arab bus No 60 from Bethlehem).

The large reservoir and Turkish fort at **Solomon's Pools** lie 8km south of Beit Jalla. To get there from Bethlehem, take Arab bus No 23 or Arab minibus No 1 to Dashit.

HEBRON   חברון الخليل
☎ 02

Currently, Hebron is extremely volatile, and visitors are advised to steer clear. If you ignore that advice, strive to look like a tourist and avoid wearing a yarmulke, Star of David or any other suggestion of Judaism.

The main stress point is the disputed **Cave of Machpelah**, which is the presumed burial site of father Abraham, and the **Ibrahimi Mosque**, which overlays it. For Jews, it's a highly revered site and to Muslims, its importance in the region is second only to that of Jerusalem's Dome of the Rock.

In the early 1970s, Jewish settlers established a community on the fringes of this largely Arab town, and their incursion inflamed strong – and often violent – passions. The result was an IDF guard posted to protect the 500 settlers from their unhappy Palestinian neighbours. Tragically, in February 1994, a disgruntled Jewish settler stepped into the mosque and opened fire on the Muslims at prayer. The building is now segregated into Muslim and Jewish sections, and security is tight.

Hebron's souq is a blend of Crusader and Mamluk facades, vaulted ceilings, tiny shops and narrow alleyways; it winds up at around 6am and continues until the afternoon. Also, don't miss the Ein Sara St factories that produce Hebron's fabulous blue glass.

Getting There & Away
Arab bus No 23 operates between Jerusalem and Hebron (3NIS), via Bethlehem, but service taxis (5NIS) from Damascus Gate are faster and more frequent. Public transport will drop you on HaMelekh David St, at the northern edge of the market. To the south lies the aforementioned Ibrahimi Mosque.

NABLUS   שכם نابلس
☎ 08

The typically bustling and quite attractive Arab town of Nablus, scenically situated between the Gerizim and Ebal peaks, is the largest West Bank population centre and is known for its production of soap, olive wood and olive oil. The central Palestine/Al-Hussein Square has the bus stops, service taxi ranks and a small market. Immediately to the south, the Old Town stretches eastward along Nasir St.

Things to See
From Al-Hussein Square head south toward the minaret of **An-Nasir Mosque** (Nasir St) – one of 30 minarets punctuating the Nablus skyline. Nearby is the privately owned old Turkish mansion known as **Touqan Castle**, where visitors will normally be able to admire the architecture and garden. From Nasir St walk south through Al-Beik Gate and the entrance is up the slope on your left.

East of the An-Nasir Mosque on An-Nasir St is **Al-Shifa** (☎ 09-838 1176; open to men only 8am-10pm daily, to women only 8am-5pm Wed), the country's oldest functioning **Turkish bath**. Built around 1480 at the start of the Ottoman period, Al-Shifa has been lovingly restored, and along with the hot rooms, you can enjoy the cushion-strewn central hall where guests can recline, sip black coffee or mint tea and puff on a *sheesha*. Baths and massage cost 10NIS each.

The nearby Arab village of **Sebastiya** stands about 15km northwest of Nablus up on the scenic slopes of the Samarian hills. Just above it on the summit of the peak lie the impressive ruins of Samaria, the capital of the ancient Israelite kingdom.

Places to Stay & Eat
Al-Istiqlal Pension (☎ 238 3618; 11 Sharia Hitteen), at the bottom of the scale, offers male-only dormitory accommodation.

Al Qasr Hotel (☎ 238 5444, 238 5944; e alqasr@netvision.net.il; Sharia Omar ibn al-Khatib; singles/doubles US$70/95) charges the same rates, regardless of the season.

Along with soap, the Nablus speciality is sweets, including Arabic pastries, halvah, Turkish delights, and especially *kanafe* (cheese topped with orange wheat threads soaked in honey). The best bakery at which to try this delicious delicacy is **Al-Aqsa** (Nasir St), in the Old City beside the An-Nasir Mosque.

Getting There & Away
Arab buses run to Nablus from East Jerusalem (9NIS, 2½ hours) via Ramallah, making the service taxis (11NIS, 1¼ hours) more appealing.

Jordan   الأردن

Jordan is a delightful place to visit, made more so by its truly friendly people, who continually call out to you 'Welcome to Jordan!' – and they really mean it. In the midst of a very tough neighbourhood, Jordan retains a calmer air, a peacefulness not prevalent in surrounding countries.

One thing that overwhelms is the sense of history, with seemingly every stone carrying some historical significance. Amman, Jerash and Umm Qais were cities of the ancient Roman Decapolis, while biblical legends abound throughout the country. This is especially the case in the Jordan Valley (including Bethany where Jesus was baptised), the Dead Sea and atop Mt Nebo, from where Moses is said to have looked out over the Promised Land. Most grandly of all, before Christ was born Nabataean stonemasons carved out their beautiful city of Petra from towering rock walls.

Jordan is also a place where the old blends peacefully with the new, with Amman's Roman ruins of antiquity coexisting alongside the trendy cafés of its upmarket districts.

In comparison with other Middle Eastern countries, travelling in Jordan can be expensive, but it's compact and has enough attractions (including some spectacular landscapes) to keep you interested for a couple of weeks. On no account miss it.

Facts about Jordan

HISTORY

Jordan has always been a crossroads for the great civilisations of the Middle East, although usually only as a means of securing more prized possession elsewhere.

In 333 BC, Alexander the Great stormed through Jordan on his way to Egypt. After his death in 323 BC, Ptolemy I gained Egypt, Jordan and parts of Syria. In southern Jordan, the Nabataeans, a once nomadic tribe who controlled lucrative trade routes, built their splendid city at Petra, while the Roman Empire controlled much of the country.

After periods of occupation by the Seleucids, Sassanians and Byzantines, Jordan was overrun by the armies of Islam in the 7th century AD. In the late 7th century, Jor-

Hashemite Kingdom of Jordan

Area: 89,206 sq km
Population: 5.3 million
Capital: Amman
Head of State: King Abdullah II
Official Language: Arabic
Currency: Jordanian dinar (JD)

- Best Dining – enjoying a Bedouin meal of *mensaf* (spit-roasted lamb), served on a bed of rice and eaten on the floor

- Best Nightlife – watching nature's planetarium from your open-air desert bed in Wadi Rum

- Best Walk – hiking through the labyrinthine Siq to the spectacular facades of ancient Petra

- Best View – admiring the Golan Heights (Syria) the Sea of Galilee (Israel) and the Jordan Valley from Umm Qais

- Best Activity – hiking through the spectacular gorges of Dana Nature Reserve

dan came under the Umayyad Empire centred in Damascus.

In AD 747 an earthquake devastated much of Jordan, ushering in the rule of the Abbasids who were in turn followed in AD 969 by the Cairo-based Fatimids and then, from 1037, by the Seljuk Turks.

In the 11th century, Pope Urban II launched the Crusades, capturing Jerusalem in 1099, slaughtering countless inhabitants and causing devastation. The Crusaders took control of most of Jordan by about

What to See

One week is the minimum required to truly explore Jordan on any form of transport, two weeks is ideal and in one month you could see almost everything covered by this book. Even if you use public transport most of the time, it's still worth hiring or chartering a vehicle for a few days to visit remote places.

If you only have three days, head to **Petra** for one or two days and use the remaining time in **Jerash** and **Amman**. In a week you could spend more time in Amman, combine a trip to Jerash with a visit to **Umm Qais**, **Madaba**, the **Dead Sea** or **Karak**, and maybe even spend a night under the stars at **Wadi Rum** or snorkelling around **Aqaba**.

Two weeks is an ideal amount of time, allowing longer at each of the above places, as well as excursions to the **Desert Castles, Machaerus (Mukawir)** and **Dana Nature Reserve**.

Any additional time, up to one month, could be used for a longer exploration of Wadi Rum, trekking around Dana and making your way down the **King's Hwy**, including **Shobak Castle**.

1115, and built fortresses at Karak and Shobak.

In the 12th century, the armies of Nur ad-Din and later Saladin reunited the Arab and Islamic world and occupied most of the Crusader strongholds in Jordan. The Mamluks, former soldier-slaves, expelled the Crusaders in 1250. The Ottoman Turks defeated the Mamluks in 1516 and ruled until WWI.

In June 1916 the Arabs, with the assistance of TE Lawrence, launched the Arab Revolt and helped the British drive the Turks from the region. In return, the Arabs were given British assurances that they would be allowed to establish an independent Arab state.

The newly formed League of Nations instead gave Britain a mandate over Palestine, and shortly afterwards the state of Transjordan, lying between Iraq and the East Bank of the Jordan River, was made a separate entity under King Abdullah. What remained of Palestine corresponded more or less to present-day Israel & the Palestinian Territories.

Immediately after WWII, the British gave up and referred the mess to the United Nations (UN), which voted in favour of the partition of Palestine into separate Arab and Jewish states. Agreement could not be reached and the Arab-Israeli War broke out in 1948, ending with a comprehensive victory for Israel, and Jewish occupation of the zones allocated to them under the UN partition plan as well as virtually all those assigned to the Palestinian Arabs. Transjordan took advantage of the situation and occupied the West Bank and part of Jerusalem. This done, King Abdullah shortened his fledgling country's name to Jordan.

King Abdullah was assassinated in 1951. He was succeeded the following year by his grandson Hussein, who took the throne at the age of just 17 and managed to hold it for 48 years through insurrection attempts, two wars with the Israelis and a virtual civil war with the Palestinians. He reigned until his death in 1999.

In the 1960s aid poured in from the USA and Jordan enjoyed a boom in tourism, mainly in Jerusalem's old city. The situation was radically altered by the Six Day War of 1967, in which Jordan lost the West Bank and its half of Jerusalem to occupying Israeli forces. In return they gained a huge influx of Palestinian refugees.

As the Palestinians, particularly the Palestine Liberation Organisation (PLO), became more militant against the Israeli occupation in the early 1970s they also posed a danger to King Hussein, given that most of them operated from Jordanian territory. They came to contest power in the kingdom, angered in part by Hussein's claim to be the leader of the Palestinian people. After some bloody fighting in 1971, the bulk of the radicals were forced to cross the border to Lebanon, where they would later become one part among many of that country's woes.

Hussein's diplomatic skills were stretched to the fullest when, during the 1991 Gulf War, the king refused to side against Iraq, largely out of fear of unrest among Jordan's Palestinian populace. Misunderstood in the West as support for Saddam, Hussein's neutral stance placed him in a precarious situation. The country avoided total isolation by playing the role of mediator and complying,

JORDAN

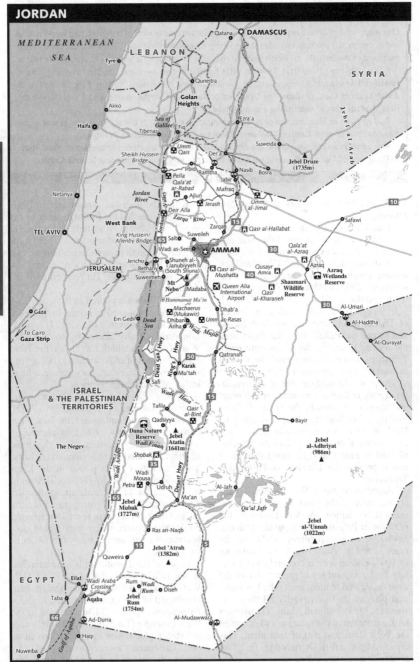

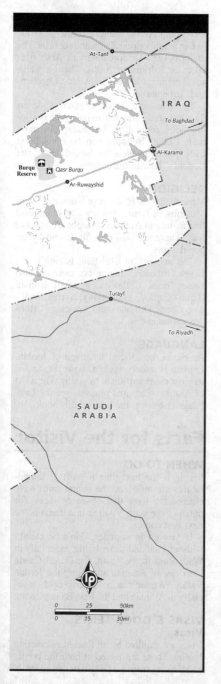

officially at least, with the UN embargo on trade with Iraq. For the third time in 45 years, Jordan experienced a massive refugee inflow, with as many as 500,000 Palestinians previously working in the Gulf states fleeing to Jordan.

Jordan recovered remarkably well from that conflict and, despite fears of the threat of Islamic extremism, Hussein went ahead and signed a full peace treaty with Israel in 1994.

Jordan Today

Peace with Israel came with the dividend of a huge upsurge in tourism in Jordan. When in February 1999, King Hussein finally succumbed to the cancer that had been ailing him for so long, it was a comparatively stable and prosperous country that was passed on to his son and nominated heir King Abdullah II. The new king has impressed most observers with his ability to protect the moderate and largely democratic legacy of his diplomatically adept father. The conflict in Palestine and Israel and the growing uncertainty over the situation in Iraq have hit Jordan's tourism industry hard and stirred passions among Jordan's population, suggesting that Jordan's future stability may rest on events largely beyond its control.

GEOGRAPHY

Jordan can be divided into three major regions: the Jordan Valley, the East Bank plateau and the desert. The fertile valley of the Jordan River is the dominant physical feature of the country's west, running from the Syrian border in the north, down the border with the Palestinian Territories and Israel. The valley continues as Wadi Araba down to the Gulf of Aqaba. The majority of the population live in a narrow 70km-wide strip running the length of the country on the East Bank plateau. The remaining 80% of the country is desert, stretching to Syria, Iraq and Saudi Arabia.

CLIMATE

Average daily maximum temperatures in Amman range from 12°C in January to 32°C in August. The weather in the Jordan Valley is oppressive in summer: daily temperatures are well in excess of 36°C and have been recorded as high as 49°C. The desert areas, with less than 50mm of rain annually, also have extremely hot summers.

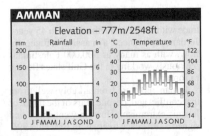

AMMAN
Elevation – 777m/2548ft

At the other extreme, snow in Amman and Petra is not unheard of in winter when desert nights can be very cold.

GOVERNMENT & POLITICS

Jordan is a constitutional monarchy with a democratically elected government. King Abdullah II came to power in February 1999 following the death of his much-admired father King Hussein. Hussein was widely respected at home and abroad and his encouragement of parliamentary democracy has been continued by Abdullah II. However, as the Israeli-Palestinian conflict escalated in early 2002, there were concerns among human rights activists that freedom of expression was being restricted with all demonstrations in support of the Palestinians strictly controlled by the government.

The National Assembly (Majlis al-Umma) is bicameral, the Senate having half as many members as the House of Representatives. The king is vested with wide-ranging powers, although his power of veto can be overridden by a two-thirds majority of both houses of the National Assembly. The 80-member lower house is elected by all citizens over the age of 18 years, but the prime minister is appointed by the king, as are the 40 members and president of the Senate.

Elections take place every four years, although the first elections since Jordan lost the West Bank in the 1967 Six Day War were held in November 1989. This was the first time that women were allowed to vote.

POPULATION & PEOPLE

The population of Jordan stood at about 5.3 million in 2001. Some 900,000 of these were registered as refugees (primarily from the wars of 1948 and 1967) with the United Nations Reliefs & Works Agency (UNRWA) on the East Bank.

Approximately 1.8 million people live in the capital Amman, and a further 700,000 live in neighbouring Zarqa and suburbs. The majority (98%) of Jordanians are Arab; over 60% are Palestinian Arabs. There are also small communities of Circassians, Chechens and Armenians.

The Bedouin were originally desert dwellers and form the majority of the indigenous population, but today not more than 40,000 Bedouin can be considered truly nomadic (see the boxed text 'The Bedouin' later in the chapter).

RELIGION

More than 92% of the population are Sunni Muslims. A further 6% are Christians who live mainly in Amman, Madaba, Karak and Salt. There are also tiny Shiite and Druze populations.

The majority of Christians belong to the Greek Orthodox Church, but there are also some Greek Catholics, a small Roman (Latin) Catholic community, Syrian Orthodox, Coptic Orthodox and Armenian Orthodox communities.

LANGUAGE

Arabic is the official language of Jordan. English is widely spoken, however, and is in most cases sufficient to get by. For a list of Arabic words and phrases, see the Language chapter at the back of this book.

Facts for the Visitor

WHEN TO GO

Spring is the best time to visit as temperatures are mild and the winter rains have cleared the haze that obscures views for much of the year. Visiting in autumn is the next best choice.

If you go in summer, don't be caught without a hat and water bottle, especially in Wadi Rum in the south, the Desert Castle loop east of Amman and along the Jordan Valley. Winter can be bitterly cold, especially in Amman and the East Bank plateau.

VISAS & DOCUMENTS
Visas

Visas are required by all foreigners entering Jordan. These are issued at both the border and airport on arrival (JD10) or can be easily obtained from Jordanian embassies or consulates outside the country. The cost is usually around US$20/40 for single-/multiple-entry visas, two photos are typically required, and the visa is issued within 24 hours. Visas are generally available at Jordanian embassies in all countries which share a border with Jordan (for addresses see the relevant chapter). The only reason to apply for a visa from a Jordanian embassy or consulate is if you wish to obtain a multiple-entry visa, as these are not issued at the border, or if you plan to arrive from Israel via the King Hussein Bridge where visas are not issued.

One exception worth knowing about is that if you arrive in Aqaba by sea from Nuweiba (Egypt), your visa may be free. This is because Aqaba has been designated as a Special Economic Zone set up for free trade. Before you get too excited, you will still have to pay the JD10 visa fee when you leave Jordan or re-enter Aqaba; the free visa applies only if you remain in Aqaba and do not visit anywhere else in Jordan.

Tourist visas are valid for three months for stays of up to two weeks from the date of entry, but can be easily extended for stays of up to three months (see Information in the Amman section later in the chapter).

For details of visas for other Middle Eastern countries, see the 'Visas at a Glance' table under Visas & Documents in the Regional Facts for the Visitor chapter.

Other Documents
Keep your passport handy, especially along the border area with Israel & the Palestinian Territories where you'll encounter a number of military checkpoints. International Driving Permits are not needed. If you're driving, keep your driving licence, rental or ownership papers and car registration in an easily accessible place.

The policy with regard to student cards was being inconsistently applied at the time of research. Officially, student discounts of 50% are available at most tourist sites, including Petra, but many places do not honour this.

Note that the card must be an international student card such as ISIC and not just your university ID card. At the time of writing the Jordanian government was undecided as to whether the discounts would be continued beyond July 2002.

EMBASSIES & CONSULATES
Jordanian Embassies & Consulates
Following are the Jordanian embassies and consulates in major cities around the world. For addresses of Jordanian embassies and consulates in neighbouring Middle Eastern countries, see the relevant chapter.

Australia (☎ 02-6295 9951) 20 Roebuck St, Redhill, Canberra, ACT 2603
Canada (☎ 613-238 8090) 100 Bronson Ave, Suite 701, Ottawa, Ontario ON K1R 6G8
France (☎ 01 46 24 23 78) 80 Blvd Maurice Barres, 92200 Neuilly-Seine, Paris
Germany (☎ 030-36 99 60 0) Heerstrasse 201, 13595 Berlin (Hanover also has a consulate)
Netherlands (☎ 070-416 7200, e info@jordanembassy.nl) Badhuisweg 79, 2587 CD The Hague
UK (☎ 020-7937 3685) 6 Upper Phillimore Gardens, London, W8 7HB
USA (☎ 202-966 2664, e HKJEmbassyDC@aol.com) 3504 International Drive NW, Washington DC 20008
 Consulate: (☎ 212-832 0119) 866 Second Ave, 4th floor, New York, NY 10017

Embassies & Consulates in Jordan
Foreign embassies and consulates are in Amman (Egypt also has a consulate in Aqaba). In general, offices open 9am to 11am Sunday to Thursday for visa applications and from 1pm to 3pm for collecting your visa.

Australia (☎ 06-5930246, fax 5931260) 13 Ameen Mar'i St, between 4th & 5th Circles
Bahrain (☎ 06-5664149) 11 Fares al-Khouri Street, Shmeisani
Canada (☎ 06-5666124) Abdul Hameed Shoman St, Shmeisani
Egypt (☎ 06-5605175, fax 5604082) 22 Qurtubah St, between 4th & 5th Circles
 Consulate in Aqaba (☎ 03-2016171) Cnr Al-Istiqlal & Al-Akhatal Sts
France (☎ 06-4641273, fax 4659606) Al-Mutanabi St, Jebel Amman
Germany (☎ 06-5930367, fax 5685887) 31 Benghazi St, between 4th and 5th Circles, Jebel Amman
Iran (☎ 06-4641281) 28 Tawfiq Abu Al-Huda St
Iraq (☎ 06-4623175, fax 4619172) Near 1st Circle, Zahran St, Jebel Amman
Israel Consulate (☎ 06-5524686) Maysaloon St, Shmeisani
Kuwait (☎ 06-5930745) 88 Zahran St, Jebel Amman
Lebanon (☎ 06-5922911, fax 5929113) Mohammed Ali Bdeir St, Abdoun

JORDAN

Netherlands (☎ 06-5930525) Al-Safarat St, between 4th & 5th Circles, Jebel Amman
New Zealand Consulate (☎ 06-4636720, fax 4634349) 4th floor, Khalas Bldg, 99 Al-Malek al-Hussein St, Downtown
Oman (☎ 06-5686155) 100 Zahran St, Jebel Amman
Qatar (☎ 06-5607311) 124 Zahran St, Jebel Amman
Saudi Arabia Consulate (☎ 06-5920154, fax 5921154) 1st Circle, Jebel Amman
Syria (☎ 06-4641953, fax 4651945) Afghani St, between 3rd and 4th Circles, Jebel Amman
Turkey (☎ 06-4641251) 36 Al-Kulliyah al-Islamiyah St, Jebel Amman
UAE (☎ 06-5934780) 73 Bu Maydan St
UK (☎ 06-5923100, fax 5913759) Wadi Abdoun, Abdoun
USA (☎ 06-5920101, fax 5820123) 20 Al-Umaywiyeen St, Abdoun
Yemen (☎ 06-4642381) Prince Hashem bin al-Hussein St, 150m south of Abdoun Circle

CUSTOMS

You can import 200 cigarettes and up to 1L of wine or spirits into Jordan duty free. There are no restrictions on the import and export of Jordanian or foreign currencies.

MONEY
Currency

The currency in Jordan is the dinar (JD) – known as the *jay-dee* among hip young locals – which is made up of 1000 fils. You will often hear *piastre* or *qirsh* used, which are both 10 fils. Often when a price is quoted, the ending will be omitted, so if you're told that something is 25, it's a matter of working out whether it's 25 fils, 25 piastre or 25 dinars! Although it sounds confusing, most Jordanians wouldn't dream of ripping off a foreigner, so just ask for clarification.

Exchange Rates

Below are the rates for a range of currencies when this book went to print.

country	unit		dinar
Australia	A$1	=	JD0.384
Canada	C$1	=	JD0.450
Egypt	E£1	=	JD0.150
euro zone	€1	=	JD0.630
Japan	¥100	=	JD0.540
New Zealand	NZ$1	=	JD0.320
Syria	S£10	=	JD0.140
UK	UK£1	=	JD1.030
USA	US$1	=	JD0.708

Exchanging Money

It's not difficult to change money in Jordan, with most hard currencies being accepted. American Express travellers cheques seem to be the most widely accepted.

Outside banking hours, there are plenty of foreign exchange bureaus in Amman, Aqaba and Irbid. Many only deal in cash but some take travellers cheques, usually for a commission. Always check the rates at banks or in the English-language newspapers before changing.

Syrian, Lebanese, Egyptian, Israeli and Iraqi currency can all be changed in Amman, usually at reasonable rates though you may have to shop around. Egyptian and Israeli currency is also easily changed in Aqaba. It's a good idea to talk to travellers arriving from across the border you're about to cross, to find out the in-country rates, so you know how much to change.

ATMs & Credit Cards It is possible to survive in Jordan almost entirely on cash advances and ATMs abound in all but the smaller towns. This is certainly the easiest way to travel if you know your pin number. Visa is the most widely accepted card.

Among others, banks which accept both Visa and MasterCard include the Arab Bank and Jordan Gulf Bank, while the Housing Bank for Trade and Finance, Cairo-Amman Bank and Jordan Islamic Bank have numerous ATMs for Visa. The Jordan National Bank and HSBC ATMs allow you to extract dinars from your MasterCard and are Cirrus compatible.

If an ATM swallows your card, call ☎ 06-5669123 (Amman).

International Transfers Western Union operates in Jordan through the Cairo-Amman bank.

Costs

One of the biggest sightseeing expenses in Jordan is the admission fee to Petra (up to JD26 for two days, depending on the season), but it's still great value. At other sites such as Jerash, they can cost as much as JD5 in high season. To encourage more tourists, 50% discounts are often available during low season (the dates of which change depending on the prevailing conditions). Most other sites cost between 500 fils and JD2.

If you're sleeping in the most basic hotels, eating felafel and shwarma, drinking tea and using shared transport (service taxis and minibuses), and factoring in visa costs and admission fees, you could survive on US$15 to US$20 per day in Jordan. For another US$15 you could live quite comfortably and eat well.

Tipping & Bargaining
Tips of 10% are generally expected in the better restaurants and loose change is usually appreciated by low-paid workers in cheaper places. Bargaining, especially when souvenir hunting, is essential, but shop owners are unlikely to shift a long way from their original asking price.

POST & COMMUNICATIONS
Post
Letters to the USA and Australia cost 400 fils, postcards 300 fils. To Europe, letters are 300 fils and postcards 200 fils, and to Arab countries 200 fils and 150 fils respectively. Parcel post is ridiculously expensive but efficient. A 1kg parcel to Australia will cost around JD13, with each subsequent kilogram JD7.500. To the UK, the first kilogram is JD10 and each kilogram thereafter JD3.500.

For express mail services, **Federal Express** (☎ 06-5511460, fax 5531232; *Nasser bin Jameel St, Amman*) and **DHL** (☎ 06-5857136, fax 5827705, e *info@amm-co.jo.dhl.com*), behind C-Town Shopping Centre on 7th Circle in Amman, are typically reliable but expensive. DHL also has an office in Aqaba (☎ 03-2012039) on Al-Petra St.

Telephone
The country code for Jordan is ☎ 962, followed by the local area code (minus the zero), then the subscriber number. Local area codes are given at the start of each city or town section. The international access code (to call abroad from Jordan) is ☎ 962. The local telephone system is quite reliable. For directory assistance, call ☎ 121. Local calls cost around 100 fils and the easiest place to make a call is your hotel.

Overseas calls can be made easily throughout the country, although from smaller centres like Wadi Rum, prices are exorbitant. Calls from hotels or private telephone agencies will generally cost around JD1.750 per

minute to Australia and JD1.250 to the USA or Europe. It is best to call overseas and then get the recipient to call you back at your hotel.

Alo, a local telephone company, has prepaid phonecards (from JD1 to JD15) that allow you to make local and international calls from their public cardphones, which abound in most towns. The cards, however, do get eaten up rapidly on international calls.

Mobiles Jordan is covered by the GSM Cellular Network and mobile telephones can be rented from companies such as **Mobile Zone** (☎/fax 06-5818294; e *thezone@nets.com.jo*) or contact **Fastlink** (☎ 06-5512010). Rates for signing up can start at JD60 including 20 minutes mobile-to-mobile time or 50 minutes mobile-to-land time. If you have your own phone and purchase a local sim card, expect to pay around JD25 to get started.

Email & Internet Access
There are Internet cafés in Amman, Irbid, Aqaba, Wadi Musa (Petra), Madaba and Ma'an, with costs ranging from 750 fils to JD2 per hour – see the relevant sections later in the chapter.

Connecting to the Internet from your hotel room is possible, although usually only at top-end and a few mid-range hotels that have direct-dial phones. **AOL** (w www.aol.com) and **Internet Gateway Services** are among the international service providers with local access numbers as part of their global roaming services. AT&T doesn't have a Jordan access number.

DIGITAL RESOURCES
For a comprehensive list of Middle East/Arab world websites see the Regional Facts for the Visitor chapter; otherwise among the better websites about Jordan are:

AmmanNet Radio station which broadcasts in Arabic live from Amman
　w www.ammannet.net
Baladna Excellent general information, links and chat lines
　w www.baladna.com.jo
Jordan Jubilee Probably the best website about Jordan, this wonderful window onto Jordanian society is loaded with practical tips
　w www.jordanjubilee.com

Jordan Tourism Board Reasonable links to range
of Jordan-related websites
W www.see-jordan.com/links.html
Madaba Excellent description of Madaba's
attractions and other nearby sites
W www.madaba.freeservers.com
RSCN Accessible information about Jordan's
environment and ecotourism
W www.rscn.org.jo

BOOKS

As well as this book, Lonely Planet publishes
a comprehensive country guide, *Jordan*. In
LP's travel literature series 'Journeys' there's
Kingdom of the Film Stars: Journey into Jordan by Annie Caulfield. This novel unravels
some of the tightly woven Western myths
about the Arab world, and it does so within
the intimate framework of a moving love
story.

The Seven Pillars of Wisdom by TE
Lawrence describes Lawrence's adventures
in Jordan before, during and after WWI (he
wrote a substantial portion of the book in
Amman).

For useful guides on hiking and climbing,
see Tony Howard and Di Taylor's *Walks &
Scrambles in Rum* or *Walks, Treks, Caves,
Climbs & Canyons in Pella, Ajloun, Moab,
Dana, Petra & Rum*.

More general Middle East titles, some of
which cover Jordan, are listed in the Books
section in the Regional Facts for the Visitor
chapter.

NEWSPAPERS & MAGAZINES

The press in Jordan is given a relatively free
reign by the government. The *Jordan Times*
(200 fils), the daily English-language newspaper, has good coverage of events in Jordan, elsewhere in the Middle East and
worldwide.

The Star (500 fils) is similar but published
only every Tuesday.

Some major European daily newspapers,
such as the *International Herald Tribune*
(surprisingly reasonable value at JD1.250),
The Times and *Guardian Weekly* (both from
the UK) and *Le Monde* from France
(JD1.500) are available in bookshops and
upmarket hotels in the capital, and at the
two major bookshops in Aqaba.

These newspapers are generally not more
than two days old, but it can cost as much
as JD6 for a copy of the hefty *Sunday
Times*.

RADIO & TV

Radio Jordan transmits in both Arabic and
English. The English-language station is on
855 kHz and 96.3 kHz FM in Amman, and
98.7 kHz FM in Aqaba. It's mostly a music
station.

Jordan TV broadcasts on three channels:
two in Arabic, and Channel 2 is almost exclusively in French and English.

Uncensored international satellite stations, such as the BBC, CNN, MTV and Al-Jazeera can be found in the homes of most
wealthy Jordanians, all rooms in luxury,
top-end hotels as well as in many mid-range
hotels.

PHOTOGRAPHY & VIDEO

Reputable brands of film (including black
& white and slide film) are widely available
in Jordan, but prices tend to be cheaper in
Amman, Madaba and Aqaba. Don't expect
to pay less than you would at home (anything up to JD8 for a roll of 36-exposure
slide film).

Check the use-by dates before buying. In
Amman, there are places on Al-Malek al-Hussein, Hashemi, Al-Makel Talal and
Quraysh Sts where you can get passport
photos taken immediately.

Always ask permission before photographing anyone, particularly women,
and be careful in any border areas, including Aqaba. Photographing military areas is
forbidden.

LAUNDRY

There are good laundries and dry cleaners
in Amman and Aqaba, although it's often
easier to get your hotel to arrange it.

Be prepared to pay JD3 for a 5kg load of
washing – it comes back smelling better and
folded more neatly than you could ever
have hoped.

TOILETS

Many hotels and restaurants, except those
in the budget category, have Western-style
toilets. Otherwise, you'll be using squat toilets with either a hose or water bucket provided for flushing.

There is also usually a receptacle for toilet paper – use it or the toilet's contents will
return to you as an overflow on the floor.
Public toilets are to be avoided except in
cases of emergency.

HEALTH

The water in Jordan is generally safe to drink but health scares (often only reported after the event) have occurred from time to time, so it's better to stick to bottled water.

Medical services in Jordan are well developed in the larger towns and cities and many of the doctors have been trained overseas and speak English. Your embassy will usually be able to recommend a reliable doctor or hospital should the need arise.

Many drugs normally sold only on prescription in the West are available over the counter in Jordan, but as the price of antibiotics in Jordan can be prohibitive, you may want to bring a supply with you. If you do, make sure you bring a prescription or a letter from your doctor.

For more general health information see the Health section in the Regional Facts for the Visitor chapter.

WOMEN TRAVELLERS

Most women who travel around Jordan experience no problems, although there have been some reports of varying levels of sexual harassment. Women will feel uncomfortable on any of the public beaches in Aqaba. A few restaurants have family areas where single men are not permitted. Women travellers should avoid hitching and be careful at some of the budget hotels in Wadi Musa (Petra) – see Places to Stay in the Wadi Musa section later in the chapter. For both men and women, dress should be modest with baggy trousers/skirts and modest shirts/blouses acceptable in most circumstances.

Attitudes to women vary greatly throughout the country. In the upmarket districts of Amman, women are treated the same as they would in any Western country, whereas in rural areas more traditional attitudes and dress codes prevail.

GAY & LESBIAN TRAVELLERS

Although the gay and lesbian scene is very much underground, there are a few places in Amman that are gay-friendly, such as the multi-purpose Books@cafe (see Bookshops & Places to Eat in the Amman section later in the chapter). Thursday nights at the Irish Pub or the trendy cafés in Abdoun, such as the Blue Fig Cafe (see Entertainment in the Amman section later in the chapter), pull in a young mixed gay and straight crowd.

BUSINESS HOURS

Government offices are open from 8am to 2pm Saturday to Thursday. Banks are open from 8.30am to 12.30pm and 4pm to 6pm Saturday to Thursday. Private businesses keep similar hours but are more flexible. Museums are generally closed on Friday, and sometimes either Saturday or Tuesday.

Small shops are open for long hours, from about 9am to 8pm or 9pm. Some close for a couple of hours mid-afternoon. Friday is pretty quiet although a few shops open. The souqs and street stalls are open daily.

Jordan operates a system of daylight-saving time, with the clocks moving forward one hour at the end of March and then back an hour at the end of September or early October.

PUBLIC HOLIDAYS

In addition to the main Islamic holidays described in Public Holidays & Special Events in the Regional Facts for the Visitor chapter, Jordan observes the following holidays:

Tree Day (Arbor Day) 15 January – school children are encouraged to get out and plant trees
Arab League Day 22 March – a low-key affair
Labour Day 1 May – also a low-key affair
Independence Day 25 May – speeches and flag waving
Army Day & Anniversary of the Great Arab Revolt 10 June – military parades and remembrance services
King Hussein's Birthday 14 November – usually turns into a lively three day weekend, with pictures of the kings (former and present) everywhere, car horns honking and a gathering at the Amman stadium

Following the death of King Hussein, and the succession of King Abdullah II, the exact number of public holidays, and the dates on which they fall, is likely to slowly change. King Abdullah's Throne Day (9 June) and his birthday (30 January) will probably replace King Hussein's Throne Day (August 11). King Hussein's Birthday (14 November) will remain a public holiday, however, and the death of King Hussein (7 February) will also probably be a holiday.

ACTIVITIES

Diving and snorkelling are popular pastimes in the Gulf of Aqaba – see the Aqaba section later in the chapter for more details. Hiking is a great way to get off the beaten track, with Dana Nature Reserve, Wadi Rum Protected Area and Wadi Mujib particularly worth the effort. For more details, see the relevant sections later in the chapter or contact the **Royal Society for the Conservation of Nature** (RSCN; ☎ 06-5350456, fax 5347411; e relation@rscn.org.jo).

COURSES

The **University of Jordan** (☎ 06-5343555; University St), in Shmeisani, Amman, offers summer courses in Modern Standard Arabic as well as more leisurely courses throughout the rest of the year. Inquiries should be addressed to the director of the Language Centre in the Arts Faculty. Some of the foreign cultural centres also have Arabic courses, including the **British Council** (☎ 4636147, fax 4656413; e registrar@britishcouncil.org.jo; Rainbow St), southeast of 1st Circle in Amman; and the **Centre Culturel Francais** (☎ 4637009; Kulliyat al-Sharee'ah St) in Jebel Weibdeh, Amman.

WORK

Work is not really an option for most foreigners passing through Jordan. Those hoping to work with Palestinian refugees should contact the public information office of the **United Nations Reliefs & Works Agency** (UNRWA; ☎ 06-5607194, ext 166, fax 5685476; e m.saqer@unrwa.org; Mustapha bin Abdullah St, Shmeisani, Amman). It focuses on health, education and relief. There is no organised volunteer programme; however, if you make contact at least three months in advance, you may be able to arrange something.

The only other alternative is occasional vacancies for English teachers at the British Council or the American Language Center (☎ 06-5859102).

ACCOMMODATION

A bed in a shared room in a cheap hotel will cost around JD3 to JD5. It's sometimes possible to sleep on the hotel roof, which in summer is a good place to be, and will cost JD1.500 to JD2.

There is a good choice of mid-range and top-end hotels in Amman, Aqaba and Wadi Musa (Petra) and usually at least one or two in other towns. A single will cost from JD12 to JD24, although discounts are often available when things are quiet.

FOOD

For those on a tight budget, there is plenty of street food although not much variety – felafel, shwarma, *fuul*, chicken and hummus are the staples. In mid-range restaurants, the most common way for a group to eat is to order mezze – a variety of small starters followed by several mains to be shared by all present. Amman and, to a lesser extent, Aqaba have a great selection of top-end restaurants serving local and international cuisine.

The Bedouin speciality is *mensaf* which is delicious. It is spit-roasted lamb that is continually basted with spices until it takes on a yellow appearance. It is served on a bed of rice and pine nuts, sometimes with the head of the lamb plonked in the centre and the cooking fat mixed into the rice. Honoured guests get the eyes, less honoured guests the tongue.

The dish is served with a sauce of cooked yoghurt that has been mixed with the leftover cooking fat. Another local favourite is *maqlubbeh* – steamed rice topped with grilled slices of eggplant or meat, grilled tomato and pine nuts.

Dessert here, as in many parts of the Middle East, may be baklava or *mahalabiyya wa festaq* (a milk pudding containing pistachio nuts).

DRINKS

The universal drink of choice is tea (followed a close second by coffee) – as soon as you enter a compound you are sat down on the floor and offered tea, then tea, then more tea. Other options include *yansoon*, an aniseed-based hot drink, and *zatar* (thyme-flavoured tea).

Bottled mineral water (500 fils) is widely available, as are the usual soft drinks, Amstel beer and wine. Imported liquors are sold in Amman, Madaba and Aqaba but are expensive.

SPECTATOR SPORTS

Watching football in the bars and coffeehouses is free and can be lots of fun. Amman's two main teams are Wahadat (generally supported by Palestinians) and Faisaly (supported by other Jordanians). Games are mostly played on Friday at the Amman International Stadium near Sports City in Shmeisani (JD1.500 to JD2).

Eating and drinking tea in public is a time-honoured way of keeping up with what's new. City workers exchange stories in an Aden café, Yemen (top left); vendors in the Grand Bazaar, İstanbul, Turkey, compare notes (top right); and men play *okey*, a tile game, in an İstanbul café, Turkey.

NEIL SETCHFIELD

All that glitters really *is* gold: shopping in the Deira Dubai gold market, United Arab Emirates

ANDREW BURKE

Jalabiyya-clad men in a Damascus souq, Syria

CHERYL CONLON

Polishing brassware, Cairo, Egypt

SARA-JANE CLELAND

A cobbled alleyway in the Muslim quarter of Jerusalem's old city, Israel & the Palestinian Territories

Getting There & Away

AIR

The main international airport is Queen Alia International Airport, 35km south of Amman. Occasionally a flight to Cairo also takes off from the smaller Aqaba airport.

Royal Jordanian (☎ 06-5678321; W www .rja.com.jo) is the national carrier, but from the main European capitals you can generally get cheaper deals with other airlines. There are direct flights to Amman from many European capitals (from UK£250 return) and most major cities of the Middle East. From the USA (around US$600/750 from east/west coast USA), you may have to get a connection in a European city or a neighbouring capital. From Australia or New Zealand, expect to pay at least A$1600. Air fares vary extensively by season.

Departure Tax

At the time of research, the departure tax from Jordan was JD5, (although rates used to vary depending on whether you left by land, sea or air). If you are in the country for less than 72 hours, you are usually exempt from the tax.

LAND

Middle Eastern politics being what it is, all border crossing information should be considered highly perishable – things can alter at short notice so always check the situation before setting out.

Iraq

Buses leave from **JETT's international office** (☎ 5696152; Al-Malek al-Hussein St, Amman) for Baghdad (JD12.500) three times a week. The bus companies which surround the Abdali station in Jebel Amman offer daily services (usually around 2pm) for a little less. Service taxis are faster (because you'll spend less time at the border) but the buses are more comfortable. It is worth remembering that all foreigners entering Iraq must undertake an HIV/AIDS blood test at the border (bring your own syringe) but some travellers are able to get around this with a small financial inducement.

It is very difficult to get an Iraqi visa in Jordan; see the Iraq chapter for details.

Israel & the Palestinian Territories

Since the peace treaty between Jordan and Israel was signed in 1994, there are three border crossings open to foreigners, detailed below.

Trust International Transport has services from Irbid, Amman and Aqaba to Nazareth (JD18), Haifa (JD18) and Tel Aviv (JD21) on every day except Saturday.

It is also worth noting that Israeli visas of one month's duration are issued at the Wadi Araba (Rabin) and Sheikh Hussein Bridge crossings, but those issued at the King Hussein Bridge are usually for three months.

King Hussein Crossing Also known as Jisr al-Malek Hussein or Allenby Bridge, this border crossing point offers travellers the most direct route between Amman and Jerusalem or Tel Aviv. It's open 8am to 6pm Sunday to Thursday and 8am to 2pm Friday and Saturday, but transport doesn't run during the Jewish Shabbat (sunset Friday to sunset Saturday).

Due to the ongoing *intifada* (uprising) and Israeli army action in the Palestinian Territories, no Jordanian buses were offering services across the King Hussein Bridge at the time of research, using instead the other crossings to avoid the West Bank. Instead you must take a service taxi from Amman's Abdali bus station *to* the King Hussein Bridge (JD6.500, 45 minutes, and they run throughout the day) or the sole daily JETT bus (JD6.500). Once at the crossing service taxis then shuttle you over the border (JD1). The ride to the Israeli side, although extremely short, can seem to last an eternity with repeated stops for passport and bag checks. At the time of research, it was not possible to walk, hitch or take a private car across. There are money changing facilities on your way to the exit.

If you wish to return to Jordan while your present Jordanian visa is still valid, you need only keep the stamped exit slip and present it on returning by the same crossing (it sometimes won't work at the other crossings). At the Israeli border post, plead with officials to stamp the Jordanian exit slip rather than your passport, especially if you intend going on to Syria and/or Lebanon – if you are, there must be no evidence of any trip to Israel in your passport, including any evidence at all that you have used any of Jordan's border crossings with Israel.

To get to Jerusalem from the border, shared taxis *(sherut)* go to Damascus Gate or take a cheaper bus to Jericho and then a *sherut* on to Damascus Gate. Be warned, much of the public transport in the West Bank was not running when we were there recently.

Wadi Araba Crossing This handy crossing (formerly Arava to the Israelis, but now renamed by them Rabin) in the south of the country links Aqaba to Eilat. The border is open from 6.30am to 10pm Sunday to Thursday and from 8am to 8pm Friday and Saturday. To get there from Aqaba, service taxis (JD1.250, 10km) leave from the main bus/minibus station, but more frequently early in the morning. Chartering a taxi between central Aqaba and the border costs about JD5. Once at the border you just walk across (the only cross-border service is offered by Trust International Transport – see earlier in the section – although they sometimes use a different crossing). Once on the other side, central Eilat is only 2km away. Bus No 16 runs from the crossing to Eilat's central bus station then on to the Taba crossing into Egypt.

Sheikh Hussein Bridge Also known as Jisr Sheikh Hussein or Jordan Bridge, this northernmost crossing into Israel is the least used of the three crossings. It links northern Jordan with Beit She'an in Galilee. The crossing is open from 6.30am to 10pm Sunday to Thursday and from 8am to 8pm Friday and Saturday.

From Irbid, regular service taxis leave the West bus station for the border (750 fils, 45 minutes). From the bridge it's a 2km walk (or hitch) to the Israeli side from where you take a taxi to the Beit She'an bus station for onward connections inside Israel.

Saudi Arabia

There are daily **Hijazi buses** (☎ 06-4625664) from Amman's Abdali bus station, and from its office on Al-Malek al-Hussein St there are **JETT buses** (☎ 06-5696152) to cities in Saudi Arabia, including Jeddah, Riyadh and Dammam (all JD25). Many of these buses continue on to the cities of the Gulf, including Dubai (JD52), Manama (JD35) and Doha (JD44).

Syria

Bus The border crossings between Jordan and Syria are at Ramtha and Jabir in Jordan and Der'a in Syria. Air-con JETT buses travel between Amman and Damascus (JD5, seven hours) twice a day in either direction; book at least a day in advance. Buses are the most comfortable way to cross the border although you may have to wait longer than in a shared taxi at the border.

Train The quaint old station for the Hejaz Railway is on King Abdullah I St, about 2.5km east of the Raghadan station in Amman. The train leaves Amman for Damascus on Monday and Thursday at 8am and costs JD2.500. The **ticket office** (☎ 06-4895413) is really only open from 7am on the morning of departure, although you may find someone around at other times. To get to the station, take a service taxi from Raghadan, or a private taxi (around 800 fils).

Service Taxi Enormous yellow shared taxis (JD6) or *servees* leave regularly throughout the day for Damascus (Baramke terminal) from the lower (eastern) end of the Abdali bus station. From Irbid's South bus station, service taxis go to Damascus (JD4.500).

SEA

There are two boat services to Nuweiba in Egypt. With both, departure times can be subject to change so call the passenger terminal (☎ 2013240) on the morning of the day you wish to travel. For noon departures, you should always get there by around 10.30am.

The fast boat, which leaves most days at noon, covers the distance in about an hour and costs US$30; children between the ages of five and 12 pay US$18, while those under five pay US$12. One reliable place that sells tickets for the fast boat in Aqaba is **International Traders** (☎ 03-2013757, fax 201 5316; e aqaba.office@traders.com.jo; Al-Hammamat al-Tunisieh St). Alternatively, buy your ticket at the ferry port.

There is also a slower ferry service which officially leaves at noon but often quite a few hours later. Some days it doesn't leave at all. The cost is US$22, or US$13/8 for children over/under five. Some agencies in Aqaba sell tickets but they never sell out and you can purchase them at the ferry terminal when departing.

Minibuses occasionally leave from near the admission to Aqaba castle on King Hussein St for the Saudi border and pass the terminal (350 fils). A private taxi from central Aqaba shouldn't cost more than JD2.

Getting Around

AIR
In addition to Queen Alia International Airport, there is also a smaller airfield in the outlying Amman suburb of Marka.

Royal Wings, a subsidiary of Royal Jordanian Airlines, flies between Aqaba and Amman (JD33.550/67 one-way/return, or JD62 for same day return) at least once every day. At the time of research, flights leave Amman in the morning, and return from Aqaba in the evening. These flights alternate between Marka airport or the Queen Alia International Airport depending on demand.

BUS & MINIBUS
The blue-and-white JETT buses run from Amman to Aqaba, King Hussein Bridge border crossing, Petra and Hammamat Ma'in. See Getting There & Away in the Amman section later in the chapter.

Other companies with regular services from Amman include: Trust International Transport and Afana (both to Aqaba) and Hijazi (Irbid).

Just about all towns in Jordan are connected by 20-seat minibuses, although the King's Hwy and Eastern Jordan are less well-served. The minibuses leave when full. The correct fare is nearly always posted in Arabic inside the front of the minibus and charging tourists more is rare, although drivers on the Amman to Wadi Musa (for Petra) run like to charge travellers JD1 for their baggage.

SERVICE TAXI
Service taxis (in Arabic, *ser-***vees**) are more expensive than minibuses and don't cover as many routes, but they're generally faster and take less time to fill up. Inside cities like Amman, service taxis offer extensive coverage and are a good alternative to walking or taking private taxis. For more details, see Getting Around and Getting There & Away in the Amman section later in the chapter.

TAXI
Private (yellow) taxis are quite cheap although only those in Amman use the meters (something most Amman taxi drivers do as a matter of course but always check it's switched on before setting out). The only exception is sometimes when you are laden with bags and obviously looking for a hotel.

CAR & MOTORCYCLE
Vehicles drive on the right side of the road in Jordan, at least most of the time. The speed limit is 50km/h in built-up areas, 90km/h on the open road and 110km/h on the Desert Hwy. Indicators are seldom used, rules are occasionally obeyed, the horn is a useful warning signal and pedestrians must take their chances. The condition of the roads varies, with unsigned speed humps common, as are shallow ditches across the road.

Petrol is available along the Desert and King's Hwys and in most sizable towns. Expect to pay about 300 fils for a litre of regular, 370 fils for super, and best of luck if you're looking for unleaded. Diesel is about 150 fils a litre.

Motorcyclists should be aware that there are precious few mechanics in Jordan able to deal with the average modern motorcycle and its problems.

Rental
Renting a car is an ideal way to get the most out of Jordan. Listed below are some of the more reliable agencies. Charges, conditions, insurance costs and waiver fees in case of accident (CDW) vary considerably so shop around. Always read your contract carefully before signing, remember that many places require a minimum three days rental and all require a deposit of up to JD400 payable upon pick-up and refunded upon the return of the car.

Budget (☎ 06-5698131, fax 5673312, e budget@ go.com.jo) 125 Al-Shareef Abdulla Hameed Sharaf St. Charges from JD33 per day including unlimited kilometres and insurance.

Eurodollar Rent a Car (☎ 06-5693399, fax 5687233, e info@eurodollar-jo.com) Al-Shareef Abdulla Hameed Sharaf St. Rates start from JD20 per day plus JD10 CDW per day with unlimited kilometres.

Firas Car Rental (Alamo Car Rental) (☎ 06-4612927, fax 4616874, e alamo@nets.com.jo) 1st Circle. Highly recommended; charges from

JD15 per day with unlimited kilometres. CDW is JD7 per day.

National Car Rental (☎/fax 5601350, e nation alcar@joinnet.com.jo) Amman Marriott and Le Meridien Hotels in Shmeisani. Charges from JD25 per day (including CDW). Rates include 200km free for the first three days (150 fils per additional kilometre) or unlimited kilometres for more than three days rental.

BICYCLE

Cycling is an option in Jordan but not necessarily a fun one. The desert in summer is not a good place to indulge in strenuous activity, and cyclists on the King's Hwy have reported stone-throwing by groups of young children. Cycling north or south can be hard work as there is a strong prevailing western wind that can wear you down. Anywhere from the East Bank plateau down to the Dead Sea or Jordan Valley makes for exhilarating descents, but coming the other way will really test your calf muscles. Bring plenty of spare parts (see Bicycle in the Getting Around the Region chapter).

ORGANISED TOURS

Amman is an ideal place to base yourself while exploring anywhere north, east and west of Amman, and even as far south as Karak. It's easy enough to day trip to these places using public transport, although you'll need weeks to see them all in this way.

Budget hotels in Amman which cater to independent travellers (eg the Cliff or Farah Hotels) offer day trips from Amman which cost anywhere from JD10 to JD25 per person depending on the places visited and number of people involved. Popular destinations include: Madaba, Mt Nebo and the Dead Sea; Jerash, Ajlun and Umm Qais; or the Desert Castles to the east. We've received varying reports about the quality of such tours so it's worth asking other travellers before deciding.

One option that has been recommended by readers is the tour offered by some hotels which leaves Amman at 8.30am and travels to Petra (around 6pm) via Madaba, Wadi Mujib, Karak, Shobak and Dana with time spent at each of the various sites. The hotels from Madaba offer a similar service.

Of the tour companies with a good reputation for comprehensive (but more expensive) tours around Jordan, try **International**

Traders (☎ 06-5607075) or alternatively call **Petra Moon** (☎ 03-2156665, fax 215 6666; e eid@petramoon.com).

Amman عمان

☎ 06

Amman is not one of the great cities of antiquity. Indeed for those arriving from Syria or Egypt, it can feel disappointingly modern and Westernised. Its obvious tourist attractions – the 6000-seat Roman Theatre, Odeon and Citadel with its great views – can be easily visited in a few hours.

But Amman has lots to offer the visitor, not least the balance it strikes between the demands of the past and the vision for the future of its next generation. Residents of Amman talk openly of two Ammans, although in truth there are many. Eastern Amman (which includes Downtown) is home to the urbanised poor, conservative, more Islamic in its sympathies and with vast Palestinian refugee camps on its fringe. Western Amman is a world apart, the preserve of leafy residential districts, trendy cafés and bars, impressive contemporary art galleries and young men and women walking openly arm in arm.

Don't come to Amman looking for medieval souqs and bazaars, or grand mosques. But do come to Amman to catch a glimpse of a tolerant and thoroughly modern Arab city, embracing an international and culturally diverse vision of the future. Whether you're in the urbane suburbs of the west, or the earthy and chaotic Downtown district, the welcome you receive will undoubtedly be warm.

History

Excavations in and around Amman have turned up finds from as early as 3500 BC. Occupation of the town, called Rabbath Ammon or 'Great City of the Ammonites' in the Old Testament, has been continuous.

Biblical references are numerous, and indicate that by 1200 BC Rabbath Ammon was the capital of the Ammonites. During David's reign, he sent Joab at the head of Israelite armies to besiege Rabbath, after being insulted by the Ammonite king Nahash. After taking the town, David burnt many inhabitants alive in a brick kiln.

AMMAN

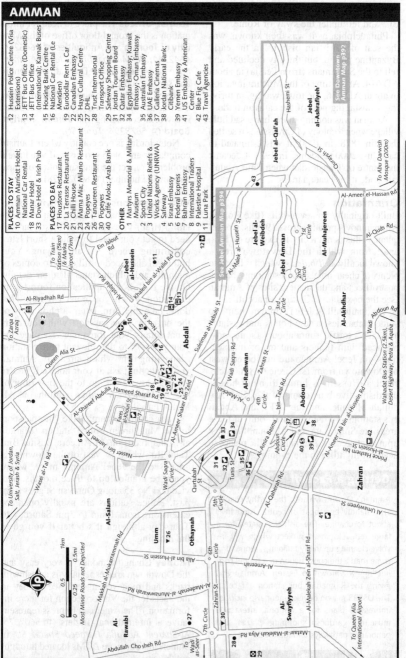

PLACES TO STAY
10 Amman Marriott Hotel;
   Manar Hotel
18 Manar Hotel
33 Dove Hotel & Irish Pub

PLACES TO EAT
17 Houstons Restaurant
20 La Terrasse Restaurant
21 Chili House
23 Mama Mia; Milano Restaurant
24 Popeyes
26 Tanouren Restaurant
30 Popeyes
40 Caffe Moka; Arab Bank

OTHER
1 Martyrs Memorial & Military
   Museum
2 Sports City
3 United Nations Reliefs &
   Works Agency (UNRWA)
4 Safeway
5 Israel Embassy
6 Federal Express
7 Bahrain Embassy
8 International Traders
9 Palestine Hospital
11 Luna Park
12 Hussein Police Centre (Visa
   Extensions)
13 JETT Bus Office (Domestic)
14 JETT Bus Office
   (International); Karnak Buses
15 Housing Bank Centre
16 National Car Rental (Le
   Meridien)
19 Eurodollar Rent a Car
22 Canadian Embassy
25 Haya Cultural Centre
27 DHL
28 Trust International
   Transport Office
29 Safeway Shopping Centre
31 Jordan Tourism Board
32 Qatar Embassy
34 Egyptian Embassy; Kuwait
   Embassy; Oman Embassy
35 Australian Embassy
36 UAE Embassy
37 Galleria Cinemas
38 Jordan National Bank;
   Citibank
39 Yemen Embassy
41 US Embassy & American
   Center
42 Blue Fig Cafe
43 Travel Agencies

JORDAN

Amman was taken by Herod around 30 BC, and fell under the sway of Rome.

Philadelphia, as it was then known, was the seat of Christian bishops in the early Byzantine period, but the city declined and fell to the Sassanians (from Persia) in about AD 614. At the time of the Muslim invasion in about AD 636, the town was again thriving as a staging post of the caravan trade.

Amman was nothing more than a sad little village when a colony of Circassians resettled there in 1878. In 1900, it was estimated to have just 2000 residents. In 1921 it became the centre of Transjordan when Emir Abdullah made it his headquarters.

Orientation

Built originally on seven hills (like Rome), Amman now spreads across 19 hills. Consequently, this is not a city to explore on foot, apart from within the Downtown area – known locally as *il-balad* – which is home to plenty of cheap hotels and restaurants, banks, post offices and the ancient sites of Amman (see the boxed text 'Getting a Facelift').

The main hill is Jebel Amman, home to some embassies, a few hotels and restaurants. The traffic roundabouts (some now replaced with tunnels and major intersections) on Jebel Amman are numbered west of Downtown from 1st Circle to 8th Circle. Jebel al-Hussein is home to more hotels, the distinctive blue dome of the King Abdullah Mosque, and the JETT and Abdali bus stations. To the west and south of these areas are Shmeisani and Abdoun, the most upmarket areas of Amman and the places to head for nightlife in the evening.

Getting a Facelift

Amman's Downtown area, the earthy, chaotic and friendly heartbeat of central Amman is about to change. The district is slated for a large redevelopment project which will involve cleaning up many buildings, reorienting some roads, the construction of a tunnel connecting Downtown to Eastern Amman and giving the Raghadan bus station a facelift. The US$33 million development also includes impressive plans for a national interactive museum, gardens, shopping plazas and panoramic pathways and lookouts.

Information

Tourist Offices The place to head for information is the ground floor office of the **Ministry of Tourism and Antiquities** (☎ 4646264, 4642311; Al-Mutanabbi St, Jebel Amman; open 8am-11pm daily). The staff are friendly and speak good English.

If you're after brochures and more information about Jordan's tourist attractions, it's worth contacting the **Jordan Tourism Board** (☎ 5678294; Tunis St).

Note: Jordan is one country where tourism complaints are taken seriously. If you have a problem, contact the tourism police on their nationwide number (☎ 80022228).

Visa Extensions If you are staying in Jordan for longer than 14 days, you must obtain a (free) visa extension. First you will need to get your hotel to write a short letter confirming where you are staying. Your hotel will also need to fill out two copies of a small card which states all their details. On the back is the application form for an extension which you must fill out. That done, take the form, letter, a photocopy of the page in your passport with your personal details, your Jordanian visa page and your passport to the relevant police station (depending on which area of Amman you're staying; ask at your hotel). If you're staying Downtown, go to the first floor of the Al-Madeenah police station on Al-Malek Faisal St.

After getting a stamp, take your passport to the Muhajireen Police Station (Markez al-Muhajireen) on Al-Ameera Basma Bint Talal Rd, which is west of the Downtown area (see the Jebel Amman map), where you'll be granted up to three months. Service taxi No 35 along Quraysh St goes right past. Police stations are usually open for extensions from 10am to 3pm Saturday to Thursday although it's better if you go in the morning.

Money Changing money is very easy and the Downtown area especially is awash with banks and moneychangers. (See Money in the Facts for the Visitor section for more information.) The American Express representative is **International Traders** (☎ 5607075; Al-Shareef Abdulla Hameed Sharaf St) in Shmeisani. There are ATMs located throughout the city.

Post & Communications The central post office (☎ 4624120; Al-Amir Mohammed St; open 7am-7pm Sat-Thur, May-Sept, 7am-5pm Sat-Thur Oct-Apr, 7am-1.30pm Fri) is in Downtown. To make a telephone call, use a telephone in your hotel, or one of the numerous payphones operated by Alo; telephone cards are available at grocery stores around town. There are also private telephone agencies along Omar al-Khayyam St.

Email & Internet Access Amman has plenty of Internet cafés, especially in Shmeisani. In Downtown, try **Internet Yard** (e dweib@joinnet.com.jo; Al-Amir Mohammed S, Downtown; open 24 hours); **Yahoo Internet** (☎ 4647215; Al-Jaza'er St) behind the Raghadan bus station; and **Books@cafe** (☎ 4650457; e contact@books-cafe.com; Omar al-Khattab St, Jebel Amman).

Bookshops Among Amman's better bookshops are: **Books@cafe** (☎ 4650457; e contact@books-cafe.com; Omar al-Khattab St); **Amman Bookshop** (☎ 4644013; Al-Amir Mohammed St); and **Al-Aulama Bookshop** (☎ 4636192; Al-Amir Mohammed St, Downtown). For international newspapers, try the bookshops of the top-end hotels (the **Jordan InterContinental** is especially good) and **Bustami's Library** (☎ 4622649; Al-Amir Mohammed St, Downtown).

Cultural Centres & Libraries All of the following cultural centres regularly organise film nights, exhibitions and concerts.

British Council (☎ 4636147, fax 4656413, w www.britishcouncil.org/jordan) Rainbow St, southeast of 1st Circle. Has a library with current English newspapers. Open noon to 6pm Sunday to Wednesday and 11am to 3.30pm Thursday.
Centre Culturel Francais (☎ 4637009) On Kulliyat al-Sharee'ah at the top of Jebel Weibdeh. Has a useful library. Open 11am to 2pm & 4pm to 8pm Sunday to Wednesday, 4pm-8pm Saturday.
Goethe Institut (☎ 4641993, fax 4612383, e giammvw@go.com.jo) 5 Abdul Mun'im al-Rifa'l St, northwest of 3rd Circle. Open 9am to 1pm Sunday to Thursday, 4.30pm to 6.30pm on Sunday, Tuesday and Wednesday, and 4.30pm to 6.30pm on Monday.
Haya Cultural Centre (☎ 5665195) Ilya Abu Mahdi St, Shmeisani. Designed for children, there's a library, playground and museum and the centre regularly organises activities for children. Open 9am to 2pm and 4pm to 6pm daily.

Medical Services Among the better hospitals are **Italian Hospital** (☎ 4777101; Italian St, Downtown); **Palestine Hospital** (☎ 5607071; Queen Alia St, Shmeisani); and **University Hospital** (☎ 5353444; University of Jordan complex) in northern Amman. The two English-language daily newspapers list the current telephone numbers of doctors and pharmacies on night duty throughout the capital. **Jacob's Pharmacy** (☎ 4644945; 3rd Circle; open 9am-3am daily) is central.

Things to See

The restored **Roman Theatre** (admission free; open 8am-5pm daily winter, 8am-7pm daily summer) is the most obvious and impressive remnant of ancient Philadelphia. The theatre is cut into the northern side of a hill that once served as a necropolis, and can hold 6000. The theatre was built in the 2nd century AD during the reign of Antoninus Pius, who ruled the Roman Empire from AD 138 to 161. Performances are sometimes staged here in summer.

The row of columns immediately in front (north) of the theatre is all that's left of the **Forum**, once one of the largest public squares (about 100m by 50m) in Imperial Rome. On the eastern side of what was the Forum stands the 500-seat **Odeon** (admission free; open 8am-5pm daily winter, 8am-7pm daily summer). Built about the same time as the Roman Theatre, it served mainly as a venue for musical performances. Philadelphia's chief fountain or **Nymphaeum** (admission free, open daylight hours Sat-Thur) (AD 191) stands with its back to Quraysh St, west of the theatre and not far from King Hussein Mosque.

The **Citadel** (admission free; open 8am-5pm daily), on Jebel al-Qala'a, has some excavated ruins of an **Umayyad Palace**, dating from about AD 720, of which the domed **audience hall** is the most impressive. There is also an **Umayyad Cistern**; a **Byzantine Basilica** from the 6th or 7th century AD; and the pillars of the **Temple of Hercules** which was constructed during the reign of Marcus Aurelius (AD 161–80). Next to the temple is a **lookout** with great views of the Downtown area.

Nearby, the **National Archaeological Museum** (☎ 4638795; admission low/high season JD1/2; open 8am-5pm Sat-Thur & 10am-4pm Fri) is one of the best museums in Jordan with

JORDAN

DOWNTOWN AMMAN

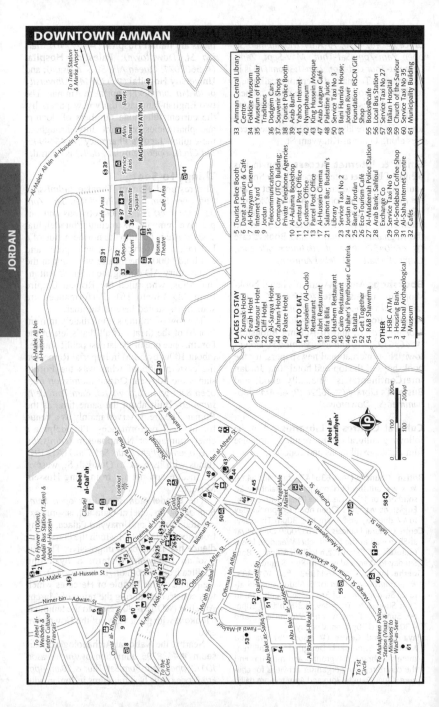

PLACES TO STAY
2 Karnak Hotel
16 Farah Hotel
19 Mansour Hotel
22 Cliff Hotel
40 Al-Saraya Hotel
44 Zahran Hotel
49 Palace Hotel

PLACES TO EAT
14 Jerusalem (Al-Quds)
   Restaurant
15 Jabri Restaurant
18 Bifa Billa
20 Hashem Restaurant
45 Cairo Restaurant
46 Shaher's Penthouse Cafeteria
51 Batata
52 Get Together
54 R&B Shawerma

OTHER
1 HSBC ATM
3 Housing Bank
4 National Archaeological
   Museum
5 Tourist Police Booth
6 Darat al-Funun & Café
8 Al-Khayyam Cinema
9 Internet Yard
9 Jordan
   Telecommunications
   Company (JTC) Building;
   Private Telephone Agencies
10 Al-Aulama Bookshop
11 Central Post Office
12 Customs Office
13 Parcel Post Office
17 Al-Hussein Cinema
21 Salamon Bar; Bustami's
   Library
23 Service Taxi No 2
24 Jordan Bar
25 Bank of Jordan
26 Eco-Tourism Café
27 Al-Madeenah Police Station
28 Arab Bank; Sahloul
   Exchange Co
29 Service Taxi No 6
30 Al-Sendebad Coffee Shop
31 Al-Saha Internet Centre
32 Cafés
33 Amman Central Library
   Centre
34 Folklore Museum
35 Museum of Popular
   Traditions
36 Dodgem Cars
37 Souvenir Shops
38 Tourist Police Booth
39 Arab Bank
41 Yahoo Internet
42 Nymphaeum
43 King Hussein Mosque
47 Arab League Café
48 Palestine Juice
50 Service Taxi No 3
53 Bani Hamida House;
   Jordan River
   Foundation; RSCN Gift
   Shop
55 Books@cafe
56 Local Bus Station
57 Service Taxi No 27
58 Italian Hospital
59 Church of the Saviour
60 Service Taxi No 35
61 Municipality Building

an interesting collection of items spanning all eras of Jordanian history.

The **Folklore Museum** (☎ 4651742; admission winter/summer JD0.5/1 (combined ticket); open 8am-5pm Wed-Mon winter, 8am-7pm Wed-Mon summer) is one of two small museums housed in the wings of the Roman Theatre. The other is the **Museum of Popular Traditions** (☎ 4651670; admission winter/summer JD0.5/1 (combined ticket); open 8am-5pm Wed-Mon winter, 8am-7pm Wed-Mon summer) which has well-presented displays of traditional costumes, jewellery, utensils and a mosaic collection.

The **Martyrs Memorial & Military Museum** (☎ 5664240; admission free; open 9am-4pm Sat-Thur), out by the Sports City, is a simple and solemn memorial to Jordan's fallen with an interesting museum chronicling Jordan's military history from the Arab Revolt in 1916 to the Arab-Israeli wars.

The small but excellent **Jordan National Gallery of Fine Art** (☎ 4630128; Hosni Fareez St; admission JD1; open 9am-5pm Sat-Mon & Wed-Thur) exhibits contemporary Jordanian works, including painting, sculpture and pottery.

Darat al-Funun (☎ 4643251, fax 464 3253; e darat@shoman.org.jo; w www.daratalfunun.org; Nimer bin Adwan St; admission free; open 10am-7pm Sat-Wed & 10am-8pm Thur) is a superb, tranquil complex dedicated to contemporary art. It features a small art gallery, an art library, artists' workshops and a regular programme of exhibitions, lectures, films and public discussion forums.

The attraction at the **King Hussein Mosque** (Hashemi St, Downtown) is the whole precinct rather than the building – as usual, prayer times are busy, but at other times the front of the mosque and the surrounding streets exude an altogether Arab flavour. The first mosque was built on this site in AD 640 by Omar, the second caliph of Islam. The latest version was built by King Abdullah I in 1924 and was restored in 1987.

The **King Abdullah Mosque** (Suleiman al-Nabulsi St; admission JD1; open 8am-11am & 12.30pm-2.30pm Sat-Thur, 10am-noon Friday) can house up to 7000 worshippers inside, and another 3000 in the courtyard area. This is the only mosque in Amman which openly welcomes non-Muslim visitors. Women are required to wear something to cover their hair.

Hashemite Square, between the Roman Theatre and the Raghadan station, is a place to stroll, sip tea, smoke the *sheesha* (water pipe) and simply watch the world go by. It can be packed on a summer's evening.

Turkish Bath

The **Al-Pasha Turkish Bath** (☎/fax 4633002; Al-Mahmoud Taha St, Jebel Amman) is the perfect antidote to the hills and bustle of Amman. The full service (JD13.500) includes a steam bath, sauna, Jacuzzi, scrubbing, 40-minute massage and two soft drinks, all done in a superb building architecturally faithful to the tradition of Turkish *hammams*. It's open 10am to midnight daily.

Places to Stay – Budget

Downtown Amman is overflowing with cheap hotels. All budget places mentioned below come with shared bathroom facilities unless stated otherwise; all promise hot water and some even deliver.

Note: Don't believe taxi drivers who tell you that your hotel is closed, they can't find it or it has suffered some other inglorious fate; they're usually looking for commission from hotel owners. Don't let them accompany you to your hotel, as the commission will be added to your bill.

Zahran Hotel (☎ 4625473; Al-Muhajereen St; beds JD1.500-3) is basic, noisy and not for lone women travellers.

Cliff Hotel (☎ 4624273, fax 46238078; Al-Amir Mohammed St; singles/doubles JD5/6) is a long-standing backpacker favourite with friendly staff in the heart of Downtown. Rooms are generally tidy and simple although some beds are better than others.

Mansour Hotel (☎ 4621575; Al-Malek Faisal St; singles JD5.500, doubles JD7.700-8.800) is central and quieter than most because it's a little back from the busy main road.

Farah Hotel (☎ 4651443, fax 4651437, Cinema al-Hussein St; singles/doubles JD7/9) is a backpacker-savvy place which gets consistently good reports from travellers. The rooms are tidy and the staff friendly and eager to help.

Palace Hotel (☎ 4624326, fax 4650603; Al-Malek Faisal St; singles/doubles JD8/14) is probably the best in the area and worth a little splurge. The rooms are clean, large, and some have balconies.

JEBEL AMMAN

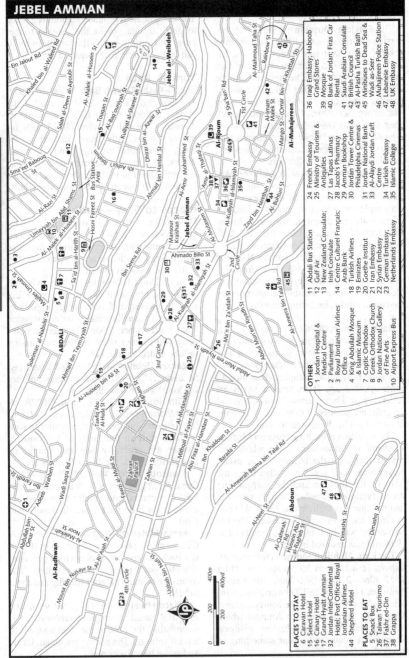

PLACES TO STAY
6 Caravan Hotel
15 Select Hotel
16 Canary Hotel
17 Grand Hyatt Amman
32 Jordan InterContinental Hotel; Post Office; Royal Jordanian Airlines
44 Shepherd Hotel

PLACES TO EAT
5 Snack Box
26 Taiwan Tourismo
37 Fakhr ed-Din
38 Grappa

OTHER
1 Jordan Hospital & Medical Centre
2 Parliament
3 Royal Jordanian Airlines Office
4 King Abdullah Mosque & Islamic Museum
7 Coptic Orthodox
8 Greek Orthodox Church
9 Jordan National Gallery of Fine Arts
10 Airport Express Bus

11 Abdali Bus Station
12 Gulf Air
13 New Zealand Consulate; Irish Consulate
14 Centre Culturel Français; Arab Bank
18 Turkish Airlines
19 Emirates
20 Goethe Institut
21 Iran Embassy
22 Syrian Embassy
23 German Embassy; Netherlands Embassy

24 French Embassy
25 Ministry of Tourism & Antiquities
27 Las Tapas Latinas
28 Jacob's Pharmacy
29 Amman Bookshop
30 Jordan Tower Centre & Philadelphia Cinemas
31 Jordan National Bank
33 Al-Alaydi Jordan Craft Centre
34 Turkish Embassy
35 Islamic College

36 Iraqi Embassy; Haboob Grand Stores
39 Mosque
40 Bank of Jordan; Firas Car Rental
41 Saudi Arabian Consulate
42 British Council
43 Al-Pasha Turkish Bath
45 Minibuses to Dead Sea & Wadi as-Seer
46 Muhajireen Police Station
47 Lebanese Embassy
48 UK Embassy

Karnak Hotel *(☎/fax 4638125; Al-Malek al-Hussein St; singles/doubles JD7/10)* is excellent value, well run and friendly. The rooms are very comfortable and a few have balconies.

Select Hotel *(☎ 4637101, fax 4637102; e sales@amman-select.com; Al-Baq'ouniyah St; singles/doubles JD11/18)* is excellent upper-budget value. Its rooms are clean and spacious and come with TV, air-con and spotless bathrooms. Prices include breakfast.

Places to Stay – Mid-Range

Al-Saraya Hotel *(☎ 4656791, fax 4656792; e sayara-hotel@index.com.jo; Al-Jaza'er St; singles/doubles/triples JD14/18/22)* is the best mid-range option in Downtown with clean, spacious rooms. It's opposite the eastern end of Raghadan bus station.

Canary Hotel *(☎ 4638353, fax 4638353; e canary_h@hotmail.com; off Kulliyat al-Sharee'ah St; singles/doubles JD24/32)* has a welcoming, homely feel. The rooms are more comfortable than luxurious although the bathrooms sparkle.

Caravan Hotel *(☎ 5661195, fax 5661996; e caravan@go.com.jo; Al-Ma'moun St; singles/doubles JD18/24)*, almost opposite the King Abdullah Mosque, is similarly good value with pleasant rooms. Add 13% tax to quoted room prices.

Dove Hotel *(☎ 5697601, fax 5674676; e dove@go.com.jo, Qurtubah St; singles/doubles JD24/28)*, between 4th and 5th Circles, is one of the best in this price range with nice rooms and excellent service.

Shepherd Hotel *(☎/fax 4639197; e shepherdhtl@joinnet.com.jo; Zayd bin Harethah St; singles/doubles/suites JD25/35/60)* has come warmly recommended by readers. The rooms are great value and very comfortable.

Manar Hotel *(☎ 5662186, fax 5684329; Al-Shareef Abdulla Hameed Sharaf St; singles/doubles JD25/35)* is excellent value in the Shmeisani area, especially in summer when it's one of the cheapest places in Amman with a swimming pool.

Places to Stay – Top End

Grand Hyatt Amman *(☎ 4651234, fax 4651634; e info@ammgh.com.jo; Al-Hussein bin Ali St; doubles JD65)* is excellent top-end value; rates change on a daily basis. It's quite a complex with seven restaurants, a book-shop, nightclub, expensive boutiques, business centre, exhibition centre and an Internet deli.

Jordan InterContinental Hotel *(☎ 4641361, fax 4645217; e ammha@interconti.com; Al-Kulleyah al-Islamiyah St; doubles JD65)*, midway between 2nd and 3rd Circles, is suitably luxurious and has a shopping arcade and deli.

Amman Marriott *(☎ 5607607, fax 567 0100; e jomariot@marriott.com.jo; Isam al-Ajlouni St; singles/doubles from JD65/75)* is also typically good top-end value.

Places to Eat

Amman's budget restaurants are concentrated in Downtown and, to a lesser extent, Jebel Amman, while the more upmarket restaurants are concentrated in Shmeisani and Abdoun.

Local Food There are plenty of felafel and shwarma stalls in Downtown, especially around the Raghadan Bus Station. **Palestine Juice** *(Al-Malek Faisal St; open 7am-11pm daily)* is a good juice stand which serves refreshing carrot or orange juice and banana with milk (500 fils/JD1 for a small/large).

Hashem Restaurant *(Al-Amir Mohammed St; meals around JD1; open 24 hours daily)*, which overflows into the alley, is very popular with locals for felafel, hummus and *fuul*.

Cairo Restaurant *(☎ 4624527; Al-Malek Talal St; mains from JD1; open 6am-10pm daily)* serves large, good-value meals with *mensaf* a lot cheaper here (JD1.500) than elsewhere.

Jerusalem (Al-Quds) Restaurant *(☎ 463 0168, fax 4649101; Al-Malek al-Hussein St; mains from JD2; open 7am-10pm daily)* specialises in sweets and pastries, but has a large restaurant at the back. It's the sort of place where a tip is expected and usually warranted.

Jabri Restaurant *(☎ 4624108; Al-Malek al-Hussein St; mains from JD1.800; open 8am-8pm Sat-Thur)* is also predominantly a pastry place but the restaurant upstairs is good with views over the street and attentive service.

Shahers Penthouse Cafeteria *(☎ 4627354; Al-Muhajereen St; mains from JD2.500; open 9.30am-11pm daily)* has an atmospheric indoor dining area and an outdoor terrace overlooking the street.

Bifa Billa *(Cinema al-Hussein St; mains from 500 fils; open noon-midnight daily)* is one of the best places in Downtown for hamburgers and shwarmas and it also does excellent milkshakes.

Get Together *(☎ 4617216; e GT_JO@ yahoo.com; Rainbow St; mains from JD1.5; open noon-midnight Wed-Mon)* serves good sandwiches, crepes and salads but this place also carries a creative twist – a menu of over 135 board games with which to pass the time.

Batata *(☎ 4656768; Rainbow St; fries JD0.6-1.5; open noon-midnight Sat-Thur & 4pm-midnight Fri)* does little but French fries but it does them well and they come with a choice of eight sauces (100 fils).

R&B Shawerma *(☎ 4645347; Rainbow St; shwarmas from 750 fils; open noon-midnight daily)* is not your average shwarma place with Chinese, chicken and cheese varieties. Meals including great fries and a soft drink cost no more than JD2.500.

Snack Box *(☎ 5661323; Suleiman al-Nabulsi St; meals JD1.750-2.500; open noon-10pm Sat-Thur)* is the best of its kind in Jordan with a delicious takeaway menu that includes superb burgers and sandwiches, not to mention Mexican, Chinese, Thai and other international dishes.

Fakhr el-Din *(☎ 4652399, fax 4641792; w www.fakhreldin.com; 40 Taha Hussein St; mains JD2-6.500; open 1pm-4pm & 7pm-11pm daily)* does highly recommended Lebanese food in a classy setting.

Kan Zaman *(☎ 4128391, fax 4128395; buffet lunch/dinner JD6/11; open 1pm-4.30pm & 6.30pm-1am daily)* is a bit of a hike, around 10km south of 8th Circle, but it is one of Amman's longest-standing top-end restaurants.

Western Food Amman also has a number of excellent restaurants if you're willing to pay a little more.

Books@cafe *(☎ 4650457; Omar bin al-Khattab St; mains from JD2.655; open 10am-11.30pm daily)* serves genuine Italian pizzas and pasta as well as good salads. The food is excellent and the atmosphere super-cool. Hot drinks are a steep JD1 to JD1.250 although the 'hot strawberry' may just be worth it.

Grappa *(☎ 4651458, fax 4650295; Abdul Qader Koshak St; mains JD2.500-7.500;*

open 6pm-1.30am daily) does decent Italian food in a superb setting with a terrace and beer garden overlooking the valley.

Blue Fig Cafe *(☎ 5928800, fax 5929988; e bluefig@nets.com.jo; Prince Hashem bin al-Hussein St; mains around JD4; open 8.30am-1am daily)* is a super-cool place not far from Abdoun Circle. It has an extensive and imaginative menu with a delicious range of pastry and pizza-type dishes.

Taiwan Tourismo *(☎ 4641093; Mithqal al-Fayez St; mains from JD1.800; open noon-3.30pm & 6.30pm-midnight daily)* is much classier than its name suggests and, with reasonable prices and over 100 menu items to choose from, is a good choice.

Mama Mia *(☎ 5604620; Ilya Abu Mahdi St; mains JD2-5; open noon-midnight daily)* does excellent pasta and pizza.

Milano Restaurant *(☎ 5680670; Ilya Abu Mahdi St; mains from JD2.200; open noon-midnight daily)* is another pizza and pasta place which is popular with young locals in the evening.

The classy and expensive places are often in remote suburbs, such as Shmeisani. Remember that most top-end places add a whopping 23% tax to the quoted prices.

La Terrasse *(☎ 5662831, fax 5601675; 11 August St; mains JD3.500-8.500; open noon-1am daily)* does decent European cuisine in a pleasant setting. There is live Arab music most nights after 10pm.

Houstons *(☎ 5620610; off Abdul Hameed Shoman St, Shmeisani; mains JD5-9; open noon-midnight daily)* is a popular restaurant that gets good reviews from expats. It specialises in Mexican dishes, but also does top-quality steaks as well as burgers, sandwiches and pasta.

Tannoureen Restaurant *(☎ 5515987, fax 5523908; Shatt al-Arab St; mains JD4.800-8; open 12.30-4.30pm & 7.30-11.30pm daily)* is good for Lebanese food, especially mezze, but it also does Western dishes.

Fast Food If you must, many of the major international fast-food chains have outlets in Amman, especially in Shmeisani. They include: **Pizza Hut; KFC, Burger King, Dunkin Donuts, Chilli House, Popeyes** and **McDonalds.**

Self-Catering Of the larger supermarkets, **Safeway** has an outlet *(☎ 5685311; Nasser* *bin Jameel St; open 24 hours)*, around 500m southwest of the Sports City junction, and just southwest of 7th Circle *(☎ 5815558)*. More central is **Haboob Grand Stores** *(☎ 4622221; Al-Kulleyah al-Islamiyah St; open 7am-midnight daily)*, between 1st and 2nd Circles, just up from the Iraqi embassy.

Entertainment

There is plenty of nightlife in the evenings in Amman, although little that's salubrious in the Downtown area. Shmeisani, Abdoun and, to a lesser extent, Jebel Amman have numerous trendy cafés, bars and a few nightclubs which stay open late.

Bars & Clubs Several bars in Downtown, visited almost exclusively by men, are tucked away in the alleys near the Cliff Hotel.

Jordan Bar *(☎ 079796352; off Al-Amir Mohammed St; open 10am-midnight daily)* is the place to go if your drinking day starts early. It's a cosy place with an earthy charm which hasn't changed in years. A large Amstel costs JD1.750.

Salamon Bar *(☎ 079902940; off Al-Amir Mohammed St; open noon-midnight daily)*, a lane or two to the north, has beer on tap, but it's tiny and full of smoke. A large Amstel costs JD1.900.

Las Tapas Latinas *(☎ 4615061, fax 461 5060; off Al-Kulleyah al-Islamiyah St near 3rd Circle; open 6pm-late daily)* is the only salsa bar in Amman. You can get tapas, just about any drink you could want and salsa dance the night away. Things don't start happening until after 10pm.

Irish Pub *(☎ 5697601; Qurtubah St; open 7pm-late daily)*, downstairs from the Dove Hotel (see Places to Stay earlier), is something of an Amman institution among the city's hip young things, and stays open until the last patrons stagger out. The dance floor is often packed, especially on a Thursday night when this place rocks.

Blue Fig Cafe *(☎ 5928800; Prince Hashem bin al-Hussein St; open 8.30am-1am daily)* is a great café/bar to spend an afternoon or evening with a trendy crowd, pleasant atmosphere and live music on Saturday nights.

Cafés Some of the cafés in Downtown are great places to watch the world go by, smoke a nargileh (or *sheesha*), meet locals and play cards or backgammon.

One of the best places for the uninitiated to try the nargileh is the **Eco-Tourism Cafe** *(☎ 4652994; Al-Malek Faisal St; open 10am-11pm Sat-Thur & 1-11pm Fri)*. Its first floor balcony is *the* place to pass an afternoon and survey the chaos of the Downtown area down below.

Al-Sendabad Coffee Shop *(☎ 4632035; open 10am-midnight daily)* is 150m west of Roman Theatre and has great views over the city. It's a great place to smoke nargileh (JD1), especially on the roof in summer.

A dozen or more cafés can be found around Hashemite Square and along Hashemi St. They're good for people-watching, as the flow of pedestrians never seems to diminish here, especially in summer.

One of the places in Amman to be seen at night is anywhere around Abdoun Circle and there are plenty of popular cafés with a decidedly chic ambience. You could probably take your pick – fashions change frequently in this part of Amman – but one of the better ones is **Caffe Moka** *(☎ 5926285; Al-Qaherah Rd; open 7.30am-11pm daily)* which serves pastries (from 500 fils) and delicious cakes (from JD1.200).

Cinemas A few cinema complexes offer recent releases in a not-too-censored form: **Philadelphia** *(☎ 4634144)*, in the basement of the Jordan Tower Centre, just down from 3rd Circle; and **Galleria** *(☎ 5939238)*, on Abdoun Circle (see the Amman map) are among the best. Tickets cost about JD4, but the quality of sound, vision and chairs are superior to the other cinemas. Programmes for these cinemas are advertised in the two English-language newspapers.

Shopping

Amman is one of the better places to shop for souvenirs in Jordan with everything from unimaginable tourist kitsch to superb and high-quality handicraft boutiques, many shops are run to benefit vulnerable communities and the environment.

Among the better places in Amman (generally open 9am to 6pm Saturday to Thursday and all fixed price) are: **Al-Alaydi Jordan Craft Centre** *(☎/fax 4644555;* e *alaydi48@ hotmail.com; off Al-Kulliyah al-Islamiyah St)*; **Jordan River Foundation** *(☎ 4613081, fax 4613083; Bani Hamida House;* e *show room@jrf.org.jo; Fawzi al-Malouf St)*; **Royal**

Society for the Conservation of Nature (RSCN) Shop (☎ 5337931; *Fawzi Al-Malouf St*); and the **Jordan Design & Trade Centre** (☎ 5699141; e *jdtc@nets.com.jo; 5 Abdullah bin Abbas St*) run by the nationwide Noor al-Hussein Foundation.

Getting There & Away

Air The only domestic air route is between Amman and Aqaba. For prices and times, see Air in the Getting Around section earlier in this chapter.

Bus & Minibus The three main bus stations in Amman are Abdali station for transport to the north and west; Wahadat station for the south; and Raghadan station for Amman and nearby towns.

Tickets for private buses should be booked at least one day in advance. The **JETT office** (☎ 5664146) is on Al-Malek al-Hussein St, about 500m northwest of the Abdali bus station. Regular services include:

destination	frequency	one-way (JD)	duration (hrs)
Aqaba	5 daily	4.200	3½ to 4
Hammamat Ma'in	1 weekly	4.200*	2
King Hussein Bridge	1 daily	6.500	¾
Petra	3 weekly	6	3

*return trip

Trust International Transport (☎ 5813428) also has six daily buses to Aqaba (JD4, four hours), the first at 7.30am and the last at 6pm. **Hijazi** (☎ 4625664, *Abdali station*) has regular buses to Irbid (870 fils, 90 minutes), while **Afana** (☎ 4614611), at the Abdali station, also has frequent services to Aqaba (JD3).

From Abdali station (scheduled to move in the next few years), minibuses leave regularly for the following destinations:

destination	cost (fils)	duration (hrs)
Ajlun	500	2
Deir Alla (for Pella)	600	1
Fuheis	150	¾
Irbid	600	2
Jerash	350	1¼
Madaba	270	¾
Ramtha	500	2
Salt	200	¾

From Wahadat, minibuses depart regularly for:

destination	cost (JD)	duration (hrs)
Aqaba	3	5
Karak	0.800	2
Ma'an	1.100	3
Tafila	1	2½

They also go a few times a day to Wadi Musa (JD1.750, three hours), for Petra, via Shobak (JD1.500, 2½ hours); and a few times a day to Qadsiyya (JD1.350, about three hours), for Dana Nature Reserve.

For the Dead Sea, minibuses leave from the small station opposite the Muhajireen Police Station (the corner of Al-Ameera Basma bin Talal Rd and Ali bin Abi Taleb Rd) for Shuneh al-Janubiyyeh (South Shuna; 500 fils, 45 minutes). From South Shuna, you'll probably have to change for Suweimeh (200 fils), although occasionally the minibuses go right to the Dead Sea Rest House.

Train See Train in the Getting There & Away section earlier in the chapter for information about the train between Amman and Damascus.

Service Taxi Most service taxis depart from the same stations as the minibuses and departures are more frequent in the morning than afternoon.

From Abdali, there are service taxis to Irbid (JD1), Ramtha (JD1) and Salt (450 fils). Service taxis to the King Hussein Bridge cost JD2.

From Wahadat, there are departures to Karak (JD1.400, two hours); Wadi Musa (JD2.750, three hours), for Petra, via Shobak (JD2.250, 2½ hours); Ma'an (JD1.200, 2½ hours) and also to Aqaba (JD5, five hours).

Getting Around

To/From the Airport Queen Alia International Airport is some 35km south of the city centre.

The Airport Express bus (☎ 5858874) runs between the airport and the upper end of the Abdali bus station, passing through the 7th to the 4th Circles en route. The service (JD1.500, 30 minutes) runs every half hour between 6am and 10pm with three further services at midnight, 2am and 4am.

The only other option (apart from staying in Madaba) is a private taxi which should cost JD12 to JD15.

Service Taxi Most fares on service taxis cost between 100 and 150 fils and you usually pay the full amount regardless of where you get off. After 8pm, the price for all service taxis goes up by 25%.

Some of the more useful routes are: No 2 (from Basman St for 1st and 2nd Circles); No 3 (from Basman St for 3rd and 4th Circles); No 6 (from Cinema al-Hussein St going past the Abdali station and JETT international and domestic offices); No 27 (from near the Italian Hospital and continuing to Middle East Circle for Wahadat station) and No 35 (from near the Church of the Saviour, passing close to the Muhajireen Police Station).

Private Taxi The flag fall in a standard taxi is 150 fils, and cross-town journeys should never cost more than JD2, usually much less. Make sure your driver uses the meter although most will without being asked to do so.

Around Amman

WADI AS-SEER & IRAQ AL-AMIR
وادي عسير   عراق الأمير

The narrow, pretty and fertile valley of Wadi as-Seer is quite a contrast to the bare treeless plateau around Amman to the east. The caves of Iraq al-Amir (Caves of the Prince) and the ruins of Qasr al-Abad (Palace of the Slave) are another 10km down the valley from the largely Circassian town of Wadi as-Seer.

The caves are arranged in two tiers – the upper one forms a long gallery along the cliff face. The palace is a further 700m down the road, and can be seen from the caves.

The small but impressive ruins of Qasr al-Abad, thought to have been a villa or minor palace, can found around 700m further down the valley.

Most scholars believe that it was built in the 2nd century BC. The palace is unique because it was built out of some of the biggest blocks of any ancient structure in the Middle East – the largest measures 7m by 3m.

Getting There & Away
Minibuses leave Amman regularly for Wadi as-Seer (200 fils, 30 minutes) from the station opposite the Muhajireen Police Station (the corner of Al-Ameera Basma bin Talal Rd and Ali bin Abi Taleb Rd). From the town of Wadi as-Seer, take another minibus (100 fils) – or walk about 10km, mostly downhill – to the caves.

North & West of Amman

JERASH   جرش
☎ 02

This beautifully preserved Roman city, 51km north of Amman, is deservedly one of Jordan's major attractions. Excavations began in 1920, but it is estimated that 90% of the city is still unexcavated. In its heyday, the ancient city of Jerash *(admission low/high season JD2.500/5; open 7am-5.30pm daily Oct-Apr & 7am-7.30pm May-Sept)*, known in Roman times as Gerasa, had a population of around 15,000.

In July and August, Jerash hosts the Jerash Festival, featuring local and overseas artists, performances inside the ancient city and displays of traditional handicrafts. There's a visitors' centre with informative displays.

History
Although there have been finds to indicate that the site was inhabited in Neolithic times, the city really only rose to prominence from the time of Alexander the Great (333 BC).

In the wake of the Roman general Pompey's conquest of the region in 64 BC, Gerasa became part of the Roman province of Syria and, soon after, a city of the Decapolis (the commercial league of cities formed by Pompey after his conquest). Gerasa reached its peak at the beginning of the 3rd century AD, when it was bestowed with the rank of Colony, after which time it went into a slow decline.

By the middle of the 5th century, Christianity was the major religion of the region and the construction of churches proceeded at a startling rate. With the Sassanian invasion from Persia in 614, the Muslim conquest in 636 and the devastating earthquake in 747, Jerash's days of prosperity were

JERASH

PLACES TO EAT
29 Janat Jerash Restaurant
30 Al-Khayyam Restaurant
34 Jerash Rest House

OTHERS
1 Synagogue Church
2 Church of Bishop Isaiah
3 North Theatre
4 Northern Tetrapylon
5 Western Baths
6 Propylaeum Church
7 Propylaeum (Gateway to the Temple of Artemis)
8 Temple of Artemis
9 Church of Bishop Genesius
10 Church of St Cosmos & St Damianus
11 Church of St John the Baptist
12 Church of St George
13 Church of St Theodore
14 Nymphaeum
15 Cathedral
16 Umayyad Houses
17 Church of St Peter & St Paul
18 Mortuary Church
19 Agora (Macellum)
20 Southern Tetrapylon
21 Mosque
22 Eastern Baths
23 Bus Station
24 Market
25 Museum
26 Oval Plaza (Forum)
27 South Theatre
28 Temple of Zeus
29 South Gate
31 Tourist Police
32 Visitors Centre
33 Jerash Festival Ticket Office
35 Parking
36 Hippodrome
37 Hadrian's Arch
38 Ticket Office (Site Entrance); Souvenir Shops

To Pella, Irbid (42km) & Syria (40km)

North Gate

North Decumanus

Cardo Maximus (Colonnaded Street)

South Decumanus

Jerash Township

Ancient City Wall

Al-Qayrawan St
Wadi Jerash
Al-Malek Abdullah St

South Gate

Bab 'Amman St

Car Park

0   100   200m
0   100   200yd

To Mafraq (38km) & Amman (51km)

To Olive Branch Resort (7km), Ajlun (22km), Dibbeen National Park & Qala'at ar-Rabad (25km)

To Amman (51km)

JORDAN

over and its population shrank to about one-quarter of its former size.

Things to See
At the extreme south of the site is the striking **Hadrian's Arch**, also known as the **Triumphal Arch**, which was built in AD 129 to honour the visit of Emperor Hadrian. Behind the arch is the **hippodrome**, which hosted chariot races and could seat 15,000 spectators. The **South Gate**, originally one of four along the city wall and built in AD 130, leads into the city proper.

The **Oval Plaza** or **Forum** is one of the most distinctive images of Jerash, unusual because of its oval shape and huge size (90m long and 80m at its widest point). Some historians attribute this to the desire to gracefully link the main north-south axis (the cardo maximus) with the Temple of Zeus. Some 56 Ionic columns surround the plaza and the centre is paved with limestone.

On the south side of the Forum, the **Temple of Zeus** was built in about AD 162 over the remains of an earlier Roman Temple. The **South Theatre** was built in the 1st century and could seat 5000 spectators. From the upper stalls, there are excellent views of ancient and modern Jerash, particularly the forum, and the acoustics are wonderful.

Northeast from the Forum is the **cardo maximus** (the city's main thoroughfare), also known as the **colonnaded street**, which stretches for 800m from the Forum to the North Gate. The street is still paved with the original stones, and the ruts worn by thousands of chariots can be clearly seen.

Halfway along the colonnaded street is the elegant **nymphaeum**, the main fountain of the city. The nymphaeum is followed by the imposing **Temple of Artemis**, reached via a fine **propylaeum** or monumental gateway, and a staircase. The Temple of Artemis was dedicated to the patron goddess of the city.

Further to the north is the **north theatre**, built originally in AD 165 and now wonderfully restored.

The small **museum** (☎ 6322267; admission free; open 8.30am-6pm daily Oct-Apr & 8.30am-5pm May-Sept) contains a good collection of artefacts from the site.

Places to Stay & Eat
Surprisingly, there is still no hotel in Jerash, but it's an easy day trip from Amman.

Olive Branch Resort (☎ 6340555, fax 6340 557; e olivekh@go.com.jo; singles/doubles JD25/35), is around 7km from Jerash, off the Ajlun road. It has modern, comfortable rooms (add 20% tax to quoted prices) with satellite TV and good bathrooms, as well as great views, a swimming pool, games room, and a highly recommended **restaurant**. You can camp here in your/their tent for JD4/5.

Jerash Rest House (☎ 6351437; e kha der@jerashrest.com; mains JD2.500-3.500; open 11am-5pm daily Oct-Apr & 11am-7pm May-Sept) has expensive à la carte meals but a good daily buffet (JD5).

You'll find cheaper meals outside the site, including at **Al-Khayyam Restaurant** or the **Janat Jerash Restaurant** on Al-Qayrawan St, opposite the visitors centre. For cheap shwarma and felafel, try the perimeter of the bus station.

Getting There & Away
From Abdali bus station in Amman, public buses and minibuses (350 fils, 1¼ hours) leave regularly for Jerash. From Jerash, minibuses travel regularly to Irbid (350 fils, 45 minutes) and Ajlun (300 fils, 30 minutes). If you're still in Jerash after about 5pm, be prepared to hitch back to Amman because most buses and minibuses stop running soon after that.

AJLUN   عجلون
☎ 02
Ajlun is another popular and easy day trip from Amman, and can be combined with a trip to Jerash. The attraction of the town is the nearby **Qala'at ar-Rabad** (admission low/high season JD0.500/1; open 8am-5pm daily Oct-Apr & 8am-7pm May-Sept), 3km west of town. It was built by the Arabs as protection against the Crusaders, and is a fine example of Islamic military architecture. The castle commands unparalleled views of the Jordan Valley and was one in a chain of beacons and pigeon posts that allowed messages to be transmitted from Damascus to Cairo in one day. The castle is a tough uphill walk (3km) from the town centre. Occasional minibuses (100 fils) and private taxis (JD1 one-way) go to the top from Ajlun.

Places to Stay & Eat
Ar-Rabad Castle Hotel (☎ 6420202, fax 4630414; singles/doubles JD24/32), about

500m before the castle, is probably the pick of the hotels near Ajlun. Add 10% tax to room prices.

Ajlun Hotel (☎/fax 6420542; singles/doubles JD24/32) is about 400m down the road from the castle and also isn't bad. Again, there's 10% tax on top of room prices.

With a tent, you could camp in the small patch of forest west of the castle. There are felafel and shwarma places around the town centre.

Getting There & Away

Minibuses travel regularly from Ajlun to Jerash (300 fils, 30 minutes) and Irbid (320 fils, around 45 minutes). From Amman direct minibuses (500 fils, 1½ hours) leave from the Abdali bus station. You'll have difficulty finding anything in either direction after 5pm.

IRBID   إربد
☎ 02

Irbid is a university town and is one of the more lively and progressive of Jordan's large towns. Jordan's second largest city is also a good base from which to explore Umm Qais, Al-Himma and even Jerash, Ajlun and Pella. There's little to see apart from the excellent **Museum of Jordanian Heritage** (☎ 7271100 ext 4260; admission free; open 9am-5pm Sun-Thur) in the grounds of Yarmouk University. In the area around the university, the streets are lined with outdoor restaurants, Internet cafés and pedestrians out strolling, particularly in the late afternoon.

Places to Stay & Eat

The cheapest hotels are in the city centre in the blocks immediately north of King Hussein (Baghdad) St, all of which have shared bathrooms.

Abu Baker Hotel (☎ 7242695; Wasfi al-Tal St; dorm beds JD2) has a mostly local (male) clientele and some of the dorms have great views over Irbid.

Al-Ameen al-Kabir Hotel (☎ 7242384; e al_ameen_hotel@hotmail.com; Al-Jaish St; singles/doubles JD5/8) is probably the best of the cheapies, with friendly management and simple but tidy rooms and good bathrooms.

Omayed Hotel (☎/fax 7245955; King Hussein (Baghdad) St; singles/doubles with bathroom and satellite TV JD15.400/19.800) is a cut above the rest in the centre. The rooms are sunny, clean and most have nice

views. The staff are friendly and it's probably the only budget place where women will feel comfortable.

Al-Joude Hotel (☎ 7275515, fax 7275517; off University Street; singles/doubles/triples JD31/37/42, suites JD65) is Irbid's finest with a classy ambience, attractive rooms and friendly staff. Room prices include bath, satellite TV and buffet breakfast.

There are ample choices in the centre of town if your budget extends no further than felafel and shwarma.

Al-Saadi Restaurant (☎ 7242354; King Hussein (Baghdad) St; mains from JD2.500; open 7.30am-9.30pm daily) is one of the better places in the centre; it also does breakfast (750 fils to JD1.500).

Umayyad Restaurant (☎ 7240106; King Hussein (Baghdad) St; mains from JD3; open 8am-10.30pm daily) is another good choice with pretty decent food and superb views over the city.

Along the southern end of university street are dozens of **restaurants** to suit most budgets.

Getting There & Away

From the North bus station, minibuses go to Umm Qais (250 fils, about 45 minutes) and Mukheiba (for Al-Himma; 300 fils, one hour).

From the large South bus station, air-conditioned Hijazi buses (870 fils, 90 minutes) leave regularly for Amman. Alternatively there are minibuses (700 fils, about two hours) and plenty of service taxis (JD1). Minibuses also leave the South station for Ajlun (320 fils, 45 minutes) and Jerash (350 fils, 45 minutes). Trust International Transport also has two daily services to Irbid (JD6, 5½ hours).

From the West bus station, just off Palestine St, minibuses go to Al-Mashari'a (350 fils, 45 minutes) for the ruins at Pella.

UMM QAIS & AL-HIMMA
أم قيس الحمى(مخيبا)
☎ 02

Tucked in the far northwest corner of Jordan, and about 25km from Irbid, are the ruins of Gadara (Umm Qais). This is the site of both an ancient Roman city and an Ottoman-era village. The hill-top site offers spectacular views over the Golan Heights in Syria and the Sea of Galilee (Lake Tiberias) in Israel to the north, and the Jordan Valley to the south.

Things to See

The **museum** (☎ 7500072, fax 7500071; admission free; open 8am-5pm daily Oct-Apr & 8am-6pm daily May-Sept) is set around a tranquil courtyard and contains mosaics, statues and other artefacts from around the site. The **West Theatre** has been nicely restored using black basalt rocks as in the original.

The baths at **Al-Himma** (entry JD1.500; open 2pm-8pm daily) are in the village of Mukheiba about 10km north of Umm Qais. The hot springs were famous in Roman times for their health-giving properties.

Places to Stay & Eat

Umm Qais Hotel (☎ 7500080, fax 724 2313; singles/doubles JD6/12, with bathroom JD8/16) is a comfortable place about 400m west of the Umm Qais ruins. The rooms are clean, quiet and sunny and the management is friendly. It also has a small **restaurant**.

The **Government Rest House** (☎ 750 0055, fax 7500059; mains from JD2; open 10am-9pm daily), inside the ruins, is a pleasant (but expensive) place to linger with tables commanding spectacular views.

In Al-Himma, there are **chalets** (☎ 750 0505) overlooking the public baths (JD9 per person). Alternatively, try **Sah al-Noum Hotel** (☎ 7500510; singles/doubles JD10/12) which has simple and bright rooms and a **restaurant**. Room prices include bath, fan and breakfast.

Getting There & Away

Minibuses leave Irbid's North bus station for Umm Qais (250 fils, 45 minutes) on a regular basis and continue on to Al-Himma (350 fils, one hour). You'll need to bring your passport as there are military checkpoints in the area.

JORDAN VALLEY غور الأردن

Forming a geographical part of the Great Rift Valley of Africa, the fertile valley of the Jordan River was of considerable significance in biblical times.

The river rises from several sources, mainly the Anti-Lebanon Range in Syria, and flows down into the Sea of Galilee (Lake Tiberias), 212m below sea level, before draining into the Dead Sea, the lowest point on earth at over 400m below sea level. The Jordan River marks the frontier between Jordan and Israel & the Palestinian Territories.

The hot dry summers and short mild winters make for ideal growing conditions, and (subject to water restrictions) two or three crops are grown every year. Thousands of tonnes of fruit and vegetables are produced annually, with the main crops being tomatoes, cucumbers, melons and citrus fruits, all watered by ambitious irrigation projects.

Apart from the Dead Sea and Pella, there is little to attract visitors to the valley today, although the views over it from the East Bank plateau are magnificent.

Pella (Tabaqat Fahl) بيلا
☎ 02

Near the village of Al-Mashari'a are the ruins of the ancient city of Pella, 2km east of the road. The ruins require considerable imagination but the setting is superb.

Pella flourished during the Greek and Roman periods, and was one of the cities of the Decapolis. The city also came under the rule of the Ptolemaic dynasty, Seleucids and Jews who largely destroyed Pella in 83 BC. It was to Pella that Christians fled persecution from the Roman army in Jerusalem in the 2nd century AD. The city reached its peak during the Byzantine era and there were subsequent Islamic settlements until the site was abandoned in the 14th century.

Of most interest are the ruins atop the hill on your right as you enter through the main gate. These include an **Umayyad settlement** with shops, residences and storehouses, the small **Mamluk mosque** (14th century) and the **Canaanite temple** which was constructed in around 1270 BC and was dedicated to the Canaanite god Baal.

Also of interest is the Byzantine **civic complex church** or **middle church** which was built atop an earlier Roman civic complex; and the **east church**, up the hill to the southeast.

Places to Stay & Eat There's a lovely family feel at **Pella Countryside Hotel** (☎ 0795 574145, fax 6560899; singles/doubles JD12/15), and a nice outlook towards the ruins. The three rooms are well-kept.

Government Rest House (☎ 0795574145, fax 6560899; meals JD5 plus cost of drinks)

JORDAN

commands exceptional views over Pella and towards the Jordan Valley.

Getting There & Away From Irbid's West bus station there are minibuses to Al-Mashari'a (350 fils, 45 minutes). Pella is a steep 2km walk up from the highway which can be punishing in summer. Minibuses (200 fils) run reasonably regularly up to the main entrance of Pella.

Bethany

Claimed by Christians to be the place where Jesus was baptised by John the Baptist, access to the River Jordan at Bethany has recently been opened to the public (it was long closed because of its proximity to the Israeli-Palestinian border). The site was still being developed with an extensive visitors centre nearing completion when we visited.

Among the more interesting of the excavations at the site are on **Elijah's Hill**, where Elijah is said to have ascended to heaven, containing three caves, baptismal pools and churches, as well as the **Rhotorius Monastery** which dates from the Byzantine period and has a mosaic floor. The hills look down into the reeds of one of the Jordan River's tributaries, the baptism site, and across the Jordan Valley to the city of Jericho.

Getting There & Away Take any minibus to the Dead Sea Rest House (see Getting There & Away in the Dead Sea in the following section). About 5km before the Rest House, the road forks; the Dead Sea (and military checkpoint) is to the left, the baptism site well-signposted to the right. From the turn-off, you'll need to walk or hitch the 5km to the visitors centre and a further 750m to the site proper.

The Dead Sea البحر الميت
☎ 05

The Dead Sea is a lake at one of the lowest points on earth and, with such high salinity, your body is remarkably buoyant. (For more information see the 'Dead Sea' special section in the Israel & the Palestinian Territories chapter.)

Most visitors (foreigners and Jordanians) head for the Dead Sea Rest House complex on the northeastern shore of the lake in Suweimeh. The admission fee (JD4) provides visitors with access to the Dead Sea

and showers (very necessary because after a dip in the Dead Sea, you'll find yourself with an uncomfortable coating of encrusted salt that is best washed off in fresh water as soon as possible). The beach and showers are open from 6am to sunset daily.

A free alternative is the popular **Herodus Spring**, about 15km south of the Rest House. Fresh (but undrinkable) water runs down its narrow canyon – ideal for washing afterwards. The Dead Sea is a short walk down the hill, under the bridge.

Places to Stay & Eat With no budget accommodation at the Dead Sea, most travellers choose to take a day trip from either Amman or Madaba.

Dead Sea Rest House (☎ 3560112; doubles from JD35) offers comfortable but overpriced air-con doubles and bungalows with a sitting room, TV and fridge (but no views). Set meals at the **restaurant** cost JD6.

Mövenpick Resort and Spa (☎ 3561111, fax 3561122; e resort.deadsea@moeven pick.com; singles/doubles from JD128/156) is an ever-expanding luxury complex, including a spa centre offering a range of treatments and massages, and its own private beach. It also has nine **restaurants** (including Asian and Italian) and **bars**.

Dead Sea Spa Hotel (☎ 3561000, fax 3561012; e dssh@nets.com.jo; singles/ doubles US$100/120, suites from US$220), about 200m further south, is also luxurious and has a swimming pool.

Getting There & Away Some budget hotels in Amman organise day trips so ask around. From Amman (see Getting There & Away in the Amman section earlier in the chapter for details), minibuses leave regularly throughout the day for Shuneh al-Janubiyyeh (South Shuna; 500 fils, 45 minutes), from where you'll probably have to change for Suweimeh (200 fils).

From Madaba, minibuses leave from the bus/minibus station to South Shuna (350 fils, 45 minutes), from where another minibus for Suweimeh (250 fils, 30 minutes) should take you right to the door of the Rest House. Returning to Madaba, you'll need to take a minibus (before 5pm) for Amman and ask the driver to let you out just before Na'ur, from where a minibus will take you to Madaba (total of JD1.250, 1½ hours).

East of Amman

UMM AL-JIMAL

This strange black basalt city in the south of the Hauran (also called Jebel Druze) is only 10km from the Syrian border and 20km east of Mafraq.

Umm al-Jimal is thought to have been founded in about the 2nd century AD and to have formed part of the defensive line of Rome's Arab possessions. It continues to flourish into Umayyad times but was destroyed by an earthquake in AD 747 and never recovered. Much of what remains is simple urban architecture and assorted **churches**. Buildings which have been identified include a **barracks** and **chapel**, and the building known as the **Western Church**.

Getting There & Away

It's possible to see Umm al-Jimal in a day trip from Amman. Take a local minibus from Raghadan station to Zarqa (150 fils, 20 minutes), a minibus from there to Mafraq (350 fils, 45 minutes) and then another minibus to the ruins (200 fils, 20 minutes).

THE DESERT CASTLES   قصور الصحراء

A string of what have become known as 'castles' lies in the Desert east of Amman. Most of them were built or taken over and adapted by the Damascus-based Umayyad rulers in the late 7th and early 8th centuries. Many of the castles can be visited in a loop from Amman via Azraq. It is just feasible to visit all the main castles along this loop in one long day using a combination of public transport and hitching. A private car would simplify matters (approximately JD35 return for a private taxi from Amman), or some budget and mid-range hotels in the capital arrange tours if there are enough travellers. Also get a copy of the Jordan Tourism Board's free *Desert Castles*.

Qasr al-Hallabat & Hammam as-Sarah   قصر الحلابات حمام الصرح

Qasr al-Hallabat was originally a Roman fort built as a defence against the raiding desert tribes. During the 7th century it was a monastery and then the Umayyads fortified it into a country estate. It is now crumbling walls and fallen stone, but worth a visit for the great views around sunset.

Some 2km down the road heading east is the Hammam as-Sarah, a bathhouse and hunting lodge built by the Umayyads. It has been almost completely reconstructed and you can see the channels that were used for the hot water and steam.

Getting There & Away From Amman's Raghadan station, take a minibus to Zarqa (150 fils, 20 minutes), from where you can get another to Hallabat (250 fils, 30 minutes). The bus should drive right past the two sites.

Azraq   الأزرق
☎ 05

The oasis town of Azraq (which means 'blue' in Arabic) lies 103km east of Amman. Once an important meeting of trade routes, it performs a similar function today as a junction of roads heading northeast to Safawi and Iraq, and southeast to Saudi Arabia.

Azraq is home to the **Azraq Wetland Reserve** (☎ 383 5017; admission JD3, combination ticket with Shaumari Reserve JD4; open 9am-sunset daily), which is administered by the RSCN and is good for birdwatching. The Azraq Basin was originally 12,710 sq km (an area larger than Lebanon), but over-pumping of ground water saw the wetlands dry up entirely in 1991. The RSCN is attempting to rehabilitate a small section (12 sq km) of the wetlands.

Qala'at al-Azraq This large castle is built out of black basalt and its present form dates to the beginning of the 13th century. It was originally three storeys high, but much of it crumbled in an earthquake in 1927. Greek and Latin inscriptions date earlier constructions on the site to around AD 300 – about the time of the Roman emperor Diocletian. The Umayyads maintained it as a military base, as did the Ayyubids in the 12th and 13th centuries. In the 16th century the Ottoman Turks stationed a garrison here.

After the 16th century, the only other recorded use of the castle was during WWI when Sherif Hussein (father of King Hussein) and TE Lawrence made it their desert headquarters in the winter of 1917, during the Arab Revolt against the Ottomans. Lawrence's room was directly above the southern entrance.

JORDAN

Shaumari Wildlife Reserve This reserve (*admission JD3, combination ticket with Azraq Wetland Reserve JD4; open 8am-4pm daily*), about 10km south of Azraq, was established in 1975 to reintroduce wildlife which had long since disappeared from the region. Shaumari is home to the Arabian oryx (87 now in the reserve), the blue-necked and red-necked ostrich (40), gazelles (six) and the Persian onager or wild ass (seven).

For more on the Arabian oryx see the boxed text 'Saving the Arabian Oryx' in the Facts about the Middle East chapter.

Places to Stay & Eat The only budget accommodation is at **Zoubi Hotel** (*☎ 3835012; singles/doubles with bathroom JD10/20*) where there are comfortable rooms. It's about 800m south of the T-junction where the Amman road intersects with the roads to Saudi Arabia and Iraq.

Azraq Resthouse (*☎ 3834006, fax 383 5215; singles/doubles/triples with bathroom & breakfast JD17.500/21.500/28.500*) is surprisingly good value with very tidy and comfortable rooms with satellite TV and there's a pleasant swimming pool. The turn-off is about 2km north of the T-junction.

A bunch of small eateries lines the 1km stretch of road south of the T-junction.

Azraq Palace Restaurant (*☎/fax 439 7144; buffets JD6; open 8am-11pm daily*) is probably the best place to eat in town. The setting is pleasant and the food is tasty. The buffet runs most days from noon to 4pm and 6pm to 11pm.

Getting There & Away Minibuses (650 fils, 1½ hours) travel between the post office (north of the castle in Azraq ash-Shomali), and the Old Station in Zarqa, which is well connected to Amman and Irbid.

Qusayr Amra قصر عمرا

Heading north towards Amman on Hwy 40, the road branches left (southwest), to Qusayr (Little Palace) Amra (*admission free; open 7am-7.30pm Oct-Apr & 8am-4.30pm May-Sept*), the best preserved of the desert 'castles'. The walls of the three halls are covered with frescoes and the castle's plain exterior belies the beauty within. It was once part of a greater complex that served as a caravanserai, with baths and a hunting lodge, possibly predating the Umayyads. It

is now a Unesco World Heritage site. The excellent visitors centre at the entrance has informative displays explaining the frescoes and a relief map of the site. To reach here, you'll probably need to hitch.

Qasr al-Kharaneh قصر الكرانه

This well-preserved castle or caravanserai is a further 16km southwest of Qusayr Amra, standing as a lonely sentinel in a vast treeless plain. It was also built by the Romans or Byzantines, although what you see today is the result of renovations carried out by the Umayyads in AD 710. Around 60 rooms surround the central courtyard and there are good views from the roof. Again, you'll need to hitch to reach this site.

South of Amman

There are three possible routes south of Amman to Aqaba: the Desert Hwy, the Dead Sea Hwy and the King's Hwy. The last is by far the most interesting of the three, passing through the historic centres of Madaba, Karak, Shobak and Petra, and the wonderful landscapes of Wadi Mujib and past the beautiful Dana Nature Reserve.

Unfortunately, public transport along the King's Hwy is infrequent and stops altogether between Dhiban and Ariha, meaning that you'll have to hitch or take a private vehicle for at least part of the way. The Farah Hotel in Amman and the hotels in Madaba can organise transport along the highway.

MADABA مأدبا
☎ 05
This easy-going town is best known for its superb and historically significant Byzantine-era mosaics. Madaba is the most important Christian centre in Jordan, and has long been an example of religious tolerance.

Madaba is worth considering as an alternative place to stay to Amman: Madaba is far more compact, has some excellent hotels and restaurants, and is less than an hour by regular public transport from the capital. Madaba is also a good base for exploring the Dead Sea, Bethany and other sites such as Mt Nebo, Mukawir (Machaerus) and Hammamat Ma'in.

Among the better Internet cafés are: Internet Café (*☎ 079842036*) on Al-Nuzha St, which is open 10am to 2am daily and charges 750 fils per hour; and Let's Go Internet Café which was to move to the Haret Jdoudna complex soon after we visited – it charges JD1 per hour.

Things to See

Madaba's most famous site is the **Mosaic Map** in the 19th-century Greek Orthodox **St George's Church** (Talal St; entry JD1; open 7am-6pm Sat & Mon-Thur, 10.30am-6pm Fri & Sun). The mosaic was once a clear map with 157 captions (in Greek) of all major biblical sites from Lebanon to Egypt. The mosaic was constructed in AD 560 and once contained more than two million pieces, but only one-third of the whole now survives.

For the following places, admission is on a combination ticket which covers all three sites.

The **Archaeological Park** (☎ 3246681; Hussein bin Ali St; admission low/high season JD1/2 (combination ticket); open daily 8am-5pm Oct-Apr & 8am-7pm May-Sept) contains more exceptional mosaics from the Madaba area. The large roofed structure in front of you as you enter contains **Hippolytus Hall** and the 6th-century **Church of the Virgin Mary**. The mosaic on the floor, thought to date from AD 767, is a masterpiece of geometric design. There are also remains of the **Roman Road**.

The **Church of the Apostles** (Al-Nuzha St; admission low/high season JD1/2 (combination ticket); open 8am-5pm daily Oct-Apr & 8am-7pm daily May-Sept) contains a remarkable mosaic dedicated to the 12 apostles.

Madaba Museum (☎ 3244056; Al-Baiqa St; admission low/high season JD1/2 (combination ticket); open 8am-5pm daily Oct-Apr & 8am-7pm daily May-Sept) was created from several old Madaba houses and contains a number of folklore exhibits and more good mosaics.

Places to Stay

Queen Ayola Hotel (☎/fax 3244087; Talal St; singles/doubles from JD10/16) is decent value with well-kept rooms.

Lulu's Pension (☎ 3243678, fax 3247617; Hamraa al-Asd St; singles/doubles/triples with shared bathroom JD10/20/30) has a lovely family feel and the rooms are certainly very comfortable and the welcome

warm. Doubles with private bathroom and balcony are JD25. You can also set up a tent in the garden for JD5.

Mariam Hotel (☎/fax 3251529; e mh@ go.com.jo; Aisha Umm al-Mumeneen St; singles/doubles JD18/22) is perhaps the best place to stay in town with spotless rooms, some of the most comfortable beds in Jordan and a super-friendly owner. It's two blocks northeast of the Al-Mouhafada Circle.

Black Iris Hotel (☎/fax 3241959; Mouhafada Circle; singles/doubles JD15/20) is another classy place with very reasonable prices and comes warmly recommended by readers. It's easy to spot from Mouhafada Circle.

Moab Land Hotel (☎/fax 3251318; Talal St; singles/doubles without balcony JD15/20, doubles with balcony JD25) is directly opposite St George's Church. It's an attractive, clean and airy place, staff are friendly and the location is excellent.

Places to Eat

Most of Madaba's restaurants serve alcohol and there are liquor stores dotted around town.

Madaba Modern Restaurant (King's Hwy; meals around JD2; open 8am-11pm daily) is the best of the cheap eateries near the bus/minibus station.

Coffee Shop Ayola (☎ 3251843; Talal St; snacks around JD1; open 8am-11pm daily), almost opposite St George's Church, is a charming, relaxed place too small to attract large tour groups. It serves delicious toasted sandwiches (JD1), all types of coffee (500 fils to JD1), tea (500 fils) and cans of cold beer (JD1.5).

Haret Jdoudna (☎ 3248650; Talal St; mains JD3.5-7; open noon-midnight daily) is a charming complex of craft shops and places to eat, all set in one of Madaba's restored old houses. The classy **restaurant** upstairs serves delicious food while downstairs is a more informal **café** where you can enjoy good pizzas either indoors or in the pleasant courtyard.

Getting There & Away

The grotty bus/minibus station-cum-market is just off the King's Hwy, a few minutes' walk down from the town centre.

From Amman's Raghadan, Wahadat and, less often, Abdali bus stations, there are regular buses and minibuses (270 fils, one hour) throughout the day for Madaba.

For details about getting to the Dead Sea from Madaba, see the Dead Sea section earlier in the chapter.

It is possible to travel to Karak on a daily university minibus (JD1.500, two hours) from the main bus/minibus station, although it travels via the less interesting Desert Hwy. From near or in the bus/minibus station in Madaba, minibuses go to Mukawir (for Machaerus castle; 350 fils, one hour) several times throughout the day, the last at around 5pm.

If there are three or more people, the hotels in Madaba will arrange transport to Petra via the King's Hwy for around JD12 per person.

AROUND MADABA
Mt Nebo   جبل نيبو

Mt Nebo, on the edge of the East Bank plateau and 9km from Madaba, is where Moses is said to have seen the Promised Land. He died and was later buried in the area, although the exact location of the burial site is the subject of conjecture.

The entrance to the complex (admission 500 fils; open 7am-5am daily Oct-Apr & 7am-7pm daily May-Sept) is clearly visible on the Madaba to Dead Sea road.

The first church was built on the site in the 4th century AD but most of the **Moses Memorial Church** you'll see today was built in the 6th century. The impressive mosaic, which covers the floor, measures about 9m by 3m, and is very well preserved, as are the others dotted around the sanctuary.

From the **lookout**, the views across the valleys to the Dead Sea, Jericho and the domes and spires of Jerusalem are superb, but they're often concealed by the haze and pollution.

Getting There & Away From Madaba, minibuses (250 fils, 15 minutes) going to South Shuna pass right by the main gate to Mt Nebo.

Hammamat Ma'in
حمامات معن (معن الزرقاء)

☎ 05

The hot springs and luxury resort of Hammamat Ma'in lie 27km southwest of Madaba, reached via a scenic road that drops steeply into the valley. The therapeutic qualities of the spring waters have been enjoyed by such luminaries as Herod the Great. The water is hot (at least 45°C), and contains potassium, magnesium and calcium, among other minerals.

The complex at Hammamat Ma'in was taken over by the French Mercure group in 2000 and it has redeveloped the site with a luxury hotel and spa centre. The gate to the complex (admission per person JD7, JD5 per vehicle; open 6am-midnight daily) is a few hundred metres up the hill. Day trippers are welcome to use (free of charge after paying the admission fee) the Roman baths, the family pool at the base of the waterfall closest to the entrance, and the swimming pool.

Places to Stay & Eat Next to the first waterfall and family pool, the **chalets** (☎ 3245500, fax 3245550; singles/doubles with bathroom JD24/35) are fairly uninspiring but the cheapest you'll get in Hammamat Ma'in.

Mercure Ma'in Spa Resort (☎ 3245500, fax 3245550; e H2174@accor-hotels.com; singles/doubles from US$132/149) is everything you'd want from a luxury spa resort with supremely comfortable rooms and a superb, tranquil setting.

For meals, your only option is the **Shallal Restaurant** in the Mercure Resort which looks out onto the main waterfall. Expect to pay at least JD5 for a meal and usually much more. Visitors are not allowed to bring food onto the site.

Getting There & Away From Amman, the JETT bus company has buses (JD4.500, two hours) between Hammamat Ma'in and Amman on Friday. It is possible to leave Amman in the morning (8am), spend the day at the springs, and return on the 5pm bus back to the capital; book your return ticket at the JETT office in Amman.

From Madaba, minibuses regularly go to Ma'in village (200 fils, 15 minutes) but the driver will only go down the steep road to Hammamat Ma'in if there is sufficient demand or financial incentive from passengers.

MACHAERUS (MUKAWIR)
مكور (ماشيروس)

Just beyond the village of Mukawir is the spectacular 700m-high hilltop perch of

Machaerus, the castle of Herod the Great. The ruins themselves are only of moderate interest but the setting is breathtaking and commands great **views** out over the surrounding hills and the Dead Sea.

Machaerus is known to the locals as **Qala'at al-Meshneq** (Gallows Castle). The ruins consist of the palace of Herod Antipas, the low-lying remains of the baths and defensive walls. Machaerus is renowned as the place where John the Baptist was beheaded by Herod Antipas, the successor to Herod the Great. The castle is about 2km past the village and easy to spot.

Getting There & Away

From Madaba, minibuses (350 fils, one hour) go to the village of Mukawir four or five times a day (the last around 5pm). Unless you have chartered a taxi from Madaba, you'll probably need to walk the remaining 2km (downhill most of the way). Otherwise, your minibus driver may, if you ask nicely and sweeten the request with a tip, take you the extra distance.

WADI MUJIB وادي مجيب

Stretching across Jordan from the Desert Hwy to the Dead Sea is the vast and beautiful Wadi Mujib, sometimes known as the 'Grand Canyon of Jordan'. The valley is about 1km deep and over 4km from one edge to the other and is home to some of the most spectacular scenery in Jordan.

Dhiban is where almost all transport south of Madaba stops. The only way to cross the mighty Wadi Mujib from Dhiban to Ariha (about 30km) is to charter a taxi for JD5/10 return. Hitching is possible, but expect a long wait.

KARAK الكرك
☎ 03

The evocative ancient Crusader redoubt of Karak is 900m above sea level. The fortified castle which dominates the town became a place of legend in the battles between the Crusaders and the Muslim armies of Saladin. Although among the most famous, the castle at Karak was just one in a long line built by the Crusaders stretching from Aqaba in the south to Turkey in the north.

The **castle** (admission low/high season 500 fils/JD1; open 8am-5.30pm daily) is entered through the **Ottoman Gate**, at the end

of a short bridge over the dry moat. The path leading up to the left from inside the entrance leads to the **Crusader Gallery** or **stables**. At the end of the gallery, a long passageway leads southwest past the **soldiers' barracks** and **kitchen**. Emerging from the covered area, the overgrown **upper court** is to your right, while straight ahead leads past the castle's main **Crusader church**. At the far southern end of the castle is the impressive **Mamluk keep**, in front of which some stairs lead down to the **Mamluk Palace** which was built in 1311 using earlier Crusader materials. More stairs lead down to the delightful **marketplace** which leads back to the entrance.

Places to Stay & Eat

New Hotel (☎ 2351942; Al-Maydan St; bed in shared room JD3), also known as Al-Kemmam Hotel, is the cheapest place and the only one in the modern town centre.

Towers Castle Hotel (☎ 2352489, fax 2354293; Al-Qala'a St; singles/doubles JD10/12, with private bathroom JD12/16) is quiet and the rooms, many with great views, are large, bright and clean.

Karak Rest House (☎ 2351148, fax 2353148; Al-Qala'a St; singles/doubles with bathroom & breakfast 15 Feb-15 May JD18/30, rest of year JD15/25) is next to the main entrance of the castle. Most of the good rooms have outstanding views.

Al-Fid'a Restaurant (☎ 2352677; Al-Mujamma St; meals JD3; open 8am-midnight daily) is a popular place and excellent value with main course, dips and salad for JD3.

Kir Heres Restaurant (☎ 079640264, fax 2355595; Al-Qala'a St; mains JD4.850-6.250; open 9am-10pm daily) has a pleasant ambience, good food and attentive service.

Turkey Restaurant (☎ 079730431; Al-Umari St; mains JD1.500; open 7am-9.30pm daily), next door, does roast chicken and hummus among other standard local fare.

Getting There & Away

From the bus/minibus station in Karak, reasonably regular minibuses go to Amman's Wahadat Station (800 fils, two hours) via the Desert Hwy. Minibuses also run every hour or so along the King's Hwy from Karak to Tafila (700 fils, 1½ hours), the best place for connections to Qadsiyya (for Dana Nature Reserve) and Shobak. To

Wadi Musa (for Petra), take a minibus to Ma'an (JD1.350, two hours) which leaves three times a day (around 7am and either side of lunchtime) and travels via the Desert Hwy. Minibuses to Aqaba (JD1.900, three hours) travel via the Dead Sea Hwy about four times a day.

TAFILA الطفيله

Wadi Hasa, the second river gorge to cut through the King's Hwy, lies halfway between Karak and Tafila. Tafila is a busy transport junction. The only reason to come here is for an onward minibus connection. Minibuses from Karak (500 fils, one hour) cross Wadi Hasa. There are also direct minibuses to/from the Wahadat station in Amman (JD1, 2½ hours) via the Desert Hwy, Aqaba (JD1.200, 2½ hours) via the Dead Sea Hwy, Ma'an (JD1, one hour) via the Desert Hwy, and down the King's Hwy to Shobak and Qadsiyya (for Dana Nature Reserve; 350 fils, 30 minutes).

DANA NATURE RESERVE
حديقة دانا الطبيعية

☎ 03

Dana Nature Reserve (also known as Dana Wildlife Reserve) is one of Jordan's hidden gems. It also represents an impressive project involving environmental protection and ecotourism, and most of the reserve is only accessible on foot. The charming 15th-century stone village of Dana clings to a precipice overlooking the valley and commanding exceptional views. It's a great place to spend a few days hiking and relaxing.

The reserve includes a variety of terrain, including peaks over 1500m high and the sandstone cliffs of Wadi Dana which leads to the Dead Sea about 14km to the west. The escarpments and valleys protect a surprisingly diverse ecosystem, and the reserve is also home to almost 100 archaeological sites.

The visitors centre (☎ 2270497, fax 2270499; e dhana@rscn.org.jo; w www.rscn .org.jo; open 8am-8pm daily) is in the Guest House complex in Dana village and it's here you must go before setting off hiking.

Places to Stay & Eat

Rummam Campground (JD18.50 per person) is reached via turn-off on the King's Hwy around 5km north of Qadsiyya.

Dana Tower Hotel (☎/fax 2270237; singles/doubles JD5/10) is a welcoming place and the rustic rooms are well kept. Meals are available for JD3 per person.

Dana Hotel (☎ 2270537; singles/doubles with breakfast JD8/16) also has very tidy rooms and is another friendly, well-run place. Meals cost JD5 per person.

Dana Guest House (☎ 2270497, fax 2270499; e dhana@rscn.org.jo; doubles/ triples with balcony JD36.050/46.350) is highly recommended. The rooms are very comfortable and those with balcony have breathtaking views.

Getting There & Away

Minibuses run reasonably often throughout the day from Tafila to Qadsiyya (350 fils, 30 minutes). The turn-off to Dana village is just north of Qadsiyya; from here it's a 2.5km (downhill) walk to Dana village. From Amman's Wahadat station, a few minibuses go to Qadsiyya (JD1.350, about three hours) every day.

SHOBAK شوبك

The commanding Shobak Castle (entry free, open daylight hours) is another renowned Crusader fortress and some readers prefer it to the more frequented Karak Castle.

Excavation on the castle's interior is ongoing and has revealed two **Crusader churches**; a **market**; and, at the northern end of the castle, a semi-circular **keep** whose exterior is adorned with **Quranic inscriptions**, possibly dating from the time of Saladin. The **court of Baldwin I** is also worth a look, as are the **catacombs**.

Occasional minibuses link Shobak village with Amman's Wahadat station (JD1.500, 2½ hours), and there are occasional minibuses to Karak from Aqaba via the Shobak turn-off (ask the driver before setting out).

PETRA & WADI MUSA
بترا وادي موسى

☎ 03

If you can only go to one place in Jordan, make it Petra. Hewn from a towering rock wall, the imposing facades of the great buildings and tombs of Petra are an enduring testament to the grandeur of the

[Continued on page 414]

PETRA

This spectacular rose-stone city was built in the 3rd century BC by the Nabataeans who carved palaces, temples, tombs, storerooms and stables from the rocky cliffs. From here they commanded the trade route from Damascus to Arabia, with great spice, silk and slave caravans passing through. In a short time, the Nabataeans made great advances – they mastered hydraulic engineering, iron production, copper refining, sculpture, stone-carving. Archaeologists believe that several earthquakes, including a massive one in AD 555, forced the inhabitants to abandon the city.

Entry to Petra

The ticket office is located in the visitors centre and tickets are sold between 6am and 4.30pm from October to April and 6am to 5.30pm from May to September.

The official admission fees are JD21/26/31 for one-/two-/three-day passes. When we visited, these rates had been reduced by 50% to JD10.500/13/15.500 and were applicable until (but may be continued after) July 2002. Importantly, student discounts of 50% of the relevant prices were also available. Multiday tickets are nontransferable and signatures are checked. Children under 15 years get in free.

The Site

Petra is approached through an incredibly narrow 1.2km-long defile known as the **Siq**. This is not a canyon (a gorge carved out by water) but

Inset: An ancient mosaic hints at past glories (Photo by Jane Sweeney)

Right: A glimpse of the fabled Al-Khazneh through the narrow corridor of the Siq

MARK PARKES

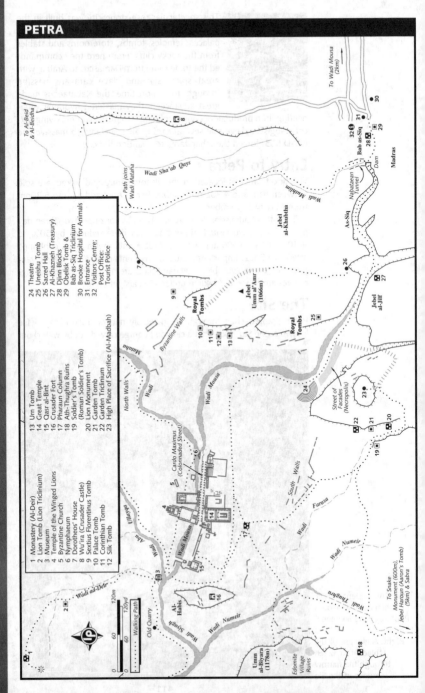

PETRA

1 Monastery (Al-Deir)
2 Lion Tomb (Lion Triclinium)
3 Museum
4 Temple of the Winged Lions
5 Byzantine Church
6 Nymphaeum
7 Dorotheos' House
8 Wu'ira (Crusader Castle)
9 Sextius Florentinus Tomb
10 Palace Tomb
11 Corinthian Tomb
12 Silk Tomb
13 Um Tomb
14 Great Temple
15 Qasr al-Bint
16 Crusader Fort
17 Pharaun Column
18 Ath-Thughra Ruins
19 Soldier's Tomb
   (Roman Soldier's Tomb)
20 Lion Monument
21 Garden Tomb
22 Garden Triclinium
23 High Place of Sacrifice (Al-Madbah)
24 Theatre
25 Uneishu Tomb
26 Sacred Hall
27 Al-Khazneh (Treasury)
28 Djinn Blocks
29 Obelisk Tomb &
   Bab as-Siq Triclinium
30 Brooke Hospital for Animals
31 Entrance
32 Visitors Centre;
   Post Office;
   Tourist Police

rather one block that has been rent apart by tectonic forces. Just as you start to think there's no end to the Siq, you catch breathtaking glimpses ahead of the most impressive of sights, the **Al-Khazneh** (Treasury). Carved out of solid, iron-laden sandstone to serve as a tomb, the Treasury gets its name from the misguided local belief that pirates hid their treasure here. The elegant pillars, alcoves and plinths are masterpieces.

Further into the site is the **Street of Facades**, the highlight of which is the weather-worn 7000-seat **theatre**. Further north above the path are the **Royal Tombs**, standing elegantly in various stages of erosion. Their evocative names – the Urn, Corinthian, Silk and Palace tombs – speak volumes for the Nabataean sense of grandeur.

The main path turns west along the **colonnaded street** which was once lined with shops, passing the rubble of the **nymphaeum** en route to the elevated **Great Temple**, staring across the wadi to the **Temple of the Winged Lions**. At the end of the colonnaded street is the imposing and (unusually for Petra) free-standing **Qasr al-Bint**. The path turns west towards the **museum** and the start of the winding path which climbs to the monastery.

High Places

Although all of Petra's high places are worth visiting, **Ad-Deir** (the monastery) shouldn't be missed. It's reached by a long rock-cut staircase leading north from the museum. The monastery has a similar facade to the Khazneh, but is far bigger and the views from the nearby cliff-tops are stunning, especially towards Jebel Haroun in the late afternoon. On the way up, look out for the **Lion Tomb**.

The **High Place of Sacrifice** is reached by stairs (45-minute climb) from off the Street of Facades and affords stunning views. Other more challenging hikes (both five hours return) to **Umm al-Biyara**, thought by some scholars to be the biblical Sela, and **Jebel Haroun** with **Aaron's Tomb** are not to be missed; the rewards include unparalleled views.

The walk along **Wadi Muthlim** from the Siq to near the Royal Tombs (45 minutes) is also recommended.

[Continued from page 410]

Nabataean vision. The Nabataeans – Arabs who controlled the frankincense trade routes of the region in pre-Roman times – chose as their city a place concealed from the outside world and made it into one of the Middle East's most memorable sites.

Orientation

The village that has sprung up around Petra is Wadi Musa (Moses' Valley), a mass of hotels, restaurants and shops stretching about 5km down from 'Ain Musa to the main entrance to Petra. The village centre is at the Shaheed roundabout, with its shops, restaurants and budget hotels, while other hotels are strung out all along the main road – known as Tourist St.

Information

The Petra **visitors centre** (☎ 2156020, fax 2156060; open 6am-9pm daily), just before the entrance to Petra, has a helpful information counter, several souvenir shops and toilets. The tourist police centre is opposite and there is a small post office behind the visitors centre. The **Housing Bank** (Visa) and **Jordan Islamic Bank** (Visa & MasterCard), up from the Shaheed roundabout, are good places to change money and both have an ATM. There are a couple of banks (but no ATMs), at the lower end of town near Petra. There are at least three Internet cafés in Wadi Musa near the Shaheed roundabout.

Places to Stay

Prices for hotels in Wadi Musa fluctuate wildly, depending on the season and amount of business.

Women travellers must be aware that allegations of sexual harassment have been made against some (but not all) of the budget hotels in the streets around the Shaheed roundabout. There have also been allegations of rape from at least one hotel. Women should exercise great caution at any of the budget hotels. In particular, we do not recommend the Valentine Inn (formerly Twaissi Inn).

Places to Stay – Budget

Mussa Spring Hotel (☎ 2156310, fax 2156910; e musaspring_hotel@yahoo.co.uk; singles/doubles JD6/8, with bathroom JD8/10) is a pleasant place far removed from the clamour of the village centre; there are daily free shuttles to/from the gate at Petra 5km away.

Al-Anbat Hotel I (☎ 2156265; e alanbath@joinnet.com.jo; singles/doubles JD8/10) is on the road between Ain Musa and Wadi Musa and is excellent value. The rooms with satellite TV are better than some mid-range hotels and the prices include free transport to/from Petra.

Cleopetra Hotel (☎/fax 2157090; singles/doubles with bathroom & breakfast JD10/14) has reasonable, small rooms and it has an extensive range of movies on DVD in the lobby.

Places to Stay – Mid-Range

Al-Rashid Hotel (☎ 2156800, fax 2156801; Shaheed roundabout; singles/doubles JD12/20) has sterile but spacious and comfortable rooms right in the centre of town.

Amra Palace Hotel (☎ 2157070, fax 215 7071; e amrapalace@index.com.jo; singles/doubles JD20/35) has very comfortable rooms with satellite TV.

Al-Anbat Hotel II (☎ 2156265, fax 2156888; e alanbath@joinit.com.jo; singles/doubles JD11/22) has generally quiet, well furnished rooms with satellite TV.

Petra Moon Hotel (☎/fax 2156220; singles/doubles JD15/25) is up behind the Mövenpick Hotel and is therefore convenient for the entrance to Petra. The rooms are spacious and comfortable and the staff helpful.

Places to Stay – Top End

Petra Palace (☎ 2156723, fax 2156724; e ppwnwm@go.com.jo; singles/doubles in low season US$52/62, in high season US$57/79) is superb value, especially in low season. There's a swimming pool.

Mövenpick Resort (☎ 2157111, fax 2157112; e hotel.petra@moevenpick.com; singles/doubles with half board JD150/190) is the closest top end place to the gate into Petra.

Petra Marriott (☎ 2156408, fax 2157096; e petra@marriott.com.jo; singles/doubles in low season with half-board JD45/50, in high season JD60/75), on the road to Tayyibeh, is superb luxury value. There's a swimming pool, restaurants, Turkish bath and a cinema.

Places to Eat

The main road, especially in Wadi Musa, is dotted with **grocery stores** where you can stock up on food, munchies and drinks for

Petra, although the selection is fairly uninspiring.

There are a few places offering felafel and shwarma, especially in the streets around the Shaheed roundabout.

Al-Wadi Restaurant (☎ 2157163; mains JD1.500-3.500; open 7am-11pm daily) is right on Shaheed roundabout. It does pasta and pizza, as well as a range of vegetarian dishes and local Bedouin specialties.

Al-Arabi Restaurant (☎ 2157661; mains from JD1; open 6am-midnight daily), almost next door, is a bright place with helpful staff and good meals.

Petra Nights Restaurant (☎ 079894543; meals from JD2.500; open 6am-11pm daily) is rustic and there's no menu but the owner's friendly and can cook just about any local dish you desire.

Rose City Restaurant (☎ 2157340; mains from JD2.750; open 6.30am-10pm daily) is one of the few budget places near the entrance to Petra. The food and service get consistently good reports from readers.

Red Cave Restaurant (☎ 2157799; mains from JD2.50; open 9am-10pm daily) is cavernous, cool and friendly and the menu has a good selection.

Papazzi (☎ 2157087; mains JD2-5; open 11am-9.30pm daily) is a Western-style pizza place which does good pasta and Italian (thin) or American (thick) pizzas.

Entertainment

There's not a lot to do in the evening, other than recover from aching muscles and plan your next day in Petra. Some hotels organise videos or other entertainment.

Cave Bar (☎ 2156266; open 3pm-midnight daily) is housed in a 2000-year-old Nabataean rock room, next to the entrance to the Petra Guest House (see Places to Stay), behind the visitors centre. It has a classy ambience and the novelty value is high, as are the prices.

Getting There & Away

The JETT bus company operates three buses a week (JD6, 3½ hours) between its domestic office in Amman and Petra. It departs Amman at 6.30am, and leaves from Wadi Musa around 5pm.

All minibuses to/from Wadi Musa pass through the Shaheed roundabout. Minibuses officially travel every day between Amman (Wahadat bus station) and Wadi

Musa (JD1.750, three hours) along the Desert Hwy. Minibuses leave Wadi Musa for Ma'an (600 fils, 45 minutes) regularly throughout the day (more frequently in the morning). Minibuses also leave Wadi Musa for Aqaba (JD3, two hours) at about 6.30am, 8am and 4pm – ask around the day before.

For Wadi Rum (JD3, 1½ hours), there is a daily minibus at around 6am but making a 'reservation' the day before is strongly encouraged; the bus sometimes doesn't leave until 9am. Alternatively get a minibus to Aqaba, and get off at, and hitch a ride from, the turn-off to Wadi Rum.

WADI RUM وادي رم
☎ 03

Wadi Rum offers some of the most extraordinary desert scenery you'll ever see, and is a definite highlight of any visit to Jordan. This area, made famous by the presence of the Arab Revolt and TE Lawrence in the early 20th century, has lost none of its forbidding majesty. Its myriad moods, dictated by the changing angle of the sun, make for a memorable experience. Unless you're really pushed for time, linger for a few days here, slowing down to the timeless rhythm of desert life, enjoying the galaxy of stars overhead at night with Orion chasing Scorpio across the sky, and the spectacular sunrises and sunsets.

The camel-mounted **Desert Patrol** was originally established to keep dissident tribes in order. Today they drive armoured patrol vehicles and their evocative traditional uniforms are now reserved for ceremonial occasions. They nonetheless still revel in their photogenic nature and will pose for those who sit with them, discuss the inconsequential and pass the time with a tea.

Information

Wadi Rum recently came under the management of the Royal Society for the Conservation of Nature and in 1998 it established the Wadi Rum Protected Area to promote tourism in balance with the imperative to protect fragile ecosystems. As a result, admission to Wadi Rum (JD2/5 per person/vehicle) is strictly controlled and all vehicles, camels and guides must be arranged either through, or with the approval of, the RSCN. The shortest excursions

The Bedouin

These desert dwellers, the *bedu* (the name means nomadic), number several hundred thousand, but few can still be regarded as truly nomadic. Some have opted for city life, but most have, voluntarily or otherwise, settled down to cultivate crops.

A few retain the old ways. They camp for a few months at a time in one spot and graze their herds of goats, sheep or camels. When the sparse fodder runs out, it is time to move on again, which allows the land to regenerate. All over the east and south of the country, you'll see black goat-hair tents (*beit ash-sha'ar* – literally 'house of hair') set up. Such houses are generally divided into a *haram* (forbidden area) for women and another section for the men. The men's section is also the public part of the home. Here guests are treated to coffee and sit to discuss the day's events.

The Bedouin family is a close-knit unit. The women do most of the domestic work, including fetching water, baking bread and weaving clothes. The men are traditionally providers and warriors. There is precious little warring to do these days, and the traditional intertribal raids that for centuries were the staple of everyday Bedouin life are now a memory.

Most of those still living in the desert continue to wear traditional dress, and this includes, for men, a dagger – a symbol of a man's dignity but rarely used in anger now. The women tend to dress in more colourful garb, but rarely do they veil their tattooed faces.

Although camels, once the Bedouin's best friend, are still in evidence, they are now often replaced by the Landrover or Toyota pick-up – Wilfred Thesiger would definitely not approve. Other concessions to modernity are radios (sometimes even TVs), plastic water containers and, occasionally, a kerosene stove.

The Jordanian Government provides services such as education, and offers housing to the 40,000 or so Bedouin estimated to be truly nomadic, but both are often passed up in favour of the lifestyle that has served them so well over the centuries.

The Bedouin are renowned for their hospitality and it is part of their creed that no traveller is turned away. This is part of a desert code of survival. Once taken in, a guest will be offered the best of the available food and plenty of tea and coffee. The thinking is simple: today you are passing through and they have something to offer; tomorrow they may be passing your camp and you may have food and drink – which you would offer them before having yourself. Such a code of conduct made it possible for travellers to cross the desert with some hope of surviving in such a hostile natural environment.

One has to wonder, if large numbers of tourists continue to pass through (and 99 times out of 100 in no danger of expiring on a sand dune), how long outsiders can expect to be regaled with such hospitality. After all, the original sense of it has largely been lost. Perhaps the moral for travellers is not to deliberately search out the Arab 'hospitality experience', reducing it to a kind of prefab high to be ticked off from the list of tourist excitements automatically claimed as a virtual right. There is a world of difference between the harsh desert existence that engendered this most attractive trait in Arab culture and the rather artificial context in which most of us experience this part of the world today.

start from JD2/7 per camel/4WD vehicle and cost up to JD20/45 for a full day. Prices are regulated, but do not include food or tents if you intend to stay overnight.

Until sometime in 2003, the RSCN has a makeshift **visitors reception centre** (☎/fax 2032918; e rum@nets.com.jo) just outside the Rest House. The new visitors centre on the road into Rum (about 2km north of the Rest House) was due for completion in 2003. The helpful **tourist police** (☎ 2018215) are in a small office in the Rest House complex.

If you intend some serious hiking, it's worth picking up a copy of *Walks & Scrambles in Rum* by Tony Howard and Di Taylor.

The Bedouin are a conservative people, so please dress appropriately. Baggy trousers/skirts and modest shirts/blouses will, besides preventing serious sunburn, earn you more respect from the Bedouin, especially out in the desert.

Things to See

The enormous and dramatic **Jebel Rum** (1754m) towers above Rum Village. Of the sites closest to Rum Village (distances in brackets from the Rest House), there is a 1st century BC **Nabataean temple** (400m) and **Lawrence's Spring** (1.2km), named after TE Lawrence because he wrote about it in the *Seven Pillars of Wisdom*, but it's more properly known locally as **'Ain ash-Shallaleh**. A rather steep, 20-minute scramble up some rocks brings you to a small pool with startling **views** to Jebel Khazali and beyond.

Further a field, the highlights include: **Barrah Siq** (14km), a long, narrow canyon; the **Burdah Rock Bridge** (19km) precariously perched about 80m above the ground; **Jebel Khazali** (7km), a superb and serene spot with welcome shade and a narrow *siq*; **Lawrence's House/Al-Qsair** (9km) which is worthwhile for its remote location and supreme views of the red sands; **Qattar Spring** (8km), a beautiful spring; **Sand Dunes/Red Sands** (6km) with superb red sand up the slope of Jebel Umm Ulaydiyya; **Sunset & Sunrise Points** (11km) with superb views from near Umm Sabatah; **Umm Fruth Rock Bridge** (13km), another small and remote rock bridge; and **Wadak Rock Bridge** (9km) with magnificent views across the valley.

Places to Stay & Eat

Most travellers who stay overnight prefer to sleep out in the desert.

Government Rest House (☎ *2018867; 2-person tent per person JD3)* has tents out the back. The price includes access to the toilets and hot showers in the Rest House. The tents can be locked so bring a small padlock and keep your valuables with you at all times. The **restaurant** at the Rest House is surprisingly good value. A main dish of kebabs or *shish tawouq* with French fries, and salads and dips costs JD3.600. Sandwiches cost 720 to JD1.200, an omelette is JD1.200 and a continental breakfast costs JD3. It is also possible to find a bed with some of the families in Rum village. Try **Restaurant Wadi Petra** (☎/*fax 2019135, mobile ☎ 0795539956;* Ⓔl *Difallahz@yahoo.com; mattress per person JD2).* This place is also good for food.

Getting There & Away

Check at the visitors centre or Rest House when you arrive in Wadi Rum for the prevailing departure times. At the time of research, there was at least one minibus a day to Aqaba (JD1.500, one hour); 7am is the most reliable departure time. From Sunday to Thursday, you should also find one leaving around 12.30pm and possibly again at 3pm, ferrying teachers from the school back to Aqaba. To Wadi Musa (JD3, 1½ hours), there is a daily minibus at 8.30am.

If you're wanting to head to Ma'an, Karak or Amman, the minibuses to either Aqaba or Wadi Musa can drop you along the Desert Hwy (750 fils, 20 minutes), from where it's easy enough to hail onward transport.

AQABA　　　　　　　　　　العقبة
☎ 03

The balmy winter climate and idyllic setting on the Gulf of Aqaba make this Jordan's aquatic playground, with mild temperatures even as Amman is experiencing snow flurries. In summer, it gets very hot.

The diving and snorkelling south of Aqaba is the region's main attraction, and Aqaba itself is a relaxed place with a good range of hotels and restaurants.

Information

The **tourist office** (☎/*fax 2013363; open 7.30am-2.30pm Sun-Thur)* is in the visitors centre next to Aqaba Castle. The Egyptian consulate north of the centre issues single-/multiple-entry tourist visas for JD12/15 with a minimum of fuss. You'll need one photo and be prepared to wait for one to two hours. It's open from 10am to 3pm Sunday to Thursday. There are plenty of banks (with ATMs) and moneychangers around town. The post office is in the centre of town and open from 7.30am to 7pm Saturday to Thursday and 7.30am to 1.30pm on Friday. Aqaba has a good sprinkling of Internet cafés, most of which charge JD2. Two recommended places are in the building to the west of the Aqaba Gulf Hotel on King Hussein St: **Samir Internet Cafe** (☎ *2033413),* which has superfast ASDL connections; and **City Internet** (☎ *2018732)* which is open 24 hours. There are also a couple of excellent bookshops.

Things to See

Along the Corniche, and squeezed between the marina and the Mövenpick Resort, is the site of **Ayla (Old Aqaba)**, the early medieval port city. The ruins are limited, but worth a quick look if you're in the area. Of more interest is **Aqaba Castle** (*admission low/high season 500 fils/JD1 (combination ticket with*

AQABA

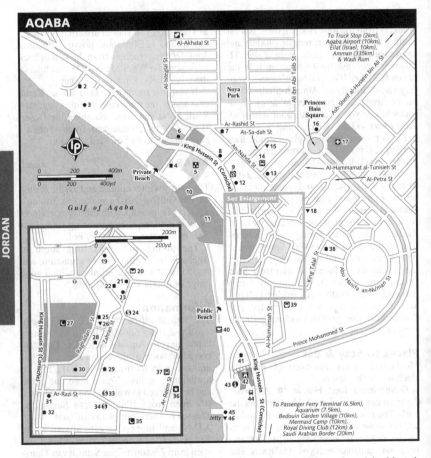

*museum); open 7am-5pm daily Oct-Apr &
7am-7pm daily May-Sept)*, built originally by
the Crusaders and expanded by the Mamluks
in the early 16th century. The Ottomans occupied the castle until World War I when it
was substantially destroyed by shelling from
the British. The Hashemite Coat of Arms
above the main entrance was raised soon afterwards as the Great Arab Revolt swept
through Aqaba.

In the visitors centre nearby is the small
but interesting **Aqaba Museum** *(admission
low/high season 500 fils/JD1 (combination
ticket with castle); open 7am-5pm daily Oct-
Apr & 7am-7pm May-Sept)*.

Part of the Marine Science Station complex, the **aquarium** *(☎ 2015145; admission
JD2; open 8am-5pm Sat-Thur)*, 7.5km south

of central Aqaba, is worth a visit although
there are very few labels.

Swimming

The beaches of Aqaba are fairly unappealing and women are likely to feel very uncomfortable. It's slightly better at the
private beaches of the upmarket hotels,
such as the Aquamarina Beach, Radisson
SAS and Mövenpick Resort, but you'll pay
anywhere between JD2.500 and JD10.

Diving & Snorkelling

There are some superb sites for diving and
snorkelling in the Gulf of Aqaba, south of the
town centre and ferry passenger terminal. To
arrange the diving, speak to one of Aqaba's
very professional dive agencies, which in-

AQABA

PLACES TO STAY		OTHER		21	Yamani Library (Bookshop)
2	Radisson SAS Hotel	1	Egyptian Consulate	23	Redwan Library (Bookshop)
4	Mövenpick Resort Hotel	3	Aquamarina Beach Hotel	24	Arab Bank
7	Al-Cazar Hotel	5	Ayla (Old Aqaba) Ruins	27	Sherif al-Hussein bin Ali
22	Dweikh Hotel 1	6	JETT Bus Office;		Mosque
25	Al-Amer Hotel;		Part of Ayla Ruins	30	Produce Souq
	Syrian Palace Restaurant;	8	Aqaba Golf Hotel	31	Avis Car Rental;
	Al-Tarboosh Restaurant	9	Samir Internet Cafe;		Peaceway Tours;
28	Al-Khouli Hotel; National		City Internet		Housing Bank
	Restaurant	10	Royal Yacht Club of Jordan	33	Jordan National Bank
29	Jordan Flower Hotel	11	Navy Docks	34	Moneychangers
32	Nairoukh 2 Hotel;	12	Aqaba International Dive	35	Mosque
	Arab Divers		Centre	36	Police Station
38	Al-Zatari Hotel	13	Hertz Car Rental; Coffee Shops	37	Main Bus/Minibus Station
41	Moon Beach Hotel	14	Trust International Transport	39	Minibus/Service Taxi Station
			Bus Office		(to Karak & Safi)
PLACES TO EAT		16	Royal Jordanian Airlines	40	Public Beach; Cafes; Paddle
15	Silk Road		Office		& Glass-Bottom Boats
	Restaurant	17	Princess Haya Hospital	42	Aqaba Castle (Mamluk Fort)
18	China Restaurant	19	International Traders (Ameri-	43	Visitors Centre; Tourist
26	Al-Shami Restaurant		can Express)		Office; Aqaba Museum
46	Mina House Floating	20	General Post Office;	44	Minibuses (to Saudi Arabia)
	Restaurant		Telephone Booths; ATM	45	Speedboat Dock

JORDAN

clude: **Aqaba International Dive Centre** (☎/fax 2031213; e diveaqaba@yahoo.com; off King Hussein St); **Arab Divers** (☎ 2031808, fax 2012053; e arabdivers@hotmail.com; King Hussein St, next to Nairoukh 2 Hotel); and the **Royal Diving Club** (☎ 2032709, fax 2017097; e rdc@jptd.com.jo), around 12km south of the city. All can arrange transport to the dive sites for no extra cost.

For snorkelling, all of the above places rent out flippers, mask and snorkel for JD3 per day, as do a couple of the campsites along the southern beach (see Places to Stay).

Places to Stay – Budget

Bedouin Garden Village (☎ 079602521, fax 201 2989; e bedwinjamal@yahoo.com; per person in tent or cabin JD2, half-board around JD12) is a wonderful place to stay. It's located about 10km south of the town centre on the east side of the road.

Mermaid Camp (☎ 0795567761; per person JD2) is another place along the beach south of Aqaba with a laid-back atmosphere, good snorkelling nearby and friendly staff.

Jordan Flower Hotel (☎/fax 2014378; singles/doubles JD5/8, with bathroom JD8/10) is simple but the best in this area.

Al-Khouli Hotel (☎ 2030152, fax 2030664; Zahran St; singles/doubles from JD8/10) is also good value. It's worth paying an extra JD2 for a balcony as these rooms are nicer.

Dweikh Hotel I (☎ 2012984, fax 201 2985; e Dweikhotel@firstnet.com.jo; singles/doubles JD10/15) has exceptionally tidy rooms with satellite TV.

Al-Amer Hotel (☎/fax 2014821; Raghadan St; singles/doubles JD12/18) is excellent value, with sunny, clean rooms. Ask for one at the front where the views are superb.

Places to Stay – Mid-Range & Top End

Every place listed below has a fridge, air-con, satellite TV, telephone and hot water, and prices include breakfast.

Al-Zatari Hotel (☎ 2022970, fax 202-2974; King Talal St; singles/doubles/triples JD20/28/32) is highly recommended with spacious, well-appointed rooms and su-perlative views. The staff are also friendly.

Nairoukh 2 Hotel (☎ 2012980, fax 201 5749; King Hussein St; singles/doubles in low season JD14/20, in high season from 16/25) is similarly good value with modern rooms, helpful staff and decent views.

Moon Beach Hotel (☎ 2013316, fax 2016500; e amsaad77@yahoo.com; King Hussein St; singles/doubles JD17/30) is re-moved from (but easy walking distance to) the bustle of central Aqaba. The rooms are lovely and most have great sea views.

Al-Cazar Hotel (☎ 2014131, fax 2014 133; e alcsea@alcazar.com.jo, An-Nahda St;

singles/doubles JD34/54) has very pleasant rooms, a swimming pool, pub and an on-demand DVD cinema with over 200 movies. Significant discounts can be negotiated.

Radisson SAS Hotel (☎ 2012426, fax 2013426; e aqizh_gm@go.com.jo; singles/doubles JD60-80) is typically luxurious with the added advantage of its own beach.

Mövenpick Resort Hotel (☎/fax 2034020; e resort.aqaba@moevenpick.com; singles/doubles JD60/65) is arguably Aqaba's finest, with a high-class complex including a private beach.

Places to Eat

Syrian Palace Restaurant (☎/fax 2014788; Raghadan St; mains JD2-7; open 10am-midnight daily) offers good local food at moderate prices.

Al-Shami Restaurant (☎ 2016107; Raghadan St; mains JD2-6; open 10am-1am daily), in a lane between Raghadan and Zahran streets, is another popular place with an extensive menu and an air-conditioned dining area with good views.

Al-Tarboosh Restaurant (☎ 2018518; Raghadan St; meals around JD1; open 7.30am-midnight daily) does good shwarma, as well as small pastry pizzas with meat or cheese (200 fils apiece).

National Restaurant (☎ 2012207; Zahran St; mains from JD2.500; open 7.30am-midnight daily) is a busy place and deservedly so. The meat and chicken dishes come with salads and hummus, and it's one of the cheapest places around for fish dishes (JD3.250).

China Restaurant (☎ 2014415; Al-Petra St; mains JD1.300-6; open 11.30am-3pm & 6.30-11pm) is a Chinese restaurant with a long-standing reputation. The cook is Chinese, prices are reasonable and it has a bar.

Mina House Floating Restaurant (☎ 201 2699; mains from JD3.500; open 12.30pm-4pm & 6.30pm-11.30pm daily) serves fish dishes from JD6.500, which isn't bad considering it is always freshly caught, and not frozen as in some other Aqaba restaurants. The setting is very pleasant.

Silk Road Restaurant (☎ 2033556; As-Sa'dah St; mains JD2.750-12.500; open noon-4pm & 6pm-2am daily) is one of Aqaba's finest restaurants with a lovely atmosphere and delicious seafood. There are live performances most nights after 10pm.

Getting There & Away

Air For details of flights between Aqaba and Amman, see the Getting Around section earlier in the chapter.

Bus & Minibus From the JETT office (☎ 2015222), on King Hussein St, buses (JD4.200) run five times daily to Amman.

Trust International Transport (☎ 2032200), on An-Nahda St, has six daily buses (JD4) to the capital. It also has two daily buses to Irbid (JD6, 5½ hours).

To Wadi Musa (for Petra), minibuses (JD3, two hours) leave at around 8.30am, 10.30am, 12.30pm and 1.30pm, but the exact departure times depend on the number of passengers going in both directions. Otherwise, get a connection in Ma'an (JD1.500, 80 minutes).

Two minibuses go to Wadi Rum (JD1.500, one hour) at 6am and 6.30am, ostensibly to ferry teachers to the school there. On Friday there is only one minibus a day. At other times, catch a minibus towards Ma'an, disembark at the turn-off to Wadi Rum and then hitch a ride to Rum village from there.

All of the above minibuses leave from the main bus/minibus station on Ar-Reem St. Minibuses to Karak (JD1.850, three hours), via Safi and the Dead Sea Hwy, are the exception, leaving from the small station next to the mosque on Al-Humaimah St.

Sea For details of boat services between Aqaba and Nuweiba in Egypt, see the main Getting There & Away section earlier in the chapter.

Israel For information about crossing the border to/from Israel, see the Getting There & Away section earlier in the chapter.

Kuwait

الكويت

Kuwait's rapid transformation into a wealthy oil emirate is something of a contradiction. While the gleaming shopping malls, flashy cars, and massive villas that are now the average home to your average Kuwaiti family certainly add glitter to this tiny desert state, if you take the time to look behind the finery you will also find a conservative, family-oriented society where tradition and typical Arabian hospitality are still very much alive.

Facts about Kuwait

HISTORY
The first inhabitants of Kuwait settled on the northern shores of Kuwait Bay at Sabiyah some 7000 years ago. Recovered shards of pottery, stone walls, tools, a small drilled pearl and remains of what is perhaps the world's earliest seafaring boat, link this site to the Mesopotamian Ubaid civilisation and indicate that the area today known as Kuwait has been on a trade route since the Stone Age.

Over time, Kuwait's main settlements shifted. The main town around 1500 years ago was believed to have been Khazimah, near Al-Jahra, while history reveals that 400 years ago a southern village known as Al-Qurain was the main centre. The headland now occupied by Kuwait City was settled only 300 years ago and in the early 18th century the Kuwait as we know it today was nothing more than a few tents clustered around a storehouse-cum-fort.

Eventually the families living around the fort divided among themselves the responsibilities attached to the new settlement. The Al-Sabah family, whose descendants now rule Kuwait, were appointed to handle local law and order. The small settlement grew quickly. By 1760, when the town's first wall was built, Kuwait's dhow fleet was said to number 800 and camel caravans based there travelled often to Baghdad and Damascus.

By the early 19th century Kuwait was a thriving trading port. But trouble was always, quite literally, just over the horizon. It was often unclear whether Kuwait was part of the Ottoman Empire. Though the 19th century Kuwaitis generally got on well

The State of Kuwait

Area: 17,818 sq km
Population: 2.2 million
Capital: Kuwait City
Head of State: The Emir, Sheikh Jaber al-Ahmed al-Sabah
Official Language: Arabic
Currency: Kuwaiti dinar (KD)

- Best Dining – eating at one of the outdoor restaurants overlooking Kuwait Bay
- Best Nightlife – strolling along the Corniche on Arabian Gulf St and stopping for Turkish coffee and a *sheesha* (water pipe)
- Best Walk – wandering through the old souq in Kuwait City
- Best View – watching the sunset from the viewing platform of Kuwait Towers
- Best Activity – diving in the clear waters off Kubar Island

Kuwait City p432
Kuwait City Centre p434

with the Ottomans, official Kuwaiti history is adamant that the sheikhdom always remained independent. As the Turks strengthened their control of Eastern Arabia (then known as Al-Hasa) the Kuwaitis skilfully managed to avoid being absorbed by the empire. The Al-Sabah did, however, agree to take the role of provincial governors of Al-Hasa on the Ottomans' behalf.

That decision led to the rise of the pivotal figure in Kuwait's modern history: Sheikh Mubarak al-Sabah al-Sabah, commonly known as Mubarak the Great (r. 1896–1915).

What to See

Kuwait is not usually on a traveller's agenda, but if you do get to visit this tiny country, and it doesn't happen to be in the middle of a typically fierce summer, it's quite easy to spend several days taking in the sights.

To get an idea of the country's architectural history, take a long morning walk down **Arabian Gulf St**. The old houses and mosques hint at Kuwait's pre-oil past while buildings such as the **National Assembly** and **Sharq Souq** are testament to the wealth oil has brought the country. If you're interested in politics, it's also possible to take in an Assembly session (English translation available). In the afternoon, chill out at the **Scientific Centre**, with its giant aquarium and IMAX theatre, or catch a movie at one of the city's many luxury cinemas.

Venturing further out to the 'suburbs', a morning wandering around the **Tareq Rajab Museum**, with its small but excellent collection of Islamic art and artefacts, is definitely a must-do. An afternoon at the **Maritime Museum** and *Al-Hashemi* II, the world's largest wooden dhow, will give you an insight into the country's maritime heritage.

If you tire of the city and have access to a car, a whole day can be spent in the northern desert, along **Al-Mutla Ridge**. It may not be Mt Everest, but reaching a height of 145m it is Kuwait's highest point and is particularly pretty during the cooler winter months, when rainfall has turned the desert green.

Driving south of Kuwait City will take you to **Al-Ahmadi**, the birthplace of the country's oil industry. Here you can visit the **Kuwait Oil Company's Display Centre** to learn about the history and development of the industry, and take a look at the **Japanese Gardens** – a display garden containing bioremediated soil from the oil lakes left after the Iraqi invasion.

Mubarak was deeply suspicious of Turkey and convinced that Constantinople planned to annex Kuwait. He overthrew and murdered his brother the emir, did away with another brother and installed himself as ruler.

In 1899 Mubarak signed an agreement with Britain. In exchange for the British navy's protection he promised not to give territory to, take support from or negotiate with any other foreign power without British consent. The Ottomans continued to claim sovereignty over Kuwait, but they were now in no position to enforce it. Britain's motive for signing the treaty was a desire to keep Germany, then the main ally and financial backer of Turkey, out of the Gulf.

Kuwait spent the early 1920s fighting off the army commanded by Abdul Aziz bin Abdul Rahman al-Saud (Ibn Saud), the founder of modern Saudi Arabia. In 1923 the fighting ended with a British-brokered treaty under which Abdul Aziz recognised Kuwait's independence, but at the price of most of the emirate's territory.

An oil concession was granted in 1934 to a US-British joint-venture known as the Kuwait Oil Company (KOC). The first wells were sunk in 1936 and by 1938 it was obvious that Kuwait was virtually floating on oil. WWII forced the KOC to suspend its operations, but when oil exports took off after the war so did Kuwait's economy.

Sheikh Abdullah al-Salem al-Sabah (r. 1950–65) became the first 'oil sheikh'. His reign was not, however, marked by the kind of profligacy with which that term later came to be associated. As the country became wealthy, health care, education and the general standard of living improved dramatically. In 1949 Kuwait had only four doctors; by 1967 it had 400.

On 19 June 1961 Kuwait became an independent state. Elections for Kuwait's first National Assembly were held the following year. Although representatives of the country's leading merchant families won the bulk of the seats, radicals had a toehold in the parliament from its inception. Leftists in the National Assembly almost immediately began pressing for faster social change and the country had three cabinets between 1963 and 1965.

In August 1976 the cabinet resigned, claiming that the assembly had made day-to-day governance impossible, and the emir suspended the constitution and dissolved the assembly. It wasn't until 1981 that the next elections were held, but then parliament was dissolved again in 1986.

In December 1989 and January 1990 an extraordinary series of demonstrations took place calling for the restoration of the 1962 constitution and the reconvening of parliament. Despite these political and economic tensions, by early 1990 the country's (and the Gulf's) economic prospects looked bright, particularly with an end to the eight year Iran-Iraq War. In light of this, the events that followed were even more shocking to most people in the region.

On 16 July 1990 Iraq sent a letter to the secretary-general of the Arab League accusing Kuwait of exceeding its OPEC quota and of stealing oil from the Iraqi portion of an oil field straddling the border. The following day Iraqi president Saddam Hussein repeated these charges in a speech and vaguely threatened military action.

When the tanks came crashing over the border at 2am on 2 August, the Kuwaitis

never had a chance. The Iraqis were in Kuwait City before dawn and by noon they had reached the Saudi frontier. The emir and his cabinet fled to Saudi Arabia.

On 8 August Iraq annexed the emirate. Western countries, led by the USA, began to enforce a UN embargo on trade with Iraq, and in the months that followed more than half a million foreign troops flooded into Saudi Arabia.

On the 15th January, after a deadline given to Iraq to leave Kuwait had lapsed, Allied (mostly US) aircraft began a five week bombing campaign over Iraq and Kuwait. The Iraqi army quickly crumbled and on 26 February 1991 Allied forces arrived in Kuwait City to be greeted by jubilant crowds and clouds of acrid black

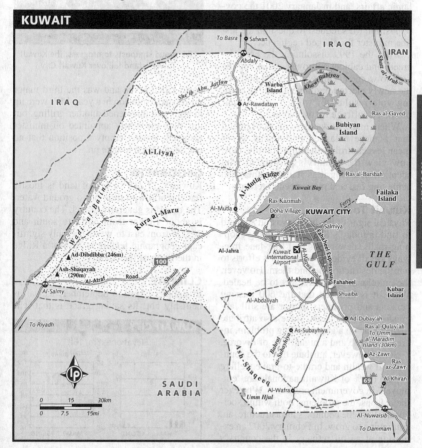

smoke which came from the hundreds of oil wells the retreating Iraqis had torched.

In keeping with a promise the opposition had extracted from the emir during the occupation, elections for a new National Assembly took place in October 1992. The opposition shocked the government by winning more than 30 of the new parliament's 50 seats. Elections in 1996 produced a parliament more to the government's liking, though the country's MPs zealously exercised their right to question ministers about anything and everything.

Dissolution of parliament is still as popular a solution as it was when it first occurred in 1963: in 1999 the emir dissolved parliament and called snap elections after MPs threatened to grill the minister for Islamic affairs, and in January 2001 the government resigned en masse following an opposition MPs request to question the justice minister for alleged negligence.

After the 1999 dissolution the emir decreed, and cabinet approved, extending the vote to women. This was debated hotly by the newly elected parliament and the ensuing vote resulted in women losing their promised suffrage by two votes.

Where many Kuwaitis were once hopeful that a more balanced parliament would mean less control by the ruling family, most now view the country's parliament with scepticism, seeing it as stalling rather than achieving real and much needed reforms.

Kuwait Today

Physical signs of the Iraqi invasion are hard to find in today's Kuwait. Gleaming shopping malls, new hotels and four-lane freeways are all evidence of Kuwait's efforts to put the destruction behind them. However, the emotional scars have yet to be healed. While it is believed that the 600 missing persons and prisoners of war are still languishing in Iraqi gaols, some also attribute to the invasion a growing drug problem, increased crime and a higher rate of divorce.

Some, however, attribute this to the country's oil wealth and cradle-to-grave welfare system (94% of Kuwaiti nationals are 'employed' in government positions). Whatever the reasons, the problems, both within society and with the country's infrastructure, are continuing to grow. In February 2002 an explosion at an oil refinery in the country's

CHRIS MELLOR

Like proud signposts to progress, the Kuwait Towers stand tall over Kuwait City

north killed seven and was the third major oil-related explosion in a year. MPs were up in arms and threatened another grilling, but this time the newly appointed oil minister resigned, leaving empty a position that no one seems keen to take on.

GEOGRAPHY

Kuwait's 17,818 sq km of land is mostly flat and arid with little or no ground water. The desert is generally gravel. The country is about 185km from north to south and 208km from east to west. The only significant geographic feature is Al-Mutla Ridge in the north of the country.

CLIMATE

In summer (April to September) Kuwait is hellishly hot. Its saving grace is that it is

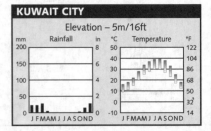

KUWAIT CITY

Elevation – 5m/16ft

nowhere near as humid as Dhahran, Bahrain or Abu Dhabi. The winter months usually see some rainfall and it can get fairly cold, with daytime temperatures hovering around 18°C and nights being genuinely chilly. Sandstorms occur throughout the year, but are particularly common in spring.

GOVERNMENT & POLITICS

Under Kuwait's 1962 constitution the emir is the head of state. By tradition the crown prince serves as prime minister. The prime minister appoints the cabinet, usually re-serving key portfolios (such as interior, and foreign affairs and defence) for other members of the ruling family.

The powers of the emir, crown prince and cabinet are tempered by the 50-member National Assembly, which must approve the national budget and also has the power to question cabinet members. The emir has the power to dissolve the assembly whenever he pleases, but is required by the constitution to hold new elections within 90 days of any such dissolution (a requirement that, historically, has not always been honoured).

While Kuwait boasts an 'elected' national assembly, only a small proportion of Kuwaitis are actually eligible to vote. Women are not allowed to vote or run for parliament, and only Kuwaiti males aged over 21 and who are not in prison or serving in the military are eligible. Only 'original' Kuwaiti nationals over the age of 30 are eligible to contest parliamentary seats.

POPULATION & PEOPLE

While no exact figures are available, Kuwait's population is thought to be around 2.2 million people. Of these, about 800,000 (around 37%) are Kuwaitis and the remaining 63% are expatriates from the Indian subcontinent, Asia, other Arab countries and, to a lesser extent, Western countries.

SOCIETY & CONDUCT

Kuwait's society is still fairly conservative when it comes to matters of public conduct. As well as immodest dress (skirts above the knee, halter tops, shorts and singlets etc), open displays of affection (kissing and hugging, for example) between men and women are also frowned upon. Alcohol is illegal and heavy penalties apply to anyone caught consuming it.

Non-Muslims should not enter mosques – the exception being the Grand Mosque and this only on a supervised tour (refer to the Kuwait City section later for details).

RELIGION

Kuwait's brand of Islam is not as strict as that practised in Saudi Arabia, but the country is not as liberal as Bahrain. Most Kuwaitis are Sunni Muslims, though there is a substantial Shiite minority.

LANGUAGE

Arabic is the official language. English is widely spoken and understood in commercial offices, large shopping centres and hotels. For Arabic words and phrases, see the Language chapter at the back of this book.

Facts for the Visitor

WHEN TO GO

The best time to visit Kuwait is during the cooler months between October and April. Avoid visiting the country during Ramadan, when most places are closed during daylight hours and the entire population is on 'Ramadan Timing', which makes it extremely frustrating and difficult to get anything done.

VISAS & DOCUMENTS
Visas

Everyone except nationals of the other Gulf States needs a visa to enter Kuwait. Kuwait does not issue tourist visas per se, but mid-range and top-end hotels can sponsor 'visit' visas for travellers.

To obtain a visa this way, send a fax to the hotel with your passport data, arrival and departure dates, flight numbers and reason for visit (generally 'business', though sometimes 'tourism' will be acceptable). Most people will receive a single-entry visa valid for 90 days from the date of issue and for a one-month stay.

The hotel will charge you KD5 for sponsoring the visa, but be sure to ask about the cost when you are making your visa arrangements. Hotels usually require that you stay with them for the duration of your visit. It usually takes three to four working days for a hotel to process a visa, though it may take mid-range hotels a bit longer.

Visas are usually picked up at a Kuwaiti embassy (though in some countries it is possible to mail your passport in) and include two sheets of paper; one to be handed in upon arrival and the other upon departure. While visas, once approved, can be picked up at any Kuwaiti diplomatic mission, the pick-up point has to be specified at the time the papers are filed. Large hotels can also arrange for the original visa to be picked up at the airport. If they do this, be sure that the hotel faxes you a copy of the visa prior to your departure, otherwise the airline may not let you fly.

Multiple-entry visas valid for anything from one to 10 years are generally only given to those coming in and out of the country for business on a regular basis and who have Kuwaiti sponsorship, though you can only stay in the country for one month at a time.

For details of visas for other Middle Eastern countries, see the 'Visas at a Glance' table under Visas & Documents in the Regional Facts for the Visitor chapter.

Transit Visas A transit visa can be obtained from any Kuwaiti consulate and is valid for a maximum of seven days and costs KD2. To be eligible you must have a valid visa for your next country of destination and a confirmed onward ticket.

If your passport contains an Israeli or Iraqi stamp you will be refused entry to Kuwait.

Visa Extensions It is sometimes possible to obtain up to two one-month extensions on a visit visa. To do this, you need to apply to the Immigration Department in Shuwaikh before your visa expires.

Driving Licences

Driving licences from most Western and Arab (and all GCC) countries are valid in Kuwait, though visitors will need to obtain 'insurance' for their licence before renting a car. See Getting Around in the Kuwait City section for details on car rental.

EMBASSIES
Kuwaiti Embassies

Following are the Kuwaiti embassies in major cities around the world. For Kuwaiti embassies in neighbouring Middle Eastern countries, see the relevant chapters.

Canada (☎ 613-780 9999) 80 Elgin St, Ottawa, ON, K1P IC6
France (☎ 17 50 47 23 54 25) 2 rue Lubeck, Paris 75116
Germany (☎ 49 228 378 081/4) Griegstrasse 5-7 D, Berlin 14193
Netherlands (☎ 31 70 3603 81316) The Hague
UK (☎ 020-7590 3400) 2 Albert Gate, Knightsbridge, London SW1X 7JU
USA (☎ 202-966 0702) 2940 Tilden St NW, Washington DC 20008

Embassies in Kuwait

Most embassies are usually open from around 8am to 1pm Saturday to Thursday.

Bahrain (☎ 531 8530) Surra district, St 1, Block 1, Bldg 24
Canada (☎ 256 3025) Da'iya district, Al-Mutawakil St, Area 4, House 24; adjacent to the Third Ring Rd
Egypt (☎ 251 9956) Diplomatic Area, Dai'ya, Block 5
France (☎ 257 1061) Mansouria district, St 13, Block 1, Villa 24
Germany (☎ 252 0857) Bahiya district, St 14, Block 1, Villa 13
Iran (☎ 256 0694) Diplomatic Area, Dai'ya, Block 5
Jordan (☎ 253 3271) Nuzha, Block 3, Akkah St, Bldg 20
Lebanon (☎ 256 2103) Diplomatic Area, Dai'ya, Block 5
Netherlands (☎ 531 2650) Jabriya district, St 1, Block 9, House 76
Oman (☎ 256 1956) Udailia district, St 3, Block 3, House 25; by the Fourth Ring Rd
Qatar (☎ 251 3606) Istiqlal St, Diplomatic Area; south of the centre off Arabian Gulf St
Saudi Arabia (☎ 240 0250) Al-Sharq district, Arabian Gulf St
Syria (☎ 539 6560) Mishref, Block 6, Al-Khos St, Bldg 1
Turkey (☎ 253 1785) Diplomatic Area, Dai'ya, Block 5
UAE (☎ 252 8544) Istiqlal St, Diplomatic Area; south of the centre off Arabian Gulf St
UK (☎ 240 3336) Arabian Gulf St, near Kuwait Towers and Dasman Palace
USA (☎ 539 5307) Al-Masjid al-Aqsa St, Plot 14, Block 14, Bayan; about 17km south of the centre
Yemen (☎ 534 9417) Jabriya, Block 11, Opp St 101, Bldg 38

CUSTOMS

No alcohol is permitted in the country, yet you are able to import up to 500 cigarettes and 2lbs of tobacco!

Duty free items are on sale at the duty free shop in the arrivals and departures section of the airport.

MONEY
Currency

Kuwait's currency is the Kuwaiti dinar (KD). The KD is divided into 1000 fils. Coins are worth five, 10, 20, 50 or 100 fils. Notes come in denominations of KD0.25, KD0.5, KD1, KD5, KD10 and KD20. The Kuwaiti dinar is a hard currency and there are no restrictions on taking it into or out of the country.

Exchange Rates

Below are the rates for a range of currencies when this book went to print.

country	unit		Kuwaiti dinar
Australia	A$10	=	KD1.640
Bahrain	Bdh1	=	KD0.813
Canada	C$10	=	KD1.913
euro zone	€10	=	KD2.967
Japan	¥100	=	KD0.247
New Zealand	NZ$10	=	KD1.417
Oman	OMR1	=	KD0.785
Qatar	Qr10	=	KD0.830
Saudi Arabia	SAR10	=	KD0.805
UAE	UAR10	=	KD0.822
UK	UK£1	=	KD0.472
USA	US$1	=	KD0.302

Exchanging Money

Money changers are dotted around the city centre and main souqs and change all major and regional currencies. Only banks and the larger money exchanges will change travellers cheques.

If you're changing cash, moneychangers will give you a far better rate than banks, but note that moneychangers' rates vary wildly, so it's worth shopping around.

ATMs & Credit Cards Visa and American Express (AmEx) are widely accepted in Kuwait and all major banks accept most credit cards and are linked to the major networks. ATMs at the National Bank of Kuwait, Commercial Bank of Kuwait and Gulf Bank all accept Visa (Electron and Plus), MasterCard and Cirrus.

Costs

Kuwait is expensive. While it's quite easy to eat for KD3 (US$9) or less per day, sleeping cheap is another matter. Because visas are generally only sponsored by main hotels you will be hard pressed to get away with spending less than KD46 (US$150) per night on accommodation. Add to this other costs such as transport, dining out and admission prices to museums and other attractions, and you will need to plan for an average daily budget of at least KD40 (US$132).

Tipping & Bargaining

A tip is only expected in fancier restaurants. Note, however, that the service charge added to your bill in such places goes into the till, not to staff.

Bargaining is *de rigueur* in Kuwait; in souqs, many Western-style shops and some hotels. It is always acceptable to ask for a discount on the original price offered.

POST & COMMUNICATIONS
Post

Post boxes are a rare sight around Kuwait City, so you will probably have to brave the lines at post offices if you need to send anything and do not already have stamps.

The postal rate for aerograms and for letters or postcards weighing up to 20g is 150 fils to any destination outside the Arab world. Postage for cards or letters weighing 20g to 50g is 280 fils. Ask at the post office for parcel rates as these vary significantly from country to country.

There is no poste restante service in Kuwait. Large hotels will usually hold mail for their guests only.

Telephone

The country code for Kuwait is ☎ 965, and is followed by the local seven-digit number. There are no area or city codes. The international access code (to call abroad from Kuwait) is ☎ 00.

Kuwait's telephone system is very good, though if you're trying to call overseas on weekends and public holidays it can take a while to get connected. Local calls are free, but international calls can be expensive: per minute to Australia will cost around 600 fils, New Zealand, the Netherlands and Japan 800 fils, Canada and the UK about 500 fils, and the US 200 fils. Payphones take 50 and 100 fil coins, though they are increasingly giving way to cardphones, for which cards are available in units of KD3, KD5 or KD10.

KUWAIT

Mobiles Users of mobile phones can link into the GSM services of Mobile Telecommunications Company or Wataniya. Prepaid SIM-cards are available from Wataniya (there's a booth at the airport) for KD10.

Fax
Fax services are available from government communications centres, though there are usually long queues. Your best bet is the business centres in the larger hotels, which charge according to their IDD rates.

Email & Internet Access
All top-end hotels have Internet access and there are a few Internet cafés in the city centre. **Kuwait Internet Café** (☎ 240 5005; mezzanine, Al-Dawlia Centre), behind the Kuwait Airways building, has reasonably fast connections for 500 fils per half-hour; next door, the **Princess Diana Internet Café** offers the same.

If you are travelling with your own laptop, Internet access is easy, provided you have a modem and phone line. While major hotels provide Internet access, it's also possible (and cheaper) to purchase prepaid dial-up Internet cards. Alphanet cards come in denominations of KD3, KD5 and KD10 and can be purchased at *bakalas* (corner shops) and supermarkets. A KD3 card will give you around 50 hours of Internet access in the mornings and around 25 hours in the evenings. When keying in the dial-up number from a hotel room be sure to include the hotel's outside line number first.

DIGITAL RESOURCES
For a comprehensive list of Middle East/ Arab world websites see the Regional Facts for the Visitor chapter; otherwise some useful Kuwait-specific websites include the following.

The Kuwait Information Office Contains lots of information and links on Kuwaiti history, culture and lifestyle
  W www.kuwait-info.org
The Kuwait Oil Company Gives a run-down on the nation's number-one resource and industry – oil
  W www.kockw.com
Kuwait Tourism Services Company Provides information on accommodation, the sights of Kuwait and specific tours as well as Kuwaiti lifestyle
  W www.ktsc-q8.com

BOOKS
As well as this book, Lonely Planet also publishes the detailed country guide *Bahrain, Kuwait & Qatar*.

Otherwise, there are several excellent, recently published books on Kuwait available.

Pearling in the Arabian Gulf by Saif Marzooq al-Shamlan is an interesting collection of memoirs and interviews on Kuwait's pearling industry.

Women in Kuwait by Haya al-Mughni paints a clear and illuminating picture of the lives and roles of Kuwaiti women as well as society's attitudes towards them.

Sheikha Altaf al-Sabah's *Traditions & Culture* is a beautifully produced coffee-table book with excellent photographs depicting old Kuwait, its people and traditional culture.

The Ministry of Information publishes a number of books on the Iraqi invasion and the Gulf War. These include a rather gruesome collection of photographs of Iraqi atrocities in occupied Kuwait called *The Mother of Crimes against Kuwait in Pictures*.

More general Middle East titles, some of which contain coverage of Kuwait, are listed in the Books section in the Regional Facts for the Visitor chapter.

NEWSPAPERS & MAGAZINES
Arab Times and *Kuwait Times* are Kuwait's two English-language newspapers. Both provide adequate foreign coverage, largely reprinted from British newspapers and the international wire services. The *Kuwait Pocket Guide* covers everything from doing business in the country to where to find horse riding lessons, and is essential for anyone intending to spend any length of time in the country.

International newspapers and magazines are available (usually a day or two late) at major hotels. Expect glossy magazines to come complete with large tracts of black texta or even with pages torn out, censoring anything that is deemed 'un-Islamic'.

RADIO & TV
Radio Kuwait – also known as the Super Station – broadcasts on 99.7 FM; it plays mostly rock and roll with a bit of local news and features mixed in. The US military's Armed Forces Radio & Television Service (AFRTS) can be heard on 107.9 FM; it

broadcasts a mixture of music, news and chat shows.

Kuwait TV's Channel 2 broadcasts programmes in English each evening from around 5pm to midnight. Many hotels, even the smaller ones, have satellite TV.

PHOTOGRAPHY & VIDEO

Provided you exercise a modicum of common sense, taking photographs in Kuwait is not really a problem. Photographing obvious 'tourist' sites, such as the Kuwait Towers or the Red Fort in Al-Jahra, is OK, but aiming your camera at military installations, embassies or palaces will more than likely get you into trouble. Always remember to ask before taking anyone's picture; photographing women is considered *haram* (forbidden).

Film is developed quickly (often in an hour or two) and cheaply, so long as it is colour print film. B&W or slide film takes a lot longer and often yields mixed results. Small photo studios throughout the centre of Kuwait City can do passport photos for about KD4.

HEALTH

Health care in Kuwait is equivalent to what is available in most Western countries, and many prescription drugs are available over the counter.

The drinking water comes from desalination plants, and while there is nothing wrong with it per se you're probably better off sticking to bottled water.

For more general health information see the Health section in the Regional Facts for the Visitor chapter.

WOMEN TRAVELLERS

Women travellers may find the increased attention afforded them by men more of a nuisance than anything. From being tailgated whilst driving to being followed around shopping centres, the men who engage in this sort of behaviour see it as harmless (read mindless) fun. The best advice is to dress conservatively, not to respond to approaches and to avoid eye contact with men. Even so, you'll more than likely find that you still attract attention – simply because you're a woman.

For some useful tips on avoiding or dealing with harassment from males, see the Women Travellers section in the Regional Facts for the Visitor chapter.

DANGERS & ANNOYANCES

Land Mines

Because of the difficulty in detecting landmines, wadi bashing is still a very dangerous sport in Kuwait and you ought to think long and hard before indulging yourself. Desert camping in organised camping areas is a better bet. The wisest course is to camp with someone who knows the area and has been there before.

Kuwait City and the residential sections of other urban centres like Al-Jahra and Al-Ahmadi may have been cleared of mines but it's still important to bear in mind the number-one rule: *don't pick up any unfamiliar object*.

Kuwait is no longer the frighteningly unsafe place it once was – but people who keep track of these things emphasise that stuff still blows up every month. When in doubt, play it safe.

Driving

Kuwait has one of the highest road accident rates in the world; one-third of all deaths in Kuwait are driving-related. The many spectacularly flattened and twisted bits of metal (that were once cars) left by the roadside are testament to this (to get an idea of how spectacular and numerous, check out **w** www .crazyshit.org/crash). While the traffic authorities have long since recognised and tried to address this problem, there are still a large number of drivers who like to drive *very* fast and without regard for others. If you are driving while you're in Kuwait the best tack is to drive defensively.

Iraqi Border

If you are going north, the Iraqi border is now pretty hard to miss. A trench, fence, earth wall and various other border fortifications have replaced the open desert across which the Iraqis rolled in August 1990.

That said, the unsettled situation between Iraq and Kuwait means that you really should *not* be anywhere north of the Kuwaiti army checkpoint on the Al-Mutla Ridge without a very good reason.

If you do run into trouble with the Iraqis (who have been known to cross into Kuwaiti territory and snatch the odd foreigner) you should keep it in mind that the UN troops who patrol the border zone have no authority to help you.

KUWAIT

BUSINESS HOURS

Shops are open from 8am or 9am to about 1pm and then again from about 4pm to 6pm or 7pm Saturday to Thursday. Large shopping centres usually stay open until 10pm and are open seven days a week. On Thursday most businesses will only be open in the morning. Friday is the weekly holiday, when almost nothing is open during the day, though by late afternoon and early evening many shops do open for business.

PUBLIC HOLIDAYS

In addition to the main Islamic holidays described in the Regional Facts for the Visitor chapter, Kuwait celebrates the following public holidays:

New Year's Day 1 January
National & Liberation Day 25th & 26th February

ACTIVITIES
Diving

While it may not be as spectacular as the Red Sea, diving in Kuwait's warm shallow waters is a pleasant way to spend a day or two. There are several dive outfits, such as **Dive Caroline** (☎ 562 4111; e *divecarolina@eudocamail .com*) at the Messilah Beach Hotel and **BBR** (☎ 562 7515; e *info@bbrdive.com*; w *www .bbrdive.com*; *Street 5, Area 6, Salwa*), that offer trips to the outer islands of Kubar and Umm al-Maradim for around KD20.

ACCOMMODATION

Because of visa restrictions your choice of accommodation is restricted to the hotel that sponsors you. Budget hotels do not arrange visas so most travellers are limited to staying in mid-range and top-end hotels.

FOOD & DRINKS

Kuwait's indigenous cuisine is much the same as that of other Gulf countries (see the special section 'Middle Eastern Cuisine' in the Regional Facts for the Visitor chapter).

Expect the likes of lentil soup, *majboos laham* (rice with lamb), *majboos dajaj* (rice with chicken), and fish dishes such as *mutabaj zubaidi* (fish and rice), *marabeen* (shrimp) and *mehamer* (sweet rice).

All or some of these dishes are usually served at the smaller (and cheaper) Arabic-style restaurants.

You can enjoy a host of international cuisines in Kuwait: from Iranian stews to Japanese sushi. There is also the usual array of Western fast-food joints and cafés.

All drinks are nonalcoholic. The selection includes soft drinks (sodas), mineral water, fruit juice, coffee and tea.

SHOPPING

Kuwait is fast becoming something of a shoppers' paradise and, some would argue, is beginning to rival the likes of Dubai for prices and its variety of goods. Indeed, the country's only real claim to 'tourism' is the annual **Hala February shopping festival** where discounts and very attractive 'special deals' can be found in shops throughout the country during the month of February.

If you're looking for something a little more traditional and locally produced then you can view and buy Kuwaiti Bedouin weavings at **Sadu House**, a cultural foundation dedicated to preserving Bedouin art. Alternatively, check out the offerings at **Souq al-Jum'a**.

See Sadu House and Shopping in the Kuwait City section for further details.

Diwaniyas

The *diwaniya* (Kuwaiti gathering) is a Kuwaiti institution and if you get invited to one, go!

Once referring to the section of a Bedouin tent where the men and their (male) visitors would sit apart from the rest of the family, today it can be anything from a few benches outside the family home to grandiose reception halls complete with chandeliers and marble floors.

In the evenings, men sit around on soft cushions or on benches, sipping tea or Arabic coffee, smoking *sheesha*, sometimes playing cards, to discuss any manner of things – from the latest soccer scores to the day's debates in parliament. Some are more formal than others and host specialised meetings with guest speakers. As political parties are effectively illegal in Kuwait, the *diwaniya* has also become the core of the country's political system. Indeed, some could even argue that Kuwait's National Assembly, where talk, talk and more talk is the norm, is the ultimate *diwaniya*!

Getting There & Away

AIR

Kuwait is not a particularly cheap place to fly into or out of. The airlines and travel agents tightly control prices, and few discounted fares are available.

Return fares from the USA start at around US$1260 (flying from Kuwait to the USA is cheaper, around US$950 return). Australia can be a bargain (relatively speaking), with return fares as low as KD300 (about A$1800) sometimes available. The cheapest airfares from London start at UK£285.

Airfares to the Indian subcontinent are among the better deals. The cheapest regular fare to New Delhi is KD230 for a return ticket allowing a four-month stay (seven-day minimum).

The cheapest return fares to some other Gulf destinations include KD80 to Abu Dhabi or Dubai, KD44 to Bahrain, KD113 to Muscat and KD63 to Riyadh.

Departure Tax

There is an airport departure tax of KD2. Tickets sold outside Kuwait often don't include this tax, meaning that you'll have to pay it in cash at the airport. Look for 'KWD 2.000' or something similar in the 'tax' box just below the part of the ticket that shows the cities between which you are travelling.

LAND

Buses operate between Kuwait and Cairo via Aqaba in Jordan and Nuweiba in Egypt. Agents specialising in these tickets (the trip takes about two days) are in the area around the main bus station. See Getting Around in the Kuwait City section for information on services.

If you're planning on driving through Saudi Arabia you'll first need to obtain a three-day transit visa. Inquire at the Saudi embassy (☎ 240 0250; Al-Sharq district, Arabian Gulf St) for more details.

SEA

The **Kuwait and Iran Shipping Company** (☎ 241 0498, fax 241 6685; Ahmed al-Jaber St, Al-Sharq), opposite Warba Insurance, operates a service three times a week from Kuwait's port of Shuwaikh to the Iranian port

of Bushehr and back. A one-way economy passage costs KD37 and if you are taking a car you will need to pay an extra KD150.

Getting Around

Kuwait has a very cheap and extensive local bus system. You can also use taxis to get around, though these are more expensive. See the Kuwait City Getting There & Away and Getting Around sections for details.

If you're renting a car expect to pay anywhere from KD8 to KD12 per day. This rate usually includes unlimited kilometres and full insurance. **Al-Mulla** (☎ 242 1660; e amrl@almulla.com.kw) is one of the better local agencies and has desks at the airport, Radisson SAS Hotel (☎ 562 6490), Messilah Beach Hotel (☎ 561 8864) and the Ritz Hotel (☎ 251 0999).

If you hold a driving licence and residence permit from another Gulf country you can drive in Kuwait without any further paperwork. Otherwise you can drive on an International Driving Permit or a local licence from any Western country, but you'll also be required to purchase 'insurance' for your licence at KD10 per month.

Kuwait City مدينة الكويت

Kuwait City started out as a *kout* (small fort), built in 1672 by the Bani Khalid tribe. By 1760, and after the arrival of the Utub tribe in 1711, a wall was built around the city, with subsequent walls being erected in 1814 and 1920. Today, while the walls have long been demolished and there remains very little of the old buildings of Kuwait, the city still retains its five original districts – Qibla, Mirqab, Sharq, Dasman and Salhya.

Kuwait can be a surprisingly relaxed place to visit – if you remember to take it easy and don't expect to get too much done!

Orientation

The commercial centre is the area from the bay inland to Al-Soor St between the Al-Jahra Gate and Mubarak al-Kabir St. The main shopping and commercial street is Fahad al-Salem St, which becomes Ahmed al-Jaber St north of Al-Safat Square. The souq is the area between the municipal park

KUWAIT CITY

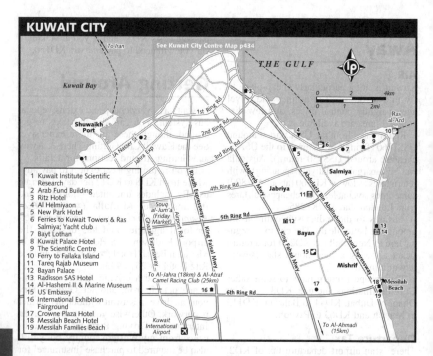

To Iran

See Kuwait City Centre Map p434

THE GULF

Kuwait Bay

Shuwaikh Port

1st Ring Rd

2nd Ring Rd

3rd Ring Rd

JA Nasser St

Jahra Exp

Ras al-Ard

Salmiya

Riyadh Expressway

4th Ring Rd

Jabriya

Maghreb Mwy

Abdulaziz Bin Abdulrahman Al Saud Expressway

Souq al-Jum'a (Friday Market)

Airport Rd

5th Ring Rd

Bayan

Ghazali Expressway

King Faisal Mwy

King Fahad Mwy

Mishref

To Al-Jahra (18km) & Al-Atraf Camel Racing Club (25km)

6th Ring Rd

Kuwait International Airport

To Al-Ahmadi (15km)

Messilah Beach

1 Kuwait Institute Scientific Research
2 Arab Fund Building
3 Ritz Hotel
4 Al Helmiyaon
5 New Park Hotel
6 Ferries to Kuwait Towers & Ras Salmiya; Yacht club
7 Bayt Lothan
8 Kuwait Palace Hotel
9 The Scientific Centre
10 Ferry to Failaka Island
11 Tareq Rajab Museum
12 Bayan Palace
13 Radisson SAS Hotel
14 Al-Hashemi II & Marine Museum
15 US Embassy
16 International Exhibition Fairground
17 Crowne Plaza Hotel
18 Messilah Beach Hotel
19 Messilah Families Beach

and Mubarak al-Kabir St. Upmarket shopping places are clustered along the lower end of Fahad al-Salem St (near Kuwait Sheraton Hotel), behind the Meridien Hotel, along Arabian Gulf St and further south in the shopping district of Salmiya.

From the centre the city spreads inland becoming ever broader as it goes. The main arteries are a series of numbered ring roads and Arabian Gulf St, which continues along the coast to Salmiya and beyond.

Information

Money You will find banks evenly distributed throughout the city. Moneychangers can offer slightly better rates than banks (and usually charge lower commissions. **Al-Muzaini Exchange** (☎ 242 4882; Fahad al-Salem St) and **UAE Exchange** (☎ 245 0852; Fahad al-Salem St), in the basement of Burgan Bank building, both change travellers cheques.

AmEx (☎ 241 3000) is represented in Kuwait by **Al-Ghanim Travel** (2nd mezzanine level, Salhiya Commercial Centre; open 8am-1pm & 4pm-7pm Sat-Thur). AmEx card holders can cash personal cheques, but the office will not hold mail for AmEx clients.

Post The **main post office** (Fahad al-Salem St; open 7.30am-7.30pm Sat-Wed, 7.30am-3.30pm Thur, 9am-11am & 3.30pm-7.30pm Fri) is by the intersection with Al-Wattiya St.

Telephone & Fax The **main telephone office** (cnr Abdullah al-Salem & Al-Hilali Sts; open 24hr daily) is at the base of the telecommunications tower. Cardphones (for which cards are on sale) are available for international calls. You can also book international calls and pre-pay the cost, but this is more expensive than using the cardphones. Fax services are also available.

Travel Agencies Fahad al-Salem and Al-Soor Sts between Al-Jahra Gate and the Radio & TV building both have lots of small travel agencies.

There are also many travel agencies in the Al-Dawliah Commercial Centre, behind the Kuwait Airways building on Al-Shuhada Street, as well as several around the corner on Fahad Al-Salem Street. Despite a theoretical ban on the discounting of published air fares, shopping around might save you some money. **Al-Ghanim Travel** (☎ 802 112;

e travel@alghanim.com; Fahad Al-Salem St) and **Al-Hogal Travels** (☎ 243 8741; Al-Dawliah Centre) and **Sanbouk Travels and Tours** (☎ 245 7267; Arabian Gulf St), opposite Sharq Souq, are all very helpful.

Bookshops The **Kuwait Bookshop** (☎ 242 3945; basement level, Al-Muthanna Centre, Fahad al-Salem St) is the best place to look for English-language books.

Cultural Centres There are several foreign cultural centres in Kuwait City.

British Council (☎ 251 5512) On Al-Arabi St in Al-Mansouria district, next to Nadi al-Arabi stadium. The library is open from 4pm to 8pm Saturday to Wednesday and 9am to 1pm Thursday.
Centre Culturel Francais de Koweit (☎ 257 4803) Located at the French embassy (Al-Mansouria District, St 13, Block 1, Villa 24), it has a library and videotheque and organises concerts, plays and exhibitions.
Indian Arts Circle (☎ 390 4817) The main office is in Funaitees. It hosts regular performances by artists from India, both at the centre and the Indian embassy.
US Cultural Center Located at the US embassy (☎ 539 5307; Al-Masjid al-Aqsa St, Plot 14, Block 14, Bayan), it sometimes hosts exhibitions and concerts of visiting US artists.

Laundry Most hotels offer reasonably priced, 24-hour-turn-around laundry services. Otherwise, try **Al-Shurouq Laundry** (cnr Abu Bakr al-Siddiq & Al-Wattiya Sts) in the city centre or **Fajr Kuwait Laundry** (Al-Soor St). Washing and ironing a medium-sized load at either place will probably cost KD2 to KD4.

National Museum
This museum (Arabian Gulf St; admission free; open 8.30am-12.30pm & 4pm-7pm Sat-Wed, 8.30am-11am & 4pm-7pm Thur & Fri) was once the pride of Kuwait; its centrepiece, the Al-Sabah collection, was one of the most important collections of Islamic art in the world. During the occupation, however, the Iraqis systematically looted the exhibition halls. Having cleaned out the building, they smashed everything they could and then set what was left on fire.

Most of the museum's collection was eventually returned by the Iraqis, but many pieces had been damaged during transit to Iraq or had been poorly stored while they were there.

A hall at the back of the museum complex's courtyard has a few items on display. The upper floor is a gallery devoted to the work of Kuwaiti artists.

Bus Nos 12 and 16 will get you to within a couple of blocks of the museum.

At the time of writing the museum was closed for renovation.

Tareq Rajab Museum
This museum (☎ 531 7358, fax 533 9063; W www.trmkt.com; House 16, St 5, Block 12, Jabriya district; admission free; open 9am-noon & 4pm-7pm Sat-Thur, 4pm-7pm Fri), which is housed in the basement of a large villa, is a private collection of Islamic art assembled by Kuwait's first minister of antiquities. The collection is all the more important given the fate that befell the National Museum's treasures.

The museum is in the Jabriya district, near the intersection of the Fifth Ring Motorway and the Abdulaziz Bin Abdilrahman al-Saud Expressway (also known as the Fahaheel Expressway). There is no sign on the building, but it is easily identified by its entrance – a carved wooden doorway flanked by two smaller doors on each side. All four of the door panels are worked in gilt metal.

Bus Nos 25 and 32 serve Jabriya, though neither stops within easy walking distance of the museum.

Al-Hashemi Marine Museum
This museum (☎ 575 6000 ext 3235/3250; Radisson SAS Hotel, Gulf Rd; admission free) has an impressive collection consisting of 12 large model dhows and various traditional seafaring equipment. It's part of the much larger complex attached to **Al-Hashemi** II – the world's largest, and most opulent, dhow. Tours are available for the museum and the dhow. Call first to arrange a time.

Scientific Centre
Kuwait's newest addition to its growing list of attractions is the Scientific Centre (☎ 848 888; W www.tsck.org.kw; Arabian Gulf St, Salmiya; open 9am-12.30pm & 5pm-9.30pm Sun-Wed, 9am-9.30pm Thur, 2pm-9.30pm Fr). The centre's Arabian Gulf ecodisplay has a fabulously mesmerising **aquarium**, and there's a walk-through section where you can view some of the wildlife (once) native to the country. The **IMAX cinema** shows a

KUWAIT CITY CENTRE

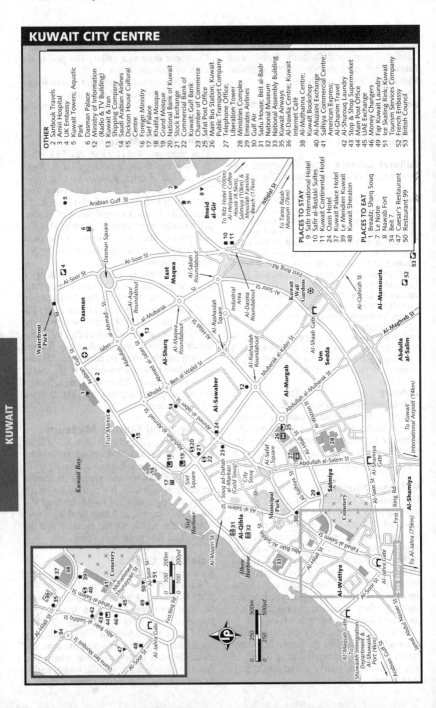

OTHER
2 Sanbouk Travels
3 Amin Hospital
4 UK Embassy
5 Kuwait Towers; Aquatic Park
6 Dasman Palace
12 Ministry of Information (Radio & TV Building)
13 Kuwait & Iran Shipping Company
14 Saudi Arabian Airlines
15 Dickson House Cultural Centre
16 Foreign Ministry
17 Sief Palace
18 Khalifa Mosque
19 Grand Mosque
20 National Bank of Kuwait
21 Stock Exchange
22 Commercial Bank of Kuwait; Gulf Bank
23 Chamber of Commerce
25 Safat Post Office
26 Main Bus Station; Kuwait Public Transport Company
27 Telephone Office; Liberation Tower
28 Ministries Complex
29 Emirates Airlines
30 Gulf Air
31 Sadu House; Beit al-Badr
32 National Museum
33 National Assembly Building
35 Kuwait Airways
36 Al-Dawlia Centre; Kuwait Internet Café
38 Al-Muthanna Centre; Kuwait Bookshop
40 Al-Muzaini Exchange
41 Salhiya Commercial Centre; American Express; Al-Ghanim Travel
42 Al-Shurouq Laundry
43 Stop & Shop Supermarket
44 Main Post Office
45 Money Changers
46 UAE Exchange
49 Fajr Kuwait Laundry
51 Ice Skating Rink; Kuwait Tourism Services Company
52 French Embassy
53 British Council

PLACES TO STAY
9 Safir International Hotel
10 Safir al-Bastaki Suites
11 Kuwait Continental Hotel
24 Oasis Hotel
37 Kuwait Palace Hotel
39 Le Meridien Kuwait
48 Kuwait Sheraton

PLACES TO EAT
1 Breadz; Sharq Souq
7 Le Notre
8 Nawab Fort
34 Beit 7
47 Caesar's Restaurant
50 Restaurant 99

selection of films (including some in 3D), and the **Discovery Place** is an interactive learning centre for children. There is a **coffee shop** and **restaurant** and a pleasant **dhow harbour** where the *Fateh al-Khair*, the last surviving wooden dhow of the pre-oil era, is moored. Admission prices vary, depending on what you see. A combination ticket to the aquarium and IMAX, for example, will cost KD5/3.5 per adult/child.

Sadu House
Sadu House (☎ 243 2395; Arabian Gulf St; admission free; open 8am-1pm & 5pm-7pm Sat-Thur) is a museum and cultural foundation dedicated to preserving Bedouin arts and crafts, and is the best place in Kuwait to buy Bedouin goods. Pillows cost around KD15 and small bags are KD7 to KD15. The house is built of gypsum and coral – note the carved decorative work around the courtyard.

The **Kuwait Textile Association** (☎ 541 2067; e Kuwait_Textile_association@hotmail .com) holds *sadu* (Bedouin-style) weaving courses, taught by Bedouin women, at the centre. The six-lesson courses cost KD40 and run for three weeks.

Al-Corniche
To watch one of Kuwait's spectacular desert sunsets, take a walk along Al-Corniche, a several-kilometre-long stretch of winding paths, parks and beaches on Arabian Gulf St that follows the Kuwait Bay coastline. Stop off at any one of the many restaurants or coffee houses here for a bite to eat or a *sheesha*. During the hot summer evenings, the Corniche is a busy thoroughfare with people flocking to the coast to enjoy the (slightly) cooler temperatures.

National Assembly Building
This distinctive white building (☎ 245 5422; Arabian Gulf St; parliamentary sessions occasionally open to the public) with its sloping roofs was designed by Jørn Utzon, the Danish architect who designed the Sydney Opera House. The two sweeping roofs were designed to evoke Bedouin tents.

Sief Palace
This is the official seat of the emir's court. The oldest parts of the building (Gulf Rd, Sharq) date to the early 20th century while the new and ponderously opulent palace

was completed around the beginning of 2000. It is not open to the public and photography is prohibited.

The Grand Mosque
Also known as Masjed Al-Kabir, the Grand Mosque (☎ 241 8448; Mubarak al-Kabeer St) was opened in 1986 and cost KD14 million. It boasts Kuwait's highest minaret (74m) and can accommodate up to 5000 worshippers in the main hall with room for another 7000 in the courtyard. It offers tours between 9am and 4pm Saturday to Wednesday, but book a day or two in advance.

Kuwait Towers
This is Kuwait's most famous landmark (☎ 244 4021; Arabian Gulf St; observation deck admission 500 fils; observation deck open 9am-11pm daily). Designed by a Swedish architectural firm and opened in 1979, the largest of the three towers rises to a height of 187m and houses a two-level revolving observation deck, restaurant, coffeehouse and private banquet room. The lower globe on the largest tower and the single globe on the middle tower each store around 4.5 million gallons of water. The smallest tower is used to light up the other two.

Stock Exchange
Kuwait's stock exchange (Mubarak al-Kabir St; trading 9.30am-noon Sat-Wed), the Gulf's largest, is the big brown building a block or so inland from the Grand Mosque. The exchange is an electronic market, so you'll see lots of people sitting around tracking their investments on the tally boards hanging from the roof, but none of the running about and shouting usually associated with Western financial markets.

Liberation Tower
This is Kuwait's tallest building (cnr Al-Hilali & Abdullah al-Salem Sts) and at a height of 372m claims to be the fifth-tallest communications tower in the world. There is an observation deck about two-thirds of the way up the tower and a revolving restaurant, though at the time of writing it was not clear whether it was open to the public.

Arab Fund Building
This is an impressive building (☎ 484 4500; Airport Rd, Shuwaikh) with exceptionally

KUWAIT

beautiful interiors. Each room represents a regional style of traditional architecture. The main foyer is exceptionally beautiful.

Dixon House Cultural Centre

This modest, white building (☎ 243 7450; Arabian Gulf St; open 8am-12.30pm & 4pm-7.30pm Sat-Wed; admission free) with blue trim was the home of former British political agent Harold Dixon and his wife Violet, who lived here until the Iraqi invasion. Now a heritage museum, in honour of the couple whose love of and contribution to Kuwait, its environment and Bedouin culture was well-documented, the building has been restored to as close to its original design as possible. It houses a collection of photographs taken during Kuwait's British protectorate era; a replica museum of the Dixons' living quarters; and an archive of Kuwaiti-British relations that dates from the 19th century to the 1960s, when Kuwait was granted independence.

Bayt al-Badr

This traditional house (☎ 242 9158; Arabian Gulf St; admission free), next to Sadu House, was built between 1838 and 1848. Its doors are a good example of the old doors of Kuwait. Call for opening times.

Khalifah Mosque

This mosque (Arabian Gulf St), opposite the Ministry of Foreign Affairs, was built in AD 1737 (AH 1126) and is Kuwait's oldest surviving mosque.

Bayt Lothan

This cultural centre (☎ 575 5866; e lothan@hotmail.com; Gulf Rd, Salmiya) promotes the work of Kuwaiti and Gulf artists. The house was originally the home of the country's late emir, Sheikh Sabah al-Salem al-Sabah, and is a well-preserved example of 1930s Kuwaiti architecture.

Old City Gates

Al-Shaab, Al-Shamiya, Al-Jahra and Al-Maqsab are the names of Kuwait City's gates on Al-Soor St, the street that follows the line of the old city wall (soor is the Arabic word for 'wall'). Despite their ancient appearance the wall and gates were only constructed around 1920. The wall was torn down in 1957.

Organised Tours

The **Kuwait Tourism Services Company** (☎ 245 1734; e ktsc@qualitynet.net; Ice Skating Rink, Al-Soor St) runs tours around the various city sights and out to the oil fields. It mainly caters for large tour groups, but can arrange similar tours for individuals.

Places to Stay – Mid-Range

All of the hotels mentioned here have air-con and private bathrooms. Satellite TVs are also standard, as are minifridges. Prices quoted are inclusive of the 15% service charge that most hotels add to their tariff – though you may be able to negotiate this away as a 'discount'.

Kuwait Continental Hotel (☎ 252 7300, fax 252 9373; Al-Dasma Roundabout; singles/doubles KD25/30) is a popular option for budget-minded business travellers.

New Park Hotel (☎ 563 4790, fax 563 4858; e nphotel@qualitynet.net; Maidan Hawally; singles/doubles KD28/36) is a decent mid-range hotel with friendly and helpful staff. The outdoor restaurant is popular, though it tends to get noisy on weekends.

Oasis Hotel (☎ 246 5489, fax 246 5490; e sales@oasis.com.kw; cnr Ahmad al-Jaber & Mubarak al-Kabir Sts; singles/doubles KD30/40) is a centrally located hotel that's very popular with budget-minded business travellers.

Safir al-Bastaki Suites (☎ 255 5081, fax 255 5082; Al-Dasma Roundabout; singles/doubles 25/30, suites KD45/50) only has six standard rooms available, so book ahead. The rooms are clean and comfortable and there is a small coffee shop downstairs, which serves breakfast.

Kuwait Palace Hotel (☎ 571 0301, fax 571 9520; e salmiya@salmiyapalace.com; Salem Mubarak St, Salmiya; singles/doubles KD35/45) is an extraordinary Yemeni-style building in the shopping district of Salmiya. The Middle Eastern–style lobby is tasteful and the rooms try to be special – split level with kitchenette – but in reality they are a little dirty and shabbily constructed. There is a billiard room and Internet café downstairs, and a swimming pool on the rooftop.

Places to Stay – Top End

If money is no object then Kuwait is an easy place to spend a lot of it. Five-star hotels offer the fastest and most reliable service for visa seekers, and charge accordingly. The prices quoted here are rack rates and even if you can negotiate some sort of 'corporate' rate you should not count on knocking more than KD5 or so off these prices.

Ritz Hotel (☎ 252 8335, fax 252 8334; Arabian Gulf St, Bneid al-Gir; singles/doubles KD49/55) is a small and tasteful boutique-style hotel with wonderful views of Kuwait Bay. It's by far the best value of the top-end hotels and therefore often full.

The following five-star hotels operate under a price cartel with singles/doubles (including breakfast) at KD66/77.

Kuwait Sheraton (☎ 242 2055, fax 244 8032; cnr Fahad al-Salam & Al-Soor Sts) is luxurious.

Le Meridien Kuwait (☎ 245 5550, fax 243 8391; Al-Hilali St) is another luxury option.

Safir International Hotel (☎ 253 0000, fax 256 3797; Arabian Gulf St), in the Bneid al-Gir district opposite the old US embassy, has been undergoing renovations for some time so only a small part of the hotel is being used. It's overpriced at these rates.

Radisson SAS Hotel (☎ 575 6000, fax 575 0155; www.radissonsas.com.kw; Arabian Gulf St, Rumaithiya) is quiet and has its own private beach.

Places to Eat

Dining out is a favourite pastime (alongside shopping) in Kuwait and Kuwait City is full of restaurants of varying styles, cuisines and prices. Here are only a few of the many to try.

Restaurant 99 (Al-Soor St; sandwiches from 300 fils) near Al-Jahra Gate is one of the city's best bets for cheap eats. Hummus, shwarma and a wide variety of things stuffed into Lebanese-style bread are on offer for a few hundred fils.

Caesar's (Abu Bakr al-Saddiq St; mains KD1.2-3) near Kuwait Sheraton Hotel is the centre's best bet for Chinese food. Note that there is another Caesar's a few blocks up the street toward the Kuwait Airways building, that serves only Indian food.

Breadz (☎ 240 7707; ground floor, Sharq Souq; sandwiches & salads from KD1.5) serves a deliciously fresh selection of pastries, sandwiches and salads as well as fresh fruit juices, tea and coffee. The outdoor terrace overlooking the Sharq marina is pleasant and the dessert bar is decadent and well worth a look.

Bayt 7 (☎ 245 0871; Behbehani Houses No 7, Al-Wattiya; mains KD5-7) is a wonderful restaurant serving international fare, set in an old Kuwaiti coral-and-gypsum house. The house was built in 1949 and is on the government's list of heritage sites.

Nawab Fort (☎ 242 7404; Al-Messilah Complex, Bneid al-Gir; mains KD3-5) offers delicious northwest Indian cuisine amidst a pleasant interior decorated with an array of Indian antiques.

Al-Helmiyaon (Arabian Gulf St; sandwiches 250 fils-KD1), a block north of the New Park Hotel, is a great place to sit and enjoy the view overlooking Kuwait Bay. A modern version of a traditional Egyptian coffeehouse, it offers kebabs and ta'amiyya (deep-fried bean-paste ball) sandwiches for 250 to 500 fils, shish tawouk (chicken kebab) for KD1 and sheesha for 500 fils. The sign is in Arabic, but the complex is large, so easy to find. There is no bus service down this part of Arabian Gulf St. A taxi from the centre costs KD1.5 to KD1.75.

Shabestan (☎ 473 2100; Crowne Plaza Hotel, Farwaniya; mains KD3-6) is an up-market restaurant serving delicious and typically rich Iranian cuisine with matching decor. It's a fair way out of town, but well worth making the trip.

Le Notre (☎ 805 050; Arabian Gulf St; lunch buffet KD3, mains KD2-5) has fantastic views of the Kuwait Towers and bay. A French café and restaurant in a two-storey glass building, it's one of Kuwait's most chic restaurants. The buffet lunch is particularly filling and fresh.

The modern **Sultan Centre** chain of supermarkets is your best bet for self catering. The closest store to the city is in Sharq Souq.

Entertainment

Beach Clubs Some 18km south of the centre, the **Messilah Families Beach** (☎ 565 0642; adult/child 500/250 fils), next to the Messilah Beach Hotel, is a good place to go if you have children or you are a woman wanting to swim without prying eyes following you. Some days are reserved for women only (call to check which days).

Camel Races A fun weekend outing is a trip to the camel races at the **Al-Atraf Camel Racing Club** (Salmi Rd; admission free). The races are held every Thursday and Friday during the cooler winter months. The track is located 7km west of Al-Jahra on the Salmi Rd. To get there from Kuwait City, take any of the main arterial roads and then turn-off onto the 6th Ring Rd. Take the turn-off where there is a faded sign of a camel.

Cinema Considering its size, Kuwait has an overwhelming number of cinemas, which unfortunately show the same films (usually heavily edited to exclude kissing, nudity and sex – violence, however, is left uncensored!). The more popular and modern of the cinemas are located at Sharq Souq on Arabian Gulf St, and in the Al-Fanar shopping complex at Salmiya. Admission to all films costs KD2.5. Check the *Arab Times* for show times.

Ferry Trips Ferries to Kuwait Towers and Ras Salmiya depart from the **marina** (☎ 564 1114) at the Sultan Centre Restaurant complex on Arabian Gulf St, Salmiya. Boats leave all day every day from 9am to 9pm. The one-hour round-trip to the towers costs around KD10 for a minimum of two people, while to Ras al-Ard expect to pay about KD2 per person.

Shopping

City Souq *(open 9am-1pm & 4pm-9pm Sat-Thur, 4pm-9pm Fri)* is a labyrinth of stalls and shops between the municipal park and Mubarikiya St. Here you can find everything from traditional clothing to carpets. It's a wonderful place to spend a few hours. Parts of the souq have been restored in a traditional style. The covered **Souq al-Hareem** is part of the larger complex and is where generations of Bedouin women have come to sell their wares. Close by is the indoor and air-con **Souq ad-Dahab al-Markazi**, the city's central gold market. **Souq al-Jum'a** *(open 8am-4pm Fri)* is on the corner of the 4th Ring Rd and Airport Rd in Shuwaikh (enter from the 4th Ring Rd) and, as the name suggests, is open only on Friday. Anything from kitsch plastic pot plants to tribal Afghani rugs and local Bedouin weavings can be found here.

Salmiya is undoubtedly *the* shopping district of Kuwait. Its main street, Hamad al-Mubarak St, is filled with glitzy shopping malls, with more on the way. **Sharq Souq**, on Arabian Gulf St, Al-Sharq, is another modern complex, and boasts its own marina.

The **International Exhibition Fairground** at Mishrif holds a mind-boggling number of shopping exhibitions throughout the year. Check the local dailies or the *Kuwait Pocket Guide* for the latest, or visit Ⓦ www.kif.net.

Getting There & Away

Air The **Kuwait international airport** (☎ 433 5599, 433 4499) is 16km south of the city centre. Check-in time is officially two hours before your flight is due to depart, but some carriers insist you be there three hours in advance; call the airline to double check.

Bus Kuwait has only a handful of intercity bus routes. All long-haul trips cost 250 fils. Route 101 runs from the main bus station in the city centre to Al-Ahmadi and Fahaheel. Route 103 goes to Al-Jahra.

International bus services to Cairo and Dammam (Saudi Arabia) can be booked through any of the small travel agencies around the intersection of Abdullah al-Mubarak and Al-Hilali Sts. There is no formal service-taxi system operating in Kuwait.

Getting Around

To/From the Airport Taxis charge a flat KD5 between the airport and the city. Bus No 501 runs between the main bus station and the airport every 30 minutes from 5.30am to 9pm daily. The fare is 250 fils. Car rental agencies have booths on the ground floor of the airport.

Bus The **main bus station** is near the intersection of Al-Hilali and Abdullah al-Mubarak Sts. On printed timetables the station is referred to as 'Mirqab bus station'.

Buses start running at around 5am and continue to around 10pm. Fares are 100, 150 or 200 fils, depending on how far you travel. An office on the ground floor of the Kuwait Public Transport Company building at the main station sells a route map for 150 fils.

Taxi Kuwait's taxis have no meters: negotiate a fare at the beginning of the trip. The orange-coloured taxis and the privately owned 'call taxis' charge the same, though the call taxis are a little more reliable. In general, any trip within the city centre is about KD1. Longer trips outside the city centre (eg, from Kuwait Sheraton Hotel to Salmiya) will cost you about KD3. Some reliable taxi companies are **Al-Salmiyah Taxi** (☎ 572 2931) and **Al-Ghanim Taxi** (☎ 481 1824).

Around Kuwait

FAILAKA ISLAND جزيرة فيلكا

The home of Kuwait's most significant archaeological site, Failaka has a history that
goes back to the Bronze Age Dilmun civilisation, which was centred on Bahrain. The
Greeks arrived in the 4th century BC in the
form of a garrison sent by Nearchus, one of
Alexander the Great's admirals. A small settlement existed on the island prior to this, but
it was as the Greek town of Ikaros that the
settlement became a real city.

Sadly, the Iraqis established a heavily fortified base on Failaka, and since liberation
not much has been done to clean up the mess
they left behind. The ancient ruins consist
largely of a **temple** and not much else.

Ferries to Failaka depart daily between
8am and 10am from Ras Salmiya (also
known as Ras al-Ard) on Arabian Gulf St,
southeast of the city centre. The schedule
varies from day to day so it's best to call the
KPTC Ferry Company (☎ 574 2664) to check
for departure times. It's a long trip out there
(1½ hours) and there's not really that much
to see. The fare is KD2.5 return or KD20 if
you take a car. The terminal can be reached
via bus Nos 14, 15, 24, 34 and 200.

AL-AHMADI الأحمدى

Built to house Kuwait's oil industry in the
1940s and '50s, Al-Ahmadi was named for
the then emir, Sheikh Ahmed. It remains, to
a great extent, the private preserve of the
Kuwait Oil Company (KOC).

The **oil display centre** (☎ 398 2747; Mid
5th St; admission free; open 7am-3pm Sat-
Wed) is a well-organised and self-congratu-
latory introduction to KOC and oil business.

To reach the town, take the King Fahad
Hwy south out of Kuwait City until you
reach the Al-Ahmadi exit. First follow the
blue signs for North Al-Ahmadi, and then
the smaller white signs for the display centre and the public garden. Bus No 101 runs
from the main bus station in Kuwait City to
Al-Ahmadi (passing by the oil display centre as it enters town).

AL-JAHRA الجهراء

Al-Jahra, 32km west of Kuwait City, is the
site where invading troops from Saudi Arabia were defeated (with British help) in

Kuwait's Japanese Garden

When retreating Iraqi troops set alight over
700 oil wells, an estimated 65 million barrels
of oil spilled into the Kuwaiti desert. Three
hundred oil lakes covering an area of around
50 sq km was the result, and Kuwait had an
environmental catastrophe on its hands.

In a joint project between the Kuwait Institute of Scientific Research (KISR) and the
Japanese Petroleum Energy Center (PEC), a
bioremediation project was launched to rehabilitate the oil-polluted soil from the lake beds.
Through a variety of biological processes,
which included composting and bioventing, the
KISR-PEC team treated more than 4000 cu metres of contaminated soil. The result? Soil of
such a high quality it could be used for land-
scaping and as topsoil.

The Japanese Garden in Al-Ahmadi is, in reality, part showcase research garden, where
over 3000 cubic metres of the remediated 'oil
soil' was used to create bio-soil–only garden
beds, and part Japanese-style garden, complete with gazebo, ceremonial tea area and
raked pebble gardens. The park is closed to
the public while scientists continue monitor-
ing the now-flourishing garden beds, but this
unique garden in the desert will always be a
reminder of Kuwait's gratitude to the assistance given it by Japan.

1920. It was also the site of the Gulf War's
infamous 'turkey shoot' – the Allied destruction of a stalled Iraqi convoy as it attempted to retreat from Kuwait.

The town's only sight is the **Red Fort**
(☎ 477 2559; open 7.30am-1.30pm &
3.30pm-6.30pm Sun-Fri, 7.30am-1.30pm Sat
winter; 7am-1pm & 4pm-7pm Sun-Fri, 7am-
1pm Sat summer), also known as the Red
Palace, a low rectangular mud structure near
the highway. The fort played a key role in the
1920 battle. Coming from Kuwait City, take
the second of the three Al-Jahra exits from
the expressway. The Red Fort is on the right,
about 200m south (inland) of the highway,
though you can't see it until you are right in
front of it. Still photography is permitted, but
videos are not. Al-Jahra can be reached on
bus No 103, which passes directly in front of
the Red Fort.

Lebanon

الكويت

Lebanon, with its unique blend of the ancient and the ultramodern, is one of the most fascinating countries in the Middle East. Visiting its extraordinary array of historical sites – from the world-famous Roman temple at Baalbek and the unique Umayyad city of Aanjar to the sprawling souqs in Tripoli and the charming Crusader Sea Castle at Sidon – gives the traveller a wonderful overview of the tides of history that have swept over this and nearby countries.

If preserving the past is one of the main objectives of Lebanon's heritage and tourist authorities, rebuilding and redirecting the country's future after decades of civil war is what's occupying the minds of its people, planners and government. The rejuvenation of the Beirut Central District, for example, is one of the largest and most ambitious urban redevelopment projects ever undertaken, and visitors to the city will find the excitement around this and other regeneration projects palpable.

Those travelling in Lebanon inevitably comment on the extraordinary generosity and goodwill of the Lebanese people and then end up asking themselves how such charming and friendly people could have spent years inflicting horrendous damage – both physical and psychological – on each other during the civil war. The answer is elusive but the bottom line is that the war is over and the Lebanese go out of their way to make travellers feel welcome.

Facts about Lebanon

HISTORY

Lebanon was another country that emerged from the break-up of the Ottoman Empire after WWI – events covered in the general history of the Middle East in the Facts about the Region chapter earlier in this book. Between the wars it was under a French mandate and then became fully independent during WWII. Its strategic Middle Eastern location and relatively stable, West-leaning government made it a major trade and banking centre, with many Western multination-

The Republic of Lebanon

Area: 10,400 sq km
Population: 3.6 million
Capital: Beirut
Head of State: President Emile Lahoud
Official Language: Arabic
Currency: Lebanese lira (LL)

- Best Dining – sampling an extraordinary range of mezze at Beit Mary's Restaurant Mounir while looking down on Beirut and the Mediterranean

- Best Nightlife – checking out the nightclubs and bars on Beirut's ultrafunky Rue Monot

- Best Walk – exploring the fascinating medieval souqs in Tripoli's old city

- Best View – marvelling at the spectacular Qadisha Valley from any of the vantage points in and around Bcharré

- Best Activity – spending a day wandering around the extraordinary Roman ruins at Baalbek

als basing their Middle Eastern head offices in Beirut.

But Lebanon had a fatal flaw in its national make-up: power and control rested with the right-wing Christian part of the population, while the Muslims (almost half the population) felt they were excluded from real government. Add large numbers of displaced and restive Palestinians and the result was a recipe for conflict. In 1975 civil war broke out between a predominantly Muslim leftist

440

What to See

Beirut has restaurants, nightclubs and museums that are the best in the Middle East. You'll need at least three days here. If your time is limited and you can only afford two other destinations, make sure they are **Baalbek**, the home of Lebanon's number-one archaeological attraction; and **Sidon**, a charming town to the south of Beirut with a fascinating souq and the Crusader Sea Castle. You'll need a night at Baalbek, but Sidon is easily visited on a day trip from Beirut.

If you have 10 days, you should also travel north and visit the spectacular caves at **Jeita Grotto**; the ancient city of **Byblos**, with its Roman ruins and picturesque harbour; and **Tripoli**, Lebanon's second city, famous for its totally delectable pastries and for its medieval souqs and monuments. Byblos and Jeita can be visited on day trips from Beirut, but Tripoli deserves a stay of at least one night.

With two weeks you'd have time for a side trip from Tripoli to the **Qadisha Valley**, home of the picturesque town of **Bcharré** and the famous **Cedars of Lebanon**. This can be done in one full day. At the other end of the country is the coastal town of **Tyre**, with its World Heritage–listed Roman ruins. You'll probably need to devote one night if you intend to visit here. Also south of Beirut are the **Chouf Mountains**, home of the impressive **Beiteddine Palace** (Beit ad-Din), a lavish Ottoman-style building set in a beautiful landscape. This can be easily visited on a day trip from Beirut.

If you're travelling from Beirut into Syria in good weather, consider stopping off at **Zahlé,** a town in the Bekaa Valley famous for its outdoor eateries. You should also be sure to stop at **Aanjar**, the only significant Umayyad site in Lebanon. To do this you would probably need to base yourself in Zahlé for one night en route to Damascus.

---

coalition (allied with Palestinian groups) and Christian right-wing militias. In April 1976 Syrian forces intervened at the request of the Lebanese president, Suleiman Franjieh, to halt the defeat of the Christian forces.

Subsequently, an uneasy peace was forced upon the two sides by the Syrians. Then in 1978 the Israelis marched into southern Lebanon and set up a surrogate militia, the South Lebanon Army (SLA), to protect northern Israel from cross-border attacks by the Palestine Liberation Organisation (PLO). Following United Nations (UN) pressure, the Israelis withdrew three months later and were replaced by an interim UN peacekeeping force (Unifil). Meanwhile in Beirut, both the Christian and Muslim militias continued building up their arsenals. In the absence of a political solution acceptable to all parties, fighting erupted frequently, only to be stopped by Syrian intervention. At the same time, the Christians started demanding that Syria withdraw its troops from Lebanon.

In June 1982 Israeli troops again marched into Lebanon, this time with the stated aim of eradicating the PLO. They laid siege to Beirut and for seven weeks relentlessly bombarded the Muslim half of the capital by air, sea and land. In August the USA arranged for the evacuation of PLO fighters to other Arab countries, and a Multinational Force (MNF) of US and Western European troops was deployed in Beirut to protect Palestinian and Muslim civilians. After the assassination of Lebanese president-elect Bashir Gemayel, who was also a Christian militia leader, Israeli troops entered west Beirut. Two days later the Israeli-backed Christian militias massacred Palestinian civilians in the Shatila and Sabra camps in this area. Gemayel's brother, Amin, was elected president.

More than a year later Israeli troops withdrew to southern Lebanon. No sooner had they left than fighting broke out between Druze Muslim militias and Christian forces who had been deployed in the Chouf Mountains east of Beirut under Israeli protection. At the same time, fighting erupted between Lebanese army units and Muslim militia in the capital. The MNF came under repeated attack and suffered heavy casualties; it withdrew in early 1984 following suicide bombings of the US and French contingents in October 1983.

In mid-1985 the Israelis withdrew from the rest of Lebanon, except for a 60km-long border strip which remained under Israeli and SLA control. Over the next couple of years the country descended into more chaos as rival factions within both the Christian and the Muslim camps fought each other,

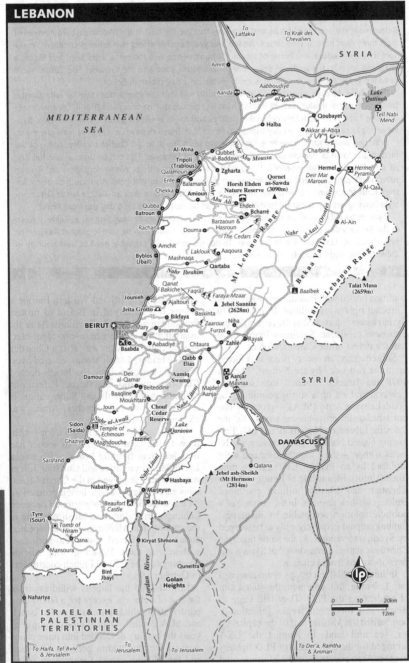

LEBANON

and Iranian-backed Muslim fundamentalists (the Islamic Jihad) resorted to taking foreigners hostage. At the request of the then prime minister, Selim al-Hoss, Syrian troops returned to west Beirut in February 1987 to end fighting between rival Muslim militias. The Syrians slowly brought the Muslim areas of Lebanon under their control.

At the end of his term, in September 1988, President Gemayel appointed a transitional military government led by General Michel Aoun to succeed him. Aoun disbanded the Christian militias and then launched a 'war of liberation' against the Syrians in Lebanon. Following fierce fighting Aoun was defeated and sought refuge in France in August 1991. In the meantime, a majority of Lebanese MPs met in Taif, Saudi Arabia, to sign an Arab-brokered 'accord for national reconciliation'. The MPs elected a new president, René Mouawad, who was assassinated 17 days later. He was replaced by Elias Hrawi, a moderate Maronite Christian who had good relations with Syria.

With the help of the Syrians the Lebanese army took control of Beirut and by late 1991 had spread its presence to most Lebanese areas. By early 1992 all surviving foreign hostages had been released and Syrian troops began withdrawing from the Beirut area.

In August 1992 parliamentary elections were held in Lebanon for the first time in 20 years, and Muslim fundamentalists of the Iranian-backed Hezbollah (Party of God) won the largest number of seats. A few months later the Cabinet resigned and Rafiq Hariri was appointed prime minister.

As the new Cabinet began rebuilding Beirut's infrastructure and rehabilitating the country, the security situation remained tense in southern Lebanon. Israeli forces continued to attack the south during 1991 and 1992 as skirmishes between Israeli soldiers in the border strip and Hezbollah fighters increased in frequency. After Hezbollah fighters killed seven Israeli soldiers in July 1993, Israeli forces launched week-long air, sea and land bombardments on some 80 villages in southern Lebanon, killing 113 people and causing more than 300,000 civilians to leave for safer areas.

Trouble flared up again in April 1996 when Israel mounted a wave of air strikes on Hezbollah positions in the southern suburbs of Beirut and southern Lebanon. After

Hezbollah responded, the Israelis launched another campaign, 'Operation Grapes of Wrath'. Their action attracted wide condemnation when media reported that 102 refugees sheltering in a UN base at Qana had been massacred when the base was bombed by the Israelis.

Lebanon Today

In late May 2000, the Israelis and the SLA withdrew from Lebanon, leading to great rejoicing throughout the region. Nevertheless, relations between the two countries remain tense, and many Lebanese fear that their country will once again be dragged into the volatile and seemingly unresolvable conflict between the Israelis and the Palestinians.

GEOGRAPHY

There are four main geographical areas, running more or less parallel to each other from north to south. They are (from west to east): the coastal plain, the Mt Lebanon Range, the Bekaa Valley and the Anti-Lebanon Range.

The coastal plain is quite narrow, except in the north, and is broken at several points by the cliffs and buttresses of the Mt Lebanon Range which run into the sea. Lebanon's main cities and towns, including Beirut and Tripoli (Trablous), are along this plain.

The Mt Lebanon Range rises from the coastal plain in limestone terraces. It is cut by deep gorges and numerous rivers and streams and includes Lebanon's highest summit, Qornet as-Sawda (3090m), and the famous Cedars of Lebanon.

The eastern slopes of the Mt Lebanon Range are rocky and arid and fall steeply into the Bekaa Valley, Lebanon's main agricultural region.

The Anti-Lebanon Range is an arid massif rising from the eastern side of the Bekaa Valley and marks the border between Lebanon and Syria. Its highest summit is Jebel ash-Sheikh (Mt Hermon), at 2814m.

CLIMATE

Lebanon has a Mediterranean climate – hot and dry in summer (June to August), cool and rainy in winter (December to February). About 300 days of the year are sunny.

In summer the humidity is very high along the coast and daytime temperatures average 30°C, with night temperatures not much lower. Winter is mild, with daytime

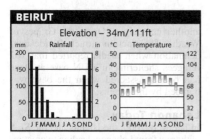

temperatures averaging 15°C. In the mountains, summer days are moderately hot (26°C on average) and the nights cool. Winters are cold, with snowfalls above 1300m.

ECOLOGY & ENVIRONMENT

Like many other Middle Eastern countries, Lebanon's record when it comes to protecting/respecting the environment is a disgrace. The concept of recycling is totally foreign to most Lebanese and litter (particularly plastic) is everywhere, even in the most picturesque parts of the country. There are no effective systems for waste management, meaning that beaches and valleys become unofficial tips; and waterways and the ocean are heavily polluted, with untreated industrial and sewage waste being pumped directly into them.

Sadly, deforestation has taken an enormous toll (there are, for instance, hardly any of the famous Cedars of Lebanon left). Another major problem is air pollution, particularly in Beirut and largely due to the number of diesel- and leaded petrol-fuelled vehicles on the road.

GOVERNMENT & POLITICS

Lebanon is a republic with a president, a Cabinet and a unicameral National Assembly of 128 members. The parliament has legislative powers and elects the president for a six-year nonrenewable term. The president appoints a prime minister and cabinet; both have executive powers. Under a National Covenant agreed to in 1943, the president is a Maronite Christian, the prime minister a Sunni Muslim, the deputy prime minister a Greek Orthodox, the speaker of parliament a Shiite Muslim and the armed forces chief of staff a Druze. Emile Lahoud was elected president in November 1998 and Rafiq Hariri was appointed to the prime-ministerial post, one that he has held before, in November 2000.

ECONOMY

The Lebanese see tourism, banking, agriculture, trade and education as being the industries that will take their country into the future. They bemoan the 'brain drain' which is seeing educated, talented, young Lebanese leaving the country, particularly when threatened with compulsory military service, to make their careers elsewhere in the world.

The poorly performing electricity and communications sectors, which are only now recovering from the civil war, have held back the country's economic development, but the country is optimistic that their rejuvenation (though still not complete) will assist its economic development.

Public debt increased by 19.15% between 2000 and 2001 to reach LL39 billion (155% of GDP) and this is increasing. The government has acted to address this by, among other things, introducing a value-added tax (VAT) and signalling its intention to privatise some government-owned industry, eg, Middle East Airlines (MEA) and Electricite du Liban.

Unemployment is rife (some estimates put it as high as 25%).

POPULATION & PEOPLE

Lebanon has an estimated population of 3.6 million people, 85% of whom live in urban areas – more than one million of them in Beirut. It is one of the most densely populated countries in the Middle East. Although the Lebanese are of mixed ancestry, around 95% of the population is of Arab descent.

There are an estimated 400,000 Palestinian refugees living in the country.

RELIGION

It's estimated that about 70% of the population is Muslim and about 30% Christian. The majority of Lebanon's Muslims are Shiite, although there are also significant numbers of Sunni and Druze. The largest Christian group is the Maronite sect.

LANGUAGE

Arabic is the official language of Lebanon, but French and English are widely spoken around the country. For a list of Arabic words and phrases, see the Language chapter at the back of this book.

Facts for the Visitor

WHEN TO GO
Spring (March to May) and autumn (September to November), when the climate is warm but not uncomfortable, are the best times to travel in Lebanon.

WHAT TO BRING
A hat, sunglasses and sunblock are essential in summer, while some warm clothes and a waterproof jacket are needed in winter. A torch is useful for walking around at night and dealing with the power failures that regularly occur throughout the country.

VISAS & DOCUMENTS
Visas
All nationalities require a visa for Lebanon. Nationals of Australia, Austria, Belgium, Canada, Cyprus, Denmark, Finland, France, Germany, Greece, Gulf Cooperative Council (GCC) countries, Ireland, Italy, Japan, Luxembourg, Malaysia, Monaco, Netherlands, New Zealand, Norway, Portugal, South Korea, Spain, Sweden, Switzerland, the UK and the USA can get a tourist or business visa on arrival at Beirut International Airport, or at the border with Syria.

At the airport, visa stamps are sold at a window on the right, just before passport control. Forty-eight–hour transit visas are issued free of charge, a two-week visa costs US$15 and a three-month visa costs US$34. Visas (including multiple-entry visas, which are useful if you're planning to go in and out of Lebanon from Syria) can also be obtained in advance at any Lebanese embassy or consulate. For addresses of Lebanese embassies in the Middle East see the relevant country chapters.

If you have an Israeli stamp in your passport or any other evidence of a visit to Israel you will be refused a visa and denied entry into the country.

For details of visas for other Middle Eastern countries, see the 'Visas at a Glance' table under Visas & Documents in the Regional Facts for the Visitor chapter.

Visa Extensions Visas can be extended at the *maktab amn al-aam* (general security office), a block to the west of the Cola transport hub in Beirut. The office is on the first floor and is open Monday to Saturday mornings. The procedure can take up to two weeks and is complicated – if you think you are likely to stay for a long period, get a multiple-entry visa before you arrive instead.

EMBASSIES & CONSULATES
Lebanese Embassies & Consulates
Following are the Lebanese embassies and consulates in major cities around the world. Irish and New Zealand nationals should apply to the UK consulate for visas. For addresses of Lebanese embassies in neighbouring Middle Eastern countries, see the relevant country chapter. Note: there is no Lebanese embassy in either Israel or Syria.

Australia (☎ 02-6295 7378, fax 6239 7024) 27 Endeavour St, Red Hill, Canberra, ACT 2603
  Consulate: (☎ 03-9529 4588,
  Ⓔ toun@alphalink.com.au) 117 Wellington St, Windsor, Victoria 3181. Issues visas to Victorian residents only.
  Consulate: (☎ 02-9361 5449) Level 5, 70 William St, Kings Cross, Sydney, NSW 2010. Issues visas to NSW residents only.
Canada (☎ 613-236 5825, fax 232 1609) 640 Lyon St, K1S 3Z5 Ottawa, Ontario
  Consulate: (☎ 514-276 2638, Ⓔ consuliban@qc.aira.com) 40 Chemin Côte Ste Catherine, Outremont, Quebec 153
France (☎ 01 40 67 75 75, fax 40 67 16 42) 2 Rue Coperic, 75116 Paris
Germany (☎ 30-474 9860, fax 474 98666) Berlinerstrasse 126–127, 13187 Berlin
Netherlands (☎ 70-365 8906, fax 362 0779) Frederick Straat 2, 2514 LK The Hague
UK (☎ 020-7227 6696, fax 7243 1699) 21 Kensington Palace Gardens, London W8 4QM
USA (☎ 202-939 6300, Ⓔ emblebanon@aol.com) 2560 28th St, Washington, DC 20008
  Consulate: (☎ 323-467 1253, Ⓔ lebmission@aol.com) Suite 510, 7060 Hollywood Blvd, Hollywood, CA 90028
  Consulate: (☎ 212-744 7905,
  Ⓔ lebconny@aol.com) 9 East 76th St, New York, NY 10021

Embassies in Lebanon
Opening hours are generally from 8am or 9am to 12.30pm or 1pm Monday to Friday. Some, such as the Jordanian embassy, are also closed on Friday. Note that many embassies were planning moves to the Beirut Central District while this book was being researched. Nationals of Ireland and New Zealand should contact the UK embassy. There is no Syrian or Israeli embassy in

Lebanon; however, most nationalities will have no problem obtaining a visa on the Syrian border for US$13. This should take approximately 30 minutes.

Western nationals wanting to travel from Lebanon to Turkey will have no trouble obtaining a Turkish visa at any of the country's international airports or at the Turkish border. Depending on your nationality, they cost US$20 to US$45. The Turkish embassy in Beirut will only issue visas to Lebanese nationals.

Australia (☎ 01-374 701, fax 374 709, e austemle@cyberia.net.lb) Farra Bldg, Rue Bliss, Ras Beirut

Canada (☎ 04-713 900, fax 710 595, e berut@dfait-maeci.gc.ca) 1st floor, Coolrite Bldg, Autostrade, Jal ad-Dib

Egypt (☎ 01-868 295, fax 863 751) Rue Thomas Edison, Ramlet al-Beida

France (☎ 01-420 200, fax 420 207, e ambafrance@cyberia.net.lb) Rue de Damas (near the National Museum)

Germany (☎ 04-914 444, fax 914 450, e germanemb@germanembassy.org.lb) Mtaileb, Rabieh

Iraq (☎ 05-459 940/452 823, fax 459 850, e iraq@terra.net.lb) Diere Houlou St, Hazmieh

Jordan (☎ 05-922 500, fax 922 502) Rue Elias Helou, Baabda

Netherlands (☎ 01-204 663, fax 204 664, e nlgovbei@sodetel.net.lb) 9th floor, ABM Amro Bldg, Achrafiye

Oman (☎ 01-856 555/855 757, fax 855 454, e omanemb@dm.net.lb) Tyseer Bldg, Zen-zwella St, Ramlet al-Bayda (next to Marriot Hotel), Summerland

Qatar (Qatar Airways ☎ 01-797 430/1, fax 810 460, e Qatar@cyberia.net.lb) Debs Bldg, Chouran, Raouché

Turkey (☎ 04-406 776, fax 407 557, e trebeyr@intracom.net.lb) Toubi Bldg, Zone 2, 3rd St, Rabieh

UAE (☎/fax 01-857 000, fax 857 009, e embassy@uae.org.lb) Near Summerland Hotel, facing Eden Rock

UK (☎ 04-715 9001/2/3, fax 715 904) Coolrite Bldg, Autostrade, Jal ad-Dib

USA (☎ 04-543 600, fax 544 209) Autostrade, Aoucar

Yemen (☎ 01-852 682/688/91/692, fax 821 610, e yemenblb@cyberia.net.lb)

CUSTOMS

Travellers can bring most items, including unlimited currency, into Lebanon. The duty-free allowance is up to two bottles of alcohol per person and 400 cigarettes.

MONEY
Currency

The official currency in Lebanon is the Lebanese lira (LL), also known locally as the pound. There are coins of LL50, 100, 250 and 500, and notes of LL1000, 10,000 and 50,000. US dollars act as a second currency and are accepted almost everywhere. It's not unusual to pay in lira and get some of the change in US dollars, and vice versa.

Exchange Rates

Exchange rates are as follows:

country	unit		Lira
Australia	A$1	=	LL820
Canada	C$1	=	LL952
euro zone	€1	=	LL1492
Japan	¥100	=	LL1238
New Zealand	NZ$1	=	LL709
UK	UK£1	=	LL2374
USA	US$1	=	LL1512

Exchanging Money

Most banks will only change US dollars and UK pounds in cash and travellers cheques. Moneychangers, found throughout Lebanon, will deal in almost any convertible currency. They also usually offer better rates than the banks.

It's often difficult to find places willing to exchange travellers cheques; those that do usually charge a commission ranging from US$3 to US$4 per cheque. It pays to shop around. You're much better off using credit/debit cards to access cash via ATMs.

Credit Cards & ATMs Travellers cheques and most international credit cards (AmEx, Visa, Diner's Club, MasterCard) are accepted in most mid-range and top-end hotels and restaurants.

Automatic Teller Machines (ATMs) accept credit cards or co-branded home banking cards for Cirrus, Diner's Club, Maestro, MasterCard, Visa and Visa-Electron and are found throughout the country. All dispense cash in both Lebanese lira and US dollars.

Costs

Compared with neighbouring Syria, and other traveller favourites like Egypt and Turkey, Lebanon is not cheap. The main expenses are accommodation and nightlife, but it's possible to get by on a tight budget of about US$20 per day. That means basing yourself in Beirut and Tripoli at budget hotels where a dorm bed costs about US$5, living on the likes of felafel and shwarma for about US$9 per day, and spending your remaining few dollars getting around on buses and paying entry fees to museums and historic sites.

A more comfortable budget of US$40 a day will get you a basic single room (about US$20), simple meals at cafés for around US$10, bus trips, entry fees, the odd service taxi and an occasional drink at a nightclub.

Beyond the budget range, a room in a mid-range hotel and meals at restaurants will set you back around US$80 per day. And if you've got more to spend than that, the sky's the limit!

Tipping & Bargaining

Most restaurants and nightspots include a 16% service charge in the bill, but it is customary to leave an extra tip of 5% to 10% of the total.

Most things, from taxi fares to hotel charges, can be bargained down in Lebanon. If you feel you're being overcharged while shopping, offer a price lower than what you're really willing to pay, to leave room for negotiation.

Many hotels will give you a discount or offer to throw in a free breakfast if there are a few of you or if you're staying for more than three days.

POST & COMMUNICATIONS

Post offices are generally open from 8am to 1pm Monday to Saturday, however, the closing time can vary between noon and 2pm. Lebanon's postal system has a history of unreliable service, though since it has been taken over by Libanpost it has improved dramatically.

Telephone

The country code for Lebanon is ☎ 961, followed by the local area code (minus the zero), then the subscriber number. Local area codes are given at the start of each city or town section in this chapter. The area code when dialling a mobile phone is ☎ 03. The international access code (to call abroad from Lebanon) is ☎ 00.

Local calls (LL1000–LL5000) can be made at public phones in shops and in the street. Otherwise, there are private telephone offices all over the country where you can make local and international calls. These private offices are often significantly cheaper than the government-run alternatives, called *centrales*. At centrales, you give your number to an operator who will then direct you to a booth. Calls to the UK and USA cost LL2100 per minute, to Australia LL2400, New Zealand LL3600 and Syria LL500; pay at the counter after the call.

Mobiles Travellers should check in their country of origin as to whether they can use their home-country mobile phone in Lebanon. The Lebanese themselves are voracious users of mobile services, largely as a result of the historical inefficiency of the local landline service.

Email & Internet Access

There are Internet cafés all over Lebanon, usually filled with teenagers and students playing the latest computer games or checking out the Web. See under Information in each town or city section for contact details.

The major ISP in Lebanon is **Cyberia** (☎ 01-355 156; @ info@cyberia.net.lb).

Some, but not all, top-end hotels have facilities whereby you can connect up your own laptop in the hotel room, but this is really expensive (around US$1 per minute). It's much better to use the hotel's business centre or an Internet café. Budget hotels often offer cheap Internet access.

DIGITAL RESOURCES

Useful websites include:

Daily Star On-Line News, views and links
W www.dailystar.com.lb
Lebanon On-Line Resources Local news and links to hotels, travel agencies and bookshops
W www.lebanon.com
United Nations Interim Force In Lebanon Information on UN peace-keeping measures
W www.un.org/Depts/DPKO/Missions/unifil.htm

Other relevant websites are mentioned throughout this chapter.

BOOKS

As well as this book, Lonely Planet publishes a comprehensive country guide, *Lebanon*.

People from every side of the political spectrum have written about the civil war. Among the many books worth reading are *A House of Many Mansions: The History of*

Lebanon Reconsidered by Kamal Salibi, *The Formation of Modern Lebanon* by Meir Zamir, and *Pity the Nation: Lebanon at War* by Robert Fisk.

The comprehensive *Projecting Beirut: Episodes in the Construction and Reconstruction of a Modern City* edited by Peter Rowe & Hashim Sarkis focuses on the rebuilding of Beirut. A glossier, more pictorial version of events is *Beirut Reborn: The Reformation and Development of the Central District* by Angus Gavin & Ramez Maluk.

If you're interested in prewar travel accounts, try *The Hills of Adonis* by Colin Thubron or *Touring Lebanon* by Philip Ward. For ancient history, *The Phoenicians* by Donald Harden is comprehensive and authoritative.

William Dalrymple's *From the Holy Mountain*, an account of his travels throughout the Middle East tracing the history of Eastern Christianity, has a fabulous section set in Lebanon. Brian Keenan's *An Evil Cradling* is a frank and extremely moving memoir of his four-and-a-half-year ordeal as a prisoner of the Islamic Jihad during the civil war.

More Middle East titles, some of which also contain coverage of Lebanon, are listed under Books in the Regional Facts for the Visitor chapter.

NEWSPAPERS & MAGAZINES

The English-language daily newspaper the *Daily Star* provides a good coverage of local events; it's included as an insert in the *International Herald Tribune*. There's also a local French-language daily newspaper, *L'Orient Le Jour*.

International newspapers and magazines are available at most large bookshops.

LAUNDRY

There are dry cleaning and laundry services in all the major cities and towns, but no do-it-yourself laundrettes. Both laundry and dry cleaning are expensive, with some places charging by the piece and others by the load. Though the price varies considerably throughout the country, expect to pay around LL1500 for a small load.

HEALTH

Medical services in Lebanon have the reputation of being among the best in the Middle East. The best-equipped hospitals are usually the private ones; a medical-insurance policy is essential as these hospitals are expensive. Pharmacists can prescribe medicines for minor ailments; most drugs are available over the counter.

The main precaution to take is with food and water. Tap water is *not* drinkable in Lebanon; either drink bottled spring water, which is widely available, or sterilise your water. Always thoroughly wash fruit and vegetables and avoid eating salads in cheap snack bars.

For more health information see Health in the Regional Facts for the Visitor chapter.

WOMEN TRAVELLERS

Women should have few hassles travelling in Lebanon. The worst they'll be subjected to is leers or zealous attempts at conversation. Revealing clothes are common in Beirut and Jounieh, but outside the main centres long-sleeved, loose clothing is preferable. This is particularly the case in the south and the Bekaa Valley, both of which are predominantly Shiite areas.

GAY & LESBIAN TRAVELLERS

Although homosexuality is officially illegal in Lebanon, there's a thriving (if clandestine) scene in Beirut. Gay travellers should be discreet, particularly in predominantly Muslim areas. For further information, check out ⓦ www.surf.to/gay.lebanon or ⓦ ://content.gay.com/channels/travel/neareast2_991101.html.

DANGERS & ANNOYANCES

The main danger spot in Lebanon is the south near the Israeli border. See the boxed text 'The Scars of War' later in this chapter for more details.

One of the few annoying things about travelling in Lebanon is the frequency of power failures. It's not unusual to be sitting in a small hotel or restaurant and suddenly find oneself in total darkness (larger places tend to have back-up generators).

BUSINESS HOURS

Government offices are open from 8am to 2pm Monday to Saturday and from 8am to 11am Friday. Banks are open from 8.30am to 12.30pm Monday to Saturday. Sunday is the end-of-week holiday in Lebanon.

Shops and private businesses open from 8am or 9am to 6pm Monday to Friday, and until 1pm or 2pm Saturday. Many grocery stores keep later hours and also open on Sunday. In summer many places close around 3pm.

PUBLIC HOLIDAYS
Most holidays are religious, and with so many different sects in Lebanon there are quite a few events to celebrate:

New Year's Day 1 January
Feast of Mar Maroun 9 February – feast of the patron saint of the Maronites
Easter March/April – Good Friday to Easter Monday inclusive
Qana Day 18 April – commemorates the massacre at the UN base at Qana
Labour Day 1 May
Martyrs' Day 6 May
The Day of Resistance and Liberation 25 May – celebrates the Israeli withdrawal from South Lebanon in 2000
Assumption 15 August
All Saints Day 1 November
Independence Day 22 November
Christmas Day 25 December

Also observed are the Muslim holidays of Eid al-Fitr, Eid al-Adha, Prophet's Birthday, Islamic New Year and Ashura. For more information on these Muslim holidays and dates see Public Holidays & Special Events in the Regional Facts for the Visitor chapter.

SPECIAL EVENTS
There are five major arts festivals in Lebanon:

February/March
Al-Bustan Festival The country's newest music festival; held at the Al-Bustan Hotel in Beit Mary
W www.albustanfestival.com

July/August
Baalbek Festival Lebanon's most famous arts festival; held at the Roman ruins
W www.baalbek.org.lb
Beiteddine Festival Arts festival held at the Beiteddine Palace in the Chouf Mountains
W www.beiteddine.org.lb
Byblos Festival Arts festival held in the town's old city

October
Beirut Film Festival This high-profile film festival has a growing reputation as the best in the Middle East

ACTIVITIES
Eco-tourism is a new but fast-growing industry in Lebanon. Companies such as **Lebanese Adventure** (☎ 01-389 982, 398 996; W www.lebanese-adventure.com) and **Ibex Eco-Tourism** (☎ 01-216 299, fax 339 629; e ibex_sarl@hotmail.com) offer trekking, cross-country skiing, rafting, off-road driving, snowshoeing, biking and caving 'adventures' lasting anywhere from an afternoon to nine days.

Lebanon is also one of the few countries in the Middle East to offer skiing. Its many snowfields including **Faraya Mzaar** (☎ 09-341 034/5), **Faqra** (☎ 01-257 220), **Lalouq** (☎ 01-200 019) and the **Cedars** (☎ 06-671 073/2) offer good skiing over the months of December–March.

Biking enthusiasts should head to **Cyclo Sport** (☎ 01-446 792; e cyclspor@cyberia.net .lb; Rue Gouraud, Gemmayze, Beirut), a well-respected company that hires out mountain bikes and roller blades for LL15,000 per day or LL45,000 per week. It also runs organised biking tours around Lebanon.

COURSES
The **American Language Center** (☎ 01-704 717, 343 403; 1st floor, Choueiry Bldg, Rue Bliss, Beirut) offers colloquial and classical Arabic courses for beginners and advanced students over a period of a month (25 hours). The courses cost US$320 and run each month from January to August. The centre also runs courses in Tripoli and Zahlé.

The **American University of Beirut** (☎ 01-374 444, fax 744 461; W www.aub.edu/lb/cames) offers a six-week intensive Arabic course during summer. Check out the website for more details.

ACCOMMODATION
There's a reasonable range of accommodation options in most parts of Lebanon, the only exceptions being the limited budget options in Beirut, the lack of any decent mid-range options in Tripoli and Baalbek, and the lack of any choice at all in Sidon.

The prices in this chapter include service charges and government taxes.

FOOD
One of the best things about a holiday in Lebanon is the food. Lebanese cuisine has a reputation as being the best in the Middle

LEBANON

East and a visit will soon demonstrate how this is indeed the case. Beans, fruits and vegetables are plentiful, and mutton and chicken are the favourite meats. A typical Lebanese meal consists of a few mezze dishes (selection of hot and cold starters); a main dish of meat, chicken or fish; and a dessert. There are two kinds of bread: *khobz*, the flat, pocket variety found everywhere in the Middle East, and *marqouk* (mountain bread), a very thin bread baked on a domed dish on a wood fire.

It is very rare to find stews (of any description) in Lebanese restaurants and the same applies to rice. Seafood is prohibitively expensive and not usually of very high quality.

Self-catering is easy, with a wide range of imported and local products available in supermarkets and groceries throughout the country. Travellers can also take advantage of bakeries, hummus stands and patisseries in every town and city.

Mid-range and top-end restaurants will often add a 9% to 16% service charge to the bill, as well as the VAT.

Mezze & Snacks

Dishes in this category include *fatayer bisbanikh* (spinach pies), hummus (chickpea paste), *baba ghanoug* or *moutabbal* (puree of grilled aubergines (eggplants) with tahini and olive oil), *labneh* (thick yogurt with olive oil), felafel (croquettes made with chickpeas and fava beans spiced with coriander), *manaeesh bi-zaatar* (flat bread seasoned with a mixture of thyme and sesame, drizzled with olive oil), *shanklish* (mature goat's cheese with onions, oil and tomatoes), *lahma bi-ajeen* (spicy meat pizza), *soujuk* (spicy Armenian sausages), *wara ainab* (stuffed vine leaves), aubergines and peppers (capsicums) cooked in oil and served cold, and *loubieh bi-zeit* (string beans cooked with tomatoes, onions and garlic).

Main Dishes

The national dish is *kibbeh* (meat-filled cracked-wheat croquettes). There's also a great variety of kebabs, including the almost-ubiquitous *shish tawouq* (marinated chicken grilled on skewers) and shwarma (meat sliced off a spit and stuffed in a pocket of pita-type bread with chopped tomatoes and garnish).

The two favourite salads are tabouleh and *fattoush*. *Tabouleh* consists of parsley, onions and tomatoes mixed with burghul and dressed with vinegar, olive oil and/or lemon juice. *Fattoush* has parsley, lettuce, tomatoes, radishes, onions, cucumbers and toasted bread pieces, and is seasoned with *sumac*, a spice with a sour taste.

Desserts & Sweets

In addition to the syrupy baklava varieties, sweets include *mahallabiye* (milk custard with pine nuts and almonds), *maamoul* (crisp, white biscuits stuffed with a paste of either pistachio or walnut), *ktayef* (small half-moon shaped pastries with a nut paste filling, or sometimes cream cheese), *nammoura* (squares of sweet semolina cake topped with nuts) and *ruz bi-laban* (rice pudding).

DRINKS
Nonalcoholic Drinks

Arabic coffee is popular in Lebanon. It's quite strong and is served in small coffee cups. You can have it *sadah* (without sugar), *wassat* (medium sugar) or *hilweh* (sweet). Tea is also available but is not as popular and is almost inevitably a Lipton's teabag in a cup. Western-style coffee is usually called Nescafé and comes in small sachets with a pot of hot water and a jug of milk.

Other popular nonalcoholic drinks include freshly squeezed vegetable and fruit juices, *limonada* (fresh lemon squash), *jellab* (a delicious drink made from raisins and served with pine nuts) and *ayran* (a yogurt drink). All kinds of foreign-brand soft drinks are also available.

Alcoholic Drinks

Alcohol is widely available in Lebanon – you'll find everything from local beers and wines to imported whisky and vodka. The most popular alcoholic drink is arak, which is mixed with water and ice and usually accompanies meals. Good local brands include Ksarak and Le Brun. There are a few wineries in Lebanon, such as Chateaux Musar, Ksara and Kefraya, producing a variety of red, rosé and white wines. The best local beer is Almaza; it lives up to its name ('diamond' in Arabic). For more information on Middle Eastern food and drinks see the Regional Facts for the Visitor chapter and the 'Middle Eastern Cuisine' special section.

SHOPPING

Local handicrafts include pottery, blown glass, embroidered materials, caftans, copperware, brass bowls and trays, rugs, and mother-of-pearl inlaid boxes and backgammon sets. If you don't have any moral qualms about buying ancient artefacts (it's legal) there are plenty on sale in Byblos, as well as in other parts of the country.

There's a state-sponsored shopping festival around Eid al-Adha in February/March called 'Fab Feb', during which there are countrywide 50% discounts on airline tickets, hotel rooms and shopping.

Getting There & Away

You can travel to Lebanon by air, by land from Syria and, from May to October, by boat from Limassol in Cyprus.

AIR

Beirut international airport (☎ 01-628 000) is Lebanon's only airport. The national carrier, Middle East Airlines (MEA), connects Beirut with most European capitals, other parts of the Middle East and some African capitals. In addition, many European, Middle Eastern and Asian airlines have services to Beirut.

Airline tickets bought in Lebanon are expensive. A one-way fare to Amman from Beirut on MEA costs a ridiculous US$210 (US$165 students). Due to lack of demand, MEA no longer flies between Beirut and Damascus. No other carrier flies this route.

Several airlines have their offices in the Gefinor Center in Ras Beirut, including **British Airways** (☎ 01-747 777), **Egypt Air** (☎ 01-741 402/3), **Malaysia Airlines** (☎ 01-741 344/5/6), **Emirates** (☎ 01-739 042/3), **Gulf Air** (☎ 01-323 332), **Lufthansa** (☎ 01-347 007), **Turkish Airlines** (☎ 01-741 391/7) and **MEA** (☎ 01-737 000). Most are open between 8.30am and 3pm Monday to Friday and 8.30am and 12.30pm Saturday.

Airlines with offices in Beirut include:

Air Canada (☎ 01-811 690)
Air France (☎ 01-200 700/9)
Air India (☎ 01-336 109)
Cathay Pacific (☎ 01-741 391/2)
KLM (☎ 01-744 803)
Royal Jordanian (☎ 01-493 320)

Departure Tax

Airline passengers departing from Beirut International Airport must pay a steep US$33 if travelling economy and US$49 if travelling business class.

LAND

The only way into Lebanon by land is through Syria; the border with Israel is closed and will be for the foreseeable future. There is no departure tax when leaving by land. If you're bringing your car into Lebanon, you must have an International Driving Permit and a *carnet de passage*.

If you want to go to Syria from Beirut, head to Zones A and B of the Charles Helou bus station. To organise a bus ticket, go straight to the **Beirut Pullman Terminal office** (☎ 587 467) on the border of the two zones, which sells tickets for all the private and government buses going to Syria. The buses aren't luxurious, but they're clean and have allocated (numbered) seats. Make sure you book the day before you plan to depart and if you're travelling with others, specify that you want to sit together.

Buses go to Damascus (LL7000, nearly four hours, every hour from 5.30am to 8.30pm), Aleppo (Halab; US$7, seven hours, every 30 minutes from 7.30am to 12.30am) and Lattakia (LL9500, four hours, three times a day at 10am, 2pm and 5.30pm). The services run every day of the week. You must have a Syrian visa or you will not be allowed on the bus.

A service taxi from Charles Helou will cost you US$10 to Damascus and US$14 to Aleppo. Don't worry about finding a seat in one of these – the Syrian drivers are famous for pouncing on potential customers the minute they enter the bus station!

SEA

It's possible to arrive in Lebanon by sea from Limassol in Cyprus during the summer. **Louis Tourist Company** (☎ 357-2 678 000 in Nicosia, Cypress) can supply you with more information.

Getting Around

There are no air services or trains operating within Lebanon, but there is a bus and minibus network which is cheap and covers most city neighbourhoods and major destinations around the country.

BUS

At first the bus system seems completely chaotic, but after a couple of days you'll start to get into the swing of things and be able to navigate yourself around Beirut and into other parts of the country. Most towns have an area where buses and private minibuses (which are cheaper but considerably less comfortable) congregate.

In Beirut there are three major transport hubs: the central Charles Helou bus station services Tripoli and the north; the Dawra (AKA Dora) transport hub in the city's northeast services Jounieh, Byblos and Tripoli; and the Cola transport hub in the city's south, services Sidon, Tyre, the Chouf Mountains and the Bekaa Valley.

Charles Helou is divided into three signposted zones: Zone A is for buses to Syria; Zone B is for buses servicing Beirut (where the route starts or finishes at Charles Helou); and Zone C is for express buses to Jounieh, Byblos and Tripoli. Zones A and C have ticket offices where you can buy tickets for your journey.

See the relevant town and city sections for further details about getting there by bus.

TAXI & SERVICE TAXI

Taxis are recognisable by their red number-plates and, on some cars, a white sign with 'TAXI' written in red letters. Most of the cars are old and extremely decrepit Mercedes, although some of the taxi companies in Beirut have brand-new cars driving around the city. Travellers considering hiring a taxi for a trip out of Beirut, or even to Syria, should think about organising one of these cars, as they are comfortable and have seat belts, a rare thing in Lebanon.

Though slightly confusing at first, the taxi system becomes clear to travellers pretty quickly. There are two options: the taxi can function as a service taxi (known as *servees*), which means that it will usually follow an established route and stop to pick up or drop off passengers anywhere along the way. These taxis can be flagged down from any street corner or pavement. Passengers specify where they want to go (eg, Rue Hamra in Beirut) and check that the taxi is functioning as a servees. If the driver

indicates that he'll accept a servees fare and that the destination is on his route, the passenger hops into the taxi, often joining up to four other passengers. When the destination is reached, the passenger signals the driver to stop (usually saying *anzil huun*, which means 'I get out here'). Payment can be made at any point during the trip, though people tend to pay as soon as they get in. To take you anywhere in central Beirut, a service taxi charges LL1000 (LL2000 to outlying districts). You may sometimes have to take more than one service taxi if your destination is not straightforward, ie, if it includes more than one of the service-taxi routes. Outside of Beirut, the fares range from LL2000 to LL8000, depending on the destination. Although the fares are not listed anywhere, the driver will usually ask for the correct fare.

The same service taxi can become a taxi if you pay for the fare of the four other empty seats in the car. This avoids the delay of stopping to let other passengers in or out and the driver will deposit you right at your destination.

CAR & MOTORCYCLE

You should think very, very seriously indeed before deciding to drive in Lebanon. The average Lebanese drives like a lunatic who has only recently – and illegally – escaped from an asylum.

Despite the attempts of traffic police to organise the flow of cars, very few drivers follow road regulations. Some intersections in Beirut do have traffic lights, but they are usually treated as give-way signs at best.

Driving in the cities is frustrating because of the traffic jams, the double parking and service taxis which stop without warning in the middle of the road to let passengers in or out. On the highways it can be a pretty scary experience, as drivers will zigzag among the cars at crazy speeds.

In the mountains many roads are narrow, with hairpin bends, and it's not unusual for drivers to recklessly overtake on hidden road bends. In addition, you have to keep an eye out for pedestrians, who often walk in the middle of the streets or haphazardly cross highways and roads. Accidents are frequent occurrences.

If you're intent on risking life and limb, car rental companies in Beirut include:

Avis (☎ 01-611 000, e avis.labanon@
kurban.com.lb) Rue Amin Gemayel,
Achrafiye
City Car (☎ 01 803 308, e citycar@citycar
.com.lb) Al Oraifi Bldg, Rue Kalaa, Ras Beirut
Speedy Car Rental (☎ 01-741 574/5,
e rental@speedycar.com) Rue Kuwait, Manara

Car hire starts at around US$35 per day for
a Renault Clio, and can climb to US$400 per
day for a brand-new Mercedes. If you decide
to hire the services of a driver with your hire
car (not a bad option if you're planning a day
trip outside Beirut), this will usually cost
around US$25 per day on top of the car hire.

ORGANISED TOURS

There are a few Lebanese operators organising tours within Lebanon and to Syria and
Jordan from Lebanon. They're a good option, as the tours cover most of Lebanon's
places of interest and are reasonably priced
(most include lunch in the deal). All transport is by air-con coaches. The itineraries
vary from company to company but they all
cover Baalbek, Aanjar, Byblos, Tripoli, the
Cedars, Sidon and Tyre. A day trip costs
about US$55. The main tour operators are
in Beirut:

Kurban Tours (☎ 01-753 432, fax 363 851)
Phoenicia Intercontinental Hotel, Minet al-Hosn
Nakhal & Cie (☎ 01-389 389, e tours@
nakhal.com.lb) Av Sami as-Solh, Ghorayeb
Bldg
Tania Travel (☎ 01-739 679, e taniatvl@cyberia
.net.lb) 1st floor of building opposite Cinema
Jeanne d'Arc, Rue Sidani, Hamra; and Sodeco
Square, Achrafiye

Beirut   بيروت

☎ 01

Beirut is the capital of Lebanon and is its
largest city. It's a city of contrasts: cosmopolitan and glitzy in parts and a bombed-
out shell of its former self in others.
Expensive new cars vie for the right of way
with 40-year-old dented petrol-guzzlers, elegant Ottoman houses are sited next to
jerry-built concrete tower blocks, and
members of Beirut's ultrawealthy ruling
class share the pavements with poverty-
stricken Palestinian refugees. Still clearly
showing the scars of the civil war, it is
nonetheless undergoing an enormously op-

timistic and exciting rebirth and has all but
achieved its aim of regaining its former status as 'the jewel of the Middle East'.

History

Beryte, as Beirut was originally known, was
a modest port during Phoenician times (2nd
millennium BC). It became famous in
Roman times for its School of Law, one of
the first three in the world, which made it a
cultural centre until the 6th century AD.
Then it went into a long period of decline,
and even during Arab times (from the 7th
century on), when mosques, *hammams* and
souqs were built, it was still relatively obscure. In the 19th century Beirut gained importance as a trading centre and gateway to
the Middle East and its port became the
largest on the eastern Mediterranean coast.
The city soon became a major business,
banking and publishing centre and remained so until the civil war undermined its
position.

Since the war ended, the rehabilitation of
the city's infrastructure has been the major
focus of the local and national government.
One positive thing to have come out of all
the destruction is the uncovering of archaeological sites from Phoenician and classical
times which would otherwise never have
been found.

Orientation

Though you're likely to be a bit confused at
first, Beirut is actually an easy city to navigate, as there are strategically located landmarks all over town.

For most visitors, the Hamra district of
Beirut is the hub of the city. It's where you'll
find many hotels, the Ministry of Tourism,
shops of every description, major banks and
a wide range of restaurants and cafés. To the
immediate north and east of Hamra is Ras
Beirut, home of both the American University of Beirut (AUB) and the Gefinor Center,
a fabulous International-Style office block
that's home to AmEx, most airline offices, a
number of travel agencies and some of the
funkiest 1960s interiors in the Middle East.
To the southwest are the seaside suburbs of
Manara and Raouché, where you'll find the
landmark Pigeon Rocks and a host of cafés
overlooking the Mediterranean.

The Corniche (Av de Paris and Av du
Général de Gaulle) runs along the coast east

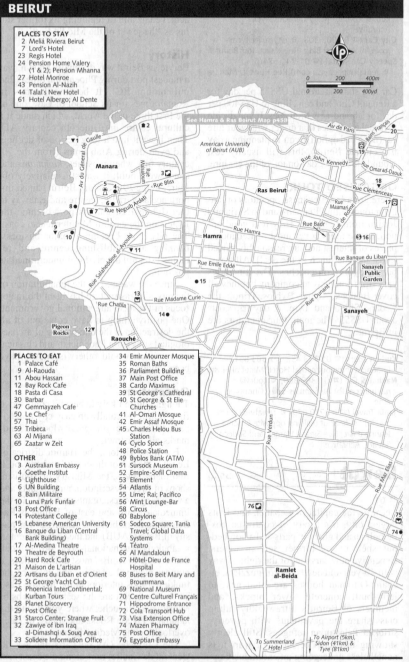

BEIRUT

PLACES TO STAY
2 Meliá Riviera Beirut
7 Lord's Hotel
23 Regis Hotel
24 Pension Home Valery (1 & 2); Pension Mhanna
27 Hotel Monroe
43 Pension Al-Nazih
44 Talal's New Hotel
61 Hotel Albergo; Al Dente

PLACES TO EAT
1 Palace Café
9 Al-Raouda
11 Abou Hassan
12 Bay Rock Cafe
21 Pasta di Casa
30 Barbar
47 Gemmayzeh Cafe
50 Le Chef
57 Thai
59 Tribeca
63 Al Mijana
65 Zaatar w Zeit

OTHER
3 Australian Embassy
4 Goethe Institut
5 Lighthouse
6 UN Building
8 Bain Militaire
10 Luna Park Funfair
13 Post Office
14 Protestant College
15 Lebanese American University
16 Banque du Liban (Central Bank Building)
17 Al-Medina Theatre
19 Theatre de Beyrouth
20 Hard Rock Cafe
21 Maison de L'artisan
22 Artisans du Liban et d'Orient
25 St George Yacht Club
26 Phoenicia InterContinental; Kurban Tours
28 Planet Discovery
29 Post Office
31 Starco Center; Strange Fruit
32 Zawiye of ibn Iraq al-Dimashqi & Souq Area
33 Solidere Information Office
34 Emir Mounzer Mosque
35 Roman Baths
36 Parliament Building
37 Main Post Office
38 Cardo Maximus
39 St George's Cathedral
40 St George & St Elie Churches
41 Al-Omari Mosque
42 Emir Assaf Mosque
45 Charles Helou Bus Station
46 Cyclo Sport
48 Police Station
49 Byblos Bank (ATM)
51 Sursock Museum
52 Empire-Sofil Cinema
53 Element
54 Atlantis
55 Lime; Rai; Pacifico
56 Mint Lounge-Bar
58 Circus
60 Babylone
61 Sodeco Square; Tania Travel; Global Data Systems
64 Téatro
66 Al Mandaloun
67 Hôtel-Dieu de France Hospital
68 Buses to Beit Mary and Broummana
69 National Museum
70 Centre Culturel Français
71 Hippodrome Entrance
72 Cola Transport Hub
73 Visa Extension Office
74 Mazen Pharmacy
75 Post Office
76 Egyptian Embassy

Manara

American University of Beirut (AUB)

See Hamra & Ras Beirut Map p458

Ras Beirut

Hamra

Raouché

Pigeon Rocks

Sanayeh Public Garden

Sanayeh

Ramlet al-Beida

To Summerland Hotel

To Airport (5km), Sidon (41km) & Tyre (81km)

Av du Général de Gaulle

Av de Paris

Rue John Kennedy

Rue Omar ad-Daouk

Rue Clémenceau

Rue Maamari

Rue de Rome

Rue Badr

Rue Hamra

Rue Banque du Liban

Rue Emile Eddé

Rue Madame Curie

Rue Dunant

Rue Chatila

Rue Bliss

Rue Neguib Ardati

Rue Salaheddine al-Ayoubi

Rue Maslaboum

Rue Verdun

Rue Mar Elias

Bains Français

0   200   400m
0   200   400yd

LEBANON

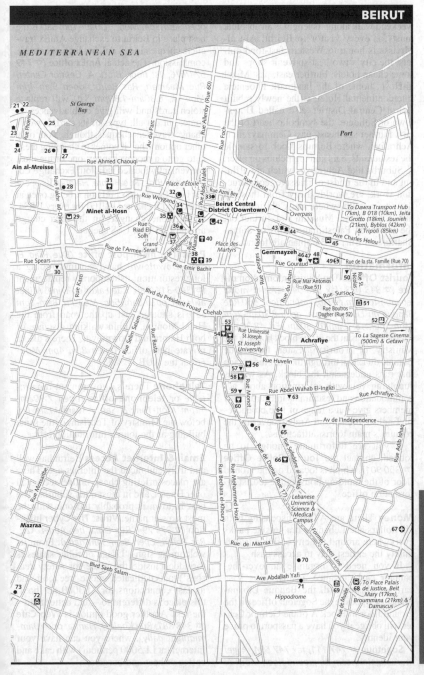

BEIRUT

MEDITERRANEAN SEA

St George Bay

Port

Rue Phoenicia

Ain al-Mreisse

Rue Fakhr ad-Dine

Av du Parc

Rue Allenby (Rue 60)

Rue Foch

Rue Ahmed Chaouqi

Rue Weygand

Minet al-Hosn

Rue Riad El Solh

Place d'Étoile

Rue Azmi Bey

Rue Abdel Malek

Rue Trieste

Beirut Central District (Downtown)

Overpass

To Dawra Transport Hub (7km), B 018 (10km), Jeita Grotto (18km), Jounieh (21km), Byblos (42km) & Tripoli (85km)

Grand Serail

Rue de Parlement

Rue Maarad

Place des Martyrs

Rue Georges Haddad

Ave Charles Helou

Rue Emir Bachir

Gemmayzeh

Rue Gouraud

Rue du Liban

Rue de la sta. Famille (Rue 70)

Rue Spears

Rue Kasti

Blvd du Président Fouad Chehab

Rue Mar Antonios (Rue 51)

Rue Sursock

Rue St. Nicolas

Rue Selim Salam

Rue Basta

Rue Boutros Dagher (Rue 52)

Rue Universitié St Joseph

St Joseph University

Achrafiye

To La Sagesse Cinema (500m) & Getawi

Rue Huvelin

Rue Monot

Rue Abdel Wahab El-Inglizi

Rue Achrafiye

Av de l'Indépendance

Rue Adib Ishaq

Mazraa

Rue Mossaitbe

Rue Bechara el-Khoury

Rue Mohammed Hout

Rue de Damas (Rue 7)

Rue Selladine el-Khatib

Lebanese University Science & Medical Campus

Rue de Mazraa

Former Green Line

Blvd Saeb Salam

Ave Abdallah Yafi

Hippodrome

Rue de Musée

To Place Palais de Justice, Beit Mary (17km), Broummana (21km) & Damascus

LEBANON

from Raouché to Ain al-Mreisse; a leisurely weekend walk along its length is an absolute must for every visitor to Beirut. Ain al-Mreisse is home to Western fast-food outlets, the city's two best souvenir shops and some cheap hotels. Further east, past Minet al-Hosn, home of the landmark Phoenicia Intercontinental Hotel, is the newly rebuilt Beirut Central District, also called Downtown or Solidere, the symbolic heart of the city. Further southeast, past Gemmayzeh, is Achrafiye, where Beirutis flock to sample the restaurants, bars and nightclubs on offer.

Suburbs like Achrafiye, which are affluent and in the midst of massive reconstruction work, are worlds away from those in the city's south, where the Cola transport hub, the National Museum and, further on, the infamous Palestinian camps of Sabra-Shatila and Burj al-Barajnah are found.

Information

Tourist Offices The **tourist information office** (☎ 343 073, fax 340 945/279; e mot@lebanon-tourism.gov.lb; ground floor, 550 Rue Banque du Liban, Hamra; open 8.30am-2pm Mon-Thur, 8.30am-11.30am Fri, 8.30am-12.30pm Sat) is in the office block housing the Ministry of Tourism. Enter from Rue Banque du Liban through the covered arcade that runs underneath the block. As well as supplying you with information about accommodation and restaurants in Beirut, staff members give out a range of free brochures (in English, French and Arabic) covering the country's main tourist attractions.

If you are unfortunate enough to be robbed, contact the **Tourist Police Office** (☎ 350 901), which is located on the ground floor of the building housing the tourist information office.

Money There are ATMs dispensing both US dollars and Lebanese lira outside banks everywhere around the city and this is definitely the easiest way to access cash.

If you need to organise an over-the-counter cash advance against your Visa card or MasterCard, the Banque Libano-Française opposite the Sogetour office on the ground floor in Block A of the Gefinor Center will oblige if you have a passport to prove your identity.

Sogetour (☎ 747 111, fax 747 594; e gefinor@sogetour.com.lb; ground floor, Block A,

Gefinor Center, Rue Maamari, Ras Beirut; open 9am-3pm Mon-Fri, 9am-1pm Sat) is the best place in Beirut to exchange AmEx travellers cheques in US dollars. It charges a 2% commission. The actual **AmEx office** (☎ 749 574/5/6; 1st floor, Block A, Gefinor Center, Rue Maamari, Ras Beirut; open 9am-4pm Mon-Fri, 8.30am-1.30pm Sat) will replace stolen cards and will give cash advances on some, but not all, types of its card. It won't change travellers cheques, though. Your only other option when it comes to changing these is to go to a moneychanger; one of the most conveniently located is **Jalloul Exchange Co.** (Rasamny Bldg, Rue Hamra, Hamra). Its opening hours vary (don't rely on it being open at night) and it charges LL100 for every US$4. Other moneychangers in the area charge around US$3 per US$ cheque.

Post The **main post office** (Rue Riad El Solh, Downtown) has been undergoing a long restoration; its temporary replacement (☎ 360 314/285; Rue Fakhr ed-Dine, Minet al-Hosn; open 8am-5pm Mon-Fri, 8am-1pm Sat) is situated just up the road from the Hotel Monroe, within walking distance of both Hamra and Downtown. There's also a private post office (open 8am-4pm Mon-Fri) at the AUB.

Telephone There's a government-run *centrale* or **telephone office** (open 7.30am-11pm Mon-Thur & Sat, 7.30am-11am Fri) below the Ministry of Tourism, in the same building as the tourist information office.

Email & Internet Access Beirut has well and truly embraced the Internet age. There are places offering cheap online access all over Hamra, and in most other suburbs. The best in town is probably the one with the most sinister name: **Virus: The Cyber Infection** (☎ 374 794; Rue Omar ben Abdel-Aziz, Ras Beirut; open 8am-3am daily). From its welcoming sign ('Usage of roller skates is forbidden inside the place for safety reasons') to its dedicated smoke-free room and its fast connections for LL3000 per hour, this place is different to – and better than – the rest. Another good option is **Web Cafe** (☎ 348 881; Rue Khalidy, Hamra; open 9am-midnight daily), where you can have your Internet (at LL5000 per hour) with cake and coffee or beer and burgers.

Other options include the popular **PC Club** (☎ 745 338; *Rue Mahatma Gandhi; open 8.30am-6am daily*), and, almost next door, smoke-filled **The Net** (☎ 740 157; *LL3000 per hour; open 24hr daily*), only recommended here because it never closes. Both offer access for LL3000 per hour. If you're in Achrafiye, try **Global Data Systems** (☎ 615 578; *ground floor, Sodeco Square; open 11am-11pm Mon-Sat, 5am-11pm Sunday*); though lacking ambience, it has fast connections for LL4000 per hour.

Travel Agencies There are travel agencies all over Beirut. Among the better ones are Tania Travel, with offices in both Hamra and Sodeco (see Organised Tours in the Getting Around section earlier in this chapter for more details), and **Campus Travel** (☎ 744 588, fax 744 583; e *campus@campus-travel .net; Maktabi Bldg, Rue Makhoul, Ras Beirut*), a travel agency specialising in cheap international flights.

Bookshops Beirut has a good selection of foreign-language bookshops stocked with academic books, dictionaries, novels, travel guides and European newspapers. These include **Librairie Antoine** (☎ 341 470; *Rue Hamra, Hamra*), **Four Steps Down** and **Way In** (☎ 353 675, 345 856; *Rue Hamra, Hamra*), **Librairie du Liban** (☎ 373 204; *Rue Bliss, Ras Beirut*), **Books & Pens** (☎ 741 975; *Rue Jeanne d'Arc, Hamra*) and **Librairie Internationale** (☎ 743 285/6; *ground floor, Block D, Gefinor Center, Ras Beirut*). All are open during usual business hours.

Medical Services There are a number of hospitals with outpatient clinics in Beirut. The **American University of Beirut Medical Center** (☎ 340 460, 350 000; *Rue du Caire, Ras Beirut; open 8am-1pm & 2pm-5pm Mon-Fri except holidays*) is considered to be the best.

Museums
National Museum This totally fabulous museum (☎ 612 295/7; *cnr Rue de Damas & Ave Abdallah Yafi*; w *www.beirutnational museum.com; adult/student/child LL5000/ 1000/1000; open 9am-5pm Tues-Sun except some public holidays*) has an impressive collection of archaeological artefacts, statuettes and sarcophagi. Housed in a 1930s building

that was badly damaged during the war but has since been sumptuously renovated, the collection is displayed in chronological order. Highlights include marble statues of baby boys from Echmoun, a beautiful 5th-century-BC marble sarcophagi from Ain al-Helwa, a 4th-century-BC mosaic from Baalbek depicting the birth of Alexander the Great, Byzantine gold jewellery found in a jar under the floor of a Byzantine villa in Beirut and an amazing marble head of Dionysus from Tyre.

The museum screens a free 15-minute video of its history, featuring a fascinating account of how curators saved the collection during the war, on the hour in its theatrette.

American University of Beirut (AUB) Museum The AUB museum (☎ 340 549; *AUB campus;* w *http://ddc.aub.edu.lb/pro jects/museum/; admission free; open 9am-5pm Mon-Fri except university & public holidays*), just inside the university's main gate, was founded in 1868 and is one of the oldest in the Middle East. On display is its collection of Lebanese and Middle Eastern artefacts dating back to the early Stone Age, a fine collection of Phoenician glass and Arab coins dating from as early as the 5th century BC. There are also terracotta statuettes, including fertility goddesses, and a large collection of pottery dating back to 3000 BC.

Sursock Museum Owned by the Sursock family, one of the country's most illustrious dynasties, this building looks more like a giant wedding cake than a museum. It's located in an amazing street of luxurious modern apartment blocks and beautiful Ottoman- and French Mandate–era mansions, making a walk around the neighbourhood almost mandatory. Lit up at night, so that the full glory of its colourful stained glass is on show, the museum (☎ 334 133; *Rue de l'Archevéché Grec-Orthodoxe, Achrafiye; admission free; open 10am-1pm & 4pm-7pm daily when exhibitions are scheduled*) is a truly extraordinary sight. Unfortunately, its exhibitions of contemporary Lebanese art don't usually live up to their location. Make sure you phone ahead to confirm that the museum is open.

Downtown
In the 1970s the Beirut Central District (now usually called Downtown or Solidere) was exalted as the Paris of the Middle East.

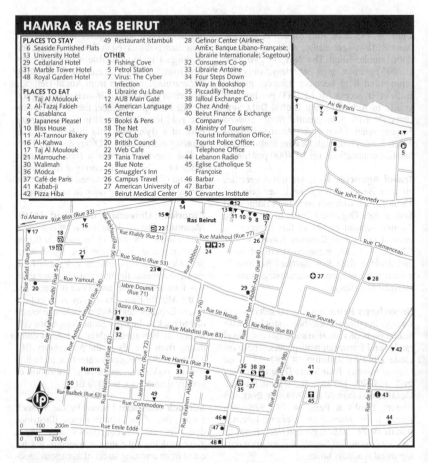

HAMRA & RAS BEIRUT

PLACES TO STAY
6 Seaside Furnished Flats
13 University Hotel
29 Cedarland Hotel
31 Marble Tower Hotel
48 Royal Garden Hotel

PLACES TO EAT
1 Taj Al Moulouk
2 Al-Tazaj Fakieh
4 Casablanca
9 Japanese Please!
10 Bliss House
11 Al-Tannour Bakery
16 Al-Kahwa
17 Taj Al Moulouk
21 Marrouche
30 Walimah
36 Modca
37 Café de Paris
41 Kabab-ji
42 Pizza Hiba

49 Restaurant Istambuli

OTHER
3 Fishing Cove
5 Petrol Station
7 Virus: The Cyber Infection
8 Librairie du Liban
12 AUB Main Gate
14 American Language Center
15 Books & Pens
18 The Net
19 PC Club
20 British Council
22 Web Cafe
23 Tania Travel
24 Blue Note
25 Smuggler's Inn
26 Campus Travel
27 American University of Beirut Medical Center

28 Gefinor Center (Airlines; AmEx; Banque Libano-Française; Librairie Internationale; Sogetour)
32 Consumers Co-op
33 Librairie Antoine
34 Four Steps Down Way In Bookshop
35 Piccadilly Theatre
38 Jalloul Exchange Co.
39 Chez André
40 Beirut Finance & Exchange Company
43 Ministry of Tourism; Tourist Information Office; Tourist Police Office; Telephone Office
44 Lebanon Radio
45 Eglise Catholique St Françoise
46 Barbar
47 Barbar
50 Cervantes Institute

In the 1980s it was the centre of a war zone, and in the 1990s it became the focus of one of the world's most ambitious rebuilding programs. Today, with much of the rebuilding finished, its spotlessly clean and traffic-free streets are so unlike the rest of the city that it has an almost surreal feel. Indeed, the whole area, though impressive, has a Disneyesque flavour, with ersatz Ottoman and French Mandate–era architecture almost indistinguishable from the restored real thing. In defence of the architects and planners who have worked on the project, though, it must be said that the area is well and truly taking off as the newest to-be-seen-in suburb in the city. On weekend evenings the area around the Place d'Étoile (AKA Nejemah Square) is awash with people sitting in the outdoor cafés, drinking arak or beer and smoking *sheeshas* stuffed with fragrant apple-flavoured tobacco.

The **Solidere information office** (☎ 980 650/60; e solidere@solidere.com.lb; Bldg 149, Rue Saad Zaghloul; admission free; open 9am-3pm & 4pm-6pm Mon-Fri) has display models and information boards outlining the redevelopment of the area. Information officers are usually on hand to answer questions or suggest walking-tour routes around the area.

If you devise your own walking tour, make sure you don't miss the **Al-Omari Mosque** (currently being renovated), originally built in the 12th century as the Church of John the Baptist of the Knights Hospitaller and converted into a mosque in 1291; **St**

The New Beirut

The rebuilding of Beirut's Central District is one of the world's largest and most ambitious urban re-development projects. This area was one of the worst-affected areas in the civil war and its rebuilding is seen as being important for both practical and symbolic reasons. The project covers 1.8 million sq metres of land, as well as 608,000 sq metres of land reclaimed from the sea, and has attracted tens of millions of dollars in investment.

In 1992 the Lebanese parliament formed the Lebanese Company for the Development and Reconstruction of Beirut Central District, known by its French acronym Solidere. Solidere became an incorporated company in 1994, with stock capital of US$1.82 billion.

The rebuilding is a two-phase project. Phase One, which has been completed, is 40% residential and 30% office buildings. One of its main features is the old souq area, which is now home to up-market shops, innumerable cafés and some of the most fashionable restaurants in town. Phase Two, now under way but progressing slowly due to Lebanon's economic slowdown, involves a new marina and construction work on reclaimed land.

The rebuilding work has unearthed archaeological finds from just about every period of Beirut's history – traces of the Canaanite, Phoenician, Persian, Hellenistic, Roman, Byzantine, Umayyad, Abbasid, Crusader, Mamluk, Ottoman and French Mandate eras have all been revealed and are now major features of the district. This archaeological work has led Beirutis to celebrate their city's ancient heritage as never before, and enjoying a coffee at one of the cafés on Rue al-Maarad overlooking the excavated remains of the cardo maximus has become one of the most popular activities in the city.

George's Cathedral (☎ 561 980; services 7.15am & 6.60pm Mon-Thur & Sat, 9am & 11am Sun), a Maronite church dating back to the Crusades; the magnificently restored Roman baths; the cardo maximus, evocative remains of a Roman-era market area; and the Grand Serail, a majestic Ottoman-era building which has been restored and now houses government offices.

The Corniche

The Corniche is a favourite promenade spot, especially late in the afternoon and on weekends. Families, couples and groups of young people dressed up to the nines saunter along its length, stopping to greet friends, buy food and drinks from vendors pushing handcarts full of local goodies, or to have a coffee-and-nargileh break at one of the water's-edge cafés along the route. Old men meet their cronies for hours-long games of backgammon, locals fish from upturned oil drums on the shore, extended families picnic at Pigeon Rocks and ultrafit AUB students zoom along on Rollerblades. This is Beirut at its best – a few hours of people-watching here will be one of the best things you do in Lebanon.

Places to Stay – Budget

Cheap accommodation isn't easy to find in Beirut. The only places offering rooms under US$20 per person per night are found in Ain al-Mreisse and near Charles Helou bus station – of the two, Ain al-Mreisse is the more pleasant location, though the area around Charles Helou is closer to Rue Monot, the city's main nightclub and eating strip.

Talal's New Hotel (☎/fax 562 567; e ZSA L72TNH@yahoo.com; dorm/singles/doubles without air-con US$4/8/10, with air-con US$6/12/14) is a clean, friendly place near Charles Helou which offers beds at bargain-basement prices. Run by a guy who speaks five languages (Arabic, English, French, Japanese and Spanish), its rooms are slightly claustrophobic, but at these prices, who's complaining? All rooms have satellite TV and hot showers are free. There's a communal kitchen, laundry facilities (LL3000 per load) and Internet access (first 15 minutes free, LL1500 per hour after that).

Pension al-Nazih (☎ 564 868; dorm beds/singles/doubles/triples/quads LL6000/10,000/15,000/18,000/20,000, doubles with toilet & handbasin LL20,000) is another budget place near the bus station. To find it, turn off Rue al-Arz into Rue Chanty – it's on the right towards the end of the street. On two floors, it's clean and comfortable. Most of the small rooms have washbasins and all have fans and satellite TV. Free hot showers and use of the washing machine, comfortable beds and a communal kitchen make this an option well worth considering.

Pension Home Valery (*Saab Bldg, Rue Phoenicia, Ain al-Mreisse*) is a Beirut institution and is one of those places that every backpacker in the Middle East seems to have heard about. There are actually three pensions in the building, which is located next to the Wash Me car wash. To find them, go into the slightly dingy hallway and walk to the rear, where you'll find a lift and stairs. On the 2nd floor is the pick of the bunch (*☎ 362 169; e homevalery@hotmail.com; beds in 2-bed/3-bed dorm US$6, singles US$8*), which is clean and has very pleasant English-speaking staff. Hot showers are free, Internet access is offered at LL5000 per hour, there are cooking facilities available and all rooms have fans. At the 3rd-floor version (*☎ 364 906*), prices, facilities and general friendliness levels are the same, although it doesn't offer Internet access. On the 4th floor, **Pension Mhanna** (*☎ 365 216; e pension-mhanna@hotmail.com; dorm beds/singles US$5/7*) is slightly cheaper, and only LL4000 for an hour's Internet access, but it charges LL1500 for a hot shower and isn't quite as welcoming or comfortable as the others. Off-season discounts are offered by the pensions on the second and third floors, but not by Pension Mhanna.

Regis Hotel (*☎ 361 845, fax 562 567; Rue Razi, Ain al-Mreisse; doubles with bathroom US$20*) is located in the middle of what looks like – and probably was – a bomb site, but the owners are very friendly and it does have the advantage of sea breezes. Very basic but reasonably clean rooms have air-con or fan, plus a fridge and TV. Only two rooms have hot water. Discounts are offered for stays of three or more nights and from October to May.

Places to Stay – Mid-Range

Seaside Furnished Flats (*☎ 363 200/1, fax 363 222; e seaside@cyberia.net.lb; George Post St, Ain al-Mreisse; without/with sea views US$39/50*) is possibly the best-value accommodation option in town. Owned by an urbane and totally charming fellow who goes out of his way to be helpful to guests, these fully furnished one-bedroom flats are in a fabulous position just near the AUB and almost on the waterfront. Each is basic but clean and has a balcony, kitchen, bathroom

and lounge with satellite TV. Most flats have sea views, all have air-con and there's underground parking for visitors with cars.

University Hotel (*☎ 365 391, fax 365 390; 19 Rue Bliss, Ras Beirut; singles/doubles/ suites with bathroom US$32/44/57*) is situated just near the main gate of AUB. In fact, it's also known as the Main Gate Hotel. You'll find it down the laneway and above the McDonald's. Though recent renovations and a resulting hike in prices have moved it out of the budget category, most of its small rooms are still rented by students from the university. All rooms have air-con, satellite TV and fridge and quite a few have balconies with sea views. The top-floor 'Royal Suite' has extraordinary panoramic views and, at US$198 per night, a price tag to match.

Cedarland Hotel (*☎ 340 233/4, fax 853 579; e cedarland_lb@yahoo.com; Rue Omar ben Abdel-Aziz, Hamra; singles/doubles/ suites with bathroom US$33/39/50*) is in a particularly bustling part of Hamra, making its rooms quite noisy. Most of its clients are student doctors from the nearby AUB Hospital and perhaps as a consequence it has a vaguely institutional feel, though the 1960s-style suites are pretty funky. Breakfast is available for US$5 and discounts are offered for those staying for more than a week.

Marble Tower Hotel (*☎ 354 586, 346 260, fax 346 262; e marble@marbletower.com.lb; Rue Makdissi, Hamra; singles/doubles/suites with bathroom LL130,000/149,000/290,000*) is located smack-bang in the centre of Hamra and is a popular choice for many travellers familiar with Beirut. Its well-known though spotlessly clean rooms can be a bit noisy but the service is excellent, the price includes breakfast, the beds are comfortable and the suites are extraordinarily good value. From October to May its prices drop considerably.

Royal Garden Hotel (*☎ 350 010, fax 353 241; e rogarden@dm.net.lb; Rue Emile Eddé, Hamra; doubles with bathroom US$66*) is on one of Beirut's busiest streets, so it can be noisy, but the fact that it offers facilities such as a swimming pool, health club and bar at these prices make it an option worth considering.

Lord's Hotel (*☎ 740 382/3, fax 740 385; the Corniche, Manara; basic singles/doubles with bathroom US$38.50/49.50, renovated rooms with sea views & bathroom US$55/66*) has an undeniable, if slightly frayed-around-the-edges, charm. Clean and serviceable, it's a particularly good summer choice. The prices include breakfast and the renovated rooms are slightly cheaper in winter.

Places to Stay – Top End

Hotel Monroe (☎ 371 122, fax 371 112; e info@monroebeirut.com; Rue Kennedy, Minet al-Hosn; singles/doubles/suites with bathroom US$110/127/174) is one of the newest hotels in town. One of that breed of oh-so-stylish places that adorn the pages of international design magazines such as *Wallpaper*, the Monroe features Scandinavian designer furniture, staff members who look as though they'd be more at home on the catwalk, and supercool locals. Despite all this, its attitude is friendly rather than pretentious and the rooms, though small, are among the most comfortable in town.

Meliá Riviera Beirut (☎ 373 210, fax 365 239; e info@meliariviera.com; the Corniche, Manara; singles/doubles with sea views & bathroom US$214/220, with garden views & bathroom US$164/189) is the type of place we'd all like to stay at but few of us can afford. On the Corniche, it has the best hotel beach club in Beirut, a gorgeous garden, posh restaurants, and rooms with every comfort you could possibly desire. If you're in Beirut during the summer season and have deep pockets, this is most definitely the place to stay. The prices include breakfast.

Hotel Albergo (☎ 339 797, fax 339 999; e albergo@relaischateaux.com; 137 Rue Abdel el-Inglizi, Achrafiye; double/junior suites with bathroom US$270/308) is one of the best hotels in the Middle East. Each of its 33 rooms is individually and extremely opulently decorated, the service is exemplary and the rooftop pool/bar has to be seen to be believed. This is the type of place that the truly stylish – rather than the vulgarly ostentatious – choose to stay in.

Places to Eat

Beirut is famous for its eating places, and no wonder – fabulous restaurants, cafés and food stalls are around every corner. As is the case with everything in the city, prices aren't cheap, but even those on the tightest budget will feel compelled to undo the purse strings at least once to indulge in the favourite pastime of most Beirutis: having

a good conversation while indulging in a lavish and totally delectable array of mezze and grills. For those self-catering, the fresh produce on offer in the shops is of a very high quality and supermarkets such as **Consumers Co-op** (Rue Makdissi, Hamra; open 7am-11pm daily) offer all of the products you're likely to need.

Street & Fast Food Every suburb has a multitude of stalls offering felafel, *manaeesh bi-zaatar*, kebabs, *fuul*, fresh juices, *fatayer bi-sbanikh* and shwarma; the best way to get a feel for where to eat is to wander around and choose the busy ones, as they are likely to be offering the freshest food. Most of these places work to a system whereby you choose what you want, order your food, pay at the till and then take your receipt to the food counter to collect your meal or snack. Prices are on a par: a felafel will cost around LL2500, a *manaeesh* LL2000, a kebab LL3000, a large fresh juice LL2500 and a shwarma LL3000. Sit-down places are both harder to find and, in many cases, less satisfying; some of the better ones are listed here with a few of the city's most famous street-food stands:

Bliss House (Rue Bliss, Ras Beirut; open 7am-5am daily) is one of the most popular takeaways in Beirut and is always packed with AUB students grabbing a quick snack on their way to/from class. Its three shop fronts offer cheap and filling shwarma, kebabs, fresh juice and ice cream.

Al-Tannour Bakery (Rue Bliss, Ras Beirut; open 24hr daily) is one of the best places around to sample delicious *manaeesh* with the basic *zaatar* topping or something more exotic, eg, haloumi cheese.

Japanese Please! (☎ 361 047; Rue Bliss, Ras Beirut; open 11am-11pm Mon-Sat) is a stylish takeaway serving sushi at reasonable prices. Customers can take away, eat at the bar or take advantage of the free delivery service.

Marrouche (☎ 743 185/6; Rue Sidani, Hamra; open 24hr daily) specialises in *shish tawouq* and chicken shwarma.

Pizza Hiba (Rue de Rome, Hamra) is a tiny food stand that offers good, fresh *manaeesh* and *fatayer bi-sbanikh*.

Al-Tazaj Fakieh (the Corniche, Ain al-Mreisse; open noon-late daily) is another popular choice. Its pleasant outdoor terrace is a great place to sit and eat the extra-tasty

BBQ chicken on offer while watching Beirutis promenade along the Corniche.

Kabab-ji *(Rue Hamra, Hamra)* is a branch of the Lebanon-wide chain. It's an extremely popular place to sit and sample fresh and delicious kebabs.

Barbar *(☎ 379 778/9; Rue Spears; open 24hr daily)* is the granddaddy of them all. This phenomenally popular chain, which also has a branch on Rue Baalbek, sells *manaeesh*, shwarma, pastries, mezze, kebabs, ice cream and fresh juice. Join the hordes of people gobbling their snacks on the street in front or organise to have food delivered to your hotel or apartment.

Zaatar w Zeit *(Rue Nasra, Sodeco, Achrafiye; open 24hr daily)* is busiest late at night, when patrons from the nearby nightclubs flock here to re-energise over cheap and delicious *manaeesh* with a multitude of toppings.

Cafés One thing's for sure: Beirutis have perfected the art of drinking coffee. The city has a wealth of places where it's possible – indeed, almost obligatory – to while away hours over a coffee and pastry or nargileh. The most pleasant of these are along the waterfront or overlooking the cardo maximus in the Downtown area. In most places listed here an Arabic coffee costs between LL1500 and LL2500, pastries around LL3000 and a nargileh around LL8000.

Modca *(☎ 345 501; Rue Hamra, Hamra)* is overpriced and the waiters have more attitude than aptitude. It's listed here purely because, like the **Café de Paris** on the opposite side of the road, it is a Beirut institution. If footsore and weary in Hamra, you may decide that the building's history and its over-the-top interior is worthy of a coffee stop.

Al-Kahwa *(☎ 362 232; Al-Kanater Bldg, Rue Bliss, Ras Beirut; open 10am-1am daily)* is a stylish hangout popular with students from the nearby AUB. Its friendly atmosphere, good Western and Arabic menu choices and reasonable prices make it a great choice for breakfast, lunch or dinner. An Arabic breakfast here costs LL6000, cooked English breakfast is LL6000, a club sandwich with fries is LL6500 and a Caesar salad is LL5000.

Taj Al Moulouk *(☎ 370 096; the Corniche, Ras Beirut)* is heaven for sweet-tooths. Great Arabic coffee and the most

amazing array of pastries you're likely to see anywhere in the Middle East make a visit here essential. This branch has a terrace and indoor café, so it makes a perfect pit stop when walking the length of the Corniche; the other branch, on Rue Bliss, is sit-down in its ice-cream parlour only.

Palace Café *(☎ 03-753 887; the Corniche, Manara; open 24hrs daily)* has an unprepossessing entrance behind a chaotic construction site, but its location right on the water makes it a pleasant place to drink coffee or have a snack. There's an outdoor terrace and after 10pm each night there's live Arabic music.

Al-Raouda *(☎ 743 348; the Corniche, Manara; open 8am-midnight daily)* is another hard-to-find place on the waterfront. Walk down the lane closest to the Luna Park entrance – don't take the lane to the right, which leads to a depressing-looking copy – and you'll come to a large, shabby but very welcoming garden café that has a misspelt 'El Rawda' sign at the front. A favourite with local families, it's particularly busy on Sunday.

Bay Rock Cafe *(☎ 796 700; Ave du Générale de Gaulle, Raouché; open 7am-2.30am daily)* is fabulously situated overlooking Pigeon Rocks. Meals, snacks, coffee and drinks are pricey but good quality and the outdoor terrace is a particularly attractive place to spend an afternoon.

Tribeca *(☎ 339 123; Rue Abdel Wahab El-Inglizi, Achrafiye; open 8am-1am daily)* serves bagels good enough to stand up and be counted in New York. A cooked breakfast here costs LL4500 and a bagel goes for anything between LL4750 and LL10,000, depending on the filling.

Gemmayzeh Cafe *(☎ 580 817; Rue Gouraud, Gemmayzeh; open 8am-3am daily)*, a Beiruti institution, has recently been renovated and has lost some of its former atmosphere. In its favour, though, is the fact that it has become one of the most popular places to hear live Arabic music in Beirut. Evening bookings for the live music are essential, but it's possible to pop in here any time of the day for a coffee.

Restaurants There are so many wonderful restaurants in Beirut that it seems a sin to single out only a few here. Those wanting to sample what's on offer should note that

Beirutis dress for dinner and eat quite late: most won't arrive at the restaurant until 9.30pm. Most of the options listed here accept credit cards and serve alcohol (exceptions are noted).

Abou Hassan (☎ 741 725; Rue Salaheddine al-Ayoubi, Manara; open noon-midnight daily) is a cosy neighbourhood eatery with only six tables, serving great food at bargain-basement prices. Choose from the ultrafresh range of dips and grills on display and you'll be in seventh heaven. Expect to pay LL12,500 for mezze, grill and beer. Note, no credit cards.

Thai (☎ 329 313; 191 Rue Monot, Achrafiye; mains from LL10,000; open noon-4pm & 6pm-11pm Mon-Thur, noon-4pm & 6pm-midnight Fri, 1pm-4pm & 6pm-midnight Sat) is an extremely hip addition to the oh-so-cool Monot eating scene. Its novelty value comes from the fact that it serves Thai food and also happens to be cheap, a rare combination in Beirut. Check out the lunch specials of a starter, main and soft drink; priced from LL10,000 they're a mega bargain.

Le Chef (☎ 445 373, 446 769; Rue Gouraud, Gemmayzeh; 2-course meal around LL10,000; open 6am-6.30pm Mon-Sat) is one of the most beloved eating places in Beirut. Only open during the day, it serves huge plates of home-style Arabic food in a simple setting. Daily specials are listed in Arabic but the helpful waiters are always happy to translate or make recommendations. No credit cards or alcohol.

Restaurant Istambuli (☎ 352 049, 353 029; Rue Commodore, Hamra; mezze around LL3500, grills around LL8000; open 12.30pm-midnight daily) serves traditional Lebanese food that's extremely well priced, meaning that it's always jam-packed with local families. Make sure you try the totally delicious cheese pastries (LL3500).

Walimah (☎ 745 933, 343 128; Rue Makdissi, Hamra; mezze around LL4000, mains around LL8500; open 8am-midnight Mon-Sat) is an oasis in the middle of bustling Hamra. Its totally gorgeous interior, which overlooks a garden, features antique wall hangings, richly upholstered banquettes and a colourful tiled floor. The healthy home-style dishes, which change daily, are both delectable and reasonably priced.

Pasta di Casa (☎ 366 909, 363 368; Ashkar Bldg, just off Rue Clemenceau, Ras Beirut; mains around LL10,000; open noon-midnight daily) is an unpretentious local eatery. Its charming staff and home-made pasta make it a good choice for those wanting an evening's break from Arabic food. It only has 10 tables and doesn't accept credit cards.

Al Dente (☎ 202 440, 333 333; 137 Rue Abdel Wahab El-Inglizi, Achrafiye; mains around LL28,000; open 12.30pm-3pm & 8.30pm-11pm Mon-Fri, 8.30pm-11pm Sat) is an Italian restaurant in a very different league to Pasta di Casa. With its lavish decor and lengthy wine list, it's the favoured eating place of the Beirut establishment. The fabulous food carries an equally fabulous price tag, but if you've got the dosh it's highly recommended.

Al Mijana (☎ 328 082, 334 675; Rue Abdel Wahab El-Inglizi, Achrafiye; mezze LL5500, grills LL11,000; open noon-3pm & 8pm-11.30pm Sun-Fri, 8pm-11.30pm Sat) is possibly Beirut's best restaurant. Housed in a restored and opulently decorated Ottoman house with both indoor and outdoor eating areas, it serves Arabic food that is to die for. If you only have one splurge in Beirut, this should be it. A bottle of Chateau Ksara will set you back LL52,000. The à la carte menu is better value than the set menus.

Casablanca (☎ 369 334; Rue Ain al-Mreisse, Ain al-Mreisse; brunch LL25,000, set-menu lunch LL27,000, dinner LL50,000; open 12.30pm-4pm & 8pm-1.30am Tues-Sat, 11am-4pm & 8pm-1.30am Sun) is one of the city's funkiest eateries. In a renovated Ottoman villa overlooking the Corniche, it's the favoured spot for the ultrafashionable to brunch on the weekend. Also open for lunch, dinner and late-night drinks.

Entertainment

Put on your glad rags, brace yourself with a preliminary cocktail or two and get ready to party, because Beirut is *the* place for nightlife in the Middle East. Thursday, Friday and Saturday are the big nights, but there's something happening every night of the week. Though there are a few bars worth visiting in Hamra, most of the popular spots are around Rue Monot in Achrafiye. Downtown has only just kicked off as a popular nightspot but it's bound to become a rival to Monot, and there are a couple of popular clubs a 10km taxi ride out of the centre at La Quarantaine. Further out, at Jounieh, there's the famous Maameltein nightclub strip, which is always superbusy in summer.

Bars Beirut has an embarrassment of riches when it comes to bars and night spots. Some of the best include:

Blue Note (☎ 743 857; Rue Makhoul, Hamra; admission LL8000-18,000; open 11am-1am daily) is one of the best places to hear jazz in Beirut. Thursday, Friday and Saturday are the only nights when the music is live; it's probably not worth a visit for the rest of the week. Admission is only charged on evenings when live music is being performed. There's food and a wide range of drinks on offer.

Smuggler's Inn (☎ 476 775; Rue Makhoul, Hamra; admission free; open 7pm-late daily), a few doors down from Blue Note, is a laid-back pub popular with AUB students and backpackers. Drinks are ultracheap at LL3000 for a local beer and LL2000 for a shot. There's also a limited food menu.

Chez André (☎ 740 777; Rue Hamra, Hamra; admission free; open 8am-4am Mon-Sat) is a tiny place that is always jam-packed in the evening. A favourite drinking spot of local academics, artists and journalists, it's great fun and highly recommended. At night, access is via the small gap in the arcade door on Rue Hamra; it's the third shop on the left.

Téatro (☎ 616 617; Av de L'Indépendence, Sodeco; admission free; open 8pm-late daily) is described as a 'pub restaurant'. It's in an attractive Ottoman house and features live music every Wednesday and Thursday. On occasion it programmes a special Sunday featuring Lebanese music luminaries such as Ziad Rahbani, the jazz-musician son of Lebanon's most-famous female vocalist, Fairouz. Reservations are recommended here from Wednesday to Sunday.

Babylone (☎ 219 539; 33 Rue Abdel Wahab El-Inglizi; admission free; open 8pm-3am Mon-Sat) is a great place for a late-night drink. Functioning as a **restaurant** (11am-3.30pm & 8pm-11.30pm Mon-Sat) during the day and early evening, it's in a renovated Ottoman house and has a particularly eccentric ersatz-Roman interior. It's a favourite watering hole of Beirut's gay community.

Mint Lounge-Bar (☎ 339 637; Rue Monot, Achrafiye; admission free; open 5pm-8am daily) is the hippest of the hip. Small and mega stylish, it's a perfect place for drinking

Martinis and listening to up-to-the-minute music chosen by the in-house DJ.

Rai (☎ 338 822; Rue Monot, Achrafiye; minimum charge US$20 mid-week, US$35 Fri-Sat; open 10.30pm-3.30am Tues-Sun) is at the epicentre of the Monot scene. In a basement, its Arabian-Nights interior is both exotic and comfortable, but overall the place is just a tad pretentious. Despite this and the over-the-top prices (LL10,000 for a local beer and US$10 for a spirit), it's extremely popular, so make sure you book.

Pacífico (☎ 204 446; Rue Monot, Achrafiye; admission free; open 7pm-late daily) is number one with the local 30-something crowd despite – or because of? – its music (way too many 1980s hits). A local beer will set you back LL6000, less between 7pm and 8pm when happy hour is held.

Lime (☎ 03-348 273; Rue Monot, Achrafiye; admission free; open 7.30pm-late daily) is a popular drinking spot and has an outdoor terrace. Ambience outweighs attitude here, which is a nice change on Monot, and at LL5000 the local beer is reasonably priced.

Nightclubs As is the case in every corner of the world, the 'in' places in Beirut change quickly and new places open up all the time, so ask around and check the social page of the *Daily Star* for new venues. Also make sure you ring ahead and reserve a place at all of the nightclubs mentioned here, especially on Friday and Saturday – the popular places get so busy they'll only open their doors to people on the reservation list. Note that the dress code is smart and things usually don't kick off in earnest until after 11pm.

B 018 (☎ 03-800 018; Beirut-Jounieh Hwy at La Quarantaine; admission free; open 9pm-late daily), next to Forum de Beyrouth, is the most famous nightclub in town. With its movable roof, mock-horror baroque interior and slightly sinister underground entrance in the middle of a car park, it's certainly a place to remember. On top of that, its liberal reputation means that gays and lesbians will feel comfortable here. You'll find it about 10km from Beirut Central District; ask a taxi driver for the club or the Forum de Beyrouth.

Strange Fruit (☎ 373 765; Starco Center, Downtown; 2-drink minimum (US$10 per drink) Fri & Sat; open 9pm-late Mon-Sat) is new, mega hip and a great place to spend a night. In a converted cinema, its sloping floor means that customers often think they're drunk a long time before this actually eventuates! Monday is movie night and every 15 days there's a highly publicised 'event'. The toilets need to be seen to be believed: they feature specially designed urinals for women and a dedicated shot bar (yes, in the toilets).

Element (☎ 338 700; Rue Université St Joseph, Achrafiye; admission free; open 8pm-late daily) is where the beautiful young things hang out. Loud music meets frantic dancing here, and the drinks aren't too expensive. Bookings essential.

Atlantis (☎ 203 344; Rue Université St Joseph, Achrafiye; admission free; open 10pm-late daily) is where James Bond would party if he were to visit present-day Beirut. Its circular tank of piranhas in the middle of the dance floor regularly lifts into the air with people gyrating on top of it. Seriously! Though some of its customers no doubt drink martinis stirred, not shaken, lesser mortals usually drink local beer at LL8000. To find the entrance, walk down Rue Boutros Karane, go past 'The 5 Room' club and then turn right. Atlantis is a few doors down on the right.

Circus (☎ 332 523; 243 Rue Monot, Achrafiye; admission free; open 8.30pm-late daily) is one of the city's most popular nightclubs. Don't let the dreadful exterior put you off – behind it is a good, fun atmosphere, excellent meals (around US$30), live music and reasonably priced local beer (LL4000). Don't even think of turning up if you haven't booked.

Al Mandaloun (☎ 611 311; Secteaur Nazareth, Achrafiye; admission free; open 9pm-late Mon-Sat) is where the wealthy, young and glitzy hang out. They must be wealthy to afford the drinks (US$12). If you want to join this crowd and dance the night away, make sure you book.

Shopping

Beirutis love to shop and there are plenty of places where they can indulge their passion. For fashion, try Downtown or Verdun; for food and practical items, try Hamra; and for gourmet foodstuffs and wine, try Achrafiye. Listed here are the two best souvenir shops in town; neither is cheap but both stock quality merchandise.

Artisans du Liban et d'Orient (☎ 362 610; the Corniche, Ain al-Mreisse; open 10am-6pm Mon-Thur, 10am-2pm Sat) is one of the most gorgeous shops you're likely to encounter anywhere in the world. Enter via the path of fragrant bay leaves and be tempted by the array of quality, locally made fabrics, cosmetics, clothes, toys and home wares on offer.

Maison de L'artisan (☎ 368 461/2; branches on the Corniche, Ain al-Mreisse & Rue Clémenceau, Hamra; open 9.30am-7.30pm Mon-Sat) sells a wide range of handicrafts made by locals. You're unlikely to leave here without indulging in at least a few mementos or gifts to take home.

Getting There & Away

For information about getting to Syria from Beirut, see Land in the Getting There & Away section earlier in this chapter. Buses, minibuses and service taxis to destinations north of Beirut leave from Charles Helou bus station and the Dawra (AKA Dora) transport hub. To the south and southeast they leave from the Cola transport hub on the opposite side of town. See the relevant town and city sections for further details.

Getting Around

To/From the Airport Beirut international airport is approximately 5km south of Beirut. From here it's possible to catch a bus into the city, but the fact that the airport bus stop is at the roundabout at the airport exit, a 1km walk from the terminal, is a major pain. The red-and-white LCC bus No 1 will take you from the airport roundabout to Rue Sadat in Hamra; bus No 5 will take you to Charles Helou bus station. The blue-and-white OCFTC buses No 7 and 10 also stop at the airport roundabout en route to the city centre; bus No 10 goes to Charles Helou bus station and bus No 7 goes to Raouché, from where you can take bus No 9 to Hamra. Fares are LL500. The buses operate between 5.30am and 6pm daily and the maximum wait should be 10 minutes.

Taxis from the airport are notoriously expensive, usually charging US$25 for the trip into town. It's possible to bargain this down to as little as US$10, but only if the supply of taxis is greatly outstripping demand when you want to travel. A cheaper option is to walk 1km to the highway and hail a service taxi into town for LL2000.

It's cheaper to catch a taxi from Beirut to the airport; the average fare is LL10,000.

Make sure you confirm this price with the driver before you get into the taxi.

Bus Beirut is well serviced by its network of buses. The red-and-white buses are run by the privately owned Lebanese Commuting Company (LCC) and the large blue-and-white OCFTC buses are government owned.

The buses operate on a 'hail-and-ride' system: just wave at the driver and the bus will stop. The only official bus stops are where the bus starts and finishes. There are no timetables, but buses come frequently during the day. Both companies stop their service in the early evening.

The bus routes most useful to travellers are listed below. A trip will almost always cost LL500.

LCC Buses
No 1 Hamra–Khaldé Rue Sadat (Hamra), Rue Emile Eddé, Hotel Bristol, Rue Verdun, Cola roundabout, Airport roundabout, Kafaat, Khaldé

No 2 Hamra–Antelias Rue Sadat (Hamra), Rue Emile Eddé, Radio Lebanon, Sassine Square, Dawra, Antelias

No 3 Ain al-Mreisse–Dawra Ain al-Mreisse, Bain Militaire, Raouche, Verdun, Museum, Dawra

No 4 Wardieh–Sfeir Radio Lebanon, Riad as-Solh Square, Place des Martyrs, Fouad Chehab, Yessoueieye, Sfeir

No 5 Charles Helou–Hay as-Saloum Place des Martyrs, Fouad Chehab, Yessoueiye, Airport roundabout, Hay es-Seloum

No 6 Dawra–Byblos Antelias, Jounieh, Jbail (Byblos)

No 7 Museum–Baabda Museum, Beit Mary, Broummana, Baabda

No 13 Charles Helou–Cola Place des Martyrs, Riad al-Solh Square, Cola roundabout

OCFTC Buses
No 1 Bain Militaire–Khaldé Bain Militaire, Unesco, Summerland, Khaldé

No 4 Dawra–Jounieh Dawra, Dbayé, Kaslik, Jounieh

No 5 Ministry of Information–Sérail Jdeideh Ministry of Information, Sodeco, Bourj Hammoud, Sérail Jdeideh

No 7 Bain Militaire–Airport Bain Militaire, Summerland, Bourj Brajné, Airport

No 8 Ain al-Mreisse–Sérail Jdeideh Ain al-Mreisse, Charles Helou, Dawra, Sérail Jdeideh

No 9 Bain Militaire–Sérail Jdeideh Bain Militaire, Rue Bliss, Rue Adbel Aziz, Rue Clemanceau, Rue Weygand, Tabaris Square, Sassine Square, Hayek roundabout, Sérail Jdeideh

No 10 Charles Helou–Airport Charles Helou, Shatila, Airport roundabout

No 15 Ain al-Mreisse–Nahr al-Mott Ain al-Mreisse, Raouché, Museum, Nahr al-Mott

No 16 Charles Helou–Cola Charles Helou, Downtown, Cola

No 23 Bain Militaire–Dawra Bain Militaire, Ain al-Mreisse, Charles Helou, Dawra

No 24 Museum–Hamra Museum, Barbir, Hamra

Taxi & Service Taxi Private taxi companies usually have meters and can quote you an approximate fare on the phone. If you hail a taxi on the street, chances are it won't have a meter and you have to agree on the fare before getting into the car. Always make sure you do this to avoid any arguments at the end. Within Beirut, taxis charge anywhere from LL5000 to LL10,000, depending on your destination.

Service taxis cover the major routes in Beirut. They can be hailed anywhere around town and will drop you off at any point along their established route. The fare is LL1000 on established routes within the city and LL2000 to outlying suburbs.

Around Beirut

BEIT MARY & BROUMMANA
بيت مرعي و بروممانا
☎ 04

Set in pine forests some 800m above and 17km east of Beirut, Beit Mary offers panoramic views over the capital. It dates back to Phoenician times and is home to Roman and Byzantine ruins, including some fine **floor mosaics** in a Byzantine church dating from the 5th century. The site is currently home to a Syrian army company, but the soldiers seem happy to allow visitors to wander around. Ask locals for directions. Nearby and also worth a visit is the 17th-century Maronite monastery of **Deir al-Qalaa**, built with the remains of a Roman temple.

The ultraposh Al-Bustan Hotel in Beit Mary hosts an annual music festival in February. See Special Events in the Facts for the Visitor section earlier in this chapter for more details.

About 4km northeast of Beit Mary is Broummana, a bustling town full of hotels, eateries, cafés, shops and nightclubs. In summer, it's extremely popular with Beirutis escaping the heat of the city and has a carnival-like atmosphere, particularly on weekends.

Perhaps the best way to enjoy the two towns is to catch a bus or service taxi to Broummana, spend an hour or so there, and then walk or catch a service taxi (LL1000) to **Restaurant Mounir** (☎ 873 900; mezze LL5000, grills LL8000; open noon-midnight daily), one of the most popular restaurants in Lebanon. The range and quality of mezze served here is simply astounding. To get here from Broumanna, make your way towards Beit Mary and turn right into the downhill street just before the 'Supermarko' sign at the entrance to town. There's also a green 'Mounir' sign here. The restaurant is at the bottom of the street. Its unparalleled reputation for mezze, its spectacular views over Beirut and the Mediterranean, and its charming staff mean that bookings are advisable, particularly on weekends and over summer. Make sure you ask for a table with a view. After lunch, walk into Beit Mary and have a leisurely look at the ruins and monastery before making your way back to Beirut.

Service taxis from the National Museum or Dawra charge LL2000 to either Beit Mary or Broummana. The No 7 LCC bus (LL500, 40 minutes) leaves from just east of the museum.

JEITA GROTTO مغارة جعيتا
☎ 09

Visiting this grotto (☎ 220 840/3; W www .jeitagrotto.com; adult/child aged 4-11 LL16,500/9250; open 9am-6pm Mon-Fri, 9am-7pm Sat & Sun July-Aug, 9am-6pm Tues-Fri, 9am-7pm Sat & Sun May-June & Sept-Oct, 9am-5pm Tues-Sun Nov-April, closed for 4 weeks late Jan-early Feb), with its extraordinary stalactites and stalagmites, seems to be the closest the Lebanese come to appreciating the natural environment. And even then this extraordinary natural attraction has been debased by unnecessary and unsympathetic additions such as a cable car, piped outdoor music, snack bars and a Disney-style toy train. The attractive valley in which the grotto is situated has also been ruined by development (a monstrously ugly country club nearby, for instance) and the fast-flowing river at its bottom is full of rubbish, particularly plastic. Despite all this, the grotto, par-

ticularly the upper cavern, is totally amazing and is most definitely worth a visit. The vast honeycomb of galleries and ravines has been known to humans since Palaeolithic times, but was first surveyed in the 19th century and opened to the public in 1958.

Visitors walk through the upper cavern and take a boat ride through the lower cavern (in winter, the lower cavern is closed when rainfall is high, because of flooding). Photography is forbidden. There's a good, clean **restaurant** serving cheap mezze, pizza and grills.

Jeita is 18km northeast of Beirut. To get there, catch a minibus (LL1000) or No 6 LCC/No 4 OCFTC bus (LL500) from Dawra and ask the driver to drop you at the Jeita turn-off on the Beirut-Jounieh Hwy, where taxis congregate. The 15-minute trip uphill to the grotto will cost LL5000, but you're much better off negotiating a return price with the driver (who can wait while you visit) because taxis from the grotto back to the highway/Dawra are exorbitantly expensive (US$10/20).

JOUNIEH جونيه
☎ 09

Once a sleepy fishing village, Jounieh, 21km north of Beirut, is now a high-rise strip mall hemmed in by the sea on one side and the mountains on the other. Famous as the home of unfettered urban development, nightclubs and glitzy shops, it has the reputation as being *the* party town in Lebanon. On summer weekends and nights, half of Beirut's population seems to decamp here and the atmosphere, though crazy, is great fun.

Orientation & Information
The town is roughly divided into three parts: Maameltein, home to most of the nightclubs, the famous casino and some of Lebanon's best restaurants; Centre Ville with its hotels, supermarket and banks; and Kaslik, a posh area where every second shop seems to be selling chic – and extraordinarily expensive – little Versace numbers just begging to be worn to the Maameltein nightspots. Rue Mina, which runs through Centre Ville and is home to the only buildings dating from Jounieh's fishing-village days, eventually turns into Rue Maameltein; a walk along its length, particularly on a summer evening when

LEBANON

traffic is blocked from entering and live music and street stalls take over the road, is highly recommended.

Cafe Net offers the only Internet access in town but is closed on Sunday. To get there head down Rue Mina from Centre Ville towards Kaslik; go left at the Kaslik, up the hill, then turn first right (at the 'Beyrouth' sign). It's about 50m up the hill off a side street on the left.

The **HSBC Bank** in Rue Mina will change travellers cheques for a charge of US$3 per US$100 cheque. It also has an ATM.

Teleferique

There's a cable car *(teleferique;* ☎ *914 324, 936 075; adult/student/child return LL7500/ 6000/3500; operates 1pm-11pm Tues, 10am-11pm Wed-Sun June-Oct, 1pm-7pm Tues, 10am-7pm Wed-Sun Nov-May)* running from Maameltein up to the mountain-top Basilica of Our Lady of Lebanon. The views are quite spectacular. To get there, walk from Centre Ville and make your way past the army position to the clock-tower roundabout; the teleferique is about 10 minutes further on.

Places to Stay & Eat

Hotel St-Joseph *(☎ 931 189; Rue Mina; basic/large rooms US$20/30),* about 100m north of the HSBC Bank in Centre Ville, is a shabby but character-filled pension run by a charming English woman. It offers basic small rooms (for one or two people) and large rooms (for two or three people), all with shower and toilet. A mayor's residence in days gone by, it has high vaulted ceilings, 14 spacious rooms, and a common lounge, kitchen and outdoor terrace.

Mercure Hotel Beverly Beach *(☎ 643 333, 639 999, fax 916 637;* e *beverly@inco.com .lb; Rue Maameltein; singles/doubles with bathroom US$60/80 June-Sept, US$50/70 Oct-May)* is probably the best hotel in Jounieh. Slap-bang in the middle of the Maameltein strip, its very comfortable, well-appointed rooms have large balconies offering sea views. The rates quoted here must be negotiated directly with hotel management; they include breakfast. Whether you stay here or not, the hotel's Italian restaurant, **Prego**, is well worth a visit.

Makhlouf *(☎ 645 192; Rue Maameltein; shwarma LL3500, mains LL11,000, large fresh juice LL3000; open 24hr daily)* is a branch of the popular Lebanese chain. This one, which is always packed with locals, has a great outdoor terrace overlooking the sea. Just down the road is **Snack al-Karkour**, which offers a similar menu and prices.

Chez Sami *(☎ 646 064/164; Rue Maameltein; meals around US$30 plus drinks; open noon-midnight daily)* has the reputation of being the best seafood restaurant in Lebanon. Its stylish interior offers great views and its menu offers treats such as squid in its own ink and fresh fried calamari. During summer and on weekends this is a place to be seen, so make sure you book ahead. If you're keen to move on elsewhere for coffee and dessert, **Patisserie Rafaat Hallab & Fils** is conveniently positioned directly opposite.

Entertainment

Jounieh is famous for its nightlife. Your best bet is to walk down Rue Maameltein and choose the bars and nightclubs with the biggest crowds around their entrances; these will inevitably be the clubs of the minute. When doing this, steer clear of the 'super nightclubs', places with tacky dance shows and plenty of female escorts.

Amor Y Libertad *(☎ 640 881; ground floor, Debs Center, Kaslik; admission US$20)* is a popular Cuban club-restaurant that's been going for years and shows no sign of closing its doors in the near future. The cover charge entitles you to two drinks.

Casino du Liban *(☎ 855 888, 853 222; slot-machine area open noon-4am, gaming rooms open 8pm-4am)* is Jounieh's most famous nightspot. If your notion of what a casino should be comes straight from James Bond movies, you're likely to be disappointed here, though. Gaming machines, middle-aged Lebanese couples having a big night out and girls wearing lots of spangles and very few clothes are more in evidence than dinner-suited secret agents striking attitudes over the roulette wheel. Guests must be over 21 and wearing smart casual gear (no jeans or sports shoes) to get in.

Getting There & Away

The OCFTC No 4 bus runs from Dawra to Centre Ville, stopping at Kaslik on the way. Also leaving from Dawra is the LCC No 6 bus to Byblos, which stops at Maameltein en route. Both services charge LL500 and take approximately 30 minutes. The trip from Jounieh to Byblos on the No 6 costs LL500. Minibuses to/from Dawra charge LL1000 and service taxis LL2000. Taxis to/from Jounieh to Hamra cost LL15,000 during the day and LL20,000 at night. A taxi to Byblos will cost LL10,000 and a service taxi LL2000.

North of Beirut

BYBLOS (JBAIL)
☎ 09

بيبلوس

Travellers inevitably fall in love with Byblos. With its picturesque ancient fishing harbour, Roman site, Crusader castle and restored souq area, it's a great place to visit overnight or on a day trip (it's only 42km from Beirut). In summer, when crowds flock to the harbour to eat at the famous seafood restaurants or soak up the ambience (and a drink or two!) on the terrace of the internationally famous Byblos Fishing Club, it's a truly magical place to be.

There's an annual arts festival in Byblos. See Special Events in the Facts for the Visitor section earlier in this chapter for more details.

History
Excavations have shown that Byblos (biblical name Gebal) was probably inhabited as early as 7000 years ago. In the 3rd millennium BC it became the most important trading port on the eastern Mediterranean under

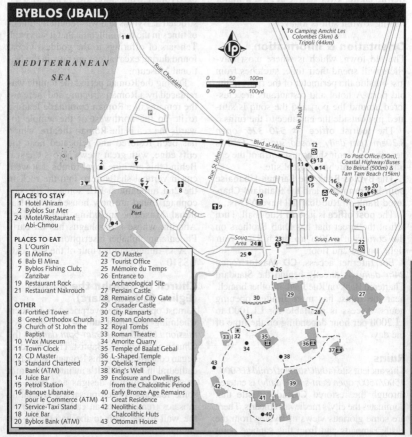

BYBLOS (JBAIL)

MEDITERRANEAN SEA

To Camping Amchit Les Colombes (3km) & Tripoli (44km)

Rue Cheralam

0   50   100m
0   50   100yd

Rue Jbail

Blvd al-Mina

To Post Office (50m), Coastal Highway/Buses to Beirut (500m) & Tam Tam Beach (15km)

Rue Sfoha

Rue Jbail

Old Port

Souq Area

Souq Area

PLACES TO STAY
1 Hotel Ahiram
2 Byblos Sur Mer
24 Motel/Restaurant Abi-Chmou

PLACES TO EAT
3 L'Oursin
5 El Molino
6 Bab El Mina
7 Byblos Fishing Club; Zanzibar
19 Restaurant Rock
21 Restaurant Nakrouch

OTHER
4 Fortified Tower
8 Greek Orthodox Church
9 Church of St John the Baptist
10 Wax Museum
11 Town Clock
12 CD Master
13 Standard Chartered Bank (ATM)
14 Juice Bar
15 Petrol Station
16 Banque Libanaise pour le Commerce (ATM)
17 Service-Taxi Stand
18 Juice Bar
20 Byblos Bank (ATM)

22 CD Master
23 Tourist Office
25 Mémoire du Temps
26 Entrance to Archaeological Site
27 Persian Castle
28 Remains of City Gate
29 Crusader Castle
30 City Ramparts
31 Roman Colonnade
32 Royal Tombs
33 Roman Theatre
34 Amorite Quarry
35 Temple of Baalat Gebal
36 L-Shaped Temple
37 Obelisk Temple
38 King's Well
39 Enclosure and Dwellings from the Chalcolithic Period
40 Early Bronze Age Remains
41 Great Residence
42 Neolithic & Chalcolithic Huts
43 Ottoman House

LEBANON

the Phoenicians, sending cedar wood and oil to Egypt in exchange for gold, alabaster, papyrus rolls and linen. The city was renamed Byblos by the Greeks, who ruled from 333 BC and named the city after their word for papyrus, *bublos*, because the papyrus shipped from Egypt to Greece via its port was famed throughout the Greek world. The Romans under Pompey took over Byblos in 64 BC, building large temples, baths, colonnaded streets and public buildings. In AD 1104 the city fell to the Crusaders, who built the castle and moat visited by many travellers today with stone and columns from the Roman temples. Subsequent centuries under Ottoman and Mamluk rule saw Byblos' international reputation as a trading port wane, with Beirut taking over as the region's major port, and it settled into life as the small local fishing town it still is today.

Orientation & Information

The old town, which is where most travellers will spend their time, stretches from just outside the perimeter of the ruins to the old port. A hotel and restaurants are clustered around the port and the souq is situated just outside the entrance to the ruins.

The **tourist office** (☎ 540 325; open 8.30am-1pm daily, closed Sun Dec-Feb) is near the souvenir shops just north of the entrance to the archaeological site.

The **Byblos Bank**, the **Banque Libanaise pour le Commerce** and the **Standard Chartered Bank** on Rue Jbail all have ATMs.

The **post office** is just off Rue Jbail. Turn left at the street that has Diab Brothers on the corner; it's 20m up the hill on your right, on the 2nd floor.

For Internet access, **CD Master** (open 24hr daily) is directly behind the Standard Chartered Bank on Rue Jbail. Its other branch, near the ruins, has more limited opening hours. Access is available for LL1000 to LL2000 per hour depending on the time of the day.

Ruins

This ancient site (adult/student/child LL6000/1500/1500; open 8am-sunset daily) is entered through the restored **Crusader castle** that dominates the city's medieval ramparts. There are some glorious views of Byblos from the castle ramparts and from this vantage point you're also able to get a very clear idea of the layout of the ancient city. From the castle, follow the path to the left until you reach a **temple** dating from the third millennium. From here, move on to marvel at the **Obelisk Temple** from the early 2nd millennium BC, where offerings of human figurines encrusted in gold leaf were discovered (now in the National Museum).

Following the path west, go past the **King's Well**, a spring that supplied the city with water until the end of the Hellenistic era, to the site of the **Great Residence**. From here, make your way to the earliest remains at the site, the **Neolithic and Chalcolithic huts** from the 5th and 4th millenniums BC. Past the site of the adjacent **Amorite Quarry** is the **Temple of Baalat Gebal** (the Mistress of Byblos) from 3000 BC. This was the largest and most important temple constructed at Byblos and was rebuilt a number of times in the two millennia that it survived. Ten jars of offerings to the goddess Gebal found during excavations are now in the National Museum.

During the Roman period the temple was replaced by a Roman structure and there are the remains of a **Roman colonnade** leading to it. To the northwest of the temple towards the sea is the **Roman theatre**, which has been restored and relocated near the cliff edge, with great views across the sea. Behind this are nine **royal tombs** that were cut in vertical shafts deep into the rock in the 2nd millennium BC; some of the sarcophagi found are now housed in the National Museum, including that of King Aharim, whose sarcophagus has an early Phoenician alphabet inscription.

A 45-minute guided tour of the site costs US$10.

Church of St John the Baptist (Église St Jean Marc)

Almost opposite the overpriced and underwhelming **Wax Museum** (☎ 540 463; admission LL5000; open 9am-5pm daily) is the Church of St John the Baptist. The Crusaders began construction of this Romanesque-style cathedral in AD 1115. It's an interesting mix of Arab and Italian designs and there are some reasonably well-preserved Byzantine mosaics (remnants of an earlier church) on the wall to the path to the harbour at the church's rear.

Places to Stay

Camping Lebanon's only camping ground, **Camping Amchit Les Colombes** (☎ 540 322, 943 782; camp sites US$3, 'tungalows' US$20, 3-4 person chalets with/without air-con US$27/30) is in Amchit, 3km north of Byblos. This friendly place is on a promontory overlooking the sea. It has all the necessary amenities, including showers, toilets, kitchen with gas burners, and electrical points for caravans (220V), although these aren't as well maintained as they could be. In addition to tent and caravan sites, there are also fully furnished chalets and 'tungalows' (claustrophobic bungalows in the shape of a tent, with two beds and a Portaloo-type shower and toilet) sleeping two people. The camping ground is set on a wooded cliff-top with steps down to its own rocky beach and the chalets and tungalows have fabulous views. It's a 25-minute walk from Byblos; a service taxi costs LL1000.

Hotels Motel/Restaurant **Abi-Chmou** (☎/fax 540 484; doubles/twins/triples US$40/50/65) is the best-value sleeping option in town. Its three rooms run off a huge communal living area with TV that is comfortable and has the 'wow factor' in spades (check out the chandelier!). There's also a spotlessly clean kitchen and shared bathroom. The triple and twin rooms have views over the ruins and the double room has a private shower. The owners also operate a café serving a set menu of mezze, main course, fruit and coffee for US$10.

Hotel Ahiram (☎ 540 440, fax 944 726; singles/doubles US$50/72 July-Aug, US$40/50 Sept-June) on the beach just north of town has most certainly seen better days. Its none-too-clean rooms have air-con, balcony with sea views and a small bath. The only reason we recommend it here is its great position behind a popular public swimming beach. Prices include breakfast.

Byblos Sur Mer (☎ 548 000, fax 944 859; e byblos.mer@inco.com.lb; singles/doubles/suites with bathroom LL99,000/110,000/173,000 low season, LL116,000/139,000/185,000 high season) has comfortable though small rooms with sea views and air-con. It also has its own sea-front swimming pool. There's no denying that its position is sensational, but the rooms are overpriced for what is offered. The hotel has its own restaurant

(breakfast LL11,500) and also operates **L'Oursin** restaurant in summer.

Places to Eat & Drink

There are a number of good, cheap fast-food places on and around Rue Jbail. The best of these are probably **Restaurant Nakrouch**, a stylish place serving burgers, BBQ chicken and pizza; and **Restaurant Rock**, which claims to serve the best felafel in town and, going by its popularity with the locals, probably does so. Restaurant Rock is near the Byblos Bank and Restaurant Nakrouch is on the other side of Rue Jbail, towards the ruins. Both are open from early morning until 1am; Nakrouch is closed on Sunday.

Byblos Fishing Club (☎ 540 213; meals around US$25 per person plus drinks; open 11am-midnight daily) is in a great location overlooking the port. Famed for the stream of film stars and politicians that have passed through over the decades, its charm is still palpable. Though the food and service can be average, its outdoor terrace and eccentric 'boat bar' make a visit almost obligatory.

Bab el Mina (☎ 540 475; set menu LL45,000; open 11am-midnight daily) is next to the Fishing Club. Its terrace is nicer and its food is better, but it just doesn't have the atmosphere of its neighbour. Despite this, it's incredibly popular, so make sure you book.

El Molino (☎ 541 555; meal with two margaritas about LL35,000; open noon-midnight Tues-Sun) offers Mexican food and a good, fun atmosphere.

Zanzibar (☎ 541 516; open 6pm-late Tues-Sun) is the most popular bar in town. It has a big bar and loud music – what more can we say?

Shopping

Mémoire du Temps (☎ 547 083; w www.memoryoftime.com; open 8am-5.30pm daily) is without doubt the best place in Byblos to buy a souvenir of your visit. Its stock of fossils and ancient artefacts should probably be in a museum, but their sale is totally legal and certificates of authenticity are supplied. Be prepared to cough up serious dollars for the offerings here.

Getting There & Away

The service-taxi stand in Byblos is near the Banque Libanaise pour le Commerce. A service taxi to/from Beirut (the hub in Beirut is

Dawra) costs LL3000. The LCC bus No 6 (LL500, one hour) and minibuses (LL1000) also leave from Dawra and travel regularly along the coast road between Beirut and Byblos, stopping on Rue Jbail. It's a scenic and very pleasant trip.

TRIPOLI (TRABLOUS) طرابلس
☎ 06

Tripoli, 85km north of Beirut, is Lebanon's second-largest city and is the main port and trading centre for northern Lebanon. Famous for its medieval Mamluk architecture, including a large souq area that's acknowledged as being the best in Lebanon, it's a great point from which to explore the northern part of the country. Tripoli is also famous as the sweets capital of Lebanon, so

any trip to the city is not complete without a visit to one of its Arabic sweet shops. The main speciality is *halawat al-jibn*, a sweet made from cheese and served with syrup.

History
Like other Phoenician cities along the eastern Mediterranean coast, Tripoli's early expansion reflected its suitability as a trading post. Its name, taken from the Greek word *tripolis* (three cities), derives from the 8th-century arrival of traders from the three ports of Sidon, Tyre and Arwad (off Tartus in Syria). Conquered in turn by the Seleucids, Romans, Umayyads, Byzantines and Fatimids, it was invaded by the Crusaders in 1102 and ruled by them for 180 years. In 1289, the Mamluk sultan Qalaun took control and embarked

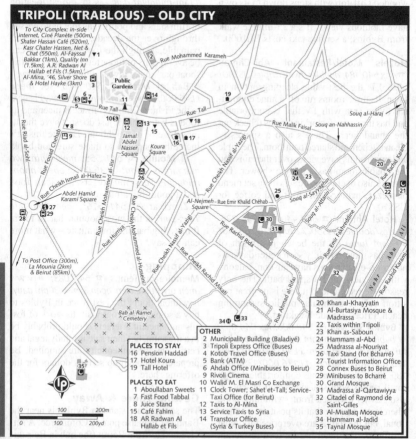

TRIPOLI (TRABLOUS) – OLD CITY

To City Complex: in-side
internet, Ciné Planète (500m),
Shater Hassan Café (520m),
Kasr Chater Hassen, Net &
Chat (550m), Al-Fayssal
Bakkar (1km), Quality Inn
(1.5km), A.R. Radwan Al
Hallab et Fils (1.5km),
Al-Mina, '46, Silver Shore
& Hotel Hayke (3km)

Public Gardens

Rue Mohammed Karameh

Rue Tall

Rue Tall

Souq al-Haraj

Rue Malik Faisal   Souq an-Nahhassin

Jamal
Abdel
Nasser
Square

Koura
Square

Rue Riad al-Solh

Rue Fouad Chehab

Rue Cheikh Ismail al-Hafez

Rue Cheikh Mohammed al-Jisr

Rue Cheikh Nassif al-Yazigi

Khan al-Khayyatin

Abdel Hamid
Karami Square

Al-Nejmeh –
Square

Rue Emir Khalid Chéhab

Souq al-Sayyaghin

Souq al-Attarin

Rue Humya

Rue Rachid Rida

Rue Cheikh Nassif al-Yazigi

Rue Cheikh Mohammed al-Husseini

Rue Rachid Mikati

Rue Emir Fakhreddine

To Post Office (300m),
La Mounia (2km)
& Beirut (85km)

Rue Ahmad al-Rifai

Nahr   Abu Ali

Rue Rachid Karami

Bab al-Ramel
Cemetery

OTHER
2 Municipality Building (Baladiyé)
3 Tripoli Express Office (Buses)
4 Kotob Travel Office (Buses)
5 Bank (ATM)
6 Ahdab Office (Minibuses to Beirut)
9 Rivoli Cinema
10 Walid M. El Masri Co Exchange
11 Clock Tower; Sahet et-Tall; Service-
    Taxi Office (for Beirut)
12 Taxis to Al-Mina
13 Service Taxis to Syria
14 Transtour Office
    (Syria & Turkey Buses)

PLACES TO STAY
16 Pension Haddad
17 Hotel Koura
19 Tall Hotel

PLACES TO EAT
1 Aboullaban Sweets
7 Fast Food Tabbal
8 Juice Stand
15 Café Fahim
18 AR Radwan Al
    Hallab et Fils

20 Khan al-Khayyatin
21 Al-Burtasiya Mosque &
    Madrassa
22 Taxis within Tripoli
23 Khan as-Saboun
24 Hammam al-Abd
25 Madrassa al-Nouriyat
26 Taxi Stand (for Bcharré)
27 Tourist Information Office
28 Connex Buses to Beirut
29 Minibuses to Bcharré
30 Grand Mosque
31 Madrassa al-Qartawiyya
32 Citadel of Raymond de
    Saint-Gilles
33 Al-Muallaq Mosque
34 Hammam al-Jadid
35 Taynal Mosque

0   100   200m
0   100   200yd

upon an ambitious building programme; many of the mosques, souqs, madrassas and khans in the old city date from this era. The Turkish Ottomans took over the city in 1516 and ruled quite peacefully until 1920, when it became part of the French mandate of Greater Lebanon.

Orientation & Information

There are two main parts to Tripoli: the city proper, which includes modern Tripoli and the old city; and Al-Mina (the port area), a promontory 3km to its west. The geographical centre of town is Saahat et-Tall (pronounced 'at-tahl'), a large square by the clock tower where you'll find the service taxi and bus stands, as well as most of the cheap hotels.

The old city sprawls east of Sahet et-Tall, while the modern centre is west of the square, along Rue Fouad Chehab. Between Rue Fouad Chehab and Al-Mina are broad avenues with residential buildings, modern shopping malls, Internet cafés and restaurants. In Al-Mina you'll find the Corniche, shops and some of the city's best restaurants and cafés.

The **tourist information office** (☎ 433 590; open 8am-5pm Mon-Sat) is on Abdel Hamid Karami Square, the first main roundabout as you enter Tripoli from the south. Staff members are friendly and helpful, but not all speak English (all seem to speak French).

Most of the large banks have ATMs and you can change US-dollar travellers cheques in any denomination at the **Walid M al-Masri Co Exchange** (Rue Tall). It charges US$2 per cheque. Enter via the watch and phone shop; the exchange is on the first floor.

There are two **post offices** in town; the main one (Rue Fouad Chehab) is near the tourist office and there's also a branch in Al-Mina (Rue ibn Sina).

There are Internet cafés scattered around the new part of town. **Net & Chat** (open 10am-midnight daily) is off Rue Riad al-Solh and has access for LL1500 per hour. To find it, turn off the main street at the Pain d'Or and walk one block. You'll see Net & Chat on the northwest corner. In the City Complex, you'll find **in-side internet** (open 10.30am-11pm daily), where the connections are slower and cost LL2000/3000 per 30 minutes/hour, but the atmosphere is more welcoming.

The Old City

Dating from the Mamluk era (14th and 15th centuries), the Old City is a maze of narrow alleys, colourful souqs, *hammams*, khans, mosques and madrassas. It's a lively and fascinating place where craftspeople, including tailors, jewellers, soap makers and coppersmiths, continue to work as they have done for centuries.

The **Grand Mosque**, built on the site of a Crusader cathedral and incorporating some of its features, has a magnificent entrance and minaret. Opposite the mosque's northern entrance is the **Madrassa al-Nouriyat**, which has distinctive black-and-white stonework and a beautiful inlaid mihrab. This madrassa is still in use today. Attached to the east side of the Grand Mosque is the **Madrassa al-Qartawiyya**, built between 1316 and 1326. Its elegant black-and-white facade and honeycomb-patterned half-dome above the portal are well worth a look.

You have to look up to see the **Al-Muallaq Mosque**, which is suspended over the street. This simple 14th-century building is a fair distance south of the Grand Mosque, very close to the **Hammam al-Jadid**, a palatial ruin of a bathhouse with glass-studded cupolas that cast shafts of light down into the rooms.

The **Khan as-Saboun** (soap khan) is in the centre of the medina, just off the gold souq. Built in the 16th century, it was first used as an army barracks, though it's been functioning as a market for centuries. In the 18th century, when Tripoli's soap industry was world famous, the khan was at its centre. Today, it's home to **Bader Hassoun** (☎ 03-438 369), a local business selling traditional handmade soap. The charming owners are happy to show visitors around the khan and demonstrate how the soap is made; the owners also sell their products from a stall at the front.

To the west of the Khan as-Saboun is the 300-year-old **Hammam al-Abd** (open 8am-11pm daily), the city's only functioning bathhouse. Unfortunately, it's only open to men – the full treatment costs LL16,000. To find it, turn into the passageway marked 'Sona-Massage'.

One of the most beautiful buildings in the old city is the **Khan al-Khayyatin**, a beautifully restored 14th-century tailors' souq lined with small workshops. Close to the souq is the **Al-Burtasiya Mosque & Madrassa**, with its particularly fine mihrab inside.

To the south of the souqs on the outskirts of the old city, but well worth the walk, is the restored **Taynal Mosque**. This dates from 1336 and has a magnificent inner portal.

Citadel of Raymond de Saint-Gilles

Towering above Tripoli, this Crusader fortress *(admission LL7500; open 8am-5pm)* was originally built in AD 1103–4. It was burnt down in AD 1297 and partly rebuilt the following century by a Mamluk emir. Since then it has been altered many times.

The most impressive part of the citadel is the imposing entrance, with its moat and three gateways (one Ottoman, one Mamluk, one Crusader). The rest of the site is a bit disappointing, largely due to the lack of any interpretive displays. Guided tours are available for LL20,000.

Places to Stay – Budget

Oddly enough, there's plenty of budget accommodation in Tripoli but nothing decent in the mid-range price bracket and not much in the top end. It's probably the only place in Lebanon where this is the case.

Pension Haddad *(☎ 624 392, 629 972; e haddadpension@hotmail.com; dorm beds/singles/doubles US$7/10/16)* uses the advertising slogan 'Miss your Grandma? Stay with us!', and the spotlessly clean rooms, solicitous owners and plethora of doilies mean that it lives up to its promise. A breakfast of croissant and tea is included in the price. The pension provides dinner for LL5000 if requested, does laundry for LL500/1000 large/small load, has a satellite TV and offers free tea. To find it, look for the inconspicuous stencil of its name high on the building, go past the stationer and to the back stairs when you reach the 1st floor.

Tall Hotel *(☎ 628 407; Rue Tall; singles/doubles LL13,000/25,000, with bathroom LL30,000/30,600)* is signposted high on the building but can be difficult to locate from the street. It has 14 rooms, three with bathroom, air-con and TV; seven with bathroom, fan and TV; and four with fan and TV only. It's reasonably clean but not as welcoming as the other budget options listed here.

Hotel Koura *(☎ 03-371 041; singles/doubles/triples with bathroom US$20/30/45, dorm beds/doubles are US$10/15 per person)* is a spotless small hotel run by a charming brother and sister. The rooms with bathroom also have air-con and there's a central shared lounge area. This is probably a summer-only option as the rooms are damp in winter. Breakfast is included in the price.

Hotel Hayke *(☎ 601 311; Rue ibn Sina; dorm beds/singles/doubles/triples US$15/20/30/35)* in Al-Mina is a friendly, family-run business offering clean, basic rooms with sea views. The hotel is above a billiard parlour/café on a street running parallel behind the Corniche. Use the boats for hire as your locator. The entrance is at the back of the building. Breakfast is included in the price.

Places to Stay – Top End

La Mounia Hotel *(☎ 401 801, fax 401 883; e info@lamounia-hotel.com; singles/doubles with bathroom US$80/100)* offers five-star service and amenities for four-star prices, probably because it's located in Kalamoun, a seaside suburb 2km to the south of Tripoli. Breakfast is included, and there's a restaurant, bar and pool, all of which are popular with the package groups that stay here. Travellers without their own transport will find it difficult to stay here and commute into Tripoli.

Quality Inn *(☎ 211 255, fax 211 277; e qualityinn1@inco.com.au; singles/doubles/suites with bathroom US$76/101/126)* is the best hotel in town. Adjacent to the Oscar Niemeyer–designed fairgrounds at the end of Rue Riad al-Solh on the left-hand side, it's strategically situated between Al-Mina and the Old City and is extremely comfortable. Rooms are large, clean and well appointed, and the price includes a delicious breakfast. Like La Mounia, it offers five-star service at a four-star price.

Places to Eat

There are a number of fast-food places located around Saahat at-Tall, the best of which is probably **Fast Food Tabbal**, which serves good felafel (LL1000) and has tables to sit at. Another popular sit-down fast-food option is **Shater Hassan Café**, in the new part of town, which serves up pizzas (LL9000) and burgers (LL4000) in a McDonald's-like atmosphere. Extremely popular with young Tripolitanians, it's open from 6am to 1am daily. To find it, turn off Rue Riad al-Solh into Rue Nadimal Jisr (almost directly opposite the City Complex).

Then turn into the third street on the left. Shater Hassan is down the street a little on the right-hand side.

The most atmospheric café in town is **Cafe Fahim**, with its extraordinary vaulted interior and crowd of local men smoking *sheeshas* and playing backgammon. It's opposite the clock tower, has an outdoor terrace and charges LL1500 for a tea. The best places to sample Tripoli's famous sweets are **AR Radwan Al-Hallab et Fils**, which has branches near the fairgrounds, on Riad al-Solh and on Rue Tall; and **Aboullaban**, on Rue Fouad Chehab. Both have sit-down areas where you can enjoy a tea or coffee with your sweets.

Al-Fayssal Bakkar *(☎ 202 203, 200 555; mezze around LL2000, grills around LL5000; open noon-midnight daily)* is a large, family-style restaurant very popular with locals. Its reasonable prices and friendly waiters make it a good option, although ordering can be a challenge, as staff speak Arabic only. You'll find it towards the end of Rue Riad al-Solh. Look for the mosque and the garden island in the middle of the road (Al-Fayssal Bakkar is on the opposite side).

Kasr Chater Hassen *(☎ 208 208; Rue Mounla; meals around LL40,000; open noon-midnight daily)* offers a good range of Lebanese dishes in very posh surrounds. The food doesn't quite match the truly over-the-top exterior, which would fit in well on the main strip in Las Vegas, but a meal here is recommended nonetheless. No credit cards. Follow the directions to Shater Hassan Café (see earlier), continue to the next intersection and then turn right. Kasr Chater Hassen is in front of you on the left-hand side.

'46 *(☎ 212 223, 03-586 737; the Corniche, Al-Mina; mains LL16,500; open 7am-1am Tues-Sun)* has great Italian food, very friendly waiters, a stylish interior and big windows overlooking the Corniche. There's live jazz on Saturday night. The restaurant is near the public gardens; enter from the rear of the building rather than from the Corniche.

Silver Shore *(☎ 601 384/5; the Corniche, Al-Mina; meals around US$35 plus drinks; open 10.30am-6.30pm daily)* is the best seafood restaurant in town, specialising in dishes with a special-recipe hot sauce. Only open during the day, it's a great place to visit on a weekend. You'll find it next door to '46. Make sure you book.

Entertainment

Tripoli is not renowned for its nightlife – to be frank, there is none – but it does have a good cinema complex showing the latest-release English-language movies, with Arabic subtitles. **Ciné Planète** *(☎ 442 471; City Complex, Rue Riad al-Solh; tickets LL10,000)* charges half-price on Monday, Wednesday and all afternoon.

Getting There & Away

From/To Beirut There are three companies running coach services from Beirut to Tripoli. **Connex** *(☎ 611 232/3, 587 507)* runs daily express 'luxury coaches' (LL2500, 90 minutes, every 30 minutes from 7am to 8.30pm). **Tripoli Express** runs smaller buses (LL2000, 90 minutes, every 20 minutes from 7am to 8.30pm). **Kotob** *(☎ 443 986)*, which runs older buses, is the cheapest option and takes longer (LL1500, two hours, every 15 minutes from 6am to 6.30pm), stopping to let passengers off and on at Jounieh (LL1500, 30 minutes), Byblos (LL1500, one hour) and Batroun (LL1500, 90 minutes). All three services leave from Zone C of Charles Helou bus station, where there's a dedicated ticket booth. There's no need to book ahead.

From Tripoli, the Connex service starts at 5.15am, running every 30 minutes until 5pm; the Tripoli Express service starts at 5.30pm and runs every 15 minutes until 5.30pm (the 6.30am, 7.30am and 9am services are on larger buses); and the Kotob service starts at 5am and runs every 15 minutes until 5.30pm. Prices and stops are the same as those outlined above.

Ahdab runs minibuses from Tripoli to Beirut every 10 minutes from 6am until 6pm daily (LL1000, around two hours). Service taxis to Beirut cost LL4000 and leave from just outside the clock tower.

To Bcharré, the Cedars & Baalbek Minibuses (LL2500, 80 minutes) from Tripoli to Bcharré leave from outside the travel agency near the tourist information office on Abdel Hamid Karami Square. The first service leaves at 7.30am, followed by 8.30am and 10am, after which minibuses leave on the hour until 4pm. From Bcharré, they leave hourly from 6am until 2pm. Those wanting to travel on to the Cedars will need to organise a taxi at Bcharré, which will cost LL7500.

A service taxi from Tripoli to Bcharré costs LL5000 and one to the Cedars will cost LL10,000; service taxis leave from Al-Koura Square.

When there's no snow or ice and the mountain road is open, it's possible to get a taxi from Bcharré to Baalbek (around US$50, 90 minutes).

To Syria, Turkey, Jordan & Saudi Arabia
Daily **Kotob** buses leave for Aleppo in Syria (LL7500, almost five hours) every 30 minutes from 9am until midnight, stopping in Homs (LL6000, two hours) en route. Kotob also runs a daily bus from Tripoli to Riyadh in Saudi Arabia, stopping in Damascus (US$5, four hours) and Amman in Jordan (US$25, 10 hours) en route. It leaves from the Kotob office at 3am.

Daily **Transtour** (☎ 03-411 015) buses leave for Aleppo in Syria (US$5, almost five hours) every hour from 9am to midnight. Its daily buses to Homs in Syria (LL5000, two hours) run hourly from 5am until midnight. There are two Transtour services daily to Damascus in Syria (LL7000, four hours), leaving at 5am and 3pm, and one daily bus to İstanbul in Turkey (US$45).

Service taxis to Homs cost LL7700, to Hama LL3000 and to Aleppo LL15,000. They leave when full from Saahat at-Tall. Service taxis don't go to Damascus.

Getting Around
Service taxis within the old and new parts of Tripoli cost LL1000; to Al-Mina they're LL2000.

BCHARRÉ
☎ 06
The trip to Bcharré takes you through some of the most beautiful scenery in Lebanon. The road winds along the mountainous slopes, continuously gaining in altitude and offering spectacular views of the Qadisha Valley. Villages of red-tile-roofed houses perch atop hills or cling precariously to the mountainsides; the Qadisha River, with its source just below the Cedars, runs along the valley bottom; and Lebanon's highest peak, Qornet as-Sawda (3090m), towers overhead. It's a truly magnificent area.

Bcharré is the main town in the Qadisha Valley. Famous as the birthplace of Kahlil Gibran and the stronghold of the right-wing

Maronite Christian Phalange party, it's a very relaxing place to spend a couple of days.

Orientation & Information
The town itself, dominated by the St Saba Church in the main street, is quite small. There are a few shops on the main street, as well as the **Blue Star Internet Cafe & Bar** *(open 8am-4am daily)*, which has access for LL4000 per hour.

Gibran Museum متحف جبران
Fans of the famous poet and artist Kahlil Gibran (1883–1931) will no doubt love this museum *(☎ 671 137; adult/student LL3000/ 2000; open 9am-5pm daily, closed Mon Nov-Mar)*. In keeping with his wishes, Gibran, who emigrated to the USA in the 19th century and published his most famous work, *The Prophet*, in 1923, was buried in a 19th-century monastery built into the rocky slopes of a hill overlooking Bcharré. The museum, which has been set up in this monastery, houses a large collection of Gibran's paintings, drawings and gouaches, and also some of his manuscripts. His coffin is in the monastery's former chapel, which is cut straight into the rock. The views of the valley from the museum's terrace are quite amazing.

Cedars of Bcharré بشرى الأرز
From Bcharré the road climbs around 4km along a tortuous road to the last remaining forest of biblical cedars in Lebanon. Known locally as Arz ar-Rab (Cedars of the Lord), they are on the slopes of Jebel Makmel at an altitude of more than 2000m. It's a small forest, as the cedar tree, which once covered most of Lebanon's high summits, has been overexploited throughout the centuries. The forest is classified as a national monument; in good weather, it's possible to walk through it for LL2000 (closed Monday). A taxi from outside the St Saba Church in Bcharré costs LL7500/15,000 one way/return.

Skiing
Near the Cedars is the eponymous ski resort *(☎ 671 073; open 8.30am-4pm daily during ski season)*, which is open in winter for both downhill and cross-country skiing. On weekends a full day costs US$23, while weekdays are cheaper at US$17. There are ski-hire shops and accommodation in the village below the forest.

Qadisha Grotto مغارة قاديشا

This small grotto (admission LL4000; open 8am-5pm daily June until first snow) extends about 500m into the mountain and has some great limestone formations. Though not as extraordinary as Jeita Grotto, its spectacular setting makes it well worth a visit. The grotto is a 7km walk from Bcharré; to get there follow the signs to the L'Aiglon Hotel and then take the footpath opposite. It's then a 1.5km walk to the grotto.

Places to Stay & Eat

Palace Hotel (☎/fax 671 460; singles/doubles/triples with bathroom US$37/49/59) is just below the main road, about 100m west of St Saba Church. It offers clean, basic rooms, some with views over the valley. There's also a large restaurant, which charges US$4.50 for breakfast.

Hotel Chbat (☎ 671 270, 672 672, fax 671 237; e schbat@cyberia.net.lb; Rue Gibran; singles/doubles/triples with bathroom US$72/86/97), in the upper part of Bcharré, looks like it should be in Switzerland rather than Lebanon. Its chalet-style building is geared towards accommodating large package-tour groups and has a slightly institutional feel, but all guests will find the pool, gymnasium, restaurant and large lounge welcoming. There's a restaurant and large outdoor terrace with spectacular views. Breakfast is included in the price. The owners also run a programme of guided walks through the Qadisha Valley.

Makhlouf (☎ 671 092, 672 585; uncertain opening hours) serves standard Lebanese fast food and has tables on an outdoor terrace overlooking the valley. The only place in town to get a budget meal, it's on the main street opposite the local school.

Restaurant River Roc (☎ 671 169; mezze LL2000, grills LL7000; open 11am-10pm daily) is an enormous place with an outdoor terrace commanding great views of the Qadisha Valley. Unfortunately, the food doesn't quite live up to the setting. It's on the road to Tripoli at the entrance to town, among a number of similar establishments.

Getting There & Away

The bus and service-taxi stop is outside the St Saba Church in the centre of town. For details about getting to Bcharré from Tripoli and from Bcharré to Baalbek see Getting There & Away under Tripoli earlier in this section.

South of Beirut

SIDON (SAIDA) صيدا
☎ 07

Sidon is a small port city, set amid citrus orchards and banana groves 45km south of Beirut. It's a very old settlement, going back 6000 years, and was once a prominent and wealthy Phoenician city. Like other Phoenician capitals, Sidon was built on a promontory facing an island to shelter its fleet. It had a succession of invaders, from the Persians to the Greeks, the Romans, the Byzantines, the Arabs (who gave it the name Saida), the Crusaders and the Mamluks. With its charming Crusader Sea Castle and its fine mosques, khans and vaulted souqs, it is one of the most attractive and historically significant towns in Lebanon. Easily visited on a day tour from Beirut, it should be high on every traveller's 'must-see' list.

Orientation & Information

The centre of town is around Saahat an-Nejmeh, where you'll find the bus and service-taxi stands, the municipality building and the police station. Rue Riad as-Solh, which runs south off Saahat an-Nejmeh (a huge roundabout), has banks, moneychangers, travel agencies etc. The old city, the harbour, the Sea Castle and the one hotel are west of Saahat an-Nejmeh and Rue Riad as-Solh, while the city's modern shopping centres and residential buildings are to the east.

There's no tourist information office in town, but the Audi Foundation (see Soap Museum later) provides free maps of the old city that have directions to many of Sidon's heritage buildings.

Most of the banks along Rue Riad as-Solh have ATMs, but neither they nor any of the moneychangers in town will change travellers cheques.

The post office is on Rue Riad as-Solh. To get there, walk north from Saahat an-Nejmeh towards the green mosque; it's a bit further down.

PC Net (☎ 03-464 985; open 24hr daily), further down from the post office, is the best Internet café in town, with access for LL2000 per hour.

The Old City

Old Sidon is behind the buildings fronting the harbour, just across from the wharf. It's a fascinating labyrinth of vaulted souqs, tiny alleyways and old buildings dating back to the Middle Ages.

In the **souqs** you'll find shops selling everything from electrical appliances to orange water; you'll also see craftspeople – many of whom live above their stalls – at work. There seem to be discoveries around each corner and visitors should make sure they devote at least a few hours to exploring every nook and cranny.

Highlights include the **Khan al-Franj** (Inn of the Foreigners), a graceful limestone khan built by Fakhreddine (Fakhr ad-Din al-Maan II) in the 17th century. Beautifully restored, it consists of vaulted galleries surrounding a large rectangular courtyard with a central fountain. Just behind the Khan al-Franj is the **Bab as-Saray Mosque**, the oldest in Sidon, dating from 1201. Another gem is the **Debbané Palace**, entered via a tall unmarked staircase directly opposite a jewellery shop with a large yellow sign in the shape of a ring. This Ottoman building, with its inner courtyard, *iwan* (vaulted hall, opening into a central court) and *qa'a* (reception room) with fountain, has intricate Mamluk decoration, including inlays and wooden ceilings, and is well worth a visit. Both buildings have free admission and inconsistent opening hours.

Further inside the old city is the **Great Mosque al-Omari**, a beautiful building with vaulted prayer areas surrounding a central courtyard. It is said to be one of the finest examples of Islamic religious architecture of the 13th century and was constructed around a church built by the Crusaders. Severely damaged by the Israeli bombings of 1982, it underwent a long restoration and was awarded the Aga Khan Architecture Prize in 1989.

Sea Castle

Built by the Crusaders in the early 13th century, the Sea Castle *(Qasr al-Bahr; admission LL4000; open 9am-6pm daily, closes earlier in winter)* sits on a small island that was formerly the site of a temple to Melkart, the Phoenician Hercules. It is connected to the mainland by an Arab fortified stone bridge (of a later date). One of many coastal castles built by the Crusaders, like many others it was largely destroyed by the Mamluks to prevent the Crusaders from returning to the region. Fortunately, its substantial renovation was ordered by Fakhreddine II in the 17th century.

Soap Museum

Who would have thought that soap, a mundane product that we all take for granted, would provide the subject matter for such an interesting museum? In a complex housing an old soap factory, the Audi family's residence and typical dwellings of the old city built in different periods, this museum *(☎ 733 353; Rue al-Moutran; admission free; open 9am-6pm Sat-Thur)*, funded by the Audi Foundation, proves that soap and style can be synonymous. An interesting display and interpretive installation, along with extremely helpful multilingual staff, make for a totally satisfying museum experience.

Echmoun

About 5km northeast of Sidon, Echmoun *(admission free; open 7.30am-sunset daily)* is Lebanon's only Phoenician site with more than just foundations. There are temple remains and lots of mosaics, though most are damaged. The temple complex to Echmoun, god of the city of Sidon, was begun in the 7th century BC and other buildings were added later by the Persians, Romans and Byzantines. The temples clearly catered for plenty of worshippers, as testified by the row of ancient shops. The highlight of the site is the throne of Astarte, guarded by winged lions.

From Sidon you can take a taxi to the site for LL5000 or get a service taxi (LL1000) or minibus (LL500) to the turn-off on the highway at the funfair and then walk the 1.5km past orchards to the ruins.

Places to Stay & Eat

Hotel d'Orient *(☎ 720 364; Rue Shakrieh; singles/doubles US$15/20)* is dirty, rundown and spectacularly overpriced for what it offers; the only reason we mention it here is that it's the one hotel in Sidon. You'll find it above a shop selling toiletries and kitchenware a couple of minutes' walk towards the harbour from the soap museum, not far from the Muslim cemetery in the old city. It's a bit hard to spot, so look out for the red 'Orient Hotel' banner on a 1st-floor balcony across the road from Pizza Abu al-Ezz.

There are lots of sandwich stalls and cheap cafés around Saahat an-Nejmeh and the harbour. A good choice is **Abou Rami**, a felafel shop opposite the Sea Castle.

Next to the Bab as-Saray Mosque is an atmospheric café that serves large glasses of fresh juice for LL2000.

To sample *sanioura*, the crumbly biscuit that's a speciality of Sidon, try **Patisserie Kanaan** (☎ 729 104; open 6am-11pm daily). It's on Saahat an-Nejmeh and is a good place for a rest and a cup of coffee.

The best place for a meal in Sidon is undoubtedly **The Rest House** (☎ 722 469; mezze LL4000, grills LL8500; open 11am-11pm). On the seafront overlooking the Sea Castle, it has indoor and outdoor eating areas and serves good Lebanese food.

Getting There & Away

From/To Beirut Buses and service taxis from Beirut to Sidon leave from the Cola bus station. To Sidon, OCFTC buses (LL750, one hour, every 10 minutes from 6am to 8pm daily) leave from the southwest side of the Cola roundabout. There is also an express bus service to Sidon (LL1500, 40 minutes, every 20 minutes from 7am to 8pm daily). Minibuses to Sidon cost LL1000 and service taxis, which congregate near the buses, cost LL2500.

Luxury coaches leave Sidon for Beirut (LL1500, 40 minutes, every 20 minutes from 6am to 6.30pm daily) from the Lebanese Transport Office on Saahat an-Nejmeh; OCFTC buses (LL750, one hour, every 10 minutes from 5am to 6.30pm) also leave from here.

To Tyre The bus from Sidon to Tyre (LL750, one hour, every 20 to 30 minutes from 6am to 6pm daily) leaves from the Lebanese Transport Office at the southern end of the town on Rue Fakhreddine, the continuation of Rue Riad as-Solh, near the Castle of St Louis. A service taxi from Sidon to Tyre costs LL3000 and a minibus (leaving from Saahat an-Nejmeh) costs LL1000.

TYRE (SOUR)   صور
☎ 07

Like much of the predominantly Shiite south, Tyre, 81km from Beirut, has traditionally suffered neglect at the hands of Beirut's Maronite power brokers. It suf-

fered dreadfully during the civil war and Israeli incursions, and seems to emanate an aura of barely restrained resentment mixed with resignation and sadness. Travellers may not feel as comfortable here as in the rest of Lebanon, but it's quite safe, and the extraordinary Roman sites of Al-Bass and Al-Mina make it well worth a visit.

History

Tyre's origins are still being investigated by historians. According to Herodotus, the city was already 2300 years old when he wrote his histories, which dates it back to approximately 2750 BC. Ruled by the Egyptians and then the famous King Hiram, who sent cedar wood and skilled workers to Jerusalem so that the Hebrew king Solomon could build the temple of Jerusalem, it prospered. Later colonised by the Assyrians, Neo-Babylonians, Greeks, Seleucids, Romans (it was the capital of the Roman province of Syria-Phoenicia), Byzantines, Arabs, Crusaders, Mamluks and Ottomans, it lost much of its early profile and prosperity. Today, it is home to a number of squatter settlements and Palestinian refugee camps and is trying to rebuild its economy and infrastructure and regain its position as one of Lebanon's major cities.

Orientation & Information

The old part of Tyre is on the peninsula jutting out into the sea and covers a relatively small area. The modern town is on the left-hand side as you arrive from Beirut. The coastal route goes all the way to Tyre's picturesque old port, around which are a few cafés and restaurants. Behind the port is the Christian quarter, with its tiny alleys and old houses behind shaded courtyards.

To the left of the port the road forks southwards and goes around the excavation site of one of the Roman archaeological sites. There are several streets running parallel between the northern and southern coastal roads, and that's where you'll find banks, moneychangers, sandwich stalls, travel agencies and the souq.

There's no tourist information office in Tyre and the only guidebooks to the archaeological sites on offer in town and at the sites themselves are in Arabic. A brochure with information on the sites and basic map of the city is available at the tourist information office in Beirut.

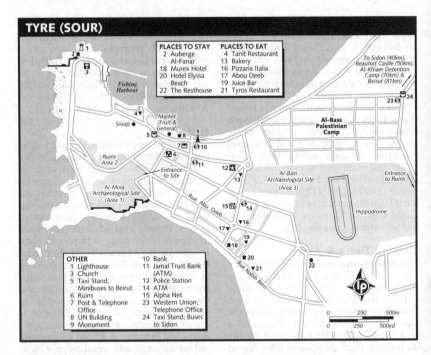

TYRE (SOUR)

PLACES TO STAY
2 Auberge Al-Fanar
18 Murex Hotel
20 Hotel Elyssa Beach
22 The Resthouse

PLACES TO EAT
4 Tanit Restaurant
13 Bakery
16 Pizzaria Italia
17 Abou Deeb
19 Juice Bar
21 Tyros Restaurant

To Sidon (40km), Beaufort Castle (50km), Al-Khiam Detention Camp (70km) & Beirut (81km)

Fishing Harbour

Souqs

Market (Fruit & General)

Ruins Area 2

Entrance to Site

Al-Mina Archaeological Site (Area 1)

Rue Abu Deeb

Al-Bass Palestinian Camp

Al-Bass Archaeological Site (Area 3)

Entrance to Ruins

Hippodrome

Rue Nabih Berri

OTHER
1 Lighthouse
3 Church
5 Taxi Stand; Minibuses to Beirut
6 Ruins
7 Post & Telephone Office
8 UN Building
9 Monument
10 Bank
11 Jamal Trust Bank (ATM)
12 Police Station
14 ATM
15 Alpha Net
23 Western Union; Telephone Office
24 Taxi Stand; Buses to Sidon

0   250   500m
0   250   500yd

Alpha Net (☎ 347 047; open 10am-1am daily) is just north of the main roundabout on Rue Abu Dib and is the best place in town for Internet access at LL3000 per hour. Banks with ATMs and the **post office/telephone bureau** are near the service-taxi stand in the town centre.

Roman Ruins

The excavated ruins at Tyre, listed as a World Heritage site by Unesco, are in three parts. The **Al-Mina excavations** (Area 1; adult/student/child LL6000/3500/3500; open 8.30am-30 mins before sunset daily) is a large site leading down to the ancient Egyptian harbour. It features colonnades, public baths, Roman and Byzantine mosaics and an unusual rectangular arena.

The second site, known as Area 2, is a five-minute walk to the north of the first site. It is fenced off and closed to the public, but you can see the ruins of a **Crusader cathedral**, including massive granite columns, from the road.

The **Al-Bass site** (Area 3; adult/student/child LL6000/3500/3500; open 8.30am-30 mins before sunset daily) has a well-preserved Roman road made of big blocks of paving stones and lined in many parts with marble columns. The road stretches in a straight line for about 1.6km, passing through a monumental archway. It's lined on one side by an aqueduct, and on both sides there are hundreds of ornate stone and marble sarcophagi of the Roman and Byzantine periods which are intricately carved with the names of the occupants or reliefs drawn from the *Iliad*. There's also a U-shaped **hippodrome** built in the 2nd century AD for chariot racing. One of the largest of the Roman period, it had a capacity for more than 20,000 spectators.

Places to Stay & Eat

Auberge al-Fanar (☎ 741 111, fax 740 111; e salwalid@inco.com.lb; double with bathroom US$40) is an annexe of the overpriced and to-be-avoided restaurant near the lighthouse. Its shabby and overpriced rooms are in the owner's home. There's also a more-expensive double room (US$50) with sea views. Prices include breakfast and are US$10 cheaper from October to May.

Hotel Elyssa Beach (☎/fax 347 551; singles/doubles with bathroom US$45/50,

LEBANON

with bathroom & TV US$55/60) is on the southern side of the peninsula. The rooms, decorated with matching psychedelic curtains and bedspreads, are clean though basic. All have air-con and balcony. There's a great communal lounge and a restaurant (only in the summer months). All rooms are $10 cheaper from October to May.

Murex Hotel (☎ 347 111, fax 347 222; Rue Nabih Berri; e info@murexhotel.com; singles/doubles/suites with bathroom & balcony US$77/94/143) offers well-appointed, if slightly cramped, rooms in a newly constructed building. The management is very helpful, there's a restaurant, the price includes breakfast and generous discounts are offered from October to May.

The Rest House (☎ 740 667/8, fax 345 163; e info@resthouse-tyr.com.lb; doubles/suites with bathroom US$98/135 Mon-Thur, US$256/311 Fri-Sun) is a light and airy luxury hotel with a private beach, pool, health club, bakery, restaurant and bar. It's popular with wealthy Beirutis on weekends, hence the over-the-top prices. Breakfast is included and rooms are half price from October to May.

Put simply, Tyre is a wasteland when it comes to food. There are a few fast-food places at the roundabout on Rue Abou Deeb, including **Abou Deeb**, which serves good felafels and shwarmas, and **Pizzaria Italia**, which serves up pizza from LL4000. Close by are a number of juice bars where a large fresh juice will set you back LL2000 or so.

Tyros Restaurant (☎ 741 027; Rue Nabih Berri; mezze LL4000, grills LL6000; open 24hr daily) is an enormous, tent-like place that's extremely popular with locals. It's got a great atmosphere, though the ambience and reasonably cheap prices don't really mitigate the unimpressive food on offer.

Tanit Restaurant (☎ 740 987; mezze LL4000, grills LL15,000; open 24hr daily except for one month over Ramadan) serves the best food in town, including some Chinese-style dishes. It's a small, friendly place that's very popular with the local Unifil staff. If you don't want to eat, the owner is happy for you to sit at the bar and have a drink or two while watching the satellite TV.

Getting There & Away
No buses or express coaches travel directly to Tyre from Beirut; all passengers must travel

via Sidon. For information about getting to Tyre by bus see Getting There & Away under Sidon earlier in this section. The first bus from Tyre to Sidon (LL750, one hour) leaves daily from the roundabout near the entrance to the Al-Bass site at 6am and the last at 8pm.

A service taxi from Beirut (Cola) costs LL5500 and from Sidon LL3000. Minibuses leave from the Cola transport hub in Beirut and cost LL2000; from Sidon they're LL1000. The service-taxi and minibus stand is about 50m before the port on the northern coastal road.

CHOUF MOUNTAINS   جبال الشوف
These spectacular mountains, just southeast of Beirut, are the southern part of the Mt Lebanon Range. In some parts they're wild and beautiful; in others they're dotted with small villages and terraced for easy cultivation. Olives, apples and grapes, the major crops, are fed by numerous springs and wells. A day trip to see the Chouf village of Deir al-Qamar and the nearby Beiteddine Palace should be high on every traveller's itinerary.

Beiteddine Palace (Beit ad-Din)
بيت الدين
The main attraction in the Chouf is the **Beiteddine Palace** (Beit ad-Din; ☎ 05-500 078; adult/student LL7500/5000; open 9am-6pm Tues-Sun Jun-Sept, 9am-4pm Oct-May), 50km southeast of Beirut. Sitting majestically atop a terraced hill and surrounded by terraced gardens and orchards, the palace was built by Emir Bashir over a period of 30 years, starting in 1788. Its name means 'House of Faith' and it was built over and around a Druze hermitage. During the French mandate the palace was used for local administration, but after 1930 it was declared an historic monument and placed under the care of the Department of Antiquities, which set about restoring it. In 1943 it became the official summer residence of the president. The palace was extensively damaged during the Israeli invasion; it's estimated that up to 90% of the original contents were lost during this period. When fighting ended in 1984, it was taken over by the Druze militia, led by Walid Jumblatt. Jumblatt ordered its restoration and declared it be a 'Palace of the People'. In 1999 the Druze handed it back to the government.

LEBANON

The Scars of War

The withdrawal of the Israeli armed forces and their Lebanese militia, the South Lebanon Army (SLA), from the south of Lebanon on 25 May 2000 was occasion for great rejoicing throughout Lebanon. Indeed, the government declared a public holiday – the Day of Resistance and Liberation – to mark its significance. A visit to the area formerly occupied by the Israelis will make all travellers appreciate just how great a cause for celebration the withdrawal was for the Lebanese people, particularly those living in the south, and is one of the most rewarding – if upsetting – experiences to be had during any visit to Lebanon.

A drive through the area's innumerable small villages is a sobering experience due to the presence of myriad multicoloured billboards featuring portraits of young local men 'martyred' during the occupation. The landscape itself is spectacular, and the two highlights of the region are undoubtedly the Al-Khiam Detention Camp and Beaufort Castle. Don't miss either.

The **Al-Khiam Detention Camp** (*admission free; open daily, hours vary*) is a notorious hilltop prison that was run by the SLA during the occupation. When the Israeli army withdrew in May 2000, the SLA guards fled and the local population flooded in to rescue the remaining 140 prisoners. The prison is now run as a museum by Hezbollah (Party of God) and a visit is a truly shocking experience. The totally appalling conditions provide a stark reminder of the horror of the invasion – the conditions before the Red Cross was allowed to inspect the centre in 1995 almost beggar belief – and the minimal but eloquent interpretation (innumerable signs denoting where prisoners were 'martyred') is extremely moving. This place truly redefines one's understanding of what a museum can be.

Beaufort Castle (*The Beaufort Outpost; admission free; always open*) is an isolated and windswept military outpost. Its craggy and weathered exterior, perched atop one of the highest ridges in the area, can be seen from miles away. Fought over by almost every invading army to pass through the area over the past 1000 years, and most recently occupied by the Israelis, it was most probably built in three stages by the Byzantines, Arabs and Crusaders. Not much of the castle remains, but it's possible to climb up a stone path to the very top of the structure and enjoy extraordinary views over Lebanon, Syria and Israel.

There's no public transport to this part of Lebanon, but it's possible to hire a taxi from Tyre for a half or full day. A five-hour trip should cost around LL60,000, but you'll have to haggle to get this price.

Warning

The security situation in this part of Lebanon changes constantly. Before embarking on a visit, travellers should read the *Daily Star* to keep abreast of the current situation and, if worried, contact either their national embassy or Unifil in Beirut for advice. Travellers should also be aware that one of the many unfortunate legacies of the years of warfare is the innumerable land mines and unexploded ordnance scattered throughout the countryside in this part of Lebanon. Make sure you don't walk anywhere off well-worn paths or sealed roads and if you see any suspicious objects in the landscape, be sure not to touch them.

Although conceived by Italian architects, the palace incorporates all the traditional forms of Arab architecture. The gate opens onto a vast, 60m-wide courtyard (Dar al-Baraniyyeh) walled on three sides only; the fourth side has great views out over valleys and hills.

A double staircase on the western side leads into a smaller central courtyard (Dar al-Wousta) with a central fountain. Beyond this courtyard is the third – and last – courtyard (Dar al-Harim). This was the centre of the family quarters, which also included a beautiful *hammam* and huge kitchens. Both these courtyard areas contain vast, vaulted rooms decorated and paved with multicoloured marble or mosaics and richly decorated doorways with exquisite calligraphic inscriptions.

Underneath the Dar al-Wousta and Dar al-Harim are the former stables, now home to an extraordinary collection of **Byzantine mosaics** dating from the 5th and 6th centuries. These were found at Jiyyeh, 30km south of

Beirut, and were brought to Beiteddine in 1982 by Walid Jumblatt. Don't miss them.

There is no information available at the entrance so it's worth picking up a free brochure at Beirut's tourist information office beforehand. Guided tours are available (price negotiable).

The palace hosts an annual music festival in July. See Special Events in the Facts for the Visitor section earlier in this chapter for more details.

Places to Stay & Eat On the hill overlooking both the palace and the village of Beiteddine is the **Mir Amin Palace** (☎ 05-501 315/6/7/8; e miramin@cyberia.net.lb; singles/doubles/junior suite with bathroom US$204/242/358), which was built by Emir Bashir for his eldest son. It is now one of the most beautiful and luxurious hotels in Lebanon, with 22 rooms, a swimming pool, three restaurants and spectacular views over the hills and valleys. Even if you don't stay here, make sure you stop for a drink or meal. Prices from the end of September to the end of March (except Christmas and New Year) are discounted by as much as 40%, making it a real bargain.

There's nowhere to stay in Beiteddine village, and very few places to eat. Travellers should either splurge on a meal at the Mir Amin or grab a felafel or shwarma at one of the fast-food places on Deir al-Qamar's main square (see the following entry).

Deir al-Qamar ﺩﻳﺮ ﺍﻟﻘﻤﺮ

This picturesque town, 5km downhill from Beiteddine, was the seat of Lebanon's emirate during the 17th and 18th centuries. The main square has some fine examples of Arab architecture, including the **Mosque of Fakhreddine** built in 1493; a **silk khan** built in 1595 that now houses the French Cultural Centre and can be visited; and **Fakhreddine's Palace**, built in 1620 and now functioning as an underwhelming wax museum.

There's nowhere to stay in Deir al-Qamar and few places to eat. Those on offer are around the main square or at the entrance (Beirut side) to town.

Getting There & Away

Buses leave Cola at regular intervals for the Chouf Mountains. Travellers wanting to visit Beiteddine should go to the northwest junc-

tion of the big roundabout at Cola (look for the derelict building) and ask for the bus to Niha (LL1500, 90 minutes, every hour from 8.15am until early evening). On the bus, tell the driver you're going to Beiteddine; you'll be dropped off at a roundabout with a statue of two soldiers with rifles. Take the road opposite the Al-Dalwa restaurant and walk approximately 200m (don't take the first turn right). A bit further on and around a bend is the road leading to the Mir Amin Palace Hotel, and from there it's a short walk downhill to Beiteddine. All up, the walk should take 15 minutes. From Beiteddine, it's a 6km downhill walk to Deir al-Qamar. (A service taxi from Beiteddine to Deir al-Qamar costs LL2000.) If this all sounds too complicated, you can pay LL5000 for a service taxi direct from Cola to Beiteddine.

Travellers wanting to go to Deir al-Qamar first can catch the No 18 OCFTC bus from Cola to Damour and then a service taxi from Damour (LL2000). A service taxi from Cola to Deir al-Qamar costs LL4000.

Travellers should note that service taxis on the Beirut–Deir al-Qamar route travel reasonably infrequently, and rarely after dark.

The Bekaa Valley
ﻭﺍﺩﻱ ﺍﻟﺒﻘﺎﻉ

A high plateau between the Mt Lebanon and the Anti-Lebanon Ranges, the Bekaa Valley is famous for its magnificent archaeological sites at Baalbek and Aanjar and for the fact that it is the base of Hezbollah (Party of God). Heavily cultivated over millennia (it was one of Rome's 'breadbaskets'), it's now deforested and not as fertile as it was, leading to a greater degree of poverty than is the case in other parts of the country. A drive through can be depressing due to this and to the fact that Lebanese disregard for the environment has led to the entire valley being littered with plastic bags and other rubbish.

The major transport hub in the valley is the town of Chtaura, on the Beirut to Damascus Hwy.

ZAHLÉ ﺯﺣﻠﻪ
☎ 08

Zahlé is known within Lebanon for its open-air, riverside eateries and general holiday feel. Very busy during the hot weather, it's like a ghost town in winter and is really not worth a visit from November to April, when most of its restaurants are closed. In summer, it makes a nice lunch stop en route from Beirut to Baalbek, and is a good place to stay if you intend to spend a few days exploring the valley.

Information

Most of the town's banks, ATMs and exchange bureaus are on Rue Brazil, the main street. There's nowhere in town to change travellers cheques.

The **tourist information office** (☎ 802 566, fax 803 595; open 8.30am-1.30pm Mon-Sat) is signposted about 1km from the highway turn-off and is on the 3rd floor of the Chamber of Commerce building, just off Rue Brazil.

Dataland Internet (☎ 814 825; Rue Brazil; open 8am-midnight daily) offers online access for LL3000 per hour. You'll find it opposite the clock tower.

The **post office** (Rue Brazil) is about 750m from the highway turn-off on the right-hand side.

Places to Stay & Eat

Hotel Akl (☎ 820 701; Rue Brazil; singles/doubles US$17/20, doubles/triples with bathroom US$33/40) is the best budget choice in town. In a dilapidated but character-filled old house, its clean rooms have balconies and loads of natural light. The rooms at the rear overlook the river. There's a large communal lounge with TV and piano and the manager is very helpful.

Arabi Hotel (☎ 821 214, fax 812 445; e sarabi@inco.com.lb; singles/doubles US$55/ 66 Apr-Oct, closed Nov-Mar) is right at the heart of the outdoor eating scene on the Bardouni River, making its rooms quite noisy. The price includes breakfast. Its attached **restaurant** is one of the most famous in Zahlé; a meal of mezze on its outdoor terrace (meals US$20 to US$40) is a wonderful way to spend an afternoon or evening.

Hotel Monte Alberto (☎ 810 912/3/4, fax 801 451; e info@montealberto.com; doubles/ triples with bathroom US$55/66) is located high above town and commands amazing views. Management recently installed a funicular, making it easy for guests to travel between the town and the hotel. Its rooms don't

have too many frills but they're clean and comfortable and the price includes breakfast. There's also an enormous **restaurant** with outdoor terrace serving up mezze feasts with the best views in town for around US$15 to US$25 per person including drinks.

Grand Hotel Kadri (☎ 813 920, fax 803 314; e info@kadrihotel.com; Rue Brazil; singles/doubles/suite with bathroom US$132/ 158/202) is huge, classy and expensive. It advertises itself as being at 'the throbbing heart' of Rue Brazil and, like all the hotels along this strip, can be noisy on summer nights. There is a 50% discount in winter and a special US$65 double weekend package rate (though not during July/August or the Christmas, New Year and Eid breaks). Prices include breakfast and hotel facilities include a health club, tennis court, nightclub and four restaurants.

Getting There & Away

Minibuses from Beirut to Zahlé (LL2000, 90 minutes) leave from the southwest side of the roundabout at the Cola transport hub. Service taxis (LL5000) leave from the same spot. Both will drop you off at the highway turn-off, which is over 1km from the centre of town. If you want to be dropped at the centre of town, you'll need to get off at Chtaura (LL2000, one hour) and catch a service taxi (LL1000); specify that you want to be dropped in town and not at the highway turn-off.

To get to Baalbek from Zahlé by government bus, take the OCFTC bus No 4 or 5 (LL500, 30 minutes) from the bus stop just below the car park midway along Rue Brazil. A service taxi to Baalbek will cost LL2000 and take around 30 minutes; you'll find one at the main taxi stand on a square off Rue Brazil.

BAALBEK   بعلبك
☎ 08

The town of Baalbek, 86km northeast of Beirut, was originally named after the Phoenician god Baal. The Greeks later called it Heliopolis, or City of the Sun, and the Romans made it a major worship site for their god Jupiter. The remains of their temples, sited against the backdrops of the majestic Mt Lebanon and Anti-Lebanon Ranges, constitute one of the Middle East's most spectacular archaeological sites and should be on the itinerary of every visitor to Lebanon.

Each July, Lebanon's most famous arts festival is held here. See Special Events in the Facts for the Visitor section earlier in this chapter for more details.

Orientation & Information

The town of Baalbek is small and thus easily explored on foot. The main road, Rue Abdel Halim Hajjar, is the one by which you'll enter town if travelling from Zahlé or Beirut. You'll see the Roman ruins on your left-hand side and the Palmyra Hotel across the road on your right. It's also the street on which you'll find the town's two banks, a few fast-food places and the Al-Shams Hotel. Rue Abdel Halim Hajjar intersects with the other main road, Ras al-Ain Blvd, where you'll find the Pension Shouman, more fast-food places, the service-taxi office and riverside restaurants.

The **Jamal Bank** has an ATM, and there's another ATM next to the Palmyra Hotel, but there's nowhere in town to cash travellers cheques and none of the hotels or restaurants accept credit cards.

Network Center *(open 8am-2am daily)* is the only place in town offering Internet access (LL3000 per hour). It's up a side street near the Palmyra Hotel.

Places to Stay & Eat

Al-Shams Hotel *(☎ 373 284; Rue Abdel Halim Hajjar; bed in 5-bed room US$6, bed in 2-bed or 3-bed room US$6)* has three very basic rooms with washbasins. Beds are uncomfortable and the overall impression is dusty. There's a shared toilet and shower. Enter via a stone staircase next to the mobile-phone shop; the hotel is on the 1st floor.

Pension Shouman *(☎ 370 160; Ras al-Ain Blvd; dorm beds/doubles/doubles in 3-bed room LL10,000/20,000/25,000)* is close to the ruins and three of its rooms enjoy great views. There are hard beds and a simple-but-clean shared bathroom. Enter via a stone staircase; the pension is on the 1st floor.

Hotel Jupiter *(☎ 376 715, 370 151; Rue Abdel Halim Hajjar; singles/doubles/triples with bathroom US$10/20/25)* is the new kid on the Baalbek hotel block. Entered via an arcade next to Restaurant Chich Kabab near the Palmyra Hotel, it has large rooms off a central courtyard. These are light and all have

fans. The helpful owner, who seems to run half the small businesses in town, is always happy to have a chat and provide directions.

Palmyra Hotel *(☎ 376 101/2/3, 370 011, fax 370 305; Rue Abdel Halim Hajjar; singles/doubles/triples with bathroom US$40/ 56/66)* is one of those wonderful colonial-era relics that dot the Middle East. Opposite the ruins on the right-hand side of the road at the entrance to town, it's set in shady gardens and has rooms with balconies overlooking the ruins. The hotel has a bar and restaurant, but be warned: when we were there, the food was dreadful. Breakfast costs US$5 per person.

Those not keen on the Gothic house-of-horrors atmosphere at the Palmyra may feel more comfortable at its new, beautiful **extension** a few doors down. Rooms are slightly more expensive (US$75), but are lavishly furnished and have ultracomfortable beds. The only drawbacks are that the hot-water system isn't efficient, there's no generator in case of power failure and the management isn't as gracious as one would like.

There are quite a few cheap eateries on Rue Abdel Halim Hajjar; the best is **Al Khayam Restaurant**. This small place serves absolutely delicious felafels (Ll750) and shwarma (LL1500) and has a few tables.

Further up Rue Abdel Halim Hajjar are a number of shops selling totally delicious sweets and meat pastries. One of these is **Cafeteria el-Shams**, a spotlessly clean place with tables. It serves pastries, filled rolls, sweets, coffee and tea. You'll find it on the souq side of the road.

In the summer months the **Riviera Restaurant** *(☎ 370 296; Ras al-Ain Blvd; mezze around LL2000)*, on the way to the spring, serves basic but tasty food in its outdoor eating area.

Getting There & Away

The only public-transport options from Beirut to Baalbek are minibuses and service taxis. From the Cola transport hub, a minibus to Baalbek costs LL3000 and takes two hours; a service taxi costs LL5000. Be warned that the drive over the Mt Lebanon Range can be totally hair-raising, particularly in winter. The bus stop in Baalbek is opposite the Palmyra Hotel and the service-taxi office is in the souq area.

[Continued on page 488]

LEBANON

BAALBEK

Baalbek, the 'Sun City' of the ancient world, is the most impressive ancient site in Lebanon and arguably the most impressive Roman site in the Middle East. Its temples, built on an extravagant scale that outshone anything in Rome, enjoyed a reputation as one of the wonders of the world. Today, the World Heritage–listed site is Lebanon's number-one tourism attraction.

In the car park near the ticket office there is a museum with a voluminous amount of information about the history of Baalbek in English, French, German and Arabic. The chronology of the information is a little unclear but it's definitely worth spending a while wandering through. At the corner of the Temple of Bacchus there is another museum, housed in the 15th-century tower added by the Mamluks. Entrance to both museums is included in the cost of entrance to the site.

The best time to visit the site is early morning, when there are few people around. Allow a few hours to wander through the museum and the ruins and consider taking food and drink with you as there is none

Inset: Detail of a carving among the ruins (Photo by Bethune Carmichael)

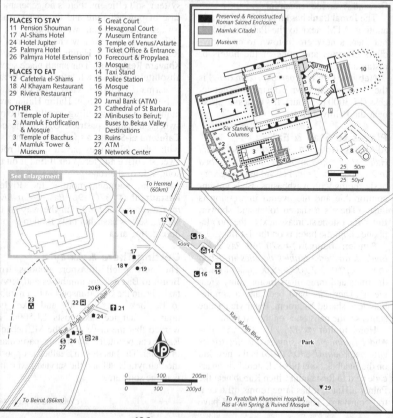

BAALBEK

PLACES TO STAY
11 Pension Shouman
17 Al-Shams Hotel
24 Hotel Jupiter
25 Palmyra Hotel
26 Palmyra Hotel Extension

PLACES TO EAT
12 Cafeteria el-Shams
18 Al Khayam Restaurant
29 Riviera Restaurant

OTHER
1 Temple of Jupiter
2 Mamluk Fortification & Mosque
3 Temple of Bacchus
4 Mamluk Tower & Museum

5 Great Court
6 Hexagonal Court
7 Museum Entrance
8 Temple of Venus/Astarte
9 Ticket Office & Entrance
10 Forecourt & Propylaea
13 Mosque
14 Taxi Stand
15 Police Station
16 Mosque
19 Pharmacy
20 Jamal Bank (ATM)
21 Cathedral of St Barbara
22 Minibuses to Beirut; Buses to Bekaa Valley Destinations
23 Ruins
27 ATM
28 Network Center

Preserved & Reconstructed Roman Sacred Enclosure
Mamluk Citadel
Museum

Six Standing Columns

0   25   50m
0   25   50yd

See Enlargement

To Hermel (60km)

11
12
13
Souq
14
17
18   19
16
15

20
23
22   24
21
25   26
27   28

Rue Abdel Halim Hajjar

To Beirut (86km)

Ras al-Ain Blvd

Park

0   100   200m
0   100   200yd

To Ayatollah Khomeini Hospital, Ras al-Ain Spring & Ruined Mosque

29

BETHUNE CARMICHAEL

available at the site. Guides can be organised at the ticket office and cost US$14 for one hour. A ticket to the site costs LL12,000 for adults. Student tickets are meant to be available for LL7000, though readers have reported that this is not always the case. Children under eight years are admitted at no cost. The site is open daily from 8am until 30 minutes before sunset (3.30pm in winter).

The Site

From the ticket office, you'll enter the ruins via a monumental staircase leading up to the propylaea. Next to this is the hexagonal court, where a raised threshold separates the propylaea from the sacred enclosure. Beyond this is the Great Court, or Sacrificial Courtyard, which leads to the remains of the Temple of Jupiter. This temple was originally completed around AD 60, and its remaining six columns are a massive, spectacular and oft-photographed reminder of the size and majesty of the original structure.

TRUDI CANAVAN

Adjacent to the Temple of Jupiter is the Temple of Bacchus, known in Roman times as the 'small temple'. This was, in fact, dedicated to Venus/Astarte rather than to Bacchus. Completed around AD 150, it's amazingly well preserved and gives a whole new meaning to the word 'small'. Its features include an ornately decorated interior, a monumental doorway and a portico with columns supporting a rich entablature with a frieze depicting lions and bulls. On this is a ceiling of curved stone decorated with scenes of gods and goddesses.

When you leave the site, check out the exquisite Temple of Venus near the entrance. It's closed to visitors but you can have a good look by wandering around the perimeter fence.

Top: Splendid even in ruins, the Temple of Bacchus

Right: Bronze statue from the Temple of Jupiter

[Continued from page 485]

For information about how to get to Baalbek from Zahlé, see Getting There & Away under Zahlé earlier in this section.

For information about how to get to Baalbek from Tripoli or Bcharré, see Getting There & Away under Tripoli earlier in this chapter.

AANJAR عنجر

Lebanon's best-preserved Islamic archaeological site *(admission LL6000; open 8am-sunset daily)*, Aanjar is the only significant Umayyad site in Lebanon. It was discovered by archaeologists as recently as the 1940s and is a wonderful place to spend a day.

The Umayyads ruled briefly but energetically from AD 660–750 and Aanjar is thought to have been built by the sixth Umayyad caliph, Walid I (r. AD 705–715). It was an important inland commercial centre, located on intersecting trade routes. The walled and fortified city was built along symmetrical Roman lines; the layout is in four equal quarters, separated by two 20m-wide avenues, the cardo maximus and the decumanus maximus. There is a **tetrapylon**, a four-column structure, where the two streets intersect that is interesting due to its alternating layers of large blocks and narrow bricks, a typically Byzantine effect.

In the city's heyday, its main streets were flanked by palaces, baths, mosques, shops (600 have been uncovered) and dwellings. The remains of these can be seen today. Perhaps the most impressive remains at the site are those of the **great palace**, one wall and several arcades of which have been reconstructed.

There are no brochures or guidebooks available at the site, so it's worth picking up a copy of the free Aanjar brochure, which includes a map and details about the site, from the Zahlé or Beirut tourist information offices before you arrive. A one-hour guided tour costs US$10.

Getting There & Away

Aanjar is 15km from Chtaura on the Beirut–Damascus Hwy. You can catch a service taxi (LL1000) or a No 12 bus (LL500) from Chtaura, which will drop you at the turn-off with the 'Welcome to Aanjar' sign, leaving you with a 2km walk. Take the road on the left-hand side, walk for approximately 10 minutes and turn left at the road opposite the Shams and Le Soleil restaurants. Follow that road until you reach the entrance to the ruins. Alternatively, hire a taxi to take you all the way to the site from Chtaura, have the cab wait an hour while you admire the site and then return. This will cost around US$13.

Oman

Since the present sultan came to power in 1970, Oman has been treading a careful path between controlling outside influence while enjoying some of the benefits that it brings, tourism in particular. The result has been an unusually successful adoption of the best parts of the Gulf, marked by a tolerance of outside 'customs and manners', without the disappointing sacrifice of national identity that often characterises rapid modernisation. Even the casual observer will notice the obvious pride Oman takes in its long history, witnessed in the conscious maintenance of tribal customs, dress, architecture and rules of hospitality as much as in the meticulous restoration of historical monuments.

Geographically, Oman is large and diverse, with an untrammelled coastline, rugged mountains patrolled by a remarkable network of forts and castles, a share of the Empty Quarter and a unique monsoon catchment. Unfortunately, it's an expensive country for the independent traveller, particularly as a 4WD is required to visit many of the places of interest. Camping equipment can help justify the expense of hiring a 4WD by saving on costly hotels and allowing access to some of the most beautiful and unexplored parts of the Middle East. If hiring a vehicle is not an option, there are plenty of tours available from Muscat and Salalah.

Oman is not an easy destination, particularly if you are alone, on a tight budget and solely reliant on public transport, but this safe and peaceful country is sure to reward the extra effort.

Facts about Oman

HISTORY

'Renaissance' is a term any visitor to Oman is sure to hear. It refers not to some dim and distant past, however, but to the current period under the leadership of Sultan Qaboos, a leader whom much of the population holds responsible for easing the country into the modern world. Before he came to the throne, after a bloodless palace coup in 1970, there were no secondary schools in Oman and only two primary schools; there were two hospitals, run by American mis-

The Sultanate of Oman

Area: 309,500 sq km
Population: 2.4 million
Capital: Muscat
Head of State: Sultan Qaboos bin Said
Official Language: Arabic
Currency: Omani rial (OR)

- Best Dining – feasting at Friday brunch at the charismatic Al-Bustan Palace Hotel

- Best Nightlife – watching turtles nest on the beach at Ras al-Jinz

- Best Walk – wading and hiking through gorgeous Wadi Shab

- Best View – watching birds of prey spiral above Wadi Ghul, the Grand Canyon of Oman, from the top of Jebel Shams

- Best Activity – camping under the stars in the Wahiba Sands

sionaries, and a meagre 10km of sealed roads. In addition, the country was in a state of civil war. Oman has since caught up with its more affluent neighbours and it boasts universities, modern hospitals, electricity to remote villages, and an ever-improving infrastructure of roads. Furthermore, Oman is now a peaceful and stable country with an enviably low crime rate and a well-trained local workforce.

The term 'renaissance' is an appropriate one as it is suggestive of equally rich periods in Oman's long history. As far back as 5000 BC, southern Oman was the centre of the lucrative frankincense trade. This highly

OMAN

What to See

With a week to spare in Oman, bargain for *dishdashas* and gold in Muscat's **Mutrah Souq**, sip a mixed fruit juice along the Muscat's **Mutrah Corniche** and learn about whales at the **Natural History Museum**, before heading out of the capital on the coast road to Sur.

Stop to wade in **Wadi Shab** and picnic under the date palms of **Wadi Tiwi** along this wild and beautiful route. At **Sur** watch planks being nailed by hand in the dhow **boatyards** before hitting Oman's best nightlife at the famous turtle nesting site at **Ras al-Jinz**. Eat camel kebabs and fall asleep counting the stars in the **Wahiba Sands** then head back to Muscat or add in a trip to **Nizwa**, gateway to the mountains. Buy a carpet on top of **Jebel Shams**, pick petals and pomegranates on **Jebel Akhdar** or imagine Beau Geste riding into the fort at **Jabrin**.

With two weeks to spend, spot wolf traps on the stunning **mountain drive** from Nizwa to Wadi Bani Awf, dip your toe into hot springs in the fort towns of **Rustaq** and **Nakhal**, and have a martini and a snorkel at the laid-back beach resort in **Sawadi** on your return to Muscat.

With three weeks or more, go round the bend off the **Musandam Peninsula** or take a shower in the **Dhofar** drizzle if time, money and season permits.

---

prized commodity, traded for spices with India and taken by camel caravan across Arabia, grew best in the monsoon-swept hills of Dhofar. Legend maintains that the semi-mythical Queen of Sheba hand-delivered Dhofari frankincense to King Solomon.

The golden-pillared city of Ubar, built by the people of Ad, grew out of that trade to become one of the most powerful in the region. The remains of the city were rediscovered in the 1990s and the presumed descendents of that remarkable civilisation still occupy the surrounding desert, speaking a distinct and ancient language known as Jibbali.

Oman enjoyed further periods of prosperity in pre-Islamic times through the trading of copper, indeed, Oman is referred to in some sources as 'the Mountain of Copper'. Then for unknown reasons the country slipped into a long isolation that prevailed until the coming of Islam in the 7th century AD. Islam was brought to Oman by Amr ibn al-As, a disciple of the Prophet Mohammed, and Oman was quick to embrace the new faith.

For approximately 500 years, Oman came under the leadership of the Bani Nabhan dynasty (1154–1624). Frequent bouts of civil war between the sultan's forces and tribal factions left the country vulnerable to outside hostilities that eventually came in the form of the Portuguese. Alarmed by Oman's naval strength, and anxious to secure Indian Ocean trade routes, the Portuguese launched a succession of attacks against the ports of Oman; by 1507 they

managed to occupy the major coastal cities of Qalhat, Muscat and Sohar. Ironically it was a sailor from Sohar, Ahmed bin Majid, who helped Vasco de Gama navigate the Cape of Good Hope in 1498 and thereby discover the route to Oman.

For the next 150 years, Oman struggled to oust the occupying forces but it was only under the guidance of the enlightened Ya'aruba dynasty (1624–1743) that they were able to build up a big enough fleet to succeed. The Portuguese were ousted by 1650 and Oman became a settled, unified state of considerable wealth and cultural accomplishment, the influence of which extended as far as Asia and Africa. Most of Oman's great castles and forts were built during this period.

By the 19th century, under Sultan Said bin Sultan (1804–56), Oman had built up a sizeable empire, controlling strategic parts of the African coast, including Mombasa and Zanzibar. It also controlled parts of what are now India and Pakistan.

When Said died the empire was divided between two of his sons. One became the sultan of Zanzibar, and ruled the African colonies, while the other became known as the sultan of Muscat and Oman. The division of the empire cut Muscat off from some of its most lucrative domains, and by the end of the century the country had stagnated economically, not helped by British pressure to end its sizeable slave and arms trade.

The new century was marked by a rift between the coastal areas, ruled by the sultan,

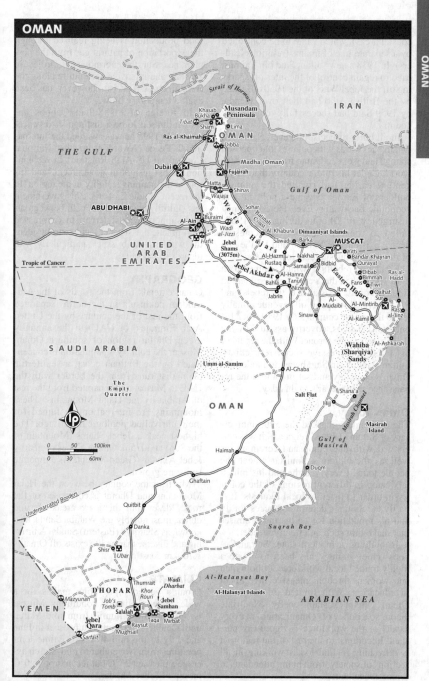

OMAN

and the interior (the name used for non-coastal areas), which came to be controlled by a separate line of imams (religious leaders). In 1938 a new sultan, Said bin Taimur, tried to regain control of the interior, sparking off the Jebel Wars of the 1950s. Backed by the British, who had their own agenda, by 1959 Said had successfully reunited the country.

In all other respects, however, Said took Oman backwards with policies that opposed change and isolated Oman from the modern world. Under his rule, a country that only a century earlier had rivalled the empire-builders of Europe became a political and economic backwater. Even the communist insurgency in Dhofar during the 1960s failed to rouse Said from his reclusive palace existence in Salalah and by the end of the decade his subjects lost patience.

Escalating rebellion (which simmered on until 1982 when the Yemeni government in Aden cut off its assistance to the rebels) and Said's refusal to spend oil revenues finally led to the palace coup in July 1970 when his only son, Qaboos, covertly assisted by the British, seized the throne. With the repeal of his father's oppressive social restrictions, Sultan Qaboos bin Said began to modernise Oman's economy and set in motion the renaissance that prevails to this day.

Oman Today

The millennium marked the 30th anniversary of Sultan Qaboos' reign and it was celebrated with due pomp and ceremony as well as the Sultan's familiar 'meet the people tour'. Every year he and his ministers camp in different regions of the country in order to listen to local requests. It is partly the Sultan's determined accessibility and his reputation for delivering promises that make him such an effective leader.

In building a modern state, Sultan Qaboos' chief strategy has been to create a highly trained local workforce, of both men and women, through intensive investment in education. With limited oil revenues, Oman cannot sustain costly expatriate labour so a policy of 'Omanisation' in every aspect of the workforce is rigorously pursued. In contrast to the rest of the region, it is refreshing to find locals working in all sections of society, from pump attendants to senior consultants.

Diversification and self-sufficiency in food production is being realised through the exportation of natural gas from the new plant near Sur, the enormous port project in Salalah, and intensive agriculture along the Batinah coast. Tourism, however, has been dealt a temporary blow.

In foreign affairs Sultan Qaboos has shown himself to be a distinguished peacemaker. In 1998 he was awarded the International Peace Award from the National Council on US-Arab Relations in recognition of his insightful government, and his role in maintaining stability in the region. In the recent Middle East crisis, his government has skilfully navigated the path between allied support against terrorism (expressed with practical assistance) and a strong identity with pan-Arab issues, particularly with regards to Palestine.

GEOGRAPHY

Oman extends from the fjords of the Musandam peninsula in the north (separated from the rest of the country by the United Arab Emirates, or UAE) to the annually green Dhofar region of southern Oman. Most of the country's population is concentrated on the Batinah coast, a semifertile plain that runs from the border with the UAE to Muscat and separated from the rest of Arabia by the Hajar Mountains. These mountains are internationally famed for their unrivalled geological heritage. The highest peak is Jebel Shams (Mountain of the Sun) at 3075m. On the slopes of nearby Jebel Akhdar (Green Mountain) temperate fruits are grown.

Much of the country between the Hajar Mountains and Dhofar is comprised of flat rocky desert but there are areas of sand dunes, most notably the Wahiba Sands, also known as Sharqiya (Eastern) Sands. A thriving and diverse marine life exists off Oman's 1,700km coastline.

CLIMATE

Oman's varied topography makes for a wide range of climatic conditions. Muscat is hot and often humid from mid-March until October, and temperatures soar in June and July to the mid-40°Cs. Daytime temperatures from November to mid-March average a pleasant 25°C but it can drop to 0°C on top of Jebel Akhdar.

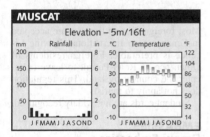

MUSCAT
Elevation – 5m/16ft

The Dhofar region has its own microclimate. During the summer, from mid-June to mid-September, the *khareef* (monsoon) arrives in the form of a persistent daily drizzle; the temperature in Salalah at this time drops to 25°C from the year-round average of 30°C.

GOVERNMENT & POLITICS

The sultan is the ultimate authority with jurisdiction over even minor policy decisions. In January 1992 an elected Majlis ash-Shura (Consultative Council) was convened as a first step towards broader participation in government.

Sultan Qaboos is not married and has no children. The constitution stipulates that an heir to the throne must be chosen by the royal family within three days of the throne falling vacant, an event that most people in Oman hope will be delayed for many a year yet.

POPULATION & PEOPLE

Oman's population is predominantly Arab, although the country's imperial history has resulted in intermarriage with other ethnic groups, particularly from eastern Africa. An Indian merchant community has existed in Muscat for at least 200 years, and people of Persian or Baluchi ancestry inhabit the Batinah coast. The Jibbali people (see the History section earlier in this chapter) form an intriguingly distinct ethnic and linguistic group in the Dhofar region. They live a mostly nomadic life with their own distinct customs.

SOCIETY & CONDUCT

Omanis show great tolerance towards foreign customs, but there are nonetheless strict mores governing their own, particularly in matters of dress. Men and women respect public modesty and cover their heads, arms and legs when in company. In the capital, women wear a headscarf, and the silk *abeyya* (black outer robe), often

worn over Western clothing, has become a refined fashion item. In the interior, women wear a much more colourful costume, and at feast times sisters often wear clothes cut from the same cloth. Men wear a *dishdasha* (a shirt-dress, usually light purple) and on official occasions wrap a turban around their cap and tuck a silver *khanjar* (ceremonial dagger) into their belt.

RELIGION

Most Omanis follow the Ibadi sect of Islam. Omanis are tolerant of other forms of Islamic worship, however, and allow expatriates to express their own religions at churches and temples in and around Muscat.

LANGUAGE

Arabic is the official language, though English is enthusiastically spoken. A large number of expatriates speak Farsi or Urdu. Many Omanis who returned from Africa in the early 1970s speak Swahili. Language buffs would find Jibbali, or the 'language of the birds', interesting and similarly Kumzari, the compound language spoken in parts of the Musandam Peninsula.

For a list of Arabic words and phrases, see the Language chapter at the back of this book.

Facts for the Visitor

WHEN TO GO

November to mid-March is the best time to visit Oman when the cooler air brings the mountain scenery sharply into focus. For the rest of the year much of Oman is oppressively hot and hazy, particularly between May and August. Without transport with air-con it is uncomfortable, if not dangerous, travelling at this time.

Oman's redeeming summertime feature, however, is the *khareef*, the rainy season that lasts from mid-June to mid-September in southern Oman. Many visitors from the Gulf flock to this area to picnic under the drizzle on the grassy slopes of Jebel Samhan. The rain (and therefore the green) vanishes by mid-September.

In the peak season (November to mid-March) it is feasible to take public transport to Nizwa, Sur or Sohar – only accessible by private transport at other times of the year (and arrange local tours to reduce the cost of these excursions). That option is not always available for the rest of the year, however, as there is so little demand.

VISAS & DOCUMENTS
Visas
In a bid to encourage tourism, Oman has recently relaxed its visa regulations considerably. Visas are still required (except for citizens of other Gulf countries) but it is now possible for many foreign nationals (including those from the EEC, the Americas, Australia and New Zealand) to obtain a visa at Seeb International Airport in Muscat, or at any border crossing.

For details of visas for other Middle Eastern countries, see the 'Visas at a Glance' table under Visas & Documents in the Regional Facts for the Visitor chapter.

On-arrival visas cost OR5 and are valid for two weeks. Tourist visas obtained through the Sultanate's embassies abroad are valid for three weeks. Visas are still obtainable through Oman's bigger hotels and tour companies. A nominal fee of OR1 is payable at the border of the Musandam Peninsula from the UAE. Despite talk of a joint UAE-Oman visa, such a thing is yet to materialise.

Multiple-entry visas cost OR10. They are valid for two years with maximum stays of six months permitted. Intended primarily for people on business, they can only be obtained once resident in Oman. You can, however, enter on a tourist visa and apply for a multiple re-entry visa from the Immigration and Passports Directorate in Qurm.

To work in Oman you have to be sponsored by an Omani company before you enter the country (ie, you have to have a job). Although it is illegal to work on a tourist visa, some expatriates take a short-term contract and hope their employer will arrange a labour card for them. The reality is a fretful experience best avoided.

For details of visas for other Middle Eastern countries, see the 'Visas at a Glance' table under Visas & Documents in the Regional Facts for the Visitor chapter.

Visa Extensions One-week extensions are available for both on-arrival and tourist visas from the Immigration & Passports Directorate in Qurm, Muscat. Overstaying a visa will incur hefty charges on departure.

Other Documents
Most foreign driving licences are accepted in Oman but an International Driving Licence is preferable. Foreign residents of Oman need a Road Permit to leave or re-enter the country by land. This regulation does not apply to tourists.

Student cards are not widely recognised.

EMBASSIES
Omani Embassies
Following are the addresses of Omani embassies in major cities around the world. Canadian travellers should contact the embassy in the USA. Australian or New Zealand travellers should contact the Omani embassy in Japan. For addresses of Omani embassies in neighbouring Middle Eastern countries see the relevant country chapter.

France (☎ 01 47 23 01 63, fax 01 47 23 77 10) 50 Ave de Lena, 75116 Paris
Germany (☎ 228-35 70 31, fax 35 70 40) Lindenallee 11, D-53173 Bonn
Japan (☎ 334020877, fax 334041334) 2-28-11 Sendagaya, Shibuya-Ku, Tokyo, 151-0051
Netherlands (☎ 70-361 5800, fax 360 7277) Koninginnegracht 27, 2514 AB Den Haag
UK (☎ 020-7225 0001, fax 7589 2505) 167 Queen's Gate, London SW7 5HE
USA (☎ 202-387 1980, fax 745 4933) 2535 Belmont Rd NW, Washington DC 20008

Embassies in Oman
Unless indicated otherwise, all the embassies listed are on Jameat ad Duwal al-Arabiyah St in the district of Shatti al-Qurm, Muscat. The British embassy looks after Irish nationals, processes visas and handles emergencies for Canadian citizens. Australians should contact the Australian embassy in Riyadh, Saudi Arabia (for details see the Embassies & Consulates section in the Saudi Arabia chapter). Consular sections of the embassy often close an hour or two earlier than the rest of the embassy so try to go as early in the day as possible or ring first to check.

Bahrain (☎ 605075, fax 605072) Way No 3017, Shatti al-Qurm; open 8am-2.30pm Sat-Wed
Egypt (☎ 600411, fax 603626); open 9am-12.30pm Sat-Wed
France (☎ 681800, fax 681843); open 9am-2.30pm Sat-Wed
Germany (☎ 702164, fax 735690) An-Nahdha St, Ruwi; open 9am-12 noon Sat-Wed

Iran (☎ 696944, fax 696888); open
7.30am-4pm Sat-Wed
Iraq (☎ 604178 fax 605112), near Al-Fair
supermarket, Madinat as-Sultan Qaboos;
open 8am-2pm Sat-Wed
Jordan (☎ 692760, fax 692762); open
8am-noon Sat-Wed
Kuwait (☎ 699627, fax 699628); open
8am-12.30pm Sat-Wed
Lebanon (☎ 695844, fax 695633) Way No
3019, Shatti al-Qurm; open 8am-2.30pm
Sat-Wed
Netherlands (☎ 603706, 603719, fax 603397)
Villa 1366, Way 3017, Shatti al-Qurm; open
9am-noon Sat-Wed
New Zealand (☎ 794932, fax 706443) Mutrah
High St, Mutrah
Qatar (☎ 691152, fax 691156) open
8am-2.30pm Sat-Wed
Saudi Arabia (☎ 601744, fax 603540); open
8.30am-2pm Sat-Wed
Syria (☎ 697904, fax 603895) Al-Inshirah St,
Madinat as-Sultan Qaboos; open 9am-2pm
Sat-Wed
Turkey (☎ 697050, 697053) Way No 3047,
Shatti al-Qurm; open 8am-noon Sat-Wed
UAE (☎ 600988, fax 602584); open
8am-1.30pm Sat-Wed
UK (☎ 693077, fax 693087); open
7.30am-2.30pm Sat-Wed
USA (☎ 698989, fax 604316); open 8am-4pm
Sat & Mon-Wed
Yemen (☎ 600815, fax 609172) Bldg No 2981,
Way No 2840, Shatti al-Qurm; open
9am-1.30pm Sat-Wed

CUSTOMS
Non-Muslims travelling by air can bring in
one bottle of alcohol but it is illegal to cross
from Oman into the UAE and vice versa carrying alcohol. A 'reasonable quantity' of cigars, cigarettes and tobacco can be imported.

MONEY
Currency
The official currency is the Omani rial (OR
but also spelt RO). One rial is divided into
1000 baisa (also spelt baiza). There are
coins of five, 10, 25, 50, 100 baisa and
notes of 100 and 200 baisa. There are notes
of a half, one, five, 10, 20, 50 rials. UAE
dirhams can be used in many towns at an
exchange rate of Dh10 to OR1.

Exchange Rates
Following are the rates for a range of currencies when this book went to print:

country	unit		Omani rial
Australia	A$1	=	OR0.209
Canada	C$1	=	OR0.243
euro zone	€1	=	OR0.378
Japan	¥100	=	OR0.314
New Zealand	NZ$1	=	OR0.182
UK	UK£1	=	OR0.601
USA	US$1	=	OR0.384

Exchanging Money
Most banks will change US dollar travellers
cheques for a commission. Banking hours are
from 8am to noon Saturday to Wednesday,
and from 8am to 11am Thursday. Moneychangers keep similar hours but are often
open from around 4pm to 7pm as well. They
often offer a slightly more competitive rate
than the banks and most charge only a nominal commission of 500 baisa per transaction
on cash. If you find a moneychanger who will
accept travellers cheques (generally only
AmEx or Thomas Cook cheques are recognised) you may be able to negotiate a lower
rate of commission than charged by the bank.

ATMs & Credit Cards Automated Teller
Machines (ATMs) are widespread in Oman
and many of them, particularly those belonging to HSBC, are tied into international
systems. The most popular credit card is
Visa, but MasterCard is also widely accepted. AmEx is not accepted in many shops
and you may incur a merchant fee of 5% for
using it in restaurants and hotels.

Costs
The cost of living is high in the capital and
a budget of OR15 (US$38) per day is the
minimum required. While general living
expenses are lower outside Muscat, high accommodation costs and off-road destinations limit the ability to see much of Oman
for less than OR25 (US$64) per day.

Tipping & Bargaining
Tipping of 10% is customary only in large
hotels and restaurants unless a service fee
has been charged. Bargain over are taxi
fares and souvenirs.

POST & COMMUNICATIONS
Post
Post office opening times vary but most
open from 8am to 1.30pm Saturday to
Wednesday, or until 11am Thursday.

Sending a postcard to any destination outside the Gulf Corporation Council (GCC) costs 150 baisa. Postage for letters is 200 baisa for the first 10g and 350 baisa for 11g to 20g. Mailing small packets to countries outside the GCC costs OR2 to OR4. For parcels of 1kg it costs OR4 to OR6.

Poste restante service is available at the post office in Ruwi. Mail should be addressed to: Your Name, Poste Restante, Ruwi Central Post Office, Ruwi, Sultanate of Oman.

Parcels received in Oman incur a 250 baisa customs charge.

Telephone

The country code for Oman is ☎ 968, followed by the local six-digit (or occasionally seven) subscriber number. There are no area or city codes. The international access code (to call abroad from Oman) is ☎ 00968.

There are central public telephone offices, offering fax services, in both Muscat and Salalah though the latter only has card phones. Phonecards are available from grocery stores and petrol stations. International phone calls can be made with a phonecard by dialling direct from most public phone booths throughout Oman. The cost of a two-minute call to Europe and the US is approximately OR1.

Mobiles Oman's mobile phone network runs on the GSM system used in Europe. It is therefore possible to use your GSM phone in Oman providing you have a roaming account.

Omantel is the only mobile phone company in Oman. Temporary local GSM connections can be made through the purchase of a SIM card, known as a Hayyak card. These Hayyak cards can be purchased on arrival at the airport and from shopping centres in Muscat for OR15 including OR5 worth of local calls. Transmission is tricky in remote wadis unless you have a Thurya phone (a satellite/GSM that automatically switches to satellite when GSM is not available).

Email & Internet Access

Internet access is available now throughout Oman and many towns have at least one Internet café. For addresses see the relevant city sections. Using a laptop computer in Oman presents few problems as hotels have

standard UK BT connections and adaptors are readily available in supermarkets. There is only one ISP in Oman, called Omantel. If you have an account with Omantel, the countrywide access number is ☎ 1311. For dialling on without an account, the number is ☎ 1312 and the service is paid for through the cost of the call. Their Internet help desk is ☎ 1313. The Omantel homepage (W www.omantel.net.om) provides up-to-date details and instructions for using the service. An account with Omantel costs OR2 per month for five hours (check the Omantel website for details as the service is improving all the time).

DIGITAL RESOURCES

For a comprehensive list of Middle East and Arab world websites, see the Regional Facts for the Visitor chapter. Some Oman-specific websites include the following:

Amateur Home Page An interesting insight into the way an Omani citizen views his country's place in the world with some excellent photographs and useful links to other Omani sites.
W www.geocities.com/siliconvalley/program/4707

Official Web Site The official website of the Ministry of Information provides a useful handbook of facts and figures about the Sultanate. It covers politics, economics, foreign affairs, commerce and media and indicates links to other websites on Oman.
W www.omanet.com

Oman Observer This popular English-language daily newspaper is available online.
W www.omanobserver.com

Oman Studies Centre This is an excellent resource for travellers and researchers alike with lively information on 'customs and manners' and a comprehensive bibliography.
W www.oman.org

BOOKS

As well as this book, Lonely Planet publishes a detailed country guide, *Oman & the UAE*. Otherwise, *Oman – a Comprehensive Guide* (OR12), published under the auspices of the Directorate General of Tourism, includes interesting anecdotal information. Other specialist guides and coffee-table books are available from hotel or city bookshops and cover diverse subjects from caving to camels.

An interesting account of life before the 'renaissance' is included in *The Doctor and* the Teacher: Oman 1955–1970 by Donald Bosch. *Travels in Oman: On the Track of the Early Explorers* by Philip Ward combines modern travel narrative with the accounts of earlier travellers. The final part of Wilfred Thesiger's 1959 classic, *Arabian Sands*, describes Oman's interior. *Atlantis of the Sands* by Ranulph Fiennes gives an account of the Dhofar insurgency in the 1960s while at the same time describing the search for the lost city of Ubar.

Of a more practical nature, some great hikes are listed in *Adventure Trekking in Oman* by Jerry Hadwin, while *Off-Road in Oman* by Heiner Klein and Rebecca Brickson is a must for 4WD exploration in Oman. Several roads it mentions have now been sealed, but it is still the most accessible guide with a useful set of maps. The *Maverick Guide to Oman* by Peter Ochs covers similar territory.

More general Middle East titles, some of which contain coverage of Oman, are listed in the Books section in the Regional Facts for the Visitor chapter.

NEWSPAPERS & MAGAZINES

The *Times of Oman* and *Oman Daily Observer* are the local English-language newspapers. Foreign newspapers and magazines, available only in top-end hotels in Muscat and Salalah and in Muscat's shopping centres, are usually three days old.

Oman Today is a bimonthly pocket-sized handbook with what's-on listings and some interesting features of interest to the tourist. It is widely available throughout the Sultanate for OR1.

RADIO & TV

The local English-language radio station broadcasts on 90.4 FM (94.3 FM from Salalah) every day from 7am to 11pm, and you can hear news bulletins at 7.30am, 2.30pm and 6.30pm.

Oman TV broadcasts a daily newscast in English at 8pm and shows English-language films two or three nights a week (usually around 11pm). Satellite TV is widely available.

PHOTOGRAPHY & VIDEO

Film is available in most towns but if you take slides or like a particular type of film, it's better to buy it in Muscat. Film processing is quick and reliable but expensive at OR5 for 36 colour prints.

HEALTH

Since his ascension Sultan Qaboos has made improving standards of health and hygiene in Oman a top priority. Life expectancy has now jumped from under 50 years of age in 1970 to over 70. For the visitor, Oman is one of the cleanest countries in the region: even small restaurants are inspected regularly.

Tap water is drinkable throughout the country and no special vaccinations are advised. Malaria, endemic only 30 years ago, has almost been eradicated and prophylactics are no longer necessary. Western medicine and healthcare products are widely available in Muscat but less so out of the capital.

Visitors from yellow-fever areas will need proof of a vaccination on arrival in Oman.

WOMEN TRAVELLERS

Travellers (especially backpackers) are a novelty in Oman and as a result women travelling alone are likely to feel uncomfortable, particularly on public transport and eating in public outside Muscat, and when visiting public beaches. Travelling beyond Muscat can be a lonely experience. The interior is sparsely populated, and with no established circuit of travellers' meeting places, bumping into other foreigners is difficult. Omani men mostly ignore women (out of respect) and it's hard to meet Omani women. Many of the country's attractions lie off-road and going solo in such situations is inadvisable unless you are highly resourceful and, if driving, strong enough to change a tyre. Beware, also, that it is not possible for women travelling solo (ie, without a bona fide husband!) to cross land borders unless travelling on public transport. Harassment is not a big problem except near tourist resorts where local attitudes are, rightly or wrongly, influenced by the sight of women in bikinis. Outside hotel resorts, it helps (in addition to being more culturally sensitive) to be discreetly dressed in loose-fitting clothing and to wear shorts and a T-shirt for swimming – see the What to Wear advice in the Women Travellers section in the Regional Facts for the Visitor.

DISABLED TRAVELLERS

Other than a few disabled parking slots, few other facilities exist in Oman. The **Oman**

Association for the Disabled (☎ 605566, e oadisable@omantel.net.om) is set up primarily to assist nationals, obviously, but it seems willing to be emailed with inquiries.

DANGERS & ANNOYANCES

Oman is a very safe country and even the driving isn't that bad. Two dangers that may escape the attention of visitors, however, are flash floods – don't camp or park in a wadi (dry river bed) especially if there's any sign of cloud – and the isolation of many off-road destinations. Always carry water and spend the extra on a 4WD if going off-road. People have baked alive waiting for assistance that never came.

BUSINESS HOURS

Most businesses are open from 8am to 1pm and again from 4pm to 7pm or 7.30pm daily, except Thursday afternoon and Friday. Shops in the Mutrah Souq and in some of Muscat's more upmarket shopping centres stay open until 9pm or 9.30pm nightly. Government departments and ministries are open from 7.30am to 2.30pm Saturday to Wednesday closing an hour earlier during Ramadan. (See also the boxed text 'Open Sesame' in the Regional Facts for the Visitor chapter.)

PUBLIC HOLIDAYS

In addition to the main Islamic holidays described in the Regional Facts for the Visitor chapter, Oman observes the following public holidays:

Lailat al-Mi'raj (Ascension of the Prophet)
October – the exact date is dependent on the lunar calendar
National Day 18 November – marked by at least two days of holiday, flags decorating the highway, a spectacular military tattoo, camel races and fireworks

SPECIAL EVENTS

One special event that is gaining momentum in Oman is the **Khareef Festival** in Salalah. Check a June, July or August edition of *Oman Today* for a programme of the festival's cultural activities.

ACTIVITIES

Off-road exploration of the country's mountains, wadis and sand dunes, particularly in a 4WD with some camping equipment, is a highlight of a visit to Oman. Essential guides for this activity are listed under Books, earlier in this chapter. Hiring a 4WD can be very expensive but the big tour companies offer all the destinations mentioned in this chapter as day trips or overnight tours.

Rock climbing, hiking and caving are increasingly popular activities, but they tend to be conducted on a 'go-it-alone' basis. *Rock Climbing in Oman* by RA McDonald lists some exciting routes in wild terrain but you will need to bring your own climbing partner and equipment.

Oman has some rich cave systems, many of which have never been explored. The 160m-deep Majlis al Jinn or 'Meeting Place of the Spirits' is the second-largest underground chamber on earth but you will need to arrange specialist tour assistance to organise a descent. Popular Hoti Cave is one of the few caves that is readily approached but it is currently being developed to allow easier access for visitors.

Caves of Oman by Samir Hanna and Mohamed al-Belushi gives an excellent account of speleology in Oman and points out some local safety advice.

With a pair of stout boots, a map, plenty of water and Jerry Hadwin's *Adventure Trekking in Oman*, you can descend the plane in Muscat and hike through superb walking territory all the way to Nizwa! Unless you are an accustomed outbacker, however, it is advisable to see the Organised Tours section later for details of companies that can help tailor a trip to suit your interests.

There are some excellent snorkelling and diving opportunities in Oman and the 1700km coastline is virtually unexplored in many places. Diving courses are available in Muscat (see Dive Centres, Dolphin-Watching & Boat Trips in the Muscat section, later) and Al-Sawadi Beach Resort (see the entry under Sawadi in The Batinah Plain section, later).

Oman is a great country for naturalists with dolphins and whales found in great numbers off the coast (see Dive Centres, Dolphin-Watching & Boat Trips under Muscat); important turtle nesting sites (see Ras al-Jinz in the Sharqiya Region section); a great diversity of shells (see Sawadi in the Sharqiya Region section); migration routes carrying unusual birds across the territory, and relatively easy sightings of gazelle (see Coast Road to Sur in the Shar-qiya Region section). A pair of binoculars and a set of wheels is all that's necessary, although tour companies can arrange specialist tours (for details see the Organised Tours section later).

ACCOMMODATION

Accommodation in Oman is limited and expensive, though generally good value for money (rooms always tend to come with private bathroom and air-con). In many places, there's no alternative to the one mid- to top-end hotel, and smaller towns may have no hotels at all.

Room rates quoted in this chapter include the mandatory 17% tax.

There are no camp sites in Oman except at Ras al-Jinz and some expensive 'camping experience' resorts in Ras al-Hadd and Wahiba Sands. That said, wild camping is one of the highlights of this country and providing you are discreet and don't require any creature comforts, a beach of your own, a dune top or wadi cave is yours for the taking; in fact, one gets quite indignant having to share.

FOOD

Most restaurant food is of Lebanese origin and not particularly exciting. Omani home cooking, however, is delicious and varied and reflects the diversity of Oman's ethnicity. Fish is important and made into curries and soups. Goat, mutton or camel are stewed to make a spicy curry (such as *qabooli*) or a stew (such as *makbousa*).

Another typical dish is *harees*, made of steamed wheat and boiled meat to form a porridge. It is often garnished *ma owaal* (with dried shark) and laced with lime, chilli and onions. Try *shuwa* (marinated meat cooked in an earth oven) if you have the chance. It is served with the wafer-thin Omani bread (known as *rukhal*) and rice. Cardamom, saffron and turmeric are essential ingredients but Omani cooking is not exceptionally spicy.

A surprisingly delicious traditional dish from southern Oman is *rabees*. It is made from boiled baby shark, stripped and washed of the gritty skin and then fried with the liver.

Lunch is the most important meal of the day but it's invariably prepared at home and many cheaper eateries are closed after 1pm before the afternoon nap. Omanis like to go out later in the evening for snacks, especially shwarma.

Indian restaurants are the best bet for wholesome, hot, vegetarian food as many cater for the nonmeat-eating expatriate community.

DRINKS

Laban (a yogurt drink) is very popular. Camels' milk is available fresh and warm from the udder in Bedouin encampments. Together with mares' milk, it's an experience many prefer to miss! Alcohol cannot be purchased 'over the counter' in Oman without a resident's permit. It is available, however, in most of the more expensive hotels and restaurants.

Omanis are developing a passion for fast food and you'll find at least a Pizza Hut in the big towns.

For information on regional cuisine see also the special section 'Middle Eastern Cuisine' in the Regional Facts for the Visitor chapter.

SPECTATOR SPORTS

Camel races are held on Friday mornings at camel tracks around the country from mid-October until mid-April. Races are announced in the Arabic dailies but not necessarily in the English-language newspapers. Alternatively, contact one of the tour companies – or check with the **Directorate-General of Camel Affairs** (☎ 893804, fax 893802).

Bull-butting involves pitting Brahmin bulls in a push-and-shove around a dirt arena. It doesn't involve blood or injury. The best place to see bull-butting is at Barka, 45km west of Muscat, on Friday between November and March from 4pm to 6pm (but timings are erratic).

Football (soccer) is a national obsession, especially since an Omani footballer, Hani Adhabet, was named top goal-scorer in the world in 2001. The Bawshar stadium in Muscat hosts regular games.

SHOPPING

Oman is not a great centre for handicrafts. However, it does have expertise in certain areas, including silversmithing. Exquisitely crafted *khanjars* can cost up to OR500 but tourist versions are available from OR30. Genuine Bedouin silver is becoming scarce (read a copy of *Disappearing Treasures of Oman* by Avelyn Foster). Silver Maria Theresa dollars, used as Oman's unit of currency for many years, make a good buy from OR2. Wooden *mandoos* (dowry chests) studded with brass tacks cost OR15 for a new one and start at OR50 for an antique.

Other items commonly for sale include coffee pots (not always made in Oman), baskets woven with leather, camel bags, rice mats and cushion covers. Many items are imported, as per centuries of tradition, from India and Iran.

Frankincense is a 'must-buy' from Salalah, together with a pottery incense burner (both available in Muscat). Amouage (OR50), currently the most valuable perfume in the world, is made in Muscat partially from frankincense. Omani dates make another excellent gift.

Getting There & Away

AIR

Other than Seeb International Airport in Muscat the only functioning airports are at opposite ends of the country in Salalah and Khasab; and these both handle domestic flights only. Services may resume to Sur and the island of Masirah if demand increases. (See Getting Around in the Muscat section for details.)

The national carrier is Oman Air. It services the domestic airports and a selection of Middle Eastern and subcontinental destinations. Oman has a 25% share in Gulf Air, which services all Middle Eastern cities and many long-haul destinations.

Buying Tickets in Oman

Oman is not a particularly good place to buy international tickets although some cheap return fares to Europe are available, particularly to London (OR250 return). Fares to Colombo and other destinations on the Indian subcontinent are about OR80/180 one way/return. Fares to nearby Gulf cities start from around OR45/OR65 one way/return. Fares to Los Angeles are around OR450 return; New York OR390; and Sydney OR420. A minimum of OR50 is levied on top of these fares for airport taxes.

Departure Tax

You will be require to pay an international departure tax of OR5.

LAND

Oman shares borders with the UAE, Saudi Arabia and Yemen but it is not possible to cross into Saudi Arabia.

The UAE

There are several options for crossing from Oman into the UAE. The **Oman National Transport Company** (ONTC; ☎ 590046) has buses to Dubai (OR5, six hours, daily) departing from **Ruwi bus station** (☎ 708522) in Muscat at 7am and 4.30pm.

Comfort Line (☎ 702191) also has a service to Dubai at 6.30am and 4.30pm (OR5, five hours, daily). The bus leaves from a parking lot outside Moon Travels, two blocks behind the bus station on Way 2985.

The ONTC service from Muscat to Abu Dhabi (OR5, six hours, daily) leaves at 6.30am. There is also a bus service from Muscat to Buraimi (a few minutes from Al-Ain in the UAE) but the new competition in fares means you won't save much by taking this route. You can cross into the UAE at any of the border posts but it's advisable to enter and exit Oman through the same border post.

If you want to visit Musandam Peninsula, your best bet is to fly to Khasab from Muscat (or visit the region from Dubai) otherwise it involves an exasperating and expensive process of exit and re-entry.

Foreign residents in Oman need a road permit obtainable through their sponsor to use a land crossing but tourists do not.

Yemen

You need to be determined to make the border crossing into Yemen. If you have a visa for Yemen, you can cross by road through Sarfait (although you may not be able to get very far on the Yemeni side through this crossing due to a complete lack of infrastructure and transport) and Mazyunah. Both posts are open 24 hours. You cannot re-enter Oman on a tourist visa, however, and note also that as a tourist in Oman, you cannot obtain a visa for Yemen from the embassy in Muscat.

The only access to either border post is in your own vehicle (4WD needed for the

Yemeni side) or by long and expensive taxi rides from Salalah or Thumrait. The road from Thumrait to Mazyunah is graded but not blacktopped. On the other side of either border post, the going really gets tough.

Note that it is usually prohibitive to take a hire car across any Omani border because of the extra cost of insurance. It is also forbidden for single women to enter or leave Oman by land unless they are travelling on a public transport bus.

SEA

There are currently no passenger services to or from Oman although Muscat is a port of call for cruise liners.

Getting Around

AIR

The only domestic flights currently available are on **Oman Air** (☎ 707222) between Muscat and Salalah (OR36/72 one way/return, 1½ hours) twice daily at variable times, and between Muscat and Khasab (OR20/40 one way/return, 1½ hours) every Monday, Wednesday and Saturday at variable times. Tickets can be booked through any travel agent.

BUS

Intercity buses are operated by **ONTC** (☎ 590 046), which has daily services to and from most of the main provincial towns for OR5 or less, with the exception of Salalah which costs OR6 one way or OR11 return from Muscat. Buses are usually on time, comfortable and safe. Tickets are available from the bus driver. See individual destinations for more details.

LONG-DISTANCE TAXI & MICROBUS

Oman has a comprehensive system of cheap but slow long-distance taxis (painted orange and white and shared by a number of passengers) and microbuses. Oman's taxis and microbuses do not wait until they are full to leave. Instead, drivers pick up and drop off extra passengers along the way.

To visit certain places of interest, you will have to take a taxi 'engaged' (ie, privately, not shared) but this is generally four times the price of a shared taxi as you have to pay

for all the seats. Bargain hard before you get in and try to avoid hailing a taxi from a hotel. Fares quoted in this chapter are for shared taxis unless prefaced by the word 'engaged'.

CAR

Traffic laws are strictly enforced, especially in Muscat. Seatbelt use is mandatory for passengers and there is a fine of OR10 for not wearing one.

Drink-driving is forbidden and so is the use of mobile phones while driving. Vehicles are fitted with a beeping device for Oman's maximum speed limit of 120km/h. Right turns are not allowed at red lights.

Road signs are written in English (albeit with inconsistent spelling), as well as in Arabic, throughout Oman. Helpful brown tourist signs are making an appearance near many sites of interest. Petrol, all of which is now unleaded, costs 120 baisas per litre.

Rental

International rental chains in Oman include Avis, Budget, Europcar and Thrifty, but dozens of local agencies offer a slightly reduced rate. Two-wheel-drive (2WD) cars start at about OR14 and four-wheel-drive (4WD) vehicles at OR35, and both come with about 200km of free mileage. Always carry water with you (a box of 12 1.5L bottles costs OR1.500 from petrol stations) and a tow-rope (OR4 from any large supermarket – try Al Fair in Madinat as-Sultan Qaboos). If you buy three large 'freezer packs' at the same time (600 baisa each) they will keep your cool box cold for a day even in summer and you can ask hotels to refreeze the packs for you at night. Alternatively, ice is available at fish factories all along the coast.

Note that it's illegal to drive a dirty car – the fine is OR5!

2WD versus 4WD Travellers comment that some roads indicated in this book as '4WD only' are passable in a 2WD. Often they are right – until something goes wrong. 2WD cars are not built to withstand potholes, washboard surfaces and steep, loose-gravel inclines, let alone long distances to the next petrol station.

If travellers letters are anything to go by then who knows over what terrain the previous driver dragged your car! Bear in mind, you'll get no sympathy from hire

OMAN

companies if your 2WD breaks down off-road and with virtually zero traffic on some routes you are very vulnerable, especially in extreme summer temperatures. Failing brakes on mountain roads and beguiling soft sand and a salty crust called *sabkha* that looks and feels hard until you drive on it are further common hazards.

In short, saving on the cost of a 4WD might cost more than you bargained for.

ORGANISED TOURS

Due to the low volume of visitors, tours in Oman are generally tailor-made for the customer in private vehicles with an English-speaking driver-guide. This is great for the itinerary but painful on the pocket unless you can muster a group of four to share your vehicle.

The following all-inclusive prices are average for a full-day tour from Muscat: Nizwa, Bahla and Jabrin (OR70); Nakhal and Rustaq (OR70); Jebel Shams (OR110); Wadi Shab and Wadi Tiwi (OR110); Wahiba Sands (OR120). Dolphin and other boat trips start from OR5 with a local fisherman to OR90 for an all-day cruise on a dhow.

Tour companies abound in Muscat and Salalah; they offer camel safaris, 4WD touring, camping, city tours, caving, rock climbing and combinations thereof. Recommended agencies include **Arabian Sea Safaris** (☎ 693223; e arabseas@omantel.net .om) for boat trips; **Desert Discovery Tours** (☎ 593232; e tours@omantel.net.om) for trips to the Wahiba Sands and **Sunny Day Tours** (☎ 590055; e sunnyday@omantel.net .om) for outward bound activities.

National Travel & Tourism (☎ 566046; e nttoman@omantel.net.om) offers an excellent, friendly and comprehensive tour service.

Heide Beale Tours (☎ 799928) offers expensive but informative tours.

Oman Today has a complete listing of tour operators.

Muscat مسقط

Muscat has a character quite different from neighbouring capitals. There are few high-rise blocks and even the most functional building is required to reflect tradition in a dome or an arabesque window. The result of these strict building policies is an attractive, clean and whimsically uniform city.

There's plenty to interest a visitor, from the historical port areas of Muscat and Mutrah, to the beaches of Qurm and Al-Bustan. Muscat may not be the nerve-centre of the Middle East but it is a forward-thinking, progressive city much loved by its citizens and a beacon for those who live in the interior.

Orientation

Wedged between the mountains and the sea, Muscat comprises a string of suburbs, each with its own attractions. It's too far, generally, to walk between one area and another but there is plenty of public transport. Muscat's well-marked highway originates at the border with the UAE, parallels the coast and passes through or close to most of the capital's areas of interest. The road is a feature in itself, lined for long sections with grass verges and planted with petunias in winter.

Muscat proper is a small area that until 1970 was gated at night. With few shops and no hotels, it is given over to the Diwan, or palace administration. Most travellers stay in the neighbouring port of Mutrah.

Giant sculptures of coffeepots and miniature forts in the middle of Muscat's roundabouts make good navigational aids. A clock tower and mural marks the Rusayl (Risail) roundabout (an important transport hub). Muscat has set a trend in roundabouts and now the tiniest, unpaved *willayat* (village) can't take itself seriously without one.

Note, street names are a novelty in Muscat and in most of the towns in Oman. Many roads don't have names at all or are called 'Way' plus a random string of numbers. Few people know what street their house is on, let alone their offices, and addresses are given as PO Box numbers. Find your way around by reference to landmarks, eg, HSBC in Qurm, or the Sultan's palace in Mutrah.

Information

Tourist Offices The **Directorate General of Tourism** (☎ 7717085, fax 7714213) can answer limited telephone inquiries but it is better to call one of the government-accredited tour operators for more detailed information. **National Travel & Tourism** (☎ 566046, e nttoman@omantel.net.om; Ar-Rumaylah St, Wattayah; open 8am-1pm & 4pm-7pm Sat-Thur) is one of the best with

GREATER MUSCAT

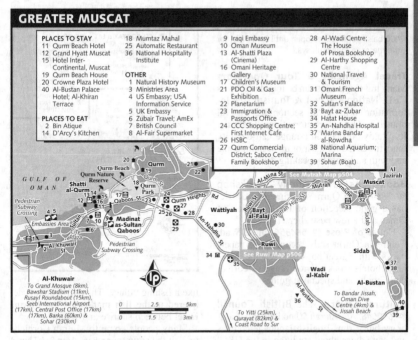

PLACES TO STAY
11 Qurm Beach Hotel
12 Grand Hyatt Muscat
15 Hotel Inter-
 Continental, Muscat
19 Qurm Beach House
20 Crowne Plaza Hotel
40 Al-Bustan Palace
 Hotel; Al-Khiran
 Terrace

PLACES TO EAT
2 Bin Atique
14 D'Arcy's Kitchen

18 Mumtaz Mahal
25 Automatic Restaurant
36 National Hospitality
 Institute

OTHER
1 Natural History Museum
3 Ministries Area
4 US Embassy; USA
 Information Service
5 UK Embassy
6 Zubair Travel; AmEx
7 British Council
8 Al-Fair Supermarket

9 Iraqi Embassy
10 Oman Museum
13 Al-Shatti Plaza
 (Cinema)
16 Omani Heritage
 Gallery
17 Children's Museum
21 PDO Oil & Gas
 Exhibition
22 Planetarium
23 Immigration &
 Passports Office
24 CCC Shopping Centre;
 First Internet Cafe
26 HSBC
27 Qurm Commercial
 District; Sabco Centre;
 Family Bookshop

28 Al-Wadi Centre;
 The House
 of Prosa Bookshop
29 Al-Harthy Shopping
 Centre
30 National Travel
 & Tourism
31 Omani French
 Museum
32 Sultan's Palace
33 Bayt az-Zubar
34 Hatat House
35 Al-Nahdha Hospital
37 Marina Bandar
 al-Rowdha
38 National Aquarium;
 Marina
39 Sohar (Boat)

experienced and helpful staff. Its main office is in Wattayah, next to the Daewoo showroom. Brochures and maps are available from larger hotel foyers.

Money The big banks, including **HSBC** (☎ 799920), are centred in Ruwi's central business district (CBD) but there are numerous branches with ATM facilities throughout Muscat able to give cash advances on international credit cards. The Qurm branch of HSBC is open in the evening from 5pm to 8pm Saturday to Thursday. The most convenient money-changers are in Qurm, along Souq Ruwi St in Ruwi and on the Mutrah Corniche at the entrance to the Mutrah Souq. Most are open 8am to 1pm, and some from 5pm to 7pm; all are open Saturday to Thursday.

AmEx (☎ 708035; Dawhat al-Adab St; open 8am-1pm & 4pm-6.30pm Sat-Thur) is represented by Zubair Travel in Madinat as-Sultan Qaboos, behind the large, department store called City Plaza.

Travellers cheques can be cashed at most major banks in Muscat, which charge a large commission; cash is a better option.

Post The **main post office** (☎ 519922; Al-Matar St; open 8am-3pm & 5pm-midnight Sat-Wed, 8am-11am & 8pm-11pm Thur) is off the airport roundabout. Ruwi's CBD has an important **branch post office** (☎ 701651; Markaz Mutrah al-Tijari St; open 7.30am-2.30pm & 4pm-6pm daily).

Telephone & Fax There are numerous cardphones around the city for making local and international calls. The **telephone office** (Al-Burj St; open 7.30am-10.30pm daily) is in Ruwi's CBD. You can send faxes from the main lobby. Hayyak cards, for making international and local calls from a mobile, can be bought at the airport and from the shopping centre in Qurm. (See the Telephone section earlier in this chapeter for more details.)

Email & Internet Access Internet cafés are springing up all over Muscat. The standard rate is 400 to 500 baisa per hour.

First Internet Café (☎ 560800) In the CCC shopping centre in Qurm, First is surprisingly popular given its hefty rates (OR1.300 per hour). It's open 9am-2pm & 5pm-10pm daily.

Cyber Point (☎ 7717179) In Ruwi, off Bayt al-Falaj St near the BP station, Cyber Point charges 400 baisa per hour. It's open until 2am daily, for the message that can't wait.

Travel Agencies & Tour Operators

Many travel agencies can be found in Ruwi's CBD. **National Travel & Tourism** (see Information earlier in this section) has a useful branch in Qurm for international ticketing. Its Wattiya office can arrange half-day city tours for OR30 for a car of up to four people and with an English-speaking driver.

Bookshops

The **Family Bookshop** (☎ 786461) in Qurm's commercial district has a good selection of English titles on Oman and a few bestsellers.

House of Prose (☎ 564356) in Al-Wadi Centre in Qurm sells second-hand paperbacks with a great buy-back scheme. Most large hotels stock a wide range of coffeetable books and specialist guides.

Cultural Centres

The **British Council** (☎ 600548; Al-Inshirah St) no longer has a library but it runs English-language courses and can advise about studying in the UK.

The **USA Information Service** (☎ 698989 ext 201; Jameat ad Duwal al-Arabiyah St; open 9am-3pm Sat-Wed), in the US embassy, maintains a comprehensive resource centre regarding studying, working and travelling in the USA.

Medical & Emergency Services

You can expect an international standard of health care in Muscat at the main city hospitals, including **An-Nahdha Hospital** (☎ 707800; An-Nahdha St) in Wattiyah. There is no ambulance service except between hospitals, although one is being introduced at the end of 2003.

The **Royal Oman Police** (☎ 560099) organises emergency care at the scene of an accident. Initial emergency treatment may be free but all other health care is charged.

Mutrah   مطرح

Mutrah stretches along an attractive **corniche** of latticed buildings and mosques; it looks particularly spectacular at sunset when the light casts shadows across a toothy crescent of mountains. Despite being the capital's main port area, Mutrah feels

MUTRAH

PLACES TO STAY & EAT
1 Al-Nahda Hotel;
   Sindebad Restaurant
2 Marina Hotel;
   Marina Restaurant
4 Corniche Hotel
11 Coffee Shop

OTHER
3 Bus Station
5 Post Office
6 Taxi Stand
7 Taxi Stand
8 HSBC
9 Exchange House
   (Money Exchange)
10 Souq Entrance
12 Mutrah Fort
13 Post Office

like a fishing village. The daily catch is delivered to the **fish market** by the Marina Hotel between sunrise and 10am.

Many people come to Mutrah Corniche to visit the **souq** (open 8am-1pm Sat-Thur & 5pm-9pm daily), which retains the chaotic interest of a traditional Arab market albeit housed under modern *barasti* (palm-leaf) roofing. There are some good antique shops selling a mixture of Indian and Omani artefacts among the usual textile, hardware and gold shops, but don't expect to find any bargains.

Mutrah Fort, built by the Portuguese in the 1580s, dominates the eastern end of the harbour. It is closed to visitors.

Beyond the fort, the corniche leads to **Al-Riyam Park** which is open erratically in the morning and late afternoon. Walk up to the ornamental incense burner for fine views of the harbour. Further along the corniche, **Kalbuh Bay Park** juts into the sea and makes a good place for an evening stroll from Mutrah.

Walled City of Muscat

The main road leads via the corniche to the tiny, gated city of Muscat, home now to the palace and Diwan. Muscat sits on a natural harbour surrounded by a jagged spine of hills. If you stand by the harbour wall on Mirani St, the building to the right with the delightful mushroom pillars is the **Sultan's Palace**. Guarding the entrance to the harbour to the east and west are two forts called **Al-Jalali** and **Al-Mirani**. They were built during the Portuguese occupation in the 1580s on Arab foundations and are still used by the military. They are closed to the public but photographs are permitted. From the harbour wall on Mirani St, look across the water at the rocks in front of you: you should be able to make out graffiti scratched into them by foreign naval crews.

There are two museums in this area. **Bayt az-Zubair** (*☎ 736688; As-Saidiyah St; admission OR1; open 9.30am-1pm & 4pm-7pm Sat-Thur*) is a beautifully restored house with exhibits of Omani heritage in photographs, and displays of traditional handicrafts and furniture. The **Omani-French Museum** (*☎ 736613; Qasr al-Alam St; admission 500 baisa; open 9am-1pm Sat-Thur & 5pm-7pm daily*) has galleries detailing relations between the two countries.

Al-Bustan & Bandar Jissah

The main road from Muscat leads to Bandar al-Rowdha. The **National Aquarium**, which is off Sidab St, is currently closed with only rumours regarding its reopening. The **marina** next door has plans to build a rival exhibit.

The road continues to Al-Bustan roundabout which is home to the **Sohar**, a boat named after the hometown of the famous Omani seafarer, Ahmed bin Majid. The boat is a replica of one sailed by Abdullah bin Gasin in the mid-8th century to Canton in China. It was built in Sur from the bark of over 75,000 palm trees and four tonnes of rope and without nails. It was launched in 1980 on a journey of 6000 nautical miles that took eight months to complete.

The sumptuous **Al-Bustan Palace Hotel**, set in lush gardens, was built as a venue for the GCC summit in 1985. Remarkable for its enormous domed atrium, the hotel has won numerous awards as the best hotel in the Middle East. It's worth coming to have a look at the building's interior and enjoy the location.

The marina and Al-Bustan can only be reached by engaged taxi (OR3 from Mutrah Souq).

If you have your own transport, follow the signs from Al-Bustan roundabout for Bandar Jissah. It's a long, steep drive to a

spectacular **viewpoint**. Picturesque **Jissah Beach** offers perfect bathing although it gets quite crowded on Thursday and Friday. For a couple of rials, entrepreneurial fishermen will take visitors on a five-minute boat ride to see the famous rock arch. **Oman Dive Centre** lies over the next headland.

Ruwi

Oman's 'Little India' is the commercial and transport hub of the capital with plenty of places to eat and socialise. The **National Museum** (*☎ 701289; An-Noor St; admission 500 baisa; open 9am-1pm & 4pm-6pm daily Oct-Mar, 5pm-7pm Apr-Sept*) has displays of jewellery, costumes and dowry chests. A mural and a collection of boats celebrates Oman's seafaring heritage.

Don't be put off visiting the **Sultan's Armed Forces Museum** (*☎ 312648; admission 500 baisa; open 8am-1pm daily*) as this excellent museum is far more than just a display of military hardware. The museum is housed in Bayt al-Falaj, built in 1845 as a royal summer home but used mostly as the headquarters of the sultan's armed forces. The lower rooms give a comprehensive outline of Oman's history to the present day and the upper rooms explore Oman's international relations and military prowess. The museum is on the itinerary of visiting dignitaries and you'll be given a mandatory military escort.

Qurm

Most of this area comprises modern shopping centres and residences but there are several places to visit. Surprisingly, one of the best places to buy Omani silver and handicrafts is the little souq inside the **Sabco Centre**. Bargaining is recommended although prices are reasonable.

In addition to the small displays of artefacts and interesting rooms on Omani architecture, **Oman Museum** (*☎ 600946; admission 500 baisa; open 9am-1pm Sat-Thur, 4pm-6pm daily Oct-Mar, 5pm-7pm daily Apr-Sept*) is worth trying to find for the sake of the view over dazzlingly white suburbs and sea. Although the way through a wealthy residential area is signposted from Al-Inshirah St it is probably better to take an engaged taxi from Qurm for OR1 up the steep 1.3km climb and ask the driver to wait, or walk down.

OMAN

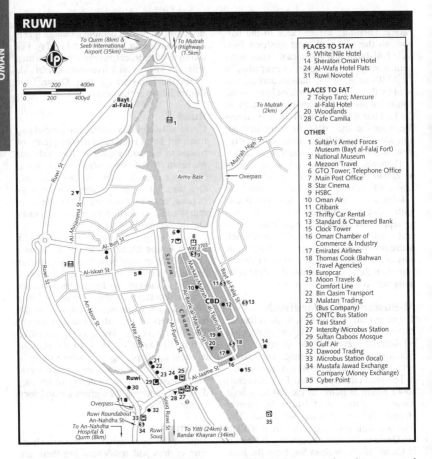

RUWI

To Qurm (8km) &
Seeb International
Airport (35km)

To Mutrah
(Highway)
(1.5km)

0   200   400m
0   200   400yd

Bayt
al-Falaj

To Mutrah
(2km)

Army Base ———— Overpass

Mutrah High St

Al-Mujamma St

Ruwi St

Al-Burj St

Al-Iskan St

An-Noor St

Al-Funan St

Al-Jaame St

Souq Ruwi St

Storm

Channel

Markaz Mutrah al-Tijari St

Bayt al-Falaj St

Al-Bank al-Markazi St

CBD

Ruwi

Overpass

Ruwi Roundabout
An-Nahdha St
To An-Nahdha
Hospital &
Qurm (8km)

Ruwi
Souq

To Yitti (24km) &
Bandar Khayran (34km)

PLACES TO STAY
5   White Nile Hotel
14 Sheraton Oman Hotel
24 Al-Wafa Hotel Flats
31 Ruwi Novotel

PLACES TO EAT
2   Tokyo Taro; Mercure
    al-Falaj Hotel
20 Woodlands
28 Cafe Camilia

OTHER
1   Sultan's Armed Forces
    Museum (Bayt al-Falaj Fort)
3   National Museum
4   Mezoon Travel
6   GTO Tower; Telephone Office
7   Main Post Office
8   Star Cinema
9   HSBC
10 Oman Air
11 Citibank
12 Thrifty Car Rental
13 Standard & Chartered Bank
15 Clock Tower
16 Oman Chamber of
    Commerce & Industry
17 Emirates Airlines
18 Thomas Cook (Bahwan
    Travel Agencies)
19 Europcar
21 Moon Travels &
    Comfort Line
22 Bin Qasim Transport
23 Malatan Trading
    (Bus Company)
25 ONTC Bus Station
26 Taxi Stand
27 Intercity Microbus Station
29 Sultan Qaboos Mosque
30 Gulf Air
32 Dawood Trading
33 Microbus Station (local)
34 Mustafa Jawad Exchange
    Company (Money Exchange)
35 Cyber Point

Petroleum Development Oman (PDO) is responsible for much of the rapid growth of infrastructure throughout the country, as outlined in the **PDO Oil & Gas Exhibition** (☎ 677044; admission free; open 8am-noon & 1pm-4pm Sat-Wed, 8am-noon Thur). The neighbouring **Planetarium** (☎ 675542) is open for two shows per week in English (Wednesday at 7pm and Thursday at 10am). To reach both, follow the signs for the Crowne Plaza Hotel and turn at the first right along Sayh al-Malih St.

Qurm Park makes a good place for a picnic; the adjacent **Nature Reserve** (closed to visitors) protects a rare stretch of mangrove. A road runs along the edge of the reserve towards the Crowne Plaza Hotel giving access to a long sandy **beach**. Women bathing on their own have sometimes been accosted here so avoid minimalist swimwear.

Shatti al-Qurm & Al-Khuwair

Near to the Hotel Inter-Continental, Muscat, along Way 2817, there is a small shopping complex where you'll find the **Omani Heritage Gallery** (☎ 696974), a nonprofit organisation set up to encourage cottage industries through the sale of handicrafts. Prices are high but so is the quality.

The Ministry of National Heritage houses the lovely little **Natural History Museum** (☎ 604957; Way 3413; admission 500 baisa; open 9am-1pm Sat-Thur, 4pm-6pm daily Oct-Mar, 5pm-7pm daily Apr-Sept). The museum is a must for anyone interested in the local flora and fauna, and there are also some excellent displays regarding Oman's geography and geology.

It's worth driving around the elaborate **ministry and embassy buildings** bunched in this area. Stop at the **Grand Hyatt, Muscat** to enjoy a Yemeni prince's flight of fancy: love it or hate it, tea in the foyer is a delight.

Al-Ghubrah

Also known as the Grand Mosque *(Sultan Qaboos St; open 8am-11am Sat-Wed for non-Muslims)*, this glorious piece of modern Islamic architecture was a gift to the nation from Sultan Qaboos to mark the 30th year of his reign. Completed in 2001, it took six years to build. Quietly imposing from the outside, the main prayer hall is breathtakingly rich. The Persian carpet alone is 70m x 60m wide, making it the largest carpet in the world; it took 600 women four years to weave.

When visiting the mosque, long sleeves and trousers (not jeans) or long skirts should be worn and women should cover their hair. (For more details on mosques see the special section 'Mosques' in the Facts about the Middle East chapter.)

Beach Facilities

Many of the big hotels have attractive beachside facilities open to nonguests for a fee. Women may feel more comfortable at one of these than on the public beaches. **Al-Bustan Palace Hotel** is on a beautiful secluded bay *(per day Sat-Wed OR8.400, Thur & Fri OR10.500)*. An engaged taxi from Mutrah should cost about OR3. Sheraton Oman Hotel has a **beach club** in Shatti al-Qurm for a more modest OR3 per day.

Dive Centres, Dolphin-Watching & Boat Trips

Diving and snorkelling facilities are available from **DivEco** *(☎ 602101; e diveco@omantel.net.om)*, outside the Grand Hyatt, Muscat. It also offers a number of water sports. **Marina Bander al-Rowdha** *(☎ 737288, e marina@omantel.net.om; Sidab St)* offers similar activities and a full range of boating amenities and boat trips.

Perhaps the most easy-going place to enjoy these activities is at the **Oman Dive Centre** *(☎ 950261; e diveoman@omantel .net.om)* at Bandar Jissah. The centre offers half-day snorkelling trips (OR9.500 including equipment hire), dolphin and whale-

watching trips (OR15) and coastal tours of Muscat (OR15). You can enjoy its peaceful beach (and club facilities) for the day for a nominal OR1 (OR3 on Thursday and Friday). Unless you're staying at Al-Bustan Palace Hotel, you'll need your own transport or an engaged taxi to get there (OR6 from Mutrah Souq).

Camping Equipment

Most of what you will need for a night under the stars is sold at Al-Fair supermarkets. For more specialised equipment, try **Dawood Trading** *(☎ 703295, fax 713553)* on Ruwi roundabout.

Places to Stay – Budget

Al-Nahda Hotel *(☎ 712385, fax 714994; Mutrah Corniche, Mutrah; singles/doubles/triples OR8.700/12.800/14.600)*, near the fish market, is a familiar travellers haunt but is in need of a facelift.

Naseem Hotel *(☎ 712418, fax 711728; Mutrah Corniche, Mutrah; singles/doubles OR10/14)* has large, clean, comfortable rooms, many facing the harbour and is recommended.

Qurm Beach House *(☎ 564070, fax 560 761; Way 1622, Qurm; singles/doubles OR10/20)* is in a quiet location and within walking distance of the beach on the approach to the Crowne Plaza Hotel. Don't be put off by the appearence of the lobby: the rooms are clean and appealingly odd.

Qurum Beach Hotel *(☎ 564070; e qbhotel@omantel.net.om; Shatti al-Qurm; singles/doubles OR14/18)* confusingly next door to the Beach Hotel, is a friendly place with a range of services, including boat trips.

Places to Stay – Mid-Range

Marina Hotel *(☎ 711711, fax 711313; Mutrah Corniche, Mutrah; singles/doubles OR14.40/OR29.250)* is a new hotel opposite the fish market with bright rooms and a restaurant overlooking the harbour. Rates include continental breakfast. (See also Places to Eat.)

Al-Wafa Hotel Flats *(☎ 786522, fax 786 534; Al-Jaame St; 1-bedroom/2-bedroom flats OR20/25)*, beside Ruwi bus station, is recommended for an early bus.

Beach Hotel *(☎ 696601, e beachhtl@omantel.net.om; Way 2818, Shatti al-Qurm; singles/doubles OR24/26.500)* has large rooms and a swimming pool.

OMAN

Places to Stay – Top End

Prices quoted here are rack rates and you can almost certainly arrange a discount of some sort.

Al-Bustan Palace Hotel (☎ 799666; e albustan@interconti.com; Al-Bustan; singles/doubles from OR113.00/129) is in a wonderful location and is a top-notch place to stay. In comparison with similar hotels in other countries it is good value for money. (See also the Al-Khiran Terrace entry in Places to Eat.)

Grand Hyatt, Muscat (☎ 641234; e hyatt mct@omantel.net.om; Shatti al-Qurm; singles/doubles OR91.570/103) is pure kitsch. The exterior owes much to Disney, while its stained glassed and marbled interior is a cross between Art Deco and a royal Bedouin tent. Watch out for the Arab on horseback – the statue rotates.

Hotel Inter-Continental, Muscat (☎ 600 500; e muscat@interconti.com; Shatti al-Qurm; singles/doubles from OR76.050/81.900) has been recently modernised and the gardens and pools extended to make it an attractive and popular resort. The hotel hosts international bands from September until April.

Crowne Plaza Hotel, Muscat (☎ 560100; e cpmct@omantel.net.om; Qurm St, Qurm; singles/doubles OR56.160/67.860), on a promontory overlooking Qurm beach, has a more relaxed atmosphere than many of the other top hotels.

Sheraton Oman Hotel (☎ 799899; e sher aton@omantel.net.om; Bayt al-Falaj St, Ruwi; singles/doubles OR41.090/46.960) is well located for business travellers and has a great seafood night (see also Places to Eat).

Places to Eat

Restaurants The **Bin Atique** (Al-Khuwair; meals OR2) serves a variety of local dishes. The restaurant caters mainly for homesick Omani traders, consequently you'll be seated on an old carpet in a private room. If you can put up with the surroundings, the food is generally good quality and authentic.

Marina Restaurant (Marina Hotel; Mutrah Corniche, Mutrah; dishes OR5) has a great view and serves Asian dishes.

Sindebad Restaurant (Al-Nahda Hotel; Mutrah; dishes OR1) serves good curries and biryanis.

National Hospitality Institute (☎ 771 3141; An-Nuzha St, Al-Wadi al-Kabir; 3-course lunch OR2; open Sat-Wed) is where nervous students practise their culinary and waiting skills. Ring to book a table as it gets surprisingly busy.

Woodlands (☎ 700192; Al-Bank al-Markazi St, Ruwi; mains OR1.500-2.200) is a cosy Indian restaurant in Ruwi's CBD with cheap bar prices.

Automatic Restaurant (mains OR2) in Qurm, behind the Sabco Centre, has good Lebanese food for casual dining.

Mumtaz Mahal (☎ 605907; Way 2601, Qurm; dishes OR10) is a wonderful Indian restaurant on a hill overlooking Qurm Nature Reserve. Try the snake coffee, which the head waiter performs by setting fire to an orange peel.

Tokyo Taro (☎ 702311; top floor Mecure al-Felaj Hotel, Ruwi; dishes OR10), with good views, offers a fun display of Filipino-style Japanese cooking, performed at the table. Try the fried ice cream.

Al-Khiran Terrace (☎ 799666; Al-Bustan Palace Hotel, Al-Bustan) serves an excellent Friday brunch for around OR10.530 in gorgeous surroundings. Al-Khiran has a bar licence after 2pm.

Sheraton Oman Hotel (☎ 799899 ext 5127; seafood night OR14.100) has a sumptuous seafood buffet night every Wednesday. You can try, among other local catches, swordfish and hamour, shark and kingfish, or sample the caviar and oysters. It's a worthwhile experience. Reservations are necessary for this popular evening.

Cafés Dozens of cafés sell a variety of largely Indian snacks, such as samosas and curried potatoes. You won't find good coffee here though, only tea and soft drinks. Arabic coffee is usually served with dates and is surprisingly hard to find in Muscat outside of an Omani home or a hotel lobby.

The **coffee shop**, left of the entrance to the Mutrah Souq, sells excellent mixed fruit juices from 500 baisa.

Cafe Camilia (Al-Jaame St; snacks 200 baisa), opposite Ruwi bus station, is a good for a quick sandwich or shwarma.

Women are less likely to be stared at in Western-style cafés in the big shopping centres. **D'Arcy's Kitchen** (☎ 600234;Shatti al-Qurm; dishes from OR1), next to the Omani Heritage Gallery on Way 2817, serves Western favourites at reasonable prices and is open when most other cafés are taking a siesta.

Each of the big hotels has an elegant café, but the Grand Hyatt, Muscat, is probably the best venue for afternoon tea and snacks.

Entertainment

Muscat is rather thin on entertainment although the five-star hotels and some of the smaller ones have bars and nightclubs, usually with live acts. *Oman Today* is your best source for this information.

Star Cinema (☎ 791641; Way 2703; tickets OR2.500) shows both Western and Indian films. It occupies the unmistakable round building with flashing lights near the telephone office in Ruwi. There's a newer cinema, **Al-Shatti Plaza** (☎ 692656; tickets OR2.500) in Shatti al-Qurm.

Getting There & Away

Air Seeb International Airport is 37km from Mutrah. For airport **flight** information call (☎ 519223 or 519456). The only domestic flights currently available are on **Oman Air** (☎ 707222) between Muscat and Salalah and Muscat and Khasab. (For more details, see the Getting Around section at the beginning of this chapter.)

Bus The national bus company **ONTC** (☎ 590046) provides comfortable intercity services throughout Oman. Its main depot is the **ONTC bus station** (☎ 708522) in Ruwi. Luggage can be stored beside the ticket office, free of charge. Timetables in English are available and a summary is printed in the *Oman Daily Observer*.

ONTC buses for Salalah (OR6/11 one way/return, 12 hours) depart at 6am and 7pm daily. However, there is some competition on this route. **Malatan Trading** (☎ 707896) has a 4.30pm daily service to Salalah and Bin **Qasim Transport** (☎ 785059) OR6/11 has a 3pm daily service. Both companies charge OR6/11 one way/return; both are around the corner from the bus station on Way 2985 near Moon Travels.

For buses to the UAE see Getting There & Away at the beginning of this chapter.

Taxi & Microbus Taxis and microbuses leave for all destinations from Al-Jaame St, opposite the main (ONTC) bus station in Ruwi. There is an additional departure point

at Rusayl roundabout, the next one west of the airport roundabout.

A shared taxi from Ruwi to Rusayl roundabout costs 500 baisa. Microbuses charge 300 baisa for the same trip. From Mutrah Corniche to Rusayl roundabout the taxi/microbus fare is 700/400 baisa.

Some sample taxi/microbus fares are:

to	engaged taxi (OR)	shared taxi (OR)	microbus (OR)
Barka	3	1	0.300
Buraimi	7	n/a	n/a
Nakhal	6	2	1
Nizwa	12	1.500	1
Rustaq	10	2	1
Samail	2.500	1	0.500
Sohar	8	2.500	1.700
Sur	16	4	3

Car There are several rental agencies in the area around the Ruwi roundabout as well as the usual desks in big hotels and at the airport. See Car in the Getting Around section earlier in this chapter for costs.

Getting Around

To/From the Airport Taxis between the airport and Qurm, Al-Khuwair and Ruwi cost OR5, and OR6 for Mutrah and Muscat. Alternatively, walk 300m to the airport roundabout outside the airport and wait for a microbus. They pass the airport fairly frequently between 7am and 7pm and cost 500 baisa to Ruwi, Mutrah or Muscat. There is no direct bus service to or from the airport.

Bus ONTC's system of local buses covers greater Muscat fairly thoroughly. Fares are either 200 or 300 baisa depending on the distance. Destinations are displayed on the front of the buses in Arabic and English. Timetables in English are available at the main bus station in Ruwi. Bus Nos 2, 4, 23, 24, 28, 31 and 32 all run between the Mutrah and Ruwi stations for 200 baisa. Other main routes include: Nos 23 and 24 to Qurm, and No 26 to Qurm and Al-Khuwair.

Microbus In Mutrah, local microbuses cruise the corniche, and congregate around the Mutrah bus station. In Ruwi they park en masse across Al-Jaame St, opposite the main bus station. Trips from one suburb to the next cost 200 to 300 baisa. No microbus journey within greater Muscat should cost more than 500 baisa.

Taxi Muscat's taxis, like all others in Oman, are orange and white and do not have meters. Even if you bargain you will inevitably pay two or three times the going rate for locals. Fix the rate before you get in. A taxi between suburbs in Muscat should cost no more than OR3 engaged or 800 baisa shared (getting to and from the airport excepted). Expect to be charged double the going rate to and from hotels. There are no regular microbuses from Ruwi to Mutrah but if you find one it should cost 100 baisa; an engaged taxi costs OR1.

Around Muscat

YITTI & BANDAR KHAYRAN
يتي بندر خيران

About 25km from Ruwi, this popular **beach** lies in the middle of a set of *khors* (rocky inlets) that are more usually visited by boat from Muscat.

If driving, from Souq Ruwi St follow the signs for Yitti through a maze of houses to a steep hill. Yitti is signposted again after 15.7km, soon after the road runs out of the hills.

Alternatively, follow the signs for As-Sifah to reach **Bandar Khayran**, a large, mangrove-fringed lagoon. It is a beautiful drive late in the afternoon when the sandstone seems to glow. There is no public transport.

QURAYAT
قريات

There are a number of features to enjoy in this attractive fishing village, an hour east of Muscat. It includes the 19th-century **castle** *(admission 500 baisa; open 8.30am-2.30pm Sun-Thur)* and a unique triangular **watchtower** overlooking the corniche. The sandy **beach** to the east of the tower extends for many miles with only the occasional football team to interrupt it.

Qurayat is well signposted from the Wadi Aday roundabout by Hatat House in Muscat, an 82km drive through the Eastern Hajar foothills. Taxis cost OR2 and microbuses cost OR1 from the Wadi Aday roundabout. An engaged taxi costs OR8.

Sharqiya Region
المنطقة الشرقيه

This easternmost corner of the Arabian Peninsular holds some of Oman's main attractions, including beautiful beaches, spectacular wadis, turtle nesting sites, and the sand dunes of Wahiba. As many of the sites of interest lie en route rather than in town, it's worth having your own vehicle, though tours cover the whole area. (For details see Organised Tours in the Getting Around section earlier in this chapter.)

COAST ROAD TO SUR

The five-hour drive from Muscat to Sur is very scenic and has many points of interest along the way. You can just about manage in a 2WD if it hasn't been raining but a 4WD is safer, as parts of the road are very steep.

To reach the coast road to Sur, take the blacktop from Muscat to Qurayat but turn right at the Toyota showroom on the Daghmar roundabout before you reach the town centre. After 6km turn right for Fans, Tiwi and Sur.

Hitching (not advisable for women, as the route is isolated) may be possible from here but make sure your ride takes you at least to Fans and carry plenty of water.

The blacktop soon runs out and the route continues along the bottom of Wadi Dayquat before meandering across the jebel (mountain) for 30km. A small watchtower signals a sharp descent into **Dibab** and arrival at the coast road to Sur.

Bimmah Sinkhole
بما سنخول

The blue-green, brackish water at the bottom of this peculiar 40m x 20m limestone hole invites a swim and a snorkel. Look out for the elusive, blind cave-fish.

The sinkhole is 1km inland, 6km after Dibab. It's not signposted but look for a ring of *barasti* (palm leaf) shelters on your right. Don't be put off by the padlocked gate: entry is permitted.

Wadi Shab
وادي شعب

This wadi is arguably one of the most gorgeous destinations in Oman; beyond the breathtaking entrance, the wadi rewards even the most reluctant walker with views

OMAN

of aquamarine pools, waterfalls, and terraced plantations; kingfishers add glorious splashes of colour. For the adventurous, there are plenty of opportunities for (discreet) swimming and a visit to a partially submerged cave.

To begin the walk, take the small rowing boat to the right of the wadi (OR1 return, payable to the local children) and follow the path through the oleanders. Be prepared to wade up to your knees in places and beware of algae-covered rocks. The path has been concreted (not very sympathetically) for part of the way. To reach the cave, allow up to two hours of walking and look for a ladder descending into a pool. Duck through a short underwater channel to find the cavern.

From Dibab, Wadi Shab is 40km southeast along the coast road. Keep an eye out for grazing gazelle along the route. You can't miss Wadi Shab: the dramatic vista of mountains opening into a pea-green lake is rather sublime after the barren plain. Vehicles, thankfully, cannot navigate the wadi beyond a small parking area.

Wadi Tiwi وادي طيوي

With its string of emerald pools and thick plantations, Wadi Tiwi can be accessed in a 4WD but take care to drive sensitively through the hidden villages. The road is narrow and steep in parts towards the upper reaches and it is easy to get stuck between the plantation walls.

To reach the wadi, continue along the coast road, past Wadi Shab and through the village of Tiwi. Turn right at a small roundabout by the block factory at the Sur end of the village.

Tiwi, and the two wadis either side of it, makes an easy day trip from Sur, 48km to the southeast. Alternatively, there is plenty of ad hoc camping along nearby beaches. The most popular is Tiwi Beach (White Beach), a large sandy bay, 9km northwest of Tiwi towards Dibab.

Qalhat قلهات

Built around 2nd century AD, there is not much left of one of the oldest settlements in Oman except the picturesque **Tomb of Bibi Miriam**, a water cistern and remnants of the city walls. As the coast road to Sur passes right through the middle of Qalhat, however, it is worth getting out to have a look:

you'll be in good company as both Marco Polo and Ibn Battuta stopped here on their travels. The sea here often boils with huge shoals of sardines.

Qalhat is 22km from Tiwi and 26km from Sur. To reach Sur skirt round the gas works and keep close to the sea. Turn left onto a blacktop road near the water tower, passing Sur Beach Hotel on the left.

SUR سور

With an attractive corniche, two forts, excellent beaches nearby and a long history of dhow-building, there is much to commend Sur to the tourist. In addition to its own attractions, Sur is a convenient base for day trips to some of the country's top destinations, including Wadi Tiwi and Wadi Shab, the turtle reserve at Ras al-Jinz and Wahiba Sands.

Orientation & Information

The blacktop road from Muscat (via Ibra) is a few kilometres inland and ends at a clock tower with a marine mural. The main road, running parallel with the coast and punctuated by five roundabouts, begins at the clock tower (Roundabout 1) and ends at the souqs and Sur Hotel. Sur Mecure Hotel, the forts, banks, museum and restaurants lie off this road.

Bilad Sur Castle

Built to defend the town against marauding tribes from the interior, 200-year-old Bilad Sur Castle *(admission 500 baisa; open 8.30am-2.30pm Sun-Thur)* is the more interesting of the town's two fortresses. To reach the castle, turn left 1.3km from Roundabout 1 at an elaborately kitsch residence. There is a small post office behind the castle.

Sunaysilah Castle

Perched on a rocky eminence, this 300-year-old castle *(admission 500 baisa; open 8.30am-30pm Sun-Thur)* is built on a classic square plan with four round watchtowers. The entrance is a few metres off Roundabout 3 but access is via Roundabout 4.

Marine Museum

The highlight of this small exhibit is a collection of photographs of Sur in 1905. The museum *(admission free; open randomly)* is inside the Al-Arouba Sports Club (look for

OMAN

the green and white flags opposite Sunaysi-lah Castle).

Corniche & Dhow Yard

The corniche affords a wonderful view across to the picturesque village of **Ayajh** with its distinctive **lighthouse**. Dhows used to be led to safe haven by Ayajh's three **watchtowers**, which mark the passage into the lagoon. It is still possible to see the boats being made by hand alongside this passage.

To reach the dhow yards turn left at the T-junction at the end of the main road and follow the road in a semicircle past the corniche to the great lagoon. The road circles back eventually to the new souq, passing by **Fatah al-Khair**, a beautifully restored dhow, built in Sur 70 years ago and recently brought back from retirement in Yemen.

Places to Stay & Eat

The top two hotels in Sur publish a 'rack rate' at greatly inflated prices; the following prices should be available if you ask, with some seasonal variation. All three hotels can arrange trips to see the turtles at Ras al-Jinz.

Sur Hotel (☎ 440090, fax 443798; singles/doubles OR10.500/15) in the middle of the new souq area has noisy rooms close to the bus stop.

Sur Beach Hotel (☎ 442 031; e surb htl@omantel.net.om; singles/doubles OR12/15, with seaview OR18/22) is a friendly Best Western hotel, which benefits from a beach location and a 2km path along the shore. Watch for phosphorescent waves at night. It offers free transportation to a sister hotel at Ras al-Hadd (near the turtle reserve).

Sur Mercure Hotel (☎ 443777; e resvnsur@ omantel.net.om; singles/doubles OR24/29) has a good bar with live entertainment but it is several kilometres inland. The hotel is on the right of the main road, 2.6km after Roundabout 1. Access, however, is via Roundabout 2.

Arabian Sea Restaurant (☎ 9746423; mains OR1-1.500) on the ground floor of the Sur Hotel (the entrance faces the other side of the block) is cheap and cheerful.

Zaki Restaurant (mains OR1) between Roundabout 4 and 5, next to the BP station, has rotisserie chickens and serves good dhal.

Pizza Hut (☎ 445388) is located just off Roundabout 3.

Getting Away & Around

Public transport leaves from or near the Sur Hotel. Buses to Muscat (OR3.400, 4¼ hours, twice daily) depart at 6am and 2.30pm. Taxis for Muscat cost OR4 to the Rusayl roundabout in Muscat (OR16 engaged). Microbuses make the same trip for OR3 and leave early in the morning. Taxis cost 150 baisa per ride anywhere in Sur.

RAS AL-JINZ رأس الجنز

Ras al-Jinz (Ras al-Junayz), the easternmost point of the Arabian Peninsula, is an internationally important **turtle nesting site** for the endangered green turtle. Over 20,000 females return annually to the beach where they hatched in order to lay eggs, a process that takes up to two hours.

Turtles are easily disturbed, especially when first emerging from the sea, and so the area is under government protection. A warden escorts visitors to the beach at about 9.30pm every evening throughout the year.

Five different species of turtle can be spotted along Oman's coastline but July is the peak laying season for the Greens. September to November, however, is the best time to witness both laying and hatching at Ras al-Jinz.

A permit (OR1 per person) is purchased at the park entrance and includes the guided tour to the beach.

Places to Stay

There is a small camp site of basic wooden huts that can be reserved through the **Directorate General of Nature Reserves** (☎ 692574, fax 602283; OR3).

Desert Discovery Tours (☎ 9317874, e tours@omantel.net.om; per person OR15) offers accommodation in barasti huts with shared bathroom and communal meals 4km outside the reserve.

Getting There & Around

Ras al-Jinz can be visited as an evening trip from Sur (organised through any of the hotels, and with a one-hour journey time each way). There is no public transport.

If you have a 4WD, turn right at Roundabout 4 in Sur and follow the signs to Ayajh. At the village roundabout, follow the graded coast road for 16km. At this point, two signs for Ras al-Jinz point in opposite directions! Take the right fork to see spectacular zebra-coloured rock formations. Having a 4WD is not strictly necessary but the washboard surfaces will shake the ball bearings off a tractor. The two forks rejoin after 15km to 20km and skirt a large lagoon and Ras al-Jinz is signposted from there. Don't leave the track: mirages of water can lead you into the shallow-crusted *sabkha* (salt plain).

RAS AL-HADD

A **castle** (admission 500 baisa; open 8.30am-2.30pm Sun-Thur), some shops and attractive lagoon scenery nearby make this fishing village a useful supply point or alternative stopover to camping at Ras al-Jinz.

Ra's al-Hadd Beach Hotel (☎ 442031/32, fax 442228; singles/doubles OR21/26) has surprisingly good portacabins with showers set back from an active turtle beach and opposite a pretty lagoon; a permanent building with a swimming pool was due to open in October 2002. To reach this Best Western hotel, turn left just after the castle and follow the signs.

Turtle Beach Resort (☎ 440068, fax 443900; OR15 per person) offers *barasti* huts with shared bathroom and meals included. It is situated on another glorious lagoon but the huts are so close together you are at the mercy of noisy neighbours. Turn left immediately after entering Ras al-Hadd; the resort is 7km along a bumpy road.

To reach Ras al-Hadd, follow the signs for Ras al-Jinz but veer left after Khor Garame. It is clearly signposted. There is no public transport to this area.

WAHIBA (SHARQIYA) SANDS
رمال وهيبه (الشرقية)

A destination in its own right, or a stopover between Muscat and Sur, these copper-coloured sand dunes could keep the visitor occupied for days. Home to the Bedu (Bedouins) and their racing camels, the sands offer the visitor a glimpse of a traditional way of life that is fast disappearing as modern conveniences limit the need for a nomadic existence. There are regular **camel races** throughout the region from mid-October to mid-April (see the boxed text 'Pet Camel').

It is essential to have a 4WD and knowledge of off-road driving to enter the sands. Alternatively there are plenty of tours available (see Places to Stay in this section for details).

Places to Stay

Al-Qabil Rest House (☎ 593232, fax 590 144; singles/doubles OR13.900/17.500) offers comfortable rooms around a courtyard with close access to the sands, if camping isn't quite your thing.

Desert Discovery Tours (☎ 9317874, fax 590144; singles/doubles OR13.900/17.500) can organise transport (OR15 per person) from Al-Qabil Rest House on the Muscat-Sur highway to their spectacular camp on the edge of a sand dune. Accommodation is in tents with shared bathroom and the price includes meals.

Al-Raha Tourism Camp (☎ 9343851; per person OR15) has been recommended by travellers.

Golden Sands (☎ 9428728; per person OR15) has cosy stone accommodation deeper into the dunes, but call first for navigational assistance.

All camps offer the full desert experience, including camel rides, camel racing, dune-driving, sand-skiing and trips to Bedouin settlements.

Al-Sharqiya Sands Hotel (☎ 9205112, fax 9207012; singles/doubles OR18.700/21) on the Muscat-Sur highway just south of Ibra is new and attractive and makes another good base.

Getting There & Around
To get to Wahiba by public transport, take a Muscat-Sur bus (OR1.800/1 from Muscat/Sur) and ask to be dropped off at the Al-Qabil Rest House. It takes three hours from Muscat and 1½ hours from Sur. There are two buses per day in either direction.

Pet Camel

A she-camel from Wahiba, known as Al-Ghuzail, has become something of a national celebrity. Her owner, Mohammed bin Said al-Wahibi, was offered half a million US dollars for her by an Emirati neighbour but he was too attached to the prize-winning animal to sell. The sultan heard of the touching story and bought the camel himself, allowing her to continue in residence with her affectionate owner.

The sands run parallel to the Muscat-Sur highway and the easiest access (with your own vehicle) is made 43km south of Ibra at Al-Mintirib.

The Western Hajar Mountains جبل الحجر الغربية

This dramatic mountainous region is probably the biggest tourist destination in Oman and for good reason. The area has some spectacular scenery, including Jebel Shams (Oman's highest mountain), Wadi Ghul (the Grand Canyon of Arabia), and Jebel Akhdar (the fruit bowl of Oman). In addition some of the country's best castles can be seen in Nizwa, Bahla and Jabrin.

If you have 4WD and want to make a round trip from Muscat, drive to Nizwa, cross the mountains from nearby Al-Hamra and descend to the Batinah plain near Rustaq.

SAMAIL سمائل

If you have your own vehicle, it's worth making a detour to visit Samail. A fort and Oman's oldest mosque are hidden in the plantations but the real attraction is the lush **oasis** through which the road passes.

Masjid Mazin bin Ghadouba Mosque, with wooden lintels and stained-glass windows, has been completely rebuilt and is constructed from blocks of stone. To find the mosque turn right off the main road through Samail at the sign for 'Sefalat Samail'. After 500m there is a T-junction. Turn left and follow the narrow street through town for 1.5km. The mosque is on the right opposite a grocery store.

Samail is signposted off the Muscat-Nizwa highway and off the Muscat-Sur highway as it cuts between the two. You can get to the souq area of Samail by public transport but to explore the oasis you'll have to walk. Microbuses charge 500 baisa for the trip from Rusayl roundabout (800 baisa from Ruwi intercity microbus station), while the taxi fare is OR1.

NIZWA نزوى

Nizwa lies on a plain surrounded by a thick palm oasis and some of Oman's highest mountains. About two hours from Muscat along a picturesque new highway, the town is not only an interesting destination in its own right, it is a gateway to the historic sites of Bahla and Jabrin, and for excursions up Jebel Akhdar and Jebel Shams.

The seat of factional imams until the 1950s, Nizwa is still a conservative town and appreciates a bit of decorum from its visitors.

Orientation & Information

Nizwa's fort dominates the town centre and all of Nizwa's sites of interest are either inside or within walking distance of the fort. The hotels, however, lie along the Muscat-Nizwa highway, a few kilometres (100 baisa by microbus) from the town centre.

Coming from Muscat, the bus stop and taxi stand are situated in the middle of the wadi in front of the fort complex, 800m past the *khanjar* roundabout. When the wadi is flowing, the road is impassable at this point, hence the bridge further upstream that leads to the book roundabout (ie, the roundabout with the stack of books in the middle). Buses for Ibri leave from the book roundabout.

Banks and moneychangers are along the main street that runs from the fort complex to the book roundabout. The post office is inside the souq, next to the No 14 bus stop.

Nizwa Fort

Built in the 17th century by Sultan bin Saif al-Yaruba, the first imam of the Ya'aruba dynasty, the fort (*admission 500 baisa; open 9am-4pm Sat-Thur & 8am-11am Fri*) is famed for its enormous round tower. It is worth climbing to the top of the tower to appreciate the extent of the date plantations encircling the town and to enjoy the view of the Hajar Mountains.

Nizwa Souq

The fruit and vegetable, meat and fish markets are housed in new buildings, behind the great, crenulated piece of city wall that overlooks the wadi. If you're not put off by the smell of heaving Brahmin bulls and irritable goats, the characterful **livestock souq** (in full swing between 7am and 9am every Thur) is worth a look. It occupies a small plot of land beyond the souq walls, left of the entrance.

Prices for antiques and silver at the other end of the souq (nearest the fort) were greatly inflated until September 2001 dealt a blow to the country's tourism industry. Even now you will have to try hard to find a bargain but local craftsmanship is good.

Places to Stay & Eat

All the following hotels are on the Muscat-Nizwa road.

Nizwa Guest House (☎/fax 412402; rooms OR14) has huge, rather dingy rooms, 3km from the *khanjar* roundabout.

Majan Hotel (☎ 431910, fax 431911; singles/doubles OR12/15) caters for local business clientele but is clean and serviceable, 5km from the *khanjar* roundabout.

Tanuf Residency (☎ 411601, fax 411059; singles/doubles OR10/12) has huge rooms with a view and a new restaurant about to open. It is next door to the Arab World restaurant, 4.5km from the *khanjar* roundabout.

Falaj Daris Hotel (☎ 410500; e fdhnizwa@ omantel.net.om; singles/doubles OR21.800/ 29.500) offers up to 50% discount from May to August. It has recently been enlarged to include a second swimming pool, gym and a bar. The rooms are more pleasant in the new block but the older courtyard and pool has some welcome shade. The hotel can arrange permits to visit Jebel Akhdar. The hotel is 4km from the *khanjar* roundabout.

Nizwa Hotel (☎ 431616; e nizhotel@ omantel.net.om; singles/doubles OR41.200/ 47.100) also offers up to 50% discount from May to August. It is situated near the turning for Jebel Akhdar, 18km from the *khanjar* roundabout.

Bin Atique Restaurant (☎ 410466; mains OR1.300) is part of a small chain of Omani-style restaurants that offer local dishes for reasonable prices.

Al-Zuhul Restaurant opposite the fort complex has great night-time views of the illuminated fort and mosque from seating on the pavement. It sells shwarma and kebabs and is popular with the locals.

Getting There & Away

ONTC buses between Muscat and Nizwa (OR1.600, two hours 20 minutes, daily) leave at 8am and 2.30pm. They leave Nizwa for Muscat at 8.40am and 5.50pm. You can catch the southbound bus from Muscat to Salalah at the roundabout on the edge of Nizwa. The buses come through Nizwa every day at approximately 9am and 9pm. The fare from Nizwa to Salalah is OR6 one way and OR11 return, and the journey takes ten hours. Telephone the **Ruwi bus station** (☎ 708522) in Muscat to reserve a seat.

Taxi/microbus fares from Nizwa to Rusayl roundabout in Muscat are OR1.500/ 1 (to Ruwi add 500 baisa). Microbuses go to Samail for 700 baisa while taxis charge OR1.500 for the same trip. Nizwa to Ibri is OR2 by taxi or OR1.500 by microbus.

AROUND NIZWA

Tanuf تنوف

Much of Oman's bottled water comes from this small village at the foot of the jebel. The old town was destroyed during the Jebel Wars of the 1950s but this is a good place to see a working *falaj* (irrigation channel).

To reach Tanuf, take the Bahla road from Nizwa for 18km, and turn right at the green water bottle sign. Turn left after 3km and follow the road behind the old village to reach the *falaj*.

BAHLA بهلا

Ask historians what is famous about Bahla and they will say the fort; ask expats and retailers and they will say the potteries; but ask any Omani not resident in Bahla and they will be sure to say, 'jin'. These devilishly difficult spirits have been blamed for all manner of evil-eye activities but you are unlikely to encounter them unless you understand Arabic, as they are carried as living legend in the folklore of the country.

What you will encounter in Bahla is a remarkable set of **battlements**, they are evident at every turn in the road and run impressively for a kilometre or more along the wadi. The battlements belong to a huge **fort** complex that is still currently being restored as a Unesco World Heritage site and is closed to the public.

There is a traditional **souq** (open 6am-10am daily) with homemade ropes and *fadl* (large metal platters used for feeding the whole family) for sale and a beautiful tree shading the tiny, central courtyard. To find it, turn off the main Nizwa-Ibri highway, opposite the fort. Its opening is 100m on the right.

Water on Tap

It may not have pipes and U-bends, but Oman's ancient *falaj* (irrigation channel) system is as sophisticated as any Western water mains. The channels, cut into mountainsides, running across miniature aqueducts and double-deckering through tunnels, are responsible for most of the oases in Oman. The precious water is diverted firstly into drinking wells, then into mosque washing areas and at length to the plantations, where it is siphoned proportionately among the village farms. There are over 4,000 of these channels in Oman, some of which were built more that 1500 years ago. The longest channel is said to run for 120km under Wahiba Sands.

To find Bahla's famous **potteries**, follow the main road through town towards the plantations. After 500m you will come to a number of potteries; the traditional unglazed water pots that hang in the tree cost a couple of rials.

The area's only hotel, the quirky **Bahla Motel** (☎ 420211, fax 420212; doubles OR15) has huge twin rooms only. The hotel could be dubbed the 'Loo with a View' as the rather run-down rooms sport lavish bathrooms with enormous porthole windows overlooking the mountains.

Microbuses to Nizwa cost 300 baisa and taxis 500 baisa. An engaged taxi should be OR2 – if you can haggle like a local! The trip takes about 45 minutes. There is an excellent branch of the Nizwa-based **Al-Huzaily Travel** (☎ 419313, fax 419009) opposite the bus stop on the corner of the road that leads to the souq. It acts as an ad hoc information centre.

JABRIN   جبرين

Rising without competition from the surrounding plain, **Jabrin Castle** (admission 500 baisa; open 9am-4pm Sat-Thur & 8am-11am Fri) is an impressive sight. Even if you have had a surfeit of fortifications at Nizwa and Bahla, make the effort to climb one more keep as Jabrin is one of the best preserved and whimsical of them all.

Look out for the **date store**, to the right of the main entrance on the left-hand side. The juice of the fruit would have run along

the channels into storage vats, ready for cooking or to help women in labour. Note the elaborately **painted ceilings** with original floral motifs in many of the rooms.

Head for the flagpole for a bird's-eye-view of the **latticed-window courtyard** at the heart of the keep. Finding these hidden rooms is part of the fun – and the defensive mechanism – of Jabrin. Before leaving, try to locate the **burial chambers**, remarkable for the carved vaults. The **falaj system** was used as an early air-con.

From Bahla, turn left off the Bahla-Ibri road after 7km and Jabrin is clearly signposted from there. Beware of hitching from the junction as it is an exposed 4km walk if you're out of luck. It may be better to engage a return taxi (OR2) from Bahla.

JEBEL SHAMS   جبل شمس

Oman's highest mountain, Jebel Shams (Mountain of the Sun; 3075m) is ironically best known not for its peak but for the spectacularly deep **Wadi Ghul** that lies alongside it. It is not known locally as the grand canyon for nothing and the road allows frighteningly close views over the edge.

Watch out for the **carpet sellers** who appear from nowhere across the barren landscape clutching piles of red-and-black goat-hair rugs. Weaving is a profitable local industry but don't expect a bargain: The cheapest 1.5m rug will leave you with not much change from a OR20 note.

Jebel Shams makes a feasible day trip from Nizwa but to savour the eerie beauty of the place you could consider camping at the plateau near the canyon rim. Alternatively, the brand new **Jebel Shams Hotel** (☎ 9382639; doubles OR16) has attractive stone cabins with bathroom, veranda and heater/air-con. The hotel is situated close to the canyon rim, 39km from the start of the road.

The junction for Jebel Shams is clearly signposted off the Nizwa-Ibri road, 31km from the book roundabout in Nizwa. Turn right at the BP station then left after 11.8km at a Shell station. A blacktop road follows the bottom of the wadi to the start of the ascent. Notice the vacant **village of Ghul**, 9.1km after the Shell station, at the entrance of the Wadi Ghul canyon.

From the end of the blacktop, it is a steep and often loose climb to the canyon rim,

28km above. It is possible but foolhardy to attempt the drive without a 4WD and car rental agencies won't thank you for the abuse of their car! There is no public transport.

JEBEL AKHDAR الجبل الأخضر

Without a guide or some inside information Jebel Akhdar (Green Mountain) may seem something of a misnomer to the first-time visitor who climbs expectantly from the desert floor hoping to see Switzerland at the top. Firstly, Jebel Akhdar refers not to a mountain as such but to an area that encompasses the great **Saiq Plateau**, at 2,000m above sea level. Secondly, the jebel keeps its fecundity well hidden in a labyrinth of wadis and terraces where the cooler mountain air and greater rainfall encourages prize pomegranates, apricots, and other temperate fruit.

With a day or two to explore this 'top of the beanstalk' the determined visitor will soon stumble across the gardens and **orchards** that make this region so justly prized.

Jebel Akhdar is particularly famous for its fragrant, pink roses from which is made that all-important, post-dinner courtesy: rosewater. Every April the petals are harvested and steamed (not boiled) over wood fires and the condensed vapours collected and filtered before bottling. The process is still conducted as a cottage industry and if you are here in season ask a local guide for a visit.

Temperatures during December to March can drop to as little as -5°C and hail stones are not uncommon.

The area was the centre of fierce fighting during the Jebel Wars of the 1950s and until recently access was restricted to residents and the military. A permit is still necessary before making the ascent (for details see Places to Stay in this section).

A walking trail through the terraced villages of Wadi al-Muaydin to the Saiq Plateau (allow six hours from the Shell station at the start of the road) does not require a permit, but you'll need a guide.

Places to Stay

Jebel al-Akhdar Hotel (☎ 429009, fax 429119; e jakhotel@omantel.net.om; singles/ doubles OR21.800/29.500) will fax the necessary **visitor's permit** providing you come by 4WD and stay at least one night at the

hotel. Once the new road is completed (June 2003) these restrictions will probably be relaxed. The hotel, on the Saiq Plateau just before the town of Saiq, is new, with an open fire in the lobby in winter and two rather whacky stained-glass domes. Make sure you pick up a hand-drawn map of the area to locate the best viewpoints and villages.

Getting There & Away

Access to Jebel Akhdar is via the town of Birkat al-Mawz, which lies on the Muscat-Nizwa highway, 111km from the Rusayl roundabout in Muscat and 24km from the *khanjar* roundabout in Nizwa. Following the signs for Wadi al-Muaydin, turn left in the village and pass the Birkat al-Mawz fort on your right. After 6km you will reach the second of two checkpoints where you will have to show your permit. The hotel is 28km beyond the checkpoint and providing you keep to the main road you shouldn't have difficulty in finding it.

There is as yet no public transport to the area but several tour companies, including **NTT** (☎ 566046), offer day trips, including permit, for a hefty OR110. (See Organised Tours at the start of this chapter for details.)

AL-HAMRA TO WADI BANI AWF الحمراء الروادي بني عوف

This newly opened road over the Hajar Mountains is truly spectacular and affords some of the best views in Oman. It can be accomplished as a long day trip from Muscat. Alternatively, it can be used to bridge the sites of interest around Nizwa with those of the Batinah plain without having to return to Muscat. Although the road has been well graded, you need a 4WD to negotiate the sustained descent into Wadi Bani Awf.

The route begins near Al-Hamra, one of the oldest mud-brick villages in Oman. From the roundabout in Nizwa, take the road to Bahla and turn right to Al-Hamra after 30.6km and zero the odometer. At 3.5km turn right again for Hoota Cave (Hoti Cave) and Balad Seet.

Access to the mountain road is a bit confusing but you are heading for the zigzag ascending the jebel in front of you. At 8.1km take the right fork for Balad Seet and right again at 8.3km. At 9km turn left then follow the signs heading up the mountain.

Ignore signs to Hoti Cave (closed for development until further notice) or you will ascend the mountain on the wrong side of the wadi. At 14.6km, take the right fork and continue following the signs for Balad Seet. At 21.6km you will come to the saddle of the ridge and the highest point in the road. It's worth spending time here to enjoy the scenery and to look for wolf traps before the long descent into the enchanting village of Hatt.

After Hatt, the road continues for another six kilometres towards Balad Seet but skirts past the village which is off the road to the left. At 43.8km, the road passes the entrance to aptly named Snake Gorge, a popular destination for adventure hikers. From here the main track meanders round the mountain to the exit of Snake Gorge at 49.6km, signalled by a neat row of trees. Continue along the main track into Wadi Bani Awf (a destination in its own right) ignoring the left fork at 57.2km. At 59.4km you will pass through the small wadi village of Al-Teekah and eventually end up on the Rustaq-Nakhal road at 69.7km

Turn right for Barka and, when you reach Barka roundabout on the main Sohar-Muscat highway, turn right again for Muscat.

The Batinah Plain

This flat and fertile strip of land between the Hajar Mountains and the Gulf of Oman is the country's most populous area and renowned as the bread-basket of Oman. There are a number of interesting sites for the visitor, including the old castle towns of Nakhal and Rustaq, a couple of interesting fishing towns, Barka and Sohar, and an attractive resort at Sawadi.

BARKA برقح

The main reason for visiting Barka, 80km west of Muscat, is to see **bull-butting**. To get to the bullring take the turning for Barka off the Muscat-Sohar highway and turn left at the T-junction in the centre of town. After 3.4km you will see the shallow, concrete ring on your right.

Barka's **fort** (admission 500 baisa; open 8.30am-2.30pm Sun-Thur), right at the T-junction and 300m on the left, has an unusual octagonal tower.

Barka's other point of interest is 18th-century **Bayt Nua'man** (admission 500 baisa; open 8.30am-2.30pm Sun-Thur), a restored merchant house. The turning for the house is signposted off the Muscat-Sohar highway, 7km west of Barka roundabout.

Barka is famous for its *halwa*, a uniquely Omani confection laboriously made from a glutenous mixture of boiled sugars, rosewater and cardamom, among other ingredients. It is quite distinct from the sesame confection, halvah, found across the rest of the region. The sticky Omani sweet is served with coffee on all official occasions. A pot from dedicated *halwa* shops in town costs from OR3.

Getting There & Away

ONTC buses between the Barka roundabout and Muscat's Ruwi bus station (400 baisa) take one hour express, 1½ hours regular and leave four times daily. Taxis and microbuses can be found both around the T-junction in town and at the Barka roundabout. A taxi from Rusayl roundabout to Barka costs OR1 per person and around OR3 engaged. Microbuses charge 300 baisa.

NAKHAL نخل

Nakhal is a picturesque town dominated by the Hajar Mountains and one of Oman's most dramatic **forts** (admission 500 baisa; open 7am-5pm daily). There are excellent views of the Batinah plain from the ramparts.

Continue past the fort through date plantations for a couple of kilometres to find the hot **spring** of Ath-Thowra. The spring emerges from the wadi walls and is channelled into a *falaj* for the irrigation of the surrounding plantations. There are usually some children, or some goats, or both, splashing in the overspill. Picnic tables with shelters make it a popular place on Thursday and Friday.

Microbuses and taxis are the only viable transport to Nakhal and leave from the junction with the main road and in the area below the fort. Microbuses charge OR1 for the trip to Rusayl roundabout and 300 baisa to/from the Barka roundabout. Taxis charge about OR2 for the same trip if you can find one that isn't local-only.

RUSTAQ الرستاق

Some 175km west of Muscat, Rustaq is best known today for its imposing **fort**, though it once enjoyed a spell as Oman's capital. The small **souq** near the entrance to the fort has a few antiques and souvenirs but the smart **new souq** on the main street, about 1.5km from the highway, has left the old one for dead.

Microbuses can be found a few hundred metres from the fort on the main road to Nakhal (500 baisa), the Barka roundabout (400 baisa) and Muscat (OR1). The taxi fare to Muscat is OR2.

Alternatively, you can head for Sohar by taxi or bus for OR1.

SAWADI السوادي

A sandy spit of land and some **islands** scattered off the shore make Sawadi a popular day trip, an hour or so's drive west of Muscat. At low tide, you can walk to one of the islands, but beware: the tide returns very quickly. There's good **snorkelling** off the islands and local fishermen will take you around for OR4.

Shells abound at Sawadi, including pen-oysters, figs and sundials and the beach is carpeted with *Umbonium vestiaria*, a tiny, pink, snail-like mollusc. The resort shop sells a handy volume called *Collectable Eastern Arabian Seashells* if you want help identifying the booty on the beach.

Al-Sawadi Beach Resort (☎ 895545, fax 895595; w www.alsawadibeach.com; singles/doubles OR20/23) is a friendly and relaxing place if you want to make a weekend of it. The resort has a good pool, gym, restaurant and café, and an excellent dive centre. Only 40 minutes from the airport, the resort makes an alternative place to stay to Muscat especially as the tour desk can organise car rental and competitive tours.

To get to Sawadi, take a right turn 16.7km west of the Barka roundabout off the main Sohar-Muscat highway (signposted almost opposite the Yokohama billboard) and drive a further 12km to the coast. The resort is 1km before the end of the headland. A microbus from Muscat to the junction costs 700 baisa, but hitching is the only option to reach the coast – unless you can hail a passing taxi (OR1).

SOHAR صحار

Home of two famous sailors, the historical Ahmed bin Majid (see History earlier in this chapter) and the fictional Sinbad, Sohar is one of those places where history casts a shadow over modern reality. A thousand years ago it occupied three times its present area and was the largest town in the country. Now it is an attractive provincial town but with little more than legend to keep the visitor amused. It is best visited en route to Dubai or as part of a tour of the Batinah coast.

Orientation & Information

Most of Sohar's sites of interest lie along or near the gleaming corniche. To get there, take the city centre exit off the highway, turn right at the An-Nahdah roundabout and head for the fort.

Things to See

Sohar's distinctive white **fort** (admission 500 baisa; open 8am-2pm & 4pm-6pm Sat-Wed, 8am-noon & 4pm-6pm Thur & Fri) is worth a visit. There's a small **museum** in the fort's tower and the **tomb** of one of Oman's 19th-century rulers, namely, Sayyid Thuwaini bin Said bin Sultan al-Busaid, the ruler of Oman from 1856 to 1866.

The **fish market** next to the corniche is fun early in the morning. The **handicraft souq** (open 8am-noon & 4pm-9pm Sat-Thur) is signposted after the An-Nahdah roundabout and has workshops selling a variety of traditional Omani items.

Places to Stay & Eat

Al-Wadi Hotel (☎ 840058, fax 841997; singles/doubles OR24/27.500) is the cheaper of the two hotels in Sohar. To get there from Muscat, turn left off the highway at the dome-on-stilts roundabout. It's about 10km from the town centre.

Sohar Beach Hotel (☎ 841111, fax 843776; singles/doubles OR35/41) offers big ad hoc discounts so ask before making a reservation. This rather gracious hotel is situated north of the corniche, on a long sandy beach.

There are a number of good biryani restaurants within easy walking distance of the fort.

Getting There & Away

ONTC buses from Muscat (OR2.300, three hours, four times daily) drop passengers off at Sohar hospital and then continue to Buraimi or Dubai. Check with **Ruwi bus station** (☎ 708522) for accurate times.

Microbuses and taxis come and go from a car park across the street from the hospital. Microbuses charge OR1.700 for the trip to Rusayl roundabout in Muscat and OR2 to Ruwi. Taxis charge OR2.500 to Rusayl roundabout and OR3 to Ruwi. Expect to pay around OR8 for an engaged taxi to Rusayl roundabout. An engaged taxi from Sohar to Rustaq or Nakhal costs OR15.

BURAIMI البريمي

Buraimi is not part of the Batinah plain but it is most easily reached from Sohar. Buraimi is the Omani portion of the border town of Al-Ain, which belongs to the UAE. To approach the town, you have to exit the Omani checkpoint, 53km from the border. While technically still in Oman for the first 53km, you are free to visit any part of the UAE from here. Both the Omani and Emirati sides of the oasis are covered in the UAE chapter.

Two daily buses run a service between Buraimi and Muscat (OR3.600, 4½ hours) and engaged taxis make the trip for OR7.

Dhofar

The southernmost province of Oman is a world away from the industrious north and separated from it geographically by an interminable rock desert. With its historic frankincense trade, great beaches, a laid-back atmosphere and an interesting ethnic mix, it is worth making the effort to get there if time allows, particularly during or just after the *khareef* or rainy season.

There are many intriguing sites to visit as day trips from the provincial capital of Salalah, including Job's Tomb, hidden in the hills behind the city; the heroic town of Mirbat with its beautiful adjacent beaches; and Mughsail, famed for the violent blowholes in the undercliff and for nearby groves of wild frankincense.

SALALAH صلاله

Salalah, the capital of Dhofar and the birthplace of Sultan Qaboos, is a colourful, subtropical city that owes much of its character to Oman's former territories in East Africa. Flying into Salalah from Muscat, especially during the *khareef*, it is hard to imagine that Oman's first and second city

share the same continent. From mid-June to mid-September, monsoon clouds from India bring a constant drizzle to the area and, as a result, the grey stubble of Salalah's surrounding jebel is transformed into an oasis of misty pastures shared by cows and camels. Year round, Salalah's coconut-fringed beaches and plantations of bananas and papayas offer the visitor a taste of Zanzibar in the heart of the Arabian desert.

If you are travelling during the *khareef* and can put up with the unremittingly tedious journey from Muscat (or Nizwa), it is worth going overland to Salalah and returning by plane. This is the best way to sense the full spectacle of the *khareef* with its ruler-line precision across the top of the jebel; after eight hours of featureless rocky plain, Dhofar seems like a little miracle. There are several motels along the 1047km route, including **Al-Ghaftain Resthouse** (*☎/fax 956872; singles/doubles OR10.900/ 15.300)*, which lies just over halfway.

Orientation & Information

The intersection of An-Nahdah and As-Salam Sts forms the commercial hub of the Salalah. Both the ONTC bus station and the Redan Hotel are a 10- to 15-minute walk from this intersection and the gold souq is around the corner.

Money There are several banks and a few exchange houses around the intersection of An-Nahdah and As-Salam Sts. Cash advances are available from the **HSBC** ATM on As-Salam St. **AmEx** is represented by **Zubair Travel** (*☎ 235581, 235582; open 8am-1pm & 4pm-6pm Sat-Thur)* in the lobby of the Holiday Inn Salalah (see Places to Stay later in this section). It cannot cash cheques for clients but it will hold mail. Mail should be addressed to: American Express (Clients' Mail), c/o Zubair Travel & Services Bureau – Salalah Branch Office, PO Box 809, Postal Code 211, Oman.

Post & Communications The entrance to the **main post office** (*☎ 292933; An-Nahdah St; open 8am-2pm Sat-Wed, 9am-11am Thur)* is from the rear of the building.

The **telephone office** (*cnr An-Nahdah & Al-Montazah Sts; open 8am-2.30pm & 4pm-10pm daily)* has fax and telex facilities.

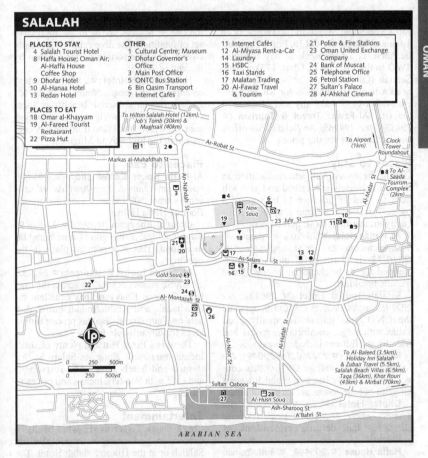

SALALAH

PLACES TO STAY
4 Salalah Tourist Hotel
8 Haffa House; Oman Air;
   Al-Haffa House
   Coffee Shop
9 Dhofar Hotel
10 Al-Hanaa Hotel
13 Redan Hotel

PLACES TO EAT
18 Omar al-Khayyam
19 Al-Fareed Tourist
   Restaurant
22 Pizza Hut

OTHER
1 Cultural Centre; Museum
2 Dhofar Governor's
   Office
3 Main Post Office
5 ONTC Bus Station
6 Bin Qasim Transport
7 Internet Cafés

11 Internet Cafés
12 Al-Miyasa Rent-a-Car
14 Laundry
15 HSBC
16 Taxi Stands
17 Malatan Trading
20 Al-Fawaz Travel
   & Tourism

21 Police & Fire Stations
23 Oman United Exchange
   Company
24 Bank of Muscat
25 Telephone Office
26 Petrol Station
27 Sultan's Palace
28 Al-Ahkhaf Cinema

ARABIAN SEA

Email & Internet Access There are numerous Internet cafés, particularly along 23 July St, charging between 500 and 800 baisa per hour.

Things to See & Do
Salalah's **museum** (admission free; open 8am-2pm Sat-Wed) is in the Cultural Centre, the large white building on Ar-Robat St (access, if you are driving, is from the back, via Markaz al-Muhafdhah St). There's not much to see but an exhibit on Khor Rouri (see Around Salalah later in this chapter) is helpful and don't miss Wilfred Thesiger's photographs in the lobby of Arabia in the 1940s and '50s.

Al-Husn Souq is the best place to buy genuine Dhofari frankincense and be daubed with locally made perfumes. Quality silver *khanjar*s, swords and jewellery are also on sale here. *Halwa* shops selling Oman's traditional confection monopolise the corner of Al-Hafah and Sultan Qaboos Sts.

The ruins of **Al-Baleed**, site of the 12th-century trading port of Zafar, are currently closed to tourists but you can peer over the fence at the site on the way to the Holiday Inn Salalah.

Organised Tours
Zubair Travel (☎ 235581, fax 235582; open 8am-1pm & 4pm-6pm Sat-Thur), in the lobby of the Holiday Inn Salalah, offers three-hour city tours for OR30. (All prices quoted are for a vehicle with an English-speaking driver and a maximum of four

people.) It also offers a half-day tour to Job's Tomb and Mughsail blowholes, or to Taqa and Mirbat for OR36. For the romantic, there is a backbreaking day trip in a 4WD to the lost city of Ubar, 175km from Salalah (OR 110), but be warned, you'll need a lively imagination (or Ranulph Fiennes' book) to make any sort of sense of the site. **Al-Fawaz Travel & Tourism** (*☎ 294324, fax 294265; An-Nahdah St*) offers similar tours for similar prices.

Places to Stay
During the *khareef* all accommodation in Salalah is heavily subscribed and you will need to book in advance to be sure of a room. Prices at that time may be significantly greater than those quoted here.

Al-Hanaa Hotel (*☎ 298305; e msarawas@ omantel.net.om; 23 July St; singles/doubles OR10/13*) is characterful and is recommended for its bright, clean rooms. Rates include breakfast.

Salalah Tourist Hotel (*☎ 295332, fax 292145; singles/doubles OR10/12*), opposite the ONTC bus station, is equally good value with large, comfortable rooms and friendly staff. Rates include breakfast.

Redan Hotel (*☎ 292266, fax 290491; As-Salam St; singles/doubles OR10/12*) is conveniently central. The lobby and lift are a bit grim but the rooms are large and clean.

Dhofar Hotel (*☎ 29048; e dhfhotel@ omantel.net.om; Al-Matar St; singles/doubles OR10/13*) has definite pretensions of grandeur!

Haffa House (*☎ 295444; e haffa@oman tel.net.om; cnr Al-Matar & Ar-Robat Sts; singles/doubles OR19.800/22*) comprises a small commercial complex and hotel near the clock tower roundabout. Rooms are large and comfortable and there is a pool and a restaurant with a view.

The **Salalah Beach Villas** (*☎ 235999; e beachspa@omantel.net.om; singles/doubles OR18.530/26.160*) on the beach one block east of the Holiday Inn Salalah is a friendly and comfortable place with a pool and lovely views out to sea. Rates include breakfast. Car hire (2WD/4WD OR14/35, including 200km free mileage) is available at reception.

The **Holiday Inn Salalah** (*☎ 235333; e hinnsll@omantel.net.om; singles/doubles OR38.610/48.555*) is in the process of up-

grading to a Crowne Plaza Resort similar to the one in Muscat and with an impressive set of facilities. The dive centre is currently closed. The extension was due to open by the end of 2002.

Hilton Salalah Hotel (*☎ 211234; e sllbc@ omantel.net.om; singles/doubles OR70.200/ 79.560*) has an attractive beachfront location despite being in view of the new port area of Raysut. It is 12km from the city centre along the highway to Mughsail.

Places to Eat
Al-Haffa House Coffee Shop (*☎ 295444; open 7am-11am & 4pm-8pm daily*) sells snacks from 500 baisa; it's on the ground floor of Haffa House.

Omar al-Khayyam (*☎ 293004; 23 July St; mains OR1.500-2*) has good Chinese and Indian food. This is a popular place in the evening.

Al-Fareed Tourist Restaurant (*☎ 292382; 23 July St; mains OR1.200-2*) across the road from Omar al-Khayyam, has excellent Indian meals and Arabic/Indian buffet dinners on Thursday. It also has private dining areas for Omani-style food.

There is a Pizza Hut and plenty of small Indian restaurants along As-Salam St. All the top-end hotels have good restaurants and café with Western menus and prices to match.

Entertainment
Check *Oman Today* to see what bands or dancers are performing at the Holiday Inn Salalah or at the Hilton Salalah Hotel. The **Al-Ahkhaf Cinema** (*☎ 290318; Sultan Qaboos St; 1st-class/balcony seats 700/900 baisa*) adjoining the Al-Husn Souq shows films in English (unlike the two modern cinemas in town). During the *khareef*, the Ittin road comes alive with the **Khareef Festival**. Check *Oman Today* for a programme of traditional dancing and music among other activities.

Shopping
Among Dhofar's most distinctive souvenirs are small, bead-covered kohl (black eyeliner) bottles (OR3 to OR5 from the new souq). Baskets made of rush and camel's leather from the fishing village of Shwaymiya, 100km (as the crow flies) from Salalah, make another good souvenir buy.

They cost anywhere between OR5 and OR30 depending on intricacy of weaving and can be found in the new souq.

Don't visit Dhofar without treading in the paths of ancient traders! A small bag of locally-harvested frankincense from Al-Husn Souq costs 500 baisa and a decorative pottery incense burner costs between OR1.500 and OR10.

Salalah is famous for its silversmiths. Ash-Sharooq St, behind Al-Husn Souq, is one of the best places in Oman to buy a new silver *khanjar*. They are beautifully crafted and cost between OR100 and OR250. Try the gold souq for Salalah's distinctive silver necklaces and bracelets, which cost between OR4 and OR20.

Alongside the plantations that line Sultan Qaboos St you can buy locally grown coconuts, bananas and papayas for a few baisa from a colourful string of stalls.

Getting There & Away

Air National carrier **Oman Air** (☎ 295747) flies to Muscat (OR36/72 one-way/return, 1½ hours, twice daily) at variable times; its office is in Haffa House.

Bus To Muscat, **ONTC** (☎ 292773) buses (OR6/11 one way/return, 12 hours, twice daily) leave at 7am and 7pm from the bus station in the new souq. You can store luggage in the adjoining ticket office free of charge. There are also services to Nizwa and Buraimi.

Malatan Trading (☎ 293574; *As-Salam St*) has a 4.30pm service (OR6/11, 12 hours, daily) that leaves from near the cemetery. Also try **Bin Qasim Transport** (☎ 291786), which has a 4pm service (OR6/11 one way/return, 12 hours, daily) that leaves from near the new souq.

Taxi & Microbus Salalah's taxis and microbuses hang out in front of HSBC on As-Salam St. Taxis will generally make only intercity trips on an engaged basis, which is invariably expensive (OR10 to Taqa, for example). Microbus fares from Salalah include: Mirbat (500 baisa), Mughsail (OR1) and Muscat (OR8).

Getting Around

There is no public transport from the airport and taxis charge a fixed price of OR3 from the airport to anywhere in Salalah. A microbus ride within the city costs around 300 baisa and a taxi about 800 baisa. Expect to pay OR2 to the Holiday Inn Salalah and OR3.500 to Hilton Salalah Hotel.

Renting a car in Salalah is recommended for exploring the beautiful coast and driving into the jebel, especially during the *khareef*. Unless you want to enjoy some of the country's best camping, or explore the more rugged roads, you don't strictly need a 4WD but beware of the soft sand on the beaches.

A further word of warning: during the *khareef* the roads into the jebel are notoriously dangerous. They are slippery and local drivers fail to make allowances for the fog. Camels often cause accidents by wandering onto the road and if you hit one you can be sure it's an extremely expensive female, prize-winning, racing camel.

Al-Miyasa Rent-a-Car (☎ 296521; *As-Salam St*), next door to the Redan Hotel, has 2WD cars for OR10, including insurance and 200km free per day. **Salalah Beach Villas** (☎ 235999) offers 2WD/4WD for rent for OR14/35, with 200km free. **Budget** (☎ 235581) and **Avis** (☎ 235160) have desks at the Holiday Inn Salalah.

AROUND SALALAH
Beaches

There are very good beaches along the entire coastal plain of Salalah. For the most beautiful, head beyond Mirbat (4WD advisable) and follow any graded road going east. After 5km to 10km there are a string of glorious bays of striking red rock and white sand suitable for protected camping. Beware of strong currents anywhere along the coast during the *khareef*.

Khor Rouri خور روري

Looking across the estuary at grazing camels and flocks of flamingos it's hard to imagine that 2000 years ago Khor Rouri was the trading post of the frankincense route and as such one of the most important ports on earth. Today, little remains of the city except some nondescript ruins, currently closed to visitors. It is worth making the trip to Khor Rouri, however, to enjoy the bird-watching and to take a cautious swim in one of the coast's prettiest bays.

Khor Rouri is about 35km from Salalah. Take the Mirbat road and turn right 5km beyond the Taqa roundabout at the signpost. The site is 2.5km along a graded road and the beach is a further 3km to 4km. A microbus to the junction on the highway is 400 baisa.

Wadi Dharbat

A popular picnic site in the *khareef* and a great place to enjoy the jebel in any season, Wadi Dharbat is the source of the estuary that flows into Khor Rouri. During a good *khareef*, an impressive waterfall spills over the cliff face, 300m to the plain below. Above the fall, water collects in limestone pools ideal for a swim. In the dry months, October to May, the Jibbali tribes people (for details see History at the start of this chapter) set up their distinctive round camps in this area. Look out for guinea fowl and rock hyrax (a fur-clad relative of the elephant) on the steep slopes of the surrounding jebel. The caves in this area were used by the sultan's forces, together with the British SAS, to infiltrate areas of communist insurgency.

To get to Wadi Dharbat, take the turning for Tawi Attair 4km after the Taqa roundabout and climb 3km to the Wadi Dhabat junction. A potholed 3km track leads to the top of the waterfall and the pools beyond.

MIRBAT مرباط

The town of Mirbat, just over 70km east of Salalah, has seen better days but it has considerable historical significance. The town's main **fort** *(admission 500 baisa; open 8.30am-2.30pm Sun-Thur)* was the site of brave fighting in the well-documented Battle of Mirbat during the Dhofari insurrection of the 1970s. The attack and defence of a fortress was a rare event for modern times.

Notice the old **merchant houses** with their wooden, latticed windows. The onion-domed **Bin Ali Tomb**, 1km off the main road, marks the entrance to the town. Microbuses charge 700 baisa for the trip from Salalah.

JOB'S TOMB قبر النبي أيوب

In religious terms Job's Tomb (referred to in Arabic simply as 'An-Nabi Ayyub' – Prophet Job) is probably the most important site in Dhofar. Regardless of your religious convictions, the tomb – situated on an isolated hilltop overlooking Salalah – is a must-see for the beautiful drive, especially during the *khareef* and for the excellent view over the Salalah plain on a clear day. Look out for weaver-bird nests in the surrounding trees.

The tomb is just over 30km from Salalah. Take the main west-bound road towards Mughsail and turn right along the Ittin road, after passing the Hamilton Plaza Hotel. Turn left at the signpost for An-Nabi Ayyub after 22km. A small restaurant below the tomb has wonderful views. There is no public transport.

If you are visiting Job's Tomb in the *khareef*, return to the main road and turn left for another 10km or so to reach the end of the monsoon catchment. The contrast between the green slopes and the desert floor beyond is remarkable. Continue along this road until you meet the Thumrait road and turn right for Salalah.

MUGHSAIL مغسيل

Mughsail is 48km west of Salalah on a spectacular bay, ending in a set of sheer cliffs that reach towards the Yemeni coast. Immediately below the start of the cliffs the rock pavement is potholed with **blowholes**

Boswelia sacra – The Frankincense Tree

It is hard to imagine that a gorgeous empire was built from the bark of such an unprepossessing tree. With its peeling bark and tufts of coarse leaves, the frankincense tree looks more like something out of the *Day of the Triffids* than the source of the most precious aromatic sap in the world. Although the tree grows in neighbouring Yemen, the specimens of Dhofar have been famed since ancient times for producing the finest quality sap. Small beads of white or amber-coloured sap form from incisions made in the bark. Tradition dictates that the tree is a gift from Allah, and is thus not to be propagated, bought or sold, only harvested if it happens to be within your lucky plot of land. Nature helps in this regard as the tree favours the unique weather system of this corner of Dhofar and is notoriously difficult to root elsewhere.

that are active year round but particularly volatile during the high seas of the *khareef*.

Camping on the beach here is not permitted but **Al-Mughsail Beach Tourist Resthouse** (☎ *9495913, fax 290643; cabins OR20*) has a few cabins on the beach with air-con, bathroom, TV and sitting room, and a small restaurant from which to enjoy the superb views. Watch out for amber blobs of jellyfish on the shore.

Microbuses charge OR1 in either direction for the trip between Salalah and Mughsail.

SARFAIT ROAD   طريق صرفيت

If you have your own transport, it is worth continuing from Mughsail towards the Yemeni border. The road is an impressive feat of engineering, zigzagging 1000m to the top of the cliff. Look out for a wadi full of **frankincense trees**, 8km from Mughsail (see the boxed text '*Boswelia sacra* – The Frankincense Tree'). Three or four kilometres after the top of the road, there are stunning views back towards Mughsail and inland across some of the wildest wadis in Arabia. The vegetation in this area is entirely different from that on the Salalah plain with yuccas and succulents clinging to the limestone ledges.

Musandam Peninsula   شبه جزيرة المسندم

Separated from the rest of Oman by the east coast of the UAE, and guarding the southern side of the strategically important Strait of Hormuz, the Musandam Peninsula is a land of beautiful khors, small villages and dramatic, mountain-hugging roads. Difficult to reach and even more difficult to travel around, it rewards the effort if you are on an extended tour of Oman, or if you're after a taste of the wilderness from Dubai. Be prepared to pay for a boat trip as this is the only way to see the best of the area. Avoid May to August when the heat and humidity are overpowering.

KHASAB   خصب

The capital of the province is small but far from sleepy. Its harbour bursts with activity, much of it involving the smuggling of US cigarettes to Iran in return for goats, and the

souq resounds to a babel of different languages, including Kumzari, a combination of Farsi, Hindi, English, Portuguese and Arabic.

Orientation & Information
The harbour area occupies the western end of the bay. The old souq, comprising dozens of dubious shipping offices packaging cigarettes, is 1.5km to the east. The town's new souq, consisting of a few restaurants and grocery stores, the post office, a couple of banks and the Oman Air office, is 1.5km inland from the centre of the bay. Khasab Hotel is 3km and the airport 6km further inland.

Things to See & Do
Khasab Fort (*admission free; open 7.30am-2.30pm Sat-Wed*) commands the mud flats on the edge of the bay.

There is a small **beach** with palm umbrellas just outside Khasab. Follow the road from the port towards Bukha for 2km or so.

Organised Tours
For most visitors, using the services of a tour company may be the only way of seeing the Musandam Peninsula. **Khasab**

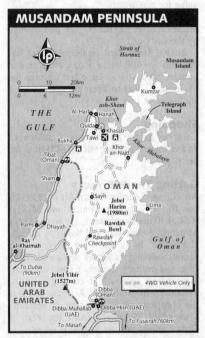

MUSANDAM PENINSULA

Strait of Hormuz

Musandam Island

Kumzar

THE GULF

Khor ash-Sham

Al-Harf • Hanah

Telegraph Island

Quida • Khasab

Bukha • Tawi

Khor an-Najd

Khor Habalayn

Tibat (Oman)

Sham

OMAN

Sayh

Jebel Harim ▲ (1980m)

Lima

Rawdah Bowl

Rams • Dhayah

Rawdah Checkpoint

Gulf of Oman

Ras al-Khaimah

To Dubai (90km)

Jebel Yibir (1527m)

UNITED ARAB EMIRATES

Dibba (Oman)

Dibba Muhallab (UAE) • Dibba Hisn (UAE)

To Masafi

=== 4WD Vehicle Only

To Fujairah (60km)

0   10   20km
0   6   12mi

OMAN

Travel & Tours (☎ 830464, fax 830364, e khastour@omantel.net.om) in the old souq offers full-day dhow trips around the khors for OR40, or OR60 to Kumzar. If you share the boat, the price is OR25 per person. This agency also offers a two-night bed-and-breakfast package at the Khasab Hotel, with a full-day dhow trip, a half-day 4WD visit to the mountains and a city tour for OR180, or OR140 for two or more people.

Places to Stay & Eat

Al-Kaddar Hotel (☎ 831664, fax 831676; singles/doubles OR16/21), near the fort on the harbour, is a new and friendly place. Ask management if they'll offer you a free transfer to Dubai next time they're heading that way. The hotel runs daily dhow trips (OR25 per person).

Khasab Hotel (☎ 830267, fax 830989; singles/doubles OR21/34), 1km south of the new souq roundabout, is small and reservations are needed between November and March.

Khasab Travel & Tours (☎ 830464; villas OR40) has two three-bedroom villas, about 200m from Khasab Hotel, which are good value for groups.

Qada Hotel (☎ 831665, fax 831676; singles/doubles OR16/21) has just opened by the harbour.

Bukha Restaurant in the old souq has biryanis for 600 baisa. Roast chicken and kebabs are also available but only in the evening. Expect to keep company with a smuggler or two.

Shopping

Look out for the Shihuh tribe's emblem of an axe-topped walking stick (OR2) from the old souq.

Getting There & Away

Air National carrier **Oman Air** (☎ 830543) has flights between Khasab and Muscat (OR20/40 one way/return, 1½ hours) every Monday, Wednesday and Saturday at variable times. Its office is on the new souq roundabout and its planes depat and arrive from the military airbase. Expect an exciting landing approach if coming over the mountains from Muscat! Arriving by air is the cheapest and easiest way of reaching Musandam Peninsula from the rest of Oman, unless you are a GCC resident.

Car The only border post currently allowing access to the Musandam Peninsula is at Tibat (also known as Sham), on the western coast of the UAE. Remember not to travel with alcohol when crossing any Oman-UAE border. There is a Dh20 road tax to leave the UAE and OR1 visa charge to enter Musandam Peninsula. A 4WD vehicle is only necessary to explore the mountainous area around Jebel Harim.

Long-Distance Taxi Public transport is erratic at best, if not nonexistent. You can try to engage a taxi in Khasab's old souq to Bukha (OR5), Tibat or Khor an-Najd (OR10), Dibba (OR25) and Muscat (OR70).

Though it is only about 70km from Ras al-Khaimah in the UAE to Khasab there are no taxis making the run on a regular basis. The Khasab pick-up truck drivers charge OR15 for the trip to Ras al-Khaimah but you may get marooned at the border in the opposite direction.

Car Rental There is no car rental in Musandam Peninsula. Khasab Hotel can sometimes arrange rental with one of the locals for OR30 per day. A 4WD with a driver costs OR80 per day from Khasab Travel & Tours.

Getting Around

To/From the Airport Arrange transfers with your hotel in advance as there are no taxis near the airport.

Taxi The orange-and-white taxis in town are almost permanently booked by locals. The only other form of public transport is 4WD pick-up trucks with benches in the back. If either stop for you, trips around town cost 200 to 300 baisa.

KHASAB-TIBAT ROAD
طريق خصب - طيبات

The cliff-hugging 90-minute drive from Khasab to Tibat is a highlight of a trip to Musandam. The road, now sealed, is a feat of engineering and affords spectacular views across the Strait of Hormuz.

There are a few sites of interest along the way and you could spend a day pottering along the empty road, enjoying a swim – and watching very large sharks basking in the shallows.

Tawi طاوي

About 10km from Khasab harbour lies the village of Tawi, site of a few prehistoric **rock carvings**. To reach the carvings, follow a track up Wadi Quida, just before Quida village, for 2.3km. The carvings are etched into two rocks on the left, just before a large white house.

Bukha بوخا

Scenically positioned **Bukha Fort** is closed to the public. A nearby beach with shelters and drinking water makes a good unofficial **camp site**.

THE MUSANDAM KHORS أخوار المسندم

A dhow trip around the khors of Musandam, flanked by dolphins and flocks of cormorants, is a must and well worth the expense. Trail a fishing line from the back of the boat, and your skipper will cook your catch for lunch.

Khor ash-Sham حور الشم

This beautiful inlet is interesting for its stone **fishing villages**, accessible only by boat, and for **Telegraph Island** (see the boxed text 'Going Round the Bend'). For OR10 a fisherman may take you to Khor ash-Sham from Khasab. Otherwise, make a day trip of it with Khasab Travel & Tours (see Organised Tours under Khasab, earlier, for details).

Khor an-Najd حورنيد

At 24.5km from Khasab, this is the only khor accessible by car, but beware the steep approach.

Head out of Khasab towards the mountains for 8km or so and follow the sign for 'Khor an-Najd 10km'. After 5.6km turn left again for 1.5km and head for the road that winds up the mountain. After 2.3km there's

Going Round the Bend

A small island in the middle of Khor ash-Sham was home to a British telegraphic relay station in the 19th century. The utter isolation of the island, tucked around the bend of this remote khor, drove many of the workers stationed there to madness. The saying 'going round the bend' persists to this day.

a great outlook after which a steep 2.8km descent brings you to the water's edge.

Kumzar كمذار

Set on an isolated khor at the northern edge of the Musandam Peninsula, the surprisingly modern town of Kumzar is accessible only by boat. The villagers speak their own language, known as Kumzari, a combination of Farsi, Hindi, English, Portuguese and Arabic.

Water taxis travel between Khasab and Kumzar most days, charging OR3 per person. This can be a pretty harrowing trip, however. Most of the speedboats used as water taxis have no seats and boast maximum clearance between deck and gunwale of 15cm. Khasab Travel & Tourism is a safer option (see under Khasab, earlier).

RAWDAH BOWL مدرّج الروضة

If you have a 4WD, the rural settlements of the **Sayh plateau** and the mountain scenery around **Jebel Harim** make a good half-day trip. Beyond the telecommunications tower, the descent towards the Omani checkpoint is via a narrow ridge with views of terraced gardens and the acacia-strewn **Rawdah Bowl**. The distances from Khasab are not great but allow a full day to enjoy the spectacular scenery.

Qatar

قطر

New-found gas wealth, big-moneyed sports tournaments, business conferences on a global scale and glitzy new hotels may have helped put Qatar on the map in recent years, but it's the towering sand dunes, ancient rock carvings, unique architecture and friendly people that make Qatar a rewarding place to visit.

Facts about Qatar

HISTORY

In the 5th century BC Greek historian Herodotus referred to the seafaring Canaanites as the original inhabitants of Qatar, while the geographer Ptolemy showed in his map of the Arab world, 'Qatara', which possibly refers to the northern town of Al-Zubara – the country's main trading port until the 19th century. Archaeologists have also uncovered flint spearheads, pottery shards and rock carvings which date back to the Ubaid civilisation in the 4th century BC.

Qatar's pearling industry had been long established by the time the present rulers, the Al-Thani family, arrived in the mid-18th century. They became the peninsula's rulers about 100 years later.

In 1915 the emir of Qatar expelled the Turkish garrison that was based in Doha. With Britain and Turkey on opposite sides in WWI, and the British controlling the rest of the Gulf, a switch in alliances seemed wise. After expelling the Turks, Qatar's emir signed an exclusive agreement with the British, under which Britain guaranteed Qatar's protection in exchange for a promise that the ruler wouldn't deal with other foreign powers without British permission.

Even before the collapse of the pearl market around 1930, life in Qatar was rough. With poverty, hunger, malnutrition and disease all widespread, the emir welcomed the oil prospectors who first arrived in the early 1930s. A concession was granted in 1935 and the prospectors struck oil in 1939. Because of WWII, however, production did not begin for another 10 years.

When the British announced they would withdraw by the end of 1971, Qatar entered talks with Bahrain and the Trucial States

The State of Qatar

Area: 11,437 sq km
Population: approx 744,000
Capital: Doha
Head of State: The Emir, Sheikh Hamad bin Khalifa al-Thani
Official Language: Arabic
Currency: Qatari riyal (QR)

- Best Dining – enjoying a meal at one of the many restaurants overlooking Doha Bay
- Best Nightlife – taking a night-time dhow cruise
- Best Walk – strolling at sunset along Doha's picturesque Al-Corniche
- Best View – watching the sun set behind the silent sand dunes of southern Qatar
- Best Activity – sand-skiing on the towering dunes of Khor al-Adaid

(now the United Arab Emirates) with the intention of forming a confederation. When Bahrain pulled out of the talks, Qatar followed suit and declared independence on 1 September 1971. Six months later Sheikh Khalifa bin Hamad al-Thani, a cousin of the emir, and for many years Qatar's ruler in all but title, took power in a coup.

Qatar Today

In June 1995, Sheikh Khalifa was unexpectedly replaced as emir by his son Hamad, who quickly set about remaking the country. Reforms included allowing women to drive and vote, encouraging education and training among Qataris, and opening the country to tourism. The discovery of huge quantities of natural gas in 1971, estimated at 5.8% of the world's gas reserves, has certainly helped boost the 'new Qatari economy'. In 2001 Qatar hosted the World Trade Organisation Conference and plans are well under way for its staging of the 15th Asian Games in 2006.

GEOGRAPHY

The Qatar peninsula is 11,437 sq km, about 160km long and 55km to 80km wide. Most of the land is flat, gravel-covered desert with little natural vegetation, but there are also kilometres of towering sand dunes in the southeast, interesting rocky outcrops in the west and mangroves in the north.

CLIMATE

Summer (May to September) temperatures generally average 35°C, but it's not uncommon for the mercury to get up to 50°C. The 90% humidity also means that summers can be very uncomfortable. The winter months are much milder with pleasant, cool evenings. Sandstorms are common throughout the year, especially in the

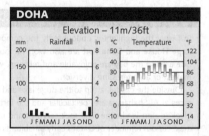

spring. Although it doesn't rain much, there are a few weeks of wet weather in December and January.

GOVERNMENT & POLITICS

Qatar is ruled by an emir: Sheikh Hamad bin Khalifa al-Thani, who is also minister of defence and commander-in-chief of the armed forces. His third son, Sheikh Jasim bin Hamad al-Thani, is the official heir apparent. The prime minister and minister of the interior is Sheikh Abdullah bin Khalifa al-Thani.

POPULATION & PEOPLE

With about 744,000 people, Qatar is one of the most sparsely populated countries in the Arab world. Of these, only 25% are indigenous Qataris. Most nationals are of Najdi (central Arabian) ancestry, though there are also people of Persian descent. The foreign population is a mix of people from the Arab world, Southeast Asia, the Indian subcontinent and a steadily growing number of Western expatriates.

RELIGION

Most Qataris adhere to the austere Wahhabi sect of Islam, which is less severe than that followed in Saudi.

LANGUAGE

The national language is Arabic. English is also widely spoken, and is a lingua franca among the foreign population, but is not widely understood by less educated Qataris. For a list of Arabic words and phrases, see the Language chapter at the back of this book.

Facts for the Visitor

WHEN TO GO

Because the heat is fierce in summer, and sandstorms are common in spring, the best

What to See

In Doha, the highlight is undoubtedly the comprehensive **Qatar National Museum**, but the **Heritage House** and **Doha Fort** are also worth a look. An evening stroll along **Al-Corniche** or a **boat ride** around the bay are enjoyable and relaxing, while a trip out to the vegetable and animal souqs makes for an interesting diversion.

Outside the capital, a trip to the huge lake and sand dunes at **Khor al-Adaid** is a must. The **camel races** at Al-Shahaniya are spectacular and the **fort museum** at Al-Zubara is interesting if only for the bleak, desert landscape. The **rock carvings** and rocky outcrops at Jebel Jassassiyeh and Bir Zekreet are a curious reminder of Qatar's early inhabitants and the nearby beaches are suitable for swimming.

time to visit is winter (October to early March). In December and January, it rarely rains for more than a few days at a time so this need not be a consideration in planning your trip.

VISAS & DOCUMENTS
Visas
All nationalities other than citizens of Gulf Cooperation Council (GCC) countries need a visa to enter Qatar. However, since Qatar opened its doors to tourism a growing number of nationalities can now obtain a visa at the airport; at the time of writing citizens of the European Union (EU), UK, USA, Australia, New Zealand, Canada, Singapore, South Korea, Japan, Brunei and Hong Kong were eligible for a two-week, single-entry tourist visa, which is issued on arrival at the airport and costs QR55.

An agreement recently penned between Oman and Qatar means that anyone with a visa for Oman can now enter Qatar (and vice versa) free of charge.

Nationalities who don't qualify for the painless and quick airport visa will need to make arrangements through mid-range and top-end hotels – for a variable fee (QR120 to QR200). Contact a hotel (preferably by fax or email), book a room and request sponsorship. Send your passport details, reason for visit (business, tourism etc), arrival and departure dates and flight numbers. The hotel will in turn send you acknowledgement of your reservation and a copy of your visa, which you then present to the immigration counter at Doha International Airport. Unfortunately, the hotel then 'controls' your visa and stay, so it's almost impossible to change hotels after you arrive. Allow at least six (Qatari) working days (nothing will get done on Thursday afternoon and Friday) for its issue.

Multi-entry tourist and business visas need to be applied for through a Qatari embassy or consulate. You must fill out three forms and provide three passport-sized photos. Anyone requesting a business visa needs to supply a letter from the company they will be visiting. These visas are issued within 24 hours.

For details of visas for other Middle Eastern countries, see the 'Visas at a Glance' table under Visas & Documents in the Regional Facts for the Visitor chapter.

Visa Extensions Tourist visas can be extended for an additional 14 days and business visas for seven days. The charges for overstaying are very high: between QR200 and QR500 *per day* for any type of visa. If you were originally sponsored by a hotel, the hotel must arrange your extension, which costs QR50 plus hotel fees. If you obtained your visa at the airport on arrival or through an embassy/consulate, go to the **Passports & Immigration Building** (☎ 488 2882; cnr Khalifa & 22nd February Sts) in Doha.

Other Documents
No other special permits are required. Student cards are worthless. See Car & Motorcycle in the Getting Around section later in this chapter for information about driving permits and licences in Qatar.

EMBASSIES & CONSULATES
Qatari Embassies & Consulates
Following is a list of Qatari embassies and consulates in major cities around the world. For addresses of Qatari embassies in neighbouring Middle Eastern countries see the relevant chapter or visit the government's website **w** www.mofa.gov.qa.

France (☎ 01 45 51 90 71, e paris@mofa
.gov.qa) 57 Quai D'Orsay, 75007, Paris
Germany (☎ 228-957 520, e bonn@mofa
.gov.qa) Brunnen alle 6, 53177 Bonn
UK (☎ 0891-633 233, e london@mofa.gov.qa)
1 South Audley St, London, W1Y 5DQ
USA (☎ 202-274 1603, fax 237 0061,
e washington@mofa.gov.qa) 4200 Wisconsin
Ave, NW, Suite 200, Washington DC 20016
Consulate: (☎ 212-486 9335) 809 UN Plaza,
4th floor, New York, NY 10017

Embassies & Consulates in Qatar

Most embassies are in the 'Diplomatic Area',
north of the Doha Sheraton Hotel, and few
have specific addresses. All are open from
8am to 2pm Saturday to Wednesday.

Bahrain (☎ 483 9360) Diplomatic Area
France (☎ 483 2283, fax 483 2254)
Diplomatic Area
Germany (☎ 487 6959, fax 487 6949) Al-Jezira
al-Arabiyya St
Iran (☎ 483 5300, fax 467 3347) Diplomatic Area
Kuwait (☎ 483 2111, fax 483 2042) Diplomatic
Area
Oman (☎ 467 0744, fax 467 0747)
41 Ibn al-Qassem St, Villa 7, Hilal district
Saudi Arabia (☎ 483 2030, fax 483 2720)
Diplomatic Area
UAE (☎ 483 8880, fax 488 2837) Off Al-Khor
St, Khalifa Town district
UK (☎ 442 1991, fax 443 8692) Al-Istiqlal St,
Rumailiah district
USA (☎ 488 4101, fax 488 4298) 149 Ahmed
bin Ali St
Yemen (☎ 443 2555, fax 442 9400) Near the
As-Saad roundabout, Al-Jezira district

CUSTOMS

The duty-free allowances on arrival are 800
cigarettes, 100 cigars or 500g of tobacco,
and 250ML of perfume.

MONEY
Currency

The currency is the Qatari riyal (QR). One
riyal is divided into 100 dirhams. Notes
come in one, five, 10, 50, 100 and 500 denominations, and coins are worth 25 dirhams
and 50 dirhams. The Qatari riyal is fully
convertible.

Exchange Rates

The Qatari riyal is fixed against the US dollar. Following are the rates for a range of
currencies when this book went to print:

country	unit		Qatar riyals
Australia	A$1	=	QR1.97
Bahrain	BD1	=	QR9.65
Canada	C$1	=	QR2.29
euro zone	€1	=	QR3.59
Japan	¥100	=	QR2.97
Kuwait	KD1	=	QR12.06
New Zealand	NZ$1	=	QR1.70
Oman	OR1	=	QR9.45
Saudi Arabia	SR1	=	QR0.97
UAE	Dh10	=	QR9.91
UK	UK£1	=	QR5.71
US	US$1	=	QR3.64

Exchanging Money

Moneychangers will offer about QR3.64 for
US$1, banks about QR3.63 for US$1, and
top-end hotels QR3.50 for about US$1.
Currencies from Bahrain, Saudi Arabia and
the United Arab Emirates are easy to buy
and sell at banks and moneychangers. Travellers cheques can be changed at all major
banks and the larger moneychangers.

ATMs & Credit Cards All major credit
cards and ATM cards are accepted in large
shops, and can be used in most ATMs. Visa
(Plus & Electron), MasterCard and Cirrus
are accepted at ATMs at HSBC, the Qatar
National Bank and The Commercial Bank of
Qatar, which also accepts American Express
(AmEx) and Diners Club.

Costs

If you're on a tight budget, Qatar is probably not the cheapest of places to visit. Still,
if you stay in the cheapest hotel, eat in the
cheapest restaurants and are prepared to
walk everywhere you could probably get by
on about QR170/120 (US$46/32) per per-
son per day if travelling as a single/double.
For those on a mid-range budget with costs
that include car hire, mid-range accommodation, admission fees, entertainment, a
desert safari and the odd splurge on some
fine dining, a more realistic budget would
be around QR520/470 (US$143/129) per
day if travelling as a single/double.

Tipping & Bargaining

A service charge is usually added to restaurant (and top-end hotel) bills, but this rarely
goes to staff. Local custom does not require
that you leave a tip though it would certainly be appreciated – 10% is fine.

Bargaining is expected in the local souqs but the Western-style shopping centres have fixed prices.

POST & COMMUNICATIONS
Post
There is a **general post office** in northern Doha and another in central Doha (see that section for details). Postal rates are standard for most Western countries: postcards and regular letters cost 200 dirhams, and letters weighing 10g cost QR2 plus a further QR2 for every subsequent 10g. The first 1kg for parcels costs QR73 to the USA or Canada and the UK or Europe, and QR88 to Australia or New Zealand. Every subsequent kilogram costs QR57 to the USA or Canada, QR27 to the UK or Europe, and QR50 to Australia or New Zealand.

Major international express mail and package delivery services are available from post offices.

Poste restante is not available and AmEx does not keep mail for clients. Your hotel will probably hold mail for a short time prior to your arrival.

Telephone
The country code for Qatar is ☎ 974. There are no specific area or city codes. The international access code (to call abroad from Qatar) is ☎ 0.

All communications services are provided by the **Qatar Public Telecommunication Corporation** (Q-Tel), and the telephone system is excellent. Local calls are free, except from payphones – QR1 per minute. To make a local or international call from a payphone you must buy a phonecard (which come in denominations of QR30, QR50 and QR100), available in many shops around Doha.

The cost of a direct-dial call to the USA or Canada and the UK or Europe is about QR4.6 per minute, while to Australia or New Zealand it's about QR4. Rates are cheaper between 7pm and 7am, all day Friday and on holidays. An additional QR4 is charged for operator-assisted calls.

Mobiles Qatar's mobile phone network runs on the GSM system through the government-run Q-Tel. Visitors can present their passports to purchase prepaid sim cards for QR300. Recharge cards come in denominations of QR30, QR50 and QR100.

Email & Internet Access
There are email and Internet facilities at all top-end hotels, and there are several Internet cafés around the capital (see the Doha section later in this chapter for details). The only local ISP is **Internet Qatar** (☎ 125; **w** www.qatar.net.qa), part of Q-Tel. It's possible to use this service on your own computer as long as you have a modem and telephone line with either GSM or international access. Prepaid dial-up cards can be purchased in supermarkets for QR30, QR50 and QR100 and are valid for six months. A QR30 card will give you five hours of Internet access.

DIGITAL RESOURCES
For a comprehensive list of Middle East and Arab world websites see Digital Resources in the Regional Facts for the Visitor chapter; otherwise some useful Qatar-specific websites include:

Destination Qatar A virtual traveller's newsletter of what's on and what to do
   w www.destinationqatar.com
Ministry of Foreign Affairs A comprehensive site covering everything from getting a visa to what to see in Qatar
   w www.mofa.gov.qa
Qatar Internet Has useful links to various Qatari sites – from ministries and embassies to schools and media sites
   w www.qatar.net.qa
Qatar National Hotels Company Information on some of the country's hotels as well as tour companies
   w www.qnhc.com

BOOKS
As well as this book, Lonely Planet also publishes a detailed country guide, *Bahrain, Kuwait & Qatar*. Otherwise, there are few up to date or available books on Qatar. If you can find a copy, Helga Graham's *Arabian Time Machine: Self-Portrait of an Oil State*, is an interesting collection of interviews with Qataris about their lives and traditions, before and after the oil boom. Also, *Qatari Women Past and Present* by Abeer Abu Said explains the changing and traditional roles of women in Qatar. More recent is Byron Augustin's *Qatar – Enchantment of the World*, which gives an overall view of life in Qatar.

Some, more general, Middle East titles also contain coverage of Qatar; see Books in the Regional Facts for the Visitor chapter.

NEWSPAPERS & MAGAZINES

Qatar's two English-language newspapers, *Gulf Times* and *The Peninsula*, are published daily (except Friday). The monthly magazine *Marhaba* is a good source of information for what's on in Qatar. International newspapers and magazines are available one or two days after publication at major bookshops in Doha.

RADIO & TV

The Qatar Broadcasting Service (QBS) offers radio programmes in English, German and French on 97.5FM and 102.6FM. The BBC and Armed Forces Radio are also available on local FM frequencies.

Channel 2 on Qatar Television (QTV) broadcasts programmes in English, while most international satellite channels are available at the majority of hotels (see also the boxed text 'Al-Jazeera').

PHOTOGRAPHY & VIDEO

Shops selling print film and video cassettes are plentiful in Doha. A roll of 24/36 print film costs about QR6/8, and about QR31/43 to develop (including a free film). Slide film is hard to find and very difficult to get developed so bring your own. Many photographic shops also arrange passport photos.

LAUNDRY

Most hotels offer a laundry service for guests. There are also cheaper laundries that charge about QR2 to QR3 for a shirt, and QR4 to QR5 for trousers or a skirt.

Al-Jazeera

Established five years ago with funding from Qatar's emir, Al-Jazeera satellite channel gained international media recognition during its 2001 coverage of the air strikes in Afghanistan and its uncensored broadcasting of Osama bin Laden's recorded statement praising the September 11 hijackers – for which American officials accused the station of being Bin Laden's mouthpiece. The Qatar-based channel, with its 24-hour news broadcasts and often controversial interviews, boasts an audience of millions across the Middle East and is recognised as one of the most independent and outspoken broadcasters in a region known for its government censors.

HEALTH

Vaccination certificates are not required, unless you're arriving from an area where cholera, yellow fever or a similar disease is endemic.

The standard of health care in Qatar is very high, and medical care is well subsidised for residents *and* tourists. A list of up-to-date contact details for hospitals and pharmacies appears in the two daily English-language newspapers and *Marhaba*.

For more general health information see Health in the Regional Facts for the Visitor chapter.

WOMEN TRAVELLERS

Qatar is a surprisingly safe place for women to travel. While it's still a largely conservative society, women can move about freely, without any of the harassment or restrictions that are often experienced in other parts of the region. Indeed, harassment of women is not looked kindly upon by officials and women are treated with respect and courtesy.

BUSINESS HOURS

Qataris love their 'siesta', and Doha resembles a ghost town in the early afternoon. Government departments are open between 7am and 2pm Saturday to Wednesday. Commercial business hours are generally from around 7.30am to noon Saturday to Thursday, opening again from 3.30pm to 7.30pm Saturday to Wednesday, while shops are open from 8.30am to 12.30pm and 4pm to 9pm every day except Friday. The modern, Western-style shopping centres are open from about 9am to 10pm daily, Friday included.

PUBLIC HOLIDAYS

In addition to the main Islamic holidays described in Public Holidays & Special Events in the Regional Facts for the Visitor chapter, Qatar observes the following public holidays:

National Day 3 September

Eid Festival Qatar's own brand of Eid festivities (date changeable) includes 'traditional-style' markets, various entertainment for both adults and children and shopping festivals (see Public Holidays & Special Events in the Regional Facts for the Visitor chapter for dates)

ACCOMMODATION

There's something of a hotel boom in the capital and this, combined with easy-to-get, no-fuss airport visas, means that travellers now have more choice when it comes to hotel accommodation. Prices for most rooms are negotiable and weekend (Thursday/Friday) specials and other deals are commonly offered.

There are no hostels in Qatar and camping in the desert is not really advised unless it's done on an organised tour or with someone who is familiar with the terrain.

FOOD

Qatar's indigenous cuisine is basically the same as that of other Gulf countries (see the special section 'Middle Eastern Cuisine' in the Regional Facts for the Visitor chapter). There are several restaurants in the capital that serve decent Arabic food and there are also some excellent restaurants serving a variety of international and Western cuisine. Apart from the usual glut of well-known fast-food joints and Indian/Pakistani eateries, the cheapest places are the 'cafeterias', which serve sandwiches and burgers, and the 'juice stalls', with their felafel-style snacks.

DRINKS

Alcohol is now widely available in all top-end hotel restaurants and bars. While the rule is that it's only available to hotel guests and 'members', at the time of writing this rule seemed to be somewhat relaxed.

SPECTATOR SPORTS

Qatar is fast becoming a very popular venue for a host of international sports events.

The Qatar Masters golf tournament (March), the Qatar Open tennis tournament (February) and the Tour of Qatar (cycle race) are just some of the annual draw cards that are attracting competitors and spectators alike. In 1998 Qatar hosted an international grand prix athletics meeting, the IAAF Grand Prix, the first in the GCC to allow foreign and local women to participate. In 2006 Qatar will stage the 15th Asian Games.

SHOPPING

While there is little in the way of locally made souvenirs, some interesting titbits can still be found. See the Doha section later in this chapter for information about souqs, markets and shopping centres.

Getting There & Away

AIR

The national carrier **Qatar Airways** (☎ 462 1717; ᴡ www.qatarairways.com; Al-Matar St), near the airport, has daily direct services from London to Doha, and several direct flights a week from Paris, Munich, Jakarta, Kuala Lumpar and from most cities in the Middle East. Qatar is also serviced by several major airlines: British Airways flies direct from London to Doha daily, KLM flies direct from Amsterdam, while Emirates flies to Doha from most major hubs via Dubai.

The new **Doha International Airport** (☎ 465 6666) is only 2.5km from the city centre. There is no departure tax for Qatar.

LAND

There are no international bus or taxi services to Saudi Arabia or the United Arab Emirates (UAE). Residents of Qatar, Saudi Arabia and the UAE can drive across the Qatar-Saudi border, but foreigners are normally not allowed to because visas must be collected at Doha International Airport.

SEA

The **Qatar National Navigation Company** (QNNC; ☎ 443 7417; Al-Corniche; open 7am-noon & 4pm-7pm Sat-Thur) is the agent for the Iranian Valfare-8 Shipping Company, which has a ferry service between Doha and the Iranian port of Bushehr. A one-way passage will cost QR180 and passage for a car will cost you an additional QR1255. Check with QNNC for departure times.

Getting Around

BUS

The local bus services that supposedly link Doha with major towns, such as Dukhan, Ar-Ruweis and Mesaieed, are infrequent and unreliable – so much so that locals don't even know if or when the buses are running.

TAXI

For short trips, taxis are useful, but to visit most sights around the countryside you're better off hiring a car. Taxi drivers will use the meter, but need a little encouragement.

The flag fall is QR2 during the day (QR3 at night), and then 10 dirhams per 200m (15 dirhams for trips outside of Doha and double those rates at night). For travel outside the capital you may want to negotiate a fixed fare. The easiest way to catch a taxi is to get your hotel to arrange the pick-up.

CAR & MOTORCYCLE

If you're driving around Doha, you'll discover that roundabouts are common, disorientating and large. Finding the right way out of Doha can also be difficult: if you're heading south towards Al-Wakrah or Mesaieed, take the airport road (Al-Matar Rd); the main road to all points north is 22nd February Rd (north from Al-Rayyan Rd); and to the west, continue along Al-Rayyan Rd.

Driving in Qatar is on the right-hand side. There are two grades of petrol: regular costs 65 dirhams per litre; super costs 70 dirhams. Numerous reputable service stations are located around Doha and along the highways.

Authorities don't take lightly to anyone caught speeding, not wearing a seat belt or not carrying a drivers licence: heavy on-the-spot fines are handed out freely.

Rental

A foreigner can rent a car (there is nowhere to rent a motorcycle) with his/her normal driving licence from home – but *only* within seven days of arriving in Qatar. After that, a temporary licence must be obtained. This is issued by the Traffic Licence Office, costs QR50 and lasts three months – rental companies can arrange this. The minimum rental period for all agencies is 24 hours and drivers must be at least 21 years old.

Rental costs (which include unlimited kilometres, but not petrol) do vary, so shop around. Major rental agencies charge about QR120/700 per day/week for the smallest sedan, though cheaper rates can be found at some of the local agencies. Most rental companies have a compulsory Collision Damage Waiver of around QR10 per day, which is a good idea anyway to avoid an excess of QR1500 to QR2500 in case of accidents. A few companies also add a compulsory Personal Accident Insurance Fee.

Al-Muftah Rent a Car (☎ 432 8100, fax 441 4339; e rntcar@qatar.net.qa; Al-Mushereib St) is a reliable and cheaper alternative to the major agencies, which include **Avis** (☎ 466 7744; e avis@qatar.net.qa); **Budget** (☎ 468 5515, fax 468 5051; e budget@qatar.net.qa); **Europcar** (☎ 443 8404); and **Hertz** (☎ 462 2891; e hertz@qatar.net.qa).

ORGANISED TOURS

There are several excellent tour companies that organise tours around Doha, to the desert, Khor al-Udaid and camel farms. They all offer similar sorts of packages, but two of the better ones are the friendly and knowledgeable **Gulf Adventures** (☎ 431 5555, fax 431 5161; e gf_adventure@qatar.net.qa; w www.gulfadventures.com; B Ring Rd) and **Arabian Adventures** (☎ 436 1461, fax 436 1471), which also has a desk at the Doha Sheraton Hotel. German-speaking guides can also be arranged, and prices for tours range from QR65/200 for half/full-day tours to QR375 for overnight desert safaris.

Doha   الدوحة

Doha (where 80% of Qatar's population lives) is rapidly developing into a modern, easy-going city, albeit one that is determined to retain its traditions and culture. With its picturesque bay, blend of old and new Islamic-style architecture, and a reputation for being one of the safest cities in the region, it's a pleasant place to spend a few days and an obvious base for day trips around the country.

Information

Money There are plenty of **moneychangers** dotted around central Doha; there's a small collection just south of the Doha Fort. AmEx is represented by **Darwish Travel & Tourism** (☎ 443 3120; Al-Rayyan Rd; w www.darwishtravel.com). There are ATMs at all banks, the Doha Club, the airport, the City Centre Shopping Complex and Mall shopping centre, and the Doha Marriott and Doha Sheraton hotels.

Post The **general post office** (open 7am-1pm & 4pm-7pm Sat-Thur, 8am-10am Fri), off Al-Corniche near the Oryx roundabout, is in the West Bay area. Another more central **post office** (open 7am-1pm & 4pm-7pm Sat-Thur, 8am-10am Fri) can be found on Abdullah bin Jasim St.

CENTRAL DOHA

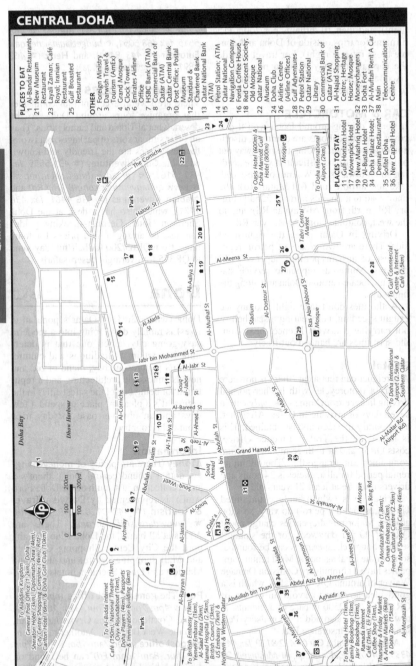

PLACES TO EAT
1 Al-Bandar Restaurants
21 New Museum Restaurant
23 Layali Zaman; Café Royal; Iranian Restaurant
25 Gulf Broasted Restaurant

OTHER
2 Foreign Ministry
3 Darwish Travel & Tourism (AmEx)
4 Grand Mosque
5 Clock Tower
6 Emirates Airline Office
7 HSBC Bank (ATM)
8 Commercial Bank of Qatar (ATM)
9 Qatar Central Bank
10 Post Office; Postal Museum
12 Standard & Chartered Bank
13 Qatar National Bank (ATM)
14 Petrol Station; ATM
15 Qatar National Navigation Company
16 Forda Coffee House
18 Red Crescent Society; Qatar National Museum
22 Old Mosque
24 Doha Club
26 Airline Centre (Airline Offices)
27 Petrol Station
29 Qatar National Library
30 Commercial Bank of Qatar (ATM)
31 Al-Najad Shopping Centre; Heritage House; Mosque
32 Moneychangers
33 Doha Fort
37 Al-Muftah Rent A Car
38 Main Telecommunications Centre

PLACES TO STAY
11 Gulf Horizon Hotel
17 Movenpick Hotel
19 New Mashriq Hotel
20 Al-Bustan Hotel
34 Doha Palace Hotel; Desman Restaurant
35 Sofitel Doha
36 New Capital Hotel

Telephone The **main telecommunications centre** *(Al-Musheireb St; open 24 hrs daily)* also offers fax, telex and telegram services.

Email & Internet Access At the business centres of all the top-end hotels Internet access costs about QR20 per hour. **Internet Cafe** *(open 7am-12.30am Sat-Thur, 12.30pm-midnight Fri)* charges QR10 per hour and has several branches around town including:

Al-Bidda (☎ 435 0060, **e** albidda@internetcafe
  .com.qa) Abu Firas St
Gulf (☎ 435 0070, **e** gulf@internetcafe.com.qa)
  Al-Khaleej St
Ramada (☎ 437 3905, **e** ramada@internet
  .com.qa) Salwa Rd

Bookshops The **Family Bookshop** *(☎ 442 4148, fax 432 0828; Al-Mirghab St • Doha Sheraton Hotel)* and the impressively large **Jarir Bookshop** *(☎ 444 0212; Salwa Rd)* both offer a wide selection of titles.

Cultural Centres Some of the cultural centres in Doha include:

American Cultural Center (☎ 488 4101, ext
  4241; **e** usisdoha@qatar.net.qa) 22nd February
  St, Al-Luqta
British Council (☎ 442 6193;
  w www.britishcouncil.org/qatar) 93 Al-Sadd St,
  Istiqlal
French Cultural Centre (☎ 467 1037;
  w www.qatar.net.qa/ambadoha/ccf) 207 Al-
  Muntazah St, Al-Hilal

Medical Services The **Hamad Hospital** *(☎ 439 4444;* **w** *www.hmcqa.org.qa)* is a well-equipped government-run centre, and offers subsidised medical and dental treatment for tourists on a walk-in basis.

Qatar National Museum

The highlight of Doha is unquestionably the Qatar National Museum *(☎ 444 2191; Al-Corniche; admission QR2; open 8am-noon & 4pm-7pm Sun-Thur, 4pm-7pm Fri)*. The large number of varied exhibits are well labelled in English and it's easy to get around. The main museum features exhibits and films about Qatar's climate, history, environment and archaeology. Next to the large 'lagoon', the **marine museum** has informative displays about fishing, pearling and

boat building. Underneath is a small but impressive **aquarium**.

Heritage Centre

Formerly known as the Ethnographic Museum, this restored heritage building *(Al-Najada Shopping Centre courtyard; admission free; open from 9am-noon & 4pm-7pm Sun-Thur)* is one of Qatar's few remaining *badghir* (wind tower) houses. The wind tower was commonly used as a form of pre-electrical air-conditioning throughout the Gulf, and the house itself is an excellent example of the ingenuity of traditional Gulf architecture.

Doha Fort

This interesting little fort *(☎ 441 2747; Jassim Bin Mohammed St; admission free; open from 7am-noon & 4pm-7pm Sun-Thur, 4pm-6.30pm Fri)* is also known as Al-Koot Fort and was built during the Turkish occupation in the 19th century.

The interior consists of a large, paved courtyard with a fountain. The exhibits range from model dhows to paintings and displays of Qatari life, but most of the topics are covered much more thoroughly in the Qatar National Museum.

The fort is officially open the hours stated here, but in reality opening hours are pretty erratic.

Al-Corniche

The 7km corniche is delightful, and one of the nicest in the region. It starts opposite the Qatar National Museum and peters out at the Doha Sheraton Hotel. There are walkways, cycling and jogging tracks, plenty of shade and enchanting views. From several points along Al-Corniche, after about 4pm, speedboats and dhows take passengers on **boat trips** for a negotiable fare.

Palm Tree Island

This tiny speck of land in the bay *(open 9am-11pm daily)* has a beach, corniche, swimming pool and activities such as horse riding and water sports. There's also the **Fish Market Restaurant** *(☎ 585 9865; 3-course set meals QR30)*.

Boats *(return tickets QR25; daily from 9am-noon & 4pm-midnight)* leave from a jetty next to the Doha Sheraton Hotel on Al-Corniche.

Activities

The **Doha Golf Club** (☎ 483 2338, fax 483 4790; e e@qatar.net.qa; West Bay) is an internationally recognised 18-hole course which hosts the annual Qatar Masters in March. A sight to behold amid the surrounding barren desert, the club also boasts an opulent, marble-rich clubhouse with an excellent restaurant, **Il Mediterraneo**.

Places to Stay – Budget

All the rooms at these hotels have air-con, a TV (normally satellite), fridge and bathroom (with hot water). As in other parts of the Gulf, most budget hotels are not suitable for, nor will they accept, solo women travellers.

Safeer Hotel (☎ 435 3999, fax 435 3888; Al-Muthaf St; singles/doubles QR130/180) is close to the national museum and is a cheap option (for men only) with large and reasonably furnished rooms.

Gulf Horizon Hotel (☎ 443 2525, fax 441 0435; e ghorizon@qatar.net.qa; Al-Jabr St; singles/doubles QR175/200) is a new and friendly budget hotel tucked away behind Al-Jabr Souq. Its spacious, clean and well-furnished rooms make it great value, and it's also suitable for solo women travellers.

New Mashriq Hotel (☎ 441 1776, fax 441 0687; Al-Muthaf St; singles/doubles QR120/160) is popular with Arab families. Rooms are basic and reasonably clean. The management speak Arabic only.

Doha Palace Hotel (☎ 436 0101, fax 442 3955; e dpalace@qatar.net.qa; Al-Musheireb St; singles/doubles QR150/180) has a large number of comfortable rooms in a convenient (but noisy) location.

Places to Stay – Mid-Range

New Capital Hotel (☎ 444 5445, fax 444 2233; Al-Musheireb St; singles/doubles QR230/260) is overpriced – probably because it boasts a swimming pool and is in the centre of town. Discounts are usually available. The rooms, though a little dated, are neat and clean, and the hotel staff friendly and helpful.

Al-Bustan Hotel (☎ 432 8888, fax 443 6111; e albustan@qatar.net.qa; Al-Muthaf St; singles/doubles QR250/300) is only a short walk from the museum. It's a small and very popular boutique-style hotel. Book ahead!

Movenpick Hotel (☎ 429 1111, fax 429 1100; e hotel.doha@moevenpick.com.qa;

w www.moevenpick.com; off Al-Corniche; standard room QR260) is another new hotel, close to the museum and with sea views. It has large and comfortable rooms with all the luxuries you usually find in top-end hotels.

Oasis Hotel (☎ 442 4424, fax 432 7096; e oasis_hotel@hotmail.com; Ras Abu Aboud St; singles/doubles QR240/320) is an older-style hotel with pleasant sea views. The rooms could do with some renovation but they're well furnished and discounts can often be negotiated.

Places to Stay – Top End

Prices quoted here are rack rates and include the mandatory 17% tax and service charge. Discounts and special deals can often be negotiated, especially during summer.

Doha Sheraton Hotel (☎ 485 4444, fax 483 2323; e sherdoha@qatar.net.qa; w www.sheraton.com/doha; Al-Corniche; singles/doubles QR660/760) is the oldest of Doha's five-star hotels but still boasts one of the better locations and views. The breezy, split-level rooms with balconies are everything you'd expect from a top-end hotel. Rates include breakfast.

Doha Marriott Gulf Hotel (☎ 443 2432, fax 441 8784; e marriott@qatar.net.qa; Ras Abu Aboud Street; standard room QR510) was formerly the Gulf Sheraton. It has been recently renovated and is close to the airport.

Sofitel Doha (☎ 446 2222, fax 443 9186; e sofisale@qatar.net.qa; singles/doubles QR330/380) is a busy hotel in a central location. It's popular with tour groups so is often full.

Ritz-Carlton (☎ 484 8000, fax 484 8310; e sales@ritzcarlton.com.qa; w www.ritzcarlton .com; West Bay Lagoon; singles/doubles QR700) has spared no expense in ensuring it is Doha's most opulent hotel. It's a fair way out of town, but with its own private beach and marina, a host of excellent restaurants and bars, a lobby lounge that serves a high tea to die for, and luxuriously appointed rooms, it's a perfect choice if you want to stay somewhere special.

Places to Eat

Snacks Doha is rife with the usual Western fast-food outlets. Try the string of **restaurants** at the intersection of C Ring and Salwa Rds, opposite the Ramada Hotel, or the food halls at the City Centre Shopping Complex and Mall Shopping Centre.

The cheapest places for a snack are cafeterias, such as the **New Museum Cafeteria** *(Al-Muthaf St)*, which serves fresh juices, felafel sandwiches and shwarma. One of the best bakeries is **Eli France** in the City Centre Shopping Complex and on Salwa Rd.

Restaurants For tasty burgers (QR6 to QR8) and chicken meals (from QR12) try **Gulf Broasted Restaurant** *(Ras Abu Aboud St; meals QR6-12)*.

Al-Bustan Tent *(Al-Muthaf St; juices & coffee QR10, sheesha QR15, grills QR40; open 6pm-1am daily)* is a popular and lively 'tent' restaurant next to Al-Bustan Hotel where you can enjoy delicious Arabic fare in a traditional setting.

Layali Zaman is the extraordinary place at the southern end of Al-Corniche. The **Iranian Restaurant** *(☎ 441 1177; open noon-late daily)* serves tasty and reasonably priced food while the adjoining **Cafe Royal** *(☎ 436 7036; open 6pm-late daily)* is a pleasant place to enjoy (cold or hot) drinks, snacks, views and occasionally live music.

Al-Bandar *(☎ 431 1818; dishes QR6-40; open 12.30pm-3.30pm & 7.30pm-10.30pm daily)* is an atmospheric collection of restaurants at the end of the fishing harbour jetty. Choose from Middle Eastern, seafood and Western dishes.

Admiral's Club *(☎ 484 8000; Ritz-Carlton; open 6.30pm-midnight daily)* is a decidedly upmarket restaurant overlooking West Bay Lagoon, and offers sushi and freshly caught seafood – for a price. The bar stays open until 1am each morning.

Al-Shaheen *(☎ 485 4444; Doha Sheraton Hotel rooftop)* is one of Doha's most exclusive restaurants and boasts fabulous views of the city and the sea. Apart from its nightly à la carte menu, it also offers Friday brunch (from 8am to 3pm) for QR69.

Entertainment
Check the events sections in the two English-language daily newspapers to find out what's going on.

Bars & Coffee Houses Hotel bars are generally only open to guests and 'members' (who pay 'membership' of about QR100 per year). However, there seems to be a relaxing of these rules and even Qataris can now be seen in some places (once strictly forbidden). Some of the more popular bars are: **The Library** *(Ramada Hotel; open 6pm-1am)*, **The Cigar Divan** *(Ritz-Carlton; 6pm-late)*, **Al-Mina Sports Bar** *(Doha Marriott Gulf Hotel; 4.30pm-late; happy hour until 8.30pm)* and **The Watering Hole** *(Doha Sheraton Hotel; 6pm-1am)*.

For a good coffeehouse try **Forda** *(Al-Corniche)*, which has good views, simple meals and hot and cold drinks in a reasonably authentic atmosphere.

Cinemas & Theatres The best cinemas are located in **The City Centre** *(☎ 488 1674)* and **The Mall** *(☎ 467 8666)* shopping complexes. They show the latest Hollywood blockbusters and the occasional film from Iran or Europe. Tickets cost about QR15.

Qatar National Theatre *(☎ 483 1250; Al-Corniche)* is housed in an impressive building in northern Doha and infrequently features Arabic plays. The expatriate **Doha Players** stage more regular shows at a small theatre *(☎ 487 1196; Ar-Rayyan al-Jedid Rd)*.

Kids' Stuff If you're travelling with children, there are several fun things to do around town: The City Centre Shopping Complex is home to **Winter Wonderland** *(☎ 483 9164; basement level)* which consists of an **ice-skating rink**, **ten-pin bowling alley** and **waterpark**. On the top level of the complex is **X-treme World** *(☎ 483 9501)*, a whizz-bang collection of virtual rides, go-kart racing, merry-go rounds and an indoor ski slope...with snow! Both Winter Wonderland and X-treme World are open from 9am to midnight Saturday to Thursday and from 10am to 10pm on Friday. **Aladdin's Kingdom** *(☎ 483 1001; West Bay; QR 25; open 4pm-10pm Sun-Thur)* is an outdoor entertainment park, which has a roller coaster, dodgem cars and go-karts (for which you need a driving licence!). Some days are allocated for women or families only, so ring first.

Shopping
Souq Watif *(open 9am-1pm & 4pm-8pm Sat-Thur, 4pm-8pm Fri)*, behind Souq Ahmad on Grand Hamad St, is a maze of covered alleyways where you can find anything from Iranian sweets and Indian spices to the national

Qatari dress, the *thobe al-nashl* (floor-length shirt-dress worn by men) and the embroidered *bukhnoq* (girl's head covering).

The **Falcon Souq** is really just a few shops scattered throughout the larger **Thursday and Friday Market**, selling falconry equipment such as *burkha* (hoods) and *hubara* (feathers). Come falcon season (October to March), however, and the shops are filled with falcons of all shapes and sizes, and would-be buyers. Shop owners are usually quite happy to show off their birds to anyone who shows some interest.

At the small **Omani Market**, located across from the Thursday and Friday Market on Wholesale Market St, you will find a curious mishmash of items such as Saudi dates and hand-woven baskets, Omani dried fish, tobacco and lemons, and Iranian honey and pots. The **Central Market** *(Salwa Rd)*, also in this area, has a range of fresh fruit, vegetables, meat and fish.

For Western-style malls, the two main shopping complexes are **The City Centre Shopping Complex** *(West Bay, open 9am-midnight Sat-Thur, 10am-10pm Fri)* and **The Mall Shopping Centre** *(D Ring Rd; open 9am-10pm Sat-Thur, 3.30pm-10pm Fri)*.

Getting There & Away

Doha International Airport *(☎ 462 2999)* has offices for **Qatar Airways** *(☎ 462 1681)* and **Gulf Air** *(☎ 445 5444)*. Many airlines have offices in the **Airline Centre** *(Ras Abu Abboud St)*, and **Al-Saad Plaza** *(C Ring Rd)* south of the city centre.

Getting Around

To/From the Airport If you have arranged your accommodation with a top-end hotel, it should provide free transport to and from the airport. A taxi between the airport and central Doha costs about QR25.

Taxi There are lots of taxis in the city – gently persuade the driver to use the meter.

Around Qatar

AL-SHAHANIYA الشحانية
Al-Shahaniya, 60km west of Doha along the Dukhan Rd, is a good place to see camels roaming around the desert, and to see **camel races** in a purpose-built stadium. If you have

a car – a 4WD is not necessary – it's fun to drive along the 18km racetrack during the race. Check the two English-language daily newspapers for race times.

There is also an oryx farm called **Almaha Sanctuary** where the Arabian Oryx – Qatar's national emblem – is being bred. To enter the farm you need a permit from the Ministry of Municipal Affairs & Agriculture *(☎ 443 5777)*, but it's easier to just go with a tour operator).

The village and stadium are well signposted on the main Doha-Dukhan road.

AL-WAKRAH الوكره
Al-Wakrah and the village of Al-Wukair have several interesting **mosques** and **traditional houses**. Al-Wakrah also has a small **museum** *(officially open 8am-noon & 3pm-6pm Sun-Fri)*, which keeps unpredictable hours. Behind the museum are the **ruins** of what is thought to be a palace.

There are some good **beaches** south of Al-Wakrah. Plenty of **flamingos** roost along the coast between Al-Wakrah and Mesaieed during winter.

Al-Wakrah is easy to reach by car from Doha; follow Al-Matar Rd past the airport.

MESAIEED أم سعيد
Mesaieed (formerly known as Umm Said) is an industrialised town about 45km south of Doha, but it does boast some of the best beaches in Qatar.

Sealine Beach Resort *(☎ 477 2722, fax 477 2733; e sbr@qatar.net.qa)* is wonderfully located on a pleasant beach near some awesome sand dunes. It's a great base from which to explore Khor al-Adaid. Ring the resort for current rates, and ask about any special offers.

Mesaieed is easy to reach by car from Doha; follow the road past the airport and through Al-Wakrah.

KHOR AL-ADAID خور العديد
Understandably touted as the major attraction in Qatar, this 'inland sea' is actually a huge lake jutting into the desert and surrounded by kilometres of towering sand dunes. These sand dunes are considered the best in Qatar for sand-skiing. The best time to visit the dunes is in the late afternoon, but to really appreciate the changing landscapes between day and night it's best to camp overnight.

QATAR

This region is *only* accessible by 4WD, and independent travellers should accompany someone who knows the area, and who can really drive a 4WD.

Going on an organised tour is probably the best and safest way to see Khor al-Adaid (see the Getting Around section earlier in this chapter). From Doha, head towards Salwa for about 60km and look for the turn-offs to Khor al-Adaid. You can also do a day trip from Sealine Beach Resort in Mesaieed.

UMM SALAL ALI   أم صلال علي

This field of very old **grave mounds** probably dates from the 3rd millennium BC and is worth visiting if you haven't seen the more impressive collections in Bahrain. A small mound field lies just north of the town and more mounds are scattered among the buildings in the town centre. Umm Salal Ali is easy to reach from along the main road north from Doha.

AL-KHOR   الخور

Al-Khor is a pleasant town with a nice corniche. The small **museum** (☎ 472 1866; *open 8am-noon Sun-Fri, 3pm-6pm Sat-Thur*), on the corniche, has some archaeological and cultural artefacts from the region, but is often closed.

A number of old **watchtowers** are scattered around the town; several have been restored to their original form. From the old mosque, the **view** of the ocean is splendid.

Ain Helaitan Restaurant & Coffee Shop and **Pearl of Asea**, both along the corniche, serve decent food.

Al-Khor is easy to reach from Doha. Along the road into Al-Khor, follow the signs to the corniche. The road then passes

the museum and mosque, about 700m further along the coast.

JEBEL JASSASSIYEH   جبل الجساسية

On the road to Al-Huwailah, about 60km north of Doha, lies the rocky ridge known as Jebel Jassassiyeh where **rock carvings** thought to date back several thousand years can be seen. Unless you're with an organised tour, it can be a little difficult to find.

Driving towards Al-Huwailah, take the dirt road to the left just before the abandoned date farm and drive until you come to the low-lying ridge.

AL-ZUBARA   الزبارة

Al-Zubara, 105km northwest of Doha, occupies an important place in Qatari history, and was a large commercial region in the 18th century. All that remains is a fort, which has been restored and converted to the **Al-Zubara Regional Museum** (*admission by donation QR1-2; open 9am-noon & 4pm-7pm Sun-Fri in summer*). It has some mildly interesting exhibits of archaeology and pottery, and some bleak **views** from the towers.

The fort is at the intersection of a road from Doha and Ar-Ruweis. From Doha, follow the signs; from Ar-Ruweis, follow the road to Abu Dhalouf and keep going.

BIR ZEKREET   بئر زكريت

Across Qatar's peninsula in the northwest are the spectacular **limestone outcrops** of Bir Zekreet. With shallow waters and sandy beaches, it's an excellent destination for a day trip or overnight camp.

To reach Bir Zekreet from Doha, head west past Al-Shahaniya and take the signposted turn-off on the right about 10km before Dukhan.

Saudi Arabia

المملكة العربية السعودية

Saudi Arabia, the birthplace of Islam and the cradle of the Arab race and Arabic language, has an abundance of attractions, including Petra's sister city Medain Saleh, traditional souqs, the largest oasis in the world and one of the last great unspoiled landscapes. For so long strictly a business destination, the Kingdom is gradually waking up to its tourism potential. The Saudi government established the Supreme Commission for Tourism in April 2000, and since that date thousands of Westerners and Japanese have visited the Kingdom on expensive, carefully choreographed educational tours.

However, the Kingdom remains for the time being almost completely closed to independent travel – a situation that is highly unlikely to change in the near future.

Facts about Saudi Arabia

HISTORY

In the Gulf, history goes as far back as any yet recorded. Parts of what is now eastern Saudi Arabia were first settled in the 4th or 5th millennium BC by migrants from what is now southern Iraq.

The best known of the western Arabian kingdoms was that of the Nabataeans, who left behind the tombs of Medain Saleh (and Petra in Jordan). At one point their empire, which thrived in the 1st century BC, stretched as far north as Damascus.

The Prophet Mohammed was born in Mecca into a family so humble that he never learned how to read or write. However, in AD 610 he received his first revelations of the Holy Quran and two years later began to preach. As a result, hostilities broke out between the Prophet and his followers and local tribes, and in 622 the Prophet and some 70 Muslim families were forced to make the Hejira, or migration, from Mecca to Medina – thus marking the beginning of the Muslim era (see the boxed text 'The Holy Cities of Mecca & Medina').

Bent on revenge, a series of battles ensued between Mohammed and his followers and local tribes. The most important were the dra-

The Kingdom of Saudi Arabia

Area: 1,960,582 sq km
Population: 21 million
Capital: Riyadh
Head of State: King Fahd ibn Abdul Aziz as-Saud
Official Language: Arabic
Currency: Saudi riyal (SR)

- Best Dining – admiring the view from Il Terrazzo on the 1st-floor balcony of Riyadh's new landmark skyscraper, the Faisaliya Tower

- Best Nightlife – relaxing at Al-Nakheel Beach in Jeddah, a favourite hang-out for Western expatriates

- Best Walk – wandering for a few hours through Jeddah's old city

- Best View – taking the local cable car to the 'hanging village' of Habalah, 'suspended' 300m off a cliff face in Asir National Park

- Best Activity – diving the Red Sea: Saudi Arabia has some of the best and least-spoiled reefs in the world

matic Muslim defeat of the Meccans at the Battle of Badr in 624, and the severe Muslim defeat by the Meccan army at the Battle of Uhud, outside Medina, in 625. However, in 627 the Muslims proved finally victorious against the Meccan army at the Battle of the Trench, and in the years until his death in 632 Mohammed made a series of daring peace initiatives which secured the spread of Islam

The Holy Cities of Mecca & Medina

Saudi Arabia is home to Islam's two holy cities, **Mecca**, where the Grand Mosque (which Muslims around the world pray toward five times a day) is located, and **Medina**, where you can find the Prophet's Mosque (the prophet's home in exile). Since the birth of Islam both cities have only been accessible to Muslims, and roadblocks continue to prevent all non-Muslims from entering them.

All able Muslims are obliged to perform a pilgrimage to these holy sites at least once in their lifetime, and such pilgrims have their own guides and are given services and information by specialist haj organisations.

For these reasons, the two holy cities themselves are not covered in this guide.

over the following centuries way beyond the borders of what is now Saudi Arabia.

In the early 18th century the Sauds, the royal family of modern Saudi Arabia, were the ruling sheikhs of the oasis village of Dir'aiyah, near modern Riyadh. The first Saudi empire grew from an alliance, cemented c. 1744, between Mohammed bin Saud, the ruler of Dir'aiyah, and Mohammed bin Abdul Wahhab (b. 1703), a preacher who espoused a simple, unadorned and strict form of Islam. The result of this was Wahhabism, which remains the form of Islam in Saudi Arabia today (although Saudis themselves continue to be deeply offended by the use of this term and reject it as a form of idolatry forbidden by Islam itself).

Wahhab's religious fervour and Saud's military skill proved to be a potent combination. After conquering and converting most of the tribes of Najd (central Arabia) to the Wahhabi doctrine, the Saudi forces swept out across the peninsula. By 1806 they controlled most of the territory of today's Kingdom of Saudi Arabia, as well as a large section of what is now southern Iraq.

As western Arabia was then part of the Ottoman Empire, a Turkish expedition to retake Arabia was inevitable. The Turks arrived in 1812, and the Saudis were driven back to Dir'aiyah, which also fell in 1818.

The Saud family's revival began in 1902 when Abdul Aziz bin Abdul Rahman as-Saud recaptured Riyadh from the Saud family's traditional rivals, the Rashids, beginning a string of conquests that built the modern Kingdom of Saudi Arabia.

In 1933 Abdul Aziz granted an oil concession to Standard Oil of California (Socal, the precursor of today's Chevron). Oil was found in commercial quantities in 1938 and by 1950 the Kingdom's royalties

were running at about US$1 million per week. By 1960, 81% of the Kingdom's national revenues came from oil.

Under the charismatic and hugely popular King Faisal, Saudi Arabia was a central player in the 1973 to 1974 Arab oil embargo. In its wake the price of oil increased fourfold and Faisal, who controlled 30% of OPEC's overall production, became a force to be reckoned with on the world stage. Between 1973 and 1978 the country's annual oil revenues increased from US$4.35 billion to US$36 billion. A building boom began: money poured into utility and infrastructure projects, and construction of a petrochemical industry commenced. Faisal, however, did not live to see it. In 1975 he was assassinated by a deranged nephew. He was succeeded by his half-brother, Khaled, with another half-brother, Fahd, as crown prince.

It is difficult today to appreciate the extent to which Saudi Arabia was modernised during King Khaled's reign (1975–82). Most accounts of Riyadh and Jeddah in the late '70s describe the cities in terms of huge construction sites. Their physical growth was staggering: everyone seemed to be making easy money. Some Saudis, however, were troubled by the outside influences and in November 1979 some 300 radicals seized control of the Grand Mosque in Mecca. It took government troops 10 days to retake the mosque, an operation in which over 250 people died.

King Khaled died in June 1982 and his half-brother, Fahd, became the fourth of Abdul Aziz's sons to rule Saudi Arabia. Fahd was well prepared for the job. Khaled's health had long been poor and for much of his reign Fahd, then crown prince, had been king in all but name.

What to See

For those who have a seven-day transit visa and are driving through the west and south of the kingdom, Petra's sister city of **Medain Salah** should be at the top of your itinerary. Also a must is a day or two in Jeddah's historic Al-Balad district, where the houses are built of coral from the Red Sea. The southwest offers a number of attractions well worth the one-day road trip from Jeddah: the mountain city of **Abha**, gateway to the spectacular **Asir National Park**, and **Habalah** the 'hanging village' with its cable cars affording spectacular views of this mountainous region; and further south, **Najran**, one of the Kingdom's many undiscovered gems. The **Farasan Islands**, 50km off the extreme southwest coast but accessible by car ferry, are an idyllic retreat, and visitors should try their utmost to make the most of this little bit of paradise before tourism changes it forever.

For those travelling through the oil-rich eastern region there is much to see, including the gold souq of **Dammam** and that city's modern twin city of **Khobar**, a diner's paradise. A short drive away in **Jubail** is a Nestorian site, where there are the remains of a pre-Islamic Christian church. **Hofuf**, a short drive inland, is the largest oasis in the world, and is host to a massive camel market every Thursday.

Saudi Arabia Today

In 1995 King Fahd suffered a stroke and his half-brother, Crown Prince Abdullah bin Abdul Aziz, took over the running of the country on a day-to-day basis. The challenges he faces are formidable. Over half the Saudi population is under the age of 20, and unemployment is conservatively estimated at 15%. There is a constant budget deficit. Oil revenues, which bankrolled the Saudi economy for three decades, are at an all-time low, and it is estimated that the oil itself will run dry within 30 years.

In response, the Saudi government has begun to radically diversify the economy, inviting Western corporations to sign multibillion dollar deals to tap the Kingdom's huge gas reserves while at the same time negotiating entry into the World Trade Organization (WTO). A campaign of 'Saudization' (replacing foreign workers with Saudi nationals) is also well under way, and millions of dollars are being spent on the domestic tourism infrastructure.

Perhaps the biggest challenge now facing Saudi Arabia is repairing the damage done to its international image in the West after it was revealed that 15 of the 11 September hijackers were Saudis – as is Osama bin Laden (although he was stripped of his citizenship long before 11 September due to his anti-Saudi stances). Saudi-US relations on the diplomatic level have not been significantly affected, as the Kingdom offered the US its full support in Afghanistan.

Domestically, there is frustration among the poor and unemployed; a yearning for greater openness in the media and government among Westernised intellectuals; and a 'back-to-basics' movement among conservative Muslims. However, Saudi Arabia remains stable, and a very safe destination.

GEOGRAPHY

Saudi Arabia is about 1,960,582 sq km in area, most of it desert. Western Saudi Arabia is dominated by the Hejaz and Asir mountain chains running the entire length of the country, which generally become higher and broader as one moves south towards Yemen. About half of the country is taken up by the Rub' al-Khali, or Empty Quarter. Much of the country's central and northern region is a gravel-covered desert plain. The extreme northwest of the Kingdom contains Arabia's second great sand desert, the Nafud. The Eastern Province is a low-lying area containing a number of *sabkhas* (salt flats). Its main geographical feature is the gigantic Al-Hasa Oasis, centred on the town of Hofuf.

CLIMATE

Daytime temperatures rise to 45°C or more from mid-April until October throughout the Kingdom, with high humidity in the

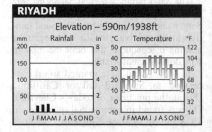

RIYADH

Elevation – 590m/1938ft

coastal regions. In the dead of winter (December to January) temperatures in the main cities will drop into the teens during the day and even hit zero in some places, particularly in the central deserts, overnight.

GOVERNMENT & POLITICS

The basic principles governing the work of the Shura Council, Saudi Arabia's parliament, come from the Quran and the sayings and traditions of Prophet Mohammed. Shura (literally 'consultation') means in practice that the chief executive, or ruler, of the country seeks out the views of his subjects, particularly scholars and wise men, while running its affairs. The members of the Shura Council, and the cabinet, are appointed by the king.

POPULATION & PEOPLE

Official figures say that of the 21 million people who live in the Kingdom, 15.5 million are Saudi citizens. The remaining 5.5 million are expatriates who come mainly from the Indian subcontinent, Afghanistan, other Arab countries and the West.

The Saudi heartland is Najd, the central Arabian region centred on Riyadh. The people of Najd pride themselves on their pure Bedouin ancestry. In contrast, the Hejaz (the western coastal region, centred on Jeddah) has, after 14 centuries of receiving Muslim pilgrims, an extraordinarily mixed population. Hejazis may be as dark skinned as sub-Saharan Africans or as pale as someone from northern Europe. Natives of the Gulf fall somewhere between these extremes. Saudis of the southwestern Asir region are distinctly Yemeni in appearance, dress and lifestyle.

SOCIETY & CONDUCT

Saudi Arabia is probably the most conservative country on earth and social life here is determined by an adherence to strict Islamic doctrine. Everything closes for prayer time five times a day, for instance, and men and women are strictly segregated in all forms of public life. Women cannot drive, and cannot travel intercity or internationally without permission from a male relative.

Older Saudi men and women for the most part wear traditional clothing – the *thobe* and *abeyya* respectively – although most teenage boys in the big cities prefer to dress in Western clothing on informal occasions.

Almost two million of the 5.5 million expatriates are from the Indian subcontinent, and they constitute most of the taxi drivers, shop owners and menial workers. Although based on generalisations, the following list does for the most part hold true. Afghans tend to run the souqs. Filipinos run many of the restaurants and shopping malls. Other Arabs are found in most walks of life, with Egyptians and Yemenis forming the largest groups.

Westerners live in walled-off compounds, completely shut off from Saudi society. The main reason for this is they are able to offer, women especially, an environment more like what they are used to in the West.

The Committee for the Propagation of Virtue and the Prevention of Vice – the *matawwa*, or religious police – is a government-sponsored squad of moral vigilantes out to enforce Islamic orthodoxy. They have become less visible in Jeddah and Khobar over the past few years. Elsewhere, if you find yourself confronted by them, they will be asking something reasonable of you (by local standards), like covering your head if you are a woman or not using a public phone during prayer time.

RELIGION

Most Saudis are Sunni Muslims. The country's Shiite minority constitutes between 5% and 10% of the population, most of whom live in the Eastern Province.

LANGUAGE

Arabic is the official government language of Saudi Arabia. English, however, is very widely spoken, both by Saudis and non-Western expatriates, especially in the major towns and cities.

For Arabic words and phrases, see the Language chapter at the back of this book.

Facts for the Visitor

WHEN TO GO

The best time to visit is between November and February when the climate is mild. The Asir mountains are at their best a bit earlier and a bit later than the rest of the country – during the winter they are often blanketed in fog.

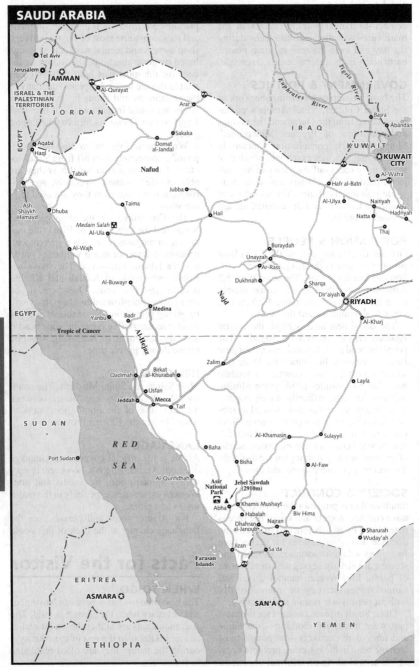

SAUDI ARABIA

ISRAEL & THE PALESTINIAN TERRITORIES

EGYPT

EGYPT

JORDAN

IRAQ

KUWAIT

SUDAN

ERITREA

ETHIOPIA

YEMEN

RED SEA

Nafud

Najd

Al-Hejaz

Tropic of Cancer

Tel Aviv
Jerusalem
AMMAN
Al-Qurayat
Arar
Sakaka
Domat al-Jandal
Tabuk
Jubba
Taima
Dhuba
Ash Shaykh Hamayd
Medain Salah
Al-Ula
Al-Wajh
Al-Buwayr
Yanbu
Badr
Medina
Qadimah
Birkat al-Khurabah
Usfan
Jeddah
Mecca
Taif
Zalim
Baha
Bisha
Port Sudan
Al-Qunfidhah
Asir National Park
Jebel Sawdah (2910m)
Abha
Khamis Mushayt
Habalah
Dhahran al-Janoub
Najran
Biv Hima
Jizan
Sa'da
Farasan Islands
ASMARA
SAN'A

Aqaba
Haql
Hail
Buraydah
Unayzah
Ar-Rass
Dukhnah
Sharqa
Dir'aiyah
RIYADH
Al-Kharj
Al-Khamasin
Sulayyil
Layla
Al-Faw
Sharurah
Wuday'ah

Basra
Abadan
KUWAIT CITY
Al-Wafra
Hafr al-Batn
Al-Ulya
Nairiyah
Abu Hadriyah
Natta
Thaj

Euphrates River
Tigris River

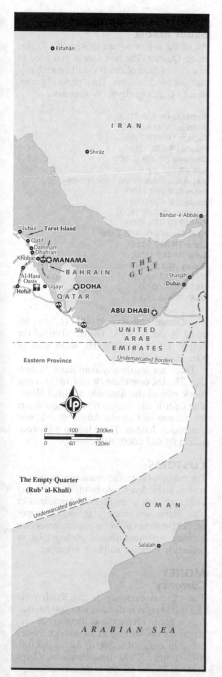

Esfahán

I R A N

Shíráz

Bandar-é Abbás

Jubail Tarut Island
Qatif
Damman
Dhahran
Khobar **MANAMA**
B A H R A I N   T H E
G U L F
Al-Hasa   Sharjah
Oasis Uqayr **DOHA** Dubai
Hofuf   Q A T A R

ABU DHABI

Sila

U N I T E D
A R A B
E M I R A T E S

Eastern Province   *Undemarcated Borders*

0   100   200km
0   60   120mi

The Empty Quarter
(Rub' al-Khali)

Undemarcated Borders

O M A N

Salalah

A R A B I A N   S E A

VISAS & DOCUMENTS
Visas
Saudi Arabia has a well-deserved reputation as one of the hardest places in the world to visit. However, visas for those willing to travel on fixed-itinerary, high-end package tours are now being issued under the sponsorship of Saudi Arabian Airlines. The tours – often educational in conception – are organised by reputable, independent travel agents and major museums or research centres.

In the US, contact **Peter Voll Associates** (☎ *800 795 5700*; ⓦ *www.pvatravel.com*).

In the UK, **Bales Worldwide Travel** (☎ *0870-241 3208*; ⓔ *inquiries@balesworld wide.com*, ⓦ *www.balesworldwide.com*) organises tours and visas.

Other tour operators specialise in Red Sea diving packages.

Desert Sea Divers (☎ *02-656 1807*; ⓔ *info@desertseadivers.net*; ⓦ *www.desert seadivers.net*), in Jeddah, can organise visit visas through London-based travel agents.

Arac Yanbu Resort (☎ *04-826 0097*, fax *825 0281*; ⓔ *info@arac.com.sa*; ⓦ *www.arac .com.sa*) located in Yanbu, another popular location for diving 350km north of Jeddah, is a very well-run outfit, which provides on request a list of the Western tour operators it deals with.

Unless you are a Muslim, your other options consist of a visitor's visa or a transit visa. The rules for obtaining these are the same for all nationalities.

To obtain a visitor visa (ie, a business visa), you must have a Saudi sponsor. This can be a company or an individual. The sponsor is issued a visa number by the Saudi Chamber of Commerce and Industry, and then passes it on to you. (There is no longer a requirement for this visa to be verified by the Ministry of the Exterior.) You go with the number and your passport to a Saudi embassy or consulate. If you show up in the morning, you usually get the visa the same afternoon. Visitor visas can be picked up at any Saudi diplomatic mission, but the pick-up site must be specified by the sponsor when the visa application is filed.

People driving between Jordan and either Kuwait or Yemen are usually issued three-day transit visas. People driving between Jordan and Bahrain or the United Arab Emirates (UAE) often get seven-day transit visas. You have to go to the embassy with your carnet and proof that you already have a visa for the country at the other end of the road.

From the first of Ramadan each year Saudi embassies in Muslim countries issue only haj visas until the haj is over about three months later. Note that all official business in Saudi Arabia is conducted according to the Muslim Hejira calendar. When you pick up the visa, be certain to ask someone at the embassy to write down the Western date on which it will expire.

For details of visas for other Middle Eastern countries, see the 'Visas at a Glance' table under Visas & Documents in the Regional Facts for the Visitor chapter.

Site Permits

To visit virtually any fort, ruin or archaeological site you must first obtain a permit from the Director General of the Department of Antiquities at the **National Museum in Riyadh** (fax 01-411 2054; PO Box 3734, Riyadh 11418).

File the permit application in the morning and return a day later to collect it. If you are not in Riyadh, fax your details, and include a fax number to which the permit can be faxed back. Resident foreigners must present their *iqama*, or residence permit, but those in the country on a visitor visa need only their passport (including the page containing your visa if faxing).

EMBASSIES & CONSULATES
Saudi Embassies & Consulates

Following are the Saudi embassies and consulates in major cities around the world. For addresses of Saudi embassies in neighbouring Middle Eastern countries, see the relevant chapter.

Australia (☎ 06-286 2099) 12 Culgoa Circuit, O'Malley, Canberra 2606 ACT
Canada (☎ 613-237 4100) 99 Bank St, Suite 901, Ottawa, Ontario, K1P 6B9
France (☎ 4766 0206) 5 Ave Hoche, 75008, Paris
Germany (☎ 810900) Godesburger Allee 40-42, 5300, Bonn 2
Ireland Apply through Saudi embassy in UK
The Netherlands (☎ 361 4391)
New Zealand Apply through Saudi embassy in Australia
UK (☎ 020-7917 3000) 30 Charles St, London W1
USA (☎ 202-342 3800) 601 New Hampshire Ave NW, Washington, DC, 20037

Embassies & Consulates in Saudi Arabia

All of the following are in Riyadh's Diplomatic Quarter. The best idea if you need to visit one of these places is to call the embassy and ask for directions. They generally open 9am to 4pm Saturday to Wednesday.

Australia (☎ 488 7788)
Bahrain (☎ 488 0044)
Canada (☎ 488 2288)
France (☎ 488 1255)
Germany (☎ 488 0700)
Iran (☎ 488 1916)
Iraq Apply through the Syria embassy
Ireland (☎ 488 2300)
Jordan (☎ 488 0051)
Lebanon (☎ 465 3800)
Kuwait (☎ 488 3500)
New Zealand (☎ 488 7988)
Qatar (☎ 482 5544)
Syria (☎ 465 3800)
Turkey (☎ 482 010)
UAE (☎ 482 6803)
UK (☎ 488 0077)
USA (☎ 488 3800)

The **Omani embassy** (☎ 482 3120) is located in the Al-Ra'id District, behind the petrol station opposite the main gate of King Saud University.

There are also many consulates in Jeddah. The **UK consulate** (☎ 654 1811) is one block east of the Sheraton al-Bilad Hotel. The British also handle diplomatic matters for citizens of Canada, Australia and New Zealand in Jeddah. There is also a **US consulate** (☎ 667 0000; Palestine St).

CUSTOMS

The import of anything containing alcohol or pork is forbidden. Customs officers also pay close attention to any books, magazines or photographs you are carrying, and videotapes are held without fail by the airport censors for viewing. Anything deemed pornographic or politically sensitive will be confiscated.

MONEY
Currency

The official currency is the Saudi riyal (SR). One riyal is divided into 100 halalas. It is a hard currency and there are no restrictions on its import or export. Notes come in one, SR5, SR10, SR50, SR100, SR200 and SR500 denominations. Coins come in 25 and 50 halala denominations.

Exchange Rates

The riyal is pegged to the US dollar, so while the US$/SR rate rarely moves by more than a halala or so either side of SR3.75, the rates against other Western currencies change constantly.

Below are the rates for a range of currencies at the time this book went to press.

country	unit		Saudi rial (SR)
Australia	A$1	=	SR2.03
Bahrain	BD1	=	SR9.94
Canada	C$1	=	SR2.37
euro zone	€1	=	SR3.68
Japan	¥100	=	SR3.05
Jordan	JD1	=	SR5.29
New Zealand	NZ$1	=	SR1.77
Qatar	QR1	=	SR1.03
UAE	Dh1	=	SR1.00
UK	UK£1	=	SR0.17
USA	US$1	=	SR0.26

Exchanging Money

All major cities, and even smaller towns, have an abundance of international ATMs. The Saudi British Bank, with hundreds of branches across the Kingdom, readily exchanges travellers cheques.

You can change all hard currencies at any bank, and since there is not a significant difference between private exchange bureau rates and bank rates it is best to just stick to the latter.

Costs

Saudi Arabia is not cheap. However, it is possible to travel relatively cheaply. Filling your stomach for SR15 (US$4) or less is never a problem. Beds generally bottom out at SR8 (US$2.50) in youth hostels, SR85 to SR115 (US$22 to US$30) in hotels. It is possible to cross the peninsula for less than SR250 (US$67). Travelling around the Kingdom can be done on about SR75 (US$20) a day, though SR125 (US$34) is a more realistic low-budget estimate (SR250 if you don't stay in the youth hostels).

Tipping & Bargaining

Tips of about 10% are expected in mid- and top-end restaurants. Elsewhere, all other prices are fixed – apart from in the souqs, where the tradition of haggling is still very much alive.

POST & COMMUNICATIONS
Post

The postal service has been opened to competition, meaning there are many small and efficiently run post offices. However, as there are no poste restante facilities and AmEx does not hold mail, you will have to ask a friend to let you receive letters through his or her company. Post offices open 8.30am to 1pm and 5pm to 9pm Saturday to Thursday.

Telephone

The country code for Saudi is ☎ 966, followed by the local area code (minus the zero), then the subscriber number. Local area codes are given at the start of each city or town section. The international access code (to call abroad from Saudi) is ☎ 00.

The privately run Saudi Telecom Company (STC) enjoys a monopoly. It has at least one cabin providing all international call facilities on every major street in the Kingdom; you pay in cash after making your call. Local calls cost SR1 per minute.

Mobiles The mobile phone network run by STC operates on the GSM system. Rechargeable prepaid chips are available locally in SR100 and SR200 denominations. However, you need to be a permanent resident to apply for one of these. There is presently no way to rent a mobile phone in the Kingdom short-term.

Email & Internet Access

Internet cafés are now everywhere (for addresses see individual town and city sections). Access, however, can be tediously slow. Those bringing their laptop into the Kingdom can buy local prepaid Internet access cards.

DIGITAL RESOURCES

There is a great deal about Saudi Arabia on the web. The following addresses are especially useful because they provide extensive links to other related sites which deal with travel and tourism.

Saudi Online Schedules and bookings for the national carrier
Ⓦ www.saudia-online.com
Sino Net Travel information and an on-line reservation service
Ⓦ www.sino.net/saudi.html
World Travel Guide News, reviews and travel tips
Ⓦ www.travel-guide.com/data/sau/sau.asp

SAUDI ARABIA

BOOKS

Personal Narrative of a Pilgrimage to Al-Madinah & Meccah by Richard Burton, originally published in 1855, is one of the few accounts of the Holy Cities written by a non-Muslim. A more recent Arabian travel classic is Wilfred Thesiger's 1959 memoir *Arabian Sands* in which he recounts his two journeys across the Empty Quarter in the late 1940s. *At the Drop of a Veil* by Marianne Alireza, a Californian who married into a Jeddah-based merchant family in the 1940s, is a good read. *The History of Saudi Arabia* by Alexei Vassiliev is objective, thorough and up-to-date.

More general Middle East titles, some of which contain coverage of Saudi, are listed under Books in the Regional Facts for the Visitor chapter.

NEWSPAPERS & MAGAZINES

Arab News (**W** www.arabnews.com) and the *Saudi Gazette* are the country's main English-language newspapers. Major foreign newspapers and magazines are available in the Kingdom's main cities a day or two after publication, by which time they have been heavily censored.

RADIO & TV

Saudi Arabian TV's Channel 2 broadcasts exclusively in English, except for a French-language newscast every night at 8pm. However, almost nobody watches it, because satellite TV is universally available.

Jeddah Radio (96.2 FM) broadcasts English and French programmes on topics of local interest.

PHOTOGRAPHY & VIDEO

As a rule, *don't* photograph any palaces, mosques, military or government buildings. Also, be careful not to focus your lens deliberately on local women. There are no other hard and fast rules: simply take photographs and hope that no petty official bothers you. All city centres have an abundance of Kodak and Fuji Film shops, which can usually process your colour or black-and-white film in about an hour.

HEALTH

The standard of health care in Saudi Arabia is very high and almost any ailment can be treated inside the country. Many diseases which were once endemic, such as malaria, are now virtually unknown. Those coming to live in the Kingdom undergo a series of medical tests, including an AIDS test, as part of the process of obtaining a visa. However, those just passing through on a visit visa do not need to have any vaccinations.

Almost all medication is available without a prescription, and all cities have 24-hour pharmacies. Even in small villages, you will find a well-equipped hospital.

Officially, the drinking water is okay. In practice, the quality varies greatly, and visitors should stick to bottled water.

WOMEN TRAVELLERS

Men and women are strictly segregated in Saudi society. Women are not allowed to drive, and unaccompanied women may not travel by intercity bus or train. Nor can an unaccompanied woman check into a hotel without a letter from her sponsor. Saudi Arabia's youth hostels are entirely off-limits to women.

Given this situation, women should consider travelling to the Kingdom alone *only* if they will be shuttled everywhere by their sponsor (and his family).

It is absolutely necessary, even in cosmopolitan Jeddah and Khobar, for foreign women to wear the *abeyya* (a long, black cloaklike garment) at all times in public – whether they are visitors or resident expatriates. There are no exceptions to this rule.

While there is generally no need for foreign women to cover their heads, it would be advisable for foreign women at least to carry a veil in case they are told to wear it by the religious police.

DANGERS & ANNOYANCES

Although the days when Saudi Arabia could boast to being a 'crime-free' society are long gone, official statistics show that violent crime still constitutes less than 2% of all crime. Muggings and other violent street crime is virtually nonexistent.

The main danger is the way people drive, and Saudi Arabia, unsurprisingly, has the highest road death rate in the world. You may as well throw away your highway code before coming here, because nobody else will be following the rules. The driving gets worse the further west you go, and is particularly reckless in Jeddah.

The most obvious annoyance visitors are likely to face are the gangs of Afghan children begging at traffic lights and in market places, all of whom belong to organised syndicates. They can be very persistent.

A spate of car bombings in the capital Riyadh, in which Westerners were killed and injured, have been attributed by the Saudi authorities to rival gangs fighting for control of the highly lucrative local black market in illegal alcohol.

BUSINESS HOURS

Banks and shops are open from 8am or 8.30am until 2pm and again from 4pm to 7pm Saturday to Thursday. Big shopping centres stay open until 11pm. Almost everything is shut on Friday mornings. However, on Friday evenings the downtown and Corniche areas throughout the Kingdom bustle with shoppers and promenaders.

At prayer time *everything* closes for about 25 minutes. If you are already inside a restaurant and eating, the staff may let you hang around and finish your meal. Then again, they may throw you out. A list of prayer times appears daily on page two of *Arab News*.

LEGAL MATTERS

Saudi Arabia imposes strict Sharia'a (Islamic law). The death penalty is imposed for murder, rape and drug trafficking, and is carried out by public beheading. The consumption of alcohol is strictly prohibited, and if you are caught in public with a drink (or with it stinking on your breath after a private gathering), expect to be jailed and then deported. There are no exceptions to this rule, and the Saudi authorities will not listen to excuses.

If you are involved in a traffic accident you must get a police report immediately, before you leave the scene. In the cities, this will not be difficult because there are traffic policemen on just about every main street corner. Elsewhere, wait for a police car to drive past, or in remote areas take down the number plate of the other person's vehicle and photograph the scene (if you have a camera).

Note that you will not be able to get your car repaired locally (by law you must provide a police report), and may even be prevented from leaving the kingdom, if you cannot explain serious damage to your car's body work.

PUBLIC HOLIDAYS

No holidays other than Eid al-Fitr (Festival of Breaking the Fast, celebrated at the end of Ramadan) and Eid al-Adha (Feast of Sacrifice, marking the pilgrimage to Mecca) are observed in the Kingdom. Saudi National Day is 23 September.

SPECIAL EVENTS

The kingdom's only cultural and folkloric festival, the Jinadriyah National Festival, takes place every February (dates change annually) at a special site about 45km northeast of central Riyadh.

ACTIVITIES
Diving

The Red Sea coast off Jeddah offers superb diving. All year, reef fish – triggerfish, wrasse grouper and surgeonfish – abound. Pelagic fish – jacks, tuna, Spanish mackerel and barracuda – have extensive breeding grounds, unspoiled by overfishing and virtually un-dived. April to June is whaleshark season.

A short boat trip off Jeddah lie numerous wrecks, many of which offer adventurous diving. The *AnAn* – a virtually complete wreck – has safe dives from 15 to 35 meters. The *Boiler* wreck, a dive that includes cathedral-like coral tunnels through the reef that supports it, is a local favourite.

The best shore diving and facilities are found at **Al-Nakheel Beach** (☎ 02-656 1177, fax 656 2597; e nakheel@naseej.com.sa; admission SR50). This seaside compound has superb reef-wall dives. Soft corals, clownfish, yellow monos and Spanish dancers all occupy the reef within 100m north of the entry point.

To get there, take Medina Road north out of Jeddah to Obhur. Pass Burger King on your left and then the Inter-Continental Hotel. One kilometre further, a small mosque behind a 2m-high wall marks the beginning of the beach.

For information on organised Red Sea Diving tours, see the Visas & Documents section earlier in this chapter.

ACCOMMODATION

Saudi Arabia's youth hostels (*beit ash-shabab* in Arabic) are excellent and, at SR8 per night, very cheap. The down side is that they are open only to men. Saudi Arabia is a Hostelling International (HI) member and hostel cards are always required.

All cities and most towns have at least one budget or mid-range hotel, and even in these a separate bathroom and satellite TV can be taken for granted. There is an abundance of five-star hotels in the provincial capitals, often offering great deals for those booking in advance.

Saudi law requires the presentation of proper documents to check in at any hotel or hostel. For visitors, this means a passport. Expatriates will require their *iqama* (residence permit). Women travelling alone must present a letter from their sponsor, and should stick to five-star hotels.

FOOD & DRINKS

Grilled chicken, *fuul* (fava bean paste) and shwarma are the most common cheap dishes. For more upmarket dining, every large city has a selection of moderately priced Asian restaurants. Filipino food is the cheapest, Chinese the most expensive. Jeddah, Riyadh and Khobar also have hundreds of up-market places, and most Saudi families eat at an international restaurant at least once a week.

The Kingdom is the biggest consumer of American junk food in the world outside the US itself – and as a result now has a serious obesity problem, especially among teenagers.

Saudi Arabia is 'dry', so beverages consist of soft drinks, mineral water and fruit juice. However, nonalcoholic beers are sold in restaurants and grocery stores.

SHOPPING

Among the best buys is silver Bedouin jewellery in Najran. The woven Bedouin bags in Hofuf's souq also make great souvenirs. The range of Oriental rugs in Jeddah's Afghan Souq is massive. Most of the other souvenirs you will see in shops – incense burners, for example – usually come from Pakistan.

Getting There & Away

AIR

Saudia (*Saudi Arabian Airlines;* w *www* *.saudiairlines.com.sa*) flies to dozens of cities in Europe, the USA and Asia and to just about every place worth mentioning in the Middle East. Riyadh, Jeddah and Dhahran airports are also served by most of the major European carriers, a few Asian airlines and the major carriers from the subcontinent (Air India, PIA etc).

Departure Tax

The departure tax is included in the air fare.

LAND

There are regular daily buses from Dammam/Khobar to Bahrain. It is also easy to get to capital cities throughout the Gulf and Middle East. On all routes, Saptco, the Saudi Arabian bus company, has the best fares and the best-maintained buses.

From Riyadh, Saptco runs services to Cairo every day (SR360; 8am). Fares on this service include ferry transit between Dhuba (KSA) and Safaga (Egypt), and onward bus transit in Egypt. There are daily services from Riyadh to Damascus (SR200, 10am), Amman (SR200, 10 am), Kuwait (SR150, 10am), Doha in Qatar (SR125, 10am) and Abu Dhabi in UAE (SR370; 10am). Services to İstanbul (SR260, 8am) from Riyadh run Wednesdays, Thursdays and Fridays. A new daily service has been established to Sana'a (SR280; 10am) and there are five trips to Bahrain (SR50; 1hr) daily from Dammam operated by Saptco's business partner, the Saudi-Bahraini Transport Company. (See w www.saptco.com.sa for up-to-date information on all these routes.)

The Kingdom has working border crossings with Jordan (Harat Amar), Bahrain (the causeway linking the island with Khobar), Kuwait (Al-Khalfji), Qatar (Salwa), the United Arab Emirates (Sila), and Yemen (At-Tawal). The border crossing with Iraq (Arar) is open, but only for pilgrims performing haj.

SEA

The car ferry connecting Jeddah with Suez is the main sea route in and out of the country. There are also passenger services from Jeddah to Port Safaga (Egypt), Port Sudan and to Musawwa (Eritrea), although the types of services available frequently change. For current schedules and prices contact **Ace Travel** (☎ 665 1254; Palestine St; open 9am-1.30pm & 4.30pm-8pm Sat-Wed, 9am-1.30pm Thur) in Jeddah, near the intersection with Al-Hamra St.

Getting Around

AIR

All domestic air services in the Kingdom are operated by Saudia, which covers the whole kingdom. It's reliable and tickets are reasonably priced. See the individual city listings for information on direct air connections to and from each city. Sample one-way economy fares include Jeddah-Riyadh (SR280), Riyadh-Dammam (SR150) and Dammam-Jeddah (SR390).

BUS

Bus fares are one-half to two-thirds of the equivalent air fare. Buses are operated by the **Saudi Arabian Public Transport Company** (Saptco; W www.saptco.com.sa), which has good, air-con buses that run on time (see individual city entries for local branches). Be sure to buy the tickets one day in advance, especially during haj or the summer.

TRAIN

Saudi Arabia has the only stretch of train track in the entire Arabian peninsula – one line from Riyadh to Dammam, via Hofuf and Abqaiq. See the relevant city entries for fares and the timetable.

CAR

Driving in Saudi Arabia is on the right. Petrol is cheap, but not (as myth has it) virtually free. If the road is sealed, there will be a petrol station sooner rather than later.

Rental

If you are in the country on a visitors visa you must have an international license to rent a car. Insurance and the collision-damage waiver are mandatory. Rates start at SR80 for a Toyota Corolla with the first 100km free for each day rented (75 halala per km after that).

Najd (Central Region) نجد (المنطقة الوسطى)

Najd consists solely of sedimentary plateaus interspersed with sand deserts and low, isolated mountain ranges. Its main city, Riyadh ('Garden' in Arabic), is the ultramodern capital of Saudi Arabia.

RIYADH الرياض
☎ 01

While Riyadh, and the nearby oasis town of Dir'aiyah, are the ancestral homes of the Saud family, it is only in the last generation that Riyadh has become the centre of government. Two spectacular new skyscrapers on King Fahd Rd – the Kingdom Tower and Faisaliya Tower – now dominate the skyline. They can be seen from anywhere in the city, and have given the capital a new, modern focus and identity.

Orientation

Riyadh, in effect, has two centres. Historic Al-Bathaa district, the cheapest part of town where the bus station and budget hotels are located, is almost exclusively populated by Bangladeshis.

In the modern downtown area, centred on King Fahd Rd and the surrounding streets, the range and size of the malls means the area now rivals Singapore's Orchard Road as a shoppers' paradise.

Although many of the city's streets have been renamed in recent years, people on the street have stubbornly stuck to using the old names. And things are made more complicated by the fact that almost all the city's street signs are written only in Arabic.

Information

Money The main branch of the **Saudi British Bank** (☎ 273 4459; Olaya St; open 8.30am-1pm & 5pm-8pm Sat-Thur) is in the Faisaliya Tower.

AmEx is represented by **Ace Travel** (☎ 464 8813; Makkah Rd; open 9am-1.30pm & 4.30pm-8pm Sat-Thur). Cheques are cashed for card holders through a nearby bank.

Street Names in Riyadh

new name	old name
Al-Malek Abdul Aziz St	Old Airport Rd
Al-Malek Faisal St	Al-Wazir St
Al-Amir Mohammad ibn Abdul Aziz St	Tahlia St
Al-Amir Sultan ibn Abdul Aziz St	Setteen St
Al-Imam Faisal ibn Turki ibn Abdullah St	Al-Khazan St
Al-Ihsa St	Pepsi Cola St

SAUDI ARABIA

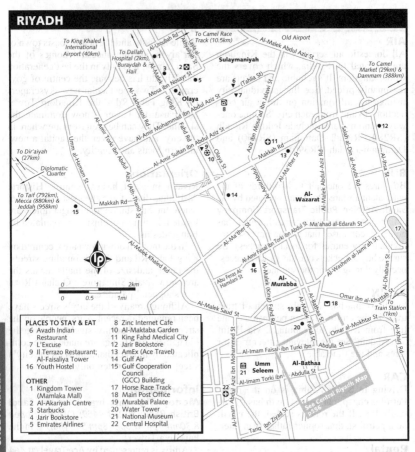

RIYADH

PLACES TO STAY & EAT
6 Avadh Indian
    Restaurant
7 L'Excuse
9 Il Terrazo Restaurant;
    Al-Faisaliya Tower
16 Youth Hostel

OTHER
1 Kingdom Tower
    (Mamlaka Mall)
2 Al-Akariyah Centre
3 Starbucks
4 Jarir Bookstore
5 Emirates Airlines

8 Zinc Internet Cafe
10 Al-Maktaba Garden
11 King Fahd Medical City
12 Jarir Bookstore
13 AmEx (Ace Travel)
14 Gulf Air
15 Gulf Cooperation
    Council
    (GCC) Building
17 Horse Race Track
18 Main Post Office
19 Murabba Palace
20 Water Tower
21 National Museum
22 Central Hospital

Post The **main post office** *(Al-Malek Abdul Aziz St; open 7.50am-2.50pm & 4pm-10.30pm Sat-Wed)* is near the intersection with Al-Bathaa St.

Telephone There are hundreds of international call cabins around the city, including dozens in the streets surrounding Al-Bathaa Hotel. Prepaid phonecards are available from any grocery in various denominations, and can be used with any private or public phone.

Email & Internet Access The **Zinc Internet Cafe** *(☎ 465 7993; Al-Amir Mohammad ibn Abdul Aziz St; SR10 per hr; open 5.30am-1am daily)* is a good choice located in the downtown area.

Bookshops There is a very wide range of English, French and German books at the **Jarir Bookstore**, which has two branches in Riyadh (on Olaya St, just south of the intersection with Mosa ibn Nosayr St, and on Al-Ihsa St in Al-Malaz District, near the Safeway Tamimi supermarket). They both stock Lonely Planet titles.

Medical Services The **Dallah Hospital** *(☎ 454 5277; cnr King Fahd Rd & Al-Imam Saud ibn Abdul Aziz ibn Mohammad Rd)* takes emergency cases on a walk-in basis. To get there, take King Fahd Road north past the Riyadh Sheraton and the Sports Village, then take the exit to Al-Owais and Taiba markets. Turn left at the traffic lights and continue 500m. The hospital is on the right.

Things to See

Start your tour of Riyadh at the extraordinary **National Museum** (☎ 403 9961; admission SR15; open 9am-noon for men & schools, 4.30pm-9pm for families, Sun-Thur & Fri evenings), located just southwest of the landmark water tower and set in a landscaped complex of 360,000 sq metres. This contains not just the museum, but also the **King Abdul Aziz Historical Complex**. Set up with assistance from the Smithsonian Institute, its exhibits are truly world class. Eight galleries provide an epochal sweep of the Arabian Peninsula, from prehistoric times through to the Islamic period and the development of the modern Saudi state, with an emphasis on the history and archaeology of the Kingdom from the Stone Age to early Islam. The galleries are particularly thorough on geography, archaeology, Islamic architecture, the haj and ethnography.

Masmak Fortress (Al-Imam Turki ibn Abdullah St; admission free; open 8am-noon & 4pm-8pm Sat-Wed, families only Sun & Tues) was the citadel in the heart of Old Riyadh that Abdul Aziz took in January 1902 to regain control of the city. During the raid, one of the future king's companions heaved a spear at the door with such force that the head is still lodged in the doorway (look just to the right of the centre panel of the small door set in the main door). The fortress, built of dried mud, is now a museum honouring Abdul Aziz. (No permit required.)

Murabba Palace (Al-Malek Faisal St; open 8am-2pm Sat-Wed) is a combination fortress and palace built by King Abdul Aziz in 1946.

Al-Thumairi Gate, near the Middle East Hotel (Al-Malek Faisal St), is an impressive restoration of one of the nine gates that used to lead into the city before the wall was torn down in 1950.

The **Camel Market** (open 7am-7pm daily), 30km from the centre, is one of the largest in the Middle East. Trading is heaviest in the late afternoon. To reach it, take the Dammam Rd to the Thumamah exit.

Places to Stay

The **Youth Hostel** (☎ 405 5552; Shabab al-Ghansani St; dorm beds SR8) is on a side street off Al-Amir Sa'ad ibn Abdul Aziz in the Al-Muralla District. The hostel is not on any bus route; nor is it within walking distance of the bus station.

The budget hotels are all in the vicinity of the bus station.

Hotel Alrajehi (☎ 412 3557; singles/doubles with bathroom SR80/120) is good value and located up an alley behind the Al-Rawdah Hotel. Room rates include breakfast.

Al-Bathaa Hotel (☎ 405 2000, fax 405 3536; Al-Bathaa St; singles/doubles SR100/170) has huge carpeted rooms with satellite TV, minibar and private bathroom, and is by far the best option in the historic downtown area, both in terms of location (in the heart of the souq) and value.

Mamora Hotel (☎ 401 2111; Al-Bathaa St; singles/doubles with shower SR90/130) is an excellent option if you're looking for something a bit more upmarket in the Al-Bathaa area.

Safari Hotel (☎ 405 5533; singles/doubles with shower SR100/140), another good mid-range option, is in an alley a block east of Al-Bathaa St, and is a good choice for families.

Places to Eat

Manila Plaza, behind Al-Bathaa Hotel, has a food court on the top floor with a dozen or so Chinese, Japanese, Thai, Indian and Filipino stalls. The best deal is at the **Mandarin Restaurant** (set meal SR6; open 10am-1am daily).

Eating out is the capital's favourite pastime, and in the modern downtown area the choice of restaurants is very extensive – and the cost of a meal invariably pricey. All those listed below have 'family' and 'male-only' sections, and be prepared if you are with your family to sit inside what feels like a train compartment – so that you are unable to see, or be seen by, the other families. Even the waiter may back into the 'compartment', offering a menu in an outstretched hand!

L'Excuse (☎ 465 7648; Al-Amir Mohammad ibn Abdul Aziz St; dishes from SR45) is a high-class seafood restaurant with luxurious, but homely decor.

Avadh Indian Restaurant (☎ 461 2200, fax 462 0509; Al-Amir Mohammad ibn Abdul Aziz St; dishes from SR38) has established itself as the leading traditional northern Indian restaurant.

Il Terrazo (☎ 273 2552; buffet SR135; dinner May-Oct, lunch Nov-April), on the large 1st-floor balcony in Al-Faisaliya Tower, is by far the best dining option in the capital. After you've finished at the salad

SAUDI ARABIA

CENTRAL RIYADH

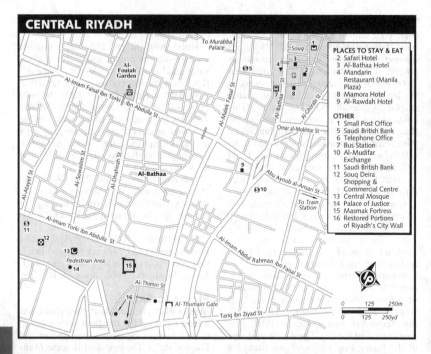

PLACES TO STAY & EAT
2 Safari Hotel
3 Al-Bathaa Hotel
4 Mandarin
   Restaurant (Manila
   Plaza)
8 Mamora Hotel
9 Al-Rawdah Hotel

OTHER
1 Small Post Office
5 Saudi British Bank
6 Telephone Office
7 Bus Station
10 Al-Mudifar
   Exchange
11 Saudi British Bank
12 Souq Deira
   Shopping &
   Commercial Centre
13 Central Mosque
14 Palace of Justice
15 Masmak Fortress
16 Restored Portions
   of Riyadh's City Wall

SAUDI ARABIA

bar, the Kenyan waiters cut you a varied selection of meat straight from the skewer, and serve an assortment of vegetables. You can eat as much as you like to the sound of African drum beats in the shadow of Riyadh's most famous landmark. This is the place to sample 'liberal' Riyadh society: the family and singles sections officially exist, but are in reality right next to one another, and not separated by barriers.

Shopping

The **souq** around Al-Bathaa Hotel is a good place to get lost for a few hours, but ther's little to buy here. The stores, run by Bangladeshis, sell mainly cheap or fake famous brand clothes and watches. The main advantage of walking around here is to get a sense of how Riyadh was before the oil boom.

The modern shopping area is centred on Olaya St and the surrounding streets, where there are dozens of malls. **Mamlaka Mall** in the Kingdom Tower has three levels of shops (the 2nd level reserved for women). There is a food court in the basement. This ultramodern shoppers' paradise, spread over 41,000 sq metres, has Marks & Spencer's and Debenhams, Saks Fifth Avenue and London's Gadget Shop.

Faisaliya Mall is always bustling and has become a main hangout for Riyadh's *shebaab*, or teenage boys. Harvey Nichols has a massive branch here. The top level has an excellent food court, and in the basement is a children's entertainment centre called **Toy Town**. Outside the north side of the mall is **Dr Cafe**, a gourmet coffee place that is a rave among the locals.

Getting There & Away

Air The **King Khaled International Airport** (☎ *222 1700*) is 40km north of Al-Bathaa. Saudia's main reservations office (☎ *488 4444*) is on Olaya St.

Saudia operates frequent flights to all the Kingdom's other airports, including: Jeddah, Dhahran, Hofuf, Buraydah, Hail, Taif and Medina, Abha and Najran and Tabuk. See Saudia's website for schedules and prices: **w** www.saudiairlines.com.sa.

Bus The **bus station** (☎ *222 1700*), just off Al-Bathaa St, is Saptco's intercity depot. There are 11 buses every day to Jeddah

(SR130, 13 hours) via Taif (SR100, 10 hours). Other routes include: 11 daily to Dammam (SR60, 4½ hours); three daily to Hofuf (SR45, four hours) with an extra bus on Thursday. To Buraydah (SR60, 4½ hours) there are nine buses daily. There are three buses daily to Hail (SR100, eight hours), ten daily to Abha (SR125, 13 hours), two daily to Jizan (SR160, 18 hours), three daily to Najran (SR115, 12 hours), two daily to Tabuk (SR200, 17 hours) and two daily to Sakaka (SR175, 14 hours).

Saptco run services to Egypt, Syria, Jordan and Turkey. See the Land entry in Getting There & Away for more details.

Train The **train station** (☎ *473 1855; Al-Amir Abdul Aziz ibn Abdullah ibn Torki St)* is 2.5km east of the bus station. Trains leave for Dammam via Hofuf and Abqaiq five times daily (9.11am, 12.09pm, 3.24pm, 5.44pm, and 8.44pm). Fares in 1st/2nd class are SR60/40 to Dammam, SR52/34 to Abqaiq and SR45/30 to Hofuf.

Car Rental Expect to pay SR110 per day, including insurance, for a Toyota Corolla. Most big hotels also have a car-hire desk and you can find a number of car-hire offices, including **Budget**, along Olaya St, near the Al-Khozama Hotel.

Getting Around
By law, all taxis (white limousines) should use meters. In practice, they do not. The unofficial rate is SR15 for a short ride, SR20 for a trip across town (ie, from Al-Bathaa to King Fahd Rd). A taxi to/from the airport should cost no more than SR50 to/from anywhere in the city.

AROUND RIYADH
Dir'aiyah الدرعية
☎ 01
Riyadh's most interesting site is outside the city. On the capital's northern outskirts, about 30km from Al-Bathaa, lie the ruins of Dir'aiyah *(admission free; open 7am-6pm Sat-Thur, 1pm-6pm Fri)*, the first capital of the Saud clan and the Kingdom's most popular and easily accessible archaeological site (no permits required). An old mud-brick city built along the edge of Wadi Hanifa, Dir'aiyah is the largest and best-preserved example of its kind in the kingdom. Worth

seeing are the fully restored bathhouse and two Al-Saud palaces. Internally, all have been restored to their original condition with decorative friezes and covered courtyards. A maze of winding streets and very photogenic ruins perch over lush gardens (which is where Riyadh gets its name).

To reach Dir'aiyah from Riyadh, leave the city centre, following the signs for the airport. Once you're on the expressway to the airport look for signs for Dir'aiyah. Once you exit the expressway you should see the ruins in the distance to your left. Follow the road until you reach a T-junction. Turn left, and left again when you reach a roundabout. Go straight, and look for the small white signs indicating a right turn to reach the ruins.

The Hejaz (Western Region) (المنطقة لغربية) لحجاز

The western region, known as the Hejaz ('barrier' in Arabic), extends from the Jordanian border on the Gulf of Aqaba in the north to the resort city of Taif in the south. It includes the two most holy cities in Islam, Mecca and Medina, the Kingdom's commercial capital Jeddah, and the Nabataean tombs at Medain Saleh.

JEDDAH جدة
☎ 02
Once a modest port living mostly off the pilgrim trade, Jeddah (Jiddah, Jidda) has evolved into one of the Arab world's most important commercial centres. It is the Gulf's most cosmopolitan city, and Saudi Arabia's most liberal.

Orientation
Al-Balad is the historic downtown district; everything centres on King Abdul Aziz St and the old city, which lies directly inland from it. However, when Jeddah expanded in the 1970s, it did so exclusively northwards, and North Jeddah is now a series of distinct, bustling suburbs – and, for Jeddah's fun-loving, fast-driving male teenagers, *the* place to hang out. Medina Rd, the city's main artery, runs from Al-Balad straight through North Jeddah and then on for 25km to King Abdul Aziz International Airport.

NORTH JEDDAH

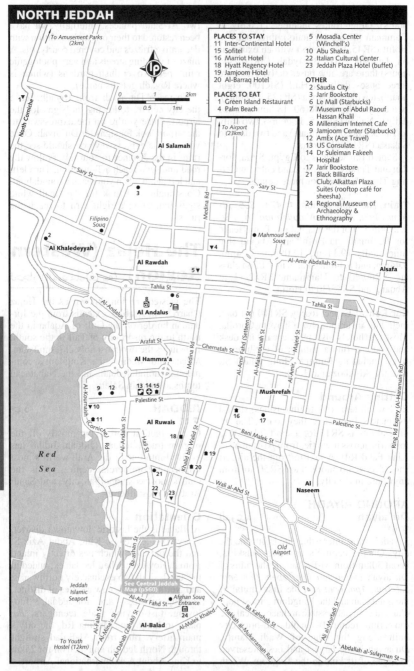

PLACES TO STAY
11 Inter-Continental Hotel
15 Sofitel
16 Marriot Hotel
18 Hyatt Regency Hotel
19 Jamjoom Hotel
20 Al-Barraq Hotel

PLACES TO EAT
1 Green Island Restaurant
4 Palm Beach

5 Mosadia Center
   (Winchell's)
10 Abu Shakra
22 Italian Cultural Center
23 Jeddah Plaza Hotel (buffet)

OTHER
2 Saudia City
3 Jarir Bookstore
6 Le Mall (Starbucks)
7 Museum of Abdul Raouf
   Hassan Khalil
8 Millennium Internet Cafe
9 Jamjoom Center (Starbucks)
12 AmEx (Ace Travel)
13 US Consulate
14 Dr Suleiman Fakeeh
   Hospital
17 Jarir Bookstore
21 Black Billiards
   Club; Alkattan Plaza
   Suites (rooftop café for
   sheesha)
24 Regional Museum of
   Archaeology &
   Ethnography

Information

Money The **Saudi British Bank** (☎ 643 2277, fax 642 7008; King Abdul Aziz St) changes travellers cheques and has an international ATM outside. AmEx is represented by **Ace Travel** (☎ 665 1254; Palestine St; open 9am-1.30pm & 4.30pm-8pm Sat-Wed, 9am-1.30pm Thur) near the intersection with Al-Hamra St. It can replace lost and stolen cards and cash personal cheques for AmEx clients, but will not hold mail.

Post The **main post office** (open 7.30am-9.30pm Sat-Wed, Mumtaz Post express mail windows open 7.30am-2pm Thur) is the large red-and-white building opposite the bus station, between Ba'ashan and Al-Bareed Sts. The entrance is on the Al-Bareed St side of the building.

Telephone The main international call cabin in Al-Balad is just near the Al-Mahmal Centre in the pedestrian area. Alternatively, prepaid phonecards are sold in all grocery shops and bookstores, which can be used from any phone.

Email & Internet Access The **Millennium Internet Cafe** (☎ 661 4664; Al-Rahman al-Tubajoti St; SR15 per hr) is a good place to access the Internet.

Bookshops The city's two **Jarir Bookstores** (☎ 682 7666; Sary St • ☎ 673 2727; Palestine St) have a wide selection of English, French and German titles, a section devoted to Saudi Arabia, and many Lonely Planet guides.

Medical Services Dr Suleiman Fakeeh Hospital (☎ 665 5000, 660 3000; Palestine St), near the US consulate, is centrally located and has a good accident-and-emergency department.

Things to See & Do

Jeddah's **Regional Museum of Archaeology & Ethnography** (Al-Amir Fahd St; admission free; open 8am-noon Sat-Wed) is near the Al-Khozam Palace and the Islamic Development Bank. The displays are quite similar to those at the Riyadh Museum, making this museum well worth a visit.

Many of Jeddah's sites can be covered in a **walking tour** that takes in the course of the old city walls torn down in the late 1940s. A circuit of these streets should take less than an hour on foot. Along the route are the three reconstructed city gates – all that remains of the wall. Near the North City Gate are several good examples of traditional Jeddah architecture in various states of preservation. Many of the older houses within the old city walls are constructed not of stone but of coral quarried from reefs in the Red Sea. For the last 12 years, a major project – under the auspices of the Jeddah Historical Preservation Society, basically a one-man show in the form of Jeddah local Sami Nowar – has been listing buildings and renovating whole streets in the area, and in 2002 was finally given a grant of SR20 million to make a reality of its ideals.

Just east of the North City Gate, **Shorbatly House** is one of the best-known examples of the city's traditional architecture. In the immediate area around it you will see several other old houses, also in various states of repair.

The **Municipality Museum** (☎ 642 4922; Al-Malik Abdul Aziz St; admission free; open 7.30am-1.30pm Sat-Wed) is in the restored traditional house opposite the National Commercial Bank's headquarters. To visit you must first make an appointment. Approximately 200 years old and built of Red Sea coral, this is the only surviving building of the WWI-era British Legation in Jeddah. TE Lawrence stayed at the Legation when he visited in 1917.

Along the old city's main thoroughfare, Souq al-Alawi, stands **Naseef House** (admission SR20; open 5pm-9pm daily), one of the city's most famous houses. The Naseefs are one of Jeddah's old-line merchant clans. The larger of the two trees to the left of the house's front door was, as recently as the 1920s, the only tree in all of Jeddah and thus an indicator of the family's wealth and importance.

Further down the souq is **Ash-Shafee Mosque**, the oldest in the city.

In North Jeddah is the private **Museum of Abdul Raouf Hassan Khalil** (☎ 665 8487; Al-Mathaf St; admission SR20; open 9am-noon & 5pm-9pm Sat-Thur). Once you get over the cartoonlike architecture of the four 'houses' that constitute the museum, lose yourself in the series of rooms linked by lobbies and sitting areas designed in extravagant Arabesque styles. This private

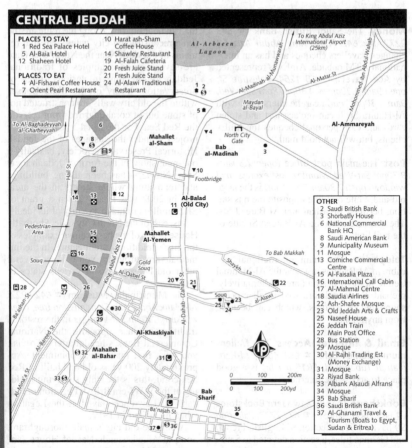

CENTRAL JEDDAH

PLACES TO STAY
1 Red Sea Palace Hotel
5 Al-Baia Hotel
12 Shaheen Hotel

PLACES TO EAT
4 Al-Fishawi Coffee House
7 Orient Pearl Restaurant

10 Harat ash-Sham
   Coffee House
14 Shawley Restaurant
19 Al-Falah Cafeteria
20 Fresh Juice Stand
21 Fresh Juice Stand
24 Al-Alawi Traditional
   Restaurant

OTHER
2 Saudi British Bank
3 Shorbatly House
6 National Commercial
  Bank HQ
8 Saudi American Bank
9 Municipality Museum
11 Mosque
13 Corniche Commercial
   Centre
15 Al-Faisalia Plaza
16 International Call Cabin
17 Al-Mahmal Centre
18 Saudia Airlines
22 Ash-Shafee Mosque
23 Old Jeddah Arts & Crafts
25 Naseef House
26 Jeddah Train
27 Main Post Office
28 Bus Station
29 Mosque
30 Al-Rajhi Trading Est
   (Money Exchange)
31 Mosque
32 Riyad Bank
33 Albank Alsaudi Alfransi
34 Mosque
35 Bab Sharif
36 Saudi British Bank
37 Al-Ghanami Travel &
   Tourism (Boats to Egypt,
   Sudan & Eritrea)

Al-Arbaeen Lagoon

To King Abdul Aziz
International Airport
(25km)

Al-Madinah al-Munawwarah

Al-Matar St.

Mohammed ibn Abdul Wahab

Maydan al-Bayal

To Al-Baghadeyyah
al-Gharbeyyah

Mahallet al-Sham

North City Gate

Bab al-Madinah

Al-Ammareyah

Hail St

Pedestrian Area

Souq

King Abdul Aziz St

Al-Balad (Old City)

Mahallet Al-Yemen

Gold Souq

Al-Qabel St

Al-Dahab (Zahab) St

Footbridge

Shaykh La

To Bab Makkah

Souq

al-Alawi

Ba'ashan St

Al-Bareed St

Al-Khaskiyah

Mahallet al-Bahar

Al-Mina St

Ba'najah St

Bab Sharif

0   100   200m
0   100   200yd

---

collection of art and artefacts, comprising 10,000 pieces, is a rich feast for the eyes. To get there coming from Medina Rd, turn left onto Al-Amir Mohammad ibn Abdul Aziz St, take the second left and then go right at the bottom of the road. It's in a tricky location, but if you get lost just head for the only white minaret in the area (usefully lit up at night) belonging to a mosque situated right next to the museum.

The 35km-long sea-front road, known as the **Corniche**, constitutes an open-air museum. The 400 sculptures dotted along it are breathtakingly diverse: from Mustafa Sunbal's flying seagulls to the curvaceous Henry Moore; from the concrete Arabic engraving 'In the name of God' to the signs of the zodiac.

Organised Tours
Red Sea Palace Hotel (☎ 642 8555; King Abdul Aziz St) offers a 1½-hour city tour at 10am every Friday for SR35. You do not have to be staying in the hotel to take the tour.

Places to Stay
Youth Hostel (☎ 688 6692; dorm beds SR12) is at the stadium, 12km east of the city centre on the Mecca Expressway. The hostel is behind the green buildings of the Sporting City. There is no access by bus. The easiest way to reach it by car is to take exit No 8 from the expressway, *not* the stadium exit, which is further on.

Shaheen Hotel (☎ 642 6582, fax 644 6302; singles/doubles with shower SR80/110), in an alley between Al-Malek Abdel Aziz St and the Corniche Commercial Centre in Al-Balad, has long been one of Jeddah's best budget buys.

Al-Baia Hotel (☎ 644 4446; Al-Malek Abdul Aziz St; single/doubles with separate bathrooms SR115/195), right next to the roundabout, is brand new, and recommended for those with families.

There's little to choose between the two good-value budget options in North Jeddah. They are near one another and offer similarly spotless, fully carpeted and furnished rooms (satellite TV, fridge with minibar and spotless bathroom). These are the **Al-Barraq Hotel** (☎ 650 3366, fax 651 1322; e htl_barraq@hotmail.com; Khalid bin Walid St; singles/doubles SR110/150) and the **Jamjoon Hotel** (☎/fax 651 4300; Al-Tawbah St; singles/doubles SR140/190).

Sunset Hotel (☎ 660 5000, fax 667 6048; e sunsethotel@hotmail.com; Prince Abdullah St; singles/doubles SR260/340), a new five-star hotel, is by far the best option in Jeddah for families. The two kinds of suites (each with fitted kitchen, living room and bathroom, and one or two bedrooms) are extremely comfortable. The price includes continental breakfast and airport pick-up.

Places to Eat
In Al-Balad, all the cheap eateries are concentrated on the pedestrian walkway on the eastern side of the **Corniche Commercial Centre**. The best is the Filipino-run **Shawly Restaurant** (☎ 644 7867) where soup, rice, two meat/vegetable dishes and a soft drink cost SR12. All the eateries along this strip have tables outside, and the real attraction of this area is the fact that it's the only place in Saudi Arabia where families dine al fresco.

Palm Beach (☎ 6394074; Medina Rd; sandwiches/meals SR4/25), next to the H-Bridge, is popular with locals and has seafood, European and Oriental selections.

Jeddah Plaza Hotel (☎ 651 4121; Medina Rd; buffet SR50) offers the best lunch deal in town.

Italian Cultural Centre (☎ 643 0134; Al-Lazegeyah St; pasta dishes from SR35; open lunch noon-3pm daily) is a wonderful place to have lunch. The menu changes with the (Italian) seasons.

Abu Shakra (☎ 660 4049; Palestine St; dishes from SR35), a well-established Egyptian restaurant, is in a stunning location. Sit

by the window and watch the sun set over the Red Sea. Then see the tallest fountain in the world burst into life (and light).

The Green Island (☎ 694 0999; North Corniche; buffet SR120) is the place to head for if money is no object. Although the buffet is nothing to write home about, you may find yourself awed into writing a postcard home from the wooden chalets that branch out into the Red Sea. This is the most romantic place in Jeddah. Watch the sun set as the waves break under your feet and the Corniche flickers gradually into life.

Entertainment
Officially, there is no **cinema** in Saudi Arabia. However, the **Italian Cultural Centre** (see Places to Eat earlier) in Jeddah has a makeshift one, which regularly screens both classics and the latest blockbusters. Check out the notice board in the courtyard.

The resort at **Al-Nakheel Beach** (☎ 656 1177, fax 656 2597; e nakheel@naseej.com .sa; admission SR50) has a very relaxed nighttime atmosphere that's very popular with expats. For further details see Activities earlier in this chapter.

Saudi youth hang out until the early hours of the morning at the Filipino-staffed café **Winchell's** (☎ 660 8923; Mosadia Centre, Medina Rd). A wide range of light drinks and snacks are served; particularly good are the hot beef/chicken croissants for SR5. **Starbucks** (Le Mal, Al-Amir Mohammad ibn Abdul Aziz St) has arrived. It's on your right after the first traffic lights coming from Medina Rd.

If it's *sheesha* (water pipe) you're into, head for the traditional hang-out on top of **Alkattan Plaza Suites** (☎ 651 3111; Hail St; sheesha SR12). It has a magnificent view of the port, and both 'family' and 'male-only' sections.

Pool (billiards) is immensely popular in Saudi Arabia. The best club in Jeddah (males only) is the **Black Billiards Club** (Hail St; open 6pm-2am daily). Here, young Saudis play for hours to the accompaniment of blasting music in the closest to a legitimate nightclub that can be found.

There are two **amusement parks** located next to one another on the North Corniche (just keep driving north until you see the Big Wheel on your right). And after dusk, opposite on the Corniche itself visitors are welcome to settle down where many local families regularly enjoy a **picnic**.

Shopping

The **gold souq** in Al-Balad, where 24-carat gold is the norm, has an extensive range of traditional Arabic jewellery and ornaments. Also in Al-Balad, the **street market** (open 10am-1pm & 5pm-11pm daily) in the streets to the south of Al-Mahmal Centre in front of the **Jeddah Train** (a restored and brightly painted locomotive that used to ride the Hejaz Railway line) is good for electronic items, local artefacts and pirated DVDs (SR15).

The **Afghan souq** (Al-Bokharia St; open 10am-11pm daily), to the east of Bab Mecca, is a must-see. The shops – in a narrow, dusty street – are managed by Afghans, and on breezy days the aroma of freshly baked Afghan bread fills the air. There are old and new carpets from Iran, Russia, Afghanistan, Turkmenistan, Turkestan and Kashmir; a wide choice of woven tribal artefacts from Afghan Balouch weavers; and needlepoint work from Uzbekistan.

Renovation has turned the **Filipino Souq** (junction Prince Sultan St & Al-Amir Abdullah St; open 10am-12pm daily), opposite Saudia City, into a rather sterile mall. Nevertheless, it's still bustling during the evenings and remains the place to buy cheap Western clothes.

Mahmoud Saeed Souq (Al-Amir Faud St; open 9am-noon & 5pm-11pm daily), north of the bicycle roundabout, is the best and biggest general market in Jeddah. Jam-packed with local bargain hunters, the hundreds of stalls here sell just about everything under the sun.

Getting There & Away

To/From the Airport Jeddah is the Kingdom's commercial capital, so there are flights to almost everywhere from **King Abdul Aziz International Airport** (☎ 684 1707, 688 5526). Within the Kingdom, **Saudia** (☎ 632 3333) has regular flights to Dammam, Riyadh, Taif and Abha.

Bus The most comfortable and reliable intercity service is run by **Saptco**. There are six buses daily to Taif (SR30, three hours), four to Abha (SR100, nine hours), hourly services to Riyadh (SR135, 10 hours) and

four buses a day to Dammam (SR20, 15 hours). The bus station is in Al-Balad.

Car There are car-rental offices all along Medina Rd offering pretty much the same deals. The best are **Jama Rent a Car** (☎ 698 4048) and **Best Rent a Car** (☎ 2320754), both on the Western side of the H-Bridge. Rates start at SR110 a day or SR2700 a month.

Sea There are also passenger services from Jeddah to Port Safaga (Egypt), Port Sudan and to Musawwa (Eritrea), although the types of services available frequently changes. For current schedules and prices contact **Ace Travel** (☎ 665 1254; Palestine St; open 9am-1.30pm & 4.30pm-8pm Sat-Wed, 9am-1.30pm Thur), near the intersection with Al-Hamra St in Jeddah.

Getting Around

Taxis (white limos) don't use meters. The unofficial rate for any destination is SR15. A taxi to/from King Abdul Aziz Airport to/from Al-Balad should cost SR40 to/from the south terminal (all Saudia flights) or SR50 to/from the north terminal (all other airlines).

TAIF   الطائف
☎ 02

Taif (Tai'if, Al-Taif), nestled in the mountains above Mecca, is the Kingdom's capital in the summer, when it is cooler and less humid than Jeddah. The town's other attractions are its scenery, its relaxed atmosphere and, in April, the harvesting of more than a million locally grown roses.

Orientation & Information

Taif centres on a nameless square formed by the intersection of King Faisal and Shubra Sts. Most of the budget hotels are a bit east of this intersection. Cheap restaurants are all over the central area. The bus station and airport are some distance north of the centre.

There are a number of banks around the main intersection, and just to the south is the post office (opposite the international call cabin). The main post office is north of town, near the bus station.

Things to See & Do

Abdallah bin Abbas Mosque (Abdullah bin Abbas St), Taif's central mosque, is a good

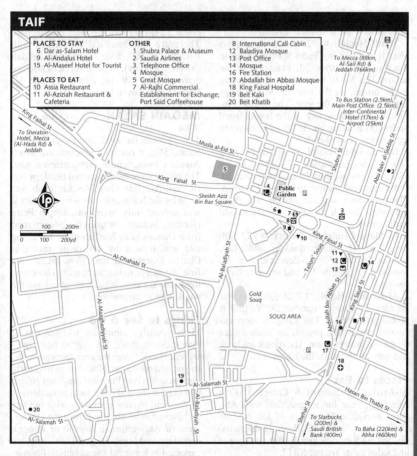

TAIF

PLACES TO STAY	OTHER	
6 Dar as-Salam Hotel	1 Shubra Palace & Museum	8 International Call Cabin
9 Al-Andalus Hotel	2 Saudia Airlines	12 Baladiya Mosque
15 Al-Maseef Hotel for Tourist	3 Telephone Office	13 Post Office
	4 Mosque	14 Mosque
PLACES TO EAT	5 Great Mosque	16 Fire Station
10 Assia Restaurant	7 Al-Rajhi Commercial	17 Abdallah bin Abbas Mosque
11 Al-Aziziah Restaurant &	Establishment for Exchange;	18 King Faisal Hospital
Cafeteria	Port Said Coffeehouse	19 Beit Kaki
		20 Beit Khatib

SAUDI ARABIA

example of simple, refined Islamic architecture. The mosque is named for a cousin of the Prophet who was also the grandfather of the founder of the Abbasid dynasty.

The **Tailor's Souq** (*open 9am-noon & 5pm-11pm daily*), one of the few surviving bits of traditional Taif, can be found just off the main square at the intersection of Shubra and King Faisal Sts around the corner from the post office. Next to a Turkish restaurant and several small grocery stores is an archway of sand-coloured stone. The short alleyway behind this arch, part of the tailor's souq, is a quick trip into old Taif.

Shubra Palace (*admission free; open 7.30am-2.30pm Sat-Wed*), a beautifully restored house on the edge of the centre, doubles as the city's museum. The palace itself

was built around the turn of the century with marble imported from Italy and timber from Turkey.

Two other old houses that have also been maintained (sort of) are **Beit Kaki** and **Beit Khatib**, once the summer residences of two of Mecca's leading merchant families. You can only view them from the outside.

The new **Cable Car** (*SR20 one way; 10am-6pm Thur-Sat Oct-Mar, daily Apr-Sept*) has a station at both the top and bottom of Al-Hada Mountain. The ride takes about 25 minutes and offers spectacular views.

Places to Stay

Taif is very crowded on summer weekends (ie, from Wednesday afternoon until Friday afternoon), so from June to September reservations are absolutely essential.

Youth Hostel (☎ 725 3400; dorm beds SR8) is at the King Fahd Sporting City in the Hawiyah district, 22.5km north of the centre. The No 10 bus runs from the centre to the hostel via the bus station and stops about 100m from the gate. The hostel is infinitely superior to any of the hotels listed under this heading and is far more likely to have space at weekends.

Dar as-Salam Hotel (☎ 736 0124; King Faisal St; singles/doubles SR40/60, summer SR50/70), just west of the main intersection, is the only real cheapie to be found in town. The hotel does not have air-con, though all the rooms do at least have ceiling fans and bathrooms.

Al-Maseef Hotel for Tourist (☎ 732 478; King Saud St; singles/doubles SR80/125, summer SR100/170) is a decent choice. All rooms have satellite TV and separate bathrooms.

Al-Andalus Hotel (☎ 732 8491; singles/ doubles SR100/150, summer SR150/180) is probably the best of Taif's slightly more expensive places. It's just off the main square by the Assia Restaurant. The rooms are large and very clean, as are the bathrooms.

Places to Eat
Al-Aziziah Restaurant & Cafeteria (King Faisal St), near the intersection with Abu Bakr as-Siddiq St, is one of the best of Taif's many small Turkish restaurants. Grilled chicken or a kebab with rice, bread and salad costs around SR12.

Assia Restaurant (King Faisal St) is a friendly place, though not quite as good. The prices are about the same as those at the Al-Aziziah.

Entertainment
Port Said Coffeehouse, above the Al-Rajhi Commercial Establishment for Exchange office on the main square, is the place to go for traditional coffeehouse pursuits (backgammon, TV etc).

Getting There & Away
The **airport** (☎ 685 5527) is 25km north of the town. Daily flights operate to Riyadh and Dhahran. Direct flights are also available to Jeddah, Abha, Medina, Tabuk and Sharurah.

The **bus station** (☎ 736 9924; Al-Matar Rd) is 2.5km north of the main intersection. There are numerous daily buses to both Riyadh (SR100, nine hours) and Jeddah (SR90, 2¾ hours). Regular services also operate to Abha (SR110, 10½ hours) and Al-Baha (SR70, seven hours).

MEDAIN SALAH   مدائن صالح
☎ 04
The spectacular rock tombs at Medain Salah, 340km north of Medina, are Saudi Arabia's most famous archaeological site. The tombs were mostly carved between 100 BC and AD 100 when Medain Salah was ruled by the Nabataeans, in whose empire it was second only in importance to Petra (Jordan). In later centuries the pilgrim road from Damascus to Medina passed near the site and it was by following this that Charles Doughty, in the 1880s, became the first Westerner to see the tombs. Those visiting now are almost guaranteed to have the whole site to themselves.

Things to See & Do
Medain Salah's tombs are less spectacular than those at Petra; but they're better preserved. The distances between them are large, so you will need a car. However, two recently opened hotels (see Places to Stay) run guided tours to the site and other local attractions

You will require permits to visit the site and these can be obtained from the Department of Antiquities in Riyadh or through one of the two hotels in Al-Ula. Visitors are expected to leave the site at sunset. Photography is permitted, but the use of video and movie cameras is forbidden without a special permit.

Be sure to see **Qasr Farid**, the largest tomb at Medain Salah, carved from a single large outcrop of rock standing alone in the desert. **Qasr al-Bint** is another important site. If you step back and look up near the northern end of its west face, you'll see a tomb that was abandoned in the early stages of construction and would, if completed, have been the largest in Medain Salah.

The Diwan, or 'meeting room', is carved into a hillside a few hundred meters northeast of Qasr al-Bint. The name owes more to modern Arab culture than to the Nabataeans, who probably used the area as a cult site. As you pass through this small siq (a narrow

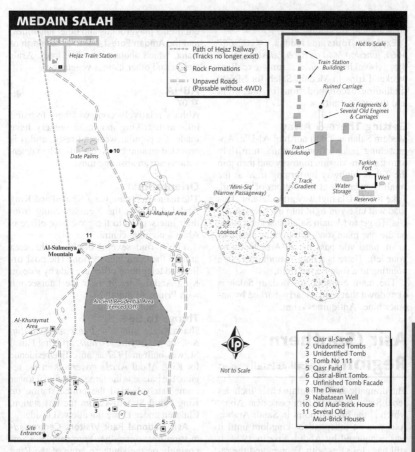

MEDAIN SALAH

See Enlargement

Hejaz Train Station

Date Palms ● 10

Al-Mahajar Area

'Mini-Siq' (Narrow Passageway)

Lookout

Al-Sulmenya Mountain ▲ 11

9

Al-Khuraymat Area

Ancient Residential Area (Fenced Off)

7 ■

■ 6

Area C-D

Site Entrance

Not to Scale

●●●●● Path of Hejaz Railway (Tracks no longer exist)

Rock Formations

= = = Unpaved Roads (Passable without 4WD)

Not to Scale

Train Station Buildings

Ruined Carriage

Track Fragments & Several Old Engines & Carriages

Train Workshop

Track Gradient

Water Storage

Turkish Fort

Well

Reservoir

Qasr No 111

1 Qasr al-Saneh
2 Unadorned Tombs
3 Unidentified Tomb
4 Tomb No 111
5 Qasr Farid
6 Qasr al-Bint Tombs
7 Unfinished Tomb Facade
8 The Diwan
9 Nabataean Well
10 Old Mud-Brick House
11 Several Old Mud-Brick Houses

SAUDI ARABIA

passageway or defile) note the small altars carved into the cliff face and the channels that brought water down into several small basins. After passing through the *siq* go straight for 150m to 200m and then climb up and to the right for a good view over the site.

On the northern edge of the site is an abandoned station from the **Hejaz Railway**. The complex of 16 buildings includes a large workshop building where a restored WWI-era engine is on display.

The **Department of Antiquities Provincial Museum** (*Al-Ula's main street; admission free; 8.30am-2pm Sat-Wed*) is well worth a visit. It has informative displays on the area's history and prehistory and provides a useful orientation before venturing to the sites themselves.

Organised Tours

Arac Hotel Al-Ula (☎ 884 4444, fax 884 0000; e hotelalula@arac.com.sa; chalets SR350) is the newest and most professionally run of Al-Ula's two hotels. All chalets come with separate bathroom. It is 4km west of Al-Ula, the nearest town to Medain Salah.

Medain Saleh Hotel and Resort (☎ 884 2888, fax 04 884 2515, e Medainsale halula@hotmail.com; all rooms SR370) is located on the edge of Al-Ula. Rooms have separate bathrooms and satellite TV. There is a swimming pool and a 300 sq m grand tent, where guests can relax and enjoy light snacks and drinks.

Both these hotels arrange permits for Medain Salah free of charge for guests, as well as guided tours (minimum six people) of the numerous other historical and archaeological sites in the area.

Explorer Tours in Jeddah (☎ 02-667 5669; junction Madina Rd & Palestine St), in the Al-Nakheel Center, runs excellent weekend trips to Medain Salah for SR600 (including accommodation for one night and the site permit).

Getting There & Away

Medain Salah is 25km north of Al-Ula. Approaching Jeddah from Medina, turn right onto the Non-Muslim highway and then join the Tabuk highway by turning right at the small roundabout at the bottom of the hill. Take the Al-Ula highway after 220km. This road will take you right into the heart of Al-Ula. To get to Medain Salah, just keep going on the one main road, through the centre of town, until you pass the **Al-Arac Hotel** on your left. There is a blue 'Antiquities' sign pointing to a road on the right.

The main entrance to Medain Salah is 4km down that road, clearly marked by another blue 'Antiquities' sign.

Asir (Southern Region) (المنطقة الجنوبي) عسير

The dramatic Asir mountain chain includes Jebel Sawdah, the 2910m peak near Abha, which is the highest point in Saudi Arabia. Asir was an independent kingdom until it was conquered by Abdul Aziz in 1922. It still has close ties with Yemen, and the region's architecture is distinctly Yemeni. Throughout the region, wild colonies of Hamadryas baboons can often be seen.

BAHA الباحت
☎ 07

Baha, 220km south of Taif and 240km north of Abha, is the secondary tourist hub of the Asir region. The area's attraction has mainly been that it is a lot less developed than Abha. Tribes in the region trace their origin to the famous pre-Islamic state of Saba, whose rule extended to areas presently known as Syria and Lebanon. Historians also report that they established the famous state of Aksum, in Abyssinia. The area has no fewer than 53 forests. They include the **Raghdan Forest**, which covers an area of

600,000 sq km, 5km from Baha, and has children's playgrounds and other amenities; and the **Amdan Forest**, 55km to the north of Baha, which abounds in olive trees, Ara'r shrubs and other natural vegetation.

ABHA أبها
☎ 07

Abha's relatively cool weather, forested hills and striking mountain scenery have made it a popular weekend resort and it is crowded on summer weekends, when reservations are an absolute must.

Orientation

The main streets are King Khaled and King Abdul Aziz Sts; the area stretching from their intersection to the governate office is Abha's nominal centre.

You'll find several **banks** in the area around the main intersection. The **post office** and **telephone office** are side by side on King Abdul Aziz St, near the intersection with Prince Abdullah St.

Things to See

Shada Palace (admission free; open 9am-1pm & 4.30pm-7.30pm Sat-Thur), off King Faisal St, was built in 1927 as an office/residence for King Abdul Aziz's governors in the region, the palace is the large, traditional tower immediately behind the police station on King Faisal St across from the bus station. Children under 12 are not allowed inside.

Asir National Park Visitors Centre (admission free; open 4pm-8pm daily) sits imposingly on the southern edge of the Ring Rd. It serves as an introduction to Asir National Park, but is rather a shoddy place and not a reliable option for those seeking guided tours of the area.

Places to Stay

Abha's **Youth Hostel** (☎ 227 0503; dorm beds SR8) is at the Sporting City, 20km west of Abha and 8km off the Abha-Khamis road. There is no bus service.

Shamasan Hotel (☎ 225 1808; singles/doubles with shower SR150/180), just outside the centre, is probably the best value for money in Abha after the hostel.

Abha Palace Hotel (☎ 229 4444; fax 229 5555, e abhapalace@hotmail.com; Nahran Rd; singles/doubles SR495/SR632), about 1.5km from city centre, is a five-star hotel

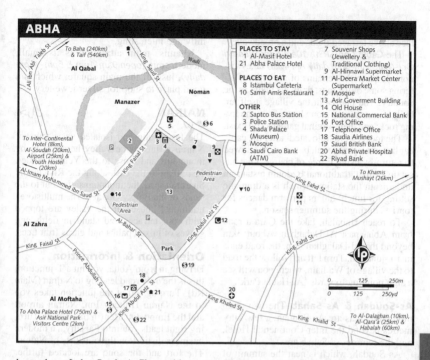

ABHA

To Baha (240km)
& Taif (540km)

Al Qabal

Wadi

King Saud St

Al Ibn Abi Taleb St

Manazer

Noman

To Inter-Continental
Hotel (8km),
Al-Soudah (20km),
Airport (25km) &
Youth Hostel
(20km)

King Faisal St

Al-Imam Mohammed ibn Saud St

Pedestrian
Area

Al Zahra

Al-Bahar St

Pedestrian
Area

King Abdul Aziz St

King Faisal St

Park

Prince Abdullah St

Al Moftaha

King Abdul Aziz St

To Abha Palace Hotel (750m) &
Asir National Park
Visitors Centre (2km)

King Khaled St

To Khamis
Mushayt (26km)

King Fahd St

King Fahd St

King Khaled St

To Al-Dalaghan (10km),
Al-Qara'a (25km) &
Habalah (60km)

PLACES TO STAY
1 Al-Masif Hotel
21 Abha Palace Hotel

PLACES TO EAT
8 Istambul Cafeteria
10 Samir Amis Restaurant

OTHER
2 Saptco Bus Station
3 Police Station
4 Shada Palace
(Museum)
5 Mosque
6 Saudi Cairo Bank
(ATM)

7 Souvenir Shops
(Jewellery &
Traditional Clothing)
9 Al-Hinnawi Supermarket
11 Al-Deera Market Center
(Supermarket)
12 Mosque
13 Asir Goverment Building
14 Old House
15 National Commercial Bank
16 Post Office
17 Telephone Office
18 Saudia Airlines
19 Saudi British Bank
20 Abha Private Hospital
22 Riyad Bank

0   125   250m
0   125   250yd

located on Lake Saad. A 7km cable car passes close to the hotel complex and provides stunning views over the escarpment and across the city. The hotel arranges excellent guided tours of the city and region.

Inter-Continental Hotel (☎ 224 7777), up in the mountains, was completely renovated in 2002. Originally designed as a palace for a Saudi prince, it's worth dropping by to marvel at its sheer scale.

Places to Eat

Samir Amis Restaurant (King Abdul Aziz St) has good kebabs and grilled chicken.

Green Mountain Restaurant (dishes from SR30), reached by Cable Car from Abha Palace Hotel, sits atop the Green Mountain after which it is named. While the food is not that special, the panoramic view of Abha it offers certainly is. You can also smoke sheesha or just enjoy a drink on the outside terrace. Highly recommended.

Getting There & Away

The airport is 25km from town. To get there, take the Abha-Khamis road to the turn-off just beyond the turn for the Sporting City.

There are several flights each day to Jeddah and Riyadh and one per day to Dhahran.

The **Saptco station** (King Faisal St) is in the big car park, a couple of blocks north of the intersection of King Khaled and King Abdul Aziz Sts. Buses to Jeddah (8½ hours) leave nearly hourly during the day. There are also several buses per day to Taif and Jizan.

Local buses run between the Abha and Khamis bus stations every 30 minutes from 6.30am to 10.30pm. The trip takes about 35 minutes and the fare is SR2.

AROUND ABHA
Asir National Park

حديقة عسير الوطنية

This park covers some 450,000 hectares of land from the Red Sea coast to the desert areas east of the mountains.

Habalah The deserted village of Habalah (Habella) – 'the ropes' in Arabic, from the fact that the only access to it was once by rope from the surrounding cliff tops – is about 60km from the centre of Abha and one of the most dramatic sites in the Asir National Park.

It appears to hang from a 300m-high cliff face above terraced fields and a broad valley.

The **Cable Car** *(SR30; 10am-6pm Wed-Fri Oct-Mar, 9am-9pm daily Apr-Mar)* takes visitors down to the remains of the village, offering some of the most dramatic views in the country. The houses in the village itself are built from trimmed stone hewn from the living rock; and their original gardens still exist.

The locals were 'relocated' after the cable car became operational, but are now allowed to return by using it free of charge. One has set up a small, traditional Bedouin restaurant underneath the station, which is a dramatic setting for lunch; others perform dances for tourists during the summer season.

To reach Habalah, take the Qara'a road from Abha past Al-Dalaghan. About 3km beyond the Al-Dalaghan turn, the road ends in a T-junction. Turn left and follow the road to the village of Wadiain, where you will see a sign pointing towards 'Al-Habla Park'.

As-Soudah & As-Sahab The two main mountain areas are As-Soudah, a few kilometres beyond the Inter-Continental Hotel, and the remote As-Sahab area.

As-Soudah, which is near the summit of Jebel Sawdah (2910m), is the most spectacular part of the park. The only access to these sites are by car.

As-Sawdah Cable Car *(☎ 229 1111; SR40 return; 2pm-5pm Thur-Fri Oct-Mar, 9am-9pm daily Apr-Sept)*, signposted as you ascend As-Soudah mountain, descends over the escarpment. Special reservations can be made outside normal operating hours. The only way to get there is by car.

From the foot of the As-Sawdah Cable Car, it's a 15-minute bus or taxi ride to **Rijal Alma**, a 1000-year-old traditional village of multistorey, stone fortress houses. One of them has been converted into the **Rijal Alma Museum** *(open 9am-8pm Sat-Thur, 2pm-8pm Fri; admission SR20, SR50 book/ catalogue)*. Its 2,000 exhibits, all related to local customs and traditions, fill the 19 rooms, and the museum is run by locals.

KHAMIS MUSHAYT   خميس مشيط
☎ 07

Khamis Mushayt (Khamis, for short) is 26km east of Abha. Khamis is usually spoken of as Abha's twin city, though it is a bit difficult to see what the two places have in common. It is as flat and dull as Abha is hilly and interesting.

Khamis' main attraction is its small, modern **souq** *(open 9am-1pm & 5pm-11pm daily)*, just off the main square, which is a good place to shop for silver jewellery.

NAJRAN   نجران
☎ 07

The fascinating and isolated oasis town of Najran is in a wide valley hemmed in by mountains and close to the Yemen border. Just 50km to the east, along the Riyadh and Sharurah road, the mountains give out to the sands of the Empty Quarter. The multistorey traditional houses in the valley are topped with roof terraces and stand in fields and groves of mixed palms and citrus fruit trees.

Orientation & Information

Driving in from Abha, you hit a T-junction; this is the only road leading to Najran (Main Rd). Turning left at the junction takes you to the Najran Holiday Inn, Najran airport and the Empty Quarter (in that order). Turning right leads you into Faisaliya, a modern business district on the outskirts of Najran. The fort and the souq are located further down the same road, in the centre of Najran.

Things to See

Parts of **Najran Fort** *(Qasr al-Imara; admission free; open 8am-sunset daily)* are said to date from pre-Islamic times, but the present fort was begun in 1942 as a royal residence. The fort is more or less in the centre of town, across from the fruit and vegetable market. You don't need a permit to get in.

Some 5km west of Najran's centre, **Al-Aan Palace** (also known as the Saadan Palace) is a five-storey tower dominating the oasis from an outcrop of rock. The building is a private residence and is not open to the public. The best way to see it is to backtrack towards Faisaliya along the Main Rd and turn (left if coming from Najran, right if coming from Faisaliya) at the sign for Maratah. Follow the road for 7km.

Najran's **museum** *(☎ 542 5292, fax 542 5120; open 8.30am-2pm Sat-Wed)* is several kilometres off the Main Rd, next to the **Al-Ukhdood archaeological site** *(admission free; open dawn-dusk daily)*. A Department of Antiquities permit is required to visit this site (unless you do it via a local hotel). To reach the museum, turn off the Main Rd at the sign for 'Okhdood'. After 3km you will reach a T-junction. Turn right. The museum is to your left after 2km.

Places to Stay

Najran's **Youth Hostel** (☎ 522 5019; beds DR8) is about 9km from the fort. As you pass through Faisaliya watch out for the Najran Municipality on your right. Main Rd swings around to the left while a smaller street continues on straight. Keep going straight on the smaller road. Take the first right (immediately after the first petrol station) and then take the second right. The hostel will be on your right after less than 200m. It's across the street from a school.

Najran Holiday Inn (☎ 522 5222, fax 522 1148; singles/doubles SR460/598) is a great base from which to explore the city. From the airport, turn left onto the main road into town. The hotel is on the left after 20km. The friendly staff can set up trips into the surrounding desert and mountains, and to historical and archaeological sites (SR100 per person), including fine examples of southern Arabian pre-Islamic rock art and the inscriptions that pepper this region (see the boxed text 'Rock Art', later).

Places to Eat

In Faisaliya there are a number of good places in the general vicinity of the youth hostel.

Cafeteria al-Beek has very good shwarma served, unusually, in submarine sandwich rolls. It's on the south side of the road, about 500m before the turn for the youth hostel. The sign is in Arabic only.

Al-Ramal ash-Shaabi, around the corner from the youth hostel, is one of the Najran area's best bets. The kebabs and grilled chicken dishes are excellent, as is the rice. At breakfast they do great, sizzling *hadas* (a spicy bean dish eaten with pita bread) for SR5. The restaurant's sign is in Arabic only. Look for the models of two Yemeni-style houses framing the entrance.

Getting There & Away

The airport is 30km to the northwest of Najran. The **Saudia office** (Main Rd) is about 1km towards the centre from the turn for the youth hostel. There are daily flights to Riyadh and Jeddah. The **bus station** is on

the Main Rd, 1.7km from the turn for Abha. There is direct service to Riyadh and Jeddah via Abha and Khamis Mushayt. There is also one bus each day to Sharurah.

SHARURAH
شرورة
☎ 07

The town of Sharurah lies deep in the Empty Quarter, about 340km east of Najran. The desert scenery on the road to Sharurah is spectacular and includes a drive of about 60km through what can only be described as a canyon of sand dunes rising to heights of 100m or more on each side of the road.

There is nothing to see in Sharurah itself. If you need to eat, try **Naseef al-Qamar**, an Egyptian-run restaurant on the main street.

The local **airport**, on the outskirts of town, has three flights a week to Riyadh (SR420) and Jeddah (SR360).

JIZAN & THE FARASAN ISLANDS
جزان جزر فرسان
☎ 07

The southern Red Sea port and provincial capital Jizan (Jazan, Gizan) is the gateway to the laid-back and easy-going Farasan Island archipelago, some 50km off the coast. This little bit of unspoiled paradise is Saudi Arabia's jewel in the crown. If the Kingdom ever opens up to independent travel, this is where most of the tourists will be heading.

Things to See & Do

Jizan itself is rather a grubby port with no attractions for the visitor.

The plankton-rich water around the Farasan Islands is shallow and marine life includes rays, sharks (including the giant whale shark), dolphins and a huge variety of smaller fish.

On land, the Farasan and several of the larger islands are home to a distinct island species of small striped gazelle. Birds provide another draw for get-away nature-lovers, as the islands lie on major migratory routes and are a bird spotter's paradise. The islands also have some of the few stretches of coastal mangrove – the habitat of the endangered dugong – on the Red Sea.

The small town of Farasan has several surviving traditional houses built from coral with intricately decorated and carved facades. These were the homes of former merchants and pearl dealers, and one – the **House of Rifai** – is now a small museum.

There is also a small **Turkish Fort** on the edge of the main town.

Both of these attractions are accessible only if you arrange a visit with the Farasan Hotel (see the following Places to Stay entry).

Places to Stay

Hayat Hotel (☎ 322 1055, fax 07 317 1774; singles/doubles SR230/SR300), next to the sea port and opposite the coast guard on the Corniche Rd in Jizan, arranges transfers to the port.

Farasan Hotel (☎ 316 0876, fax 316 0873; e farasanhotel@yahoo.com; rooms SR250), on the island itself, is next to the General Hospital in the town centre. It organises land tours, beach picnics, sea excursions and full-day and overnight guided sea trips for fishing, snorkelling and reef diving off the 70 islands (from SR250 per person inclusive; minimum six passengers).

Getting there & Away

Jizan's **airport** has daily flights to Riyadh and Jeddah.

From the fishing port in Jizan, fast, covered **launches** cross to the central town of the Farasan Islands in 55 minutes (SR350 divided by the number of passengers; maximum of seven; 24-hour service).

A **car ferry** sails from the main harbour to the Farasan Island (free of charge; four hours; 7am Saturday to Wednesday).

Northern Region

Northern Saudi Arabia extends along the Kingdom's northern frontiers with Iraq and Jordan. Its major cities are Hail, Al-Jouf, Sakaka and Domat Al-Jandal. The largest city, Tabuk, is a military town.

HAIL
☎ 06

حائل

Hail, 640km northwest of Riyadh, was formerly the seat of the Rashid family, the Saud clan's most formidable rivals. It is now the centre of the Kingdom's vast agricultural programme, and most of Saudi Arabia's wheat crop comes from the surrounding area.

Hail's main street runs north-south and centres on Commercial District Square next to the Saudi Holland Bank building. Old Hail is roughly east of this street and the newer areas are west of it, except for the Al-Qashalah Fortress. The **bus station** is at the Al-Qashalah Fortress, three blocks south of Commercial District Square.

Things to See

Before doing any sightseeing, your permit has to be validated at the Antiquities Section of the **Ministry of Education office** (open 8am-1pm Sat-Wed) in town (ask for maktab al-athaar). The office is on the 1st floor. These are also more or less the hours during which you can visit the sites.

The **Al-Qashalah Fortress**, next to the bus station, was built in the 1930s and was used mostly as a barracks for Abdul Aziz's troops in Hail. The small square building in the courtyard contains a display of artefacts from Hail and the surrounding desert region. **Airif Fort**, on a hill just outside the centre, is much older. It was built about 200 years ago as a combination observation post and stronghold. Also in the centre, on Barazan Square, you can see two restored **towers**, all that remain of another of Hail's palaces.

Places to Stay & Eat

Youth Hostel (☎ 533 1485; dorm beds SR8) is at the stadium, a short drive along Hail's main street.

Hail Hotel (☎ 532 0180, fax 532 7104; King Khaled St; singles/doubles with bathroom SR140/180) is another choice. To reach the hotel walk west from Commercial District Square and turn left at the first set of traffic lights. The hotel will be on your right.

Lahore Restaurant, across from the Hail Hotel, is a decent and clean place with the usual selection of chicken dishes and curries. Another good bet is **Ababa Sera's**, a small Indian place across from the Al-Bank al-Saudi al-Fransi office, offering cheap samosas (50 halalas apiece) and other quick eats. For shwarma and fresh juice try **Fast Food** (Main Rd), across from the southern edge of the park.

Getting There & Away

Hail's small **airport** is southwest of the centre. There are two or three flights a day to/from Riyadh, daily service to Jeddah and one or two flights a week to Dhahran.

Saptco runs three buses a day to Riyadh (SR110, eight hours) via Buraydah (SR45, four hours). There are daily buses to Medina and Tabuk.

TABUK تبوك
☎ 04

Tabuk (Tabouk), the largest city in northwestern Saudi Arabia, is largely a military town, so be careful where you point your camera. It also has a conservative reputation – another reason to tread carefully.

Most of Tabuk's essential services are on or near Prince Fahd bin Sultan St. The local antiquities office is in the education ministry building 400m west of the Al-Balawi Hotel. Moving from the hotel towards the centre you will see two white buildings opposite each other on either side of the street. Coming from the hotel the education building is the one on the right. The antiquities office is on the 2nd floor.

The main attractions are **Tabuk Fort** *(open dusk-dawn daily)*, a 17th-century Ottoman structure, once a stop on the pilgrim's road from Damascus to Mecca, and the reconstructed **Hejaz Train Station** a few blocks away.

DOMAT AL-JANDAL دومت الجندل
☎ 04

Domat al-Jandal is one of the Kingdom's many little-known gems. This modest town boasts two of the country's most interesting antiquities – the ruined **Qasr Marid** and the still-in-use **Mosque of Omar**, both of which are a short walk from the **Jouf Regional Museum** *(admission free; open 8am-1pm Sat-Wed)*.

The museum is 1.2km off the main road from Tabuk to Sakaka. Coming from Sakaka, turn right off the main road just past the second Domat al-Jandal petrol station and 350m beyond the police station. Follow this road for 1.2km. The museum will be on the right.

Rock Art

A little-known fact is that Saudi Arabia is one of the richest regions in the world for rock art, having around 2000 sites. In addition, there are countless rock inscriptions from various literate ages scattered throughout the Kingdom.

Much of the country's rock art is on ancient sandstone. Over long stretches of time the rock surface is covered with a wind-smoothed accretion of manganese and iron salts, a patina called 'desert varnish'. Where successive cultures over millennia have pecked and incised images onto the same rock panel, this varnish can help determine the relative chronology of the different works of art: the darker images are older than the lighter ones.

In the southern region, there are plenty of accessible sites, especially around the town of Najran and in the highlands of Asir. In the northern region, there are concentrations around Al-Ula, Domat al-Jandal, Tabuk and Hail.

The area around Najran has the largest number of sites. Scattered among the sandstone hills and valleys of an area 160km to the north, towards Riyadh, are countless remarkable human and animal images. The **Najran Holiday Inn** in Najran organizes day trips to rock-art sites (see Najran, Places to Stay).

More recent rock-art images extending back some 3000 years include ostrich, Arabian oryx and ibex as well as camels and lance-wielding horseback riders in hunting and war scenes. Further back in time, providing a fascinating window on Neolithic times when a wetter Arabian climate supported savannah grasslands, there are images of lions, cheetah, hyenas, dogs, long- and short-horned cattle. There are also human figures – males with headdresses and long-haired females – symbols and carved-out foot and handprints.

On the edge of the town of Jubba, 140km north west of Hail, a mountain massif contains a panoply of rock art enclosed within several large, fenced areas. Here, numerous images of early domesticated dogs, long-horned cattle and human figures suggest a transition from hunter-gatherer to agricultural communities.

Peter Harrigan

Qasr Marid is immediately adjacent to the museum. Its foundations date to Nabataean times, and Roman-era records mention Marid by name. The fortress was repaired in the 19th century and again served as the regional seat of government in the early years of the 20th century. The Mosque of Omar, on the far side of Marid from the museum, is one of the oldest in the Kingdom.

Outside the centre a portion of Domat al-Jandal's once-formidable **city wall** has been restored and can be viewed without a permit. The wall is 3.6km from the museum. Ask at the museum for directions. The best way to get to this remote corner of the Kingdom is to fly. The regional **airport** appears in Saudia's domestic timetables as 'Jouf'.

Places to Stay & Eat

Actually, there isn't anywhere to stay in Domat al-Jandal.

You'll have to stay 50km down the road in the regional capital, Sakaka.

Sakaka's **Youth Hostel** (☎ 624 1883, fax 624 8341; dorm beds cost SR8) is around 1.5km west of the town's main intersection on the big street immediately to the west of the mosque. Look for a green sign with white lettering in Arabic and a small blue-and-white IYHF logo in the upper left hand corner.

Al-Nusl Hotel (☎ 625 0353; fax 625 0408; singles/doubles SR345/450) is the most unique and tastefully designed hotel in Saudi Arabia. From the airport, turn right onto King Abdul Aziz road and you'll see the hotel after 30km. The rooms surround glass-domed courtyards cooled by traditional wind towers. Throughout the public areas there are displays of antiquities and artefacts. The hotel is an ideal base to explore the rich antiquities in the area and offers package tours that include tour guides, transportation and visits.

Al-Buraq Restaurant-3 (meals SR9-20), near the youth hostel, is an excellent cheap eatery. The surroundings are good and the kebabs are especially well-seasoned.

Eastern Region

المنطقة الشرقية

The Eastern Region – more commonly known as the Eastern Province – is located on the Arabian Gulf and contains the towns of Dhahran, Khobar, Dammam, Qatif, Hofuf and Jubail. It was here that oil was first discovered in Saudi Arabia in the 1930s. Before then, Dammam and Khobar were small fishing villages, and Dhahran did not even exist.

KHOBAR الخبر
☎ 03

Khobar (Al-Khubar or Alkhobar) is the newest of the cities, and has taken on the air of an expatriate village. It's also the most modern, and the most liberal, city in the Eastern Region, and with its gardens, picnic spots and kilometres of beaches has become the region's main vacation centre.

Orientation

Prince Turky St becomes Corniche Rd as you head towards Dammam. In Khobar itself, Dammam Rd is the main artery, and all the other main streets are either off it or run through it.

Information

The **Saudi British Bank** (☎ 882 6000; King Abdul Aziz St) is at the junction of the Khobar-Dammam Hwy. The **main post office** (☎ 864 2305) is on Prince Turky St. Every main street has at least one international call cabin. Alternatively, pre-pay telephone cards are available in all grocery shops and bookstores. **Sahara Internet Cafe** (☎ 897 6448; SR10 per 1hr) is located on the second floor of Rasheed Mall.

King Fahd University Hospital (☎ 894 3600; 30th St), off Hofuf St, has a good accident and emergency department.

Things to See & Do

Rasheed Mall (Dammam St) claims to be the largest in the Middle East. It has an extraordinary musical fountain, which is great entertainment for the kids, and just about every brand name has an outlet here.

Khobar Corniche is the main centre for entertainment, particularly its **Outside Sports and Health Centre** (admission free), with a track and fitness centre, which stretches for some 5km. It is open to the public, but unfortunately 'public' here predictably means 'men only' in practice.

The **Steamer Boat** (SR40, 10am to 7pm on the hour daily) takes tourists on a scenic, 40-minute ride to King Fahd Causeway and back again every hour on the hour for SR40.

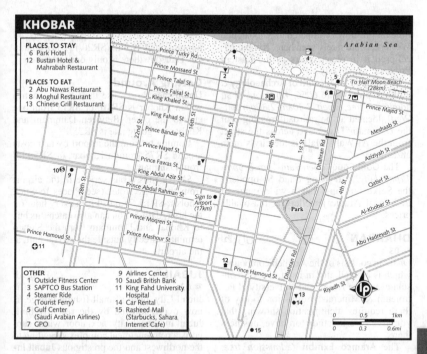

KHOBAR

PLACES TO STAY
6 Park Hotel
12 Bustan Hotel &
   Mahrabah Restaurant

PLACES TO EAT
2 Abu Nawas Restaurant
8 Moghul Restaurant
13 Chinese Grill Restaurant

OTHER
1 Outside Fitness Center
3 SAPTCO Bus Station
4 Steamer Ride
  (Tourist Ferry)
5 Gulf Center
  (Saudi Arabian Airlines)
7 GPO
9 Airlines Center
10 Saudi British Bank
11 King Fahd University
   Hospital
14 Car Rental
15 Rasheed Mall
   (Starbucks, Sahara
   Internet Cafe)

Arabian Sea

Half Moon Beach, 28km from downtown Khobar, is the main tourist attraction, and its popularity is due both to its clean beaches and smart holiday chalets (SR300 per day off-season, SR1,000 July to August).

The tourist villages of **Al-Khaleej Village** and **Palm Village** offer all water activities and tourist facilities, but people value most their liberal atmosphere. For kids, there is the massive **Prince Mohammed Amusement Park** (☎ 8109652).

Places to Stay & Eat

Bustan Hotel (☎ 894 6550, fax 895 4405; Prince Hamoud St; singles/doubles SR80/150) is the best budget deal. The staff are friendly, and every room has a separate bathroom, satellite TV and minibar.

Park Hotel (☎ 8950005, fax 8987271; Prince Turki St; singles/doubles SR180/ SR280) is a local institution, and a great base from which to explore Khobar. The rooms are large and all have separate bathrooms.

Eating out well and cheaply is one of the great joys of Khobar.

Chinese Grill (☎ 864 8865; Dhahran St; meals from SR25) specialises in Chinese food, but also has Indian, Arabic and continental dishes.

Marahaba (☎ 895 1671; Prince Hamoud St; dishes from SR15-35), right next to the Bustan Hotel, has excellent Indian Mughlai and Arabic cuisine. You can have your meal outside, next to the hotel pool.

Fish Market Restaurant (☎ 899 3900; Khobar Corniche) is a must for those who love seafood. Set up as a kind of supermarket, you get a trolley, choose live or prepared fish, pay for it and then have it prepared for you at your table. A typical meal for two costs SR150.

Getting There & Away

Khobar's **Saptco bus station** (☎ 899 6724) has regular services to Qatif and Safwa (SR2) and Tarut Island (SR5). Buses also depart regularly for Hofuf and Riyadh. Saptco also runs a service to Bahrain (SR60, about two hours) four times a day from here.

DAMMAM   الدمام
☎ 03

The provincial capital, Dammam, is the longest settled and largest town of the

Dhahran-Dammam-Khobar group. It is a little bit run-down compared to Khobar, and Westerners are rarely seen here. Khobar has eclipsed it in recent years as the Eastern Province's main city.

The **Regional Museum of Archaeology & Ethnography** (☎ 826 6056; 4th floor, 1st St; admission free; open 7.30am-2.30pm Sat-Wed), located at the railroad crossing near the Dammam Tower and across the street from the Al-Waha Mall, is the city's main attraction.

The **Gold Souq** (open 9am-1pm & 5pm-11pm daily), off King Saud St opposite the Seiko building, has a wide range of traditional Arabic jewellery at reasonable prices.

DHAHRAN لظهران
☎ 03

Dhahran consists of the Aramco compound, which is a small city in itself, the US consulate, and the King Fahd University of Petroleum & Minerals. Admission to any of these requires identification showing that you live, work, study or have business there.

The **Aramco Exhibit** (admission free; open 8am-6.30pm Sat-Wed, 9am-noon & 3pm-6.30pm Thur, 3pm-6.30pm Fri, families only Thur-Fri) is the Kingdom's best museum bar none. For the layperson, the centre is a comprehensive guide to the oil industry with a minimum of pro-Big Oil preaching and an emphasis on explaining the technical side of the industry.

Getting There & Away
Air Dhahran's **King Fahd International Airport** is 75km north of Dammam. It has regular flights to all the Kingdom's main cities, and direct flights to many international destinations.

There is a **Saudia Office** (☎ 894 3333; Gulf Centre, Prince Turky St) in Khobar. The **Airline Centre** (King Abdul Aziz St), next to the Saudi British Bank, has representatives from every major airline operating flights from King Fahd International Airport.

Train The **train station** is southeast of the city centre, near the Dammam-Khobar Expressway and Dammam Housing Development (a series of drab, high-rise apartment blocks). Trains leave three times daily (ex-

cept Thursday) for Riyadh (SR60/40 1st/2nd class, four hours) via Abqaiq (SR10/6, 45 minutes) and Hofuf (SR20/15, 1½ hours). On Thursday there is only one train.

Getting Around
Limousines do not use their meters. A trip within Khobar is SR10, or SR15 from one end to the other. Between Dammam and Khobar the going rate is SR25.

Coming to/from the airport by taxi costs around SR75 from/to Khobar, or SR50 to/from Dammam.

Saptco runs a bus service to the airport from the Park Hotel (see Places to Stay, Khobar; SR15, 7am to 11pm every hour on the hour, daily). You can also catch this bus to Khobar and Dammam from the Saptco terminal, directly outside the arrival hall, at the airport.

JUBAIL الجبيل
☎ 03

Jubail City, once a small fishing village, is now overshadowed by the recently built Jubail Industrial City, next door, which supports a petrochemical complex sprawling to the northwest and the prestigious **Jubail Industrial College**.

Jubail City is a port that handles fleets of wooden and fibreglass fishing dhows, and is a mix of fishing village, office and shopping areas.

Things to See
At the southern end of Jubail City is a new and lively **Fresh Fish Market**, best visited at sunrise.

A **Nestorian site** (not officially open to the public) was discovered in Jubail in 1986. Although only the walls are left, the shape of the rooms is clearly visible. There are the remains of a **pre-Islamic church** and a number of houses. There is also some pottery lying around.

The site was fenced off shortly after it was discovered, and access is now limited; most of the religious symbols were also removed from the masonry.

To get to the site, take the Khobar-Dammam Hwy and leave it directly behind the petrol station after the exit for Jubail North. Drive west, cross the pipelines after about 400m, continue straight for 200m, and you'll come to the fenced-in areas.

Places to Stay

Ash-Sharq Hotel (☎ *362 1155, fax 362 4161; Jeddah St; singles/doubles with bathroom SR230/154*) is in the heart of Jubail City and a local expat hang-out. It's a great place to have lunch or a (nonalcoholic) beer, if you are passing through town.

Getting There & Away

The only way to get to and from Jubail is by taxi, which costs SR20 to Khobar.

TARUT ISLAND   جزيرة تاروت
☎ 03

For centuries the small island of Tarut has been one of the most important ports and military strongholds on the Arabian side of the Gulf.

Tarut Fort is one of Saudi Arabia's most photographed ruins. What you see today was built by the Portuguese in the 16th century on top of a site that has been used since the 3rd millennium BC. Tarut's other site is **Qasr Darin** – so exposed and so thoroughly ruined that you do not need a permit to see it. It was built in 1875 to guard the sea approaches to the island.

Tarut is connected to the mainland by a causeway off the Dammam-Qatif Hwy passing through Dammam Corniche. Once you're on the island turn right at an intersection-cum-roundabout. Follow a narrow road through Tarut town for about 1km and you will see Tarut Fort on the right. To reach Qasr Darin continue on the same road for 2km until it swings around to the right. At that point just keep hugging the coastline for another 6km and you'll see the ruins on the right, near the pier.

HOFUF   الهفوف

The Al-Hasa Oasis, centred on the town of Hofuf, is the largest in Arabia and one of the largest in the world. The oasis seems to go on and on and, if you have time and a car, exploring the small villages scattered through this large, lush area can be a pleasant way to spend an afternoon or two.

Orientation & Information

King Abdul Aziz St is the main commercial street and intersects with Al-Khudod St to form a central square containing the bus station. Both of the centre's hotels are an easy walk from this intersection.

There are several banks, moneychangers and call cabins around this main area.

Things to See

The **Hofuf Museum** (*admission free; open 8am-2pm Sat-Wed*) is especially good on Eastern Province archaeology. It is about 5km from the main intersection. From the main intersection head west on Al-Khudod St and turn left at the first traffic signal past Qasr Ibrahim. Follow this road for 1.2km and turn left at the third set of traffic lights (Al-Safir supermarket will be across the intersection from you). Go about 100m and turn right at the next traffic signal. Follow this road for 1.8km and turn left at the second traffic signal. Go left again after 700m (at the first traffic signal). The museum will be on your left after a further 600m.

In the centre is Hofuf's best known site, the Ottoman fortress of **Qasr Ibrahim** (*admission free; open dawn-dusk*). You'll need a site permit to visit the interior. Once inside, take a look at the jail, next to the mosque, and the underground cells inside it. The Turkish bath near the northwest corner of the compound was used during Abdul Aziz's time to store dates, the smell of which still lingers inside. The stairs along the eastern wall lead to what were the commanding officer's quarters.

Hofuf's wonderful **souq** (*open 9am-1pm & 5pm-11pm daily*) is just off King Abdul Aziz St, about 300m south of the main intersection. Several shops also have good collections of **Bedouin weaving** and a few have old **silver jewellery**. You will also find a few shops selling woven materials near Qasr Ibrahim.

The **Hofuf Camel Market**, on the ring road on the way to the Omani border, is the Thursday feature and a wonderful opportunity to experience part of a tradition extending back many centuries. It's a working market and not a tourist attraction, trading in camels, sheep and goats. Sightseers are rare, but are able to wander around freely and with no sense of threat; Western females, however, should expect to be the object of persistent but in no way threatening curiosity. It's best to arrive around 6am and stay for a few hours to experience the build up of trading.

Pass by the traders to the main body of the camel markets, marked by a spread of wooden and wire fenced pens. Inside the trading area, wide sandy paths separate the

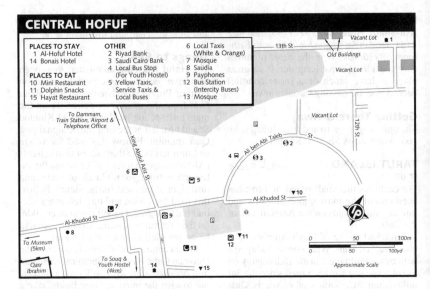

CENTRAL HOFUF

PLACES TO STAY
1 Al-Hofuf Hotel
14 Bonais Hotel

PLACES TO EAT
10 Mini Restaurant
11 Dolphin Snacks
15 Hayat Restaurant

OTHER
2 Riyad Bank
3 Saudi Cairo Bank
4 Local Bus Stop
 (For Youth Hostel)
5 Yellow Taxis,
 Service Taxis &
 Local Buses

6 Local Taxis
 (White & Orange)
7 Mosque
8 Saudia
9 Payphones
12 Bus Station
 (Intercity Buses)
13 Mosque

Approximate Scale

pens. Colourful stalls laden with the halters, bridles, blankets and other paraphernalia of camel saddlery and breeding dot the walkways and are usually run by veiled ladies.

If you buy the halters or camel blankets for sale, you can be sure they have not been made just for the tourist trade.

Places to Stay

Youth Hostel (☎ 580 0028; dorm beds SR8) is at the stadium. To reach the hostel take bus No 2 to the large T-junction by the prison. There is a stadium behind it, but that's not the one you need. Turn right at the junction and follow the road for 500m until it forks. Keep left at the fork and follow the road for another 2.5km. A cab from the bus station costs SR15.

Bonais Hotel (☎ 582 7700; King Abdul Aziz St; singles/doubles SR110/165) is your best bet in town.

Al-Hofuf Hotel (☎ 587 7082; 13th St; 2-star singles/doubles SR140/210) also has a four-star section for triple the price.

Places to Eat

Al-Haramein Restaurant is a good small place across the main intersection from the bus station. A meal of chicken, rice and salad costs SR14.

Sargam Restaurant, just west of the bus station, serves up good, cheap Indian food; chicken or mutton curry and a serve of rice costs only SR9.

Getting There & Away

The town's **bus station** (☎ 587 3687; cnr King Abdul Aziz & Al-Khudod Sts) has buses travelling to Dammam throughout the day as well as a regular service making the trip to Riyadh.

The **train station** (information ☎ 582 0571) is a long way from the town centre. To reach it, head north along the Dammam Rd and then turn west onto Hajer Palace Rd at the telephone office.

There are daily services to Riyadh and Dammam.

Syria

سورية

Changes are afoot in Syria. With the ascendance to power of the young, urbane and Western-educated Bashir al-Assad, the country is undergoing something of a thaw. The US state department may still regard Syria as an addendum to its perceived 'axis of evil', but major political and economic reforms are already having a visibly modernising effect. Suddenly, everybody is online; chic bars and restaurants are opening in the capital at breakneck pace; a new wave of boutique hotels in Aleppo are being readied for the onslaught of mass tourism... Expect Syria's profile as a travel destination to experience a steady climb, beginning now.

Not that travelling here was ever a problem. Despite the misguided perception of Syria as a place full of terrorists and other nasties, the truth is that most visitors are charmed by the locals, who are among the most gentle and hospitable in the Middle East, or anywhere else for that matter. The historic sights rival those of neighbouring Turkey or Jordan, ranging from hilltop Crusader castles to a ruined Roman city at a desert oasis. Damascus and Aleppo both vie for the title of the oldest continuously inhabited city in the world, and both have extensive souqs that rank as the best to be found in the region. Added to which, the food is superb, good accommodation is plentiful, and the prices are a bargain compared to the West. In sum, Syria is one of the highlights of any Middle Eastern trip.

Facts about Syria

HISTORY

Historically Syria included the territories that now make up modern Jordan, Israel and the Palestinian territories, Lebanon and Syria itself. Due to its strategic position, its coastal towns were important Phoenician trading posts and later the area became an equally pivotal part of the Egyptian, Persian and Roman empires – and many others in the empire-building business, for that matter. For more details on these eras see the History section in the Facts about the Region chapter.

Arab Republic of Syria

Area: 185,180 sq km
Population: 17 million
Capital: Damascus
Head of State: President Bashir al-Assad
Official Language: Arabic
Currency: Syrian pound (S£)

- Best Dining – feasting in fantastic restaurants in beautifully restored 18th-century townhouses in Aleppo and Damascus
- Best Nightlife – seeking out the narrow alleys of Damascus' old Christian quarter
- Best Walk – ambling at sunrise or sundown through the ambient ruins of the desert city of Palmyra
- Best View – standing on top of the world on Jebel Nasiriyya and looking out over the Al-Ghaba plain
- Best Activity – making like Indiana Jones and exploring the overgrown Dead Cities, such as Apamea, south of Aleppo

Syria finally ended up as part of the Ottoman domains ruled from İstanbul and (along with Lebanon) was dished out to France when the Turkish empire broke up after WWI. This caused considerable local resentment, as the region had been briefly independent from the end of WWI until Paris took over in 1920.

The French never had much luck with their Syria-Lebanon mandate and during WWII agreed to Syrian and Lebanese independence. The French proved reluctant to

What to See

Damascus is a thoroughly charming capital with an old city that can keep you enraptured for days, although you should drag yourself away for at least a day trip south to **Bosra** for the Roman theatre. Syria's premier, must-see attractions are the ruins of the desert city of **Palmyra** and the Crusader castle **Crac des Chevaliers**, the latter of which is best visited from **Hama**, a small town with good food and accommodation. From a Hama base it's certainly also worth visiting the ancient site of **Apamea**.

Aleppo is Syria's second great city, a historical commercial centre with a fabulous souq. It also makes a good base from which to explore the surrounding countryside and its littering of Byzantine sites, the best of which is undoubtedly **Qala'at Samaan**.

---

make good on the proposal and it was only in 1946 that they finally withdrew.

A period of political instability followed and by 1954, after several military coups, the nationalist Ba'ath party (*Ba'ath* means 'renaissance') rose and took power virtually unopposed. A brief flirtation with the Pan-Arabist idea of a United Arab Republic (with Egypt) in 1958 proved unpopular and coups in 1960, '61 and '63 saw the leadership change hands yet again. By 1966 the Ba'ath were back in power, but they were severely weakened by loss in two conflicts – the Six Day War with Israel in 1967 and the Black September hostilities in Jordan in 1970. At this point, defence minister Hafez al-Assad seized power.

Assad maintained control longer than any other post-independence Syrian government with a mixture of ruthless suppression and guile. In 1998, he was elected to a fifth seven-year term with a predictable 99.9% of the vote. It took a failing of health to finally remove the man from power: his death was announced on 10 June 2000.

Syria Today

The sporting playboy Basel al-Assad had been the heir apparent until he was killed in a car crash in 1994. Therefore, following death of Assad senior, the younger son Bashir, a 35-year-old trained ophthalmolo-

gist, acceded to power. Early signs have been encouraging. A new government was formed in December 2001 with a mandate to push forward new reforms aimed at dismantling the creaking socialist systems of old and replacing them with private enterprise. However, improving the country's relations with the international community may prove more tricky. The sticking point is the stand-off between Syria and Israel. Neither side is willing to make sufficient concessions to the other on the subject of security: Syria demands complete Israeli withdrawal from the Golan Heights (lost in 1967); Israel demands Syria use its influence in keeping the radical Hezbollah movement in check. Stalemate. But so long as Washington sides with Israel, Syria remains an international pariah.

GEOGRAPHY

Syria is a bit over half the size of Italy. It is bordered in the southwest by Lebanon and Israel (with whom it contests possession of the Golan Heights), in the south by Jordan, in the east by Iraq and in the north by Turkey. The country has four geographical regions: a fertile 180km-long coastal strip between Lebanon and Turkey; the Jebel Ansariyya (also known as Jebel an-Nasiriyya) mountain range, which runs north-south inland from the coast; the cultivated steppes that form an arc on the inland side of the mountain range and include the main centres of Damascus, Homs, Hama and Aleppo; and the stony Syrian desert in the southeast.

CLIMATE

Syria has a Mediterranean climate with hot, dry summers and mild, wet winters close to the coast. Inland it gets progressively drier and more inhospitable. On the coast average daily temperatures range from 29°C in summer to 10°C in winter and the annual rainfall is about 760mm. Temperatures on

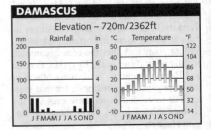

DAMASCUS

Elevation – 720m/2362ft

the cultivated steppe area average around 35°C in summer and 12°C in winter. Rainfall varies from about 250mm to 500mm. In the desert the temperatures are high and rainfall is low. In summer the days average 40°C and highs of 46°C are not uncommon.

GOVERNMENT & POLITICS

Although presidential elections took place once every seven years, the decades-long rule of Hafez al-Assad was never challenged by any kind of democratic process. His rule was absolute. Similarly, on his death there was never any question over the succession of his son, Bashir. As president and leader of the Arab Ba'ath Socialist Party, Bashir al-Assad has the power to appoint ministers (including the prime minister, who is charged with forming the cabinet), declare war, issue laws and appoint civil servants and military personnel. At the time of the promulgation of the constitution, which guarantees freedom of religious thought and expression, there was outrage that Islam was not declared the state religion. Bowing (but not all the way) to the pressure, the former President Assad and his government amended it to say that the head of state must be Muslim.

POPULATION & PEOPLE

Syria has a population of somewhere just under 17 million. It's annual growth rate of 2.7%, while down from the 3.4% of not long ago, is one of the region's highest and means that over 40% of Syrians are under 14 years of age. Most of the population lives in the western, more humid, part of the country.

About 90% of the population are Arabs, which includes some minorities such as the Bedouin (about 100,000). The remainder is made up of smaller groupings of Kurds (about one million), Armenians, Circassians and Turks.

RELIGION

Islam is practised by about 86% of the population – 20% of this is made up of minorities such as the Shiite, Druze and Alawite, while the remainder are Sunni Muslims.

Christians account for most of the rest and belong to various churches including the Greek Orthodox, Greek Catholic, Syrian Orthodox, Armenian Orthodox, Maronite, Roman Catholic and Protestant.

Since the government started issuing them passports in 1992, all but a handful of the several thousand Jews who lived in Damascus have emigrated, mostly to the USA.

LANGUAGE

Arabic is the majority mother tongue of the majority. Kurdish is spoken in the north, especially towards the east, Armenian in Aleppo and other major cities, and Turkish in some villages east of the Euphrates.

English is widely understood and increasingly popular as a second language, while French, although waning, is still quite common among older people.

For Arabic words and phrases, see the Language chapter at the back of this book.

Facts for the Visitor

WHEN TO GO

Spring is the best time to visit as temperatures are mild and the winter rains have cleared the haze that obscures views for much of the year. April is made glorious by blossoming wild flowers. Autumn is the next best choice.

If you go in summer, don't be caught without a hat, sunscreen and water bottle, especially if visiting Palmyra or the north-east. Winter can be downright unpleasant on the coast and in the mountains.

VISAS & DOCUMENTS
Visas

All foreigners entering Syria should obtain a visa in advance. The most sure way to get your visa is to apply for it in your home country well before you intend travelling. Avoid applying in a country that is not your own or that you don't hold residency for as the Syrian authorities don't like this. At best they will ask you for a letter of recommendation from your own embassy (which is often an expensive proposition); at worst, they'll turn you down flat. US citizens should be aware that many US embassies abroad have a policy of not issuing letters of recommendation – exceptions include the US embassy in Athens, which issues letter of recommendation for free. It's also worth knowing that the Syrian embassy in Cairo does not require such a letter – just fill in three forms and you're away. If your home

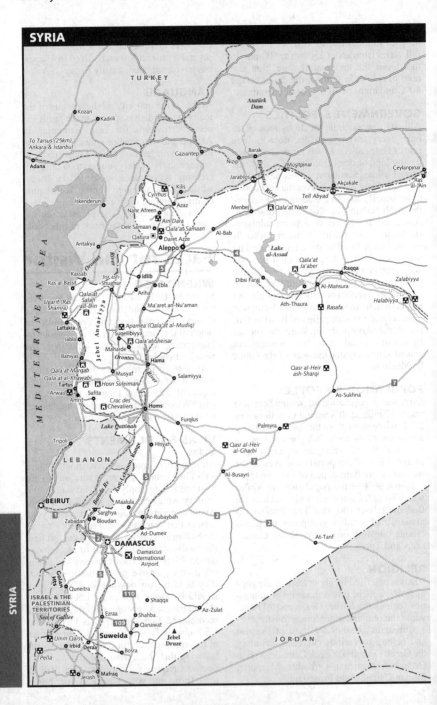

SYRIA

TURKEY

Atatürk Dam

Kozan

Kadrili

To Tarsus (25km), Ankara & Istanbul

Adana

Iskenderun

Gaziantep

Nizip

Barak

Müşitpinar

Euphrates River

Akçakale

Ceylanpinar

Ras al-'Ain

Kilis

Cyrrhus

Azaz

Jarablos

Tell Abyad

Antakya

Nahr Afreen

Ain Dara

Deir Samaan

Qala'at Samaan

Qatura

Daret Azze

Al-Bab

Menbej

Qala'at Najm

Aleppo

Lake al-Assad

Qala'at Ja'aber

Raqqa

Zalabiyya

Kassab

Ras al-Bassit

Jisr ash-Shughur

Idlib

Ebla

Dibsi Faraj

Al-Mansura

Halabiyya

Ugarit (Ras Shamra)

Qala'at Salah ad-Din

Ariha

Ma'aret an-Nu'aman

Ath-Thaura

Rasafa

Lattakia

Jabla

Apamea (Qala'at al-Mudiq)

Suqeilbiyya

Qala'at Sheisar

Baniyas

Maharde

Orontes

Hama

Salamiyya

Qasr al-Heir ash-Sharqi

Qala'at Marqab

Qala'at al-Khawabi

Musyaf

Tartus

Hosn Suleiman

Arwad

Amrit

Safita

Crac des Chevaliers

Homs

Furqlus

Palmyra

As-Sukhna

Qattinah

Lake Qattinah

Hisyah

Qasr al-Heir al-Gharbi

Al-Busayri

Tripoli

LEBANON

Anti-Lebanon Range

BEIRUT

Barda Ry

Maalula

Ar-Rubaybah

At-Tanf

Sarghya

Bloudan

Zabadani

Ad-Dumeir

DAMASCUS

Damascus International Airport

ISRAEL & THE PALESTINIAN TERRITORIES

Golan Heights

Quneitra

Shaqqa

Az-Zulat

JORDAN

Sea of Galilee

Fio

Ezraa

Shahba

Umm Qais

Qanawat

Irbid

Suweida

Jebel Druze

Pella

Deraa

Bosra

Jerash

Mafraq

MEDITERRANEAN SEA

Orontes River

Jebel Ansariyya

SYRIA

country doesn't have a Syrian embassy or consulate, then there's no problem with you applying anywhere else.

The Syrian embassy in Amman issues visas only to nationals and residents of Jordan and to nationals of countries that have no Syrian representation. So, if you are from a country like the UK, the USA or France, which has a Syrian embassy, then you cannot get a Syrian visa in Jordan. Of course, as there will always be, there is the odd traveller who has proved the exception (but you cannot count on it). In Turkey, you can get Syrian visas in both Ankara and İstanbul without too much of a problem.

There are two types of visa issued: single entry and multiple entry, but both are valid only for 15 days inside Syria and must be used within three months of the date of issue (six months for multiple-entry visas). Don't be misled by the line on the visa stating a validity of three months – this simply means the visa is valid *for presentation* for three months.

The cost of visas varies according to nationality and on where you get them. There seems to be little rhyme or reason in deciding which nationalities pay what, except in the case of UK passport-holders, who always pay a lot.

If there is any evidence of a visit to Israel in your passport (see the boxed text 'Israeli Stamp Stigma' in the Regional Facts for the Visitor chapter), your application will be refused.

For details of visas for other Middle Eastern countries, see the 'Visas at a Glance' table under Visas & Documents in the Regional Facts for the Visitor chapter.

Visas at the Border The official line is that if there is no Syrian representation in your country, you are entitled to be issued a visa on arrival at the border, airport or port. That said, there's no Syrian embassy or consulate in New Zealand yet we've had letters from Kiwi passport holders who were turned back at the border. Conversely, there is Syrian representation in Australia but we've had more than one email from Aussie travellers who managed to get a visa at the Turkey-Syria border with no probs mate. Even so, it's chancy and our advice has got to be that you should make all attempts to secure your visa in advance.

SYRIA

Holders of single-entry Syrian visas who wish to visit Lebanon can do so and be issued a new Syrian visa at the border when returning. Costs and regulations change frequently (check with your hostel/hotel in Damascus for the latest info), but at the time of research the new visa was US$50.

Visa Extensions If your stay in Syria is going to be more than 15 days you have to get a visa extension while in the country. This is done at an immigration office, which you'll find in all main cities. The length of the extension appears to depend on a combination of what you're willing to ask for and the mood of the official you deal with. They are usually only granted on the 14th or 15th day of your stay, so if you apply earlier expect to be knocked back. The specifics vary from place to place but there are always several forms to complete and you need from three to five passport photos. The cost is never more than US$1. For addresses and further details see the individual city sections.

Other Documents
Student cards get massive discounts on site admissions. However, it must be an internationally recognised card such as ISIC. If you don't have one you can probably pick one up in Syria for about US$15 – make inquiries at hostels/hotels frequented by backpackers.

EMBASSIES & CONSULATES
Syrian Embassies & Consulates
Following are addresses of Syrian embassies and consulates in cities around the world. There is no Syrian representation in New Zealand, and citizens are advised to contact one of the Syrian honorary consulates in Australia. For the addresses of Syrian embassies and consulates in the Middle East, see the relevant chapter.

Australia Consulate: (☎ 03-9347 8445, fax 9347 8447) 57 Cardigan St, Carlton, Victoria 3053
Consulate: (☎ 02-9597 7714, fax 9597 2226) 10 Belmore St, Arncliffe, NSW 2205
Canada (☎ 613-569 5556, fax 569 3800) 151 Slater St, Ottawa, Ontario K1P 5H3
France (☎ 01 40 62 61 00) 20 rue Vaneau, 75007 Paris
Germany (☎ 030-220 20 46) Otto Grotewohl Str 3, Berlin
Consulate: (☎ 228-81 99 20, fax 81 92 99)

Andreas Hermes Str 5, D-53175 Bonn
Consulate: (☎ 40-30 90 54 14, fax 30 90 52 33)
Brooktor 11, 20457 Hamburg
Netherlands Consulate: (☎ 070-346 9795)
Laan van Meerdervoort 53d, The Hague
UK (☎ 020-7245 9012, fax 7235 4621)
8 Belgrave Square, London SW1 8PH
USA (☎ 202-232 6313, fax 234 9548) 2215 Wyoming Ave NW, Washington DC 20008
Consulate: (☎ 212-661 1313) 820 Second Ave, New York NY 10017

Embassies & Consulates in Syria
Most embassies and consulates are open from around 8am to 2pm and are closed on Friday, Saturday and any public holidays. All the following are in Damascus. Note, the Canadian embassy currently provides emergency consular services to Australian citizens, while Irish interests are looked after by the UK.

Egypt (☎ 011-333 3561, fax 333 7961) Sharia al-Jala'a, Abu Roumaneh
France (☎ 011-332 7992/3/4/5) Sharia Ata Ayyubi, Salihiyya
Germany (☎ 011-332 3800/1/2, fax 332 3812) 53 Sharia Ibrahim Hanano, Immeuble Kotob
Iran (☎ 011-222 6459, fax 222 0997) Autostrad al-Mezzeh, about 4km west of the city centre
Jordan (☎ 011-333 4642, fax 333 6741) Sharia al-Jala'a, Abu Roumaneh
Netherlands (☎ 011-333 6871, fax 333 9369) Sharia al-Jala'a, Abu Roumaneh
Saudi Arabia (☎ 011-333 4914) Sharia al-Jala'a, Abu Roumaneh
Turkey (☎ 011-333 1411) 58 Sharia Ziad bin Abi Soufian
UK (☎ 011-371 2561/2/3, fax 371 3592) 11 Sharia Mohammed Kurd Ali, Malki
USA (☎ 011-333 1342, fax 224 7938) 2 Sharia al-Mansour, Abu Roumaneh

CUSTOMS
We've never been able to ascertain what the customs allowances are for Syria, but foreign visitors are almost never stopped so it's almost a moot point. Passengers arriving by air can also avail themselves of cigarettes and alcohol at the airport's duty-free shop at bargain prices. About the only thing customs officials really seem interested in is high tech electronic gear. Items such as video cameras, laptops and palmtops can excite a lot of interest and attract heavy taxes or, at the very least, they result in an entry being written into your passport to make sure that you leave the country with

these items and don't sell them while in Syria. To avoid complications keep it all out of sight.

MONEY
Currency
The official currency is the Syrian pound (S£), also called the *lira*. There are 100 piastres *(qirsh)* to a pound but this is redundant because the smallest coin you'll find now is one pound. Other coins come in denominations of two, five, 10 and 25. Notes come in denominations of 50, 100, 200, 500 and 1000.

Exchange Rates
Exchange rates at the time of writing are as follows:

country	unit		Syrian pounds
Australia	A$1	=	S£27.81
Canada	C$1	=	S£32.41
euro zone	€1	=	S£50.70
Israel	1NIS	=	S£10.53
Japan	¥100	=	S£42.06
Jordan	JD1	=	S£72.62
Lebanon	LL1	=	S£00.03
UK	UK£1	=	S£80.63
USA	US$1	=	S£51.40

Exchanging Money
There's at least one branch of the Commercial Bank of Syria (CBS) in every major town and most of them will change cash *and* travellers cheques in most major currencies, although each branch has its own quirks – some charge commission, some don't: some require the bank manager's signature to authorise transactions, some just hand over the cash without any form filling whatsoever. There are also a small number of officially sanctioned private exchange offices. These change cash and *sometimes* travellers cheques at official bank rates, and generally don't charge any commission. The other advantage is that whereas banks usually close for the day at 12.30pm or 2pm, the exchange offices are often open until 7pm.

Many hotel owners, shop keepers and touts in the souq are also keen to change your hard currency for Syrian pounds, but given that the black market rate is usually exactly the same as the official bank rate there is no advantage to be gained here, except perhaps convenience (for example, if you're short on cash and it's out of bank hours).

ATMs & Credit Cards While there are no ATMs in Syria at present, major credit cards such as AmEx, Visa, MasterCard and Diners Club are increasingly being accepted by bigger hotels and some restaurants and shops – particularly those that enjoy the custom of foreigners.

Cash advances are officially not possible as the Commercial Bank of Syria has no links with any credit card companies, however, ask around and you will find a shop willing to carry out the transactions via a Jordanian or Lebanese bank. The exchange rate offered may not be too great, on top of which you can also expect to pay a hefty commission.

Costs
It is possible to get by on as little as S£750 (US$15) a day if you are willing to stick to the cheapest hotels (you can get a bed for as little as S£150, or US$3), make felafel, shwarma and juice the mainstay of your diet, and carry a student card to offset the site admission costs. If you stay in a modest hotel room with fan and private bathroom, eat in regular restaurants, with the odd splurge, and aim to see a couple of sites each day, you'll spend around US$20 to US$30 a day.

To give an indication of daily costs, a felafel or shwarma costs well under US$1, while a meal in an average restaurant ranges from anything from S£60 (just over a dollar) to S£250 (US$5). A beer costs S£50 to S£100 (US$1 to US$2) depending on where you drink it.

Getting around the country is cheap: the four-hour bus ride between Damascus and Aleppo costs only S£150 (US$3) on a luxury air-con bus, while if you want to slum it on an old battered bus you can do it as cheaply as S£60 (US$1.20).

Admission fees are the killer. Many museums, castles and other sites cost S£300 (US$6). While such a fee is justified at sites such as Crac des Chevaliers, there will be times when you have to ask yourself if a sight is worth paying such money. Often it's not. Note that a student card slashes prices by up to 90%.

Tipping & Bargaining

Tipping is expected in the better restaurants and occasionally waiters deduct it themselves when giving you your change. Whatever you buy, remember that bargaining is an integral part of the process and listed prices are always inflated to allow for it. If you are shopping in the souqs, bargain – even a minimum amount of effort will almost always result in outrageous asking prices being halved.

POST & COMMUNICATIONS
Post

The Syrian postal service is slow but effective enough. Letters mailed from the main cities take about a week to Europe and anything up to a month to Australia or the USA. Mailing letters to the UK and Europe costs S£17, while to the USA and Australia it's S£18; stamps for postcards to the UK and Europe cost S£10, while to Australia and the USA they're S£13. In addition to post offices, you can also buy *tawaabi* (stamps) from most tobacconists.

The poste restante counter at the main post office in Damascus is more or less reliable. You must take your passport as identification and be prepared to pay an S£10 pick-up fee.

Telephone

The country code for Syria is ☎ 963, followed by the local area code (minus the zero), then the subscriber number. Local area codes are given at the start of each city or town section. The international access code (to call abroad from Syria) is ☎ 00.

Calling from Damascus and Aleppo is straightforward – you just use one of the direct-dial Easycomm card phones dotted about town (plentiful in Damascus, less so in Aleppo). Phonecards are bought from shops – just ask at the nearest shop, no matter what kind of shop it is, and if they don't have them, they'll point you to someone who does. The cards come in denominations of S£200 (local and national calls only), S£350, S£500 and S£1000.

For cheap rates to Australia call from 2pm to 7pm; to the USA from 3am to 8am; and to Europe from 1am to 7am.

Elsewhere in the country international calls have to be made from cardphones inside or just outside the local telephone office.

You buy the necessary card either from a booth within the office or from a vendor who'll be hovering around the phones. Cards bought in Damascus or Aleppo will not work in phones anywhere else and vice versa.

Mobile Phones You should now be able to use your mobile phone in Damascus and Aleppo. In October 2001 Syrian providers introduced roaming services for subscribers from neighbouring countries, and plans were to quickly extend this to all GSM services.

Email & Internet Access

Since the new president opened the flood gates and allowed Syrians access to the Internet for the first time in 2000, online activity has taken off in a huge way. Every town now has at least two or three venues, with more certainly on the way. For addresses see individual town and city sections. Bear in mind though that almost all these places are just a few months old and some of them are bound to fail and disappear.

Another problem is overloaded servers (there are only four national ISPs), meaning information transfer is painfully slow. Costs are typically S£100 per hour. Direct access to certain sites, including Hotmail and Yahoo, is blocked by the authorities but the kids running the Internet cafés have their ways around this and you'll have no problems logging on to check email, whatever the service.

If you are lugging around your own laptop then you can get connected in some of the better hotels by using an RJ-11 standard telephone connector.

DIGITAL RESOURCES

For a comprehensive list of Middle East and Arab world websites see the Regional Facts for the Visitor chapter; otherwise some useful Syria-specific websites include:

Cafe Syria Lots of general background info on sightseeing, the economy, history etc, plus practical stuff like links to airlines, banks, hotels. Plus it's updated regularly.
w www.cafe-syria.com

Goodbye Assad One for political perverts, a hagiographic tribute to the reign of former president Hafez al-Assad. Includes pictures of the funeral procession and tributes from world leaders.
w www.assad.org

Souria Online Youth oriented and gossipy social site devoted to hanging out in the Syrian capital. Want to cast a vote for your favourite Arab world mobile phone tone, well here's where to go.
w www.souria.com

Syria Online Gateway site with dozens of links organised by category (travel & tourism; media; society & culture). Check out the hints and tips page with postings from travellers.
w www.syriaonline.com

BOOKS

As well as this book, Lonely Planet publishes a highly detailed country guide, *Syria*. In LP's travel literature series 'Journeys' is *The Gates of Damascus* by Lieve Joris. Through her friendship with a local woman and family, Joris paints a grim and claustrophobic picture a million miles from the Syria most visitors will encounter – which is perhaps all the more reason to read the book.

Otherwise, there are two fine architectural guides to Syria; the better of them is *Monuments of Syria: An Historical Guide* by Ross Burns, which is a wonderfully comprehensive and opinionated gazetteer of Syria's castles, Islamic monuments and archaeological sites. It's widely available in Syria in a cheap locally published edition. The other guide is *Syria: A Historical and Architectural Guide* by Warwick Ball.

Cleopatra's Wedding Present by Robert Tewdwr Moss is a very individual take on Syria. His experiences (including an affair with a Palestinian commando) are unlikely to be shared by many but they do make for entertaining reading.

Of the various coffee-table titles *Hidden Damascus: Treasures of the Old City* by Brigid Keenan is a gorgeous volume illustrating the fantastic wealth of historic buildings in Damascus, most currently hidden away behind closed doors.

NEWSPAPERS & MAGAZINES

The English-language daily newspaper the *Syria Times* is published under direct government control and is predictably big on anti-Zionist, pro-Arab rhetoric and short on news. A limited selection of foreign newspapers and magazines is irregularly available in Damascus and Aleppo. Any articles on Syria or Lebanon are so lovingly torn out you'd hardly notice there was anything missing.

RADIO & TV

The Syrian Broadcasting Service seems to have dropped much of its foreign language broadcasting. For news of the world, you can tune into retransmitted BBC and VOA broadcasts. Try 9.41 MHz, 9.51 MHz, 21.7 MHz and 15.31 MHz for the BBC and 11.84 MHz for VOA. If you have a shortwave set you'll have no trouble.

Syrian TV reaches a large audience and programmes range from news and sport to American soaps. There is news in English on Syria 2 at around 10pm. An increasing number of hotels, even at the budget end, now have satellite TV with CNN and BBC World.

PHOTOGRAPHY

In Damascus and Aleppo there's a good choice of film available including Ektachrome, Elite, Kodak Gold and K-Max film, sold at specialist photo shops which seem to take pretty good care of their stock. Film generally costs as much as, if not more than, it does in the West.

Colour print processing costs vary depending where you go but in Damascus we paid S£25 for processing plus S£10 per print and the quality was fine.

TOILETS

Western toilets are standard but in some budget hotels and restaurants, and in cafés, especially outside Damascus and Aleppo, you will encounter the hole-in-the-floor variety. Toilet paper is not always available so it's a good idea to carry tissues.

HEALTH

No inoculations are required in order to enter Syria unless you are coming from a disease-affected area, but it is a good idea to have preventative shots for hepatitis A, polio, tetanus and typhoid before you go. If you plan on spending a great amount of time along the Euphrates River in the north of Syria, your doctor may also recommend that you take anti-malarial tablets such as chloroquine.

In the major towns the tap water is safe to drink but if your stomach is a bit delicate or you find yourself in out-of-the-way places, bottled water is widely available.

Medical services in Syria are well developed in the larger towns and cities, and many of the doctors have been trained overseas and speak English. Your embassy will usually be able to recommend a reliable doctor or hospital if the need arises.

For more information see the Health section in the Regional Facts for the Visitor chapter.

WOMEN TRAVELLERS

Compared to countries like Egypt, Turkey and parts of Israel, women travellers will experience comparatively little hassle in Syria. Foreign women are generally treated with courtesy. Even so, there will still always be a certain amount of unwanted predatory male attention. We've also had letters relating alarming experiences in Palmyra (voyeurism and groping), so look out there. To minimise the chance of any unpleasant encounters follow the advice given on clothing and behaviour in the Women Travellers section in the Regional Facts for the Visitor chapter.

BUSINESS HOURS

Government offices, such as immigration and tourism, are generally open from 8am to 2pm daily except Friday and holidays. Other offices and shops keep similar hours and often open again from 4pm to 6pm or 7pm. Most restaurants and a few small traders stay open on Friday.

Banks generally follow the government office hours but there are quite a few exceptions to the rule. Some branches keep their doors open for only three hours from 9am, while some exchange booths are open as late as 7pm.

Museums and sites tend to be closed on Tuesday.

PUBLIC HOLIDAYS

In addition to the main Islamic holidays described in the Regional Facts for the Visitor chapter, Syria celebrates the following public holidays:

New Year's Day 1 January – an official national holiday, but many businesses stay open

Christmas 7 January – a fairly low-key affair and only Orthodox-run businesses are closed for the day

Commemoration of the Revolution 8 March – celebrates the coming to power of the Arab Ba'ath Socialist Party

Commemoration of the Evacuation 17 April – celebrates the end of French occupation

Easter Different dates each year – the most important date in the Orthodox Christian calendar

May Day 1 May – an official national holiday

Martyrs' Day 6 May – honours all political martyrs who have died for Syria

SPECIAL EVENTS

There are probably only two special events worth most visitor's attention:

Bosra Festival This is a festival of music and theatre held every other September. It offers the chance to be part of an audience in the town's spectacular Roman amphitheatre.

Palmyra Festival Every April/May the desert ruins are the venue for this popular folk festival. There is horse and camel racing during the day, and music and dance performances are held in the ancient theatre by night.

COURSES

For would-be students of the Arabic language, there are several options in Damascus. The **Arabic Teaching Institute for Foreigners** (☎ 222 1538; PO Box 9340, Jadet ash-Shafei No 3, Mezzeh-Villat Sharqiyya), runs two courses: a short one in summer (June to September) and another in winter (October to May). The **Goethe Institut** and the **Centre Culturel Français** also run courses in colloquial Arabic.

ACCOMMODATION

There is only one so-called youth hostel in Syria, at Bosra, and the camping options are very limited. For the most part, it's hotels. The choice is reasonable; every town or city has at least one or two good budget options (typically charging S£400 to S£600 for a double, which is US$8 to US$12), with a fair number of reasonable back ups. If you can stretch to US$20 to US$30 for a double (which is the two- and three-star bracket) then there are some excellent value places. Surprisingly, it's at the top-end of the range that choices thin out; in many places it's one of the state-run Cham hotels (not recommended) or nothing. Sheraton and Le Meridien have a minor presence (a hotel each in Damascus and Aleppo, plus another Le Meridien in Lattakia) but they do no credit to the chains. The one bright spot is Aleppo, which has several beautiful 'boutique' hotels occupying converted old houses in the old quarters. If you're going to splash out, do it here.

In the low season (December to March) you should be able to get significant discounts at all hotels including those at the top end – we were told that even the hotels in the Cham chain will drop a double room rate by as much as US$50. Conversely, during the peak season months of July and August it can be extremely difficult to get a room in Damascus, Hama or Lattakia as these towns are flooded with Saudis fleeing the summer heat of the Gulf. At such times you really need to book in advance.

Most hotels will want to keep your passport overnight, usually in a drawer at the reception desk, so that they can fill in a standard police registration slip (sounds more sinister than it is).

Hotels rated two-star and up generally require payment in US dollars. The more expensive hotels sometimes accept credit cards and with some it is possible to change travellers cheques for the appropriate amounts.

FOOD

The food of its neighbours is well known through the worldwide proliferation of Lebanese and Turkish restaurants, but very little is ever heard of Syrian cuisine. Which makes it such as a pleasant surprise to discover just how good dining here can be. Syrian cuisine is very similar to that of Lebanon – which actually shouldn't come as any surprise considering the two countries only split 50 years ago.

Street-food staples are the ubiquitous felafel and shwarma, but even the cheapest of restaurants can usually lay on an excellent spread of various mezze, typically rounded off with meat from the grill. There are also a few local specialities to look out for, including *maqlubbeh*, which is steamed rice topped with grilled slices of eggplant or meat, grilled tomato and pine nuts, and *batorsh*, which is a base of *baba ghanoug* on top of which is lamb in a tomato sauce sprinkled with pistachios and peanuts. Also look out for regional specialities, like *kebab halebi* (Aleppan kebab), a standard kebab but served in a heavy, chopped tomato sauce, and *cherry kebab*, another Aleppan speciality served only in season and hard to find but extremely beautiful: balls of minced lamb served in a rich, thick cherry sauce.

A dessert native to the town of Hama, and well worth seeking out, is *halawat al-jibna* – a soft doughy pastry filled with cream cheese and topped with syrup and ice cream.

DRINKS

Copious amounts of both tea and coffee are consumed daily by the average Syrian – taken as described in the Drinks section of the Regional Facts for the Visitor. Syria produces its own beer (two kinds: Barada in the south; Ash-Sharq in the north), wine (quite drinkable, but pricey), and arak (like the French pastis or Greek ouzo). The latter is commonly drunk as an accompaniment to a meal.

Getting There & Away

AIR

Syria's main international airport is just outside Damascus. There's also a second international airport at Aleppo, but this is most frequently used by flights to and from countries of the ex-Soviet Union. Damascus has regular connections to Europe, other cities in the Middle East, Africa and Asia.

As it's not a popular destination you won't find much discounting on fares to Syria. Nevertheless, prices do vary from one agency to the other, so take the time to call around. At the time of writing the best deals were with either Air France, Alitalia or Turkish Airlines.

If you're planning to tour either Jordan or Turkey as well as Syria, you should consider flying to Amman or İstanbul, as a greater range of airlines serve those cities with a wider spread of fares. Another option worth looking into is taking a charter plane to Adana in southern Turkey and a local bus from there.

Departure Tax

There's a departure tax of S£200 payable at the airport.

LAND

Syria has land borders with Lebanon, Turkey, Jordan and Iraq. It also shares a border with Israel, namely the hotly disputed

Golan Heights but this is a definite no-go zone that's mined and is patrolled by UN peacekeepers.

Lebanon

There are plenty of buses from Damascus to Beirut (the journey take about four hours), although to travel direct to Baalbek the only option is a service taxi. You can also travel to Beirut via Tripoli from Homs and Lattakia by bus or service taxi; see the relevant city entries later in this chapter.

While the Lebanese have no embassies or consulates in Syria (because the Syrians don't recognise Lebanon as an independent entity) holders of passports from the following countries can get a visa at the border: Australia, Austria, Belgium, Canada, Denmark, Finland, France, Germany, Greece, Holland, Ireland, Italy, Japan, Malaysia, New Zealand, Norway, Portugal, South Korea, Spain, Switzerland, the UK and the US. A 48-hour transit visa is free, while a standard 15-day visa costs the equivalent of US$16 and a three-month visa is US$32. All other nationalities must obtain their Lebanese visa before arriving in Syria. Note that unless you have a multiple-entry Syrian visa in your passport you will have to buy a new visa to get back into Syria. Regulations on this are constantly changing but on our most recent visit the cost was US$50.

Turkey

There are several border crossings between Syria and Turkey. The busiest and most convenient links Antakya in Turkey with Aleppo via the Bab al-Hawa border station. This is the route taken by all cross-border buses including those direct from Damascus and Aleppo bound for İstanbul and all other Turkish destinations (for details of fares see the Getting There & Away sections for those cities).

An interesting alternative to the bus might be the weekly train from Aleppo to İstanbul (again, see the Aleppo section for details).

You can also make your way by microbus from Lattakia, on the Syrian coast, to the border post on the outskirts of the village of Kassab and on via Yayladağ to Antakya. Over in the far northeast of Syria there's another crossing at Qamishle for the southeastern Turkish town of Nusaybin.

This latter border crossing is open 9am to 3pm only.

While Turkish visas are issued at the border, you must already be in possession of a valid visa to enter Syria – unless you hold a passport of a country without Syrian representation, in which case you can get your visa at the border (see Visas earlier in this chapter).

Jordan

The main border crossing between Syria and Jordan is at Deraa/Ramtha. You can cross by direct bus, service taxi or by using a combination of local transport and walking – for details of the latter see the Deraa section later in this chapter.

From Damascus there are a couple of daily buses, for which you need to book in advance as demand for seats is high, or you can catch a service. There's also a twice-weekly train service – slow but interesting. For details of departure times and prices see the Getting There & Away part of the Damascus section.

Jordanian visas are issued at the border (JD10) or can be obtained in advance from the embassy in Damascus (see earlier in this chapter for the address). It's cheaper to get it at the border.

Iraq

The only open border crossing with Iraq is just south of Abu Kamal in the extreme east of the country. We have yet to hear of any foreigners making this crossing, although presumably if you possess a valid visa there's no reason why you can't.

SEA

There are no passenger boats operating between Syrian ports and any port in Europe or elsewhere at present.

Getting Around

AIR

Syrianair operates a reasonable internal air service and flights are cheap by international standards. Bear in mind that, given the time taken to get to and from airports, check in and so on, you're unlikely to save much time over the bus; the Damascus-Qamishle run is the only exception to this.

There are air services from Damascus to Aleppo (S£900/1800 one way/return), Deir ez-Zur (S£742/1484), Lattakia (S£532/1064) and Qamishle (S£1200/2400).

BUS

Syria has a well-developed road network and public transport is frequent and cheap. Distances are short and so journeys rarely take more than a few hours. Carry your passport at all times as you may need it for ID checks; you definitely will need it to buy tickets.

Several kinds of buses ply the same routes, but by far the most comfortable way to travel is by 'luxury' bus.

Luxury Bus

At one time the state-owned bus company Karnak had a monopoly on the road, but since the early 1990s it's been overtaken by a crop of private companies. Routes are few and the operators are all in fierce competition for passengers. Every city bus station (known locally as 'karaj', ie, garages) has a row of prefab huts which serve as booking offices for the various companies. Annoyingly, there's no central source of information giving departure times or prices so it's simply a case of walking around and finding out which company has the next bus to your desired destination. Fares vary little and the buses are all pretty much the same (large, newish, air-con). Seats are assigned at booking. A rigid no-smoking rule is imposed on most buses, and in the course of the journey a steward will distribute sweets and the occasional cup of water. A handful of companies do have the edge when it comes to the cleanliness of their vehicles and timekeeping, and we particularly recommend travelling with Qadmous, Al-Ahliah and Al-Rayan.

Karnak & Other Buses Karnak does still operate a shrinking network of services, but their distinctive orange-and-white buses are old and none too clean. Fares are usually about a third cheaper than those charged by the luxury buses but given that you're only talking a difference perhaps of less than a dollar...

There's also a third, even cheaper category of buses. These are really old, battered buses – rust buckets for which a punt on a ticket is akin to a gamble on whether the vehicle's going to make it or not. Needless to say, this is the cheapest way of covering long-distances between towns. These vehicles have their own garages separate from those of the luxury buses.

Minibus & Microbus

Minibuses operate on many of the shorter routes, eg, Hama–Homs, Homs–Lattakia, or Damascus–Deraa. They take about 20 people, are often luridly decorated (especially on the inside) and have no schedule, departing only when full. This means that on less popular routes you may have to wait quite some time until one fills up. Journey times are generally longer than with the other buses, as they set people down and pick them up at any and all points along the route – hence their other common name of 'stop-stops'.

The term microbus is blurred, but in general refers to the little white vans (mostly Japanese) with the sliding side-door. These are used principally to connect the major cities and towns with surrounding small towns and villages. They are replacing the clattering old minibuses with which they compete, and are more expensive. They follow set routes but along that route passengers can be picked up or set down anywhere. The fare is the same whatever distance you travel; pay the driver whatever the other passengers are paying.

TRAIN

Syria has a fleet of fairly modern trains made in Russia. They are inexpensive and punctual but the main disadvantage is that the stations are usually several kilometres from the town centres and services only ever seem to pass through in the dead of night.

First class is air-con with aircraft-type seats; 2nd class is the same without air-con.

The main line connects Damascus, Aleppo, Deir ez-Zur, Hassake and Qamishle. A secondary line runs from Aleppo to Lattakia, along the coast to Tartus and again inland to Homs and Damascus. For further details see the relevant Getting There & Away sections.

SERVICE TAXI

The service taxis (shared taxis; pronounced ser-**vees**) only operate on the major routes

Hostage to Hospitality

The number one rule of travel in Syria is to be flexible. It's not that the transport system is bad – on the contrary, all manner of four-wheeled vehicles go wherever you need to go, frequently, and for very little money. But you share your journey with local Syrians and that adds an element of unpredictability. As a foreigner – a guest – you can expect to receive frequent invitations to talk, share in food, and often to come back home or accompany your fellow passenger to wherever it is they're going. Depending on how open you are to this proffered hospitality, you can find yourself alighting from the bus several stops earlier than anticipated in the company of a new companion heading off to go for tea, meet the family, look at some photos, watch some TV... We've had letters from readers who've spent days with such spontaneous hosts.

All of this is wonderful as long as you're not in any kind of hurry. Anybody with rigid schedules and a strict quota of four sites a day should probably stick to luxury buses, but for anyone with a more relaxed attitude to sightseeing, then taking the locals up on their offers of tea and such is a fine way to experience the country through its people rather than just its old stones.

and can cost three times the microbus fare – sometimes more. Unless you're in a tearing hurry, there's really no need to use them.

CAR

Traffic runs on the right-hand side of the road in Syria. The speed limit in built-up areas is 60km/h, 70km/h on the open road and 110km/h on major highways. The roads are generally quite reasonable, but when heading off into the backblocks you will find that most signposting is in Arabic only. Night driving can be dangerous and is best avoided. A lack of street lighting combined with the poor state of the roads makes it potentially lethal.

Rental

Europcar has been joined by Budget and Avis, as well as a gaggle of sometimes dodgy local companies. With the latter, keep your eye on insurance arrangements, which seem quite lackadaisical. Budget's cheapest standard rate is US$45 a day for a Ford Fiesta or something similar, including all insurance and unlimited mileage. Rental for a week comes out at US$259. The local companies can be cheaper, but it's best to look around.

HITCHING

Hitching is easy as few people have private cars and it is an accepted means of getting around. Some payment is often expected, as drivers will take passengers to subsidise their own trip. As always, women should think twice before hitching alone. It's been done without incident, but it is risky.

Damascus   دمشق

☎ 011

Damascus (Ash-Sham to locals) is the capital of Syria and, with an estimated population of six million, its largest city. It owes its existence to the Barada River, which rises high up in the Jebel Libnan ash-Sharqiyya (Anti-Lebanon Range). The waters give life to the Ghouta oasis, making settlement possible in an otherwise uninhabitable area.

It retains much of the mystery of the oriental bazaars and the gracious, somewhat decayed charm of some of the Islamic world's greatest monuments. Exuding just a hint of its more remote past too, Damascus is well worth spending a few days exploring. Many travellers find themselves caught up in its spell and stay much longer.

HISTORY

Damascus is claimed to be the oldest continuously inhabited city in the world – there was an urban settlement here as long ago as 5000 BC. Later it was a Persian capital, fell to Alexander the Great, became a Greek centre and then a major Roman city. In AD 635, with Byzantine power on the decline, Damascus fell to the armies of Islam and rose to primacy in the rapidly expanding Muslim Arab empire. In 1200 it was sacked by the Mongols and then endured centuries of slow decline under the Mamluks and the Ottomans before eventually passing to the French mandate and finally achieving independence.

ORIENTATION

The city centre is compact and finding your way around on foot is no problem. The heart of the city is Martyrs' Square (known to locals as Al-Merjeh), and many of the cheap hotels and restaurants are close by.

The main street, Sharia Said al-Jabri, begins at the Hejaz train station and runs northeast, changes its name a couple of times and finishes at the Central Bank building. The entire street is about 1km long and on it you'll find the central post office, tourist office, various airline offices and many mid-range restaurants and hotels.

Half a mile east of Martyrs' Square is the old city, still ringed by its old Arab walls. For visitors, this is where most of the city's attractions lie.

INFORMATION
Immigration Office

For visa extensions, the **central immigration office** (*Sharia Filasteen; open 8am-2pm Sat-Thur*) is one block west of the Baramke bus station. Go to the 2nd floor to begin filling in the three forms, for which you'll need three photos (the Kodak Express just west of Hejaz train station can do them in 10 minutes; S£200). You can get extensions of up to one month. It costs S£25 and takes a working day to process – pick up your passport at 1pm the following day.

Re-entry visas are acquired at another **immigration office** (*Sharia al-Furat; open 8am-2pm Sat-Thur*), just west of Martyrs' Square.

Tourist Offices

The **main tourist office** (*☎ 232 3953; Sharia 29 Mai; open 9.30am-2pm, 4pm-7pm*) is just up from Saahat Yousef al-Azmeh in the centre of town. There's a second, smaller **office** (*☎ 221 0122; Ministry of Tourism Bldg*) by the Takiyya as-Suleimaniyya, near the National Museum. Take the given opening times with a pinch of salt.

Money

There are several branches of the **Commercial Bank of Syria** around town, as well as exchange booths where you can change money fairly easily. The offices on Martyrs' Square and across from Hejaz station will change travellers cheques.

The local **AmEx agent** (*☎ 221 7813, fax 222 3707, e amexrep@net.sy; Sharia Balkis*)

is on the 1st floor above the Sudan Airways office, on the small street running between Sharias al-Mutanabi and Fardous. It can't give advances against your credit card or cash cheques, it can only replace stolen ones. Thomas Cook is represented by **Nahas Travel** (*☎ 223 2000, fax 223 6002, e nahasent@net.sy; Sharia Fardous*). Again, it can't cash travellers cheques, only arrange for replacements for any stolen. Nahas also represents MasterCard and Visa in Syria; although it can't give cash advances against credit cards the office can probably point you in the direction of a business that can.

Post & Communications

The **central post office** (*Sharia Said al-Jabri; open 8am-7pm Sat-Thur, 8am-1pm Fri & holidays*) is just downhill from the Hejaz train station, but if you just want stamps you can also get them at the bookshop at the Cham Palace hotel.

The **telephone office** (*Sharia an-Nasr; open 24 hrs*) is a block east of the Hejaz train station, but given that there are card phones on almost every street corner, you're only likely to need this place if you have a fax to send (for which it's necessary to present your passport).

Internet & Email Access

The following are a few of the many Internet cafés in Damascus:

Amigo Net (*☎ 542 1694*) Sharia al-Kassaa, north of Bab Touma; open 24 hours, except for cleaning 8am to 10am. S£50 per half hour.
@ural Internet Service (*☎ 231 1253*) Ash-Sharq al-Awsat Building, 1st floor, Sharia al-Itehad, north of Martyrs' Square; open 10am to 11pm daily. S£50 per half hour.
Zoni Internet (*☎ 232 4670*) Abdin Building, 3rd floor, Sharia Hammam al-Ward, off Sharia Souq Saroujah; open 10am to 11pm Saturday to Thursday, 1pm to 11pm Friday; S£40 per half hour. On the 1st floor of the same building is also Internet Privacy, which is supposedly cheaper but was closed when we visited.

Bookshops

Librairie Avicenne (*☎ 224 4477; 4 Sharia Attuhami; open 9am-6m Sat-Thur*), a block southeast of the Cham Palace hotel is possibly the best bookshop in the country as far as foreign-language publications are concerned – though that's not saying much. It

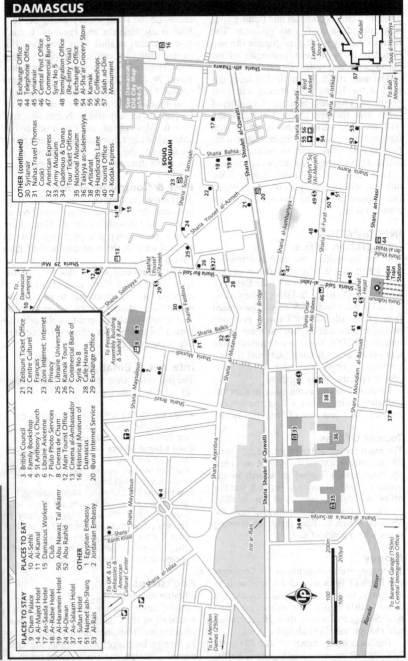

DAMASCUS

PLACES TO STAY
9 Cham Palace
14 Al-Majed Hotel
17 As-Saada Hotel
18 Ar-Rabie Hotel
19 Al-Haramein Hotel
24 Al-Diwan
37 As-Salaam Hotel
41 Sultan Hotel
51 Najmet ash-Sharq
53 Al-Rais

PLACES TO EAT
10 Al-Sehhi
11 Al-Kamal
15 Damascus Workers'
   Club
50 Abu Nawas; Tal Alkamr
52 Abu Rashid

OTHER
1 Egyptian Embassy
2 Jordanian Embassy

3 British Council
4 Family Bookshop
5 St Anthony's Church
6 Librairie Avicenne
7 Pluto Photo Services
8 Cinema de Cham
12 Main Tourist Office
13 Cinema al-Ambassador
16 @ural Internet Service

21 Zeitouni Ticket Office
22 Centre Culturel
   Français
23 Zoni Internet; Internet
   Privacy
25 Librairie Universalle
26 Karnak Tours
27 Commercial Bank of
   Syria No 8
28 Cafe Havana
29 Exchange Office

OTHER (continued)
30 Syrianair
31 Nahas Travel (Thomas
   Cook)
32 American Express
33 Army Museum
34 Qadmous & Damas
   Tour Ticket Offices
35 National Museum
36 Takiyya as-Suleimaniyya
38 Artisanat
39 Handicrafts Lane
40 Tourist Office
42 Kodak Express

43 Exchange Office
44 Telephone Office
45 Syrianair
46 Central Post Office
47 Commercial Bank of
   Syria No 5
48 Immigration Office
   (Re-Entry Visas)
49 Exchange Office
54 Al-Sha'ar Grocery Store
55 Karnak
56 Coffeeshops
57 Salah ad-Din
   Monument

also has a selection of days-old international press. The **Family Bookshop** (☎ 222 7006; Saahat al-Najmeh; open 9am-6pm Sat-Thur), **Librairie Universalle**, just off Sharia Yousef al-Azmeh, plus the bookshops at the Cham Palace, Sheraton and Le Meridien Damas hotels also all have a small selection of airport novels, and coffee-table type books on Syria and the Islamic world. The hotel bookshops also carry Time and Newsweek, plus, if you're lucky, a few two- or three-day-old international newspapers.

Cultural Centres

Bring your passport as many cultural centres require ID before they'll let you enter.

American Cultural Center (☎ 333 8413, w www .usembassy.state.gov/damascus) 87 Sharia Ata al-Ayyoubi. Open 1pm-5pm Sun-Thur.
British Council (☎ 333 0631, fax 332 1467, w www.britishcouncil.org/syria) Sharia Karim al-Khalil, off Sharia Maysaloun. Open 9am-8pm Sun-Thur, 10am-5pm Sat.
Centre Culturel Français (☎ 224 6181, fax 231 6194) off Sharia Yousef al-Azmeh. Open 9am-9pm Mon-Sat.

OLD CITY

Most of the sights of Damascus are in the old city, which is surrounded by what was initially a **Roman wall**. The wall itself has been flattened and rebuilt several times over the past 2000 years. The best preserved section is between Bab as-Salaama (the Gate of Safety) and Bab Touma (Thomas's Gate – named for a son-in-law of Emperor Heraclius), best experienced by following the road that runs along the outside of the wall.

Next to the **citadel** (closed to the public) is the entrance to the main covered market, the **Souq al-Hamidiyya**, constructed in the late 19th century and recently restored to its original state. At the far end of this wide shop-lined avenue is an arrangement of Corinthian columns supporting a decorated lintel – which is the remains of the **western gate** of the old Roman Temple of Jupiter dating from the 3rd century AD. Beyond the columns, across a flagged square, is the Umayyad Mosque.

Umayyad Mosque

Converted from a Byzantine cathedral (which occupied the site of the former Roman Temple of Jupiter), the mosque (ad-mission S£50) was built in AD 705. The outstanding feature is the golden mosaics, which adorn several facades around the central courtyard. The three minarets, although subsequently altered, date back to the original construction. The tourist entrance to the mosque is from the north side, which is also where you'll find the small ticket office. All women, and men in shorts, have to don the black robes supplied. Photography is permitted.

In the small garden north of the mosque's walls is the modest, red-domed **Mausoleum of Saladin**, the resting place of one of the greatest heroes of Arab history (see the boxed text 'Saladin' in the Facts about the Region chapter). The mausoleum was originally built in 1193 and restored with funds made available by Kaiser Wilhelm II of Germany during his visit to Damascus in 1898. Admission is included in the price of the Umayyad Mosque ticket.

North of the Mosque

Northwest of Saladin's mausoleum is the 13th-century **Madrassa az-Zahiriyya** (open 9am-5pm daily), within which is buried Sultan Beybars, another Islamic warrior hero, this time of the Mamluk dynasty. It was Beybars who won several decisive victories over the Crusaders, driving them from the region.

Also near the Umayyad Mosque is the modern Iranian-built Shiite **Sayyida Ruqayya Mosque**, which is dedicated to the daughter of the martyr Hussein, son of Ali. It stands out for its decoration (covered in gold and shades of blue) and overall style, a quite alien, but very striking, Persian introduction.

South of the Mosque

The **Azem Palace** (adult/student S£300/15; open 9am-4pm Wed-Mon in winter, 9am-6pm Wed-Mon rest of year), south of the Umayyad Mosque, was built in 1749 by the governor of Damascus, As'ad Pasha al-Azem. It's fashioned in typical Damascene style of striped stonework, achieved by alternating layers of black basalt and limestone. The rooms of the modest palace are magnificent, decorated with inlaid tile work and the most exquisite painted ceilings.

Swinging back to the west, the **Madrassa an-Nuri** is the mausoleum of Saladin's predecessor Nureddin. Just south of the Souq

DAMASCUS – OLD CITY

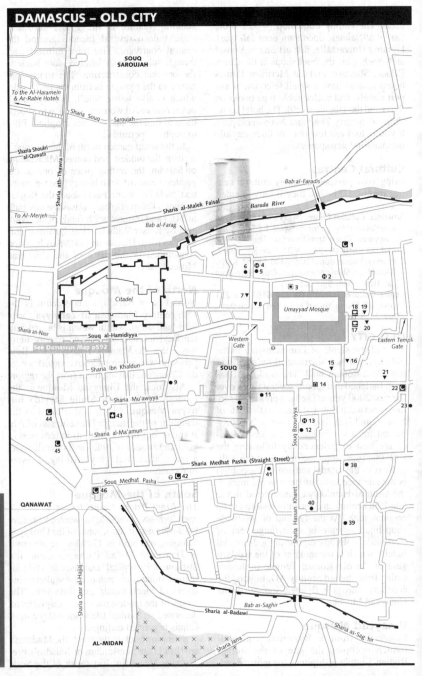

SOUQ
SAROUJAH

To the Al-Haramein
& Ar-Rabie Hotels

Sharia Souq - Saroujah

Sharia Shoukri
al-Quwatli

Sharia ath-Thawra

To Al-Merjeh

Bab al-Faradis

Sharia al-Malek Faisal   Barada River

Bab al-Farag

Citadel

Sharia an-Nasr

Souq al-Hamidiyya

Western
Gate

Eastern Temple
Gate

Umayyad Mosque

Sharia ibn Khaldun

SOUQ

Sharia Mu'awiyya

Sharia al-Ma'amun

Souq Bzouriyya

Sharia Medhat Pasha (Straight Street)

Souq Medhat Pasha

QANAWAT

Sharia Qasr al-Hajjaj

Sharia Hassan Kharet

Bab as-Saghir

Sharia al-Badawi

Sharia Jarra

Sharia as-Saghir

AL-MIDAN

SYRIA

See Damascus Map p592

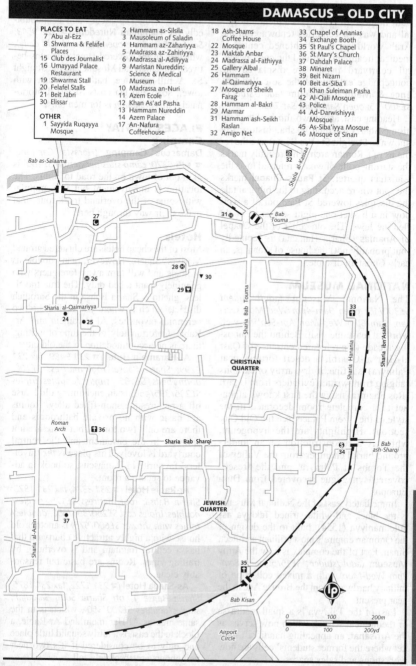

DAMASCUS – OLD CITY

PLACES TO EAT
7 Abu al-Ezz
8 Shwarma & Felafel Places
15 Club des Journalist
16 Umayyad Palace Restaurant
19 Shwarma Stall
20 Felafel Stalls
21 Beit Jabri
30 Elissar

OTHER
1 Sayyida Ruqayya Mosque
2 Hammam as-Silsila
3 Mausoleum of Saladin
4 Hammam az-Zahariyya
5 Madrassa az-Zahiriyya
6 Madrassa al-Adiliyya
9 Maristan Nureddin; Science & Medical Museum
10 Madrassa an-Nuri
11 Azem Ecole
12 Khan As'ad Pasha
13 Hammam Nureddin
14 Azem Palace
17 An-Nafura Coffeehouse
18 Ash-Shams Coffee House
22 Mosque
23 Maktab Anbar
24 Madrassa al-Fathiyya
25 Gallery Albal
26 Hammam al-Qaimariyya
27 Mosque of Sheikh Farag
28 Hammam al-Bakri
29 Marmar
31 Hammam ash-Seikh Raslan
32 Amigo Net
33 Chapel of Ananias
34 Exchange Booth
35 St Paul's Chapel
36 St Mary's Church
37 Dahdah Palace
38 Minaret
39 Beit Nizam
40 Beit as-Siba'i
41 Khan Suleiman Pasha
42 Al-Qali Mosque
43 Police
44 Ad-Darwishiyya Mosque
45 As-Siba'iyya Mosque
46 Mosque of Sinan

Bab as-Salaama

Sharia al-Kassaa

Bab Touma

Sharia al-Qaimariyya

CHRISTIAN QUARTER

Sharia Bab Touma

Sharia Hanania

Sharia Ibn'Asaka

Roman Arch

Sharia Bab Sharqi

Bab ash-Sharqi

JEWISH QUARTER

Sharia al-Amin

Bab Kisan

Airport Circle

0   100   200m
0   100   200yd

SYRIA

al-Hamidiyya, the **Maristan Nureddin** was built in the 12th century as a mental hospital and was for centuries renowned in the Arab world as an enlightened centre of medical treatment. Around the cool, peaceful courtyard inside are displayed the hodgepodge exhibits of the so-called **Science & Medical Museum** (adult/student S£300/15; open 8am-2pm Sat-Thur).

Heading east, about two-thirds of the way along Sharia Medhat Pasha, historically known as **Straight St** (Via Recta), are the remains of a **Roman arch**. This roughly marks the starting point of what's referred to as the Christian quarter. **St Paul's Chapel** marks the spot where according to the biblical tale the disciples lowered St Paul out of a window in a basket one night so that he could flee the Jews. The old cellar of the **Chapel of Ananias** (Sharia Hanania) is reputedly (but probably not) the house of Ananias, an early Christian disciple.

NATIONAL MUSEUM

The National Museum (adult/student S£300/15; open 9am-4pm Wed-Mon Oct-Jan, 9am-6pm Wed-Mon Apr-Sept) is well worth at least one visit. Behind the imposing facade (the relocated entrance of Qasr al-Heir al-Gharbi, a desert fortress near Palmyra) is a fine, if dry, array of exhibits ranging from written cylinders from Ugarit (Ras Shamra) using the first known alphabet to a complete room decorated in the style of the Azem Palace (see the Old City section). Highlights are the hypogeum, which is a reconstruction of an underground burial chamber from the Valley of the Tombs at Palmyra, and the fresco-covered synagogue recovered from Dura Europos.

Immediately east of the National Museum is the black-and-white striped **Takiyya as-Suleimaniyya** (1554), built to the design of the Ottoman empire's most brilliant architect, Sinan. Part of the complex is now the **Army Museum** (adult/student S£15/5; open 8am-2pm Wed-Mon) with a mixed collection of military hardware from the Bronze Age to the near present.

East of the Takiyya is a small madrassa or theological school, which now serves as the **Artisanat**, an appealing handicraft market where the former students' cells are now workshops and sales spaces.

HAMMAMS

The best of the Damascus baths is undoubtedly the **Hammam Nureddin** (☎ 222 9513; Souq al-Bzouriyya; open 9am-midnight daily), which is in the covered street that runs between the Umayyad Mosque and the Straight St. A full massage, bath and sauna with towel, soap and tea costs S£240. Unfortunately, this hammam is for men only.

PLACES TO STAY
Camping

Damascus Camping (Harasta Camping; ☎ 445 5870; camp sites per person S£250) is 4km out of town on the road to Homs. The location is inconvenient but it is popular with some of the overland truck tours that make their way through here.

Hotels

Most of the cheap hotels are clustered around Martyrs' Square. However, many double as brothels and will turn away foreigners who genuinely want a bed only. The true travellers' ghetto is Sharia Bahsa in the Saroujah district, which is where you'll find the two perennial favourites, Al-Haramein and Ar-Rabie. Unfortunately, at the time of writing, there is no accommodation in the old city.

Al-Haramein Hotel (☎ 231 9489, fax 231 4299; Sharia Bahsa; roof mattress S£100, dorm beds S£185, singles/doubles/triples S£235/395/450) is an enchanting old house off a picturesque shop-filled alley. Rooms are basic with no private bathrooms and there are only two toilets, but there are hot showers in the basement and the central courtyard is lovely. This place is *the* travellers' favourite in Damascus, so book in advance to secure a room.

Ar-Rabie Hotel (☎ 231 8374, fax 231 1875; Sharia Bahsa; roof mattress S£175, singles/doubles/triples cost S£250/395/550, doubles/triples with shower S£600/675) is another old house with a highly attractive courtyard that has a central fountain and is overhung by trailing vines. Rooms are basic but reasonably clean.

As-Saada Hotel (☎ 231 1722, fax 231 1875; Sharia Bahsa 1, off Sharia Souq Saroujah; singles/doubles S£200/350), which is in the same area as Al-Haramein and Ar-Rabie, a block to the east, is a fairly squalid little place and only to be considered if it's two near neighbours are absolutely full.

Najmet ash-Sharq (☎ 222 9139; Martyrs' Square; singles/doubles S£300/500) is perhaps the best bet if the two Sharia al-Bahsa favourites are full. The rooms are basic but clean and most have immaculate en suite bathrooms. The location is great, right on the square. Clientele are predominantly Arab and little or no English is spoken.

Al-Rais (☎ 221 4252; Sharia as-Sandjakdar; doubles with bathroom S£500), one block east and south of Martyrs' Square, has basic rooms which have recently benefited from a fresh paint job. Some have also gained sparkling new en suite bathrooms. Again, clientele are predominantly Arab and little or no English is spoken.

Sultan Hotel (☎ 222 5768, fax 224 0372; Sharia Mousalam al-Baroudi; singles/doubles US$21/27, breakfast US$3), just west of the Hejaz train station, is justifiably the most popular (with Western travellers) of the mid-range hotels. Some of the rooms are shabby (although most are air-con with en suite bathrooms), but the desk staff and level of service are exceptional: they speak several languages, will reconfirm flights at no cost, make bus, train or onward hotel bookings, arrange car rentals and offer all-round good advice on travel in Syria. There's a small library of books to borrow, a guests' notice board and a reception/breakfast area with satellite TV. The hotel offers a pick-up service from the airport for US$15.

Al-Diwan (☎ 231 8567; Sharia Souq Saroujah; singles/doubles US$24/28) had just been refitted when we visited and the rooms were immaculate – almost Scandinavian in their white-pine pristineness. All come with gleaming en suite bathroom, air-con and TV. The rates include breakfast – it's exceptional value. Not to be confused with the nearby Iwan.

As-Salaam Hotel (☎ 221 6674, fax 221 5031; Sharia ar-Rais; singles/doubles US$22/29) is in a quiet location, just south of the Takiyya as-Suleimaniyya and National Museum. It's extremely clean and all rooms come with en suite bathroom, air-con and fridge. It's a good mid-range fall back if the Sultan is full.

Al-Majed Hotel (☎ 232 3300, fax 232 3304; doubles US$40) just off Sharia 29 Mai, behind the Cinema al-Ambassador, is new and modern with spacious air-con rooms with fridge, satellite TV and spotless

new en suite bathrooms. For the quality the price is hard to beat.

PLACES TO EAT

The following restaurants are ordered approximately by cost, starting with the cheapest. None of these places accept credit cards unless stated otherwise.

New City

The side streets off Martyrs' Square are crowded with cheap eateries, mostly offering shwarma and felafel, while some of the pastry shops also do some good savouries – we particularly recommend **Abu Rashid**, which is at the top of the steps down the alley at the southeast corner of the square.

Abu Nawas (☎ 2229139; Martyrs' Square; meals S£150; open 7am-2am daily) and **Tal Alkamr** (☎ 221 0764; Martyrs' Square; meals S£150; open 7am-2am daily) are two adjacent restaurants on the southwest corner of the square. Both are clean, efficiently run and open for breakfast. They serve near identical selections of mezze, kebabs and grilled chicken. Beer is served.

Al-Arabi off the southwest corner of the square, is the name of two adjacent cheap restaurants, both run by the same management and sharing the same extensive menu with an unusually wide range of meat and vegetable dishes. The food is hit and miss and there are no prices given, but for a main dish plus a couple of mezze you can expect to pay S£200. Seats out on the pavement are preferable to being inside. No alcohol.

Al-Sehhi (☎ 221 1555; Sharia al-Abed, off Sharia 29 Mai; open noon-midnight daily) is a modest family restaurant that confines itself to the basics – mezze, grilled meats and very good *fattah* (an oven-baked dish of chickpeas, minced meat or chicken and bread soaked in *tahina*; S£70). It's clean and efficient and, even better, it's one of the few places that has a menu (in English and Arabic) with the prices given. No alcohol.

Al-Kamal (☎ 222 1494; Sharia 29 Mai; open 11am-midnight daily; mezze S£15-30, mains around S£90), which is next to the main tourist office, has a menu that features many home-style dishes like mixed vegetable stews but the best are on the changing daily menu – try the *kabsa*, spiced rice with chicken or lamb. Expect to pay around S£100 to S£150 per head. No alcohol.

Damascus Workers' Club (*open 5pm-late Sat-Thur*) is a garden restaurant in the middle of the city. Food is the standard fare of mezze and grilled meats at decent prices. Expect to pay about S£150 per head for a full meal, without drinks (alcohol is served). Hard to find, it's through a modest door in a wall opposite the Majed Hotel, behind the Cinema al-Ambassador.

Old City

In the small alley east of the Umayyad Mosque, just past the two coffee houses, are a couple of very good shwarma places and a stall that does probably the best value felafel in town – a truly fat felafel with salad will cost you S£25. There's another collection of felafel and shwarma hole-in-the-wall eateries in the covered market lane that runs north off Souq al-Hamidiyya, just before you reach the mosque.

The real joy are the numerous restaurants in renovated old Damascene houses; the settings are superb, often with a gurgling fountain and tables under jasmine or orange trees. The food is usually equally excellent.

Beit Jabri (*Jabri House*; ☎ 544 3200; 14 Sharia as-Sawwaf; open 9.30am-12.30am daily) is an informal café in the partially restored courtyard of an old Damascene house. The menu runs from breakfasts and omelettes to oriental mezze and mains. The lamb *fattah* is excellent. Fresh juices are served as well as nargileh (water pipe). Alcohol is not served, but most credit cards are accepted.

Club des Journalist (☎ 223 6543; Sharia Hamrawi; open noon until late) is a relaxed restaurant, again in the courtyard of an old house which has been sympathetically restored. The food is standard fare (no menu), but it's very good and also very cheap – when we dined here four mezze, two grilled meat dishes, two fresh juices, coffee and nargileh resulted in a bill of just under S£550. No alcohol.

Umayyad Palace Restaurant (☎ 222 0826; Sharia Masbagha al-Khadra; open noon-2am daily) is a large atmospheric basement venue, down an alley just south of the Umayyad Mosque. It's set up for tour groups, offering a decent buffet lunch at S£350 a head or dinner at S£600, plus performances by whirling dervishes at 9pm nightly, and makes for a fun night out. No alcohol.

Elissar (☎ 542 4300; Sharia ad-Dawamneh, Bab Touma; open noon until late daily) offers perhaps the best dining in Damascus. It's an enormous old house with tables filling the courtyard and two upper levels of terraces. While the menu of typical Syrian cuisine offers few surprises, the food is sublime. You can expect a meal for two of several mezze, two grilled meat dishes and a quarter bottle of arak to cost around S£700. It's money well spent. Reservations are recommended. Accepts AmEx, Diners Club, MasterCard, Visa.

ENTERTAINMENT

The finest place to relax in Damascus is at either of the two coffee houses, **An-Nafura** or **Ash-Shams**, nestled in the shadow of the Umayyad Mosque's eastern wall. **Gallery Albal** (☎ 544 5794; Sharia Shaweesh; open 9.30am-12.30am daily), which is about a five-minute walk from the coffeehouses east along Qaimariyya, is a loud and studenty Western-style café with an art gallery above.

Bar-wise, the most convenient haunt for backpackers is the **Karnak**, above the Hotel Siyaha on Martyrs' Square – just head up the stairs in the street entrance off the square. You can eat here, but really it's more a serious drinking place with patrons knocking back the beers (S£75) or arak until 2am. You wouldn't bring your mother here. On the other hand, she'd probably love **Damascus Workers' Club** – see Places to Eat. Though people do eat here, plenty take a table and just order a beer (S£55).

In the old city, the area around Bab Touma is a big nightlife hang-out. The most popular place at the time of writing was **Marmar** (☎ 544 6425; Sharia ad-Dawanneh; open 8pm until late) a bar/restaurant that turns club, complete with DJ and heaving sweaty bodies on Thursday and Friday nights.

Most of the cinemas around show pretty appalling fare. **Cinema de Cham** (Sharia Maysaloun; tickets S£150), at the Cham Palace hotel, is the exception. It regularly screens mainstream Hollywood fare in its two wide-screen auditoriums. The only way to find out what's showing is to drop by.

GETTING THERE & AWAY

Air

There are several **Syrianair offices** (☎ 223 2154, 223 2159, 222 9000) scattered about the city centre (for example, in Sharia Fardous and on Sharia Said al-Jabri across from the post office). The telephone number for Damascus airport is ☎ 543 0201/9.

From Damascus Syrianair flies to Aleppo (S£900 one way, one hour, once or twice daily), Deir ez-Zur (S£742, one hour, thrice weekly), Qamishle (S£1200, 80 minutes, thrice weekly) and Lattakia (S£532, 45 minutes, twice weekly).

Most of the other airline offices are grouped across from the Cham Palace hotel on Sharia Maysaloun or one block south on Sharia Fardous.

Bus & Microbus

There are two main bus stations in Damascus: **Harasta** (karajat Harasta), which has luxury bus services to the north, and **Baramke** (karajat Baramki), which has services to the south, plus international services to Jordan, Lebanon, Egypt and the Gulf. In addition there are several other minibus and microbus stations serving regional destinations.

Harasta station is about 6km northwest of the city centre. All the big private bus companies have their offices here, including Al-Ahliah and Qadmous. Prices are much of a muchness and average one-way fares include Aleppo (S£150, five hours), Deir ez-Zur (S£175, six hours), Hama (S£85 to S£90, 2½ hours), Homs (S£70, two hours), Lattakia (S£120 to S£150, 4½ hours), Palmyra (S£130, four hours) and Tartus (S£100 to S£110, 3½ hours). To get up to Harasta you can take a microbus from Martyrs' Square for S£5 or a taxi will cost S£50 maximum.

Baramke, which is about a 15- to 20-minute walk southwest of Martyrs' Square, is where you go for services to Bosra, Deraa and Suweida, as well as to Jordan and Lebanon. The station occupies a square block, which is organised in four quarters; as you approach from the north, in front to the left are local microbus services and behind are the buses to the south; the front right quarter is for service taxis to Beirut and Amman, behind is the Karnak lot.

From here Karnak runs buses to Beirut (S£175, 4½ hours, eight daily) between 7am and 6.30pm, plus two buses a day at 7am and 3pm to Amman (US$6 or JD5, no Syrian pounds accepted).

Buses to İstanbul (S£1500, 30 hours) and other Turkish destinations such as Antakya

(S£350) and Ankara (S£1200) all go from Harasta. There are frequent departures during the day – just show up and book a ticket on the next bus out.

Note that if you are on a tight budget it's cheaper to get local transport to Aleppo and then to the border from where there are Turkish buses.

The Aman bus company has a daily service to Riyadh (S£1500) at 11am, one to Jeddah (S£1000) on Tuesday, Thursday and Saturday, and buses to Kuwait (S£2500) on Saturday, Wednesday and Thursday. These buses go from the Baramke terminal and tickets should be bought in advance.

Train

Although one of the landmarks of central Damascus is the Hejaz station, few trains actually depart from there. Instead, they go from the **Khaddam station** (☎ 888 8678), about 5km southwest of the centre (you'll have to take a taxi to get there). Trains are very infrequent and slow. There's service to Aleppo (1st/2nd class S£85/57, six hours, once daily) departing at 4pm and travelling via Homs and Hama, and Lattakia (S£90/60, six hours, once weekly) departing at 3pm Thursday and travelling via Tartus. There's also a train to İstanbul (sleeper/1st-class seat US$66/33, 42 hours, once weekly) departing at 5.30am Tuesday; tickets should be bought in advance.

The only trains leaving from the **Hejaz station** (☎ 221 7247) are the summer season (June to October) services up to the hill resorts northwest of the capital, and the twice weekly services to Amman (S£160, eight to 10 hours), which depart at 8am Monday and Thursday. Book your ticket at least a day in advance.

Service Taxi

There is a service-taxi station which is part of the Baramke garage. Taxis leave throughout the day and night for Amman (S£385 or JD5.500, five hours) and Beirut (S£191 to S£291, three hours).

GETTING AROUND
To/From the Airport

The airport is 26km southeast of Damascus. There's a Karnak airport service that runs between the airport forecourt and the southwest corner of the Baramke garage (S£20, 30 minutes). Departures are every half hour between 6am and midnight.

A taxi into the city centre organised at the desk in the arrivals hall costs US$10. If you're taking a taxi from the centre out to the airport, expect to pay anything from S£250 to S£500 (US$5 to US$10), depending on your bargaining skills.

Bus & Taxi

Damascus is well served with a local bus and microbus network, but as the centre is so compact you'll rarely have to use them. All the taxis are yellow and there are hundreds of them. A ride across town should never cost more than S£25.

South of Damascus

Much of the area from Damascus south to the Jordanian border, which is about 100km away, is intensively farmed, fertile agricultural land.

Around the border and to the southeast, the good soil gives way to an unyielding black basalt plain, and the region is known as the Hauran. The capital of the Hauran is **Suweida**, 75km south of Damascus. It has a good **museum** with some fine mosaics, and a 15-minute bus ride to the northeast is **Qanawat**, a small village studded with Roman remains including those of a Roman temple complex. You get to Suweida (S£40, 1¾ hours) with Damas Tours, Al-Muhib or Al-Wassim, all of whom operate out of Damascus' Baramke garage.

To the west of Suweida the land rises to the Golan Heights, occupied by Israel since 1967 and the principal bone of contention in the on-again off-again Israeli-Syrian peace talks.

DERAA درعا
☎ 015

There's not a lot of interest in this southern town, 100km from Damascus, although most travellers have to pass through to get to the ruins at Bosra or to the border with Jordan. We do not recommend staying here overnight but if you have to then there is a clutch of grotty hotels on the main drag, Sharia Ibrahim Hanano. Of these, **Orient Palace Hotel** (Ash-Sharq; ☎ 238 304; doubles US$24) is easily the best.

Getting There & Away

The bus station lies about 3km east of the centre of town. Buses operated by Al-Wassim and As-Soukor run between Deraa and the Baramke garage in Damascus, costing S£50 and taking just under 1½ hours.

Jordan Service taxis shuttle between the bus stations in Deraa and Ramtha (on the Jordanian side), and cost S£150 or JD2 per person. Alternatively, you can hitch a ride or walk.

BOSRA بصرة
☎ 015

The town of Bosra is 40km east of Deraa. Once important for its location at the crossroads of major trade and, under the Muslims, pilgrimage routes, it is now little more than a backwater. But what a weird and wonderful backwater it is. Apart from having possibly the best preserved Roman theatre in the Middle East, the rest of the town is built in, around and over old sections of Roman buildings, and made almost entirely out of black basalt blocks.

Bosra makes for an easy day trip from Damascus.

Things to See

The **citadel** (adult/student S£300/15, open 9am-6pm daily Apr-Sept, 9am-4pm daily Oct-Mar) is a curious construction as it is largely a fortified **Roman theatre**. The two structures are in fact one – the fort was built around the theatre to make it an impregnable stronghold. The first walls were built during the Umayyad and Abbasid periods, with further additions being made in the 11th century by the Fatimids.

The big surprise on entering the citadel is the magnificent 15,000 seat theatre – a rarity among Roman theatres in that it is completely freestanding rather than built into the side of a hill.

Other sites around the small town include various monumental gates, colonnades, Roman baths, vast cisterns, and the Mosque of Omar, which dates to the 12th century.

Places to Stay & Eat

Bosra has the most unusual accommodation in all Syria – a **hostel** in one of the towers inside the citadel. It's extremely basic, just a room with some beds in it, and you'd be wise to bring a sleeping bag or at least your own sheets, but it's a unique experience and you're free to wander the fortress and citadel all night. There's a shower and toilet available and the cost is S£100 per person (in addition to the S£300 entrance).

Bosra's only other accommodation option is the expensive yet unappealing **Bosra Cham Palace** (☎ 790 882/3, fax 790 446; singles/ doubles US$100/120).

Getting There & Away
Two companies run buses between Bosra and Damascus (S£50, 1¾ hours): Damas Tours and Al-Muhib, whose offices are in the southeast quarter of Baramke garage. Both have departures every two hours starting at 8am, then 10am and through until 8pm. If you've just missed a bus then take a minibus or microbus via Deraa. The whole trip, Damascus-Deraa-Bosra, takes around two hours and costs S£34 by minibus or S£65 by smaller, faster microbus.

Mediterranean Coast شاطرء البحر المتوسط

The 180km-long Syrian coastline is dominated by the rugged mountain range that runs along its entire length. The extremely fertile and heavily cultivated coastal strip is narrow in the north and widens towards the south.

The beaches along the coast are nothing to rave about as the water is murky and the sand is littered with garbage, but they are popular with Syrians on holiday.

LATTAKIA اللاذقية
☎ 041
Lattakia is not a typical Syrian town. A busy port since Roman times, the place is less inward-looking than the rest of the country. With wide, tree-lined boulevards and pavement cafés it feels almost European (Greek, perhaps). Its comparative liberalism aside, the city itself has no real attractions but it makes a good base for visits to the ruins of the ancient city of Ugarit and the Crusader castle of Qala'at Saladin.

Information
The **tourist centre** (☎ 416 926; Sharia 14 Ramadan; open 8am-8pm Sat-Thur) is in the foyer of a severe municipal building a kilometre northeast of the centre.

For visa extensions, the **immigration office** (Saahat Jumhuriyya; open 8am-2pm Sat-Thur) is some distance from the centre, beyond the tourist information centre, on the far side of a large traffic roundabout. You need an absurd *six* passport photos, although after much shuffling between desks you will get your extension issued within an hour or so.

At the **Commercial Bank of Syria** (Sharia Baghdad; open 8.30am-1.30pm, 5pm-8pm Sat-Thur) you can change cash and travellers cheques and no commission is charged on either.

The **main post office** (open 8am-6pm daily) is some distance out of the centre, just north of the train station in a little alley off Sharia Suria. The **telephone office** (Sharia Seif al-Dawla; open 8am-11pm daily) is west of Sharia Baghdad. To make an international call buy a phonecard then wait your turn for a free phone. Phonecards bought in Damascus or Aleppo will not work here.

Email & Internet Access Of the several places we visited around town **Center Net** (☎ 465 310; Sharia al-Mutanabi; open 11am-11pm daily) and **Internet Cafe Clic** (☎ 466 113; 12 Sharia 14 Ramadan, 1st floor; open noon-midnight daily) had the best set ups. Both charge S£50 per half hour.

Things to See
There's a small **museum** (Sharia Jamal Abdel Nasser; adult/student S£300/15; open 8am-6pm Wed-Mon Apr-Sept, 8am-4pm Wed-Mon Oct-Mar) down near the waterfront housed in what was once an old khan, but its contents are sparse and few will find it worth the steep admission.

Places to Stay
The cheapest accommodation is around the central Saahat al-Sheikh Daher area (the square with the Assad statue).

Hotel Lattakia (☎ 479 527; Sharia Yousef al-Azmeh; dorm beds/doubles S£125/200) is the current backpackers' favourite. It's tucked away down a narrow alley north of the mosque and has a variety of rooms from dorms to doubles with or without en suite bathroom and even a complete apartment.

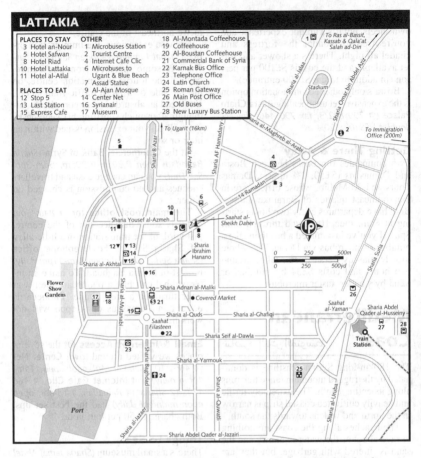

LATTAKIA

PLACES TO STAY
3 Hotel an-Nour
5 Hotel Safwan
8 Hotel Riad
10 Hotel Lattakia
11 Hotel al-Atlal

PLACES TO EAT
12 Stop 5
13 Last Station
15 Express Cafe

OTHER
1 Microbuses Station
2 Tourist Centre
4 Internet Cafe Clic
6 Microbuses to
  Ugarit & Blue Beach
7 Assad Statue
9 Al-Ajan Mosque
14 Center Net
16 Syrianair
17 Museum

18 Al-Montada Coffeehouse
19 Coffeehouse
20 Al-Boustan Coffeehouse
21 Commercial Bank of Syria
22 Karnak Bus Office
23 Telephone Office
24 Latin Church
25 Roman Gateway
26 Main Post Office
27 Old Buses
28 New Luxury Bus Station

Hotel al-Atlal (☎ 476 121; Sharia Yousef al-Azmeh; beds per person S£250) is a quiet, family-run establishment with freshly laundered sheets and a pleasant common area with a fridge stocked with soft drinks. It charges a per person rate and hot water is available at all times in the common showers.

Hotel Safwan (☎ 478 602, ✉ mziadeh22@excite.com; Sharia Mousa bin Nosier; singles/doubles/triples S£300/500/700) is just a little north of the centre close to the seafront. The place is a bit rundown (especially reception) but some of the rooms are fine and most have their own en suite bathrooms.

Hotel Riad (☎ 479 778; fax 476 315; Sharia 14 Ramadan; singles/doubles US$13/19) is a modernish two-star with a good location right on the main square. Some of the rooms are a little shabby but the sheets are clean. Some rooms have balconies, but there is no air-con, only fans.

Hotel an-Nour (☎ 423 980, fax 468 340; Sharia 14 Ramadan; singles/doubles US$13/19) is similar in standard to the nearby Riad but given a choice between the two we go for this one because of its comfortable lounge area and breakfast room. Breakfast is included in the price.

Places to Eat

As with accommodation, the cheapest source of dining is around the Saahat al-Sheikh Daher area. A quick hunt will turn up the old faithfuls – felafel, kebabs and shwarma, as well as a good, clean spit-rotisserie chicken place (S£100 for a whole chicken plus salad, hummus and bread) next door to the Hotel Riad. Otherwise, head for Sharia al-Mutanabi, home to so many Western-style food outlets that it's acquired the nickname the 'American Quarter'.

Express Cafe (☎ 456 200; 22 Sharia al-Mutanabi; dishes S£80-150; open 9.30am-midnight daily) is a gleaming new US-style diner offering burgers, steaks, pizza and hot and cold sandwiches. The menu is in English. It also does great milkshakes and there's a bar downstairs.

Stop 5 (☎ 477 919; 27 Sharia al-Mutanabi; dishes S£75-125; open noon-late daily) more resembles a bar than a restaurant with shelves of spirits, posters advertising happy hours, and a TV tuned in to MTV. The food (burgers, escalopes, pizza, pasta) is good and very affordable.

Last Station (☎ 468 871; 20 Sharia al-Mutanabi; per person S£200; open noon-late daily) is a little more formal than Stop 5, which is opposite, and caters for a more mature crowd. It's a definite restaurant, as opposed to a bar/restaurant (though it does serve alcohol), with a menu of international and Middle Eastern standards.

Getting There & Away

Air There's a flight once a week to Damascus from Lattakia's airport, about 25km south of the town. The local office of **Syrianair** (☎ 476 863) is at 8 Sharia Baghdad.

Bus The luxury bus station is on Sharia Abdel Qader al-Husseiny about 200m east of the train station. All the numerous private companies have their offices here and between them they operate frequent services to Damascus (S£150, four hours), Aleppo (S£100, 3½ hours) and Tartus (S£35, under an hour). In addition buses go from here to Antakya, İskenderun, Ankara and İstanbul in Turkey, and to Amman, Beirut and Cairo.

Karnak buses also depart from this station, but the **booking office** (☎ 233 541; Sharia Seif al-Dawla) is just off Sharia Baghdad. Prices are slightly cheaper than the luxury buses but you need to book one day in advance.

There's a second bus station between the luxury station and the train station from where really old, clapped out vehicles totter forth for Damascus (S£55) and Aleppo (S£40) – cheap yes, but recommended, no.

Microbus The main congregation of microbuses is 1.5km north of the town centre, near the sports stadium. From a great big lot, services (just walk around and listen for your destination being shouted) depart frequently for Baniyas (S£10, 45 minutes), Tartus (S£35, one hour), Homs (S£60, two hours) and Kassab (S£20, 1½ hours) for the Turkish border.

Microbuses for Ugarit (Ras Shamra) go from a back alley down the side of the big white school on Saahat al-Sheikh Daher.

Train The train station is about 1.5km east of the city centre on Saahat al-Yaman. There are four daily departures for Aleppo (S£67/40 1st/2nd class) at 6.40am, 1.30pm, 3.20pm and 5pm. The trip takes 3½ hours and the scenery is stunning.

AROUND LATTAKIA
Ugarit   راس شمرا

Ugarit (adult/student S£300/15; open 9am-4pm Nov-May, 9am-6pm June-Oct), also known as Ras Shamra, was once the most important city on the Mediterranean coast. From about the 16th to the 13th century BC, it was a centre for trade with Egypt, Cyprus, Mesopotamia and the rest of Syria. Writing on tablets found here is widely accepted as being the earliest known alphabet. The tablets are on display in the museums in Lattakia, Aleppo and Damascus, as well as the Louvre in Paris. Today, the masonry left behind shows you the layout of the streets and gives you some vague idea of where the most important buildings were.

Getting There & Away Microbuses make the trip to Ugarit regularly from Lattakia.

Qala'at Saladin   قلعة صلاح الدين

Although less celebrated than Crac des Chevaliers, TE Lawrence was moved to write of Qala'at Saladin, 'It was I think the most sensational thing in castle building I have seen'. The sensational aspect is largely due to the site – the castle is perched on top of a heavily wooded ridge with near precipitous sides dropping away to surrounding ravines.

The castle (adult/student S£300/15; open 9am-4pm Wed-Mon Nov-Mar, 9am-6pm Wed-Mon Apr-Oct) is 24km east of Lattakia and is a very easy half-day trip.

Getting There & Away Take a microbus from Lattakia to Al-Haffa (S£20, 45 minutes). From here the castle is a further 6km and you'll have to hire a taxi; the local price is S£20 per person but expect to pay more like S£50.

Qala'at Marqab قلعة مرقب

This citadel (adult/student S£300/15; open 9am-4pm Wed-Mon Nov-Mar, 9am-6pm Wed-Mon Apr-Oct) was originally a Muslim stronghold, possibly founded in 1062. After falling into Crusader hands in the early 12th century, the fortifications were expanded. The main defensive building, the donjon, is on the southern side, as the gentler slopes made that aspect the castle's most vulnerable. After several attempts, Saladin gave up trying to take Marqab. It eventually fell to the Mamluks in 1285.

The walls and towers are the most impressive element of what is left today, and the interior of the citadel is rapidly being overrun with vegetation.

Getting There & Away To get there, take a microbus (S£5) from Baniyas on the coast towards Zaoube – it goes right past.

TARTUS طرطوس
☎ 043

Tartus is Syria's second port. It's a very easy going place, and if there's little in the way of 'sights' it's a comfortable place to hang out and rest-up for a couple of days. The compact remnants of the old city (known to the Crusaders as Tortosa) warrant exploration as does the once fortified island of Arwad.

Information
The **immigration office** (open 8am-2pm Sat-Thur) for visa extensions is just south of Sharia Jamal Abdel Nasser, one block east of the park (it's well signposted). The **tourist office** (☎ 223 448; Sharia 6 Tichreen; open 8am-2pm Sat-Thur) is inconveniently stuck out on the southeast edge of town on the main Homs highway, 2km south of the train station.

The **telephone office** (open 24 hours) is just north of the junction of Sharias Khaled ibn al-Walid and Ath-Thawra; buy a phonecard from the desk and queue for a phone.

The local branch of the **Commercial Bank of Syria** (open 8am-noon Sat-Thur) is northeast of the old city on Sharia Khaled ibn al-Walid. It changes cash or travellers cheques (S£40 commission).

Things to See
From the outside the 12th-century **Cathedral of Our Lady of Tortosa** (adult/student S£300/15; open 9am-6pm Wed-Mon Apr-Oct, 9am-4pm Nov-Mar) looks more like a fortress, and that is no coincidence as its construction was conceived with its own defence in mind. It's a splendid piece of Crusader construction; inside is a rather less impressive archaeological museum.

Head north from the cathedral and cut toward the waterfront for the remains of the **old city walls**. The area of the old city is small and crowded but fascinating for the way homes have been burrowed into the old fortifications.

The island of **Arwad**, visible from the seafront off to the southwest, was also a Crusader stronghold. Small motor launches leave from the fishing harbour every 15 minutes (pay on the return voyage; S£20). There are ship building yards, fish restaurants and the remnants of sea walls on the island – plus an unfortunate amount of garbage.

Places to Stay
There are several cheapies (around S£150 a bed) around the junction of sharias Ath-Thawra and Al-Wahda but these are very, very dire – bedding down on one of the mattresses in these places could be the start of a long-term relationship with a dermatologist.

Daniel Hotel (☎ 312 757, fax 316 555; Sharia al-Wahda; singles/doubles S£300/600) is the town's choice accommodation. Rooms are large with large beds (with crisp, white sheets) and new en suite bathrooms. It also benefits from a very central location. The management are helpful and speak English.

Hotel Raffoul (☎ 220 616 or 220 097; Saahat Manchieh; beds per person S£200), across from the cathedral, is a converted apartment with 10 rooms. Two of the rooms have en suites, the rest share facilities. It's quiet and very well looked after. If the hotel is locked up you need to go to the grocers on the corner, which is owned by the same guy who runs the hotel.

Hotel Shahine (☎ 222 005, fax 221 703; Sharia Ahmed al-Azawi; singles/doubles US$24/30) is a modern, eight-storey place one block back from the sea – rooms on the 3rd floor and above have good sea views. Rooms have air-con, en suite and fridge.

Places to Eat

The usual cheap restaurants and snack places (for felafel, shwarma, grilled chicken) are clustered around the clock tower and Sharia al-Wahda and south down Ath-Thawra. There's also a cluster of cheap eats places along Sharia Ahmed al-Azawi (south of Sharia al-Wahda), which is where the local kids hang-out.

Al-Ayounak (☎ 326 086; 7 Sharia Ahmed al-Azawi; open noon-midnight daily) is a small snack bar at the sea-front end of the street run by a friendly guy who lived for 17 years in Sydney – the pizzas here are excellent and it sells beer (S£50).

Al-Nabil (Sharia al-Amara) one block back from the fishing harbour (just round the corner from the Daniel Hotel), specialises in heavily spiced and salted baked fish but also does more regular dishes like chicken and kebabs for around S£100. Local beer (S£50) is available too.

Tec Tac (Sharia al-Corniche al-Bahr; open 10am-2am daily) is one of a string of coffee shops along the seafront between the fishing harbour and old city – it's notable though for serving food (cheap local fare) and beer. It's also very female friendly, attracting plenty of local girls sharing nargileh.

The Cave (☎ 220 408; Sharia al-Corniche al-Bahr; meals S£300-400; open noon-late daily) occupies a vaulted hall burrowed into the sea wall of the old city. It's got atmosphere in spades and the food's excellent too. The house speciality is seafood (pricey) but there are also grilled meat dishes. Alcohol is served and Diners Club, MasterCard and Visa are all accepted.

Getting There & Away

The luxury bus company Qadmous has a station just off the big roundabout north of the park. It has frequent services to Damascus (S£110, four hours), Aleppo (S£115, four hours), Lattakia (S£35, one hour) and Homs (S£40, one hour).

Microbuses depart from Sharia 6 Tichreen, east of the centre by the train station, to Lat-

takia (S£35, one hour) and Baniyas (S£11, 30 minutes). There are also plenty of buses heading for Homs (S£23, 1½ hours) and Damascus (S£53, four hours).

CRAC DES CHEVALIERS
قلعة الحصن

☎ 031

For a description of the castle see the special section 'Crac des Chevaliers'.

Places to Stay & Eat

Accommodation choices are few; given that Crac is only just over an hour from Tartus, Homs or even Hama, most people visit on a day trip.

Restaurant/Hotel La Table Ronde (☎ 734 280, fax 741 400; rooms S£500), about 200m south of the castle's main entrance, has a few grubby rooms with squat toilets that are vastly overpriced. You can also camp. The food is better value at S£175 per person for shish kebab/tawouq plus salad, hummus and French fries, but mediocre in quality.

Bebers Hotel (☎ 741 201; singles/doubles US$20/25) was still partially under construction when we visited but when finished 24 of its 31 rooms will have stunning unobstructed views of the castle. The hotel is on the next hill over from the castle (west) – about a 15-minute walk from the main entrance.

Restaurant al-Qalaa (☎ 740 493, 740 003; meals S£250) is the lone white two-storey building immediately west of the castle, on the next hill top. It's worth dining here for the views alone. Food is grilled chicken and mezze, and if you ask nicely owner Anran might show you the guest book signed by Sean Connery.

Getting There & Away

Crac des Chevaliers lies some 10km north of the Homs-Tartus highway. From Homs there are several microbuses to the village of Hosn (S£20) before noon. They will drop you right at the castle.

The other alternative, and the only choice from Tartus, is to catch one of the buses, minibuses or microbuses that shuttle between the two cities and alight at the turn-off for the castle. From there you will have to hitch or flag down a local microbus (S£10) heading up the hill.

[Continued on page 608]

CRAC DES CHEVALIERS

Author Paul Theroux described the Crac des Chevaliers as the epitome of the dream castle of childhood fantasies; of jousts and armour and pennants. TE Lawrence simply called it 'the finest castle in the world'. Take their word for it, the remarkably well-preserved Crac des Chevaliers (in Arabic Qala'at al-Hosn) is one of Syria's prime attractions. Impervious to the onslaught of time, it cannot have looked a great deal different 800 years ago, and such is its size and state of completeness that you could easily spend several hours here absorbed in exploring.

The first fortress known to have existed on this site was built by the Emir of Homs in 1031 but it was the Crusader knights around the middle of the 12th century who largely built and expanded the Crac into the form in which it exists today. Despite repeated attacks and sieges the castle held firm. In fact, it was never truly breached. Instead, the Crusaders just gave it up. By 1271, when the great Muslim warlord Beybars marched on the castle, the knights at the Crac were a last outpost. Jerusalem had been lost and the Christians were on the retreat.

Numbers in the castle, which was built to hold a garrison of 2000, had fallen to around 200. Surrounded by the armies of Islam and with no hope of reprieve, the Crac must have seemed more like a prison than a stronghold. Even though they had supplies to last for five years, after a month under siege the Crusaders agreed to depart the castle in return for safe conduct.

Inset: The view through one of the archways (Photo by Troy Flower)

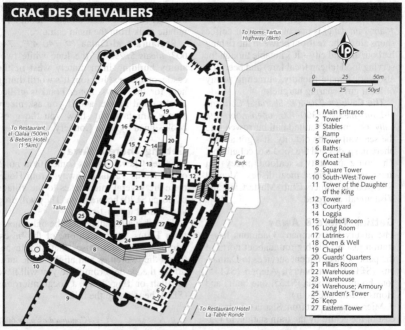

CRAC DES CHEVALIERS

To Homs-Tartus Highway (8km)

To Restaurant al-Qalaa (500m) & Bebers Hotel (1.5km)

Car Park

Talus

Talus

To Restaurant/Hotel La Table Ronde

1 Main Entrance
2 Tower
3 Stables
4 Ramp
5 Tower
6 Baths
7 Great Hall
8 Moat
9 Square Tower
10 South-West Tower
11 Tower of the Daughter of the King
12 Tower
13 Courtyard
14 Loggia
15 Vaulted Room
16 Long Room
17 Latrines
18 Oven & Well
19 Chapel
20 Guards' Quarters
21 Pillars Room
22 Warehouse
23 Warehouse
24 Warehouse; Armoury
25 Warden's Tower
26 Keep
27 Eastern Tower

PATRICK BEN LUKE SYDER

The Castle

The castle comprises two distinct parts: the outside wall with its 13 towers and main entrance; and the inside wall and central construction, which are built on a rocky platform. A moat dug out of the rock separates the two walls.

A suggested route for exploration is to walk from the main entrance up the sloping ramp and out to the moat. Visit the **baths**, which you can get down to by a couple of dogleg staircases over in the corner off to your left, then on to the **great hall**, from where you can gain access to the three towers that punctuate the southern wall.

Continue around and enter the inner fortress through the tower at the top of the access ramp into an open courtyard. The **loggia**, with its Gothic facade, on the western side of the yard, is the most impressive structure in the Crac. Opposite is a **chapel** that was converted to a mosque after the Muslim conquest (the *minbar*, or pulpit, still remains). The staircase that obstructs the main door is a later addition and leads to the upper floors of the fortress. You can make your way over to the round tower in the southwest corner, which is known as the **Warden's Tower** – on a clear day there are magnificent views from the roof.

Crac des Chevaliers is open from 9am to 6pm daily from April to October (until 4pm November to May) except public holidays. Admission is S£300 (students S£15).

Top: The 800-year-old Crusader castle in its present glory

[Continued from page 605]

Orontes Valley

The Orontes River (Nahr al-Assi in Arabic) has its headwaters in the mountains of Lebanon near Baalbek. The river flows through the industrial city of Homs before reaching Hama, where the only obstruction to the flow are the ancient *norias*, or water wheels. The Orontes once used to flow northwest from Hama and seep away in the swamps of Al-Ghab, but those swamps have long been drained to form one of the most fertile plains in Syria.

HOMS
حمص

☎ 031

There's little of interest in Homs but it is one of those crossroads most travellers have to pass through at some stage. Roads head north to Hama, east to Palmyra and the Euphrates, south to Damascus and west to Tartus and the coast. You will find a small **information booth** (open 8.30am-2pm, 4pm- 9pm Sat-Thur) beside the footpath along Sharia Shoukri al-Quwatli, the town's main east-west street. For **visa renewals**, go to the 3rd floor of a multistorey administration building at the end of a tiny side lane north of Shoukri al-Quwatli.

The only building of great note is the **Khaled ibn al-Walid Mosque** on the Hama road about 600m north of the town centre. It holds the tomb of the commander of the Muslim armies who brought Islam to Syria in AD 636.

Places to Stay & Eat

The cheap hotels are on or around Shoukri al-Quwatli between the tourist office and the souq. They're a pretty foul bunch and if you have to spend the night in Homs we recommend shelling out the extra for Al-Mimas or even, if you can afford it, the five-star **Safir** (☎ 412 400; singles/doubles US$110/125).

An-Nasr al-Jedid Hotel (☎ 227 423; Sharia Shoukri al-Quwatli; singles/doubles S£200/300), entered from a side street just off Sharia al-Quwatli, is about the best of the lot. It's a bit grubby and basic but the sheets are clean and one of the showers along the corridor can be cranked up to give out some hot water (S£50 per shower).

Grand Basman Hotel (☎ 225 009; Sharia Abu al-Ala al-Mari; singles/doubles US$15/22) has rooms with bathroom and fan. The entrance is in the middle of a small shopping arcade. It's not bad, but as is so often the case with the lower end hotels charging US dollars, it's well overpriced and tends to be a haunt for some dubious passing trade.

Hotel al-Mimas (☎/fax 220 224; Sharia Malab al-Baladi; singles/doubles US$24/30) offers the best value in town. It's modern, clean and the rooms come with big plump beds, fridge, balcony, en suite bathrooms and air-con. The drawback is that it's about 2km northwest of the centre.

The cheap restaurants are all in a group one block south of Sharia al-Quwatli and have the same old stuff – kebabs, chicken, felafel, hummus and salad.

City Cafe (☎ 239 755; Sharia Abu al-Ala al-Mari; open 24hr) may be the best of the lot – same food as the rest but with a pleasant shaded terrace facing the clock tower.

Getting There & Away

There are two bus stations: the Karnak station, about 1.5km north of the city centre up the Hama road, and the luxury bus station, 1km farther on. At the latter are the usual bus companies (Qadmous, Al-Ahliah etc) and between them they have buses for Damascus (S£70, two hours), Aleppo (S£75 to S£85, 2½ hours), Tartus (S£40, one hour) and Palmyra (S£75, two hours). The quickest way to Hama is to jump in a microbus (S£17, 40 minutes) – they leave every 10 minutes or so. Battered old minibuses go from the Karnak station to all over for fares that are considerably cheaper than the bigger buses, but they're generally cramped and uncomfortable with nowhere to put baggage. The fare to Aleppo on one of these is S£30, Tartus is S£17, Palmyra S£22 and Hama S£10.

For Crac des Chevaliers catch a 'Hosn' minibus (mornings only) from the Karnak bus station, or a Tartus-bound bus or minibus from either bus station and ask to be let off on the highway at the castle junction – tell the driver you want 'Qala'at Hosn'.

HAMA
حماه

☎ 033

This is one of the most attractive towns in Syria with the Orontes River flowing through the town centre, its banks lined

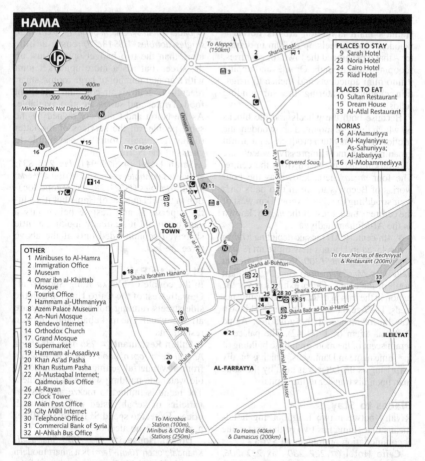

HAMA

PLACES TO STAY
9 Sarah Hotel
23 Noria Hotel
24 Cairo Hotel
25 Riad Hotel

PLACES TO EAT
10 Sultan Restaurant
15 Dream House
33 Al-Atlal Restaurant

NORIAS
6 Al-Mamuriyya
11 Al-Kaylaniyya;
As-Sahuniyya;
Al-Jabariyya
16 Al-Mohammediyya

To Aleppo
(150km)

Sharia Ziqar

Orontes River

The Citadel

AL-MEDINA

Covered Souq

Sharia Said al-A'as

OLD TOWN

Sharia al-Mutanabi

Sharia Abu al-Feda

To Four Norias of Bechriyyat
& Restaurant (200m)

Sharia al-Buhturi

Sharia Ibrahim Hanano

Sharia Soukri al-Quwatli

ILEILYAT

Sharia Badr ad-Din al-Hamid

Sharia Jamal Abdel Nasser

Souq

Sharia al-Murabet

AL-FARRAYYA

To Microbus,
Minibus & Old Bus
Stations (250m)

To Homs (40km)
& Damascus (200km)

OTHER
1 Minibuses to Al-Hamra
2 Immigration Office
3 Museum
4 Omar ibn al-Khattab Mosque
5 Tourist Office
7 Hammam al-Uthmaniyya
8 Azem Palace Museum
9 An-Nuri Mosque
12 An-Nuri Mosque
13 Rendevo Internet
14 Orthodox Church
17 Grand Mosque
18 Supermarket
19 Hammam al-Assadiyya
20 Khan As'ad Pasha
21 Khan Rustum Pasha
22 Al-Mustaqbal Internet;
Qadmous Bus Office
26 Al-Rayan
27 Clock Tower
28 Main Post Office
29 City M@il Internet
30 Telephone Office
31 Commercial Bank of Syria
32 Al-Ahliah Bus Office

0   200   400m
0   200   400yd
Minor Streets Not Depicted

with trees and gardens. There's not a lot to see, but the town's peaceful atmosphere and excellent accommodation makes it a pleasant base for excursions to Crac des Chevaliers and other sights in the area.

Information

For visa extensions the **immigration office** *(Sharia Ziqar; open 8am-2pm Sat-Thur)* is on the north edge of town, near the new museum, in a modern building with 'Passport' written in English above the main entrance. The **tourist office** *(☎ 511 033; Sharia Said al-A'as; open 8.30am-5pm Sat-Thur)* is in a small building in the gardens in the centre of town just north of the river. The **Commercial Bank of Syria** *(Sharia Shoukri al-Quwatli; open 8.30am-12.30pm Sat-Thur)* is just east of the

clock tower (next to the **post office**). It accepts cash and travellers cheques (no commission) at the exchange counter (1st floor).

Email & Internet Access The Cairo and Riad hotels both offer online computer access to their guests, otherwise try one of the following:

City M@il (☎ 214 466) 8 Sharia Abdel Alwani, right behind the post office; open 10.30am-midnight daily. S£50 per half hour.

Al-Mustaqbal (☎ 210 135) Sharia al-Buhturi, in the Afamia Restaurant along from the Qadmous bus office – look for the sign saying 'Future'; open 8am-midnight daily. S£30 per half hour.

Rendevo (☎ 211 686) Sharia al-Qalaa, beside the Citadel; open 11am-2am daily. S£30 per half hour.

Things to See

Hama's main attraction are its **norias** – wooden water wheels up to 20m in diameter – that have graced the town for centuries, scooping water from the Orontes and tipping it into mini aqueducts and thence to irrigation channels watering the surrounding fields.

Because both the wheels and the blocks on which they are mounted are wooden, the friction when they turn produces a mournful groaning. The most impressive wheels are about 1km east, upstream from the centre. The four *norias* here, known as the Four Norias of Bechriyyat, are in two pairs on a weir straddling the river. About 1km west of the centre is the largest of the *norias*, known as the Al-Mohammediyya.

A 4th-century AD mosaic depicting a *noria* is displayed in Hama's new **museum** *(Sharia Ziqar; adult/student S£300/15; open 9am-4pm daily Nov-Mar, 9am-6pm Apr-Oct)*, 1.5km north of the centre. Other exhibits cover the region in the iron age, Roman and Islamic periods. The **Azem Palace** in the small old town was the residence of the governor, As'ad Pasha al-Azem (r. 1700–42). The palace is reminiscent of the more grandiose building of the same name in Damascus, which is hardly surprising as the latter was built by the same man upon his transfer to the capital.

Places to Stay

Rivalry between two neighbouring hotels means that Hama has two of the best value accommodation options in all Syria.

Cairo Hotel *(☎ 222 280, fax 237 206; e cairo_hotel@ayna.com; Sharia Shoukri al-Quwatli; mattress on the roof S£100, dorm bed S£125, singles/doubles/triples S£300/400/550)* has rooms that are spotlessly clean with fridge, satellite TV and en suite bathrooms, all for a budget price. There's also a good little breakfast area, online terminals, free tea on arrival, and a small library of books to borrow. Staff are extremely friendly and speak English. The hotel also runs a range of trips around the region. Fantastic.

Riad Hotel *(☎ 239 512, fax 517 776; e riadhotel@scs-net.org; Sharia al-Quwatli; dorm beds S£150, singles S£300, doubles S£350-550)* is next door but one to the Cairo Hotel and is identical in almost all respects. Equally fantastic.

Noria Hotel *(☎ 512 414, fax 511 715, e bader@mail.sy; Sharia Shoukri al-Quwatli; singles/doubles US$18/28)* costs a little more than the two budget options just up the street, but it's a more upmarket joint with a greater number of large rooms, smart reception, central air-con and excellent food. Triples and suites are also available. As the Noria and Cairo are owned by the same people, all the services of the latter (online terminals, tours) are available to guests of the Noria.

Sarah Hotel *(☎ 515 941, fax 235 831, w www.sarahhotel.com; Sharia Abu al-Feda; singles/doubles US$21/28)* has a good location in the old quarter of Hama but it's a little impersonal and despite being only a year or so old it's already looking a little shabby. Recommended only if the above three are full.

Places to Eat

In the couple of blocks along Shoukri al-Quwatli west of the Cairo Hotel and in the side streets running north to the river are all the usual cheap kebab and chicken restaurants.

Sultan Restaurant *(☎ 235 104; off Sharia Abu al-Feda; open noon-midnight)* benefits from a wonderful setting in a characterful old waterside building with *noria* attached. The menu is limited to mezze and several varieties of kebab, listed in English with prices. Expect to spend S£100 to S£150 per head. There's no alcohol.

Dream House *(☎ 411 687; Sharia al-Khandak; open 10am-1am)* is a smart modern place in the Al-Medina quarter, west of the Citadel. The menu's in English and includes pizzas, burgers, salads and various steak and chicken dishes. Expect to pay S£100 to S£200. Alcohol is served. Accepts AmEx, MasterCard and Visa.

Al-Atlal *(☎ 222 234; Sharia al-Buhturi; open noon-late)* is the first restaurant on the left as you walk east from the Al-Ahliah bus office. It has a lovely riverside terrace and an indoor dining hall, but the main thing is the food, which is said to be the best in town. Expect Syrian standards and expect to pay S£150 to S£250 per head – but we didn't check it out because it doesn't serve booze.

Four Norias *(Sharia al-Buhturi; meals S£300; open noon until late)* is around a mile east of the centre on the banks of the river beside, what else, four norias. It's a large open-air place popular with (often rowdy) groups. It gets particularly lively on summer evenings. The food is the standard mezze and kebabs, but it's very good. Alcohol is served.

Getting There & Away

Hama has no central station for luxury buses. Instead, the main bus companies (including Al-Ahliah, Qadmous and Al-Rayan) have their offices in the town centre – see the map for locations. Al-Ahliah have the most frequent departures (the times are posted up in English) with services to Damascus (S£85 to S£90, 2½ hours) departing every half hour between 5am and 9am then hourly until 11.30pm; services to Aleppo (S£65, 2½ hours) are hourly between 6.30am and 11.15pm. Other fares include Homs (S£20, 45 minutes), Tartus (S£70, two hours) and Lattakia (S£100, three hours). There are no direct services to Palmyra from Hama.

The main microbus station is a 10-minute walk from the centre of town at the southwest end of Sharia al-Murabet. It's in a triangular lot at the junction with the main Damascus road. The old minibus station is a further 200m left and along the Damascus road.

APAMEA أفاميا

If it weren't for the unsurpassable magnificence of Palmyra, Apamea (pronounced a-**fam**-ia) would be considered a wonder and one of the unmissable highlights of Syria. As it is, Apamea is like a condensed version of the pink sandstone desert city, but executed in grey granite and transposed to a high, wild grassy moor overlooking the Al-Ghaba plain. The city was founded in the 2nd century BC by Seleucus I, one of Alexander the Great's generals. It prospered until the Byzantine period but then the city was sacked by the Persians in AD 540 and again in 612. Barely a quarter of a century later Syria was seized by the Muslims and Apamea fell into decline. The city was all but flattened in a devastating earthquake in 1157.

Beside the site is the village of Qala'at al-Mudiq, sheltered in a medieval castle, while down below, beside the main road is a **mosaic museum** (*adult/student S£150/15; open 9am-2.30pm Wed-Mon*) housed in a grand old khan with a massive grassy courtyard.

The site of Apamea has no set opening hours as it's unfenced and there's nothing to stop anyone wandering across it at any time, however, there is an admission fee of S£300/25. Officials patrol the site checking tickets. You can purchase a combined ticket good for both museum and site for S£350.

Getting There & Away

Minibuses (S£10) and microbuses (S£20) regularly run the 45km from Hama to Suqeilibiyya, and from there microbuses go on to Qala'at al-Mudiq (S£10). The whole trip usually takes about an hour.

Aleppo حلب

☎ 021

Called Haleb by the locals, Aleppo, with a population of about three million, is Syria's second-largest city. Since Roman times it has been an important trading centre between the countries of Asia and the Mediterranean. With its fascinating covered souqs, the citadel, museum and khans (merchants' inns), it is a great place to spend a few days. There are also interesting sights in the vicinity such as the Basilica of St Simeon (Qala'at Samaan), which was the largest Christian building in the Middle East when built in the 4th century.

Orientation

The area where most of Aleppo's cheap hotels are clustered is a compact zone centred on Sharias Al-Quwatli and Al-Baron. A lot of the restaurants, the National Museum and places to exchange money are also here. Southeast is the citadel and old city, while northeast of the centre are the main Christian quarters. To the west is the modern commercial centre, the newer suburbs and the university district.

Information

Immigration Office Visit the **immigration office** (*open 8am-1.30pm Sat-Thur*) for visa extensions, on the 1st floor of a building just north of the citadel. You must bring four passport photos and then fill out forms in quadruplet. The processing takes one to 1½ hours and there's a fee of S£25, but you may be given an extension of up to two months.

SYRIA

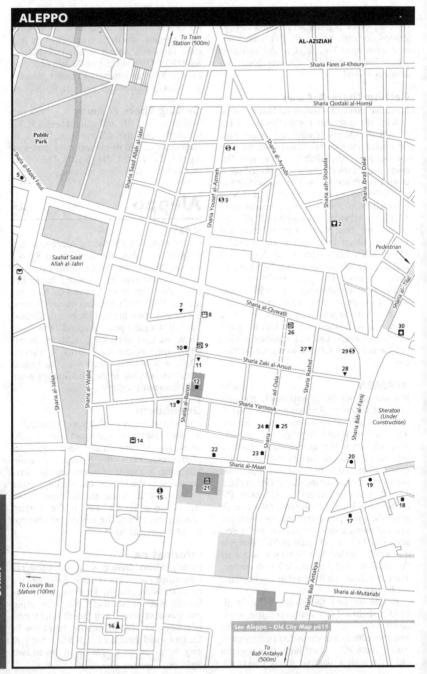

ALEPPO

AL-AZIZIAH

Sharia Fares al-Khoury

Sharia Qostaki al-Homsi

Public Park

To Train Station (500m)

Sharia al-Malek Faisal

5

Saahat Saad Allah al-Jabri

6

Sharia Saad Allah al-Jabri

Sharia Yousef al-Azmeh

Sharia al-Ayyubi

Sharia ash-Shohada

Sharia Ibrail Dalal

4

3

2

Pedestrian

Sharia al-Tilal

7

8

Sharia al-Quwatli

26

10

9

27

29

30

11

Sharia Zaki al-Arsuzi

Sharia Rashid

28

12

Sharia ad-Dala

Sheraton (Under Construction)

13

Sharia Yarmouk

Sharia al-Jalaa

Sharia al-Walid

Sharia al-Barron

14

24

25

Sharia Bab al-Faraj

22

23

Sharia al-Maari

20

19

15

18

21

17

16

To Luxury Bus Station (100m)

Sharia Bab Antakya

Sharia al-Mutanabi

See Aleppo – Old City Map p615

To Bab Antakya (500m)

SYRIA

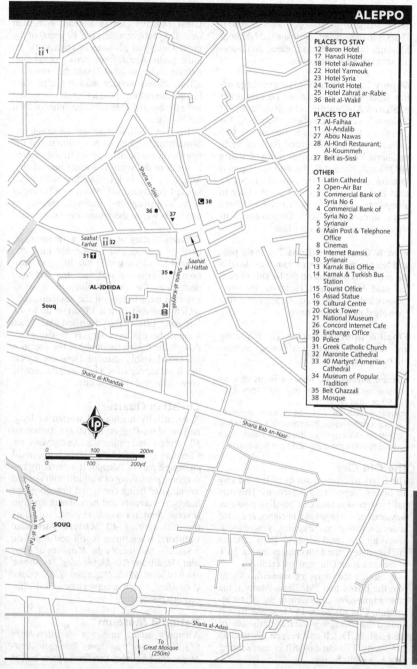

ALEPPO

PLACES TO STAY
12 Baron Hotel
17 Hanadi Hotel
18 Hotel al-Jawaher
22 Hotel Yarmouk
23 Hotel Syria
24 Tourist Hotel
25 Hotel Zahrat ar-Rabie
36 Beit al-Wakil

PLACES TO EAT
7 Al-Faihaa
11 Al-Andalib
27 Abou Nawas
28 Al-Kindi Restaurant;
   Al-Koummeh
37 Beit as-Sissi

OTHER
1 Latin Cathedral
2 Open-Air Bar
3 Commercial Bank of
   Syria No 6
4 Commercial Bank of
   Syria No 2
5 Syrianair
6 Main Post & Telephone
   Office
8 Cinemas
9 Internet Ramsis
10 Syrianair
13 Karnak Bus Office
14 Karnak & Turkish Bus
   Station
15 Tourist Office
16 Assad Statue
19 Cultural Centre
20 Clock Tower
21 National Museum
26 Concord Internet Cafe
29 Exchange Office
30 Police
31 Greek Catholic Church
32 Maronite Cathedral
33 40 Martyrs' Armenian
   Cathedral
34 Museum of Popular
   Tradition
35 Beit Ghazzali
38 Mosque

Sharia as-Sissi

38

36 37

Saahat
Farhat   32

31

AL-JDEIDA

Saahat
al-Hattab

35

Souq

34

33

Sharia al-Kayyali

Sharia al-Khandak

0 ___ 100 ___ 200m
0 ___ 100 ___ 200yd

Sharia Bab an-Nasr

Sharia Hamma m al-Tal

SOUQ

Sharia al-Adasi

To
Great Mosque
(250m)

Tourist Office The tourist office (☎ 222 1200; Sharia al-Baron; open 9am-2pm Sat-Thur) is in the gardens opposite the National Museum but it's next to useless, and doesn't seem to be staffed often.

Money There's a convenient **exchange office** (open 9am-7.30pm daily) on the corner of Sharias Al-Quwatli and Bab al-Faraj, but it doesn't accept travellers cheques – for these you'll have to go to one of the two branches of the Commercial Bank of Syria on Sharia Yousef al-Azmeh, north of Sharia al-Quwatli. Note that you will be required to show the receipts for your cheques (the ones that you are advised to always keep in a separate place). At both branches there is a commission of S£25. Or you could always try reception at your hotel.

Post & Communications The **main post and telephone office** (open 8am-5pm daily) is the enormous building on the far side of Saahat Saad Allah al-Jabri. However, for international calls use the card phones you'll find sparsely dotted around town.

Email & Internet Access The following are a couple of Internet cafés open to travellers in Aleppo.

Concord Internet Cafe Above a pastry café on Sharia al-Quwatli; open 9am to 11pm daily. S£50 per half hour.

Internet Ramsis (☎ 224 1545) Sharia al-Baron, above a coffeehouse in a converted cinema just a few doors along from the Baron Hotel; open 11am to midnight daily. S£50 per half hour.

The Old City

The fabulous covered **souqs** of the old city are one of Aleppo's big attractions. This partially covered network of bustling passageways extends over several hectares, and once under the vaulted stone ceiling, you're swallowed up into another world. Parts of these markets date to the 13th century but the bulk of the area is an Ottoman-era creation.

In among the souqs are numerous khans (see the boxed text 'Medieval Malls'), the most impressive of which is the **Khan al-Jumruk**. Completed in 1574, at one time it housed the consulates and trade missions of the English, Dutch and French, as well as 344 shops. The khan is still in use, serving now as a cloth market.

On the northern edge of the souqs is the **Great Mosque** (Jamaa al-Kebir; admission free), the younger sibling (by 10 years) of the great Umayyad Mosque in Damascus. Its most impressive feature is its freestanding minaret dating to 1090. Inside the mosque is a fine, carved wooden *minbar* (pulpit) and behind the railing to the left of it is supposed to be the head of Zacharias, the father of John the Baptist.

It's also worth seeking out the wonderful **Bimaristan Arghan** (it has railings out the front with a little nameplate affixed), which is south of the souq. A former mental asylum, it's a lovely little building with a tree shaded courtyard off which is a series of tight, claustrophobic passages leading to tiny cells where the insane were confined.

Citadel Sitting atop a huge (man-made) earthen mound east of the old city, the **citadel** (adult/student S£300/15; open 9am-6pm Wed-Mon Apr-Sept, 9am-4pm Oct-Mar) dominates the city skyline. Its moat is spanned by a bridge on the southern side, which then climbs at a 45° angle up to the imposing 12th-century fortified gate. Once inside, the castle is largely in ruins, although the throne room above the entrance has been lavishly restored. However, by far the best aspect of a visit are the terrific views afforded over the city.

Christian Quarter

A beautifully maintained warren of long, narrow stone-flagged alleyways, occasionally arched, and with walls like canyons, the Christian quarter of Al-Jdeida is the most charming part of Aleppo. It's currently undergoing something of a rebirth with age-old townhouses being converted into gorgeous hotels, restaurants and bars. There are also several churches worth visiting, including the 15th-century **40 Martyrs' Armenian Cathedral** where mass is still performed on a Sunday, and there's the **Museum of Popular Tradition** (Le Musee des Traditions; adult/student S£150/10; open 8.30am-2pm Wed-Mon), which occupies a beautiful 18th-century residence.

National Museum

Aleppo's main museum (adult/student S£300/15; open 9am-1pm, 4pm-6pm Wed-Mon) could be mistaken for a sports hall if

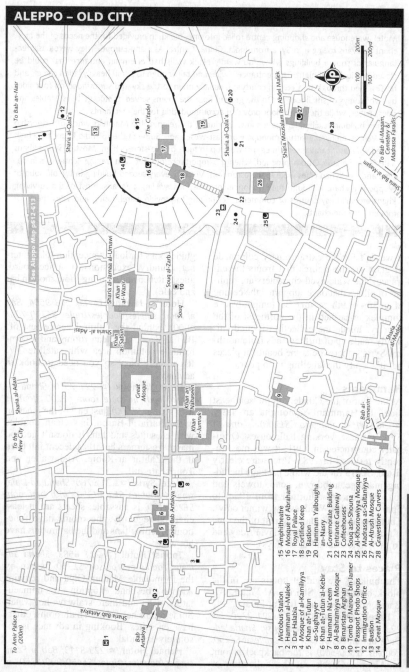

ALEPPO – OLD CITY

1 Microbus Station
2 Hammam al-Maleki
3 Dar Halabia
4 Mosque of al-Kamiliyya
5 Khan at-Tutun as-Sughayyer
6 Khan at-Tutun al-Kebir
7 Hammam Na'eem
8 Al-Bahramiyya Mosque
9 Bimaristan Arghan
10 Tomb of Marouf bin Jamer
11 Passport Photo Shops
12 Immigration Office
13 Bastion
14 Great Mosque
15 Amphitheatre
16 Mosque of Abraham
17 Royal Palace
18 Fortified Keep
19 Bastion
20 Hammam Yalbougha an-Nasry
21 Governorate Building
22 Entrance Gateway
23 Coffeehouses
24 Souq ash-Shouna
25 Al-Khosrowiyya Mosque
26 Madrassa as-Sultaniyya
27 Al-Atrush Mosque
28 Gravestone Carvers

Medieval Malls

Motel, warehouse and shopping centre rolled into one, the khan provided for the needs of the merchant caravans rolling into Syria from India, China, Central Asia and Europe. They were basic rectangular or square buildings whose outwardly blank walls had one main entrance that could be closed and locked at night. That entrance – wide and tall enough to admit heavily laden camels and horses – led through to a central courtyard, usually open to the sky and surrounded on four sides by two storeys of small rooms. On the ground floor the rooms served as storage bays, stables and sales spaces, while the upper floor provided accommodation for the merchants.

Khan building reached its apogee in Cairo during the reign of the Mamluks who, in partnership with Venice, enjoyed a virtual monopoly on east-west trade. Some of the splendid khans they built (called *wikala* or caravanserai in Egypt) were up to four- or five-storeys high. Most of Syria's khans date from the later Ottoman period, when the importance of Cairo as a trading centre was in decline and the Syrian cities were in the ascendant. Virtually every second building in the old souq of Aleppo is a khan. Although they no longer provide for travelling caravans, most of the surviving khans are still busy centres of commerce, continuing to provide warehousing and sales space for modern-day merchants.

it weren't for the extraordinary colonnade of giant granite figures that fronts the entrance. The wide-eyed characters are replicas of pillars that once supported the ceiling of an 8th- or 9th-century BC temple-palace complex unearthed in the northeast of the country. Inside the collection is predominantly made up of further finds from northern Syria – there are some beautiful pieces but it's a pity the labelling is so poor.

Hammams

At the foot of the Citadel, on the southeast side, the **Hammam Yalbougha an-Nasry** (☎ 362 3154; admission S£200) is one of Syria's finest working bathhouses. Originally constructed in 1491, it was most recently restored in 1985. Prices are clearly listed: S£415 for the whole package including massage, rubdown, soap, towels and tea. Women are admitted from 10am to 5pm on Monday, Wednesday (winter only), Thursday and Saturday; the rest of the time it's men only (Sunday, Tuesday, Friday and from 5pm to 2am all other days).

Places to Stay

The bulk of the budget hotels are in the block bounded by Sharias Al-Maari, Al-Baron, Al-Quwatli and Bab al-Faraj.

Hotel Zahrat ar-Rabie (☎ 221 2790, fax 223 5898; e 373hotur@mail.sy; Sharia ad-Dala; dorm beds S£175, one single at S£250, doubles S£300-500) is *the* backpacker joint in Aleppo. Check out the collection of

guidebooks for loan at reception (plus Internet, laundry, excursions, a notice board, guest kitchen and, coming soon, rooftop bar and café).

Hotel al-Jawaher (☎/fax 223 9554; Bab al-Faraj; singles/doubles/triples S£350/700/1050), behind the cultural centre just off Bab al-Faraj, has clean rooms and a comfortable common area with satellite TV. It's usually busy so you need to book in advance.

Hotel Yarmouk (☎ 221 7510; Sharia al-Maari; beds in share room S£200, doubles with shower S£500), just east of the junction with Sharia al-Baron, has clean doubles with en suites and fan. It doesn't get too many Westerners so it's a decent fall back if the Zahrat ar-Rabie, Al-Jawaher and Tourist are full.

Hotel Syria (☎ 221 9760; Sharia ad-Dala; singles/doubles S£200/350, with bathroom S£250/400) is passable: sheets are at least changed regularly, the rooms have functioning ceiling fans and the bathrooms have hot water.

Tourist Hotel (☎ 221 6583; Sharia ad-Dala; rooms per person S£350) is run by the formidable Madam Olga and remains Aleppo's best budget option – it's immaculately clean and there's always hot water. Some rooms have shared bathrooms, others have en suites. Booking in advance is absolutely essential.

Hanadi Hotel (☎ 223 8113; Bab al-Faraj; singles/doubles/triples S£450/900/1350) is extraordinary – what a hotel might look like if it was decorated by Barbie. Pink, pink and more pink. But it's well looked after, clean, and all rooms have en suite bathrooms (albeit with squat toilets).

Dar Halabia (☎ 332 3344, fax 332 3344, e halabiatour@net.sy; singles/doubles US$20/35) is the only hotel in the Old City. It has 12 rooms on two levels round a central courtyard. Although lonely at night when the whole quarter is deathly silent, its quite lovely and great value.

Baron Hotel (☎ 221 0880, fax 221 8164, e hotelbaron@mail.sy; Sharia al-Baron; singles/doubles US$30/40) has in the past hosted TE Lawrence and Agatha Christie. You have to be prepared for a bit of a trade-off: for its character and air of Gothic romance, you have to let go any attachments to more physical luxuries – the beds are old and squeaky, the air-con clatters like it was powered by diesel. That said, rooms are being renovated and an extra US$5 per night now gets you a brand new bathroom and comfy mattress.

Beit al-Wakil (☎ 221 7169, fax 224 7083, Sharia as-Sissi; singles/doubles US$80/100) in the Al-Jdeida quarter may be Syria's most romantic hotel. Opened only in 1998, it's a 450-year-old house lovingly restored and converted into a 19-room boutique hotel.

Places to Eat

In the block bounded by Sharias Al-Maari, Bab al-Faraj, Quwatli and Al-Baron are the cheapies offering the usual stuff – the price is more variable than the food so check before you sit down. A row of excellent juice stands lines up at the Bab al-Faraj end of Sharia Yarmouk. Just off Sharia al-Baron, **Al-Faihaa** is a clean and immensely popular felafel place.

Across from the juice stands are the kebab restaurants **Al-Kindi Restaurant** and **Al-Koummeh**. They are none too hot on hygiene but offer reasonable food at budget prices.

Abou Nawas (☎ 224 0290; Sharia Rashid) has a menu that stretches way beyond the basics to include the kind of dishes that are usually only ever served up at home (patrons are often invited into the kitchen to see what's cooking). A two-course meal will come in at about S£150 to S£200.

Al-Andalib (Sharia al-Baron; set menu S£200) is a rooftop restaurant one block

north of the Baron Hotel. The atmosphere is boisterous and the place is packed most evenings with locals. It serves a set menu – a platter of kebab, huge amounts of salads, hummus, baba ghanoug and fries.

Beit al-Wakil (☎ 221 7169, fax 224 7083; Sharia as-Sissi) and **Beit as-Sissi** (☎ 221 9411), in the Al-Jdeida quarter, both have courtyard dining areas complete with jasmine and lemon trees and gently splashing fountains. Both specialise in local variations on Levantine cuisine; the dishes change according to the season and the food is stunningly good. Expect to pay S£250 to S£350 per person, wine not included. Credit cards are accepted.

Getting There & Away

Air Aleppo has an international airport with some connections to Turkey, Europe and other cities in the Middle East. Internally, there is a daily flight to Damascus (S£900, one hour).

Bus The main station, as far as most travellers are concerned, is the one for luxury, long-distance buses, on Sharia Ibrahim Hanano, about 800m west of the National Museum.

From here a variety of companies run buses to Damascus (S£150, five hours), Deir ez-Zur (S£125, five hours), Hama (S£65, 2½ hours), Homs (S£100, 3½ hours), Lattakia (S£100, 3½ hours), among others. In addition there are seven daily buses from here to Beirut (S£300, six hours).

North of the tourist office is another garage shared between state-owned Karnak buses and several private companies running services to Turkey and a handful of other international destinations. There are at least five buses a day to İstanbul (approximately S£950, 22 hours) and more to Antakya (S£200 to S£250).

Train The train station, about 15 minutes' walk from the central hotel area, is north of the big public park. Local trains run daily to Damascus, Lattakia, Deir ez-Zur and Qamishle in the northeast.

AROUND ALEPPO
Qala'at Samaan   قلعة سمعان

This is the **Basilica of St Simeon** (adult/student S£300/15; open 9am-6pm daily

Apr-Sep, 9am-4pm Oct-Mar), also known as St Simon of Stylites, who was one of Syria's most unusual early Christians.

In AD 423, he climbed to the top of a 3m pillar and went on to spend the next 36 years atop this and other taller pillars. After his death in 459, an enormous church was built around the most famous pillar. The church today is remarkably well preserved, with the arches of the octagonal yard still complete, along with much of the four basilicas.

Getting There & Away Microbuses from Aleppo leave every hour or so from the main microbus station. The trip to the village of Daret' Azze takes somewhere in the order of one hour (S£10). It is about a farther 8km from Daret' Azze to Qala'at Samaan and it's a matter of negotiating with a local for transport or hitching.

Palmyra

تدمر

☎ 031

Known to the locals as Tadmor (which is its ancient Semitic name), Palmyra is Syria's prime attraction and one of the world's great historical sites.

If you're only going to see one thing in Syria, make it Palmyra. Although mass tourism is making itself felt and the place's popularity is growing, there's still a good chance you'll be able to enjoy it with relatively few other people about.

The oasis is really in the middle of nowhere – 150km from the Orontes River to the west and 200km from the Euphrates to the east.

The ruins of the 2nd century AD city have been extensively excavated and beautifully restored. They cover some 50 hectares. The new town is rapidly growing around it, spreading out with particular speed towards the west.

History

Palmyra was at one time a Greek outpost of considerable importance. It was an Assyrian caravan town for over 1000 years but only enjoyed its later Greek period of glory for two centuries. It was annexed by Rome in AD 217 and became a centre of unsurpassed wealth.

The city's most famous character was Zenobia, the half-Greek, half-Arab queen who claimed descent from Cleopatra. She was a woman of exceptional ability and ambition, and after the death in suspicious circumstances of her husband Odenathus, she became ruler of Palmyra from AD 267. She set her sights on Rome, but her troops were soundly beaten by the forces of Aurelian in 271, and the city was put to the torch by him two years later.

This was the beginning of the end for Palmyra. It fell to the Muslims in 634 and was finally and completely destroyed by an earthquake in 1089.

Information

Palmyra's new **tourist office** is across from the museum, although when we visited it hadn't yet opened for business. There's an **exchange office** *(open 8am-8pm Sat-Thur)* in a kiosk in front of the museum. At the time of our last visit, there was no Internet available anywhere in town.

Museum

With no labelling to speak of and poor presentation, it's debatable whether Palmyra's modest museum *(adult/student S£300/15; open 8am-1pm & 4pm-6pm Wed-Mon Apr-Sep, 8am-1pm & 2pm-4pm Wed-Mon Oct-Mar)* is worth a visit or not.

However, there is a very good, large-scale model of the Temple of Bel that gives an excellent idea of how the complex would have looked in its original state, as well as a couple of very dynamic mosaics that were found in what are presumed to be nobles' houses, just east of the Temple of Bel. There are also countless busts and carved portraits that formed part of the panels used to seal the tombs in Palmyra's many funerary towers.

Places to Stay

Prices vary seasonally and according to trade. This is one place where it pays to haggle.

Baal Shamin Hotel *(☎ 910 453; mattress on roof S£100, singles/doubles/triples/quad S£200/300/400/500)* is run by mountain of mirth Mohammed Ahmed, who camps in the lobby and entertains guests with tea, coffee and booze. Many travellers who aren't staying here end up hanging out in reception with Mohammed until all hours. Rooms are basic but serviceable with clean en suites.

New Tourist Hotel (☎ 910 333; Sharia al-Quwatli; beds in share room S£150, singles/doubles S£175/275, with bathroom S£200/325) was at one time about the only hotel in town. It's failed to keep up with the times and is looking a bit grotty and battered, although the communal lounge is still quite cosy.

New Afqa Hotel (☎ 791 0386; roof mattress S£100, singles/doubles S£250/500) would be a decent option (although rooms are a little spartan) if staff weren't so pushy with the tours. Room prices seemed to be very negotiable. The reception area has satellite TV and beer.

Umayyad Palace (☎/fax 910 755; Saahat al-Jamarek; doubles S£400) has potential with rooms (most with en suite bathrooms) arranged around a pleasant courtyard area, but we have received complaints about sleazy behaviour by staff, so female travellers beware.

Citadel Hotel (☎ 910 537; Sharia As'ad al-Amir; beds in share room S£200, doubles S£500), faces the side of the museum. There's a wide range of rooms, some new with air-con, good bathrooms and views of the ruins. Check a few out before choosing. It accepts Visa.

Palace Hotel (☎ 791 3941, fax 911 707; singles/doubles with bathroom US$17/24) is not bad at all. It's quiet and well looked after, and some of the rooms have good views of the ruins. The place is used a lot by French groups but manager Khaled also speaks English.

Orient Hotel (☎ 910 131, fax 910 700; singles/doubles US$20/25) is favoured by some of the adventure tour companies and rightly so – air-con rooms are spotlessly clean with gleaming en suites complete with towels and toiletries. Good value for the money.

Ishtar Hotel (☎ 913 073, fax 913 260; Sharia al-Quwatli; singles/doubles US$20/28) is about the first place you come to, on the left, as you enter the town. Rooms – all with air-con and en suites – have benefited from a recent refit (new carpets, mattresses, furniture). There's also a basement bar.

Hotel Zenobia (☎ 910 107, fax 912 407, **e** zenobia-hotel@net.sy; singles/doubles US$60/78), although built around 1900, is short on any kind of charm, period or otherwise, but owes its popularity to a location right on the very edge of the ruins. However, be sure to get one of rooms 101 to 106, which are the only ones with views, otherwise it's just not worth the money.

Places to Stay

Most travellers seem to end up at one of two restaurants on the main drag, Sharia al-Quwatli: **Traditional Palmyra** or **Spring Restaurant** across the street. There's little to choose between them. The food is variable although the *mansaf* at the Traditional Palmyra is reasonably good (S£250 for two). Both restaurants have a pleasantly laid back atmosphere and both greatly benefit from the fact that there's little to do at night in Palmyra except take a street-side table and linger over a meal and several teas.

Pancake House (☎ 913 733; Sharia an-Nasr; open 8am-3pm, 6pm-11pm daily), just north of the main drag, is the best place in town. The menu is limited to a handful of savoury and sweet options (plus the ubiquitous *mansaf*) but all ingredients are fresh, and boy is the food good. Excellent milkshakes and juices too.

Palmyra Restaurant, on the main square, opposite the museum, serves fairly average food but the garden setting with fountains and plenty of leafy shade is extremely pleasant and it's a good place to linger over beers (S£75).

Getting There & Away

Palmyra doesn't have a bus station. The government-run Karnak bus company has its office on the main square opposite the museum, but its services are infrequent – including just one bus a day to Damascus (S£125, three hours).

It's better to go by Qadmous. Its buses stop at the Sahara Cafe on the edge of town (2km from the museum; a taxi should cost S£25); services in both directions – Damascus (S£135, four hours) and Deir ez-Zur (S£100, three hours) – are frequent and the ticket office is in front of the café.

Bus times are posted on a board in front of the Traditional Palmyra Restaurant in town.

[Continued on page 622]

PALMYRA

Bel was the most important of the gods in the Palmyrene pantheon and the **Temple of Bel** is the most complete structure and single most impressive part of the ruins. Once inside, you'll see that the complex consists of two parts, a huge walled courtyard and at its centre, the temple proper, or **cella**, which dates from AD 32.

Formerly connected to the temple by a colonnade – of which only some column stubs remain – the **monumental arch**, now serves as the entrance to the site proper. The arch is interesting in that it is actually two arches joined like a hinge to pivot the main street through a 30° turn. This slight direction switch, and a second one just a little farther west, are in themselves evidence of the city's unique development – a crooked street like this would be quite unimaginable in any standard Roman city.

South of the main **colonnaded street** (impressively restored in the section immediately east of the arch) is the city's theatre, which until the 1950s was buried by sand. Since its discovery it has been extensively restored but large sections now look just a bit too shiny and new.

About one-third of the way along the colonnaded street is the reconstructed **tetrapylon**, a monumental structure that served to mark a junction of thoroughfares. From here the main street continues northwest, and another smaller pillared street leads southwest to the **agora**, or forum, and northeast to the **Temple of Baal Shamin**, a small shrine dedicated to the god of storms and fertilising rains.

Inset: Grapevine bas-relief motif among the ruins of the Temple of Bel (Photo by Corey Wise)

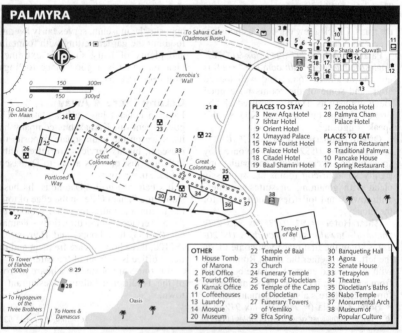

PALMYRA

PLACES TO STAY
3 New Afqa Hotel
7 Ishtar Hotel
9 Orient Hotel
12 Umayyad Palace
15 New Tourist Hotel
16 Palace Hotel
18 Citadel Hotel
19 Baal Shamin Hotel
21 Zenobia Hotel
28 Palmyra Cham Palace Hotel

PLACES TO EAT
5 Palmyra Restaurant
8 Traditional Palmyra
10 Pancake House
17 Spring Restaurant

OTHER
1 House Tomb of Marona
2 Post Office
4 Tourist Office
6 Karnak Office
11 Coffeehouses
13 Laundry
14 Mosque
20 Museum
22 Temple of Baal Shamin
23 Church
24 Funerary Temple
25 Camp of Diocletian
26 Temple of the Camp of Diocletian
27 Funerary Towers of Yemliko
29 Efca Spring
30 Banqueting Hall
31 Agora
32 Senate House
33 Tetrapylon
34 Theatre
35 Diocletian's Baths
36 Nabo Temple
37 Monumental Arch
38 Museum of Popular Culture

620

TROY FLOWER

Beyond the tetrapylon the main street continues for another 500m. This stretch has seen much less excavation and reconstruction and the way is littered with tumbled columns and assorted blocks of masonry. The road ends in the impressive, portico of a **funerary temple**, dating from the 3rd century. The area around here is also littered with broken and tumbled masonry, in places just heaped up into small hillocks of fragments of statuary and decorated friezes and panels – it gives you a chance to look at the intricacy of the carving at close quarters.

South of the funerary temple along the porticoed way is **Diocletian's camp**, erected after the destruction of the city by Aurelian, possibly on the site of what had been the palace of Zenobia, although excavations so far have been unable to prove this. The camp lay near what was the Damascus Gate, which led on to a 2nd-century colonnaded street that supposedly linked Emesa (Homs) and the Euphrates.

Over to the south at the foot of some low hills are a series of tall, free-standing square-based towers; these are funerary towers. The towers contain coffins – or rather, did contain coffins – in niches like pigeon holes that rise for up to five levels.

Although there is no admission fee to the site, you pay S£300/15 to enter the Temple of Bel, S£300/15 to get into the Arab castle up on the hill overlooking the site (a good place to be at sundown) and S£150 to have the funerary towers unlocked for investigation (payable at the museum, where you also have to arrange transport).

Top: Visitors now take centre stage at the amphitheatre in the old city

[Continued from page 619]

The Euphrates River

نهر الفرات

The Euphrates River (Al-Furat in Arabic) starts out high in the mountains of eastern Anatolia in Turkey and winds through northeastern Syria into Iraq, finally emptying into the Shatt al-Arab waterway and the Gulf – a total distance of over 2400km.

One of the few tributaries of the Euphrates, the Kabur, flows down through northeastern Syria to join it below Deir ez-Zur. These two rivers make it possible to irrigate and work the land, and wheat and cotton grown here are an important source of income for the country.

RAQQA
الرقة

☎ 022

From AD 796 to 808, the city of Raqqa (then Ar-Rafika) reached its apex as the Abbasid caliph, Haroun ar-Rashid, made it his summer residence.

Practically nothing of the city's old glory has been preserved, except the partly restored **Baghdad Gate**, about a 15-minute walk to the east of the clock tower. The old Abbasid city **wall**, restored at some points to a height of 5m, runs north from the gate past the **Qasr al-Binaat** (Daughters' Palace), which served as a residence under the Ayyubids.

A small **museum** (*adult/student S£300/150; open 9am-6pm Wed-Mon Apr-Sept, 9am-4pm Wed-Mon Oct-Mar*), roughly halfway between the Baghdad Gate and the clock tower, has some interesting artefacts from excavation sites in the area.

There are a few hotels around the clock tower, all of them amazingly expensive. **Ammar Hotel** (*☎ 222 2612; Sharia al-Quneitra; doubles S£400*), just north of the clock tower, is the best of a bad lot, with very basic, grotty rooms with shared shower and toilet facilities. Food-wise, the **Al-Rashid** (*☎ 241 919; Sharia al-Malek Faisal*), just west from the clock tower, is about the best there is.

Getting There & Away

There's a new bus station about 300m south of the clock tower. Several companies have their offices here and between them there are regular services to Aleppo (S£85, 2½ hours), Damascus (S£225, seven hours) and Deir ez-Zur (S£60, 2½ hours).

RASAFA
رصافا

This startling walled city lies in the middle of nowhere, and seems to rise up out of the featureless desert as you approach it. The city was first fortified by the Romans; Byzantine emperor Justinian gave it much of its present look, a religious basilica complex devoted to St Sergius and a military outpost. The Umayyads later built a palace here, which was subsequently destroyed by the Abbasids.

Getting There & Away

Catch a microbus from Raqqa to Al-Mansura (S£15, 20 minutes) – that's the easy bit. Now it's just a matter of waiting at the signposted turn-off for a pick-up to take you the 35km to the ruins for about S£20. The alternative is to hitch.

DEIR EZ-ZUR
دير الزور

☎ 051

This is a pleasant town on the Euphrates and a crossroad for travellers visiting the northeast of Syria. It has prospered recently with oil discoveries in the surrounding areas.

There's not much to see, apart from a reasonable new **museum** (*Sharia Ali ibn Abi Taleb*) about a kilometre west of the centre, but a stroll along the riverbank is a popular activity. On the other side of the suspension bridge is a small recreation ground where you can swim with the locals, though this is probably not advisable for women travellers.

Places to Stay & Eat

Budget accommodation is not good in Deir ez-Zur and this is a place where it might be worth considering an upgrade.

Al-Arabi al-Arabiyya (*☎ 222 070; Sharia Khaled ibn al-Walid; singles/doubles S£200/300*), east of the square, is very basic but clean. Rooms have fans and fresh sheets, and a couple have balconies, but showers and toilets (squat) are shared.

Hotel Raghdan (*☎ 222 053, fax 221 169; Sharia Abu Bakr as-Siddiq; singles/doubles US$14/20, with bathroom US$17/23*) overlooking the canal has grotty air-con rooms and is otherwise another choice.

Ziad Hotel (*☎ 214 596, fax 211 923; singles/doubles US$20/30*) is a great newly constructed place, just west of the main square on the canal. The air-con rooms are tasteful, large, comfortable and have satellite TV, and the price includes breakfast. Excellent value.

Layalty (☎ 226 388; Sharia Ali ibn Abi Taleb), 400m west of the main square, is a smart new restaurant in a converted function hall. The menu is a mis of Syrian standards plus international dishes including pizza. The food's not bad at all and prices are low (and listed on the English-language menu). No alcohol.

There are also a couple of restaurants on the south bank of the Euphrates – **Tourist Blue Beach**, just to the north of the suspension bridge, and **Al-Jisr al-Kebir** (Big Canal), just to the south. Both are little more than open-air terraces but enjoy excellent riverside settings that go some way to compensating for indifferent, overpriced food.

Getting There & Away

The airport is about 7km east of town and the weekly flight between Deir ez-Zur and Damascus costs S£600.

The **luxury bus station** (Sharia 8 Azar) is about 2km south of town, at the end of Sharia 8 Azar. Several companies have their offices here and between them they offer regular services to Damascus (S£175, seven hours) via Palmyra (S£100, three hours) and to Aleppo (S£135, five hours) via Raqqa (S£60, two hours). There's little need to book in advance (just show up and get a ticket for whichever bus is going out next). Services to Hassake (S£75, two hours) and Qamishle (S£110, three hours) are less frequent – in fact, to the latter there's only one service a day, operated by Qadmous. Better to take a minibus.

The **minibus station** (Sharia 8 Azar) is about 1km south of the main square. From here there's an hourly minibus to Raqqa (S£60, two hours) and plenty to Hassake in the northeast (S£75, 2½ hours) and on to Qamishle on the Turkish border (S£125). There are also frequent departures to Abu Kamal (often pronounced buka-**mel**) by minibus (S£30, two hours) and by microbus (S£50, two hours).

SOUTH OF DEIR EZ-ZUR
جنوبدير الزور

The route southeast of Deir ez-Zur follows the Euphrates down to the closed Iraqi bor-

der. It is dotted with sites of archaeological and historical interest.

Dura Europos
تل صالحية

For the uninitiated, the extensive, largely Hellenistic/Roman fortress city of Dura Europos is by far the most intriguing site to visit on the road from Deir ez-Zur to Abu Kamal. The riverside walls overlook the left bank of the Euphrates, 90m below. The city was renowned for its apparent religious tolerance, seemingly confirmed by the presence of a church, synagogue and other Greek, Roman and Mesopotamian temples side by side.

Mari
تل حريري

The ruins of Mari (Tell Hariri), an important Mesopotamian city dating back some 5000 years, are about 10km north of Abu Kamal. Although fascinating for their age, the mud-brick ruins do not grab the imagination as much as you might hope.

The **Royal Palace of Zimri-Lim** was enormous, measuring 200m by 120m with over 300 rooms. The palace is the main point of interest; it is now sheltered from the elements by a modern protective roof.

Getting There & Away Local microbuses run alongside the Euphrates from Deir ez-Zur to Abu Kamal (S£50, two hours).

The Northeast
الشمال الشرقى

Bordered by Turkey and Iraq, there are no major monuments or sights in the northeastern corner of the country, but this does not mean it is empty of attractions. Perhaps the greatest is the chance to meet the Kurds, a people without a country, who have yet to give up their struggle. Only about one million of a total of around 20 million Kurds live in Syria.

The numerous *tells* (artificial hills) dotted around the place are a sign that the area has been inhabited since the 3rd millennium BC.

HASSAKE
الحسكة
☎ 052

The capital of the governorate of the same name, Hassake doesn't offer the visitor an awful lot to do, but it's not a bad base from which to explore the area, unless you're planning on entering Turkey here, in which case you may as well push on to Qamishle.

Hassake is best reached by microbus from Deir ez-Zur (S£75, 2½ hours).

QAMISHLE الحسكة
☎ 053

Situated right at a crossing point on the Turkish border in the northeast, Qamishle is full of Kurds and Turks, and the cheaper hotels will sometimes quote prices in Turkish lira rather than Syrian pounds.

There is nothing to see in Qamishle, but the mix of people makes the place interesting. Because of its proximity to the border, you can expect passport checks at the hotels (even during the night), and when getting on or off buses or trains.

Places to Stay & Eat
Among the cheapest and worst is **Umayyad Hotel** *(beds S£100)* in a side street across from **Hotel Semiramis**. Just around the cor-

ner is **Chahba Hotel** *(beds S£100)*, which is nothing to write home about (women must take a double). The upstairs terrace is OK.

Mamar *(singles/doubles S£300/400)*, a block south, is better value, although a tad more expensive. The rooms with balconies are quite good and they have hot water.

Opposite the Chahba is a pleasant **restaurant** with an outdoor section. A good meal of kebabs and the usual side orders will cost about S£200.

Getting There & Away
The Turkish border is only about 1km from the centre of Qamishle.

There are three flights a week to Damascus (S£900).

Several private companies operate buses to Damascus (S£340, 10 hours) and Aleppo (S£175, five hours). More rickety buses do the trips for half the price.

There are three daily trains that go as far as Aleppo, and one or two of them go all the way to Damascus (S£740/198/132 sleeper/ 1st class/2nd class).

Turkey

Turkey is the bridge between Europe and the Middle East, both physically and culturally. The Ottoman sultans ruled the entire Middle East for centuries, and traces of Turkish influence remain in all the countries once controlled from İstanbul.

Turkey was the first formerly Ottoman Muslim land to establish a republic and achieve democracy, as well as the first to look westward, to Europe and North America, for cultural models. The tourism boom of the 1990s brought even more European influence, from rock music to topless beaches. But although Turkey may be one of the least exotic countries you encounter in this region, it's much more than just an imitation Europe. With a famously hospitable people, more ancient cities than any other country in the region, over 6000km of glorious coastline, varied countryside and excellent food, Turkey has lots to offer, especially if you try to take in a few more off-the-beaten-track destinations.

Facts about Turkey

HISTORY

By 7000 BC a Neolithic city, one of the oldest ever recorded, was already established at Çatal Höyük, near Konya. The greatest of the early civilisations of Anatolia (Asian Turkey) was that of the Hittites, a force to be reckoned with from 2000 to 1200 BC with their capital at Hattuşus, north of Ankara.

After the collapse of the Hittite empire, Anatolia splintered into several small states and it wasn't until the Graeco-Roman period that parts of the country were reunited. Later, Christianity spread through Anatolia, carried by the apostle Paul, a native of Tarsus (near Adana).

In AD 330 the Roman emperor Constantine founded a new imperial city at Byzantium (İstanbul). Renamed Constantinople, this strategic city became the capital of the Eastern Roman Empire and was the centre of the Byzantine Empire for 1000 years. During the European Dark Ages, the Byzantine Empire kept alive the flame of Western culture, although it was occasionally threatened by

Turkish Republic (Türkiye Cumhuriyeti)

Area: 788,695 sq km
Population: approx 68 million
Capital: Ankara
Head of State: President Ahmet Necdet Sezer
Official Language: Turkish
Currency: Turkish lira (TL)

- Best Dining – tucking into a fish supper in İstanbul's Kumkapı neighbourhood
- Best Nightlife – soaking up the atmosphere of the Chimaera at Olympos beneath a full moon
- Best Walk – strolling through the Ihlara Gorge in Cappadocia
- Best View – looking down on Cappadocia from the citadel at Uçhisar
- Best Activity – relaxing in a *hamam,* or Turkish bath

the powerful empires of the east (Persians, Arabs, Turks) and west (the Christian powers of Europe).

The beginning of the Byzantine Empire's decline came with the arrival of the Seljuk Turks and their defeat of the Byzantine forces at Manzikert, near Lake Van, in August 1071. The Seljuks overran most of Anatolia and established a provincial capital at Konya. Their domains included today's Turkey, Iran and Iraq.

With significantly reduced territory, the Byzantines endeavoured to protect Constantinople and reclaim Anatolia, but the

625

Fourth Crusade (1202–04) proved disastrous for them when a combined Venetian and Crusader force took and plundered Constantinople. They eventually regained the ravaged city in 1261.

A Mongol invasion of the late 1200s put an end to Seljuk power, but small Turkish states soon arose in western Anatolia. One, headed by Osman (1258–1326), grew into the Ottoman Empire, and in 1453 Constantinople finally fell to the Ottoman sultan Mehmet the Conqueror (Mehmet Fatih).

A century later, under Süleyman the Magnificent, the Ottoman Empire reached the peak of its power, spreading deep into Europe, Asia and North Africa. Ottoman success was based on military expansion. When the march westward was stalled at

Vienna in 1683, the rot set in and by the 19th century the great European powers had begun to covet the sultan's vast domains.

Nationalist ideas swept through Europe after the French Revolution, and in 1829 the Greeks won their independence, followed by the Serbs, the Romanians and the Bulgarians. Then Italy took Tripolitania in North Africa from Turkey, and in 1913 the Ottomans lost Albania and Macedonia.

The Turks emerged from WWI stripped of their last non-Turkish provinces: Syria, Palestine, Mesopotamia (Iraq) and Arabia. Most of Anatolia itself was to be parcelled out to the victorious Europeans, leaving the Turks virtually nothing.

At this low point, Mustafa Kemal, the father of modern Turkey, took over. Atatürk,

as he was later called, made his name by repelling the Anzacs in their heroic, but futile, attempt to capture Gallipoli. Rallying the tattered remnants of the Turkish army, he pushed the last of the weak Ottoman rulers aside and out-manoeuvred the Allied forces in the War of Independence, which the Turks finally won in 1923 by pushing the invading Greeks into the sea at Smyrna (İzmir). In the ensuing population exchange over a million Greeks left Turkey and nearly half a million Turks moved in. The two countries were left with grievances that have festered for more than 75 years.

After renegotiation of the WWI treaties a new Turkish Republic, reduced to Anatolia and part of Thrace, was born. Atatürk then embarked on a rapid modernisation

programme: establishing a secular democracy, introducing the Latin script and European dress, and adopting equal rights for women – at least in theory. The capital was also moved from İstanbul to Ankara. Such sweeping changes did not come easily and some of the battles (eg, over women's head covering) are still being fought today (see the boxed text 'Atatürk').

Since Atatürk's death, Turkey has experienced three military coups and considerable political turbulence. During the 1980s and '90s it was also wracked by the conflict with the Kurdistan Workers Party (PKK; led by Abdullah Öcalan), which aimed to create a Kurdish state in Turkey's southeast corner. This conflict led to an estimated 35,000 deaths and huge population shifts, and it

What to See

Set on the Bosporus, İstanbul is one of the world's great romantic cities and could keep you entertained for days. Heading south along the Aegean from İstanbul, top places to stay include Çanakkale for the battlefields of Gallipoli and the ruins of Troy; and Selçuk, for excursions to the ruins at Ephesus, Priene, Miletus and Didyma. Along the Mediterranean coast, inviting small resorts include Dalyan, Kaş and Olympos, perfect bases for exploring local Graeco-Roman and Lycian archaeological sites. The beach at Patara is simply superb.

Inland, Turkey's premier attraction is the spectacular landscape of Cappadocia, where the village of Göreme makes a popular base. From there you can travel west to Konya to see the beautiful tomb of the Mevlana; east to Mt Nemrut to see the giant Commagene heads; and south to the exotic bazaars of Sanlıurfa.

wreaked havoc on the economy. In 1999 Öcalan was sentenced to death, a sentence that was being reviewed by the European Court of Human Rights at the time of writing.

Turkey Today

While it may not be obvious on a short visit, modern Turkey suffers from an acute identity crisis. Hopes that it could move quickly to full membership of the European Union (EU) are looking increasingly forlorn, and the festering dispute with Greece, symbolised by the seemingly insoluble problem of Cyprus (invaded and partitioned in 1974), is no nearer resolution. Worse, perhaps, the

secular society established by Atatürk is coming under strain as a result of resurgent Islamic fundamentalism; the man most tipped to succeed Prime Minister Ecevit is Recep Tayyip Erdoğan, who has served a jail sentence for inciting religious hatred.

Some commentators had been forecasting a brighter future for the southeast as the PKK insurgency wound down. However, the economic collapse of 2001 (see Economy later in this section) dimmed that hope in the short term. Hopes of closer trading links with the Turkic-speaking republics of Central Asia also seem to be fading fast.

GEOGRAPHY

The Dardanelles, the Sea of Marmara and the Bosphorus strait divide Turkey into Asian and European parts, but Eastern Thrace (European Turkey) makes up only 3% of the 788,695 sq km land area. The remaining 97% is Anatolia, a vast plateau rising eastward towards the Caucasus Mountains. Turkey's 6000km-long coastline is almost entirely given over to tourism except where mountains come too close to the sea to squeeze in even the smallest hotel.

CLIMATE

The Aegean and Mediterranean coasts have mild, rainy winters and hot, dry summers. In İstanbul, summer temperatures average around 28° to 30°C; the winters are chilly but usually above freezing, with rain and perhaps a dusting of snow. The Anatolian plateau can be boiling hot (although less humid than the coast) in summer and freezing in winter. The Black Sea coast is mild and wet in summer, chilly and wet in winter.

Atatürk

You'll see him here, you'll see him there, you'll see him just about everywhere. Those busts and statues gracing the main square in every town and village are all reminders of Turkey's national hero Mustafa Kemal Atatürk.

Every schoolchild learns Atatürk's life story off by heart, and on 10 November every year the whole country comes to a standstill on the stroke of 9.05am to commemorate his death in 1938.

As the years go by, Atatürk is becoming even more of a hero, as the secular establishment fights to keep 'Kemalism' – Atatürk's antireligious philosophy of modernisation – centre stage. Inevitably, therefore, the most fervently religious Turks can get heartily sick of him.

Atatürk was a great orator and many of his sayings embellish public buildings countrywide. Look out in particular for the phrase 'Ne Mutlu Türküm Diyene' ('How happy I am that I can call myself a Turk'), which goes down like a lead balloon in the Kurdish parts of the country.

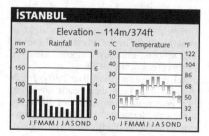

İSTANBUL

Elevation – 114m/374ft

Rainfall — Temperature

Mountainous eastern Turkey is icy cold and snowy in winter, and only pleasantly warm in high summer. The southeast is dry and mild in winter and baking hot in summer, with temperatures above 45°C not unusual.

ECOLOGY & ENVIRONMENT

Turkey's embryonic environmental movement is making slow progress, and you may well be shocked by the amount of discarded litter and half-built properties disfiguring the west in particular.

Recently, the noisiest environmental ding-dongs have been fought over big dam projects. One such scheme that would have drowned the historic town of Hasankeyf in southeastern Turkey seems (thankfully) to have been derailed, but white-water rafting on the Çoruh River around Yusufeli in north-eastern Turkey looks likely to vanish, along with Yusufeli itself, for the sake of a dam.

Other skirmishes are fought over how to supply the country's rapidly growing electricity demands. Plans for a controversial new nuclear power station seem to be safely on the back burner but other grandiose schemes to pipe fuel from Iran or under the Black Sea from Russia seem unlikely to do much to enhance the landscape. Meanwhile, argument rages over whether Turkey should have to permit ever more giant oil tankers to transit the Bosphorus, potentially endangering the residents of İstanbul.

The **Society for the Protection of Nature** (☎ 212-281 0321, fax 279 5544; Doğal Hayat 1/2 Koruma Derneği, PK 18 Bebek, 80810 İstanbul) and **Greenpeace Mediterranean** (☎ 236 4238, fax 236 4215; PO Box MBE 109, Dolapdere Caddesi 283, Pamgaltı, İstanbul) have information on many other environmental issues.

See also Ecology & Environment in the Facts about the Region chapter at the beginning of this book.

GOVERNMENT & POLITICS

In theory Turkey is a multiparty democracy on the Western European model, although in practice it has proved more of a semi-democracy, with the military wielding considerable power behind the scenes. There have been 57 governments since the republic's creation in 1923.

During the 1990s no one political party was able to win absolute control of parliament in elections based on proportional representation. This resulted in a series of weak coalition governments with increasing representation from parties of the extremes.

In 1999 an unlikely coalition government made up of representatives of the right-wing MHP (National Unity Party), the right-of-centre ANAP (Motherland Party) and the left-wing DSP (Democratic Socialist Party) came to power. To most people's amazement it is still clinging to power despite mishandling the aftermath of the twin earthquakes of 1999 and presiding over the worst economic disaster in the republic's history. It says everything for the parlous state of Turkey's democracy that it hangs on at least in part because most of the alternatives look even less appealing.

The current prime minister is veteran left-winger Bulent Ecevit, while the president is Ahmet Necdet Sezer, who emerged, seemingly from nowhere, to replace the equally veteran Süleyman Demirel. So far Sezer is proving very popular because he seems untainted by the whiff of corruption that lingers over many Turkish politicians. Likewise, Kemal Derviş, the outsider finance minister brought in to try to sort out the economic mess in 2001, gets popular support as much for what he isn't as for what he is.

In 2002 the coalition government was struggling in the face of the EU's demands for greater freedom of speech and the total abolition of the death penalty – demands that find little support among nationalists.

ECONOMY

In February 2001 the Turkish economy collapsed in spectacular fashion; more than one million people lost their jobs as the economy contracted by 9.5%. One of the few sectors of the economy to see out the year in good shape was tourism, which was then knocked for six by the events of 11 September. However, Turkey is the only Muslim member-state of NATO, a fact that, combined with its vital strategic position, meant that it could not be allowed to collapse completely. By late 2001 the IMF (International Monetary Fund) was pumping in funds to refloat the economy. It remains to be seen how quickly tourism can recover from yet another body blow.

POPULATION & PEOPLE

Turkey's roughly 68 million people are predominantly Turks, with a large Kurdish minority (perhaps 12 million) and much smaller groups of Laz, Hemsin, Arabs, Jews, Greeks and Armenians. The Laz and Hemsin people are natives of the northeastern corner of the Black Sea, while Arab influence is strongest in the Hatay area abutting Syria. Southeastern Turkey is pretty solidly Kurdish, although the problems of the last 20 years have led many to head west in search of a better life.

SOCIETY & CONDUCT

As a result of Atatürk's reforms, republican Turkey has largely adapted to a modern Westernised lifestyle, at least on the surface. In the big cities, the coastal resorts and among the well educated, you will not feel much need to adapt in order to fit in. In smaller towns and villages, however, you may find people warier and more conservative. There is also a small but growing group of 'born-again' Muslims who may make you feel uncomfortable, especially about alcohol, skimpy clothing and anything pertaining to religion.

To keep everyone smiling, try to remember that public drunkenness is not particularly acceptable in Turkey, and that most people prefer women to keep their legs, upper arms and neckline covered except on the beach. Be particularly careful when going into a mosque: women should cover their heads and shoulders; both men and women should cover their legs and remove their shoes.

RELIGION

Turkey is 99% Muslim, overwhelmingly Sunni, with small groups of Shiites and larger groups of Alevis mainly in the east. But Turkey espouses a more relaxed version of Islam than many other countries in the Middle East; many women uncover their heads and many men drink alcohol (although almost no-one touches pork).

İstanbul still has a tiny Jewish community and the Greek Orthodox Ecumenical Patriarch is also based in İstanbul, although Turkey refuses to recognise his right to speak for all of Greek Orthodoxy. However, the Orthodox minority dwindled after the Cyprus crisis of the 1970s.

Religious minorities live fairly freely provided they keep their heads down but there is increasing intolerance of difference in the east, fermented by Turkey's home-grown Hezbollah (Party of God) movement.

LANGUAGE

Turkish is the official language and almost everyone understands it. It has been written in the Latin script since Atatürk rejected Arabic in 1928.

However, language is one of contemporary Turkey's very hot potatoes. Although an earlier ban on spoken Kurdish has been lifted, battle royal is still being waged over people's right to study in Kurdish, to watch locally produced Kurdish television and to read Kurdish-language newspapers. It's wise not to get involved in this argument, but if you spend any time in the southeast you will almost certainly hear Kurdish (and Arabic) being spoken alongside Turkish.

In big cities and tourist areas, many locals will speak passable English, French, German or Japanese – or all of these.

For words and phrases in Turkish, see the Language chapter at the back of this book.

Facts for the Visitor

WHEN TO GO

Spring (late April/May) and autumn (late September/October) are the best times to visit; the weather will be warm and dry but not too hot, and the crowds have yet to appear. In the high season (July to mid-September) the weather can be very hot and/or humid, and major tourist destinations are crowded and overpriced. Although winter is generally rainy and cold, accommodation prices are low and there are no crowds. Try to avoid travelling during Kurban Bayramı, Turkey's biggest public holiday, when half the country is on the move.

VISAS & DOCUMENTS
Visas

Nationals of the following countries don't need to obtain a visa to visit Turkey for up to three months: Belgium, Denmark, Finland, France, Germany, Holland, Japan, New Zealand, Norway, Sweden and Switzerland. Although nationals of Australia, Austria, Canada, Greece, Ireland, Israel, Italy, Portugal, Spain, the UK and the USA need a visa, this is just a sticker, which you buy on arrival at the airport or at an overland border rather than at an embassy in advance. Make sure to join the queue to buy your visa before the one for immigration. How much you pay depends on your nationality; at the time of writing British citizens paid UK£10, Australians US$20 and citizens of Canada and the USA a hefty US$45. You *must* pay in hard currency (ie, not Turkish lira).

The standard visa is valid for three months and, depending on your nationality, usually allows for multiple entries.

For details of visas for other Middle Eastern countries, see the 'Visas at a Glance' table under Visas & Documents in the Regional Facts for the Visitor chapter.

Visa Extensions In theory a Turkish visa can be renewed once after three months, but the bureaucracy and costs involved mean that it's much easier to leave the country (usually to a Greek island) and then come back in again on a fresh visa.

Work Permits
You normally need a sponsoring employer to organise a work permit for you, and you must apply for it from abroad. As a result, most Westerners working in Turkey do so illegally and have to leave the country and come back in again every three months.

Other Documents
Fewer museums seem to be giving discounts to holders of International Student Identity Cards (ISICs), although it's still worth brandishing them hopefully.

An international driving permit (IDP) may be handy if your driving licence is from a country likely to seem obscure to a Turkish police officer.

EMBASSIES & CONSULATES
Turkish Embassies
Following are the Turkish embassies and consulates in major cities around the world. For addresses of Turkish embassies in

neighbouring Middle Eastern countries see the relevant country chapters.

Australia (☎ 02-6295 0227, fax 6239 6592) 60 Mugga Way, Red Hill ACT 2603
Canada (☎ 613-789 4044, fax 789 3442) 197 Wurtemburg St, Ottawa, Ontario KIN 8L9
France (☎ 01 53 92 71, fax 01 45 20 41 91) 16 Ave de Lamballe, 75016 Paris
Germany (☎ 49-228 95 38 30, fax 228 34 88 77) Utestr 47, 53179 Bonn 2
Ireland (☎ 01-668 5240, fax 668 5014) 11 Clyde Rd, Ballsbridge, Dublin 4
Netherlands (☎ 70-360 4912, fax 361 7969) Jan Evenstraat 2514 BS, The Hague
New Zealand (☎ 4-472 1290, fax 472 1277) Level 8, 15-17 Murphy St, Wellington
UK (☎ 020-7393 0202, fax 7393 0066) 43 Belgrave Square, London SW1X 8PA
USA (☎ 202-659 8200, fax 659 0744) 1714 Massachusetts Ave, NW Washington, DC 20036

Embassies & Consulates in Turkey
Foreign embassies are in Ankara but many countries also have consulates in İstanbul. In general they are open from 9.30am to 3.30pm Monday to Friday, although there's usually an hour off for lunch. The offices of some Islamic countries (notably Iran) close on Friday, but may be open on Sunday.

Australia (Avustralya) (☎ 446 1180, fax 446 1188) Nenehatun Caddesi 83, Gaziosmanpaşa, Ankara
   Consulate: (☎ 257 7050, fax 257 7054) Tepecik Yolu 58, Etiler, İstanbul
Bulgaria (☎ 426 7455, fax 427 3178) Atatürk Bulvarı 124, Kavaklıdere, Ankara
Canada (☎ 436 1275, fax 446 4437) Nenehatun Caddesi 75, Gaziosmanpaşa, Ankara
Egypt (☎ 0312-426 1026, fax 427 0099) Atatürk Bulvarı 126, Kavaklıdere, Ankara
   Consulate: (☎ 0212-263 6038, fax 257 4428) Cevdet Paşa Caddesi 173, Bebek, Istanbul
France (☎ 468 1154, fax 467 9434) Paris Caddesi 70, Kavaklıdere, Ankara
   Consulate: (☎ 293 2460, fax 249 9168) İstiklal Caddesi 8, Taksim, İstanbul
Germany (☎ 426 5465, fax 426 6959) Atatürk Bulvarı 114, Kavaklıdere, Ankara
   Consulate: (☎ 334 6100, fax 249 9920) İnönü Caddesi 16-18, Taksim, İstanbul
Greece (☎ 436 8860, fax 446 3191) Ziya-ur-Rahman Caddesi (Karagöz Caddesi) 9-11, Gaziosmanpaşa, Ankara
   Consulate: (☎ 245 0596, fax 252 1365) Ağahamam Turnacıbaşı Sokak 32, Beyoğlu, İstanbul
Iran (☎ 468 2820, fax 468 2823) Tahran Caddesi 10, Kavaklıdere, Ankara

TURKEY

Consulate: (☎ 513 8230, fax 511 5219)
Ankara Caddesi 1/2, Cağaloğlu, İstanbul
Consulate: (☎ 442-218 3876, fax 316 1182)
off Atatürk Bulvarı, Erzurum
Iraq (☎ 468 7421, fax 468 9821) Turan Emeksiz
Sokak 11, Gaziosmanpaşa, Ankara
Ireland (☎ 446 6172, fax 446 8061) Uğur
Mumcu Caddesi, MNG Binasi B-Bl 88/3,
Gaziosmanpaşa, Ankara
Consulate: (☎ 246 6025, fax 248 0744)
Cumhuriyet Caddesi 26/A, Harbiye, İstanbul
Israel (☎ 446 3605, fax 446 8071) Mahatma
Gandhi Caddesi 85, 06700 Gaziosmanpaşa,
Ankara
Consulate: (☎ 317 6500, fax 317 6555) YK
Plaza C Blok K 7, 4 Levent, İstanbul
Jordan (☎ 0312-440 2054, fax 440 4327) Mes-
nevi Ded Korkut Sokak 18, Çankaya, Ankara
Consulate: (☎ 0212-230 1221, 241 4331)
Kalıpcı Sokak 119/6, Teşvikiye, İstanbul
Kuwait (☎ 0312-445 0576, fax 446 6839) Reşit
Galip Caddesi, Kelebek Sokak 110, Gazios-
manpaşa, Ankara
Lebanon (☎ 0312-446 7485, fax 446 1023)
Kıkulesi Sokak 44, Gaziosmanpaşa, Ankara
Consulate: (☎ 0212-236 1365, fax 227 3373)
Teşvikiye Caddesi 134/1, Teşvikiye, İstanbul
Netherlands (☎ 446 0470, fax 446 3358) Uğur
Mumcu Caddesi 16, Gaziosmanpaşa, Ankara
Consulate: (☎ 251 5030, fax 251 9289) İstiklal
Caddesi 393, Beyoğlu, İstanbul
New Zealand (☎ 467 9056, fax 467 9013) İran
Caddesi 13/4, Kavaklıdere, Ankara
Oman (☎ 0312-447 0630, fax 447 0632)
Mahatma Gandhi Caddesi 63, Gaziosmanpaşa,
Ankara
Qatar (☎ 0312-441 1364, fax 441 1544) Karaca
Sokak 19, Gaziosmanpaşa, Ankara
Saudi Arabia (☎ 0312-468 5540, fax 427 4886)
Turan Emeksiz Sokak 6, Gaziosmanpaşa,
Ankara
Consulate: (☎ 0212-275 4396, fax 274 9995)
Akıncı Bayırı Sokak 8, Mecidiyeköy, İstanbul
Syria (☎ 440 9657, fax 438 5609) Sedat Simavi
Sokak 40, Çankaya, Ankara
Consulate: (☎ 232 6721, fax 230 2215)
Maçka Caddesi 59/5, İstanbul
UAE (☎ 0312-447 6861, fax 447 5548) Reşit
Galip Caddesi, Şairler Sokak 28, Gaziosman-
paşa, Ankara
Consulate: (☎ 0212-279 6348, fax 278 0570)
Altzeren Sokak 7, 1 Levent, İstanbul
UK (☎ 468 6230, fax 468 3214) Şehit Ersan
Caddesi 46/A, Çankaya, Ankara
Consulate: (☎ 293 7546, fax 245 4989)
Meşrutiyet Caddesi 34, Beyoğlu, İstanbul
USA (☎ 455 5555, fax 467 0019) Atatürk
Bulvarı 110, Kavaklıdere, Ankara
Consulate: (☎ 229 0075, fax 323 2037) Şehit
Halil İbrahim Caddesi 23, İstiniye, İstanbul
Yemen (☎ 0312-446 2637, fax 446 1778)
Fethiye Sokak 2, Gaziosmanpaşa, Ankara

CUSTOMS

Two hundred cigarettes, 50 cigars or 200g of
tobacco, one litre of liquor and four litres of
wine can be imported duty-free. Duty-free
items can be bought both on arrival and departure from Turkey's international airports.

It's strictly illegal to buy, sell or export
antiquities. Customs officers spot-check
luggage and will want proof that you have
permission before letting you leave with an
antique carpet.

MONEY
Currency

The Turkish lira (TL) comes in coins of
25,000, 50,000 and 250,000 lira, and notes
(bills) of 100,000, 250,000, 500,000, one
million, five million, 10 million and 20 million lira. Hopes that the zeros could be
lopped off these unwieldy denominations
once inflation was under control have been
abandoned in the wake of the economic crisis, which saw inflation soar to around 90%.
Prices in this chapter are quoted in more
stable US dollars.

Exchange Rates

During 2001 the Turkish lira devalued
steadily in line with inflation. At the time of
writing, however, it had regained some of its
value. Check exchange rates shortly before
your visit and be prepared for fluctuations.

Below are the rates for a range of currencies when this book went to print.

country	unit		Turkish lira
Australia	A$1	=	TL901,683
Canada	C$1	=	TL1,051,440
euro zone	€1	=	TL1,632,609
Japan	¥100	=	TL1,365,511
New Zealand	NZ$1	=	TL778,313
UK	UK£1	=	TL2,599,141
USA	US$1	=	TL1,660,000

It's easy to buy Iranian rials in Doğubeyazıt
and Syrian pounds in Antakya, but changing them back again is unlikely to land you
a profit.

Exchanging Money

It's easy to change major currencies in most
exchange offices, post offices (PTTs),
shops and hotels, although banks may make
heavier weather of it. Cashing even major

travellers cheques is less easy (post offices in tourist areas are a good bet) and the exchange rate is usually slightly lower. Places that don't charge a commission usually offer a worse exchange rate instead.

Although Turkey has no black market, foreign currencies are readily accepted in shops, hotels and restaurants in main tourist areas. If the currency is fluctuating particularly wildly it can be in your own interest to settle hotel bills in hard currency.

ATMs & Credit Cards ATMs readily dispense Turkish lira to Visa, MasterCard, Cirrus, Maestro and Eurocard holders; there's hardly a town that lacks a machine. Provided that your home banking card only requires a four-digit personal-identification number (PIN), it's perfectly possible to get around Turkey with nothing else. But remember to draw out money in the towns to tide you through the villages, and keep some cash in reserve for the inevitable day when the ATM decides to throw a wobbly.

Visa and MasterCard/Access are quite widely accepted by hotels, restaurants, carpet shops etc, although not by pensions and local restaurants. You can also get cash advances on these cards. AmEx (American Express) cards are rarely useful.

International Transfers For info on **Western Union** call ☎ 0212-212 6666. Branches of several big international banks (including HSBC) operating in İstanbul may also be able to transfer money for you (slowly). If you're expecting to receive cash you may have to be very persistent; while interest rates are high it is often in the bank's interest to delay handing funds over.

Costs

Turkey is still relatively cheap, especially away from İstanbul and the coast. It's still possible to travel on as little as US$15 to US$20 per person per day if you use buses or trains, stay in pensions and eat only one restaurant meal daily. For US$20 to US$35 per day you can upgrade to one- and two-star hotels with private bathrooms, eat most meals in restaurants and manage some of the heftier monument admission fees. On more than US$50 per person per day you can luxuriate in three- and four-star hotels, take the occasional flight and dine out constantly. Costs are lowest in small eastern towns off the tourist trail, but Cappadocia, Selçuk, Pamukkale and Olympos still offer bargain prices.

Unfortunately, since the economic crisis (see Economy in the Facts about Turkey section earlier in this chapter), frequent price increases have become a fact of life in Turkey; the prices given in this chapter should be treated as a guideline only.

Tipping & Bargaining

Turkey is fairly European in its approach to tipping and you won't be pestered by demands for baksheesh as elsewhere in the Middle East. Leave waiters and bath attendants around 10% of the bill; a hotel porter US$0.50 to US$1; and a cinema usher a few coins. You might round up your taxi fare but there's absolutely no need to tip *dolmuş* drivers.

Taxes & Refunds

Value-added tax of 15% to 20% is included in the price of most items and services: look for signs saying *'KDV dahil'* (VAT included). Some hotels and shops discount the price if you agree to forego the official receipt.

If you buy an expensive item like a carpet, ask the shopkeeper for a *'KDV iade özel fatura'* (special VAT refund receipt). Get it stamped as you clear customs, then try to get a refund at a bank in the airport departure lounge. Alternatively, you can mail the receipt and one distant day a cheque may conceivably arrive.

POST & COMMUNICATIONS
Post

Turkish *postanes* (post offices) are indicated by black-on-yellow 'PTT' signs.

Postcards to Europe cost US$0.30; to Australia, New Zealand and the USA US$0.45. Letters to Europe cost US$0.45; to Australia, New Zealand and the USA US$0.55.

It's best to post letters in the post-office slots rather than in street letter boxes. The *yurtdışı* slot is for mail to foreign countries, the *yurtiçi* for mail to other Turkish cities and *şehiriçi* for local mail.

Main post offices operate a courier-type *acele posta servisi* (APS), which is supposed to be a cheaper alternative to the international express carriers like Federal

Express. If you must get something somewhere quickly, ask for this rather than the slower *ekspres* (special delivery) service.

Although mailing packages abroad is fairly straightforward, your package may have to be opened for customs inspection, so it's best to anticipate some delay. To be sure that a parcel will get to its destination intact, send it by *kayıtlı* (registered mail). Better still, use APS, DHL, FedEx, UPS or TNT.

Most post offices in tourist areas offer a poste restante service. To collect your mail, go to the main post office and show your passport. Letters sometimes take several weeks to arrive (packets even longer), so plan ahead accordingly. Parcels are often opened by customs and then resealed. There are too few AmEx offices to use them as a mail service.

Telephone

The country code for Turkey is ☎ 90, followed by the local area code (minus the zero), then the seven-digit subscriber number. Local area codes are given at the start of each city or town section. Note that İstanbul has two codes: ☎ 0212 for the European side and ☎ 0216 for the Asian side. The international access code (to call abroad from Turkey) is ☎ 00.

Phoning home from Turkey is surprisingly expensive, mainly because of taxes; it costs around UK£1 to phone Britain for one minute, US$3 per minute to phone the USA and even more to call Australia. The cheapest rates operate from 10.30pm to 7am and from 7am on Sunday to 7am on Monday; it's also slightly cheaper to phone on Saturday or after 8pm on weekdays. Hotels often levy exorbitant surcharges, even on local calls. Wherever possible, try to make collect (reverse-charge) calls, although this facility is not currently available to New Zealand.

These days all Türk Telekom's public telephones require telephone cards, which can be bought at telephone centres or, for a small mark-up, at some shops. If you're only going to make one quick call, it's easier to look for a booth with a sign saying '*köntörlü telefon*', where the cost of your call will be metered.

Mobiles The Turks just love mobile *(cep)* phones. However, calling a mobile costs roughly three times the cost of calling a land line, no matter where you are. If you set up a roaming facility with your home phone provider you should be able to connect your own mobile to the Turkcell or Telsim network. At the time of writing US-bought mobile phones couldn't be used in Turkey.

Fax

Türk Telekom centres have faxes but require lots of paperwork and often insist on retaining your original! It's easier to use your hotel fax, although you should always check the cost first.

Email & Internet Access

Wherever you go, you'll never be far from an Internet café. Lots of hotels, pensions, tour operators and carpet shops are also hooked up. Fees are usually around US$1 for an hour, and less in areas with lots of competition and/or few tourists.

CompuServe has nodes (9600 bps) in Ankara (modem 468 8042) and İstanbul (modem 234 5168). **AOL**'s İstanbul node is 234 5158 (28,800 bps). Consult your online service for more information on charges etc.

Many phones use US-style RJ11 modular plugs (common in expensive hotels). For cheaper hotels you must buy a three-prong *telefon fişi* (Turkish phone plug) and make an adapter.

DIGITAL RESOURCES

Many websites feature Turkey, and many hotels, bus companies and other travel services have their own sites. The following are worth looking at:

Transport Detailed public transport information but no fares
  ⓦ www.neredennereye.com
Turkish Airlines (Türk Hava Yolları; THY) Lists all THY's flight schedules
  ⓦ www.thy.com
Turkish Daily News The latest news as well as ads for teaching jobs etc
  ⓦ www.turkishdailynews.com
Turkish Embassy The Turkish embassy in Washington, DC's site is good for visa, consular and economic information and email addresses of Turkish diplomatic missions; it also has links to other Turkey-related sites
  ⓦ www.turkishembassy.org

BOOKS

As well as this book, Lonely Planet publishes a detailed country guide, *Turkey*, and a separate city guide, *İstanbul*, complete with colour maps. Other products that might be of use include LP's *Turkish phrasebook*.

The most accessible introduction to modern Turkey is probably Hugh & Nicole Pope's *Turkey Unveiled: A History of Modern Turkey*. However, for the low-down on Turkey's national hero you should dip into Lord Kinross's definitive *Atatürk: The Rebirth of a Nation* or Andrew Mango's more recent doorstopper, also called *Atatürk*. Noel Barber's *Lords of the Golden Horn* is a gripping account of the decline of the Ottoman Empire. Recent Turkey-focused travelogues include Jeremy Seal's entertaining *A Fez of the Heart* and Tim Kelsey's more sober *Dervish*.

Barbara Nadel's gripping detective novels *Balthazar's Daughter*, *A Chemical Prison*, *Arabesk* and *Deep Waters* are all set in modern İstanbul.

General Middle East titles, some of them covering Turkey, are listed under Books in the Regional Facts for the Visitor chapter at the beginning of this book.

NEWSPAPERS & MAGAZINES

Of the two local English-language newspapers, the *Turkish News* is more readily available since it is distributed with the *Turkish Star*. It's also marginally more lively than the longer-established *Turkish Daily News*, although that's not saying much.

In major tourist areas you'll find day-old European and US newspapers and magazines. Fez Travel's free magazine *Fark Etmez*, available in the big tourist gathering points, is full of tips for travellers.

Although from the way the Turks slag their governments off in print it may look as though there's little censorship, certain subjects (especially discussion of the 'Armenian genocide' or 'Kurdish problem') invite retribution against the journalists and editor responsible. Because some have wound up jailed (or even dead), hefty doses of self-censorship undoubtedly take place.

RADIO & TV

Most hotels and pensions in tourist areas subscribe to cable or satellite TV services that offer programmes in English, French and German as well as all the myriad Turkish channels. The Cine5 (Cine Beş) channel offers some English-language films, but is

rapidly being replaced by Digiturk, which offers more than 300 different channels (including CNN and the BBC).

Turkish Radio & Television (TRT) provides short news broadcasts in English on the radio each morning and evening.

PHOTOGRAPHY & VIDEO

Film costs about US$5, plus developing, for 24 Kodacolor exposures. Kodachrome is scarce, pricey and can't be developed in Turkey, though the simpler E-6 process films such as Ektachrome and Fujichrome are readily available and speedily processed in city photo shops. Watch the prices in popular tourist resorts.

Most big towns have camera shops that can take passport photos on the spot for about the same price you'd pay at home.

You must usually pay to use cameras or videos in museums. To use a flash or tripod, you usually need written permission from the Ministry of Culture, which is unlikely to be readily forthcoming.

LAUNDRY

Laundrettes and dry-cleaners can be found in the larger cities, but most çamaşır (laundry) is done in hotels; expect to pay around US$3.50 a load.

TOILETS

Although most hotels and public facilities have familiar Western toilets, you'll also see enough traditional hole-in-the-ground models to be able to join in the 'healthy' debate over which is the more hygienic. The Turkish custom is to wash yourself with water from a jug or a pipe attached to the toilet, using the left hand. Doesn't appeal? Then always carry toilet paper and don't forget to place it in the bin provided to avoid inadvertently flooding the premises.

Almost all public toilets require payment of about US$0.20.

HEALTH

In general, Turkey is a pretty healthy country to travel in, although many people experience the odd day of stomach upset. It's wise to stick with bottled water and to take the usual precautions over food hygiene, especially in July and August. There's a small but growing risk of contracting malaria in southeastern Turkey, where the lakes created by the GAP project have made it easier for mosquitoes to breed, but the average visitor is unlikely to linger long enough near the water to need to take precautions.

An *eczane* (pharmacy) can advise on minor problems and dispense many drugs for which you would need a prescription at home. Emergency medical and dental treatment is available at simple *sağlık ocağı* (dispensaries), *klinik* (clinics) and *hastane* (government hospitals; look for signs with a red crescent or big 'H'). You'll have to pay but fees are generally low.

The standard of hygiene and care in Turkey's state hospitals is not always high; make sure you have insurance that will cover treatment in a private hospital (those listed under Information in the İstanbul section later in this chapter have a good reputation) or repatriation in an emergency.

For more detailed information, see Health in the Regional Facts for the Visitor chapter.

WOMEN TRAVELLERS

Most women, whether travelling alone or with a friend, will find Turkey to be one of the easier Middle Eastern countries to deal with. There are no laws regulating how they should dress, for example, although it makes sense to wear modest clothing that covers the upper legs and arms, and to put on a headscarf before going into a mosque. Unrelated men and women are usually separated on buses and there are separate sections in most restaurants for women and families (although in tourist areas they won't mind where you sit).

In traditional society men and women still live very separate lives, although that is changing fast in İstanbul and the western coastal areas. This relative unfamiliarity with women is the usual excuse given for the pestering which drives many of us to despair as we try to go about our business in peace and quiet. Most men give up if asked to desist, but a few can turn nasty if their attentions are shunned, so be a bit careful what you say.

Although there have been occasional instances of rape and murder, in general tourist women are probably safer in Turkey than in their own home towns, even after dark.

GAY & LESBIAN TRAVELLERS

Although not uncommon in a culture that traditionally separates men and women,

overt homosexuality is not socially acceptable except in a few small pockets of İstanbul, Bodrum and other resorts. Laws prohibiting 'lewd behaviour' can be turned against homosexuals if required, so be discreet. Some *hamams* are known to be gay meeting places.

For more information, contact Turkey's own gay and lesbian support group, **LAMBDA İstanbul** (**e** *lambda@lambdaistanbul.org*).

DANGERS & ANNOYANCES

Although Turkey is one of the safest countries in the region, the number of ne'er-do-wells seems to be on the increase, so you must take precautions. Wear a money belt under your clothing and be wary of pickpockets in buses, markets and other crowded places. Keep an eye out for anyone suspicious lurking near ATM machines. And remember that a Western passport can be a valuable commodity.

In İstanbul, single men are sometimes lured to a bar (often near İstiklal Caddesi) by new Turkish 'friends'. The man is then made to pay an outrageous bill, regardless of what he drank. Drugging is also becoming a serious problem, especially for lone men. Sometimes the person in the seat next to you on the bus buys you a drink, slips a drug into it and then makes off with your luggage. However, it can also happen in hostels, pensions and especially in bars, so be a tad wary of whom you befriend, especially when you're new to the country.

More commonly, the hard-sell tactics of carpet sellers can drive you to distraction. Be warned that 'free' lifts and suspiciously cheap accommodation often come attached to near-compulsory visits to carpet showrooms.

At the time of writing travelling in the southeast seemed to be safe, provided you stick to the places mentioned in this book.

BUSINESS HOURS

Government and business offices/banks usually open from 8.30am to noon and 1.30pm to 5pm Monday to Friday. During the hot summer months the working day in some cities begins at 7am or 8am and finishes at 2pm. Also, during the holy month of Ramazan the working day gets shortened.

In tourist areas food and souvenir/carpet shops are often open virtually round the clock. Elsewhere, grocery shops and markets are usually open from 6am or 7am to 7pm or 8pm Monday to Saturday. Most markets close on Sunday, although one or two neighbourhood grocery shops stay open. It's increasingly rare for shops to close for lunch except in the most out-of-the-way places.

Friday, the Muslim Sabbath, is a normal working day in Turkey. The day of rest, a secular one, is Sunday.

PUBLIC HOLIDAYS

In addition to the main Islamic holidays described in Public Holidays & Special Events in the Regional Facts for the Visitor chapter, Turkey observes the following national holidays:

New Year's Day 1 January – decorated shops, gift-swapping and cards in a sort of surrogate Christmas

Children's Day 23 April – international festival with children invited to Turkey from all over the world

Youth & Sports Day 19 May – sports festival to commemorate Atatürk's birth

Victory Day 30 August – parades to commemorate victory over the Greeks during the War of Independence in 1922

Republic Day 29 October – commemorates the founding of the Turkish Republic in 1923

Atatürk's Death 10 November – a minute's silence observed at 9.05am in memory of Atatürk's death in 1938

SPECIAL EVENTS

Following are some of the major annual festivals and events in Turkey:

Anzac Day The great battle at Gallipoli is commemorated with a dawn ceremony (25 April)

International İstanbul Music Festival Concerts are held in a wide variety of venues, including Aya İrini; it runs from early June to early July

Kırkpınar Oil Wrestling Championship Huge crowds watch oil-covered men wrestling in a field near Edirne (June)

Mevlana Festival The dervishes whirl in Konya from 10 to 17 December

ACTIVITIES

Popular activities include hiking and trekking in the Kaçkar Mountains and other national parks. With the opening of the 500km Lycian Way from Fethiye to Antalya, Turkey also has its first marked national trail.

All sorts of water sports, including diving, water-skiing, rafting and kayaking, are available in the Aegean and Mediterranean

resorts. You can also try tandem paragliding at Ölüdeniz.

Skiing is becoming more popular, with the best facilities at Uludağ, near Bursa, on Mt Erciyes, near Kayseri, and at Palendöken, near Erzurum. However, even at these sites the facilities would not meet the standards of the better European resorts.

Those of a lazier disposition may want to take a *gület* (yacht) trip along the coast, stopping off to swim in bays along the way. The laziest 'activity' of all consists of paying a visit to a *hamam*, or Turkish bath, where you can get yourself scrubbed and massaged for a fraction of what it would cost in most Western countries. The sexes were always segregated in traditional Turkish baths and this remains the case if you frequent one of the inland baths. Along the coast, however, mixed bathing has become the norm – along with inflated prices – in response to the perceived preferences of Westerners.

For more details on all of these activities, see Lonely Planet's *Turkey*.

COURSES

A great place to learn Turkish is **Dilmer** (☎ 252 5154; *İnönü Caddesi, Prof Dr Tarık Zafer Tunaya Sokak 18, Taksim, İstanbul*). One- and two-month courses are available (morning, afternoon and evening) at a variety of different levels. Another possibility is **International House** (☎ 282 9064, fax 282 3218; *Nispetiye Caddesi, Güvercin Durağı, Erdölen İşhani38, Kat 1, Levent, İstanbul*).

The *Turkish Daily News* sometimes carries ads for private tutors. Alternatively, try advertising for one yourself at Yağmur Internet Café in Beyoğlu, which has a good notice board.

ACCOMMODATION
Camping

Camping facilities are dotted about Turkey, although not perhaps as frequently as you might hope. The best are usually on Forestry Department land. Some hotels and pensions will also let you camp in their grounds and use their facilities for a small fee (US$2 to US$4). A few resorts boast well-equipped European-style camp sites.

Hostels

Given that pensions are so cheap, Turkey has no real hostel network, although a few places now claim to be affiliated to Hostelling International. Some are real hostels with dormitories, others little different from the cheapest pensions.

Pensions & Hotels

Most tourist resorts offer simple pensions with a good, clean bed for around US$7 a night. These places usually offer a choice of simple meals (including breakfast), book exchanges, laundry services, international TV services etc. In comparison, the hotels in more traditional Turkish towns, however clean and comfortable, normally offer only Turkish TV in the rooms, only Turkish breakfast and none of the other 'extras'.

The cheapest nonresort hotels (around US$4 a night) are mostly used by working Turkish men travelling on business and are not always suitable for lone women, unless they're up for stares whenever they enter the lobby. Moving up a price bracket, one- and two-star hotels may cost US$15 to US$30 for a double room with shower, but are less oppressively masculine in atmosphere, even when the clientele remains mainly male. Three-star hotels are usually accustomed to women travellers as well.

Not surprisingly, the most difficult places to find really good cheap rooms are İstanbul, Ankara, İzmir and package-holiday resort towns like Alanya. In most other cities and resorts good, inexpensive beds are readily available. Note that breakfast is normally included in the room rates of all two- and three-star hotels, although you usually pay extra for it in one-star hotels and pensions.

In smaller tourist towns like Fethiye, Pamukkale and Selçuk, touts for the pensions may accost you as you step from your bus and string you whatever line they think will get you to their lair most quickly. For everyone's sake, do your best to avoid letting them make your choices for you.

FOOD

Not without reason is Turkish food regarded as one of the world's greatest cuisines. No-one need fear going hungry here, although vegetarians will need to look closely to make sure meat-based stock hasn't slipped into even an ostensibly 'lentil' soup.

Kebabs (kebaps) are, of course, the mainstay of restaurant meals and you'll find lokantas selling a wide range of kebabs everywhere

you go. Try the ubiquitous durum döner kebap – lamb packed onto a vertical revolving spit, sliced off and tucked into bread and rolled up in pide bread. Laid on a bed of pide bread and with a side serving of yogurt, döner kebab becomes delicious İskender kebap, a primarily lunch-time delicacy.

For a quick, cheap fill you could hardly do better than a freshly cooked pide or Turkish pizza topped with cheese or meat.

Fish dishes, although excellent, are often expensive – always check the price before ordering.

For vegetarians a meal of mezzes (hors d'oeuvres) can be an excellent way to ensure a varied diet. Most restaurants will be able to rustle up at least beyaz peynir (white sheep's-milk cheese), börek (flaky pastry stuffed with white cheese and parsley), kuru fasulye (beans) and patlıcan tava (fried aubergine).

For dessert, try fırın sütlaç (baked rice pudding), aşure ('Noah's Ark' pudding made from up to 40 different ingredients), baklava (honey-soaked flaky pastry stuffed with walnuts or pistachios), or kadayıf (shredded wheat with nuts in honey).

The famously chewy sweet called lokum, or Turkish Delight, has been made here since the 18th century; there's not a bus station in the country that doesn't sell it.

In this chapter, the suggested price of a 'meal' should be taken to cover a soup or starter followed by a main dish and a soft drink. For more information on Turkish cuisine, look out for Lonely Planet's World Food Turkey guide.

DRINKS

The Turkish liquor of choice is rakı, a fiery aniseed drink like the Greek ouzo or Arab arak; do as the Turks do and cut it by half with water if you don't want to suffer ill effects. Turkish wine, both red and white, is improving in quality and is well worth the occasional splurge. You can buy Tuborg or Efes Pilsen beers everywhere, although outside the resorts you may need to find a Tekel store to buy wine.

Not a day will go by without your being offered a glass of çay. Turkish tea is grown on the eastern Black Sea coast and served in tiny tulip-shaped glasses with copious quantities of sugar. If it's too strong for you, ask for the milder but wholly chemical elma çay (apple tea).

If you're offered a tiny cup of traditional Turkish *kahve* (coffee), order it *sade* (no sugar), *orta* (medium-sweet) or *çok şekerli* (very sweet) and take care not to swig the grains. But these days Nescafé is fast replacing *kahve*. In tourist areas it usually comes *sütlü* (ie, with milk). Elsewhere expect it to be served black.

Bottled water is sold everywhere, as are all sorts of packeted fruit juices and canned soft drinks.

SPECTATOR SPORTS

Turks are fanatical football fans and barely a day goes by without a match on TV. To soak up the atmosphere of the real thing, try to get a ticket for one of the three İstanbul biggies: Galatasaray, Fenerbahçe or Beşiktaş.

More unusual sports include camel and oil wrestling. The main camel-wrestling bouts take place near Selçuk and Kuşadası from January to March, with oil wrestling near Edirne in June, but it's worth keeping an eye out for details of smaller local events too.

SHOPPING

As well as the legendary Turkish carpets, you may also want to buy clothes, jewellery, onyx or carved meerschaum as souvenirs. The widest choice of everything is available in İstanbul, but many people find the hard-sell tactics of the carpet salespeople off-putting. Bargaining is absolutely essential. You may prefer to postpone your purchases until you reach the more easygoing atmosphere of Cappadocia. The coastal resorts are great places to stock up on leather jackets, although classy, individual handicrafts are also sold in Bodrum and Kaş.

Getting There & Away

AIR

Turkey's most important airport is İstanbul's **Atatürk International Airport**. The cheapest fares are almost always to İstanbul, and to reach other Turkish airports, even Ankara, you usually have to transit İstanbul. In the last few years Turkey has built an increasing number of new domestic airports, all of them accessible on flights from İstanbul, some also accessible from Ankara.

Turkish Airlines and European carriers like Aeroflot, Air France, Alitalia, Austrian Airlines, British Airways, Finnair, KLM, Lufthansa and SAS fly to İstanbul. One-way, full-fare tickets from London to İstanbul can cost as much as US$425; it's usually advisable to buy an excursion ticket (from US$300) even if you don't plan to use the return portion. If you're planning a two- or three-week stay, it's also worth enquiring about cheaper charter flights, especially from Britain, France, Germany and the Netherlands.

Turkish Airlines offers flights to İstanbul from New York from about US$625/649 one way/return. From Los Angeles fares start at US$757/740 one way/return. It's also worth checking Delta, North Western, KLM and British Airways' fares, which can sometimes be quite competitive.

The cheapest flights to İstanbul from Sydney or Melbourne (Australia) are on Egypt-Air via Singapore and Cairo; one way/return fares start at A$985/1695. Japanese Airlines, Malaysian Airlines and Singapore Airlines offer fairly competitive fares or there are connecting flights via Athens, Amsterdam, London and Rome.

Fares to İstanbul from Auckland (New Zealand) start at NZ$1440/2400 one way/return on Air New Zealand, but Singapore Airlines, Qantas and British Airways' fares are also worth checking.

Turkish Airlines offers daily nonstop flights to İstanbul from Athens (1½ hours) and Tel Aviv (two hours). It also has several flights a week from Beirut (one hour), Tunis (two hours), Amman (2¼ hours), Cairo and Damascus (2½ hours), Kuwait (4¼ hours), Tehrān (4½ hours), Jeddah (5½ hours), Riyadh (5¾ hours) and Dubai (6¼ hours). It also has direct flights from İstanbul to Bangkok, Karachi, Singapore and Tokyo.

Buying Tickets in Turkey

Travel agencies in İstanbul, especially along Divan Yolu in Sultanahmet, specialise in selling cheap air tickets. Some agencies in popular resort areas have links that enable them to sell these same tickets, but in general you'll need to head for the big city to shop for bargains. One-way tickets start at US$140 to Frankfurt or London and US$260 to New York.

Departure Tax

A departure tax of US$12 is usually included in the cost of tickets bought in Turkey.

LAND

Since Turkey has borders with eight countries there are plenty of ways to get into and out of the country by rail or bus, although you'll need a transit visa for all of them except Greece. For details see the regional Getting There & Away chapter.

Turkey's relationship with most of its neighbours tends to be tense, which can affect the availability of visas and when/where you can cross overland. Always check with the relevant embassy for the most up-to-date information before leaving home. For the addresses of embassies and consulates in Turkey see Embassies & Consulates in the Facts for the Visitor section earlier in this chapter.

Iran

Once a week the *Trans-Asya Espresi* leaves İstanbul's Haydarpaşa train station at 10.55pm. Two nights later you'll arrive in Tehrān (US$42) at 6.45pm via Tatvan and Van. Alternatively, there are long, exhausting bus services from İstanbul and Ankara to Tehrān via Tabriz (US$30).

It probably makes more sense to make your way to Doğubayazıt and then catch a local bus onto the Gürbulak/Bāzārgān border, cross on foot and pick up a shared taxi on to Maku or Tabriz from the other side. This will avoid delays while everyone on the bus is searched at the border. There is also a border post at Esendere/Serō, southeast of Van, which brings you to Orumiyeh on the Iranian side. However, this border keeps shorter hours than the one near Doğubayazıt.

Syria

Daily buses connect Antakya with the Syrian cities of Aleppo (US$4, four hours) and Damascus (US$7, eight hours), and Amman in Jordan (US$20, 10 hours) via the border at Reyhanlı/Bab al-Hawa. You can also buy tickets direct from İstanbul to Aleppo (US$24, 24 hours) or Damascus (US$30, 30 hours). There are usually five or six daily departures between about 11am and the early evening.

For details of local transport to the border, see Getting There & Away under Antakya in the Mediterranean Coast section later in this chapter.

A train for Damascus (via Aleppo) leaves İstanbul's Haydarpaşa station at 8.55pm every Thursday (US$50).

SEA

Turkey has passenger shipping connections with Greece, Italy and northern Cyprus. For details see the regional Getting There & Away chapter.

Getting Around

AIR

Turkish Airlines (Türk Hava Yolları, THY) links all the country's major cities but domestic flights fill up rapidly, so try to book in advance. Smoking is prohibited on domestic flights.

A one-way ticket from İstanbul to Ankara (50 minutes) or Kayseri (for Cappadocia; one hour) costs US$76.

BUS

Turkish buses go just about everywhere you could possibly want to go, and what's more they do so cheaply and comfortably (around US$2.25 to US$2.75 per 100km). **Kamil Koç**, **Metro**, **Ulusoy** and **Varan** are the premium companies, offering greater speed and comfort for slightly higher fares. They have a better safety record than most companies, an important consideration in a country where traffic accidents claim hundreds of lives every year.

A town's otogar (bus station) is often on the outskirts, but the bigger bus companies usually have free *servis* minibuses to ferry you into the centre and back again. Most otogars have an *emanet* (left-luggage room) with a small charge, or you can sometimes leave luggage at the bus company's ticket office. Don't leave valuables in unlocked luggage.

Local routes are usually operated by midibuses or *dolmuşes*, minibuses that sometimes run to a timetable but more usually set off when they're full.

All Turkish bus services are officially smoke-free. However, you may want to avoid the front seats near the driver and conductor, the only people still allowed to puff away freely.

Fez Bus

The Fez Bus (☎ 516 9024, fax 517 1626; W www.feztravel.com; Aybıyık Caddesi, Sultanahmet, İstanbul) is a hop-on, hop-off bus service linking the main tourist resorts of the Aegean and the Mediterranean with İstanbul and Cappadocia.

A Northern Zone travel pass (İstanbul-Gallipoli-Ephesus-Cappadocia-İstanbul) starts at US$99; a Southern Zone travel pass (Ephesus-Köceğiz-Fethiye-Olympos-Capadocia-Ephesus) starts at US$85. A Turkish Delight Pass, combining the two, starts at US$199.

TRAIN

The **Turkish State Railways** (TCDD) has a hard time competing with the long-distance buses for speed and comfort, although trains are usually a bit cheaper than buses. Unfortunately, the stations are not always in the city centre. Only the special express trains such as the *Fatih* and *Başkent* are faster than the bus.

Ekspres and *mototren* services often have only one class; if they have 2nd class it costs 30% less. Return fares are cheaper than two one way fares. These trains are a little slower than buses, but they are sometimes more pleasant because you can get up and move around. On *yolcu* and *posta* trains you could grow old and die before reaching your destination. Trains east of Ankara are not as punctual or comfortable as those to the west.

Sleeping-car trains linking İstanbul, İzmir and Ankara are good value; the cheaper *örtülü kuşetli* carriages have four simple beds per compartment.

CAR & MOTORCYCLE

You can get help from **Türkiye Turing ve Otomobil Kurumu** (TTOK, Turkish Touring & Automobile Association; ☎ 0212-282 8140, fax 282 8042; Oto Sanayi Sitesi Yanı, Seyrantepe, 4 Levent, İstanbul).

Carnets are not required for stays of less than three months, but details of your car are stamped in your passport to ensure it leaves the country with you.

Mechanical services are easy to find, reasonably competent and cheap. The most common and therefore most easily serviced models are Fiat, Renault and Mercedes, but Volkswagens and Toyotas are starting to show up in large numbers as well.

In the west, petrol stations have been sprouting like cabbages recently and the new places usually come equipped with flashy *dinlenme tesisleri* (rest facilities). Further east you shouldn't expect such splendour. There are also some roads with fewer petrol stations than you might hope to find – the road from Eğirdir to Konya is one example.

In the major cities plan to leave your car and use public transport – traffic is terrible and parking impossible.

Rental

All the main car-rental companies are represented in İstanbul, Ankara and İzmir, but car hire in Turkey is pricey (often around US$35 a day) and driving hazardous. For a list of the main car-hire company offices, see Getting Around in the İstanbul section later in this chapter.

BOAT

Every Monday from June to early October a **Turkish Maritime Lines** (TML; ☎ 0212-249 9222; information ☎ 244 0207; Rıhtım Caddesi, Karaköy, İstanbul) car ferry departs from İstanbul, heading for Trabzon and Rize via Zonguldak and Samsun. It departs from Trabzon on Wednesday, arriving in İstanbul on Friday. Fares from İstanbul to Trabzon (per person, no meals) range from US$35 for a reclining seat to US$160 for a bed in the best cabin. A car costs US$56.

TML also operates a year-round car ferry service between İstanbul and İzmir, departing İstanbul every Friday afternoon and arriving the next morning in İzmir. In the other direction it departs from İzmir every Sunday afternoon, arriving in İstanbul on Monday morning. Fares range from US$17 for a reclining seat to US$164 for a luxury cabin, plus US$28 for a car.

ORGANISED TOURS

Most independent travellers find tours around Turkey expensive, especially since many of them park you in a carpet shop for an hour or so (the guide gets a kickback). In general, it's faster and cheaper to make your own travel arrangements. Be particularly careful if booking a tour out of İstanbul; some of these are ludicrously expensive compared with doing it yourself, especially if you still end up travelling on the same bus services and staying in the same pensions.

To guard against getting ripped off, use this book to work out the approximate cost of doing it yourself, add on a reasonable profit margin and take it from there.

Visitors who want to see the Gallipoli battlefield sites in a hurry may need to take a tour; see the Gallipoli entry later in this chapter for details.

If you're on a whistlestop tour of Cappadocia you may need to take a tour to see all the sights quickly; see Organised Tours in the Cappadocia (Kapadokya) section later in this chapter for details of some good local operators.

İstanbul

☎ 0212 (European side) • ☎ 0216 (Asian side)

A city of some 12 to 16 million individuals (depending on who's counting), modern İstanbul is the capital of the Turkish Republic in all but name. Ankara may hog the embassies, but it's İstanbul that has the palaces, the Bosphorus, the labyrinthine bazaars. It's a veritable treasure trove of things to see and do, a place to come back to time and time again.

İstanbul also boasts Turkey's best choice of places to eat and some of its finest hotels. It's from here, too, that trains fan out across the country and buses set off on their long journeys south, east and west. The coastal re-

---

İstanbul Highlights

- Best Dining – eating fish alfresco in Kumkapı; but be careful to ask the price of everything you order and to check the bill afterwards

- Best Nightlife – ducking down the side streets off İstiklal Caddesi in Taksim to find small live-music bars where you can listen to folk songs updated for a modern clientele

- Best Walk – strolling along Divan Yolu from the square between Aya Sofya and the Blue Mosque

- Best View – watching the floodlit Blue Mosque on a winter evening from Rami restaurant

- Best Activity – smoking a nargileh in the Çorlulu Ali Paşa Medresesi, off Divan Yolu

---

sorts aside, İstanbul is also the place with the liveliest nightlife, whether your tastes fall to clubbing, cinema-going or concert-catching.

History

Late in the 2nd century AD, the Roman Empire conquered the small city-state of Byzantium, which was renamed Constantinople in AD 330 after Emperor Constantine moved his capital there.

The city walls kept out barbarians for centuries as the western part of the Roman Empire collapsed before invasions of Goths, Vandals and Huns. When Constantinople fell for the first time it was to the misguided Fourth Crusade in 1204. Bent on pillage, the Crusaders abandoned their dreams of Jerusalem, instead ravaging Constantinople's churches, shipping out the art and melting down the silver and gold. By the time the Byzantines regained the city in 1261 it was a mere shadow of its former glory.

The Ottoman Turks attacked in 1314, but then withdrew. Finally, in 1453, after a long and bitter siege, the walls were breached just north of Topkapı Gate on the western side of the city. Mehmet II, the Conqueror, marched to Aya Sofya (Hagia Sofia) and converted the church into a mosque. Bar a tiny enclave on the Black Sea, the Byzantine Empire had ended.

As capital of the Ottoman Empire the city experienced a new golden age. During the glittering reign of Süleyman the Magnificent (1520–66), the city was graced with many beautiful new buildings. Even during the empire's long decline, the capital retained much of its charm. Occupied by Allied forces after WWI, it came to be thought of as the decadent capital of the sultans, just as Atatürk's armies were shaping a new republican state.

When the Turkish Republic was proclaimed in 1923, Ankara became the new capital. Nevertheless, İstanbul remains the centre for business, finance, journalism and the arts.

Orientation

The Bosphorus strait, between the Black and Marmara Seas, divides Europe from Asia. On its western shore, European İstanbul is further divided by the Golden Horn (Haliç) into Old İstanbul in the south and Beyoğlu in the north.

İstanbul's otogar is at Esenler, about 10km west of the city. Aksaray, midway between the city walls and Sultanahmet, is a major traffic intersection and heart of a chaotic shopping district. East of Aksaray, the boulevard called Ordu Caddesi runs uphill to İstanbul University, where it changes names to become Yeniçeriler Caddesi as it passes the Covered Market or Grand Bazaar (Kapalı Çarşı). As it heads downhill again past other historic sites to Sultanahmet it becomes the famous Divan Yolu.

Sultanahmet is the heart of Old İstanbul (a Unesco World Heritage site) and boasts many of the city's most famous sites, including the ancient Hippodrome (Atmeydanı), the Blue Mosque (Sultan Ahmet Camii), Aya Sofya and the Topkapı Palace (Topkapı Sarayı). The adjoining area, with hotels to suit all budgets, is actually called Cankurtaran, although if you say 'Sultanahmet' most people will understand where you mean.

North of Sultanahmet, on the Golden Horn, is Sirkeci train station, terminus for European train services. Ferries for Üsküdar, the Princes Isles and the Bosphorus leave from nearby Eminönü, the bustling waterfront.

Across the Galata Bridge from Eminönü is Karaköy, where cruise ships dock. Ferries also depart from Karaköy for Kadıköy and Haydarpaşa on the Asian shore. If you continue along the waterfront until you reach the big Beşiktaş football stadium you'll find the grandiose Dolmabahçe Palace, where Atatürk breathed his last.

Beyoğlu, on the northern side of the Golden Horn, was once the 'new' or 'European' city. These days it's a good area to scout out a cheap meal and some Turkish nightlife. An underground railway (Tünel) runs uphill from Karaköy to the southern end of Beyoğlu's pedestrianised main street, İstiklal Caddesi. A tram runs all the way to the north end, which is Taksim Square, the heart of 'modern' İstanbul, with many luxury hotels and airline offices.

On the Asian side, Haydarpaşa station is the terminus for Anatolian trains and those to Syria and İran. There's an intercity bus station at Harem, a 10-minute taxi ride north.

Information
Tourist Offices There are **tourist offices** in the Atatürk International Airport arrivals

hall (☎ 663 0793); in Sirkeci train station (☎ 511 5888); at the northwestern end of the Hippodrome in Sultanahmet (☎ 518 1802; tram: Sultanahmet); and near the UK consulate in Beyoğlu (☎ 243 2928; Meşrutiyet Caddesi 57, Tepebaşı; tram: Galatasaray Lisesi). In general, only the one in Sultanahmet is much use and many of them close between October and April.

Money Divan Yolu has several **foreign-exchange offices** and **travel agencies** offering speedy, hassle-free exchange facilities at fairly good rates. Most exchange offices are open daily from 9am to 9pm. Better rates are often available around the Grand Bazaar or you can try around Sirkeci station or along İstiklal Caddesi. The rates offered at the airport are usually as good as those offered in town, and sometimes better.

Most of the **banks** along Divan Yolu and along İstiklal Caddesi in Taksim have ATMs. There are also several ATM booths in Sultanahmet Meydanı between Aya Sofya and the Blue Mosque. They're certainly handy, although if the machine swallows your card it can be tricky getting it back again.

Post & Telephone For poste restante go to the **Merkez Postane** (main PTT; Sehinşah Pehlevi Sokak; tram: Sirkeci), just west of Sirkeci station. There are branch PTTs in the Grand Bazaar, and in Beyoğlu at Galatasaray and Taksim, as well as in the domestic and international departure areas at Atatürk airport. For much of the year a small PTT booth also opens in Sultanahmet Meydanı.

All phone numbers in this section use the ☎ 0212 area code unless otherwise indicated.

Email & Internet Access You can check your email at several hostels and cafés in Sultanahmet/Cankurtaran, including at the **Orient Youth Hostel** and **Mavi Guesthouse** (see Hostels under Places to Stay – Budget later in this section); and at **Yağmur Cyber-café** (☎ 292 3020; Şeyh Bender Sokak 18/2, Asmalımescit, Tünel; tram: Tünel). Expect to pay around US$1 per hour.

Travel Agencies Divan Yolu in Sultanahmet boasts several travel agencies that sell cheap air and bus tickets; some can also arrange train tickets and minibus transport to the airport but you will need to shop around

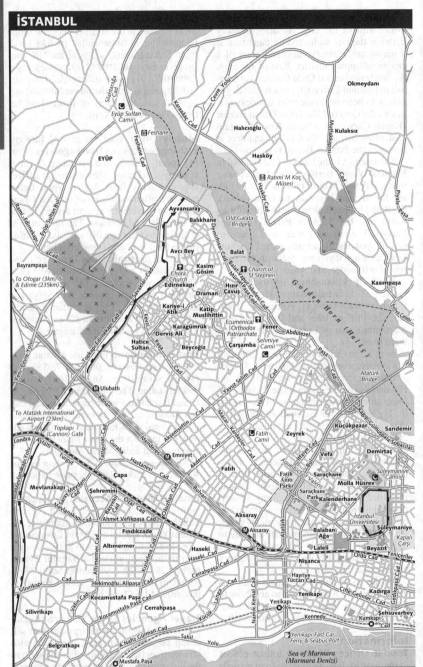

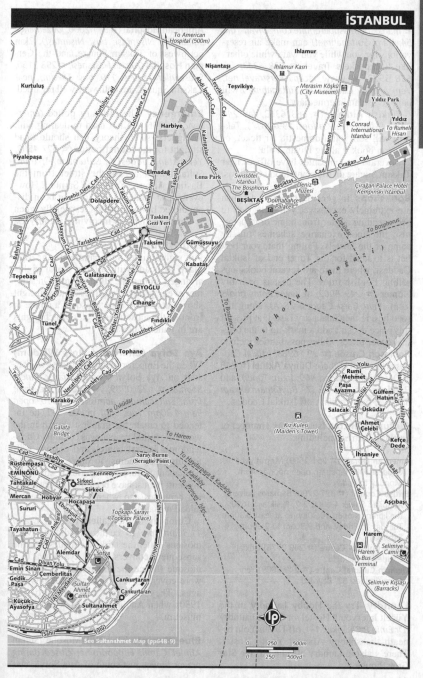

İSTANBUL

Kurtuluş

To American
Hospital (500m)

Ihlamur

Nişantaşı

Ihlamur Kasrı

Teşvikiye

Merasim Köşkü
(City Museum)

Yıldız Park

Harbiye

Piyalepaşa

Conrad
International
İstanbul

Yıldız
To Rumeli
Hisarı

Elmadağ

Çırağan Cad

Luna Park

Swissôtel
İstanbul
The Bosphorus

Beşiktaş

Çırağan Palace Hotel
Kempinski İstanbul

Yenişehir Dere Cad

Dolapdere

Deniz
Müzesi

BEŞİKTAŞ

Dolmabahçe
Palace

To Üsküdar

To Bosphorus

Tarlabaşı

Taksim
Gezi Yeri

Taksim

Gümüşsuyu

Tepebaşı

Galatasaray

BEYOĞLU

Kabataş

Cihangir

B
o
s
p
h
o
r
u
s
(
B
o
ğ
a
z
i
)

Tünel

Fındıklı

Necatibey

To Bostancı

Tophane

To Üsküdar

Karaköy

Yolu

Rumi
Mehmet
Paşa
Ayazma

Gülfem
Hatun

Galata
Bridge

To Harem

Kız Kulesi
(Maiden's Tower)

Salacak

Üsküdar

Ahmet
Çelebi

Kefçe
Dede

İhsaniye

Saray Burnu
(Seraglio Point)

To Haydarpaşa & Kadıköy

To Kadıköy

To Prince Isles

Rüstempaşa

Sirkeci

EMİNÖNÜ

Sirkeci

Tahtakale

Hocapaşa

Mercan

Hobyar

Topkapı Sarayı
(Topkapı Palace)

Aşçıbaşı

Sururi

Tayahatun

Aya
Sofya

Alemdar

Harem

Emin Sinan

Divan Yolu

Cankurtaran

Harem
Bus
Terminal

Selimiye
Camii

Gedik
Paşa

Çemberlitaş

Küçük
Ayasofya

Sultan
Ahmet
Camii

Cankurtaran

Sultanahmet

Selimiye Kışlası
(Barracks)

See Sultanahmet Map (pp648-9)

0   250   500m
0   250   500yd

for the best deals. **Marco Polo** (☎ 519 2804; e marco_polo@superonline.com; Divan Yolu 54; tram: Sultanahmet) can make air reservations for you while you wait, while others like **Backpackers Travel** (☎ 638 6343, fax 638 3922; w www.backpackerstravel.net; Yeni Akbıyık Caddesi 22, Sultanahmet) will have to use an intermediary.

Turkish Airlines (☎ 663 6363, fax 240 2984; Cumhuriyet Caddesi 199-201/3, Taksim) will sell you a domestic air ticket, or you can book it along Divan Yolu.

Several bus companies have offices near Taksim Square on Mete and İnönü Caddesis.

Bookshops In general, books in English are extremely expensive; you'd do well to bring reading matter from home or to patronise the book-exchange schemes run by some of the hostels. Failing that, your best bet is to head for the Tünel end of İstiklal Caddesi, where there are several bookshops selling English titles. The best is probably **Homer** (☎ 249 5902; w www.homerbooks .com; Yeni Carşı Caddesi 28/A), along the road beside the Galatasary Lisesi; at present this place doesn't add a mark-up to the original cover prices. Other possibilities include **Robinson Crusoe** (☎ 293 6968; İstiklal Caddesi 389; tram: Tünel); **Dünya Aktüel** (☎ 249 1006; İstiklal Caddesi 469; tram: Tünel); and **Pandora** (☎ 245 1667; Büyükparmakkapı Sokak 3; bus: Taksim), off İstiklal Caddesi.

Cultural Centres İstanbul has a number of cultural centres, including:

American Library (☎ 251 2589) Meşrutiyet Caddesi 108, Tepebaşı; open noon to 4pm Monday to Friday
British Council (☎ 327 2700) Barbaros Bulvarı, Akdoğan Sokak 43, Kat 2-7, Beşiktaş 81690; the library is open 10.30am to at least 5.30pm Tuesday to Friday, and 9.30am to 2.30pm Saturday
French Cultural Centre (☎ 249 0776) İstiklal Caddesi 8, Beyoğlu
German Cultural Centre (☎ 249 2009) Yeni Çarşı Caddesi 52, Beyoğlu

Laundry Try the **Hobby Laundry** in the Yücelt Interyouth Hostel, or **Active Laundry** (Dr Emin Paşa Sokak 14), off Divan Yolu beneath the shabby Arsenal Youth Hostel. There's also a laundry attached to the **Star Guesthouse**.

Medical Services In an emergency the **American Hospital** (☎ 311 2000; Güzelbahçe Sokak 20, Nişantaşı; bus: Nişantaşı), 2km northwest of Taksim Square, and the **German Hospital** (Alman Hastanesi; ☎ 293 2150, Sıraselviler Caddesi 119; bus: Taksim), near Taksim Square, are both very well regarded.

Emergency The ordinary **police** (emergency ☎ 155) are not used to dealing with foreigners, so in theory you should head straight for the **tourist police** (☎ 527 4503; Yerebatan Caddesi 6, Sultanahmet; tram: Sultanahmet) across the street from the Basilica Cistern (Yerebatan Sarnıcı). However, most readers seem to have been disappointed by their efforts, especially when it comes to disputes involving taxi drivers.

Old İstanbul

For sightseeing, Sultanahmet is the first place to head, with all the major sights arranged around the Hippodrome. On summer evenings there's a free sound-and-light show outside the Blue Mosque; a notice in front of the mosque indicates which nights are in which language.

Aya Sofya (Church of Holy Wisdom)

When the Emperor Justinian ordered work to start on Aya Sofya (Hagia Sofia or Sancta Sophia; ☎ 522 0989; Aya Sofya Meydanı; tram: Sultanahmet; admission US$10; open 9am-4.30pm Tues-Sun) in AD 532, he intended to create the grandest church in the world. For 1000 years it was certainly Christendom's largest church and despite scaffolding that seems to have become a permanent feature, the interior is still magnificent; it must have been truly overwhelming centuries ago when it was covered in gilded mosaics.

Climb up to the **gallery** (US$10; closed 11.30am-1pm) to see the splendid surviving mosaics. After the Turkish conquest and the subsequent conversion of Aya Sofya to a mosque (hence the minarets), the mosaics were covered over, as Islam prohibits images. They were not revealed until the 1930s when Atatürk declared Aya Sofya a museum.

Blue Mosque

The Blue Mosque (Sultan Ahmet Camii; Hippodrome; closed during prayer times), just south of Aya Sofya, was built between 1609 and 1619 and is light and delicate compared with its squat ancient neighbour. The exterior is notable for its six slender minarets and a cascade of domes and half-domes; inside, you'll find the luminous blue impression created by the tiled walls and painted dome. You're expected to make a small donation and to leave your shoes outside.

Up the ramp on the northern side of the Blue Mosque is a **Carpet & Kilim Museum** (admission US$1.25; open 9am-noon & 1.30pm-4pm Tues-Sat). Rents from the row of shops called the **arasta** on the street to the east provide support for the Blue Mosque's upkeep. Near the *arasta* is the entrance to the **Great Palace Mosaic Museum** (Büyük-saray Mozaik Müzesi; admission US$2; open 9am-4.30pm Tues-Sun), a spectacular stretch of ancient Byzantine pavement showing scenes of nature and the hunt.

Hippodrome In front of the Blue Mosque is the Hippodrome (Atmeydanı), where chariot races and the Byzantine riots took place. While construction started in AD 203 the Hippodrome was later added to and enlarged by Constantine.

The **Obelisk of Theodosius** is an Egyptian column from the temple of Karnak with 3500-year-old hieroglyphics, resting on a Byzantine base. The 10m-high **Obelisk of Constantine Porphyrogenitus** was once covered in bronze (the Crusaders stole the metal plates). The base rests at the former level of the Hippodrome, now several metres below the ground. Between these two monuments are the remains of a **spiral column** of intertwined snakes. Erected at Delphi by the Greeks to celebrate their victory over the Persians, it was later transported to the Hippodrome, where the snakes' heads disappeared.

Turkish & Islamic Arts Museum On the western side of the Hippodrome, the Turkish & Islamic Arts Museum (Türk ve İslam Eserleri Müzesi; ☎ 518 1805; Hippodrome; tram: Sultanahmet; admission US$2; open 9.30am-5.30pm Tues-Sun) is housed in the former palace of İbrahim Paşa, grand vizier and son-in-law of Süleyman the Magnificent. The building itself is one of the finest surviving examples of 16th-century Ottoman secular architecture. Inside, the most spectacular ex-

hibits are probably the wonderful floor-to-ceiling Turkish carpets, the beautifully illuminated Qurans and some of the mosque fittings, but don't miss the fascinating ethnographic collection downstairs either.

Basilica Cistern Across the tram lines from Aya Sofya is the entrance to the Basilica Cistern (Yerebatan Sarnıcı; ☎ 522 1259; Yerebatan Caddesi 13; tram: Sultanahmet; admission US$2.75; open 9am-4.30pm daily), which was built by Constantine and enlarged by Justinian. This vast, atmospheric cistern filled with columns held water not only for regular summer use but also for times of siege. It's sometimes open later on summer evenings when there may also be concerts inside.

İstanbul Archaeology Museum Down the hill from the outer courtyard to the west of Topkapı Palace is the İstanbul Archaeology Museum (İstanbul Arkeoloji Müzesi; ☎ 520 7740; Osman Hamdi Bey Yokuşu; tram: Gülhane; admission US$3.40; open 9.30am-5pm Tues-Sun). The main building houses an outstanding collection of Greek and Roman statuary, including the magnificent sarcophagi from the royal necropolis at Sidon in Lebanon, while a separate building on the same site (the Museum of the Ancient Orient) houses Hittite and other older archaeological finds. Also in the grounds is the graceful **Tiled Pavilion** (Çinili Köşk), built on the orders of Sultan Mehmet the Conqueror in 1472 and one of İstanbul's oldest Turkish buildings. Although it houses a museum of Turkish tile work you'll be lucky to find it open.

Divan Yolu Walk or take a tram (US$0.30) westward along Divan Yolu from Sultanahmet, looking out on the right for a complex of **tombs** for 19th-century sultans, including Mahmut II (1808–39), Abdülaziz (1861–76) and Abdülhamid II (1876–1909).

A bit further along, on the right, is the **Çemberlitaş** (Banded Stone), a monumental column erected by Constantine the Great some time during the 4th century. Within a century it had to be strengthened with iron bands. During a storm in 1105 Constantine's statue toppled off the top, killing several people sheltering below. In 1779 the column was badly damaged by a fire, and was further

SULTANAHMET

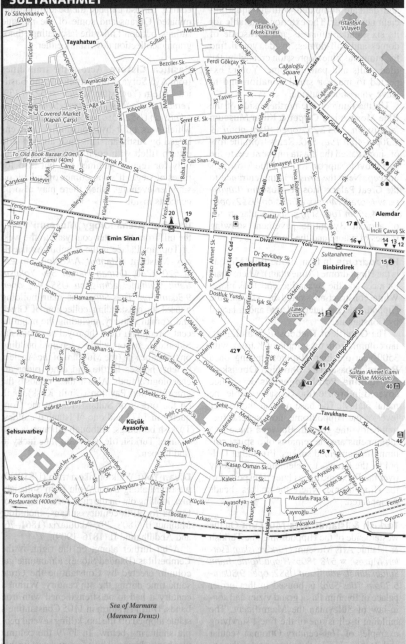

To Süleymaniye (20m)

Tayahatun

Covered Market (Kapalı Çarşı)

To Old Book Bazaar (20m) & Beyazıt Camii (40m)

Çarşıkapı Hüseyin

To Aksaray

Emin Sinan

İstanbul Erkek Lisesi

İstanbul Vilayeti

Cağaloğlu Square

Alemdar

Yerebatan

İncili Çavuş Sk

Sultanahmet

Divan Yolu

Çemberlitaş

Binbirdirek

Law Courts

Atmeydanı (Hippodrome)

Sultan Ahmet Camii (Blue Mosque)

Küçük Ayasofya

Şehsuvarbey

Işık Sk

To Kumkapı Fish Restaurants (400m)

Nakilbent

Tavukhane

Sea of Marmara
(Marmara Denizi)

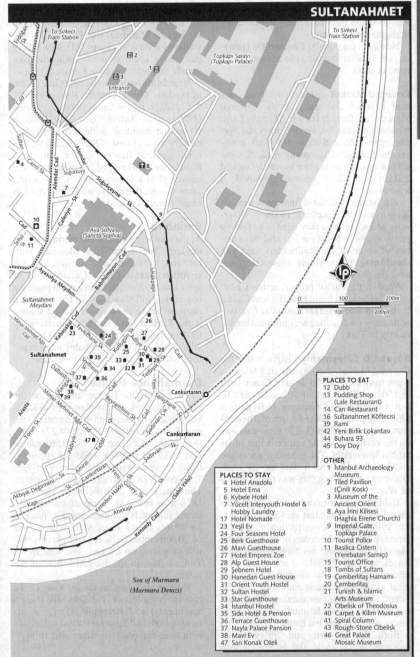

SULTANAHMET

To Sirkeci Train Station

To Sirkeci Train Station

Topkapı Sarayı (Topkapı Palace)

Entrance

Aya Sofya (Sancta Sophia)

Sultanahmet Meydanı

Sultanahmet

Ayasofya Meydanı

Sultanahmet

Cankurtaran

Cankurtaran

Sea of Marmara (Marmara Denizi)

0 — 100 — 200m
0 — 100 — 200yd

PLACES TO STAY
4 Hotel Anadolu
5 Hotel Ema
6 Kybele Hotel
7 Yücelt Interyouth Hostel & Hobby Laundry
17 Hotel Nomade
23 Yeşil Ev
24 Four Seasons Hotel
25 Berk Guesthouse
26 Mavi Guesthouse
27 Hotel Empress Zoe
28 Alp Guest House
29 Şebnem Hotel
30 Hanedan Guest House
31 Orient Youth Hostel
32 Sultan Hostel
33 Star Guesthouse
34 İstanbul Hostel
35 Side Hotel & Pension
36 Terrace Guesthouse
37 Nayla Palace Pansion
38 Mavi Ev
47 Sarı Konak Oteli

PLACES TO EAT
12 Dubb
13 Pudding Shop (Lale Restaurant)
14 Can Restaurant
16 Sultanahmet Köftecisi
39 Rami
42 Yeni Birlik Lokantası
44 Buhara 93
45 Doy Doy

OTHER
1 İstanbul Archaeology Museum
2 Tiled Pavilion (Çinili Kosk)
3 Museum of the Ancient Orient
8 Aya İrini Kilisesi (Haghia Eirene Church)
9 Imperial Gate, Topkapı Palace
10 Tourist Police
11 Basilica Cistern (Yerebatan Sarnıçı)
15 Tourist Office
18 Tombs of Sultans
19 Çemberlitaş Hamamı
20 Çemberlitaş
21 Turkish & Islamic Arts Museum
22 Obelisk of Theodosius
40 Carpet & Kilim Museum
41 Spiral Column
43 Rough-Stone Obelisk
46 Great Palace Mosaic Museum

strengthened with the iron hoops you see today. At the time of writing it was being strengthened yet again.

Nearby is the popular **Çemberlitaş Hamamı** (see Turkish Baths later in this section for more details).

Covered Market Just north of Divan Yolu, near İştanbul University, is the Covered Market, or Grand Bazaar *(Kapalı Çarşı;* w: *www.mygrandbazaar.net; tram: Universite; open 8.30am-6.30pm Mon-Sat)*, a labyrinthine medieval shopping mall of some 4500 shops. It's a fun place to wander around and get lost – which you will certainly do at least once.

The bazaar is divided into areas specialising in carpets, jewellery, clothing, silverware and so on. You may need to be feeling pretty strong to resist the forceful sales tactics of some of the stallholders, and you should never buy anything without haggling over the price first.

West of the bazaar proper, across Çadırcılar Caddesi and beside the Beyazıt Camii, is the **Old Book Bazaar** (Sahaflar Çarşısı), with many stalls selling second-hand books, mostly in Turkish.

Beyazıt & Süleymaniye Right beside the Covered Market, the Beyazıt area takes its name from the graceful **Beyazıt Camii**, built in 1506 on the orders of Sultan Beyazıt II, son of Mehmet the Conqueror. In Byzantine times this plaza was the **Forum of Theodosius**, laid out in AD 393. The great gateway on the north side of the square is that of **İstanbul University**. The gateway, enclosure and buildings behind it date mostly from Ottoman times when this was the Ministry of War.

Behind the university to the northwest rises İstanbul's grandest mosque complex, the **Süleymaniye**. Construction was completed in 1557 on the orders of Süleyman the Magnificent; he and his foreign-born wife Roxelana (Hürrem Sultan) are buried in a mausoleum behind the mosque. Süleyman's great architect, Sinan, is entombed near the sultan. The buildings surrounding the mosque originally served as a hospital, *medrese* (seminary), soup kitchen and baths.

Both the Beyazıt and Süleymaniye mosques are open to the public outside prayer times in return for a small donation.

Theodosian Walls & Chora Church
Stretching for 7km from the Golden Horn to the Sea of Marmara, the Theodosian city walls date back to about AD 420. Many parts have been restored during the past decade and work continues apace.

Near **Edirnekapı** (Adrianople Gate) is the marvellous **Chora Church** *(Kariye Müzesi;* ☎ *523 3009; Kariye Camii Sokak; admission US$10; open 9am-4.30pm Thur-Tues)*, a Byzantine building with the best 14th-century mosaics east of Ravenna, as well as some glorious frescoes of the same age. Built in the 11th century, it was restored and converted to a mosque, and is now a museum. To get there, take an Edirnekapı bus along Fevzi Paşa Caddesi.

Eminönü

At the southern end of **Galata Bridge** looms the large **Yeni Cami** (New Mosque), built between 1597 and 1663. Beside it is the **Egyptian Bazaar** (Mısır Çarşısı), full of spice and food vendors and a great place for last-minute gift shopping. To the west, on a platform above the fragrant market streets, is the **Rüstem Paşa Camii**, a small, richly tiled mosque designed by the great Ottoman architect Sinan; you'll probably need to ask someone to help you find the entrance.

Dolmabahçe Palace

Cross the Galata Bridge and follow the shore road along the Bosphorus from Karaköy towards Ortaköy and you'll come to the grandiose Dolmabahçe Palace *(☎ 236 9000; Dolmabahçe Caddesi; bus: Kabataş; admission US$5 for Selamlik, US$5 for Haremlik, US$8 for combined ticket; open 9am-3pm Tues-Wed & Fri-Sun)* right on the waterfront. The palace was built between 1843 and 1856 as a home for some of the last Ottoman sultans. It was guaranteed its place in the history books when Atatürk died there on 10 November 1938. A highlight of a visit will be gazing on his bed, shrouded in the Turkish flag, in the Haremlik part of the palace.

Visitors are taken on guided tours of the two main buildings: the **Selamlik** (men's apartments) and **Haremlik** (family apartments). Both buildings are stuffed to the gills with over-elaborate furniture and fittings.

[Continued on page 655]

TOPKAPI PALACE

Near Aya Sofya stands the sprawling, world-famous Topkapı Palace (*Topkapı Sarayı;* ☎ 512 0480; *Soğukçeşme Sokak; tram: Sultanahmet; admission: US$10 plus US10 for Treasury, US$10 for Harem & US$3 for Adalet Kulesi; open 9.30am-5pm Wed-Mon, 9.30am-noon & 1pm-3.30pm for Harem, 11am-noon & 1pm-2pm for Adalet Kulesi*). Allow at least half a day to see everything.

Mehmet the Conqueror built the first palace here shortly after the Conquest in 1453 and lived in it until his death in 1481. Many sultans followed him until the 19th century, when Mahmut II (1808–39) was succeeded by sultans who preferred living in European-style palaces like the Dolmabahçe.

The Site

Unlike European-style palaces, Topkapı is not one large building with outlying gardens. Instead it's a series of pavilions, kitchens, audience chambers and kiosks built around a central enclosure. You enter through the **Middle Gate** (Orta Kapı), which leads to the Second Court, which was used for the business of running the empire. It was constructed by Süleyman the Magnificent in 1524.

The second courtyard has a beautiful park-like setting. On the left-hand side is the ornate **Imperial Council Chamber** (Kubbealtı), beneath the **Justice Tower** (Adalet Kulesi). The imperial council met here to discuss matters of state while the sultan eavesdropped through a grille high on the wall.

Inset: A fanciful flower motif features on this decorative tile in the palace (Photo by Greg Elms)

Right: Twin turrets beckon one to the fairytale entrance of the palace and its sumptuous interiors

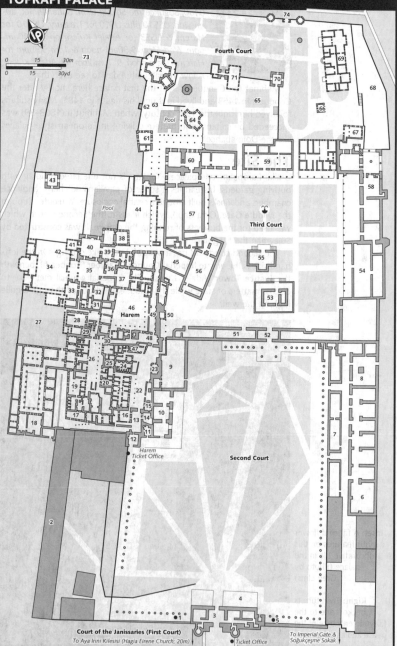

TOPKAPI PALACE

Fourth Court

Third Court

Harem

Pool

Pool

Second Court

Harem
Ticket Office

Court of the Janissaries (First Court)
To Aya Irini Kilesisi (Hagia Eirene Church; 20m)

Ticket Office

To Imperial Gate &
Soğukçeşme Sokak

TOPKAPI PALACE

SECOND COURT
1 Book & Gift Shop
2 Imperial Stables
3 Middle Gate (Orta Kapı)
4 Models of Palace
5 Imperial Carriages
6 Chinese & Japanese Porcelain
7 European Silverware
8 Confectionery Kitchen
9 Inner Treasury
10 Imperial Council Chamber (Kubbealtı)
11 Guard Room

HAREM
12 Carriage Gate; Dome with Cupboards
13 Hall with Şadırvan
14 Justice Tower (Adalet Kulesi)
15 Harem Eunuchs' Mosque
16 Black Eunuchs' Mosque
17 Laundry Room
18 Harem Hospital
19 Women's Dormitory
20 Women's Hamam
21 Black Eunuchs' Dormitories
22 Black Eunuchs' Courtyard
23 Harem Chamberlain's Room
24 Imperial Princes' School
25 Harem Kitchen
26 Concubines' & Consorts' Courtyard

27 Harem Garden
28 Valide Sultan's Quarters
29 Sultan Ahmet's Kiosk
30 Concubines' Corridor
31 Sultan's Hamam
32 Valide Sultan's Hamam
33 Chamber of Abdül Hamit I
34 Terrace of Osman III
35 Emperor's Chamber
36 Room with Hearth; Room with Fountain
37 Consultation Place of the Genies
38 Double Kiosk
39 Beautifully Tiled Antechamber
40 Privy Chamber of Murat III
41 Library of Ahmet I
42 Dining Room of Ahmet III
43 Private Prison
44 Favourites' Courtyard & Apartments
45 Harem Mosque
46 Courtyard of the Valide Sultan
47 Chief Black Eunuch's Room
48 Main Gate; Second Guard Room
49 Golden Road
50 Birdcage Gate

THIRD COURT
51 White Eunuchs' Quarters
52 Gate of Felicity

53 Audience Chamber
54 Dormitory of the Expeditionary Force
55 Library of Ahmet III
56 Mosque of the Eunuchs & Library
57 Gallery of Sultans' Portraits
58 Imperial Treasury
59 Treasury Dormitory
60 Sacred Safekeeping Rooms

FOURTH COURT
61 Circumcision Room
62 Moonlight Canopy (for breaking fast)
63 Marble Terrace & Pool
64 Erivan Kiosk
65 Tulip Garden
66 Bookshop
67 Sofa or Terrace Mosque
68 Cafe Terraces
69 Mecit Kiosk; Konyalı Restaurant
70 Tower of Chief Tutor
71 Kiosk of Mustafa Pasha
72 Baghdad Kiosk
73 Lower Gardens of the Imperial Terrace
74 Gate of the Privy Gardens

A bronze lion guards the delights of the palace gardens

TOPKAPI PALACE

ANDERS BLOMQVIST

Beside the Kubbealtı is the entrance to the 300-odd sumptuously decorated rooms that make up the **harem**. The harem is usually imagined as a place where the sultan could engage in debauchery. In fact, these were the family quarters where every detail of daily life was governed by tradition, obligation and ceremony.

Many of the rooms were constructed during the reign of Süleyman the Magnificent but others were added or reconstructed over the years. In 1665 a fire destroyed much of the complex, which was rebuilt by Mehmet IV and later sultans. You can only visit the harem on a guided tour. In summer head straight for the ticket booth when the palace opens; individual travellers can't always get in as tour groups pre-book all the slots.

The main gate into the Third Court leads into what was the sultan's private domain. Just inside is the **Audience Chamber**, constructed in the 16th century, but refurnished in the 18th century. Important officials and foreign ambassadors came here to conduct the business of state.

In the Third Court are the sultan's ceremonial robes and the fabulous **Imperial Treasury**, containing an incredible wealth of gold and gems and some truly stupendous thrones. The **Sacred Safekeeping Rooms** hold a solid-gold casket containing the Prophet Mohammed's cloak and other Islamic relics.

The Fourth Court contains four pleasure pavilions set amid gardens. The **Mecit Kiosk** was designed according to 19th-century European models.

Up the stairs at the end of the tulip garden are two particularly enchanting kiosks. Sultan Murat IV (1623–40) built the **Erivan Kiosk** in 1635, and the **Baghdad Kiosk** in 1638. Just off the terrace overlooking the Bosphorus is the **Circumcision Room**.

Top: Visitors to the harem inside the Emperors Chamber

[Continued from page 650]

Because the tour is very rushed not everyone will want to put aside the two hours required to see both parts. If you decide to opt for just one part, make it the Haremlik.

Any bus heading out of Karaköy along the Bosphorus shore road will take you to Dolmabahçe.

Beyoğlu

Cross the Galata Bridge and cut uphill from Karaköy towards the circular **Galata Tower**, from whose roof an intrepid, 17th-century 'birdman' launched himself on the first intercontinental flight to Asian İstanbul.

In its present form the tower dates from 1348, when Galata was a Genoese trading colony. Later it served as a prison, an observatory, then a fire lookout before it caught fire itself in 1835. In 1967 it was completely restored as a supper club. The **observation deck** (Galata Kulesi Sokak; tram: Tünel; admission US$3.50, Mon US$1.75; open 9am-8pm daily) is an excellent place for views and photos. Unfortunately, a set meal at the **restaurant** (☎ 293 8180, fax 245 2133) costs a rather prohibitive US$75!

İstiklal Caddesi & Taksim At the top of the hill is İstiklal Caddesi, once called the Grand Rue de Péra, now a pedestrian street served by a picturesque restored tram (US$0.30). The famed **Pera Palas Oteli**, patronised by the likes of Atatürk, is off to the west; huge consulates – embassies in Ottoman times – line the avenue, which is being slowly but steadily restored. Near the big Galatasaray Lisesi (high school) are the colourful **Fish Market** (Balık Pazar) and **Çiçek Pasajı** (Flower Passage), and an assortment of fish-and-beer restaurants where a fun night out is normally guaranteed.

Taksim Square, with its huge hotels, park and Atatürk Cultural Centre, is the hub of modern İstanbul and the scene of many a demonstration – a place best avoided when political tensions are running hot.

Rumeli Hisarı & the Bosphorus

The shores of the Bosphorus north of İstanbul are home to some beautiful old Ottoman buildings, including Rumeli Hisarı (Rumeli Castle; admission US$2; open 9.30am-5pm Thur-Tues), the huge castle built by Mehmet the Conqueror on the European side to complete his stranglehold on Constantinople.

There are also many small and surprisingly peaceful villages that have been engulfed to form the city's suburbs. Towns on the Asian side in particular have charm, open space and good food.

To get to Rumeli Hisarı, take any bus or dolmuş going north along the European shore of the Bosphorus to Bebek, Emirgan, Yeniköy or Sarıyer.

In summer a ferry ride up the Bosphorus is de rigueur for all İstanbul tourists, and is likely to prove a highlight of your trip. Organised excursion ferries depart from Eminönü daily at 10.35am, 12.35pm and 2.10pm each weekday, and stop at Beşiktaş on the European shore, Kanlıca on the Asian shore, Yeniköy, Sarıyer and Rumeli Kavağı on the European shore; and Anadolu Kavağı on the Asian shore (1¾ hours). Extra trips are added on Sunday and holidays, with boats departing from Eminönü at 10 and 11am, noon, 1.30pm and 3pm.

The weekday round-trip fare is US$3. Hold on to your ticket, as you need to show it to re-board the boat for the return trip.

Can't afford the time? Then you can take the 'poor-person's sunset cruise' across the Bosphorus and back by boarding any boat from Eminönü for Üsküdar.

The Princes' Isles

Once the site of monasteries and a haven for pirates, this string of nine spotless islands makes a popular getaway for İstanbul's middle class, many of whom migrate to live there in the summer. With good beaches, open woodland and transport by horse-drawn carriages, the islands, especially Büyükada (the biggest), make a pleasant escape from the noise and hustle of İstanbul. Ferries (US$3.50) to the islands leave from the special Adalar Iskelesi (Islands' Harbour) on the waterfront near Sirkeci station. Try to go midweek, when the queues for the horse-drawn carriages will be shorter.

Turkish Baths

İstanbul's most interesting historical Turkish baths (hamams) are pretty touristy, with prices to reflect their non-Turkish clientele. The best one to try if you're a first-timer is the beautiful **Çemberlitaş Hamamı** (Vezirhan Caddesi 8; tram: Çemberlitaş; admission

US$18; open 6am-midnight daily), just off Divan Yolu beside the Çemberlitaş monument. There are separate baths for men and women in a building possibly designed by the great Sinan himself. Prices would be outrageous anywhere else in Turkey, but the service here is experienced and hassle-free.

Organised Tours

In summer, tickets for open-top bus tours of the city's main sites are sold from a booth in Sultanahmet Meydanı, but most people will find they can get around perfectly well using the normal buses and trams.

Few of the city's tour operators bother with tours of their own city. **Kirkit Voyage** *(☎ 518 2282, fax 518 2281; ⓦ www.kirkit .com; Kutlugün Sokak 24; tram: Sultanahmet)* organises city walking tours, especially at weekends, but you need to check whether they will be led in French or English. **Senkron Tours** *(☎ 638 8340, fax 517 4524; Arasta Caddesi 51, Sultanahmet)* has a programme of half-day (US$30) and full-day (US$60) city tours, taking in all the main sites.

Special Events

The **İstanbul International Music Festival** from early June to early July attracts top-name artists from around the world, who perform in venues (like Aya İrini Kilisesi) which are not always open to the public.

Places to Stay

Hostels and camp sites aside, İstanbul's accommodation is becoming quite pricey. For the time being, the best area to stay remains Cankurtaran, immediately southeast of Sultanahmet, where the quiet streets play host to a range of cheap and moderate hotels, mostly with stunning views from their roof terraces. However, property values there are rising so fast it seems unlikely that room prices will not continue rising in tandem.

Most four- and five-star chain hotels are across the Bosphorus in Taksim, although the few luxury places in Cankurtaran are well worth frequenting.

Places to Stay – Budget

Camping In İstanbul camping is inconvenient and costs almost as much as staying in a cheap hotel (around US$10 for a tent and two people), on top of which you must pay fares in and out of the centre.

Londra Kamping *(☎ 560 4200; Çoban-çeşme-Kuleli Mevkii, Bakırköy; tent sites US$7)* is a truck stop with a large camping area behind it on the south side of the Londra Asfaltı, between the Topkapı district and the airport (coming east from the airport, follow the *servis alanı* signs).

Ataköy Mokamp *(☎ 559 6000; Ataköy Sahil Yolu, Bakırköy; tent sites US$11)*, on the shore southeast of the airport, is a holiday beach hotel–bungalow complex with camping facilities. To get there, take the No 81 bus from Eminönü.

Hostels İstanbul's hostels charge around US$8 (depending on demand) for a bed in summer, less in winter. In high summer even the hostels fill up (with the inevitable problems of noise and overstretched facilities), and roof space becomes available for around US$5. These days most of the hostels boast a few private single and double rooms for a few dollars more than the dorm prices, Internet access and extras like cafés and games rooms.

Yücelt Interyouth Hostel *(☎ 513 6150, fax 512 7628; Caferiye Sokak 6/1, Sultanahmet)*, a little way from the other hostels, is a big, brash place with lots of facilities including a mini-gym and laundry. Some rooms look onto Aya Sofya, right beside it.

İstanbul Hostel *(☎ 516 9380, fax 516 9384; ⓦ www.istanbul-hostel.com; Kutlugün Sokak)*, in Cankurtaran, is new and immaculate, and shows movies in its basement bar.

Further along and not to be confused with the expensive Mavi Ev nearby, **Mavi Guesthouse** *(☎ 516 5878, fax 517 7287; ⓦ www.maviguesthouse.com; Kutlugün Sokak 3)* is small and welcoming. Rates include breakfast, and the cosy ground-floor lounge is a plus.

One block over is Akbıyık Caddesi, with lots of places to stay, eat and drink.

Orient Youth Hostel *(☎ 518 0789, fax 518 3894; ⓦ www.hostels.com/orienthostel; Akbıyık Caddesi 13)* is a popular place with some newly decorated rooms, a top-floor café with marvellous Bosphorus views and a basement bar that features belly dancers and nargilehs (see the boxed text 'Return of the Nargileh' later in this section).

Sultan Hostel *(☎ 516 9260, fax 517 1626; ⓦ www.sultanhostel.com; Terbıyık Sokak 3)* is used as a base by Fez Bus and boasts Marmara views from its roof.

Hotels Yerebatan Caddesi runs northwest from Aya Sofya. A block past the Sunken Palace Cistern, turn right on Salkım Söğüt Sokak to find a couple of simple if uninspiring budget-priced hotels. **Hotel Ema** (☎ 511 7166; rooms without shower US$15) is on the left, while **Hotel Anadolu** (☎ 512 1035; singles/doubles without shower US$15/20) is down the street on the right.

Places to Stay – Mid-Range
Many Cankurtaran pensions are gradually upgrading into classy small hotels.

Side Hotel & Pension (☎/fax 517 6590; W www.sidehotel.com; Utangaç Sokak 20; singles/doubles in pension from US$20/35, in hotel from US$40/50) is one of those places where you arrive knowing no-one and leave with a whole bunch of new friends. To find it, head down from Aya Sofya and you'll come to Utangaç Sokak on the right. Breakfast is included in the prices.

Walk down past the Four Seasons Hotel and turn into Kutlugün Sokak for a couple more good options. **Berk Guesthouse** (☎ 516 9671; Kutlugün Sokak 27, Sultanahmet; doubles with shower from US$45) is a homely place with comfortable rooms and a family-run atmosphere. From the roof terrace and lounge you can eyeball goings-on in the grounds of the Four Seasons.

The tiny **Terrace Guesthouse** (☎ 638 9733, fax 638 9734; Kutlugün Sokak 39; doubles US$50) has only six rooms. They're cheerful enough and the carpets are very likely to be for sale. Across the road the **Nayla Palace Pansion** (☎ 516 3567, 516 6306; Kutlugün Sokak 22; doubles with shower US$25) has simple rooms with air-conditioning in a beautiful old building.

Star Guesthouse (☎ 638 2302, fax 516 1827; Akbıyık Caddesi 18; doubles with shower from US$30) is in the heart of an outdoor drinking area in summer, so it's likely to be noisy, although convenient if you're a night owl yourself.

Three small places in Adliye Sokak, a turn-off from Akbıyık Caddesi, are likely to be quieter than those right on it. **Hanedan Guest House** (☎ 516 4869, fax 517 4524; singles/doubles with shower US$25/35) is simplest, but does have a small rooftop café,

and **Alp Guest House** (☎ 517 9570; Adliye Sokak 4; singles/doubles with shower US$35/50) has pleasingly decorated rooms. But smartest is **Sebnem Hotel** (☎ 517 6623, fax 638 1056; W www.sebnemhotel.com; singles/doubles with shower from US$45/55), across the road, which has comfortable, colour-coordinated rooms.

Hotel Empress Zoe (☎ 518 2504, fax 518 5899; W www.emzoe.com; Akbıyık Caddesi, Adliye Sokak 10; singles/doubles with shower from US$55/70) is built around a Byzantine cistern next to an old Ottoman hamam. Rooms are tiny but stylish, although you must navigate a spiral staircase to access them. The rooftop bar/lounge/terrace affords good views of the sea and the Blue Mosque.

Sarı Konak Oteli (☎ 638 6358, fax 517 8635; W www.sarikonak.com; Mimar Mehmet Ağa Caddesi 42; singles/doubles with shower from US$59/79) is immaculate, has comfortable rooms, a mosaic-floored breakfast room and a rooftop dining room with sweeping Marmara views.

Hotel Nomade (☎ 511 1296, fax 513 24 04; Divan Yolu, Ticarethane Sokak 15; Sultanahmet; singles/doubles with shower US$50/60) is just off busy Divan Yolu but has pleasant decor and good views from the roof terrace.

Kybele Hotel (☎ 511 7766, fax 513 4393; W www.kybelehotel.com; Yerebatan Caddesi 35, Sultanahmet; singles/doubles with shower US$50/80) is a gem of a place, a reflection of its owner's taste, with 3000 glass lamps decorating every corner of a colourful hotel.

Places to Stay – Top End
Cankurtaran also harbours some wonderful hotels in restored Ottoman mansions or buildings designed to imitate them.

Yeşil Ev (Green House; ☎ 517 6785, fax 517 6780; Kabasakal Caddesi 5; singles/doubles with shower from US$120/160), probably the classiest, is a 22-room Ottoman house furnished with period pieces and antiques. Behind it is a shady garden restaurant.

Mavi Ev (Blue House; ☎ 638 9010, fax 638 9017; W www.bluehouse.com.tr; Dalbastı Sokak 14; singles/doubles with shower US$120/140) offers comfortable rooms and excellent morning views of the Blue Mosque from its rooftop restaurant.

Four Seasons Hotel *(☎ 638 8200, fax 638 8530; Tevkifhane Sokak 1; singles/doubles with shower US$360/450)* must, of course, be *the* place to stay. This gorgeous luxury hotel used to be a prison (the one in *Midnight Express*, what's more), but even at these prices it's often full.

Places to Eat

Once a legend among travellers, the **Pudding Shop**, also called Lale Restaurant, is now just one of a string of cheapish restaurants along Divan Yolu opposite the Hippodrome. At any of them a typical if unmemorable kebab meal costs around US$4 to US$6. The **Can Restaurant** is worth trying, and **Sultanahmet Köftecisi** is famed for its delicious grilled meatballs with salad, bread and a drink for US$3 or less – not surprisingly, it heaves with Turks at lunch time.

Yeni Birlik Lokantası *(Üçler Sokak 46; meals US$3-5; open 8am-3pm)*, favoured by lawyers from the nearby courts, is a good place to find a choice of stews at lunch time. At the far (southwestern) end of the Hippodrome, walk up Üçler Sokak one block to find it.

Doy Doy *(Sifa Hamamı Sokak 13; meals US$3.50)*, a long-time favourite, is downhill from the southeastern end of the Hippodrome. Offering cheap, simple Turkish staples, it's usually busy with a mixture of locals and travellers. Across the road, **Buhara 93** *(Nakilbent Sokak 15/A)* has similarly cheap and appetising meals.

Rami *(☎ 517 6593; Utangaç Sokak 6; meals about US$20-30)*, in a restored house offering fine views of the Blue Mosque from its terrace, is perfect for that special occasion and serves interesting Ottoman specialities like paper kebap and *hünkär beğendi* (lamb stew on pureed eggplant).

Dubb *(☎ 513 7308, İncili Çavuş Sokak 10; meals around US$15)* is that rare thing for Sultanahmet – a restaurant selling something other than Turkish food (in this case, delicious Indian meals). Be sure to book at weekends.

The Kumkapı neighbourhood following the shoreline 800m south of Beyazıt along Tiyatro Caddesi boasts dozens of good **seafood restaurants**. On summer evenings the whole place turns into one big party. A meal of fish and rakı is likely to cost US$14 to US$22, but you need to be careful to check the price of everything you order before eating. For a cheaper lunch, US$1 buys you a delicious fish sandwich from one of the boats moored near the Galata Bridge.

Although there's a reasonable selection of places to eat in Sultanahmet, for a bigger choice you must head across town to Beyoğlu. Just hop on a bus to Taksim Square (T4 from the Hippodrome) and start walking along İstiklal Caddesi and you'll be spoilt for choice, from the takeaway döner places right at the start of the street to the flashier, Westernised bar-cafés at the Tünel end.

Konak *(İstiklal Caddesi 259)*, near the big Galatasaray Lisesi, is a great place to tuck into an *İskender kebap* (döner kebap with yogurt, served on pide bread and topped with tomato sauce and browned butter). You sit beneath plaster ceilings and chandeliers that hint at Pera's past glory. A meal with cold drink will cost around US$4, a pide even less.

Saray *(İstiklal Caddesi 102)* is a great place to try out one of Turkey's myriad puddings; a bowl of *aşure* (Noah's Ark pudding), for example, should cost just US$1.50.

Entertainment

Coastal resorts aside, İstanbul is one of the few places in Turkey offering real nightlife, with a range of cinemas, theatres and concert halls, as well as plenty of pubs and clubs. In

Return of the Nargileh

Not so long ago the only Turks smoking water pipes were flat-capped, moustachioed older men who frequented the sort of traditional teahouses few tourists even ventured into. But in the last five years or so there has been a startling revival of interest in the pipes – and not just among tourists either. These days you can join young Turkish students over a pipe even in towns as notoriously conservative as Konya.

Not surprisingly, İstanbul was quick off the mark in catering for the new fashion and one of the most atmospheric places to try a puff is the courtyard of the Çorlulu Ali Paşa Medresesi, off Divan Yolu. You pay more to smoke and drink at Meşale, right in front of the Blue Mosque. Or if you're really up for it, hop on a bus from Eminönü to Tophane, duck behind the big mosque and try any one of the small local cafés there.

summer Akbıyık Caddesi in Cankurtaran really hops, with people drinking at tables set out on the pavements until the early hours. At other times of the year you may want to head across to Beyoğlu and investigate the small bars and clubs in the side streets off the Taksim end of İstiklal Caddesi, but be careful – many of İstanbul's pickpockets and scammers have the same idea.

For an excellent night out, head for **Babylon** *(☎ 292 7368; Şehbender Sokak 3, Beyoğlu; tram: Tünel)* where big-name bands occasionally play to rapturous audiences.

Getting There & Away

Air Most people fly into İstanbul's **Atatürk International Airport**, Turkey's international flight hub. Most foreign airlines have their offices north of Taksim, along Cumhuriyet Caddesi.

Bus A monster of a place, **İstanbul Otogar** *(Uluslararası İstanbul Otogarı; ☎ 658 0036, fax 658 2858; Esenler)* has 168 ticket offices, and buses leaving for all parts of Turkey and beyond. To get to it from Sultanahmet take the tram to Aksaray, switch to the metro and get out at Otogar.

Buses depart for Ankara (US$12 to US$24, six hours) roughly every 15 minutes, day and night; buses for most other cities depart at least every hour. Heading east to Anatolia, you might want to board at the smaller **Harem Otogar** *(☎ 216-333 3763)*, north of Haydarpaşa on the Asian shore, but the choice of service there is more limited.

Train For services to Edirne, Greece and Eastern Europe go to the station at **Sirkeci** *(☎ 520 6575)*. There are three express trains a day to Edirne (US$3, 6½ hours), but the bus is faster (US$6, three hours). The nightly *Bosfor Expresi* goes to Bucharest (US$26, 18 hours) and Budapest (US$95, 32 hours).

Haydarpaşa *(☎ 0216-336 4470)*, on the Asian shore, is the terminus for trains to Anatolia, Syria and İran. There are seven express trains a day to Ankara (US$10 to US$28, seven to 10 hours); the fastest is a sleeper only.

Boat For information on car ferries to İzmir and along the Black Sea coast to Trabzon, see Boat in the Getting Around sec-

tion earlier in this chapter. Buy tickets at the **Turkish Maritime Lines** (Denizyolları) office, just east of the Karaköy ferry dock.

Yenikapı, south of Aksaray Square, is the dock for *hızlı feribot* (fast car ferries) across the Sea of Marmara. Heading for Bursa, take a Yalova ferry or catamaran, which will get you to Yalova in less than an hour for US$35 (car and driver). The voyage to Bandırma takes less than two hours and costs US$70 (car and driver) or US$12 (pedestrian/passenger).

Ferries for the Princes' Isles depart from the waterfront near Sirkeci station (see Princes' Isles earlier in this section).

Getting Around

To/From the Airport The fastest way to get into town from the airport is by taxi. During the day *(gündüz)* it costs US$10 to Sultanahmet (20 minutes), US$12 to Taksim (30 minutes) and US$8 to the otogar (20 minutes), although fares are higher at night *(gece)*.

A cheaper but slower alternative is the Havaş airport bus (US$2, 30 to 60 minutes), which departs from the international terminal, stops at the domestic terminal, then goes to Taksim Square via Aksaray. Buses leave every 30 minutes from 5am to 11.30pm.

It's even cheaper to find other thrifty travellers and share a taxi (US$3 total; make sure the driver runs the meter) from the airport to the Yeşilköy or Yeşilyurt *banliyö tren istasyonu*, the nearest suburban train stations, from where battered trains (US$0.50) run every 30 minutes or so to Sirkeci station. Get off at Cankurtaran for Sultanahmet, or at Eminönü (end of the line) for Beyoğlu.

Many Divan Yolu travel agencies and Sultanahmet hostels book minibus transport from the hotels to the airport for about US$4 a head. Unfortunately, this option only works going *from* town to the airport and not vice versa.

Air Most domestic flights with **Turkish Airlines** *(☎ 663 6363, fax 240 2984; ⩊ www.thy .com)* cost under US$100. See the table Turkish Airfares for details.

Bus City buses are crowded but useful. Destinations and intermediate stops are indicated at the front and side of the bus. On most

TURKEY

Turkish Air Fares

route	duration (hrs)	frequency (one way)	fare
İstanbul-Ankara	1	hourly	US$76
İstanbul-Antalya	1¼	7 flights daily	US$83
İstanbul-Bodrum	1¼	1 flight daily	US$76
İstanbul-Erzurum	1½	3 flights daily via Ankara	US$82
İstanbul-İzmir	1	10 flights daily	US$76
İstanbul-Trabzon	1¾	3 flights daily	US$76

routes you must have a ticket (US$0.30) before boarding, so stock up on tickets in advance from the white booths near major stops or nearby shops.

Ferries The cheapest and nicest way to travel any distance in İstanbul is by ferry. The main ferry docks are at the mouth of the Golden Horn (Eminönü, Sirkeci and Karaköy) and at Kabataş, 3km northeast of the Galata Bridge, just south of Dolmabahçe Palace. Short ferry hops cost US$0.60, most longer ones US$1.20.

Train To get to Sirkeci station, take the *tramvay* (tram) from Aksaray or Sultanahmet, or any bus for Eminönü. Haydarpaşa station is connected by ferry to Karaköy (US$0.60, at least every 30 minutes).

Every 20 minutes suburban trains from Sirkeci (US$0.40) run along the southern walls of Old İstanbul and west along the Marmara shore. There's a handy station in Cankurtaran for Sultanahmet.

Tram The useful *hızlı tramvay* (fast tram) network has three lines. The first runs between Eminönü and Aksaray via Divan Yolu and Sultanahmet; the second runs west from Aksaray via Adnan Menderes Bulvarı through the city walls to the otogar. A third line runs from Taksim to 4 Levent. Another restored tram trundles along İstiklal Caddesi to Taksim. All tram tickets cost US$0.30.

Underground The Tünel, İstanbul's ancient underground train, mounts the hill from Karaköy to Tünel Square and İstiklal Caddesi (US$0.40, every 10 or 15 minutes from 7am to 9pm).

Car Rental It makes no sense to drive around İstanbul itself and have to deal with the traffic and parking problems. However, if you're heading out of the city all the main rental agencies have desks in the international terminal of Atatürk International Airport:

Avis (☎ 663 0646)
Europcar (☎ 663 0746)
Hertz (☎ 663 0807)

Taxi İstanbul has 60,000 yellow taxis, all of them with meters – even if not every driver wants to run them. From Sultanahmet to Taksim costs around US$5; to the otogar around US$10.

Around İstanbul

Since İstanbul is such a vast city, few places are within easy reach by day trip. However, if you make an early start it's just possible to see the sites of Edirne in Thrace (Trakya), the only bit of Turkey that is geographically within Europe. The fast ferry link means that you can also just make Bursa and back in a day, although it's much better to plan to overnight there.

EDİRNE
☎ 0284
Edirne is a surprisingly pleasant if sleepy town, with several fine old mosques. If you're passing through, have a look at the **Üçşerefeli Cami**, the **Eski Cami** and especially the **Selimiye Camii**, the finest work of Süleyman the Magnificent's master architect, Sinan. The impressive **Beyazıt II Camii** complex is on the outskirts. There are several good, cheap hotels a few blocks from the **tourist office** (☎/fax 225 1518; Hürriyet Meydanı 17) in the town centre. Buses from İstanbul run every 20 minutes (US$5, three hours).

BURSA

☎ 0224

Sprawling at the base of Uludağ, Turkey's biggest winter-sports centre, Bursa was the Ottoman capital before İstanbul. It retains several fine mosques and pretty neighbourhoods from early Ottoman times, but its biggest attractions are the thermal springs in the village-like suburb of Çekirge. Bursa's wonderful **covered market** should also delight anyone who finds İstanbul's version too touristy.

Orientation & Information

The city centre, with its **banks** and **shops**, is along Atatürk Caddesi between the Ulu Cami (Grand Mosque) to the west and the main square, Cumhuriyet Alanı, commonly called Heykel ('statue'), to the east. The **PTT** is on the southern side of Atatürk Caddesi, opposite the Ulu Cami. Çekirge, with its hot springs, is around about 6km west of Heykel.

Bursa's **otogar** is an inconvenient 10km north of the centre on the Yalova road.

The **tourist office** (☎ 251 1834; Orhangazi Altgeçidi, Ulu Cami Parkı) is opposite the Koza Han (Silk Market).

Yeşil Cami

About 1km east of Heykel is the early Ottoman Yeşil Cami (Green Mosque), built in 1424, with its beautifully tiled **Yeşil Türbe** (Green Tomb; admission free; open 8.30am-noon & 1pm-5pm daily). Also here is the **Turkish & Islamic Arts Museum** (admission US$0.75; open 8.30am-noon & 1pm-5pm Tues-Sun), which was closed for restoration at the time of writing.

A few hundred metres further east is the **Emir Sultan Mosque** (1805). To get there, take a dolmuş or bus No 18 ('Emir Sultan') east from Heykel.

Other Mosques

Right in the city centre, the largest of Bursa's mosques is the 20-domed **Ulu Cami** (Grand Mosque; Atatürk Caddesi), built in 1399.

Uphill and west of the Ulu Cami, on the way to Çekirge, are the 14th-century **tombs of Osman & Orhan**, the first Ottoman sultans. A kilometre beyond lies the delightful **Muradiye Mosque Complex**, with 12 decorated tombs dating from the 15th and 16th centuries.

Uludağ

Whether it's winter or summer, it's worth taking a cable car ride up Uludağ (Great Mountain, 2543m). From Heykel take bus No 3 or a dolmuş east to the **teleferik** (cable car; US$3 return to the summit). Alternatively, take a dolmuş (US$6) from the otogar for the 22km to the top. Bear in mind that the skiing facilities, while some of Turkey's best, are not up to those of the best European ski resorts.

Places to Stay

Bursa hotels tend to be pricey, although a few cheapies can be found in the Tahtakale/İnebey district just south of the Ulu Cami.

Otel Güneş (☎ 222 1404; İnebey Caddesi 75; singles/doubles with shared bathrooms US$5/8), in an old wooden building, is clean and simple, if somewhat squashed.

Otel Çamlıbel (☎ 221 2565, fax 223 4405; İnebey Caddesi 71; singles/doubles US$9/13, with shower US$12/17) has quite good rooms, although some are a bit cell-like and the hot water 'iffy'. Breakfast costs extra.

Hotel Çeşmeli (☎ 224 1511, fax 224 1511; Gümüşçeken Caddesi 6; singles/doubles with shower US$19/30), north of Atatürk Caddesi, is friendly, fairly quiet and very clean.

Hotel Efehan (☎ 225 2260, fax 225 2259; Gümüşçeken Caddesi 34; singles/doubles with shower US$20/30) has the advantage of newness – the decor is immaculate. Rooms come with mod cons like hair driers, minibars and TVs.

Safran Oteli & Restaurant (☎ 224 7216, fax 224 7216; Kale Sokak, Tophane; singles/doubles with shower US$30/50), opposite the Osman and Orhan tombs, is a smart replica Ottoman house in a historic neighbourhood. Mod cons like TVs come with quirks like knee-level light switches.

Çekirge's main street is 1 Murat Caddesi (Birinci Murat Caddesi). In some ways it's nicer to stay here, despite having to bus back and forth. The plusses include the relative quiet and the fact that your hotel may have private or public bathing facilities in the hotel basement to take full advantage of the mineral water. To get here, take a bus or dolmuş from Heykel or along Atatürk Caddesi to 'Çekirge'.

Öz Yeşilyayla Termal Otel (☎ 239 6496; Selvi Sokak 5; singles/doubles with shared bathroom US$15/20), between the Boyugüzel and Yıldız II hotels at the upper end of the village, is a quaint old wooden building – everything creaks as you walk across the floor. There's free use of the basement mineral baths.

Boyugüzel Termal Otel (☎/fax 233 9999; *Selvi Sokak; singles/doubles with shower US$20/30*) is smart and modern and the room price includes 30 minutes in the mineral bath downstairs.

Termal Hotel Gönlüferah (☎ 233 9210, fax 233 9218; 1. *Murat Caddesi 24; singles/ doubles with shower US$45/60*), in the very centre of the village, has the air of an English country-house hotel and is the place to go for real luxury. Some of the 62 rooms have fine views over the valley and there's a private *hamam* (US$2 extra).

Places to Eat

Bursa, birthplace of the *İskender kebap*, at the time of writing had kebabs of questionable quality.

Kebapçı İskender (*Ünlü Caddesi 7; full meals US$6*), just east of Heykel, dates back to 1867 and is beginning to show its age, although the *İskender kebap* is still tasty. **Adanur Hacıbey**, opposite, costs the same but is less fancy.

Çiçek Izgara (*Belediye Caddesi 15; full meals US$2.50; open from 11am-3.30pm & 5.30pm-9pm daily*), just north of the half-timbered Belediye in the flower market, is bright, modern, super-popular and good for lone women.

Çınar Izgara (*Atatürk Caddesi, Ulucami Yanı; full meals US$4*) is housed in what was the old toilet block of the Ulu Cami and has pictures of old Bursa on the walls. Service is attentive and the food tasty.

For a jolly evening of seafood and drinks, head straight for Sakarya Caddesi, off Altıparmak Caddesi. It pays to dip in and out of the different restaurants to check for the buzz on any given evening, but **Arap Şükrü** (☎ 221 1453; *Sakarya Caddesi 6; meals US$10*) is usually inviting and the calamaris (US$2) and grilled mackerel (US$3.50) enjoyable.

Getting There & Away

The fastest way to get to İstanbul is to take the hourly bus to Yalova (US$2, one hour), then a catamaran to İstanbul's Yenikapı docks (US$5, one hour, at least seven a day). Get a bus that departs at least 1½ hours before the scheduled boat departure; you can pick up the timetable on the 1st floor of the new Zafer Plaza shopping centre.

Karayolu ile (by road) buses to İstanbul take four hours and drag you all around the Bay of İzmit. Those designated *feribot ile* (by ferry) take you to Topçular, east of Yalova, and drive aboard the car ferry to Eskihisar, a much quicker and more pleasant way to go.

Getting Around

To/From the Otogar There are no *servis* buses to the otogar, so you must take the grey-and-blue 'Terminal' bus (US$0.30) to travel the 10km between the otogar and the city centre. Allow at least three-quarters of an hour. A taxi costs US$5.

City Bus Bursa's city buses (BOİ; US$0.30) have destinations and stops marked on the front. The bus stops also have the numbers and destinations clearly marked. The best place to pick up buses is on Atatürk Caddesi just before Heykel.

Dolmuş Many *dolmuşes* wait in front of Ulu Cami Parkı, although the Çekirge *dolmuş* waits at the northeasterly end of Feraizcizade Sokak.

Aegean Coast

While the coastal scenery of the Aegean Coast is not as spectacular as that of the Mediterranean, this is the part of Turkey that was once Asia Minor and it is studded with fantastic historic sites, including the ruins of Troy, Ephesus and Pergamum. This is also where you come to see the battlefield sites at Gallipoli.

ÇANAKKALE
☎ 0286

Çanakkale makes a good base for visiting Troy and Gallipoli (Gelibolu), across the other side of the Dardanelles. It was here that Leander swam across what was then called the Hellespont to his lover Hero, and here, too, that Lord Byron did his Romantic bit and duplicated the feat.

The defence of the straits during WWI led to a Turkish victory over Anzac (Australian and New Zealand Army Corps) forces on 18 March 1916, which is now annually remembered with a big local holiday.

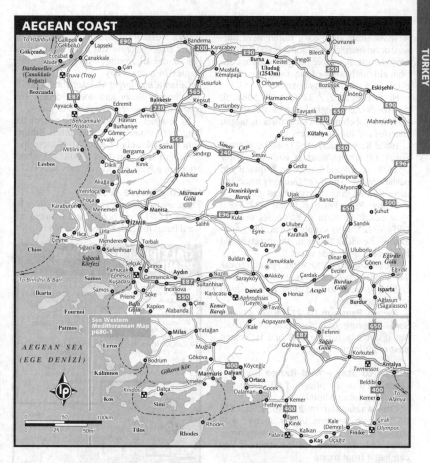

AEGEAN COAST

But even more people flock to town on 25 April for Anzac Day, when a dawn service commemorates the anniversary of the Allied landings on the peninsula in 1915.

Orientation & Information

The **tourist office** (☎ 217 1187), all the cheap hotels and a range of reasonable restaurants are within a block or two of the ferry pier, near the town's landmark clock tower.

Things to See

Built by Sultan Mehmet the Conqueror in 1452, the **Ottoman castle** now houses an **Army Museum** (*Askeri Müze; admission US$0.75; open 9am-noon & 1.30pm-5pm Fri-Sun & Tues-Wed*), with some wonderful drawings of old Çanakkale. Just over 2km

south of the ferry pier on the road to Troy, the **Archaeological Museum** (*admission US$0.75; open 9am-5pm daily*) holds artefacts found at Troy and Assos.

Places to Stay

Places to Stay – Budget In summer, camping is available at **Mocamp Trova** (☎ 232 8025; *Güzelyalı Beach*), 15km south of Çanakkale, off the road to Troy and accessible by city bus from the town centre.

Except on Anzac Day, Çanakkale has hotels to fit all pockets. Unfortunately, the stresses and strains of 25 April seem to result in more complaints from readers about Çanakkale hotels than about anywhere else in the country. Check prices carefully before settling in.

Anzac House (☎ 213 5969, fax 217 2906; e www.anzachouse.com; Cumhuriyet Bulvarı; dorm beds/singles/doubles US$5/9/14) provides clean, simple budget accommodation, although some of the rooms are claustrophobic, windowless boxes.

Hotel Efes (☎ 217 3256; Aralık Sokak 5; dorm beds US$5, singles/doubles with shower US$10/14), behind the clock tower, is bright, cheerful and run by women.

Hotel Kervansaray (☎ 217 8192; Fetvane Sokak 13; singles/doubles without shower US$5/9) is a good choice in a quaint old pasha's house. The rooms are very basic, but there's an inviting courtyard and garden.

Yellow Rose Pension (☎/fax 217 3343; Yeni Sokak 5; dorm beds/singles/doubles US$4/6/12) offers simple rooms 50m southeast of the clock tower in an attractive old house on a quiet side street.

Hotel Konak (☎ 217 1150; Fetvane Sokak 14; singles/doubles US$6/8, with shower US$6/10) looks to be fading fast, but will still do at a push.

Avrupa Pansiyon (☎ 217 4084; Matbaa Sokak 8; singles/doubles US$6/8) is basic, but it's handy for the bars and is located next to an Internet café.

Places to Stay – Mid-Range Breakfast is included in the prices of all of the following mid-range hotels.

Otel Anafartalar (☎ 217 4454, fax 217 2622; İskele Meydanı; singles/doubles with shower US$25/34) is a high-rise, waterfront hotel with fine views of the straits if you can bag a front room.

Anzac Hotel (☎ 217 7777, fax 217 2017; w www.anzachotel.com; Saat Kulesi Meydanı 8; singles/doubles with shower US$20/30), more or less facing the clock tower, is a presentable two-star place in a central location.

Hotel Temizay (☎ 212 8760, fax 217 58 85; Cumhuriyet Meydanı 15; singles/doubles with shower US$20/30) makes a good choice because it's clean and new.

Hotel Bakır (☎ 217 2908, fax 217 4090; singles/doubles/triples with shower US$40/50/60) is another good choice, with splendid views, right on the waterfront near the ferry terminal.

Otel Kestanbol (☎ 243 0466; Dörtyöl; singles/doubles with shower US$25/40) is a little less central, but ready to discuss rates for its fairly simple rooms when it's quiet.

Places to Eat

Trakya Restaurant (Cumhuriyet Meydanı; meals US$5), across the road from Anzac House, can fill you up with pide and other staples 24 hours a day.

Gülen (Cumhuriyet Meydanı; meals US$5) has cheerier decor and does a decent İskender kebap as well as a range of pides.

In summer it's fun to eat at one of the long-lived waterfront restaurants – **Rıhtım**, **Yeni Entellektüel** or **Çekic**. All of them specialise in fish, but you should ask about prices in advance to avoid nasty shocks.

Getting There & Away

There are hourly buses to Çanakkale from İstanbul (US$11, six hours), and frequent onward buses to İzmir (US$8, five hours).

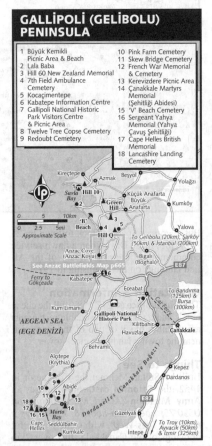

GALLİPOLİ (GELİBOLU) PENINSULA

1 Büyük Kemikli Picnic Area & Beach
2 Lala Baba
3 Hill 60 New Zealand Memorial
4 7th Field Ambulance Cemetery
5 Kocaçimentepe
6 Kabatepe Information Centre
7 Gallipoli National Historic Park Visitors Centre & Picnic Area
8 Twelve Tree Copse Cemetery
9 Redoubt Cemetery
10 Pink Farm Cemetery
11 Skew Bridge Cemetery
12 French War Memorial & Cemetery
13 Kerevizdere Picnic Area
14 Çanakkale Martyrs Memorial (Şehitliği Abidesi)
15 'V' Beach Cemetery
16 Sergeant Yahya Memorial (Yahya Çavuş Şehitliği)
17 Cape Helles British Memorial
18 Lancashire Landing Cemetery

GALLİPOLİ (GELİBOLU)

☎ 0286

Always the first line of defence for İstanbul, the Dardanelles defences proved their worth in WWI.

Atop the narrow, hilly Gallipoli Peninsula, Mustafa Kemal (Atatürk) and his troops fought off a far superior but badly commanded force of Anzac and British troops. After nine months and having suffered horrendous casualties, the Allied forces were withdrawn.

For most people a visit to the battlefields and war graves of Gallipoli (now a national historic park) is a moving experience.

The easiest way to see the sights, particularly if time is tight, is on a minibus tour from Çanakkale with **Troyanzac Tours** (☎ 217 5849) or **Hassle Free Tours** (☎ 213 5969) for about US$20 per person. **Down Under Travel** (☎ 814 2431; Eceabat) also garners lots of praise from readers.

With time on your hands, it's cheaper to take a ferry from Çanakkale to Eceabat and a dolmuş to Kabatepe, and follow the trail around the sites described in a booklet sold at the visitors centre there.

Places to Stay

Most people use Çanakkale as a base for exploring Gallipoli, but you could also stay at Eceabat on the Thracian side of the straits. **TJs Hostel** (☎ 814 2940, fax 814 2941; e tjs_tours@mail.excite.com; Cumhuriyet Caddesi 5; bed with shower US$5) gets fond reviews from its guests. The rooms may be basic but the beers are cheap.

Getting There & Away

Car ferries cross the straits hourly from Çanakkale to Eceabat and from Lapseki to Gallipoli (US$0.50 per person).

Small private ferries cross more frequently than the car ferries and are faster (US$0.30, 15 to 20 minutes); they leave for Kilitbahir from in front of the Hotel Bakır in Çanakkale.

Many travellers prefer to use **Hassle Free Tours** (☎ 213 5969) or **Trooper Tours** (☎ 516 9024). These outfits pick people up in İstanbul, ferry them to Çanakkale and show them the battlefields and Troy, then either return them to İstanbul or drop them in İzmir or Selçuk, for U$49 including one night's accommodation.

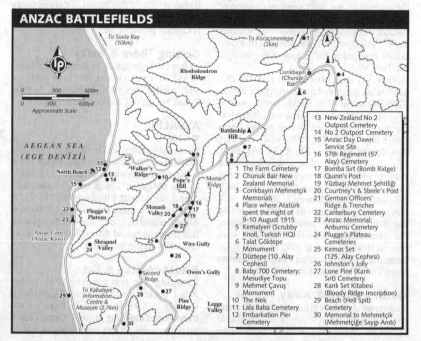

ANZAC BATTLEFIELDS

1 The Farm Cemetery
2 Chunuk Bair New Zealand Memorial
3 Conkbayırı Mehmetçik Memorials
4 Place where Atatürk spent the night of 9-10 August 1915
5 Kemalyeri (Scrubby Knoll, Turkish HQ)
6 Talat Göktepe Monument
7 Düztepe (10. Alay Cephesi)
8 Baby 700 Cemetery; Mesudiye Topu
9 Mehmet Çavuş Monument
10 The Nek
11 Lala Baba Cemetery
12 Embarkation Pier Cemetery
13 New Zealand No 2 Outpost Cemetery
14 No 2 Outpost Cemetery
15 Anzac Day Dawn Service Site
16 57th Regiment (57. Alay) Cemetery
17 Bomba Sırt (Bomb Ridge)
18 Quinn's Post
19 Yüzbaşı Mehmet Şehitliği
20 Courtney's & Steele's Post
21 German Officers' Ridge & Trenches
22 Canterbury Cemetery
23 Anzac Memorial; Arıburnu Cemetery
24 Plugge's Plateau Cemeteries
25 Kırmızı Sırt (125. Alay Cephesi)
26 Johnston's Jolly
27 Lone Pine (Kanlı Sırt) Cemetery
28 Kanlı Sırt Kitabesi (Bloody Ridge Inscription)
29 Beach (Hell Spit) Cemetery
30 Memorial to Mehmetçik (Mehmetçiğe Saygı Anıtı)

TRUVA (TROY)

According to Homer, Paris abducted the beautiful Helen from her husband, Menelaus, King of Sparta, and whisked her off to Troy, thus precipitating the Trojan War. When 10 years of carnage failed to end the war, Odysseus came up with the idea of a wooden horse filled with soldiers, against which Cassandra warned the Trojans in vain. It was left outside the west gate for the Trojans to wheel inside the walls.

Today the approach to Troy lies across low, rolling grain fields, dotted with villages. This is the ancient Troad, all but forgotten until German-born treasure-hunter and amateur archaeologist Heinrich Schliemann (1822–90) got permission to dig there in 1871. At that time it was assumed that Homer's poetry was based on legend, but as Schliemann unearthed the remains of four ancient towns he proved that its roots lay in real history.

Since then excavations have revealed nine ancient cities, one on top of another, dating back to 3000 BC. The cities called Troy I to Troy V (3000–1700 BC) had a similar culture, but Troy VI (1700–1250 BC) took on a different character, with a new population of Indo-European stock related to the Mycenaeans. Archaeologists argue over whether Troy VI or Troy VII was the city of Priam which engaged in the Trojan War; most go for Troy VI.

Troy VII lasted from 1250 to 1050 BC. The Achaeans may have burned the city in 1240 BC; an invading Balkan people moved in around 1190 BC and Troy sank into a torpor for four centuries. It was revived as a Greek city (Troy VIII, 700–85 BC) and then as a Roman one (Troy IX, 85 BC–AD 500).

A huge replica of the **wooden horse** catches your eye as you approach the ruins (*admission US$7; open 8.30am-5pm daily Nov-May, 8am-7.30pm daily Jun-Oct*). You can see **walls** from various periods, including the five oldest still standing in the world; the **Bouleuterion** (Council Chamber), built around Homer's time (c. 800 BC); the stone **ramp** from Troy II; and the **Temple of Athena** from Troy VIII, rebuilt by the Romans.

Getting There & Away

In summer *dolmuşes* ply back and forth along the 32km between Troy and Çanakkale (US$1.50, 35 minutes). Walk inland from the ferry pier to Atatürk Caddesi, and turn right towards Troy; *dolmuşes* wait by the bridge.

BEHRAMKALE (ASSOS)
☎ 0286

Behramkale, 19km southwest of Ayvalık, consists of a beautiful hilltop village, with the ruins of a **Temple of Athena** (*admission US$0.75; open 8am-5pm Tues-Sun*) looking across the water to Lesbos in Greece, and a small *iskele* (port), 2km further on. Both get overcrowded in summer, especially at weekends, so visit in low season if possible.

Places to Stay

Camping There's **Çakır Camping** (*☎ 721 7048; tent sites US$5*) right on the beach, but there are other possibilities in the olive groves nearby.

Pensions & Hotels In Behramkale itself, **Dolunay Pansiyon** (*☎ 721 72710*) and other pensions can put you up for around US$12.50 a head. The lovely port hotels charge around US$45/60 a single/double with half board in summer. The following places fill up quickly, so phone ahead: **Behram** (*☎ 721 7016*), **Kervansaray** (*☎ 721 7093*), **Assos Şen** (*☎ 721 7076*) and **Nazlıhan** (*☎ 721 7385*).

Getting There & Away

You get to Behramkale by infrequent *dolmuş* (US$1.50) from Ayvacık (not to be confused with nearby Ayvalık). Ayvacık is, in turn, linked by bus to Çanakkale and Ayvalık.

AYVALIK
☎ 0266

Inhabited by Ottoman Greeks until 1923, this small, pleasant fishing port and beach resort is the departure point for ferries to Lesbos.

The **otogar** is 1.5km north of the town centre, the **tourist office** (*☎/fax 312 2122*) 1km south, opposite the marina. Offshore is **Alibey Island** (Cunda), lined with open-air fish restaurants and linked by ferries and a causeway to the mainland.

Places to Stay & Eat

Camping The best camping is on Alibey Adası, but at the southern end of Çamlık, on the way to Sarımsaklı beach, there's a **national forest camping ground** (Orman Kampı) and several private camping grounds.

Pensions & Hotels In a renovated Ottoman house, Taksiyarhis Pansiyon (☎ 312 1494; Mareşal Çakmak Caddesi 71; beds with shared shower US$7) is the most interesting place to stay. It's five minutes' walk east of the PTT, behind the former Taxiarkhis church, and is often full in summer; book ahead if possible. Breakfast costs US$2.50.

Bonjour Pansiyon (☎ 312 8085; Fevzi Çakmak Caddesi, Çeşme Sokak 5; singles/ doubles with shower US$12/20; open May-Sept) is in the fine, restored house of a French ambassador to the sultan. Breakfast is included in the prices.

Chez Beliz Pansiyon (☎ 312 4897, fax 312 2948; Mareşal Çakmak Caddesi 28; beds from US$10; open May-Nov) boasts a gorgeous garden, an exuberant hostess and excellent food.

Hüsnü Baba'nin Yeri (Tenekeciler Sokaği 16; meals US$4), just off İnönü Caddesi in a shady alley, doesn't look much decorwise, but offers excellent mezzes to wash down with raki. Anyone for sea urchins? In season only, of course.

Kardeşler (meals US$10-12), on the waterfront, is pricier but good for seafood and atmospheric views. 15 Kardeşler (Talatpaşa Caddesi; meals US$4.50), in the street behind, offers cheaper soup and kebab suppers.

Getting There & Away
There are frequent direct buses from İzmir to Ayvalık (US$3.50, three hours). Coming from Çanakkale (US$5, 3½ hours) the buses will probably drop you on the main highway to hitch to the centre.

To get to Alibey Adası take the red 'Ayvalık Belediyesi' bus north (US$0.50).

Daily boats operate to Lesbos (Greece) from late May to September (US$40/50 one way/return). There's at least one boat a week even in winter.

BERGAMA
☎ 0232
From the 3rd century BC to the 1st century AD, Bergama (formerly Pergamum) was a powerful and cultured kingdom. A line of rulers beginning with a general under Alexander the Great ruled over this small but wealthy kingdom, famous now for its extensive ruins.

The tourist office (☎ 633 1862; İzmir Caddesi 57) is midway between the otogar

and the market. Taxis waiting here charge US$4 to the Acropolis, US$8 total if they wait and bring you back down.

Things to See
The Asclepion (Temple of Asclepios; admission US$4; open from 8.30am-5.30pm daily), 3.5km from the city centre, was a famous medical school with a library that rivalled that of Alexandria in Egypt. The Acropolis (admission US$4; open from 8.30am-5.30pm daily), 6km from the city, has a spectacular sloping theatre. If you're a walker, follow the pretty path marked by dots down through the ruins to get back to town. The excellent Archaeology & Ethnography Museum (admission US$2; open 8.30am-5.30pm daily) contains finds from both of these sites.

Places to Stay & Eat
Hotel Berksoy (İnönü Caddesi) has sites for tents, caravans and camper vans.

Pension Athena (☎ 633 3420; İmam Çıkmazı 5; beds without/with shower US$5/7), in an old Ottoman house, is run by natural-born host Aydın Şengül. A great breakfast is US$2 extra. To find Pension Athena, look for the Tabak Bridge at the Acropolis end of town and then follow the sign.

Böblingen Pension (☎ 633 2153; Asklepion Caddesi 2; singles/doubles with shower US$10/20), spotless and family-run, is at the start of the road to the Asclepion. Prices include breakfast.

Acroteria (☎ 633 2469; Bankalar Caddesi; doubles/triples with shower US$6/10) has a pleasant terrace and courtyard but fairly simple rooms. Breakfast is extra.

Anıl Hotel (☎ 631 3031, fax 632 1615; Hatuniye Caddesi 4; singles/doubles with a shower US$37/50) has cheerful modern rooms with TVs. Ask for one at the back for the sake of quietness.

Meydan Restaurant (İstiklal Meydanı; meals US$5), near the Basilica (Red Hall) on the main street, serves meals on a vine-shaded terrace. Sarmaşık Lokantası (meals US$3) compensates for a lack of outdoor seating with cheaper prices.

Sağlam 3 Restaurant (Cumhuriyet Meydanı 29; meals US$4) serves a range of kebabs at indoor and outdoor tables, while Sağlam 2 (İstiklal Meydanı 3; meals US$3) offers cheaper soups and pides, with live music upstairs to round off the evening afterwards.

Getting There & Away

Buses shuttle between Bergama and İzmir every half-hour in summer (US$3, two hours). Fairly frequent buses also connect Bergama with Ayvalık (US$2.50, 1¾ hours).

Getting Around

A taxi tour of the Acropolis, the Asclepion and the museum costs US$15.

İZMİR

☎ 0232

Turkey's third-largest city, İzmir (once Smyrna) was the birthplace of Homer in about 700 BC. Today it's the main transport hub for the Aegean coast, but it's a good place to skip on a short trip; it's spread out and baffling to find your way around, its sites are relatively minor and its hotels overpriced.

Orientation

Central İzmir is a web of *meydanlar* (plazas) linked by streets that aren't at right angles to each other. Instead of names the back streets have numbers. You'll go mad without a map (the tourist office supplies a good free one).

Budget hotels cluster near Basmane train station, a district sometimes called Çankaya. To the southwest, Anafartalar Caddesi twists and turns through the labyrinthine bazaar to the waterfront at Konak, the commercial and government centre. Atatürk Caddesi (Birinci Kordon) runs northeast from Konak along the waterfront 1.4km past Cumhuriyet Meydanı with its equestrian statue of Atatürk, the main PTT, luxury hotels and tourist and airline offices.

At Atatürk Caddesi's northern end is the harbour, Alsancak İskelesi, and the smaller, mostly suburban Alsancak train station. İzmir's flashy new **otogar** is 6km northeast of the town centre.

Information

The **tourist office** (☎ 484 2147; fax 489 9278; Gaziosmanpaşa Bulvarı 1/C, Cumhuriyet Meydanı) is next to the **Turkish Airlines** office (☎ 484 1220; Büyük Efes Oteli, Gaziosmanpaşa Bulvarı 1/F, Cumhuriyet Meydanı).

Things to See

Since most of old İzmir was destroyed by earthquakes there's little to see here compared with other Turkish cities. However, it does boast the remains of an extensive 2nd-century-AD Roman **agora** (admission US$1.40; open 8.30am-noon & 1pm-5pm daily), right inside the sprawling, atmospheric modern **bazaar**. It's also worth taking a bus to the hilltop **Kadifekale** fortress, where women still weave kilims on horizontal looms and the views are spectacular. The **Archaeology & Ethnography Museums** (combined admission US$2.75; open 9am-noon & 1pm-5pm Tues-Sun) are both quite interesting, although it's rare for both to be open.

Places to Stay

For the cheapest places to stay, walk out of the front of Basmane train station, turn left, cross the main road and walk up shady Anafartalar Caddesi, the bazaar area.

Otel Hikmet (☎ 484 2672; 945 Sokak No 26; singles/doubles with shared bathroom US$3.50/5.50), near the Hatuniye Camii, is clean, comfortable and dirt cheap, although the owner seems unsure whether he really wants guests. There's a great teahouse, **Emin Çay Salonu**, right on the street corner.

Otel Antik Han (☎ 489 2750; Anafartalar Caddesi 600; singles/doubles with shower US$20/30), a new hotel in a restored house right in the bazaar, is another good choice. Rooms have TVs, ceiling fans and plenty of character but can be noisy because of nearby music halls.

Hotel Baylan (☎ 483 1426; 1299 Sokak No 8; singles/doubles with shower US$35/55) is a professionally managed and comfortable two-star place. To find it, cross the road outside the station, turn left and then immediately right. **Hotel Imperial** (☎ 483 9771; 1296 Sokak 54; singles/doubles with shower US$10/14) is another welcoming place very close to the Baylan.

For other hotels, walk straight down Fevzipaşa Bulvarı from Basmane station and turn right (north). The streets 1368 Sokak and its westward continuation, 1369 Sokak, host a few clean, quiet hotels. Two of the best are **Çiçek Palas** (☎ 446 9252; 1368 Sokak 10; singles/doubles without shower US$5/8, with shower US$12/18) and **Hotel Oba** (☎ 441 9605; 1369 Sokak 27; singles/doubles with shower & air-con US$7/14).

Places to Eat

For bargain-basement meals, especially at lunch time, head straight into the bazaar and take your pick of what's cooking, or head

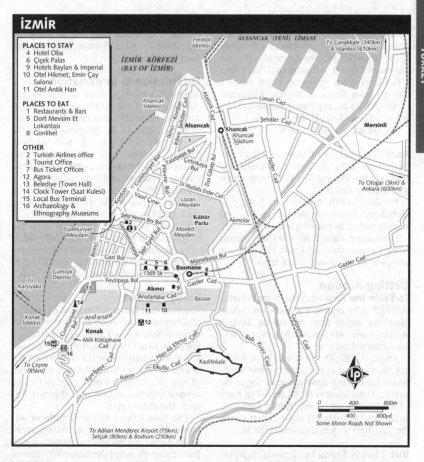

İZMİR

PLACES TO STAY
4 Hotel Oba
6 Çiçek Palas
9 Hotels Baylan & Imperial
10 Otel Hikmet; Emin Çay Salonu
11 Otel Antik Han

PLACES TO EAT
1 Restaurants & Bars
5 Dort Mevsim Et Lokantası
8 Gonlibel

OTHER
2 Turkish Airlines office
3 Tourist Office
7 Bus Ticket Offices
12 Agora
13 Belediye (Town Hall)
14 Clock Tower (Saat Kulesi)
15 Local Bus Terminal
16 Archaeology & Ethnography Museums

İZMİR KÖRFEZİ
(BAY OF İZMİR)

Feribot İskelesi

ALSANCAK (YENİ) LİMANI

To Çanakkale (340km) & İstanbul (610km)

Alsancak İskelesi

Liman Cad

Alsancak

Alsancak Stadium

Şehitler Cad

Mersinli

To Otogar (3km) & Ankara (600km)

Kültür Parkı

Montrö Meydanı

Akıncılar

Gaziler Cad

Basmane

1369 Sk

Akıncı

Bazaar

Kadifekale

0   400   800m
0   400   800yd
Some Minor Roads Not Shown

To Adnan Menderes Airport (15km),
Selçuk (80km) & Bodrum (250km)

towards Konak and eat at one of the many döner kebap stalls there.

Gönlibel (*Anafartalar Caddesi 878; full meals US$4*) is clean, cheap and handy for Basmane station. Try the delicious piping-hot *kiremitte tavuk* (chicken baked on a tile) for just US$2.

Dört Mevsim Et Lokantası (*1369 Sokak 51/A; meals US$5-6*) is an excellent place with an open *ocakbaşı* grill, a full range of kebabs and cheerful, welcoming service.

For something more Westernised, head for the tiny streets of restored houses near Alcancak train station. **Aditya Sanat Evi** (*1453 Sokak 14/B; meals US$7*) is that rare thing for Turkey – a combined bookshop and café. It's deservedly popular with local students.

Alternatively, hit the waterfront café-bars, great, atmospheric places for hanging out.

Getting There & Away
Air There are nonstop flights with **Turkish Airlines** to İstanbul (US$82, 50 minutes) and Ankara, with connections to other destinations.

Bus Many bus companies have ticket offices around Dokuz Eylül Meydanı, just north of Basmane, and west along Gazi Bulvarı. They usually provide a *servis* (free minibus) to the otogar. From İzmir there are frequent buses to Selçuk (US$1.75, one hour) Çanakkale (US$8, five hours) and Pamukkale (US$4, four hours), as well as many other destinations.

670 Turkey – Aegean Coast

Train The evening *Mavi Tren* (US$10, 14 hours) hauls sleeping cars from Basmane station to Ankara; or you can take the *İzmir Express* for US$8. For İstanbul, take the *Marmara Express* to Bandırma (US$2), then a fast ferry. Four pokey but cheap trains a day go from Basmane to Selçuk/Ephesus (US$1.50, 2½ hours); three continue to Denizli (for Pamukkale; US$3, six hours).

For İzmir train times, call ☎ 484 5353.

Boat For details of summer-only ferry services from İzmir to Venice, Brindisi and Bari, see the Getting There & Away chapter earlier in this book.

For details of the ferry service linking İstanbul and İzmir, see the Getting Around section earlier in this chapter.

In summer, daily ferries to Chios depart from Çeşme, west of İzmir (US$30 one way, US$40 same-day return trip).

Getting Around

To/From the Airport A bus going to Havaş (US$2.50, 30 minutes) departs for Adnan Menderes airport from outside the Turkish Airlines office 1½ hours before every Turkish Airlines departure.

Trains (US$0.50) run hourly from Alsancak train station to the airport; some southbound trains from Basmane also stop at the airport. From Montrö Meydanı, 700m north of Basmane, southbound 'Adnan Menderes Belediyesi' buses travel to the airport during the day (US$1). A taxi can cost US$30.

Bus There is a local bus terminal right beside Konak Meydanı. Local bus tickets cost US$0.40 and must be bought before boarding. Catch bus No 33 to Kadifekale or bus No 601, 603 or 605 to the otogar.

Train İzmir's new metro runs from Üçyöl to Bornova via Konak. You're most likely to use it to get from Basmane station to Konak (US$0.30).

Boat Frequent ferries connect Konak with Alsancak (US$0.30), a great way of moving from one part of town to the other.

SELÇUK & EPHESUS
☎ 0232

Selçuk is an easy one-hour bus trip south of İzmir. Almost everybody comes here to visit the splendid Roman ruins of Ephesus (Efes); in its heyday only Athens was more magnificent, and in Roman times this was Asia's capital.

Orientation & Information

Although touristy, Selçuk is a backwater compared with coastal playpens like Kuşadası and Marmaris, and most backpackers prefer it. Most of the pensions are on the quieter western side of the highway (Atatürk Caddesi) behind the museum, but others are on the eastern side along with the otogar, restaurants and train station. There's a **tourist office** (☎/fax 892 1328) and town map in the park on the western side of the main street, across from the otogar.

Ephesus is a 3km walk west from the otogar along a shady road – turn left (south) at the Tusan Restaurant. Alternatively, there are frequent minibuses from the otogar to the junction, leaving you just a 1km walk.

Things to See

The excellent **Ephesus Museum** *(admission US$2; open 8.30am-noon & 12.30pm-4.30pm daily)* in Selçuk has a striking collection of artefacts. Don't miss the exquisite figure of a boy on a dolphin in the first room; the marble statues of Cybele/Artemis with rows of egg-like breasts, which may in fact be severed testicles; and several effigies of Priapus, the phallic god.

The foundations of the **Temple of Artemis** *(Artemision; open 8.30am-5.30pm daily)*, between Ephesus and Selçuk, are all that remain of one of the Seven Wonders of the Ancient World. In its prime, with 127 columns all with figures carved around the base, it was larger than the Parthenon at Athens. Unfortunately, little more than one pillar remains now.

The **Basilica of St John** *(admission US$2; open 8am-6pm daily)*, on Ayasuluk Hill, was erected in the 6th century AD on the site where it was believed St John the Evangelist had been buried. Recently restored, it's a fine place to while away an hour or so.

Places to Stay

Selçuk has almost 100 small pensions, mostly charging US$7 per person with perhaps another US$2 or so for breakfast.

[Continued on page 674]

EPHESUS (EFES)

Ephesus is the best-preserved classical city in the eastern Mediterranean and is one of the best places in the world to get a feel for what life was like in Roman times.

Ancient Ephesus was a great trading and religious city, a centre for the cult of Cybele, the Anatolian fertility goddess. In time Cybele became Artemis, the virgin goddess of the hunt and the moon, and a fabulous temple was built in her honour. When the Romans took over and made this the province of Asia, Artemis became Diana and Ephesus became the Roman provincial capital.

As a busy Roman town, Ephesus quickly acquired a sizable Christian congregation and St Paul wrote the most profound of his epistles to the Ephesians.

The site *(admission US$10; open 8am-5pm daily, 8.30am-7pm in summer)* seems to be permanently swamped with coach groups and gets extremely hot in high summer. Start exploring early in the morning, then retire to a shady restaurant to avoid the midday heat. Unfortunately, since this is what the coach parties also do, lunch time is when you're most likely to avoid the groups. Allow at least half a day for looking around, and more if you're keen on ruins.

The Site

As you walk into the site you pass the **Gymnasium of Vedius** (2nd century AD) on your left. The road descends to the car park. To the

Inset: Carved relief of Winged Victory on the Gate of Hercules (Photo by Christina Dameyer)

Right: Now empty, the Library of Celcus still pulls crowds of patrons from afar

IZZET KERIBAR

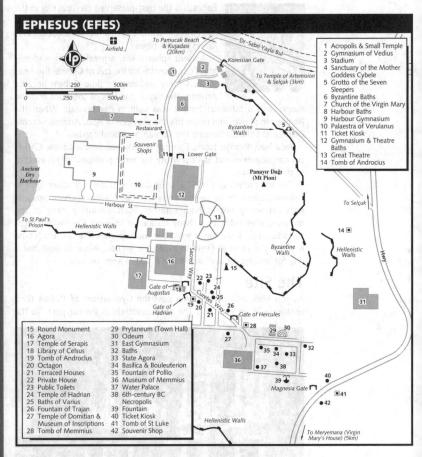

EPHESUS (EFES)

To Pamucak Beach & Kuşadası (20km)

Dr Sabri Yayla Bul

Airfield

Koressian Gate

To Temple of Artemision & Selçuk (3km)

Restaurant

Byzantine Walls

Souvenir Shops

Lower Gate

Ancient Dry Harbour

Panayır Dağı (Mt Pion)

Harbour St

To Selçuk

To St Paul's Prison

Hellenistic Walls

Byzantine Walls

Hellenistic Walls

Sacred Way

Gate of Augustus

Curetes Way

Gate of Hadrian

Gate of Hercules

Prytaneum

Magnesia Gate

Hellenistic Walls

To Meryemana (Virgin Mary's House) (5km)

1 Acropolis & Small Temple
2 Gymnasium of Vedius
3 Stadium
4 Sanctuary of the Mother Goddess Cybele
5 Grotto of the Seven Sleepers
6 Byzantine Baths
7 Church of the Virgin Mary
8 Harbour Baths
9 Harbour Gymnasium
10 Palaestra of Verulanus
11 Ticket Kiosk
12 Gymnasium & Theatre Baths
13 Great Theatre
14 Tomb of Androcius

15 Round Monument
16 Agora
17 Temple of Serapis
18 Library of Celsus
19 Tomb of Androclus
20 Octagon
21 Terraced Houses
22 Private House
23 Public Toilets
24 Temple of Hadrian
25 Baths of Varius
26 Fountain of Trajan
27 Temple of Domitian & Museum of Inscriptions
28 Tomb of Memmius

29 Prytaneum (Town Hall)
30 Odeum
31 East Gymnasium
32 Baths
33 State Agora
34 Basilica & Bouleuterion
35 Fountain of Pollio
36 Museum of Memmius
37 Water Palace
38 6th-century BC Necropolis
39 Fountain
40 Ticket Kiosk
41 Tomb of St Luke
42 Souvenir Shop

right are the ruins of the **Church of the Virgin Mary**, site of the third Ecumenical Council (AD 431), which condemned the Nestorian heresy.

Continue on and you'll see remains of the **Harbour Gymnasium** to the right before you reach the marble-paved **Harbour St**, Ephesus' grandest street, which had water and sewer lines beneath the marble flagstones, 50 streetlights along its colonnades and shops along its sides. It was a legacy of the Byzantine emperor Arcadius (AD 395–408).

At the eastern end of Harbour St is the **Great Theatre**, skilfully reconstructed by the Romans between AD 41 and AD 117 to seat 25,000 people and still used for performances.

From the theatre, walk along the marble-paved **Sacred Way**, noting the remains of the city's water and sewer systems beneath the paving stones and the ruts made by wheeled vehicles. The large open space to the right of the street was the **agora** or marketplace, the heart of Ephesus' business life.

In AD 114, Consul Tiberius Julius Aquila erected a huge **library** nearby in memory of his father Celsus Polemaenus. The fine building you see now used to hold 12,000 scrolls in niches around its walls. Architectural trickery was used to make it look bigger than it really was.

On the left is the **Gate of Augustus**, leading into the agora.

As you turn into **Curetes Way**, look out for an elaborate building once thought to be a brothel but now believed to be a house. Shortly afterwards, a passage on the left leads to the communal men's toilets. The famous figure of Priapus, with the penis of most men's dreams, was found nearby. It's now in the Ephesus Museum.

Opposite the toilets is the entrance to the **Terraced Houses** *(Yamaç Evleri; admission US$20)*, a group of wonderful restored houses complete with frescoed walls and mosaic floors. Pompeii aside, there are few other places where you have such a strong sense of what the homes of the wealthy might really have been like. Shame, then, about the off-putting entry charge.

Further along Curetes Way you can hardly miss the impressive Corinthian-style **Temple of Hadrian** on the left. Dedicated to Hadrian, Artemis and the people of Ephesus in AD 118, it was reconstructed in the 5th century. Curetes Way ends at the two-storey **Gate of Hercules**, constructed in the 4th century AD.

TURKEY

[Continued from page 670]

They're modest, friendly places, and in some cases it's you can sleep on the roof or camp in the garden for US$2 to US$3 per person.

Camping West of Ayasuluk Hill is **Garden Motel & Camping** (☎ 892 1163; *tent sites US$7*). Walk past the Basilica of St John and down the hill, then turn right at the İsa Bey Camii to find tent and caravan sites in an idyllic location amid fruit orchards.

Pensions & Hotels There's a good roof terrace and free use of bikes at **Homeros Pension** (☎ 892 3995; *Asmalı Sokak 17*), which has some simple pension rooms across the road from a set of beautiful, individually decorated rooms.

Akgüneş Pension (☎ 892 3869; *Turgutreis Sokak 14*), nearby, has a few simpler rooms and a family atmosphere. **Barım Pansiyon** (☎ 892 6923; *Turgutreis Sokak 34*), also nearby, has whimsical external decor added to an attractive old house.

Australia & New Zealand Pension (☎ 892 1050; W *www.anzturkishguesthouse.com;* *Profesör Mitler Sokak 17*) has very comfortable rooms with showers set round a courtyard, and excellent meals on its roof terrace. It also has a dormitory.

Artemis Guest House (*Jimmy's Place;* ☎ 892 6191; W *www.artemisguesthouse .com; 1012 Sokak 2*) is in the newer part of town, near an aqueduct where storks nest in spring. It offers a multitude of services for travellers, including a library of information on Turkey to put the so-called official tourist information offices to shame. **All Blacks** (☎ 892 3657, fax 892 9406; e *abnomads@ egenet.com.tr; 1011 Sokak 1*), nearby, has clean rooms in a high-rise block with a fine roof terrace.

Kiwi Pension (☎ 891 4892; W *www.ki wipension.com; Kubilay Caddesi 8*) is a spotless place, run by an English woman, just south of the centre. It has a lovely swimming pool 1km away in an orange orchard.

Otel Kalehan (☎ 892 6154; *singles/doubles with shower & air-con US$30/50*), on the main road just north of the Shell petrol station, has pleasantly decorated rooms in three separate buildings set round a pool and garden. The restaurant is especially inviting.

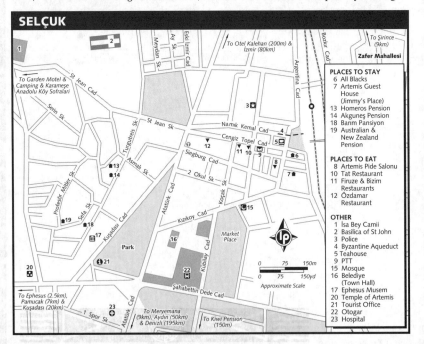

SELÇUK

PLACES TO STAY
6 All Blacks
7 Artemis Guest House (Jimmy's Place)
13 Homeros Pension
14 Akgüneş Pension
18 Barım Pansiyon
19 Australian & New Zealand Pension

PLACES TO EAT
8 Artemis Pide Salonu
10 Tat Restaurant
11 Firuze & Bizim Restaurants
12 Özdamar Restaurant

OTHER
1 Isa Bey Camii
2 Basilica of St John
3 Police
4 Byzantine Aqueduct
5 Teahouse
9 PTT
15 Mosque
16 Belediye (Town Hall)
17 Ephesus Musem
20 Temple of Artemis
21 Tourist Office
22 Otogar
23 Hospital

To Otel Kalehan (200m) & İzmir (80km)

To Şirince (9km)

Zafer Mahallesi

To Garden Motel & Camping & Karameşe Anadolu Köy Sofraları

To Ephesus (2.5km), Pamucak (7km) & Kuşadası (20km)

To Meryemana (9km), Aydın (50km) & Denizli (195km)

To Kiwi Pension (150m)

Market Place

Park

Approximate Scale
0   75   150m
0   75   150yd

Places to Eat

Cengiz Topel Caddesi has many outdoor restaurants and cafés; **Özdamar Restaurant**, facing the fountain, is perennially popular.

Artemis Pide Salonu *(Cengiz Topel Caddesi; meals US$1.50-2.50)*, a half-block south of the tea garden, is a great place for a hit-and-run type meal.

On the next block, **Firuze** and **Bizim** are a bit simpler, with slightly lower prices. Also popular is a place called **Tat** *(meals with wine cost around US$6)*.

In a lovely location opposite the İsa Bey Camii, **Karameşe Anadolu Köy Sofraları** *(☎ 892 0466; meals US$5)* serves averagely good kebabs amid water and greenery. There's a small zoo attached.

Getting There & Away

Selçuk's notoriously hassley **otogar** is across from the tourist office. Buses from İzmir (US$1.75, one hour) usually drop you on the main highway nearby.

Frequent minibuses head for Kuşadası (US$0.90, 30 minutes) and the beach at Pamucak (US$0.75, 10 minutes), passing the Ephesus turn-off (US$0.50, five minutes). Taxis to Ephesus charge US$4; ask for the *güney kapısı* (southern gate) so you can walk downhill back towards the north gate.

KUSADASI

☎ 0256

This cruise-ship port is a shameless tourist trap and you will probably want to linger just long enough to catch a boat to Samos (Greece). If you do decide to stay, there are several attractions nearby, and a raging nightlife.

Information

The **tourist office** *(☎ 614 1103, fax 614 6295)* is beside the pier. Three lines sail to Samos (Sisam) daily in summer for US$30 (one way), US$35 (same-day round-trip), or US$55 (open round-trip); all have ticket offices near the tourist office.

The **otogar** is 1.5km southeast of the centre on the highway, although you may only need to use the *dolmuş* stand on Adnan Menderes Bulvarı.

Things to See

Kuşadası is short on specific sights, although there's a 16th-century **castle** once

used by pirates on an island in the harbour, and an old **caravanserai**, now a hotel, in the older part of town.

Kuşadası also makes a good base for visits to the ancient cities of **Priene**, **Miletus** and **Didyma** *(admission to all 3 sites US$1)* to the south; if you're pushed for time, a 'PMD' tour from the otogar costs around US$20. To get to the beaches of **Dilek National Park**, take a *dolmuş* south to Güzelçamlı.

Places to Stay

Camping The **Önder** and **Yat Mocamp** *(tent sites US$8)* camp sites are north of town on the waterfront near the marina.

Pensions & Hotels Most cheaper pensions have pleasant rooms, usually with private bathroom, for US$16 to US$24 a double in high season. When coming from the harbour, walk up Barbaros Hayrettin Caddesi, turn right towards the Akdeniz Apart-otel, and take Yıldırım Caddesi, the road to the left of the Akdeniz, or Aslanlar Caddesi, the road to the right. These take you into the neighbourhood with most of the small pensions and inexpensive hotels.

The historic **Hotel Kervansaray** *(☎ 614 4115; singles/doubles with shower US$50/80)*, near the harbour, doubles as a carpet shop and nightclub, which hardly guarantees a peaceful stay.

Places to Eat

Kuşadası is fish-and-chips and 'full English breakfast' country. For something more Turkish, cut into the Kaleiçi district behind the harbour and try somewhere like **Avlu** *(Cephane Sokak; meals US$3)*, with indoor and outdoor tables and tasty soups and stews.

Good seafood places facing the harbour charge US$15 to US$25 for a fish dinner, depending on the fish and the season. Try **Toros** *(Balıkée Limanı; meals US$10-15)* for friendly service and excellent sea bream.

For drinks and snacks, the Kaleiçi district shelters several charming café-bars, a million times more sophisticated than the crass offerings of Barlar Sokak (Bar Lane).

Getting There & Away

Kuşadası's **otogar** is out on the bypass at the southern end of Kahramanlar Caddesi. Direct buses depart for several far-flung parts of the country, or you can transfer at

İzmir (US$2.50, every 30 minutes) or Söke. In summer there are frequent buses to Bodrum (US$4, two hours) and Denizli (for Pamukkale; US$6, three hours).

For Selçuk (US$0.90, 30 minutes), pick up a minibus on Adnan Menderes Bulvarı.

PAMUKKALE
☎ 0258

Way inland east of Selçuk, Pamukkale is renowned for the brilliant white ledges (travertines) with pools that flow down over the plateau edge. Sadly, in recent years the water supply has dried up and you can only swim in odd corners here and there. Behind this natural wonder lie the extensive ruins of the Roman city of **Hierapolis**, an ancient spa resort.

If time allows, on your way back to Selçuk or Kuşadası it's well worth detouring to **Afrodisias** (Geyre), near Karacasu south of Nazilli. A beautiful ruined city, Afrodisias is thought by many to rival Ephesus.

Travertines & Hierapolis Ruins
As you climb the hill above Pamukkale village you pay to enter the **travertines and Hierapolis** (admission US$3; open ticket valid from 9am to 9am next day). The ruins of Hierapolis, including a theatre, a colonnaded street with public toilet and a vast necropolis, are spread over a wide area; allow at least half a day to do them justice.

Afterwards you can swim amid sunken Roman columns at **Pamukkale Termal** (admission US$3), on top of the ridge, and visit **Hierapolis Archaeology Museum** (admission US$0.75; open 9am-noon & 1pm-5pm Tues-Sun), which contains some spectacular sarcophagi and friezes from Hierapolis and nearby Afrodisias. As you return to the village keep looking back for great views of the glittering travertines.

Places to Stay
Over 60 bargain pensions and hotels lurk below the travertines in Pamukkale village (the further from the highway, the cheaper they become).

For cheerful service and decent rooms, good bargains are **Kervansaray Pension** (☎ 272 2209, fax 272 2143; e kervansaray@superonline.com; singles/doubles with shower US$12/18) and the nearby **Aspawa** (☎ 272 2094, fax 272 2631; e aspawa@mail.koc

.net.tr; singles/doubles US$8/12). Breakfast is included in the room rates at both places. **Weisse Burg Pension** (☎ 272 2064; singles/doubles US$6/12) comes recommended by readers. Excellent breakfast costs US$2, dinner US$5.

Meltem Motel (☎ 272 2413; e meltemmotel@superonline.com; dorm beds/singles/doubles US$4/5/8) is big and popular with backpackers. It has its own pool and a rooftop terrace.

Koray Motel (☎ 272 2300, fax 272 2095; w www.korayhotel.com; Fevzi Çakmak Caddesi 27; doubles with shower US$20, with full board US$30) is an inviting place a few streets south, with a pool-side restaurant and bar, and tour services.

Places to Eat
Eating in your pension or hotel is usually the best option. Of the restaurants in the town, **Gürsoy** (meals US$4-6), opposite the Yörük Motel in the village centre, has the nicest terrace, but **Han** (meals US$4-6), around the corner facing the square, offers best value for money. Or you can hop on the bus to Denizli and eat for even less at the small places ringing the otogar.

Getting There & Away
Frequent buses run from İzmir to Denizli (US$4, four hours), and also from Denizli to Konya (US$10, seven hours).

Municipal buses and dolmuşes make the half-hour trip between Denizli and Pamukkale every 30 minutes or so (US$0.50), more frequently on Saturday and Sunday; the last bus runs at around 10pm.

BODRUM
☎ 0252

Bodrum (formerly Halicarnassus) is the site of the Mausoleum, the monumental tomb of King Mausolus, which was another of the Seven Wonders of the Ancient World. By some miracle Bodrum has managed to avoid the urban sprawl that has so damaged Kuşadası and Marmaris – in spring and autumn it's still a delightful place to stay.

Orientation & Information
The **otogar** is 500m inland along Cevat Sakir Caddesi from the Adliye (Yeni) Camii, a small mosque at the centre of the town. The **PTT** and several **banks** are on Cevat Sakir.

The **tourist office** (☎ 316 1091, fax 316 7694) is beside the Castle of St Peter.

Things to See
There's little left of the **Mausoleum** (admission US$2; open 8am-noon & 12.3pm-5pm Tues-Sun), although the **Castle of St Peter**, built in 1402 and rebuilt in 1522 by the Crusaders, using stones from the tomb, makes up for its shortcomings. The castle houses the **Museum of Underwater Archaeology** (admission US$7; open 8am-noon & 1pm-5pm Tues-Sun), containing finds from the oldest Mediterranean shipwreck ever discovered (admission US$2; open 10am-11am & 2pm-4pm); and a model of a Carian princess' tomb (admission US$2; open 10am-noon & 2pm-4pm).

West past the marina and over the hill, **Gümbet** has a nicer beach than Bodrum proper but is solid package-holiday territory; you may prefer less-developed **Ortakent**. **Gümüşlük**, to the west of the Bodrum peninsula, is the least spoilt of the many smaller villages nearby. Hourly *dolmuşes* run there (US$1).

Places to Stay
The narrow streets north of Bodrum's western harbour have pleasant family-run pensions, generally charging around US$18 to US$25 a double in high season. Those behind the western bay tend to be quieter than those on the eastern bay because they're further from the famously noisy Halikarnas Disco. Prices drop between November and March, but few places stay open in winter.

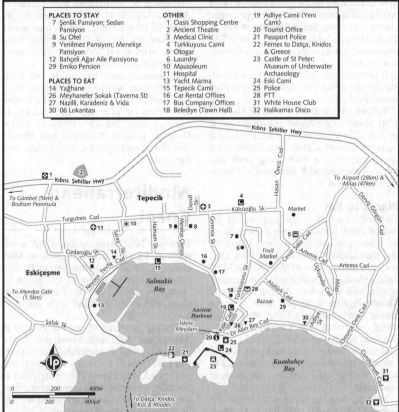

BODRUM

PLACES TO STAY	OTHER	19 Adliye Camii (Yeni
7 Şenlik Pansiyon; Sedan	1 Oasis Shopping Centre	Cami)
Pansiyon	2 Ancient Theatre	20 Tourist Office
8 Su Otel	3 Medical Clinic	21 Passport Police
9 Yenilmez Pansiyon; Menekşe	4 Turkkuyusu Camii	22 Ferries to Datça, Knidos
Pansiyon	5 Otogar	& Greece
12 Bahçeli Ağar Aile Pansiyonu	6 Laundry	23 Castle of St Peter;
29 Emiko Pension	10 Mausoleum	Museum of Underwater
	11 Hospital	Archaeology
PLACES TO EAT	13 Yacht Marina	24 Eski Cami
14 Yağhane	15 Tepecik Camii	25 Police
26 Meyhaneler Sokak (Taverna St)	16 Car Rental Offices	27 PTT
27 Nazilli, Karadeniz & Vida	17 Bus Company Offices	28 Eski Cami
30 06 Lokantası	18 Belediye (Town Hall)	31 White House Club
		32 Halikarnas Disco

Two quiet, modern places are tucked away down a narrow alley that begins between Neyzen Tevfik 84 and 86: **Yenilmez** (☎ *316 2520; Menekşe Çıkmazı 30; doubles with shower US$18)* and **Menekşe** (☎ *316 5890; Menekşe Çıkmazı 34; doubles with shower US$18)*.

Bahçeli Ağar Aile Pansiyonu (☎ *316 16 48; doubles with shower US$18)* has quiet, basic rooms set back from the seafront at the end of a passage.

Emiko Pension (☎/fax *316 5560; Atatürk Caddesi, Uslu Sokak 11; beds with shower US$5)* is spotless, quiet and run by a Japanese woman.

Türkkuyusu Sokak starts just north of the Adliye Camii and cuts up past several good, cheap, convenient pensions, mostly with shady courtyards. **Şenlik Pansiyon** (☎ *316 63 82; Türkkuyusu Sokak 115; beds with showers from US$6)*, right on the street, could do with buying new mattresses but it stays open when other places close. **Sedan Pansyon** (☎ *316 03 55; Türkkuyusu Sokak 121; beds from US$6)*, just behind it, is a family-run place with some newer rooms.

If both of these are full, just keep prowling up and down the street until you find somewhere else.

Su Otel (☎ *316 6906; Turgutreis Caddesi, 1201 Sokak; singles/doubles with shower & air-con US$40/65)* is best of all, a colourful oasis set around a charming flower-filled courtyard, with a swimming pool and rooms decorated with local crafts. Follow the signs to find it.

Places to Eat

The grid of small streets just east of the Adliye Camii harbours several cheap eateries where you can grab a döner kebap for less than US$2 at a street-side buffet. Otherwise, continue eastward to Kilise Meydanı, a plaza filled with open-air restaurants serving pide and kebab. At both **Nazilli** and **Karadeniz** a pide topped with meat or cheese should cost only US$3. **Vida** (meals US$5), just round from Karadeniz, does an excellent tomato soup for US$0.75.

Heading further east, look out for **06 Lokantasi** (Cumhuriyet Caddesi; meals US$4), which is deservedly popular with locals at lunch time.

In warm weather, check out Meyhaneler Sokak (Taverna St), off İskele Caddesi.

Wall-to-wall tavernas serve food, drink and live music to rapturous crowds for US$10 to US$15. **İbo** seems particularly good and offers mezzes like stuffed vine leaves and octopus salad.

Yağhane (☎ *313 4747; meals around US$20)*, on the western bay, is atmospherically housed in an old olive-oil factory. At the time of writing it was the 'in' place with the upmarket yachting clientele. Alternatively, head for the serial fish restaurants lining the eastern bay, making sure to check all prices before ordering.

Getting There & Away

Bodrum international **airport** (☎ *523 0129)* is actually nearer to Milas and has disappointingly few flights. Havaş buses meet arrivals and charge US$4.50 for the Bodrum run. The taxi fare is US$32.

Bodrum offers frequent bus services to Antalya (US$10, 11 hours), Fethiye (US$6, about 4½ hours), İzmir (US$10, four hours), Kuşadası and Selçuk (US$4, about three hours), Marmaris (US$5, about three hours) and Pamukkale (US$6, five hours).

In summer daily hydrofoils and boats link Bodrum with Kos (İstanköy; from US$14 one way, US$18 day return); in winter services shrink to three times weekly. In summer there are also boats to Datça, Didyma, Knidos, Marmaris and Rhodes (Rhodos); check with the ferry offices near the castle.

Mediterranean Coast

Turkey's Mediterranean coastline winds eastward for more than 1200km from Marmaris to Antakya on the Syrian border. From Marmaris to Fethiye the gorgeous 'Turquoise Coast' is perfect for boat excursions, with many secluded coves and quiet bays.

The rugged peninsula east of Fethiye to Antalya and the Taurus Mountains east of Antalya are wild and beautiful. Further east you pass through fewer seaside resorts and more workaday cities. The entire coast is liberally sprinkled with impressive ruins, studded with beautiful beaches and washed by glittering sea ideal for sports.

MARMARİS
☎ 0252

Like Bodrum, Marmaris sits on a beautiful bay at the edge of a hilly peninsula. Unlike Bodrum, however, Marmaris has succumbed to unplanned, haphazard development, which has robbed it of much of its charm – although you may still want to drop by to sample the nightlife and the shopping.

The Greek island of Rhodes (Rodos) is a short boat trip south.

Orientation & Information
İskele Meydanı (main square) and the **tourist office** (☎ 412 1035) are by the ferry pier northeast of the castle, near the waterfront. The **PTT** (Fevzipaşa Caddesi) is in the bazaar. The centre is mostly a pedestrian precinct, but new development stretches many kilometres to the southeast. Hacı Mustafa Sokak, also called Bar St, runs inland from the bazaar; action here keeps going until the early hours.

The **otogar** is 2km north of town, off the road to Bodrum.

Things to See & Do
The small **castle** (admission US$0.75; open 8am-noon & 1pm-5pm Tues-Sun) has a few unexciting exhibition rooms but offers fine views of Marmaris.

Numerous boats along the waterfront offer day tours of the harbour, its beaches and islands. Before deciding on your boat, talk to the captain about where the excursion goes, what it costs, whether lunch is included and, if so, what's on the menu. A day's outing usually costs around US$16 to US$20 per person, much less in the low season, when boats also leave later in the day.

The most popular daily excursions are to **Dalyan** and **Kaunos** or to the bays around Marmaris, but you can also take longer, more serious boat trips to Datça and Knidos. It's also worth asking for a boat heading for **Cleopatra's Island,** which offers silky-soft sand and water as warm as a Jacuzzi.

Places to Stay
Unlike Kuşadası and Bodrum, Marmaris lacks a network of small, welcoming pensions. Indeed, almost all the cheaper places have been squeezed out by the relentless growth of hotels serving package holiday-makers. The cheapies that remain may be fairly central but are often noisy and unin-

spiring. There are several moderately priced hotels a short walk from İskele Meydanı. Most of the really pricey places are well around the bay from the town or in neighbouring İçmeler.

The **Interyouth Hostel** (☎/fax 412 7823; Tepe Mahallesi, 42 Sokak 45) is deep in the bazaar right at the town centre. In season it's a good travellers hangout, with lots of services and atmosphere. Out of season, it charges more for grim rooms without shower than some of the cheaper hotels.

Otherwise, to find the cheapest accommodation stroll along the waterfront to Abdi İpekçi Park and turn inland just past the park, then left at the first street, and right past Ayçe Otel. **Maltepe Pension** (☎ 412 1629; rooms with shower US$20), across a wooden footbridge, is serviceable. The **Özcan Pension** (☎ 412 7761; Çam Sokak 3) next door is bigger but similarly priced.

Hotel Aylin (☎ 412 8283, fax 413 9985; 1 Sokak 4; singles/doubles with a shower from US$5/9) offers reasonably comfortable rooms even at times of the year when most places close.

Hotel Begonya (☎ 412 4095; Hacı Mustafa Sokak 71; singles/doubles with shower US$20/35) is potentially delightful, with a breakfast courtyard filled with plants. But Hacı Mustafa is wall-to-wall bars – good news if you're up for a big night, not so great if you want to catch up on your beauty sleep.

Places to Eat
There are literally hundreds of restaurants all along the harbour, along Kordon Caddesi and out along the shore to Uzunyalı, with yet more places to eat in the bazaar and along Hacı Mustafa Sokak.

For the cheapest fare, explore the bazaar and the streets beyond it, looking for 'untouristy', local Turkish places selling pide, kebabs and fast food. Head for the PTT on 51. Sokak in the bazaar. Just inland from it are several good, cheap restaurants including **Sofra** (36 Sokak 23; meals US$3.50) and **Liman Restaurant** (40 Sokak 32; meals US$5) off 51 Sokak. Both of these places heave with happy diners at lunch time.

Cut inland from the Atatürk statue along Ulusal Egemenlik Bulvarı and turn right opposite the Tansaş shopping centre to find **Kırçiçeği Pide-Pizza Çorba ve Kebap Salonu** (Yeni Yol Caddesi 15; meals US$3),

TURKEY

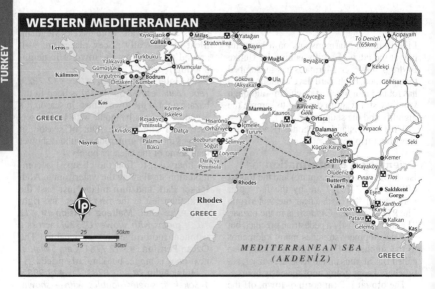

WESTERN MEDITERRANEAN

Kiyikişlacık, Güllük, Milas, Yatağan, Acıpayam, Leros, Stratonikea, Bayir, To Denizli (65km), Yalıkavak, Turkbuku, Muğla, Beyağaç, Kelekçi, Gümüşlük, Mumcular, Gölhisar, Kálimnos, Turgutreis, Bodrum, Ören, Ula, Ortakent, Gumbet, Gökova (Akyaka), Kos, Körmen İskelesi, Köyceğiz, Reşadiye Peninsula, Marmaris, Kaunos, Köyceğiz Gölü, Ortaca, GREECE, Knidos, Hisarönü, İçmeler, Dalyan, Dalaman, Arpacık, Orhaniye, Turunç, Göcek, Seki, Datça, Bozburun, Selimiye, Küçük Kargı, Nisyros, Palamut Büku, Söğüt, Simi, Loryma, Fethiye, Kemer, Daraçya Peninsula, Kayaköy, Rhodes, Ölüdeniz, Pınara, Tlos, Butterfly Valley, Eşen, Sakhkent Gorge, Xanthos, Kınık, Letoon, Rhodes, Patara, Kalkan, Gelemiş, Kaş, GREECE, MEDITERRANEAN SEA (AKDENİZ), GREECE

0 25 50km
0 15 30mi

---

which is always crowded with locals tucking into soups and filling pides.

The **waterfront restaurants** south and east of the tourist office have pleasant outdoor dining areas, but prices are higher than those inland, and the extra pays for the setting rather than the food. Assume you'll spend between US$10 and US$20 per person for a full meal with wine.

Kartal Restaurant & Terrace Bar (☎ 412 3308; Eski Cami Sokak; meal with drinks US$12-18) is in the attractive castle area; follow the signs from the waterfront to find it.

Keyif (Netsel Marina Çarşısı; meals from US$4) is upstairs inside the big marina at the eastern end of town. On Sunday it offers a good-value open-buffet breakfast for a fixed US$4.50 from 9.30am to 1pm.

Getting There & Away
The nearest airports to Marmaris are at Bodrum and Dalaman.

Marmaris' **otogar** has frequent buses and minibuses to Antalya (US$9.50, about seven hours), Bodrum (US$4, three hours), Dalyan (via Ortaca; US$2, two hours), Datça (US$3, 1¾ hours) and Fethiye (US$4, three hours). Bozburun minibuses run at least once a day from the minibus terminal near the Tansaş shopping centre (US$2, 1½ hours). If you're heading all the way to Antalya, avoid taking the uncomfortable Mar-

maris Koop, Fethiye Koop or Antalya Tur Koop midibuses.

Car ferries run to Rhodes daily in summer (less frequently in winter) for US$32 one way and US$50 return (plus US$13 port tax at Rhodes and US$10 to re-enter Turkey). You must give your passport to the travel agency the day before you sail.

KÖYCEĞİZ
☎ 0252
In early spring Köyceğiz smells sweetly of orange blossom, a reminder that this quiet town on the edge of a placid lake still has a farming life beyond tourism. It makes a pleasant alternative to Dalyan if you want to visit Kaunos, wallow in the mud baths and laze on İstuzu beach.

Places to Stay & Eat
Tango Pansiyon (☎ 262 2501, fax 262 4345; W www.tangopension.com; Alihsan Kalmaz Caddesi; dorm beds US$5, singles/doubles/triples with shower US$10/12/16) has clean, pleasant rooms and a range of activities, from moonlight cruises to short treks. If it's full, try the nearby **Samba Pension**, which is run by the same people.

Hotel Kaunos (☎ 262 4288, fax 262 4836; singles/doubles with shower US$5/10) has a very decent waterfront location but rather faded rooms. **Hotel Alila** (☎/fax 262 1150;

Emeksiz Caddesi; singles/doubles with shower US$14/24) is newer and altogether more cheerful, with a fine pool and an inviting dining room.

Çiçek Restaurant *(meals US$5)*, on the main square, is good for people-watching while you eat standard fare, but **Colıba** *(Emeksiz Caddesi; meals US$5)* has much more flair when it comes to both its menu and its decor.

Getting There & Away
There are hourly *dolmuşes* from Ortaca (US$0.75, 25 minutes) and Muğla (US$1.50, one hour). Take a *şehiriçi* minibus from the otogar to the town centre (2km).

DALYAN
☎ 0252
Set on the banks of a placid river and backed by a cliff face cut with elegant Lycian tombs, Dalyan was always too good to remain undiscovered by the big tour operators and some people feel it has become a bit too touristy. Still, **İztuzu beach**, a short boat trip (US$5.50) along the river, is a gorgeous place to sun yourself (as well as being one of the few remaining nesting grounds of the *carretta carretta*, or sea turtle). The same boat trips usually take in a visit to the ruined city of **Kaunos** *(Caunos; admission US$2; open 8.30am-5.30pm daily)* and the **Sul-**

taniye hot springs *(Sultaniye Kaplıcaları; admission US$0.75)*, on the shores of Köyceğiz Lake.

Places to Stay & Eat
Camping About 500m southwest of the *dolmuş* stand is **Dalyan Camping** *(tent sites US$4)*.

Pensions & Hotels A simple family-run pension, **Önder Pansiyon** *(☎ 284 2605; Maraş Caddesi; singles/doubles US$12/17)* is right on the river. Its rates include breakfast.

There is a cluster of places in Yalı Sokak, northwest of Maraş Caddesi, past the school. **Hotel Caria** *(☎ 284 2075, fax 284 3046; doubles with shower US$20)* has comfortable rooms with balconies and a gorgeous, river-facing roof terrace. **Çınar Sahil Pansiyon** *(☎ 284 2117)*, across the road, is more casual about its welcome, but has an equally inviting location. **Hotel Dönmez** *(☎ 284 2107, fax 284 2201; doubles with shower US$17)*, nearby, has the added benefit of a swimming pool.

Most of Dalyan's restaurants serve a predictable menu of mezzes, kebabs and fish, but **Metin Pide & Pizza Restaurant** *(Sulungur Sokak; meals US$2)* rustles up excellent Italian-style pizzas as well as pides.

It's a shameless tourist trap, but you could also try the **Ley Ley Restaurant** *(☎ 384 4660; Dalyan Yolu; meals US$8-10)*, which looks out over storks nesting on specially created stands (March through August only). A *dolmuş* service leaving Dalyan at 8pm and returning at 11pm also serves the **Yuvarlakçay Restaurant** *(meals US$6)*, a riverside place where you can tuck into trout beneath shady plane trees.

Getting There & Away
From Dalaman airport or Marmaris, take a bus to Ortaca and change for a minibus to Dalyan (US$0.50, 30 minutes).

FETHİYE
☎ 0252
Despite its picture-postcard harbour backdrop, Fethiye still has much more of the feel of a living town than big resorts like Kuşadası and Marmaris. It can be extremely hot and crowded in summer, but is still well worth a visit and makes a good base for visiting the beautiful **Saklıkent Gorge** and the ruins at

Tlos and **Pınara**. The beach at **Calış**, 5km northeast of the centre, is many kilometres long, and is backed by hotels and pensions.

Orientation & Information

Fethiye's **otogar** is 2km east of the centre. Karagözler *dolmuşes* ply up and down the main street, taking you past the government buildings, the **PTT** and several **banks**. They then skirt the bazaar district on the left, curving round the bay past the **tourist office** *(☎/fax 614 1527)*, and cutting up by the marina on the western side of town.

Things to See & Do

Of ancient Telmessos, little more remains than the ruins of a theatre and several Lycian stone sarcophagi dating from about 400 BC. The picturesque rock-cut **Tomb of Amyntas** *(admission US$2; open 8am-7pm)* makes a perfect vantage point for watching the sun set over the harbour.

Most people succumb to the **'12 Island'** boat tour, which mixes swimming, cruising and sightseeing; prices start at around US$8 per person but ask around carefully. Don't miss the *hamam (cost around US$10; open 7am-midnight)* in the bazaar either.

Dolmuşes run to the nearby Ottoman Greek 'ghost town' of **Kaya Köy** *(admission US$2)*, abandoned after the population exchange of 1923.

Places to Stay

Most of the nicer pensions are uphill from the yacht marina along Fevzi Çakmak Caddesi; take a Karagözler *dolmuş* along the harbour road to reach them. **Yıldırım** *(☎ 614 3913)*, **Pınara** *(☎ 614 2151)* and **İrem** *(☎ 614 3985)* all charge around US$16/30 for singles/doubles with shower and breakfast.

İdeal Pension *(☎ 614 1981; Zafer Caddesi 1; singles/doubles with shower US$5/10)*, one street back from the harbour road, has superb views from its terrace and offers a full range of backpacker services: laundry, Internet access, book exchange etc.

Ferah Pension *(Monica's Place; ☎ 614 2816, fax 612 7398; w www.backpackingeu rope.com; 2 Karagözler Mahallesi, Ordu Caddesi 2; dorm beds US$5, doubles without/ with shower US$10/12)* has nicer rooms, but is a little further out, so you need to take a *dolmuş* in and out of town. Dinners are said to be impressive. Breakfast is US$2 extra.

Cennet Pansiyon *(☎ 614 2230; 2 Karagözler Mahallesi; doubles with shower US$7)*, used by the Fez Bus, has a pleasant waterside location. An on-site restaurant and bar make up for the rather remote position.

Places to Eat

Side by side on Tütün Sokak are two local favourites – **Sedir Restaurant** and **Şamdan Restaurant** – both serving excellent pizza for around US$3.50. In Eski Cami Geçidi Likya Sokak look out for the very popular **Meğri** *(meals US$5)*, with a wide range of piping-hot meals. There's another branch in the bazaar.

Right opposite the post office, **Birlik Lokantası** *(Atatürk Caddesi; meals US$4)* serves up good, big portions of lean *İskender kebap*.

On the edge of the bazaar, near the *hamam*, **Café Oley** *(Eski Meğri Sokak 4; meals US$5)* offers such unexpected delights as smoked-salmon sandwiches and cheesecake for anyone who's 'kebabed out'.

Getting There & Away

If you're heading straight for Antalya, note that the *yayla* (inland) route is shorter and cheaper (US$6) than the *sahil* (coastal) route (US$8); also, it's much more comfortable travelling in the big buses than in the short-hop midibuses offered by Fethiye Koop and Antalya Tur. The midibuses that ply the coast route also serve Patara, Kınık (for Xanthos; US$2), Kalkan (US$2) and Kaş (US$3). Minibuses to more local destinations leave from behind the big white Yeni Cami in the town centre.

In high summer a **hydrofoil** service operates between Rhodes (Greece) and Fethiye on Tuesday and Thursday (one way US$50, same-day round-trip US$75, open return US$95).

ÖLÜDENİZ

☎ 0252

Over the mountains to the south of Fethiye, lovely **Ölüdeniz** (Dead Sea) has proved a bit too beautiful for its own good. It's now one of the most famous beach spots on the Mediterranean, with far too many hotels catering for the package-holiday market backed up behind the sands. Still, the lagoon *(admission US$0.50; open 8am-8pm)* itself remains tranquillity incarnate and along its banks you'll find moderately priced bungalows and camping areas. This is a good place to try **tandem paragliding** for a cool US$100.

Places to Stay & Eat

Ölüdeniz Camping (☎ 617 0048, fax 617 0181; tree house beds/tents US$1.75/$3, bungalows from US$8) is probably the most popular choice, although there are several other similar camp sites further round the lagoon near Hotel Meri.

Hotel Meri (☎ 617 0001, fax 617 0010; W www.hotelmeri.com; doubles with shower from US$74) is the oldest and most appealing of Ölüdeniz's hotels, not least because it has gardens and a pool of its own.

When it comes to eating, you may well feel disinclined to venture further than the **cafés** attached to the camp sites, or the **restaurant** at Hotel Meri.

Getting There & Away

Frequent *dolmuşes* to Ölüdeniz (US$1, 30 minutes) run from outside Fethiye otogar or from behind the Yeni Cami.

PATARA
☎ 0242

Patara's main claim to fame is its superb 20km beach, one of the best in all of Turkey. However, there are also extensive ruins here (admission US$7; open 7.30am-7pm daily May-Oct, 8am-5.30pm Nov-March). Altogether, it's a great place to chill out for a few days.

Places to Stay & Eat

All the places to stay and most of the places to eat are in Gelemiş village, 1.5km inland from the beach.

Flower Pension (☎ 843 5164; beds with shower US$7) is one of the furthest inland but has a particularly welcoming host. **St Nicholas Pension** (☎ 843 5024; beds with shower US$7) is a bit more central and offers services like a terrace restaurant and canoe hire. **Golden Pension** (☎ 843 5162; beds with shower US$7), opposite, also boasts a restaurant. Some rooms have fans – vital in summer.

Getting There & Away

Midibuses plying the Fethiye-Antalya main road will drop you 2km from Gelemiş vil-

lage (3.5km from the beach, signposted 'Patara'). In summer there are also direct *dolmuşes* from Kaş, Kalkan and Fethiye.

AROUND PATARA

From Patara (or Fethiye) it's easy to visit two of Turkey's Unesco-listed World Heritage sites, both of them atmospheric ruins. The **Letoön** (admission US$2), just off the Fethiye-Antalya highway near Kumluova, boasts excellent mosaics, a good theatre and a sacred pool used in the worship of the goddess Leto.

With its Roman theatre and Lycian pillar tombs, **Xanthos** (admission US$2), a few kilometres southeast of Letoön above the village of Kınık, is among the most impressive sites along this part of the coast, even though many of its best sculptures are now in the British Museum in London.

KALKAN
☎ 0242

Once a quaint fishing village, but now a rather Disneyfied, upmarket tourist resort, Kalkan is 11km east of the Patara turn-off. Its narrow streets lined with pretty wood-and-stone houses tumble down a steep hillside to a marina with plenty of open-air restaurants. Kalkan itself has no good beaches, but boat tours (or minibuses) can take you to Patara and secluded coves along the coast.

Places to Stay & Eat

The cheapest **pensions** tend to be at the top of town, near where the *dolmuşes* stop. **Öz Pansiyon** (☎ 844 3444; singles/doubles with shower US$13/17) is good, as is the simple **Çelik Pansiyon** (☎ 844 2126; Yalıboyu 9; singles/doubles with shower US$8/12), which stays open when rivals are closed. **Holiday Pension** (☎ 844 3154) and, up the hill across from it, **Gül Pansiyon** (☎ 844 3099), are both more basic and slightly cheaper.

Kalamaki Pension (☎ 844 3649, fax 844 3654; doubles with shower US$24) is a popular choice with a rooftop restaurant.

Balıkçı Han (☎ 844 3075, fax 844 3640; doubles with shower US$34) was designed to look like an older building, with stone fireplaces and red-tiled floors. It's very atmospheric and breakfast is included in the price.

Daphne Pansiyon (☎ 844 3547; Kocakaya Caddesi; singles/doubles with shower US$12/25) is near the mosque on the road winding down to the harbour. It's nicely decorated and throws in breakfast on a pleasant roof terrace.

Patara Stone House (☎ 844 3076; singles/ doubles with shower US$13/25) is almost hidden beneath a veil of bougainvillea, right on the waterfront.

Çetinkaya Pension (☎ 844 3307; doubles with shower US$10), nearby, seems especially friendly.

Getting There & Away
Hourly buses connect Kalkan with Kaş (US$1, 35 minutes) and Patara (US$0.50, 25 minutes).

KAŞ
☎ 0242
Kaş is another of those places that seems to have everything: a picturesque quay, pleasant restaurants, excellent shops, a scattering of Lycian tombs and a big Sunday market. Even the **tourist office** (☎ 836 1238, fax 836 1368), on the main square, is better informed than most. It's a fine, laid-back place to hang out for a few days.

Things to See & Do
Apart from enjoying the town's ambience and a few small pebble beaches, you can walk west a few hundred metres to the well-preserved **theatre**. Lycian **sarcophagi** are dotted about the streets, and tombs are cut into the cliffs above the town.

The most popular boat trip sails round **Kekova Island** and out to beautiful **Kaleköy** (Simena), passing over Lycian ruins beneath the sea. You'll pay around US$10 per person in a glass-bottomed boat.

Other excursions take in Patara, Xanthos and the wonderful 18km **Saklıkent Gorge**, where you can eat trout on platforms over an ice-cold river. There are also less-frequent excursions to the **Mavi Mağara** (Blue Cave), to **Meis Adası** (Kastellorizo), the Greek island just off the coast, and to villages further inland.

Places to Stay
Camping In an olive grove just west of town past the theatre there's **Kaş Camping** (☎ 836 1050; tent sites US$5).

Pensions & Hotels Kaş' quietest places to stay are all on the west side of town and

tend to rise in price (and quality) the nearer you get to the sea.

Yenicami Caddesi (or Recep Bilgin Caddesi), just south of the otogar, has lots of small, family-run pensions, including **Orion Hotel** (☎/fax 836 1286), **Anıl Motel** (☎ 836 1791), the **Hilal** (☎ 836 1207) and the **Santosa** (☎ 836 1714). In high season a bed with shower in all these places is likely to cost US$10 including breakfast.

Ay Pansiyon (☎ 836 1562; singles/doubles with shower US$7/10), at the southern end of the street by the mosque, has sea views from its front rooms.

Turn right at Ay Pansiyon and follow the signs to one of Kaş best places to stay. **Kale Otel** (☎ 836 4074; Kilise Mevkii; singles/ doubles with shower & air-con US$20/33) is an immaculate place with a lawn overlooking the sea, lovely rooms and great breakfasts included in the price. It's often busy with German groups. **Kale Pansiyon** (☎ 836 4074; singles/doubles with shower & air-con US$12.50/16), opposite and with a fine roof terrace, was being turned into an extension at the time of writing.

Hotel Korsan Karakedi (☎ 836 1887, fax 836 3086; Yeni Cami Sokak 7; singles/ doubles with shower US$10/23), up the hill behind it, offers a warm welcome that compensates for slightly lumpy bedding. There's a small but inviting roof bar.

Ateş Pension (☎ 836 1393; e atespension@superonline.com; doubles with shower US$10), one more street back, rambles across two buildings but has a good rooftop terrace.

Places to Eat
Corner Café, at the PTT end of İbrahim Serin Caddesi, serves juices or a vegetable omelette for US$1, and yogurt with fruit and honey for US$1.75. **Café Merhaba**, across the street and run by two women, is good for cakes, coffee and Western newspapers.

Sympathy Restaurant (☎ 836 241; Uzunçarşı Gürsöy Sokak 11; meals around US$8) offers excellent cooking, including a fine spread of mezzes, in a cosy atmosphere.

Mercan Restaurant (meals US$12-18) is very popular because of its waterside location, but can catch out the unwary by substituting cheaper fish for what was actually ordered. **Octopus** (Öztürk Sokak 5; meals US$8) is newer but maybe tries that little bit harder. Actual octopus dishes cost around US$5 each.

For cheaper eats, cut up Atatürk Bulvarı and try **2000 Restaurant** or **Kervan Restaurant**, both of them busiest at lunch time when food is likely to be freshest.

Getting There & Away

Frequent midibuses connect Kaş with Kalkan (US$1, 35 minutes), Patara (US$1.30, one hour), Kale (Demre; US$1.30, one hour), Olympos (US$2, 2½ hours) and Antalya (US$2.75, four hours).

KALE (DEMRE)

☎ 0242

Set in a rich alluvial plain covered in greenhouses, Kale (ancient Myra) is famous for a generous, 4th-century bishop who, according to legend, gave anonymous gifts to dowryless girls, thus enabling them to marry. He was later canonised as St Nicholas, the original Father Christmas (Noel Baba in Turkish). The restored, 3rd-century **Church of St Nicholas** (admission US$4; open 8am-5.30pm daily) supposedly holds his tomb but is more interesting for the remains of Byzantine frescoes and mosaic floors.

About 2km inland from the church is a rock face honeycombed with ancient **Lycian tombs**, right next to a large **Roman theatre** (admission US$7; open 8am-5.30pm daily).

Getting There & Away

Frequent midibuses ply up and down the coast road, connecting Kale with Kaş and the turn-off for Olympos.

OLYMPOS & ÇIRALI

☎ 0242

After climbing into the mountains, the switchback coast road reaches a turn-off marked for Olympos. From there it's just over 8km down a winding unpaved road to the village, and a further 3.5km along a picturesque, but ever-worsening, road to the site of **ancient Olympos** (admission US$7). It's a wild, abandoned place where ruins peek out from forest copses, rock outcrops and riverbanks – perfect for rough camping. Note that you have to pay the admission fee for the ruins to access the beach from Olympos, although your ticket will be valid for a week.

Most people come here to stay in the tree houses set back along the road from the beach. If that's not your thing, there are pensions and hotels at neighbouring Çıralı.

Chimaera

According to legend, the Chimaera (Yanartaş), a natural eternal flame, was the hot breath of a subterranean monster. Easily sighted by mariners in ancient times, it is today a mere glimmer of its former fiery self, but no less inspiring for all that.

To get to the Chimaera, follow the signs for 3km east down a neighbouring valley. A half-hour climb along a good path leads to the flame.

Places to Stay & Eat

Olympos Lining the road to the Olympos ruins are assorted treehouse-cabin-bar complexes where prices of around US$5 per person in a tree house and US$7 in a cabin include breakfast and dinner.

Kadir's (☎ 892 1250), the grandaddy of them all and still the most visually inviting, offers rustic, ramshackle charm with Internet connections but is furthest from the beach. In summer minibuses run guests to and from the sands.

Bayram's (☎ 892 1243, fax 1399; w www .bayrams.com) doesn't look so pretty but is the sort of place where you arrive to spend a day and find yourself still there a week later.

Türkmen (☎ 892 1249) is popular with holidaying Turkish families, while **Orange** (☎ 892 1242) and **Şaban** (☎ 892 1265) are the preferred choices out of several pensions further a field.

Zeus (☎ 892 1347) suits the idle as it's one of the closest complexes to the ruins/beach.

Çıralı A separate turn-off from the Fethiye-Antalya highway less than 1km east of the Olympos turn-off leads to the more conventional pensions and hotels at Çıralı. You can also get there by walking 1km along the beach from Olympos.

Sima Peace Pension (☎ 825 7245; singles/doubles with shower US$10/15) is a pleasing group of wooden chalets set around a garden with a menagerie of resident cats, dogs and birds.

Olympos Lodge (☎ 825 7171; fax 825 7173; e olimposlodge@superonline.com; singles/doubles with shower US$87/134) is a delightful place set among citrus orchards and well-tended gardens right by the beach.

Getting There & Away

Buses and minibuses plying the Fethiye-Antalya road will drop you at the Olympos or Çıralı turn-offs. In summer regular *dolmuşes* wait to run you down to Olympos (US$0.50); if you don't want to walk the 7km to Çıralı you may need to ring a pension to collect you or take a taxi.

The nicest way to get from Olympos to Fethiye or vice versa is on a three- or four-day 'blue cruise' on a *gûlet* (wooden yacht), calling in at bays along the way. Prices for three-day cruises start at around US$100.

PHASELIS

About 2km from the highway, Phaselis is a collection of **ruins** *(admission US$7; open 7.30am-7pm daily)* framing three small, perfect bays – a good place for a swim.

ANTALYA
☎ 0242

A bustling, modern town of around half a million people, Antalya has more than just its lovely harbour setting to boast about and avoids that soullessness that tends to come over resorts that live only for tourism. It's fun to kick around in **Kaleiçi**, the old restored Ottoman town that spreads back from a beautiful marina and the sea-facing Karaalioglu Parkı.

Pebbly Konyaaltı beach spreads out to the west of town, sandy Lara beach to the east. Both are solidly backed with package-holiday hotels – you'd do best to wait until Olympos for a swim.

Orientation & Information

The **otogar** is 4km north of the centre on the D650 highway to Burdur. The city centre is at Kalekapısı, a major intersection marked by a landmark clock tower right next to Cumhuriyet Meydanı, with its dramatic equestrian statue of Atatürk. To get into Kaleiçi, head south down the hill from the clock tower or cut in from Hadrian's Gate, just off Atatürk Caddesi.

The **tourist office** *(☎/fax 241 1747; Cumhuriyet Caddesi 91)* and the **Turkish Airlines** office *(☎ 243 4383)* are in the same building, 450m west of Kalekapısı in the Özel İdare Çarşısı building – look for 'Antalya Devlet Tiyatrosu' emblazoned on it. The **PTT** is around the corner in Güllük Caddesi. The **Owl Bookshop** *(☎ 243 5718;*

Akarçeşme Sokak 21) is one of Turkey's best second-hand bookshops.

Antalya Museum

Antalya Museum *(Cumhuriyet Caddesi; tram: Müze; admission US$7; open 9am-6pm Tues-Sun)* houses finds from nearby Perge, Aspendos and Side, as well as a wonderful ethnographical collection. It's one of Turkey's finest museums.

Kaleiçi

Heading down from the clock tower you'll pass the **Yivli Minare** (Grooved Minaret), which rises above an old mosque. Further into Kaleiçi, the **Kesik Minare** (Truncated Minaret) is built on the site of a ruined Roman temple.

Just off Atatürk Caddesi, the monumental **Hadrian's Gate** (Hadriyanüs Kapısı) was built for the Roman emperor's visit in AD 130. The surrounding medieval walls were under restoration at the time of writing.

The **Suna & İnan Kıraç Kaleiçi Museum** *(☎ 243 4274; Kocatepe Sokak; admission US$0.75; open 9am-noon & 1pm-6pm Thur-Tues, 9am-noon & 2pm-7.30pm June-Sept)* houses a fine collection of Kütahya and Çanakkale pottery. There are also rooms set up to show important events in Ottoman family life: serving coffee to guests, shaving a bridegroom before his wedding and a bride's henna night.

Places to Stay

Would-be campers are best off pushing on to Olympos.

Kaleiçi is full of pensions and more seem to open (and close) every year. The ones listed here seem to be here to stay. In summer you may want to check how close the nearest bars are if you're keen to get a good night's sleep.

Pansiyon White Garden *(☎ 241 9115, fax 241 3062; Hesapçı Geçidi 9; doubles with shower US$15, with shower & air-con US$18)* is a spotless, family-run place with a pleasant courtyard bar-restaurant where Metin cooks up grills every evening. Seven rooms have air-con, the rest have fans – both very necessary in summer.

Senem Family Pension *(☎ 247 1752; Zeytingeçidi Sokak 9; singles/doubles with shower & air-con US$15-18)*, near the Hıdırlık Kulesi, offers a safe haven for women

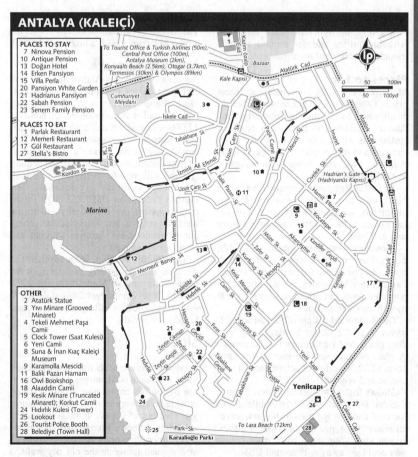

ANTALYA (KALEIÇI)

PLACES TO STAY
7 Ninova Pension
10 Antique Pension
13 Doğan Hotel
14 Erken Pansiyon
15 Villa Perla
20 Pansiyon White Garden
21 Hadrianus Pansiyon
22 Sabah Pension
23 Senem Family Pension

PLACES TO EAT
1 Parlak Restaurant
12 Memerli Restaurant
17 Gül Restaurant
27 Stella's Bistro

OTHER
2 Atatürk Statue
3 Yivi Minare (Grooved Minaret)
4 Tekeli Mehmet Paşa Camii
5 Clock Tower (Saat Kulesi)
6 Yeni Camii
8 Suna & İnan Kıraç Kaleiçi Museum
9 Karamolla Mescidi
11 Balık Pazarı Hamam
16 Owl Bookshop
18 Alaaddin Camii
19 Kesik Minare (Truncated Minaret); Korkut Camii
24 Hıdırlık Kulesi (Tower)
25 Lookout
26 Tourist Police Booth
28 Belediye (Town Hall)

travellers, with clean, simple rooms and an inviting roof terrace.

Sabah Pension (☎ 247 5345; Hesapçı Sokak 60/A; singles/doubles with shower US$10/16) is a popular backpacker place, offering tours, car hire and other useful services as well as decent evening meals. **Erken Pansiyon** (☎ 247 6092; Hıdırlık Sokak 5; doubles with shower US$10) is an old Ottoman house in need of modernisation. **Antique Pension** (☎ 242 4615, 241 5890; e antique@ixir.com; Paşa Camii Sokak 28; singles/doubles with shower US$10/17) is equally old, but has had the necessary makeover. However, it can suffer from noise in summer.

Hadrianüs Pansiyon (☎ 244 0030; Zeytin Sokak 4/A-B; singles/doubles with shower US$10/20) is a series of old, mostly unrestored buildings around a refreshingly large walled garden.

For a bit more money, Kaleiçi has many other beautiful places, including the **Doğan Hotel** (☎ 247 4654, fax 247 4006; w www.doganhotel.com; Memerli Banyo Sokak 5; singles/doubles with shower US$20/30), a beautifully rebuilt house with a sea-facing restaurant-terrace which is proving very popular with readers.

Ninova Pension (☎ 248 6114, 248 9684; Hamit Efendi Sokak 9; singles/doubles with shower US$25/40) has very comfortable rooms in a restored house, with a lovely secluded garden in which to eat breakfast.

Villa Perla (☎ 248 9793, fax 241 2917; e villaperla@hotmail.com; Hesapçı Sokak

26; singles/doubles with shower US$50/70)
is a lovely, idiosyncratic place furnished
with antiquities and set around a well-
thought-of courtyard restaurant.

Places to Eat
Many pensions serve good meals at decent
prices. Otherwise, Eski Sebzeciler İçi Sokak,
an alley near the junction of Cumhuriyet and
Atatürk Caddesis, is lined with **open-air
restaurants** where a kebab, salad and drink
can cost as little as US$4. The speciality is
Antalya's own *tandır kebap* (mutton cooked
in earthenware).

At **Parlak Restaurant** (meals US$5-10), a
block up Kazım Özalp/Sarampol Caddesi
on the left, skewered chicken and lamb kebabs sizzle in the courtyard as patrons down
rakı and beer.

Mermerli Restaurant (meals US$7-10),
perched above the eastern end of the harbour, can't be beaten for sunset views of the
bay and Bey Mountains. It's a bit heavy on
packeted food, but prices are lower than at
most harbour restaurants.

Gül Restaurant & Café (Kocatepe Sokak 1;
meals US$5-10; closed Sunday lunch) is a
cosy place run by a German-Turkish couple.
A plate of appetisers big enough for three
costs US$2.50, a dish of octopus baked with
cheese and vegetables US$3.50.

Stella's Bistro (☎ 248 6920; Fevzi Çakmak
Caddesi 3/C; meals US$10-15), while almost
too cool and trendy for its own good, serves
an interesting range of non-Turkish dishes.
If you stick with just a pasta main course
you could get away with around US$6.

Getting There & Away
Air There are daily **Turkish Airlines** flights
from Antalya to Ankara and İstanbul, and
weekly flights to Amman, Lefkoşa (Nicosia),
London, Tel Aviv and Zürich.

Bus From the otogar, buses head for Alanya
(US$3, 2½ hours), Göreme (US$12, about 10
hours), Konya (US$12, six hours), Olympos
(US$2, 1½ hours) and Manavgat/Side (US$2,
1¾ hours).

Beach buses leave from the Doğu Garaj
(Western Garage) on Ali Çetinkaya Cad-
desi – the Konyaaltı minibus goes west, the
Lara minibus east. You can get to the
nearby ruins from here too: take a *dolmuş* to
Aksu for Perge and to Manavgat for Side.

Getting Around
The airport is 10km east of the city centre; the
airport bus costs US$2, a taxi about US$10.

AROUND ANTALYA
Between Antalya and Alanya there are several spectacular Graeco-Roman ruins to explore. **Perge** (admission US$10), east of
Antalya and just north of Aksu, boasts a
12,000-seat stadium and a 15,000-seat theatre. **Aspendos** (admission US$10), 47km
east of Antalya, has Turkey's best-preserved
ancient theatre, dating from the 2nd century
AD and still used for performances during
the Antalya Festival every June/July. **Ter-
messos** (admission US$0.75), high in the
mountains off the Korkuteli road, to the
west of Antalya, has a spectacular setting
but demands some vigorous walking and
climbing to see it all.

The **Köprülü Kanyon**, 96km northeast of
Antalya, is a deservedly popular spot for
white-water rafting. **Medraft** (☎ 248 0083,
fax 242 7118; Cumhuriyet Caddesi 76/6, Işık
Apt, Antalya) offers rafting trips for around
US$55 per person.

SİDE
☎ 0242
No doubt because of its fine sandy beaches,
Side, 4km south of Manavgat, has been overrun by tourists and is now a tawdry, overcrowded caricature of its former self unless
you visit out of season. Impressive ancient
structures include a **Roman bath** (admission
US$3; open 8am-noon & 1pm-5pm daily),
now a small museum; the old **city walls**; a
huge **amphitheatre** (admission US$5); and
seaside **temples** to Apollo and Athena.

Places to Stay & Eat
The village itself is packed with pensions
and hotels, all of which fill up in summer.
Inland, **Pettino's Pension** (☎ 753 3608;
e pettino@superonline.com; beds with
shower US$8) offers rooms in a wooden
house; air-con costs US$5 extra. **Trio's**
(meals US$7), opposite, is a friendly restaur-
ant which pads out the standard kebab menu
with surprises like curried chicken.

The **Beach House Hotel** (☎ 753 1607;
singles/doubles with shower US$10.50/21)
offers pleasant rooms, some with sea views,
and a terrace and garden to relax in. The
owners also run the nearby **Soundwaves**

Restaurant *(meals around US$15)*, which offers such delicacies as garlic prawns and onion steak.

Side Hotel *(☎ 753 3824, fax 753 4671; Şarmaşık Sokak 25; singles/doubles with a shower US$15/20)* offers comfortable rooms right next to the western beach, perfect for a longer stay.

Getting There & Away Frequent minibuses connect Side with Manavgat otogar (US$0.30), where there are onward buses to Antalya (US$2, 1¾ hours) and Alanya (US$2, one hour).

ALANYA
☎ 242

Alanya is as close as Turkey gets to a no-go zone for independent travellers. It's not that there's a shortage of hotels – far from it, there are hundreds of them. However, most are firmly closed in winter and block-booked to package-holiday companies in summer. You may still want to stop by to take in the ruins of a magnificent Seljuk castle perched high on a hill above the town.

Orientation & Information
The otogar is 3km west of the centre; to get into town take a *dolmuş* or municipal bus (US$0.20) from the road leading to the sea outside the otogar and get off at the roundabout by the Küyülarönü Camii. Downhill from there lies the old waterfront area with trendy shops and good food; uphill above the harbour are the few remaining cheap hotels. The **tourist office** *(☎/fax 513 1240)* is on the western side of the promontory, where you can pick up a bus to the castle.

Things to See & Do
Alanya's crowning glory is the Seljuk **castle** *(admission US$10; open 8am-7pm daily)*, a fortress built in 1226 high above the modern town; take a bus up, then stroll back down to take advantage of the views. It's also worth visiting the **Kızıl Kule** *(Red Tower; admission US$2; open 8am-noon & 1.30pm-5.30pm Tues-Sun)*, down by the harbour and also built in 1226. Afterwards you can hire a **boat** *(US$5.50-8)* to tour caves beneath the hillside.

There are good beaches to east and west but they're solidly backed with high-rise hotels.

Places to Stay
Sadly, cheap accommodation has virtually disappeared as pensions give way to accommodation for package holidaymakers. Most of the places that do still handle passing trade do so pretty half-heartedly.

A couple of places linger on in noise-ridden İskele Caddesi, above the harbour. The first is **Baba Hotel** *(☎ 513 1032; İskele Caddesi 6; singles/doubles without shower US$6/12)*, with mundane rooms. **Hotel Temiz** *(☎ 513 1016, fax 519 1560; İskele Caddesi 12; singles/doubles with shower US$15/24)*, a little further towards the Red Tower, is more expensive but infinitely more comfortable and welcoming.

Hotel Kaptan *(☎ 513 4900, fax 513 2000; İskele Caddesi; singles/doubles with shower & sea view US$51/66)* has modern rooms and spotless bathrooms. There are slightly cheaper rooms at the rear.

Club Hotel Bedesten *(☎ 512 1234, fax 513 7934; doubles with shower US$54)* is probably the best choice, right up on the hill, with spectacular views from its terraces. Advance booking is advisable.

Places to Eat
These days, to get a cheap bite to eat you'll have to head well inland to the bazaar and beyond. Otherwise, the waterfront restaurants, especially long-lived **Mahperi** *(meals US$8-12)*, are worth frequenting for evening meals. Or you could try the **Ottoman House Restaurant** *(Kültür Caddesi; meals US$10-15)*, which serves meals in the gardens or in the atmospheric upstairs rooms of an old wooden house. A big plate of 12 mezzes as a main course costs US$5.

Getting There & Away
There are frequent buses to Alanya from Antalya (US$3, 2¾ hours) and Manavgat (US$2, one hour).

Fergün Denizcilik *(☎ 511 5565)* runs ferries to Girne (Northern Cyprus) at least twice a week for a return fare of US$57 including tax.

THE EASTERN COAST
East of Alanya the coast sheds some of its touristic freight. About 7km east of **Anamur** there is a wonderful castle, built by the emirs of Karaman in 1230, right on the beach, with pensions and camp sites nearby.

The ghostly ruins of Byzantine **Anemurium** are 8.5km west of the town.

Silifke has a Crusader castle and a ruined Roman temple, but is mostly a transport hub. At **Taşucu**, 11km southwest of Silifke, boats and hydrofoils depart daily for Girne (Kyrenia) in Northern Cyprus (see the Getting There & Away chapter for details). **Kızkalesi** (Maiden's Castle) is a growing holiday resort with a striking Crusader castle offshore.

Neither Mersin nor Adana have much to detain you, but **Tarsus**, tucked between them, was the birthplace of St Paul and the site where Antony first ran into Cleopatra.

HATAY

Southeast of Adana, Hatay turns the corner of the Mediterranean and starts to head for Syria. You'll pass several impressive castles on the way to **İskenderun**, where Alexander the Great defeated the Persians and Jonah is thought to have been coughed up by the whale. It's still an important port, although you're unlikely to want to linger.

ANTAKYA
☎ 0326

The biblical Antioch, Antakya (also confusingly called Hatay) was vilified as the Roman Empire's most depraved city. Undeterred, St Peter dropped by to preach here and you can visit the ancient **St Peter's Church** *(St Pierre Kilisesi; admission US$3.50; open 8.30-noon & 1.30pm-4.30pm Tues-Sun)*, 3km east of the centre. The magnificent Roman mosaics in the **Antakya Museum** *(admission US$3.50; open 8am-noon & 1.30pm-5pm Tues-Sun)* more than justify an overnight stop on the way to Syria.

Places to Stay

Antakya's hotels are all south of the otogar. **Jasmin Hotel** *(☎ 212 7171; İstiklal Caddesi 14; doubles US$6.50)* is about the best for basic rooms. **Divan Oteli** *(☎ 215 1518; İstiklal Caddesi 62; singles/doubles with shower US$10/20)* is a step up in quality.

Onur Hotel *(☎ 216 2210; İstiklal Sokak 10; singles/doubles with shower US$31/44)*, on the edge of the bazaar, is quiet at night and has comfortable, modern rooms.

Getting There & Away

Syrian visas are not normally issued at the border, but this depends partly upon your na-

tionality and partly upon current regulations (see the Visas section in the Syria chapter).

For information about buses from Antakya to Aleppo and Damascus, see Land in the Getting There & Away section earlier in this chapter.

If you are really determined to save money, you could take a local bus from Antakya to Reyhanli (US$2, 45 minutes) and then catch a *dolmuş* to the border. After crossing on foot (a long, sweaty couple of kilometres in summer) you can try to cadge a lift on the Syrian side. This can greatly lengthen an already tiresomely slow procedure and the cost savings are minimal.

Alternatively, you can catch a *dolmuş* south to Yayladağı (these go from behind the taxi rank across the road from the entrance to the otogar), and then pick up a taxi or hitch a few kilometres to the border. Once across (and crossing takes all of 15 minutes), you're just 2km from the mountain village of Kassab, from where regular microbuses make the 45-minute run to Lattakia (S£25).

Central Anatolia

Wanting a base that was more closely linked to the Anatolian heartland, Atatürk moved the capital from İstanbul to Ankara. Some of Turkey's most dramatic landscapes can be seen in Cappadocia, where wind and rain have eroded soft tuff into exotic rocks and cones which people have then carved into churches, houses and whole underground cities. Lovers of fine Selçuk architecture may also want to visit Konya, Kayseri and Sivas; those who prefer the Ottoman style should stop off in Safranbolu and Amasya.

ANKARA
☎ 0312

Capital of Turkey since 1923, Ankara's site was a Hittite settlement nearly 4000 years ago. The Museum of Anatolian Civilisations aside, it's not of great interest to most visitors, but because of its central location there's a good chance you'll at least pass through.

Orientation

Ankara's *hisar* (citadel) crowns a hill 1km east of Ulus Meydanı (Ulus Square), the heart of Old Ankara and near most of the cheap hotels. Nearby Opera Meydanı

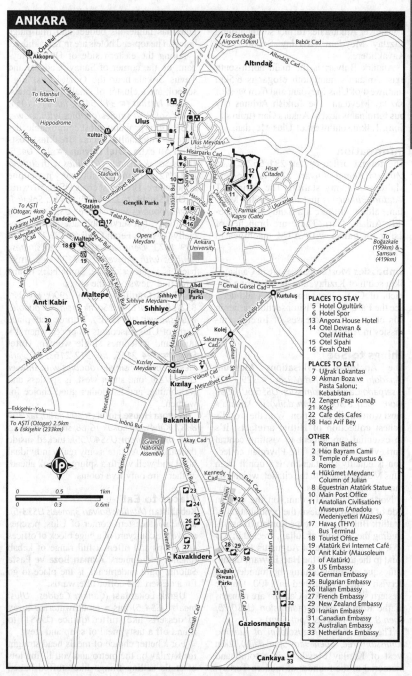

ANKARA

PLACES TO STAY
5 Hotel Ögültürk
6 Hotel Spor
13 Angora House Hotel
14 Otel Devran &
Otel Mithat
15 Otel Sipahi
16 Ferah Oteli

PLACES TO EAT
7 Uğrak Lokantası
9 Akman Boza ve
Pasta Salonu;
Kebabistan
12 Zenger Paşa Konağı
21 Köşk
22 Cafe des Cafes
28 Hacı Arif Bey

OTHER
1 Roman Baths
2 Hacı Bayram Camii
3 Temple of Augustus &
Rome
4 Hükümet Meydanı;
Column of Julian
8 Equestrian Atatürk Statue
10 Main Post Office
11 Anatolian Civilisations
Museum (Anadolu
Medeniyetleri Müzesi)
17 Havaş (THY)
Bus Terminal
18 Tourist Office
19 Atatürk Evi Internet Café
20 Anıt Kabir (Mausoleum
of Atatürk)
23 US Embassy
24 German Embassy
25 Bulgarian Embassy
26 Italian Embassy
27 French Embassy
29 New Zealand Embassy
30 Iranian Embassy
31 Canadian Embassy
32 Australian Embassy
33 Netherlands Embassy

(Opera Square) has lots more cheap hotels. The newer Ankara lies further south, around Kızılay Meydanı (Kızılay Square) and Kavaklıdere.

Atatürk Bulvarı is the main north-south axis. Ankara's mammoth **otogar** is 6.5km southwest of Ulus Meydanı and 6km west of Kızılay Meydanı. The **Turkish Airlines city bus terminal** is next to Ankara Garı (train station), 1.4km southwest of Ulus Meydanı.

Information

The **tourist office** (*☎/fax 231 5572; Gazi Mustafa Kemal Bulvarı 121*) is opposite Maltepe Ankaray station. The main **PTT** (*Atatürk Bulvarı*) is just south of Ulus Meydanı, although there's a handy branch beside Ankara Garı. There are branches of the main **banks** with ATM machines in Ulus.

Embassies Most embassies are in Çankaya, 5km south of Kızılay, and the adjoining districts of Gaziosmanpaşa and Kavaklıdere. See the Facts for the Visitor section earlier in this chapter for addresses of foreign embassies in Ankara.

Things to See

The **Anatolian Civilisations Museum** (*Anadolu Medeniyetleri Müzesi; ☎ 329 3160; Hisarparkı Caddesi; admission US$5.50, US$8 Mon; open 8.30am-5pm daily*) is Ankara's most worthwhile attraction. With the world's richest collection of Hittite artefacts, it's an essential supplement to visiting central Turkey's Hittite sites. The Phyrgian collection is equally spectacular. It's uphill from Ulus Meydanı, next to the citadel, which you can explore afterwards.

North of Ulus Meydanı, on the eastern side of Çankırı Caddesi (the continuation of Atatürk Bulvarı), are some **Roman ruins**, including the **Column of Julian**, erected in AD 363, and the **Temple of Augustus & Rome**. Next to the temple is the **Hacı Bayram Camii**, a mosque commemorating the founder of a dervish order established in 1400. On the western side of Çankırı Caddesi are remains of the **Roman baths** (*admission US$0.75; open 8.30am-noon & 1pm-5pm*).

The **Anıt Kabir** (*Mausoleum of Atatürk; admission free; open 9am-5pm daily*), 2km west of Kızılay Meydanı, is a tomb and memorial to the founder of modern Turkey.

Places to Stay

Ulus has numerous budget and mid-range hotels. The top-end hotels are in Kavaklıdere.

Along the eastern side of Opera Meydanı, on the corner of Sanayi Caddesi and Tavus Sokak near the Gazi Lisesi high school, are a cluster of small cheap hotels.

Otel Mithat (*☎ 311 5410, fax 310 1054; Tavus Sokak 2; singles/doubles with shower US$9/14*) is probably most comfortable, despite its minimalist decor. Breakfast costs US$1.50 extra. **Otel Devran** (*☎ 311 0485; Tavus Sokak 8; singles/doubles with shower US$8/12*) is friendly, with a very masculine atmosphere. Breakfast costs US$1.50 extra.

Otel Sipahi (*☎ 324 0235; Kosova Sokak 1; singles/doubles with shower US$6/8*) is old and dingy, but serviceable at a pinch, especially for men. **Ferah Oteli** (*☎ 309 1174, fax 309 1173; Denizciler Caddesi 58; singles/doubles with shower US$6/12*), one street back, is a quieter choice. Some back rooms have fine views over the city.

Hotel Oğultürk (*☎ 309 2900; fax 311 8321; Rüzgarlı Eşdost Sokak 6; singles/doubles with shower US$45/65*), a three-star place north of Ulus, discounts its prices when it's quiet and welcomes single women. **Hotel Spor** (*☎ 324 2165, fax 312 2153; Rüzgarlı Plevne Sokak 6; singles/doubles with shower US$18/25*), one street west, is spotless and welcoming, and is another good choice for women.

Angora House Hotel (*☎ 309 8380, fax 309 8381; Kalekapısı Sokak 16-68; singles/doubles with shower from US$40/55*), tucked inside the citadel, is Ankara's only really individual hotel and well worth a splurge. Book ahead, as there are only five rooms.

Places to Eat

Kebabistan (*Atatürk Bulvarı 3; meals US$3-5*), at the southeastern corner of Ulus, perches above the courtyard of a huge block of offices and shops and offers a full range of kebab lunches and dinners. **Akman Boza ve Pasta Salonu**, right underneath, is the place to go for a dessert and coffee afterwards.

Uğrak Lokantası (*Çankırı Caddesi, Ulus; meals US$4-5*) has a mouthwatering array of desserts like stuffed quince (US$1) to round off a tasty meal of soup and stew.

For a better choice of meals head straight for Kızılay on the metro and you'll find lots of stalls selling things like stuffed baked potatoes. **Kösk** *(Tuna Caddesi, İnkılap Sokak 2; meals US$4-5)* is a bright, cheerful, restaurant offering excellent *İskender kebap* (US$3) and *İnegöl köfte* (US$2.50).

Zenger Paşa Konağı *(☎ 311 7070; Doyran Sokak 13; meals US$6-12)*, an old house in the citadel with wonderful ethnographic displays, is a good place to try for a memorable dinner at very reasonable cost with live music as an accompaniment.

More Westernised (and pricier) restaurants lurk in Kavaklıdere. **Café des Cafés** *(Tunalı Hilmi Caddesi 83/A; meals US$8-10)* offers a range of pastas and crepes, as well as coffee and cake in surroundings reminiscent of a Viennese café.

Hacı Arif Bey *(Güniz Sokak 48; meals US$6-8)* is surprisingly reasonably priced for Kavalıdere, with a wide range of kebabs and pides all pictured on its table mats for easy ordering.

Getting There & Away
Air There are daily nonstop flights to most Turkish cities with **Turkish Airlines** *(☎ 419 2800; Atatürk Bulvarı 167/A, Bakanlıklar)*. International routes usually require a connection in İstanbul.

Bus Ankara's huge **otogar** (ASTİ) is the vehicular heart of the nation, with coaches going everywhere all day and night. For İstanbul (US$10 to US$18, six hours) they depart at least every 15 minutes.

Other sample fares are: Antalya (US$10, eight hours), Bodrum (US$12, 12 hours), Erzurum (US$10, 12 hours), İzmir (US$9, about nine hours) and Göreme (Cappadocia, US$7.50, five hours).

Train For details of trains to İstanbul and İzmir see Getting There & Away in those sections.

Trains heading east of Ankara are not as comfortable or punctual as those travelling westward. The *Doğu Express*, hauling carriages and sleeping cars, departs each evening for Erzurum (US$15, or US$32 for a bed, 25 hours) and Kars. On alternate mornings the *Güney Express* departs for Diyarbakır (US$10, 26½ hours), and the *Vangölü Express* departs for Tatvan. There are also daily trains to Adana (US$10).

For more information phone **Ankara Garı** *(☎ 311 0600)*.

Getting Around
To/From the Airport Ankara's **Esenboğa** airport *(☎ 398 0100)* is north of the city centre. Havaş buses (US$3, 40 minutes in light traffic) depart from outside Ankara Garı 1½ hours before domestic and two hours before international Turkish Airlines flights. A taxi costs about US$25. There are also Havaş buses from the otogar to the airport every half-hour (4am to 11.30pm).

Local Transport Many city buses run the length of Atatürk Bulvarı. Buy a *bilet* (ticket) for US$0.50 from kiosks by bus stops, or from a shop saying '*EGO Bilet(i)*'. Regular buses connect Ulus with Kızılay; a few continue direct to Kavaklıdere and Çankaya.

A taxi between the otogar and the train station costs about US$3; to Ulus or Kızılay it's about US$2.50.

The Ankaray underground train runs between ASTİ otogar in the west through Kızılay to Dikimevi in the east. Ankara's metro system runs from Kızılay northwest via Sıhhiye, Maltepe and Ulus to Batıkent, connecting with the Ankaray at Kızılay. A ticket costs US$0.50, a five-ride pass US$2 (it's valid on some buses too).

SAFRANBOLU
☎ 0372

Just off the road from İstanbul to Ankara, Safranbolu has a beautifully preserved old Ottoman quarter full of half-timbered houses. It's a place for pottering and shopping, rather than looking at specific sites.

The **tourist office** *(☎/fax 712 3863)* is next to the Köprülü Mehmet Paşa Camii mosque in the *arasta*, or bazaar.

Çarşı Pansiyon *(☎ 725 1079; singles/doubles with shower US$14/27)* offers rooms with Ottoman-style low beds, not far from the Cinci Hanı.

If you can afford to splash out on accommodation, Safranbolu is the place to do it. Why not book into the beautiful **Havuzlu Asmazlar Konağı** *(☎ 725 2883, fax 712 3824; singles/doubles with shower US$30/50)*, where you sleep in Ottoman-style rooms and eat your breakfast around a relaxing indoor pool? Or the more central **Tahsin Bey Konağı** *(☎ 712 2065; Hükümet Sokak 50; singles/doubles with shower from US$17/35)*, with lovely views from the upstairs rooms?

Note that all Safranbolu accommodation gets booked up at weekends, when prices soar accordingly.

Getting There & Away

You will need to take a bus to Karabuk and then change to a Safranbolu bus. Once at Safranbolu you will need a local bus to the 'Çarşı' part of town.

AMASYA

☎ 358

Dramatically set on riverbanks hemmed in by a cliff, Amasya features the rock-cut tombs of the Pontic kings dating back to before Christ, a lofty citadel, fine old wooden houses and imposing Seljuk buildings. The **tourist office** (☎ 218 7428; Mustafa Kemal Bulvarı 27) is on the riverbank in the centre.

Things to See

Look for the **Gök Medrese Camii** (1276), the **Burmalı Minare Camii** (Spiral Minaret; 1242), the Mongol-built **Bimarhane Medresesi** (1308), the octagonal **Büyük Ağa Medresesi** (1488) and the Ottoman **Sultan Beyazit II Camii** (1486). The **museum** houses some particularly gruesome mummies.

Places to Stay

The best place to stay is the small but exquisite **İlk Pansiyon** (☎ 218 1689, fax 218 6277; Hitit Sokak 1; singles/doubles with shower from US$13/17), with lovely Ottoman-style rooms. Also good is **Yuvam Pension** (☎ 218 1324; Atatürk Caddesi 24/5; singles/doubles with shower US$15/20). The quiet **Zümrüt Pansiyon** (☎ 218 2675; Hazeranlar Sokak 28; beds with shower US$10) has great tomb views from its roof terrace.

Getting There & Away

There are frequent buses to Tokat (US$3, two hours). To get to Safranbolu you will need to take a Karabuk bus, get out at the Safranbolu junction and flag down a bus into town.

SIVAS

☎ 0346

Once an important crossroads on the long-distance caravan route to Persia and Baghdad, Sivas has many marvellous Seljuk buildings to prove it. In 1919, Atatürk convened the second congress of the War of Independence here.

The **tourist office** (☎ 221 3535) is in the Vilayet building on the main square. The buildings to see are in the adjoining park: the **Çifte Minare Medrese** (Twin Minaret Seminary), the **Sifaiye** and **Bürüciye** seminaries, the **Ulu Cami** and the **Gök Medrese** (Blue Seminary).

Places to Stay & Eat

The better, cheap hotels are 700m southeast of Konak Meydanı, at the junction of Atatürk Caddesi and Kurşunlu Sokak.

Hotel Yavuz (☎ 225 0204; Atatürk Caddesi 86; singles/doubles with shower US$12/17) is the best of the newer places and has a handy restaurant downstairs.

Otel Çakır (☎ 222 4526; Kurşunlu Caddesi 20) and **Otel Fatih** (☎ 233 4313; Kurşunlu Caddesi 15) are similar places with averagely comfortable rooms. Both charge US$13/17 for singles/doubles with shower.

Otel Sultan (☎ 221 2986; Eski Belediye Sokak 18; singles/doubles with shower US$25/50) is beginning to show its age but still offers comfortable rooms with copious hot water. **Otel Köşk** (☎ 221 1150, Atatürk Caddesi 11; singles/doubles with shower US$25/33) is likely to be noisier so ask for a room at the back.

For cheap meals, duck down 1 Sokak, the road behind the PTT on Atatürk Caddesi.

Getting There & Away

There are hourly buses from Tokat to Sivas (US$4, 1½ hours) and fairly frequent buses to Erzurum (US$10, six hours).

KONYA

☎ 0332

South of Ankara, Konya was the capital of the Seljuk Turks and showcases some of the best Seljuk architecture. It was here that the 13th-century poet Mevlana Rumi inspired the founding of the whirling dervishes, one of Islam's most important mystical orders (see the boxed text 'When is a Whirling Dervish Not a Whirling Dervish?'). You can see the whirling dervishes perform in Konya during the **Mevlana Festival** every December.

Orientation & Information

The town centre stretches from Alaettin Tepesi, the hill topped by the Alaettin Mosque (1221), along Alaettin Caddesi and

Mevlana Caddesi to the tomb of Mevlana, now called the Mevlana Müzesi. The **otogar** is 10km northwest of the centre; free *servis* minibuses take half an hour to run you into town, or you can catch the tram from outside the otogar as far as Alaettin Tepesi (US$0.30).

The **tourist office** (☎ 351 1074; Mevlana Caddesi 21) is across the square from the Mevlana Müzesi.

Things to See
Mevlana's tomb (admission US$4; open 9am-5pm Tues-Sun, 10am-5pm Mon) is topped by a brilliant turquoise-tiled dome. It's a powerful place to visit, and popular with pilgrims; you should be especially careful about dressing modestly when you go inside.

It's also well worth visiting two outstanding Seljuk buildings near the Alaettin Tepesi: **Büyük Karatay Müzesi** (admission US$0.75; open 9am-noon & 1pm-5pm daily), once a Muslim theological seminary, now a ceramics museum; and **İnceminare Medresesi** (Seminary of the Slender Minaret; admission US$0.75; open 9am-noon & 1pm-5pm), now the Museum of Wood & Stone Carving.

Places to Stay & Eat
Hotel Ulusan (☎ 351 5004; Kurşuncular Sokak 2; singles/doubles with shared bathroom US$6/12), immediately behind the PTT, is first choice, with clean, simple rooms.

Mavi Köşk (☎ 350 1904; Bostan Çelebi Sokak 13; singles/doubles with a shower US$9/11) and **Derviş** (☎/fax 351 1688; Bostan Çelebi Sokak 11/D; singles/doubles US$10/15), side by side near the Mevlana Müzesi, are other good, cheap choices.

Kök & Esra Otel (☎ 352 0671, fax 352 0901; Yeni Aziziye Caddesi, Kadılar Sokak 28; singles/doubles with shower USS$10/15) is a step up in quality, with comfortable, if rather idiosyncratically decorated rooms.

Sifa Restaurant (Mevlana Caddesi 29; meals US$6) is a large place specialising in Konya's very own *tandir kebap*, a melt-in-your-mouth version of lamb. **Dilayla Restaurant** (Mevlana Caddesi, Altın Çarşışı Bitiği; meals US$4), nearby, is smaller but similar and stays open when other places close.

Mevlevi Sofrasi (☎ 353 3341, fax 353 4743; Şehit Nazim bey Caddesi 1/A; meals US$10) is a group-focused restaurant behind the Mevlana Müzesi where it's possible to watch dervishes dancing as you eat.

Getting There & Away
There are frequent buses from Konya to Nevşehir, some of which continue to Göreme (US$6, 3½ hours). There are also frequent buses between Konya and Pamukkale (US$10, seven hours).

Cappadocia (Kapadokya)

Cappadocia, the region between Ankara and Malatya, and between Aksaray and Kayseri, is famous for its fantastic natural **rock formations**. Over the centuries people have carved houses, churches, fortresses, even complete underground cities where early Christians sought refuge, into the soft, eerily eroded volcanic stone. Attractions include the Göreme and nearby Zelve Valleys; the rugged Ihlara Valley with a stream flowing through it; Soğanlı with its scores of stone-cut chapels; and the huge underground cities at **Kaymaklı** and **Derinkuyu** (admission US$7; open 8am-5pm daily).

When is a Whirling Dervish Not a Whirling Dervish?

Atatürk may have abolished the dervishes in 1925 but he'd reckoned without the power of the tourism industry. For many years visitors to Turkey were frustrated to discover that only those prepared to brave the Anatolian winter got to see the dervishes in action. Nowadays, however, you can hardly move for posters advertising performances. The question is, are any of these dervishes really what they seem?

As is so often the case, the answer depends on what you mean. The dervishes you see whirling in Meşale in İstanbul, those you see perform near Göreme, even those you see whirling in Konya's Mevlevi Sofrasi are all very talented professional dancers. What they are not is truly religious dervishes. To see dervishes who are whirling because of true religious conviction you need to visit one of the twice-monthly performances at the Galata Mevlevihanesi in İstanbul.

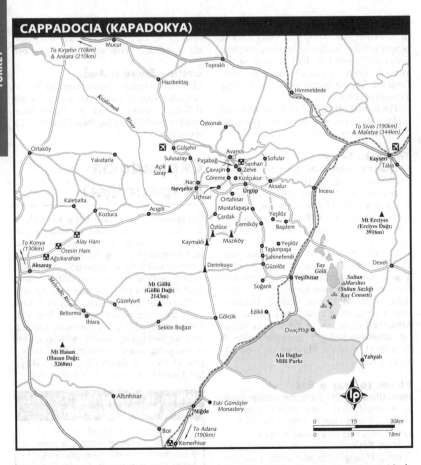

CAPPADOCIA (KAPADOKYA)

Loud, unattractive **Nevşehir** is a vital transport base for the region; catch buses here for Derinkuyu and Kaymaklı, or to **Niğde**, much further south but with another fine rock-cut monastery.

Ürgüp, Avanos and Uçhisar all have a good selection of hotels and pensions, but Göreme is most attractive to low-budget travellers.

In summer hourly buses link Nevşehir, Uçhisar and Avanos, stopping in Göreme.

ORGANISED TOURS

Good daily tours (around US$30) of local highlights, including Ihlara Gorge, are offered by **Ötuken Voyage** (☎ 271 2757), **Neşe Tour** (☎ 271 2525) and **Zemi Tour** (☎ 271 2576) in Göreme. **Kirkit Voyage** (☎ 511 3259; � www.kirkit.com), in Avanos, and **Argeus**

(☎ 341 4688; � www.argeus.com.tr), in Ürgüp, are experienced travel agents with varied programmes including horse-riding and cycling tours. **Middle Earth Travel** (☎ 271 2559), in Göreme, also offers a programme of walking tours and activities like abseiling.

GÖREME
☎ 0384

The Göreme landscape is one of Turkey's most amazing sights. Over the centuries a thick layer of volcanic tuff has been eroded into fantastic, eerie shapes, dubbed 'fairy chimneys' by the locals. Into the chimneys early Christians carved chambers, vaults and labyrinths for use as churches, stables and homes. Blow your budget and view all this drama from the air in a hot-air balloon with **Kapadokya Balloons** (☎ 271 2755; e fly@kapadokyaballoons.com; US$230).

Göreme Open Air Museum

Medieval frescoes can be seen in the rock-hewn monastery, nunnery and cave churches of **Göreme Open Air Museum** (admission US$10 plus Karanlık Kilisesi US$6; open 8am-5.30pm daily May-Oct, 8am-4.30pm Nov-Apr). Some date from the 8th century, though the best are from the 10th to 13th centuries. The churches are tiny, so try to visit at a time when the adjacent coach party is not looking too full. Don't miss the **Tokat church**, which is across the road from the main entrance and has some of the best frescoes.

Places to Stay

Camping You can camp at the **Dilek** or **Berlin** camp sites, side by side amid wonderful rock formations on the road leading to the open-air museum.

Pensions & Hotels Göreme has some of Turkey's best-value pensions, often offering the chance to try out the troglodyte lifestyle by sleeping in a cave. In most, a dorm bed costs US$3.50, a bed in a room without shower US$5, and a bed in a room with shower US$7.

Köse Pension (☎ 271 2294), near the PTT, is a very popular choice, with a gorgeous swimming pool, a book exchange and good home-cooked food for vegetarians and meat-eaters.

Kelebek (☎ 271 2531; w www.kelebek hotel.com), right up in the old village, boasts spectacular views, great food and a wide range of rooms, including a cave honeymoon suite complete with Jacuzzi (US$60).

Paradise (☎ 271 2248), tucked in amid fairy chimneys just off the Open Air Museum road, is also popular with backpackers.

Flintstones (☎ 271 2555), along the road leading to the Pigeon Valley, is quiet and secluded, with a pleasant swimming pool.

Shoestring Cave Pension (☎ 271 2450) has simple cave rooms set around a pleasant courtyard. Meals here get good reports.

Tuna Caves (☎ 271 2236) are off the road leading up into the old village and are used by the Fez Bus.

Other popular pensions include **L'Elysee** (☎ 271 2244), **Walnut House** (☎ 271 2564) and **Peri** (☎ 271 2136).

Cave Hotel Melek (☎ 271 2463; doubles without/with shower US$10/16) offers clean, simple rock-cut rooms in a quiet location. **Ottoman House** (☎ 271 2616; doubles with shower US$15) boasts of offering luxury at affordable prices in a modern building.

Places to Eat

Best of Göreme's restaurants is the **Orient** (meals from US$5), as you head up the hill towards Uçhisar; the steaks (US$4) are especially well regarded. Also popular is the **Local**, on the corner of the road leading up to the Göreme Open Air Museum and offering very tasty 'Ottoman' specials. Along the main road to Avanos, **Sedef** and **Sultan** offer a wide choice of mezzes, while **Tardelli** majors in pizzas and pides. **Mercan** and **SOS** tend to have the lowest prices.

Getting There & Away

Overnight buses connect Göreme with İstanbul (US$16, about 11 hours) and Antalya (US$14, 10 hours). Twice-hourly dolmuşes link Göreme with Nevşehir (US$0.50).

UÇHISAR

Between Göreme and Nevşehir is picturesque Uçhisar, built around a **rock citadel** (admission US$1; open 8am-sunset daily) offering panoramic views from its summit. There are many more places to stay here, although most only open from May to September.

ZELVE VALLEY

The Zelve Valley (admission US$7; open 8am-5.30pm daily), off the road from Göreme to Avanos, is less visited than the Göreme Valley, though it, too, has rock-cut churches, a rock-cut mosque and the chance to indulge in some serious scrambling. On the way back be sure to stop off to see some of the finest fairy chimneys at **Paşabağ**.

AVANOS
☎ 0384
On the northern bank of the Kızılırmak (Red River), Avanos is known for its pottery. Best of the pensions is **Kirkit Pansiyon** (☎ 511 3148; doubles without/with shower US$8/10); from the northern end of the bridge, walk east and bear left at the first alley.

Venessa Pansiyon (☎ 511 3840; Hafızağa Sokak 20; beds with shower US$10) is a beautifully restored old house, complete with its own private underground city.

Sofa Motel (☎ 511 5186; *singles/doubles with shower US$20/35)*, moving up the price and comfort scale, is near the northern end of the bridge. Its tastefully decorated rooms in several old houses are popular with groups, so you need to book ahead.

Getting There & Away
There are two buses an hour from Nevşehir to Avanos (US$0.45).

ÜRGÜP
☎ 0384
Despite being a bigger town, Ürgüp has plenty of appeal, with sandstone buildings, cobbled streets and a stone hill shot through with rooms and passages. For wine buffs, it also boasts Cappadocia's best wineries. The helpful **tourist office** (☎/fax 341 4059; *Kayseri Caddesi)* is downhill in the park.

Places to Stay & Eat
Hotel Elvan (☎ 341 4191; *Dutlu Cami Mahallesi, Barbaros Hayrettin Sokak 11; doubles with shower US$15-25)* has homely rooms arranged around a small courtyard.

Asia Minor Hotel (☎ 341 4645, fax 341 2721; *İstiklal Caddesi; doubles with shower US$40)* has stylishly decorated rooms and a pleasant garden. **Hitit Hotel** (☎ 341 4481, fax 341 3620; *İstiklal Caddesi)* is marginally cheaper, with an equally inviting garden but more-mundane rooms.

Esbelli Evi (☎ 341 3395, fax 341 8848; *singles/doubles with shower US$70/85)*, behind Club Ürgüp on the one-way system out of town, was created out of a group of lovely rock-cut rooms in a warren of inviting courtyards. Advance reservation is advisable.

Where Esbelli led, others have since followed and Ürgüp now boasts some of the finest boutique hotels around, mostly clustered together in the Esbelli Mahallesi. **Ügüp Evi** (☎ 341 3173), **Elkepi Evi** (☎ 341 6000), **Kayadam Pansiyon** (☎ 341 6673) and **Yunak Everli** (☎ 341 6920) are all guaranteed to offer a memorable stay for prices not dissimilar to Esbelli's.

Sömine Restaurant (*meals US$8-14)* is the town's most prominent eatery, right on the main square, with indoor and outdoor tables. Ürgüp-style kebabs baked on tiles are a speciality. The **Ocakbaşı** (*meals US$15)* beside

the otogar offers better food – especially grills and mezzes – if in a less immediately inviting setting. Otherwise, there's the usual range of cheap kebaberies around the otogar.

Getting There & Away
Buses run hourly to Ürgüp from Nevşshir and every two hours from Göreme (US$0.75).

IHLARA GORGE & GÜZELYURT
☎ 0382
A once-remote, beautiful canyon full of rock-cut churches dating back to Byzantine times, Ihlara Gorge (*admission US$3.50)* is now a mainstay of the day-trip excursions run out of Cappadocia. With time on your hands, you're better off staying and walking the entire 16km length of the gorge, which has a pretty stream running through it.

Places to Stay & Eat
Ihlara village is 40km southeast of Aksaray. **Anatolia Pansiyon** (☎ 453 7440; *camping US$3 per person, doubles with a shower US$16)* offers comfortable rooms on the road running along the top of the gorge between the village and the official entrance. **Akar Pansiyon** (☎ 453 7018; *doubles with shower US$16)*, on the road towards Aksaray, has a handy shop close by. There are more inviting camp sites and simple restaurants in the gorge itself, near the village of Belisırma.

About 9km from Ihlara, on the road east to Derinkuyu, is Güzelyurt, a quiet farming village of stone houses, the perfect antidote to the Göreme hustle. At beautiful **Otel Karballa** (☎ 451 2103; *fax 451 2107; B&B US$17, half board US$24)* you eat your meals in what was once a monastic refectory but with the very unmonastic luxury of a swimming pool awaiting you afterwards.

Getting There & Away
Several daily buses connect Ihlara and Güzelyurt with Aksaray otogar (US$0.75).

KAYSERİ
☎ 0352
In the shadow of Mt Erciyes, Kayseri, a conservative but rapidly modernising town, was once the capital of Cappadocia and is full of mosques, tombs and old seminaries tucked away behind the ugly high-rises.

Near the **tourist office** (☎ 222 3903, fax 222 0879) is the **Hunat Hatun mosque, tomb** and **seminary**. Opposite, behind the massive 6th-century city walls, is the **Ulu Cami** (Great Mosque), begun by the Seljuks in 1136. Inside the walls is the ancient **Vezirhanı**, once a caravanserai, now a sheepskin market. Further out are the **Gıyasiye ve Sifaiye Medreseleri** (Twin Seminaries) in Mimar Sinan Park, a Seljuk hospital now a medical museum *(admission US$0.75)*. Don't miss the **Güpgüpoğlu Konağı** *(admission US$0.75; open 8am-5pm Tues-Sun)*, a beautifully decorated, 18th-century mansion.

Places to Stay & Eat

Hunat Oteli *(☎ 232 4319; Zengin Sokak 5; beds without shower US$7)*, behind the Hunat Hatun mosque, is cheap but none the less friendly. **Hotel Sur** *(☎ 222 4367; Talas Caddesi 12; singles/doubles with shower US$20/ 30)*, tucked in behind the walls, offers more comfortable rooms.

Hotel Turan *(☎ 222 5537, fax 231 1153; Turan Caddesi 8; singles/doubles with shower US$18/28)* is a professionally run place right in the heart of the shopping centre with some sizable rooms.

Beyaz Saray *(Millet Caddesi 8)* boasts a mouthwatering *İskender kebap* (US$3), as does the older **İskender Kebap Salonu** across the road. Afterwards the **Divan Pastanesi**, immediately opposite, is just the place to round off your meal over coffee and baklava.

Getting There & Away

A *dolmuş* to Kayseri from Ürgüp costs US$2; a bus from Göreme US$3. Buses from Kayseri to Dereğli pass over Mt Erciyes.

Black Sea Coast

Turkey's Black Sea coast is steep and craggy, damp and lush, and isolated behind the Pontic Mountains along most of its length. The hazelnuts grown here make Turkey the world's biggest exporter of these nuts. The tea you drink in İstanbul probably comes from east of Trabzon; the cigarette smoke you endure probably comes from tobacco grown west of Samsun.

Partly because of heavy industry around Zonguldak, the coast west from Sinop to the Bosphorus is little visited, although the fishing port of **Amasra**, with its Roman and Byzantine ruins and small, cheap hotels, is worth a look. **Sinop**, three hours northwest of Samsun, is a fishing and boat-building town; it's a fine little backwater, with beaches on both sides of the peninsula, as well as a few historic buildings and several cheap hotels.

While there's little of interest to detain tourists, **Samsun** makes a good starting point for coastal travel as it's the first port of call for the ferry from İstanbul. Atatürk landed here on 19 May 1919 to begin the Turkish War of Independence.

There are excellent beaches around the cheerful resort town of **Ünye**, on a wide bay 85km east of Samsun. Beaches are the only reason to stop in the glum town of **Ordu**, 80km further to the east.

Europe's first cherry trees came from **Giresun** courtesy of Lucullus, the Roman general and famous epicure, and the town is still surrounded by cherry orchards.

TRABZON
☎ 0462

Trabzon is by far the most interesting place along the Black Sea coast, with lots of old Byzantine buildings and the amazing Sumela Monastery right on its doorstep. Trabzon held out against the Seljuks and Mongols and was the last town to fall to the Ottoman Turks. Today, it still feels very different from other Turkish towns, not least because its trading focus is on Russia and the Caucasus.

Orientation & Information

Modern Trabzon is centred on Atatürk Square. The **tourist office** *(☎/fax 321 4659)* is off the southern side of the square, near Hotel Nur. The **Georgian Consulate** *(☎ 326 2226, fax 326 2296; Gazipaşa Caddesi 20)* is off the northern side of the square. Minibuses plying the coastal highway wait at the foot of a hill; to reach Atatürk Square, just take the steepest climb up. About 3km to the east is the **otogar** for long-distance buses.

Things to See

A 20-minute walk west of Atatürk Square are the dark walls of the Byzantine city. The **old town**, with its timber houses and stone bridges, still looks medieval.

The main attraction in Trabzon is the 13th-century **Aya Sofya** *(admission US$0.75; open 8am-5pm Tues-Sun)*, west of town and reachable by *dolmuş* from Atatürk Square. The **Atatürk Köşkü** *(Atatürk Villa; admission*

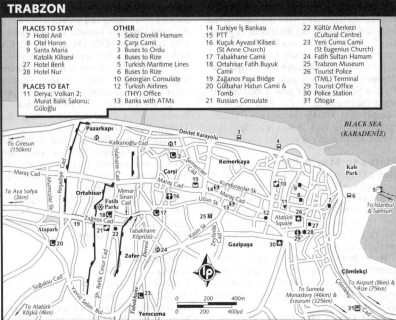

TRABZON

PLACES TO STAY	OTHER	14 Turkiye İş Bankası	22 Kültür Merkezi
7 Hotel Anıl	1 Sekiz Direkli Hamam	15 PTT	(Cultural Centre)
8 Otel Horon	2 Çarşı Camii	16 Kuçuk Ayvasıl Kilisesi	23 Yeni Cuma Camii
9 Santa Maria	3 Buses to Ordu	(St Anne Church)	(St Eugenius Church)
Katolik Kilisesi	4 Buses to Rize	17 Tabakhane Camii	24 Fatih Sultan Hamam
27 Hotel Benli	5 Turkish Maritime Lines	18 Ortahisar Fatih Buyuk	25 Trabzon Museum
28 Hotel Nur	6 Buses to Rize	Camii	26 Tourist Police
	10 Georgian Consulate	19 Zağanos Paşa Bridge	(TML) Terminal
PLACES TO EAT	12 Turkish Airlines	20 Gülbahar Hatun Camii &	29 Tourist Office
11 Derya; Volkan 2;	(THY) Office	Tomb	30 Police Station
Murat Balık Salonu;	13 Banks with ATMs	21 Russian Consulate	31 Otogar
Güloğlu			

US$0.75; open 9am-5pm daily) is a beautiful, 19th-century house set high above the town.

Sumela Monastery

Many travellers come to Trabzon just to visit Sumela Monastery *(admission US$3; open 9am-6pm, shorter hours in winter)*, built into a cliff face like a swallow's nest and dating back to Byzantine times. Inhabited until 1923 and newly restored, it boasts fine murals (damaged by vandals) and amazing views. Ulusoy buses (US$6, 45 minutes) depart for Sumela from a small terminal on Taksim Caddesi, across the street and uphill a few steps from Atatürk Square. You can also visit on a tour from Trabzon (US$6) or by taking a shared taxi (around US$30).

Places to Stay

Sadly, traders and prostitutes from the former Soviet states often fill the cheapest hotels, so you may have trouble finding somewhere affordable and tolerable. The cheapest rooms are east of Atatürk Square on Güzelhisar Caddesi and surrounding streets.

Hotel Anıl *(☎ 326 7282; Güzelhisar Caddesi 10; singles/doubles US$12/18)* has a flashy lobby and fairly clean rooms.

Hotel Benli *(☎ 321 1022; Cami Çıkmazı 5; singles/doubles with sink US$5/10, with shower US$7/12)* is uphill behind the Belediye. Small, old and drab, it has clean enough rooms. Facing it is the newly renovated **Hotel Nur** *(☎ 323 0445; Cami Sokak 4; singles/doubles with shower US$12/20)*, a good bet for single women.

Sankta Maria Katolik Kilisesi *(☎ 321 2192; Sümer Sokak 26)*, a few blocks downhill from Atatürk Square, has a hostel with spotless rooms and hot showers. Don't forget to leave a (realistic) donation.

Otel Horon *(☎ 322 6455, fax 321 6628, Sıra Mağazalar Caddesi 125; singles/doubles with shower US$30/40)*, off Güzelhisar Caddesi, is central, comfortable and modern.

Places to Eat

Lots of cheap food is available right around Atatürk Square. Try **Derya** and **Volkan 2** near the cheap hotels for *sulu yemek* (fast food). **Murat Balık Salonu**, on the northern side of the square, fries up mackerel (US$3) and *hemsi*, a Black Sea delicacy when in season. **Güloğlu** serves a wide range of meals (and baklava to follow) in cheerful surroundings.

Getting There & Away
Air With its office at the southwestern corner of Atatürk Square, **Turkish Airlines** (☎ *321 1680*) offers daily flights to Ankara and İstanbul.

Bus Westbound *dolmuşes* run to Ordu from the minibus yard on the highway below the bazaar. *Dolmuşes* to Rize, and minibuses to Maçka and Sumela, go from the yard east of Atatürk Square near the ferry terminal. From the otogar, minibuses leave for Rize, Hopa and Artvin every 30 minutes. A dozen buses a day head for Erzurum (US$8, five hours, 325km), a beautiful ride via Gümüşhane.

Boat See the Getting Around section earlier in this chapter for details on car ferries to İstanbul and the Getting There & Away chapter at the beginning of this book for details on the Karden Lines service to Sochi (Russia).

Getting Around
You'll need to take a *dolmuş* from Hotel Toros, just north of Atatürk Square, to get to the airport. *Dolmuşes* connect the otogar with Atatürk Square (US$0.30).

Eastern Turkey

The east is probably the most exciting (and toughest) part of Turkey to travel in, and certainly the part that feels least affected by mass tourism. If you're heading overland for Iran or Syria you will certainly need to transit parts of it, bearing in mind that the weather can be bitterly cold and snowy in winter – only well-equipped masochists travel this region between January and April.

Turkey's southeastern corner was once Upper Mesopotamia, a historic area drained by the Tigris (Dicle) and Euphrates (Fırat) Rivers. They are also some of the most exotic-feeling places you'll visit in Turkey, with the influence of neighbouring Syria and Iraq plain to see.

Since the capture of the PKK (Kurdistan Workers Party) leader Abdullah Öcalan in 1999, the security situation in southeastern Turkey has improved considerably. Although

it's always wise to check with your embassy for the latest information, at the time of writing there was little reason to think travellers would suffer anything worse than delays at checkpoints along the way.

ERZURUM
☎ 0442
The big town of Erzurum is famous for its harsh climate, but it has some striking Seljuk buildings that justify a stay of a day or so. It also has an Iranian consulate that likes to say 'yes' to visa requests from all but American and British travellers.

Orientation & Information
Both the **tourist office** (☎ *218 5697, fax 218 5443; Cemal Gürsel Caddesi*) and the **otogar** are inconveniently located, the tourist office far out on the main street, west of Havuzbaşı, the otogar 3km from the centre on the airport road. Luckily the centre itself is compact, with all the main sites within walking distance of each other.

The **Iranian Consulate** (☎ *218 3876, fax 316 1182; just off Atatürk Bulvarı; open 8am-1pm & 2pm-4pm Sat-Thur*) can often arrange visas in one day provided you apply from Monday to Thursday.

Things to See
The well-preserved walls of the 5th-century **citadel** loom over a maze of narrow streets, offering good views of the town's layout and the bleak surrounding plains.

The beautifully symmetrical **Çifte Minareli Medrese** (1253) is a famous example of Seljuk architecture. Its classic carved portal is flanked by twin minarets.

The oldest mosque is the **Ulu Cami** (Great Mosque; built in 1179), next to the Çifte Minareli Medrese. Further west along Cumhuriyet Caddesi is a square with an Ottoman mosque and, at the western corner, another seminary, the **Yakutiye Medresesi**, built by the local Mongol emir in 1310 and now a museum (*admission US$0.75; open 8.30am-5pm Tues-Sun*).

Places to Stay
The area around Kazım Karabekir Caddesi nurtures lots of cheapies, although some are pretty dismal.

Hitit Otel (☎ *218 1204; Kazım Karabekir Caddesi 27; singles/doubles with shower*

TURKEY

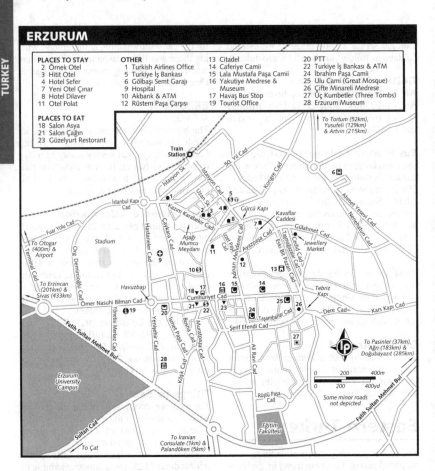

ERZURUM

PLACES TO STAY
2 Örnek Otel
3 Hitit Otel
4 Hotel Sefer
7 Yeni Otel Çınar
8 Hotel Dilaver
11 Otel Polat

PLACES TO EAT
18 Salon Asya
21 Salon Çağın
23 Güzelyurt Restorant

OTHER
1 Turkish Airlines Office
5 Türkiye İş Bankası
6 Gölbaşı Semt Garajı
9 Hospital
10 Akbank & ATM
12 Rüstem Paşa Çarşısı

13 Citadel
14 Caferiye Camii
15 Lala Mustafa Paşa Camii
16 Yakutiye Medrese &
    Museum
17 Havas Bus Stop
19 Tourist Office

20 PTT
22 Turkiye İş Bankası & ATM
24 İbrahim Paşa Camii
25 Ulu Cami (Great Mosque)
26 Çifte Minareli Medrese
27 Üç Kumbetler (Three Tombs)
28 Erzurum Museum

US$9/12) and the similarly priced **Örnek Otel** (☎ 218 1203; *Kazım Karabekir Caddesi 8*) look pretty bashed about, but would do for an overnight stay.

Yeni Otel Çınar (☎ 212 1050; *Ayazpaşa Caddesi 18; doubles with shower US$10*) is friendly and popular, with cleaner, more comfortable rooms. To find it, look for the Gürpınar Cinema in the bazaar. The street opposite leads to the Çınar.

Otel Polat (☎ 218 1623; *Kazım Karabekir Caddesi 4; singles/doubles with showers US$13/21*) is a step up in quality, with decent bathrooms and double-glazed windows. **Hotel Sefer** (☎ 218 6714; *İstasyon Caddesi; singles/doubles with shower US$15/25*), nearby, is hardly fancy but offers reasonably modern rooms and a decent restaurant.

Hotel Dilaver (☎ 235 0068; *Aşağı Mumcu Caddesi Petit Meydani; singles/doubles with shower US$70/100*) has all the three-star luxuries: minibar, TV, air-con etc.

Places to Eat
There are several reasonable choices along Cumhuriyet Caddesi near the Yakutiye Medresesi. **Güzelyurt Restorant** is cheap, good and long-lived: try the *mantarlı güveç* (lamb-and-mushroom casserole), with drinks, for less than US$10. **Salon Çağın** and **Salon Asya**, a block away, are reliable student hangouts where a kebab meal rarely tops US$4.

Getting There & Away
Air There are daily flights offered by **Turkish Airlines** (☎ 234 1516; *Kazım Karabekir*

Caddesi) to Ankara (US$85), with connections to İstanbul and İzmir.

Bus Erzurum has frequent buses to most big towns in eastern Turkey, including Doğubayazıt (US$6, four hours) and Sivas (US$10, six hours).

Train Erzurum station is at the northern end of İstasyon Caddesi, within walking distance of most hotels. The *Yeni Doğu Ekspresi* offers good rail connections with İstanbul and Ankara via Kayseri and Sivas.

Getting Around
Havaş buses to the airport leave from Cumhuriyet Caddesi (US$1.75). A taxi to the airport costs about US$6.

Bus No 2 will run you into town from the otogar (US$0.30); a taxi costs US$2.50. Buses for town depart from outside the train station every 30 minutes.

KARS
☎ 0474
About 260km northeast of Erzurum, Kars is not the most inviting town at first sight, although if you roam the back streets you soon discover its massive fortress, innumerable *hamams* and fine old Russian houses.

Ani
Most people come to Kars to visit the romantic ruins of Ani, 45km east of town. Ani was completely deserted in 1239 after a Mongol invasion, but before that it was an important city and a capital of both the Urartian and Armenian kingdoms. Fronted by a hefty wall, the ghost city now lies in fields overlooking the Arpaçay River, which forms the border with Armenia. The ruins are extremely dramatic and include several notable churches and a cathedral built between the years 989 and 1010.

In a piece of nonsense left over from Cold War days, to get permission to visit Ani you must first visit the **tourist office** *(☎ 223 2300, fax 223 8452; 1st floor, Milli Eğitim Müd. Hizmet Binası, Atatürk Caddesi)*, then visit **Emniyet Müdürlüğü** *(Faik Bey Caddesi)* to get your permit stamped, then buy a ticket at the **Kars Museum** *(Cumhuriyet Caddesi; admission US$0.75; open 8.30am-5.30pm daily)*. Only then can you set off for Ani itself *(admission US$3.50; open 8.30am-5pm)*.

Places to Stay & Eat
Otel Kervansaray *(☎ 223 1990; Faik Bey Caddesi 124)* and the neighbouring **Hotel Nur Saray** *(☎ 223 1364)* are as basic as they come, fit only for fleeting visits. Both offer singles/doubles with shower for US$5/11.

Güngören Oteli *(☎ 212 5630; Halit Paşa Caddesi, Millet Sokak 4; singles/doubles with shower US$15/25)*, with its own *hamam* and *ocakbaşı* restaurant, offers the best value for money in Kars.

Hotel Karabağ *(☎ 212 3480; Faik Bey Caddesi 84; singles/doubles with shower US$40/60)* offers comfortable three-star rooms with minibars, TVs and (supposedly) air-con.

Several shops near the Temel and Güngören hotels sell Kars honey and tasty local cheeses – perfect picnic ingredients. **Şirin Anadolu Mutfağı** *(Karadağ Caddesi 55; meals US$5)* has a bright, cheerful dining room with an upstairs café, deservedly popular with local students of both sexes. **Café Kristal** *(Atatürk Caddesi; meals US$3)* serves a wide range of ready meals, including *piti*, a local meat-and-chickpea stew (US$1.75).

Getting There & Away
Kars is not especially well served by transport, although there are a few daily minibuses to Erzurum (US$5, 3½ hours) and a few buses to Doğubayazıt (US$4, three hours).

Taxi drivers charge US$40 to ferry people around Kars getting their permit and ticket and then taking them to Ani, with around 2½ hours waiting time thrown in – fair enough if there's a group of you, but a lot if you're alone. The tourist office may be able to help assemble a group, but don't bank on it.

DOĞUBAYAZIT
☎ 0472
This drab little town is Turkey's last outpost on the road to Iran. It's dramatically sited at the far side of a sweeping grass plain that runs to the foot of Mt Ararat. Everything is within a five-minute stroll of the centre.

Things to See
Snow-capped **Mt Ararat**, a dormant volcano alongside the main road between Erzurum and the Iranian border, makes an impressive sight from the surrounding plain. When the 40 days and 40 nights finally ended, Noah and his flock are said to have landed on Mt

Ararat – a nice story but one that innumerable mountaineers have failed to confirm.

Now that the troubles in the east have died down it is once again possible to climb the mountain and check for yourself, although you need to pick your dates carefully and come equipped with suitable gear. For more information, inquire at local travel agencies.

Otherwise, most people come here to visit İshak Paşa Palace (İshak Paşa Sarayı; admission US$4; open 8am-5.30pm daily), perched romantically among rocky crags 5km east of town. Built between 1685 and 1784, this palace-fortress brings together elements of Seljuk, Ottoman, Georgian, Persian and Armenian architecture. Newly restored, it's worth visiting just for the views.

Places to Stay

Camping If you want to pitch a tent, **Murat Camping** (tent sites US$1), on the road to the İshak Paşa Palace, is very popular.

Pensions & Hotels One of the best of Erzurum's many cheap and spartan hotels is **Hotel Erzurum** (☎ 312 5080; Belediye Caddesi; doubles without shower US$7).

Ararat Hotel (☎ 312 8889; singles/doubles with shower US$12/20), near the otogar, gets good reviews from readers and boasts fine views of Ararat from some rooms. **Hotel İsfahan** (☎ 215 5289; İsa Geçit Caddesi 26; singles/doubles with shower US$20/30) could do with a makeover but the rooms are comfortable enough and the car park is handy.

Getting There & Away

Bus services to Doğubayazıt are fairly limited and usually go via Erzurum (US$4, four hours) or Iğdır (US$1.50, 45 minutes).

Minibuses to the Gürbülak border for Iran cost US$1; if your visa is in order the crossing should take about 20 minutes. A shared taxi on to Maku will cost around US$0.35.

Getting Around

If you don't want to walk, the occasional dolmuş trundles up to İshak Paşa Palace. A taxi will cost about US$4.

MT NEMRUT

Mt Nemrut (Nemrut Dağı) is one of the great must-see attractions of eastern Turkey. Two thousand years ago, right on top of the mountain and pretty much in the middle of nowhere, an obscure Commagene king chose to erect his **memorial sanctuary**. The fallen heads of the gigantic decorative statues of gods and kings, toppled by earthquakes, form one of Turkey's most enduring images.

There are several possible bases for visiting Mt Nemrut. To the north is rapidly modernising Malatya, where the **tourist office** (☎ 323 3025, fax 324 2514) organises daily minibus tours (US$30, April to mid-October) that take in a sunset visit to the heads, a night at a hotel near the summit and a second dawn visit. Alternatively, you can visit the mountain from the south via the oil-prospecting town of Kahta. Kahta is notoriously hassley, but by taking this route you do at least get to see other sites along the way.

Because of the transport difficulties many people prefer to take a three-day tour from Göreme in Cappadocia. For US$150 per person these take in other places in the east too, making them particularly good value. Or you can arrange a tour from Şanliurfa.

Places to Stay

Malatya As basic as they come is **Otel Tahran** (☎ 0422-324 3615; PTT Caddesi; singles/doubles US$5/9). **Otel Kantar** (☎ 0422-321 1510; Atatürk Caddesi 21; singles/doubles with shower US$7/12) would make a better choice, with clean if simple rooms. **Malatya Büyük Otel** (☎ 0422-321 1400; singles/doubles with shower US$17/21) is definitely the best choice in the town centre and handy for shopping in the bazaar.

Kahta In high summer the nicest places to stay, especially with your own transport, are not in Kahta itself but on the slopes of the mountain. **Karadut Pension** (☎ 0416-737 2169; beds US$7) is very basic, but makes up for its primitive facilities with views to die for. **Hotel Euphrat** (☎ 0416-737 2190; singles/doubles with shower US$30/44) shares the views, but piles on the home comforts too.

In Kahta itself, **Anatolia Pension** (☎ 0416-725 6483; singles/doubles US$5/9) will be too basic for most people. **Pension Kommagene** (☎ 0416-725 5548; singles/doubles with shower US$12/18), at the start of the Nemrut road, is a better choice. **Hotel Mezopotamya** (☎ 0416-725 5112; singles/doubles with shower & air-con US$9/18) also gets good reports from readers.

ŞANLIURFA (URFA)
☎ 0414

The former Edessa is a delightful city that claims to harbour the **cave** where the patriarch Abraham (İbrahim) was born. Pilgrims come to pay their respects, then feed fat sacred carp in a pool nearby. After doing likewise, you can visit the wonderful **bazaar**, some graceful **mosques**, a good **museum** and the **citadel**. Harran, 50km to the south, is one of the oldest continuously occupied settlements, with distinctive beehive houses.

Places to Stay

Urfa has accommodation to suit all tastes and budgets but there's a backpacker enclave in Köprübaşı Caddesi behind the Özel Sanmed Hastanesi. Try the popular **Hotel İpek Palas** (☎ 215 1546; singles/doubles with shower US$12/20), or, a few doors along, the very basic **Otel Günbay** (☎ 313 9797; singles/doubles US$5/9).

Şanlıurfa Valiliği Konuk Evi (☎ 215 9377; Vali Fuat Caddesi; singles/doubles with shower US$32/50) is a delightful 19th-century stone building and Şanlıurfa's most atmospheric place to stay, but, with only six rooms, it gets booked up fast.

Hotel Harran (☎ 313 2860; Atatürk Bulvarı; singles/doubles with shower US$60/90), directly opposite the Belediye, is another long-time favourite despite its hefty prices. The swimming pool makes it a winner in summer.

Getting There & Away

Fairly frequent buses connect Şanlıurfa with Gaziantep (US$4, 2½ hours) and Diyarbakır (US$6, three hours).

DIYARBAKIR
☎ 0412

Diyarbakır's great basalt walls ring a city of medieval mosques and churches, narrow streets and Kurdish separatist feelings. After many troubled years, the city is beginning to feel more relaxed. Long may it last.

Places to Stay

Take a *dolmuş* from the otogar to Dağ Kapısı (3.5km) to find cheap and cheerful hotels such as **Hotel Kenan** (☎ 221 6614; Süleyman Caddesi 20; singles/doubles US$7/12). **Hotel Güler** (☎/fax 224 0294; Kıbrıs Caddesi, Yoğurtçu Sokak 7; singles/doubles with shower

US$14/28) is a considerable step up in quality, offering a quiet location, clean, comfortable rooms and lots of hot water.

Getting There & Away

Several buses a day link Diyarbakır with Şanlıurfa (US$6, three hours) and Van (US$7.50, seven hours).

VAN
☎ 0432

On the southeastern shore of vast Lake Van, Van boasts a 3000-year-old **citadel** (Rock of Van; admission US$0.75) and an interesting **museum** (admission US$0.75; open 9am-6pm daily). The 10th-century church on **Akdamar Island** in the lake is a fascinating piece of Armenian architecture in a beautiful setting, with frescoes and reliefs depicting biblical scenes. To get there you need to take a *dolmuş* from Beş Yol in Van to the harbour or at least to Gevaş (US$1), then pick up a ferry from the harbour; an inclusive ticket for the crossing and admission should cost no more than US$4.50.

Places to Stay

Van has accommodation to suit all budgets. Places in the bazaar to the west of Cumhuriyet Caddesi tend to be cheapest, those to the east slightly more expensive but also cleaner and more comfortable.

Several hotels in the bazaar charge US$4.50 per person in rooms with sink and/or private shower. **Aslan Oteli** (☎ 216 2469; beds US$5) is one of the better choices.

Büyük Asur Oteli (☎ 216 8792; Cumhuriyet Caddesi, Turizm Sokak 5; singles/doubles with shower US$18/25) is an excellent choice with a helpful manager who speaks English. **Hotel Bayram** (☎ 216 1136; Cumhuriyet Caddesi 1/A; singles/doubles with shower US$15/20) is another good choice, with clean, modern rooms.

Büyük Urartu Oteli (☎ 212 0660; Cumhuriyet Caddesi 60; singles/doubles US$70/100) is Van's best, but is vastly overpriced despite such mod cons as bathtubs and a swimming pool.

Getting There & Away

There are several buses a day to Diyarbakır (US$7.50, seven hours) and several *dolmuşes* to Doğubayazıt (US$3, 2½ hours).

The United Arab Emirates

إتحاد الإمارات العربية

Once an obscure corner of Arabia, the United Arab Emirates have transformed themselves into an Arabian success story through a mix of oil profits, stability and a sharp eye for business. The UAE attracts visitors to its beaches, desert vistas and Bedouin heritage. Each of the seven emirates bears a unique character. Dubai is the Singapore of the Gulf, with bustling harbours, gigantic shopping malls and a taste for bold architecture. The oil-rich emirate of Abu Dhabi has two beautiful oases: the attractively green and orderly Al-Ain and the spectacular contrast of green farms and towering pink dunes at Liwa. Sharjah offers the country's best museums and art gallery, and a magnificent zoo, as well as the charming port of Khor Fakkan. The smaller emirates are quieter – Umm al-Qaiwain is the closest thing to what the fishing and pearling towns of 50 years ago must have been like.

With visa regulations relaxed, it has never been easier to visit this intriguing little federation.

Facts about the UAE

HISTORY

Like much of the rest of the Gulf, what is now the UAE has been settled for many centuries. The earliest significant settlements are from the Bronze Age. In the 3rd millennium BC a culture known as Umm an-Nar arose near modern Abu Dhabi. Umm an-Nar's influence extended well into the interior and down the coast of what is now Oman. There were also settlements at Bidiya (near Fujairah) and at Rams (near Ras al-Khaimah) during the 3rd millennium BC.

The Persians and to a lesser extent the Greeks were the next major cultural influence in the area. The Persian Sassanid empire held sway until the arrival of Islam in AD 636. Christianity had made a brief appearance in the form of the Nestorian Church, which had a monastery on Sir Baniyas Island, west of Abu Dhabi, in the 5th century.

During the Middle Ages much of the area was part of the Kingdom of Hormuz, which controlled the entrance to, and most of the trade in, the Gulf. The Portuguese first ar-

The United Arab Emirates

Area: 83,600 sq km
Population: 3.13 million
Capital: Abu Dhabi
Head of State: President Sheikh Zayed bin Sultan an-Nahyan
Official Language: Arabic
Currency: UAE dirham (Dh)

- Best Dining – eating the mixed grill by which all others must be judged at Fakhreddine, Dubai's finest Lebanese restaurant

- Best Nightlife – mixing with mobile-phone-toting sheikhs, pint-sized jockeys and punters of every nationality at Nad al-Sheba racecourse in Dubai

- Best Walk – exploring the cool date palm plantations in the heart of Al-Ain, the garden city

- Best View – looking out over the enormous waves of peach-tinged dunes at the Liwa Oasis

- Best Activity – watching a bullfight on a Friday afternoon in Fujairah

rived in 1498 and by 1515 they had occupied Julfar (near Ras al-Khaimah) and built a customs house through which they taxed the Gulf's flourishing trade with India and the Far East. The Portuguese stayed on in the town until 1633.

The rise of British naval power in the Gulf in the mid-18th century coincided with the rise of two important tribal confederations along the coast of the lower Gulf.

What to See

Dubai is the most vibrant city in the Gulf. The museum and Deira souqs are worth a look, but the city's real attraction is its atmosphere.

The **Al-Ain/Buraimi Oasis** is an easy trip from Dubai. There are a number of historic sites in the area, and the contrast between the Emirati and Omani sides of the oasis is greater than you think.

If you have more time, consider a trip from **Fujairah** to **Dibba** on the east coast where there is some of the country's best scenery and some great beaches. On the way there from Dubai, stop at the **Sharjah Desert Park**, which has a fantastic zoo. The scenery around the mountain town of **Hatta** is also worth exploring. For real desert aficionados, the **Liwa Oasis** on the Saudi border is remarkable for its vast dunes and sense of isolation.

These were the Qawasim and the Bani Yas, the ancestors of the rulers of four of the seven emirates that today make up the UAE.

The Qawasim, whose descendants now rule Sharjah and Ras al-Khaimah, were a seafaring clan based in Ras al-Khaimah. Their influence extended, at times, to the Persian side of the Gulf. This brought them into conflict with the British, who dubbed the area the Pirate Coast and launched raids against the Qawasim in 1805, 1809 and 1811. In 1820 a British fleet destroyed or captured every Qawasim ship it could find, imposed a General Treaty of Peace on nine Arab sheikhdoms in the area and installed a garrison. Europeans took to calling the area the Trucial Coast, a name it retained until 1971.

Throughout this period the main power among the Bedouin tribes of the interior was the Bani Yas tribal confederation, made up of the ancestors of the ruling families of modern Abu Dhabi and Dubai. The Bani Yas were originally based in Liwa, an oasis deep in the desert, but moved to Abu Dhabi in 1793. They engaged in the traditional Bedouin activities of camel herding, small-scale agriculture, tribal raiding and extracting protection money from caravans passing through their territory. The Bani Yas divided into two main branches in the early 19th century when Dubai split from Abu Dhabi.

So long as their rivals were kept out of the region and the lines of communication to India remained secure, the British, who formally established a protectorate over the Trucial Coast in 1892, did not really care what happened in the Gulf. The area became a backwater. Throughout the late 19th and early 20th centuries the sheikhdoms were tiny enclaves of fishers, pearl divers and Bedouin. Protracted rivalries between the various rulers occasionally erupted into conflict, which the British tried to subdue.

It was the prospect of oil that changed the way the British ran their affairs. After the collapse of the world pearl market in the early 20th century, the coast sank into poverty. In 1939, Sheikh Shakhbut, of Abu Dhabi, granted the first of several oil concessions on his territory. It was not until 1958, however, that oil was found in the emirate. Exports began in 1962 and, with a population at the time of only 15,000, Abu Dhabi was on its way to becoming very rich. Throughout this period Dubai was cementing its reputation as the region's busiest trading centre, until it was found to have oil of its own in 1966.

Britain's 1968 announcement that it would leave the Gulf in 1971 came as a shock to most of the sheikhs. The original plan, announced in February 1968, was to form a federation including Bahrain, Qatar and the Trucial Coast. Three years of negotiations resulted in independence for Bahrain and Qatar and the formation of the UAE. The new country came into existence when six of the emirates united on 2 December 1971; Ras al-Khaimah joined the following year.

At the time many outsiders dismissed the UAE as an artificial and largely British creation. While there was some truth in this charge, it was also true that the emirs of the smaller and poorer sheikhdoms knew that their territories had little hope of surviving as independent states. Despite the doomsayers, since independence the UAE has become one of the wealthiest and most stable countries in the Arab world.

The UAE Today

Though it is developing into a regional business centre, the UAE rarely produces much news of interest to the outside world – aside from an ever-growing list of major sporting events hosted by Dubai and Sharjah. The generosity and wit of the president, Sheikh Zayed of Abu Dhabi (he once said that he appreciated talking privately with citizens

UNITED ARAB EMIRATES

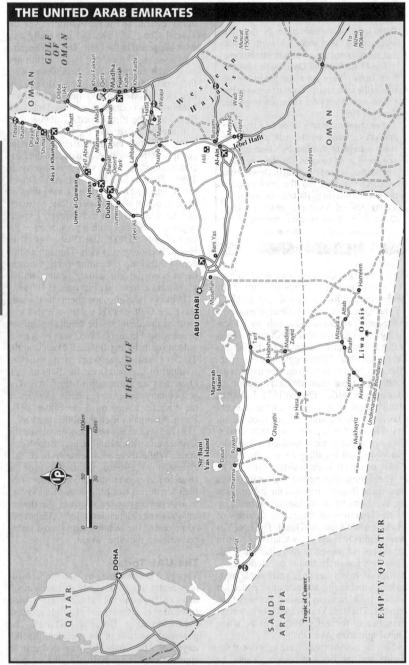

about their troubles, because the secret police got it wrong half the time), has made him one of the Arab world's more popular leaders. There are some fears that the federation may weaken once Sheikh Zayed dies.

There are some minor tensions between the various emirates. Dubai is following liberal social policies to attract tourists, while Sharjah is becoming more strictly Islamic. Abu Dhabi has large oil reserves to last 100 years or more, but the other emirates are busily competing to become centres of trade and manufacturing.

GEOGRAPHY

The UAE is about 83,600 sq km in area. The Emirate of Abu Dhabi represents over 85% of this total. Salt flats mark the coastal areas while much of the inland area is a nearly featureless desert running to the edges of the Empty Quarter (Rub al-Khali) in the south. Some of the tallest sand dunes in the world lie around the Liwa Oasis. A part of the Hajar Mountains runs through the UAE, and sections of the country's north and east are green and inviting.

CLIMATE

From May to September, daytime temperatures are in the low to mid-40°C range in Abu Dhabi and Dubai. On the east coast and in the mountainous north you're more likely to have a breeze. The inland desert areas are sometimes hotter, though without the humidity the heat here is more bearable than on the coast. In the winter months, all the emirates enjoy sunny, warm weather, though it can get windy on the Gulf coast. On average it rains only five days a year.

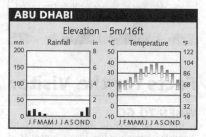

ABU DHABI

Elevation – 5m/16ft

ECOLOGY & ENVIRONMENT

In addition to the Federal Environment Agency and the Environmental Research & Wildlife Development Agency there are

many NGOs concerned with the environment, including the **Arabian Leopard Trust** (☎ 4-344 4871; PO Box 24444, Sharjah), the **Dubai Natural History Group** (☎ 349 4816; PO Box 9234) and the **Emirates Environmental Group** (☎ 331 8100; W www.eeg-uae .org; PO Box 7013, Dubai). The **Emirates Diving Association** (☎ 393 9390; W www.emirates diving.com; PO Box 33220, Dubai) is a participant in environmental campaigns.

FLORA & FAUNA

At Sharjah Desert Park, which is concerned with increasing the numbers of Arabia's endangered species, you can see Arabian oryx and gazelle. Sir Baniyas Island, west of Abu Dhabi, is a breeding ground for rare and endangered species, but access is restricted.

The UAE is well known as a birdwatcher's delight and each year the local bird population swells by over 500% when migrating birds stop over on their way from Africa and Europe to Asia. Autumn and spring are the best months for bird activity.

In Dubai, thousands of flamingos inhabit an area of swampy land along Oud Metha Rd that has been set aside as a waterbird and wildlife sanctuary. In the parks, golf courses and wadis you will see parakeets, shrikes, doves, Indian rollers and little green bee-eaters. On the coasts you'll see Socotra cormorants and swift terns. The mangrove swamp of Khor Kalba on the east coast is the only home in the world to the Khor Kalba white-collared kingfisher, and the mangroves at Umm al-Qaiwain are home to abundant bird species.

Bird-watchers can arrange tours with Colin Richardson of the **Emirates Bird Records Committee** (☎ 4-650 3398, mobile 050-650 3398; e colinR@emirates.net.ae; Dubai).

GOVERNMENT & POLITICS

Though there is a federal government over which one of the emirs presides, each ruler is completely sovereign within his emirate.

Sheikh Zayed bin Sultan an-Nahyan of Abu Dhabi has been president since the country was formed in 1971, a position he seems likely to hold for life. Sheikh Maktoum bin Rashid al-Maktoum, the ruler of Dubai, is the country's vice president and prime minister.

The degree of power that the emirs should cede to the federal government has been one of the country's hottest topics of debate since independence. The forum where these and other issues are discussed is the Supreme Council, the highest body in the country, which comprises the seven emirs. There is also a cabinet in which the posts are distributed among the emirates. Most of the population live in Abu Dhabi and Dubai so their representatives hold most of these posts.

The cabinet and Supreme Council are advised, but can't be overruled, by the Federation Council of Ministers. This is a consultative body whose members are appointed by the respective emirs. All the council's members come from leading families.

The UAE does not align itself with any country but it is committed to Arab unity. It has a long-running dispute with Iran over three islands in the Gulf.

POPULATION & PEOPLE

There's an estimated 3.1 million people living in the UAE, of whom about 27% (70,000) are UAE citizens (or 'nationals' as they are usually referred to). The population has been growing at 4% a year, bolstered by a high birth rate and ever-growing numbers of expatriate workers. The majority of the expat community are from India, Pakistan, Iran and other Arab countries. The Emiratis themselves come from a number of different backgrounds. All of the northern emirates have substantial communities of people of Persian, Indian or Baluchi ancestry.

RELIGION

Most Emiratis are Sunni Muslims subscribing to the Maliki or Hanbali schools of Islamic law. Many of the latter are Wahhabis, though UAE Wahhabis are not nearly as strict and puritanical as the Saudi Wahhabis. There are also smaller communities of Ibadi and Shiite Muslims. Other religions are tolerated, and there are a number of Christian churches throughout the country, as well as Hindu and Sikh temples in Dubai.

LANGUAGE

Arabic is the official language of the UAE but English is very widely understood. Hindi and its sister language Urdu can be useful because of the large number of Indian and Pakistani expatriates. For Arabic words and phrases, see the Language chapter at the back of this book.

Expatriates

There's a clear hierarchy among the UAE's expatriate communities. At the top are the Westerners. Then come the middle-income workers from Middle Eastern countries. At the bottom are the labourers from India, Pakistan and Bangladesh.

For the 50,000 or so Western expats, life is a fantasy world of no taxes, often no rent and a free air fare home once or twice a year. A typical expat existence is one of disposable income, sunny weather, weekend camping and 4WD trips, beach resorts, pubs and restaurants. It's a lifestyle few could maintain back home.

Nationals of the less-wealthy Middle Eastern nations also flock to the UAE, but they experience a far more parsimonious existence. They are here purely to earn. Working predominantly in professional occupations – teachers, engineers – or running small businesses, they typically stay just long enough to raise the cash to build a house back home and secure enough wealth to snag themselves a wife. In a country like Egypt, remittances from nationals working abroad constitutes the backbone of the economy.

For the two million or so Asian expats living in the UAE, life is very different again. While perhaps 10% of the Asian community have living standards similar to the Western and Emirati communities, most are employed as labourers. Working on building sites without proper safety precautions or digging roads in 45°C heat is hardly the easy life, but is preferable to poverty back home. One man is able to support an extended family back in India on his pay packet alone. Living here is not really a means to an end for many Asian expats – it is simply a better existence. Many men stay for 20 years or more, seeing their families on a trip home for one month every two years.

Facts for the Visitor

WHEN TO GO

A trip to the UAE in high summer (July/August) is simply a bad idea – however, if you do enjoy temperatures of 48°C then you will be treated to heavily discounted hotel rates. Many hotels also offer up to 50% off their normal rates during Ramadan.

VISAS & DOCUMENTS
Visas
Visit visas valid for 60 days are available on arrival in the UAE at approved ports of entry (all airports and ports) to citizens of most developed countries, including passport holders of all western European countries (except for Malta and Cyprus), plus Australia, Canada, Hong Kong, Japan, New Zealand, Singapore and the USA. This visa can be extended for another 30 days for Dh500, but only at the Department of Immigration & Naturalisation in the emirate that you arrived in.

Citizens of other Gulf Cooperative Council (GCC) countries do not need visas to enter the UAE, and can stay as long as they want.

For citizens of other countries, a transit or tourist visa must be arranged through a sponsor (a company or a resident of the UAE).

Officially, if your passport shows any evidence of travel to Israel you will be denied entry, but we have heard from travellers who have visited Israel and have had no problem entering the UAE.

For details of visas for other Middle Eastern countries, see the 'Visas at a Glance' table under Visas & Documents in the Regional Facts for the Visitor chapter.

Other Documents
Student cards are generally not recognised in the UAE and having one will not get you discounts at hotels or sites. Most foreign driving licences are accepted for car rental.

EMBASSIES & CONSULATES
UAE Embassies
Following are UAE embassies and consulates in some major cities around the world. For addresses of UAE embassies in neighbouring Middle Eastern countries, see the relevant chapter.

Australia (☎ 02-6286 8802, fax 6286 8804) 36 Culgoa Circuit, O'Malley ACT 2606
Canada (☎ 613-565 8007, fax 565 8007) Suite 1800, World Exchange Plaza, 45 O'Connor St, Ottawa K1P-1A4
France (☎ 01 45 53 94 04, fax 47 55 61 04) 3 rue de Lota, 75116 Paris
Germany (☎ 228-267 070, fax 267 0714) Erste Fahrgasse, D-54113, Bonn
UK (☎ 020-7581 1281, fax 581 9616) 30 Princes Gate, London SW1
USA (☎ 202-338 6500, fax 337 7029) Suite 600, 3000 K St, NW, Washington DC 20007

Embassies in the UAE
Core opening hours are 9am to noon Saturday to Wednesday, although many embassies either open an hour earlier or close an hour later than this.

The following are all in Abu Dhabi.

Australia (☎ 789 946, fax 779 909) 14th floor, Al-Muhairy Centre, Zayed the First St
Bahrain (☎ 631 2200, fax 631 1202) An-Najda St, behind Abu Dhabi Islamic Bank
Canada (☎ 445 6969, fax 445 8787) An-Nahyan St, near the Batin Palace
Egypt (☎ 444 5566, fax 444 9878) Diplomatic Area, Airport Rd, about 10km south of the centre
France (☎ 443 5100, fax 443 4158) An-Nahyan St, near the Batin Palace
Germany (☎ 443 5630, fax 445 5712) An-Nahyan St, near the Batin Palace
Iran (☎ 444 7618, fax 444 8714) Diplomatic Area, Airport Rd, 10km south of the centre
Iraq (☎ 665 5215, fax 665 5214) Diplomatic Area, Airport Rd, about 10km south of the centre
Jordan (☎ 444 7100, fax 444 9157), Diplomatic Area, Airport Rd, about 10km south of the centre
Kuwait (☎ 444 6888, fax 444 4990) Diplomatic Area, Airport Rd, about 10km south of the centre
Lebanon (☎ 449 2100, fax 449 3500) Diplomatic Area, Airport Rd, about 10km south of the centre
Netherlands (☎ 632 1920, fax 631 3158) 6th floor, Al-Masoud Tower (look for the Standard & Chartered Bank at street level of the same building), Sheikh Hamdan bin Mohammed St
Oman (☎ 446 3333, fax 446 4633) Al-Karamah St, behind Immigration Department, about 8km south of the centre
Qatar (☎ 449 3300, fax 449 3311) Diplomatic Area, Airport Rd, about 10km south of the centre
Saudi Arabia (☎ 444 5700, fax 444 8491) Diplomatic Area, Airport Rd, about 10km south of the centre
Syria (☎ 444 8768, fax 444 9387) Diplomatic Area, Airport Rd, about 10km south of the centre
Turkey (☎ 665 5421, fax 666 2691) 142, Al-Bateen St 16
UK (☎ 632 6600, fax 634 2676) Khalid bin al-Walid St, slightly south of the Corniche
USA (☎ 443 6691, fax 443 5441) Sudan St, between Al-Karamah St and the intersection where King Khalid bin Abdul Aziz St becomes An-Nahyan St
Yemen (☎ 444 8457, fax 444 7978) Diplomatic Area, Airport Rd, about 10km south of the centre

UNITED ARAB EMIRATES

CUSTOMS
The duty-free allowances for tobacco are huge: 2000 cigarettes, 400 cigars or 2kg of loose tobacco (this is *not* a country cracking down on smoking). Non-Muslims are allowed to import 2L of wine and 2L of spirits, unless they are arriving in Sharjah, where alcohol is prohibited. You are not allowed to bring in alcohol if you enter the country by land.

MONEY
Currency
The official currency is the UAE dirham (Dh). One dirham is divided into 100 fils. Notes come in denominations of five, 10, 20, 50, 100, 200, 500 and 1000. Coins are Dh1, 50 fils, 25 fils, 10 fils and 5 fils. The government has issued new coins that are smaller than the old ones. Both types remain legal tender.

Exchange Rates
The dirham is fully convertible and pegged to the US dollar. Below are rates for a range of currencies:

country	unit		dirham
Australia	A$1	=	Dh2.00
Canada	C$1	=	Dh2.31
euro zone	€1	=	Dh3.62
Japan	Y100	=	Dh3.00
New Zealand	NZ$1	=	Dh1.75
UK	UK£1	=	Dh5.76
USA	US$1	=	Dh3.67

Exchanging Money
Moneychangers sometimes have better rates than banks, and some do not even charge a commission. The problem with moneychangers is that some of them either will not take travellers cheques or will take only one type. Currencies of neighbouring countries are all easily exchanged.

ATMs & Credit Cards There are ATMs on major streets, in shopping centres and sometimes at hotels. ATMs at branches of HSBC are linked to the Global Access system. ATMs at Emirates Bank International and Abu Dhabi Commercial Bank are also on Global Access, as well as Cirrus, Plus and, sometimes, Switch. All major credit cards are accepted, though you may be hit with a 5% merchant fee if you use American Express (AmEx).

Costs
The UAE is not a low-budget country but it is possible to keep costs under control. Decent hotels can be found for Dh100 to Dh150 (US$30 to US$40) in Dubai but they tend to be more expensive elsewhere. Eating for Dh10 to Dh15 (US$3 to US$4) is rarely a problem though if you include alcohol the bill will be a lot higher. Getting around is cheap in shared long-distance taxis and minibuses, and admission fees to museums are minimal. Plan on spending Dh150/200 (US$40 to US$60) per day for budget/mid-range travel. In Dubai, Fujairah, Khor Fakkan and Sharjah, which have youth hostels, you might be able to keep your budget down to half that.

Tipping & Bargaining
Tips are not generally expected in the UAE as there is a service charge added to your bill. This goes to the restaurant, however, not the waiter – so if you want to leave a tip, 10% should be sufficient.

Bargaining in souqs in the country can be exhausting. Be prepared to spend some time at it and you'll find that prices may come down by as much as 50%. Even in shopping centres you can ask for a discount or for their 'best price'. The more touristy souqs in the cities will not usually offer much of a discount.

Taxes & Refunds
In Dubai most hotel and restaurant bills will have a 10% service charge added and another 10% for a municipality tax. In Abu Dhabi, hotels and restaurants have a 16% service charge added to their bills and in Sharjah it's 15%. If a price is quoted 'net', this means that it includes all taxes and service charges.

POST & COMMUNICATIONS
Post
Letters up to 20g cost Dh3 to Europe, or Dh3.50 to Australia and the USA. Postcard rates are Dh2 to Europe, Australia and the USA. Sending a 1kg package to Europe costs Dh45; to Australia or the USA it's Dh68.

Mail generally takes about a week to Europe or the USA, and eight to 10 days to Australia. Mumtaz Speed Post or Express Mail Services are available from main post offices in each emirate, but they are very expensive and you might save money by using a courier.

Poste restante is not available in the UAE. The AmEx offices in Abu Dhabi and Dubai will hold mail for clients (see city entries for addresses). If you are checking into a five-star hotel the reception desk will usually hold letters and small packages for two or three days prior to your arrival.

Telephone

The country code for the UAE is ☎ 971, followed by the area code (minus the zero), then the subscriber number. In the text, local area codes are given at the start of each city or town section. The international access code (to call abroad from the UAE) is ☎ 00.

The UAE has a splendid telecommunications system, and you can connect up with just about anywhere in the world from even the remotest areas. The state telecom monopoly is Etisalat, recognisable in each city by the giant golf ball on top of its offices. Coin phones have almost completely been taken over by cardphones. Phonecards are available from grocery stores. Local calls (within the same area code) are free.

Mobile Phones The UAE's mobile-phone network uses the GSM 900 Mhz and 1800 Mhz standard, the same as Europe, Asia and Australia. Etisalat is the sole operator. Visitors can buy a prepaid SIM card at airports or from Etisalat offices for Dh300. This lasts 60 days, or until the credit runs out. Mobile phones can also be rented from car hire companies in the airport arrival halls at Dubai, Abu Dhabi and Sharjah.

Fax

You can send faxes from Etisalat offices. They may ask for your local address and contact number before they'll send it. The service is fairly good but it is expensive at Dh10 per page to most international destinations.

Email & Internet Access

Internet connection is available through Etisalat. Internet cafés can be found in most cities (see city entries for details), and cost around Dh10 to Dh15 per hour. Five-star hotels offer Internet access to their guests, though sometimes this is only available to guests staying in executive suites.

If you're toting a laptop and want to log on, Etisalat has a dial-and-surf service; simply plug in and dial ☎ 500 5333 to get onto the Internet; charges are 15 fils (US$0.04) per minute. Check how much extra the hotel will charge for using the telephone line first, though.

DIGITAL RESOURCES

The following are just a few of the useful websites available for travellers to the UAE.

The UAE Ministry of Information and Culture This is an excellent website
W www.uaeinteract.com
Khaleej Times A site covering all the news from the local paper
W www.khaleejtimes.co.ae
Gulf News The website for the UAE's other major English-language newspaper
W www.gulf-news.com
Dubai City Guide Up-to-date information on happenings in Dubai, plus tourist information
W www.dubaicityguide.com
Time Out Cultural events and comprehensive listing of restaurants, bars and clubs for Dubai and Abu Dhabi
W www.timeoutdubai.com
W www.timeoutabudhabi.com
Dubai Tourism This is the official government tourism website
W www.dubaitourism.co.ae
Sharjah Online Useful tourism information site on everything in Sharjah
W www.sharjah-welcome.com

BOOKS

As well as this book, Lonely Planet publishes *Oman & the United Arab Emirates*, and a dedicated city guide to *Dubai*.

Otherwise, the *Abu Dhabi Explorer*, *Dubai Explorer* and *Sharjah – The Guide* include information on just about everything there is to see and do – they're particularly useful for expats. For those who have 4WDs, *UAE Off-Road Explorer* is absolutely superb and a must if you want to go exploring.

Father of Dubai: Sheikh Rashid bin Said al-Maktoum, by Graeme Wilson, is a tribute to the acknowledged founder of modern Dubai. For an intimate view of life on the Trucial Coast before oil was discovered, read Wilfred Thesiger's classic *Arabian Sands*, originally published in 1959.

For an Emirati view of local history and Britain's role in the Gulf see *The Myth of Arab Piracy in the Gulf*, by Sultan Muhammad al-Qasimi, the Emir of Sharjah. *Mother Without a Mask*, by Patricia Holton, is an easy to read account of a British woman's involvement with a family from Al-Ain.

More-general Middle East titles, some of which also contain coverage of the UAE, are listed in the Books section in the Regional Facts for the Visitor chapter.

NEWSPAPERS & MAGAZINES

Gulf News and *Khaleej Times* are the UAE's two English-language newspapers. Each costs Dh2 and carries pretty much the same international news, though *Gulf News* is widely regarded as the better of the two.

Time Out Dubai (Dh10) is an excellent magazine and listings guide, with the lowdown on hot restaurants, bars and clubs. *What's On* (Dh12) is another monthly catering to expatriates, and also covers Al-Ain and Abu Dhabi. International news magazines such as *The Economist* (Dh28) are available in Dubai and Abu Dhabi.

RADIO & TV

Abu Dhabi and Dubai each have an English-language TV channel, although outside the two main cities reception is decidedly mixed. In various parts of the country you can also pick up English-language signals from Qatar and Oman. Most hotels, even small ones, offer satellite TV with CNN, BBC World and other English-language channels.

Emirates FM 1 at 99.3 and Emirates 2 FM at 98.7 are English-language stations. Dubai and Ajman also have English-language FM radio stations. Dubai FM is at FM 92 and Ajman's Channel 4 FM is at 104.8.

PHOTOGRAPHY & VIDEO

Getting prints developed is never a problem (photo developers in every city centre advertise 20-minute services). A 36-exposure roll of film costs about Dh38 for developing. You'll also get another film and a photo album thrown in. The best place to get slides and B&W film developed is at **Prolab** (☎ 266 9766; *Abu Baker al-Siddiq Rd*) in Dubai.

LAUNDRY

There are few laundrettes in the UAE's cities, but small laundries abound and are very cheap. An average load might cost you Dh10. Dry cleaning services are also offered in most cities.

TOILETS

The best advice is to go when you can, because there is not an abundance of public toilets in the UAE. Most public toilets in shopping centres, restaurants, museums or hotels are Western style. The only toilets you're likely to find out of the cities are holes in the ground out the back of restaurants or petrol stations.

HEALTH

The standard of health care is high throughout the UAE, though it is expensive. It's important to get decent travel insurance, or risk a very hefty bill. Should you get sick consult either the hotel doctor, if you are in a big hotel, or your embassy or consulate. If this is not possible, you can go to any hospital. Western medicines are widely available in larger cities. Tap water in Abu Dhabi and Dubai is safe, but often tastes bad and is heavily chlorinated. Stick to bottled water.

See the Health section in the Facts about the Region chapter for more on health.

WOMEN TRAVELLERS

Dubai is the most liberal place in the UAE, and people here are used to Western dress and ways. That said, women should still avoid revealing clothing when walking in the souqs of Deira. In small towns the dress codes are more conservative. There's no need to wear a headscarf, but loose clothing covering the arms and legs is a good idea. Sharjah actually has laws against tight clothing. In the UAE foreign women will often be asked to take the front seat in buses or be asked to sit next to other women. This is so you can avoid the embarrassment of men's stares.

DANGERS & ANNOYANCES

The main danger is bad driving. Many drivers in the UAE don't seem to have a concept of other cars, and courtesy on the road simply does not exist. People will cut in front of you, turn without indicating, and race each other on freeways. Out of the cities, the inner lane is for speeding luxury vehicles only – block them at your own risk. Drivers have a tendency to zoom into roundabouts at frightening speeds, and try to exit them from inside lanes. Pedestrian crossings are no guarantee that drivers will stop or even slow down. Watch out! If you have an accident, even a small one, the car must remain *in situ* until the police arrive and make a report, unless it's completely blocking traffic.

BUSINESS HOURS

Government offices open from 7am or 7.30am until 1pm or 1.30pm, Saturday to Wednesday. Banks, private companies and shops open from 8am to 1pm or 1.30pm, then again from 4pm to 7pm or 8pm from Saturday to Wednesday. Shopping centres and souqs are open until about 10pm daily.

There are a few local variations: in Ras al-Khaimah, for example, all shops are required to close for about 30 minutes at prayer time.

PUBLIC HOLIDAYS

Special events include the Dubai Shopping Festival (March). You might need to book hotels in advance during this month, but major retailers have substantial discounts. Apart from the Islamic holidays (see the Regional Facts for the Visitor chapter), the UAE observes the following public holidays:

New Year's Day 1 January
Accession Day 6 August
National Day 2 December

SPECIAL EVENTS

The following special events take place in the UAE:

Dubai Tennis Open February – ATP Tournament
Dubai Shopping Festival March – retailers drop prices and the city stages performances and competitions
Dubai Rugby Sevens First weekend in December – drinking event with rugby sideshow

Each emirate may also observe its own holidays (eg, in Abu Dhabi 6 August is a holiday marking the accession of Sheikh Zayed).

ACTIVITIES

The UAE's sophisticated tourism industry offers a wide range of activities, though prices are high. Popular excursions include organised safari-style camps in the desert, 4WD trips through the Hajar Mountains, diving on the coast north of Fujairah, and water sports such as fishing, yachting and jet-skiing. Golf, tennis, rugby, cricket, horse racing and even polo feature in the local sporting calendar.

ACCOMMODATION

There are no camp sites adjacent to the UAE's cities but camping in the desert is quite common. There are youth hostels in Dubai, Sharjah and Fujairah (see these sections for details). HI cards are required at all three. Most of the country's cheap hotels are in and around the Dubai souq. There are no B&Bs, alas, but plenty of good-quality, mid-range hotels and an extraordinary number of five-star hotels.

FOOD

Eating cheap in the UAE means eating either in small Indian/Pakistani restaurants or sticking to street-food. Excellent and cheap South Indian vegetarian food is widely available; a *thali* (a kind of mini-smorgasbord of vegetarian dishes and rice) makes a cheap main meal. Inexpensive Lebanese, Chinese and Filipino food is also available, as is the usual American fast food. See the special section 'Middle Eastern Cuisine' in the Regional Facts for the Visitor chapter for a general discussion of typical Middle Eastern fare.

DRINKS

Alcohol can only be sold in restaurants and bars in hotels, or in members-only places such as country clubs and sports clubhouses (which often admit paying guests). The prices are pretty outrageous – expect to pay around Dh18 for a pint of beer. Alcohol is not available in Sharjah.

SPECTATOR SPORTS

The most popular spectator sport in the UAE is camel racing (although after 10 minutes a single race can get exceedingly boring to watch). Early Friday mornings are the best time to see races or training.

The Dubai Desert Classic is one of the richest PGA golf tournaments and is held at Dubai Creek Golf & Yacht Club in February. The Dubai Tennis Open, also held in February, is a part of the ATP world series tour. The Dubai World Cup is well known as the world's richest horse race with prize money of US$16 million. It is held at Nad ash-Sheba racecourse 5km southeast of Dubai.

Sharjah Cricket Stadium hosts regular one-day contests between international teams, vocally supported by the Indian, Pakistani and Sri Lankan communities.

SHOPPING

Dubai has a well-established reputation as a shoppers' paradise, largely because of its duty-free status. There are a few shops in Al-Ain, Abu Dhabi, Sharjah and Dubai dealing in Bedouin souvenirs, most of which come from Oman. If you have a lot of money to spend try the gold souq in Dubai or the carpet merchants in Sharjah's Central Market. Dubai is also the cheapest place outside Iran to buy Iranian caviar.

Getting There & Away

AIR
Dubai and Abu Dhabi are the country's main international airports, though an increasing number of carriers serve Sharjah as well. There are also small international airports at Fujairah, Ras al-Khaimah and Al-Ain. There is no departure tax when leaving by air.

Emirates Airlines and Gulf Air are the major airlines. There are daily services from Abu Dhabi and Dubai to major European and Middle Eastern cities.

There are no direct flights from North America; fares via either Europe or Southeast Asia start at about Dh3200. Return air fares to Europe range from Dh2500 to Dh3500. You can get to Rome for Dh1700 one way. During summer and Christmas, when many expats return home, airlines often have special fares to London, sometimes as low as Dh2000 return.

There are frequent flights from the UAE to cities in the Indian subcontinent. Return fares to Mumbai and Delhi start at Dh1400.

Sample return air fares to other destinations in the Middle East are: Amman, Dh1550 (US$422); Beirut, Dh1140 (US$310); Cairo, Dh1370 (US$373); Doha, Dh890 (US$242); Muscat, Dh705 (US$192); and Tehrān Dh570 (US$155).

Strictly speaking there are high and low seasons, but special fares are offered at any time of the year so shop around. There are no bucket shops in the UAE.

LAND
There is a daily bus service between Dubai and Muscat, though the lack of a UAE border post at Dibba, Buraimi or Hatta can present some visa problems for travellers. Essentially, you can leave the UAE this way with no problems, but if you want to enter at

these points you will not receive an entry stamp and therefore will be considered to be in transit and have 48 hours to leave – whether by air, sea or road. After that you will incur a fine of Dh100 per day when you do try to leave. Having a valid UAE visa in your passport makes no difference.

If you enter through Gheweifat, the checkpoint near the Saudi-UAE border, Sham on the UAE-Oman border north of Ras al-Khaimah, or Khatmat Malahah on the UAE-Oman border south of Kalba, you will get a border stamp and can remain in the country for as long as your visa allows.

Dozens of bus companies have services to Jordan, Syria and Egypt via Saudi Arabia and Jordan, but Saudi transit visas are not usually given to people without UAE residency papers. There are two buses a week to Amman, Jordan (Dh350 return, 38 hours).

If you leave by road, there's a Dh20 tax, though at some crossing points there are no border posts to collect it.

SEA
Two ferry services connect the UAE and southern Iran. There's a Dh20 departure tax.

The Iranian shipping company Valfajre-8 has twice weekly services between Bandar-e Abbās and Sharjah's Port Khalid (US$28 economy, eight hours). The local agent is the **Oasis Freight Company** (☎ 6-559 6325, Kayed Ahli Bldg, Jamal Abdul Nasser Rd, Sharjah).

Naif Marine Services (☎ 4-345 7878, fax 345 5570, Port Rashid, Dubai) has a fortnightly service between Dubai and Bushehr. Pullman seats cost US$45 while economy-class cabins cost US$113 for the 24-hour journey.

Getting Around

AIR
The only internal flight is between Dubai and Abu Dhabi. It costs Dh550 return with Emarat Link Aviation in nine-seater seaplanes. Flights depart 12 times daily from Dubai Creek, next to the Dubai Creek Golf & Yacht Club, and land in Abu Dhabi near the Hilton on the Abu Dhabi Corniche. The Dubai office (☎ 4-295 9779; cnr Baniyas Rd & 9 St, Deira) is in Al-Yamamah Towers, opposite Deira City Centre. The Abu Dhabi

office (☎ 2-632 3777; Corniche) is in the Hilton Baynunah Tower.

MINIBUS
Dubai transport minibuses serve all the emirates but there is no return service. Yes, that's right. The buses go back to Dubai empty.

LONG-DISTANCE TAXI
Shared taxis can be cramped but they are cheap and a great way to meet people. The main problem is often that, aside from the busy Abu Dhabi–Dubai route, they fill up slowly. You can also take them engaged if you are willing to pay for all of the seats.

CAR
Major roads in the UAE are good; dual-lane highways link the major cities, and have lighting along their entire length! Small-car rental starts at about Dh120 per day plus Dh20 to Dh30 for insurance, but you may be able to negotiate this down to a net rate of Dh100 per day, with insurance, at smaller agencies. The first 100km or 150km per day are usually free. If you rent a car for more than three days you will usually be given unlimited kilometres.

ORGANISED TOURS
There are several companies in Dubai, Abu Dhabi, Sharjah and Ras al-Khaimah offering tours of the various emirates. An overnight desert safari, including a barbecue, camel ride, sleeping in a Bedouin tent and perhaps a belly-dancing show, is one of the more popular excursions on offer. They also offer dhow cruises, camel rides and camping trips.

Major operators include **Arabian Adventures** (☎ 4-343 9966, W www.arabian-adven tures.com), **Arabian Dream Tours** (☎ 4-221 1129), **Net Tours & Travels** (☎ 4-266 8661, W www.nettoursdubai.com) and **Orient Travel & Touring** (☎ 282 8238).

Bear in mind that what you spend on a day's tour with one of these companies, you could hire a car for up to three days and take yourself to lots more places at your own pace.

Abu Dhabi   أبو ظبي

☎ 02
Everything in the UAE's island capital is modern, sleek and shiny. Abu Dhabi is often accused of being a rather soulless place, but that's probably going a bit too far. It's the classic Arabian petrodollar city, completely remodelled in less than 40 years into a wealthy metropolis filled with gardens and tall mirrored-glass buildings.

Orientation
The city of Abu Dhabi sits at the head of a T-shaped island. The airport is about 30km from the centre. The main business district is the area bounded by Sheikh Khalifa bin Zayed and Istiqlal Sts to the north, Zayed the Second St to the south, Khalid bin al-Walid St to the west, and As-Salam St to the east. Some of the streets have names that are in more common use than their official ones. See the boxed text 'Street Names'.

Information
Money In the centre, and especially along Hamdan and Sheikh Khalifa bin Zayed Sts, it often seems like every third building is a bank. If you're looking for a moneychanger instead of a bank, try Liwa St, around the corner from Hamdan.

AmEx is represented by **Al-Masoud Travel & Services** (☎ 621 3045; An-Nasr St; open 8.30am-1pm, 4pm-6.30pm Sun-Thur), near the intersection with Khalid bin al-Walid St. All the usual AmEx services are provided, including cheque cashing and holding mail. Mail should be addressed c/o American Express, PO Box 806, Abu Dhabi, UAE, and should be clearly marked 'Client's Mail'.

Post The main post office (East Rd; open 8am-midnight Sat-Wed, 8am-11pm Thur) is between Al-Falah and Zayed the Second Sts.

Telephone & Fax The Etisalat office (cnr Zayed the Second St & Airport Rd; open 24hr) offers fax, telex and telegram services.

Internet Access The Cyber Café (cnr Zayed the Second & Bani Yas Sts) is above Choithram's. There is a separate computer room for women. It costs Dh15 per hour. **Havana Café** (cnr Sheikh Hamdan bin Mohammed & As-Salam Sts) also has Internet access, and two terminals reserved for women. It costs Dh10 per hour.

Bookshops The **All Prints Bookstore** (An-Nasr St) has a selection of English-language

Street Names	
official name	common name
Sheikh Rashid bin Saeed al-Maktoum St	Airport Rd or Old Airport Rd
Zayed the Second St	Electra St
Sheikh Hamdan bin Mohammed St	Hamdan
Al-Falah St	Passport St

books. **Book Corner** is in the Liwa Centre, Sheikh Hamdan bin Mohammed St.

Cultural Centres The following cultural centres are in Abu Dhabi.

Alliance Française (☎ 626 0404) Located in the Choithram's Building on Zayed the First St in Khalidia, about 3km west of the Volcano Fountain, the Alliance is open 9am to 1pm and 4pm to 8.30pm Saturday to Wednesday, and 9am to 2pm Thursday.
British Council (☎ 665 9300) On An-Nasr St (Fifth St), off Tariq ibn Ziyad St, it's open from 9am to 1.30pm and 4.30pm to 7pm Monday to Wednesday.
US Information Service (USIS; ☎ 643 6567) At the US embassy on Sudan St.

Medical Services Abu Dhabi's **Central Hospital** (☎ 621 4666 for general switchboard, 634 4663 for emergency unit; Al-Manhal St) emergency entrance is on the corner of Al-Manhal and Karamah Sts. The pharmacy hotline on ☎ 677 7979 gives the locations of pharmacies open 24 hours.

The Cultural Foundation
This large, faceless building (Zayed the First St; admission free; open 8am-2pm, 5pm-9.30pm Sat-Thur; 5pm-8pm Fri) is more interesting inside than its outward appearance would indicate, and is worth a visit. It houses the National Archives, the National Library and the Institution of Culture & Art. There are often interesting exhibits on local history and Islamic art as well as modern art exhibits and musical concerts.

Al-Hosn Palace
Al-Hosn Palace (Old Fort or White Fort; cnr Khalid bin al-Walid & Sheikh Hamdan bin Mohammed Sts; admission free; open 7.30am-2.30pm, 5pm-9pm Sat-Thur) is one of the few buildings in Abu Dhabi that's more than 30 years old. It was built in the late 19th century and is the oldest building in Abu

Dhabi. Its interior has been completely modernised and is now used by the Cultural Foundation as a documents and research centre.

Old Souq
If you're looking for a break from the world of banks and boutiques that is modern Abu Dhabi take a walk through what remains of the old souq in the small area east of Al-Ittihad Square and north of Sheikh Khalifa bin Zayed St.

Women's Handicraft Centre
This is a government-run operation where traditional weavings and other crafts are displayed and sold. Ask taxi drivers to take you to the Women's Association Complex or the Women's Union; the centre is at the rear of this compound.

To reach the centre (admission Dh5; open 8am-12.30pm Sat-Wed) simply take Airport Rd south from the centre and exit at the small black-and-white sign pointing right (it is easy to overshoot the turn-off so watch the road closely). It is in a compound marked 'Handicraft Industrial Centre'.

Dhow Wharf & Fish Market
At the eastern end of the Corniche, near the port, lies Abu Dhabi's fish market and small dhow wharf. It is rather disappointing compared with Dubai's waterfront but it does offer good local colour and an excellent view back towards the city.

Places to Stay
There are really no cheap hotels in Abu Dhabi. The rates quoted here are the hotels' rack rates (standard high-season rates). It's usually possible to negotiate some sort of discount. Service charges have been included in the prices.

Places to Stay – Budget
Zakher Hotel (☎ 627 5300; e zakhotel@ emirates.net.ae; Umm an-Nar St; singles/

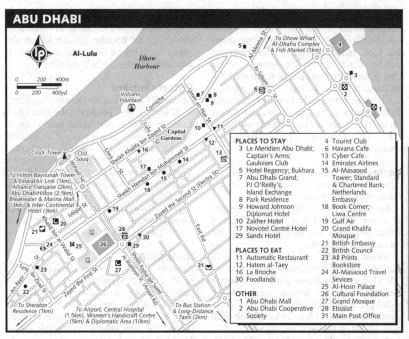

ABU DHABI

Al-Lulu

Dhow Harbour

0   200   400m
0   200   400yd

Volcano Fountain

Corniche

Capital Gardens

Clock Tower

Old Souq

To Hilton Baynunah Tower & EmaratAir Link (1km); Alliance Française (2km); Abu DhabiHilton (2.5km); Breakwater & Marina Mall (3km) & Inter-Continental Hotel (3km)

To Dhow Wharf, Al-Dhafra Complex & Fish Market (1km)

To Sheraton Residence (1km)

To Airport, Central Hospital (1.5km), Women's Handicraft Centre (5km) & Diplomatic Area (10km)

To Bus Station & Long-Distance Taxis (2km)

PLACES TO STAY
3 Le Meridien Abu Dhabi; Captain's Arms; Gauloises Club
5 Hotel Regency; Bukhara
7 Abu Dhabi Grand; PJ O'Reilly's; Island Exchange
8 Park Residence
9 Howard Johnson Diplomat Hotel
10 Zakher Hotel
17 Novotel Centre Hotel
29 Sands Hotel

PLACES TO EAT
11 Automatic Restaurant
12 Hatem al-Taey
16 La Brioche
30 Foodlands

OTHER
1 Abu Dhabi Mall
2 Abu Dhabi Cooperative Society

4 Tourist Club
6 Havana Cafe
13 Cyber Cafe
14 Emirates Airlines
15 Al-Masaood Tower; Standard & Chartered Bank; Netherlands Embassy
18 Book Corner; Liwa Centre
19 Gulf Air
20 Grand Khalifa Mosque
21 British Embassy
22 British Council
23 All Prints Bookstore
24 Al-Masaood Travel Sevices
25 Al-Hosn Palace
26 Cultural Foundation
27 Grand Mosque
28 Etisalat
31 Main Post Office

UNITED ARAB EMIRATES

doubles Dh150/200) is the cheapest hotel in Abu Dhabi, and has a dubious nightclub featuring 'entertainers from CIS countries'. Rates include the service charge.

Park Residence (☎ 674 2000; e parkres@ emirates.net.ae; singles/doubles Dh175/200) is just off Umm an-Nar St. It has 85 comfortable rooms.

Howard Johnson Diplomat Hotel (☎ 671 0000; e diplomathojo@hotmail.com; singles/ doubles Dh250/300) is next to the Park Residence. The rooms are quite good value, at least for Abu Dhabi.

Places to Stay – Mid-Range

Sands Hotel (☎ 633 5335, fax 633 5766; Zayed the Second St; singles/doubles Dh402.50/ 437) has comfortable rooms as well as the **Harvesters Pub**, a very popular expatriate's hangout.

Novotel Centre Hotel (☎ 633 3555, fax 621 0128; Sheikh Hamdan bin Mohammed St; singles/doubles Dh400/500) is in the heart of the commercial and shopping district.

Hotel Regency (☎ 676 5000, fax 677 7446; cnr Al-Meena & As-Salam Sts; singles/

doubles Dh395/450) is an excellent hotel with five-star amenities. All rooms have kitchenettes.

Places to Stay – Top End

The following hotels all have private beach clubs and health facilities as well as numerous restaurants and bars.

Abu Dhabi Hilton (☎ 681 1900; e auhitw@ emirates.net.ae; Corniche; singles/doubles Dh754/870) is an ageing five-star edifice.

Le Meridien Abu Dhabi (☎ 644 6666; e meridien@emirates.net.ae; Zayed the Second St; singles/doubles Dh1160/1276) is a luxurious hotel with the best health club and restaurant complex in town.

Abu Dhabi Grand (☎ 674 2020; e grand htl@emirates.net.ae; Umm an-Nar St; singles/ doubles Dh922/986), with its large rooms, tends to attract mostly business clientele.

Sheraton Residence (☎ 666 6220; e sher resi@emirates.net.ae; Zayed the First St; singles & doubles Dh638, large suites Dh1276) is designed for long-term guests. All rooms have cooking facilities, and the rooftop pool has some great views of Abu Dhabi from 18 floors up.

Places to Eat

Street Food If you don't want to spend much on food try the little **shwarma shops** and **South Indian vegetarian restaurants** that can be found all over the centre. Another choice for cheap snacks are the **Indian-run restaurants** where you can tuck into omelette sandwiches, burgers, chicken sandwiches and Indian snacks such as *kima* (tasty mince meat served with salad and flaky bread) and biryanis for Dh2.50 to Dh7. You can buy tea and (Nescafé) coffee for 50 fils a cup.

Restaurants Pick up a copy of *Time Out Abu Dhabi* to get a complete listing of restaurants by cuisine.

Foodlands (☎ *633 0099; Zayed the Second St; mains Dh10-25)* is a popular Chinese/Indian restaurant. The food is varied and the servings are generous.

Hatem al-Taey (☎ *633 8339; Sheikh Hamdan bin Mohammed St; mains Dh10-25)* advertises itself as a Turkish restaurant but actually serves Iranian cuisine. It's a small place with homely service, offering standards such as *chelo kebab* (lamb with rice, Dh15), plus soups and salads.

Automatic Restaurant (☎ *677 9782; Umm an-Nar St; mains Dh15-25)* is a branch of a reliable chain of Lebanese restaurants. Grills come with free salads and fruit.

Bukhara (☎ *676 5000; mains Dh15-30)* is in the Hotel Regency. It bills itself as a Central Asian restaurant which, in practice, means that the menu features mostly Indian dishes with a few Persian dishes, with the emphasis on subtle combinations of spices rather than sheer heat.

As-Sofon (☎ *681 6134; mains Dh30-70)* and **As-Safina** (☎ *681 6085; mains Dh20-40)* are both Arabic-style fish restaurants on the Breakwater. Visit at night for the spectacular views of Abu Dhabi. To get to the Breakwater turn to the right at the Hilton roundabout at the western end of the Corniche.

Fishmarket (☎ *666 6888; meals Dh140-200)* is in the Hotel Inter-Continental on Bainunah St, at the western end of Zayed the First St. It's a Thai seafood restaurant, with six-course menus from Dh140 to Dh200 including service charge – almost worth the splurge to savour some of the local seafood.

Self-Catering For fresh fruit and vegetables try the markets near the port area. For Arabic breads and sweets there are a number of bakeries around town. For European breads head straight to **La Brioche** (*Sheikh Khalifa bin Zayed St)*, where a wide selection of white and brown loaves are baked daily.

Entertainment

Abu Dhabi is no rival to Dubai's club scene. **PJ O'Reilly's**, an Irish pub at the Abu Dhabi Grand, is popular. Also at this hotel is the **Island Exchange**, which is more of a nightclub. The Le Meridien has 14 bars and restaurants set around some nice gardens, including the **Captain's Arms** and the **Gauloises Club**.

Century Cinema, a modern complex in the Abu Dhabi Mall at the end of 9th St, shows recent Hollywood releases, as does **CineStar Cinemas** at the Marina Mall on the Breakwater. Tickets at both cost Dh30.

Shopping

An-Nasr St has a number of shops with a good selection of carpets and Arabian souvenirs, though most of these are actually made elsewhere, generally in Egypt, Syria, Iran, India or Pakistan. The large complex behind the Abu Dhabi Co-op near the Le Meridien Hotel has similar items for sale. Locally made crafts are available at the Women's Craft Centre south of the city centre.

Getting There & Away

Air Abu Dhabi international airport is on the mainland, about 30km from the centre or town. You can call for **airport information** (☎ *575 7611)*. The main airline for Abu Dhabi is **Gulf Air** (☎ *633 1700; cnr Airport Rd & Sheikh Hamdan bin Mohammed St)*. **Emirates Airlines** (☎ *800 4444; Sheikh Hamdan bin Mohammed St)* is between East Rd and Bani Yas St.

Bus The **main bus terminal** (*Hazza'a bin Zayed St)* is south of the centre. Intercity service is only available within the Abu Dhabi emirate. Buses run to Al-Ain every 30 minutes from 6am to 10pm every day. Buses for Madinat Zayed leave every hour, finishing at 8pm. Both trips take 2½ hours and cost Dh10. Change at Madinat Zayed for Liwa.

Minibus These are found with the long-distance taxis next to the main bus station on East Rd. They take 14 passengers and charge Dh20 per person to Dubai and Dh25 to Sharjah. Minibuses also go to the same places within Abu Dhabi emirate as the large coaches for the same price, but only if they have a full load.

Long-Distance Taxi These leave from the same place as minibuses. To catch an engaged taxi to Dubai, Sharjah or Al-Ain costs Dh150. Don't pay more than this. A shared taxi with five to seven people costs Dh30 per person. If you have luggage you will have to pay Dh30 for that too.

Car Rental There are a number of car hire companies on An-Nasr St near the corner of Khalid bin al-Walid St. You will also find agencies in the lobbies of most four- and five-star hotels.

Getting Around
To/From the Airport Bus No 901 runs from the main bus station to the airport around the clock, departing every 20 minutes (every 30 minutes between midnight and 6am). The fare is Dh3. Airport limos and Al-Ghazal taxis charge Dh65 from the airport to the city. A regular taxi to or from the city centre costs around Dh40.

Bus You will notice large municipal buses throughout Abu Dhabi. These are cheap – fares are only Dh1 within the city – but nearly useless for travellers because they follow no fixed routes. All of the buses originate at the main bus station on Hazza'a bin Zayed Rd. From there they go down one of the three main roads and end up in various industrial zones and labourers' camps on the mainland, where they turn around and head back into the souq.

Around Abu Dhabi

LIWA
لیوا
☎ 088
Liwa Oasis is a popular weekend getaway spot. Lying on the edge of the Empty Quarter, its main attractions are its 350m-high, salmon-tinged dunes. If you could walk southwest from Liwa, you wouldn't see another soul until you reached Yemen 1000km away. The long stretches of green agricultural plots stretching from the roadside to the base of these mountains of sand make

the place quite a sight. The oasis of Liwa is actually a belt of villages and farms spread out over a 150km arc of land. The ancestors of the ruling families of Abu Dhabi and Dubai came from this region.

The bus from Abu Dhabi (Dh10, three hours) takes you as far as **Medinat Zayed**. From there you must catch another bus south, which drops you at the Liwa bus station at **Mizaira'a** (Dh3, 30 minutes). This road is bordered by oil-funded oddities such as forestry projects and a massive sprinkler-fed fodder farm.

Notice Sheikh Zayed's huge palace on the right at the first roundabout you come to in Mizaira'a. The dune it sits on has been covered in lawn. There's not much else to see except a couple of three-towered forts: one is off the Arada road and the other is in the village of Attab.

Two local routes serve the oasis communities. The more interesting route goes east to the village of **Hameem** (Dh3), where the paved road ends and the bus turns around. The other route, 40km west to **Karima** (Dh2), is flatter and more open.

The **Liwa Hotel** (☎ 22000; e liwahtl@ emirates.net.ae; singles/doubles Dh312/372) sits on a high dune opposite Sheikh Zayed's palace, 4km west of Mizaira'a. It's a handsome building with a swimming pool, bar, tennis courts and comfortable rooms. The views looking south over the dunes are quite spectacular.

Liwa Resthouse (☎ 22075, fax 29311; rooms Dh165) is an older place with slightly musty rooms. It is about 8km west of the bus station along the Arada road. Breakfast is included in the rates.

A taxi to Liwa from Abu Dhabi will cost Dh160.

AL-AIN & BURAIMI
البریمی العین
☎ 03
The Buraimi Oasis straddles the border between Abu Dhabi and Oman. In the days before the oil boom, the oasis was a five-day overland journey by camel from Abu Dhabi. Today, the trip takes about two hours on a tree-lined freeway. You can cross freely between the UAE and Oman – people driving from Muscat pass through customs 50km before reaching the Omani town of Buraimi. Al-Ain is a leafy, sprawling city, conspicuously wealthier than Buraimi.

One of Al-Ain's main attractions come summer is the dry air – a welcome change from the humidity of the coast. The cool and quiet date palm plantations are nice to wander through at any time of the year.

Orientation

The Al-Ain/Buraimi area can be confusing. All of the streets in Al-Ain look pretty much the same. The main streets in Al-Ain are Khalifa bin Zayed St (known as Khalifa St) and Zayed bin Sultan St (known as Main St). The main north-south cross streets are Abu Bakr as-Siddiq St, which extends into Buraimi, and Al-Ain St. The two landmarks you need to know for navigational purposes are the Clock Tower and Coffeepot round-abouts.

Distances in both Al-Ain and Buraimi are large. You could walk from the bus or taxi station in Al-Ain to Buraimi's cheap hotels, but with any luggage it would be a hell of a hike, especially when it's hot.

Information

There is no tourist office in either city, but it's fairly easy to find most of the things worth seeing in Al-Ain by following the big purple tourist signs.

Money There are banks in Al-Ain near the Clock Tower roundabout. The area around the Grand Mosque has several money-changers. In Oman you'll see several banks on the main road. UAE currency is accepted in Buraimi at a standard rate of OR1 for

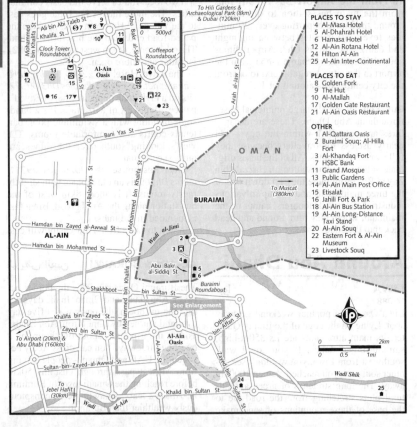

AL-AIN & BURAIMI

PLACES TO STAY
4 Al-Masa Hotel
5 Al-Dhahrah Hotel
6 Hamasa Hotel
12 Al-Ain Rotana Hotel
24 Hilton Al-Ain
25 Al-Ain Inter-Continental

PLACES TO EAT
8 Golden Fork
9 The Hut
10 Al-Mallah
17 Golden Gate Restaurant
21 Al-Ain Oasis Restaurant

OTHER
1 Al-Qattara Oasis
2 Buraimi Souq; Al-Hilla Fort
3 Al-Khandaq Fort
7 HSBC Bank
11 Grand Mosque
13 Public Gardens
14 Al-Ain Main Post Office
15 Etisalat
16 Jahili Fort & Park
18 Al-Ain Bus Station
19 Al-Ain Long-Distance Taxi Stand
20 Al-Ain Souq
22 Eastern Fort & Al-Ain Museum
23 Livestock Souq

Dh10 but you'll find that Omani currency is not as widely accepted in Al-Ain.

Post & Communications Al-Ain's **main post office** *(open 8am-1pm & 4pm-7pm Sat-Wed, 8am-4.30pm Thur, 8am-11am Fri)* is at the Clock Tower roundabout.

Eastern Fort & Al-Ain Museum

The museum *(50 fils; open 8am-1pm & 3.30pm-5.30pm Mon-Thur, 9am-11.30am Fri, 8am-1pm Sat Nov-Apr; 8am-1pm, 4.30pm-6.30pm Mon-Thur, 9am-11.30am Fri, 8am-1pm Sat May-Oct)* and fort are in the same compound, southeast of the overpass near the Coffeepot roundabout. This is one of the best museums in the country. The fort was the birthplace of the UAE's president, Sheikh Zayed. Be sure to see the *majlis* (meeting room) and the display of photographs of Al-Ain in the 1960s.

Jahili Fort & Park

This beautifully restored fort lies next to the Public Gardens, close to the Rotana Hotel. It's set inside a walled park *(admission Dh1; open 9am-10pm daily)*, but there's no entrance to the fort itself. Built in 1898, the fort is a handsome piece of traditional architecture, with the main corner tower graced with three concentric rings of serrated battlements.

Livestock Souq

You can see the entrance to this souq from the museum/fort car park. The souq, which sells everything from Brahmin cows to Persian cats, attracts people from all over the southern UAE as well as from northern Oman. The best time to be there is before 9am, when the trading is at its heaviest.

Buraimi Souq & Al-Hilla Fort

Buraimi's souq is bigger than it looks from the road. It's a very practical place selling fruit, vegetables, meat and household goods. The Al-Hilla Fort, right behind the souq, is closed to the public, but if you ask the workers nicely they may let you wander around.

Jebel Hafit

This jagged, 1160m-high, limestone mountain rears out of the plain south of Al-Ain. The views from the top, and on the winding drive up, are excellent. The summit is about 30km by road from the centre of Al-Ain.

To get there, head south from the Clock Tower roundabout and turn right at Khalid ibn Sultan St, then follow the purple tourist signs. A taxi will cost Dh50 for the round trip.

Hili Gardens

This combination public park and archaeological site *(admission Dh1; open 9am-10pm daily)* is 8km north of the centre of Al-Ain, off the Dubai Rd. The main attraction is the **Round Structure**, a 3rd millennium BC tomb, possibly connected with the Umm an-Nar culture.

Places to Stay

Al-Ain The only choices here are five-star hotels; all have bars and restaurants.

Al-Ain Inter-Continental *(☎ 768 6686; e alain@interconti.com; singles/doubles Dh671/700)* has spacious gardens, lots of sports facilities and Al-Ain's most popular expat bar, the **Horse & Jockey**.

Al-Ain Rotana Hotel *(☎ 751 5111; e alain.hotel@rotana.com; singles/doubles Dh760/814)* is probably the second-best of the three; it's bland but fairly new (it opened in 1999).

Hilton Al-Ain *(☎ 768 6666; e alhilton@emirates.net.ae; singles/doubles Dh600/670)* is the oldest of the three, and while comfortable it doesn't quite match up to its rivals.

Buraimi None of the hotels on the Omani side of the border serve alcohol.

Hamasa Hotel *(☎ 651 200, in the UAE ☎ 050-619 4248, fax 651 210; singles/doubles Dh120/150)* is the better of the two cheap hotels. It's 100m north of the border, on your right as you enter Buraimi from Al-Ain. The rooms are larger than at the Ad-Dhahrah, though not quite as clean.

Ad-Dhahrah Hotel *(☎ 650 492; e sirshirt@omantel.net.om; singles/doubles Dh130/160)* is a few doors north of the Hamasa Hotel. The rooms were clean (bathrooms spotless) but the beds seemed rather hard.

Al-Masa Hotel *(☎ 653 007, fax 653 008; singles/doubles Dh200/300)* is a new mid-range hotel 500m from the border, on the left as you enter Buraimi. All the rooms here have satellite TV as well as a small balcony.

Places to Eat

Al-Ain's main restaurant strip is on Khalifa St; finding a cheap eat is no problem.

Golden Fork (☎ 766 9033; Khalifa St; mains Dh7-15) is a branch of the popular Filipino restaurant chain, offering noodle dishes from Dh7 and mixed grills for Dh15.

Golden Gate Restaurant (☎ 766 2467; Al-Ain St; mains Dh15-25) is more upmarket and serves good Chinese and Filipino food.

Al-Mallah (☎ 766 9928; Khalifa St; mains Dh 20-40) serves generous portions of Lebanese cuisine. Mezzes cost around Dh7, shish tawouk (chicken shwarma) Dh20, but fish and prawn dishes can cost up to Dh40.

The Hut (☎ 751 6526; Khalifa St) is a Western-style coffee shop. It offers good cappuccino, latte and other coffee drinks as well as a wide selection of cakes, pastries and sandwiches. At Dh5 for a cappuccino the prices are a bit high, but the comfortable surroundings make up for it.

Al-Ain Oasis Restaurant (☎ 766 5340; Al-Ain Oasis; mains Dh15-30) is in a beautiful setting in the heart of the oasis. It's about a 500m walk from the Al-Ain Museum. The menu includes mixed grills and fish biryani (recommended).

In Buraimi your options are limited to biryani for about Dh10.

Getting There & Away

Air Al-Ain's airport is approximately 20km from the centre. Gulf Air offers direct services from Al-Ain to Bahrain, Doha and Muscat. EgyptAir, Royal Jordanian, Air India and PIA service the airport. You can call for **airport information** (☎ 785 5555).

Bus Buses run from Al-Ain to Abu Dhabi (Dh10, 2½ hours) every 30 minutes from 6am to 9.30pm. The bus station is behind the Al-Ain Co-op, near the Livestock Souq. Oman's bus company, ONTC, has three buses a day to and from the Ruwi station in Muscat (OR3.60, five hours) via Sohar. They leave from the bus station on the main street in Buraimi, just over the Al-Ain border.

Long-Distance Taxi Al-Ain's taxi station is in the big car park lot behind the Grand Mosque. There is another at the bus station near the livestock souq. It costs Dh30 to Dubai and Dh20 to Abu Dhabi.

Getting Around

Bus No 500 is an express service that runs every 30 minutes between Al-Ain's bus sta-

tion and the airport. The fare is Dh3 and the trip takes about 40 minutes. A taxi to or from Al-Ain should cost about Dh25. All of Al-Ain's buses run roughly on the 30 minutes from 6am to midnight. Most fares are Dh1. There are no local buses in Buraimi.

If you're going by taxi it's better to use the Al-Ain ones, which have meters. Al-Ain's taxis are gold-and-white, Buraimi's are orange-and-white.

Dubai دبي

☎ 04

In all the Middle East, there is no place quite like Dubai. It's a bastion of anything-goes capitalism – an Arab version of Hong Kong. You won't find a more easy-going place anywhere in the Gulf – or a place with better nightlife.

Orientation

This fast-growing city stretches for 35km along the coast between Jebel Ali and Sharjah. The new skyscraper strip along Sheikh Zayed Rd is the heart of the city. Old Dubai is two towns: Deira to the northeast, and Dubai to the southwest. They are separated by the khor (creek), an inlet of the Gulf. The Dubai side is sometimes called Bur Dubai.

Information

Tourist Office The **Department of Tourism & Commerce Marketing** (DTCM; ⓦ www .dubaitourism.co.ae) has three Welcome Bureaus you can call for information or for help in booking hotels, tours and car hire: at the airport arrivals area (☎ 224 5252; open 24 hr), in Baniyas Square in Deira (☎ 228 5000; open 9am-11pm daily) and about 40km out of town on Sheikh Zayed Rd on the way into Dubai from Abu Dhabi (☎ 884 6827; open 9am-9pm daily).

Money In central Deira, especially along Baniyas Rd and on Baniyas Square, every other building seems to contain a bank or a moneychanger. In Bur Dubai there are lots of moneychangers (though most of them only take cash) around the abra (water taxi) docks. There are many ATMs on shopping streets and at shopping malls.

AmEx is represented in Dubai by **Kanoo Travel** (☎ 336 5000, fax 336 6006; 1st floor,

Hermitage Bldg, Za'abeel Rd, Karama; open 8.30am-1pm, 3pm-6.30pm Sat-Thur), next to the main post office. It won't cash travellers cheques but will hold mail for AmEx clients. Address mail c/o American Express, Client's Mail, PO Box 290, Dubai, UAE.

Post The **main post office** (Za'abeel Rd; open 8am-11.30pm Sat-Wed, 8am-10pm Thur, 8am-noon Fri) is on the Bur Dubai side of the Creek, near 25A Rd in Karama. It has a philatelic bureau.

The **Deira post office** (Al-Sabkha Rd; open 8am-midnight Sat-Wed, 8am-1pm, 4pm-8pm Thur) is near the intersection with Baniyas Rd.

Telephone & Fax There's an **Etisalat office** (cnr Baniyas & Omar ibn al-Khattab Rds; open 24hr) in Deira, recognisable by the giant golf ball structure atop the building.

Email & Internet Access The **Internet Café** (☎ 345 3441; Al-Dhiyafah Rd; open 10am-3am Sat-Thur, 2pm-3am Fri) charges Dh15 per hour. The **Al-Jalssa Internet Café** (☎ 351 4617; Al-Ain Centre; Khalid bin al-Waleed Rd; open 9am-1am) charges Dh10 an hour, as does **Inet** (☎ 344 2602; Hamarain Centre, Abu Bakr al-Siddiq Rd, Rigga).

Bookshops One of Dubai's best bookshops, **Magrudy Books** is in the shopping centre of the same name on Jumeira Rd. In the centre, try **Book Corner** at Deira City Centre or on Al-Dhiyafah Rd in Jumeira. Most of the larger hotels have small selections in their bookshops. For second-hand books, try **Bookzone** in the Al-Rais Centre on Al-Mankhool Rd.

Medical Services Dubai's **Rashid Hospital** (☎ 371 4000) is on the Dubai side of the Creek, just east of the Al-Maktoum Bridge. The **New Dubai Hospital** (☎ 222 9171) is off Al-Khaleej Rd in Deira.

The Creek

The obvious place to start your tour of Dubai is at the waterfront. *Abras* (motorised boat taxis) make the crossing all day for 50 fils per person. The best idea is to hire one for an hour or so. For around Dh50 (for the whole boat, not per person) the captain should take you most of the way to Al-Maktoum Bridge

and back. Take a walk along the cargo docks on the Deira side of the Creek. Dhows bound for every port from Kuwait to Mumbai to Aden dock here to load and unload all sorts of interesting cargo.

Dubai Museum

Dubai's museum (adult/child Dh3/1; open 8.30am-8.30pm Sat-Thur, 3pm-9pm Fri) occupies the Al-Fahidi Fort on the Dubai side of the Creek, just southeast of the Ruler's Office. Al-Fahidi Fort was built in the early 19th century and is thought to be the oldest building in Dubai. The displays explain the pearling industry, traditional town life and local handicrafts, and there are interactive displays on the region's flora and fauna. It's well worth a visit.

The Bastakia Quarter

This waterfront area has some old windtower houses that were once the homes of wealthy merchants from southern Iran. Built between 1900 and 1930, the neighbourhood is now being restored. In a few years Bastakia will be home to cafés and cultural institutions. The **Majlis Gallery** (Al-Fahidi St) occupies an old house typical of the area, and has an excellent selection of works by local and visiting artists.

Sheikh Saeed al-Maktoum House

The house of Sheikh Saeed (adult/child Dh2/1; open 8.30am-9pm Sat-Thur, 3pm-10pm Fri), the grandfather of Dubai's present ruler, is now a museum of pre-oil times. The 30-room house was built in 1896 during the reign of Sheikh Maktoum bin Hasher al-Maktoum. The house was made a museum in 1986 and houses an **exhibition of photographs**, from the 1940s, '50s and '60s, documenting the development of Dubai. It is amazing to see how different the place looked only a few decades ago. It lies next to the Heritage and Diving villages in Dubai.

Heritage & Diving Villages

These villages (Al-Shindagha Rd; admission free; open 7.30am-2pm, 3pm-9pm daily) lie next to the Creek, in the heart of the old Shindagha neighbourhood. The Diving Village shows displays of pearl diving, once the livelihood of the city. The Heritage Village re-creates traditional Bedouin and coastal village life, complete with *barasti* homes, a

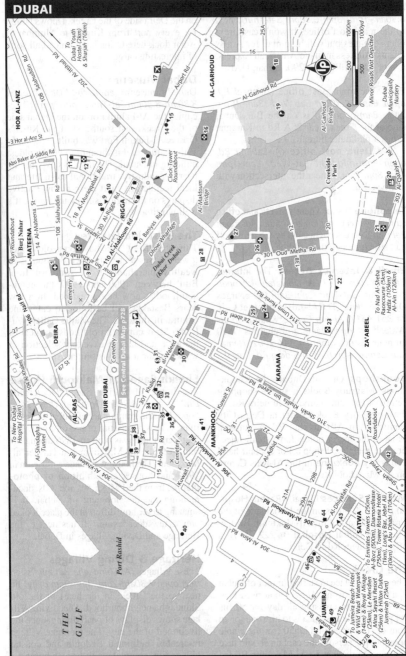

DUBAI

DUBAI

PLACES TO STAY		OTHER			
5	Hilton Dubai Creek; Verre	1	Al-Maktoum Hospital	25	Kanoo Travel; Hermitage Building
7	Avari Dubai Hotel	2	Al-Ghurair Centre	26	Rashid Hospital
8	Quality Inn Horizon	3	Deira Taxi Stand; Minibuses to Other Emirates	27	British Council
10	Holiday Inn Downtown			28	Palace
11	JW Marriott Hotel	4	Etisalat	29	British Embassy
15	Budget	6	Avis	30	Bur Juman Centre
32	Regal Plaza Hotel	12	Hamarain Centre Shopping Centre; Inet Internet Cafe	31	Banks
36	Panorama Hotel			33	Al-Jalssa Internet Cafe
38	Admiral Plaza Hotel	13	DNATA Airline Centre; Oman Transport	34	Al-Khaleej Centre; Automatic Restaurant
39	Hyde Park Hotel				
41	Golden Sands 3	14	Hertz	35	Al-Rais Centre; Bookzone
44	Rydges Plaza	15	Deira City Centre (Shopping Mall); Book Corner; Cinestar	40	Naif Marine Services
		17	Dubai International Airport	42	Dubai World Trade Centre
PLACES TO EAT		18	The Irish Village		
9	Automatic Restaurant	19	Dubai Creek Golf & Yacht Club	45	Book Corner
22	Holiday Inn Bur Dubai; Fakhreldine			46	Internet Cafe
		20	Grand Cineplex	48	The Alamo; Sho Chos; Dubai Marine Beach Resort
37	Kwality	21	Wafi City Centre; Carters		
43	Ravi Restaurant	23	Lamcy Plaza	49	Jumeira Mosque
47	Japengo	24	Main Post Office	51	Magrudy Books
50	Lime Tree Cafe				

traditional coffeehouse and a small souq where you can buy freshly made *dosa* (a flat, grilled bread made of flour and water). There are also some traditional pottery and weaving workshops. The shops here sell rather nice traditional handicrafts, Bedouin jewellery and pottery.

Souqs
The **Deira souq** *(Spice souq)*, offers a taste of traditional Dubai and is a wonderful place to take in the aroma of spices, nuts and dried fruits. The **Deira covered souq**, off Al-Sabkha Rd, sells just about anything.

Deira's **Gold souq**, on and around Sikkat al-Khail St, is probably the largest such market in Arabia and is a 'must see'.

Wild Wadi Waterpark
This 4.8-hectare water park *(Jumeira Rd; adult/child Dh95/75; open 11am-7pm daily Sept-May, 1pm-9pm June-Aug)*, next to the Jumeira Beach Hotel, is one of Dubai's most impressive leisure facilities. The 24 rides are all interconnected, and some reach speeds of 80km/h. Towels and lockers can be rented for Dh5, while body boards and tubes are free.

Nad al-Sheba Racecourse
Dubai's fine racecourse *(admission free, members' stand Dh60)* is 5km southeast of the Creek. From November to March races are held from 7pm (9pm during Ramadan).

Jockeys from all over the world compete here. Check newspapers for details. The ruling Al-Maktoum family are leading members of the international horse-racing fraternity, so a visit here is a great opportunity for people-watching.

Places to Stay – Budget
Dubai Youth Hostel *(☎ 298 8161; e uae yha@emirates.net.ae; Al-Nahda Rd; dorm beds Dh35-50, singles Dh60-80, doubles Dh120-145)* has the cheapest accommodation in town. The hostel has an old wing with two- and three-bed dorm rooms, and a new wing with very comfortable single and double rooms. Women, as well as men, can be accommodated and there are separate rooms for families.

Dubai's cheap hotels are concentrated around the Deira souqs and Bur Dubai. Some hotels advertise themselves as a 'family hotel', which basically means no prostitution. They will usually accept single women. Beware of the ultra cheap hotels: apart from probably being turned away you'll find that they are more brothel than hotel.

Deira The respectable **Al-Khayyam Hotel** *(☎ 226 4211; e khayamh@emirates.net.ae; Souq Deira St; singles/doubles Dh150/180)* is a 'family' hotel (so no 'night visitors') with only 26 rooms, which are a little on the small side, but clean.

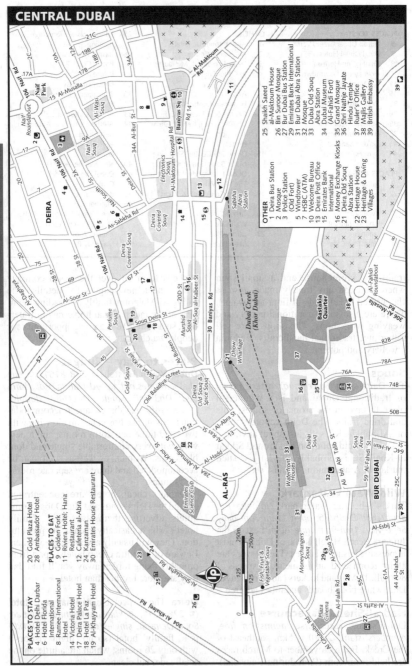

Gold Plaza Hotel (☎ 225 0240, fax 225 0259; Souq Deira St; singles/doubles with balcony Dh125/150), a family hotel, is at the entrance to the Gold Souq. The rooms are small but have tiled floors. Some of the bathrooms need renovating, but otherwise it's not bad.

Hotel La Paz (☎ 226 8800; e lapazhtl@emirates.net.ae; Souq Deira St; singles/doubles Dh120/170) is a clean family hotel with friendly English-speaking staff, but the quality of the rooms is only average.

Deira Palace Hotel (☎ 229 0120, fax 225 5889; 67 St; singles/doubles Dh130/150) is a large family hotel, with clean rooms but slightly uncomfortable beds.

Bur Dubai The Hyde Park Hotel (☎ 393 9373; e hydepark@emirates.net.ae; 38 St; singles/ doubles Dh165/220) is one of the few cheap hotels on this side of the Creek. It is basic but clean, and has a handy location near Al-Ghubaiba bus station.

Panorama Hotel (☎ 351 8518; e panhotel@emirates.net.ae; Al-Mankhool Rd; singles/doubles Dh250/350) is a rather old building, but it's in a good location and the rooms are quite large, though not noise-proofed. Rates are negotiable for longer stays. The hotel's bar is dodgy.

Places to Stay – Mid-Range

Deira Opposite the Al-Sabkha bus station, Hotel Florida International (☎ 224 7777; e floridai@emirates.net.ae; Al-Sabkha Rd; singles/doubles Dh300/400) is a new hotel in the heart of Deira. The rooms are on the small side but nicely furnished.

Ramee International Hotel (☎ 224 0222; e rameedxb@emirates.net.ae; 9C St; singles/doubles Dh250/350), a busy hotel off Bani-yas Square, is good value for money.

Victoria Hotel (☎ 226 9626, fax 226 9575; 20 St; singles/doubles Dh200/250), in an alley near the Al-Sabkha and Al-Maktoum Hospital Rds intersection, has decent rooms.

Hotel Delhi Darbar (☎ 273 3555, fax 273 3737; Naif Rd; singles/doubles Dh175/250) is an Indian-oriented establishment. It's better than most of the hotels in the area, featuring spacious clean rooms with decent bathrooms, minifridge and TV. There's an Indian restaurant on the ground floor.

Bur Dubai The Admiral Plaza Hotel (☎ 521 111; e admplaza@emirates.net.ae; Al-Nahda St; singles/doubles Dh240/350) offers well-appointed but rather cramped rooms.

Ambassador Hotel (☎ 393 9444; e amb hotel@emirates.net.ae; Al-Falah Rd; singles/doubles Dh312.50/475) is one of the oldest hotels in Dubai (established 1968).

Golden Sands 3 (☎ 355 5551; e gldn snds@emirates.net.ae; 10B St, Mankhool; rooms from Dh322) and its neighbouring building Golden Sands 5 is a good place to stay if you plan to be in Dubai for more than a week. A one-bedroom apartment is much like a three-star hotel room, except with an oven and washer-dryer. Stays of longer than a week can be negotiated down to about Dh150 per day.

Places to Stay – Top End

Deira The three-star Quality Inn Horizon (☎ 227 1919; e qualitin@emirates.net.ae; Al-Rigga Rd; singles/doubles Dh540/660) is a comfortable hotel with decent-sized rooms. There's a small rooftop swimming pool.

Avari Dubai Hotel (☎ 295 6666; e avari gst@emirates.net.ae; 45C St; singles/doubles Dh847/957, 2-room suite Dh1320) is an mid-standard hotel. It's set back off the west side of Abu Baker al-Siddiq Rd, near the Clock Tower roundabout.

Holiday Inn Downtown (☎ 228 8889; e hidowtwn@emirates.net.ae; 37 St; singles/doubles Dh550/650, suites Dh1260), north of Al-Rigga Rd, has large and luxurious rooms. It's a fairly subdued business-oriented hotel.

JW Marriott Hotel (☎ 262 4444; e marri ott@emirates.net.ae; Abu Baker al-Siddiq Rd; rooms from Dh1260, executive suites Dh3000) is one of the most impressive five-star hotels in Dubai. It is beautifully decorated and standard rooms are very luxurious and spacious.

Dubai Hilton Creek (☎ 227 1111, e hil tonck@emirates.net.ae, Baniyas Rd, Rigga; rooms from Dh1440) is a classy boutique hotel with a stunning interior – all glass, chrome, stainless steel and wood. The rooms feature curved wooden wardrobes and black leather armchairs. Some rooms overlook the dhow wharf on the Creek.

Dubai Run by a reputable Indian hotel company, Regal Plaza Hotel (☎ 355 6633; e rameedxb@emirates.net.ae; singles/doubles Dh600/700; Al-Mankhool Rd) is near the corner with Khalid bin al-Waleed Rd. It has a pub on the ground floor as well as a swimming pool.

Rydges Plaza (☎ 398 2222; e rydges@ emirates.net.ae; cnr Al-Dhiyafah & Al-Mankhool Rds, Satwa; rooms Dh850, executive suites Dh1000) has an ordinary exterior which belies the fine refurbishing job they've done on the rooms. Rates are highly negotiable (around Dh300 per night if you stay a week).

Emirates Towers (☎ 330 000; e eth@emirates-towers-hotel.com; Sheikh Zayed Rd; singles & doubles from Dh1440) is the tallest hotel in the Middle East, a slick, ultramodern monument to Dubai's confidence. The decor is Armani meets Tokyo. The pricey bar on the 51st floor has amazing views.

Beach Hotels The **Jumeira Beach Hotel** (☎ 348 0000; e reservations@jumeirahinternational.com; Jumeira Rd, Umm Suqeim; singles/doubles Dh1560/1650) is designed as a cresting wave. With 618 rooms it is one of the biggest hotels in Dubai, and has 19 bars, cafés and restaurants.

Five-star hotels run along the waterfront between Jumeira Beach Hotel and Jebel Ali. All these hotels are like mini-resorts, but they are a long way from the centre – about 25 minutes and costing up to Dh55 in a taxi.

Royal Mirage (☎ 399 9999; e royalmirage@royalmiragedubai.com; Al-Sufouh Rd; singles/doubles Dh1950/2160) is a fantasy of an Arabian palace, with date palms, burbling canals and a spectacular lobby.

Le Meridien Mina Seyahi Resort (☎ 399 3333; e reservations@lemeridien-minaseyahi.com; Al-Sufouh Rd; rooms with land/sea view Dh1200/1400) is a smallish resort hotel with all the five-star accoutrements.

Hilton Dubai Jumeirah (☎ 399 1111; e hiltonjb@emirates.net.ae; Al-Sufouh Rd; singles/doubles Dh1250/1350) is one of the nicer hotels on this strip. Opened in 2000, it has a spacious stretch of beach frontage.

Places to Eat

Budget Next to the abra dock in Deira, **Cafeteria al-Abra** is good for a quick, cheap meal while watching the activity on the Creek. It has shwarma and samosas along with fruit juice, soda, and coconut juice served fresh in the shell.

Golden Fork (☎ 224 3834; Baniyas Square) has an odd combination of oriental (mainly Filipino) and Western fast food. The Western food is cheaper and better; you can get three pieces of fried chicken with fries and bread, or a burger, salad and fries, for Dh10.

Emirates House Restaurant (☎ 352 2597; Al-Esbij St, Bur Dubai; mains Dh3-7) specialises in South Indian vegetarian dishes such as thalis and dosas. It's simple, but clean and comfortable, and certainly easy on your budget.

Kwality (☎ 393 6563; Khalid bin al-Waleed Rd; mains Dh12-20) offers good-value Indian dishes such as chicken makhani (butter chicken) and rogan josh (lamb curry), as well as many vegetarian options.

Lime Tree Café (☎ 349 8498; Jumeira Rd) is in a converted villa near the Jumeirah Mosque. Along with excellent coffee (a cappuccino costs Dh10), the kitchen serves up an ever-changing range of muffins, sandwiches and quiches.

Ravi Restaurant (☎ 331 5353; Satwa) is a Pakistani restaurant just off Al-Dhiyafah Rd. A meal consisting of a curry, biryani, or chicken tikka with bread, salad, raita (yogurt-based side dish) and a drink comes to about Dh15. Chinese dishes are also served.

Mid-Range & Top-End The **Automatic Restaurant** (☎ 227 7824; Al-Rigga Rd; mezze Dh12-15, mains Dh25-45) is a clean and comfortable Lebanese restaurant. There is also a branch on Al-Mankhool Rd in the Al-Khaleej Centre (☎ 355 0333).

Al-Borz (☎ 331 8777; Al-Durreh Tower, Sheikh Zayed Rd; kebabs Dh30-45) is a charming Iranian restaurant in a tower block next to the Crowne Plaza Hotel. The lamb, chicken or fish kebabs are deliciously tender. Soups and salads come free.

Japengo (☎ 345 4979; Palm Strip Shopping Centre, Jumeira Rd; mains Dh25-50) is a cheerfully trendy place, serving coffee, noodles and sushi in a casual environment.

Casa Mia (☎ 282 4040; mains Dh50-85; open 12.30pm-3pm, 8pm-11.30pm) is ably run by an Italian couple. The menu is interesting and the restaurant offers an excellent wine list. It's behind the Le Meridien Hotel, near the airport.

Hana (☎ 222 2131; Riviera Hotel; mains Dh30-50; open noon-3pm, 7pm-11pm) offers three different menus: Japanese, Thai and Chinese. The sushi platter (Dh45) is delicious. The food is authentic and reasonably priced, but alcohol is not served.

Fakhreldine (☎ 336 6000; Holiday Inn Bur Dubai, 19 St, Oud Metha; mains Dh40-80) gets our vote for Dubai's best restaurant. All the classic Lebanese dishes are represented. The Liwan Fakhreldine is a cheaper outdoors section, with tents to relax in and grills for around Dh30.

Kanzaman (☎ 393 9913; Heritage & Diving Village, Shindagha; starters Dh10-15, mains Dh30-50) is by the Creek, and offers a long list of mezzes, grills, steaks and seafood. The breezes off the Creek offer cool relief, but on a winter's night it pays to bring warm clothing.

Verre (☎ 227 1111; Hilton Dubai Creek; Baniyas Rd, Rigga; mains Dh80-120) is a franchise by British celebrity chef Gordon Ramsay. The emphasis is on elegant, fresh food without the frills. The decor is stark and modern – lots of chrome and glass.

Entertainment

Check *Time Out* to see what's happening each month around town. The **Irish Village** is popular, with outdoor seating and a menu featuring fish and chips. **Carters** is a bar and restaurant with a colonial Egyptian theme. The terrace is a good place to relax with a drink. **Long's Bar** (Tower Rotana Hotel, Sheikh Zayed Rd) is one of Dubai's more active music venues, with an ever-changing list of bands and DJs and a small dance floor. **Sho Chos** (Dubai Marine Beach Resort) is a groovy bar with a resident DJ, while **The Alamo** (Dubai Marine Beach Resort) is a popular drinking den.

You can catch relatively recent Western flicks at **Cinestar** (Deira City Centre) and the **Grand Cineplex**, near the Wafi City shopping centre.

Shopping

If you're looking for cheap electronics try the area at the Al-Sabkha Rd end of Baniyas Square. The **gold souq** has to be seen to be believed: even veterans of Middle Eastern gold markets are likely to be blown away be the sheer scale of it. Practically every modern consumer item is on sale somewhere at the vast **Deira City Centre** and **Wafi City** shopping centres.

If you're looking for Middle Eastern souvenirs, including Bedouin jewellery, there are

a couple of small shops along Baniyas Rd near the *abra* dock that are worth browsing around. For similar merchandise try the shops in the **Heritage Village** on Al-Shindagha Rd.

Getting There & Away

Air You can fly to almost anywhere from Dubai international airport (general ☎ 224 5555, flight inquiries ☎ 206 6666). Dubai is the base for **Emirates Airlines** (☎ 214 4444, fax 204 4040; DNATA Airline Centre, Al-Maktoum Rd, Deira).

Bus Intercity buses operate within the Dubai emirate only. To go to another emirate, you have to take a Dubai Transport minibus. There are hourly buses every day to Hatta (Dh10, 1¼ hours) between 6.10am and 9pm. The Hatta buses leave from the Deira bus station, near the gold souq, and stop at the Bur Dubai bus station on Al-Ghubaiba Rd. There are two buses a day to Muscat, Oman (adult one way/return Dh50/90, child Dh30/50, 5½ hours). These depart at 7.30am and 4.30pm from the parking lot of the DNATA Airline Centre on Al-Maktoum Rd, Deira. Tickets are available at the Oman Transport office at the DNATA Airline Centre or from the bus driver. For information, call ☎ 203 3923.

Long-Distance Taxi You can only take these to other emirates 'engaged'. You'll need to haggle over a price, but it should be roughly five times as much as the individual minibus fares in the following section.

Minibuses Dubai Transport's minibuses carry 14 passengers and run every 15 or 20 minutes depending on when they fill up. They are clean and efficient.

Minibuses leave Deira from the bus and taxi station near the intersection of Omar ibn al-Khattab and Al-Rigga Rds. Prices per person are: Sharjah, Dh5; Ajman, Dh7; Umm al-Qaiwain, Dh10; Ras al-Khaimah, Dh20; Fujairah, Dh25; and Khor Fakkan Dh30.

Minibuses for Abu Dhabi and Al-Ain leave from the Bur Dubai bus station on Al-Ghubaiba Rd. It's Dh33 to Abu Dhabi or Al-Ain.

Car Car rental starts at about Dh140 for one day (including insurance) for a small sedan such as a Mazda 626. Rates fall to about Dh120 per day for a week, and Dh90 per day for a month. You'll need a credit card and drivers licence. There are dozens of agencies listed in the phone book; the smaller ones may offer slightly better rates. Major agencies include:

Avis (☎ 295 7121, W www.avis.com) Al-Maktoum Rd; (☎ 224 5219) Airport arrivals hall, open 24 hours

Budget (☎ 282 3030) Al-Maktoum Rd just before Cargo Village; (☎ 224 5192) Airport arrivals hall, open 24 hours

Diamondlease (☎ 331 3172, W www.diamondlease.com) Sahara Towers, Sheikh Zayed Rd

Hertz (☎ 282 4422, W www.hertz-uae.com) Al-Maktoum Rd, just before Cargo Village; (☎ 224 5222) Airport arrivals hall, open 24 hours

Getting Around

To/From the Airport From the Deira bus station, bus Nos 4, 11 and 15 go to the airport about every 30 minutes for Dh1. Only the sand-coloured Dubai Transport taxis are allowed to pick up passengers at the airport, which start with a Dh20 surcharge. A ride from the Deira souq area to the airport in a metered cab costs about Dh12; from Bur Dubai it costs about Dh17.

Bus Local buses operate out of stations in both Deira and Bur Dubai. The Deira bus station is off Al-Khor St, near the intersection with Al-Soor St, and there's the Bur Dubai bus station on Al-Ghubaiba Rd. Numbers and routes are posted on the buses in English as well as Arabic. Free route maps are available at both bus stations. Fares are Dh1 to Dh3.50. The best way to get to where you're going is just to say where you want to go and someone will point you to the right bus. Tell the bus driver where you're going and he'll tell you when to get off.

Taxi Dubai has a large taxi fleet, many of which will beep you if they see you walking. Nearly all have meters, starting at Dh3. There are a handful of nonmetered taxis, with which you'll have to negotiate a fare. You can also call **Dubai Transport** (☎ 208 0808) for a taxi.

Abra Abras leave constantly from early morning until about midnight. There are two routes. The one closer to the mouth of the Creek runs between Bur Dubai Abra Dock and Deira Old Souq Abra Dock, while the

other is between Dubai Old Souq Abra Dock and Sabkha Abra Dock. The fare is 50 fils, collected once you are out on the water.

Around Dubai

HATTA   حتا
☎ 04

An enclave of Dubai nestled in the Hajar Mountains, Hatta is a popular weekend getaway. It is 105km from Dubai by road, about 20km of which runs through Omani territory. There is no customs check but remember that if you are driving a rental car your insurance does not cover accidents in Oman.

Hatta's **Heritage Village** (admission free; open 8am-8pm Sat-Thur, 2.30pm-8pm Fri), a re-creation of a traditional mountain village, includes a restored fort and displays on traditional arts and crafts. It's a pleasant place to explore for an hour or two. Opening hours can be erratic, however. The enclave's other attractions are its relatively cool, dry climate (compared with that of the coast) and the mountain scenery. It is also a good jumping-off point for off-road trips through the mountains. There's a **rug souq** about 12km west of Hatta on the main highway.

Hatta Fort Hotel (☎ 852 3211; e hfhho tel@emirates.net.ae; rooms Sat-Wed Dh524, Thur-Fri Dh780) is the only place to stay in Hatta. The chalet-style accommodation is surrounded by lush gardens, and the hotel has lots of sporting facilities. The hotel's coffee shop is a popular place for day-trippers to have lunch; mains cost around Dh30.

There are minibuses every hour from 6.10am to 9pm between Dubai's Deira bus station and Hatta (Dh10, 1¼ hours). In Hatta, the buses depart from the red bus shelter near the Hatta Mountains Restaurant.

The Northern Emirates

SHARJAH   الشارقة
☎ 06

The third largest of the seven emirates, Sharjah promotes itself as the cultural capital of the UAE and, with the proliferation of new museums, galleries and theatres in the last couple of years, it's easy to see why. Sharjah has some of the most interesting architecture in the country. Its new souq offers shopping to rival that of Dubai and its restored old souq offers a window on an older way of life that has now all but disappeared.

Sharjah has recently introduced laws banning revealing clothing (cover your arms and legs), and forbidding non-married couples from staying in the same room.

Orientation

Sharjah's business district is the area between the Corniche and Al-Zahra Rd, from the Central Market to Sheikh Mohammed bin Saqr al-Qasimi Rd (or Mohammed Saqr St). This is not a huge area and it's pretty easy to get around. Driving here is a horror though, because of the manic traffic and the many roundabouts with street signs in tiny print. The main road to Dubai, Al-Wahda Rd, suffers morning and afternoon peak-hour gridlock every weekday.

Information

On Burj Ave (also called Bank St), nearly every building contains a bank. Money-changers can be found on the small streets immediately to the east and west of it. The **main post office** (open 7.30am-8.30pm Sat-Wed, 7.30am-5.30pm Thur) is on Government House Square.

Al-Hisn Fort

This fort (admission free; open 9am-1pm & 5pm-8pm Tues-Sun, 5pm-8pm Fri), originally built in 1822, has been fully restored and houses a fascinating collection of photographs and documents, mainly from the 1930s. As you enter the fort there is a room on your left showing footage of the first Imperial Airways flights from London, which landed here on their way to India. Other rooms have displays of weapons, jewellery, currency and items used in the pearl trade. The fort sits in the middle of Burj Ave.

The Heritage Area

All the buildings in this block, just inland from the Corniche, between Burj Ave and Al-Mina St, have been faithfully constructed incorporating traditional designs and materials such as sea rock and gypsum. Coming from Burj Ave, the first place you come across is **Literature Square**. The **House of Poetry** facing the square some-

times holds public poetry readings. Across from here is **Bait al-Gharbi**, a house built around a courtyard displaying traditional costumes, jewellery, ceramics and furniture. The **Heritage Museum** (admission free; open 8am-1pm & 5pm-8pm Tues-Sun, 5pm-8pm Fri) displays much the same thing; it's worth exploring just for the traditional architecture of the building. Next door is the **Islamic Museum** (admission free; open 8am-1pm & 5pm-8pm Tues-Sun, 5pm-8pm Fri), which should definitely not be missed. It includes a large collection of coins from all over the Islamic world and a number of handwritten Qurans and writing implements. At these museums, Wednesday is usually for women only. There are more restored buildings north of the Heritage Museum, towards the Corniche, including the **Majlis of Ibrahim Mohammed al-Midfa** and **Al-Midfa House**.

The Arts Area

Tucked away on the north side of Burj Ave from the Heritage Area is the Arts Area, where there is an imposing **Art Museum** (open 9am-1pm & 5pm-8pm Sat-Thur, 5pm-8pm Fri) exhibiting modern art by local and foreign artists. It's the finest art gallery in the UAE. Upstairs is a permanent exhibition of 19th-century European paintings and lithographs.

The **Bait Obeid al-Shamsi**, next to the Art Museum, is a restored house used as artists' studios; check out the intricate pillars on the upper level. The **Arts Café**, on the main square, serves traditional hot milk with ginger for about Dh1. Next to the Arts Café are the **Very Special Arts Centre**, which is both a workshop and a gallery for disabled artists, and the **Emirates Fine Arts Society**, which also displays the works of local artists.

Souqs

Tucked away in the alleys between the Heritage Area and the Corniche is the **Al-Arsah Souq**. The *areesh* (palm frond) roof and wooden pillars give it a traditional feel and it's a lovely place to wander around and buy Arabic and Bedouin souvenirs. Despite the efforts to re-create a traditional atmosphere you can buy all kinds of non-Arabic souvenirs here too.

The **Central Market** (Blue Souq; Corniche), just south of the King Faisal Mosque,

UNITED ARAB EMIRATES

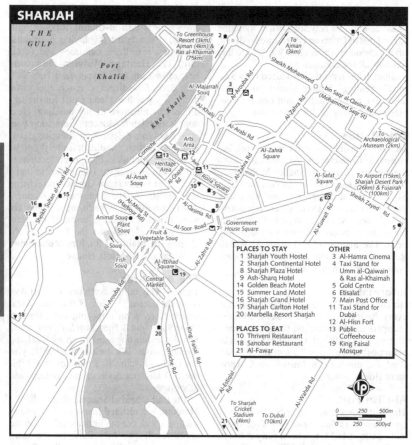

SHARJAH

THE GULF

Port Khalid

To Greenhouse Resort (3km), Ajman (4km) & Ras al-Khaimah (75km)

To Ajman (3km)

Sheikh Mohammed

bin Saqr al-Qasimi Rd (Mohammed Saqr St)

Al-Majarrah Souq

Al-Arouba Rd

Al-Khalij

Khor Khalid

Al-Arabi Rd

Al-Zahra Rd

To Archaeological Museum (2km)

Corniche

Burj Ave

Arts Area

Al-Zahra Square

Heritage Area

Al-Arsah Souq

Al-Ghazal Rd

Rolla Square

Al-Zahra Rd

Al-Safat Square

To Airport (15km), Sharjah Desert Park (26km) & Fujairah (100km)

Sheikh Zayed Rd

Al-Mina St (Harbour Rd)

Al-Qasimia Rd

Al-Kuwait Rd

Sheikh Sultan al-Awal Rd

Animal Souq

Plant Souq

Al-Soor Road

Government House Square

Fruit & Vegetable Souq

Fish Souq

Al-Ittihad Square

Al-Zahra Rd

Central Market

Al-Arouba Rd

King Faisal Rd

Corniche Rd

Al-Estiqlal Rd

Al-Wahda Rd

To Sharjah Cricket Stadium (4km)

To Dubai (10km)

PLACES TO STAY	OTHER
1 Sharjah Youth Hostel	3 Al-Hamra Cinema
2 Sharjah Continental Hotel	4 Taxi Stand for
8 Sharjah Plaza Hotel	Umm al-Qaiwain
9 Ash-Sharq Hotel	& Ras al-Khaimah
14 Golden Beach Motel	5 Gold Centre
15 Summer Land Motel	6 Etisalat
16 Sharjah Grand Hotel	7 Main Post Office
17 Sharjah Carlton Hotel	11 Taxi Stand for
20 Marbella Resort Sharjah	Dubai
	12 Al-Hisn Fort
PLACES TO EAT	13 Public
10 Thriveni Restaurant	Coffeehouse
18 Sanobar Restaurant	19 King Faisal
21 Al-Fawar	Mosque

0   250   500m
0   250   500yd

has the best selection of oriental carpets in the country, and also hundreds of shops selling souvenirs and antiques from Oman, India, Thailand and Iran. The gold-domed **Al-Majarrah Souq**, on the Corniche, has about 50 shops selling textiles, perfumes and clothes. The **Gold Centre** (cnr Sheikh Zayed & Al-Wahda Rds) has about 40 stores selling jewellery, diamonds, gold coins and everything else that glitters. The **Animal Souq**, **Plant Souq** and **Fish Souq** may also be worth a visit.

Sharjah Archaeological Museum

This museum (Al-Hizam al-Akhdar Rd near Cultural Square; admission free; open 9am-1pm & 5pm-8pm Mon-Sat, 5pm-8pm Fri, men only Sat, women only Mon) covers the earliest archaeological finds in the emirate (dating from 5000 BC) up to the beginning of the Islamic era.

Sharjah Cricket Stadium

The UAE's biggest cricket stadium (☎ 532 2991; Industrial Area 5, 2nd Industrial Rd) lies south of Al-Wahda Rd. With room for around 22,000 spectators, it sees regular one-day matches between international teams in March and April and October and November.

Matches between Subcontinental teams, such as India and Pakistan, pull the biggest crowds. Tickets cost up to Dh150 to watch a final in the members pavilion, or as low as Dh20 for seats in the North Stand during lead-up games.

Places to Stay – Budget

Sharjah Youth Hostel (☎ 522 5070; Al-Zahra Rd; dorm beds for members/nonmembers Dh30/45) is about 1.5km northeast of Al-Zahra Square, next to the Children's Hospital. The hostel is only open for men.

Sharjah Plaza Hotel (☎ 561 7000, fax 561 8000; Al-Qasimia Rd; singles/doubles Dh100/ 120), Government House Square, is basic but clean and the rates are negotiable for longer stays.

Al-Sharq Hotel (☎ 562 0000, fax 562 0011; Rolla Square; singles/doubles Dh150/ 200) is a small hotel in the centre of town, handy for transport to Dubai. The rooms are simple and on the small side.

Places to Stay – Mid-Range

Greenhouse Resort (☎ 522 4260, fax 522 4631, Al-Muntazah Rd; one-bedroom flat Dh250) is in a quiet residential area close to Ajman. Al-Muntazah Rd is an extension of the Corniche. The apartments are modern and the resort has two swimming pools and a small gymnasium.

The following hotels are all on Sheikh Sultan al-Awal Rd, southwest of the centre on the other side of Khor Khalid.

Golden Beach Motel (☎ 5281 331, fax 528 1151; rooms Dh200) has large rooms with kitchens but could use refurbishment. Each room has a balcony overlooking the beach.

Summer Land Motel (☎ 528 1321, fax 528 0745; rooms Dh200) has rooms with sitting area. It caters to a largely Russian clientele.

Places to Stay – Top End

Sharjah Continental Hotel (☎ 565 7777, fax 565 0090; Corniche; singles/doubles Dh345/ 402.50) is Sharjah's top hotel. If you are in Sharjah on a weekend this rate drops to Dh300 for a double, including tax and two breakfasts.

Marbella Resort Sharjah (☎ 5741 1111; e maresort@emirates.net.ae; Corniche; junior suites Dh517.50, master suites Dh805) has nicely decorated Spanish-style villas set among trees and gardens.

The following top-end places are outside the city centre on Sheikh Sultan al-Awal Rd.

Sharjah Grand Hotel (☎ 528 5557, fax 528 2861; singles/doubles Dh460/575) is a slightly blowzy 1980s-era beach resort with

mostly German and Russian guests on package tours.

Sharjah Carlton Hotel (☎ 528 3711, fax 528 4962; singles/doubles Dh345/460) asks more than the price quoted here for a room with a sea view. It too is stuck in 1985, the year Sharjah banned alcohol.

Places to Eat

The Public Coffeehouse, in the Al-Arsah souq, is one place that you really must visit while in Sharjah. For Dh10 you not only get a fairly large biryani, but also salad and a bowl of fresh dates for dessert. The restaurant is a traditional coffeehouse, with seating on high benches. Backgammon sets are available and sweet tea is served out of a huge urn.

Thriveni Restaurant (meals Dh5) is a cheap Indian eatery on Rolla Square. The surroundings are pleasant and you get a nice view out onto the square.

Al-Fawar (☎ 559 4662; King Faisal Rd; mezzes Dh8-12, mains Dh20-40) is a long-running Lebanese restaurant. It has a cheaper, cafeteria-style section next door, where you can get takeaway.

Sanobar Restaurant (☎ 528 3501; Al-Khan Rd; mezze Dh10, mains Dh15-40) is an excellent seafood restaurant close to the Sheikh Sultan al-Awal Rd hotel strip. The atmosphere is reminiscent of a Greek taverna, with prices far lower than what you find in Dubai. It also offers Lebanese dishes.

Getting There & Away

Sharjah international airport is 15km from the centre. The phone number for airport information is ☎ 558 1111.

There is no bus service to, from or through Sharjah but the city does have two long-distance taxi stations. Taxis for Umm al-Qaiwain (engaged/shared Dh30/8) and Ras al-Khaimah (Dh75/15) leave from Al-Arouba Rd across from the Al-Hamra cinema. Taxis for Dubai (Dh30/5) depart from a stand at the northern end of Rolla Square.

Getting Around

Since Sharjah has no bus system, getting around without your own car means either taking taxis or walking. The taxis have no meters and trips around the centre should cost Dh5 to Dh10 (agree on the fare before you get in). When the heat is not too debilitating

Sharjah's centre can be covered on foot quite easily.

AROUND SHARJAH
Sharjah Desert Park

حديقة صحراء الشارقة

Containing probably the best zoo in the Middle East, it would really be a shame to miss this remarkable complex *(Sharjah ad-Dhaid Rd; admission per person/family Dh15/30; open 9am-7pm Sat-Wed, 11am-7pm Thur, 2pm-7pm Fri)*. The problem for budget travellers is that it's 26km out of Sharjah (past Intersection No 8) towards Fujairah and there's no public transport. The main attraction is **Arabia's Wildlife Centre**, which is both a breeding centre and a zoo. One of the highlights is the indoor aviary, home to flamingos, Houbara bustards and Indian rollers. The outdoor enclosures are home to Sacred baboons, striped hyenas, Arabian wolves, and the splendid Arabian leopard. The restaurant looks out onto an open range area featuring flamingos, Nubian ibex, Arabian oryx, ostriches and sand gazelles.

The **Children's Farm** *(closed noon-4pm)* has farm animals such as goats, camels and ducks which kids can feed, and pony rides for Dh5. The third segment of the park is the **Natural History Museum**, another interesting and well-planned museum. The museum may appeal to kids more than adults, but the gardens are worth anyone's time. They include a botanical garden with more than 120 types of wildflower.

AJMAN

عجمان

☎ 06

The smallest of the seven emirates, Ajman occupies a small stretch of coast between Sharjah and Umm al-Qaiwain centred on a placid natural harbour. The emirate also has two inland enclaves at Masafi and Masfout. The public beach stretches from Sharjah to the Ajman Beach Hotel.

Things to See

The **Ajman Museum** *(admission Dh4; open 9am-1pm & 4pm-7pm Sun-Thur, 4pm-7pm Fri)* occupies the old police fort on the central square. Built in the late 18th century, the fort served as the ruler's palace and office until 1970. From 1970 to 1978, it was Ajman's main police station. It contains artifacts and reconstructions of traditional life.

Fruit and vegetables and meat and fish are sold in two souqs along the coast, off Mohamed bin Salem Bu Khamees Rd. Also here is the **Iranian souq**, an interesting place to wander around. You are unlikely to find much in the way of souvenirs (unless your idea of a souvenir is a plastic washing bucket), though you can sometimes find interesting pottery.

Places to Stay

Emirates Plaza Hotel *(☎ 744 5777, fax 744 6642; Omer bin al-Khattab St; singles/doubles Dh130/150)* has basic but clean rooms. The staff are helpful and friendly. Rooms on the right side of the building offer stunning views of the Gulf. The beach is just across the road.

Dana Beach Resort *(☎ 742 9999; e reservations@danabeach.com; Arabian Gulf St; rooms Dh185, suites from Dh325)* is an attractive new hotel with rooms facing the beach and a range of suites with kitchens for longer stays. No alcohol is served at the multicuisine restaurant.

Ajman Kempinski Hotel & Resort *(☎ 745 1555, fax 745 1222; Arabian Gulf St; singles/doubles from Dh862.50/977.50)*, at the northern end of Arabian Gulf St, is a large, package-tour-oriented resort hotel, with bars, a bowling alley and a wide stretch of beach.

Places to Eat

Dhow Restaurant, along the waterfront, is actually a coffeehouse in a traditional *barasti* shelter. Look for the blue-and-white sign with two coffee pots and a rose-water urn on it.

India House *(☎ 741 5637; Sheikh Humaid bin Abdul al-Aziz St; mains Dh10-20)* is a clean, cheap vegetarian restaurant.

Getting There & Away

Ajman has no bus service. There's a **taxi stand** *(Omar ibn al-Khattab St)* just down from the Emirates Plaza Hotel. If you want to go farther north along the coast, you'll have to go to the taxi stand at the main roundabout on the highway just out of town.

UMM AL-QAIWAIN

أم القيوين

☎ 06

For a glimpse of the slow-paced life of the old Emirati fishing ports, Umm al-Qaiwain is the place to visit. With a population of around 35,000, Umm al-Qaiwain ('Mother of Two

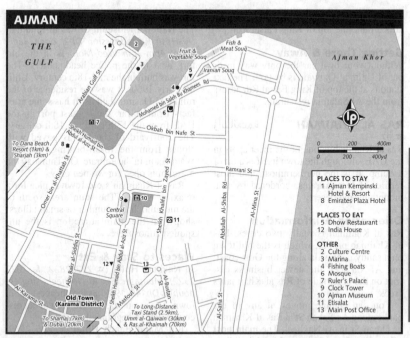

AJMAN

THE GULF

Ajman Khor

Fruit & Vegetable Souq

Fish & Meat Souq

Iranian Souq

Arabian Gulf St

Mohamed bin Saleh Bu Khamees Rd

Sheikh Humaid bin Abdul al-Aziz St

To Dana Beach Resort (1km) & Sharjah (3km)

Okbah bin Nafe St

Omer bin al-Khattab St

Ramrani St

Sheikh Khalifa bin Zayed St

Abdullah Al-Shiba Rd

Al-Mina St

Central Square

Abu Bakr al-Siddiq St

Al-Karama St

Sheikh Humaid bin Abdul al-Aziz St

Masfout St

To Sharhaj (7km) & Dubai (20km)

Old Town (Karama District)

To Long-Distance Taxi Stand (2.5km), Umm al-Qaiwain (30km) & Ras al-Khaimah (70km)

Al-Bustan St

Al-Safia St

0   200   400m
0   200   400yd

PLACES TO STAY
1 Ajman Kempinski Hotel & Resort
8 Emirates Plaza Hotel

PLACES TO EAT
5 Dhow Restaurant
12 India House

OTHER
2 Culture Centre
3 Marina
4 Fishing Boats
6 Mosque
7 Ruler's Palace
9 Clock Tower
10 Ajman Museum
11 Etisalat
13 Main Post Office

UNITED ARAB EMIRATES

Powers', referring to the emirate's power over both land and sea) is the least populous of the seven emirates. It lies on a narrow peninsula of sand jutting north from the main road linking Sharjah with Ras al-Khaimah. The old town and the emirate's small business district are at the northern tip of the peninsula, particularly along King Faisal Rd.

The small **Umm al-Qaiwain Museum** (admission Dh4; open 8am-1pm & 5pm-8pm Sat-Thur, 5pm-8pm Fri), in the heart of the old town, was once the town's fortress. The staff are friendly and might show you around the building, which includes a fine majlis room. The best activity is just to wander along the quiet **harbour**, and perhaps look at one of the unrestored **towers** which once protected the old town.

On the northern side of the peninsula, just off the Corniche, is the **Tourist Centre** at the Flamingo Beach Resort (admission Dh20) which offers a private beach, boat and jet ski hire, a swimming pool, Jacuzzi and bar. Hire a boat here for a trip around **Sinaiyah Island**, home to the UAE's largest Socotra cormorant colony and a herd of Arabian gazelles. It is not permitted to land on the island.

Dreamland Aquapark

The entertainment complex (adult/child aged 5-12 Dh30/20; open 10am-7pm) is 10km north of Umm al-Qaiwain on the main highway. It has many rides, slides and pools, as well as an open-air theatre, restaurants and kiosks. It usually closes later in summer.

Places to Stay & Eat

Pearl Hotel (☎ 766 6678, fax 766 6679; Palace Rd; rooms Dh200) is about 5km south of the town centre on the northern side of the peninsula. It has rather spartan cabins and a bar, which seems to be the favourite thing about the place for Emiratis.

Palma Beach Hotel (☎ 766 7090, fax 766 7388; singles/doubles Dh220/360), 2.5km north of the Pearl Hotel, has chalet-style accommodation, a pool and gardens enlivened with painted statues of tigers and mythological creatures.

Flamingo Beach Resort (☎ 765 0000, fax 765 0001; Corniche; singles/doubles Dh350/550) is a motel-style resort with a pool, a small beach and comfortable rooms.

All the **hotel restaurants** serve similar Western and Arabic meals (Dh20 to Dh30).

There's also a collection of **Indian restaurants** around the top of King Faisal Rd.

Getting There & Away
Without your own car the only way in or out of Umm al-Qaiwain is by taxi. The taxi stand is at the top of King Faisal Rd, across from the Al-Salamia restaurant.

RAS AL-KHAIMAH رأسالخيمة
☎ 07
Ras al-Khaimah is one of the nicer spots in the UAE, although the town itself is a bit of a dump. It is the northernmost, and most fertile, of the emirates, bordered by sea, mountains and desert.

Orientation & Information
Ras al-Khaimah is really two cities: Ras al-Khaimah proper, which is the old town on a sandy peninsula along the Gulf coast; and Al-Nakheel, the newer business district on the other side of Ras al-Khaimah's creek.

You can change money at any of the banks along As-Sabah St in Ras al-Khaimah or Oman St in Al-Nakheel. The **main post office** (King Faisal St) is a red-brick building, about 4km north of the Bin Majid Beach Hotel.

The **Etisalat office** (Al-Juwais Rd) can be found in An-Nakheel.

Things to See
The **National Museum of Ras al-Khaimah** (Al-Hosn Rd; admission Dh2; open 8am-noon, 4pm-7pm Wed-Mon) is in the old fort, next to the police headquarters. The fort was built in the mid-18th century. Until the early 1960s it was the residence of the ruling Al-Qasimi sheikhs. It has some artefacts from Julfar, the biggest port in the UAE from the 13th until the 18th century. The courtyard of the fort is paved with stones from the fossil-bearing strata of Wadi Haqil in the emirate. On Thursday the museum is open for women only.

Ras al-Khaimah's **old town** is nice for a relaxing wander. The **souq area**, south of the museum, has a number of small tailors' shops but the main attraction is the unspoiled atmosphere.

Places to Stay & Eat
Al-Nakheel Hotel (☎ 222 2822, fax 222 2922; Muntaser St, Al-Nakheel; singles/doubles Dh140/190) has the cheapest bar in town. The rooms are a bit rundown, but discounts can be negotiated.

Bin Majid Beach Hotel (☎ 235 2233; e bmbhrak@emirates.net.ae; King Faisal St; singles/doubles Dh280/380) is a fairly comfortable 1980s hotel, a favoured haunt for German and Russian tour groups. Rooms include breakfast, and the beach here is lovely.

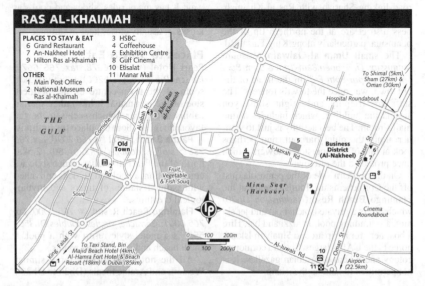

RAS AL-KHAIMAH

PLACES TO STAY & EAT
6 Grand Restaurant
7 An-Nakheel Hotel
9 Hilton Ras al-Khaimah

OTHER
1 Main Post Office
2 National Museum of Ras al-Khaimah

3 HSBC
4 Coffeehouse
5 Exhibition Centre
8 Gulf Cinema
10 Etisalat
11 Manar Mall

THE GULF

Corniche
As-Sabah St
Khor Ras al-Khaimah
Old Town
Al-Hosn Rd
Souq
Fruit, Vegetable & Fish Souq
Al-Jazirah Rd
Business District (Al-Nakheel)
Muntaser St
Mina Saqr (Harbour)
Cinema Roundabout
Oman St
Al-Juwais Rd
King Faisal St

To Shimal (5km), Sham (27km) & Oman (30km)
Hospital Roundabout
To Taxi Stand, Bin Majid Beach Hotel (4km), Al-Hamra Fort Hotel & Beach Resort (18km) & Dubai (85km)
To Airport (22.5km)

0   100   200m
0   100   200yd

Lion of the Sea

Arabia's greatest mariner, Ahmad ibn Majid, was born in the 1430s in the port city of Julfar, north of Ras al-Khaimah. Legend tells that he was the pilot who guided Vasco da Gama across the Indian Ocean in 1498 from East Africa to South India. Some experts argue that it was a pilot from Gujarat in India, not Ibn Majid, who inadvertently found the route from Europe to India for the Portuguese. Da Gama visited Julfar on the return journey from India, but regardless of whether he met the Arabian navigator, Ibn Majid's fame in the Arab world is sustained by the 40 or so works he wrote on oceanography and navigation. He drew on texts written by his father and grandfather, also navigators, and older works dating back to the 10th century. These works, such as *Book of Profitable Things Concerning the First Principles and Rules of Navigation*, describe the currents and winds of the Indian Ocean, and reports on places as far away as Madagascar and the Comoros. Intriguingly, some of his navigational experiences were written as poetry, the most beloved of the Arab arts. For his services to navigation, he was called the 'Lion of the Sea'. For centuries after his death around 1500, Arab sailors dedicated the recital of the first *surah* of the Quran to Ibn Majid's soul.

Hilton Ras al-Khaimah (☎ 228 8888; e *rkhilton@emirates.net.ae; singles/doubles Dh450/550*) has the usual five-star amenities but rather bleak views over the harbour.

Al-Hamra Fort Hotel & Beach Resort (☎ 244 6666; e *hamfort@emirates.net.ae; singles/doubles Dh550/650*) lies 18km south of Ras al-Khaimah on the Sharjah highway. Styled as an Arabian fort, it offers attractive gardens and a lovely stretch of beach.

Grand Restaurant (☎ 228 4250; *Al-Muntaser St; mains Dh12-20*) is an Indian restaurant which has vegetarian and Chinese dishes on the menu.

The enormous **Manar Mall** (*cnr Al-Juwais Rd & Al-Muntaser St*) has a Carrefour supermarket and a clutch of fast-food eateries. The restaurants at the **Hilton Ras al-Khaimah** are the only upmarket option.

You should definitely drop in at the *barasti* **coffeehouse** near Mina Saqr, overlooking the Creek. Very sweet tea costs 50 fils a cup (Dh1 with milk) and you can also get snacks.

Getting There & Away

Ras al-Khaimah's small airport is 22.5km south of Al-Nakheel. Gulf Air flies three times a week to Muscat, while Indian Airlines flies once a week to Calicut and Chennai and EgyptAir has a weekly flight to Cairo. You can call for **airport information** (☎ 244 8111).

The **taxi station** (*King Faisal St*) is just south of the Bin Majid Beach Hotel. Taxis to Dubai and Sharjah charge Dh15 per person or Dh75 engaged.

AROUND RAS AL-KHAIMAH
Shimal   سمال
The village of Shimal, 5km north of Ras al-Khaimah, is the site of some of the most important archaeological finds in the UAE. The area has been inhabited since the late 3rd millennium BC. The main attraction is the **Queen of Sheba's Palace**, a set of ruined buildings and fortifications spread over two small plateaus overlooking the village.

To reach the site travel north for about 4km from the Hospital roundabout in Al-Nakheel and turn right onto a paved road where there are a number of signs. One has a red arrow, another has red Arabic script on a white background and another has the falcon crest on it. Follow this road for 1.5km until you reach a roundabout. Turn right and follow the road for another 2.3km through a village until you come to the People Heritage Revival Association, a new building made to look like a fort. Turn left. After about 400m the sealed road ends. Continue on a dirt track through the village.

You will pass a small green-and-white mosque on the left. Keep going straight, heading for the base of the hills and get onto the paved road to your left. Continue along this road for about 1km until you see a track leading to a large green water tank. At this point you will see a gap in the fence on your right.

Walk through the gap in the fence and follow a faint track to the base of the closest hill. At the top of this hill (on your right) you should see the remains of a stone wall. The 15-minute climb is a little strenuous due to the loose rocks underfoot.

The East Coast

FUJAIRAH الفجيرة
☎ 09

The burgeoning little city of Fujairah is a bit short on attractions but it makes a good base for exploring the east coast. The town beaches suffer from pollution; the Port of Fujairah just north of the city is one of the world's busiest bunkering or refuelling ports.

Orientation & Information

The main business area is Hamad bin Abdullah Rd, between the Fujairah Trade Centre and the coast. Along this stretch of road you'll find the Etisalat office, several banks and, at the intersection with the coast road, the central souq. The **main post office** (*Al-Sharqi Rd*) is off Hamad bin Abdullah Rd.

The coastal road changes its name three times, which can be confusing. Passing through the city from south to north it is called Al-Rughailat Rd, Al-Ghorfah Rd and finally Al-Faseel Rd.

Things to See

Fujairah Museum (*admission Dh1; open 8.30am-1.30pm & 4.30pm-6.30pm Sun-Thur, 2pm-6.30pm Fri*) in the **old town** has exhibits on maritime activities, archaeological finds from around the emirate, and displays of heritage jewellery. The **fort** in the old town is being restored, but the rest of the area is dilapidated and littered.

Ain al-Madhab Garden (*admission with/ without swim Dh5/2; open 10am-10pm*) on the edge of town is nothing special, but the **swimming pools** (*open 10am-7pm Sun-Fri*) here are clean, cool and segregated into men's and women's sections. There is a small **Heritage Village** (*admission free; open 9am-6pm*) across from the garden, where you'll find a reconstructed coastal desert village.

Places to Stay & Eat

Fujairah Youth Hostel (*☎ 222 2347, mobile ☎ 050 458 4044; beds for HI members/ nonmembers Dh15/30*) is just off Al-Faseel Rd near the sports club. The hostel will only accommodate women if it is empty enough to segregate them from the men.

Ritz Plaza Hotel (*☎ 222 2202; e ritzplza@ emirates.net.ae; Hamad bin Abdullah Rd;*

doubles Dh288) is a comfortable mid-range hotel with pleasant but smallish rooms.

Fujairah Hilton (*☎ 222 2411; e shjhitwrm@ hilton.com; Al-Faseel Rd; singles/doubles Dh747.50/805*) is an attractive low-rise complex by the sea, with a number of private chalets.

There are a number of cheap restaurants on Al-Faseel Rd near the Hilton.

Diner's Inn (*☎ 222 6351; Al-Faseel Rd; mains from Dh8*) has moderately priced Indian and Chinese dishes.

Al-Meshwar (*King Faisal Rd; mezzes Dh7-12, mains Dh12-25*) is a medium-priced Lebanese restaurant. It's in the block behind the Diner's Inn.

Taj Mahal (*☎ 222 5225; Hamad bin Abdullah Rd; mains Dh10-15*) serves good Indian food, plus Chinese dishes. It's at the back of the building opposite Etisalat.

Getting There & Away

Fujairah international airport is served by Gulf Air, EgyptAir and Indian Airlines. You can call for **airport information** (*☎ 222 6222*).

The **taxi station** is on the edge of town on the road to Sharjah and Dubai. The fare to Dubai or Sharjah is Dh25 per person or Dh150 shared. Shared taxis to Dibba cost around Dh20, Dh10 to Dhaid and Dh5 to Masafi and Khor Fakkan.

AROUND FUJAIRAH

The town of **Kalba**, just south of Fujairah, is part of the Sharjah emirate. It is also the site of the oldest mangrove forest in Arabia. This conservation reserve has abundant bird life and is the only home in the world to the Khor Kalba white collared kingfisher. It's possible to hire canoes and paddle up the inlets into the mangroves. Make a deal with the fishermen on the beach.

Breeze Motel (*☎ 277 8877; e jasminede la_cruz@hotmail.com; doubles from Dh125*) is the only place to stay. The cabins are simple, but the aviaries and bougainvillea cheer the place up.

KHOR FAKKAN خورفكان
☎ 09

One of Sharjah's enclaves and the largest town on the east coast after Fujairah, Khor Fakkan (Creek of the Two Jaws) must be the most beautiful harbour in the UAE,

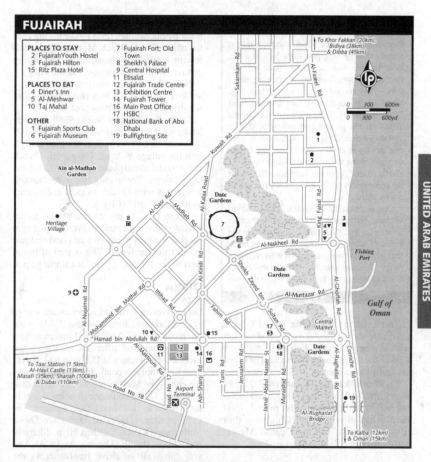

FUJAIRAH

PLACES TO STAY
2 FujairahYouth Hostel
3 Fujairah Hilton
15 Ritz Plaza Hotel

PLACES TO EAT
4 Diner's Inn
5 Al-Meshwar
10 Taj Mahal

OTHER
1 Fujairah Sports Club
6 Fujairah Museum

7 Fujairah Fort; Old Town
8 Sheikh's Palace
9 Central Hospital
11 Etisalat
12 Fujairah Trade Centre
13 Exhibition Centre
14 Fujairah Tower
16 Main Post Office
17 HSBC
18 National Bank of Abu Dhabi
19 Bullfighting Site

backed by steep rocky mountains. Tourism has been somewhat held back by Sharjah's ban on alcohol.

The sweeping Corniche is bounded by the **port** and **fish market** at the southern end and the luxury Oceanic Hotel to the north, with a nice beach in between. The fort that once dominated the coast is long gone.

With your own transport it's worth detouring to **Rifaisa Dam**, in the mountains above the town. To get there, turn inland from the main street at the Emarat petrol station, then go left at the T-intersection (at the red-and-white radio tower on your left), then turn right onto the graded track after the mosque but before the bridge. The track divides after 300m or so; stick to the right. The dam lies 4.7km up the valley. There are a

couple of ruined watchtowers atop hills along the way.

Places to Stay & Eat

Khor Fakkan Youth Hostel (☎ 237 0886; beds for members/nonmembers Dh25/40) is on the traffic circle just north of the Oceanic Hotel. It's new and clean, but there are only six rooms, and as Khor Fakkan is part of conservative Sharjah it's unlikely women can stay here.

Oceanic Hotel (☎ 238 5111; e oceanic2@ emirates.net.ae; singles/doubles Dh460/575) is a comfortable establishment at the northern end of the Corniche. The hotel has a nautical theme in '70s 'style'. The rooftop restaurant offers a view of the bay, while the beach in front is clean and secluded.

Bullfighting, Gulf Style

Every Friday, around 4.30pm, Fujairah's special brand of bullfighting gets underway at a site next to the road to Kalba, near the Al-Rughailat bridge. There are no prancing matadors – this contest is bull against bull. The horns of the opponents are blunted, and bloodshed is rare. The bulls lower their heads almost to the ground and mostly head-butt and shove each other around. Sooner or later one bull forces another out of the ring, or else one tires of the struggle and walks away. Usually there are four or five contests, after which the competitors are led into pick-up trucks and driven away.

One tradition has it that the Portuguese introduced bullfighting to Fujairah, though other sources say that the local bullfights predate the arrival of Islam. A more colourful legend holds that long ago two young men were vying to marry the same woman, so their families decided to let battling bulls settle the matter.

The **Lebanon Cafeteria** (☎ 238 5631; *Corniche; mains Dh20*) is a good option, with a range of grills, Lebanese mezze as well as the usual cheap Indian fare of biryanis and tikka dishes.

Taj Khorfakkan Restaurant (☎ 222 5995; *mains Dh10-15*) is a nicely decorated Indian restaurant with reasonably priced food, mostly Indian with some Chinese dishes. It's just inland from the Central Market, across from the Saheel Market store.

BIDIYA   بادية
☎ 09

The fishing village of Bidiya (or Badiyah), 8km north of Khor Fakkan but in the Fujairah emirate, is one of the oldest towns in the Gulf. Archaeological digs show it's been settled continuously since the 3rd millennium BC. Today, it is known mainly for its **mosque**, a small whitewashed structure of stone, mud brick and gypsum built around AD 640. It is the oldest mosque in the UAE. Non-Muslims may not enter. It is built into a low hillside along the main road just north of the village. On the hillside above and behind it are several ruined **watchtowers**.

Bidiya Beach Villa (☎ 244 5050; **e** *sbdiving@emirates.net.ae; dorm beds Dh50*) has eight bunk beds in two rooms (with shared

toilet facilities) in an old villa. You must book by phone, then drop by the diving centre at the Sandy Beach Motel (see the following entry). Someone from the diving centre will arrange transport to the villa.

Near the village market, a 10-minute walk from the villa, is a **restaurant** where wholesome, basic curries cost Dh5.

Sandy Beach Motel (☎ 244 5555; **e** *sandybm@emirates.net.ae; singles/doubles Dh302/385, chalets Dh418*) is 6km north of Bidiya, near the village of Aqqa. The gardens, beach and relaxed atmosphere compensate for the high prices. The motel has a **restaurant**, where it is wise to stick to local dishes such as the mixed grill (Dh40).

There is a diving centre at the motel where you can organise dives or just hire snorkelling gear to explore the coral reef just 100m from the beach. The stretch of beach next to the hotel is a popular **camping** spot.

DIBBA   دبا
☎ 09

Dibba lives in Islamic history as the site of one of the great battles of the Ridda wars, the reconquest of Arabia by Muslim armies in the generation after the death of the Prophet. The victory at Dibba in 633, a year after the Prophet's death, traditionally marks the end of the Muslim reconquest of Arabia.

Today, Dibba is unique in being the only town ruled by two sheikhs and a sultan. The three seaside villages of Dibba are Dibba Muhallab (Fujairah), Dibba Hisn (Sharjah) and Dibba Bayah (Oman). As in Al-Ain, you can walk or drive freely across the Omani border or explore some of the Omani villages at the southern edge of the spectacular Musandam peninsula. At the northern end of Dibba (the Omani section) is a fine deserted beach which is a popular **camping** spot.

Dibba is a lovely town; the shame is that is nowhere to stay. There is nothing much to see, but nevertheless, the quiet pace of life here makes it worth the trip.

Holiday Beach Motel (☎ 244 5540; **e** *holibemo@emirates.net.ae; singles/doubles Dh485/685*) lies 6km east of central Dibba (the Sharjah section) on the coast highway. The motel rooms are pleasant, if not luxurious, and expensive for what you get. There is a nice little crescent of sandy beach a few hundred metres west of the motel.

Yemen

All but cut off to the outside world until the 1960s, Yemen is classic, unspoiled Arabia. Because of a lack of oil, the country is poor, undeveloped and little known compared with some other parts of the region, but it's one of the undiscovered treasures of the Middle East. If you can live without beach resorts, golf courses, shopping centres and bars, but want to experience a unique culture, legendary hospitality, incredible architecture and stunning landscapes, Yemen is ideal. It's not Westernised, nor set up for mass tourism, so travelling around can be occasionally uncomfortable and inconvenient, but for many visitors this just adds to the excitement.

Although it receives negative media coverage regarding Islamic fundamentalism and kidnappings, parts of Yemen are probably safer than your own country. Be aware that some warnings are on the hysterical side, often issued by over-sensitive Western governments.

Facts about Yemen

HISTORY
Very little is known about the ancient history of southern Arabia. The area of modern-day Yemen became known during the 1st millennium BC for the production and trade of frankincense, which was controlled by the Saba empire. Originally based in eastern Yemen, the Sabaeans ruled most of the country for many centuries. Several other empires later emerged; the greatest was Himyar. The Himyarites initially ruled the central highlands, but had control of most of Yemen by the late 3rd century AD.

Due to its open coastline and proximity to Africa and central Asia, Yemen was invaded and partially occupied by, among others, the Ptolemaic dynasty (from Egypt), Abyssinians (Ethiopia) and Persians (Iran). But Yemenis proudly claim that no single foreign power has ever managed to conquer all of modern-day Yemen.

Undoubtedly, *the* major event in Yemen's turbulent history was the coming of Islam in the early 7th century AD. Most Yemenis became Sunnis, but over the next few centuries individual Shiite sects, such

Republic of Yemen

Area: 555,000 sq km
Population: 18 million
Capital: San'a
Head of State: President Ali Abdullah Salih
Official Language: Arabic
Currency: Yemeni riyal (YR)

- Best Dining – enjoying fresh fish anywhere along the coast of the Red Sea and Arabian Sea
- Best Nightlife – sipping a glass of mint tea in the old city of San'a
- Best Walk – ambling along the extensive wall surrounding the old town in Sa'da
- Best View – looking across to Shibam and Thilla from the mountain-top village of Kawkaban
- Best Activity – shopping in the souqs for jewellery, clothes, incense...and machine guns!

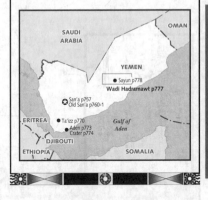

as the Zaydis, were created. (For more information see Religion later in this section, and in the Facts about the Region chapter.) Also during this time, various states were formed and run by such groups as the Sulayhids and Rasulids.

From the 15th century, the Egyptians and Portuguese vied for control of the Red Sea coast, but it was the Ottomans from Turkey who made the most impact. They occupied most of Yemen from 1535 to 1638, and again from 1872 to 1918, but ignored or failed to capture remote areas ruled by

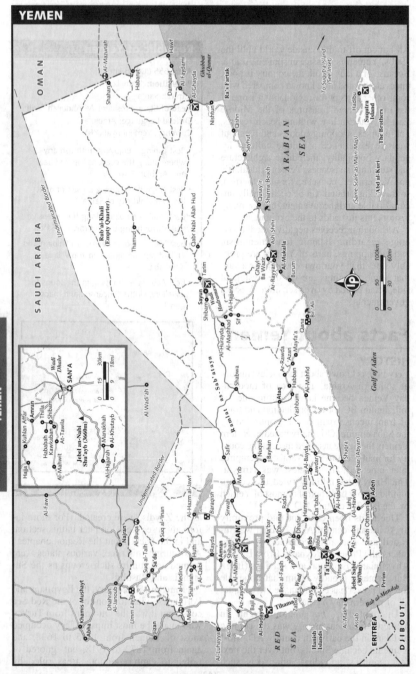

YEMEN

What to See

Nowhere on earth can you see so many remarkable villages perched on the top of hills and mountains; villages such as **Shaharah**, **Al-Hajjarah** and **Kawkaban**. The villages of Al-Hajjarah, **Hajja** and Kawkaban are also ideal for short hikes and long-distance trekking. Yemen's unique architecture can be best appreciated in the Unesco-protected old cities of **San'a**, **Shibam** (in Wadi Hadramawt) and **Zabid** – all are virtual open-air museums. Some of the better souqs for shopping are in San'a, **Ta'izz** and **Sa'da**. Parts of **Aden** offer some colonial charm, and the rock palace at **Wadi Dhahr** is enchanting.

If you only have three or four days, stick to San'a and the nearby villages. In one week, you'll also have time to visit Shibam and Kawkaban, as well as Wadi Hadramawt; and in two weeks, you'll be able to explore the **Tihama coast**, Ta'izz and Aden. If you have longer, include hiking in the **Haraz Mountains**, **Mar'ib**, northern Yemen and the **Red Sea coast**.

---

various imams. The British occupied and controlled parts of southern Yemen, including the strategic port of Aden, from 1839 to 1967 but did little to develop the region.

Various imams ruled central and northern Yemen until 1962, when an eight-year civil war commenced after the death of the influential imam Ahmad. Egypt supported army officers who had proclaimed the Yemen Arab Republic (YAR), while Britain and Saudi Arabia supported royalists, based in the north and loyal to Ahmad's son. The YAR forces eventually won.

Meanwhile, the British abandoned southern Yemen in 1967 after the National Liberation Front won a guerrilla campaign against the colonialists. Three years later the People's Democratic Republic of Yemen (PDRY) in the south became the only Marxist state in the Arab world.

In the north, President Ali Abdullah Salih ruled the YAR benevolently. Conflicts between tribes were contained, and the constitution respected both Islamic and Western- like values such as personal freedom and private property. By contrast in the south, the Yemen Socialist Party in the PDRY was in turmoil. Internal power struggles led to a two-week civil war in Aden in January 1986. The situation wasn't helped by the collapse of the Soviet Union (the major benefactor of the PDRY), throwing the south into virtual bankruptcy.

Despite the political differences, most Yemenis hated a divided country. Although there had been a few short border wars in 1972, 1978 and 1979, a unified Republic of Yemen was declared on 22 May 1990, no doubt accelerated by the discovery of oilfields in the mid-1980s. The republic was ratified following a successful referendum a year later.

The War of Unity in 1994, started by disenchanted former PDRY officials, failed to achieve any widespread support and ended after only two months.

Yemen Today

Although Yemen is crawling slowly towards stability, elements continue to destabilise the country. On 12 October 2000, a boat full of Islamic extremists bombed the US *Cole*, killing 17 American service personnel. (The vessel was stationed offshore from Aden at the time, on its way to the Gulf to help enforce the United Nations' unpopular sanctions against Iraq.) One day later a bomb exploded outside the UK embassy in San'a.

Although the USA often places Yemen in the same basket as Afghanistan and Iran with regards to Islamic extremism, many Yemen-based fundamentalists are foreign Arabs living in Yemen illegally.

GEOGRAPHY

Yemen, which lies in the southwest corner of the Arabian Peninsula, is about three-quarters the size of France. There are four distinct regions. The Tihama is a strip of land, 20km to 50km wide, along the Red Sea coast. The central western region is very mountainous and features Jebel an-Nabi Shu'ayb (3660m), the highest peak on the peninsula. The desert in the east is part of the Empty Quarter (Rub' al-Khali), which occupies most of southern Saudi Arabia. Between the mountains and the desert are fertile highlands where San'a, the capital, is located.

Yemen shares long borders with only two countries – Oman and Saudi Arabia – but both borders are disputed. And Yemen continues to squabble with the Saudis and Ethiopians over uninhabitable bits of rock in the Red Sea and the Arabian Sea.

CLIMATE

Parts of Yemen are particularly fertile because monsoons come twice a year (though they're not always reliable). Most of the limited rain along both coasts falls between July and September. In August alone, the mountains in the southwest can receive almost 500mm of rain, while San'a is lucky to get one quarter as much. Anywhere along the Tihama coastal strip is unbearably hot and humid from May to September, but tolerable at other times. The central highlands, including San'a, enjoy a mild climate most of the year, though it can get chilly in winter (December to March).

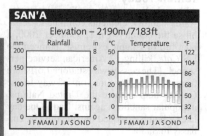

SAN'A
Elevation – 2190m/7183ft

GOVERNMENT & POLITICS

Yemen is one of the few genuine democracies in the Middle East. The ruling political party is the General People's Congress (GPC). It currently holds the majority of parliamentary seats, possibly because the main opposition party, the Yemen Socialist Party, boycotted the presidential elections in 1999. One significant opposition party is Islah, an Islamic group with some hardliners.

President Ali Abdullah Salih has been president of Yemen since unification in 1990. He was re-elected in 1999 when an admirable 66% of eligible citizens (including women) voted. Abdul al-Qadir Ba Jamal is the prime minister.

POPULATION & PEOPLE

With a population of 18 million, Yemen has one of the highest growth rates (3.4%) in the world, so the country's population has increased tenfold since 1970. About 47% of Yemenis are under 15 years old and 27% of the population lives in urban centres. Many residents along the Tihama coast have darker skin because of the area's proximity to Africa. Only 30 minutes' drive east into the mountains, the lighter Arabian complexion is more common. Bedouins inhabit the desert regions to the east.

SOCIETY & CONDUCT

Many Yemenis are inescapably linked to a tribe. Educated men working in the cities may return to their villages if their tribe is under threat or their land is encroached upon or challenged by another tribe. Disputes may involve gunfire, but injuries and deaths are very rare. However, tribal wars do flare up occasionally, mainly in the north and east, and some parts of Yemen are almost permanently off limits to tourists because of tribal problems.

Qat

Life for most Yemeni men revolves around the stimulant qat, which are leaves from *catha edulis* trees cultivated in the mountainous regions. The leaves are carefully picked, stuffed inside the cheek and masticated endlessly.

Chewing qat is an important social activity, but also a serious economic, health and social problem. While qat is not actually harmful, it is highly addictive. Some men spend 30% of their income on qat. Yemeni men – and sometimes women, but separately and in private – can easily spend four hours every afternoon doing little more than chewing qat. It's so profitable that qat is sometimes grown and/or supplied by criminal gangs, and maybe three-quarters of fertile land is used to grow it (rather than food).

Foreign males will sometimes be offered a few choice leaves or be invited to a qat party, but it's easy enough to politely decline. Foreign women may also be invited to chew qat at a *tafrita* (see the boxed text 'The Female Encounter with Yemen' in the Facts for the Visitor section).

YEMEN

RELIGION

Islam is the state religion of Yemen and the overwhelming focus of life for almost all residents. Most are Sunnis, many of whom follow the Shafa'i sect. Most Shiites follow the Ismaili or Zaydi sects.

The British converted a few Yemenis to Christianity in the southern region. Almost all Jews emigrated to Israel in the 1950s, but a few hundred remain in the north, particularly in Rayda.

LANGUAGE

The official language is Arabic, and most Yemenis speak little else. Many working in the tourist industry do speak some English (and often French), but tourists are likely to encounter problems using only English while travelling on public transport.

For a list of Arabic words and phrases, see the Language chapter at the back of this book.

Facts for the Visitor

WHEN TO GO

The best time to visit is between October and March. This is when daytime temperatures are normally pleasant and rain is usually infrequent. In summer (May to September) temperatures along both coasts regularly exceed 40°C and the humidity is very unpleasant.

Monsoons should come in March/April and August/September but will rarely disrupt your travels. In fact, this is often a preferable time to visit because the countryside is at its most attractive. When tourism picks up again, you'll need to pre-book rooms in decent hotels between 20 December and 10 January.

VISAS & DOCUMENTS

Visas

The visa situation changes regularly, so it's *imperative* to check with a Yemeni embassy or consulate, or find a reliable website (try w www.yemenembassy.org, run by the Yemeni embassy in Washington DC). At the time of writing everyone, except citizens of Gulf Cooperation Council (GCC) countries, needs a visa to enter Yemen.

If there is a Yemeni embassy/consulate in your home country you should apply there for a one-month tourist visa. If not, obtain a visa at an embassy/consulate in a neighbouring country or somewhere along the way to Yemen (eg, Oman or the UAE).

You'll need to provide your passport, one passport-sized photo, a fee (from US$50 to US$100), and a self-addressed, stamped envelope if you're not applying in person. If you're visiting on business or to study, you'll need to apply for a special visa from a Yemeni embassy/consulate and provide a letter of introduction from a sponsor within Yemen.

Alternatively, arrange a one-month tourist visa through a Yemeni travel agency (for a list of agencies see Organised Tours in the Getting Around section later in this chapter) (but this is *only* currently possible if you arrive by air in San'a). While travel agencies normally only help you obtain a visa if you book a tour or a car and driver with them, they may arrange a visa only for a fee (about US$50).

If you do arrange a visa through a travel agency in Yemen, ask the agency to fax you an application form (which can be completed in English). Send the form back with a photocopy of the personal pages from your passport and your flight details. Allow about two weeks. Your visa can be collected at the 'visa counter' at San'a airport upon arrival.

If you have evidence in your passport of a visit to Israel you'll be denied a visa for (and entry to) Yemen.

For details of visas for other Middle Eastern countries, see the 'Visas at a Glance' table under Visas & Documents in the Regional Facts for the Visitor chapter.

Visa Extensions A one-month tourist visa can normally be extended at the **Immigration, Passports & Naturalisation Authority** (☎ 01-250761) on 7th July St in San'a. It may be easier to pay a travel agency in the capital to handle the paperwork, but you may be obliged to book a tour or car through them. The passport office may require sponsorship by a travel agency anyway. Visas can be extended by two weeks on the working day before the visa expires. The cost of a visa extension seems to be at the whim of whoever is in charge.

Travel Permits

Because of tribal problems and the possibility of being kidnapped in some areas, a *tasrih* (travel permit) is required when travelling to many parts of Yemen. Permit regulations change regularly depending on the security situation, and the checkpoint officials often have no idea when the tourist police change the regulations.

The easiest option is to obtain one overall permit to cover all your travels outside San'a. Take plenty of photocopies of the permit (about five for every day of travelling) to give to checkpoint officials.

Permits are free and available in less than 10 minutes from the **tourist police** (☎ *01-202765 mornings*, ☎ *01-202764 afternoons*) in the Ministry of Tourism & Environment on Hodeida Rd in San'a. Theoretically, the office is open 24 hours but you're more likely to get the permit from 9am to 1.30pm and 3pm to 6pm Saturday and Wednesday.

The tourist police require: a photocopy of the personal pages from your passport; a photocopy of your visa; a detailed itinerary (ie, where and when you're travelling and by what mode of transport); the names of everyone travelling in your group; the name of the travel agency (if applicable); and details of the chartered vehicle (if applicable).

If you significantly change your itinerary you should inform the tourist police and/or the travel agency with 24 hours' notice. Alternatively, obtain another permit from the tourist police in San'a.

If you're on an organised tour, or hiring a car with a driver, the travel agency will arrange the permit. If your first point of arrival is not San'a, try to get a travel permit through the Yemeni embassy/consulate when you obtain your visa. Alternatively, you'll need to fly to San'a from wherever you arrive and get a permit in the usual way.

Permits are *only* required when travelling overland. Flying from San'a to Sayun, for example, and travelling around Wadi Hadramawt, does not require a permit.

Information on which places require you to have a permit, chartered vehicle and military escort is detailed in the boxed text 'Current Travel Restrictions' in the Getting Around section later in this chapter.

EMBASSIES & CONSULATES
Yemeni Embassies & Consulates
Following are the Yemeni embassies and consulates in major cities around the world. For the addresses of Yemeni embassies in neighbouring Middle Eastern countries see the relevant country chapter.

Canada (☎ 613-729 6627, fax 729 8915) 788 Island Park Dr, Ottawa
France (☎ 01-47 20 62 47, fax 49 52 04 42) 25 rue Georges Bizet, 75016 Paris
Germany (☎ 30-798 3050, fax 7322 5903) Rheinbabenllee 18, Berlin 14199
The Netherlands (☎ 70-365 3936, fax 356 3312) Surinamestraat 2585 GC, The Hague
UK (☎ 020-7584 6607, fax 7589 3350) 57 Cromwell Rd, London SW7 2Ed
US (☎ 202-965 4760, fax 337 2017) Suite 705, 2600 Virginia Ave NW, Washington DC 20037
Consulate: (☎ 212-355 1730, fax 750 9613) Room 435, 866 United Nations Plaza, New York, NY 10017

Embassies in Yemen
If you're travelling independently, you should contact your embassy in San'a to register and ask about any current security concerns. Otherwise, contact and register at your embassy in Riyadh (see the Saudi Arabia chapter for details).

Most embassies listed here are open between about 9am and 1pm from Saturday to Wednesday.

Eritrea (☎ 209422) Western Safia Bldg 68, Baghdad St
Ethiopia (☎ 208833) Al-Hamadani St, off Hadda St
France (☎ 268882) No 21 St, near Mugahed St, off Gamal Abdul Nasser St
Germany (☎ 413174) Hadda St
Netherlands (☎ 421800) 14 October St, off Ring Rd
Oman (☎ 208875) Villa 7, No 5 St, off Hodeida Rd
Saudi Arabia (☎ 240429) Bldg I, Al-Quds St, off 30m Rd
UAE (☎ 248777) Hadda St
UK (☎ 264081) cnr Hadda St & 45m Rd
USA (☎ 303155) Sa'wan St

CUSTOMS
You can bring in and take out a reasonable amount of gifts and items of a personal nature. You can also bring in the usual two boxes of duty-free cigarettes, but alcohol is strictly forbidden.

MONEY
Currency
The official currency is the Yemeni riyal (YR). Banknotes come in denominations of YR10 (rare), YR20, YR50, YR100, YR200,

YR500 and YR1000. Each note is translated into English on one side. Only YR5 and YR10 coins remain, and both sides of these coins are in Arabic only.

Rates quoted by some mid-range hotels, all top-end hotels, most travel agencies and Yemenia airlines are in US dollars, but payment is possible in US dollars or Yemeni riyals. For all other goods and services in Yemen, payment should be made in riyals, even if rates are quoted to you (and listed in this book) in US dollars.

Exchange Rates

Below are the rates for a range of currencies when this book went to print.

country	unit		YR
Australia	A$1	=	YR96.3
Canada	C$1	=	YR110.8
euro zone	€1	=	YR173.9
Japan	¥100	=	YR143.8
New Zealand	NZ$1	=	YR84.1
Oman	OR1	=	YR458.2
Saudi Arabia	SR1	=	YR47.0
UAE	Dh1	=	YR48.0
UK	£1	=	YR276.6
USA	$1	=	YR176.3

Exchanging Money

In short, cash is far easier to change than travellers cheques, and US dollars are more acceptable than any European currency.

The best places to change money are the numerous foreign-exchange offices in the cities and larger towns. The rates offered rarely vary by 1%, and commissions are seldom charged, but it pays to ask for the final amount of riyals you'll receive before handing over your cash. Foreign-exchange offices are always well signed in English and typically open from about 9am to 9pm daily except Friday. Some larger offices in the cities may change travellers cheques, but will charge commission of up to 5%.

Banks offer slightly lower rates for cash than foreign-exchange offices, but are more likely to change travellers cheques (with a commission rate of about 5%). Some of the better banks for changing cash and travellers cheques are the Crédit Agricole Indosuez, the International Bank of Yemen, the Central Bank of Yemen and the National Bank of Yemen.

There is no black market, so avoid changing any money on the street. At the very best you'll be ripped off; at worst, you'll be robbed.

ATMs & Credit Cards Visa and AmEx (American Express) are accepted by Yemenia airlines, most upmarket travel agencies and all top-end hotels, but a 10% surcharge may be added. It's not possible to obtain cash advances with any credit card at banks or foreign-exchange offices in Yemen, nor do automatic teller machines (ATMs) currently accept any Western credit cards.

Costs

If you stay in the cheapest flea-bitten hotels, catch public buses and eat basic Yemeni food at roadside stalls, it's possible to get by on about US$6 per person per day. But if you crave any comfort at all, allow US$16/13 per person per day for one/two people. This will pay for decent budget hotels, some Western food each, shared taxis and museum admission fees. On US$20/16 per person per day you will be able to buy souvenirs, charter taxis and even enjoy a beer or two in Aden. Add to this the cost of internal flights (San'a to Sayun is US$116 one way) and chartering a vehicle with a driver when required (from US$50 to US$100 per day).

Tipping & Bargaining

Tipping is not customary in restaurants. In fact, upmarket places add a 10% service charge anyway. Top-end hotels often add service charges and 'government taxes' totalling 22% to the bill. Give a tip to any child who shows you around their village (about YR20) and any adult who opens up and/or shows you around a mosque (about YR50).

Bargaining is not nearly as common as elsewhere in the region, but it's still worth haggling a little over expensive souvenirs. Rates offered at mid-range hotels are sometimes negotiable when business is quiet (which is very often).

POST & COMMUNICATIONS
Post

The cost of sending a postcard/normal-sized letter is YR70/100 to the USA, YR60/70 to the UK and Europe, and YR80/120 to Australia and New Zealand. The only reliable poste restante in Yemen is in the Tahrir Post Office in San'a. You'll find post offices in all larger towns and villages.

Telephone

The country code for Yemen is ☎ 967, followed by the local area code (minus the zero), then the number. Local area codes are given at the start of each city or town section. The international access code (to call abroad from Yemen) is ☎ 00. For inquiries, dial ☎ 118.

The national telephone system is controlled by the government monopoly, Yemen Communications Company, commonly known as TeleYemen. Every city and town has a plethora of telephone centres. Each is signposted in English as a 'telecommunications centre' or 'call centre', and most are open daily from 8am to midnight. The standard charge is about YR270 per minute to anywhere in Europe, North America, Australia and New Zealand. There are no off-peak periods with discounted rates.

Mobiles The **Spacetel** and **Sabafon** companies are the only two suppliers of mobile-phone networks. Both sell prepaid cards (YR9000) that fit most foreign mobile phones. Access is good in most populated regions, but poor in remote areas.

Fax

Faxes can be sent from any 'telecommunications/call centre'. The cost per minute is the same as a telephone call.

Email & Internet Access

TeleYemen is the only ISP. Throughout Yemen, access is slow but cheap: from YR5 per minute. Internet cafés can be found in all cities and larger towns, but they rarely serve food or drinks.

DIGITAL RESOURCES

For information about Yemen before you go, try these websites:

US Department of State Contains updates on the security situation
  Ⓦ www.travel.state.gov/travel_warnings.html
Yemen Gateway An overview of Yemen, with great links
  Ⓦ www.al-bab.com.yemen
Y Net Basic information and useful links, provided by TeleYemen
  Ⓦ www.y.net.ye

BOOKS

Lonely Planet publishes a detailed country guide, *Yemen*.

The City of Sealions by Eva Sallis is a recent novel set in Yemen and Kangaroo Island, off the coast of South Australia. *J'étais Médecin au Yemen* (I Was a Doctor in Yemen) by Claude Fayein is a classic memoir by a French female doctor who worked in Yemen in the 1950s. It has been reprinted in French, English and German. Another classic is *Motoring with Mohammed* by Eric Hansen.

Yemen: Land & People by Sarah Searight has plenty of detail about Yemeni history, geography and culture. *Yemen: Jewel of Arabia* by Charles & Patricia Aithie is probably the best of several glorious souvenir books.

Tim Mackintosh-Smith's lively journal *Yemen – Travels in Dictionary Land* is recommended and includes many vibrant illustrations.

Anyone with a serious interest in exploring Yemen's few ecotourism sites should look for the booklet, *Wild Yemen* (YR250), published by *Yemen Times* and available at larger bookshops in San'a. It lists a dozen day trips and overnight trips (by rented/chartered car) from San'a, as well as short hikes near the capital.

More general Middle East titles, some of which contain coverage of Yemen, are listed under Books in the Regional Facts for the Visitor chapter.

NEWSPAPERS & MAGAZINES

The *Yemen Observer* and the *Yemen Times* (Ⓦ www.yementimes.com) both cost YR30 and are available in San'a. Day-old copies of the *Arab News* from Saudi Arabia can also be bought in San'a. *Newsweek* is available in the capital, but other foreign newspapers and magazines are hard to find.

RADIO & TV

The two government-run television channels are so boring that most hotels (and homes) have satellite TV. However, with the exception of those in top-end hotels, most TVs only pick up soap operas from Lebanon, news broadcasts from the United Arab Emirates (UAE) and religious programmes from Saudi Arabia – all in Arabic. You may be able to find CNN or BBC, and often MTV from India.

Most international radio services can be picked up on a short-wave radio.

PHOTOGRAPHY & VIDEO

Photographing anything related to the military, including airports, is strictly forbidden. Never photograph any Yemeni women without their *express* consent. Almost without exception women loathe being photographed, so please respect their wishes. Most boys and girls, however, are keen to get in a photo.

Print film is readily available in cities and larger towns, and developing a roll of 24/36 print film costs about YR550/715. Bring your own slide film, and develop it at home.

LAUNDRY

Most mid-range and top-end hotels offer a laundry service for guests, and dry-cleaning shops are common in the old towns of major cities. Cleaning costs about YR70 per garment; your clothes often come back looking better than new!

TOILETS

Most rooms in decent hotels (including many in the budget range) that have private bathrooms contain sit-down European toilets. Toilet paper is usually provided, but it pays to carry a roll with you anyway. Communal toilets, eg, in bus stations and restaurants, and shared bathrooms in cheaper hotels, will almost always be a squat-style hole in the floor.

HEALTH

The sort of medical services expected in the West can only be found in San'a and Aden; elsewhere, facilities are poor. It's important to note that no ambulance service exists anywhere in Yemen and not all medicines are always available. Your embassy (or any Western embassy) in San'a can recommend competent English-speaking doctors, as well as preferred hospitals and clinics. Hospitals and doctors usually demand US$ cash.

Malaria is an increasing problem along both coasts and on Suqutra Island. The recommended prophylactic is Paludrine, available without prescription at pharmacies throughout Yemen.

Parts of Yemen are very mountainous and all of the country is *exceptionally* dusty, so anyone with serious respiratory and asthmatic conditions should consider this carefully before embarking on a trip to Yemen.

In late 2000, there was an outbreak of Rift Valley Fever near the Saudi border. This disease is usually carried by mosquitoes and normally only affects cattle, but it is highly infectious and can be transmitted to humans.

For detailed health information, see Health in the Regional Facts for the Visitor chapter.

WOMEN TRAVELLERS

Yemen's attitude towards and treatment of foreign (and local) women is considerably more enlightened than its northern neighbour. Female tourists can drive rented/private vehicles in Yemen and do not have to wear any head covering. However, conservative dress is mandatory.

DANGERS & ANNOYANCES

The number of possible dangers should be put into perspective. One reader deduced from official statistics that he was 97 times more likely to be robbed or killed in his home town (Kansas City, USA) than in San'a.

Price rises at the instigation of the International Monetary Fund and World Bank have recently resulted in riots, so obviously avoid

Kidnappings

About 130 foreign tourists and workers were kidnapped in Yemen between 1995 and 2000. Kidnapping is undertaken by tribesmen with economic and political grievances against the central government and *not* done by any particular fundamentalist group or directed at citizens of any particular nation.

Although kidnappers carry weapons, almost all of these hostages were released unharmed after a few days. In fact, most were treated warmly. The notable exception was in December 1998 when 16 tourists were abducted and four died in crossfire between the kidnappers and Yemeni soldiers. Yemenis were outraged at the time, and the government subsequently proved that most perpetrators were foreign Arabs (some were even citizens of the UK).

As a result of the introduction of the death penalty for kidnapping, and the recent arrest (with US military assistance) of hundreds of suspected extremists, kidnappings are far less likely to occur in the future.

YEMEN

The Female Encounter with Yemen

While one sees many women on the streets of Yemen (shopping, or simply in transit somewhere) one is struck by the invisibility of their lives. As a traveller – the observer – the woman's world is closed from view. This makes one even more curious. High walls surround houses, curtains cover windows, swathes of fabric encase bodies and faces.

Yemen is a strictly segregated society, so apart from the males of their immediate family traditional Yemeni women have no interaction with other Yemeni or foreign males. But Yemeni women are open, warm and welcoming to foreign females.

To see the woman's world one must enter the domestic sphere – invitations to homes are forthcoming, but only on an individual basis as the privacy of the home is respected. In the afternoons, groups of women all over Yemen head purposefully for the *tafrita*, where women congregate in the privacy of their homes to gossip, chew qat and smoke the *nargileh* (water pipe). The *tafrita* is often a fairly animated encounter, with much raucous chatter and singing.

A visit to the local *hammam* (bathhouse) is a more accessible way for foreign women to meet Yemeni women. (Bathhouses have alternate days for males and females.) In female company, Yemeni women appear to be quite uninhibited with nudity. It's a curious spectacle to see the transition from the totally encased dark figures that enter from the street as they peel off their layers and are transformed into the fleshy image of the bather.

When dressing, the women demonstrate remarkable dexterity; swift movements transform lengths of cloth into a range of different styles of head covering. This has been practiced from childhood, as a woman's head is always covered outside of her home.

Mariana Hardwick

areas with any civil unrest. On average there are three weapons for every Yemeni person, but most are carried by men as part of their traditional costume and are *very* rarely used. Unknown numbers of land mines were planted in the south, particularly around (but not in) Aden, during the 1994 War of Unity.

According to the US government, Yemen is home to a significant number of supporters and members of Al-Qaeda, but most are probably not Yemenis. The Yemeni government and the overwhelming majority of the population do not in any way support or condone any extremist groups or terrorist activities.

Swimming in the Red Sea and Arabian Sea is possible, but get away from urban centres to ensure privacy, security and clean water. Possibly lurking in the sea are scary but harmless sharks and stingrays. (See also the boxed text 'Kidnappings'.)

BUSINESS HOURS

Government offices are officially open from 8am to 3pm Saturday to Wednesday, but in practice many close by 1.30pm. Shops and private businesses open from about 8.30am to 1pm and about 4pm to 7pm Saturday to Wednesday. A few open on Thursday, but rarely on Friday. Banks open between 8.30am and midday from Saturday to Wednesday. Post offices generally operate daily from 8am to 1pm and 4pm to 8pm. All hotels, restaurants and public transport function every day of the week.

PUBLIC HOLIDAYS

In addition to the main Islamic holidays described under Public Holidays & Special Events in the Regional Facts for the Visitor chapter at the beginning of this book, Yemen observes the following holidays:

May/Labour Day 1 May
National/Unity Day 22 May
Victory Day 7 July
September Revolutionary/Anniversary Day 26 September
October Revolutionary/Anniversary Day 14 October
Evacuation Day 30 November

ACTIVITIES

Expensive boat trips and scuba diving around the Red Sea and Suqutra Island can be arranged with **Future Tours Industries** (☎ 01-253216; ⓦ www.ftiyemen.com) in San'a. It doesn't have an office, so just call. Scuba diving can also be organised in

Al-Mukalla and Al-Khawkha (see the relevant sections later in this chapter), and with **Moka Tours** (☎ 01-7321 2670; Az-Zubayri St; e mokatours@hotmail.com) in San'a.

Parts of western Yemen are ideal for short hikes and long-distance trekking. To avoid the heat in summer and fog in winter, hiking is better in the morning. There are no official hiking trails, and hiking maps are nonexistent, so you'll need a guide. Guides can be arranged in Kawkaban, Manakhah and Al-Hajjarah. Otherwise, try a camel trip in Zabid.

COURSES

San'a is an ideal place to learn Arabic; costs are low and the language spoken by Yemenis is close to classical Arabic. Both places listed here are open all year and also offer courses about Islam and Middle Eastern culture and history. Both can arrange accommodation for students for about US$100 per person per month.

The Center for Arabic Language & Eastern Studies (☎ 01-287078; e cales@ust.edu; Old City) in San'a is an impressive outfit. Basic training for individuals costs US$8 per hour for 40 hours (over four weeks) or US$4 per hour in a group (minimum of three) for 80 hours (eight weeks).

San'a Institute for Arabic Language (☎ 01-284330; e info@sialyemen.com, w www.sialyemen.com; As-Sailah St) in San'a is also well established, and has been recommended by readers. Courses for individuals start at US$6 per hour and group courses start at US$3 per hour.

ACCOMMODATION

There are no camp sites in Yemen, but free camping is possible along secluded beaches (eg, at Bir ' Ali) and on Suqutra Island.

A *lukanda* is a basic hostel. It offers a dirty mattress – usually on the floor with filthy blankets and no sheets – in a dormitory often shared with itinerant Yemeni men. This is obviously not an option for women and should only be considered by truly adventurous men on a very tight budget. Prices range from about YR300 to YR500 per person.

A *funduq* is usually a basic guesthouse. Private rooms often contain a mattress on the floor with blankets (but rarely two sheets), and have a shared bathroom. Rooms are normally clean and cost about YR800/1200 for

singles/doubles. Some funduqs in remote villages with no restaurants offer half board, ie, a private room with breakfast and dinner, for about YR1500 per person.

All cities and most large towns offer a range of better hotels with private bathroom, TV and air-conditioning (and/or fan) from about YR1500/2000.

FOOD

If you stay in cities and large towns you can eat Western-style meals of lamb, chicken and fish with rice and salad, and even find an occasional Pizza Hut. But it's worth trying some Yemeni food.

Breakfast is sometimes little more than *shai* (sweet tea, often with milk), bread and eggs. Lunch is the main meal of the day. At this time, Yemenis often eat chicken or mutton dishes accompanied by salad and a thin soup such as *shurba wasabi* (lamb soup). At cheaper eateries and roadside stalls *salta* is a tasty option. This piping-hot meat stew also contains eggs, vegetables and fenugreek (which has a distinctive aroma). For dinner, *fuul* (bean stew) is popular. *Fuul*, rice and salad are often the only choice for vegetarians.

Every meal is accompanied by huge slices of fresh bread. Along the coast, freshly grilled fish is a welcome change. One cheap and delicious snack is shwarma (sliced meat from a spit) in bread with salad.

For a list of typical dishes, see the special section 'Middle Eastern Cuisine' in the Regional Facts for the Visitor chpter.

DRINKS

Bottles of internationally brewed nonalcoholic beer are available throughout Yemen. Expensive imported alcoholic beer can be bought at a few hotels and bars in Aden only.

Fresh fruit juices are delicious, but at cheaper stalls it's likely to contain tap water. *Shai* is normally hot, black and sweet, and often spiced with mint or cardamom. Inevitably, tourists are offered European-style tea bags in hotel restaurants. All sorts of sugary soft drinks (sodas) are available, and bottled mineral water can be bought anywhere.

SHOPPING

A unique memento is the curved *jambiya* dagger worn by most Yemeni males. A decent blade costs about YR1500, a scabbard

YR1500 and a belt about YR2000. The best places to buy these are the souqs in San'a and Sa'da. In and around Sa'da, it's also possible to buy a machine gun (!) for about YR23,000.

A more useful souvenir might be a *futa*, the sarong-style 'skirt' often worn by Yemeni men. A quality hand-woven garment made in Yemen (rather than imported from India) will cost about YR2500. The best places to buy a *futa* or a *mashadda* (head cloth) are Zabid, Beit al-Faqih and anywhere in Wadi Hadramawt.

The Women's Products Marketing Training Association in the old city of San'a sells silver, woodcarvings, textiles and leather products. Other souvenirs from Yemen include leather goods from Amran, jewellery from Ta'izz, (expensive) honey from around Sayun and Shaharah, frankincense from Shibam (in Wadi Hadramawt) and conical (and comical) *madhalla* hats from Sayun.

Getting There & Away

AIR
Several major European airlines, such as British Airways and KLM-Royal Dutch Airlines, fly to San'a, as do some other regional airlines such as Emirates Airlines, Royal Jordanian and EgyptAir. The national carrier, Yemenia, offers regular flights between San'a and Frankfurt, London, Paris, Rome and Milan, and between San'a and most cities in North Africa and the Middle East.

Most international flights start and finish in San'a, but a few Middle Eastern airlines also fly to/from Aden, Al-Hudayda, Sayun and Ar-Rayyan (near Al-Mukalla).

Departure Tax
The international departure tax of US$13 is included in the price of all tickets bought in or outside Yemen.

LAND
See the relevant sections in the Saudi Arabia and Oman chapters for more information on border-crossing regulations.

Saudi Arabia
For many years foreigners have not been permitted to travel independently across the Saudi-Yemeni border. If you are given a Saudi visa allowing you to travel by bus from Yemen (unlikely), Yemitco operates a daily bus from San'a at 3pm to Jeddah (YR3500) and Riyadh (YR5900).

Foreigners with private vehicles (and the right visas) can cross the border at Hard al-Medina (near the coast) and Al-Buqa (northeast of San'a).

Oman
Because of bad roads and long distances there are no direct buses or shared taxis between anywhere in Yemen and Oman. Therefore, you'll have to hire a vehicle or hitch a ride across. The only border that foreigners are allowed to cross is between Shahan (Yemen) and Al-Mazunah (Oman). Foreigners are also not permitted to travel directly between this border and Wadi Hadramawt; you must go via Al-Ghayda and Al-Mukalla.

SEA
The chances of finding a passenger boat, or a cargo boat willing to take a foreigner, to Ethiopia, Sudan, Egypt or Eritrea are slim. There are no regular schedules, but you could try at Al-Makha, Al-Hudayda, Aden or Al-Mukalla.

You'll need plenty of luck with timing and some ability to speak Arabic to negotiate a fare. And make sure you get the right sort of visas (ie, stating your arrival and/or departure by sea) for both countries.

Getting Around

AIR
The only airline that offers internal flights is the national carrier, Yemenia. It flies to and from San'a, Aden, Ar-Rayyan (for Al-Mukalla), Sayun, Ta'izz, Al-Hudayda, Hadibu (on Suqutra Island) and Al-Ghayda (near the Omani border). Details are in the relevant sections later in this chapter.

It's considerably cheaper to buy Yemenia tickets in Yemen rather than through a foreign travel agency or on the Internet, and you're always likely to get a seat. Yemenia has offices in every city and major town. Payment is possible with Visa and AmEx, as well as with Yemeni riyals, US dollars and, probably in the future, euros.

Current Travel Restrictions

Places where foreigners are allowed to travel independently by public transport *without* a travel permit or military escort are:

- The road from San'a to Al-Mahwit, Wadi Dhahr, Thilla, Shibam and Kawkaban
- The road from San'a to Al-Hudayda, via Manakhah, Al-Hajjarah and Al-Khutayb
- The road from San'a to Aden, via Dhamar, Ibb and Ta'izz
- Any road to or near the Red Sea coast
- The road from Sif to Tarim, via Sayun, in Wadi Hadramawt

Places where foreigners are allowed to travel independently by public transport *with* a travel permit (but no military escort) are:

- The road from Ma'rib to Al-Mukalla, via Ataq
- The road from Aden to Al-Mukalla
- The road from Al-Mukalla to Wadi Hadramawt
- The paved road (but not the desert trails) from Ma'rib to Wadi Hadramawt, via Shabwa
- The road from Al-Mukalla to the Omani border, via Al-Ghayda

Places where foreigners are *only* allowed to travel by organised tour, or with a pre-arranged car and driver, with a travel permit (but no military escort) are:

- Unmarked desert trails (but not the paved road) from Ma'rib to Wadi Hadramawt

Places where foreigners are *only* allowed to travel by organised tour, or with a pre-arranged car and driver, with a travel permit and a military escort are:

- Road from San'a to Ma'rib
- All roads north of San'a, ie, to Amran, Hajja, Shaharah and Sa'da

Places where foreigners are *not* allowed to travel at any time in any form of transport are:

- Anywhere near the undemarcated border with Saudi Arabia
- Anywhere between Tarim and the Omani border
- Across the Arabian Sea by boat to Suqutra island

The domestic departure tax of US$3 is included in the cost of all tickets bought in or outside Yemen.

BUS

Every city and major town is accessible by public and private buses most days, but public buses are less comfortable and increasingly less common. The best private bus company is **Yemitco**. It offers comfortable seats in air-conditioned buses, but charges foreigners twice as much as locals.

Public and private buses run to a strict schedule and usually leave on time. It's often possible (and advisable) to buy tickets for private buses the day before departure. One advantage of travelling by public or private bus rather than by shared taxi is that buses are rarely stopped at checkpoints, though you should still have the correct travel permit.

Crowded minibuses ply the main roads around cities and major towns, but taxis are quicker and more comfortable, and still reasonably priced. To avoid traffic jams, you could take a ride as a passenger on a motorbike.

SHARED TAXI

You can get almost everywhere you want to go by shared taxi (known as a *sarwis*). Although rarely more comfortable than buses, shared taxis are quicker and depart at more convenient times (but only when full). Fares are fixed, and payment is always made before the journey begins. All passengers on a long-distance trip are often required to write their names and nationalities on a passenger list (in English is OK). Foreigners must show their travel permit at each checkpoint.

It's certainly a good idea to pay for the two front seats if possible. Taxis can also be chartered between cities and towns; the word 'special' is commonly used by drivers to describe chartered taxis. To charter your own taxi, you'll need to pay for all the seats (usually six or 10).

CAR & MOTORCYCLE
Car Rental

There are plenty of excellent reasons *not* to drive a rented car around Yemen, for example: maniacal drivers with a complete disregard for the few existing road rules, a lack of signposts in any language, terrible roads and troublesome checkpoints.

If you're still keen, try **Europcar** (☎ *01-270751; e europcar@y.net.ye*) next to the Sam City Hotel along Ali Abdul Mogni St in San'a, or its other office at San'a airport

(☎ 01-344495). Cars cost from US$70 per day (including 150km free, then US$0.15 per km) and a 4WD from US$80 (with 150km free, then US$0.20 per km). Rates include insurance, but not petrol. You will need a valid drivers licence from your home country and must be 21 years old or over. There is nowhere to rent a motorbike in Yemen.

Chartered Vehicles

It's *far* safer, cheaper and more comfortable to rent a car with a driver. You can still plan your itinerary and stop for photos, and the driver will know which places are safe.

The standard rate among travel agencies in San'a is US$50 per vehicle per day. This includes the driver's fee, his food and accommodation, and petrol. The rate increases to US$75 per day for longer trips (ie, more than 250km or about six hours' driving), and to US$100 per day for journeys along desert trails (eg, Ma'rib to Wadi Hadramawt).

If you're travelling in a group of three to five people it's worth asking around for a larger jeep, and always ask for a driver who speaks a language everyone understands. The driver or the travel agency should arrange all your travel permits for no extra charge. You can be dropped off at Aden, for example, from San'a, and take a bus, taxi or plane onwards, but you'll have to pay US$50 extra (ie, one day's rate) so the vehicle can be returned to San'a.

Military Escorts

When travelling in a chartered vehicle along the road from San'a to Ma'rib, and anywhere north of the capital, you're obliged to pick up one or two armed military escorts at the appropriate checkpoints. If you're on an all-inclusive organised tour, the travel agency will pay for this. If not, you'll have to pay YR300 to YR500 per guard. Guards often change at a village or checkpoint, so the cost of hiring them (and paying for their meals) will add to your travel costs.

HITCHING

While hitching is always risky and we don't recommend it, hitching in Yemen is nonetheless an accepted way of getting around remote areas. Payment is often expected and should be agreed on before you get into the vehicle. For more information see Hitching in the Getting Around the Region chapter.

ORGANISED TOURS

The following agencies are all based in San'a. They are reputable, well established and have been recommended by readers. Each can arrange all-inclusive tours around Yemen, rental of a 2WD or 4WD with driver, and guides for about US$20 per day.

Arabian Eco-tours (☎/fax 01-326 134,
 📧 aet@y.net.ye) PO Box 5420; competent,
 multilingual outfit specialising in ecotours
Ashtal Travel & Tourism (☎ 01-266412,
 📧 ashtal@y.net.ye) PO Box 1501, Hadda St;
 large and capable company
Bazara Travel & Tourism (☎ 01-279235,
 📧 bazara@y.net.ye) PO Box 2616, Az-Zubayri
 St; specialises in package tours
Soqotra Tours (☎ 01-280 212, fax 280213) Old
 City; has German-speaking staff
Universal Travel & Tourism (☎ 01-272861,
 📧 tourism@y.net.ye), office at airport
 (☎ 344057), PO Box 10473, Az-Zubayri St;
 has offices in most cities and large towns
Voyages au Yemen (☎ 01-270 716,
 📧 mashrah@y.net.ye) PO Box 3980, As-Sailah
 St; has French-speaking staff

San'a   صنعاء

☎ 01

Although the fascinating old city of San'a is some 2500 years old, the rest of the sprawling capital is comparatively new and unattractive. It's the point of arrival for most travellers and has enough attractions to occupy a few days. San'a is also a base for excellent day trips (see the Around San'a section) and the best place to organise a tour, or a car with a driver, for the rest of Yemen.

According to legend, the old city was built by Shem (also known as Sam), the son of Noah, but it was more probably the city of Azal mentioned in the Old Testament that was built by him. San'a (which means 'Protected') became the regional capital of the Himyarite empire in the 6th century AD. San'a was later used as a capital by the Abyssinians, Persians and Zaydis. After the revolution of the 1960s, San'a experienced a period of rapid growth, doubling in size every four years. It was the obvious choice for the capital of the reunited Yemen in 1990.

Orientation

The two main thoroughfares in the city centre are Ali Abdul Mogni St and As-Sailah St;

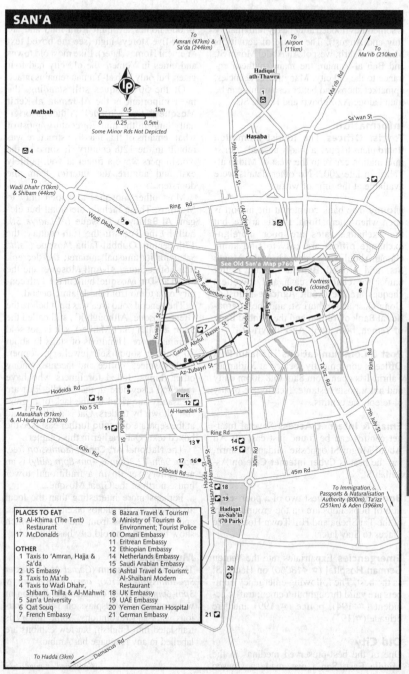

SAN'A

To Amran (47km) & Sa'da (244km)

To Airport (11km)

To Ma'rib (210km)

Matbah

0   0.5   1km
0   0.25   0.5mi
Some Minor Rds Not Depicted

Hadiqat ath-Thawra

Hasaba

To Wadi Dhahr (10km) & Shibam (44km)

Ring   Rd

See Old San'a Map p760

Old City

Fortress (closed)

Qat Souq

Park

Al-Hamadani St

Ring Rd

Djibouti Rd

Hadiqat as-Sab'in (70 Park)

To Immigration, Passports & Naturalisation Authority (800m), Ta'izz (251km) & Aden (396km)

To Manakhah (91km) & Al-Hudayda (230km)

To Yemen German Hospital

To Hadda (3km)

Damascus Rd

PLACES TO EAT
13 Al-Khima (The Tent) Restaurant
17 McDonalds

OTHER
1 Taxis to 'Amran, Hajja & Sa'da
2 US Embassy
3 Taxis to Ma'rib
4 Taxis to Wadi Dhahr, Shibam, Thilla & Al-Mahwit
5 San'a University
6 Qat Souq
7 French Embassy
8 Bazara Travel & Tourism
9 Ministry of Tourism & Environment; Tourist Police
10 Omani Embassy
11 Eritrean Embassy
12 Ethiopian Embassy
14 Netherlands Embassy
15 Saudi Arabian Embassy
16 Ashtal Travel & Tourism; Al-Shaibani Modern Restaurant
18 UK Embassy
19 UAE Embassy
20 Yemen German Hospital
21 German Embassy

YEMEN

the latter is a remarkable, paved wadi which is sometimes flooded after heavy rain (mainly July and August). The centre of activity is Midan at-Tahrir, west of Ali Abdul Mogni St, and Bab al-Yaman, the main southern entrance to the old city. Many travel agencies, upmarket shops and better restaurants can be found along Az-Zubayri and Hadda Sts.

Information

Tourist Offices The **Tourist Promotion Board** plans to open a (badly needed) tourist information centre to the west of Midan at-Tahrir in late 2002. No other details were available at the time of writing.

Money The bank counter at the airport is open when international flights arrive, but the exchange rates are poor. **Foreign-exchange offices** are easy to find along Gamal Abdul Nasser and Ali Abdul Mogni Sts, and around Bab al-Yaman. Better banks for changing cash and travellers cheques are the **Crédit Agricole Indosuez** along Qasr al-Jumhuri St, and the **International Bank of Yemen** and the **Central Bank of Yemen**, both along Az-Zubayri St.

Post & Communications The **Tahrir Post Office** is conveniently located at Midan at-Tahrir. It's open from 8am to 8.30pm daily and has a poste restante. Nearby are plenty of telephone centres.

Email & Internet Access Several Internet centres can be found just east off Ali Abdul Mogni St opposite Midan-at Tahrir, but the best is **Cyber Internet Cafe** on As-Sailah St.

Bookshops The best two of a poor selection of bookshops are on the ground floors of the Taj Sheba and Hill Town Hotels (see Places to Stay later).

Emergencies Expatriates rate the **Yemen German Hospital** (☎ 418000) on Hadda St as the best. The following emergency numbers are valid throughout Yemen: traffic accident (☎ 194), police (☎ 199) and fire brigade (☎ 191).

Old City

One of the best-preserved medinas in the Middle East, San'a was made a Unesco World Heritage Site in 1986. Many of the 14,000 homes are built from mud and are about five storeys high (see the boxed text 'Yemeni Homes' later). Like most old towns and cities in Yemen, the old city had four gates, but only Bab al-Yaman remains intact.

Of the 50 mosques still standing, the most important is the **Al-Jamaa al-Kebir Mosque** (Great Mosque). Although originally built in the mid-7th century, most of what remains of this massive structure was rebuilt in the 12th century. If some of the worshippers wave a finger at you, politely exit and admire the interior from the doorstep.

Most other mosques are open only to Muslims. These include the small but elegant **Al-Bakiliyah Mosque** (Al-Laqiya St), built by the Turks in the 16th century; the 17th-century **Qubbat Talha Mosque** (Talha St), with its unusual minaret; the decrepit mid-16th century **Al-Aqil Mosque**; and the **Salah ad-Din Mosque**, built in the 17th century on a tomb from the Islamic period.

The general souq area was built before the Great Mosque. Although it's still called the **Souq al-Milh** (Salt Market), salt is not sold there anymore. Hundreds of stalls in about 30 smaller souqs sell jewellery, copper, clothes, spices, coffee and incense, among other things. Jaded foreigners who have travelled elsewhere in the Middle East are pleasantly surprised by the lack of aggression shown by traders. Qat is sold here and at the separate **qat souq** further east (see the boxed text 'Qat' earlier in this chapter).

The **National Art Center** (admission free; open 9am-12.30pm & 4pm-8pm daily) is an art gallery set up in a traditional tower house north of the Great Mosque.

Perhaps more interesting than the local art for sale are the photos taken in the 1910s, and newer photos from the 1990s, which show how little the old city has changed.

Museums

The **Military Museum** (Gamal Abdul Nasser St; admission YR100; open 8am-11am & 3pm-6pm Sat-Wed) contains a collection of weapons and gory displays on Yemen's various wars and revolutions. Some history is translated into English, but few exhibits are labelled in any language but Arabic.

[Continued on page 762]

OLD SAN'A

The old walled city originally comprised separate western and eastern parts, connected at the present-day Ali Abdul Mogni St around the Al-Mutwakil Mosque. The eastern part is one of the largest completely preserved medinas in the Arab world.

The best remaining examples of San'a's city wall are by the western side of the Sa'ila and by Az-Zubayri St, between the Sa'ila and Bab al-Yaman. The wall was originally built of mud only; the stony lower part was built in 1990 as an act of restoration, preserving the structure but altering its spirit. On the northern side of the medina, near Bab ash-Sha'ub, restored stretches of the wall still stand.

Private gardens hide behind mud walls. There are hectares of them, with entries only from the backyards of the houses or mosques.

Inset: Gypsum plaster trimmings gleam like lacework on the mud-brick houses in Yemen's capital (Photo by Bethune Carmichael)

Right: A minaret commands the view over the old city

CHRIS MELLOR

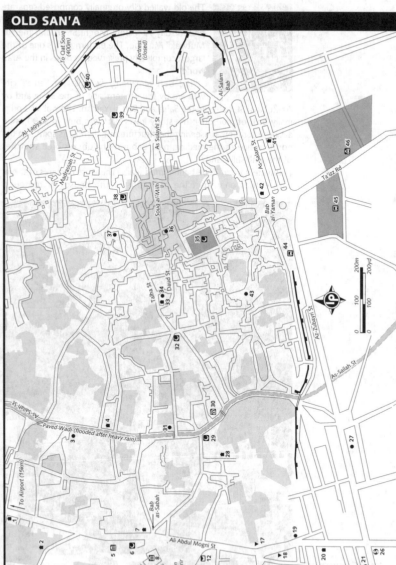

OLD SAN'A

OLD SAN'A

Traders and their clients hustle and bustle in the Old City's Souk al-Milh

Travellers can best enjoy these improbable oases from the *manzars* (attics) of palace hotels or by looking over walls. The city used to be self-sufficient in vegetables and fruit; the gardens are actively cultivated to this day.

On the southeastern tip of the walled city, the old citadel stands on an elevation, surrounded by massive walls. It is used by the military forces and cannot be entered.

[Continued from page 758]

The extensive **Museum of Arts & Crafts** (*Midan at-Tahrir; admission YR500; open 9am-12.30pm & 4pm-7pm Sat-Wed*) contains dioramas of traditional Yemeni life and displays that explore leather, jewellery and pottery crafts.

All the exhibits have explanations in English, but it's probably not worth the admission fee unless you're particularly keen on arts and crafts.

Just up from the Al-Mutwakil Mosque is the renovated **National Museum** (*Ali Abdul Mogni St; admission YR500; open 9am-1.30pm Sat-Wed*). It features a very interesting collection of pre-Islamic artefacts, and bits and pieces from various occupying empires and excavations at Ma'rib and Zabid. Most explanations are in English or German.

Places to Stay – Budget
Reidan Palace Hotel (☎ 245686; *As-Salam St; singles/doubles with shared bathroom YR500/800*) is popular. At this price the rooms are unsurprisingly basic and musty, but the hotel is in a vibrant (albeit noisy) area.

A few other places nearby offer a similar standard for the same price.

Al-Ikhwa Hotel (☎ 274909; *singles/doubles with TV & bathroom YR1000/1500*) is one of the better hotels in the quiet and convenient area to the west of the overpass Ali Abdul Mogni Street. Rooms are comfortable and clean.

Emirates Hotel (☎/fax 272812; *off Qasr al-Jumhuri St; singles without/with bath-room YR800/1000, doubles with bathroom YR1500*) is on a quiet street. Rooms are large and clean, have TV, and are good value.

Al-Aloobeh Tourist Hotel (☎ 279004; *Bab al-Yaman; singles/doubles with TV & shared bathroom YR700/1200*) overlooks the Bab al-Yaman, so the location is outstanding. It's basic but clean, and some quieter rooms are available.

Al-Nasr Hotel (☎ 273453; *Ali Abdul Mogni St; singles/doubles with TV & bathroom YR700/1400*) is also central. Rooms are clean and the staff is friendly. Some rooms are very noisy.

Sultan Palace Hotel (☎ 273766; e *ab dulkarem2000@yahoo.com; singles/doubles with shower, communal toilet & breakfast YR1300/1600*), just near the Qubbat al-Mahdi Mosque, has been recommended by a number of readers for its friendly staff. The rooms are quite small and have mattresses on the floor, but the place is very clean and comfortable.

Places to Stay – Mid-Range
Taj Talha Hotel (☎ 287130; e *taj.talha.hotel@ y.net.ye; Talha St; singles with shared bathroom YR2250, doubles/triples with bathroom YR3500/4325*) is a traditional tower house in the middle of the old city. Each room is authentically furnished, but small. The convivial mafraj and cafeteria offer outstanding views. Rates include breakfast.

The **Arabia Felix Tourist Hotel** (☎ 287 330; e *arabia-felix@y.net.ye; As-Sailah St; singles/doubles with bathroom US$18/22*) is a charming traditional tower house built around a tranquil garden. The rooms are clean and modern, but it's a little pricey. Rates include breakfast.

Yemeni Homes

The architecture of Yemen is unlike that of any country in the Middle East. Building designs are also different within Yemen depending on the local climate, available building materials (such as mud and stones) and historical links with other regions (such as India and Africa). Designs often blend in harmoniously with the environment, and all buildings have thick, high walls to counter the heat. Many rural homes are clustered together on the top of hills and mountains for defensive reasons.

The ground floor is typically made from stones and often used for storage and, in rural areas, to accommodate livestock. The next level (1st floor) is normally used for social events, and the 2nd floor is usually reserved for the use of women and children. The upper floors (often made from mud bricks) contain bedrooms, and a kitchen and bathroom. On or near the top floor is the *mafraj*. This commodious and decorative room features plenty of windows, and is where (normally) Yemeni men (and foreign men and women) relax, eat, dance, play music and, of course, chew qat.

Sam City Hotel *(☎ 270752, Ali Abdul Mogni St; singles/doubles with TV & bathroom US$15/25)* is a modern alternative. The rooms are quite comfortable and the staff are very friendly. There are lots of rooms to chose from as it's rarely full, and rates are negotiable.

Places to Stay – Top End
The following hotels offer all the luxuries and amenities (eg, private bathrooms, air-con, hot water and TV) expected at these prices.

Hill Town Hotel *(☎ 278426;* e *hilltown@y .net.ye; off Ali Abdul Mogni St; singles/ doubles US$45/60)* offers the best top-end value. It's quiet, and rooms are large and well furnished. Rates include breakfast.

Taj Sheba Hotel *(☎ 272372;* e *sheba .sanaa@tajhotels.com; Ali Abdul Mogni St; singles/doubles US$164/183)* is the most central of the luxury hotels.

Places to Eat
Palestine Restaurant *(Ali Abdul Mogni St; meals YR400)* continues to be recommended by readers. It's a cafeteria where you can order precooked (but fresh) food from a counter, so it's easy to point at what you want without ordering in Arabic. There's no menu but a large meal of chicken, salad, bread and a drink will see you right.

Al-Shazarwa *(Ali Abdul Mogni St; meals about YR300)* has a menu in English but no prices are listed, so check before you start ordering, or before the waiter starts putting down too many unwanted dishes. The food is usually tasty and always cheap.

Al-Shaibani Modern Restaurant *(Hadda St; large meals YR800)*, next to the Ashtal Travel & Tourism office, is the one most locals and expats flock to. The restaurant is noisy and unpretentious, but there's a nicer eating area at the back. There's no menu, but expect a mighty feed of meat, salads, dips, bread and drinks.

Al-Gazeera Restaurant *(26th September St; meals about YR300)* is convenient, cheap, friendly, clean and offers a menu in English. Try a grilled half chicken with salad and french fries. It opens early for breakfast.

Al-Khima (Alkhaimah) Restaurant *(☎ 440 069; off Hadda St; salads YR150, starters YR300-500, grills about YR1000)* caters mainly to tour groups. Nevertheless, 'The Tent' (as it's also known) is an ideal place to try some Yemeni food in a traditional setting. It's well known to taxi drivers if you're having any trouble finding it.

Hill Town Hotel *(☎ 278426; off Ali Abdul Mogni St; meals YR400-700)* offers a decent selection of Chinese, Indian and Italian meals, but the quality of food does vary.

Arabia Felix Tourist Hotel *(As-Sailah St; meals YR350-650)* has a small courtyard restaurant open to the public.

The best place to stock up on Western goodies is the **Al-Huda Supermarket** *(Az-Zubayri St)*. If you're hankering for a Big Mac, **McDonald's** *(Djibouti Rd)* recently opened its first outlet in Yemen.

Getting There & Away
Air The national carrier **Yemenia** has several flights a day to Aden (YR14,760), one on Friday to Suqutra (YR42,088), five weekly to Ta'izz (YR7710), four a week to Al-Hudayda (YR7710) and Sayun (YR20,050), and almost daily to Ar-Rayyan (YR20,050) for Al-Mukalla. The most convenient Yemenia offices in San'a are along Ali Abdul Mogni St *(☎ 274697)* and near Universal Travel & Tourism on Az-Zubayri St *(☎ 260834)*.

Bus On Az-Zubayri St, **Yemitco** has daily services to Aden (YR2400, eight hours) at 7am, 11am, 1pm and 3pm; Al-Hudayda (YR1800, 4½ hours) at 7.15am and 1.30pm; Al-Mukalla (YR6000, 23 hours) at 7am; Sayun (YR4000, 23 hours) via Ma'rib (YR1400, four hours) at 7.30am; and Ta'izz (YR2000, five hours) at 7am and 2pm.

The **General Land Transport Co** bus agency on Az-Zubayri St offers cheaper daily services to Aden (YR1000) at 7am and 1.30pm; Al-Hudayda (YR800) at 7am and 2pm; Al-Mukalla (YR2500) at 7am; Sayun (YR1800) via Ma'rib (YR500) at 7am; and Ta'izz (YR800) at 7am and 1.30pm.

Shared Taxi Most shared taxis to Wadi Dhahr (YR70, 30 minutes), Shibam (YR150, one hour), Thilla (YR170, one hour) and Al-Mahwit (YR400, 2½ hours) leave from a remote spot along Wadi Dhahr Rd in the northwestern suburb of Matbah. A few shared taxis to these places (and to Matbah) also leave from outside Al-Gazeera Restaurant on 26th September St.

Shared taxis to Manakhah (YR200, around three hours), Al-Hudayda (YR500), Ta'izz

YEMEN

(YR600) and Aden (YR850) leave from the main taxi station on Ta'izz Rd. Taxis to Ma'rib, and to Amran, Hajja and Sa'da, leave from specific taxi stations listed on the San'a map, but foreigners are not currently permitted to travel to these places by public transport.

Getting Around

There's no public transport between San'a International Airport and the city centre. Locals pay about YR1200 for a chartered taxi, but foreigners inevitably pay more. Alternatively, walk about 150m from the airport terminal and jump into a shared taxi to Midan at-Tahrir. Top-end hotels should provide a courtesy minibus for guests.

Minibuses and shared taxis ply the main roads, but are uncomfortable. Chartered private taxis are a better option, and motorbikes offer rides on the back for a small fee.

Around San'a

WADI DHAHR   وادي ظهر

About 14km northwest of San'a is the fertile Wadi Dhahr, along which is the marvellous rock palace known as **Dar al-Hajar** *(admission YR400; open 8am-6pm daily)*. This five-storey summer palace was built on pre-Islamic caves by an imam in about 1786 and was extended in the 1930s. Many of the 17 rooms are lavishly furnished and their former uses are explained mostly in English. The admission fee should include a guided tour. If you visit on a Friday you may witness a traditional Yemeni wedding outside the palace.

The palace is about 1km north of the taxi stop in the village and is impossible to miss. About 1.5km along the eastern road to San'a, and near a defunct petrol station, is a **lookout** offering superb views of the palace and wadi.

There's nowhere to stay, but you can buy basic items at village shops or eat at the tent **restaurant** (normally only open for tour groups) inside the palace. Shared taxis from San'a cost YR70.

SHIBAM & KAWKABAN   شبام كوكبان

☎ 07

Shibam, 48km northwest of San'a, boasts one of the oldest **mosques** in Yemen. The village is at the base of Jebel Kawkaban (2800m), home to an extensive array of **bird life**. For most travellers, however, Shibam is a transit point for Kawkaban, Thilla and Al-Mahwit (see later in this chapter). (Shibam should not be confused with the village of the same name in Wadi Hadramawt to the east.)

On top of the mountain is the extraordinary village of Kawkaban, where residents of Shibam sheltered from frequent raiders in the past. Contact the Hotel Jebel Kawkaban (see Places to Stay & Eat later) about arranging guides for **hikes** to traditional villages such as At-Tawila and Hababah, and around landscapes reminiscent of the Grand Canyon in the US. Local children will also happily show you around the village.

Places to Stay & Eat

Hameda Hotel & Restaurant *(☎ 450480; Shibam; singles/doubles with shared bathroom YR600/1200)* is about 200m down from the souq/taxi stop. Rooms are bright, clean and quiet, and the bathroom is spotless. Breakfast is included in the rates; lunch (YR500) and dinner (YR400) are available to guests.

Altaj Tourist Hotel *(☎ 450170; Kawkaban; doubles with bathroom YR2400)* is in a traditional home grandly signed 'Planets Tower'. The rooms are clean, but small and unremarkable.

Hotel Jebel Kawkaban *(☎ 450856; Kawkaban; with breakfast & dinner per person YR1000)* is the best place in town. This family-run hotel offers simple mattresses on the floor, but is clean and comfortable. The effusive English-speaking manager is an essential source of information about local hiking.

Getting There & Away

Taxis from San'a to Shibam cost YR150. From near the main mosque in Shibam, a steep path heads up to Kawkaban (one hour). Shared taxis from Shibam to Kawkaban use the circuitous 7km road (YR250, 30 minutes).

THILLA (THULA)   ثلا

About 9km north of Shibam is Thilla. This traditional village is cleaner and better preserved than others, and is renowned for its stone houses with decorative windows. Children can show you the **souq** and the impregnable **Husn Thula** fortress, as well as some **old homes** and **mosques**. Sadly, the **museum** has been closed for several years. Thilla is an easy **hike** from Shibam or Kawkaban; no guide is needed.

Thal'aa Tourist Hotel (*village square; per person with bathroom YR1200*) offers musty rooms but rates include breakfast and dinner.

The village can be reached by shared taxi (YR170, one hour) from San'a, or from Shibam.

Northwestern Yemen

This part of the country is occasionally unstable, so foreigners are allowed to visit only places listed in this section on an organised tour, or in a chartered car with a driver, from San'a. Therefore, no practical information about buses and shared taxis is provided in this section.

Some places can also only be visited with an armed military escort, but don't let the inconvenience and security requirements dissuade you from visiting this spectacular and ancient region.

AMRAN عمران
☎ 07

Amran, 52km northwest of San'a, boasts a remarkable **old town** built on flat land (so it's easy to reach). Although there are no specific sites, it's fun to wander about, especially during the Friday **souq**. The old town is about 2km west of the main San'a–Sa'da road.

Amran Tourist Hotel (☎ 61055; *doubles with shared bathroom YR600*), opposite the cemetery about 300m west of the main road, offers large but basic rooms.

Between Amran and Hajja is **Kuhlan Affar**, a friendly village with a majestic hilltop **fortress** (*admission YR150; open 9am–6pm daily*). The village is also home to a chaotic **qat souq** each morning and a general **souq** every Monday.

HAJJA حجة
☎ 07

Hajja is a large town spread over several hills 126km northwest of San'a. The main reason to visit is the magnificent (and often green) mountain **scenery** along the road

from Amran. The town centre is the roundabout in front of the Al-Jazeera Hotel.

On top of one hill is the large **Al-Qahira fortress** (*entry YR100; open daily in daylight hours*). Built by an imam about 600 years ago, it was occupied by the Turks (note the British-made cannons) and used as a gruesome prison by another imam in the 1950s. Bang loudly on the door for the caretaker.

Places to Stay & Eat
Two hotels, about 100m along Al-Hodeida St from the Al-Jazeera Hotel roundabout, offer basic rooms.

Al-Hmra Blus Tourist Hotel (☎ 223310; *singles/doubles with bathroom & TV YR1100/1600*) is the better one.

Ghamdan Hajjah Hotel (☎ 200420; *singles/doubles with bathroom YR3500/4000*), superbly located on a hilltop, has pleasant furnished rooms with TV, fridge and balcony, but is overpriced. The hotel is a steep 10-minute walk north of the main road from Amran. The expensive **restaurant** (*meals about YR500*) here is open to the public.

Hajja Tourism Hotel (☎ 220196; *singles/doubles with bathroom YR1200/1500*) is inconvenient, but quiet and good value. The rooms are clean, and most include a TV. Take a taxi from the Al-Jazeera Hotel roundabout. Guests can pre-order simple meals.

SHAHARAH (SHIHARA) شهارة
This village, 100km north of San'a, boasts one of the most spectacular vistas in the country, but half the fun is getting there! Shaharah is famous for the 17th-century **stone bridge**. It was built of limestone bricks, and links two villages previously unconnected because of the deep gorge.

Funduq Khalid (*rooms with shared bathroom per person YR1500*) offers a clean mattress in a comfortable traditional room. Rates include breakfast and dinner. The less salubrious **Funduq Francesca** has the same sort of rooms, with meals, for the same price. **Funduq Al-Shareq** (*Al-Qabi*) also charges the same but is slightly nicer.

To get to Shaharah from San'a, it's a 1½-hour trip to Al-Qabi, then another 10km (1½ hours) along a shocking road. Villagers won't allow any vehicles from San'a to go to Shaharah, so visitors are forced to charter a battered WWII-surplus jeep for an extortionate YR5500 return per vehicle from Al-Qabi.

You're allowed to wander around Shaharah, but not outside the village.

SA'DA صعدة
☎ 07

The most important town in this part of Yemen is also one of the more historical and troublesome. Many locals still adhere to the Zaydi sect, and most are fiercely independent and distrustful of the central government, but all are friendly to foreigners.

Things to See
The major attraction is the lovely **old town**. If you turn left, and left again, immediately past the southern entrance (Bab al-Yaman), you'll find steps to the wall. You can walk the 3.3km along most of the surrounding 6m-to 8m-high wall. In the midst of the old town is the elegant 12th-century **Al-Hadi Mosque**.

The daily **souq** in the old town is renowned for the quality of its *jambiyas*. Each Saturday, a massive **souq** is also held at Suq al-Talh, about 10km northwest of Sa'da. It's here that you'll find Kalashnikovs and bullets strewn across the ground like tomatoes at other souqs.

Places to Stay & Eat
Each place listed here is within 200m of the Bab al-Yaman.

Al-Aokhoah *(per person with shared bathroom YR200)* is the best of the cheapies, but don't expect any peace or too many amenities for this price.

Kaz Blankla Wings Hotel *(☎ 514505; singles/doubles with bathroom YR1000/ 2000)* is large, convenient and good value. The rooms are well furnished, with TV and fan, but not as nice as the outside suggests.

Rahban Tourism Hotel *(☎ 512856; singles/ doubles with TV & fan YR1680/2464)* has a large number of huge rooms; most with private bathrooms. Rates include breakfast.

Opposite the Rahban is the adequate **Rahban Tourism Cafeteria** and the **Sanabel Restaurant** *(meals at both about YR150)*.

Southwestern Yemen

Most of the places listed in this section are accessible by public transport from San'a,

and travel is usually allowed without a travel permit.

MANAKHAH مناخة
Manakhah is 95km southwest of San'a. There isn't a great deal to see here except the daily **souq** (best on Sunday), so you're better off continuing to Al-Hajjarah (see later in this section). A couple of places along the main road will change money.

The friendly **Al-Tawfiq Tourism Hotel** *(☎ 01-460085; per person with breakfast, dinner & shared bathroom YR2800)* is easy to spot along the noisy main road into Manakhah from San'a. It offers comfortable mattresses on the floor, and hot water, but is pricey. The views from the *mafraj* are typically gorgeous. With notice staff can arrange **traditional music** and guides for **hiking**.

Shared taxis from San'a cost YR200. Alternatively, take a bus or shared taxi towards Al-Hudayda, and get another taxi at the turn-off to Manakhah.

AL-KHUTAYB (AL-HOTEIB) الحطيب
This pilgrimage site, 6km south of Manakah, is perched on a solitary mountain. It is revered by followers of the Ismaili sect as the location of a shrine dedicated to a 16th-century preacher. You are allowed to walk around the area, but the shrine is fenced off to non-Muslims. The major pilgrimage takes place on the 16th day of the first Islamic month, Muharram.

The paved road south from Manakhah to Al-Khutayb is excellent. There's no public transport to the village, so the only option is a chartered taxi from Manakhah. Otherwise, hike from Manakhah or Al-Hajjarah.

AL-HAJJARAH الهجرة
This spectacular 11th-century hilltop village, 5km west of Manakhah, is one of the highlights of Yemen. The surrounding Haraz Mountains are ideal for **hiking**, while the less adventurous can hire donkeys. Both activities can be arranged at the hotel (see later), where knowledgeable English-speaking guides cost about YR2000 per day. Longer treks can be organised with overnight stays in village homes, or the guides may be able to find a tent with enough notice.

Interestingly, the original village was divided into two. The Al-Ba'aha quarter was inhabited by Jews until they fled to Israel in the 1950s. Above this is the 'Muslim quarter' with its huge gate, ostensibly to shut out invaders and animals. English-speaking boys will no doubt want to show you around.

Al-Hajjarah Tourist Hotel & Restaurant *(☎ 01-460210; e alhajjarah-hotel@y.net.ye; per person with breakfast, dinner & shared bathroom YR1500)* has been warmly recommended by readers. The rooms are small and contain mattresses on the floor, but are spotless. Guests can enjoy tasty meals, as well as **traditional music** and **dancing** most evenings.

The village is connected to Manakhah by a very rough track. You can jump in the back of a pick-up, but it may be quicker to walk. The track is not too steep and offers awesome **views**.

AL-MAHWIT المحويت

This bustling town has little to offer the traveller, but is worth visiting for the stunning **scenery** along the windy, 125km road west of San'a. The region attracts a fair amount of rain, and the hills are sometimes covered with fog.

The **old town**, perched on a hilltop, is where the Ottomans based their regional capital in the 16th century. Kids will show you around (whether you want them to or not). **Hiking** is possible, but not currently recommended (nor probably allowed) because of tribal problems in the area.

Friendship Hotel *(singles/doubles with shared bathroom YR600/1000)* is just off the main road about 200m down the hill from the taxi stop. It offers basic beds with no sheets in a musty room.

Mahweet Hotel *(☎ 07-404767; singles/doubles with TV & bathroom YR3050/3660)* is on the main road, 400m down the hill from the taxi stop. Rooms are modern, clean and comfortable, if a little charmless, and some offer wonderful views. The **restaurant** *(meals from YR250)* is uninspiring but serves decent Western food.

Al-Waha Restaurant *(meals from YR250)*, along the road behind the Mahweet Hotel, is the best place to eat. The grilled chicken is particularly tasty.

Shared taxis from San'a cost YR400 (2½ hours). Travel agencies in San'a charge around US$75 for a day trip from the capital.

AL-HUDAYDA (HODEIDA) الحديده
☎ 03

Yemen's fourth-largest city is a likable place at the end of a spectacular road, on the Tihama coast, 230km southwest of San'a, but there's not much to keep you there for more than a day. The city centre is the large and pleasant **Hadiqat ash-Sha'b** (People's Garden), around which you'll find Internet centres and foreign-exchange offices.

An evening walk along the unimpressive **corniche** offers some welcome breezes. The early-morning **fish souq**, 2km southeast down the corniche from the city garden, is a hive of activity. Decrepit old **Turkish houses** can be found south of Midan at-Tahrir, which is along the road between the city garden and corniche.

Places to Stay & Eat
The following hotels, along with several others, sit along the southern edge of the People's Garden. Both these places offer rooms with a TV, fridge, fan, air-con and bathroom.

Al-Burg Hotel *(☎ 201114; singles/doubles YR2000/2400)* is good value. The rooms are a bit poky and in need of some renovation, but the hotel is well furnished.

Al-Jazira Hotel *(☎ 201403; singles/doubles YR4500/6000)*, which was formerly known as The Bristol, is better but dearer. It offers large, modern and fairly unexciting rooms. The attached **restaurant** is worth trying, with meals around YR250.

Several outdoor **cafés** are squeezed into the eastern corner of the city garden. Plenty of decent eateries, such as the **Al-Khayyam Restaurant**, are dotted along the western side of the garden.

Getting There & Away
Yemenia, which has an office *(☎ 238211)* near the Al-Burg Hotel, flies four times a week to San'a (YR7710) and once a week to Ta'izz (YR7710).

Yemitco, which has an office north of the People's Garden, has daily buses to San'a (YR1800) as well as Aden (YR2000) and Ta'izz (YR3000) via Zabid. Other bus offices are located along the western side of the garden. Shared taxis leave from the corner of San'a St (the main road from the capital) and Ring Rd, about 1.2km southeast of the garden. A shared taxi from San'a costs YR500.

YEMEN

BEIT AL-FAQIH بيت الفقيه

The only reason to visit this dusty roadside town, 62km southeast of Al-Hudayda, is the massive **souq** on Friday. The epicentre of what is probably the largest souq in Yemen is about 1.5km west of the main road. This is one of the best places to buy hand-woven *futas* (see Shopping in the Facts for the Visitor section earlier in this chapter), head cloths and tablecloths, as well as mats and rugs.

There's no hotel in town, so come on a day trip from Zabid or Al-Hudayda. Both places are regularly linked to Beit al-Faqih by shared taxi and bus.

ZABID زبيد

Zabid is a charming historical town 99km south of Al-Hudayda. The circular old town, originally built in AD 820, was renowned for its Islamic university, some 200 mosques and dozens of religious schools. The old town was declared a Unesco World Heritage Site in 1993 and was transferred to the organisation's Danger List in 2000 so more funds for urgent restoration could be allocated.

This lethargic town sits along the fertile Wadi Zabid and is one of the hottest places on earth (unbearable in July and August).

Orientation & Information

The labyrinthine old town is 500m southwest of the main road along an obvious turn-off. Most sights are only a short walk from the Zabbed Tourism Rest House (see Places to Stay & Eat later in this section). Walking around with a guide (they'll find you!) is worthwhile because it's easy to get lost and miss out on the old **mosques** and **weaving workshops** behind the walls and along the narrow lanes.

Things to See & Do

The gate to the **citadel** is near the conspicuous four-storey white building (currently a government office that may be converted to a hotel at a later date). Through the gate is the **Zabid Museum** (*admission by donation; open daily during daylight hours*); if it's closed, get the keys from the caretaker at the adjacent resthouse. The collection of pottery and implements, which were excavated around the old town, is small but interesting enough. Some explanations are in English.

Nearly 90 mosques and religious schools still operate in the old town. The white, 13th-century **Al-Iskandar Mosque** is within the citadel walls. It's normally off limits to non-Muslims, though staff at the Zabid Citadel Rest House (see Places to Stay & Eat later in this section) will often show guests around (for a small fee). Outside the citadel in the western part of the old town are the **Al-Jami'a Mosque** and **Ash-Sha'ria Mosque**.

The **Old Zabid Souq** (*open daily*) is busiest on Sunday and is a great place to buy mats and hand-woven *futas*.

The Zabbed Tourism Rest House can arrange tours by **camel** or **donkey** around the old town for US$70 per person per day. More exhilarating is a four-day trip by camel from Zabid to Al-Khawkha, via Wadi Zabid and the coast, for US$280 per person.

Places to Stay & Eat

Zabbed Tourism Rest House (*☎ 03-340270; per person with breakfast & dinner YR1500*) is a comfortable hostel that caters well to backpackers. All beds are in an open-air, undercover room, so there's no peace or privacy, but most guests don't seem to mind. The staff are friendly, and the meals are usually hearty. Lunch for guests costs YR700. The hostel is signposted from the entrance to the old town.

Zabid Citadel Rest House (*YR500 per person*) is inside the citadel and next to the museum. It was established by some Canadian archaeologists, and all profits help with restoration of the citadel. It offers a similar setup to the other resthouse, but basic private rooms are also available. If the heat inside becomes too stifling, take your mattress to the rooftop.

Getting There & Away

Zabid is accessible by Yemitco bus from Al-Hudayda (YR1000, two hours) and Ta'izz (YR2000, 3½ hours). Shared taxis also ply these routes.

AL-KHAWKHA الخوخه
☎ 03

This village along the Red Sea coast is as close as Yemen gets to a resort. You can **swim** at Al-Khawkha but high tide often swallows the beach, and harmless sharks lurk past the sandbars. Alternatively, ask around for a **boat trip** (about YR1000 per hour) to watch pelicans roosting. San'a-based Moka Tours (see Activities in the Facts for the Visitor section earlier in this chapter), in conjunction with Le Village Moka Marine (see later), offers **scuba diving** for groups around the Hanish Islands. Plenty of advance notice is required. Sindibad (see later) sometimes has snorkelling gear for guests and can organise boat trips.

Le Village Moka Marine *(☎ 362770; singles/doubles with air-con YR2500/3000)* is a charming collection of bungalows, each with two bedrooms and a bathroom. Breakfast (YR350), lunch (YR700) and dinner (YR700) are available to guests.

Sindibad *(☎ 362872; per person with breakfast & dinner YR1800)* has a superb seaside location, seemingly overrun by crows, cats and, sometimes, crabs. It's reasonably clean and friendly, but has seen far better days: the rooms are rustic, the ablution blocks are rudimentary and electricity is only available in the evenings.

Several fly-blown **restaurants** in the village serve mouthwatering grilled fish.

Take a shared taxi or bus from Ta'izz or Al-Hudayda, get off at Hays and wait for a pick-up to Al-Khawkha. Plenty of taxis wait on the road from Hays. At this point a path heads south to the scruffy fishing village. Another path goes north to the hotels and beaches, which are accessible only by taxi.

TA'IZZ تعز
☎ 04

Yemen's third-largest city, 250km south of San'a, sprawls around the mighty Jebel Sabir (3070m). Ta'izz boasts a wonderful old town and plenty of great shopping, but suffers from unrestrained population growth and appalling traffic. It reached its zenith as the capital of the Rasulid empire between the early 13th and mid-15th centuries, and was briefly the capital of an imamate as recently as the 1950s.

Information
The tourist office on 26th September St is permanently closed through lack of interest, so contact **Universal Travel & Tourism** *(☎ 225 383)* on Gamal Abdul Nasser St if you have any specific questions.

Several foreign-exchange offices can be found near the junction of Gamar Abdul Nasser and At-Tahrir Sts. Otherwise, try the **Central Bank of Yemen**, opposite the Ta'izz Museum, or the **Credit Agricole Indosuez**, off 26th September St.

The **post office** is just north of 26th September St. For emailing and surfing the Net, try the classy **Everist Internet Cafe**, opposite the TeleYemen office on 26th September St, or the **Al-Khatib Internet Centre** in the jewellery souq on 26th September St.

Things to See
Dominating the surrounding countryside is the granite mountain of **Jebel Sabir** (3070m). It's now accessible by a windy and very steep 4km road, built courtesy of a US$10 million gift from a Saudi prince. Take a taxi from Bab al-Kabir, and perhaps walk down all or some of the way. More accessible **views** of the city are available from around the Mareb Hotel (see Places to Stay later in this section).

The stunning **Qalat al-Qahira** is majestically perched on a hilltop between the city centre and Jebel Sabir but, disappointingly, the fortress is occupied by the military and is off limits to tourists.

About 500m northwest of the fortress are the twin minarets of the decorative **Al-Ashrafiya Mosque**. It was originally constructed in AD 628, but extensively rebuilt in the 12th and 13th centuries. If you can find the gatekeeper, he will happily show you around for a small tip (about YR50). Other mosques which can be admired – but not entered by non-Muslims – include the pre-13th-century **Al-Muzzafar Mosque** in the old town, and the Turkish **Al-Mutabiyya Mosque**, just south of the old town.

The **Ta'izz Museum** *(26th September St; admission YR100; open 9am-noon Sat-Wed)* is a converted palace that offers unique glimpses into the personal life of an imam. Opening hours are erratic, however.

Bab al-Kabir is the main entrance to the **old town**, but only a few pieces of the walls and two gates remain. Just east of Bab al-Kabir, off 26th September St, is the **jewellery souq**. This is probably the best place to pick up anything made from gold or silver.

Places to Stay
All hotels listed here offer rooms with a fan, TV and bathroom.

YEMEN

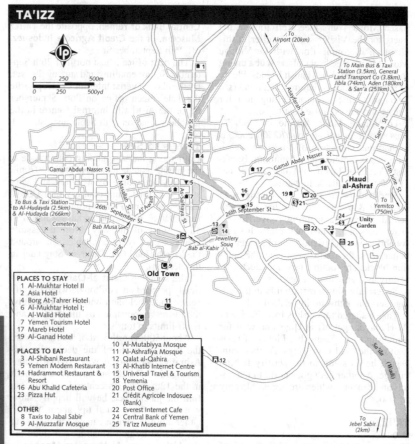

TA'IZZ

PLACES TO STAY
1 Al-Mukhtar Hotel II
2 Asia Hotel
4 Borg At-Tahrer Hotel
6 Al-Mukhtar Hotel I;
   Al-Walid Hotel
7 Yemen Tourism Hotel
17 Mareb Hotel
19 Al-Ganad Hotel

PLACES TO EAT
3 Al-Shibani Restaurant
5 Yemen Modern Restaurant
14 Hadrammot Restaurant &
   Resort
16 Abu Khalid Cafeteria
23 Pizza Hut

OTHER
8 Taxis to Jabal Sabir
9 Al-Muzzafar Mosque

10 Al-Mutabiyya Mosque
11 Al-Ashrafiya Mosque
12 Qalat al-Qahira
13 Al-Khatib Internet Centre
15 Universal Travel & Tourism
18 Yemenia
20 Post Office
21 Crédit Agricole Indosuez
   (Bank)
22 Everest Internet Cafe
24 Central Bank of Yemen
25 Ta'izz Museum

The following three places are on As-Saifraya St, a convenient and relatively quiet back street.

Yemen Tourism Hotel (☎ 253999; singles/doubles with air-con YR1850/2500), opposite the Al-Walid, is the best of the three. It has been recommended by readers and is worth the extra few riyals.

Al-Mukhtar Hotel I (☎ 222491; e dafaq@y.net.ye; singles/doubles YR1500/2500) is a bit rough around the edges, but perfectly adequate. It's worth looking at a few rooms because some are better than others.

Al-Walid Hotel (☎ 253000; singles/doubles YR1500/2500) next door is considerably classier and more comfortable. The rooms feature huge double beds and are very clean.

Al-Mukhtar Hotel II (☎ 256590; e dafaq@y.net.ye; At-Tahrir St; singles/doubles YR1350/1850) is a little inconvenient but worth trying. The rooms are large and comfortable, and feature a balcony and decent bathroom. Many rooms are situated away from the noisy road.

Asia Hotel (☎ 254453; e asiahotel@hotmail.com; At-Tahrir St; singles/doubles with air-con YR1500/2000) is reasonably convenient. The rooms are clean, comfortable and well furnished.

Borg At-Tahrer Hotel (☎ 221483; At-Tahrir St; singles/doubles YR800/1200) has large but noisy rooms. It is good value, however.

Al-Ganad Hotel (☎ 210528; 26th September St; singles/doubles YR1500/2000) is located behind a gate opposite the post office.

It offers basic, old-fashioned rooms, but they're comfortable and quiet.

Mareb Hotel (☎ 210350; off Gamal Abdul Nasser St; singles/doubles YR3000/5000) is about the only mid-range option. It's a serene place with an elevated position. Most furniture is left over from the 1960s, and rooms don't seem to have been upgraded since.

Places to Eat
Dozens of cheap **eateries** offering chicken, rice, salad and *salta* (stew), can be found within 200m (in any direction) of the corner of Gamal Abdul Nasser and At-Tahrir Sts.

Yemen Modern Restaurant (Gamal Abdul Nasser St; meals about YR350) has an upstairs dining area with views of the chaos below. The extensive menu is in English. A half chicken, salad, rice and soft drink makes a satisfying meal.

Al-Shibani Restaurant (Gamal Abdul Nasser St; meals about YR300) is famous for its fish dishes.

Hadrammot Restaurant & Resort (26th September St; salads about YR100, grills from YR300) is a rather grand name for a tiny concrete oasis set back from the street. It offers all sorts of drinks, as well as grills and salads at meal times.

Pizza Hut (Unity Garden, 26th September St; small/large pizzas YR600/1000, pasta dishes from YR500) offers a modern respite.

Abu Khalid Cafeteria (Gamal Abdul Nasser St) is a quiet, air-con spot. It's ideal for a drink, a plate of sweet treats or an ice cream.

Getting There & Away
Yemenia, which has an office (☎ 233226) along Gamal Abdul Nasser St, has five flights to San'a (YR7710) and one to Al-Hudayda (YR7710) each week.

From the main taxi station about 4km northeast of the city centre, shared taxis go to San'a (YR600), Aden (YR400) and Ibb (YR180) near Jibla.

From the terminal about 300m further up (northeast) from the main taxi station, the **General Land Transport Co** has two bus services a day to San'a (YR800, five hours). **Yemitco**, just off 13th June St, has daily buses to Al-Hudayda (YR3000, 5½ hours), San'a (YR2000) and Aden (YR1000, 3½ hours). Public buses and shared taxis to Al-Hudayda leave from a spot along Hodeida Rd about 4km west of the city centre.

JIBLA جبله
Jibla is 74km north of Ta'izz and 8km southwest of Ibb, the regional capital. This stunning hilltop village served as a capital of the Sulayhid empire in the 11th and 12th centuries, and was particularly prosperous under the benevolent Queen Arwa. Jibla is far more accessible than other similar villages and, thankfully, almost devoid of traffic. It's also famous among locals for its daily **qat souq**.

About 1.5km up from the taxi stop at the southern end of the village are the twin minarets of the 11th-century **Queen Arwa Mosque**. Non-Muslims are allowed to look around if accompanied by the gatekeeper (or someone in a similar position) for a small donation (about YR50). It's possible to climb some steps above the mosque for excellent **views**.

Across the village from this mosque – and accessible through the incredibly narrow lanes of the **souq** – is the solitary minaret of the 16th-century **As-Sunna Mosque**. The crumbling **Dar as-Sultana Palace** (admission free; permanently open) is nearby. It's possible to scramble around the ruins, but nothing is explained in any language.

Near the palace is the **Queen Arwa Museum** (admission YR100; open daily 8am-6pm). It features some dioramas about traditional life and a few musical instruments, but nothing much is captioned in English. There are wonderful **views** from the windows in the museum and from the **café** on top.

There's nowhere to stay in Jibla, so come on a day trip from Ta'izz. From Ta'izz, take a shared taxi to the dreary town of Ibb (YR180, 1½ hours), and another to Jibla (YR50, 20 minutes) from the separate taxi station in Ibb.

ADEN عدن
☎ 02
Although San'a is the administrative capital of Yemen, the commercial centre is undoubtedly Aden (ah-**dahn**). This is possibly where, according to the Bible, Noah's Ark was built and launched, but the first reliable mention of this great port was recorded in the 6th century BC.

Aden's fortunes fluctuated constantly over many centuries. By the late 13th century it was home to perhaps 80,000 people, but by the time the British occupied Aden in 1839 the population had plummeted to about 600. Within a few decades, however, Aden became the third most important port in the world.

Aden served as the capital of the PDRY from 1967 and, after the two Yemen's united, it was declared a free-trade zone, paving the way for great economic growth. Although badly damaged in the War of Unity in 1994, it has made a good recovery.

Orientation & Information

The extensive city is based around an extinct 551m-high volcano joined to the mainland by an isthmus. To the west is the port of At-Tawahi, which offers some colonial history. The quiet and not particularly old section known as Crater is below the volcano, while Ma'alla stretches along the main road between Crater and At-Tawahi. The industrial region of Sheikh Othman is to the north.

The **tourist office** (☎ 204415) along Al-Muhsen St in At-Tawahi is open between 8am and 2pm Saturday to Wednesday, but is more of a government department and not very useful. Plenty of **foreign-exchange offices** can be found along Main Bazaar Rd and Ghandhi St in Crater. The **National Bank of Yemen** is along Queen Arwa Rd in Crater.

The **main post office** is just off Esplanade Rd in Crater, and there are telephone centres all over the city. There's an Internet café to the back of the minibus/taxi station (for Sheikh Othman) in Crater, and the **Horizon Internet Centre** is along Al-Muhsen St in At-Tawahi.

Things to See & Do

The dignified **Military Museum** (Sayla Rd, Crater; admission YR100; open 9am-noon & 4pm-7pm Sat-Thur) contains numerous displays about various wars in recent Yemeni history, as well as archaeological artefacts from Ma'rib and exhibits about British colonialism. Frustratingly, everything is labelled in Arabic, but a charming lady can provide a (free) guided tour in English.

The **National Museum for Antiquities** (off Al-Aidrus St, Crater; admission YR150; open 7.30am-2pm Sat-Wed) was closed for refurbishment at the time of writing. The effusive caretaker promises a vast number of ethnological exhibits left over from the

1930s, and many archaeological items. It's housed in a colonial-period girl's school.

All mosques in Aden are closed to non-Muslims, including the **Al-Khawja Mosque** (Al-Aidrus St, Crater), and the **Al-Aidrus Mosque** (Al-Aidrus St, Crater), built in the mid-19th century on the ruins of a 600-year-old mosque. The strange little **Aden Minaret** (off Esplanade Rd, Crater) is all that remains of a mosque built in the 8th century.

At the end of Sayla Rd in Crater are about 18 cisterns or reservoirs known as the **Aden Tanks** (admission YR100; open daily during daylight hours), carved out of the rocky hills. Many possibly date from the 1st century, but were partially rebuilt by the British in the 1850s. Along the way see if the enticing **Aden Museum** (Sayla Rd) has reopened (it was closed at the time of writing). Further up the hill is the **Tower of Silence** (admission free; permanently open), which is the ruins of a former Zoroastrian burial site.

Opposite the pier in At-Tawahi is the private **Tawahi Art Gallery** (Al-Muhsen St), which features works by Yemeni artists. About 60 minutes on foot from At-Tawahi (or take a shared taxi) is **Gold Mohur Bay**, one of the better and more accessible **beaches** in the region.

It's easy enough to walk across to **Sira Island** from Crater and wander around the enticing **fortress** (admission free; open daily during daylight hours) on top of the hill.

Places to Stay – Budget

The cheapest hotels are along the streets leading southeast from Sayla Rd in Crater. **Ousan Hotel** (Sabeel St; singles/doubles with shared bathroom YR600/900) is typical of an unappealing bunch.

Rimbaud/Rambow Tourist Hotel (☎ 255 899; Esplanade Rd, Crater; singles/doubles with fan & bathroom from YR2600/3200) is in the former home of the eccentric French poet Arthur Rimbaud (see the boxed text 'Rimbaud'). The building has some crumbling colonial charm, and some rooms have sea views, as well as fridge and TV. Readers have commented favourably about helpful staff.

Al-Wafa Hotel (☎ 256340; Ghandhi St, Crater; singles/doubles with shared bathroom YR1500/1700, doubles with bathroom YR2200) is one of the better options in the city centre. It's unpretentious, but clean and

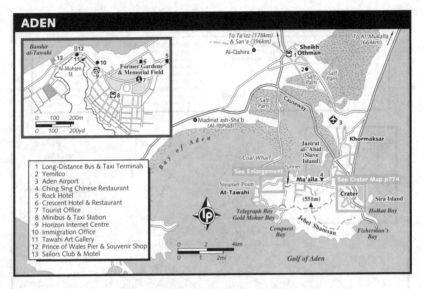

ADEN

1 Long-Distance Bus & Taxi Terminals
2 Yemitco
3 Aden Airport
4 Ching Sing Chinese Restaurant
5 Rock Hotel
6 Crescent Hotel & Restaurant
7 Tourist Office
8 Minibus & Taxi Station
9 Horizon Internet Centre
10 Immigration Office
11 Tawahi Art Gallery
12 Prince of Wales Pier & Souvenir Shop
13 Sailors Club & Motel

reasonably quiet, and some renovations were under way at the time of writing. The air-conditioning doesn't look too promising, but each room has a fan.

Aden Gulf Hotel (☎ 253900; *Ghandhi St, Crater; doubles with bathroom YR2500-YR3000*) is good value. The staff are helpful and the hotel central. Rooms are large, clean and feature a fan, air-con, fridge and TV.

Places to Stay – Mid-Range

All hotels listed here offer rooms with TV, fridge, fan, air-con and bathroom.

Al-Amer Hotel (☎ 250000; e *alamer-group@y.net.ye; doubles YR3600*), opposite the minibus/taxi station (for Sheikh Othman), is probably the best value in Crater. The hotel is convenient, reasonably quiet, and the rooms are large and nicely furnished.

City Center Hotel (☎ 257 700; *off Al-Mu'arri St, Crater; singles/doubles YR3000/3500*) is a central but quiet place. The rooms are large, modern and full of furniture.

Crescent Hotel (☎ 203471; *off Al-Muhsen St, At-Tawahi; singles/doubles with breakfast US$30/40*) claims to be the first hotel built in Yemen. This former British hotel has some atmosphere, but better value can be found elsewhere. Rates include breakfast and are negotiable.

Rock Hotel (☎ 202087; *Al-Muhsen St, At-Tawahi; singles/doubles YR3000/3500*) is a

bit run down but better value than the Crescent Hotel. Many rooms have views, and the rates, which include breakfast, are negotiable.

Places to Eat

Reem Tourist Restaurant (*Ghandhi St, Crater; salads YR100, grills YR250*) is always full of locals at lunch times. They come for the air-conditioning, tasty food and cheap prices. One reader enjoyed the 'best kebabs in Yemen' here.

Al-Amer Restaurant (*Al-Amer Hotel; salads from YR100, grilled fish YR250*), under the hotel of the same name in Crater (see Places to Stay – Mid-Range earlier in this section), is a brightly lit and charmless place. However, meals are large, tasty and surprisingly cheap. There's a menu (with prices) in English, and a large variety of nonalcoholic beers are available.

Al-Rayyan Restaurant (*off Ghandhi St, Crater; salads YR150, grills YR200*) offers a menu in English, good service and food.

Ching Sing Chinese Restaurant (☎ 243 016; *Ma'alla Main Rd, Ma'alla; meals from YR350*) is not cheap, but most diners have been more than satisfied. The menu is extensive and alcoholic beer is available. The all-you-can-eat 'seafood special', including lobster, costs about YR2000.

Pizza Hut (*Corniche Rd, Crater; small/large pizzas YR600/1000*) offers the sort of

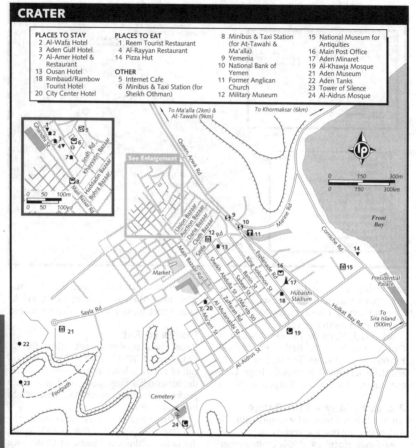

CRATER

PLACES TO STAY
2 Al-Wafa Hotel
3 Aden Gulf Hotel
7 Al-Amer Hotel &
   Restaurant
13 Ousan Hotel
18 Rimbaud/Rambow
    Tourist Hotel
20 City Center Hotel

PLACES TO EAT
1 Reem Tourist Restaurant
4 Al-Rayyan Restaurant
14 Pizza Hut

OTHER
5 Internet Cafe
6 Minibus & Taxi Station (for
   Sheikh Othman)

8 Minibus & Taxi Station
   (for At-Tawahi &
   Ma'alla)
9 Yemenia
10 National Bank of
    Yemen
11 Former Anglican
    Church
12 Military Museum

15 National Museum for
    Antiquities
16 Main Post Office
17 Aden Minaret
19 Al-Khawja Mosque
21 Aden Museum
22 Aden Tanks
23 Tower of Silence
24 Al-Aidrus Mosque

Western delights you would expect, but it's inconvenient to the city centre.

Sailors Club & Motel (*Al-Muhsen St, At-Tawahi; salads and snacks under YR200 & grills YR600-800*) is by far the best choice in Aden – and one of the best in Yemen. It offers breezy sea views, excellent meals (including pasta, curries and Western dishes) and *really* cold alcoholic beer.

Entertainment

For some, a highlight of Aden is the chance to enjoy a beer: this is the only place in Yemen where alcohol can be bought. But its not cheap: a can of beer costs about YR300. The best place for a cold one is undoubtedly the **Sailors Club & Motel** (see Places to Eat earlier) in At-Tawahi.

Getting There & Away

Yemenia has an office (☎ 253848) along Queen Arwa Rd in Crater. Every week, it flies four times to Ar-Rayyan for Al-Mukalla (YR20,050), three times to Suqutra Island (YR42,088) and twice to Sayun (YR20,050). There are also several flights a day to San'a (YR14,760).

Buses and shared taxis leave from terminals in Sheikh Othman. The best company, **Yemitco**, has daily services to Al-Mukalla (YR3400, about 15 hours) at 6.30am, Ta'izz (YR1000, 3½ hours) at 6am and 2pm, San'a (YR2400, eight hours) at 6.30am, 8am, 10am and 2pm, and Al-Hudayda (YR2000, nine hours) at 7am. The Yemitco terminal is in the grounds of the Crescent Hotel (not the one in At-Tawahi), about 1.5km southeast of the

Rimbaud

In his short and tragic life, the French poet Arthur Rimbaud (1854–91) wrote some of the greatest and most influential poetry of the modern era. Rimbaud was a child prodigy who began writing as a form of rebellion against his repressive upbringing and the depravity of his times. He repeatedly ran away from his mother's provincial home, roaming the streets and countryside during the terrible Franco-Prussian war and rise of the Paris Commune.

In his later teens, the impoverished poet tried to win the respect of the Paris literary set, but they were appalled by his ragged clothes, lice-infested hair and obvious use of hashish and opium. His scandalous homosexual affair with the married poet Verlaine sealed his fate as an outcast. During a quarrel, Verlaine shot and wounded Rimbaud.

After completing *Ma Bohème* (My Bohemian Life), and the extraordinary prose poems *Les Illuminations* and *Une Saison en Enfer* (A Season in Hell), Rimbaud, at the age of 19, abandoned writing forever. He took to the open road, travelling for many years across Europe and as far east as Java.

In 1880 Rimbaud arrived in Aden and gained employment as a clerk in the shop of a coffee exporter named Bardey. He wrote to his family: 'Aden is a frightful rock without a single blade of grass or a drop of fresh water...I am like a prisoner here.' For the next 11 years Rimbaud moved between Aden and Bardey's other store in Harar, Abyssinia (Ethiopia), and made disastrous attempts at selling guns to warring tribes. For four years Rimbaud lived in the walled Muslim city of Harar. While there, he explored the surrounding country and wrote a report on his findings that was published by the Société de Géographie in Paris.

In 1884 Rimbaud returned to Aden with a slave girl with whom he lived. In the greatest misadventure of his gunrunning career, Rimbaud used his savings to buy a large arsenal of weapons, and spent the next four years trying to sell them. His search for a buyer eventually led him on a perilous four-month journey into Abyssinia during which his caravan was repeatedly attacked by Danakil tribespeople. In the end, he was forced to sell his guns for a pittance. Rimbaud persisted in his trading endeavours until 1891, when he developed a severe knee tumour that eventually forced him to sail from Aden back to France. In Marseilles he had his right leg amputated and died soon after, at the age of 37.

Bethune Carmichael

long-distance bus/taxi terminals. Shared taxis to San'a cost YR850 and YR400 to Ta'izz.

Getting Around
Minibuses and shared taxis link Crater, Ma'alla, Sheikh Othman and At-Tawahi every few minutes from stations included on the relevant maps. Private taxis cost about YR600 from Sheikh Othman to At-Tawahi, and about YR400 from Crater to the airport.

Eastern Yemen

The most desolate part of the country is across the desert sands to the east. Ma'rib is a major attraction, while Wadi Hadramawt is unquestionably a highlight of Yemen.

MA'RIB مأرب
☎ 0630
About 214km east of San'a is Ma'rib, the former capital of the powerful Sabaean em-

pire. Ma'rib is worth visiting if you have time and money and thrive on a little adventure.

Things to See
All sights mentioned here are permanently open and free to enter.

About 3km west of the main town is the eerie silhouette of **Old Ma'rib**. Originally built before the 1st millennium BC, the village was bombed during the 1962 civil war. It's a marvellous place to wander about, but the destruction and poverty are depressing.

From the village a road leads southwest to the ruins of the **Great Ma'rib Dam**, probably built in the mid-8th century BC. Archaeologists believe it was about 700m long, 60m wide and about 35m high, and capable of irrigating about 70 sq km of desert. It sustained a population of between 30,000 and 50,000 people for over 1000 years. Most of the remaining walls were used to build the new town, so only two sluicegates (with Sabaean inscriptions) are left.

The road continues to the impressive **New Dam** built in 1986 by a sheikh from the United Arab Emirates. It's worth visiting, if only to imagine that the old dam was once three times larger than this one.

Another road leads to **'Arsh Bilqis** (also called the Bilqis Palace or Bilqis Throne). This is where the five-and-a-half columns, often seen on tourist brochures, are located. According to legend, the palace was linked to the Queen of Sheba (see the boxed text 'Who Was the Queen of Sheba?'), but archaeologists believe the temple was built in about 2000 BC as a dedication to the moon.

Further along is **Mahram Bilqis** (also known as the Bilqis Temple or Awwam Temple). It was built before 800 BC and was dedicated to the sun god. Disappointingly, both sites are fenced off and difficult to appreciate.

Places to Stay & Eat

The only two hotels are inconveniently located in the new town. Both offer rooms with TV, air-con, fan, fridge and bathroom, and both have (uninspiring) **restaurants** – which is just as well, because you're not allowed outside your hotel at night.

Hotel Al-Jannattyn (☎ 302310; singles/ doubles YR2100/2900), also called The Land of Two Paradise Hotel, is easy to reach from the main road. It has seen better days, but is clean and comfortable.

Bilqis Mareb Hotel (☎ 2372; singles/ doubles with breakfast US$73/86) is a luxurious place with, of all things, a swimming pool and an excellent **bookshop**. It's accessible only by chartered taxi.

Getting There & Away

Foreigners are only allowed to visit Ma'rib from San'a on an organised tour or in a chartered vehicle, arranged with a travel agency. You must also travel with an armed military escort. All agencies in San'a can arrange a day trip (and permits) from the capital for about US$75 per vehicle, plus about YR2000 for the escorts.

Contact any of the travel agencies along the main street in Ma'rib, or one of the hotels, about buses to Sayun and local tours (and permits). They can also organise private transport (and permits) to Wadi Hadramawt. This will cost US$100 per day per vehicle via the paved road, or US$100 per day per vehicle and US$200 for a compulsory Bedouin guide along the desert trails.

WADI HADRAMAWT

وادي حضرموت

☎ 05

Wadi Hadramawt is understandably one of the highlights of Yemen. The longest (about 200km) wadi in the Middle East was named after the people who lived there centuries ago. It's mentioned in the Quran and the

---

Who Was the Queen of Sheba?

The legend of the meeting of King Solomon (965–925 BC) and the Queen of Sheba, or Saba, appears in three holy books: the Jewish and Christian Old Testament (1 Kings 10:1-13); the Ethiopian Orthodox Kebra Nagast; and the Muslim Quran (sura of Ants, 20-44).

Today the story is well known throughout the western world, but nowhere is her legend as alive and well as on both sides of the southern Red Sea. There are many Islamicised versions of the story, with the main plot being her conversion to the faith of Solomon's God, ultimately leading to Islam. Arabian tradition also tells us that Menelik, the son of King Solomon and Queen Bilqis, became the ruler of Aksum, in today's Ethiopia. The intriguing love story between the king and the queen is not mentioned at all in the Quran and only vaguely hinted at in the Bible, but the Ethiopian Kebra Nagast is explicit about it. Indeed, Menelik's ancestry was then claimed by all Ethiopian leaders up to Haile Selassie (r. 1930–74), who traced his lineal descent from her through 237 generations.

How did the same queen live and rule both sides of the Red Sea? The legends obviously contradict each other. Actually, no hard archaeological proof exists that Saba was indeed ruled by a queen at the time of King Solomon, although Sabaean queens are mentioned in scriptures from later times. While scholars keep debating the unresolved issue, no Yemeni would ever doubt the reality of the legend, and many Yemeni girls are still named Bilqis after her.

WADI HADRAMAWT

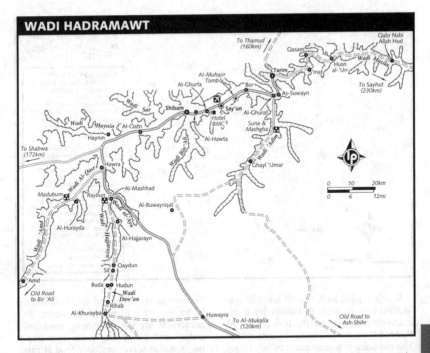

To Thamud (160km)

Qabr Nabi Allah Hud

Qasam

Husn Wadi Masila

Tarim · Inat · al-'Urr

Al-Muhajir Tomb

Al-Ghurfa

Bor

As-Suwayri

To Sayhut (230km)

Wadi Sar · Shibam · Say'un · Al-Ghuraf

Hotel BMC

Suna & Mashgha

Wadi · Haynin · Al-Qatn

Haynin

Al-Hawta

To Shabwa (172km)

Hawra

Wadi Bin 'Ali

Ghayl 'Umar

Wadi 'Idim

0 10 20km

0 6 12mi

Al-Mashhad

Madubum · Raybun

Al-Buwayriqat

Wadi 'Amd · Wadi Al-Qasr

Al-Hurayda

Al-Hajjarayn

Al-Khuraybah

Qaydun

Sif

'Amd

Old Road to Bir 'Ali

Buda · Hudun

Wadi Daw'an

Rihab

Huwayra

To Al-Mukalla (120km)

Old Road to Ash-Shihr

Bible because of the quality of the incense it produced and the fertility of its land.

Most attractions are conveniently located in the middle of the three major towns: Shibam, Sayun and Tarim.

Getting There & Away
The **Yemenia** office (☎ 402 550) is in Sayun. There are four flights a week from Sayun to Aden (YR20,050) and San'a (YR20,050).

Yemitco and the **General Land Transport Co** offer daily buses from San'a to Sayun via Ma'rib, but foreigners are not permitted to travel from San'a to Ma'rib by bus (see Getting There & Away under Ma'rib earlier in this section). However, independent travel (with a permit) is allowed from Ma'rib to Sayun (YR3500, 20 hours) along the paved road, and from Al-Mukalla to Sayun (YR1800, about six hours).

For many travellers, the trip across the desert between Ma'rib and Sayun is a highlight, but it's certainly not cheap (see under Ma'rib earlier in this section for details). **Universal Travel & Tourism** (☎ 404288) and **Abu Hafs Travel Agency** (☎ 404447) in

Sayun can arrange a car, driver, permits and, if required, a Bedouin guide to Ma'rib. Both agencies can also arrange a car with a driver for trips around Wadi Hadramawt for about US$50 per day (more for a 4WD). Alternatively, charter a shared taxi.

Sayun (Seiyun)   سيئون
Sayun is the administrative centre of Wadi Hadramawt. It's a likable, compact and comparatively clean town. It offers the best range of accommodation and is conveniently situated between Shibam and Tarim. Sayun also has the only bank, foreign exchange offices and Internet centre in the region, as well as a post office.

Things to See & Do Dominating the town centre is the opulent green-and-white **Sultan's Palace**, which has been converted into a **museum** (admission YR150; open 8am-1pm Sat-Wed). Built in 1873, this 34m-high palace contains archaeological items, displays about traditional weaving and medicine, weapons and drums. Most exhibits are explained in English. The **views** of Sayun from the windows and rooftop are superb.

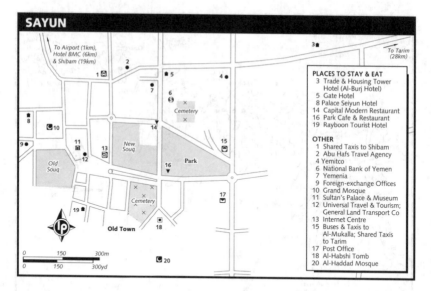

SAYUN

To Airport (1km), Hotel BMC (6km) & Shibam (19km)

To Tarim (28km)

Cemetery

New Souq

Old Souq

Park

Cemetery

Old Town

0   150   300m
0   150   300yd

PLACES TO STAY & EAT
3   Trade & Housing Tower
    Hotel (Al-Burj Hotel)
5   Gate Hotel
8   Palace Seiyun Hotel
14 Capital Modern Restaurant
16 Park Cafe & Restaurant
19 Rayboon Tourist Hotel

OTHER
1   Shared Taxis to Shibam
2   Abu Hafs Travel Agency
4   Yemitco
6   National Bank of Yemen
7   Yemenia
9   Foreign-exchange Offices
10 Grand Mosque
11 Sultan's Palace & Museum
12 Universal Travel & Tourism;
    General Land Transport Co
13 Internet Centre
15 Buses & Taxis to
    Al-Mukalla; Shared Taxis
    to Tarim
17 Post Office
18 Al-Habshi Tomb
20 Al-Haddad Mosque

Worth a quick look, but off limits to non-Muslim visitors, is the **Al-Habshi Tomb** *(opposite the cemetery)* and the 16th-century **Al-Haddad Mosque** *(just south of the cemetery)*. The **old souq** is a great place to buy honey, colourful *futas* and the sort of conical *madhalla* hats worn by rural women.

Places to Stay Each hotel listed here offers rooms with air-con, TV, fridge and bathroom.
    Palace Seiyun Hotel *(☎ 405566; singles/doubles YR1000/1300)* is not as nice as the outside would suggest. It's a bit noisy because of the thin walls and the mosque opposite, but it's good value. Ask for a corner room with a private balcony.
    Gate Hotel *(☎ 405680; singles/doubles YR1350/1750)*, opposite Yemenia, is better than the Palace Seiyun and worth a look.
    Rayboon Tourist Hotel *(☎ 402686; doubles YR2000)* boasts an excellent location in the old town. The rooms are modern, clean and comfortable, but check that the plumbing works before accepting a room.
    Trade & Housing Tower Hotel *(☎ 403575; singles/doubles YR2100/2500)*, on the road to Tarim, is also known as the Al-Burj Hotel. It's no better than other cheaper places in town, but the attraction is the clean swimming pool. Rates include breakfast.
    Hotel BMC *(☎ 428040; singles/doubles YR2500)* is about 6km southwest of Sayun.

The rooms are large and spotless, and the bathrooms have plenty of hot water. Two attractions are the swimming pool (with water) and the dining room (for guests only), which serves ordinary food at extraordinary prices.

Places to Eat There is a startling lack of acceptable places to eat in Sayun, and, incredibly, none of the hotels have public restaurants. The best idea is to sit at a café in front of the palace with a fruit shake or cup of tea and munch on some chips and samosas.
    Capital Modern Restaurant *(meals about YR150)*, in an enclosed courtyard in the middle of the road, is the best of an uninspiring bunch. It offers basic food and can rustle up same tasty kebabs in the evening.
    Park Cafe & Restaurant *(meals YR200)* is a shady spot for a drink, but the meals are nothing to get excited about.

Getting There & Away Shared taxis for Tarim (YR100, 45 minutes) and Shibam (YR60, 30 minutes) depart from separate places (as shown on the map). Buses and taxis for Al-Mukalla (YR1800, six hours) leave from a spot near the park.

Shibam شبام
This incredible walled village, 19km west of Sayun, was built in about the 4th century AD,

probably on the ruins of a far older town. The 'Manhattan of the Desert' – as it was dubbed by the intrepid adventurer Freya Stark – was declared a Unesco World Heritage Site in 1982. Millions of dollars of restoration aid is continually needed to ensure that the village, which is built along a wadi, is not permanently damaged by flooding.

Things to See & Do Most of the 500 or so buildings within the village wall are seven or eight storeys high, made from mud bricks and featuring decorative windows and doors. The wall itself is a relatively recent addition from the 17th century. The souq is particularly photogenic and the best place to stock up on frankincense.

To the right (east) as you enter the main entrance is the **Sultan's Palace**, built in about AD 1220. The dominant **Al-Jama'ia Mosque** (also known as Rashid Mosque or Great Mosque), built in AD 904, is one of eight in the village. None of the mosques are open to non-Muslims.

Places to Stay The **Shibam Motel** (☎ 420 424; singles/doubles with air-con & bathroom YR3000/5000), just outside the main entrance to the village, is the most atmospheric place in Wadi Hadramawt. This white, double-storey guesthouse features old-fashioned but renovated rooms (some with a TV and private balcony) surrounded by a shady garden. It has the monopoly and charges accordingly, but as one reader states: 'How many other places on earth can one actually stay in a museum?'. Rates include breakfast.

Getting There & Away From the bus and taxi stop outside the entrance to the village along the main road, shared taxis leave regularly for Sayun. For anywhere else, you're better off going to Sayun and getting onward transport from there.

Tarim تريم
The religious and educational centre of Wadi Hadramawt is Tarim, 28km northeast of Sayun. The architecture in this former regional capital is unique because many wealthy residents previously lived in, and were inspired by, other Islamic centres in India and Asia. Sadly, most of these buildings, such as the **Munaysurah Mansion** and

the Mogul-style **Ishshah Palace**, are neglected and not open to the public.

The town centre is the bustling **souq** (especially busy on Friday) in front of the decrepit **Sultan's Palace** (admission YR50; open 8am-1pm & 3pm-6pm Sat-Wed). Several blocks east is the dazzlingly white **Al-Muhdar Mosque**, built in 1915. It features a 40m-high minaret (the tallest in Yemen), but is only open to Muslims. Nearby, the **Al-Khaf Palace** (open sporadically) contains a library that is revered among Islamists for the number of important manuscripts.

Places to Stay & Eat The **Brothers Pension Tourist** (singles/doubles with fan & shared bathroom YR350/500), opposite the Sultan's Palace, is basic and noisy, but has some charm. The tiny **café** on the ground floor serves simple food.

Kenya Tourist Hotel (☎ 417550; doubles with air-con & shared bathroom YR1000/ 2000) is opposite the new post office and signposted from the taxi stop for Sayun. The hotel is noisy and musty, but the rooms are reasonable and the bathrooms are clean.

Getting There & Away Shared taxis to/ from Sayun stop on the main road into Tarim, about 200m south of the Sultan's Palace.

AL-MUKALLA المكلا
☎ 05
There isn't a lot of point detouring to this unattractive port city. The sole attraction is the **Mukalla Museum** (admission YR500; open 8.30am-noon Sat-Wed) at the back of the elegant, green-and-white former Sultan's Palace (built in the 1920s) along the corniche. It offers some reasonably interesting exhibits about the former sultan and local Yemeni history. Most explanations are in English.

The **diving centre** (☎ 303441) in the four-star Wadi Hadramout Hotel, about 5km east of the city centre, offers scuba diving, but give them plenty of notice.

Places to Stay & Eat
Both hotels listed here offer rooms with TV, fridge, fan and air-con.

Al-Salama Hotel (☎ 306127; doubles with shared bathroom YR1800) is located in the charming old town along the corniche. Some rooms offer views of the sea, but it's a little pricey. The **restaurant** is very popular.

YEMEN

Gulf Hotel (☎ 304147; Al-Ghar al-Ahmar St; doubles with bathroom YR1500) is comfortable, though noisy. It's conveniently located along the middle section on the western side of the very obvious wadi-cum-football field.

Opposite the Al-Salama Hotel, the **Al-Khayyam Restaurant** (meals from YR200) offers tasty fish meals. A few enticing **teahouses** are dotted along the corniche.

Getting There & Away

Yemenia, which has an office (☎ 303444) in the northern suburbs of Al-Mukalla, regularly flies to Aden, Suqutra Island and San'a. The airport is at Ar-Rayyan, about 25km northeast of Al-Mukalla. See those sections for fare details.

The **General Land Transport Co** has a bus most days to San'a (YR2500, 23 hours) via Aden (YR1800, 18 hours). Its office is under the mosque next to the Arab Bank at the lower eastern end of the wadi. **Yemitco**, which has an office at the western end of the last bridge along the wadi also offers a daily bus to San'a (YR6000) via Aden (YR3400). To Sayun, it's easier to travel by shared taxi from the station in the northern suburb of Hay ad-Dis.

BIR ' ALI   بيرعلي

About 128km south-west of Al-Mukalla is Bir ' Ali, a port historically known as Qana. It's one of the more appealing places along the Arabian Sea for **swimming**. There's nothing much to do but relax, which suits most visitors. You can **camp** along the beach for free, but there's no shade or public toilets. Also watch out for crabs, strong winds and malarial mosquitoes. There's no hotel, but a few shops sell basic supplies.

Most visitors come in a chartered vehicle. If you're relying on public transport, you'll probably have to buy a bus ticket all the way from Aden to Al-Mukalla (or vice versa) and ask to be dropped off.

SUQUTRA (SOCOTRA) ISLAND   سقطرى

☎ 05

Yemen's largest Island (3650 sq km) is about 500km southeast of the mainland. Because of its isolation, Suqutra hosts an ex-traordinary range and diversity of unspoiled flora and fauna, including six endemic species of birds and 275 endemic types of plants. The island has developed a unique culture and language, and is also the location of exciting archaeological discoveries dating back to the 3rd century AD.

The best time to visit is between mid-October and mid-May. Monsoons, winds and waves make it unpleasant at other times. The island is slowly being developed for tourism, but conservationists are desperately hoping to have some input into this development in order to save the island's unique ecology. The **Soqotra Biodiversity Project** (☎ 660132), in the main town of Hadibu, can arrange **guides** for anyone interested in the island's flora and fauna.

Some **caves** in the south contain amazing stalagmites and stalactites, and **boat trips**, **hiking** and **swimming** are possible at several places around the island (ask at the hotels for details). **Snorkelling** is occasionally spectacular, but bring your own gear.

Places to Stay & Eat

Suqutra Island is one of the few places in Yemen where **camping** is allowed – but get away from the towns, find some shade and shelter from the winds, and watch out for malarial mosquitoes.

There are only three hotels on the island (all in Hadibu), so it's worth booking a room in advance. Both hotels listed here have a **restaurant**.

Hotel Summerland (☎ 660360; singles/doubles with fan & shared bathroom US$20/30) has some charm and many large rooms, but is not great value. Rates include breakfast.

Al-Jazeera Hotel (☎ 660443; singles/doubles with shared bathroom US$10/15), close to the Summerland, is smaller, cleaner, brighter and better value.

Getting There & Away

Piracy is a serious problem in the Arabian Sea so foreigners are not allowed to travel to the island by boat.

The Yemenia office (☎ 660123) is in Hadibu. There's one flight a week from Hadibu to Aden (YR42,088), two flights to Ar-Rayyan (YR21,990) near Al-Mukalla, and one to San'a (YR42,088).

Language

ARABIC

Arabic is the official language of all Middle Eastern countries except Afghanistan, Iran, Israel and Turkey. While English (and to a lesser extent, French – mainly in Lebanon and Syria) is widely spoken in the region, any effort to communicate with the locals in their own language will be well rewarded. No matter how far off the mark your pronunciation or grammar might be, you'll often get the response (usually with a big smile), 'Ah, you speak Arabic very well!'.

Learning the basics for day-to-day travelling doesn't take long at all, but to master the complexities of Arabic would take years of constant study. For a more comprehensive guide to the language, get a copy of Lonely Planet's *Egyptian Arabic phrasebook*.

Transliteration

It's worth noting here that transliterating from Arabic script into English is at best an approximate science. The presence of sounds unknown in European languages, and the fact that the script is 'incomplete' (most vowels are not written), combine to make it nearly impossible to settle on one method of transliteration. A wide variety of spellings is therefore possible for words when they appear in Roman script – and that goes for place and people's names as well.

The matter is further complicated by the wide variety of dialects and the imaginative ideas Arabs themselves often have on appropriate spelling in, say, English. Words spelt one way in a Gulf country may look very different in Syria, which is heavily influenced by French. Not even the most venerable of Western Arabists have been able to come up with an ideal solution.

Pronunciation

Pronunciation of Arabic can be tongue-tying for someone unfamiliar with the intonation and combination of sounds.

Much of the vocabulary that follows would be universally understood throughout the Arab world, although some of it, especially where more than one option is given, reflects the region's dialects. Arabic pronunciation is not easy, and to reflect sounds unknown in English, certain combinations of letters are used in transliteration.

For best results, pronounce the transliterated words slowly and clearly.

Vowels

Technically, there are three long and three short vowels in Arabic. The reality is a little different, with local dialect and varying consonant combinations affecting their pronunciation. This is the case throughout the Arabic-speaking world. More like five short and three long vowels can be identified:

a	as in 'had'
e	as in 'bet'
i	as in 'hit'
o	as in 'hot'
u	as in 'push'

A macron over a vowel indicates that the vowel has a long sound:

ā	as in 'father' or as a long pronunciation of the 'a' in 'had'
ī	as the 'ea' in 'eagle'
ū	as the 'oo' in 'food'

Consonants

Pronunciation for all Arabic consonants is covered in the Arabic alphabet table on the following page. Note that when double consonants occur in transliterations, both are pronounced. For example, *el-hammām* (toilet), is pronounced 'el-ham-mam'.

Other Sounds

Arabic has two sounds that are very tricky for non-Arabs to produce, the 'ayn and the glottal stop. The letter 'ayn represents a sound with no English equivalent that comes even close. It is similar to the glottal stop (which is not actually represented in the alphabet), but the muscles at the back of the throat are gagged more forcefully – it has been described as the sound of someone being strangled. In many transliteration systems 'ayn is represented by an opening quotation mark, and the glottal stop by a

The Arabic Alphabet

final	medial	initial	alone	transliteration	pronunciation
ﺍ			ﺍ	ā	as the 'a' in 'father'
ﺐ	ﺒ	ﺑ	ﺏ	b	as in 'bet'
ﺖ	ﺘ	ﺗ	ﺕ	t	as in 'ten' (but the tongue touches the teeth)
ﺚ	ﺜ	ﺛ	ﺙ	th	as in 'thin'; also as 's' or 't'
ﺞ	ﺠ	ﺟ	ﺝ	j	as in 'jet'; often also as the 's' in 'measure'
ﺢ	ﺤ	ﺣ	ﺡ	H	a strongly whispered 'h', almost like a sigh of relief
ﺦ	ﺨ	ﺧ	ﺥ	kh	a rougher sound than the 'ch' in Scottish *loch*
ﺪ			ﺩ	d	as in 'den' (but the tongue touches the teeth)
ﺬ			ﺫ	dh	as the 'th' in 'this'; also as 'd' or 'z'
ﺮ			ﺭ	r	a rolled 'r', as in the Spanish word *caro*
ﺰ			ﺯ	z	as in 'zip'
ﺲ	ﺴ	ﺳ	ﺱ	s	as in 'so', never as in 'wisdom'
ﺶ	ﺸ	ﺷ	ﺵ	sh	as in 'ship'
ﺺ	ﺼ	ﺻ	ﺹ	ş	emphatic 's' *
ﺾ	ﻀ	ﺿ	ﺽ	ḍ	emphatic 'd' *
ﻂ	ﻄ	ﻃ	ﻁ	ţ	emphatic 't' *
ﻆ	ﻈ	ﻇ	ﻅ	ẓ	emphatic 'z' *
ﻊ	ﻌ	ﻋ	ﻉ	'	the Arabic letter 'ayn; pronounce as a glottal stop – like the closing of the throat when saying 'Oh oh!' (see Other Sounds, p.781)
ﻎ	ﻐ	ﻏ	ﻍ	gh	a guttural sound like Parisian 'r'
ﻒ	ﻔ	ﻓ	ﻑ	f	as in 'far'
ﻖ	ﻘ	ﻗ	ﻕ	q	a strongly guttural 'k' sound; often pronounced as a glottal stop
ﻚ	ﻜ	ﻛ	ﻙ	k	as in 'king'
ﻞ	ﻠ	ﻟ	ﻝ	l	as in 'lamb'
ﻢ	ﻤ	ﻣ	ﻡ	m	as in 'me'
ﻦ	ﻨ	ﻧ	ﻥ	n	as in 'name'
ﻪ	ﻬ	ﻫ	ﻩ	h	as in 'ham'
ﻮ			ﻭ	w	as in 'wet'; or
				ū	long, as the 'oo' on 'food'; or
				aw	as the 'ow' in 'how'
ﻲ	ﻴ	ﻳ	ﻱ	y	as in 'yes'; or
				ī	as the 'e' in 'ear', only softer; or
				ay	as the 'y' in 'by' or as the 'ay' in 'way'

Vowels Not all Arabic vowel sounds are represented in the alphabet. See Pronunciation on p.781.

*Emphatic Consonants Emphatic consonants are similar to their nonemphatic counterparts but are pronounced with greater tension in the tongue and throat.

closing quotation mark. To make the transliterations in this language guide (and throughout the rest of the book) easier to use, we have not distinguished between the

glottal stop and the 'ayn, using the closing quotation mark to represent both sounds. You should find that Arabic speakers will still understand you.

Language

ARABIC

Arabic is the official language of all Middle Eastern countries except Afghanistan, Iran, Israel and Turkey. While English (and to a lesser extent, French – mainly in Lebanon and Syria) is widely spoken in the region, any effort to communicate with the locals in their own language will be well rewarded. No matter how far off the mark your pronunciation or grammar might be, you'll often get the response (usually with a big smile), 'Ah, you speak Arabic very well!'.

Learning the basics for day-to-day travelling doesn't take long at all, but to master the complexities of Arabic would take years of constant study. For a more comprehensive guide to the language, get a copy of Lonely Planet's *Egyptian Arabic phrasebook*.

Transliteration

It's worth noting here that transliterating from Arabic script into English is at best an approximate science. The presence of sounds unknown in European languages, and the fact that the script is 'incomplete' (most vowels are not written), combine to make it nearly impossible to settle on one method of transliteration. A wide variety of spellings is therefore possible for words when they appear in Roman script – and that goes for place and people's names as well.

The matter is further complicated by the wide variety of dialects and the imaginative ideas Arabs themselves often have on appropriate spelling in, say, English. Words spelt one way in a Gulf country may look very different in Syria, which is heavily influenced by French. Not even the most venerable of Western Arabists have been able to come up with an ideal solution.

Pronunciation

Pronunciation of Arabic can be tongue-tying for someone unfamiliar with the intonation and combination of sounds.

Much of the vocabulary that follows would be universally understood throughout the Arab world, although some of it, especially where more than one option is given, reflects the region's dialects. Arabic pronunciation is not easy, and to reflect sounds unknown in English, certain combinations of letters are used in transliteration.

For best results, pronounce the transliterated words slowly and clearly.

Vowels

Technically, there are three long and three short vowels in Arabic. The reality is a little different, with local dialect and varying consonant combinations affecting their pronunciation. This is the case throughout the Arabic-speaking world. More like five short and three long vowels can be identified:

a	as in 'had'
e	as in 'bet'
i	as in 'hit'
o	as in 'hot'
u	as in 'push'

A macron over a vowel indicates that the vowel has a long sound:

ā	as in 'father' or as a long pronunciation of the 'a' in 'had'
ī	as the 'ea' in 'eagle'
ū	as the 'oo' in 'food'

Consonants

Pronunciation for all Arabic consonants is covered in the Arabic alphabet table on the following page. Note that when double consonants occur in transliterations, both are pronounced. For example, *el-hammām* (toilet), is pronounced 'el-ham-mam'.

Other Sounds

Arabic has two sounds that are very tricky for non-Arabs to produce, the 'ayn and the glottal stop. The letter 'ayn represents a sound with no English equivalent that comes even close. It is similar to the glottal stop (which is not actually represented in the alphabet), but the muscles at the back of the throat are gagged more forcefully – it has been described as the sound of someone being strangled. In many transliteration systems 'ayn is represented by an opening quotation mark, and the glottal stop by a

The Arabic Alphabet

final	medial	initial	alone	transliteration	pronunciation
ا			ا	ā	as the 'a' in 'father'
ب	ـبـ	بـ	ب	b	as in 'bet'
ت	ـتـ	تـ	ت	t	as in 'ten' (but the tongue touches the teeth)
ث	ـثـ	ثـ	ث	th	as in 'thin'; also as 's' or 't'
ج	ـجـ	جـ	ج	j	as in 'jet'; often also as the 's' in 'measure'
ح	ـحـ	حـ	ح	H	a strongly whispered 'h', almost like a sigh of relief
خ	ـخـ	خـ	خ	kh	a rougher sound than the 'ch' in Scottish loch
د			د	d	as in 'den' (but the tongue touches the teeth)
ذ			ذ	dh	as the 'th' in 'this'; also as 'd' or 'z'
ر			ر	r	a rolled 'r', as in the Spanish word caro
ز			ز	z	as in 'zip'
س	ـسـ	سـ	س	s	as in 'so', never as in 'wisdom'
ش	ـشـ	شـ	ش	sh	as in 'ship'
ص	ـصـ	صـ	ص	ş	emphatic 's' *
ض	ـضـ	ضـ	ض	ḍ	emphatic 'd' *
ط	ـطـ	طـ	ط	ţ	emphatic 't' *
ظ	ـظـ	ظـ	ظ	ẓ	emphatic 'z' *
ع	ـعـ	عـ	ع	'	the Arabic letter 'ayn; pronounce as a glottal stop – like the closing of the throat when saying 'Oh oh!' (see Other Sounds, p.781)
غ	ـغـ	غـ	غ	gh	a guttural sound like Parisian 'r'
ف	ـفـ	فـ	ف	f	as in 'far'
ق	ـقـ	قـ	ق	q	a strongly guttural 'k' sound; often pronounced as a glottal stop
ك	ـكـ	كـ	ك	k	as in 'king'
ل	ـلـ	لـ	ل	l	as in 'lamb'
م	ـمـ	مـ	م	m	as in 'me'
ن	ـنـ	نـ	ن	n	as in 'name'
ه	ـهـ	هـ	ه	h	as in 'ham'
و			و	w	as in 'wet'; or
				ū	long, as the 'oo' on 'food'; or
				aw	as the 'ow' in 'how'
ي	ـيـ	يـ	ي	y	as in 'yes'; or
				ī	as the 'e' in 'ear', only softer; or
				ay	as the 'y' in 'by' or as the 'ay' in 'way'

Vowels Not all Arabic vowel sounds are represented in the alphabet. See Pronunciation on p.781.

*Emphatic Consonants Emphatic consonants are similar to their nonemphatic counterparts but are pronounced with greater tension in the tongue and throat.

closing quotation mark. To make the transliterations in this language guide (and throughout the rest of the book) easier to use, we have not distinguished between the glottal stop and the 'ayn, using the closing quotation mark to represent both sounds. You should find that Arabic speakers will still understand you.

Greetings & Civilities

Arabs place great importance on civility, and it's rare to see any interaction between people that doesn't begin with profuse greetings, inquiries into the other's health and other niceties.

Arabic greetings are more formal than greetings in English, and there is a reciprocal response to each. These sometimes vary slightly, depending on whether you're addressing a man or a woman. A simple encounter can become a drawn-out affair, with neither side wanting to be the one to put a halt to the stream of greetings and well-wishing. As an *ajnabi* (foreigner), you're not expected to know all the ins and outs, but if you come up with the right expression at the appropriate moment, they'll love it.

The most common greeting is *salām 'alaykum* ('peace be upon you'), to which the correct reply is *wa alaykum as-salām* ('and upon you be peace'). If you get invited to a birthday celebration or are around for any of the big holidays, the common greeting is *kul sana wa intum bi-khēr* ('I wish you well for the coming year').

After having a bath or a haircut, you will often hear people say to you *na'iman*, which roughly means 'heavenly' and boils down to an observation along the lines of 'nice and clean now!'.

Arrival in one piece is always something to be grateful for. Passengers will often be greeted with *al-hamdu lillah 'al as-salāma*, meaning 'Thank God for your safe arrival'.

Spelling That Name

While we have tried to standardise all spellings in this book there are some instances in which flexibility seemed to be more appropriate than consistency. For example, while we use the more accepted 'beit' (house) throughout the book, in the Oman and The United Arab Emirates chapters we decided to go with 'bait' as this is the spelling any visitor to those countries will find on local maps and road signs.

Differences in spelling also arise through the same word appearing modified in the different languages of the region – 'square' in Arabic is traditionally transliterated as 'midan', but in Turkish it's written 'maydan' and in Persian 'meidun' (or 'meidun-é; 'the square of'). Here lies great potential for confusion, as in the case of 'hamam' which is Turkish for the famed 'bathhouse', but Arabic for 'pigeon'; if you're looking for a good steam-cleaning in Arabic you ask for 'hammam', with two distinctly sounded syllables.

We have also been forced to modify some spellings because of regional differences in Arabic pronunciation. The most obvious example of this is the hard Egyptian sounding of the letter jīm, like the 'g' in 'gate', whereas elsewhere in the Arab world it's a softer 'j' as in 'jam' – hence we have used both 'gadid' and 'jadid' (new), and 'gebel' and 'jebel' (mountain).

Hi.	*marhaba*
Hello. (literally 'welcome')	*ahlan wa sahlan/ahlan*
Hello. (response)	*ahlan bīk or ya hala*
Goodbye.	*ma'a salāma/ Allah ma'ak*
Good morning.	*sabah al-khayr*
Good morning. (response)	*sabah an-nūr*
Good evening.	*masā al-khayr*
Good evening. (response)	*masā an-nūr*
Good night.	*tisbah 'ala khayr*
Good night. (response)	*wa inta min ahlu*
Please. (request)	*min fadlak* (m)/ *min fadlik* (f)
Please. (polite, eg in restaurants)	*law samaht* (m)/ *law samahtı* (f)
Please. (come in/ go ahead)	*tafadal* (m)/*tafadalı* (f)/ *tafadalu* (pl)
Thank you.	*shukran*
Thanks a lot.	*shukran jazīlan*
You're welcome.	*'afwan or ahlan*
How are you?	*kayf hālak?* (m)/ *kayf hālik?* (f)
Fine. (literally 'thanks be to God')	*al-hamdu lillah*
Pleased to meet you. (departing)	*fursa sa'ida*
Pardon/Excuse me.	*'afwan*
Sorry!	*'assif!*
Congratulations!	*mabrūk!*

Useful Phrases

What's your name?	*shu-ismak?* (m)/ *shu-ismik?* (f)
My name is ...	*ismı ...*

Where are you from?	*min wayn inta?*
Do you speak ...?	*btah-ki ...?/*
	hal tatakallam ...?
I speak ...	*ana bah-ki .../*
	ana atakallam ...
English	*inglīzi*
French	*faransi*
German	*almāni*

I understand.	*ana af-ham*
I don't understand.	*ma bif-ham/la af-ham*
What does this mean?	*yānī ay?*
I want an interpreter.	*urīd mutarjem*
I (don't) like ...	*ana (ma) bahib/*
	ana (la) uhib ...
Yes.	*aywa/na'am*
No.	*la*
No problem.	*mish mushkila*
Never mind.	*ma'alesh*
I'm sick.	*ana marīd* (m)/
	ana marīda (f)

Questions like 'Is the bus coming?' or 'Will the bank be open later?' generally elicit the inevitable response *in sha' Allah* (God willing) an expression you'll hear over and over again. Another less common one is *ma sha' Allah* (God's will be done), sometimes a useful answer to probing questions about why you're not married yet!

Getting Around

How many kilometres?	*kam kilometre?*
airport	*al-matār*
bus station	*mahattat al-bās*
train station	*mahattat al-qitār*
car	*as-sayāra*
1st class	*daraja awla*
2nd class	*daraja thani*
here/there	*hena/henak*
left	*yasār*
right	*shimal/yamīn*
straight ahead	*'ala tūl*

Around Town

Where is (the) ...?	*wayn ...?*
bank	*al-masraf/al-bank*
hotel	*al-funduq*
market	*as-sūq*
Mohammed St	*sharia Mohammed*

mosque	*al-jāmi'/al-masjid*
museum	*al-mat'haf*
passport & immigration office	*maktab al-jawāzāt wa al-hijra*
pharmacy	*as-saydaliyya*
police	*ash-shurta*
post office	*maktab al-barīd*
restaurant	*al-mat'am*
tourist office	*maktab as-siyāHa*

Accommodation

Do you have ...?	*fi'andakum ...?*
a room	*ghurfa*
a single room	*ghurfa mufrada*
a double room	*ghurfa bı sarīrayn*
a shower	*dūsh*
hot water	*mayy harr*
a toilet	*twalet/mirhad/ hammām*
soap	*sābūn*
air-con	*kondishon/takyīf*
electricity	*kahraba*

Shopping

How much?	*qaddaysh/bikam*
How many?	*kam wahid?*
How much money?	*kam fulūs?*
money	*fulūs/masāri*
big	*kabīr*
small	*saghīr*
bad	*mish kwayyis/ mu kwayyis*
good	*kwayyis*
cheap/expensive	*rakhīs/ghāli*
cheaper	*arkhas*
closed	*maghlūq/musakkar*
open	*maftūh*

Signs – Arabic

Entrance *dukhūl*	مدخل
Exit *khurūj*	خروج
Toilets (Men) *Hammam lirrijal*	حمام للرجال
Toilets (Women) *Hammam linnisa'a*	حمام للنساء
Hospital *mustashfa*	مستشفى
Police *shurta*	الشرطة
Prohibited *mamnu'u*	ممنوع

Time

What is the time?	adaysh as-sā'a?
It's 5 o'clock.	as-sa'a khamsa
When?	mata/emta?
yesterday	imbārih/'ams
today	al-yōm
tomorrow	bukra/ghadan
minute	daqiqa
hour	sa'a
day	yom
week	usbu'
month	shaher
year	sana

Days & Months

Monday	al-itnīn yom
Tuesday	at-talāta yom
Wednesday	al-arbi'ā yom
Thursday	al-khamīs yom
Friday	al-jum'a yom
Saturday	as-sabt yom
Sunday	al-ahad yom

The Islamic year has 12 lunar months and is 11 days shorter than the western year (the Gregorian calendar), so important Muslim dates will fall 11 days earlier each (Western) year.

There are two Gregorian calendars in use in the Arab world. In Egypt and the Gulf States, the months have virtually the same names as in English (January is *yanāyir*, October *octobir* and so on), but in Lebanon, Jordan and Syria, the names are quite different. Talking about, say, June as 'month six' is the easiest solution, but for the sake of completeness, the months from January are:

January	kānūn ath-thāni
February	shubāt
March	āzār
April	nisān
May	ayyār
June	huzayran
July	tammūz
August	'āb
September	aylūl
October	tishrīn al-awal
November	tishrīn ath-thani
December	kanūn al-awal

The Hejira months, too, have their own names:

| 1st | Moharram |
| 2nd | Safar |

Numbers – Arabic

Arabic numerals are simple to learn and, unlike the written language, run from left to right. Note the order of the words in numbers from 21 to 99.

0	٠	sifir
1	١	waHid
2	٢	idhnīn
3	٣	dhaladha
4	٤	arba'a
5	٥	khamsa
6	٦	sitta
7	٧	sab'a
8	٨	dhimania
9	٩	tis'a
10	١٠	ashra
11	١١	Hda'ash
12	١٢	dhna'ash
13	١٣	dhaladhta'ash
14	١٤	arba'ata'ash
15	١٥	khamista'ash
16	١٦	sitta'ash
17	١٧	sabi'ta'ashr
18	١٨	dhimanta'ash
19	١٩	tisi'ta'ash
20	٢٠	'ishrīn
21	٢١	waHid wa 'ishrīn
22	٢٢	idhnīn wa 'ishrīn
30	٣٠	dhaladhīn
40	٤٠	arbi'īn
50	٥٠	khamsīn
60	٦٠	sittīn
70	٧٠	saba'īn
80	٨٠	dhimanīn
90	٩٠	tis'īn
100	١٠٠	imia
101	١٠١	imia wa-waHid
200	٢٠٠	imiatayn
300	٣٠٠	dhaladha imia
1000	١٠٠٠	alf
2000	٢٠٠٠	alfayn
3000	٣٠٠٠	dhaladha-alaf

Ordinal Numbers

first	awwal
second	dhānī
third	dhālidh
fourth	rābi'
fifth	khāmis

3rd	Rabī' al-Awwal
4th	Rabī' ath-Thāni
5th	Jumada al-Awwall

Emergencies – Arabic

Help me!	*sā'idūnī!*
I'm sick.	*ana marīd* (m)/
	ana marīda (f)
Call the police!	*ittusil bil bolīs!*
doctor	*duktūr/tabīb*
hospital	*al-mustash-fa*
police	*ash-shurta/al-bolīs*
Go away!	*rouh min hūn!*
Shame on you!	*istiHi a'la Hālak!*
(said by woman)	

6th	*Jumada al-Akhīra*
7th	*Rajab*
8th	*Sha'bān*
9th	*Ramadān*
10th	*Shawwāl*
11th	*Zūl-qe'da*
12th	*Zūl-hijja*

FARSI

Farsi (Persian) is the national language of Iran. Although the vast majority of Iranians can speak it, it's the first language for only about 60% of the population. The most predominant minority languages are Āzeri, Kurdish, Arabic, Baluchi and Lori.

Pronunciation
Vowels & Diphthongs

A macron over the letter a (ā) indicates a longer sound. This is very important, as the wrong vowel length can completely change the meaning of a word, or make it incomprehensible, eg, *māst* (rhyming with 'passed') means 'yogurt', while *mast* (pronounced 'must') means 'drunk'.

a	as the 'u' in 'must'
ā	as in 'far' (longer than a)
e	as in 'bed'
i	as in 'marine'
o	as in 'mole'
u	as in 'rule'

Consonants

The letters b, d, f, j, k, l, m, n, p, s, sh, t, v and z are pronounced as in English.

ch	as in 'chip'
g	as in 'go'
y	as in 'yak'
zh	as in 'Zhivago'
r	slightly trilled as in Italian *caro*

h	always pronounced; like r, it doesn't lengthen the preceding vowel
kh	as the 'ch' in Scottish loch
gh	a soft guttural sound like the noise made when gargling
'	a weak glottal stop, like the double 't' in the Cockney pronunciation of 'bottle'

Double consonants are always pronounced as two distinct sounds. Stress generally falls on the last syllable of a word (but é is never stressed).

Greetings & Civilities

Hello.	*salām*
Peace be upon you.	*salām aleikom*
Goodbye.	*khodāfez/*
	khodā hāfez (more polite)
Good morning.	*sobh bekheir*
Good night/	*shab bekheir*
Good evening.	
Please. (request, literally 'kindly')	*lotfan*
Please. (offering something)	*befarmed/befarmā'id*
Thank you.	*mersi/tashakkor/*
	motashakkeram
Don't mention it.	*ghābel nabud*
Excuse me/	*bebakhshid*
I'm sorry.	

Useful Phrases

Yes.	*bale*
No.	*nakheir/*
	na (less formal)
OK.	*dorost*
Where are you from?	*shomā ahl-e kojā hastid?*

Do you speak ...?	*shomā ... baladid?*
English	*engelisi*
French	*ferānse*
German	*ālmāni*

I'm sorry, I don't speak Farsi.	*bebakhshid, farsi balad nistam*

Getting Around

Where is the ... (to Tabriz)?	*... (betabriz) kojāst?*
bus	*otobus*
train	*ghetār*
boat	*ghāyegh*
ship/ferry	*kashti*

Signs – Farsi

Entrance	ورود
Exit	خروج
Open	باز
Closed	بسته
No Entry	ورو د ممنـوع
No Smoking	دخانيات ممنوع
Prohibited	ممنوع
Hot	گرم
Cold	سـرد
Toilets	توالـت
Men	مردانـه
Women	زنانـه

taxi (any kind)	tāksi
car (or taxi)	māshin
minibus	minibus

airport	forudgāh
jetty/dock/harbour	eskele
bus/train station	termināl/istgāh
ticket	belit
ticket office	daftar-e belit forushi
open/closed	bāz/ta'til

left	dast-e chap
right	dast-e rāst
far (from ...)	dur (az ...)
near (to ...)	nazdik (-e ...)
straight ahead	mostaghim

Around Town

Excuse me, where is the ...?	bebakhshid, ... kojāst?
church	kelisā
consulate	konsulgari
embassy	safārat
mosque	masjed
post office	postkhune
restaurant	restorān/ chelo kabābi/ sālon-e ghezā
street/avenue	kheyābun
toilet	dast shu'i
town centre	markaz-e shahr

Shopping

How many?	chand tā?
How much is it?	chand e?
cheap/expensive	arzun/gerun

Accommodation

hotel	hotel/mehmunkhune
cheap hotel/ guesthouse	mosāferkhune

Do you have a ... for tonight?	emshab ... dārid?
room	otāgh
single room	otāgh-e ye nafari
double room	otāgh-e do nafari
cheaper room	otāgh-e arzuntar
better room	otāgh-e behtar

How much is the room per night?	otāgh shabi chand e?

Time & Dates

When?	kei?
At what time?	chi vaght?
(at) ... o'clock	sā'at-e ...
today	emruz
tonight	emshab
tomorrow	fardā
(in the) morning	sobh
(at) night, evening	shab

Saturday (1st day of Muslim week)	shambe
Sunday	yekshambe
Monday	doshambe
Tuesday	seshambe
Wednesday	chahārshambe
Thursday	panjshambe
Friday	jom'e

Emergencies – Farsi

Help!	komak!
Stop!	ist!
Call ...!	... khabar konin!
a doctor	ye doktor
the police	polis o
I wish to contact my embassy/consulate.	mikham bā sefārat/ konsulgari khod am tamās begiram
Where is the toilet?	tuvālet kojā st?
Go away!	gom sho!
Shame on you! (said by a woman to a man bothering her)	khejalāt bekesh!

Numbers

1	*yek*
2	*do*
3	*se*
4	*chahār*
5	*panj*
6	*shesh*
7	*haft*
8	*hasht*
9	*noh*
10	*dah*
11	*yāzdah*
12	*davāzdah*

HEBREW

Written from right to left, Hebrew has a basic 22-character alphabet – but from there it starts to get very complicated. Like English, not all these characters have fixed phonetic values and their sound can vary from word to word. You just have to know that, for instance, Yair is pronounced 'Ya-ear' and doesn't rhyme with 'hare' or 'fire'.

As with Arabic, transliteration of Hebrew script into English is at best an approximate science. The presence of sounds not found in English, and the fact that the script is 'incomplete' (most vowels are not written) combine to make it nearly impossible to settle on one consistent method of transliteration. A wide variety of spellings is therefore possible for words when they appear in Roman script, and that goes for place names and people's names as well.

For a more comprehensive guide to Hebrew than can be given in this chapter, get a copy of Lonely Planet's *Hebrew phrasebook*.

Useful Words & Phrases

Hello.	*sha-**lom***
Goodbye.	*sha-**lom***
Good morning.	***bo**-ker tov*
Good evening.	*erev tov*
Goodnight.	*lie-la tov*
See you later.	*le-**hit**-rah-**ott***
Thank you.	*to-**dah***
Please.	*be-va-ka-**sha***
You're welcome.	*al low da-**vaar***
Yes.	*ken*
No.	*loh*
Excuse me.	*slee-**kha***
Wait.	***reg**-gah*
What?	*mah?*
When?	*mah-tye?*
Where is ...?	***aye**-fo ...?*

I don't speak Hebrew.	***ah-nee** lo m'dah-**behr** ee-**vreet***
Do you speak English?	*ah-**tah** m'dah-**behr** ang-**leet**?*

Getting Around

Which bus goes to ...?	***aye**-zeh auto-boos no-**se**-ah le ...?*
Stop here.	*ah-**tsor** kahn*
airport	*sde t'oo-**fah***
bus	*auto-boos*
near	*ka-**rov***
railway	*rah-**keh**-vet*
station	*ta-cha-na*

Food & Accommodation

food	*okhel*
water	*my-im*
restaurant	***miss**-ah-**dah***
breakfast	*ah-roo-**chat** bo-ker*
lunch	*ah-roo-**khat**-tsa-ha-**rye**-im*
dinner	*ah-rookhaterev*
menu	*taf-**reet***
egg	*bay-**tsa***
vegetables	*yeh-rah-**koht***
bread	*lekh-hem*
butter	*khem-**ah***
cheese	*g'**vee**-nah*
milk	*kha-**lav***
ice cream	*glee-**dah***
fruit	*pay-**rot***
wine	*yain*
bill	***khesh**-bon*
hotel	*ma-**lon***
room	*khe-der*
toilet	*she-ru-**teem***

Around Town

How much is it?	***ka**-mah zeh ule?*
money	***kes**-sef*
bank	*bank*
post office	*dūgh-ar*
letter	*mich-tav*
stamps	*boolim*
envelopes	*ma-ata-**fot***
postcard	*gloo-yah*
telegram	*miv-rack*
air mail	*dūgh-ar ah-veer*
pharmacy	*bait mer-kah-**khat***
shop	*kha-**noot***
expensive	*ya-**kar***
cheap	*zol*
right (correct)	*na-**chon***

Time & Days

What is the time?	*ma ha-sha-am?*
seven o'clock	*ha-sha-ahshev-vah*
minute	*da-kah*
hour	*sha-ah*
day	*yom*
week	*sha-voo-ah*
month	*kho-desh*
year	*sha-nah*
Monday	*shey-nee*
Tuesday	*shlee-shee*
Wednesday	*reh-vee-ee*
Thursday	*cha-mee shee*
Friday	*shee-shee*
Saturday	*sha-bat*
Sunday	*ree-shon*

Numbers

1	*eh-had*
2	*shta-yim*
3	*sha-losh*
4	*ar-bah*
5	*cha-maysh*
6	*shaysh*
7	*shev-vah*
8	*sh-mo-neh*
9	*tay-shah*
10	*ess-er*
11	*eh-had-ess-ray*
12	*shtaym-ess-ray*
20	*ess-reem*
21	*ess-reem v'ah-khad*
30	*shlo-sheem*
31	*shlo-sheem v'ah-khad*
50	*cha-meeshleem*
100	*may-ah*
200	*mah-tah-yeem*
300	*shlosh may-oat*
500	*cha-maysh may-oat*
1000	*alef*
3000	*shlosh-et alef-eem*
5000	*cha-maysh-et alef-eem*

TURKISH

Ottoman Turkish was written in Arabic script, but it was phased out when Atatürk decreed the introduction of Latin script in 1928. In big cities and tourist areas, many locals know at least some English and/or German. In the south eastern towns, Arabic or Kurdish is the first language.

For a more in-depth look at the language, including a comprehensive list of useful words and phrases, get a copy of Lonely Planet's *Turkish phrasebook*.

Pronunciation

The letters of the new Turkish alphabet have a consistent pronunciation; they're reasonably easy to master, once you've learned a few basic rules. All letters except ğ (which is silent) are pronounced, and there are no diphthongs.

Vowels

A a	as in 'shah'
E e	as in 'fell'
İ i	as 'ee'
I ı	as 'uh'
O o	as in 'hot'
U u	as the 'oo' in 'moo'
Ö ö	as the 'ur' in 'fur'
Ü ü	as the 'ew' in 'few'

Note that ö and ü are pronounced with pursed lips.

Consonants

Most consonants are pronounced as in English, but there are a few exceptions:

Ç ç	as the 'ch' in 'church'
C c	as English 'j'
Ğ ğ	not pronounced – it draws out the preceding vowel
G g	as in 'go'
H h	as in 'half'
J j	as the 's' in 'measure'
S s	as in 'stress'
Ş ş	as the 'sh' in 'shoe'
V v	as the 'w' in 'weather'

Greetings & Civilities

Hello.	*Merhaba.*
Goodbye/	*Allaha ısmarladık/*
Bon Voyage.	*Güle güle.*
Please.	*Lütfen.*
Thank you.	*Teşekkür ederim.*
That's fine/	*Bir şey değil.*
You're welcome.	
Excuse me.	*Affedersiniz.*
Sorry. (Excuse me/	*Pardon.*
Forgive me.)	

Useful Words & Phrases

Yes.	*Evet.*
No.	*Hayır.*
How much is it?	*Ne kadar?*
Do you speak English?	*Ingilizce biliyor musunuz?*
Does anyone here speak English?	*Kimse Ingilizce biliyor mu?*

I don't understand.	*Anlamiyorum.*
Just a minute.	*Bir dakika.*
Please write that down.	*Lütfen yazın.*

Getting Around

Where is the bus/ tram stop?	*Otobüs/tramvay durağınerede?*
I want to go to (İzmir).	*(İzmir)'e gitmek istiyorum.*
Can you show me on the map?	*Haritada gösterebilir misiniz?*
Go straight ahead.	*Doğru gidin.*
Turn left.	*Sola dönün.*
Turn right.	*Sağa dönün.*
far/near	*uzak/yakın*

When does the ... leave/arrive?	*... ne zaman kalkar/ gelir?*
ferry/boat	*feribot/vapur*
city bus	*şehir otobüsü*
intercity bus	*otobüs*
train	*tren*
tram	*tramvay*

next	*gelecek*
first	*birinci/ilk*
last	*son*

I'd like a ... ticket.	*... bileti istiyorum.*
one-way	*gidiş*
return	*gidiş-dönüş*
1st-class	*birincısınıf*
2nd-class	*ikincısınıf*

Accommodation

Where is a cheap hotel?	*Ucuz bir otel nerede?*
What is the address?	*Adres ne?*
Please write down the address.	*Adresıyazar mısınız?*
Do you have any rooms available?	*Boş oda var mı?*

I'd like ...	*... istiyorum.*
a single room	*tek kişilik oda*
a double room	*Ikıkişilik oda*
a room with a bathroom	*banyolu oda*
to share a dorm	*yatakhanede bir yatak*
a bed	*bir yatak*

How much is it per night?	*Bir gecelik nekadar?*

Signs – Turkish

Giriş	**Entrance**
Çıkış	**Exit**
Boş Oda Var	**Rooms Available**
Dolu	**Full**
Danışma	**Information**
Açık/Kapalı	**Open/Closed**
Polis/Emniyet	**Police**
Polis Karakolu/ Emniyet Müdürlüğü	**Police station**
Yasak(tır)	**Prohibited**
Tuvalet	**Toilet**

May I see it?	*Görebilir miyim?*
Where is the bathroom?	*Banyo nerede?*

Around Town

I'm looking for the/a ...	*... arıyorum*
bank	*bir banka*
city centre	*şehir merkezi*
... embassy	*... büyükelçiliğini*
hotel	*otelimi*
market	*çarşıyı*
police	*polis*
post office	*postane*
public toilet	*tuvalet*
telephone centre	*telefon merkezi*
tourist office	*turizm danışma bürosu*

beach	*plaj*
bridge	*köprü*
castle	*kale/hisar*
church	*kilise*
hospital	*hastane*
island	*ada*
lake	*göl*
mosque	*cami(i)*
old city	*tarihışehir merkezi*
palace	*saray*
ruins	*harabeler/kalıntılar*
sea	*deniz*
square	*meydan*
tower	*kule*

Food

breakfast	*kahvaltı*
lunch	*öğleyemeği*
dinner	*akşamyemeği*

I'd like the set lunch, please.	*Fiks menü istiyorum, lütfen.*

Is service included in the bill?	*Servis ücretıdahil mi?*
I don't eat meat.	*Hiç et yemiyorum.*

Health

I'm diabetic/ epileptic/ asthmatic.	*Şeker hastasıyım/ saralıyım/ astımlıyım.*
I'm allergic to antibiotics/ penicillin.	*Antibiyotiklere/ penisiline/ alerjim var.*
antiseptic	*antiseptik*
aspirin	*aspirin*
condom	*prezervatif*
contraceptive	*gebeliğiönleyici*
diarrhoea	*ishal/diyare*
medicine	*ilaç*
nausea	*bulantı*
sunblock cream	*güneş blok kremi*
tampon	*tampon*

Time

What time is it?	*Sät kaç?*
today	*bugün*
tomorrow	*yarın*
in the morning	*sabahleyin*
in the afternoon	*öğleden sonra*
in the evening	*akşamda*

Days

Monday	*Pazartesi*
Tuesday	*Salı*
Wednesday	*Çarşamba*
Thursday	*Perşembe*
Friday	*Cuma*
Saturday	*Cumartesi*
Sunday	*Pazar*

Months

January	*Ocak*
February	*Şubat*
March	*Mart*
April	*Nisan*
May	*Mayıs*
June	*Haziran*
July	*Temmuz*
August	*Ağustos*
September	*Eylül*
October	*Ekim*
November	*Kasım*
December	*Aralık*

Emergencies – Turkish

Help!/Emergency!	*İmdat!*
There's been an accident!	*Bir kaza oldu!*
(There's a) fire!	*Yangın var!*
Call a doctor!	*Doktor çağırın!*
Call the police!	*Polis çağırın!*
Could you help us, please?	*Bize yardım edebilir-misiniz lütfen?*
Go away!	*Gidin!/Git!/Defol!*
I'm lost.	*Kayboldum.*

Numbers

0	*sıfır*
1	*bir*
2	*iki*
3	*üç*
4	*dört*
5	*beş*
6	*altı*
7	*yedi*
8	*sekiz*
9	*dokuz*
10	*on*
11	*on bir*
12	*on iki*
13	*on üç*
14	*on dört*
15	*on beş*
16	*on altı*
17	*on yedi*
18	*on sekiz*
19	*on dokuz*
20	*yirmi*
21	*yirmıbir*
22	*yirmıiki*
30	*otuz*
40	*kırk*
50	*elli*
60	*altmış*
70	*yetmiş*
80	*seksen*
90	*doksan*
100	*yüz*
200	*ikıyüz*
1000	*bin*
2000	*ikıbin*
one million	*bir milyon*

Glossary

Here, with definitions, are some unfamiliar words and abbreviations you might meet in the text or on the road in the Middle East. For a list of common foods, see the special section 'Middle Eastern Cuisine' in the Regional Facts for the Visitor chapter:

Abbasid dynasty – Baghdad-based successor dynasty to the *Umayyad dynasty*; ruled from AD 750 until the sacking of Baghdad by the Monguls in 1258
abd – servant, slave
abeyya – woman's full-length black robe
abra – small motorboat
abu – father; saint
acropolis – high city; hilltop citadel and temples of a classic Hellenic city
agal – head ropes used to hold a *kufeyya* or *gutra* in place; also 'iqal
agora – open space for commerce and politics in a classic Hellenic city
ahwa – coffee, also qahwa
aile salonu (Turkish) – family room for use by couples, families and single women in a Turkish restaurant
ain – spring, well; also ein, ayn
akhbar – great
Al-Ahram – the Pyramids
arasta (Turkish) – row of shops beside a mosque
arg (Farsi) – citadel
āteshkade (Farsi) – Zoroastrian fire temple
Ayyubid dynasty – Egyptian-based dynasty founded by *Saladin* (1169–1250)
azzan – call to prayer

bab – gate
bait – see *beit*
bakala – corner shop
balad – land or city
barasti – traditional method of building palm-leaf houses; name of the house itself
barjeel – wind towers (bādgir in Iran)
bawwab – doorman
bazbort – passport; also basbut, pispot
beit – house; also bait
beit ash-sha'ar – black goat-hair tents
bijous – service taxi
Book of the Dead – ancient Egyptian theological compositions, or hymns, which were the subject of most of the colourful paintings and reliefs on tomb walls

bublos (Greek) – papyrus
bukhnoq – girl's head covering
burj – tower; *burg* in Egypt

caliph – Islamic ruler
cami(i) (Turkish) – mosque
Canopic jars – pottery jars which held the embalmed internal organs and viscera of the mummified pharaoh; these were placed in the burial chamber near the sarcophagus
caravanserai – see *khan*
carnet de passage – permit allowing entry of a vehicle to a country without incurring taxes
çarşı (Turkish) – market, bazaar
cartouche – oblong figure enclosing the hieroglyphs of royal or divine names
centrale – telephone office
chador – black, one-piece head-to-toe covering garment; worn by many Iranian women

dalla – traditional coffee pot
Decapolis – league of 10 cities, including Damascus, in the northeast of ancient Palestine
deir – monastery, convent
dervish – Muslim mystic; see also *Sufi*
dhabar – minibus in Yemen
dhuma – Yemeni nobleman's curved dagger
Diaspora – Jewish dispersion or exile from the Land of Israel; the exiled Jewish community worldwide
dishdasha – man's shirt-dress worn in Kuwait and the UAE
diwan – reception room
diwaniya – Kuwaiti gatherings, usually at someone's home
dolmuş (Turkish) – minibus that sometimes runs to a timetable but more usually sets off when it's full
doner kebab – see *shwarma*

Eid al-Adha – Feast of Sacrifice marking the pilgrimage to Mecca
Eid al-Fitr – Festival of Breaking the Fast; celebrated at the end of Ramadan
ein – see *ain*
eivān – rectangular hall opening onto a mosque's courtyard
emām (Farsi) – see imam
emir – Islamic ruler, military commander or governor; literally, prince

Eretz Y'Israel – the Land of Israel, commonly used by Israel's right wing to refer to their preferred borders for the Jewish State, which includes the Gaza Strip, the West Bank and sometimes Jordan and/or the Sinai

fadl – large metal platters for serving food
falaj – irrigation channel
Fatimid dynasty – Shiite dynasty (908–1171) from North Africa, later based in Cairo, claiming descent from Mohammad's daughter Fatima; founders of Al-Azhar, the oldest university in the world
felafel – deep-fried balls of chickpea paste with spices served in a piece of flat bread with tomatoes or pickled vegetables
fellaheen – peasant farmers or agricultural workers who make up the majority of Egypt's population; literally 'ploughman' or 'tiller of the soil'
funduq – hotel
fuul – paste made from fava beans

galabeyya – full-length robe worn by men; also jalabiyya
GCC – Gulf Cooperation Council; members are Saudi Arabia, Kuwait, Bahrain, Qatar, Oman and the UAE
gebel – see *jebel*
gutra – white headcloth worn by men in Saudi Arabia and the Gulf States

haj – annual Muslim pilgrimage to Mecca
Hamas – militant Islamic organisation which aims to create an Islamic state in the pre-1948 territory of Palestine; acronym (in Arabic) for Islamic Resistance Movement
hammam – Turkish steam bath; hamam in Turkish
hantour – horse and carriage
haram – forbidden area
hared or **hasid** – (pl *haredim* or *hasidim*) member of an ultra-orthodox Jewish sect
hejab – woman's head scarf, worn for modesty; hegab in Egypt
hejira – migration; Islamic calendar
hisar – fortress, citadel; same as *kale*
hızlı feribot – fast car ferries
hypostyle hall – hall in which the roof is supported by columns

imam – prayer leader, Muslim cleric
intifada – Palestinian uprising against Israeli authorities in the Occupied Territories and Jerusalem; literally 'shaking off'

'iqal – see *agal*
iqama – residence permit
iskele(si) (Turkish) – landing-place, wharf, quay
iwan – vaulted hall, opening into a central court in the *madrassa* of a mosque

jalabiyya – see *galabeyya*
jambiya – tribesman's ceremonial dagger
jebel – hill, mountain; also gebel
jihad – literally, striving in the way of the faith; holy war

ka – spirit, or 'double', of a living person which gained its own identity with the death of that person; the survival of the ka, however, required the continued existence of the body, hence mummification
Kabaa – see *Qaaba*
kale(si) (Turkish) – fortress, citadel; also *hisar*
kanyon – Israeli shopping plaza
khan – travellers' inn, usually constructed on main trade routes, with accommodation on the 1st floor and stables and storage on the ground floor; also *caravanserai, wikala*
khanjar – Omani curved dagger; also *khanja*
khareef – monsoon, from mid-June to mid-September in Oman
khedive – Egyptian viceroy under Ottoman suzerainty (1867–1914)
khor – rocky inlet
kibbutz – (pl *kibbutzim*) communal settlement; originally farms, but now involved in additional industries
kibbutznik – member of a *kibbutz*
kilim – flat, woven mat
kiosk – open-sided pavilion
knanqah – *Sufi* monastery
Knesset – Israeli parliament
komite – Iranian religious police
Koran – see *Quran*
kosher – food prepared according to Jewish dietary law
köy(ü) (Turkish) – village
kufeyya – head scarf
kufic – type of highly stylised old Arabic script

Likud – Israeli right-wing political party
liman(ı) (Turkish) – harbour

madrassa – Muslim theological seminary; also modern Arabic word for school

mafraj – 'room with a view'; top room of a tower house

mahalle(si) (Turkish) – neighbourhood, district of a city

mahattat servees – taxi depot

majlis – formal meeting room; also parliament

maktab amn al-aam – general security office where visas are extended (Lebanon)

Mamluk – slave-soldier dynasty that ruled out of Egypt from 1250–1517

manzar – attic; room on top of a tower house

mashrabeyya – ornate carved wooden panel or screen; feature of Islamic architecture

mastaba – Arabic word for 'bench'; mudbrick structure above tombs from which the pyramids were developed

matawwa – religious police (Saudi Arabia)

medina – old walled centre of Islamic city

medrese(si) (Turkish) – see *madrassa*

menorah – eight-pronged candelabra; an ancient Jewish symbol associated with the Hanukkah Festival

meydan(ı) (Turkish) – see *midan*

midan – town or city square

midrahov – pedestrian mall

mihrab – niche in a mosque indicating the direction of Mecca

minbar – pulpit used for sermons in a mosque

Misr – another name for Egypt and Cairo; also written as Masr

mosaferkhune (Farsi) – cheap hotel

moshav – cooperative settlement, with private and collective housing and industry

moulid – festival celebrating the birthday of a local saint or holy person

muezzin – cantor who sings the call to prayer

mullah – Muslim clergyman

nargilah – water pipe used to smoke tobacco; also nargileh, sheesha

Nilometer – pit descending into the Nile containing a central column marked with graduations; the marks were used to measure and record the level of the river, especially during the inundation

norias – water wheels

obelisk – monolithic stone pillar with square sides tapering to a pyramidal top; used as a monument in ancient Egypt

Omayyad dynasty – see *Umayyad dynasty*

OPEC – Organisation of Petroleum Exporting Countries

otogar (Turkish) – bus station

pansiyon – pension, B&B, guesthouse

PLO – Palestine Liberation Organization

PTT – Posta, Telefon, Telğraf (post, telephone and telegraph office)

pylon – monumental gateway at the entrance to a temple

qa'a – reception room

Qaaba – the rectangular structure at the centre of the Grand Mosque in Mecca (containing the Black Stone) around which haj pilgrims circumambulate; also Kabaa

qahwa – coffee; also *ahwa*

qalyan – water pipe (Iran)

qasr – castle

qat – mildly narcotic leaves commonly chewed in Yemen

Quran – the holy book of Islam; also spelt Koran

rakats – cycles of prayer during which the *Quran* is read and bows and prostrations are performed

Ramadan – Muslim month of fasting

ras – cape or headland; also head

sabil – public drinking fountain

sabkha – soft sand with a salty crust

sadu – Bedouin-style weaving

Saladin – (in Arabic *Salah ad-Din*) Kurdish warlord who retook Jerusalem from the Crusaders; founder of the *Ayyubid dynasty*

şehir (Turkish) – city; municipality

şehiriçi (Turkish) – minibus

serdab – hidden cellar in a tomb, or a stone room in front of some pyramids, containing a coffin with a life-size, lifelike, painted statue of the dead king

settler – term used to describe those Israelis who have created new communities on territory captured from the Arabs during the 1967 War

Shabbat – Jewish sabbath and shutdown, observed from sundown Friday to sundown Saturday

shai – tea

shari'a – Islamic law

sheesha – see *nargilah*

sheikh – venerated religious scholar; also shaikh

sherut – shared taxi with a fixed route (Israel)

shwarma – grilled meat sliced from a spit and served in pita-type bread with salad; also doner kebab and, in Turkish, döner kebap

siq – narrow passageway or defile such as the one at Petra

soor – wall

souq – market

stele – (pl *stelae*) stone or wooden commemorative slab or column decorated with inscriptions or figures

Sufi – follower of any of the Islamic mystical orders that emphasise dancing, chanting and trances in order to attain unity with God

sultan – absolute ruler of a Muslim state

tawaabi – stamps

ta'amiyya – see *felafel*

TC – Türkiye Cumhuriyeti (Turkish Republic); designates an official office or organisation

tell – ancient mound created by centuries of urban rebuilding

thobe – term used in Saudi Arabia, Bahrain and Qatar for man's shirt-dress; similar to a *dishdasha*, but more tightly cut

THY – Türk Hava Yolları (Turkish Airlines)

tirma – Iranian silk

tomān (Farsi) – unit of 10 rials

Torah – five books of Moses (the first five Old Testament books); also called the Pentateuch

Umayyad dynasty – first great dynasty of Arab Muslim rulers, based in Damascus (661–750); also Omayyad dynasty

velayat-e faqih (Farsi) – Iranian 'supreme leader'

wadi – dried up river bed; seasonal river

wikala – see *khan*

willayat – village

zawiya – small school dedicated to the teaching of a particular *sheikh*

ziggurat (Farsi) – Pyramid-like temple

zurkane – wrestling ground

Thanks

Many thanks to the travellers who used the last edition and wrote to us with helpful hints, useful advice and interesting anecdotes.

Moha Abdulla, Ali Abedini, R Ackermann, Nick Adlam, Von Reis Affleck, Mike Agerton, Jefley Aitken, KJ Aitken-Meehan, Francesca Albertini, Bruce Allen, Charles Allen, Danny Allen, Rene Allen, Unal Altinyay, Sheila Aly, Tore Rye Andersen, Amanda S Anderson, Lainie & Craig Anderson, Yngve Andersson, Phil & Hilary Andre, Morten Anthun, Marianne Aral, Barbara & Graham Archer, Daniel Arenas, Karin Arver, Hiroyuki Asakuno, Marzieh Asgari-Targhi, Hilmir Ásgeirsson, Ruth Ash, Cathy Atkinson, Kazuya Ayani, MJ Bache, Gordon Bailey, Steve Bailey, Renske Bakker, Bart Baltus, Anne Bancroft, Shubha Banerjee, David Barr, Grace Barran, Mark Bartolo, Billy-Jo Basinger, Taher Bazerbashi, Tony Bazouni, John Bedford, Kathryn Beer, G Beerepoot, Luca Belis, Jeff Bell, Melanie Bell, Marzia Beltrami, Tony Benfield, Kemal Berberoglu, George & Brenda Berry, Jeff Berry, W Berryman, Alain Bertallo, Sophie Berteau, SL Betania, Michelle Beveridge, Nicola Beyfus, Luisa Bezzola, Sheila Bharat, Ami Bhatt, Sylvain Biemont, Annacarin & Nils Billing, Sam Birch, Michael Birrell, Steve Blair, Jane & Steve Bland, Sherry Blankenship, Ezster Blaskovics, Roger Blesa, Cindy & Maggie Blick, Jeff Blundell, Ed Bobeff, Thomas Bocquet, Julien Bodart, Rachel Borer, Myriam Born, Frans Borst, Mahmut Boynudelik, Jack Bradshaw, Marijana Brajac, Achille Brambilla, Sonja Bregman, Lance Brendish, Melinda Brenton, Manfred Bress, Paul Brians, Evan Brinder, Eric Bringuier, Ron Broadfoot, Colin Brougham, Eric Brouwer, Gunner Brunke, Douglas Buchanan, David Bugden, Carolyn Burdette, Sandi Burford-Poole, Louis Burgers, Mr Burns, Clea Burrett, Maret Busch, Holly Byrne, Joshua Byrne, Armando Cabrera, Emma Cain, Ignacio Calvo, Andrew Cameron, Rebecca Cameron, Tui Cameron, Paola Capris, Drew Caputo, Simon Carter, Rosemary Cartmill, Curzio Casoli, Luigi Cavaleri, Michelle Cave, Luigi Ceccarini, Ali Cengiz, Lucienne Cermann, Sam Chamberlain, Beryl Chambers, Beryl & Patrick Chambers, Colleen Chan, Vinod Chandra, David Chaudoir, Tan Kwang Cheak, Gerard Chetboun, Kristina Chetcuti, Terrie Chin, Na Choo, Alfred Choy, Hanno Christ, Arthur Ciastoch, Guadalupe Cincunegui, Chrissy & Malcolm Clark, Darren Clarke, Fiona Clarkson, Charles & Anne Clayton, Lucinda Coates, Ian Coggin, Robyn Cohen, Niall Connolly, David & Astrid Cooksey, Art Corey, Ursula Cornu, Sarah Cottam, George Coulouris, Michael Counsell, Paolo Criscione, Margaret Cronin, Sarok Csaba, Linton Cull, Neil Cullen, John Curry, Rukia Daaboul, Oystein Bornes Dalijord, Shaun Daly, Anjana Das, Neil Datta, Robert D'Avanzo, Martin Davis, Susan & Stewart Davison, Irene de Charriere, Joost de Graaf, Jeannie & Keith de Jong, Waldo de Oliveira, Kristi De Vadder, Peter Debruyne, Phill Dellow, Shane Delphine, Carine Delvaux, Graeme Dempster, Sander den Haring, Carine Derch, Arati Desai, Joel Didomizio, Karlheinz dienelt, David & Alison Dixon, Mary-Lou Dixon, Geoff & Anita Doig, Matjaz Dolenc, Neil Donnelly, Michael Donovan, Luis Eduardo Dosso, Luis Eduardo & Luciana Dosso,

Petr Drbohlav, Els Drent, Jason Dressler, Pattie Dubaere, Tilman Duerbeck, Linda Dufour, Gertjan Duiker, Laurent-jan Dullaart, Andy Dunbar, Alistair Duncan, Kevin Dunshea, Ben Earl, Roland W Earl, Jason Earle, Matt Eaton, Hussein Elazm, Bruce Elliott, Antonio Elorza, Hugh Elsol, Kim Elton, Vincent Frechette Emmanuel Andre, Reinhard Enne, Bodil Enoksson, Kerrieann Enright, Gennevene Ensor, Gennaro Escobedo, Robert A Estes, Bernard Farjounel, Jerry Felix, Lyndon Ferguson, Marylene Ferguson, Jan Fischer, Tony Fisher, Hetty Fletcher, Mark Forkgen, Sia Frederick, Jonathan Freeman, Louise Fryer, Mechthild Fuchs, Reyes Moran Fuertes, Sana Fullerton, Tammo Funke, Scott Furness, Helene Gabriel, Marzia Gandini, Alexander Garcia, Matthew Garfein, Alissa Garner, Jan Garvelink, Stefan Gasser, Carol Gaston, Mark Gazia, Ben Gazzal, Sandra Geisler, Simon & Georgie, Bernhard Gerber, Sebrina Gibson, Gudrun Gielen, Ritchie Gifford, Jenny Gilbert, Kathleen Gilbert, Paul W Gioffi, David Gips, Christian Glossner, Richard Goffin, Jane Golding, Ashley Goldstraw, Barry Gore, Wynand Goyarts, Jacqueline Graf, Alain Grand, Luca Grassi, Thomas Gray, Vincent Gray, Vincent & Mary Gray, Zach Greig, Bryan Grenn, Darrin W Griffiths, Daniel Groeber, Michelle Groenvelt, Gorm Gronnevet, Richard Groom, Raphael Gruener, Agnes Grundeken, Matteo Guidotti, Cher Guldemond, Rene Gulden, Don & Marlene Gunther, Dr Arun Gupta, Arne Haaland, Shelly Habel, Oskar Habjanic, Claudia Hackh, Guy Hagan, Pamela Hagedorn, Terje Hagen, Paul Hagman, Ken Haley, James Halton, Georg Hamacher, Luc & Anja Hansenne-Geril, Mat Hardy, Ido Harpaz, Evans Harrell, Donna Harris, John Harris, Peter Harris, Stephen & Akkelin Harris, Rob Hart, Jim Hartley, Chloe Harwood, David Havelin, Brendon Hayes, Tony Hayman, Bob Hayne, David Heath, Lutz Heide, Philip Heinecke, Roos Hermans, Sandie Hernandez, John Hershkowitz, Nick Hewitt, Markus Heyme, Max Hickey, Matthew Hildebrand, Richard Hill, Simon Hill, Kym Hirst, Peter Hitchcock, Michelle Hodge, Geoff Hodgson, Tomas Homann, Erik Hoogcarspel, Lee & Mei Hook, Chong Hoong Yin, Andrea Hooper, Fran Hopkins, Kevin Hopkins, Nancy Hourani, Sue Houston, Matt Howes, Stephen Howse, John Hulme, Sharon Humphrey, Frances B Hunt, John Hunt, Tony Hylton, Jouni Hytönen, Paul Inman, J Kirby Inwood, Miki Jablkowska, Mary Jackson, Andreas Jens Jahrow, Simon James, Pete Jameson, Rok Jarc, Peter Jensen, Maria Jesus de Lope, Ola Joernmark, Adrian Jones, Chris Jones, Don Jones, John Jones, Laura Jones, Nazima Kadir, Oscar Kafati, Jesse Kalisher, A Kamberg, Jason Kane, Viktor Kaposi, Estaphan Kareh, Simone Karlhuber, Joakim Karlsson, Ayla Karmali, Wouter Karst, Gina Kattenberg, Gina & Mark-Matthijs Kattenberg, Prashanta Kaushik, Tim Kealy, Mary Kelley, Cathie Kerr, Lee Kessler, Pete Kesting, Hala Khalaf, Rafi Khankhajeh, Karen Killalea, Derek Kim, Andrea King, Brett King, Lucie Kinkorova, Klaus Kirchner, Juergen Kirst, Dr Sabine Klahr, Kees Kleinjan, Arabian Knight, Andrew Knoedler, Martin Koene, Cynthia Koens, Jolanda Koopmans, Joost Kremers, Dale & Debbie Krumreich, Felicia Kruse, Carlo Krusich, Gabriel Kuhn, Simon Kutcher, Yan Lachat, Nikolaj Ladegaard, Jesse Lainer, Chris Lambert, Gilles

Lamere, Jo Lane, Mary-Justine Lanyon, Fabio Lanzavecchia, Steffen Lars, Espen Lauritzen, Al Lawrence, Vanessa Lawrey, John Lea, Ibrahim Leadley, John Leake, Jill Ledger, Alanna Lee, Valerie & Christophe Lefebvre, Paul Lelievre, Brian Lema, Eugene Lemaire, Claire Lessard, Ruud Leukel, Robert Leutheuser, Daniel Lieberfeld, Rolf Lienekogel, Alain Liger, Henry YM Lim, Carolyn List, Zhiyu Liu, Emiliano Lo Manto, Anna Lochmann, Alex Loucaides, Christina Lowe, Janine Lucas, Marc Luetolf, Francesco Lulli, Helen Lundgaard, Scott Lusher, Damian MacCormack, Elizabeth Madigan Jost, Kjell J Madsen, Louise Mair, Pertti Malo, Delyan Manchev, Jan Mansfield, Barbara Mansvelt, Luis Garcia Marco, Susan Mares-Pilling, Delia Margherini, Brian Mariotti, Pietsch Marit, Eric Markowitz, Christine Martens, Dave Mason, Ryan Masterson, Fouad Matar, Stefano Materassi, Jason Mathwin, Paul Mattock, Bob Maysmor, Glenn McAllister, Mark McCabe, Jeff McCartney, Wendy McCarty, Bernadette McCormack, Derek McDermott, Margaret McDonnell, Sarah McElwain, Nick McGhee, Mathew McGillan, Jamie McGraw, John McKie, RN McLean, Ralph McLean, Peter McLennan, Thorsten Meier, Dan Meijer, Steve Mellor, Robert Merrision, Tale Meyer, Stefano Micchia, Karen Mickle, Markella Mikkelsen, Janet Miller, Haleema Mini, Chris Mitchinson, Galder Mitxelena, Jean-Marc Mojon, Reza Mokarram, Ray Mondo, Montvazski Anita, Edward Moore, Jake Moore, Guy Moorhouse, Jo-Ann Morris, Pedr Morris, Mariella Mosler, Szabolcs Mosonyi, Nazik Moudden, Ted & Brenda Mouritz, Daniel Muller, Brennan Mulligan, Edan Mumford, Dave Munn, Graham Munn, Patrick Murphy, Terry Murphy, Zafer Mustafaoglu, Brad Myer, Karen Myhill-Jones, Agnes Nagy, Hari Nair, Karen Nalbandyan, Joanne Nathan, Giovanni Neri, Dr Jule Neuss, Steve Newcomer, Bridget Nichols, Sina Nielsen, Mick Nolan, Thomas Nolte, Luka Novak, Klara Novakova, Padraig O'Blivion, Debbie O'Bray, Richard O'Callaghan, Julia Old, G O'Limann, Shannon O'Loughlin, Curtis Oneal, Sibren Oosterhaven, Stefanie Opper, Brett Charles Osteen, Irene Otto, Kate Overheu, Vivien Ow, Shawn Owen, Ben Owens, Laura Owens, GL & MJ Palm, Craig Palmer, Anita Paltrinieri, Meritxell Pijoan Parellada, JS Parkes, Thea Parkin, Edwin & Barbara Parks, Claudia Pasquero, Dr Janos Patai, David Patel, Debra & Bharat Patel, Rene Paulin, SR Pawley, Emily Peckham, Davide Perdomo, Erika Peron, Jane Perry, Noam Perry, Richard Perry, Rick Petkovsek, Katja & Henry Petzold, Marie-Helene Pigis, Sean Plamondon, Leo Planken, David Plested, Dimitris Ploumides, Douglas Poole, Robert Portais, Jim Potter, Pirasri Povatong, Carlo Pozzi, Marcelo Horacio Pozzo, Daniel & Catherine Price, Scott Prysi, Peter & Erika Pucsok, Steve Pyle, Leila Qizilbash, Gunter Quaisser, Therese Quin, Aliya Quraishi, Bernard Radvaner, Karen L Rae, Stephanie Ragals, Patrick Raiman, Maria Ralph, Andre Rameil, Andrew Ratcliffe, Jo Reason, Thomas Reber, Timothy Reducha, Justin Reed, Volker Reichhardt, Miriam Reichmuth, Alistair Reid, Melinda Reidinger, Jon Reimer, Patrick Reinquin, Caroline Reynolds, Charlie Rich, Benjamin Richards, Manuel Rincon, Maurice Roberts, H Roivas, Frederic Rolet, Jennifer Rooke, Hans Peter Ros, Diana Rose, Darren Ross, Maike Rudolph, Esa Ruotsalainen, Ellis Ryan, Heather Ryan, Krysztof Rybak, H Sabathy, Ali Sabetian, Sandra Saccone, Cathy Sackett, Aimee Sacks, Ali Sadeghi, Kolja Sadowski, Maja Sajovic, Errol Salvador, Sibel Samaha, Dr V Sampanther, Yusuke Sasaki, Suzanne Sataline, Keith Savory, Mike Scales, Nora Schep, Joan Schlegel, Tim Schmith, Vicki Schnaedelbach, Monique Schoone, E Schotman, Bram Schout, Jennifer Scott, Judy Sebastian, Hendrik Selle, Nicola Seu, Trevor Sewell, Dahlia Shamsuddin, Kevin Shank, Esther Shannon, Barbara Sheils, Andrew & Ingrid Shepherd, Martin Sher, Cary Shewmaker, Susie Shinaco, Stephan Siemer, Hanne Siewartz, Roger L Simon, John Simpson, Khaldoun Sinno, Annarosa Sinopoli, Rainer Sittenthaler, Jan Sjoukens, Bob Skinner, Mirjam Skwortsow, Jan & Hetty Smalheer, Christine Smith, Gavin Smith, Owen Smith, Fenwick Snowdon, Kelly Sobczak, Helena Soderlind, Frederick Soderlund, Nora Soliman, Ralph Somma, Eduardo Spaccasassi, Andy Sparrow, Jim R Speirs, Fred Spengler, Joesph T Stanik, Mike Steinbach, Hans Sterkendries, Jane Stewart, Walter Stielstra, Alison Stimpson, Greg Stitt, Elena Stocco, Knut Arne Stromme, Deanie Sultana, Marek Aziz Szymanowicz, Zara Tai, Fiona Tarpey, Maike Tausch, Kevin Taylor, Andrei Tchijov, Eric Telfer, Martin Terber, Drew Terenzini, Carl Thalbitzer, Bruce Thompson, Julie Thompson, Alan Tinay, Paul Tod, Ippolita Tolja, Stefano Tona, Bern Toomey, Julie Toth, Brian Travers, Bev & John Treacy, Derek Trowell, Eleana Tsocas, Max & Eva Tsolakis, Andrew Turner, Dean Turner, Murphy Turner, Yves Tychon, Charlotte Ulfsparre, Fabio Umehara, Yusuf Usul, Cagri Uyarer, Mike Vafai, Franco Valdes, Liselotte Van de Perre, Marco van de Sande, Marnix van den Broek, Famke van der Duin, Manon van der Hilst, Joseph van der Linden, Talitha Van der Waerden, Martine van Dusseldorp, Nootje van Gorp, Nootje & Marcel van Gorp, Bart van Meyer, Geeske van Mierlo, Peter van Nederpelt, Linda Van Schel, Muriel Vander Donckt, Balint Vaszilievits-Somjen, Thomas Vaughan, Tamara Veenendaal, Jan Veragten, Martina Vercikova, Rik Verdellen, Warren Verkerk, Haman Veyseh, Susan Viner, Gregory Viscusi, Tommaso Vistosi, Eric Voinot, Hayco J Volkers, Rob Voncken, Jan Vorsselmans, Arno Waal, Judith Waegell, Joost Wagenaar, Suraj Wagh, Leslie Waldorf, Steve Walker, Kerry Wallace, Kerry & John Wallace, Scott Wallace, Nick Walmsley, Arme T Warmington, Domenic Wasescha, Karen Watkins, Paul & Joanne Watson, Julie Webb, Felix Weber, Renee Webster, Jason Weigold, Patrick Weinrauch, Joshua Welbaum, Jan Wergeland, Johan Westman, Caroline White, Michael Whitehouse, Sarah Whitson, Jeroen Wiersma, Jeroen Wijkamp, Janne Wikman, Andy Williams, Craig Williams, George Williams, W Williams, Melissa Wilson, Debra Winters, Peter Witte, Justin Wong, Adrian Wright, Dion & Donna Wright, Ian Wright, Martin Wright, William Yates, Yoram Yom-Tov, Cheryl Young, Robin Young, Roland Young, Simon Young, Beate Ziegler, Karla Zimmerman.

LONELY PLANET

ON THE ROAD

Travel Guides explore cities, regions and countries, and supply information on transport, restaurants and accommodation, covering all budgets. They come with reliable, easy-to-use maps, practical advice, cultural and historical facts and a rundown on attractions both on and off the beaten track. There are over 200 titles in this classic series, covering nearly every country in the world.

 Lonely Planet Upgrades extend the shelf life of existing travel guides by detailing any changes that may affect travel in a region since a book has been published. Upgrades can be downloaded for free from **www.lonelyplanet.com/upgrades**

For travellers with more time than money, **Shoestring** guides offer dependable, first-hand information with hundreds of detailed maps, plus insider tips for stretching money as far as possible. Covering entire continents in most cases, the six-volume shoestring guides are known around the world as 'backpackers bibles'.

For the discerning short-term visitor, **Condensed** guides highlight the best a destination has to offer in a full-colour, pocket-sized format designed for quick access. They include everything from top sights and walking tours to opinionated reviews of where to eat, stay, shop and have fun.

CitySync lets travellers use their Palm™ or Visor™ hand-held computers to guide them through a city with handy tips on transport, history, cultural life, major sights, and shopping and entertainment options. It can also quickly search and sort hundreds of reviews of hotels, restaurants and attractions, and pinpoint their location on scrollable street maps. CitySync can be downloaded from **www.citysync.com**

MAPS & ATLASES

Lonely Planet's **City Maps** feature downtown and metropolitan maps, as well as transit routes and walking tours. The maps come complete with an index of streets, a listing of sights and a plastic coat for extra durability.

Road Atlases are an essential navigation tool for serious travellers. Cross-referenced with the guidebooks, they also feature distance and climate charts and a complete site index.

LONELY PLANET

ESSENTIALS

Read This First books help new travellers to hit the road with confidence. These invaluable predeparture guides give step-by-step advice on preparing for a trip, budgeting, arranging a visa, planning an itinerary and staying safe while still getting off the beaten track.

Healthy Travel pocket guides offer a regional rundown on disease hot spots and practical advice on predeparture health measures, staying well on the road and what to do in emergencies. The guides come with a user-friendly design and helpful diagrams and tables.

Lonely Planet's **Phrasebooks** cover the essential words and phrases travellers need when they're strangers in a strange land. They come in a pocket-sized format with colour tabs for quick reference, extensive vocabulary lists, easy-to-follow pronunciation keys and two-way dictionaries.

Miffed by blurry photos of the Taj Mahal? Tired of the classic 'top of the head cut off' shot? **Travel Photography: A Guide to Taking Better Pictures** will help you turn ordinary holiday snaps into striking images and give you the know-how to capture every scene, from frenetic festivals to peaceful beach sunrises.

Lonely Planet's **Travel Journal** is a lightweight but sturdy travel diary for jotting down all those on-the-road observations and significant travel moments. It comes with a handy time-zone wheel, a world map and useful travel information.

Lonely Planet's eKno is an all-in-one communication service developed especially for travellers. It offers low-cost international calls and free email and voicemail so that you can keep in touch while on the road. Check it out on **www.ekno.lonelyplanet.com**

FOOD & RESTAURANT GUIDES

Lonely Planet's **Out to Eat** guides recommend the brightest and best places to eat and drink in top international cities. These gourmet companions are arranged by neighbourhood, packed with dependable maps, garnished with scene-setting photos and served with quirky features.

For people who live to eat, drink and travel, **World Food** guides explore the culinary culture of each country. Entertaining and adventurous, each guide is packed with detail on staples and specialities, regional cuisine and local markets, as well as sumptuous recipes, comprehensive culinary dictionaries and lavish photos good enough to eat.

LONELY PLANET

OUTDOOR GUIDES

For those who believe the best way to see the world is on foot, Lonely Planet's **Walking Guides** detail everything from family strolls to difficult treks, with 'when to go and how to do it' advice supplemented by reliable maps and essential travel information.

Cycling Guides map a destination's best bike tours, long and short, in day-by-day detail. They contain all the information a cyclist needs, including advice on bike maintenance, places to eat and stay, innovative maps with detailed cues to the rides, and elevation charts.

The **Watching Wildlife** series is perfect for travellers who want authoritative information but don't want to tote a heavy field guide. Packed with advice on where, when and how to view a region's wildlife, each title features photos of over 300 species and contains engaging comments on the local flora and fauna.

With underwater colour photos throughout, **Pisces Books** explore the world's best diving and snorkelling areas. Each book contains listings of diving services and dive resorts, detailed information on depth, visibility and difficulty of dives, and a roundup of the marine life you're likely to see through your mask.

LONELY PLANET

OFF THE ROAD

Journeys, the travel literature series written by renowned travel authors, capture the spirit of a place or illuminate a culture with a journalist's attention to detail and a novelist's flair for words. These are tales to soak up while you're actually on the road or dip into as an at-home armchair indulgence.

The range of lavishly illustrated **Pictorial** books is just the ticket for both travellers and dreamers. Off-beat tales and vivid photographs bring the adventure of travel to your doorstep long before the journey begins and long after it is over.

Lonely Planet **Videos** encourage the same independent, tough-minded approach as the guidebooks. Currently airing throughout the world, this award-winning series features innovative footage and an original soundtrack.

Yes, we know, work is tough, so do a little bit of deskside dreaming with the spiral-bound Lonely Planet **Diary** or a Lonely Planet **Wall Calendar**, filled with great photos from around the world.

TRAVELLERS NETWORK

Lonely Planet Online. Lonely Planet's award-winning Web site has insider information on hundreds of destinations, from Amsterdam to Zimbabwe, complete with interactive maps and relevant links. The site also offers the latest travel news, recent reports from travellers on the road, guidebook upgrades, a travel links site, an online book-buying option and a lively travellers bulletin board. It can be viewed at **www.lonelyplanet.com** or AOL keyword: lp.

Planet Talk is a quarterly print newsletter, full of gossip, advice, anecdotes and author articles. It provides an antidote to the being-at-home blues and lets you plan and dream for the next trip. Contact the nearest Lonely Planet office for your free copy.

Comet, the free Lonely Planet newsletter, comes via email once a month. It's loaded with travel news, advice, dispatches from authors, travel competitions and letters from readers. To subscribe, click on the Comet subscription link on the front page of the Web site.

LONELY PLANET

Guides by Region

L onely Planet is known worldwide for publishing practical, reliable and no-nonsense travel information in our guides and on our Web site. The Lonely Planet list covers just about every accessible part of the world. Currently there are 16 series: Travel guides, Shoestring guides, Condensed guides, Phrasebooks, Read This First, Healthy Travel, Walking guides, Cycling guides, Watching Wildlife guides, Pisces Diving & Snorkeling guides, City Maps, Road Atlases, Out to Eat, World Food, Journeys travel literature and Pictorials.

AFRICA Africa on a shoestring • Botswana • Cairo • Cairo City Map • Cape Town • Cape Town City Map • East Africa • Egypt • Egyptian Arabic phrasebook • Ethiopia, Eritrea & Djibouti • Ethiopian Amharic phrasebook • The Gambia & Senegal • Healthy Travel Africa • Kenya • Malawi • Morocco • Moroccan Arabic phrasebook • Mozambique • Namibia • Read This First: Africa • South Africa, Lesotho & Swaziland • Southern Africa • Southern Africa Road Atlas • Swahili phrasebook • Tanzania, Zanzibar & Pemba • Trekking in East Africa • Tunisia • Watching Wildlife East Africa • Watching Wildlife Southern Africa • West Africa • World Food Morocco • Zambia • Zimbabwe, Botswana & Namibia
Travel Literature: Mali Blues: Traveling to an African Beat • The Rainbird: A Central African Journey • Songs to an African Sunset: A Zimbabwean Story

AUSTRALIA & THE PACIFIC Aboriginal Australia & the Torres Strait Islands •Auckland • Australia • Australian phrasebook • Australia Road Atlas • Cycling Australia • Cycling New Zealand • Fiji • Fijian phrasebook • Healthy Travel Australia, NZ & the Pacific • Islands of Australia's Great Barrier Reef • Melbourne • Melbourne City Map • Micronesia • New Caledonia • New South Wales • New Zealand • Northern Territory • Outback Australia • Out to Eat – Melbourne • Out to Eat – Sydney • Papua New Guinea • Pidgin phrasebook • Queensland • Rarotonga & the Cook Islands • Samoa • Solomon Islands • South Australia • South Pacific • South Pacific phrasebook • Sydney • Sydney City Map • Sydney Condensed • Tahiti & French Polynesia • Tasmania • Tonga • Tramping in New Zealand • Vanuatu • Victoria • Walking in Australia • Watching Wildlife Australia • Western Australia
Travel Literature: Islands in the Clouds: Travels in the Highlands of New Guinea • Kiwi Tracks: A New Zealand Journey • Sean & David's Long Drive

CENTRAL AMERICA & THE CARIBBEAN Bahamas, Turks & Caicos • Baja California • Belize, Guatemala & Yucatán • Bermuda • Central America on a shoestring • Costa Rica • Costa Rica Spanish phrasebook • Cuba • Cycling Cuba • Dominican Republic & Haiti • Eastern Caribbean • Guatemala • Havana • Healthy Travel Central & South America • Jamaica • Mexico • Mexico City • Panama • Puerto Rico • Read This First: Central & South America • Virgin Islands • World Food Caribbean • World Food Mexico • Yucatán
Travel Literature: Green Dreams: Travels in Central America

EUROPE Amsterdam • Amsterdam City Map • Amsterdam Condensed • Andalucía • Athens • Austria • Baltic States phrasebook • Barcelona • Barcelona City Map • Belgium & Luxembourg • Berlin • Berlin City Map • Britain • British phrasebook • Brussels, Bruges & Antwerp • Brussels City Map • Budapest • Budapest City Map • Canary Islands • Catalunya & the Costa Brava • Central Europe • Central Europe phrasebook • Copenhagen • Corfu & the Ionians • Corsica • Crete • Crete Condensed • Croatia • Cycling Britain • Cycling France • Cyprus • Czech & Slovak Republics • Czech phrasebook • Denmark • Dublin • Dublin City Map • Dublin Condensed • Eastern Europe • Eastern Europe phrasebook • Edinburgh • Edinburgh City Map • England • Estonia, Latvia & Lithuania • Europe on a shoestring • Europe phrasebook • Finland • Florence • Florence City Map • France • Frankfurt City Map • Frankfurt Condensed • French phrasebook • Georgia, Armenia & Azerbaijan • Germany • German phrasebook • Greece • Greek Islands • Greek phrasebook • Hungary • Iceland, Greenland & the Faroe Islands • Ireland • Italian phrasebook • Italy • Kraków • Lisbon • The Loire • London • London City Map • London Condensed • Madrid • Madrid City Map • Malta • Mediterranean Europe • Milan, Turin & Genoa • Moscow • Munich • Netherlands • Normandy • Norway • Out to Eat – London • Out to Eat – Paris • Paris • Paris City Map • Paris Condensed • Poland • Polish phrasebook • Portugal • Portuguese phrasebook • Prague • Prague City Map • Provence & the Côte d'Azur • Read This First: Europe • Rhodes & the Dodecanese • Romania & Moldova • Rome • Rome City Map • Rome Condensed • Russia, Ukraine & Belarus • Russian phrasebook • Scandinavian & Baltic Europe • Scandinavian phrasebook • Scotland • Sicily • Slovenia • South-West France • Spain • Spanish phrasebook • Stockholm • St Petersburg • St Petersburg City Map • Sweden • Switzerland • Tuscany • Ukrainian phrasebook • Venice • Vienna • Wales • Walking in Britain • Walking in France • Walking in Ireland • Walking in Italy • Walking in Scotland • Walking in Spain • Walking in Switzerland • Western Europe • World Food France • World Food Greece • World Food Ireland • World Food Italy • World Food Spain **Travel Literature:** After Yugoslavia • Love and War in the Apennines • The Olive Grove: Travels in Greece • On the Shores of the Mediterranean • Round Ireland in Low Gear • A Small Place in Italy

LONELY PLANET

Mail Order

Lonely Planet products are distributed worldwide. They are also available by mail order from Lonely Planet, so if you have difficulty finding a title please write to us. North and South American residents should write to 150 Linden St, Oakland, CA 94607, USA; European and African residents should write to 10a Spring Place, London NW5 3BH, UK; and residents of other countries to Locked Bag 1, Footscray, Victoria 3011, Australia.

INDIAN SUBCONTINENT & THE INDIAN OCEAN Bangladesh • Bengali phrasebook • Bhutan • Delhi • Goa • Healthy Travel Asia & India • Hindi & Urdu phrasebook • India • India & Bangladesh City Map • Indian Himalaya • Karakoram Highway • Kathmandu City Map • Kerala • Madagascar • Maldives • Mauritius, Réunion & Seychelles • Mumbai (Bombay) • Nepal • Nepali phrasebook • North India • Pakistan • Rajasthan • Read This First: Asia & India • South India • Sri Lanka • Sri Lanka phrasebook • Tibet • Tibetan phrasebook • Trekking in the Indian Himalaya • Trekking in the Karakoram & Hindukush • Trekking in the Nepal Himalaya • World Food India **Travel Literature:** The Age of Kali: Indian Travels and Encounters • Hello Goodnight: A Life of Goa • In Rajasthan • Maverick in Madagascar • A Season in Heaven: True Tales from the Road to Kathmandu • Shopping for Buddhas • A Short Walk in the Hindu Kush • Slowly Down the Ganges

MIDDLE EAST & CENTRAL ASIA Bahrain, Kuwait & Qatar • Central Asia • Central Asia phrasebook • Dubai • Farsi (Persian) phrasebook • Hebrew phrasebook • Iran • Israel & the Palestinian Territories • Istanbul • Istanbul City Map • Istanbul to Cairo • Istanbul to Kathmandu • Jerusalem • Jerusalem City Map • Jordan • Lebanon • Middle East • Oman & the United Arab Emirates • Syria • Turkey • Turkish phrasebook • World Food Turkey • Yemen **Travel Literature:** Black on Black: Iran Revisited • Breaking Ranks: Turbulent Travels in the Promised Land • The Gates of Damascus • Kingdom of the Film Stars: Journey into Jordan

NORTH AMERICA Alaska • Boston • Boston City Map • Boston Condensed • British Columbia • California & Nevada • California Condensed • Canada • Chicago • Chicago City Map • Chicago Condensed • Florida • Georgia & the Carolinas • Great Lakes • Hawaii • Hiking in Alaska • Hiking in the USA • Honolulu & Oahu City Map • Las Vegas • Los Angeles • Los Angeles City Map • Louisiana & the Deep South • Miami • Miami City Map • Montreal • New England • New Orleans • New Orleans City Map • New York City • New York City City Map • New York City Condensed • New York, New Jersey & Pennsylvania • Oahu • Out to Eat – San Francisco • Pacific Northwest • Rocky Mountains • San Diego & Tijuana • San Francisco • San Francisco City Map • Seattle • Seattle City Map • Southwest • Texas • Toronto • USA • USA phrasebook • Vancouver • Vancouver City Map • Virginia & the Capital Region • Washington, DC • Washington, DC City Map • World Food New Orleans **Travel Literature**: Caught Inside: A Surfer's Year on the California Coast • Drive Thru America

NORTH-EAST ASIA Beijing • Beijing City Map • Cantonese phrasebook • China • Hiking in Japan • Hong Kong & Macau • Hong Kong City Map • Hong Kong Condensed • Japan • Japanese phrasebook • Korea • Korean phrasebook • Kyoto • Mandarin phrasebook • Mongolia • Mongolian phrasebook • Seoul • Shanghai • South-West China • Taiwan • Tokyo • Tokyo Condensed • World Food Hong Kong • World Food Japan **Travel Literature:** In Xanadu: A Quest • Lost Japan

SOUTH AMERICA Argentina, Uruguay & Paraguay • Bolivia • Brazil • Brazilian phrasebook • Buenos Aires • Buenos Aires City Map • Chile & Easter Island • Colombia • Ecuador & the Galapagos Islands • Healthy Travel Central & South America • Latin American Spanish phrasebook • Peru • Quechua phrasebook • Read This First: Central & South America • Rio de Janeiro • Rio de Janeiro City Map • Santiago de Chile • South America on a shoestring • Trekking in the Patagonian Andes • Venezuela **Travel Literature:** Full Circle: A South American Journey

SOUTH-EAST ASIA Bali & Lombok • Bangkok • Bangkok City Map • Burmese phrasebook • Cambodia • Cycling Vietnam, Laos & Cambodia • East Timor phrasebook • Hanoi • Healthy Travel Asia & India • Hill Tribes phrasebook • Ho Chi Minh City (Saigon) • Indonesia • Indonesian phrasebook • Indonesia's Eastern Islands • Java • Lao phrasebook • Laos • Malay phrasebook • Malaysia, Singapore & Brunei • Myanmar (Burma) • Philippines • Pilipino (Tagalog) phrasebook • Read This First: Asia & India • Singapore • Singapore City Map • South-East Asia on a shoestring • South-East Asia phrasebook • Thailand • Thailand's Islands & Beaches • Thailand, Vietnam, Laos & Cambodia Road Atlas • Thai phrasebook • Vietnam • Vietnamese phrasebook • World Food Indonesia • World Food Thailand • World Food Vietnam

ALSO AVAILABLE: Antarctica • The Arctic • The Blue Man: Tales of Travel, Love and Coffee • Brief Encounters: Stories of Love, Sex & Travel • Buddhist Stupas in Asia: The Shape of Perfection • Chasing Rickshaws • The Last Grain Race • Lonely Planet ... On the Edge: Adventurous Escapades from Around the World • Lonely Planet Unpacked • Lonely Planet Unpacked Again • Not the Only Planet: Science Fiction Travel Stories • Ports of Call: A Journey by Sea • Sacred India • Travel Photography: A Guide to Taking Better Pictures • Travel with Children • Tuvalu: Portrait of an Island Nation

LONELY PLANET

You already know that Lonely Planet produces more than this one guidebook, but you might not be aware of the other products we have on this region. Here is a selection of titles that you may want to check out as well:

Egypt
ISBN 1 86450 298 3
US$19.99 • UK£12.99

Egyptian Arabic phrasebook
ISBN 1 86450 183 9
US$7.99 • UK£4.50

Hebrew phrasebook
ISBN 0 86442 528 7
US$5.95 • UK£3.99

Libya
ISBN 0 86442 699 2
US$16.99 • UK£11.99

Iran
ISBN 0 86442 756 5
US$21.99 • UK£13.99

Farsi phrasebook
ISBN 0 864425 581 3
US$7.99 • UK£4.50

**Black on Black –
Iran Revisited**
ISBN 0 86442 795 6
US$12.95 • UK£6.99

**Breaking Ranks: Turbulent
Travels in the Promised Land**
ISBN 1 86450 361 0
US$12.99 • UK£6.99

World Food Turkey
ISBN 1 86450 027 1
US$11.99 • UK£6.99

Diving and Snorkeling Red Sea
ISBN 1 86450 205 3
US$19.99 • UK£12.99

Istanbul map
ISBN 1 86450 080 8
US$5.95 • UK£3.99

Turkey
ISBN 1 74059 362 6
US$24.99 • UK£14.99

**Available wherever books
are sold**

Index

Abbreviations

Text

Bold indicates maps.

Bold indicates maps.

Boxed Text & Special Sections

MAP LEGEND

CITY ROUTES

Freeway .... Freeway	═ ═ ═ ═ .... Unsealed Road
Highway .... Primary Road	═══ ...... One Way Street
Road ..... Secondary Road	════ .... Pedestrian Street
Street .... Street	▭▭▭▭▭ .... Stepped Street
Lane .... Lane	⇥ ═ ═ .... Tunnel
.... On/Off Ramp	════ .... Footbridge

HYDROGRAPHY

.... River, Creek	▭ ▭ Dry Lake; Salt Lake
.... Canal	⊙ ⟶ .... Spring; Rapids
.... Lake	⊛ ↦ ≋ .... Waterfalls

REGIONAL ROUTES

══════ ...... Tollway, Freeway	
══════ .... Primary Road	
══════ .... Secondary Road	
▭▭▭▭▭ .... Minor Road	

TRANSPORT ROUTES & STATIONS

══●══ .... Train	─ ─ ─ ▭ .... Ferry
▭▭▭▭▭ ...... Underground Train	─ ─ ─ ─ .... Walking Trail
──Ⓜ── .... Metro	· · · · · · · · .. Walking Tour
══▭══ .... Tramway	.... Path
▭▭▭▭▭ .... Cable Car, Chairlift	──────── Pier or Jetty

BOUNDARIES

▬ ▪ ▬ ▪▪ .... International	
▬ ▪▪ ▬ ▪▪ .... State	
─ ─ ─ .... Disputed	
▬▭▬ .... Fortified Wall	

AREA FEATURES

▭ .... Building	▭ .... Market
▭ ⊛ ...... Park, Gardens	▭ .... Sports Ground
∵ 🐾 ∵ .... Beach	× ▪ × × .. Islamic Cemetery
+ + + . Christian Cemetery	▭ .... Campus

POPULATION SYMBOLS

○ **CAPITAL** .... National Capital	● **CITY** .... City	● Village	.... Village
◉ **CAPITAL** .... State Capital	● **Town** .... Town	▭	.... Urban Area

MAP SYMBOLS

Note: not all symbols displayed above appear in this book

▪ .... Place to Stay	▼ .... Place to Eat		● .... Point of Interest
✚ ⊠ ..... Airstrip; Airport	◲ .... Dive Site	⚓ .... Monument	▭ .... Pub or Bar
⊖ .... Bank	▭ .... Embassy	◐ .... Mosque	⊠ .... Shopping Centre
⊛ .... Border Crossing	⊓ .... Gate	⌃▲ .... Mountain/Hill	▭ .... Stately Home
▭ ▭ .. Bus Stop/Terminal	◑ .... Golf	▭ .... Museum	▭ .... Synagogue
▭ .... Camping	⊕ .... Hammam	▭ .... National Park	▭ .... Taxi
⚓ ⚐ .... Canoe; Ski	◯ .... Hospital	◎ .... Noria	▭ .... Telephone
▭ ... Castle/Fort; Ruins	▭ .... Internet Café	▭ ☂ .... Oasis	▭ .... Theatre
⌂ .... Cave	◑ .. Islamic Monument	▭ .... Parking	⊙ .... Toilet
▭ ▭ .... Church	⛪ .... Islamic Shrine	)(....................... Pass	▪ .... Tomb
▭ .... Cinema	ⓚ .... Kibbutz	◎ .... Petrol	❶ . Tourist Information
⌒ .... Cliff	⛯ ✳ Lighthouse; Lookout	▭ .... Police	▭ .... Transport
▭ ...... Coffee House	Ⓜ .... Moshav	▭ .... Post Office	▭ ▭ Zoo; Bird Sanctuary

---

LONELY PLANET OFFICES

Australia
Locked Bag 1, Footscray, Victoria 3011
☎ 03 8379 8000 fax 03 8379 8111
email: talk2us@lonelyplanet.com.au

USA
150 Linden St, Oakland, CA 94607
☎ 510 893 8555 TOLL FREE: 800 275 8555
fax 510 893 8572
email: info@lonelyplanet.com

UK
10a Spring Place, London NW5 3BH
☎ 020 7428 4800 fax 020 7428 4828
email: go@lonelyplanet.co.uk

France
1 rue du Dahomey, 75011 Paris
☎ 01 55 25 33 00 fax 01 55 25 33 01
email: bip@lonelyplanet.fr
www.lonelyplanet.fr

World Wide Web: www.lonelyplanet.com *or* **AOL keyword: lp**
Lonely Planet Images: www.lonelyplanetimages.com